McDougal Littell

CLASSZONE

Visit classzone.com and get connected.

ClassZone resources provide instruction, practice and learning support for students and parents.

Help with the Math

- @Home Tutor enables students to focus on the math and be more prepared for class, using animated examples and instruction.
- Extra examples similar to those in the book provide additional support.
- Hints and Homework Help offers assistance solving select homework exercises.

Practice, Practice, Practice

- eWorkbook includes interactive worksheets with additional practice problems.
- Problem of the Week features a new problem to solve every week.

Games and Activities

- Crossword puzzles, memory games, and other activities help students connect to essential math concepts.
- Math Vocabulary Flipcards are a fun way to learn math terminology.

Math

- Engaging activities with animated problem-solving graphics support each lesson.

Access the online version of your textbook at **classzone.com**

Your complete text is available for immediate use!

McDougal Littell

Where Great Lessons Begin

CALIFORNIA

CA

McDougal Littell

MATH

Course 1

Ron Larson
Laurie Boswell
Timothy D. Kanold
Lee Stiff

McDougal Littell
A DIVISION OF HOUGHTON MIFFLIN COMPANY
Evanston, Illinois • Boston • Dallas

Larson Boswell Kanold Stiff

About *California Math Course 1*

The content of *California Math Course 1* is organized around and offers complete coverage of California's Grade 6 Mathematics Content Standards. Mathematics standards from previous grades are reviewed to help with your understanding of the Grade 6 standards. Activities are provided to develop Course 1 concepts. Each lesson has ample skill practice so that you can master the important mathematical processes taught in Course 1. *California Math Course 1* also teaches you valuable techniques for solving purely mathematical as well as real-world problems. Throughout each chapter you will engage in error analysis and mathematical reasoning to build critical thinking skills and to construct logical arguments. *California Math Course 1* thus provides a balance between basic skills, conceptual understanding, and problem solving—all supported by mathematical reasoning.

In *California Math Course 1* you will have many opportunities to practice your understanding of the Grade 6 standards. At the end of each lesson are multiple choice exercises that review standards that you learned in previous lessons. Additionally, multiple choice exercises on chapter content appear in each lesson, on Mixed Review pages twice per chapter, and at the end of each chapter on the Multiple Choice Strategies and Multiple Choice Practice pages. Technology support for learning course content is available at classzone.com.

ISBN-13: 978-0-618-72650-9
ISBN-10: 0-618-72650-0   5 6 7 8 9-DJM-13 12 11 10 09 08

Internet Web Site: http://www.mcdougallittell.com

About the Authors

Ron Larson is a professor of mathematics at Penn State University at Erie, where he has taught since receiving his Ph.D. in mathematics from the University of Colorado. Dr. Larson is well known as the author of a comprehensive program for mathematics that spans middle school, high school, and college courses. Dr. Larson's numerous professional activities keep him in constant touch with the needs of teachers and supervisors. He closely follows developments in mathematics standards and assessment.

Laurie Boswell is a mathematics teacher at The Riverside School in Lyndonville, Vermont, and has taught mathematics at all levels, elementary through college. A recipient of the Presidential Award for Excellence in Mathematics Teaching, she was also a Tandy Technology Scholar. She served on the NCTM Board of Directors (2002–2005), and she speaks frequently at regional and national conferences on topics related to instructional strategies and course content.

Timothy D. Kanold is the superintendent of Adlai E. Stevenson High School District 125 in Lincolnshire, Illinois. Dr. Kanold served as a teacher and director of mathematics for 17 years prior to becoming superintendent. He is the recipient of the Presidential Award for Excellence in Mathematics and Science Teaching, and a past president of the Council for Presidential Awardees in Mathematics. Dr. Kanold is a frequent speaker at national and international mathematics meetings.

Lee Stiff is a professor of mathematics education in the College of Education and Psychology of North Carolina State University at Raleigh and has taught mathematics at the high school and middle school levels. He served on the NCTM Board of Directors and was elected President of NCTM for the years 2000–2002. He is a recipient of the W. W. Rankin Award for Excellence in Mathematics Education presented by the North Carolina Council of Teachers of Mathematics.

Advisers and Reviewers

McDougal Littell's *California Math* series

Program Advisory Panel

Rick Austin
Mathematics Teacher
Daniel Lewis Middle School
Paso Robles, CA

Gregory T. Miyata
EETT/IMaST II Lead Coach/Advisor
Robert Louis Stevenson Middle School
Los Angeles, CA

Karen Cliffe
Mathematics Curriculum Specialist
Sweetwater Union High School District
Chula Vista, CA

Yoshiko Okamoto
Mathematics Teacher, Department Chair
Hoover Middle School
Lakewood, CA

Stephanie Davis
Mathematics and Science Teacher
Jefferson Middle School
San Gabriel, CA

Jane Marie Smith
Mathematics Teacher
Hillview Middle School
Palmdale, CA

Barry Fox
Mathematics Teacher/Assistant Principal
Florence Nightingale Middle School
Los Angeles, CA

Gwendolyn Walker-Jennels
Mathematics Teacher
Ralph Waldo Emerson Middle School
Pomona, CA

Brent T. Kuykendall
Mathematics Teacher
Ridgecrest Intermediate School
Rancho Palos Verdes, CA

Joan Hairston
Mathematics Teacher
Francisco Bravo Medical Magnet School
Los Angeles, CA

Textbook Reviewers

José Aguilar
Mathematics Coach
Eagle Rock High School
Los Angeles, CA

Tamesha Carter
Mathematics Teacher
DeMille Middle School
Long Beach, CA

Mark Chavez
Mathematics Teacher
DeMille Middle School
Long Beach, CA

Karen Cliffe
Mathematics Curriculum Specialist
Sweetwater Union High School District
Chula Vista, CA

Ed Kohn
Professional Development Facilitator
Los Angeles Unified School District
Los Angeles, CA

Chris Martinez
Mathematics Teacher
Arden Middle School
Sacramento, CA

Rick Austin
Mathematics Teacher
Daniel Lewis Middle School
Paso Robles, CA

Gregory T. Miyata
EETT/IMaST II Lead Coach/Advisor
Robert Louis Stevenson Middle School
Los Angeles, CA

Yoshiko Okamoto
Mathematics Teacher, Department Chair
Hoover Middle School
Lakewood, CA

Mike Pacheco
Mathematics Teacher
David Wark Griffith Middle School
Los Angeles, CA

Rudy Sass
Mathematics Teacher
Orangeview Junior High School
Anaheim, CA

Teacher's Editions Advisory Panel

Edie Birbeck
Mathematics Teacher
William Hopkins Junior High School
Fremont, CA

Janet L. Bryson
Mathematics Coach,
TASEL-M
Orange, CA

Ellen Duffy
Mathematics Coach
TASEL-M
Fullerton, CA

Donna Krueger Phair
Mathematics Teacher, Department Chair
William Hopkins Junior High School
Fremont, CA

Frank Dong
Mathematics Teacher
Marina Middle School
San Francisco, CA

Ellen Fujii
7–12 Mathematics Program Facilitator
Garden Grove Unified School District
Garden Grove, CA

Douglas Harik
Mathematics Teacher
Westborough Middle School
South San Francisco, CA

Sheila Hernandez
Mathematics Teacher
Horner Junior High School
Fremont, CA

Diane Jacobs
Mathematics Teacher
Fitz Intermediate School
Santa Ana, CA

Shauna Poong
Mathematics Teacher
Marina Middle School
San Francisco, CA

Jenita Whiting-Dandridge
Mathematics Teacher
Los Angeles Academy Middle School
Los Angeles, CA

CALIFORNIA

CA

Overview
California Student Edition

Yosemite National Park

CALIFORNIA TABLE OF CONTENTS

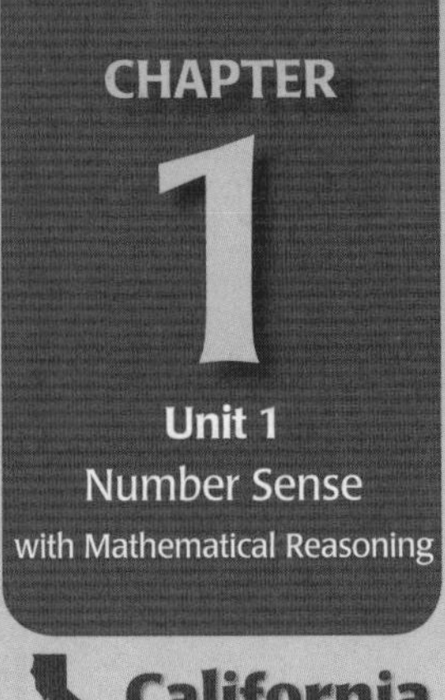

Ordering Fractions, p. 44
$\frac{780}{3} \approx \underline{\ ?\ } \times 88.4$

Number Patterns and Fractions

Chapter 1 Highlights

TECHNOLOGY

At classzone.com:
- Animated Math, 11, 16, 22, 37, 43, 48
- California @Home Tutor, 8, 13, 19, 24, 32, 38, 39, 44, 50, 56
- Online Quiz, 9, 14, 20, 25, 33, 39, 45, 52

STUDENT HELP

- Vocabulary and Reading, 4, 5, 6, 7, 10, 12, 16, 18, 21, 23, 29, 31, 35, 37, 40, 42, 44, 47, 49, 56, 61
- Notetaking, 4, 18, 56
- Another Way, 11, 29, 34, 37
- Avoid Errors, 17, 30
- Hints and Homework Help, 7, 12, 18, 23, 31, 37, 42, 49

◆ ASSESSMENT

- Multiple choice examples and exercises, 7, 8, 10, 12, 13, 18, 19, 21, 23, 24, 30, 31, 32, 38, 43, 44, 50, 51
- California Standards Spiral Review, 9, 14, 20, 25, 33, 39, 45, 52
- Writing, Open-Ended, and Short Response, 3, 7, 9, 12, 13, 14, 15, 18, 23, 24, 25, 27, 31, 32, 33, 37, 39, 42, 49, 51, 52

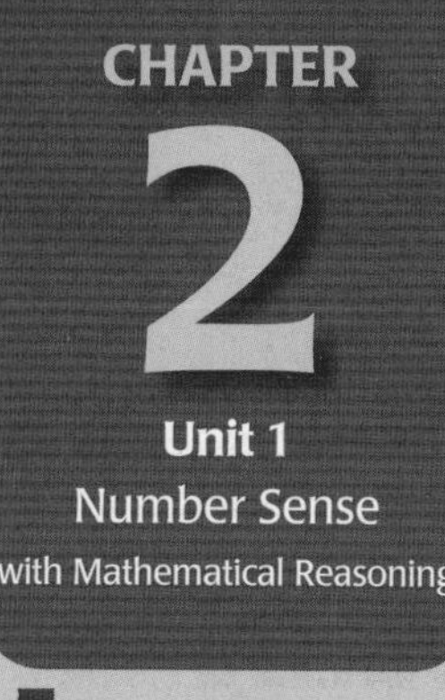

Subtracting Fractions, p. 77
$\text{Part of day not at lunch} = 1 - \frac{1}{15}$

Fraction and Decimal Operations

Chapter 2 Highlights

TECHNOLOGY

At classzone.com:
- **Animated Math,** 77, 82, 95, 101, 107
- **California @Home Tutor,** 72, 79, 84, 91, 98, 105, 111, 117
- **Online Quiz,** 73, 80, 85, 92, 99, 106, 113

STUDENT HELP

- **Vocabulary and Reading,** 68, 69, 70, 71, 75, 77, 80, 81, 83, 88, 90, 95, 97, 102, 104, 107, 110, 117, 121
- **Notetaking,** 68, 71, 117
- **Another Way,** 81, 90, 93, 103, 108
- **Avoid Errors,** 69, 109
- **Hints and Homework Help,** 71, 77, 83, 90, 97, 104, 110

◆ ASSESSMENT

- **Multiple choice examples and exercises,** 71, 73, 75, 78, 79, 83, 84, 89, 91, 97, 98, 99, 104, 106, 110, 111, 112
- **California Standards Spiral Review,** 73, 80, 85, 92, 99, 106, 113
- **Writing, Open-Ended, and Short Response,** 67, 72, 74, 77, 79, 80, 83, 84, 85, 87, 90, 92, 97, 99, 101, 104, 105, 106, 110, 111, 112

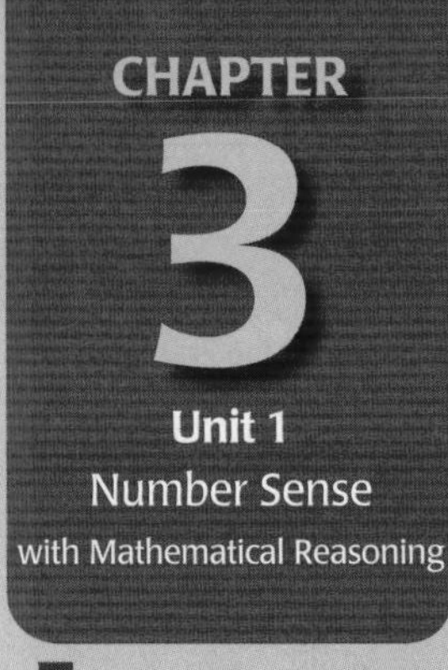

Multiplying Integers, p. 151
Distance = (−3 ft/sec) • (15 sec)

Integers

Chapter 3 Highlights

TECHNOLOGY

At classzone.com:

- **Animated Math,** 130, 137, 142, 162, 170, 174, 177
- **California @Home Tutor,** 132, 139, 146, 151, 157, 163, 164, 171, 176, 182
- **Online Quiz,** 133, 140, 147, 152, 158, 165, 172, 178

STUDENT HELP

- **Vocabulary and Reading,** 128, 129, 131, 135, 136, 138, 143, 145, 148, 149, 150, 154, 156, 160, 162, 165, 167, 168, 170, 172, 173, 175, 182, 187
- **Notetaking,** 128, 138, 182
- **Another Way,** 143, 149, 153
- **Avoid Errors,** 130, 137, 174
- **Hints and Homework Help,** 131, 138, 145, 150, 156, 162, 170, 175

◆ ASSESSMENT

- **Multiple choice examples and exercises,** 131, 132, 135, 138, 139, 140, 144, 145, 146, 150, 151, 155, 157, 161, 163, 164, 170, 171, 175, 176, 177
- **California Standards Spiral Review,** 133, 140, 147, 152, 158, 165, 172, 178
- **Writing, Open-Ended, and Short Response,** 127, 131, 132, 139, 142, 145, 147, 150, 156, 158, 162, 164, 170, 171, 175, 177

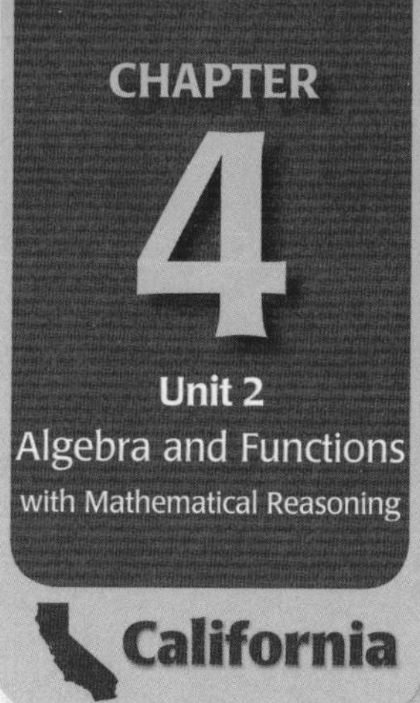

Using Mental Math, p. 223
$48 + x = 64$

Expressions and Equations

Chapter 4 Highlights

TECHNOLOGY

At classzone.com:
- **Animated Math,** 204, 216, 220, 227
- **California @Home Tutor,** 200, 205, 210, 216, 223, 230, 238, 243
- **Online Quiz,** 200, 206, 210, 217, 224, 231, 239

STUDENT HELP

- **Vocabulary and Reading,** 196, 197, 199, 202, 204, 207, 209, 212, 215, 219, 220, 221, 226, 228, 234, 236, 238, 243, 247
- **Notetaking,** 196, 236, 243
- **Another Way,** 228, 232
- **Avoid Errors,** 197, 227
- **Hints and Homework Help,** 199, 204, 209, 215, 221, 228, 236

◆ ASSESSMENT

- **Multiple choice examples and exercises,** 199, 200, 203, 204, 205, 209, 210, 213, 215, 216, 222, 223, 229, 230, 236, 237, 238
- **California Standards Spiral Review,** 200, 206, 210, 217, 224, 231, 239
- **Writing, Open-Ended, and Short Response,** 195, 199, 200, 204, 206, 209, 211, 215, 221, 223, 224, 225, 228, 230, 231, 233, 238

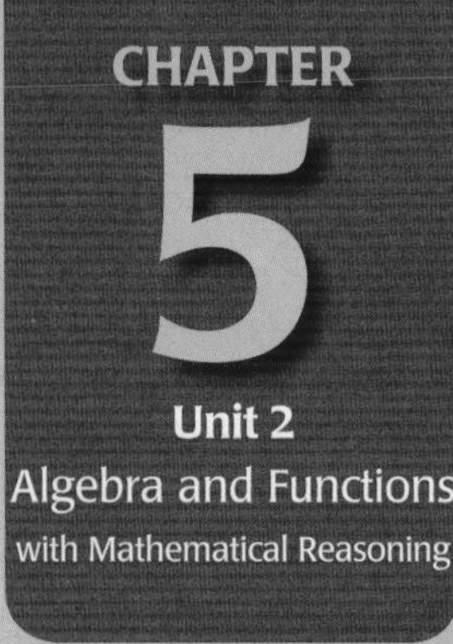

Using Proportions, p. 278

$\frac{15 \text{ mi}}{1 \text{ h}} = \frac{x \text{ mi}}{0.5 \text{ h}}$

Ratios and Proportions

Chapter 5 Highlights

TECHNOLOGY

At classzone.com:

- **Animated Math,** 257, 260, 265, 282
- **California @Home Tutor,** 258, 263, 269, 278, 284, 285, 290
- **Online Quiz,** 259, 264, 271, 279, 286

STUDENT HELP

- **Vocabulary and Reading,** 254, 255, 257, 260, 262, 266, 268, 270, 274, 276, 281, 283, 290, 293
- **Notetaking,** 254, 276, 290
- **Another Way,** 266, 267, 272, 275, 276
- **Avoid Errors,** 255, 268
- **Hints and Homework Help,** 257, 262, 268, 276, 283

◆ ASSESSMENT

- **Multiple choice examples and exercises,** 256, 257, 258, 262, 264, 268, 269, 270, 275, 277, 278, 281, 284, 285
- **California Standards Spiral Review,** 259, 264, 271, 279, 286
- **Writing, Open-Ended, and Short Response,** 253, 257, 258, 259, 262, 263, 265, 268, 278, 280, 283, 285

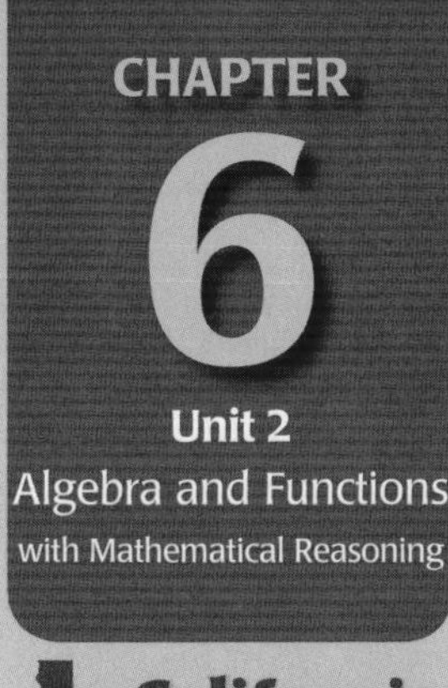

Percents and Proportions, p. 307

$\frac{a}{525} = \frac{20}{100}$

Percents

Chapter 6 Highlights

TECHNOLOGY

At classzone.com:

- **Animated Math,** 302, 309, 312, 331
- **California @Home Tutor,** 304, 310, 316, 322, 328, 329, 334, 339
- **Online Quiz,** 304, 311, 317, 323, 329, 335

STUDENT HELP

- **Vocabulary and Reading,** 300, 301, 303, 306, 308, 312, 314, 319, 320, 321, 323, 325, 327, 331, 333, 339, 343
- **Notetaking,** 300, 327, 339
- **Another Way,** 313, 327, 330
- **Avoid Errors,** 314, 326, 332
- **Hints and Homework Help,** 303, 308, 314, 321, 327, 333

◆ ASSESSMENT

- **Multiple choice examples and exercises,** 303, 304, 309, 310, 315, 316, 321, 322, 326, 328, 329, 331, 333, 334
- **California Standards Spiral Review,** 304, 311, 317, 323, 329, 335
- **Writing, Open-Ended, and Short Response,** 299, 303, 304, 308, 314, 321, 329, 333, 335

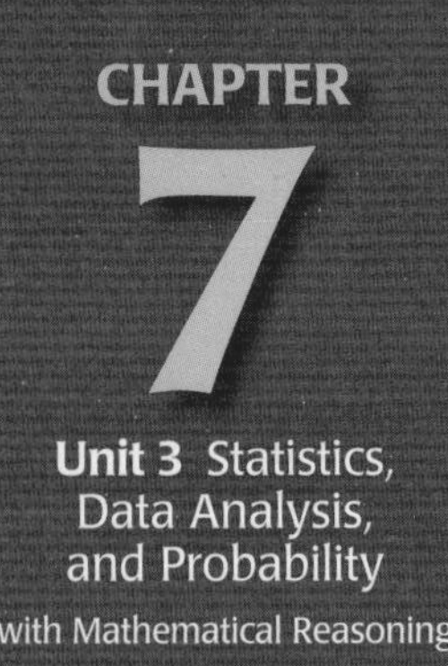

Range and Outliers, p. 376
range = 368 − 358

Analyzing Data

Chapter 7 Highlights

TECHNOLOGY

At classzone.com:
- **Animated Math,** 385, 389
- **California @Home Tutor,** 357, 358, 362, 367, 368, 376, 383, 391, 396, 403
- **Online Quiz,** 358, 363, 369, 377, 384, 391, 398

STUDENT HELP

- **Vocabulary and Reading,** 352, 354, 356, 359, 361, 364, 366, 368, 372, 375, 379, 382, 387, 389, 392, 393, 395, 403, 407
- **Notetaking,** 352, 395, 403
- **Another Way,** 366, 370
- **Avoid Errors,** 365, 372, 379, 380, 394
- **Hints and Homework Help,** 356, 361, 366, 375, 382, 389, 395

◆ ASSESSMENT

- **Multiple choice examples and exercises,** 356, 357, 361, 362, 365, 367, 368, 375, 376, 381, 382, 383, 390, 391, 395
- **California Standards Spiral Review,** 358, 363, 369, 377, 384, 391, 398
- **Writing, Open-Ended, and Short Response,** 351, 356, 357, 361, 363, 366, 369, 375, 382, 383, 384, 389, 391, 396, 398

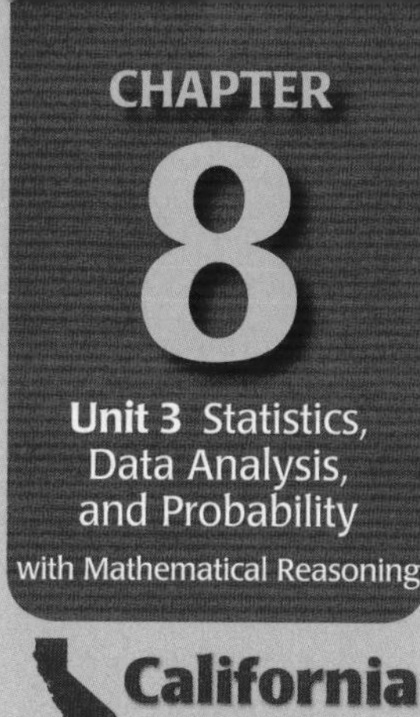

Experimental Probability, p. 425
$P(\text{bluegill}) = \frac{42}{123} = \frac{14}{41}$

Probability

Chapter 8 Highlights

TECHNOLOGY

At classzone.com:

- **Animated Math,** 422, 427, 434
- **California @Home Tutor,** 418, 419, 425, 431, 438, 445, 450
- **Online Quiz,** 419, 426, 432, 439, 446

STUDENT HELP

- **Vocabulary and Reading,** 414, 415, 417, 422, 424, 427, 430, 434, 437, 439, 441, 442, 444, 450, 453
- **Notetaking,** 414, 424, 450
- **Another Way,** 416, 429, 436, 440
- **Avoid Errors,** 415, 443
- **Hints and Homework Help,** 417, 424, 430, 437, 444

◆ ASSESSMENT

- **Multiple choice examples and exercises,** 416, 417, 419, 424, 425, 428, 430, 431, 435, 437, 438, 444, 445
- **California Standards Spiral Review,** 419, 426, 432, 439, 446
- **Writing, Open-Ended, and Short Response,** 413, 417, 425, 426, 430, 437, 444

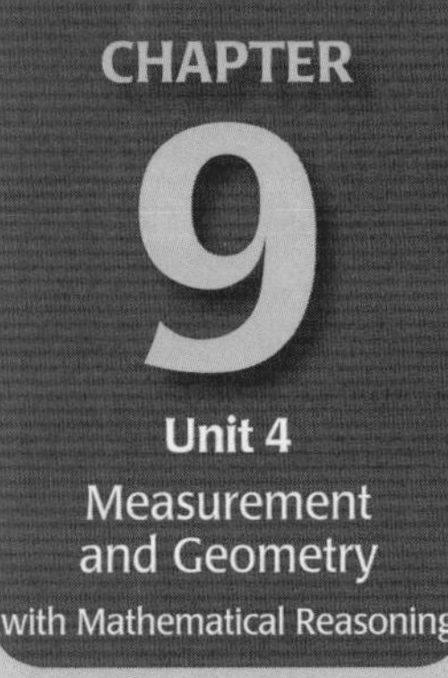

Similar Polygons, p. 494
$\frac{l}{w} = \frac{160}{360}$

Geometric Figures

Chapter 9 Highlights

TECHNOLOGY

At classzone.com:
- **Animated Math,** 463, 465
- **California @Home Tutor,** 466, 467, 471, 478, 487, 493, 498, 503
- **Online Quiz,** 467, 472, 479, 487, 494, 499

STUDENT HELP
- **Vocabulary and Reading,** 462, 463, 464, 465, 468, 470, 472, 474, 476, 477, 482, 484, 485, 490, 492, 495, 497, 503, 507
- **Notetaking,** 462, 485, 503
- **Another Way,** 469, 476, 480
- **Avoid Errors,** 484, 490, 491
- **Hints and Homework Help,** 465, 470, 477, 485, 492, 497

◆ ASSESSMENT
- **Multiple choice examples and exercises,** 464, 465, 466, 471, 475, 477, 478, 486, 487, 492, 494, 495, 497, 498
- **California Standards Spiral Review,** 467, 472, 479, 487, 494, 499
- **Writing, Open-Ended, and Short Response,** 461, 465, 467, 470, 471, 473, 477, 487, 492, 493, 494, 497

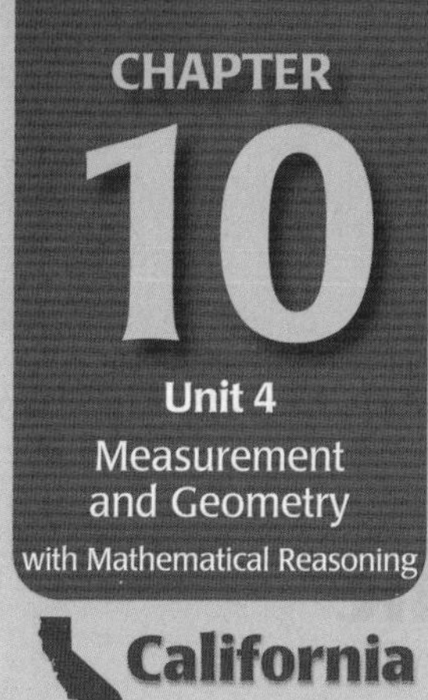

Converting Units, p. 530

$\frac{9.5 \text{ mi}}{1 \text{ h}} \times \frac{1.609 \text{ km}}{1 \text{ mi}} \times \frac{1000 \text{ m}}{1 \text{ km}}$

Measurement and Area

Chapter 10 Highlights

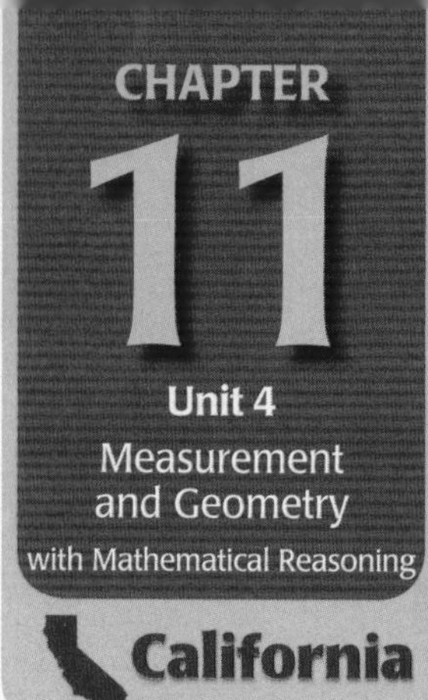

Volume of Prisms, p. 600
Volume of sand = (12 ft • 5 ft) • (3 ft)

Surface Area and Volume

Chapter 11 Highlights

TECHNOLOGY

At classzone.com:
- **Animated Math,** 596, 606
- **California @Home Tutor,** 579, 585, 592, 599, 604, 610
- **Online Quiz,** 579, 586, 593, 600, 605

STUDENT HELP

- **Vocabulary and Reading,** 574, 575, 576, 577, 581, 583, 589, 591, 596, 598, 601, 603, 604, 610, 613
- **Notetaking,** 574, 577, 610
- **Another Way,** 583, 587
- **Avoid Errors,** 589, 597, 598, 602
- **Hints and Homework Help,** 577, 583, 591, 598, 603

◆ ASSESSMENT

- **Multiple choice examples and exercises,** 578, 579, 582, 584, 585, 591, 592, 597, 599, 600, 602, 603, 604
- **California Standards Spiral Review,** 579, 586, 593, 600, 605
- **Writing, Open-Ended, and Short Response,** 573, 579, 583, 585, 591, 592, 598, 599, 600, 603, 613

Functional Relationships, p. 663
Input: 1 hour
Output: 440 calories

Graphing: Review and Preview

Chapter 12 Highlights

TECHNOLOGY

At classzone.com:
- **Animated Math,** 628, 633, 636, 643
- **California @Home Tutor,** 628, 633, 639, 646, 651
- **Online Quiz,** 629, 634, 640, 647

STUDENT HELP

- **Vocabulary and Reading,** 622, 624, 625, 626, 630, 632, 636, 637, 640, 642, 644, 651, 655
- **Notetaking,** 622, 632, 651
- **Another Way,** 631, 635, 644
- **Avoid Errors,** 643
- **Hints and Homework Help,** 626, 632, 637, 644

◆ ASSESSMENT

- **Multiple choice examples and exercises,** 624, 627, 628, 631, 632, 633, 638, 639, 645, 646
- **California Standards Spiral Review,** 629, 634, 640, 647
- **Writing, Open-Ended, and Short Response,** 621, 626, 628, 632, 637, 639, 644, 646, 647

Contents of Student Resources

Standards Review Handbook
pages 661–691

Extra Practice for Chapters 1–12

Tables

English-Spanish Glossary

Index

Credits

Selected Answers

CALIFORNIA

California Student Guide

Getting Started

The following pages will help you get started by providing a preview of the course and an introduction to your textbook.

California Standards Practice — *Pages SG2 – SG23*

Gives you an overview of the standards for this course. Lists all Grade 6 standards with two multiple choice exercises for each standard.

California Pre-Course Test — *Pages SG24 – SG25*

Tests prerequisite skills for Grade 6 with page references to the Standards Review Handbook at the back of the book.

Scavenger Hunt — *Pages SG26 – SG27*

Provides an opportunity to explore student resources at the back of the book.

Yosemite National Park

Standards Practice

As you answer each multiple choice question, you may want to turn to the page given in blue to study the mathematical concepts that the question is addressing. The symbol points out the key 6th Grade Standards.

Grade 6

Number Sense

NS 1.0 **Students compare and order positive and negative fractions, decimals, and mixed numbers. Students solve problems involving fractions, ratios, proportions, and percentages:**

NS 1.1 **Compare and order positive and negative fractions, decimals, and mixed numbers and place them on a number line.**

1. Which list of numbers is ordered from *least* to *greatest*? ***(p. 40)***

Ⓐ $0.05, \frac{1}{5}, 0.5, 1.5, 1\frac{3}{5}$

Ⓑ $0.05, 0.5, \frac{1}{5}, 1.5, 1\frac{3}{5}$

Ⓒ $\frac{1}{5}, 0.05, 0.5, 1\frac{3}{5}, 1.5$

Ⓓ $1\frac{3}{5}, 1.5, 0.5, \frac{1}{5}, 0.05$

2. Which point shows the location of $-\frac{2}{3}$ on the number line? ***(p. 167)***

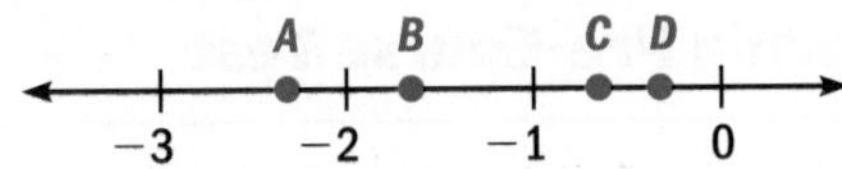

Ⓐ Point *A*

Ⓑ Point *B*

Ⓒ Point *C*

Ⓓ Point *D*

NS 1.2 **Interpret and use ratios in different contexts (e.g., batting averages, miles per hour) to show the relative sizes of two quantities, using appropriate notations (*a*/*b*, *a* to *b*, *a*:*b*).**

3. Car A travels 105 miles in 3 hours. Car B travels 120 miles in 4 hours. Which ratio shows the average speed of the faster car? ***(p. 260)***

Ⓐ $\frac{30 \text{ mi}}{1 \text{ h}}$

Ⓑ $\frac{35 \text{ mi}}{1 \text{ h}}$

Ⓒ $\frac{40 \text{ mi}}{1 \text{ h}}$

Ⓓ $\frac{45 \text{ mi}}{1 \text{ h}}$

4. During one season, a hockey team won 42 games, lost 35 games, and tied 5 games. What is the ratio of wins to losses? ***(p. 255)***

Ⓐ 6 : 5

Ⓑ 5 : 6

Ⓒ 21 : 20

Ⓓ 20 : 21

NS 1.3 Use proportions to solve problems (e.g., determine the value of N if $\frac{4}{7} = \frac{N}{21}$, find the length of a side of a polygon similar to a known polygon). Use cross-multiplication as a method for solving such problems, understanding it as the multiplication of both sides of an equation by a multiplicative inverse.

5. A recipe for 24 bran muffins requires 2.25 cups of flour. You want to make 30 bran muffins. Which proportion could be solved to find x, the total number of cups of flour needed? *(p. 266)*

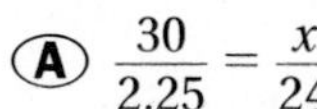

Ⓐ $\frac{30}{2.25} = \frac{x}{24}$ Ⓑ $\frac{24}{2.25} = \frac{x}{30}$

Ⓒ $\frac{2.25}{24} = \frac{30}{x}$ Ⓓ $\frac{24}{2.25} = \frac{30}{x}$

6. $\triangle RST$ is similar to $\triangle XYZ$. What is the length of $\overline{RT}$? *(p. 495)*

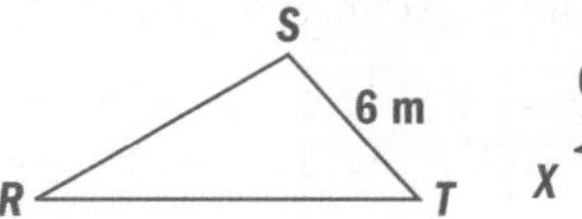

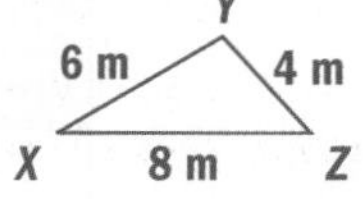

Ⓐ $5\frac{1}{3}$ meters Ⓑ 8 meters

Ⓒ 10 meters Ⓓ 12 meters

NS 1.4 Calculate given percentages of quantities and solve problems involving discounts at sales, interest earned, and tips.

7. A sweater is on sale for 75% off the original price of \$38. What is the new price of the sweater? *(p. 325)*

Ⓐ \$9.50 Ⓑ \$27.50

Ⓒ \$28.50 Ⓓ \$47.50

8. You deposit \$500 into a savings account that earns 3% simple annual interest. What will be the balance in the account after 3 years? *(p. 331)*

Ⓐ \$45 Ⓑ \$515

Ⓒ \$545 Ⓓ \$950

NS 2.0 Students calculate and solve problems involving addition, subtraction, multiplication, and division:

NS 2.1 Solve problems involving addition, subtraction, multiplication, and division of positive fractions and explain why a particular operation was used for a given situation.

9. You are building a fence that is 18 feet long. On Thursday you build $5\frac{3}{4}$ feet of the fence. On Friday you build $4\frac{2}{3}$ feet more of the fence. How many feet do you have left to build? *(p. 81)*

Ⓐ $7\frac{7}{12}$ feet Ⓑ $10\frac{5}{12}$ feet

Ⓒ $16\frac{11}{12}$ feet Ⓓ $28\frac{5}{12}$ feet

10. A recipe for chicken salad calls for 2 cups of diced cooked chicken, 1 cup of diced celery, and $\frac{1}{2}$ cup of mayonnaise. You want to make half the recipe. How many cups of ingredients will you need? *(p. 88)*

Ⓐ $\frac{1}{7}$ cup Ⓑ $1\frac{3}{4}$ cups

Ⓒ $3\frac{1}{2}$ cups Ⓓ 7 cups

Go On 

NS 2.2 Explain the meaning of multiplication and division of positive fractions and perform the calculations $\left(\text{e.g., } \frac{5}{8} \div \frac{15}{16} = \frac{5}{8} \times \frac{16}{15} = \frac{2}{3}\right)$.

11. The entire rectangle below represents one whole. Which expression represents the part that is enclosed by the red rectangle? *(p. 88)*

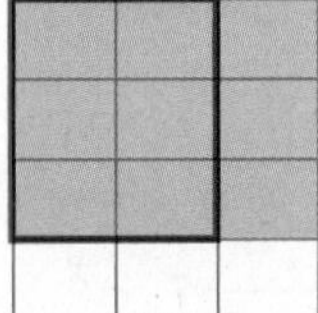

Ⓐ $\frac{3}{4} \div \frac{2}{3}$ Ⓑ $\frac{2}{3} \times \frac{3}{4}$

Ⓒ $\frac{2}{3} + \frac{3}{4}$ Ⓓ $1 \div \frac{3}{4}$

12. Which of the following expressions is *not* equivalent to the others? *(p. 95)*

Ⓐ $1\frac{2}{3} \div 2\frac{3}{4}$

Ⓑ $\frac{5}{3} \div \frac{11}{4}$

Ⓒ $\frac{5}{3} \times \frac{4}{11}$

Ⓓ $\frac{3}{5} \times \frac{11}{4}$

NS 2.3 Solve addition, subtraction, multiplication, and division problems, including those arising in concrete situations, that use positive and negative integers and combinations of these operations.

13. Emily and Alberto are playing a video game. Emily has 520 points. Alberto has −80 points. What is the difference between Emily's score and Alberto's score? *(p. 143)*

Ⓐ −600 Ⓑ −440

Ⓒ 440 Ⓓ 600

14. $-20 \div (-5) =$ *(p. 154)*

Ⓐ −25

Ⓑ −4

Ⓒ 4

Ⓓ 15

NS 2.4 Determine the least common multiple and the greatest common divisor of whole numbers; use them to solve problems with fractions (e.g., to find a common denominator to add two fractions or to find the reduced form for a fraction).

15. What is the least common multiple of 6, 9, and 12? *(p. 21)*

Ⓐ 648 Ⓑ 108

Ⓒ 36 Ⓓ 3

16. $\frac{8}{15} - \frac{1}{3} =$ *(p. 75)*

Ⓐ $\frac{7}{45}$ Ⓑ $\frac{1}{5}$

Ⓒ $\frac{7}{15}$ Ⓓ $\frac{7}{12}$

Grade 6 Algebra and Functions

AF 1.0 Students write verbal expressions and sentences as algebraic expressions and equations; they evaluate algebraic expressions, solve simple linear equations, and graph and interpret their results:

AF 1.1 Write and solve one-step linear equations in one variable.

17. The eruption of a volcano decreased its elevation by 1313 feet. The volcano now has an elevation of 8364 feet. Which equation can you use to find the original elevation, v, of the volcano? *(p. 226)*

Ⓐ $v - 1313 = 8364$

Ⓑ $8364 - v = 1313$

Ⓒ $v + 1313 = 8364$

Ⓓ $1313 - v = 8364$

18. What value of t makes the equation $\frac{t}{4} = 40$ true? *(p. 234)*

Ⓐ 0.1

Ⓑ 10

Ⓒ 36

Ⓓ 160

AF 1.2 Write and evaluate an algebraic expression for a given situation, using up to three variables.

19. Which expression gives the total value in dollars of p pennies, n nickels, and d dimes? *(p. 202)*

Ⓐ $p + n + d$

Ⓑ $0.16(p + n + d)$

Ⓒ $p + 5n + 10d$

Ⓓ $0.01p + 0.05n + 0.1d$

20. The cost of admission to a movie is \$8. A drink costs \$2.50. You buy your ticket. You also buy a drink for you and each of f friends. Which expression gives the total amount of money that you spent? *(p. 202)*

Ⓐ $8 + 2.5f$ Ⓑ $(8 + 2.5)f$

Ⓒ $8 + 2.5(f + 1)$ Ⓓ $8 + 2.5f + 1$

AF 1.3 Apply algebraic order of operations and the commutative, associative, and distributive properties to evaluate expressions; and justify each step in the process.

21. Which expression does *not* have the same value as $5 + 3(9 - 7)$? *(p. 173)*

Ⓐ $5 + 3 \times 9 - 3 \times 7$

Ⓑ $8(9 - 7)$

Ⓒ $3(9 - 7) + 5$

Ⓓ $5 + (9 - 7)(3)$

22. Jared started to evaluate the expression $6 \div 3 + 4 \times 8$ as follows:

$$6 \div 3 + 4 \times 8 = 2 + 4 \times 8$$

What should be the next operation in evaluating the expression? *(p. 160)*

Ⓐ 2 plus 4. Ⓑ 2 plus 8.

Ⓑ 2 times 8. Ⓓ 4 times 8.

Go On 

Standards Practice

AF 1.4 Solve problems manually by using the correct order of operations or by using a scientific calculator.

23. $10 - 3 \times 2 + 4^2 =$ *(p. 160)*

Ⓐ 20

Ⓑ 30

Ⓒ 64

Ⓓ 324

24. $(8 - 1)(3) + (20 + 10) \div 5 - 2 =$ *(p. 160)*

Ⓐ 9

Ⓑ 25

Ⓒ 31

Ⓓ 41

AF 2.0 Students analyze and use tables, graphs, and rules to solve problems involving rates and proportions:

AF 2.1 Convert one unit of measurement to another (e.g., from feet to miles, from centimeters to inches).

25. The formula $F = \frac{9}{5}C + 32$ relates a Celsius temperature (*C*) and a Fahrenheit temperature (*F*). What is 30°C in degrees Fahrenheit? *(p. 212)*

Ⓐ 38°F

Ⓑ 48.7°F

Ⓒ 86°F

Ⓓ 302°F

26. How many yards are in 45 inches? *(p. 520)*

Ⓐ $1\frac{1}{4}$ yards

Ⓑ $1\frac{1}{2}$ yards

Ⓒ $1\frac{9}{10}$ yards

Ⓓ $3\frac{3}{4}$ yards

AF 2.2 Demonstrate an understanding that *rate* is a measure of one quantity per unit value of another quantity.

27. Edward has a part-time job at the library and earns a fixed amount of money per hour. Last week he earned $116 for 16 hours of work. This week he earned $159.50. How many hours did he work this week? *(p. 274)*

Ⓐ 18 hours

Ⓑ 20 hours

Ⓒ 22 hours

Ⓓ 24 hours

28. You can make 6 hours of phone calls using a calling card that costs you $18. How much money are you paying per minute when using the card? *(p. 274)*

Ⓐ $.03

Ⓑ $.05

Ⓒ $.20

Ⓓ $3.00

Grade 6 | **Algebra and Functions**

AF 2.3 Solve problems involving rates, average speed, distance, and time.

29. Laura drives 160 miles from San Diego to Santa Clarita. The trip lasts 2 hours 40 minutes. What is her average speed? ***(p. 260)***

Ⓐ 40 miles per hour

Ⓑ 60 miles per hour

Ⓒ 64 miles per hour

Ⓓ $66\frac{2}{3}$ miles per hour

30. A bus travels 15 miles from Sacramento to Davis in 18 minutes. Then the bus travels from Davis to Oakland in 80 minutes. The average speed between Davis and Oakland is the same as between Sacramento and Davis. What is the approximate distance from Sacramento to Oakland? ***(p. 260)***

Ⓐ 52 miles Ⓑ 67 miles

Ⓒ 82 miles Ⓓ 96 miles

AF 3.0 Students investigate geometric patterns and describe them algebraically:

AF 3.1 Use variables in expressions describing geometric quantities (e.g., $P = 2w + 2l$, $A = \frac{1}{2}bh$, $C = \pi d$ — the formulas for the perimeter of a rectangle, the area of a triangle, and the circumference of a circle, respectively).

31. The height of a triangle is h. The base of the triangle is twice the height. What is the area of the triangle in terms of h? ***(p. 541)***

Ⓐ $\frac{1}{4}h^2$

Ⓑ $\frac{1}{2}h^2$

Ⓒ h^2

Ⓓ $2h^2$

32. A rectangle with a base of 8 and a height of 6 is inside a square with a side of s, as shown. Which expression represents the area of the shaded region in terms of s? ***(p. 212)***

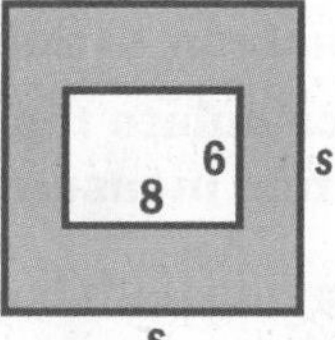

Ⓐ $s^2 - 48$ Ⓑ $s^2 + 48$

Ⓒ $4s - 28$ Ⓓ $4s + 28$

Go On

Standards Practice

AF 3.2 Express in symbolic form simple relationships arising from geometry.

33. A rectangle has a width of 10 meters and a perimeter of P meters. Which equation could be used to find the length l (in meters) of the rectangle? *(p. 212)*

Ⓐ $P = 2l + 10$ Ⓑ $P = 2l + 20$

Ⓒ $P = l + 5$ Ⓓ $P = l + 20$

34. A triangle has a base of 12 inches and an area of A square inches. Which equation could be used to find the height h (in inches) of the triangle? *(p. 541)*

Ⓐ $A = \frac{h}{12}$ Ⓑ $A = 6h$

Ⓒ $A = 12h$ Ⓓ $A = 24h$

MG 1.0 Students deepen their understanding of the measurement of plane and solid shapes and use this understanding to solve problems:

MG 1.1 Understand the concept of a constant such as π; know the formulas for the circumference and area of a circle.

35. Which equation could be used to find the area in square feet of a circle with a radius of 10 feet? *(p. 555)*

Ⓐ $A = 10 \times \pi$

Ⓑ $A = 20 \times \pi$

Ⓒ $A = 25 \times \pi$

Ⓓ $A = 100 \times \pi$

36. A circular hoop has a diameter of 30 inches. Which equation can be used to find the circumference, C, in inches? *(p. 549)*

Ⓐ $C = 15 \times \pi$

Ⓑ $C = 30 \times \pi$

Ⓒ $C = 2 \times 30 \times \pi$

Ⓓ $C = 15^2 \times \pi$

MG 1.2 Know common estimates of $\pi \left(3.14; \frac{22}{7}\right)$ and use these values to estimate and calculate the circumference and the area of circles; compare with actual measurements.

37. A circular jogging path has a radius of 15 feet. About how far will you travel if you jog around the path three times? *(p. 549)*

Ⓐ 94.2 ft

Ⓑ 141.3 ft

Ⓒ 282.6 ft

Ⓓ 706.5 ft

38. What is the area of a circle with a diameter of 14 millimeters? *(p. 555)*

Ⓐ 7π, or about 21.98 mm^2

Ⓑ 14π, or about 43.96 mm^2

Ⓒ 49π, or about 153.86 mm^2

Ⓓ 196π, or about 615.44 mm^2

MG 1.3 Know and use the formulas for the volume of triangular prisms and cylinders (area of base × height); compare these formulas and explain the similarity between them and the formula for the volume of a rectangular solid.

39. Which equation can be used to find the volume V (in cubic meters) of the cylinder below? *(p. 601)*

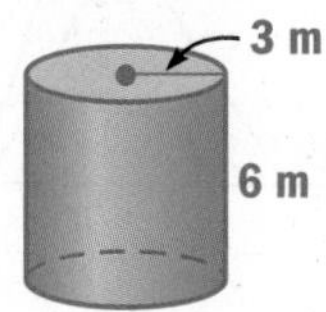

Ⓐ $V = \pi \times 3 \times 3$

Ⓑ $V = \pi \times 3 \times 6$

Ⓒ $V = \pi \times 6 \times 6$

Ⓓ $V = \pi \times 9 \times 6$

40. What is the volume of the triangular prism below? *(p. 596)*

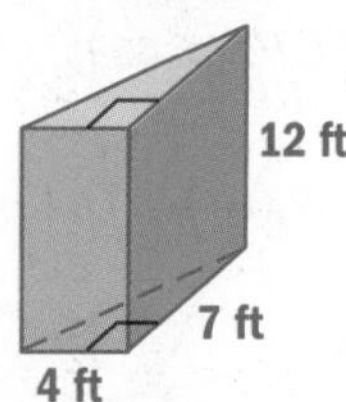

Ⓐ 23 cubic feet

Ⓑ 132 cubic feet

Ⓒ 168 cubic feet

Ⓓ 336 cubic feet

MG 2.0 Students identify and describe the properties of two-dimensional figures:

MG 2.1 Identify angles as vertical, adjacent, complementary, or supplementary and provide descriptions of these terms.

41. In the diagram below, which angle forms a vertical pair with ∠2? *(p. 468)*

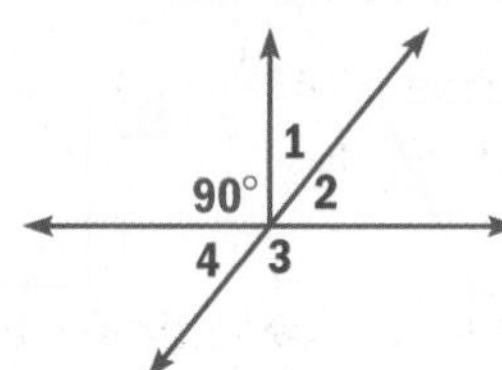

Ⓐ ∠1

Ⓑ ∠3

Ⓒ ∠4

Ⓓ the angle marked 90°

42. In the diagram below, which pair of angles are adjacent and complementary? *(p. 468)*

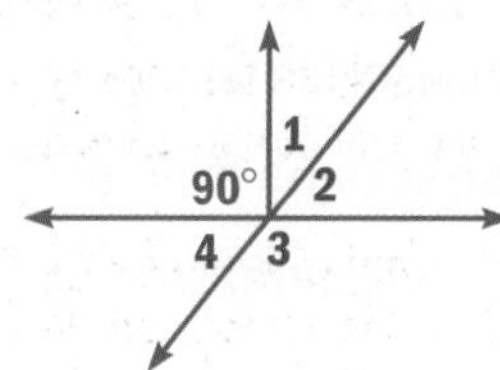

Ⓐ ∠1 and ∠2

Ⓑ ∠1 and ∠4

Ⓒ ∠2 and ∠4

Ⓓ ∠3 and ∠4

Go On 

Standards Practice

MG 2.2 Use the properties of complementary and supplementary angles and the sum of the angles of a triangle to solve problems involving an unknown angle.

43. In the figure below, $\angle BGC$ and $\angle CGD$ are complementary, $\angle CGD$ and $\angle DGE$ are complementary, and $m\angle CGD = 40°$. What is $m\angle EGF$? *(p. 463)*

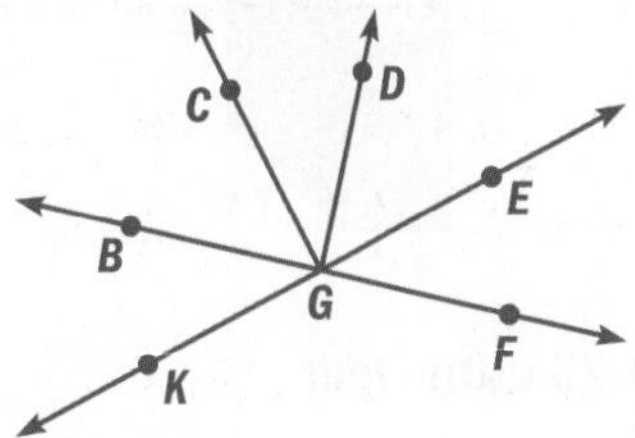

Ⓐ 20°

Ⓑ 40°

Ⓒ 50°

Ⓓ 90°

44. In the figure below, what is the measure of $\angle 2$? *(p. 474)*

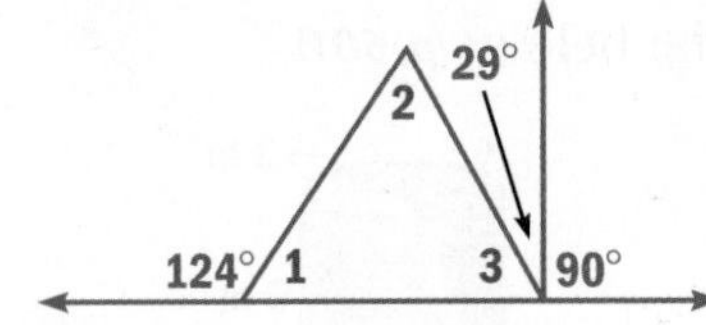

Ⓐ 56°

Ⓑ 61°

Ⓒ 63°

Ⓓ 119°

MG 2.3 Draw quadrilaterals and triangles from given information about them (e.g., a quadrilateral having equal sides but no right angles, a right isosceles triangle).

45. Which figure *cannot* be drawn? *(p. 474)*

Ⓐ Acute equilateral triangle

Ⓑ Right isosceles triangle

Ⓒ Obtuse scalene triangle

Ⓓ Right equilateral triangle

46. Which quadrilateral has exactly one pair of parallel sides? *(p. 482)*

Ⓐ 

Ⓑ 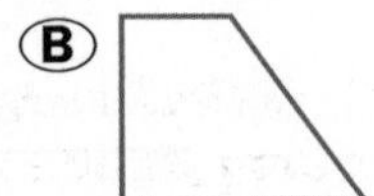

Ⓒ 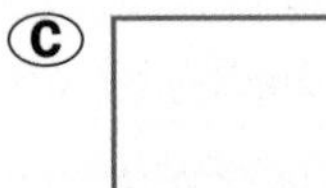

 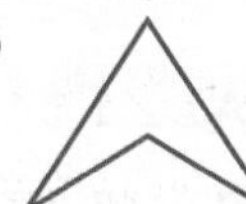

Grade 6 | Statistics, Data Analysis, and Probability

SDAP 1.0 Students compute and analyze statistical measurements for data sets:

SDAP 1.1 Compute the range, mean, median, and mode of data sets.

47. Which list of numbers has a mean that is 1 less than the median? *(p. 364)*

Ⓐ 4, 12, 7, 5, 2, 12

Ⓑ 2, 10, 4, 2, 11, 10

Ⓒ 7, 6, 11, 2

Ⓓ 8, 4, 7, 3, 8

48. Which list shows the mean, median, mode, and range—*in that order*—of the list of numbers below? *(p. 372)*

6, 8, 15, 3, 15, 11, 8, 6, 12, 6

Ⓐ 9, 8, 6, 12 Ⓑ 9, 6, 8, 12

Ⓒ 8, 9, 12, 6 Ⓓ 8, 12, 6, 9

SDAP 1.2 Understand how additional data added to data sets may affect these computations.

49. You find the mean, median, mode, and range of this list of numbers.

5, 7, 8, 8

If you add the number 6 to the list, then *(pp. 364, 372)*

Ⓐ the mean will decrease.

Ⓑ the median will increase.

Ⓒ the mode will decrease.

Ⓓ the range will increase.

50. Adding which number to the list below would decrease the mean and increase the median? *(p. 364)*

6, 9, 10, 19

Ⓐ 12

Ⓑ 10

Ⓒ 9.5

Ⓓ 8

SDAP 1.3 Understand how the inclusion or exclusion of outliers affects these computations.

51. In the data set below, 56 is an outlier.

4, 7, 9, 10, 11, 12, 12, 15, 16, 21, 22, 56

If you *exclude* the outlier, which statement about the data set will be true? *(p. 372)*

Ⓐ The range will increase.

Ⓑ The median will decrease.

Ⓒ The mean will decrease.

Ⓓ The mode will increase.

52. You find the mean, median, and mode of a data set. Then you *include* an outlier that is less than all the other values in the set. Which measure(s) of central tendency will always decrease? *(p. 372)*

Ⓐ Mean

Ⓑ Median

Ⓒ Mode

Ⓓ Mean, median, and mode

Go On 

Standards Practice

SDAP 1.4 Know why a specific measure of central tendency (mean, median) provides the most useful information in a given context.

53. The list below shows the hourly wages of six employees in an office.

$7.50, $10.50, $11.00,
$7.50, $12.50, $29.00

Which measure is *most* useful in describing the average wage of an employee? *(pp. 364, 372)*

Ⓐ Mean　Ⓑ Median

Ⓒ Mode　Ⓓ Range

54. The list below shows the ages of people at a birthday party.

5, 5, 7, 6, 8, 6, 7, 6, 35, 42

Which measure is *least* useful in describing the typical age of a person at the party? *(p. 364)*

Ⓐ Mean　Ⓑ Median

Ⓒ Mode　Ⓓ None of these

SDAP 2.0 Students use data samples of a population and describe the characteristics and limitations of the samples:

SDAP 2.1 Compare different samples of a population with the data from the entire population and identify a situation in which it makes sense to use a sample.

55. You ask two samples of 12 sixth grade students at your school how many hours per night they do homework. The list below shows their responses.

Sample A: 2, 1.5, 2, 3, 2.5, 2,
1, 2, 1.5, 2.5, 3.5, 2

Sample B: 1.5, 2, 2.5, 2, 2, 1.5,
2, 1.5, 1, 1, 1.5, 2

Suppose that the mean number of hours spent on homework per night for all sixth grade students at your school is 2. Which statement is true? *(p. 354)*

Ⓐ The mean of sample A is greater than the mean of the population.

Ⓑ The mean of sample A is less than the mean of the population.

Ⓒ The mean of sample B is greater than the mean of the population.

Ⓓ The mean of sample A is less than the mean of sample B.

56. In which situation does it make the *most* sense to survey a sample to collect the data? *(p. 354)*

Ⓐ A family wants to gather information from other residents who live on the same block about having a neighborhood picnic.

Ⓑ Your friend sends out 200 invitations for a wedding and wants to know how many people who are invited plan to attend.

Ⓒ A teacher asks students in a class which of three places they prefer for a field trip.

Ⓓ A librarian in a city library wants to know which library services that the residents would like added.

SDAP 2.2 Identify different ways of selecting a sample (e.g., convenience sampling, responses to a survey, random sampling) and which method makes a sample more representative for a population.

57. A newspaper reporter wants to find out whether people support the construction of a new mall. The reporter interviews commuters at a bus stop near the reporter's place of work. Which sampling method did the reporter use? *(p. 354)*

Ⓐ Convenience

Ⓑ Random

Ⓒ Self-selected

Ⓓ Systematic

58. The principal at a school wants to know if more vegetarian items should be added to the lunch menu. Which of the following methods is the *best* way for the principal to choose a representative sample of students at the school? *(p. 354)*

Ⓐ Asking the first 20 students in the lunch line

Ⓑ Selecting every tenth student on an alphabetized list

Ⓒ Distributing surveys and asking students to return them

Ⓓ Asking students who visit the office during the week

Go On 

SDAP 2.3 **Analyze data displays and explain why the way in which the question was asked might have influenced the results obtained and why the way in which the results were displayed might have influenced the conclusions reached.**

59. Customers at a supermarket are surveyed about their eating habits. The survey question and the results are displayed below.

Question: Do you try to eat foods that are good for your health?

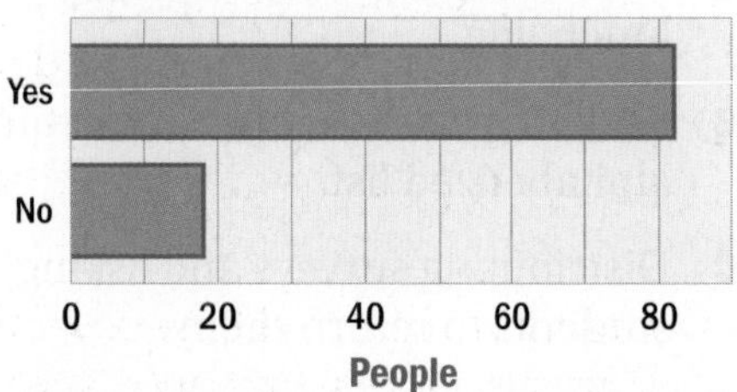

Your friend claims that most people eat foods that are good for their health. Which of the following would be the *most* likely reason for the claim to be invalid? *(p. 359)*

Ⓐ The results were displayed in a bar graph.

Ⓑ You surveyed customers at different times of the day.

Ⓒ You surveyed every tenth customer that entered the supermarket.

Ⓓ The question you asked was biased.

60. You ask 100 students to name their favorite room in which to study. The results are displayed below.

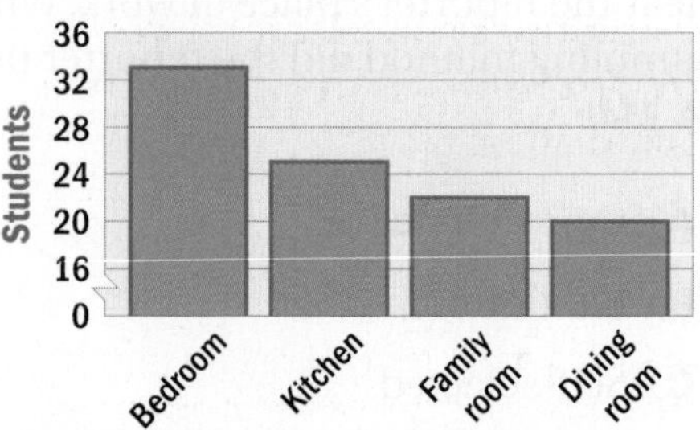

You claim that about twice as many students prefer to study in their bedroom as in the family room. What is the *most* likely reason the graph could lead to this invalid conclusion? *(p. 392)*

Ⓐ The scale on the vertical axis does not go high enough.

Ⓑ The bars are too far from one another.

Ⓒ The scale on the vertical axis is not spread out enough.

Ⓓ The break in the vertical scale distorts the relative heights of the bars.

SDAP 2.4 Identify data that represent sampling errors and explain why the sample (and the display) might be biased.

61. You want to know the opinions of voters in your city about a new convention center. You survey people who live on your street. The survey question and the results are shown below.

Question: Do you support the construction of a new convention center in our city?

Response	*People*
Yes	7
No	3

Which of the following sampling errors does *not* apply to this situation? *(p. 359)*

Ⓐ You didn't ask enough people.

Ⓑ Some of the people you asked were not voters.

Ⓒ The question is biased.

Ⓓ The people who live on your street are not representative of the entire population of voters in your city.

62. Which situation is *least* likely to produce biased results? *(p. 359)*

Ⓐ You conduct a survey about recycling. You dial the first phone number listed on every tenth page in a phone book.

Ⓑ You want to find the average number of sports events that students in your school attend per year. You survey members of the men's and women's basketball teams.

Ⓒ A teacher wants to know how long students studied for a test. The teacher includes the following as the last question on the test: How many hours did you study for this test?

Ⓓ A telephone poll about people's favorite television shows is conducted on Monday and Tuesday mornings from 9 A.M. to 12 P.M.

Go On 

SDAP 2.5 Identify claims based on statistical data and, in simple cases, evaluate the validity of the claims.

63. The table below shows the fuel economies for 20 cars.

Fuel Economy (miles per gallon)									
34	28	36	38	28	30	40	38	26	22
32	34	32	44	42	40	20	22	26	30

Which statement is valid about the fuel economies of the cars? *(pp. 364, 372)*

Ⓐ The mean fuel economy is greater than the median fuel economy.

Ⓑ The range of the fuel economies is 25 miles per gallon.

Ⓒ One fourth of the fuel economies are less than 26 miles per gallon.

Ⓓ Most of the fuel economies are less than 30 miles per gallon.

64. A restaurant manager wants to know whether customers like the food at the restaurant. The table below shows the results of an unbiased survey of 200 randomly selected customers.

Response	*Customers*
Positive	97
Negative	76
No opinion	37

Which statement is valid about the customer responses? *(p. 392)*

Ⓐ There were more negative responses than positive responses.

Ⓑ More than half of the responses were positive.

Ⓒ Less than 10% of the customers did not have an opinion.

Ⓓ Of the customers who had an opinion, more than 55% of them gave a positive response.

SDAP 3.0 Students determine theoretical and experimental probabilities and use these to make predictions about events:

SDAP 3.1 Represent all possible outcomes for compound events in an organized way (e.g., tables, grids, tree diagrams) and express the theoretical probability of each outcome.

65. The table below shows the different outcomes when flipping a fair coin and rolling a number cube.

	H	*T*
1	H1	T1
2	H2	T2
3	H3	T3
4	H4	T4
5	H5	T5
6	H6	T6

You flip a coin and roll a number cube. What is the probability that you will get tails and roll an even number? *(p. 434)*

Ⓐ $\frac{1}{2}$

Ⓑ $\frac{1}{4}$

Ⓒ $\frac{1}{6}$

Ⓓ $\frac{1}{12}$

66. You want to find all the two-digit numbers that can be formed from the digits 1, 2, and 3 without using the same digit twice. Which tree diagram can be used to find all the outcomes? *(p. 434)*

Ⓐ
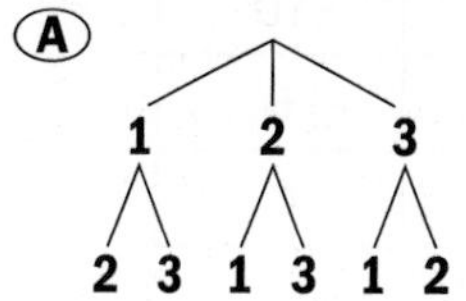

Ⓑ
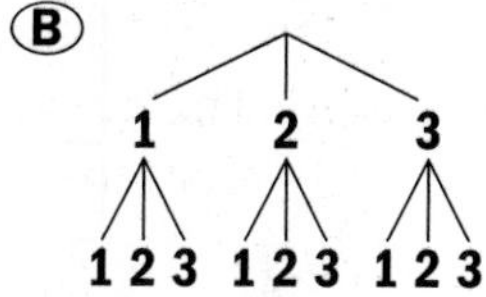

Ⓒ
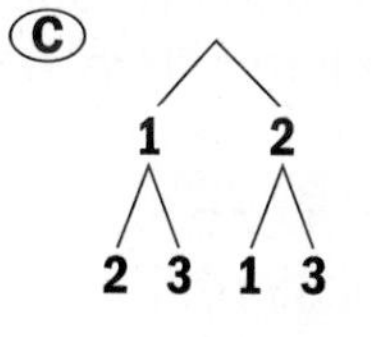

Ⓓ
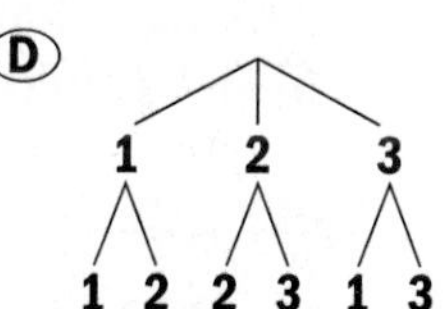

SDAP 3.2 Use data to estimate the probability of future events (e.g., batting averages or number of accidents per mile driven).

67. A company makes hand grips for bicycles. The company tests a random sample of 200 hand grips and finds 3 of them to be defective. What is the estimated probability that a randomly chosen hand grip in a large shipment will be defective? *(p. 422)*

Ⓐ 0.015%

Ⓑ 0.15%

Ⓒ 1.5%

Ⓓ 15%

68. During a basketball season, Sara makes 20 free throws in her first 25 attempts. If Sara attempts 30 more free throws, how many more free throws can she be expected to make? *(p. 422)*

Ⓐ 17

Ⓑ 20

Ⓒ 24

Ⓓ 25

Go On

SDAP 3.3 Represent probabilities as ratios, proportions, decimals between 0 and 1, and percentages between 0 and 100 and verify that the probabilities computed are reasonable; know that if *P* is the probability of an event, 1 − *P* is the probability of an event not occurring.

69. The table shows the numbers of tiles printed with different letters that are inside a bag.

Letter	Tiles
M	13
A	10
T	6
H	11

You choose a tile from the bag without looking. What is the probability that the tile is printed with the letter H? *(p. 415)*

Ⓐ 11%　Ⓑ 22%

Ⓒ 25%　Ⓓ 27.5%

70. The probability that a person chosen at random is left-handed is $\frac{1}{10}$. What is the probability that a person chosen at random is *not* left-handed? *(p. 427)*

Ⓐ 0.1

Ⓑ 0.5

Ⓒ 0.9

Ⓓ 1

SDAP 3.4 Understand that the probability of either of two disjoint events occurring is the sum of the two individual probabilities and that the probability of one event following another, in independent trials, is the product of the two probabilities.

71. A bucket contains 8 yellow, 10 green, and 2 white tennis balls. You choose a ball without looking. What is the probability that the ball will be green or white? *(p. 427)*

Ⓐ $\frac{1}{10}$

Ⓑ $\frac{1}{2}$

Ⓒ $\frac{3}{5}$

Ⓓ $\frac{9}{10}$

72. You roll a number cube twice. What is the probability that you will roll a 4 on the first roll and a number less than 3 on the second roll? *(p. 441)*

Ⓐ $\frac{1}{18}$

Ⓑ $\frac{1}{12}$

Ⓒ $\frac{2}{9}$

Ⓓ $\frac{1}{2}$

Grade 6 | Statistics, Data Analysis, and Probability; Mathematical Reasoning

SDAP 3.5 Understand the difference between independent and dependent events.

73. Which two events are dependent? *(p. 441)*

Ⓐ Flipping a coin and rolling a number cube

Ⓑ Drawing a card from a deck of cards and not putting it back in the deck, then drawing a second card

Ⓒ Spinning a spinner twice

Ⓓ Choosing a marble from a bag of marbles and putting it back in the bag, then choosing a second marble

74. A bag contains 10 red and 6 white marbles. You choose a marble at random and do not put it back in the bag. Then you choose a second marble at random. What is the probability that both marbles will be red? *(p. 441)*

Ⓐ $\frac{1}{8}$

Ⓑ $\frac{3}{8}$

Ⓒ $\frac{25}{64}$

Ⓓ $\frac{5}{12}$

MR 1.0 Students make decisions about how to approach problems:

MR 1.1 Analyze problems by identifying relationships, distinguishing relevant from irrelevant information, identifying missing information, sequencing and prioritizing information, and observing patterns.

75. Flora drives for 1.5 hours at an average speed of 52 miles per hour. She stops for 45 minutes to have lunch. Then she drives for another 1.25 hours at an average speed of 45 miles per hour. Her car can travel 24 miles per gallon of gas. What information is *not* needed to find the number of gallons of gas her car used for the trip? *(p. 212)*

Ⓐ The time she drove for each part of the trip

Ⓑ The speed at which she drove for each part of the trip

Ⓒ The time spent for lunch

Ⓓ The gas mileage of the car

Go On 

MR 1.2 Formulate and justify mathematical conjectures based on a general description of the mathematical question or problem posed.

76. The product of four integers is negative. Which of the following could be true about the integers? ***(p. 148)***

Ⓐ All four integers are negative.

Ⓑ One integer is positive, and three integers are negative.

Ⓒ Two integers are positive, and two integers are negative.

Ⓓ All four integers are positive.

MR 1.3 Determine when and how to break a problem into simpler parts.

77. Square A has a side length of 8 inches. Square B has a side length of x inches. Square B is inside square A. To find the area of the region that is inside square A but outside square B, first you find the areas of both squares. What is the next step? ***(p. 212)***

Ⓐ Add the two areas.

Ⓑ Subtract the area of B from the area of A.

Ⓒ Subtract the area of A from the area of B.

Ⓓ Find the ratio of the area of B to the area of A.

MR 2.0 Students use strategies, skills, and concepts in finding solutions:

MR 2.1 Use estimation to verify the reasonableness of calculated results.

78. Jenna's lunch bill is \$10. She leaves an 18% tip. The sales tax is 7.25%. Which is the most reasonable estimate of the total amount that Jenna will pay? ***(p. 325)***

Ⓐ \$11.50 Ⓑ \$12.00

Ⓒ \$12.50 Ⓓ \$13.00

Grade 6 | Mathematical Reasoning

MR 2.2 Apply strategies and results from simpler problems to more complex problems.

79. The tree diagram shows the four different outcomes from flipping a fair coin twice. How many different outcomes result from flipping a fair coin four times? *(p. 434)*

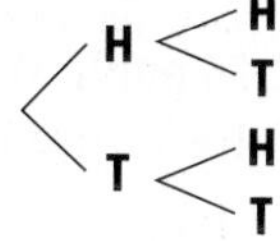

Ⓐ 4 Ⓑ 8

Ⓒ 16 Ⓓ 32

MR 2.3 Estimate known quantities graphically and solve for them by using logical reasoning and arithmetic and algebraic techniques.

80. The graph relates U.S. dollars and Mexican pesos. Which of the following best approximates the value of $20 in Mexican pesos? *(p. 527)*

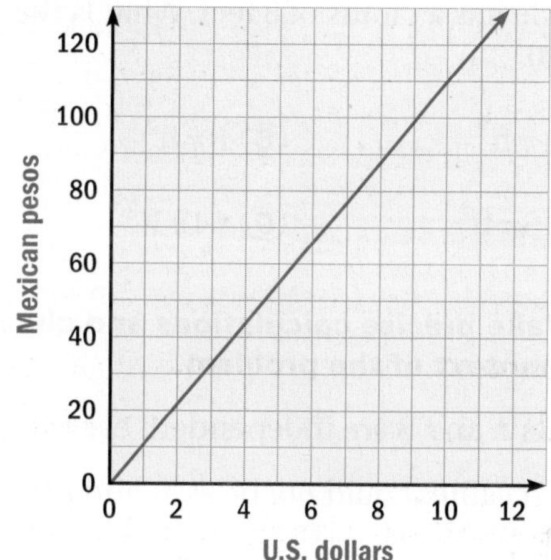

Ⓐ 2 pesos Ⓑ 120 pesos

Ⓒ 200 pesos Ⓓ 220 pesos

MR 2.4 Use a variety of methods, such as words, numbers, symbols, charts, graphs, tables, diagrams, and models, to explain mathematical reasoning.

81. The equation $x + 4 = 7$ is represented by the model below.

Which model represents the solution of the equation? *(p. 219)*

Ⓐ  Ⓑ 

Ⓒ  Ⓓ 

Go On 

Standards Practice

MR 2.5 Express the solution clearly and logically by using the appropriate mathematical notation and terms and clear language; support solutions with evidence in both verbal and symbolic work.

82. You buy 6 sandwiches for \$2.75 each. Which expression *cannot* be used to find the total cost of the sandwiches? *(p. 173)*

Ⓐ 6(2) + 6(0.75) Ⓑ 6(3) − 6(0.25)

Ⓒ 6(3 − 0.25) Ⓓ 6(3) + 6(0.25)

MR 2.6 Indicate the relative advantages of exact and approximate solutions to problems and give answers to a specified degree of accuracy.

83. A circle has a radius of 8 feet. What is the exact area of the circle? *(p. 555)*

Ⓐ 4π ft^2 Ⓑ 8π ft^2

Ⓒ 16π ft^2 Ⓓ 64π ft^2

MR 2.7 Make precise calculations and check the validity of the results from the context of the problem.

84. Events A and B are independent events with $P(\text{A and B}) = \frac{1}{4}$.

Which values could *not* be $P(\text{A})$ and $P(\text{B})$ respectively? *(p. 441)*

Ⓐ $\frac{1}{2}, \frac{1}{2}$ Ⓑ $\frac{2}{5}, \frac{5}{8}$

Ⓒ $\frac{1}{3}, \frac{3}{4}$ Ⓓ $\frac{1}{7}, \frac{7}{8}$

MR 3.0 Students move beyond a particular problem by generalizing to other situations:

MR 3.1 Evaluate the reasonableness of the solution in the context of the original problem.

85. You are buying hot dogs and hot dog buns for a picnic. Hot dog buns are sold in packages of 8. Hot dogs are sold in packages of 10. You want to have the same number of hot dogs as hot dog buns. What is the least number of packages of hot dog buns you can buy? *(p. 21)*

Ⓐ 4 Ⓑ 5

Ⓒ 40 Ⓓ 80

MR 3.2 Note the method of deriving the solution and demonstrate a conceptual understanding of the derivation by solving similar problems.

86. You run 5 miles around a high school track. Each lap of the track is $\frac{1}{4}$ mile. How many laps do you run?

Which of the following problems can be solved using the same arithmetic operation used to solve the problem above? *(p. 95)*

Ⓐ You have a part-time job mowing lawns. You earn \$9 for mowing a lawn in $\frac{3}{4}$ hour. How much money do you earn per hour?

Ⓑ You practice the piano for $1\frac{1}{2}$ hours per day. How many hours do you practice in 7 days?

Ⓒ A baking recipe calls for $4\frac{1}{4}$ cups of flour. You have $2\frac{1}{2}$ cups of flour. How many more cups of flour do you need?

Ⓓ You bike $1\frac{1}{3}$ miles from your house to the park. Then you bike $2\frac{1}{4}$ miles from the park to your friend's house. How many miles do you bike?

MR 3.3 Develop generalizations of the results obtained and the strategies used and apply them in new problem situations.

87. Judy used the following process to find the area of a trapezoid with a height of 7 inches and bases of 3 inches and 9 inches.

Step 1: Find the sum of the bases.
$3 + 9 = 12$

Step 2: Multiply the result in Step 1 by the height.
$12 \cdot 7 = 84$

Step 3: Divide the result in Step 2 by 2.
$\frac{84}{2} = 42$

The area of the trapezoid is 42 square inches.

Using this method, which expression gives the area of the trapezoid given its height h and bases b_1 and b_2? *(p. 541)*

Ⓐ $b_1 + b_2 + \frac{h}{2}$ Ⓑ $b_1 + \frac{b_2 h}{2}$

Ⓒ $\frac{(b_1 + b_2)h}{2}$ Ⓓ $\frac{b_1 + b_2 h}{2}$

Pre-Course Test

Number Sense

Whole Number Operations *(Standards Review pp. 661–664, 670–671)*

Find the sum, difference, product, quotient, or value of the power.

1. 51,285 + 769
2. 9023 − 849
3. 4244 × 1000
4. 356 × 904
5. 76,324 ÷ 8
6. 485.44 ÷ 8.2
7. 5^4
8. 3 to the sixth power

9. Tickets for a school play are $5. If $3405 was received for ticket sales, how many tickets were sold?

Rounding and Estimation *(Standards Review pp. 665–669, 674)*

Round the number to the place value of the red digit.

10. 15,829
11. 55,505,555
12. 137.999
13. 32.8618

Estimate the sum, difference, product, or quotient.

14. 449 + 481 + 512
15. 66,109 − 12,674
16. 712 × 45
17. 6267 ÷ 79

Fraction and Decimal Concepts *(Standards Review pp. 672–673, 675)*

Write a fraction or mixed number in simplest form to represent the shaded section. In Exercise 20, also write your answer as a decimal.

18. 8 circles = 1

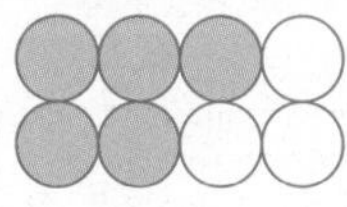

19. large triangle = 1

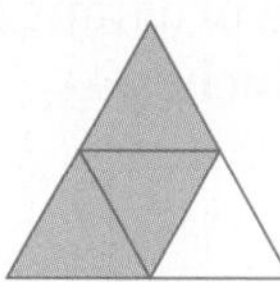

20. one 10-by-10 base-ten piece = 1

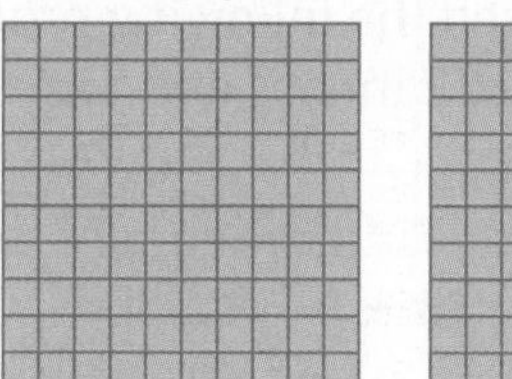

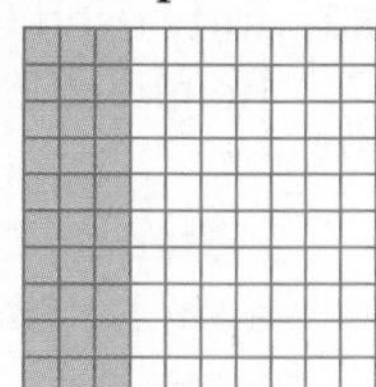

Graph the numbers on a number line.

21. 0.8 and 2
22. 3.3 and 3.14
23. $\frac{5}{6}$ and $2\frac{1}{3}$

Copy and complete the statement with <, >, or =.

24. 5.23 __?__ 5.230
25. 0.51 __?__ 0.499
26. 9.407 __?__ 9.47

Algebra and Functions

Commutative and Associative Properties *(Standards Review pp. 676–677)*

27. Use the commutative and associative properties to evaluate the expression (25 • 87) • 4. *Justify* each step.

Points in a Coordinate Plane *(Standards Review p. 678)*

28. Plot the points (4, 3) and (0, 5) in the same coordinate plane. Label the coordinates.

Measurement and Geometry

Units and Tools for Measurement *(Standards Review pp. 679–682)*

In Exercises 29–31, copy and complete.

29. 5 d 8 h = __?__ h   **30.** 64 d = __?__ wk __?__ d   **31.** 270 sec = __?__ min __?__ sec

32. How long is a trip that starts at 7:48 A.M. and ends at 2:25 P.M.?

33. Choose an appropriate customary unit and metric unit to measure the diameter of a quarter and to measure the weight or mass of a quarter.

34. Use a metric ruler to draw a segment that is 2.7 centimeters long.

35. Use a compass to draw a circle with radius 4 inches.

Identifying and Measuring Geometric Figures
(Standards Review pp. 683–685)

36. Draw $\overrightarrow{RS}$. Then identify the type of figure you drew.

37. Draw a rectangle with length 7 cm and width 3 cm. Find its perimeter.

38. Find the area of the figure at the right.

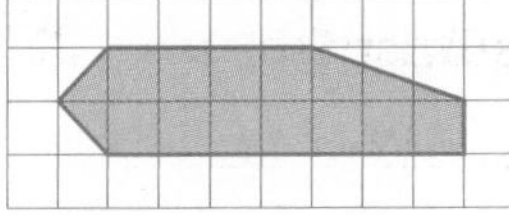

Statistics, Data Analysis, and Probability

Data Displays *(Standards Review pp. 686–688)*

Represent the survey results using the specified data display.

39. Line plot; Books read:
7, 15, 3, 4, 6, 5, 7, 5, 4, 8, 9, 6, 10, 11, 5

40. Bar graph; Favorite color:
purple (36), blue (42), green (28)

41. Use the line graph shown at the right. Between which two hours did the temperature change the most? What was the change?

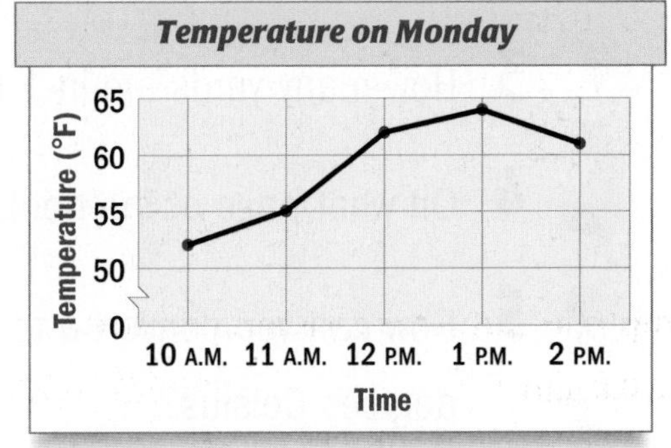

Mathematical Reasoning

Venn Diagrams and Problem Solving *(Standards Review pp. 689–691)*

42. Draw a Venn diagram and answer the questions. Identify any irrelevant information.
There are 26 families that live on Pine Lane. Twelve families own a dog only. All but two of the dogs are taller than two feet. Eight families own a cat only. Three families do not own a dog or a cat. How many families own both a dog and a cat? How many families own a dog?

Pre-Course Test

Practice using your textbook!

Use the student resources described on the next page to answer each question. Give page numbers to show where you found the answer to the question.

1 What is the population of a survey?

2 Tell what each of these symbols means: $|a|$, n^5, π.

3 How many yards are in 1 meter?

4 On what page of the book is the order of operations first discussed?

5 How can you convert a temperature in degrees Fahrenheit to degrees Celsius?

6 What is the probability of an event?

7 On what page can you review the skill of comparing decimals?

8 On what page can you find selected answers for Lesson 1.1?

9 What formula can you use to find the volume of a prism?

Student Resources in Your Textbook

Your textbook contains many resources that you can use for reference when you are studying or doing your homework.

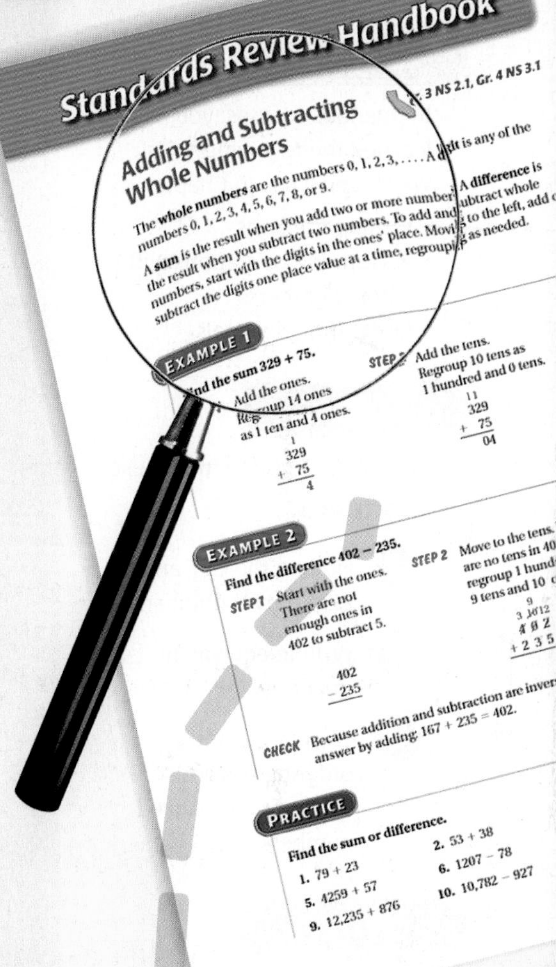

Standards Review Handbook

Adding and Subtracting Whole Numbers

Gr. 3 NS 2.1, Gr. 4 NS 3.1

The **whole numbers** are the numbers 0, 1, 2, 3, ... A digit is any of the numbers 0, 1, 2, 3, 4, 5, 6, 7, 8, or 9.

A **sum** is the result when you add two or more numbers. A **difference** is the result when you subtract two numbers. To add and subtract whole numbers, start with the digits in the ones' place. Moving to the left, add or subtract the digits one place value at a time, regrouping as needed.

EXAMPLE 1

Find the sum 329 + 75.

STEP 1 Add the ones. Regroup 14 ones as 1 ten and 4 ones.

STEP 2 Add the tens. Regroup 10 tens as 1 hundred and 0 tens.

EXAMPLE 2

Find the difference 402 − 235.

STEP 1 Start with the ones. There are not enough ones in 402 to subtract 5.

STEP 2 Move to the tens. There are no tens in 402, so regroup 1 hundred as 9 tens and 10 ones.

CHECK Because addition and subtraction are inverse operations, check your answer by adding: 167 + 235 = 402.

PRACTICE

Find the sum or difference.

1. 79 + 23
2. 53 + 38
5. 4259 + 57
6. 1207 − 78
9. 12,235 + 876
10. 10,782 − 927

Standards Review Handbook Use the Standards Review Handbook on pages 661–691 to review material learned in previous courses.

Tables Refer to the tables on pages 704–709 if you need information about mathematical symbols, measures, formulas, properties, and the squares of numbers.

English-Spanish Glossary Use the English-Spanish Glossary on pages 710–738 to look up the meanings of math vocabulary terms in both English and Spanish. Each glossary entry also tells where in your book a term is covered in more detail.

Index Use the Index on pages 739–756 as a quick guide for finding out where a particular math topic is covered in the book.

Selected Answers Use the Selected Answers starting on page SA1 to check your work or to see whether you are on the right track in solving a problem.

1 Number Patterns and Fractions

Before

In previous courses, you learned the following skills, which you'll use in Chapter 1:

- Writing fractions
- Performing operations with whole numbers
- Comparing decimals

Now

In Chapter 1 you'll study these ***Big Ideas:***

1. Finding the GCF and LCM of two numbers
2. Writing equivalent fractions
3. Comparing and ordering fractions, decimals, and mixed numbers

Why?

So you can solve real-world problems about . . .

- Rose Bowl floats, p. 13
- Mayan calendars, p. 24
- Carousels, p. 32
- Tennis, p. 33
- Kangaroos, p. 44
- Origami, p. 50

Get-Ready Games

OPERATION COVER-UP

California Standards

Review comparing whole numbers. ***Gr. 4 NS 1.2***

Prepare for comparing fractions. ***Gr. 6 NS 1.1***

Materials

- 1 deck of *Operation Cover-Up* cards
- 2 *Operation Cover-Up* game boards

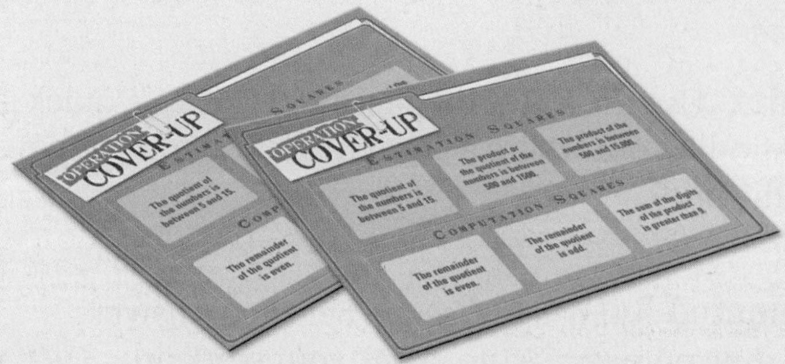

How to Play Play in pairs. Each player has a game board. Shuffle the deck of cards and place it face down where both players can reach it. Players should take turns following the steps on the next page.

CALIFORNIA STANDARDS

- **Gr. 6 NS 1.1 Compare and order positive** and negative **fractions, decimals, and mixed numbers and place them on a number line.** *(Lessons 1.5, 1.6, 1.7)*
- **Gr. 6 NS 2.4 Determine the least common multiple and the greatest common divisor of two whole numbers; use them to solve problems with fractions (e.g., to find a common denominator** to add two fractions **or to find the reduced form for a fraction).** *(Lessons 1.2, 1.3, 1.4)*

1 Draw two cards from the deck.

2 Decide whether the numbers on the cards make any statements on your board true.

3 Cover a statement with the cards if they make the statement true. If the cards do not make any of the statements true, discard them.

How To Win Be the first player to cover all six statements on your game board. Or be the player with the most statements covered when all of the cards have been used.

Games Wrap-Up

Draw Conclusions

Complete these exercises after playing the game.

1. **WRITING** Is it possible for two cards to make all three statements in the Estimation Squares true? *Explain* why or why not.
2. **REASONING** *Explain* why you do not need to calculate exactly to find if a product is between 5000 and 15,000.

Prerequisite Skills

California @HomeTutor

Prerequisite skills practice at classzone.com

REVIEW VOCABULARY

- **factor,** *p. 662*
- **product,** *p. 662*
- **power,** *p. 663*
- **exponent,** *p. 663*
- **dividend,** *p. 664*
- **divisor,** *p. 664*
- **quotient,** *p. 664*
- **remainder,** *p. 664*
- **fraction,** *p. 672*

VOCABULARY CHECK

Copy and complete using a review term from the list at the left.

1. Because $12 \times 14 = 168$, 12 and 14 are each a(n) __?__ of 168.
2. In the expression $144 \div 3$, the number 144 is the __?__.
3. In the expression 6^4, the number 4 is a(n) __?__.

SKILL CHECK

Write a fraction to represent the shaded part of the set or region. ***(p. 672)***

4.

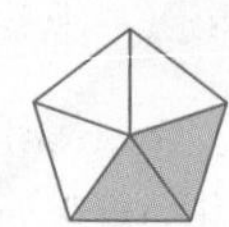

5.

6.

Find the value of the power. ***(p. 663)***

7. 4^4 **8.** 9^2 **9.** 2^4 **10.** 5^3

11. 1^7 **12.** 7^1 **13.** 0^5 **14.** 3^3

Copy and complete the statement using <, >, or =. ***(p. 675)***

15. 4.65 ? 4.194 **16.** 0.032 ? 0.13 **17.** 1.45 ? 1.450

18. 1.735 ? 1.694 **19.** 3 ? 3.000 **20.** 7.395 ? 8.147

Notetaking Skills

NOW YOU TRY

Make a *word triangle* for *quotient*. You may want to use colored pencils.

Focus on Graphic Organizers

Use a *word triangle* to organize information about a new vocabulary word, such as *dividend*.

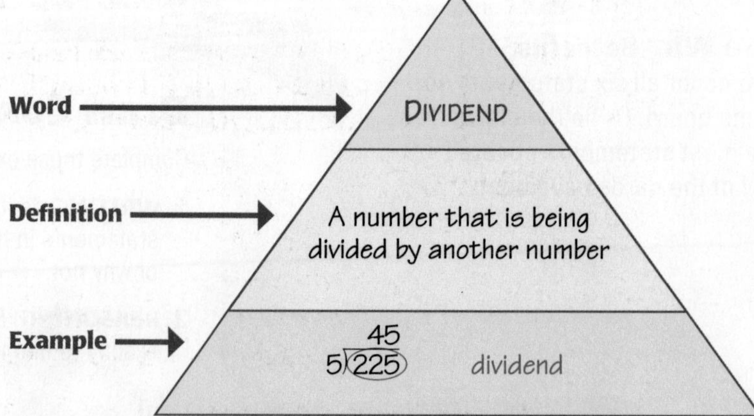

1.1 Prime Factorization

Math and EDUCATION
Example 1, p. 5

Standards Preparation **Gr. 5 NS 1.4 Determine the prime factors of all numbers through 50 and write the numbers as the product of their prime factors by using exponents to show multiples of a factor (e.g., $24 = 2 \times 2 \times 2 \times 3 = 2^3 \times 3$).**

Connect ***Before*** you multiplied whole numbers to find their product. ***Now*** you will write a number as a product of primes to prepare for Grade 6 Standard NS 2.4.

KEY VOCABULARY
- **prime number**
- **composite number**
- **prime factorization**
- **factor tree**

ACTIVITY

You can make a list of *prime numbers.*

STEP 1 **Write** the whole numbers from 2 through 48, as shown below.

STEP 2 **Circle** 2 and cross out all multiples of 2 other than 2. (The first row below has been done for you.) Then go to the next available number after 2, circle it, and cross out all its multiples other than itself. Repeat until every number is either circled or crossed out.

(2)	3	~~4~~	5	~~6~~	7	~~8~~	9	~~10~~	11	~~12~~	
13	14	15	16	17	18	19	20	21	22	23	24
25	26	27	28	29	30	31	32	33	34	35	36
37	38	39	40	41	42	43	44	45	46	47	48

In the activity, the numbers that are circled are called *prime numbers.* A **prime number** is a whole number greater than 1 whose only whole number factors are 1 and itself. A **composite number** is a whole number greater than 1 that has whole number factors other than 1 and itself. The number 1 is neither prime nor composite.

EXAMPLE 1 Writing Factors of a Number

FIELD TRIP A science class of 30 students is on a field trip at the zoo. The teacher wants to break the class into smaller groups of the same size to observe the reptiles. Find all possible group sizes by writing all factors of 30.

SOLUTION

$30 = 1 \times 30$

$= 2 \times 15$

$= 3 \times 10$

$= 5 \times 6$ **30 isn't divisible by 4. Skip to 5.**

$= 6 \times 5$ **Stop when the factors repeat.**

▶ **Answer** The possible group sizes are 1, 2, 3, 5, 6, 10, 15, and 30.

EXAMPLE 2 Identifying Prime and Composite Numbers

Tell whether the number is *prime* or *composite*.

a. 56

b. 11

SOLUTION

a. The factors of 56 are 1, 2, 4, 7, 8, 14, 28, and 56. So, 56 is composite.

b. The only factors of 11 are 1 and 11. So, 11 is prime.

✓ GUIDED PRACTICE for Examples 1 and 2

Write all the factors of the number.

1. 35 **2.** 32 **3.** 65 **4.** 23

Tell whether the number is *prime* or *composite*.

5. 47 **6.** 81 **7.** 34 **8.** 79

READING

To *factor* a number means to write the number as a product of factors.

PRIME FACTORIZATION To factor a whole number as a product of prime numbers is called **prime factorization**. You can use a diagram called a **factor tree** to write the prime factorization of a number. When a prime factor appears more than once in the prime factorization, use an exponent. An exponent shows how many times the base is used as a factor in the product.

EXAMPLE 3 Writing the Prime Factorization

Use a factor tree to write the prime factorization of 54.

One possible factor tree:

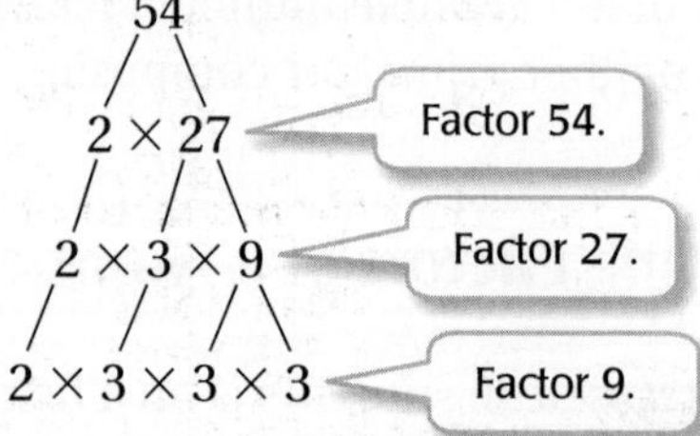

Another possible factor tree:

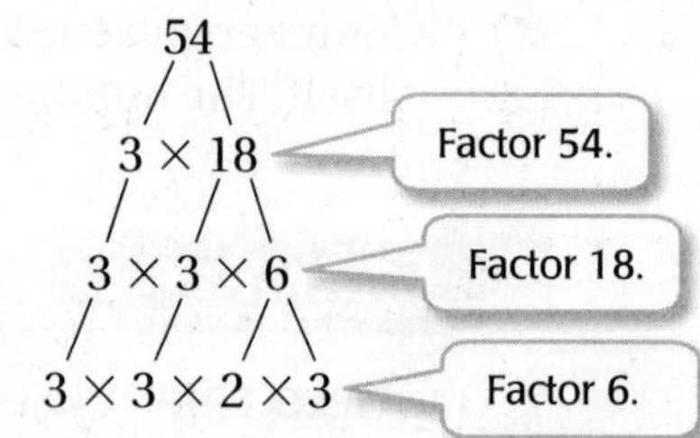

About the Standards

You will learn more about exponents in Lesson 3.6 as part of Grade 6 Standard AF 1.4.

For further review, see page 663.

Both factor trees give the same result: $54 = 2 \times 3 \times 3 \times 3 = 2 \times 3^3$.

▶ **Answer** The prime factorization of 54 is 2×3^3.

✓ GUIDED PRACTICE for Example 3

Use a factor tree to write the prime factorization of the number.

9. 30 **10.** 48 **11.** 44 **12.** 75

1.1 EXERCISES

HOMEWORK KEY

◆ = **MULTIPLE CHOICE PRACTICE** Exs. 8, 20, 31, 49, 58–60

○ = **HINTS AND HOMEWORK HELP** for Exs. 11, 27, 49 at classzone.com

SKILLS • PROBLEM SOLVING • REASONING

1. **VOCABULARY** Copy and complete: A whole number, such as 22, that has whole number factors other than 1 and itself is a ___?___ number.

2. **WRITING** *Explain* how to find the prime factorization of 20.

SEE EXAMPLE 1 on p. 5 for Exs. 3–9

WRITING FACTORS **Write all the factors of the number.**

3. 20   4. 25   5. 13   6. 84   7. 100

8. ◆ **MULTIPLE CHOICE** Which number is *not* a factor of 64?

Ⓐ 2   Ⓑ 4   Ⓒ 6   Ⓓ 8

9. **ERROR ANALYSIS** *Describe* and correct the error made in finding the factors of 48.

Factors of 48:
1, 2, 4, 6, 8, 12, 24, 48 ✕

SEE EXAMPLE 2 on p. 6 for Exs. 10–20

CLASSIFYING NUMBERS **Tell whether the number is *prime* or *composite*. *Explain* your reasoning.**

10. 88   (11.) 23   12. 39   13. 51   14. 61

15. 67   16. 41   17. 99   18. 201   19. 87

20. ◆ **MULTIPLE CHOICE** Which number is *not* prime?

Ⓐ 17   Ⓑ 21   Ⓒ 29   Ⓓ 37

SEE EXAMPLE 3 on p. 6 for Exs. 21–32

PRIME FACTORIZATION **Use a factor tree to write the prime factorization.**

21. 49   22. 68   23. 50   24. 64   25. 26

26. 144   (27.) 225   28. 588   29. 612   30. 864

31. ◆ **MULTIPLE CHOICE** What is the prime factorization of 72?

Ⓐ $2^2 \times 3 \times 6$ Ⓑ $2^2 \times 3^3$ Ⓒ $2^3 \times 3^2$ Ⓓ $2^3 \times 9$

32. **ERROR ANALYSIS** *Describe* and correct the error made in writing the prime factorization of 36.

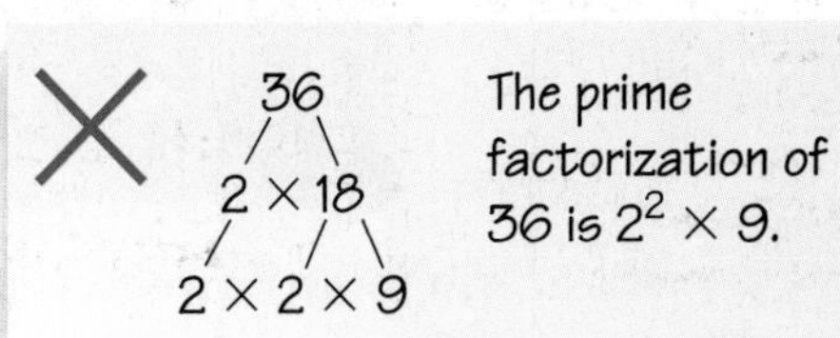

36
2 × 18
2 × 2 × 9
The prime factorization of 36 is $2^2 \times 9$.

REASONING **Is the statement *true* or *false*? *Explain* your reasoning.**

33. The prime factors of 15 are 1, 3, and 5.

34. All even numbers are composite.

35. The product of any two numbers is a composite number.

36. The product of any two prime numbers is always odd.

FINDING PRIMES **Find all the prime numbers between the given numbers.**

37. 15, 35 **38.** 50, 80 **39.** 108, 135

40. 180, 198 **41.** 230, 260 **42.** 270, 295

CONNECT SKILLS TO PROBLEM SOLVING **Exercises 43–45 will help you prepare for problem solving.**

43. A teacher wants to divide the 28 students in a class into equal groups. Find all possible group sizes by writing all the factors of 28.

44. A baker wants to divide 24 dinner rolls into equal groups to place into boxes. Find all possible group sizes by writing all the factors of 24.

45. A carpenter wants to drill equally spaced peg holes for adjustable shelves in a 42 inch high bookcase. Find all possible whole inch distances between the peg holes by writing all the factors of 42.

SEE EXAMPLE 1 on p. 5 for Exs. 46 and 48–49

46. MULTI-STEP PROBLEM You are a tour guide and want to divide 90 people into groups of the same size.

a. Find all the factors of 90. What are all the possible group sizes?

b. Each group should have from 11 to 15 people. Is more than one size for the groups possible? *Explain* your reasoning.

California @HomeTutor for problem solving help at classzone.com

47. SOUVENIRS As a volunteer at a museum, you fill small souvenir bags with several polished stones. Each bag has the same number of stones, with no stones left over. Is the total number of stones in all the souvenir bags *prime* or *composite*? *Explain.*

California @HomeTutor for problem solving help at classzone.com

48. AZALEAS One rectangular arrangement of azalea plants is shown below. Find all the other possible rectangular arrangements of the plants.

49. ◆ **MULTIPLE CHOICE** You want to display 63 baseball cards in a rectangle. Which number of rows is possible?

Ⓐ 3 Ⓑ 4 Ⓒ 5 Ⓓ 6

50. PUZZLE PROBLEM Find the composite number between 20 and 50 whose prime factors have a sum of 21.

51. **OPEN-ENDED** Find two composite numbers whose prime factors have a sum of 18.

52. **SHORT RESPONSE** One classroom in your school has 32 desks, and another classroom has 35 desks. In which classroom can more rectangular desk arrangements be made using all the desks? *Explain* your answer.

One arrangement of 32 desks is 4 rows of 8 desks.

53. **MULTI-STEP PROBLEM** List all the factors of 5 and 10, then of 27 and 54. Does the number of all factors double when you double an odd number? *Explain.* List all the factors of 10, 20, 40, and 80. Does the number of all factors double when you double an even number? *Explain.*

54. **GOLDBACH'S CONJECTURE** A *conjecture* is a statement believed to be true but not proved to be true. Christian Goldbach (1690–1764) made the following conjecture about prime numbers.

Every even number greater than 2 is the sum of two primes.

Show Goldbach's conjecture is true for every even number from 4 to 16.

55. **EXAMPLES AND NONEXAMPLES** The prime factorizations of the numbers in Group A share a common property that is *not* true of the numbers in Group B. Find another number that belongs in Group A and another number that belongs in Group B.

Group A: 1764, 1089, 1225 **Group B:** 1232, 2310, 112

56. **CHALLENGE** Find the composite number between 50 and 60 whose prime factors have a sum of 11.

57. **CHALLENGE** The lengths of the sides of a triangle are three whole numbers in a row, such as 4, 5, and 6. Can the perimeter of this triangle be a prime number? *Explain* your reasoning.

◆ CALIFORNIA STANDARDS SPIRAL REVIEW

Gr. 5 NS 1.5

58. What can the value of P be? *(p. 675)*

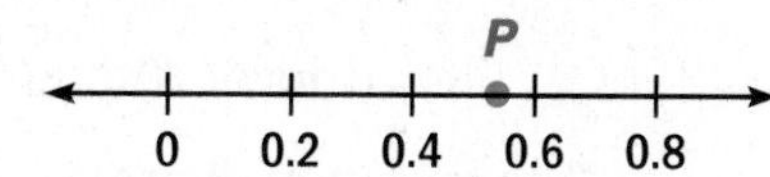

Ⓐ 0.34 Ⓑ 0.40 Ⓒ 0.54 Ⓓ 0.74

Gr. 5 NS 1.1

59. What is 12,375,486 rounded to the thousands' place? *(p. 665)*

Ⓐ 12,375,000 Ⓑ 12,375,500 Ⓒ 12,376,000 Ⓓ 12,380,000

Gr. 4 NS 3.4

60. A middle school principal wants to divide 216 students equally among 8 homerooms. How many students should be in each homeroom? *(p. 671)*

Ⓐ 23 Ⓑ 24 Ⓒ 25 Ⓓ 27

1.2 Greatest Common Factor

Math and MUSIC
Example 2, p. 11

Standards **NS 2.4** **Determine** the least common multiple and **the greatest common divisor of whole numbers**; use them to solve problems with fractions (e.g., to find a common denominator to add two fractions or to find the reduced form for a fraction).

Connect ***Before*** you found all the factors of a whole number. ***Now*** you will find the greatest common factor of two or more numbers.

KEY VOCABULARY

- **common factor**
- **greatest common factor (GCF)**

ORCHESTRA An orchestra conductor wants to divide 48 violinists, 24 violists, and 36 cellists into groups. Each group should have the same number of each instrument. What is the greatest number of groups that can be formed? How many violinists, violists, and cellists will be in each group? You will answer these questions in Example 2.

A whole number that is a factor of two or more nonzero whole numbers is a **common factor** of the numbers. The greatest of the common factors is called the **greatest common factor (GCF)**.

One way to find the greatest common factor of two or more numbers is to list all the factors of each number. Then find the greatest number that is on every list.

EXAMPLE 1 ◆ Multiple Choice Practice

READING
In Example 1, the phrase "greatest common *divisor*" means the same as "greatest common *factor*."

What is the greatest common divisor of 28, 42, and 70?

Ⓐ 2 Ⓑ 4 Ⓒ 7 Ⓓ 14

SOLUTION

Write the divisors of 28, 42, and 70.

Divisors of 28: **1**, **2**, 4, **7**, **14**, 28

Divisors of 42: **1**, **2**, 3, 6, **7**, **14**, 21, 42

Divisors of 70: **1**, **2**, 5, **7**, 10, **14**, 35, 70

The common divisors are 1, 2, 7, and 14. The greatest common divisor is 14.

▶ **Answer** The correct answer is D. Ⓐ Ⓑ Ⓒ Ⓓ

✓ GUIDED PRACTICE for Example 1

Find the greatest common factor of the numbers by listing factors.

1. 16, 28 **2.** 60, 96 **3.** 14, 70, 91 **4.** 15, 20, 75

EXAMPLE 2 Using the GCF to Solve Problems

ANOTHER WAY

List the factors of the least number. Find which of those numbers are factors of all the greater numbers, until you have checked your entire list.

In the orchestra problem on page 10, the most groups that can be formed is given by the greatest common factor of 48, 24, and 36.

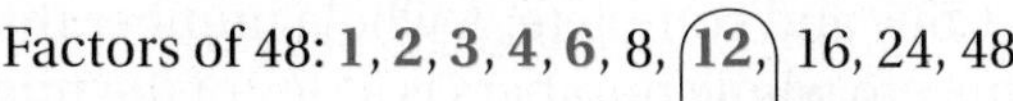

Factors of 48: **1, 2, 3, 4, 6,** 8, **12,** 16, 24, 48

Factors of 24: **1, 2, 3, 4, 6,** 8, **12,** 24

Factors of 36: **1, 2, 3, 4, 6,** 9, **12,** 18, 36

The common factors are 1, 2, 3, 4, 6, and 12. The GCF is 12.

▸ **Answer** The most groups that can be formed is 12. Dividing the number of each type of musician by 12, you find each group will have 4 violinists, 2 violists, and 3 cellists.

USING PRIME FACTORIZATION Another way to find the greatest common factor of two or more numbers is to use the prime factorization of each number. The product of the common prime factors is the GCF.

EXAMPLE 3 Using Prime Factorization to Find the GCF

Animated Math

For an interactive example of finding the GCF, go to **classzone.com.**

Find the greatest common factor of the numbers using prime factorization.

a. 180, 126

180: 10×18; $2 \times 5 \times 2 \times 9$; $2 \times 5 \times 2 \times 3 \times 3$

126: 2×63; $2 \times 3 \times 21$; $2 \times 3 \times 3 \times 7$

$180 = 2 \times 2 \times 3 \times 3 \times 5$

$126 = 2 \times 3 \times 3 \times 7$

▸ **Answer** From the factor trees you see the common factors are 2, 3, and 3. So, the GCF is $2 \times 3^2 = 18$.

b. 28, 45

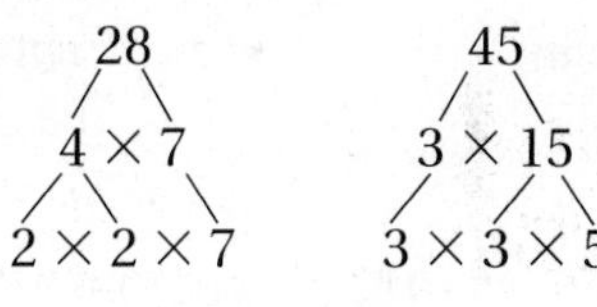

$28 = 2 \times 2 \times 7$

$45 = 3 \times 3 \times 5$

▸ **Answer** The factor trees show no common prime factors, so the GCF is 1.

✓ GUIDED PRACTICE for Examples 2 and 3

5. **WHAT IF?** What is the most groups possible with 32 violinists, 40 violists, and 16 cellists? How many of each type of musician will be in each group?

Find the GCF of the numbers using prime factorization.

6. 90, 150
7. 84, 216
8. 120, 192
9. 49, 144

1.2 EXERCISES

HOMEWORK KEY

◆ = **MULTIPLE CHOICE PRACTICE** Exs. 15, 18, 42, 54–56

○ = **HINTS AND HOMEWORK HELP** for Exs. 5, 19, 45 at classzone.com

SKILLS • PROBLEM SOLVING • REASONING

1. **VOCABULARY** Copy and complete: A whole number that is a factor of two or more nonzero whole numbers is a __?__ of the numbers.

2. **WRITING** *Describe* how to find the greatest common factor of two numbers using their prime factorizations. Include an example.

SEE EXAMPLES 1 AND 2 on pp. 10–11 for Exs. 3–16

FINDING THE GCF Find the greatest common factor of the numbers by listing factors.

3. 14, 21
4. 24, 32
5. 11, 33
6. 45, 76
7. 56, 81
8. 39, 52
9. 20, 55, 65
10. 42, 72, 84
11. 75, 90, 105
12. 48, 64, 96
13. 18, 30, 60
14. 36, 54, 135

15. ◆ **MULTIPLE CHOICE** What is the greatest common divisor of 18, 45, and 72?

Ⓐ 2 Ⓑ 3 Ⓒ 9 Ⓓ 18

ERROR ANALYSIS ***Describe*** **and correct the error made in finding the greatest common factor of the numbers.**

SEE EXAMPLE 3 on p. 11 for Exs. 17–30

16.

✗ Factors of 20: 1, 2, 4, 5, 10, 20
Factors of 32: 1, 2, 8, 16, 32
The GCF is 2.

17.

✗ 18 → 2 × 9   51 → 3 × 17
The GCF is 1.

18. ◆ **MULTIPLE CHOICE** What is the greatest common divisor of 180 and 225?

Ⓐ 9 Ⓑ 15 Ⓒ 25 Ⓓ 45

PRIME FACTORIZATION Find the greatest common factor of the numbers using prime factorization.

19. 98, 140
20. 27, 117
21. 86, 154
22. 37, 93
23. 198, 216
24. 36, 168
25. 34, 85
26. 75, 285
27. 144, 264
28. 65, 112
29. 63, 84, 126
30. 39, 65, 182

REASONING Tell whether the statement is *always, sometimes,* or *never* true. *Explain* your reasoning.

31. The greatest common factor of two even numbers is 2.
32. The greatest common factor of two composite numbers is 1.
33. The greatest common factor of two different prime numbers is 1.
34. The greatest common factor of an odd and an even number is 1.

NUMBER SENSE **Find two numbers between 200 and 300 that have the given greatest common factor. *Explain* how you found the numbers.**

35. 7 **36.** 18 **37.** 8 **38.** 13

CONNECT SKILLS TO PROBLEM SOLVING **Exercises 39–41 will help you prepare for problem solving.**

Find the greatest common factor of the two numbers to solve.

39. Molly has 40 wooden beads and 56 glass beads. She wants to place an equal number of each type into bags, with no beads left over. What is the greatest number of bags she could use?

40. Two pieces of wood, 60 inches and 36 inches long, are entirely used for shelves of equal length. What is the longest the shelves can be?

41. At an awards banquet, 80 football players and 64 soccer players will be seated at tables. An equal number of players from each team will be at each table. What is the greatest number of tables that can be used?

SEE EXAMPLES 1 AND 2 on pp. 10–11 for Exs. 42–44

42. ◆ **MULTIPLE CHOICE** For an activity the same number of students and the same number of teachers will be assigned to each group. How many groups can be formed from 40 students and 24 teachers?

Ⓐ 3 Ⓑ 5 Ⓒ 8 Ⓓ 12

California @HomeTutor for problem solving help at classzone.com

43. MULTI-STEP PROBLEM You are making bags of school supplies for your friends. You have 12 markers, 18 pens, and 30 pencils. You want to put the same number of each kind of supply into each bag.

a. List the factors of 12, 18, and 30. What is the GCF of the numbers?

b. What is the greatest number of bags you can make?

c. How many of each kind of supply will be in each bag? *Explain.*

California @HomeTutor for problem solving help at classzone.com

44. ROSE BOWL PARADE You are decorating a Rose Bowl float using bunches of roses. You have 108 red roses, 144 white roses, 48 yellow roses, and 72 purple roses. Bunches of roses should be identical with no roses left over. What is the greatest number of bunches you can make? How many roses of each color are in a bunch?

45. SHORT RESPONSE A class is making fruit baskets for a local nursing home using 162 apples, 108 oranges, and 180 bananas. The baskets should be identical with no fruit left over. What is the greatest number of baskets that can be made? *Explain* how this number would change if 54 more apples were donated.

46. PUZZLE PROBLEM A number is a common factor of 96 and 144. The sum of the number's digits is 7. Find the number.

Rose Bowl Parade float

47. **SCIENCE CLASS** A science class with 15 girls and 12 boys is divided into groups. Each group has the same number of boys and the same number of girls. What is the greatest number of groups that can be formed? How many boys are in each group? how many girls?

48. **REASONING** You are given two numbers. The lesser of the two numbers is a factor of the greater number. What can you say about the GCF of the numbers? *Justify* your reasoning.

49. **OPEN-ENDED** Name 3 pairs of composite numbers from 50 to 100 that have a GCF of 1. *Explain* how you found the pairs.

50. **SHORT RESPONSE** To find the GCF of 6, 15, 18, and 75, your friend says you need to check only the factors of 6 because the GCF cannot be greater than the least number. Is your friend correct? *Explain.*

51. **MULTI-STEP PROBLEM** A marching band has 81 trombonists, 36 flutists, 27 drummers, and 54 trumpeters. For a parade, the band is arranged into rows of equal length with a single type of instrument in each row.
    a. What is the most musicians that can be in each row?
    b. How many of the longest rows are needed for each instrument?
    c. *Explain* why adding a row of 8 tuba players would not fit the arrangement, while adding 45 clarinetists would.

Trumpeters are in the row shown.

52. **CHALLENGE** The GCF of a number and 48 is 16. The sum of the number's digits is 13. Find two numbers that satisfy these conditions.

53. **CHALLENGE** You want to use sections of fence that are all of the same length to enclose the land at the right. How long can each section be? What is the least number of sections that are needed to enclose the land? *Explain* your reasoning.

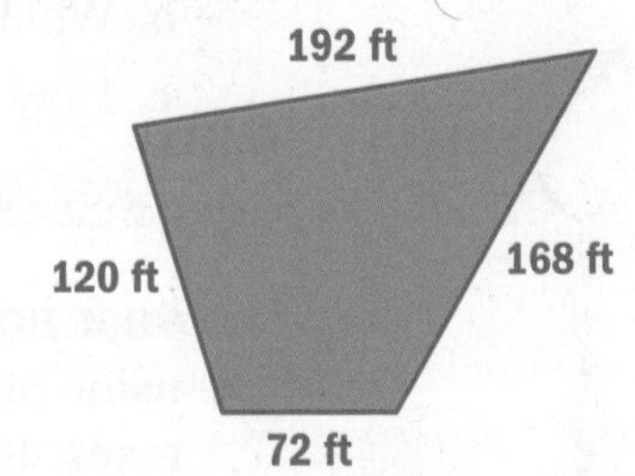

◆ CALIFORNIA STANDARDS SPIRAL REVIEW

Gr. 4 NS 3.1

54. Find the sum 1,059,472 + 963,744 + 978,304. ***(p. 661)***

    (A) 315,200 (B) 3,001,520 (C) 3,015,200 (D) 3,150,200

Gr. 5 NS 1.4

55. What is the prime factorization of 24? ***(p. 6)***

    (A) 2×3 (B) 4×6 (C) $2^3 \times 3$ (D) 2×12

Gr. 4 NS 3.3

56. A tube contains 24 lead refills for a mechanical pencil. You buy 12 tubes. How many lead refills do you have? ***(p. 671)***

    (A) 2 (B) 12 (C) 36 (D) 288

Standards Preparation

Gr. 4 NS 1.5 Explain different interpretations of fractions, for example, parts of a whole, parts of a set, and division of whole numbers by whole numbers; **explain equivalence of fractions** (see Standard 4.0).

1.3 Modeling Equivalent Fractions

MATERIALS • colored pencils or markers • paper

QUESTION How can you represent a fraction in other ways?

Equivalent fractions have the same part-whole relationship. You can use area models to represent them.

EXPLORE Represent $\frac{4}{6}$ in other ways.

STEP 1 **Draw** a rectangle on a piece of paper. Model $\frac{4}{6}$ by dividing the rectangle into 6 equal parts and shading 4 parts.

STEP 2 **Look** for other ways of dividing the original rectangle into equal parts.

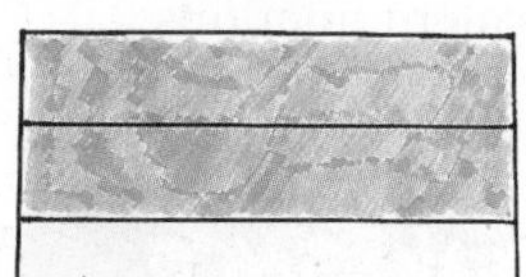

Shade 2 of 3 equal parts.

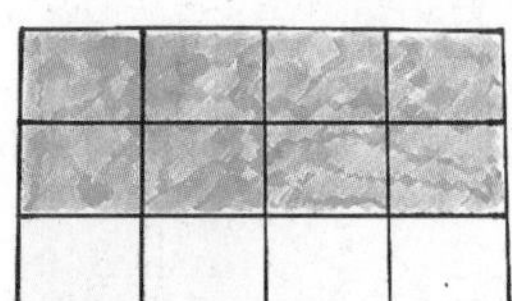

Shade 8 of 12 equal parts.

STEP 3 **Write** two other fractions that represent $\frac{4}{6}$ using the models in Step 2.

The fractions $\frac{2}{3}$ and $\frac{8}{12}$ also represent $\frac{4}{6}$.

DRAW CONCLUSIONS Use your observations to complete these exercises.

Use models to help you write two fractions equivalent to the fraction.

1. $\frac{9}{18}$ **2.** $\frac{2}{14}$ **3.** $\frac{9}{12}$ **4.** $\frac{15}{20}$

5. In the fractions $\frac{4}{6}$ and $\frac{2}{3}$, compare the numerators and then compare the denominators. In the fractions $\frac{4}{6}$ and $\frac{8}{12}$, compare the numerators and then the denominators.

6. **WRITING** *Write* a rule about the numerators and denominators of equivalent fractions. Is this rule true for the fractions you found in Exercises 1–4?

1.3 Equivalent Fractions

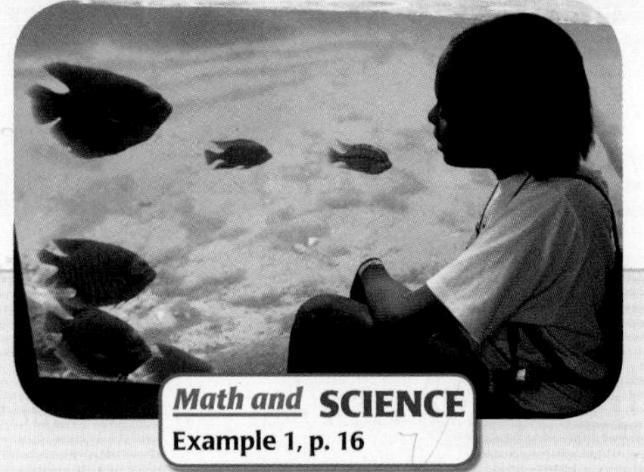

Math and SCIENCE
Example 1, p. 16

Standards **NS 2.4 Determine** the least common multiple and **the greatest common divisor of whole numbers; use them to solve problems with fractions (e.g.,** to find a common denominator to add two fractions or **to find the reduced form for a fraction).**

Connect ***Before*** you factored whole numbers. ***Now*** you will use factors to write equivalent fractions.

KEY VOCABULARY

- **equivalent fractions**
- **simplest form**
- **fraction,** *p. 674*
- **numerator,** *p. 674*
- **denominator,** *p. 674*

A *fraction* is a number of the form $\frac{a}{b}$ $(b \neq 0)$ where a is the *numerator* and b is the *denominator*. A fraction represents equal parts of a whole. Fractions representing the same part-to-whole relationship are **equivalent fractions**.

EXAMPLE 1 Writing Fractions

AQUARIUM Two fish in an aquarium are goldfish. The 10 fish in the aquarium are pictured below. What *fraction* of the fish are goldfish?

SOLUTION

Using the diagram, you can write two equivalent fractions:

$$\frac{\text{Number of goldfish}}{\text{Number of fish}} = \frac{2}{10}$$

$$\frac{\text{Number of groups of 2 goldfish}}{\text{Number of groups of 2 fish}} = \frac{1}{5}$$

READING
The fraction $\frac{2}{10}$ is read "two tenths."

The activity on page 15 and Example 1 suggest you can find an equivalent fraction by multiplying or dividing the numerator and denominator of a fraction by the same nonzero number. Because you are multiplying or dividing by 1, the value of the fraction does not change. You will see why this is true in Lesson 2.4.

EXAMPLE 2 Writing Equivalent Fractions

Write two fractions that are equivalent to $\frac{6}{8}$.

$\frac{6}{8} = \frac{6 \times 3}{8 \times 3} = \frac{18}{24}$ **Multiply numerator and denominator by 3.**

$\frac{6}{8} = \frac{6 \div 2}{8 \div 2} = \frac{3}{4}$ **Divide numerator and denominator by 2, a common factor of 6 and 8.**

▶ **Answer** $\frac{18}{24}$ and $\frac{3}{4}$ are equivalent to $\frac{6}{8}$.

AnimatedMath
For an interactive example of finding equivalent fractions go to **classzone.com.**

✓ GUIDED PRACTICE for Examples 1 and 2

1. **GROCERIES** Two eggs in a carton of a dozen eggs are cracked. Write two equivalent fractions that represent the fraction of eggs that are cracked.

Write two fractions that are equivalent to the given fraction.

2. $\frac{1}{6}$
3. $\frac{3}{10}$
4. $\frac{8}{18}$
5. $\frac{30}{45}$

About the Standards

"Simplest form" and "reduced form," used in Grade 6 Standard NS 2.4, mean the same thing.

SIMPLEST FORM A fraction is in **simplest form** if the greatest common factor of the numerator and denominator is 1. To *simplify* a fraction, you divide its numerator and denominator by their GCF.

Two fractions that do not have the same simplest form are not equivalent.

EXAMPLE 3 Simplifying Fractions

Write the fraction in simplest form.

a. $\frac{8}{28} = \frac{2 \times \cancel{4}^{1}}{7 \times \cancel{4}_{1}}$ **Divide out GCF of 8 and 28.**

$= \frac{2}{7}$

b. $\frac{8}{15}$ **The GCF is 1.**

The fraction is in simplest form.

EXAMPLE 4 Using Fractions in Simplest Form

BASKETBALL At a basketball game, the home team made 14 out of 22 free throw shots. The visiting team made 10 out of 25 free throw shots. Write fractions for the portion of free throws made by each team. Are the fractions equivalent?

Home Team $\frac{\text{Free throws made}}{\text{Free throw shots}} = \frac{14}{22} = \frac{7 \times \cancel{2}^{1}}{11 \times \cancel{2}_{1}} = \frac{7}{11}$

Visiting Team $\frac{\text{Free throws made}}{\text{Free throw shots}} = \frac{10}{25} = \frac{2 \times \cancel{5}^{1}}{5 \times \cancel{5}_{1}} = \frac{2}{5}$

▸ **Answer** No, $\frac{7}{11}$ and $\frac{2}{5}$ are not equivalent fractions.

AVOID ERRORS

Be sure that the "simplified" fraction has no common factors in the numerator and denominator. If it does, then you should simplify it further.

✓ GUIDED PRACTICE for Examples 3 and 4

Write the fraction in simplest form.

6. $\frac{12}{16}$
7. $\frac{15}{35}$
8. $\frac{7}{28}$
9. $\frac{14}{34}$

10. **WHAT IF?** In Example 4, suppose the home team made 8 out of 20 free throw shots. Is this fraction equivalent to the visiting team's? *Explain.*

1.3 EXERCISES

HOMEWORK KEY

◆ = **MULTIPLE CHOICE PRACTICE** Exs. 27, 47, 52, 61–63

○ = **HINTS AND HOMEWORK HELP** for Exs. 21, 31, 53 at classzone.com

SKILLS • PROBLEM SOLVING • REASONING

1. **VOCABULARY** Copy and complete: A fraction whose numerator and denominator have a GCF of 1 is in _?_.

2. **NOTETAKING SKILLS** Make a *word triangle,* as on page 4, for *equivalent fractions.*

SEE EXAMPLE 1 on p. 16 for Exs. 3–5

WRITING FRACTIONS **Write two equivalent fractions that describe the model.**

3. 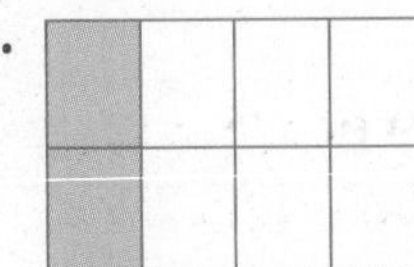

4. 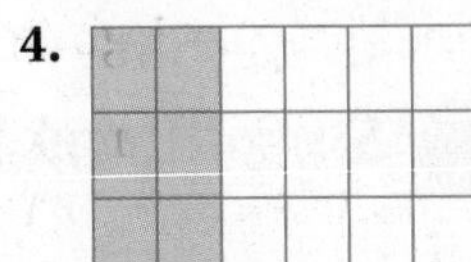

5. 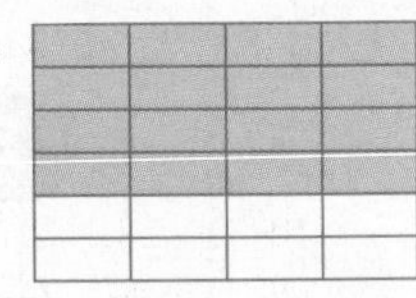

SEE EXAMPLE 2 on p. 16 for Exs. 6–16

OPEN-ENDED **Write two fractions that are equivalent to the given fraction.**

6. $\frac{25}{120}$ 7. $\frac{18}{21}$ 8. $\frac{14}{34}$ 9. $\frac{30}{52}$ 10. $\frac{28}{32}$

11. $\frac{84}{96}$ 12. $\frac{95}{126}$ 13. $\frac{54}{168}$ 14. $\frac{44}{121}$ 15. $\frac{39}{169}$

16. **ERROR ANALYSIS** *Describe* and correct the error made in writing a fraction equivalent to $\frac{4}{5}$.

$$\frac{4}{5} = \frac{4 \times 4}{5 \times 5} = \frac{16}{25}$$

SEE EXAMPLE 3 on p. 17 for Exs. 17–28

WRITING IN SIMPLEST FORM **Write the fraction in simplest form.**

17. $\frac{32}{72}$ 18. $\frac{6}{21}$ 19. $\frac{15}{21}$ 20. $\frac{12}{35}$ (21.) $\frac{28}{48}$

22. $\frac{30}{45}$ 23. $\frac{24}{32}$ 24. $\frac{22}{27}$ 25. $\frac{49}{105}$ 26. $\frac{33}{81}$

27. ◆ **MULTIPLE CHOICE** What is the simplest form of the fraction $\frac{108}{192}$?

Ⓐ $\frac{54}{96}$ Ⓑ $\frac{5}{8}$ Ⓒ $\frac{9}{16}$ Ⓓ $\frac{2}{23}$

28. **ERROR ANALYSIS** *Describe* and correct the error made in writing $\frac{24}{42}$ in simplest form.

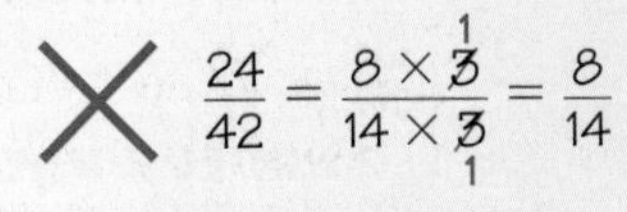

SEE EXAMPLE 4 on p. 17 for Exs. 29–38

EQUIVALENT FRACTIONS **Tell whether the fractions are equivalent.**

29. $\frac{6}{10}, \frac{9}{15}$ 30. $\frac{14}{22}, \frac{10}{35}$ (31.) $\frac{6}{15}, \frac{4}{16}$ 32. $\frac{15}{33}, \frac{25}{55}$ 33. $\frac{3}{8}, \frac{9}{64}$

34. $\frac{14}{21}, \frac{24}{36}$ 35. $\frac{15}{36}, \frac{40}{96}$ 36. $\frac{56}{196}, \frac{132}{462}$ 37. $\frac{34}{44}, \frac{136}{144}$ 38. $\frac{45}{54}, \frac{8}{18}$

MENTAL MATH **Copy and complete the equivalent fractions.**

39. $\frac{18}{24} = \frac{?}{12}$ **40.** $\frac{12}{21} = \frac{?}{7}$ **41.** $\frac{3}{7} = \frac{18}{?}$ **42.** $\frac{12}{16} = \frac{6}{?}$

43. $\frac{10}{15} = \frac{?}{3}$ **44.** $\frac{4}{14} = \frac{20}{?}$ **45.** $\frac{2}{9} = \frac{?}{45}$ **46.** $\frac{16}{14} = \frac{8}{?}$

47. ◆ **MULTIPLE CHOICE** Which fraction pairs are equivalent to three ninths?

(A) $\frac{9}{10}, \frac{1}{3}$ (B) $\frac{3}{19}, \frac{6}{38}$ (C) $\frac{1}{3}, \frac{5}{20}$ (D) $\frac{6}{18}, \frac{2}{6}$

CONNECT SKILLS TO PROBLEM SOLVING **Exercises 48–51 will help you prepare for problem solving.**

48. During the 1800s, six of the 22 different presidents of the United States were born in Virginia. Write two equivalent fractions for the portion of presidents that were born in Virginia in the 1800s.

49. During a hockey game, a goalie makes 38 saves out of 42 shots. Write two equivalent fractions for the portion of shots that were saves.

50. You read 35 pages of a chapter in a book and have 15 pages left. Write two equivalent fractions for the part of the chapter you have read.

51. Tony has 12 oranges and 28 apples. Write two equivalent fractions for the portion of fruit that is oranges.

SEE EXAMPLE 3 on p. 17 for Exs. 52–53

52. ◆ **MULTIPLE CHOICE** At one time, the highway speed limit in 18 states was 65 miles per hour. In simplest form, what fraction of the 50 states had a speed limit of 65 miles per hour at that time?

(A) $\frac{18}{65}$ (B) $\frac{9}{25}$ (C) $\frac{18}{50}$ (D) $\frac{36}{100}$

California @HomeTutor for problem solving help at classzone.com

53. **MULTI-STEP PROBLEM** The table below shows the number of bones found in four parts of the body.

Location	*Number of Bones*
Upper limbs	64
Wrists	16
Lower limbs	62
Ankles	14

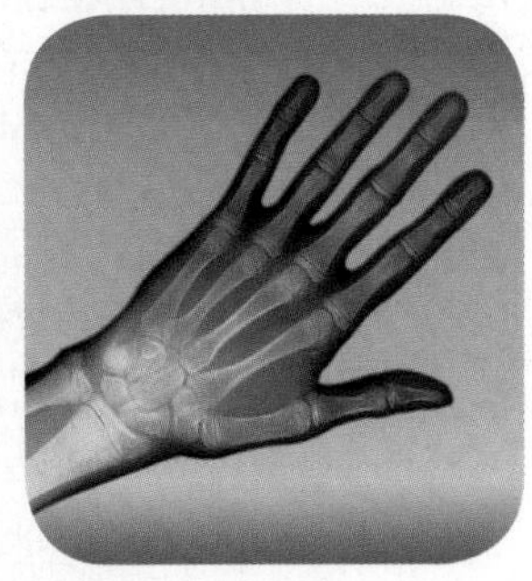

a. Represent Write a fraction that represents the part of the upper limb bones that are found in the wrists.

b. Represent Write a fraction that represents the part of the lower limb bones that are in the ankles.

c. Compare Rewrite your answers from parts (a) and (b) as fractions in simplest form. Are the fractions equivalent? *Explain.*

California @HomeTutor for problem solving help at classzone.com

54. **MULTI-STEP PROBLEM** The football diagrams show data for the two quarterbacks (QB) of one game. It compares the numbers of passes completed to the number thrown for three lengths of passes.

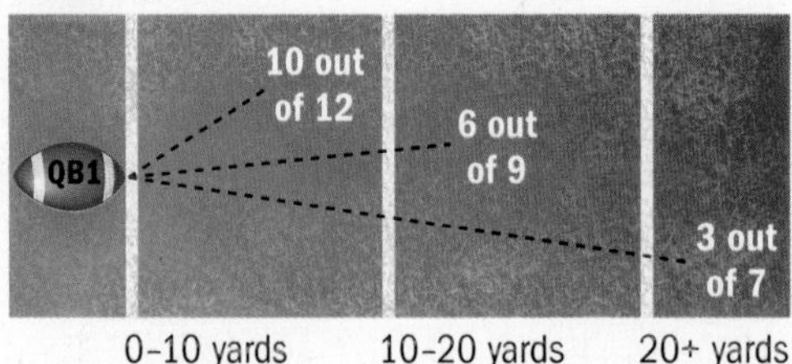

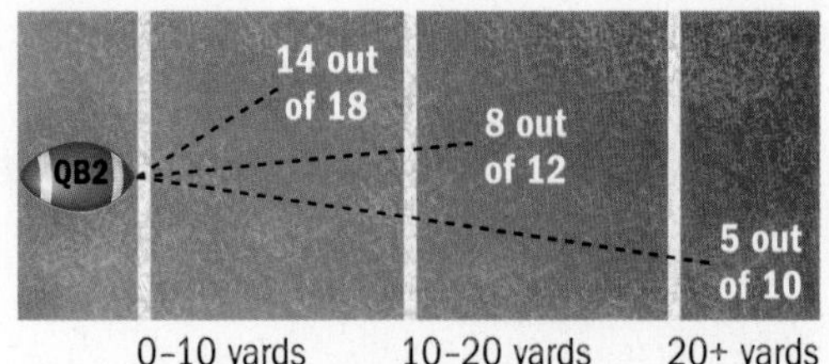

a. **Represent** Write a fraction for each of the six data pairs.

b. **Compare** For which length of pass do the two players have the same record? *Justify* your reasoning.

55. **CHALLENGE** The table below shows the number of wins and losses of three baseball coaches.

a. What part of the total games played were wins for each coach?

b. Which coach has the worst record? *Explain* your reasoning.

c. If you wanted to hire one of these coaches, which one would you choose? *Explain* your reasoning.

Name	Number of Wins	Number of Losses
Coach Samuels	35	14
Coach Turner	50	20
Coach Welsh	35	20

CHALLENGE Find an equivalent fraction with the greatest denominator less than 100. Then find an equivalent fraction with the greatest denominator less than 1000.

56. $\frac{3}{8}$ 57. $\frac{5}{9}$ 58. $\frac{6}{7}$ 59. $\frac{2}{3}$

60. **CHALLENGE** You get 7 out of 11 answers correct on a quiz. About how many correct answers could you expect on a quiz that has 8 questions? 12 questions? 16 questions? *Justify* your answers.

◆ CALIFORNIA STANDARDS SPIRAL REVIEW

Gr. 5 NS 1.3 61. What is the product $7 \times 7 \times 7 \times 7$ written as a power? ***(p. 663)***

Ⓐ 7×4 Ⓑ 7^4 Ⓒ 2401 Ⓓ 4^7

Gr. 5 NS 1.5 62. Which of the numbers are in order from least to greatest? ***(p. 671)***

Ⓐ 5.005, 5.055, 5.500, 5.505 Ⓑ 6.776, 6.767, 6.667, 6.676

Ⓒ 3.343, 3.344, 3.443, 3.434 Ⓓ 8.998, 8.899, 8.889, 8.989

Gr. 5 NS 1.1 63. The length of a crane-fly is 0.02576 meter. What is the length of the crane-fly, rounded to the thousandths' place? ***(p. 676)***

Ⓐ 0 m Ⓑ 0.03 m Ⓒ 0.026 m Ⓓ 0.0258 m

1.4 Least Common Multiple

Math and SPORTS
Ex. 31, p. 24

Standards NS 2.4 **Determine the least common multiple** and the greatest common divisor **of whole numbers**; use them to solve problems with fractions (e.g., to find a common denominator to add two fractions or to find the reduced form for a fraction).

Connect *Before* you found the GCF of two or more numbers. *Now* you will find their LCM.

KEY VOCABULARY
- **multiple**
- **common multiple**
- **least common multiple (LCM)**

A **multiple** of a number is the product of the number and any nonzero whole number. A multiple that is shared by two or more numbers is a **common multiple**. The least of the common multiples is the **least common multiple (LCM)**.

EXAMPLE 1 Finding the Least Common Multiple

Find the least common multiple of the numbers by using a list.

a. 5, 6 **b.** 4, 8

VOCABULARY
The similarity between the words "multiple" and "multiply" can help you to remember that a multiple is a product.

SOLUTION

a. Multiples of 5: 5, 10, 15, 20, 25, **30**, ...
Multiples of 6: 6, 12, 18, 24, **30**, ...
Answer The LCM of 5 and 6 is 30.

b. Multiples of 4: 4, **8**, 12, **16**, ...
Multiples of 8: **8**, **16**, 32, ...
Answer The LCM of 4 and 8 is 8.

EXAMPLE 2 ◆ Multiple Choice Practice

What is the least common multiple of 4, 10, and 12?

Ⓐ 20 Ⓑ 48 Ⓒ 60 Ⓓ 120

ELIMINATE CHOICES
Any multiple of 10 must have a zero in the ones' place. So you can eliminate choice B.

SOLUTION

Multiples of 4: 4, 8, 12, 16, 20, 24, 28, 32, 36, 40, 44, 48, 52, 56, **60**, ...

Multiples of 10: 10, 20, 30, 40, 50, **60**, ...

Multiples of 12: 12, 24, 36, 48, **60**, ...

Answer The LCM is **60**. The correct answer is C. Ⓐ Ⓑ Ⓒ Ⓓ

✓ GUIDED PRACTICE for Examples 1 and 2

Find the LCM of the numbers by listing multiples.

1. 3, 5 **2.** 12, 16 **3.** 2, 6, 14 **4.** 3, 12, 15

PRIME FACTORS The prime factorizations of the numbers in Example 2, shown below, can be used to form the LCM of the numbers.

$$4 = 2 \times 2 = \mathbf{2^2} \qquad 10 = 2 \times \mathbf{5} \qquad 12 = 2 \times 2 \times 3 = \mathbf{2^2} \times \mathbf{3}$$

The LCM of 4, 10, and 12 must be a multiple of 2, 3, and 5. But $2 \times 3 \times 5$, or 30, is not a multiple of either 4 or 12. Because 2 is used twice as a factor in 4 and 12, you need to use two 2s as factors in the LCM.

LCM of 4, 10, and 12: $\mathbf{2^2 \times 3 \times 5}$

This observation suggests that to find the LCM, you use the *greatest* exponent for each factor that appears in the prime factorizations.

Animated Math

For an interactive example of finding GCFs and LCMs, go to **classzone.com**.

EXAMPLE 3 Using Prime Factorization to Find the LCM

TOUR SCHEDULES Three trolley tours leave from the same stop at 9:00 A.M. Tour A returns to the the stop every 75 minutes, Tour B returns every 60 minutes, and Tour C returns every 40 minutes. In how many hours will all three tours return to the stop at the same time?

Tour A returns in 75 min.

SOLUTION

Find the least common multiple of 75, 60, and 40.

STEP 1 **Find** the prime factorization of each number.

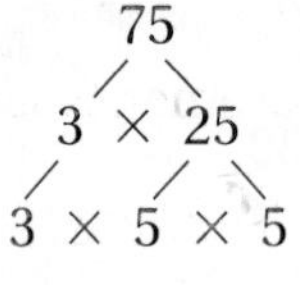

60
2 × 30
2 × 2 × 15
2 × 2 × 3 × 5

40
2 × 20
2 × 2 × 10
2 × 2 × 2 × 5

STEP 2 **Circle** the greatest power of every prime factor that appears in any of the prime factorizations.

$75 = \textcircled{3} \times \textcircled{5^2} \qquad 60 = 2^2 \times 3 \times 5 \qquad 40 = \textcircled{2^3} \times 5$

STEP 3 **Multiply** the circled powers.

$2^3 \times 3 \times 5^2 = 2 \times 2 \times 2 \times 3 \times 5 \times 5 = 600$

▶ **Answer** The tours all return at the same time in 600 minutes, or 10 hours.

REVIEW UNITS OF TIME

For help changing between units of time, see p. 678.

✓ GUIDED PRACTICE for Example 3

Find the LCM of the numbers using prime factorizations.

5. 36, 72 **6.** 24, 30 **7.** 54, 126 **8.** 20, 22, 55

9. WHAT IF? In Example 3, suppose Tour C returns every 25 minutes. In how many hours will the three tours return at the same time?

1.4 EXERCISES

HOMEWORK KEY ◆ = **MULTIPLE CHOICE PRACTICE** Exs. 13, 22, 35, 44–46

○ = **HINTS AND HOMEWORK HELP** for Exs. 7, 19, 35 at classzone.com

SKILLS • PROBLEM SOLVING • REASONING

1. **VOCABULARY** Copy and complete: The product of a given number and any nonzero whole number is a __?__ of the given number.

2. **WRITING** *Explain* how finding the LCM and finding the GCF of two numbers are similar. How are these processes different?

SEE EXAMPLES 1 AND 2 on p. 21 for Exs. 3–13

FINDING THE LCM **Find the least common multiple of the numbers by listing multiples.**

3. 9, 24
4. 12, 18
5. 16, 20
6. 30, 33
7. 5, 8, 12
8. 6, 11, 18
9. 9, 14, 21
10. 7, 20, 35

11. **WHICH ONE DOESN'T BELONG?** Which of the following is *not* a common multiple of 9, 15, and 30?

A. 720 **B.** 540 **C.** 360 **D.** 240

12. **ERROR ANALYSIS** *Describe* and correct the error in finding the least common multiple of 6 and 16.

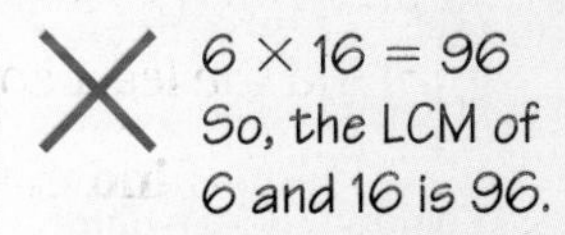

13. ◆ **MULTIPLE CHOICE** What is the least common multiple of 8 and 36?

Ⓐ 4 Ⓑ 8 Ⓒ 72 Ⓓ 288

SEE EXAMPLE 3 on p. 22 for Exs. 14–22

USING PRIME FACTORIZATION **Find the least common multiple of the numbers using prime factorization.**

14. 4, 18
15. 28, 60
16. 34, 52
17. 84, 360
18. 42, 56, 140
19. 39, 52, 169
20. 28, 40, 144
21. 16, 25, 27

22. ◆ **MULTIPLE CHOICE** The least common multiple of which pair of numbers is $3^3 \times 2^4$?

Ⓐ 12, 36 Ⓑ 9, 48 Ⓒ 27, 48 Ⓓ 16, 81

FINDING THE GCF AND LCM **Find the GCF and the LCM of the numbers. Compare the product of the GCF and LCM to the product of the numbers.**

23. 90, 165
24. 34, 66
25. 54, 132
26. 72, 168

ALGEBRA **Copy and complete the factorizations to find two numbers with the given LCM.**

27. 2 × __?__; 3 × __?__; LCM 30
28. 17 × __?__; 3 × __?__; LCM 102
29. 5 × __?__; 2 × __?__; LCM 30
30. 2 × __?__; 3 × __?__; LCM 72

CONNECT SKILLS TO PROBLEM SOLVING **Exercises 31–33 will help you prepare for problem solving.**

Find the least common multiple of the numbers to solve.

31. During track practice Pedro runs a lap in 3 minutes. David runs the same lap in 4 minutes. They both pass a point *S* at the same time. When will they next pass point *S* together?

32. A grocery store gets an order of fresh fruit every 4 days and an order of canned fruit every 10 days. The store received both orders one Monday. When will the store next receive both orders on the same day?

33. In separate rows of your garden, you plant onions 4 inches apart, peas 12 inches apart, and peppers 20 inches apart. The plants all line up at the beginning of the rows. How many inches back will all three vegetables next line up?

SEE EXAMPLES 1 AND 2 on p. 21 for Exs. 34–36

34. SUPPLIES You want to have the same number of napkins, paper plates, and plastic cups. Using whole packs, what is the fewest you could buy?

California @HomeTutor for problem solving help at classzone.com

35. ◆ **MULTIPLE CHOICE** You and a neighbor want to build brick walls of the same height. Your bricks are 5 inches tall and your neighbor's bricks are 7 inches tall. Without cutting bricks, what is the lowest wall possible?

Ⓐ 48 in. Ⓑ 35 in. Ⓒ 12 in. Ⓓ 2 in.

California @HomeTutor for problem solving help at classzone.com

36. MAYAN CALENDARS The Mayans used more than one calendar system, including using steps to represent days. One calendar had 365 days. Another calendar, thought to be sacred, had 260 days. If both calendars began on the same day, in how many days would they next begin on the same day?

Temple of Kukulcan, showing 91 of the 365 calendar steps

37. CHOOSE A STRATEGY You want to find the LCM of 32 and 49. Would you list multiples or use prime factorization? *Explain* your choice.

38. WRITING Is the product of two numbers always a common multiple of the numbers? always the least common multiple? *Explain* your reasoning.

39. REASONING Is the number $2^5 \times 3^7 \times 7^{10} \times 13^{45}$ a multiple of 15? *Explain* your reasoning.

40. **SHORT RESPONSE** While swimming, Sarah swims 7 laps in 5 minutes, and Jen swims 11 laps in 6 minutes. They start and stop at the same time and swim a whole number of laps. What is the least amount of time they swim? During this time, how many laps does each girl swim? *Explain* how you found your answer.

41. **CHALLENGE** The greatest common factor of two numbers a and b is 1. Is the least common multiple of these numbers always the product of the numbers? *Explain* your reasoning.

42. **CHALLENGE** Al has fewer than 100 trading cards. When he groups them by 2s, 3s, 4s, or 5s, he has 1 left over each time. How many cards are there?

43. **CHALLENGE** Two numbers less than 50 have a GCF of 5. If 5 is added to both numbers, the GCF is doubled but the LCM is reduced by 15. What are the two numbers?

◆ CALIFORNIA STANDARDS SPIRAL REVIEW

NS 2.4 44. What is the greatest common divisor of 6 and 21? *(p. 10)*

Ⓐ 2 Ⓑ 3 Ⓒ 42 Ⓓ 126

NS 2.4 45. What is the simplest form of $\frac{84}{116}$? *(p. 15)*

Ⓐ $\frac{28}{39}$ Ⓑ $\frac{21}{29}$ Ⓒ $\frac{7}{10}$ Ⓓ $\frac{42}{58}$

Gr. 4 NS 3.1 46. Ms. Li has $11,357 in her bank account and makes a deposit of $2966. How much money is now in her account? *(p. 670)*

Ⓐ $13,213 Ⓑ $13,223 Ⓒ $14,223 Ⓓ $14,323

QUIZ *for Lessons 1.1– 1.4*

Tell whether the number is *prime* or *composite*. If the number is composite, write its prime factorization. *(p. 5)*

1. 75 2. 53 3. 61 4. 98

5. **QUILTING** You will sew 36 quilt squares together to make a wall hanging. *Describe* all possible rectangular arrangements of these squares. *(p. 5)*

Find the greatest common factor of the numbers. *(p. 10)*

6. 12, 30 7. 10, 21 8. 28, 50 9. 30, 48, 72

Write the fractions in simplest form. Tell whether they are equivalent. *(p. 16)*

10. $\frac{15}{28}, \frac{45}{84}$ 11. $\frac{7}{56}, \frac{12}{84}$ 12. $\frac{27}{72}, \frac{36}{90}$ 13. $\frac{45}{75}, \frac{81}{180}$

Find the least common multiple of the numbers. *(p. 21)*

14. 15, 27 15. 8, 18 16. 24, 50 17. 45, 54, 72

MIXED REVIEW of Skills and Problem Solving

Multiple Choice Practice for Lessons 1.1–1.4

1. Which fraction is *not* represented by the diagram below? **Gr. 4 NS 1.5**

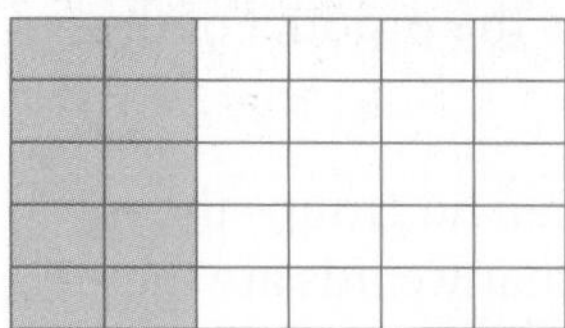

Ⓐ $\frac{1}{3}$ Ⓑ $\frac{2}{6}$

Ⓒ $\frac{5}{6}$ Ⓓ $\frac{10}{30}$

2. What is the simplest form of $\frac{54}{96}$? **NS 2.4**

Ⓐ $\frac{3}{8}$ Ⓑ $\frac{9}{16}$

Ⓒ $\frac{27}{48}$ Ⓓ $\frac{108}{192}$

3. What is the least common multiple of 28, 72, and 84? **NS 2.4**

Ⓐ 4 Ⓑ 42

Ⓒ 504 Ⓓ 2016

4. The table below shows how many students in one school are in grades 6, 7, and 8 and how many of them have traveled abroad. About what fraction of the students in grade 6 have traveled abroad? **NS 2.4, MR 2.6**

Grade	*Students*	*How Many Traveled Abroad*
6	75	9
7	72	27
8	68	16

Ⓐ $\frac{1}{10}$ Ⓑ $\frac{1}{8}$

Ⓒ $\frac{4}{17}$ Ⓓ $\frac{3}{8}$

5. A counselor wants to divide 48 boys and 30 girls into as many groups as possible. Each group must have the same number of boys, and it must have the same number of girls. How many boys and girls are in each group? **NS 2.4**

Ⓐ 6 boys and 6 girls

Ⓑ 8 boys and 5 girls

Ⓒ 16 boys and 10 girls

Ⓓ 24 boys and 15 girls

6. A store offers discounts, coupons, and prizes for its customers. How many customers will it take until a customer receives a discount, a coupon, and a prize? **NS 2.4, MR 3.3**

Ⓐ 10 Ⓑ 300

Ⓒ 480 Ⓓ 1200

7. What is the prime factorization of 216? **Gr. 5 NS 1.4**

Ⓐ $2^3 \times 3^2$

Ⓑ $2 \times 3^2 \times 7$

Ⓒ $2^3 \times 3^3$

Ⓓ $2 \times 3^3 \times 4$

8. What is the greatest common divisor of 16, 88, and 132? **NS 2.4**

Ⓐ 4 Ⓑ 22

Ⓒ 66 Ⓓ 528

1.5 Comparing Fractions

MATERIALS • colored pencils • paper

Standards

NS 1.1 Compare and order **positive** and negative **fractions**, decimals, and mixed numbers and place them on a number line.

QUESTION **How can you compare fractions with different denominators?**

You can use area models to compare fractions with different denominators.

EXPLORE 1 **Use models to compare $\frac{3}{4}$ and $\frac{5}{6}$.**

STEP 1 **Draw** two rectangles of the same size. Divide one rectangle vertically into 4 equal parts and shade 3 parts. Divide the other rectangle horizontally into 6 equal parts and shade 5 parts.

$\frac{3}{4}$ 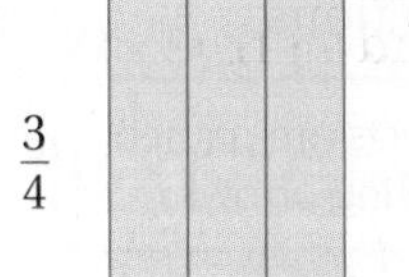

$\frac{5}{6}$ 

STEP 2 **Divide** the two rectangles into the same number of equal parts by dividing the model for $\frac{3}{4}$ horizontally into 6 equal parts and dividing the model for $\frac{5}{6}$ vertically into 4 equal parts.

$\frac{3}{4} = \frac{18}{24}$

$\frac{5}{6} = \frac{20}{24}$

STEP 3 **Compare** the fractions. Because both rectangles are divided into the same number of equal parts, $\frac{18}{24} < \frac{20}{24}$, so $\frac{3}{4} < \frac{5}{6}$.

DRAW CONCLUSIONS **Use your observations to complete these exercises.**

Model the two fractions. Then copy and complete using <, >, or =.

1. $\frac{5}{6}$? $\frac{3}{5}$ **2.** $\frac{4}{7}$? $\frac{1}{2}$ **3.** $\frac{7}{11}$? $\frac{2}{3}$ **4.** $\frac{5}{15}$? $\frac{4}{12}$

5. WRITING How is $\frac{18}{24}$ similar to $\frac{3}{4}$? How is it different?

Continued on next page

Continued from the previous page

On the previous page you compared $\frac{3}{4}$ and $\frac{5}{6}$ using models to rewrite the fractions using the same denominator of 24. You can represent what happens in Step 2 using multiplication.

$$\frac{3}{4} = \frac{3 \times 6}{4 \times 6} = \frac{18}{24} \qquad \frac{5}{6} = \frac{5 \times 4}{6 \times 4} = \frac{20}{24}$$

Notice that the 18 in $\frac{18}{24}$ is a result of multiplying the **3** in $\frac{3}{4}$ by the **6** in $\frac{5}{6}$.

Similarly, the 20 in $\frac{20}{24}$ is a result of multiplying the **5** in $\frac{5}{6}$ by the **4** in $\frac{3}{4}$.

These observations suggest a way to compare fractions using *cross products.*

EXPLORE 2 **Compare $\frac{5}{8}$ and $\frac{7}{12}$ using cross products.**

STEP 1 **Multiply** the numerator of each fraction by the denominator of the other fraction. These products are *cross products* of the fractions.

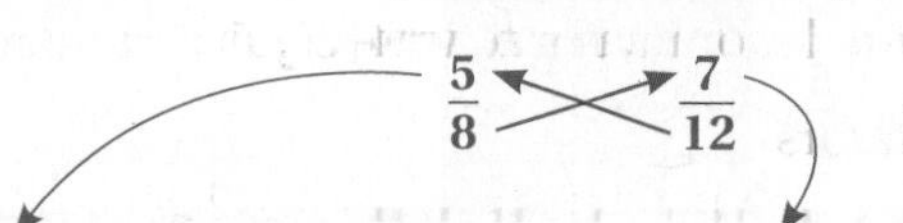

Cross products are named for the crossing arrows.

$12 \times 5 = \mathbf{60}$, the number of shaded parts in the model for $\frac{5}{8}$

$8 \times 7 = \mathbf{56}$, the number of shaded parts in the model for $\frac{7}{12}$

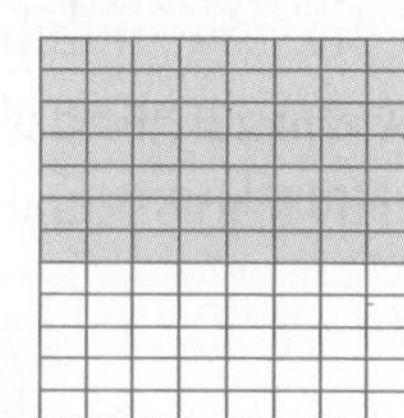

Each model has 8×12, or 96, equal parts.

STEP 2 **Compare** the two cross products.

Because 60 shaded parts > 56 shaded parts, $\frac{5}{8} > \frac{7}{12}$.

DRAW CONCLUSIONS **Use your observations to complete these exercises.**

Compare the fractions using cross products. Then copy and complete using <, >, or =.

6. $\frac{1}{6} \underset{-}{?} \frac{2}{9}$ **7.** $\frac{1}{4} \underset{-}{?} \frac{3}{10}$ **8.** $\frac{3}{7} \underset{-}{?} \frac{2}{3}$ **9.** $\frac{4}{7} \underset{-}{?} \frac{6}{11}$

10. REASONING In Explore 2, what is the common denominator used to compare the two fractions? How is it related to the original denominators?

11. REASONING Suppose you are using cross products to compare fractions. How do you know which cross product belongs to which fraction?

1.5 Comparing and Ordering Fractions

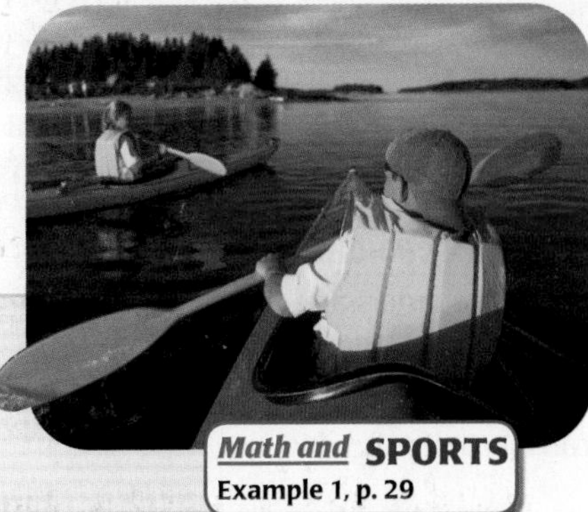

Standards **NS 1.1 Compare and order positive** and negative **fractions**, decimals, and mixed numbers **and place them on a number line.**

Connect ***Before*** you compared and ordered decimals. ***Now*** you will compare and order fractions.

Math and **SPORTS**
Example 1, p. 29

KEY VOCABULARY

- **least common denominator (LCD)**

You can compare fractions by using the *least common denominator.* The **least common denominator (LCD)** of two or more fractions is the least common multiple of the denominators.

KEY CONCEPT *For Your Notebook*

Comparing Two or More Fractions

1. Find the least common denominator of the fractions.
2. Use the least common denominator to write equivalent fractions.
3. Compare the numerators.

EXAMPLE 1 Comparing Fractions Using the LCD

KAYAKING Julie kayaks a distance of $\frac{7}{10}$ mile, and Seth kayaks $\frac{3}{4}$ mile. Who kayaks a greater distance?

SOLUTION

STEP 1 **Find** the LCD of the fractions to compare $\frac{7}{10}$ and $\frac{3}{4}$. Because the LCM of 10 and 4 is 20, the LCD of the fractions is 20.

STEP 2 **Use** the LCD to write equivalent fractions.

Julie: $\frac{7}{10} = \frac{7 \times 2}{10 \times 2} = \frac{14}{20}$ **Seth:** $\frac{3}{4} = \frac{3 \times 5}{4 \times 5} = \frac{15}{20}$

STEP 3 **Compare** the numerators: $\frac{14}{20} < \frac{15}{20}$, so $\frac{7}{10} < \frac{3}{4}$.

▶ **Answer** Seth kayaks a greater distance.

CHECK Graph the numbers on a number line.

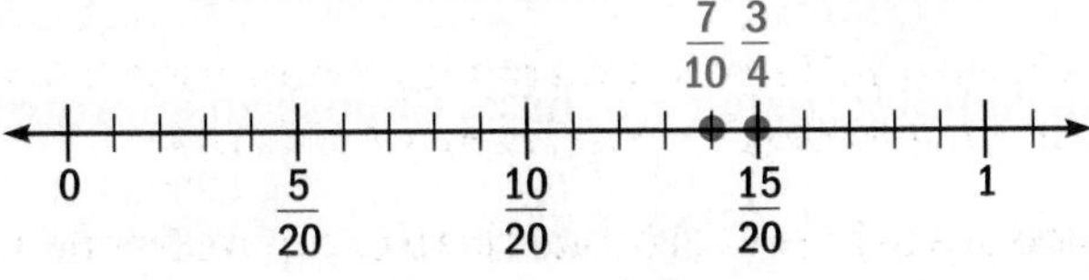

Because $\frac{14}{20}$ is to the left of $\frac{15}{20}$, $\frac{7}{10} < \frac{3}{4}$. ✓

ANOTHER WAY

For an alternate method for solving the problem in Example 1, turn to page 34 for the **Problem Solving Workshop**.

EXAMPLE 2 ◆ Multiple Choice Practice

ELIMINATE CHOICES
Because quarters are greater than eighths, $\frac{3}{4}$ is greater than $\frac{3}{8}$, so you can eliminate choice C.

Which list shows $\frac{2}{3}, \frac{3}{8}, \frac{1}{6},$ and $\frac{3}{4}$ in order from least to greatest?

Ⓐ $\frac{3}{8}, \frac{1}{6}, \frac{3}{4}, \frac{2}{3}$　Ⓑ $\frac{1}{6}, \frac{3}{8}, \frac{2}{3}, \frac{3}{4}$　Ⓒ $\frac{1}{6}, \frac{2}{3}, \frac{3}{4}, \frac{3}{8}$　Ⓓ $\frac{1}{6}, \frac{3}{8}, \frac{3}{4}, \frac{2}{3}$

SOLUTION

STEP 1 **Find** the LCD. The LCD is the LCM of 3, 8, 6, and 4, which is 24.

STEP 2 **Use** the LCD to write equivalent fractions.

$$\frac{2}{3} = \frac{2 \times 8}{3 \times 8} = \frac{16}{24} \qquad \frac{3}{8} = \frac{3 \times 3}{8 \times 3} = \frac{9}{24}$$

$$\frac{1}{6} = \frac{1 \times 4}{6 \times 4} = \frac{4}{24} \qquad \frac{3}{4} = \frac{3 \times 6}{4 \times 6} = \frac{18}{24}$$

STEP 3 **Compare** the numerators: $\frac{4}{24} < \frac{9}{24} < \frac{16}{24} < \frac{18}{24}$, so $\frac{1}{6} < \frac{3}{8} < \frac{2}{3} < \frac{3}{4}$.

▸ **Answer** The correct answer is B. Ⓐ Ⓑ Ⓒ Ⓓ

COMPARE TO ONE HALF Fractions equivalent to $\frac{1}{2}$ have numerators that are half their denominators. This fact can help you compare some fractions.

EXAMPLE 3 Comparing to One Half

AVOID ERRORS
If both fractions are greater than $\frac{1}{2}$ or less than $\frac{1}{2}$, you will need to use another method.

Which portion remaining in each box is greater, $\frac{13}{24}$ or $\frac{17}{36}$?

Compare the numerator of each fraction to half its denominator. Decide if the fraction is greater than or less than $\frac{1}{2}$.

Because $13 > \frac{1}{2}(24)$, you know $\frac{13}{24} > \frac{1}{2}$.

Because $17 < \frac{1}{2}(36)$, you know $\frac{17}{36} < \frac{1}{2}$.

▸ **Answer** You can conclude that $\frac{13}{24} > \frac{17}{36}$, so the box with $\frac{13}{24}$ of its pencils has a greater portion left.

✓ **GUIDED PRACTICE** for Examples 1, 2, and 3

Copy and complete using <, >, or =. Choose an appropriate method.

1. $\frac{4}{7} \underline{\ ?\ } \frac{7}{12}$　2. $\frac{16}{33} \underline{\ ?\ } \frac{11}{18}$　3. $\frac{23}{48} \underline{\ ?\ } \frac{31}{56}$　4. $\frac{3}{8} \underline{\ ?\ } \frac{4}{9}$

5. Order the fractions from least to greatest: $\frac{9}{14}, \frac{5}{7}, \frac{3}{4}, \frac{5}{28}$.

1.5 EXERCISES

HOMEWORK KEY

◆ = **MULTIPLE CHOICE PRACTICE** Exs. 18, 25, 27, 47–49

○ = **HINTS AND HOMEWORK HELP** for Exs. 7, 13, 39 at classzone.com

SKILLS • PROBLEM SOLVING • REASONING

1. **VOCABULARY** Copy and complete: The least common multiple of the denominators of two or more fractions is their _?_.

2. **WRITING** *Explain* how to compare fractions with unlike denominators.

SEE EXAMPLE 1 on p. 29 for Exs. 3–11

USING NUMBER LINES Use the number line. Copy and complete the statement using <, >, or =.

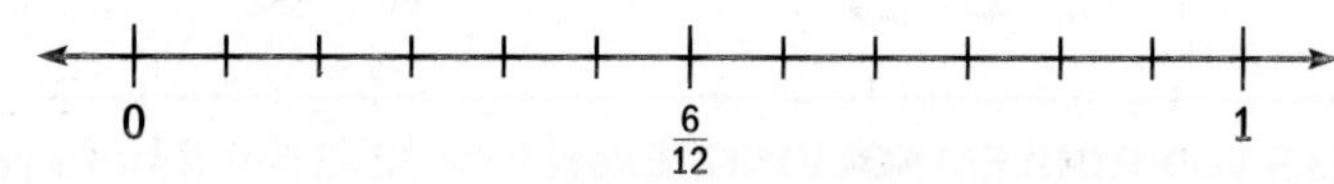

3. $\frac{1}{3}$ _?_ $\frac{2}{12}$
4. $\frac{2}{3}$ _?_ $\frac{5}{6}$
5. $\frac{3}{12}$ _?_ $\frac{1}{4}$

COMPARING FRACTIONS Copy and complete the statement using <, >, or =. Check using a number line.

6. $\frac{9}{16}$ _?_ $\frac{3}{4}$
7. $\frac{5}{6}$ _?_ $\frac{7}{8}$
8. $\frac{11}{15}$ _?_ $\frac{2}{3}$
9. $\frac{17}{34}$ _?_ $\frac{9}{18}$
10. $\frac{28}{81}$ _?_ $\frac{7}{24}$
11. $\frac{13}{14}$ _?_ $\frac{26}{28}$

SEE EXAMPLE 2 on p. 30 for Exs. 12–18

ORDERING FRACTIONS Order the fractions from least to greatest.

12. $\frac{1}{3}, \frac{2}{5}, \frac{3}{10}, \frac{11}{30}$
13. $\frac{3}{4}, \frac{2}{5}, \frac{5}{8}, \frac{7}{10}$
14. $\frac{3}{7}, \frac{1}{3}, \frac{1}{2}, \frac{9}{14}$
15. $\frac{3}{8}, \frac{9}{32}, \frac{1}{4}, \frac{5}{16}$
16. $\frac{7}{9}, \frac{32}{45}, \frac{20}{27}, \frac{2}{3}$
17. $\frac{17}{81}, \frac{5}{9}, \frac{13}{27}, \frac{2}{3}$

18. ◆ **MULTIPLE CHOICE** Which fractions are in order from least to greatest?

Ⓐ $\frac{8}{15}, \frac{5}{9}, \frac{3}{5}$ Ⓑ $\frac{7}{18}, \frac{2}{9}, \frac{5}{12}$ Ⓒ $\frac{5}{6}, \frac{13}{18}, \frac{16}{27}$ Ⓓ $\frac{3}{8}, \frac{5}{16}, \frac{15}{32}$

SEE EXAMPLE 3 on p. 30 for Exs. 19–22

COMPARING TO ONE HALF Compare to $\frac{1}{2}$ to tell which fraction is greater.

19. $\frac{10}{21}, \frac{15}{28}$
20. $\frac{15}{31}, \frac{27}{50}$
21. $\frac{40}{79}, \frac{23}{48}$
22. $\frac{9}{17}, \frac{8}{16}$

ERROR ANALYSIS *Describe* and correct the error in comparing fractions.

23. ✗ 15 > 3 and 49 > 4, so $\frac{15}{49} > \frac{3}{4}$.

24. ✗ 16 < 17, so $\frac{5}{16} < \frac{5}{17}$.

25. ◆ **MULTIPLE CHOICE** The fraction $\frac{4}{7}$ lies between which pair of fractions on a number line?

Ⓐ $\frac{7}{14}$ and $\frac{17}{28}$ Ⓑ $\frac{8}{14}$ and $\frac{18}{28}$ Ⓒ $\frac{9}{14}$ and $\frac{24}{28}$ Ⓓ $\frac{10}{14}$ and $\frac{27}{28}$

26. **CHECKING REASONABLENESS** Use the the least common denominator to tell which fraction is greater, $\frac{7}{15}$ or $\frac{15}{28}$. Approximate to check the reasonableness of your answer.

27. ◆ **MULTIPLE CHOICE** Which fraction is the best estimate of the portion of the granola bar with a yogurt coating?

Ⓐ $\frac{1}{10}$ Ⓑ $\frac{3}{13}$ Ⓒ $\frac{4}{7}$ Ⓓ $\frac{5}{6}$

CHOOSE A METHOD Copy and complete using <, >, or =. Tell whether you used *mental math* or *paper and pencil*. *Explain* your choice.

28. $\frac{15}{56} \underline{?} \frac{1}{4}$ 29. $\frac{7}{21} \underline{?} \frac{1}{3}$ 30. $\frac{13}{24} \underline{?} \frac{19}{32}$ 31. $\frac{13}{18} \underline{?} \frac{5}{9}$

CONNECT SKILLS TO PROBLEM SOLVING Exercises 32–35 will help you prepare for problem solving.

32. After a holiday dinner, $\frac{1}{4}$ of an apple pie and $\frac{3}{10}$ of a pumpkin pie are left. Which pie has a greater portion left? Use a common denominator of 20.

33. Yoko answers $\frac{3}{4}$ of the questions on a test correctly. Glen answers $\frac{13}{15}$ of the same questions correctly. Who answers more of his or her test correctly? Use a common demominator of 60.

34. Curtis and Linda are running for class president. Curtis receives $\frac{2}{5}$ of the votes and Linda receives $\frac{19}{25}$ of the votes. Who received more votes?

35. On one apple tree, $\frac{7}{12}$ of the apples fall to the ground. On another tree, $\frac{4}{9}$ of the apples fall to the ground. Which apple tree has a greater portion of apples fall to the ground?

SEE EXAMPLE 1 on p. 29 for Ex. 36

36. **CAROUSELS** Carousel horses that move up and down are called *jumpers*. The Broadway Flying Horses carousel in San Diego has 28 jumpers out of 40 horses. The carousel at the San Francisco Zoo has 24 jumpers out of 36 horses. Which carousel has the greater fraction of jumpers?

California @HomeTutor for problem solving help at classzone.com

Jumpers on a carousel

37. **WRENCHES** The sizes, in inches, of several wrenches are as follows: $\frac{11}{16}, \frac{3}{8}, \frac{3}{4}, \frac{1}{2}, \frac{5}{8}$, and $\frac{7}{16}$. Order the wrenches from smallest to largest.

California @HomeTutor for problem solving help at classzone.com

38. **SHORT RESPONSE** Alex says "You don't have to rewrite fractions using least common denominators to compare them. You can use any common denominator." Do you agree? *Explain* using examples.

39. **MULTI-STEP PROBLEM** Jon and Anne are raising money for a school project. Jon's goal is to raise \$225. Anne's goal is to raise \$275. So far, Jon has raised \$150, and Anne has raised \$190.

a. **Write fractions** Write a fraction in simplest form for the portion of his or her goal that each student has raised.

b. **Analyze** Who has raised the greater fraction of his or her goal?

c. **Compare** *Compare* the students' progress in terms of fractions and in terms of absolute dollars they still need to raise. What do you observe?

40. **TENNIS** At tennis camp, Mia won 13 games and lost 15. Audrey won 19 games and lost 18. Write a fraction for the portion of games won by each girl. Who won the greater fraction of her games? Was the fraction greater than $\frac{1}{2}$?

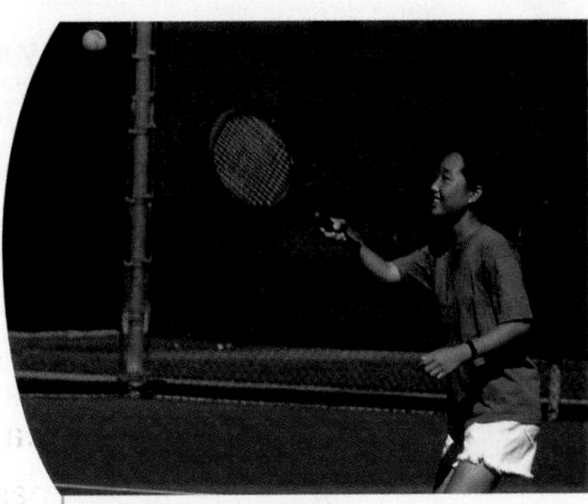
Mia won 13 games.

41. **WRITING** Write a fraction that is exactly halfway between $\frac{3}{7}$ and $\frac{3}{5}$. *Explain* how you found the fraction.

REASONING ***Explain*** **how you can compare the given fractions without using a model or writing equivalent fractions.**

42. $\frac{1}{24}, \frac{1}{36}$

43. $\frac{11}{37}, \frac{11}{42}$

44. $\frac{19}{20}, \frac{24}{25}$

45. **CHALLENGE** Suppose a and b are nonzero whole numbers and $a < b$. How do $\frac{1}{a}$ and $\frac{1}{b}$ compare? How do $\frac{a}{b}$ and $\frac{b}{a}$ compare? *Justify* your reasoning.

46. **CHALLENGE** Matt and Nina each paint an equal sized mural. One day Matt paints $\frac{2}{3}$ of his mural and Nina paints $\frac{1}{2}$ of her mural. The next day, Matt paints $\frac{2}{5}$ of the unpainted part of his mural and Nina paints $\frac{3}{4}$ of her unpainted part. Who has painted the greater amount? *Explain.*

◆ CALIFORNIA STANDARDS SPIRAL REVIEW

NS 2.4 **47.** Which fraction is equivalent to $\frac{8}{14}$? ***(p. 16)***

Ⓐ $\frac{1}{7}$ Ⓑ $\frac{7}{13}$ Ⓒ $\frac{4}{7}$ Ⓓ $\frac{14}{8}$

Gr. 5 NS 2.2 **48.** What is the quotient 4288 ÷ 134? ***(p. 664)***

Ⓐ 30 Ⓑ 32 Ⓒ 67 Ⓓ 3200

Gr. 4 NS 3.1 **49.** Jackson School has 327 students in grade 6 and 288 students in grade 7. How many more students are in grade 6 than in grade 7? ***(p. 670)***

Ⓐ 39 Ⓑ 49 Ⓒ 161 Ⓓ 615

PROBLEM SOLVING WORKSHOP
LESSON 1.5

Using ALTERNATIVE METHODS

Another Way to Solve Example 1, page 29

Standards
NS 1.1

In Example 1 on page 29, you compared kayaking distances by using the least common denominator of the fractions. You can also solve the problem by using area models.

PROBLEM

KAYAKING Julie kayaks a distance of $\frac{7}{10}$ mile, and Seth kayaks $\frac{3}{4}$ mile. Who kayaks a greater distance?

METHOD

Using Area Models An alternate approach is to use area models.

STEP 1 **Draw** two rectangles of the same size. Divide one vertically into 10 equal parts and shade 7 of the parts. Divide the other horizontally into 4 equal parts and shade 3 of the parts.

$\frac{7}{10}$ $\frac{3}{4}$

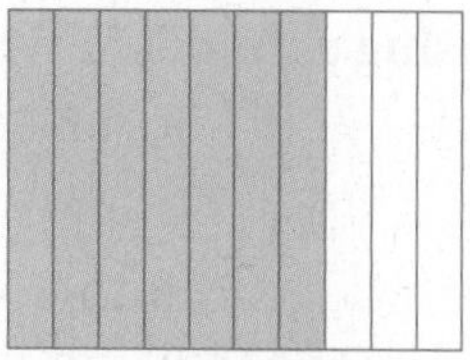

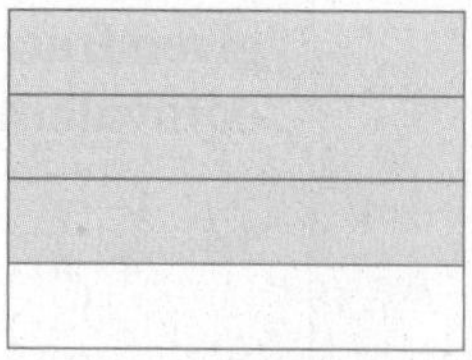

STEP 2 **Divide** the two rectangles into the same number of equal parts. First divide the model for $\frac{7}{10}$ horizontally into 4 equal parts. Then divide the model for $\frac{3}{4}$ vertically into 10 equal parts.

$\frac{7}{10} = \frac{28}{40}$ $\frac{3}{4} = \frac{30}{40}$

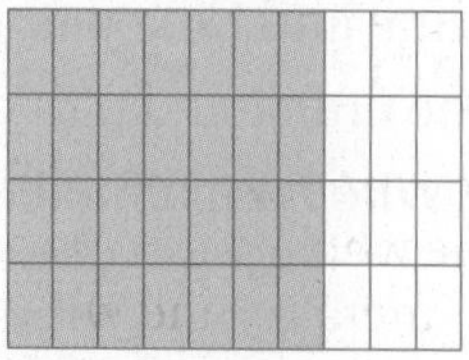

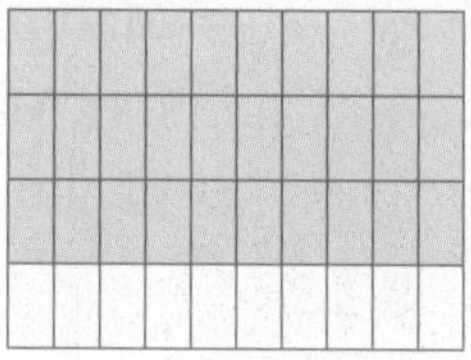

STEP 3 **Compare** the fractions. Because both rectangles are divided into the same number of equal parts, $\frac{28}{40} < \frac{30}{40}$, so $\frac{7}{10} < \frac{3}{4}$.

▶ **Answer** Seth kayaks a greater distance.

PRACTICE

1. **SNACK FOOD** Paul ate $\frac{2}{5}$ pound of grapes and Jeff ate $\frac{1}{3}$ pound of grapes. Who ate a greater portion of grapes? Use area models to solve the problem.

2. **RUNNING** Amy runs $\frac{5}{8}$ mile and Beth runs $\frac{7}{12}$ mile. Who runs farther? Solve using the least common denominator. Then use area models to check.

1.6 Comparing Fractions and Mixed Numbers

Standards **NS 1.1 Compare and order positive** and negative fractions, decimals, and **mixed numbers** and place them on a number line.

Connect ***Before*** you compared and ordered fractions. ***Now*** you will compare and order fractions and mixed numbers.

Math and **RECREATION**
Ex. 39, p. 39

KEY VOCABULARY
- **mixed number**
- **proper fraction**
- **improper fraction**

A **mixed number** has a whole number part and a fraction part. Model A represents the mixed number $2\frac{3}{4}$.

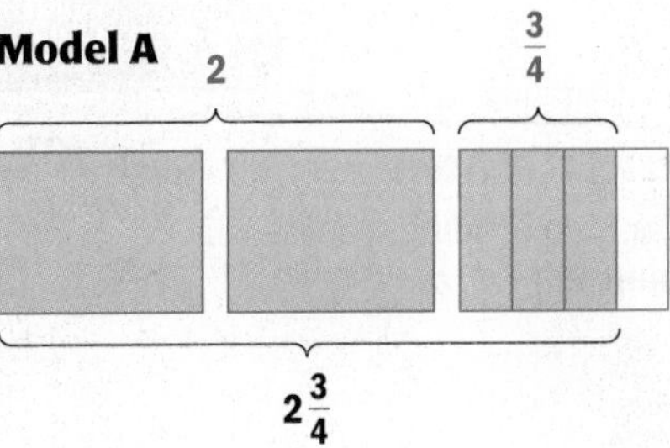

A **proper fraction** is a fraction whose numerator is less than its denominator. A fraction is called an **improper fraction** if its numerator is greater than or equal to its denominator. Model B represents the improper fraction $\frac{11}{4}$.

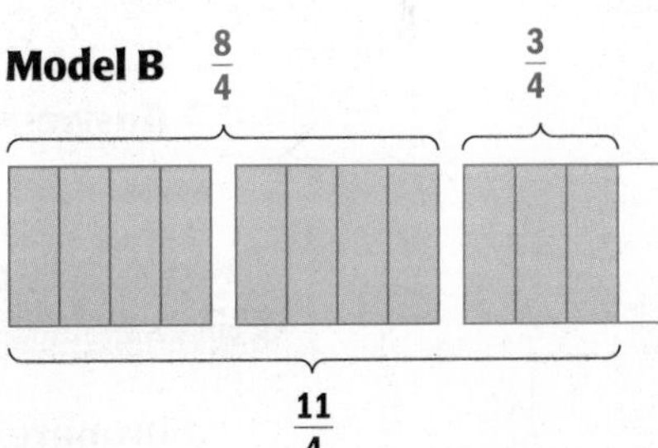

READING

The mixed number $2\frac{3}{4}$ is read "two and three fourths."

Model B shows how to write the mixed number $2\frac{3}{4}$ as an improper fraction. First divide the whole number part into 2×4, or 8, fourths. Then find the total number of fourths: $2 \times 4 + 3$, or 11. This method is summarized below.

KEY CONCEPT *For Your Notebook*

Writing Mixed Numbers as Improper Fractions

Words To write a mixed number as an improper fraction, multiply the whole number part and the denominator, add the numerator, and write the sum over the denominator.

Numbers $2\frac{3}{4} = \frac{2 \times 4 + 3}{4} = \frac{11}{4}$

EXAMPLE 1 Writing Improper Fractions

Write the mixed number as an improper fraction.

a. $3\frac{5}{6} = \frac{3 \times 6 + 5}{6}$

$= \frac{23}{6}$

b. $4\frac{7}{8} = \frac{4 \times 8 + 7}{8}$

$= \frac{39}{8}$

KEY CONCEPT — *For Your Notebook*

Writing Improper Fractions as Mixed Numbers

Words To write an improper fraction as a mixed number, divide the numerator by the denominator and write any remainder as a fraction.

Numbers $\frac{7}{3} \rightarrow 7 \div 3 = 2\text{ R1, or } 2\frac{1}{3}$

EXAMPLE 2 Writing Mixed Numbers

REVIEW DIVISION

For help dividing whole numbers, see p. 664.

Write $\frac{21}{6}$ as a mixed number in simplest form.

STEP 1 **Divide** the numerator by the denominator.

$$\frac{21}{6} = 21 \div 6 = 3\text{ R3}$$

STEP 2 **Write** the remainder R3 as a fraction: $\frac{\text{remainder}}{\text{divisor}}$.

$$3\text{ R3} \rightarrow 3\frac{3}{6}$$

▶ **Answer** $\frac{21}{6} = 3\frac{3}{6}$, or $3\frac{1}{2}$ in simplest form.

EXAMPLE 3 Comparing Mixed Numbers and Fractions

Compare $\frac{17}{6}$ and $2\frac{1}{4}$.

STEP 1 **Write** $2\frac{1}{4}$ as an improper fraction: $2\frac{1}{4} = \frac{9}{4}$.

STEP 2 **Rewrite** $\frac{17}{6}$ and $\frac{9}{4}$ using the least common denominator, 12.

$$\frac{17}{6} = \frac{17 \times 2}{6 \times 2} = \frac{34}{12} \qquad \frac{9}{4} = \frac{9 \times 3}{4 \times 3} = \frac{27}{12}$$

STEP 3 **Compare** the fractions: $\frac{34}{12} > \frac{27}{12}$, so $\frac{17}{6} > 2\frac{1}{4}$.

About the Standards

In Chapter 2, you will again use common denominators but to add and subtract fractions, as called for in Grade 6 Standard NS 2.4.

✓ GUIDED PRACTICE for Examples 1, 2, and 3

Copy and complete the improper fraction or mixed number.

1. $3\frac{3}{4} = \frac{?}{4}$
2. $1\frac{2}{5} = \frac{?}{5}$
3. $\frac{17}{3} = \underline{?}\,\frac{?}{3}$
4. $\frac{15}{7} = \underline{?}\,\frac{?}{7}$

Copy and complete the statement using <, >, or =.

5. $\frac{19}{6}\ \underline{?}\ 3\frac{5}{12}$
6. $\frac{14}{3}\ \underline{?}\ 4\frac{3}{5}$
7. $\frac{27}{4}\ \underline{?}\ 6\frac{3}{4}$
8. $\frac{49}{9}\ \underline{?}\ 5\frac{1}{2}$

EXAMPLE 4 Ordering Mixed Numbers and Fractions

ANOTHER WAY

You can also change each whole or mixed number to an improper fraction with a common denominator to compare.

FITNESS The Presidential Physical Fitness Award involves a flexibility test called the V-sit reach. The distances, in inches, that four students could reach are listed below. Order the distances from least to greatest.

Measuring distance for the V-sit reach

$3\frac{5}{8}$ $\quad 3 \quad$ $\frac{17}{4}$ $\quad 3\frac{1}{2}$

SOLUTION

Rewrite $\frac{17}{4}$ as $4\frac{1}{4}$, which is the longest distance.

The shortest distance is 3 inches.

To compare $3\frac{5}{8}$ and $3\frac{1}{2}$, compare their fraction parts: $\frac{1}{2} = \frac{4}{8} < \frac{5}{8}$, so $3\frac{1}{2} < 3\frac{5}{8}$.

▶ **Answer** From least to greatest, the distances are 3, $3\frac{1}{2}$, $3\frac{5}{8}$, and $\frac{17}{4}$ inches.

Animated Math

For an interactive example of ordering mixed numbers go to **classzone.com.**

GUIDED PRACTICE for Example 4

Order the numbers from least to greatest.

9. $2, 2\frac{7}{8}, \frac{16}{5}, 2\frac{3}{4}$ **10.** $7\frac{2}{5}, \frac{23}{4}, \frac{38}{5}, 7\frac{5}{8}$ **11.** $\frac{3}{2}, 1\frac{1}{3}, \frac{11}{8}, 1\frac{3}{7}$

1.6 EXERCISES

HOMEWORK KEY

◆ = **MULTIPLE CHOICE PRACTICE** Exs. 25, 32, 38, 48–50

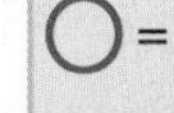

○ = **HINTS AND HOMEWORK HELP** for Exs. 9, 19, 39 at classzone.com

SKILLS • PROBLEM SOLVING • REASONING

VOCABULARY Tell whether the number is a *mixed number*, a *proper fraction*, or *an improper fraction*.

1. $\frac{12}{12}$ **2.** $\frac{12}{17}$ **3.** $8\frac{3}{8}$ **4.** $\frac{21}{20}$ **5.** $\frac{53}{54}$

6. WRITING *Explain* how proper and improper fractions are alike and how they are different.

SEE EXAMPLE 1 on p. 35 for Exs. 7–11

IMPROPER FRACTIONS Write the mixed number as an improper fraction.

7. $5\frac{1}{3}$ **8.** $2\frac{4}{9}$ **(9.)** $11\frac{3}{8}$ **10.** $8\frac{6}{7}$ **11.** $4\frac{5}{16}$

SEE EXAMPLE 2 on p. 36 for Exs. 12–16

MIXED NUMBERS Write the improper fraction as a whole number or as a mixed number in simplest form.

12. $\frac{27}{5}$ **13.** $\frac{95}{6}$ **14.** $\frac{99}{4}$ **15.** $\frac{126}{14}$ **16.** $\frac{58}{21}$

SEE EXAMPLE 3 on p. 36 for Exs. 17–25

COMPARING NUMBERS **Copy and complete the statement using <, >, or =.**

17. $\frac{3}{2}$? $3\frac{1}{2}$ 18. $\frac{8}{3}$? $2\frac{2}{3}$ 19. $8\frac{5}{12}$? $\frac{101}{12}$ 20. $\frac{29}{5}$? $6\frac{3}{5}$

21. $5\frac{7}{8}$? $\frac{43}{8}$ 22. $\frac{29}{6}$? $4\frac{7}{9}$ 23. $\frac{22}{3}$? $7\frac{1}{4}$ 24. $\frac{45}{4}$? $11\frac{7}{16}$

25. ◆ **MULTIPLE CHOICE** Which measure is *not* equivalent to the measure indicated below?

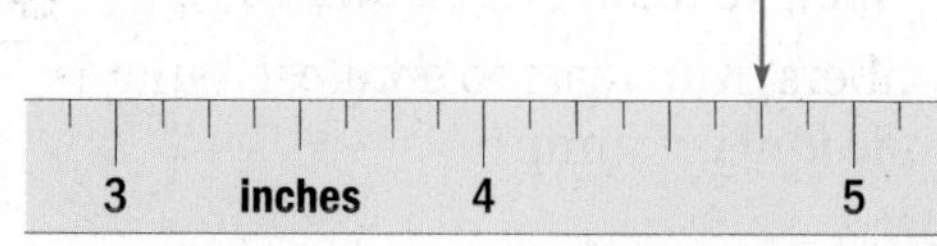

Ⓐ $4\frac{12}{16}$ in. Ⓑ $\frac{39}{8}$ in. Ⓒ $\frac{19}{4}$ in. Ⓓ $4\frac{3}{4}$ in.

SEE EXAMPLE 4 on p. 37 for Exs. 26–31

ORDERING NUMBERS **Order the numbers from least to greatest.**

26. $\frac{22}{2}, 2\frac{2}{3}, \frac{22}{11}, 2\frac{20}{33}$ 27. $\frac{40}{40}, \frac{49}{42}, \frac{22}{20}, 1\frac{1}{9}$ 28. $7\frac{1}{5}, 7, \frac{38}{5}, \frac{50}{7}$

29. $3\frac{11}{18}, \frac{65}{24}, \frac{43}{12}, 3\frac{3}{4}$ 30. $4\frac{13}{25}, \frac{27}{5}, 4\frac{11}{20}, \frac{67}{15}$ 31. $2\frac{15}{28}, \frac{35}{14}, 2\frac{3}{8}, \frac{26}{7}$

32. ◆ **MULTIPLE CHOICE** Which of the following fractions is closest to 5?

Ⓐ $4\frac{5}{6}$ Ⓑ $\frac{35}{8}$ Ⓒ $\frac{61}{16}$ Ⓓ $5\frac{2}{5}$

ERROR ANALYSIS ***Describe*** **and correct the error made in rewriting the number.**

33. ✗ $5\frac{2}{3} = \frac{5 \times 3 + 3}{3} = \frac{18}{3}$

34. ✗ $\frac{9}{5} = 1\frac{4}{9}$ because $5\overline{)9}$ = 1 R4; 9 − 5 = 4

CONNECT SKILLS TO PROBLEM SOLVING **Exercises 35–37 will help you prepare for problem solving.**

35. A recipe for banana nut bread calls for $1\frac{1}{2}$ cups of bananas. Write the amount of bananas needed as an improper fraction.

36. An adjustable wrench can open as far as $1\frac{3}{8}$ inches. Write the length as an improper fraction.

37. The Olympic marathon is $26\frac{7}{32}$ miles. Write the distance of the Olympic marathon as an improper fraction.

SEE EXAMPLE 1 on p. 35 for Exs. 38–39

38. ◆ **MULTIPLE CHOICE** At a restaurant, a serving of lasagna is one eighth of a tray. How many servings are in the remaining $2\frac{3}{4}$ lasagna trays?

Ⓐ 2 Ⓑ 11 Ⓒ 19 Ⓓ 22

California @HomeTutor for problem solving help at classzone.com

39. BUBBLE SOLUTION You are filling 5 bottles with bubble solution. To fill one bottle, you need $1\frac{1}{4}$ cups of water. You can find only a quarter cup measure. How many quarter cups of water do you need?

California @HomeTutor for problem solving help at classzone.com

40. LONG JUMPS The four best long jumps at a track meet are $18\frac{7}{12}$ feet, 18 feet, $\frac{35}{2}$ feet, and $18\frac{1}{3}$ feet. Order the numbers from least to greatest. What is the length of the longest jump?

Long Jump

41. REASONING Which type of number is greater, an *improper fraction* or a *proper fraction*? *Explain* your reasoning.

42. WRITING How could you order $3\frac{1}{4}$, $3\frac{1}{3}$, $3\frac{2}{7}$ and $3\frac{1}{8}$ from least to greatest without writing them as improper fractions? *Explain* your reasoning. Then order the mixed numbers from least to greatest.

43. WRITING Use the diagram below. *Explain* how to rearrange the shaded parts to write the fraction $\frac{7}{3}$ as a mixed number. Include a diagram.

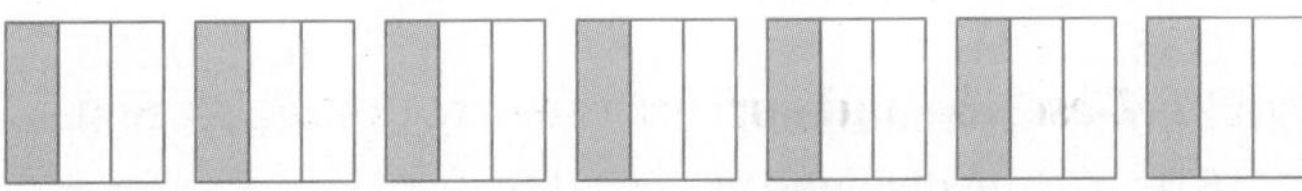

CHALLENGE **Order the given numbers from least to greatest. Then find a value for a new number so that it is third in the list.**

44. $\frac{85}{9}$, $9\frac{11}{20}$, $9\frac{21}{40}$, $\frac{245}{27}$

45. $\frac{79}{7}$, $11\frac{3}{11}$, $\frac{45}{4}$, $11\frac{17}{24}$

46. $5\frac{11}{15}$, $\frac{43}{8}$, $5\frac{17}{30}$, $\frac{17}{3}$

47. CHALLENGE Estimate the two whole numbers that the fractions $\frac{1284}{385}$ and $\frac{1520}{413}$ are between. *Explain* your reasoning.

◆ CALIFORNIA STANDARDS SPIRAL REVIEW

NS 2.4 **48.** What is the least common multiple of 32 and 40? ***(p. 21)***

Ⓐ 8 Ⓑ 20 Ⓒ 160 Ⓓ 1280

Gr. 4 NS 3.2 **49.** What is the product 162×27? ***(p. 662)***

Ⓐ 6 Ⓑ 1458 Ⓒ 4374 Ⓓ 43,740

NS 1.1 **50.** The lengths (in inches) of four grasshoppers are $\frac{9}{10}$, $\frac{4}{5}$, $\frac{11}{12}$, and $\frac{2}{3}$. Which list shows the lengths in order from least to greatest? ***(p. 29)***

Ⓐ $\frac{9}{10}, \frac{4}{5}, \frac{11}{12}, \frac{2}{3}$ Ⓑ $\frac{2}{3}, \frac{4}{5}, \frac{9}{10}, \frac{11}{12}$ Ⓒ $\frac{2}{3}, \frac{11}{12}, \frac{4}{5}, \frac{9}{10}$ Ⓓ $\frac{4}{5}, \frac{2}{3}, \frac{11}{12}, \frac{9}{10}$

1.7 Ordering Fractions and Decimals

Math and SCIENCE
Exs. 54–56, p. 44

Standards **NS 1.1 Compare and order positive** and negative **fractions, decimals, and mixed numbers** and place them on a number line.

Connect ***Before*** you compared fractions and mixed numbers. ***Now*** you will write fractions as decimals and decimals as fractions to help you compare them.

KEY VOCABULARY
- **terminating decimal**
- **repeating decimal**

You can think of the fraction $\frac{a}{b}$ as the division expression $a \div b$, which can help you write a fraction as a decimal. You can divide the numerator by the denominator as in Examples 1 and 2. In Example 4 you will use this skill to help you order numbers.

EXAMPLE 1 Writing Fractions as Decimals

Write (a) $\frac{7}{20}$ and (b) $3\frac{5}{8}$ as decimals.

SOLUTION

REVIEW DIVISION
For help dividing by a whole number, see p. 664.

a.
$$\begin{array}{r} 0.35 \\ 20\overline{)7.00} \\ \underline{6\,0} \\ 1\,00 \\ \underline{1\,00} \\ 0 \end{array}$$
← **Write zeros in dividend as placeholders.**
← **Remainder is zero.**

b.
$$\begin{array}{r} 0.625 \\ 8\overline{)5.000} \\ \underline{4\,8} \\ 20 \\ \underline{16} \\ 40 \\ \underline{40} \\ 0 \end{array}$$
← **Write zeros in dividend as placeholders.**
← **Remainder is zero.**

▶**Answer** $\frac{7}{20} = 0.35$

▶**Answer** $3\frac{5}{8} = 3 + 0.625 = 3.625$

✓ **GUIDED PRACTICE** for Example 1

Write the fraction or mixed number as a decimal.

1. $\frac{3}{10}$ **2.** $\frac{17}{200}$ **3.** $3\frac{4}{5}$ **4.** $2\frac{7}{8}$

VOCABULARY
In a terminating decimal, the digits *terminate*, or end. In a repeating decimal, the digits *repeat* with no end.

TERMINATING AND REPEATING DECIMALS When a division problem results in a remainder of 0, the quotient is a **terminating decimal**. Sometimes, long division gives a **repeating decimal**, where one or more digits repeat without end. Repeating decimals can be written with a bar over the digit(s) that repeat.

$0.4444\ldots = 0.\overline{4}$ **One digit repeats.**

$3.0505\ldots = 3.\overline{05}$ **Two digits repeat.**

EXAMPLE 2 Writing Fractions as Repeating Decimals

Write (a) $\frac{5}{3}$ and (b) $\frac{13}{33}$ as decimals.

SOLUTION

a.

$$\begin{array}{r} 1.666\ldots \\ 3\overline{)5.000} \\ \underline{3} \\ 2\,0 \\ \underline{1\,8} \\ 20 \\ \underline{18} \\ 20 \\ \underline{18} \\ 2 \end{array}$$

The digit 6 keeps repeating.

Remainder will never be zero.

▶ **Answer** $\frac{5}{3} = 1.\overline{6}$

Only the 6 repeats, so draw a bar over only that digit.

b.

$$\begin{array}{r} 0.3939\ldots \\ 33\overline{)13.0000} \\ \underline{99} \\ 31\,0 \\ \underline{29\,7} \\ 1\,30 \\ \underline{99} \\ 310 \\ \underline{297} \\ 13 \end{array}$$

The digits 3 and 9 keep repeating.

Remainder will never be zero.

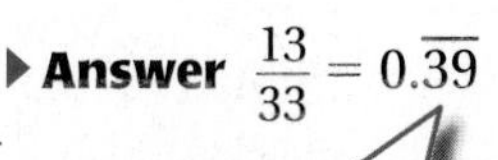

▶ **Answer** $\frac{13}{33} = 0.\overline{39}$

The digits 39 repeat, so draw a bar over both digits.

REVIEW PLACE VALUE

For help with decimal place value, see p. 676.

WRITING DECIMALS AS FRACTIONS To write a decimal as a fraction, use the place value of the last digit of the decimal as the denominator. For example, in the decimal 0.45, the digit 5 is in the hundredths' place, so write $\frac{45}{100}$.

EXAMPLE 3 Writing Decimals as Fractions

TAKE NOTES

It is useful to know these common equivalents. Write them in your notebook.

$\frac{1}{2} = 0.5$ $\quad \frac{1}{5} = 0.2$

$\frac{1}{3} = 0.\overline{3}$ $\quad \frac{2}{3} = 0.\overline{6}$

$\frac{1}{4} = 0.25$ $\quad \frac{3}{4} = 0.75$

Write (a) 0.85 and (b) 4.375 as a fraction or mixed number in simplest form.

SOLUTION

a. $0.85 = \frac{85}{100}$ **5 is in the hundredths' place.**

$= \frac{17 \times \cancel{5}^{1}}{20 \times \cancel{5}_{1}}$

$= \frac{17}{20}$

b. $4.375 = 4\frac{375}{1000}$ **5 is in the thousandths' place.**

$= 4\frac{3 \times \cancel{125}^{1}}{8 \times \cancel{125}_{1}}$

$= 4\frac{3}{8}$

✓ GUIDED PRACTICE for Examples 2 and 3

Write the fraction or mixed number as a decimal.

5. $\frac{7}{9}$ **6.** $\frac{13}{6}$ **7.** $2\frac{5}{11}$ **8.** $4\frac{3}{22}$

Write the decimal as a fraction or mixed number in simplest form.

9. 0.4 **10.** 2.65 **11.** 1.0025 **12.** 0.735

EXAMPLE 4 Ordering Numbers

GEOGRAPHY The map at the right gives the area of four states as fractions of the total area of the United States. Which of these states have the least area?

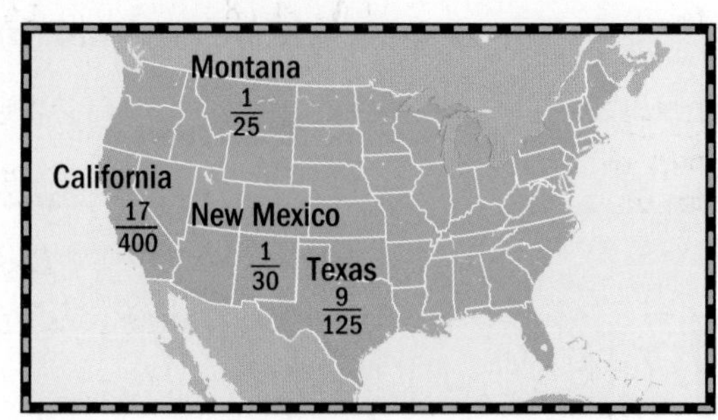

SOLUTION

Write the fractions as decimals and then compare the decimals.

California: $\frac{17}{400} = 0.0425$ **Montana:** $\frac{1}{25} = 0.04$

New Mexico: $\frac{1}{30} = 0.0\overline{3}$ **Texas:** $\frac{9}{125} = 0.072$

▶ **Answer** Because $0.072 > 0.0425 > 0.04 > 0.0\overline{3}$, the state with the least area is New Mexico.

COMPARE DECIMALS
For help comparing decimals, see p. 677.

GUIDED PRACTICE for Example 4

Copy and complete the statement using <, >, or =.

13. $2.65 \ \underline{?}\ 2\frac{13}{20}$ **14.** $\frac{7}{8}\ \underline{?}\ 0.78$ **15.** $\frac{7}{3}\ \underline{?}\ 2.3$ **16.** $0.18\ \underline{?}\ \frac{17}{40}$

17. Order the fractions $\frac{1}{40}, \frac{21}{200}, \frac{1}{16},$ and $\frac{17}{125}$ from least to greatest.

1.7 EXERCISES

HOMEWORK KEY

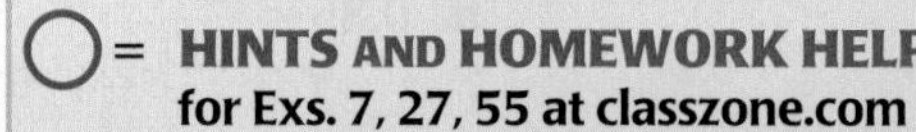

◆ = **MULTIPLE CHOICE PRACTICE** Exs. 13, 42, 53, 65–67

○ = **HINTS AND HOMEWORK HELP** for Exs. 7, 27, 55 at classzone.com

SKILLS • PROBLEM SOLVING • REASONING

1. VOCABULARY Copy and complete: If the results of long division repeat without end, the quotient is a _?_.

2. WRITING Suppose you are using division to write a fraction as a decimal. *Explain* how you know when to stop dividing.

SEE EXAMPLES 1 AND 2
on pp. 40–41 for Exs. 3–12

WRITING DECIMALS Write the fraction or mixed number as a decimal.

3. $\frac{1}{2}$ **4.** $1\frac{1}{4}$ **5.** $1\frac{1}{3}$ **6.** $\frac{5}{6}$ **(7.)** $\frac{5}{18}$

8. $2\frac{2}{3}$ **9.** $2\frac{2}{5}$ **10.** $5\frac{4}{25}$ **11.** $3\frac{4}{9}$ **12.** $9\frac{7}{11}$

SEE EXAMPLE 1 on p. 40 for Ex. 13

13. ◆ MULTIPLE CHOICE Which number is $4\frac{7}{8}$ written as a decimal?

(A) 4.78 (B) $4.7\overline{8}$ (C) 4.875 (D) 4.9

SEE EXAMPLE 2 on p. 41 for Exs. 14–18

REPEATING DECIMALS Rewrite the repeating decimal using bar notation.

14. 0.7777 . . . **15.** 3.5888 . . . **16.** 5.2121 . . . **17.** 2.358358 . . .

18. ERROR ANALYSIS *Describe* and correct the error made in writing $\frac{5}{11}$ as a decimal.

$\frac{5}{11} = 0.4\overline{5}$ ✗

SEE EXAMPLE 3 on p. 41 for Exs. 19–26

WRITING FRACTIONS Write the decimal as a fraction or mixed number in simplest form.

19. 0.8 **20.** 0.12 **21.** 0.475 **22.** 0.125

23. 6.24 **24.** 4.175 **25.** 2.245 **26.** 1.78

SEE EXAMPLE 4 on p. 42 for Exs. 27–41

COMPARING FRACTIONS Copy and complete the statement. Use <, >, or =.

27. $0.32 \ \underline{?}\ \frac{7}{18}$ **28.** $\frac{16}{9} \ \underline{?}\ 1.78$ **29.** $6\frac{8}{15} \ \underline{?}\ 6.5\overline{3}$ **30.** $4\frac{7}{24} \ \underline{?}\ 4.24$

31. $9.\overline{36} \ \underline{?}\ 9\frac{9}{25}$ **32.** $4\frac{7}{8} \ \underline{?}\ 4.875$ **33.** $\frac{17}{29} \ \underline{?}\ 0.62$ **34.** $0.04 \ \underline{?}\ \frac{2}{50}$

35. ERROR ANALYSIS *Describe* and correct the error in comparing $6\frac{1}{3}$ and 6.32.

$6\frac{1}{3} = 6.3$, so $6\frac{1}{3} < 6.32$

ORDERING NUMBERS Order the numbers from least to greatest.

36. $\frac{2}{7}$, 0.25, $\frac{5}{2}$, 0.2, $0.\overline{2}$

37. 3.67, $3\frac{4}{5}$, $3\frac{2}{3}$, $\frac{16}{5}$, $3.6\overline{7}$

38. $\frac{8}{3}$, 1.9, 1.94, $\frac{9}{4}$, $1\frac{4}{9}$

39. $\frac{9}{10}$, 0.89, $\frac{6}{7}$, $0.\overline{90}$, $\frac{15}{20}$

40. $\frac{10}{3}$, 3.36, $3\frac{1}{9}$, 3.76, $3\frac{2}{3}$

41. $5.\overline{54}$, $5\frac{7}{12}$, $\frac{11}{2}$, $5\frac{4}{9}$, 5.6

Animated Math at classzone.com

42. ◆ MULTIPLE CHOICE Which of the following is closest to 4?

(A) $4.\overline{22}$ (B) $3\frac{7}{9}$ (C) $4\frac{1}{10}$ (D) $3.\overline{90}$

MATCHING Match the number with its graph on the number line.

43. 1.75 **44.** $2\frac{1}{4}$ **45.** $\frac{6}{5}$ **46.** $1.\overline{3}$

A B C D

1.0 1.5 2.0 2.5

47. REASONING Would you change $5\frac{3}{5}$ to a decimal or 5.75 to a mixed number to compare them? *Explain* your choice.

CONNECT SKILLS TO PROBLEM SOLVING **Exercises 48–51 will help you prepare for problem solving.**

48. The distance from your home to the library is $\frac{5}{8}$ mile. Write the distance to the library as a decimal.

49. The weight of a cat is $7\frac{9}{11}$ pounds. Write the cat's weight as a decimal.

50. The length of a pencil is $5\frac{13}{16}$ inches. Write the pencil length as a decimal.

51. Joshua buys $4\frac{27}{40}$ pounds of turkey. Write the amount of turkey as a decimal.

SEE EXAMPLE 4 on p. 42 for Exs. 52–53

52. RAINBOW BRIDGE At 88.4 meters, Rainbow Bridge in Utah is the highest natural bridge in the world. The height of the Transamerica Pyramid in San Francisco is $\frac{780}{3}$ meters. Estimate how many times as high as Rainbow Bridge the Transamerica Pyramid is.

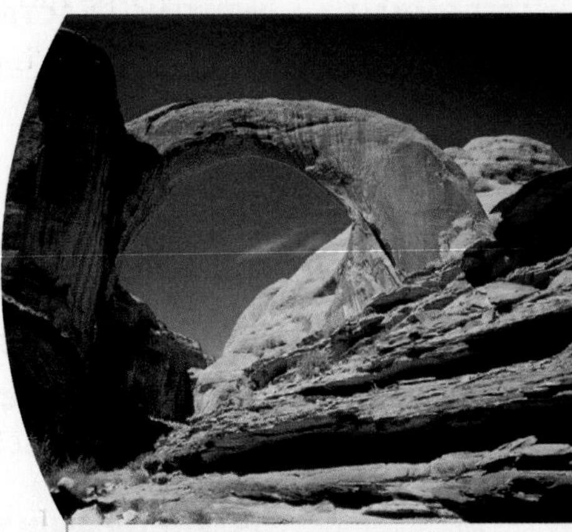

Rainbow Bridge is 88.4 m high.

California @HomeTutor for problem solving help at classzone.com

53. ◆ MULTIPLE CHOICE In your stamp collection, 13 of the 18 stamps are from the United States. What decimal is closest to the fraction $\frac{13}{18}$?

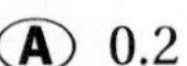

Ⓐ 0.2 Ⓑ 0.65

Ⓒ 0.7 Ⓓ 0.8

California @HomeTutor for problem solving help at classzone.com

READING *IN* MATH Read the information below for Exercises 54–56.

Marsupials Kangaroos are the best known type of marsupial, which are mammals with pouches. A newborn kangaroo can be as small as a lima bean but, depending on its species, can grow to the lengths shown in the table.

Kangaroo	*Adult Length*
Black	$3\frac{7}{10}$ ft to $4\frac{1}{2}$ ft
Eastern gray	$3\frac{1}{10}$ ft to $7\frac{3}{5}$ ft
Red	$4\frac{7}{10}$ ft to $7\frac{9}{10}$ ft
Western gray	$3\frac{1}{10}$ ft to $7\frac{2}{5}$ ft

Kangaroos are native to Australia, which is home to many other marsupials, such as koalas, wombats, and numbats. Wombats, the largest of these other marsupials, grow to a length of up to 3.8 feet. Still other marsupials are native to the Americas.

54. Rewrite Write each length in the table as a decimal number of feet.

55. Reasoning Would an adult black kangaroo normally have a length of 3.4 feet? *Explain.*

56. Reasoning Is the longest wombat as long as an adult of any type of kangaroo? If so, which type(s)? *Explain* your reasoning.

57. **INTERNET USE** A recent government report notes that the number of households in the United States using dial-up Internet service declined by about 1 in 8. Write the decline as a fraction and as a decimal. Is this greater than 0.12? *Explain.*

58. **MULTI-STEP PROBLEM** The table shows the portion of 12 to17 year olds who participated in selected sports activities in 2002.

Type of Exercise	*Fraction of 12 to 17 Year Olds*
Skateboarding	$\frac{4}{25}$
Snowboarding	$\frac{7}{100}$
Walking	$\frac{3}{16}$
Weightlifting	$\frac{1}{5}$

a. **Rewrite** Write the fractions in the table as decimals.

b. **Compare** Which sports activity had more participants, walking or weightlifting?

c. **Order** Which exercise had the greatest participation? the least participation?

59. **MULTI-STEP PROBLEM** Consider these fractions: $\frac{1}{9}, \frac{2}{9}, \frac{3}{9}$, and $\frac{4}{9}$.

a. **Calculate** Write each fraction as a decimal.

b. **Look for a Pattern** What pattern do you notice?

c. **Make a Table** Use the pattern you found in part (b) to make a table of equivalent fractions and decimals for proper fractions that are ninths.

CHALLENGE Write the decimal as a fraction or mixed number.

60. $1.\overline{3}$ 61. $0.1\overline{3}$ 62. $0.1\overline{6}$ 63. $0.02\overline{6}$

64. **CHALLENGE** A fraction in simplest form has a decimal form that terminates rather than repeats. What is true about the denominator of the fraction? *Justify* your reasoning.

◆ CALIFORNIA STANDARDS SPIRAL REVIEW

NS 1.1 65. Which list shows $6\frac{1}{4}, 6\frac{7}{18}, 6\frac{3}{8}$, and $6\frac{2}{7}$ in order from least to greatest? ***(p. 35)***

Ⓐ $6\frac{1}{4}, 6\frac{7}{18}, 6\frac{3}{8}, 6\frac{2}{7}$ Ⓑ $6\frac{3}{8}, 6\frac{1}{4}, 6\frac{7}{18}, 6\frac{2}{7}$

Ⓒ $6\frac{2}{7}, 6\frac{1}{4}, 6\frac{7}{18}, 6\frac{3}{8}$ Ⓓ $6\frac{1}{4}, 6\frac{2}{7}, 6\frac{3}{8}, 6\frac{7}{18}$

Gr. 5 NS 1.5 66. Which number represents point P on the number line? ***(p. 675)***

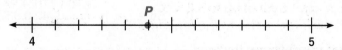

P

4 5

Ⓐ $\frac{5}{12}$ Ⓑ $\frac{5}{3}$ Ⓒ $4\frac{1}{3}$ Ⓓ $4\frac{5}{12}$

Gr. 4 NS 2.1 67. Recently the population of Long Beach was 461,522 and of Sacramento was 407,018. About how many more people lived in Long Beach? ***(p. 667)***

Ⓐ 5,500 Ⓑ 55,000 Ⓒ 87,000 Ⓓ 870,000

Technology **ACTIVITY** *Use after Lesson 1.7*

1.7 Comparing Fractions and Decimals

Standards

NS 1.1 Compare and order **positive** and negative **fractions, decimals, and mixed numbers** and place them on a number line.

QUESTION How can you use a calculator to compare fractions, mixed numbers, and decimals?

Some calculators allow you to work with fractions. You can use the ▶F key to change decimals into fractions or mixed numbers. Use the ▶D key to change fractions and mixed numbers into decimals.

EXAMPLE 1 Write the decimal as a fraction or mixed number.

a. 2.125 **b.** 0.85

The ⊔ in the display separates the whole number part from the fraction part of the mixed number.

SOLUTION

a. Keystrokes: 2.125 ▶F = **Display** 2⊔1/8

b. Keystrokes: 0.85 ▶F = **Display** 17/20

EXAMPLE 2 Compare $2\frac{3}{4}$ and $\frac{23}{9}$.

SOLUTION

Write $2\frac{3}{4}$ and $\frac{23}{9}$ as decimals.

The UNIT key is used to write a mixed number. The display for the key is ⊔.

Keystrokes: 2 UNIT **3** / **4** ▶D = **Display** 2.75

Keystrokes: 23 / **9** ▶D = **Display** 2.555555556

▶ **Answer** Because $2.75 > 2.\overline{5}$, you can conclude that $2\frac{3}{4} > \frac{23}{9}$.

PRACTICE

Write the decimal as a fraction or mixed number in simplest form.

1. 0.375 2. 1.825 3. 2.56 4. 0.9375

Write the fraction or mixed number as a decimal.

5. $15\frac{5}{6}$ 6. $11\frac{7}{11}$ 7. $\frac{20}{3}$ 8. $\frac{123}{200}$

Copy and complete the statement using <, >, or =.

9. $0.48 \underline{?} \frac{12}{25}$ 10. $1\frac{4}{9} \underline{?} 1.4$ 11. $3\frac{11}{13} \underline{?} 3.94$ 12. $6\frac{3}{16} \underline{?} 6.2$

1.8 A Problem Solving Plan

Math and MUSIC
Ex. 19, p. 51

Standards **MR 1.0** **Students make decisions about how to approach problems.**
MR 2.0 **Students use strategies, skills, and concepts in finding solutions.**
MR 3.0 **Students move beyond a particular problem by generalizing to other situations.**

Connect ***Before*** you found factors and multiples and compared fractions. ***Now*** you will apply these skills and a 4-step plan to solve many kinds of problems.

KEY VOCABULARY
- **fraction,** *p. 674*
- **decimal,** *p. 674*

BASKETBALL The table shows the number of free throws taken and made by two players on a basketball team. With Maria's next few free throws, she hopes to have a greater fraction of free throws made than Jodi. How many free throws in a row does Maria need to make to do this?

Name	*Free Throws Taken*	*Free Throws Made*
Jodi	15	6
Maria	21	6

EXAMPLE 1 Understanding and Planning

To solve the problem, you need to make sure you understand the problem. Then make a plan for solving it.

READ AND UNDERSTAND

What do you know?

Jodi has made 6 out of 15 free throws.

Maria has made 6 out of 21 free throws.

What do you want to find out?

How many free throws in a row does Maria need to make to have a greater portion of free throws made than Jodi?

MAKE A PLAN

How can you relate what you know to what you want to find out?

Find Jodi's and Maria's fraction of free throws made.

Increase the number of Maria's free throws taken and the number made by one until Maria's fraction is greater than Jodi's.

USE PROBLEM SOLVING STRATEGIES
To review problem solving strategies, see pp. 690–691.

✓ GUIDED PRACTICE for Example 1

1. In the table above, what is Jodi's fraction of free throws made?

2. What is Maria's fraction of free throws made?

EXAMPLE 2 Solving and Looking Back

To solve the problem from the previous page, you need to carry out the plan from Example 1 and then check the answer.

Free throw from foul line

SOLVE THE PROBLEM

Jodie has made $\frac{6}{15} = 0.4$ of her free throws. Maria has made $\frac{6}{21}$, or about 0.286, of her free throws. Increase Maria's free throws taken and made by 1. Then find the fraction of her free throws made. Record your results in a table. Keep increasing her free throws until her fraction is greater than 0.4.

Free Throws Made in a Row	*Total Free Throws Made*	*Total Free Throws Taken*	*Fraction of Free Throws Made*
1	7	22	$\frac{7}{22} = 0.318$
2	8	23	$\frac{8}{23} \approx 0.348$
3	9	24	$\frac{9}{24} = 0.375$
4	10	25	$\frac{10}{25} = 0.4$
5	11	26	$\frac{11}{26} \approx 0.423$

The symbol $\approx$ is read as "is approximately equal to."

About the Standards

In Example 2, you solve the problem by using a table, one of the problem solving methods mentioned in Grade 6 Standard MR 2.4.

▶ **Answer** Maria needs to make 5 free throws in a row to have a greater fraction of free throws made than Jodi.

LOOK BACK

After Maria makes 4 free throws in a row, she has the same fraction of free throws made as Jodi. So, it is reasonable that if she makes her next shot, she will have a greater fraction of free throws made than Jodi.

✓ GUIDED PRACTICE for Example 2

3. **WHAT IF?** In Example 2, suppose Maria misses her first free throw and now has made 6 of her 22 free throws. How many free throws in a row does she need to make to exceed Jodi's fraction of free throws made?

4. **PHONE CALLS** A phone card charges $2 for the first 20 minutes and $.05 for each extra minute. One call costs $3.65. How long was the call?

Animated Math

For an interactive example using problem solving strategies, go to **classzone.com**.

A PROBLEM SOLVING PLAN In Examples 1 and 2, you solved the basketball problem in four steps. These steps make up a problem solving plan summarized on page 49. This plan shows how you can use mathematical reasoning with other math skills to solve problems throughout this course.

CONCEPT SUMMARY *For Your Notebook*

A Problem Solving Plan

1. **Read and understand the problem.**
    - Distinguish between relevant and irrelevant information.
    - Identify missing information.
    - Sequence and prioritize information.

2. **Make a plan.**
    - Identify relationships.
    - Observe patterns.
    - Determine whether the problem can be broken into simpler parts.
    - Make conjectures.
    - Determine whether the answer needs to be exact or can be approximate.

3. **Solve the problem.**
    - Apply strategies/results from simpler problems.
    - Test/justify conjectures.
    - Use estimation, then make precise calculations and give the answer to an appropriate degree of accuracy.
    - Express the solution clearly; explain mathematical reasoning.

4. **Look back.**
    - Check the reasonableness of the solution using estimation and the context of the problem.
    - Generalize results.

1.8 EXERCISES

HOMEWORK KEY

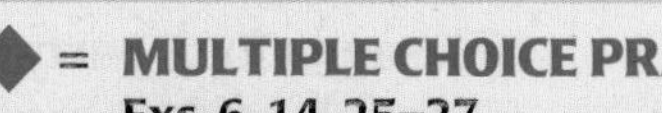
◆ = **MULTIPLE CHOICE PRACTICE** Exs. 6, 14, 25–27

○ = **HINTS AND HOMEWORK HELP** for Exs. 5, 7, 19 at classzone.com

SKILLS • PROBLEM SOLVING • REASONING

1. **VOCABULARY** *Describe* all four steps of the problem solving plan.

2. **WRITING** Why should you look back at a problem's solution after solving?

SEE EXAMPLE 1 on p. 47 for Exs. 3–4

UNDERSTAND **Identify what you know and what you need to find out.**

3. You buy a package of 12 pens for $3. What is the cost per pen?

4. You are making snack bags for school. You have 20 raisin mini boxes and 24 carrot sticks. You want to put the same number of each snack in each bag and make the most bags possible. How many bags can you make?

SEE EXAMPLE 2
on p. 48
for Exs. 5–7

5. **ERROR ANALYSIS** *Describe* and correct the error made in solving the following problem.

You spent a total of $22 for yourself and a friend at the movies. You spent $6 on snacks. How much did each movie ticket cost?

> ✗ $22 \div 2 = 11$
> The tickets cost $11 each.

6. ◆ **MULTIPLE CHOICE** Which expression could you use to find the number of raisin mini boxes in each bag in Exercise 4 on page 49?

   Ⓐ $20 \div 2$ Ⓑ $20 \div 4$

   Ⓒ $20 \div 5$ Ⓓ $20 \div 10$

7. **ORIGAMI** In origami, you can fold paper into animal shapes. The number of origami peacocks Jane makes on each of four days is given in the table. Identify the pattern. If Jane continues this folding pattern, on which day will she have a total of 70 peacocks?

Day	*Peacocks*
1	1
2	4
3	7
4	10

CONNECT SKILLS TO PROBLEM SOLVING Exercises 8–11 will help you prepare for problem solving.

Use the following problem: Chester is making a scrapbook of his 42 postcards. He is arranging them in groups of equal size. How many different size groups of two or more can he make?

8. Identify what you know and what you need to find out.
9. Make and describe a plan to solve the problem.
10. Carry out the plan and solve the problem.
11. Check that your answer is reasonable.

12. **USING THE PROBLEM SOLVING PLAN** You are ordering whole pans of lasagna for a party. One pan of lasagna serves 8 people. You expect 52 people at the party. How many pans of lasagna should you order?
   a. What are you trying to find?
   b. Why should you divide to find an answer?
   c. Write an expression to find the answer. Evaluate your expression.
   d. *Explain* why you need to adjust the quotient to make the answer reasonable. How many pans do you need?

California @HomeTutor for problem solving help at classzone.com

13. **HOMEWORK** You have to finish your homework before your favorite TV show starts at 9 P.M. You estimate it will take you 20 minutes to read the short story, 30 minutes to do the math problems, and 15 minutes to do the science lab. What is the latest time you can start your homework?

California @HomeTutor for problem solving help at classzone.com

14. ◆ **MULTIPLE CHOICE** Rob, Flo, and Jesse are writing thank you notes. To write each note Rob takes $4\frac{5}{6}$ minutes, Flo takes $\frac{24}{5}$ minutes and Jesse takes 4.75 minutes. Who takes closest to 5 minutes for each note?

Ⓐ Rob Ⓑ Flo Ⓒ Jesse Ⓓ Rob and Flo

15. **NUMBER SENSE** The sum of the digits of a two digit number is 7. The tens' digit is 3 more than the ones' digit. What is the number?

16. **WRITING** You buy a 5 pound bag of apples for $2.50. Do you have enough information to find the cost per apple? *Explain* your reasoning.

17. **REASONING** You want to place solar lanterns 3 yards apart on the perimeter of the backyard shown below.

Your friend says "You need 4 lanterns for each 9 yard side and 10 lanterns for each 27 yard side. So you need 8 + 20 = 28 lanterns." Do you agree? *Explain* why or why not. If not, how many lanterns do you need?

18. **MULTI-STEP PROBLEM** You and a neighbor are building fences of the same length. Each piece of your fence is 60 inches long, and each piece of your neighbor's fence is 45 inches long. The 60 inch fence pieces cost $30 each. The 45 inch fence pieces cost $22 each.

  a. What is the shortest possible fence length that both of you can build?

  b. How many pieces of fence do each of you need for this length of fence? Which fence costs less to build?

19. **MARCHING BAND** Your school's marching band can play for up to 14 minutes at the halftime show. The band needs to choose 3 songs from the table, and one of the songs must be the school song. What songs can the band play? *Describe* how you solved the problem.

Band Songs	*Time (min)*
School song	3
A	6
B	5
C	4
D	7

20. **JEWELRY** You are making a bracelet using two strands of beads. The strands will be the same length. One strand will have beads that are $\frac{5}{8}$ inch long. The other strand will have $\frac{3}{4}$ inch beads. What is the shortest length possible for the strands? *Justify* your reasoning.

21. **TICKETS** Marta, Emily, Stan, and Ty are standing in line for movie tickets. Ty is directly behind Emily. Stan is not last. Emily is first. In what order are they standing? *Describe* your method of solution.

22. **SHORT RESPONSE** You have a box of snack bars. If you divide the bars into groups of 3, two bars are left over. If you divide the bars into groups of 4, two bars are left over. If you divide the bars into groups of 5, no bars are left over. What is the fewest snack bars that could be in the box? *Explain* your reasoning.

23. **CHALLENGE** Sam and Elwin have lunch, and each agrees to pay half of the $30 cost (which includes tax and tip). Sam has two $10 bills, and Elwin has a $20 bill and two $5 bills. Is there a way for them to each pay half of the bill without getting change? *Explain* your reasoning.

24. **CHALLENGE** You are camping and have only a 3 cup container and a 5 cup container. You need to measure 1 cup of water. How can you do this? Is there more than one way? *Explain* your reasoning.

◆ CALIFORNIA STANDARDS SPIRAL REVIEW

NS 1.1 25. Which list shows 6.78, $6\frac{4}{5}$, 6.75, and $6\frac{5}{7}$ in order from least to greatest? ***(p. 40)***

Ⓐ $6\frac{5}{7}$, $6\frac{4}{5}$, 6.78, 6.75 Ⓑ 6.78, $6\frac{4}{5}$, 6.75, $6\frac{5}{7}$

Ⓒ $6\frac{4}{5}$, $6\frac{5}{7}$, 6.75, 6.78 Ⓓ $6\frac{5}{7}$, 6.75, 6.78, $6\frac{4}{5}$

NS 1.1 26. Which fraction is equivalent to the decimal 0.8375? ***(p. 40)***

Ⓐ $\frac{67}{200}$ Ⓑ $\frac{67}{80}$ Ⓒ $\frac{67}{40}$ Ⓓ $\frac{67}{8}$

Gr. 4 NS 4.2 27. Which of the numbers is *not* a prime number? ***(p. 5)***

Ⓐ 3 Ⓑ 7 Ⓒ 39 Ⓓ 47

QUIZ *for Lessons 1.5–1.8*

Copy and complete the statement using <, >, or =. *(p. 29)*

1. $\frac{7}{12} \underline{?} \frac{2}{3}$ 2. $\frac{3}{10} \underline{?} \frac{3}{4}$ 3. $\frac{5}{7} \underline{?} \frac{1}{3}$ 4. $\frac{22}{27} \underline{?} \frac{55}{72}$

Write the mixed number as an improper fraction or the improper fraction as a mixed number in simplest form. *(p. 35)*

5. $2\frac{3}{8}$ 6. $5\frac{5}{7}$ 7. $\frac{38}{4}$ 8. $\frac{67}{6}$

Order the numbers from least to greatest. *(p. 40)*

9. 4.45, $4\frac{11}{20}$, $\frac{27}{6}$, $4\frac{5}{9}$, 4.39 10. $\frac{3}{10}$, $0.3\overline{4}$, $\frac{5}{12}$, $\frac{17}{50}$, 0.27 11. $2\frac{2}{3}$, 2.68, $\frac{38}{15}$, $2\frac{3}{5}$, $\frac{45}{16}$

12. **TOLLS** A toll at a toll booth is $.45. Make a table to list all the ways you can pay the exact toll using nickels, dimes, and quarters. ***(p. 47)***

MIXED REVIEW *of Skills and Problem Solving*

Multiple Choice Practice for Lessons 1.5–1.8

1. At a pizza party, all the pizzas are the same size, but they are cut into different numbers of equal slices, as shown.

Type of pizza	*Number of slices*
Pepperoni	8
Vegetable	16
Mushroom	12
Cheese	6

Paul eats 3 slices of pepperoni pizza. Sita eats 4 slices of vegetable pizza. Paige eats 5 slices of mushroom pizza. Diego eats 3 slices of cheese pizza. Which list shows the people in increasing order, by the portion of a whole pizza each person ate? **NS 1.1, MR 2.2**

Ⓐ Paul, Sita, Paige, Diego

Ⓑ Sita, Paul, Paige, Diego

Ⓒ Diego, Paul, Paige, Sita

Ⓓ Paige, Sita, Paul, Diego

2. Which mixed number or improper fraction is closest to the decimal 5.27? **NS 1.1**

Ⓐ $5\frac{1}{3}$ Ⓑ $5\frac{13}{36}$

Ⓒ $\frac{46}{9}$ Ⓓ $5\frac{4}{29}$

3. The mixed number $8\frac{4}{5}$ lies between which pair of numbers on a number line? **NS 1.1**

Ⓐ $8\frac{1}{6}$ and $8\frac{11}{16}$ Ⓑ $\frac{26}{3}$ and $8\frac{3}{4}$

Ⓒ $\frac{58}{7}$ and $\frac{80}{9}$ Ⓓ $8\frac{7}{8}$ and $9\frac{1}{3}$

4. Point *R* lies between points *P* and *Q* on the number line. Which decimal could represent point *R*? **NS 1.1**

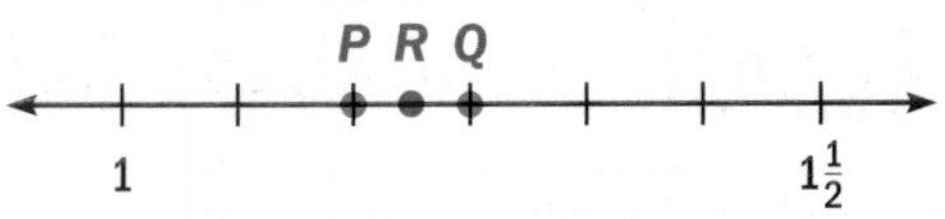

Ⓐ 1.2 Ⓑ 1.25

Ⓒ 1.3 Ⓓ 1.35

5. Hannah wants to buy between 0.375 pound and $\frac{7}{16}$ pound of spices. Which weight is *not* between these two weights? **NS 1.1**

Ⓐ $\frac{19}{50}$ lb Ⓑ $\frac{3}{7}$ lb

Ⓒ $\frac{9}{20}$ lb Ⓓ $\frac{2}{5}$ lb

6. Which list shows $\frac{1}{3}$, $\frac{4}{11}$, $\frac{4}{9}$, and $\frac{2}{7}$ in order from least to greatest? **NS 1.1**

Ⓐ $\frac{1}{3}, \frac{2}{7}, \frac{4}{9}, \frac{4}{11}$ Ⓑ $\frac{2}{7}, \frac{1}{3}, \frac{4}{11}, \frac{4}{9}$

Ⓒ $\frac{1}{3}, \frac{4}{11}, \frac{4}{9}, \frac{2}{7}$ Ⓓ $\frac{4}{11}, \frac{1}{3}, \frac{2}{7}, \frac{4}{9}$

7. A car's owner follows the maintenance schedule below. The car now has 20,550 mi on it. After how many more miles will all three things need to be done at the same time? **NS 2.4, MR 3.1**

Maintenance Schedule

Change oil: every 3000 mi

Rotate tires: every 6000 mi

Check brakes: every 7500 mi

Ⓐ 1950 miles Ⓑ 3550 miles

Ⓒ 9450 miles Ⓓ 30,000 miles

8. Tiles come in $\frac{3}{4}$ inch squares and $\frac{7}{8}$ inch squares. You want to make 2 rows of equal length for a mosaic, one row from each size of tile. What is the shortest length for a row you can make? **NS 2.4**

Ⓐ 5 in. Ⓑ $5\frac{1}{4}$ in.

Ⓒ $5\frac{3}{8}$ in. Ⓓ $5\frac{1}{2}$ in.

1 CHAPTER SUMMARY

Standards
NS 1.1, NS 2.4, Gr. 5 NS 1.4

BIG IDEAS

For Your Notebook

Big Idea 1

Finding the GCF and LCM of Two Numbers

You can find the greatest common factor (GCF) of two or more numbers by listing the factors of each number, or by using the prime factorization of the numbers.

You can find the least common multiple (LCM) of two or more numbers by listing multiples of each number, or by using the prime factorization of the numbers.

	The GCF of 36 and 54 is 18.	*The LCM of 25 and 30 is 150.*
Use a list.	36: 1, 2, 3, 4, 6, 9, 12, 18, 36 54: 1, 2, 3, 6, 9, 18, 27, 54	25: 25, 50, 75, 100, 125, 150, ... 30: 30, 60, 90, 120, 150, 180, ...
Use prime factorization.	36: $2 \times 2 \times 3 \times 3$ 54: $2 \times 3 \times 3 \times 3$ GCF is $2 \times 3 \times 3 = 18$	25: $5 \times 5 = 5^2$ 30: $2 \times 3 \times 5$ LCM is $2 \times 3 \times 5^2 = 150$

Big Idea 2

Writing Equivalent Fractions

To write an equivalent fraction, you multiply or divide the numerator and denominator of a fraction by the same nonzero number.

To write the simplest form of a fraction, you divide the numerator and denominator by their GCF.

Two fractions that are equivalent to $\frac{20}{32}$ are shown.

$$\frac{20}{32} = \frac{20 \times 4}{32 \times 4} = \frac{80}{128} \qquad \frac{20}{32} = \frac{20 \div 4}{32 \div 4} = \frac{5}{8}$$

The fraction $\frac{5}{8}$ is in simplest form because the GCF of 20 and 32 is 4.

Big Idea 3

Comparing and Ordering Fractions, Decimals, and Mixed Numbers

The table below shows three ways to compare and order fractions, decimals, and mixed numbers.

Use LCM to write equivalent fractions.	$\frac{7}{8} = \frac{7 \times 3}{8 \times 3} = \frac{21}{24}$	$\frac{5}{6} = \frac{5 \times 4}{6 \times 4} = \frac{20}{24}$	$\frac{7}{8} > \frac{5}{6}$
Write as decimals.	$\frac{7}{8} = 0.875$	$\frac{5}{6} = 0.8\overline{3}$	$\frac{7}{8} > \frac{5}{6}$
Graph on a number line.	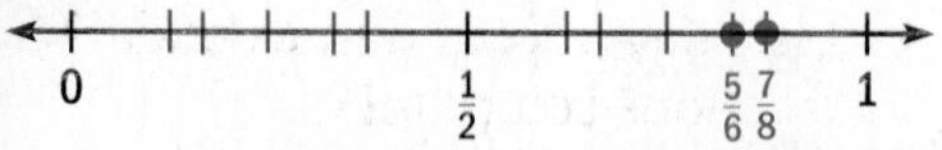		$\frac{7}{8} > \frac{5}{6}$

CHAPTER PROBLEM

Standards
NS 1.1, NS 2.4

APPLYING THE BIG IDEAS

Big Idea 1
You find the LCM in **Step 2.**

Big Idea 2
You write fractions in simplest form in **Ex. 1.**

Big Idea 3
You compare fractions in **Step 3** and **Ex. 3.**

PROBLEM How can you use least common multiples and fractions to compare a new calendar to a normal calendar?

STEP 1 **Plan a new calendar.**

Suppose you could create a new calendar. Choose new numbers for days in a week, weeks in a month, and months in a year for a new calendar. If the days in a year do not total 365, describe how to add leap days, weeks, or months. Make each year average 365 days.

> Sample calendar
>
> 1 year = 15 months of 4 weeks
>
> 1 month = 4 weeks of 6 days
>
> Leap year (every 5 years) has 1 extra month of 25 days.

STEP 2 **Make a table.**

Suppose a week begins on a Sunday on both your calendar and a normal one. In how many days will a week once again begin on a Sunday on both calendars? Copy and complete the table to find out.

My Calendar		*Normal Calendar*	
Weeks	***Total Days***	***Weeks***	***Total Days***
1	?	1	7
2	?	2	14

STEP 3 **Compare fractions.**

What fraction of the days in a year are the months in your calendar? in a normal calendar? Is any month in your calendar a greater portion of a year than any month in a normal year? *Justify* your reasoning.

BIRTHDAY MONTH
1 2 3 4 5 6
7 8 9 10 11 12
13 14 15 16 17 18
19 20 21 22 23 24

Extending the Problem

Use your results from the problem to complete the exercises.

1. What fraction of a year does a week represent in each calendar? Using simplest form, tell whether these fractions are equivalent.
2. How many days after the beginning of the year is your birthday in a normal calendar? What month and date is this in your new calendar?
3. Using your new calendar, make a page for your birthday month like the one above. What fraction of the month comes before your birthday in your new calendar? in a normal calendar? How do these fractions compare?

1 CHAPTER REVIEW

California @HomeTutor
classzone.com
• Multi-Language Visual Glossary
• Vocabulary practice

REVIEW KEY VOCABULARY

- prime number, *p. 5*
- composite number, *p. 5*
- prime factorization, *p. 6*
- factor tree, *p. 6*
- common factor, *p. 10*
- greatest common factor (GCF), *p. 10*
- equivalent fractions, *p. 16*
- simplest form, *p. 17*
- multiple, *p. 21*
- common multiple, *p. 21*
- least common multiple (LCM), *p. 21*
- least common denominator (LCD), *p. 29*
- mixed number, *p. 35*
- proper fraction, *p. 35*
- improper fraction, *p. 35*
- terminating decimal, *p. 40*
- repeating decimal, *p. 40*

VOCABULARY EXERCISES

1. The __?__ of 45 is $3^2 \times 5$.

2. A fraction whose numerator is greater than its denominator is a(n) __?__.

3. The __?__ of 2, 4, and 8 is 2.

4. The fractions $\frac{3}{10}$ and $\frac{4}{5}$ have a(n) __?__ of 10.

5. **NOTETAKING SKILLS** Make a *word triangle* for *least common multiple* like the one on page 4.

REVIEW EXAMPLES AND EXERCISES

1.1 Prime Factorization *pp. 5–9*

Gr. 5 NS 1.4

EXAMPLE

List the factors of 36. Tell whether it is *prime* or *composite*. If it is composite, use a factor tree to write the prime factorization of 36.

- The factors of 36 are 1, 2, 3, 4, 6, 9, 12, 18, and 36.
- It is composite because it has whole number factors other than 1 and itself.
- The prime factorization of 36 is $2^2 \times 3^2$.

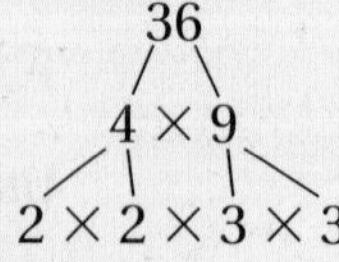

EXERCISES

SEE EXAMPLES 1, 2, AND 3 on pp. 5–6 for Exs. 6–13

Write all the factors of the number. Then tell whether the number is *prime* or *composite*.

6. 68 **7.** 43 **8.** 72 **9.** 31

Use a factor tree to write the prime factorization of the number.

10. 60 **11.** 91 **12.** 81 **13.** 726

1.2 Greatest Common Factor

pp. 10–14

NS 2.4

EXAMPLE

Find the greatest common factor of 24, 72, and 84.

Factors of 24: 1, 2, 3, 4, 6, 8, 12, 24

Factors of 72: 1, 2, 3, 4, 6, 8, 9, 12, 18, 24, 36, 72

Factors of 84: 1, 2, 3, 4, 6, 7, 12, 14, 21, 28, 42, 84

▶ **Answer** The common factors are 1, 2, 3, 4, 6, and 12. The GCF is 12.

EXERCISES

SEE EXAMPLES 1, 2, AND 3 on pp. 10–11 for Exs. 14–30

Find the GCF using a list.

14. 12, 18 **15.** 40, 51 **16.** 72, 136 **17.** 144, 192

18. 15, 35, 60 **19.** 44, 66, 121 **20.** 28, 63, 91 **21.** 27, 59, 81

Find the GCF using prime factorization.

22. 17, 85 **23.** 48, 60 **24.** 38, 45 **25.** 84, 360

26. 40, 64, 96 **27.** 13, 65, 142 **28.** 54, 108, 216 **29.** 90, 108, 135

30. CLASS SIZES An English class with 12 boys and 16 girls is divided into groups. Each group has the same number of boys and the same number of girls. What is the most groups that can be formed? How many boys and and how many girls are in each group?

1.3 Equivalent Fractions

pp. 16–20

NS 2.4

EXAMPLE

Write two fractions that are equivalent to $\frac{12}{14}$.

Multiply or divide the numerator and denominator by the same nonzero number.

$\frac{12}{14} = \frac{12 \times 4}{14 \times 4} = \frac{48}{56}$ **Multiply numerator and denominator by 4.**

$\frac{12}{14} = \frac{12 \div 2}{14 \div 2} = \frac{6}{7}$ **Divide numerator and denominator by 2, the GCF of 12 and 14. The fraction is in simplest form.**

▶ **Answer** Two fractions equivalent to $\frac{12}{14}$ are $\frac{48}{56}$ and $\frac{6}{7}$.

EXERCISES

SEE EXAMPLES 2, 3, AND 4 on pp. 16–17 for Exs. 31–35

Write two fractions that are equivalent to the given fraction. Include its simplest form, if it is not given.

31. $\frac{3}{5}$ **32.** $\frac{6}{9}$ **33.** $\frac{4}{8}$ **34.** $\frac{2}{7}$

35. TEST SCORES On one test you earn 46 out of 50 points. On another test, your friend earns 54 out of 60 points. For each test, write the fraction of possible points each of you earn. Are the fractions equivalent? *Explain.*

1.4 Least Common Multiple

pp. 21–25

NS 2.4

EXAMPLE

Use prime factorization to find the LCM of 10 and 18.

$10 = (2) \times (5)$. **Circle the 2 and circle the 5.**

$18 = 2 \times 3 \times 3 = 2 \times (3^2)$. **Circle the 3^2.**

▶ **Answer** The LCM of 10 and 18 is $2 \times 3^2 \times 5$, or 90.

EXERCISES

SEE EXAMPLES 1, 2 AND 3 on pp. 21–22 for Exs. 36–43

Find the LCM using a list.

36. 8, 20 **37.** 14, 21 **38.** 45, 81 **39.** 144, 156

Find the LCM using prime factorization.

40. 5, 35 **41.** 8, 9 **42.** 100, 250 **43.** 55, 70

1.5 Comparing and Ordering Fractions

pp. 29–33

NS 1.1

EXAMPLE

Order the fractions $\frac{4}{7}, \frac{5}{8}, \frac{5}{14}, \frac{17}{28}$ from least to greatest.

The LCD is 56. Use the LCD to write equivalent fractions.

$\frac{4}{7} = \frac{4 \times 8}{7 \times 8} = \frac{32}{56}$ $\frac{5}{8} = \frac{5 \times 7}{8 \times 7} = \frac{35}{56}$ $\frac{5}{14} = \frac{5 \times 4}{14 \times 4} = \frac{20}{56}$ $\frac{17}{28} = \frac{17 \times 2}{28 \times 2} = \frac{34}{56}$

Compare the numerators: $\frac{20}{56} < \frac{32}{56} < \frac{34}{56} < \frac{35}{56}$, so $\frac{5}{14} < \frac{4}{7} < \frac{17}{28} < \frac{5}{8}$.

▶ **Answer** From least to greatest, the fractions are $\frac{5}{14}, \frac{4}{7}, \frac{17}{28}$, and $\frac{5}{8}$.

EXERCISES

SEE EXAMPLE 2 on p. 30 for Exs. 44–51

Order the fractions from least to greatest.

44. $\frac{3}{4}, \frac{49}{52}, \frac{25}{26}, \frac{11}{13}$

45. $\frac{8}{15}, \frac{1}{2}, \frac{7}{10}, \frac{2}{3}$

46. $\frac{5}{21}, \frac{1}{3}, \frac{3}{7}, \frac{2}{9}$

47. $\frac{6}{13}, \frac{25}{39}, \frac{5}{6}, \frac{17}{26}$

48. $\frac{2}{3}, \frac{3}{5}, \frac{5}{9}, \frac{7}{12}$

49. $\frac{5}{12}, \frac{11}{18}, \frac{4}{7}, \frac{9}{20}$

50. $\frac{5}{22}, \frac{1}{12}, \frac{3}{16}, \frac{2}{9}$

51. $\frac{9}{10}, \frac{11}{12}, \frac{6}{7}, \frac{7}{8}$

1.6 Comparing Fractions and Mixed Numbers

pp. 35–39

NS 1.1

EXAMPLE

Compare $\frac{37}{4}$ and $9\frac{3}{10}$.

STEP 1 **Write** $9\frac{3}{10}$ as an improper fraction, $\frac{93}{10}$.

STEP 2 **Rewrite** $\frac{37}{4}$ and $\frac{93}{10}$ using the LCD, 20.

$$\frac{37}{4} = \frac{37 \times 5}{4 \times 5} = \frac{185}{20} \qquad \frac{93}{10} = \frac{93 \times 2}{10 \times 2} = \frac{186}{20}$$

STEP 3 **Compare** the fractions: $\frac{185}{20} < \frac{186}{20}$, so you can conclude. $\frac{37}{4} < 9\frac{3}{10}$.

EXERCISES

SEE EXAMPLES 3 AND 4 on pp. 36–37 for Exs. 52–55

Copy and complete the statement using <, >, or =.

52. $\frac{9}{2} \ \underline{?}\ \frac{23}{5}$

53. $1\frac{4}{11} \ \underline{?}\ 1\frac{2}{9}$

54. $4\frac{3}{8} \ \underline{?}\ 4\frac{5}{14}$

55. $12\frac{3}{16} \ \underline{?}\ \frac{195}{16}$

1.7 Ordering Fractions and Decimals

pp. 40–45

NS 1.1

EXAMPLE

Order the numbers $3\frac{5}{6}$, 3.75, $\frac{31}{8}$, and $3\frac{7}{9}$ from least to greatest.

Write the fractions as decimals by dividing.

$$3\frac{5}{6} = 3.8\overline{3} \qquad \frac{31}{8} = 3.875 \qquad 3\frac{7}{9} = 3.\overline{7}$$

Then compare the decimals: $3.75 < 3.\overline{7} < 3.8\overline{3} < 3.875$.

▶ **Answer** From least to greatest, the number are 3.75, $3\frac{7}{9}$, $3\frac{5}{6}$, and $\frac{31}{8}$.

EXERCISES

SEE EXAMPLES 1, 2, AND 3 on pp. 40–41 for Exs. 56–66

Write the fraction or mixed number as a decimal.

56. $\frac{11}{6}$ **57.** $4\frac{7}{9}$ **58.** $\frac{3}{20}$ **59.** $11\frac{3}{5}$

Write the decimal as a fraction or mixed number.

60. 0.06 **61.** 5.125 **62.** 3.3125 **63.** 2.25

Order the numbers from least to greatest.

64. 0.46, $\frac{7}{16}$, $\frac{12}{25}$, 0.38 **65.** $6\frac{1}{3}$, 6.24, $\frac{73}{12}$, 6.1 **66.** $\frac{17}{12}$, $1.\overline{2}$, $1\frac{2}{5}$, 1.42

1.8 A Problem Solving Plan

pp. 46–50

MR 1.0, MR 2.0, MR 3.0

EXAMPLE

CUTTING PAPER You are cutting a piece of paper that is $5\frac{3}{8}$ inches long into $\frac{1}{8}$ inch strips. How many strips will you make?

Read and Understand You want to know how many $\frac{1}{8}$ inch strips of paper you will make using a piece of paper that is $5\frac{3}{8}$ inches wide.

Make a Plan You can rewrite the length of the paper as an improper fraction to find the number of $\frac{1}{8}$ inch strips you will make.

Solve the Problem The length of the paper is $5\frac{3}{8} = \frac{43}{8}$ inches. So, you will make 43 strips that are $\frac{1}{8}$ inch wide.

Look Back A piece of paper that is 5, or $\frac{40}{8}$, inches long will make 40 strips and a piece of paper that is 6, or $\frac{48}{8}$, inches long will make 48 strips, so the answer is reasonable.

▶ **Answer** You will make 43 strips that are $\frac{1}{8}$ inch wide.

EXERCISES

SEE EXAMPLES 1 AND 2 on pp. 47–48 for Exs. 67–68

67. FIELD TRIP Your school is organizing a field trip for 81 students and 13 teachers. A bus can hold a maximum of 40 people. How many buses do you need for the field trip?

68. MAKING CHANGE You buy a pen for \$.65 and receive coins in change for a \$1 bill. What are the possible combinations of nickels, dimes, and quarters you could receive?

1 CHAPTER TEST

1. **VOCABULARY** Give an example of an improper fraction.

2. **VOCABULARY** Write all the factors of 51. Then tell whether 51 is *prime* or *composite.*

Use a factor tree to write the prime factorization of the number.

3. 96
4. 128
5. 168
6. 260

Find the GCF and the LCM of the numbers.

7. 9, 16
8. 12, 15
9. 10, 25
10. 7, 13
11. 42, 66
12. 64, 120
13. 28, 49, 84
14. 72, 144, 192

Write the fraction in simplest form.

15. $\frac{15}{80}$
16. $\frac{13}{78}$
17. $\frac{54}{81}$
18. $\frac{76}{135}$

Copy and complete the statement using <, >, or =.

19. $\frac{6}{7} \underline{?} \frac{9}{11}$
20. $\frac{5}{9} \underline{?} \frac{60}{108}$
21. $3\frac{2}{7} \underline{?} \frac{16}{5}$
22. $5\frac{5}{6} \underline{?} \frac{59}{10}$

Order the numbers from least to greatest.

23. $\frac{7}{4}, \frac{23}{12}, 1\frac{5}{6}, \frac{5}{3}$
24. $\frac{5}{6}, \frac{7}{9}, \frac{23}{27}, \frac{13}{18}$
25. $\frac{1}{2}, \frac{17}{42}, \frac{16}{21}, \frac{5}{7}$
26. $\frac{8}{5}, 1\frac{8}{15}, \frac{8}{3}, \frac{22}{15}$

Write the fraction as a decimal, or the decimal as a fraction or mixed number in simplest form.

27. $\frac{11}{25}$
28. $\frac{29}{11}$
29. 2.68
30. 0.56

Order the numbers from least to greatest.

31. $3\frac{14}{15}, 3.\overline{8}, 3\frac{7}{8}, 3.82$
32. $5\frac{9}{16}, 5.5, \frac{60}{11}, 5.52$
33. $1.286, \frac{4}{3}, 1\frac{2}{7}, 1.3$

34. **DISTANCES** Use the table at the right. It shows the distances that 4 bikers rode. Order the fractions from least to greatest. Who rode the farthest?

Rider	Suzie	Tom	Nikki	Lisa
Distance (miles)	$\frac{7}{9}$	$\frac{5}{6}$	$\frac{2}{3}$	$\frac{1}{2}$

35. **BRACELETS** You have 280 green beads, 200 yellow beads, and 240 blue beads to make identical bracelets. If you use all the beads, what is the most bracelets you can make? How many beads of each color will be on each bracelet?

1 ◆ MULTIPLE CHOICE STRATEGIES

STRATEGIES YOU'LL USE:
- **SOLVE DIRECTLY**
- **ELIMINATE CHOICES**

Standards
NS 1.1, NS 2.4

If you have difficulty solving a multiple choice problem directly, you may be able to use another approach to eliminate incorrect answer choices.

PROBLEM 1

Which point shows the location of $1\frac{3}{8}$ on the number line?

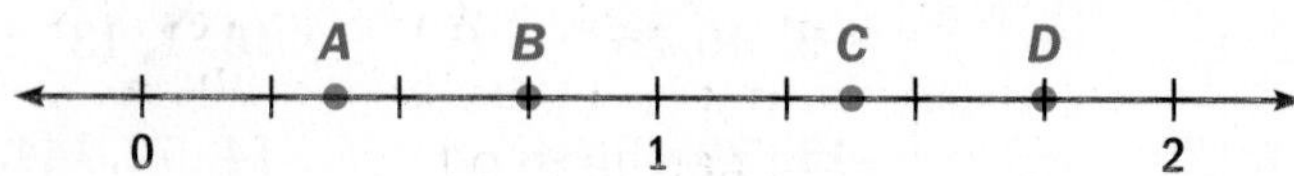

Ⓐ Point *A* Ⓑ Point *B* Ⓒ Point *C* Ⓓ Point *D*

Strategy 1 **SOLVE DIRECTLY**

Find the increments on the number line. Use these to locate the point that represents the mixed number.

STEP 1 **Find** the increments on the number line.
- Because the interval from 0 to 1 is divided into 4 sections, each increment represents $\frac{1}{4}$.

STEP 2 **Count** using the increments.
- The first mark to the right of 1 is $1\frac{1}{4}$, or $1\frac{2}{8}$.
- The second mark to the right of 1 is $1\frac{2}{4}$, or $1\frac{4}{8}$.
- Because Point *C* is halfway between $1\frac{2}{8}$ and $1\frac{4}{8}$, Point *C* shows the location of $1\frac{3}{8}$.

The correct answer is C. Ⓐ Ⓑ Ⓒ Ⓓ

Strategy 2 **ELIMINATE CHOICES**

You can use what you know about the number line to identify points that cannot be located at $1\frac{3}{8}$.

Because $1\frac{3}{8} > 1$, you can eliminate any choices less than 1, which are to the left of 1. You can eliminate choices A and B.

Because $\frac{3}{8} < \frac{1}{2}$, you know that $1\frac{3}{8}$ will be closer to 1 than to 2. Point *D* is closer to 2 than to 1, so you can eliminate choice D.

The correct answer is C. Ⓐ Ⓑ Ⓒ Ⓓ

PROBLEM 2

Jim, Maya, and Tran give walking tours of a historic district. Jim starts a tour every 30 minutes. Maya starts a tour every 60 minutes. Tran starts a tour every 40 minutes. All three start their first tour at the same time and work for 6 hours. How many times will they start a tour at the same time?

Ⓐ 1 Ⓑ 3 Ⓒ 10 Ⓓ 15

Strategy 1 SOLVE DIRECTLY

Find the least common multiple of the tour lengths. Then find how many of these time periods occur in 6 hours.

STEP 1 **Find** the multiples of 30, 40, and 60.

Multiples of 30: 30, 60, 90, **120**, ...

Multiples of 40: 40, 80, **120**, ...

Multiples of 60: 60, **120**, ...

The least common multiple of the numbers is 120. The tours start at the same time every 120 minutes.

STEP 2 **Find** how many 120 minute periods occur in 6 hours. Divide 6 hours by 120 minutes, or 2 hours.

$6 \div 2 = 3$

Over 6 hours, they will start tours at the same time 3 times.

The correct answer is B. Ⓐ Ⓑ Ⓒ Ⓓ

Strategy 2 ELIMINATE CHOICES

Look for unreasonable answer choices that you can eliminate. Some choices will be easier to eliminate than others.

Maya takes a group out every 60 minutes. She starts only 6 tours in a 6 hour period. She cannot start 10 or 15 tours. You can eliminate choices C and D.

Every time that Maya starts a tour, Jim will also. Try to find another time when Maya and Tran will start a tour at the same time.

After 60 minutes Maya will start another tour, but Tran will not. After 120 minutes, Maya will start a third tour, and Tran will start a fourth tour. The three guides will start a tour at the same time at least twice. You can eliminate choice A.

The correct answer is B. Ⓐ Ⓑ Ⓒ Ⓓ

STRATEGY PRACTICE

Explain why you can eliminate the highlighted answer choice.

1. Marcus has 28 hits in 64 at bats in baseball this season. What fraction, in simplest form, of Marcus's at bats are hits?

   Ⓐ ✗ $\mathbf{\frac{14}{32}}$ Ⓑ $\frac{16}{7}$ Ⓒ $\frac{7}{16}$ Ⓓ $\frac{1}{9}$

2. What is the greatest common factor of 45 and 75?

   Ⓐ 5 Ⓑ 15 Ⓒ ✗ **225** Ⓓ 3375

1 ◆ MULTIPLE CHOICE PRACTICE

1. Which list shows the fractions in order from least to greatest? **NS 1.1**

   Ⓐ $\frac{1}{4}, \frac{3}{14}, \frac{4}{7}, \frac{9}{28}$

   Ⓑ $\frac{7}{36}, \frac{1}{9}, \frac{7}{12}, \frac{1}{2}$

   Ⓒ $\frac{2}{7}, \frac{8}{21}, \frac{2}{5}, \frac{17}{25}$

   Ⓓ $\frac{1}{3}, \frac{5}{9}, \frac{7}{12}, \frac{8}{15}$

2. You are making gift baskets using the items in the table. You want to make identical baskets and have no items left over. What is the most gift baskets you can make? **NS 2.4**

   Ⓐ 4

   Ⓑ 10

   Ⓒ 13

   Ⓓ 26

Items for Gift Baskets	
Jars of mustard	65
Boxes of cheese	26
Scented candles	104

3. The director of a coed basketball league is placing 200 girls and 250 boys on teams. Each team must have the same number of girls and the same number of boys. What is the greatest number of teams that can be formed? **NS 2.4**

   Ⓐ 5

   Ⓑ 25

   Ⓒ 50

   Ⓓ 75

4. Which fraction is *not* equivalent to $\frac{42}{120}$? **NS 2.4**

   Ⓐ $\frac{14}{40}$

   Ⓑ $\frac{6}{17}$

   Ⓒ $\frac{56}{160}$

   Ⓓ $\frac{7}{20}$

5. The table shows the results of a survey about students' favorite pets. What fraction of the students preferred cats? **NS 2.4, MR 1.1**

   Ⓐ $\frac{1}{5}$

   Ⓑ $\frac{8}{35}$

   Ⓒ $\frac{3}{20}$

   Ⓓ $\frac{8}{15}$

Pet	*Students*
Birds	3
Cats	8
Dogs	15
Fish	6
Other	8

6. To decorate for a school dance, Alice uses two rolls of paper streamers. One roll is 64 feet long and the other is 72 feet long. She wants to cut the streamers into equal whole-foot lengths and have no paper left over. How many lengths are possible? **NS 2.4**

   Ⓐ 1

   Ⓑ 4

   Ⓒ 5

   Ⓓ 8

7. The lengths of three boards are 30 inches, 36 inches, and 96 inches. You want to cut the boards into segments of equal length without having any wood left over. What is the longest each segment can be? **NS 2.4**

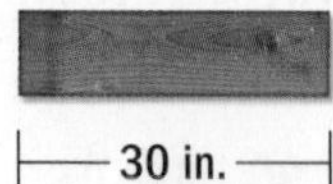

30 in.

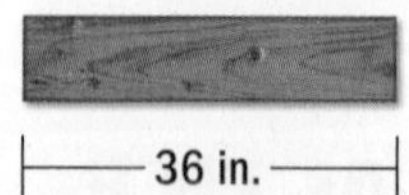

36 in.

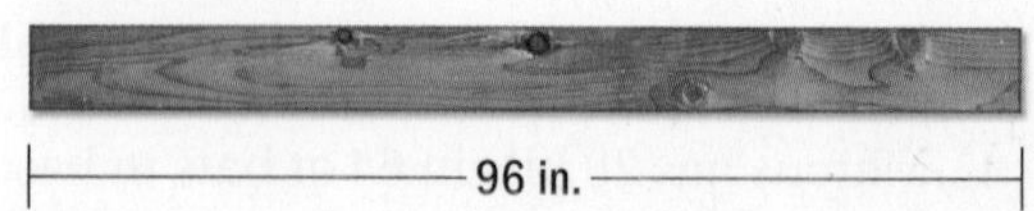

96 in.

   Ⓐ 6 in.

   Ⓑ 12 in.

   Ⓒ 24 in.

   Ⓓ 1440 in.

8. Which two numbers have a least common multiple of 168? **NS 2.4**

Ⓐ 14, 42

Ⓑ 21, 56

Ⓒ 12, 14

Ⓓ 28, 30

9. The graph shows the number of songs on 4 CDs and the number of songs Juan liked on each one. On which CD did Juan like the greatest fraction of songs? **NS 1.1, MR 2.2**

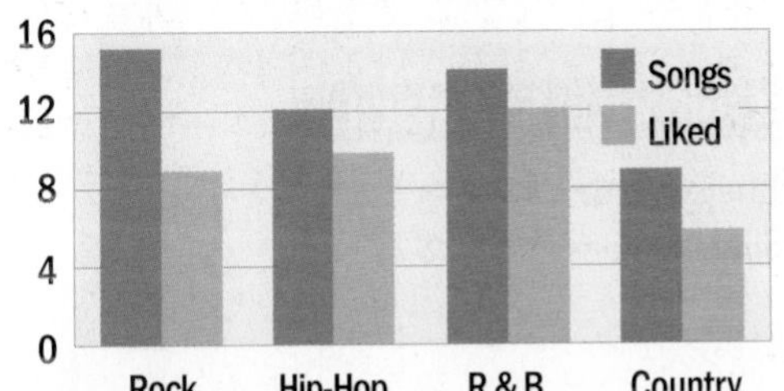

Ⓐ Rock

Ⓑ Hip-Hop

Ⓒ R & B

Ⓓ Country

10. The greatest common factor of 3 numbers is 4. The least common multiple of the same 3 numbers is 128. Which of the following could *not* be one of the numbers? **NS 2.4**

Ⓐ 8

Ⓑ 16

Ⓒ 32

Ⓓ 36

11. What is the prime factorization of 184? **Gr. 5 NS 1.4**

Ⓐ $2^2 \times 46$

Ⓑ 2×92

Ⓒ $2^3 \times 23$

Ⓓ $2 \times 3 \times 31$

12. Last week four members of a runner's club ran the distances shown below. Which member(s) ran a distance closest to Ryan's distance? **NS 1.1**

Ⓐ Kelly and Jane

Ⓑ Kelly

Ⓒ Jane

Ⓓ Alana

13. Three tour buses leave at the same time. One bus returns every 30 minutes, one returns every 60 minutes, and one returns every 90 minutes. When will all three buses first return at the same time? **NS 2.4, MR 1.2**

Ⓐ In 30 minutes

Ⓑ In 90 minutes

Ⓒ In 120 minutes

Ⓓ In 180 minutes

14. Which list shows $4\frac{3}{8}$, $\frac{25}{6}$, $4\frac{5}{16}$, and $4.\overline{2}$ in order from least to greatest? **NS 1.1**

Ⓐ $\frac{25}{6}$, $4.\overline{2}$, $4\frac{3}{8}$, $4\frac{5}{16}$

Ⓑ $4\frac{3}{8}$, $\frac{25}{6}$, $4\frac{5}{16}$, $4.\overline{2}$

Ⓒ $\frac{25}{6}$, $4\frac{3}{8}$, $4.\overline{2}$, $4\frac{5}{16}$

Ⓓ $\frac{25}{6}$, $4.\overline{2}$, $4\frac{5}{16}$, $4\frac{3}{8}$

15. Which number is not equivalent to $7\frac{5}{6}$? **NS 2.4**

Ⓐ $7\frac{15}{18}$

Ⓑ $\frac{47}{6}$

Ⓒ $\frac{41}{6}$

Ⓓ $7\frac{25}{30}$

2 Fraction and Decimal Operations

Before

In previous chapters, you learned the following skills, which you'll use in Chapter 2:

- Identifying equivalent fractions
- Writing fractions in simplest form
- Renaming improper fractions and mixed numbers

Now

In Chapter 2 you'll study these ***Big Ideas:***

1. Solving problems using addition and subtraction of fractions
2. Multiplying and dividing fractions
3. Adding, subtracting, multiplying, and dividing decimals

Why?

So you can solve real-world problems about . . .

- Alligators, p. 79
- Music, p. 80
- Running, p. 84
- Mazes, p. 105
- Scavenger hunts, p. 105
- Comets, p. 112

at classzone.com

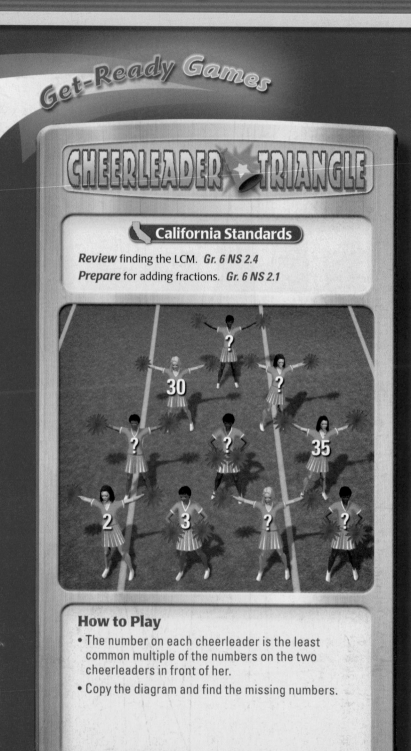

Get-Ready Games

CHEERLEADER TRIANGLE

California Standards

Review finding the LCM. ***Gr. 6 NS 2.4***
Prepare for adding fractions. ***Gr. 6 NS 2.1***

?

30 ?

? ? 35

2 3 ? ?

How to Play

- The number on each cheerleader is the least common multiple of the numbers on the two cheerleaders in front of her.
- Copy the diagram and find the missing numbers.

CALIFORNIA STANDARDS

- **Gr. 6 NS 2.1 Solve problems involving addition, subtraction, multiplication, and division of positive fractions and explain why a particular operation was used for a given situation.** *(Lessons 2.1, 2.2, 2.3, 2.4, 2.5)*
- **Gr. 5 NS 2.1 Add, subtract, multiply, and divide with decimals;** add with negative integers; subtract positive integers from negative integers; **and verify the reasonableness of the results.** *(Lessons 2.6, 2.7)*

MATH CHEERS

California Standards

Review finding the LCM. *Gr. 6 NS 2.4*
Prepare for adding fractions. *Gr. 6 NS 2.1*

How to Play

- The numbers on the shirts of the four cheerleaders in the back form a pair of equivalent fractions.
- Arrange the numbers on the eight other cheerleaders in two groups of four, so that each group consists of two equivalent fractions.

Games Wrap-Up

Draw Conclusions

Complete these exercises after playing the games.

1. **WRITING** Is the number in the back of the *Cheerleader Triangle* a multiple of all the numbers in front of it? Is it the least common multiple? *Explain* your reasoning.
2. **REASONING** Rearrange the numbers in one of your groups from *Math Cheers* to form other pairs of equivalent fractions. How many pairs are possible?

2 Getting Ready

Prerequisite Skills

California @HomeTutor
Prerequisite skills practice at classzone.com

REVIEW VOCABULARY

- **greatest common factor (GCF),** *p. 10*
- **equivalent fractions,** *p. 16*
- **simplest form,** *p. 17*
- **least common denominator (LCD),** *p. 29*
- **mixed number,** *p. 35*
- **improper fraction,** *p. 35*

VOCABULARY CHECK

Copy and complete using a review term from the list at the left.

1. Fractions that represent the same part-to-whole relationship are called __?__.
2. A number that has a whole number part and a fraction part is a(n) __?__.
3. The greatest whole number that is a factor of two or more nonzero whole numbers is the __?__ of the numbers.

SKILL CHECK

Write the fractions in simplest form. Tell whether they are equivalent. *(p. 16)*

4. $\frac{14}{28}, \frac{12}{21}$
5. $\frac{8}{12}, \frac{10}{15}$
6. $\frac{15}{24}, \frac{25}{40}$
7. $\frac{24}{27}, \frac{36}{42}$
8. $\frac{9}{36}, \frac{6}{24}$
9. $\frac{15}{18}, \frac{18}{21}$
10. $\frac{10}{15}, \frac{30}{48}$
11. $\frac{16}{32}, \frac{10}{20}$

Write an improper fraction and a mixed number to describe the model. *(p. 35)*

12. 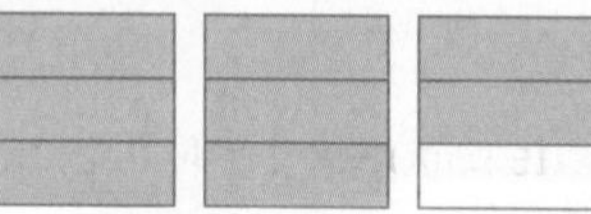

13. 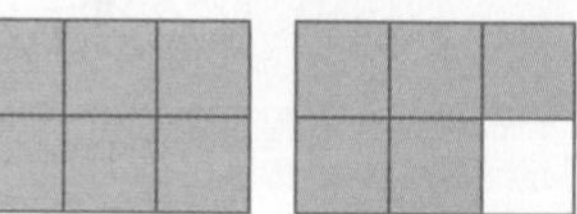

Notetaking Skills

NOW YOU TRY
Make a *concept map* for *fraction*. You may want to use colored pencils.

Focus on Graphic Organizers

Use a *concept map* to organize information about a new idea or vocabulary word, such as *least common denominator*.

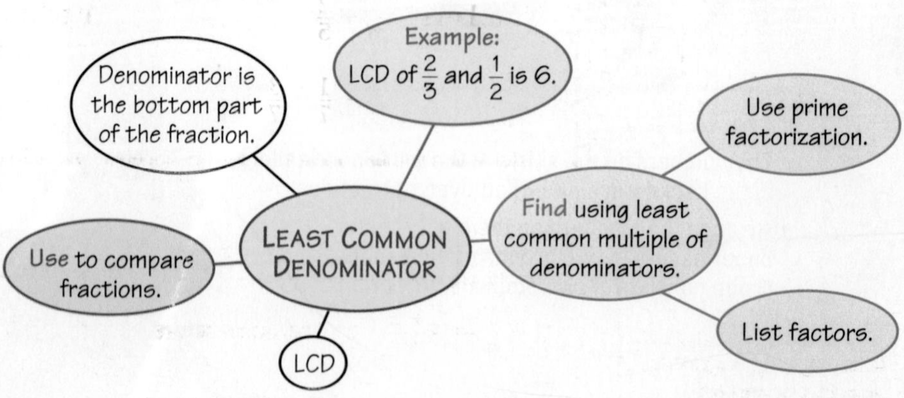

2.1 Adding and Subtracting Fractions

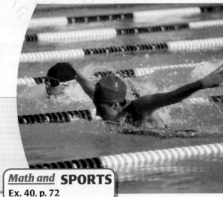

Standards **NS 2.1 Solve problems involving addition, subtraction,** multiplication, and division **of positive fractions and explain why a particular operation was used for a given situation.**

Connect ***Before*** you found equivalent fractions. ***Now*** you will add and subtract fractions to solve problems.

Math and **SPORTS**
Ex. 40, p. 72

KEY VOCABULARY
- variable
- algebraic expression
- evaluate

ACTIVITY

You can use models to add and subtract fractions.

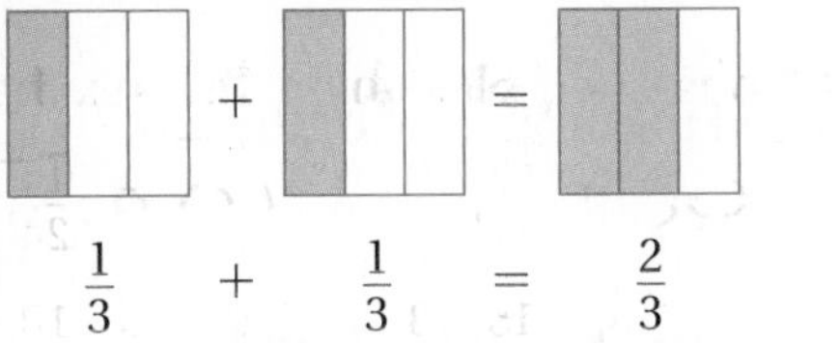

$\frac{1}{3} + \frac{1}{3} = \frac{2}{3}$

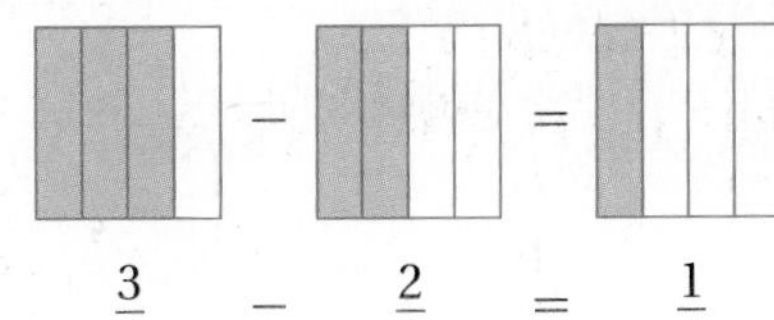

$\frac{3}{4} - \frac{2}{4} = \frac{1}{4}$

Use a model to find the sum or difference.

1. $\frac{2}{3} + \frac{1}{3}$ **2.** $\frac{1}{4} + \frac{1}{4}$ **3.** $\frac{3}{4} - \frac{1}{4}$ **4.** $\frac{2}{3} - \frac{1}{3}$

The activity suggests the following rules for adding and subtracting fractions with common denominators.

KEY CONCEPT *For Your Notebook*

Fractions with Common Denominators

Words To add or subtract two fractions with a common denominator, write the sum or difference of the numerators over the denominator.

Numbers $\frac{1}{5} + \frac{2}{5} = \frac{3}{5}$

$\frac{4}{7} - \frac{1}{7} = \frac{3}{7}$

Algebra $\frac{a}{c} + \frac{b}{c} = \frac{a+b}{c}$ $(c \neq 0)$

$\frac{a}{c} - \frac{b}{c} = \frac{a-b}{c}$ $(c \neq 0)$

EXAMPLE 1 Adding Fractions

AVOID ERRORS
When adding fractions, you do not add the denominators.

$\frac{2}{9} + \frac{5}{9} = \frac{2+5}{9}$ **Add numerators.**

$= \frac{7}{9}$ **Simplify numerator.**

EXAMPLE 2 Subtracting Fractions

CONSTRUCTION You are installing wooden trim in the window frames of a new house. At noon, there is still $\frac{7}{8}$ of the job to complete. You complete $\frac{3}{8}$ more of the job in the afternoon. What fraction of the job do you still need to complete?

$\frac{3}{8}$ of the job is completed in the afternoon.

SOLUTION

To find the part left to do, you need to subtract.

$\frac{7}{8} - \frac{3}{8} = \frac{7-3}{8}$ **Subtract numerators.**

$= \frac{4}{8}$ **Simplify numerator.**

$= \frac{1}{2}$ **Simplify fraction.**

SIMPLIFYING FRACTIONS
For help with simplifying fractions, see p. 17.

▶ **Answer** You still need to complete $\frac{1}{2}$ of the job.

✓ GUIDED PRACTICE for Examples 1 and 2

Find the sum or difference. Simplify if possible.

1. $\frac{3}{8} + \frac{1}{8}$ **2.** $\frac{3}{5} + \frac{4}{5}$ **3.** $\frac{5}{7} - \frac{2}{7}$ **4.** $\frac{5}{16} - \frac{3}{16}$

VOCABULARY
To simplify a numerical expression, perform all of the operations.

ALGEBRAIC EXPRESSIONS Sometimes you may want to evaluate an expression when one of more of the values might change. A **variable** is a letter used to represent one or more numbers. An **algebraic expression**, or *variable* expression, like $n + 6$, consists of numbers, variables, and operations. To **evaluate** an algebraic expression, you substitute values for the variables and then simplify the resulting *numerical* expression.

EXAMPLE 3 Evaluating Variable Expressions

Evaluate the expression $x + \frac{5}{9}$ when (a) $x = \frac{3}{9}$ and when (b) $x = \frac{8}{9}$.

a. $x + \frac{5}{9} = \frac{3}{9} + \frac{5}{9}$ **Substitute $\frac{3}{9}$ for x.**

$= \frac{8}{9}$ **Add.**

b. $x + \frac{5}{9} = \frac{8}{9} + \frac{5}{9}$ **Substitute $\frac{8}{9}$ for x.**

$= \frac{13}{9} = 1\frac{4}{9}$ **Add and rewrite.**

✓ GUIDED PRACTICE for Example 3

Evaluate the expression for the given values.

5. $a + \frac{7}{12}$; $a = \frac{11}{12}$, $a = \frac{2}{12}$ **6.** $b - \frac{13}{30}$; $b = \frac{23}{30}$, $b = \frac{17}{30}$

2.1 EXERCISES

HOMEWORK KEY ◆ = **MULTIPLE CHOICE PRACTICE** Exs. 28, 29, 45, 50–52

○ = **HINTS AND HOMEWORK HELP** for Exs. 7, 31, 41 at classzone.com

SKILLS • PROBLEM SOLVING • REASONING

1. **VOCABULARY** Copy and complete: To add fractions with a common denominator, add the __?__ and write the sum over the __?__.

2. **NOTETAKING SKILLS** Make a *concept map* like the one shown on page 68 for *expression*.

SEE EXAMPLES 1 AND 2 on pp. 69–70 for Exs. 3–28

INTERPRETING MODELS Write and evaluate the expression represented by the model.

3. 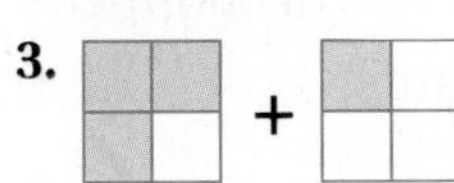

4. 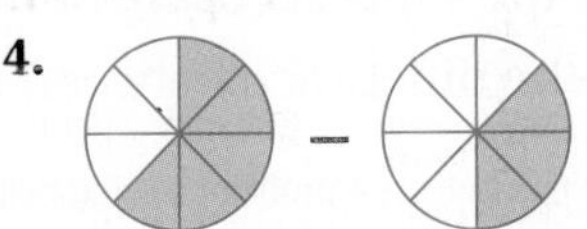

5. 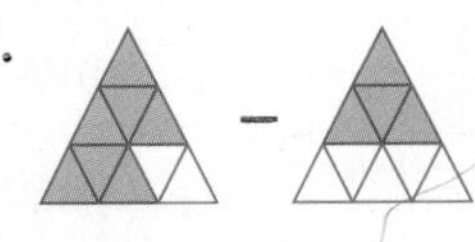

OPERATING WITH FRACTIONS Find the sum or difference. Simplify if possible.

6. $\frac{1}{3}+\frac{1}{3}$ 7. $\frac{4}{5}+\frac{2}{5}$ 8. $\frac{8}{9}+\frac{1}{9}$ 9. $\frac{7}{8}+\frac{1}{8}$

10. $\frac{1}{4}+\frac{1}{4}$ 11. $\frac{1}{9}+\frac{2}{9}$ 12. $\frac{5}{8}-\frac{1}{8}$ 13. $\frac{7}{10}-\frac{3}{10}$

14. $\frac{5}{7}-\frac{3}{7}$ 15. $\frac{5}{6}-\frac{1}{6}$ 16. $\frac{15}{16}-\frac{5}{16}$ 17. $\frac{7}{9}-\frac{4}{9}$

18. $\frac{5}{8}+\frac{1}{8}+\frac{7}{8}$ 19. $\frac{7}{12}+\frac{11}{12}+\frac{5}{12}$ 20. $\frac{9}{20}+\frac{17}{20}+\frac{9}{20}$ 21. $\frac{5}{14}+\frac{9}{14}+\frac{3}{14}$

22. $\frac{3}{4}-\frac{1}{4}-\frac{1}{4}$ 23. $\frac{9}{10}-\frac{1}{10}-\frac{3}{10}$ 24. $\frac{22}{35}-\frac{6}{35}-\frac{4}{35}$ 25. $\frac{25}{28}-\frac{5}{28}-\frac{13}{28}$

ERROR ANALYSIS ***Describe*** **and correct the error made in the solution.**

26. ✗ $\frac{6}{7}+\frac{3}{7}=\frac{9}{14}$

27. ✗ $\frac{7}{9}-\frac{4}{9}-\frac{1}{9}=\frac{7}{9}-\frac{3}{9}=\frac{4}{9}$

28. ◆ **MULTIPLE CHOICE** What is $\frac{25}{32}-\frac{13}{32}$ in simplest form?

(A) $\frac{3}{8}$ (B) $\frac{12}{32}$ (C) $1\frac{3}{16}$ (D) $1\frac{6}{32}$

SEE EXAMPLE 3 on p. 70 for Exs. 29–32

29. ◆ **MULTIPLE CHOICE** What is the value of $a+\frac{7}{18}$ when $a=\frac{8}{18}$?

(A) $\frac{1}{18}$ (B) $\frac{5}{12}$ (C) $\frac{5}{6}$ (D) 15

EVALUATING EXPRESSIONS Evaluate the expression for the given values.

30. $a+\frac{3}{7}$; $a=\frac{2}{7}$, $a=\frac{3}{7}$ 31. $r-\frac{7}{21}$; $r=\frac{16}{21}$, $r=\frac{10}{21}$ 32. $\frac{6}{14}+g$; $g=\frac{5}{14}$, $g=\frac{9}{14}$

33. $\frac{5}{26}+\frac{17}{26}-s$; $s=\frac{19}{26}$ 34. $z-\frac{7}{9}+z$; $z=\frac{8}{9}$ 35. $b+\frac{5}{24}+b$; $b=\frac{17}{24}$

CONNECT SKILLS TO PROBLEM SOLVING **Exercises 36–38 will help you prepare for problem solving.**

Write the expression you would use to solve the problem.

36. A sponge weighs $\frac{1}{16}$ ounce when dry and $\frac{13}{16}$ ounce after soaking part of it in water. How many ounces heavier is the wet sponge?

37. Two pieces of stained glass are placed together. One piece has a width of $\frac{17}{24}$ foot and the other piece has a width of $\frac{15}{24}$ foot. What is the combined width of the pieces of stained glass?

38. You buy $\frac{7}{8}$ yard of fabric to make a craft project. You use only $\frac{3}{8}$ yard. How much fabric do you have left?

SEE EXAMPLES 1 AND 2 on pp. 69–70 for Exs. 39–41

39. RECIPES A recipe suggests using between $\frac{1}{8}$ and $\frac{3}{8}$ cups of chopped nuts. What is the difference between the two amounts?

California @HomeTutor for problem solving help at classzone.com

40. MULTI-STEP PROBLEM You and two friends all compete in different races for your age group at a swim meet. Your friends each swim in $\frac{1}{5}$ of the races. You swim in $\frac{2}{5}$ of the races.

a. What is the total fraction of the races that your two friends swim in?

b. How does the total fraction of the races that they swim in compare with the fraction of the races that you swim in?

c. Are there races for your age group that none of you are in? *Explain.*

California @HomeTutor for problem solving help at classzone.com

41. AIRPORT RUNWAYS Runways A and B are being constructed at a rural airport. Runway B is to be $\frac{3}{25}$ mile shorter than Runway A.

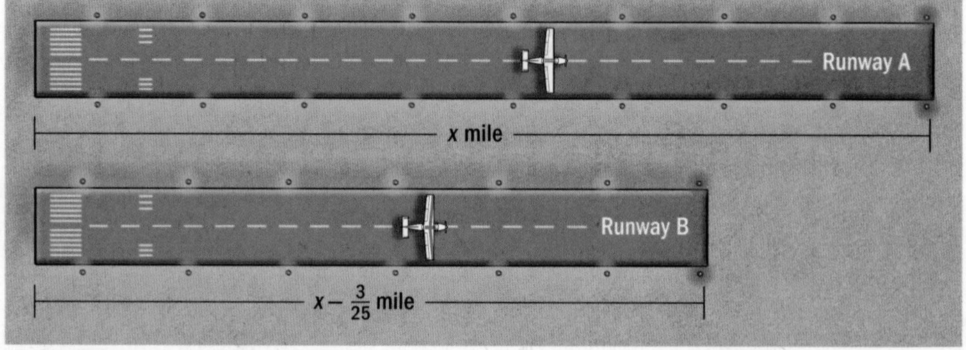

a. Calculate What is the length of Runway B if Runway A is $\frac{13}{25}$ mile long? $\frac{17}{25}$ mile long? $\frac{22}{25}$ mile long?

b. Reasoning The length of Runway A can be at most 0.92 mile long. What is the longest that Runway B can be? *Explain.*

42. WRITING How can you tell whether the sum of two fractions with a common denominator is greater than 1? less than 1? equal to 1?

43. **SNOWFALL** The weather report below shows the amount of snow that fell over a weekend and Monday's forecast. How much snow is expected Monday? *Explain* how you solved the problem.

Snowfall
Saturday
$\frac{3}{4}$ ft
Sunday
$\frac{3}{4}$ ft
Monday Forecast
$\frac{1}{4}$ ft less than weekend total

44. **SURVEYS** The table shows the results of a survey.

Hours per day online	*Fraction of students*
Less than 2.5	$\frac{16}{25}$
2.5–5	$\frac{6}{25}$
More than 5	$\frac{?}{25}$

a. **Choose the Operation** What fraction of the students spend more than 5 hours per day online? *Explain* how you solved the problem.

b. **Reasoning** Suppose $\frac{12}{25}$ of the students spend 1.5 hours or less per day online. What fraction of the students spend less than 2.5 hours, but more than 1.5 hours, per day online? *Explain.*

45. ◆ **MULTIPLE CHOICE** You make a home movie that contains $\frac{7}{15}$ hour of family trips and $\frac{4}{15}$ hour of birthday parties. If the tape can hold 1 hour of video, how much time is left on the tape?

Ⓐ $\frac{1}{5}$ hour Ⓑ $\frac{4}{15}$ hour Ⓒ $\frac{8}{15}$ hour Ⓓ $\frac{11}{15}$ hour

CHALLENGE Describe the relationship between *a* and *b* by completing the statement *a* = __?__ using an expression involving *b*.

46. $\frac{a}{c} + \frac{b}{c} = \frac{2a}{c}$ 47. $\frac{a}{c} - \frac{b}{c} = \frac{2b}{c}$ 48. $\frac{a}{c} + \frac{b}{c} = \frac{2}{c}$

49. **CHALLENGE** Copy and complete the equations below, replacing each "?" with a digit from 1 through 9. Use each digit only once.

$\frac{?}{7} + \frac{?}{7} + \frac{?}{7} = 1$ $\frac{?}{11} - \frac{?}{11} = \frac{2}{11}$ $\frac{?}{8} - \frac{?}{8} = \frac{1}{4}$ $\frac{?}{10} + \frac{?}{10} = 1\frac{1}{5}$

◆ CALIFORNIA STANDARDS SPIRAL REVIEW

NS 1.1 50. Which number is greater than 5.375? ***(p. 675)***

Ⓐ $\frac{42}{8}$ Ⓑ $\frac{29}{5}$ Ⓒ $5\frac{3}{10}$ Ⓓ $5\frac{3}{8}$

NS 2.4 51. What is the least common multiple of 18, 32, and 48? ***(p. 21)***

Ⓐ 2 Ⓑ 144 Ⓒ 288 Ⓓ 576

Gr. 4 NS 3.3 52. A factory produces 1450 packages of hair clips each day. Each package contains 5 clips. How many hair clips are made each day? ***(p. 671)***

Ⓐ 290 Ⓑ 1445 Ⓒ 1455 Ⓓ 7250

2.2 Modeling Addition of Fractions

MATERIALS • colored pencils • paper

> **Standards**
> **NS 2.1 Solve problems involving addition,** subtraction, multiplication, and division **of positive fractions** and explain why a particular operation was used for a given situation.

QUESTION **How can you add fractions with different denominators?**

You survey your class to find which type of movie they prefer. You find that $\frac{1}{2}$ the class prefers comedy and $\frac{1}{3}$ prefer action.

EXPLORE **Use models to find the fraction of your class that prefers comedy or action, $\frac{1}{2} + \frac{1}{3}$.**

STEP 1 **Draw** a model of $\frac{1}{2}$ by dividing a square vertically.

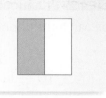

STEP 2 **Draw** a model of $\frac{1}{3}$ by dividing a square horizontally.

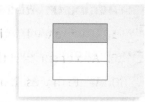

STEP 3 **Redraw** the models so that they are divided similarly.

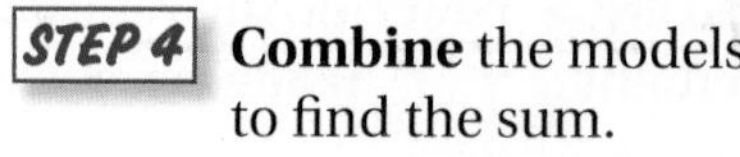

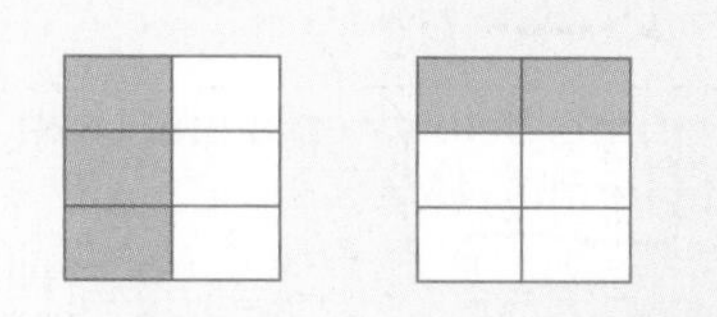

STEP 4 **Combine** the models to find the sum.

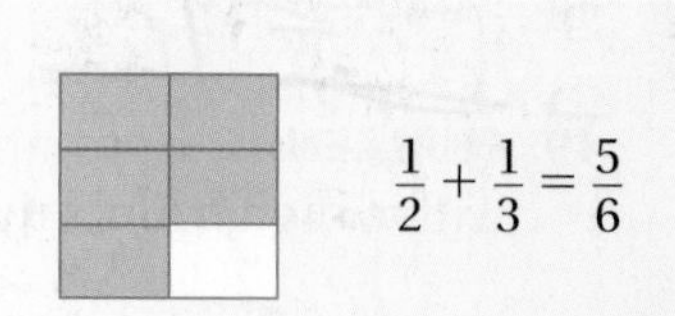

DRAW CONCLUSIONS **Use your observations to complete these exercises.**

Use models to find the sum. Write your answers in simplest form.

1. $\frac{1}{4} + \frac{1}{3}$ **2.** $\frac{3}{8} + \frac{1}{5}$ **3.** $\frac{2}{5} + \frac{1}{3}$ **4.** $\frac{3}{4} + \frac{1}{7}$

5. **WRITING** You add two fractions whose denominators are 5 and 7, such as $\frac{3}{5}$ and $\frac{1}{7}$. What denominator does their sum have? *Explain* how you can use models to answer this question.

6. **REASONING** Without drawing a model, tell what the denominator will be when you add two fractions whose denominators are 5 and 11. *Explain.*

2.2 Using a Common Denominator

Math and MUSIC
Exs. 47–50, p. 80

Standards NS 2.4 **Determine the least common multiple** and the greatest common divisor **of whole numbers; use them to solve problems with fractions (e.g., to find a common denominator to add two fractions** or to find the reduced form for a fraction).

Connect ***Before*** you added and subtracted fractions with common denominators. ***Now*** you will add and subtract fractions with different denominators.

KEY VOCABULARY

- **least common denominator (LCD),** *p. 29*
- **mixed number,** *p. 35*
- **variable,** *p. 70*
- **algebraic expression,** *p. 70*

The activity on page 74 suggests how to add or subtract fractions with different denominators. First rewrite them with a common denominator. Then add or subtract the numerators as in Lesson 2.1.

You can use any common denominator to add or subtract two fractions. Using the *least* common denominator can make the calculation easier.

KEY CONCEPT *For Your Notebook*

Adding or Subtracting with Different Denominators

1. Rewrite the fractions using the LCD.
2. Add or subtract the numerators.
3. Write the result over the LCD.
4. Simplify if possible.

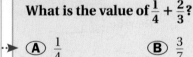

EXAMPLE 1 ◆ Multiple Choice Practice

What is the value of $\frac{1}{4} + \frac{2}{3}$?

Ⓐ $\frac{1}{4}$ Ⓑ $\frac{3}{7}$ Ⓒ $\frac{3}{4}$ Ⓓ $\frac{11}{12}$

ELIMINATE CHOICES
You are adding a positive fraction to $\frac{1}{4}$. The sum must be greater than $\frac{1}{4}$. You can eliminate choice A.

SOLUTION

$$\frac{1 \times 3}{4 \times 3} = \frac{3}{12}$$ **Rewrite each fraction using the LCD, 12.**

$$+\frac{2 \times 4}{3 \times 4} = +\frac{8}{12}$$

$$\frac{11}{12}$$ **Add the fractions.**

CHECK $\frac{1}{4} + \frac{2}{3} =$

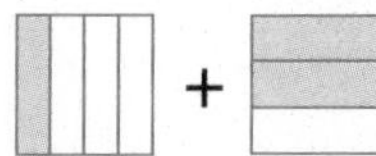

▶ **Answer** The correct answer is D. Ⓐ Ⓑ Ⓒ Ⓓ

EXAMPLE 2 Rewriting Sums of Fractions

Find the sum $\frac{5}{8} + \frac{3}{4}$.

REWRITING FRACTIONS
For help with writing equivalent fractions, see p. 16.

$\frac{5}{8} + \frac{3}{4} = \frac{5}{8} + \frac{3 \times 2}{4 \times 2}$ **Find equivalent fractions using the LCD, 8.**

$= \frac{5}{8} + \frac{6}{8}$ **Rewrite.**

$= \frac{11}{8}$, or $1\frac{3}{8}$ **Add the fractions. Rewrite as a mixed number.**

✓ **GUIDED PRACTICE for Examples 1 and 2**

Find the sum. Simplify if possible.

1. $\frac{1}{3} + \frac{1}{8}$
2. $\frac{3}{5} + \frac{5}{12}$
3. $\frac{9}{40} + \frac{1}{10}$
4. $\frac{5}{6} + \frac{2}{3}$

SOLVING PROBLEMS Be sure to read a problem carefully to understand what is being asked and which operation you should choose. When using 1 whole, you may have to rewrite 1 as an equivalent fraction, such as $\frac{5}{5}$.

EXAMPLE 3 Subtracting Fractions

RAINFALL Last week, $\frac{3}{14}$ inch of rain fell on Monday and $\frac{5}{6}$ inch fell on Tuesday. How much more rain fell on Tuesday than on Monday?

SOLUTION

About the Standards
Note that Grade 6 Standard NS 2.1 asks you to explain why a particular operation was used for a given situation.

To find out *how much more,* you need to find the *difference* of $\frac{5}{6}$ and $\frac{3}{14}$.

$\frac{5}{6} - \frac{3}{14} = \frac{5 \times 7}{6 \times 7} - \frac{3 \times 3}{14 \times 3}$ **Find equivalent fractions using the LCD, 42.**

$= \frac{35}{42} - \frac{9}{42}$ **Rewrite.**

$= \frac{26}{42}$, or $\frac{13}{21}$ **Subtract the fractions.**

▶ **Answer** On Tuesday, $\frac{13}{21}$ inch more rain fell than on Monday.

 **GUIDED PRACTICE for Example 3**

Find the difference. Simplify if possible.

5. $\frac{5}{6} - \frac{3}{4}$
6. $\frac{7}{8} - \frac{1}{4}$
7. $\frac{1}{2} - \frac{4}{9}$
8. $\frac{5}{6} - \frac{3}{10}$

9. **RACING** One lap of Speedway A is $\frac{2}{5}$ mile. One lap of Speedway B is $\frac{3}{4}$ mile. How much longer is one lap of Speedway B?

EXAMPLE 4 Rewriting 1 as a Fraction

ACTIVITIES The circle graph shows how Kate spends her school day. What fraction of her school day is *not* spent in classes?

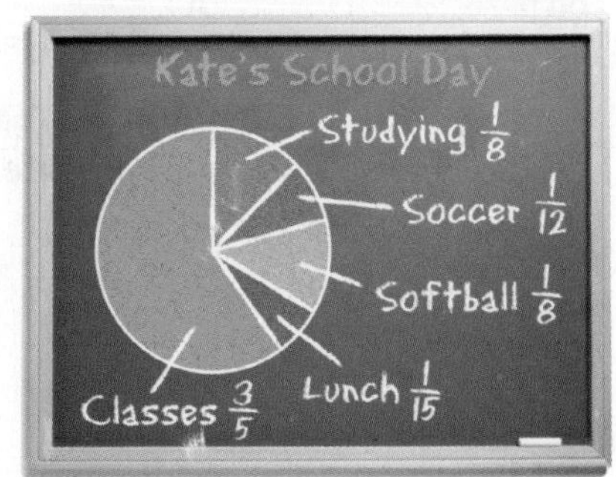

Animated Math For an interactive example of adding and subtracting fractions go to **classzone.com.**

SOLUTION

Kate's whole school day can be represented by 1. You want to find the difference between 1 and the fraction of her school day that she spends in classes, $\frac{3}{5}$, so subtract using fifths.

$1 - \frac{3}{5} = \frac{5}{5} - \frac{3}{5}$ **Rewrite 1 as $\frac{5}{5}$.**

$= \frac{2}{5}$ **Subtract the fractions.**

▶ **Answer** Kate spends $\frac{2}{5}$ of her school day not in classes.

✓ GUIDED PRACTICE for Example 4

10. **WHAT IF?** What fraction of Kate's school day does she spend *not* at lunch? *not* playing sports?

2.2 EXERCISES

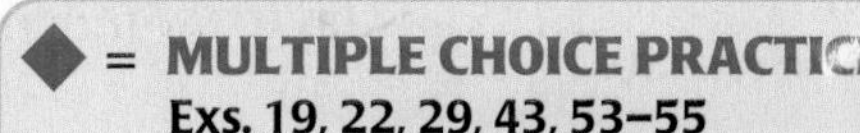

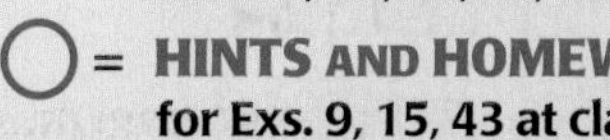

HOMEWORK KEY ◆ = **MULTIPLE CHOICE PRACTICE** Exs. 19, 22, 29, 43, 53–55
○ = **HINTS AND HOMEWORK HELP** for Exs. 9, 15, 43 at classzone.com

SKILLS • PROBLEM SOLVING • REASONING

1. **VOCABULARY** Copy and complete: To add fractions with different denominators, first rewrite the fractions using the _?_.

2. **WRITING** *Describe* how $\frac{1}{4} + \frac{1}{3}$ is related to $\frac{3}{12} + \frac{4}{12}$.

SEE EXAMPLES 1, 2, 3, AND 4 on pp. 76–77 for Exs. 3–18

USING COMMON DENOMINATORS Find the sum or difference. Simplify if possible.

3. $\frac{1}{5} + \frac{7}{10}$
4. $\frac{5}{8} + \frac{1}{4}$
5. $\frac{3}{14} + \frac{3}{4}$
6. $\frac{3}{7} + \frac{13}{28}$
7. $\frac{7}{12} + \frac{3}{5}$
8. $\frac{4}{15} + \frac{1}{2}$
9. $\frac{19}{24} - \frac{7}{16}$
10. $\frac{5}{6} - \frac{4}{9}$
11. $\frac{11}{12} - \frac{3}{4}$
12. $\frac{4}{5} - \frac{3}{10}$
13. $1 - \frac{5}{8}$
14. $1 - \frac{4}{9}$
15. $\frac{3}{8} + \frac{5}{16} + \frac{7}{8}$
16. $\frac{5}{6} + \frac{7}{12} + \frac{2}{3}$
17. $\frac{3}{4} - \frac{2}{5} - \frac{1}{3}$
18. $1 - \frac{7}{30} - \frac{2}{5}$

SEE EXAMPLES 2 AND 3 on p. 76 for Exs. 19–21

19. ◆ **MULTIPLE CHOICE** What is the value of $\frac{37}{48} - \frac{7}{16}$?

(A) $\frac{1}{3}$ (B) $\frac{5}{8}$ (C) $\frac{15}{16}$ (D) $2\frac{7}{8}$

ERROR ANALYSIS ***Describe*** **and correct the error made in finding the sum or difference.**

20. $\frac{3}{4} + \frac{2}{3} = \frac{3+2}{4+3} = \frac{5}{7}$ ✗

21. $\frac{9}{28} - \frac{2}{7} = \frac{9}{28} - \frac{2}{28} = \frac{7}{28} = \frac{1}{4}$ ✗

SEE EXAMPLE 4 on p. 77 for Ex. 22

22. ◆ **MULTIPLE CHOICE** What is the value of $1 - \frac{11}{18}$?

(A) 0 (B) $\frac{7}{18}$ (C) $\frac{5}{9}$ (D) $\frac{10}{17}$

xy **EVALUATING EXPRESSIONS** **Evaluate the expression for the given value.**

23. $a + \frac{3}{7}$ when $a = \frac{5}{14}$

24. $w - \frac{13}{45}$ when $w = \frac{5}{9}$

25. $g + \frac{5}{6}$ when $g = \frac{1}{4}$

26. $x - \frac{3}{10} - \frac{1}{5}$ when $x = \frac{6}{7}$

27. $t + \frac{7}{10} + \frac{2}{9}$ when $t = \frac{8}{27}$

28. $1 - y$ when $y = \frac{19}{24}$

29. ◆ **MULTIPLE CHOICE** The sum of $\frac{1}{4}$ and which number is *greater* than $\frac{1}{2}$?

(A) $\frac{1}{8}$ (B) $\frac{1}{6}$ (C) $\frac{1}{4}$ (D) $\frac{1}{3}$

CHOOSE A METHOD **Copy and complete the statement using <, >, or =. Tell whether you used** ***mental math, estimation,*** **or** ***pencil and paper.***

30. $\frac{9}{10} - \frac{4}{5} \ \underline{?}\ \frac{1}{10}$

31. $\frac{5}{12} + \frac{1}{6} \ \underline{?}\ \frac{13}{24}$

32. $\frac{3}{4} + \frac{1}{20} \ \underline{?}\ \frac{9}{10}$

33. $\frac{2}{3} - \frac{5}{9} \ \underline{?}\ \frac{1}{6}$

34. $\frac{5}{8} + \frac{1}{2} \ \underline{?}\ 1$

35. $\frac{13}{14} - \frac{6}{7} \ \underline{?}\ \frac{5}{7}$

36. **LOOK FOR A PATTERN** *Describe* the pattern: $\frac{1}{16}, \frac{1}{8}, \frac{3}{16}, \frac{1}{4}, \ldots$. Then write the next three fractions in the pattern.

CONNECT SKILLS TO PROBLEM SOLVING **Exercises 37–40 will help you prepare for problem solving.**

Write the expression you would use to solve the problem.

37. You run $\frac{3}{8}$ mile and your friend runs $\frac{19}{24}$ mile. What is the total distance that you and your friend run?

38. You practice piano for $\frac{3}{4}$ hour on Monday and $\frac{11}{15}$ hour on Tuesday. How many total hours do you practice on the two days?

39. You study for 1 hour before dinner and $\frac{7}{10}$ hour after dinner. How much longer do you study before dinner?

40. The thicknesses of two tabletops are $\frac{1}{4}$ foot and $\frac{1}{6}$ foot. What is the difference in the thicknesses of the two tabletops?

SEE EXAMPLES 1, 2, AND 3 on pp. 75–76 for Exs. 41–43

41. **ALLIGATORS** A recently hatched alligator is $\frac{3}{4}$ foot long. The alligator grows $\frac{5}{12}$ foot over the next 5 months. Write and evaluate an expression to find the length of the alligator when it is 5 months old. *Explain* your choice of operation.

A newborn alligator

California @HomeTutor for problem solving help at classzone.com

42. **SNACK FOOD** A recipe for trail mix calls for $\frac{3}{4}$ cup of dried mixed fruit, $\frac{1}{2}$ cup of mixed nuts, and $\frac{1}{3}$ cup of granola. How many cups of trail mix does this recipe make?
    a. **Make a Model** Draw a model to answer the question.
    b. **Write an Expression** Write and evaluate an expression to answer the question. Estimate to check your answer.

California @HomeTutor for problem solving help at classzone.com

43. ◆ **MULTIPLE CHOICE** Which expression can you use to find how much greater $\frac{9}{10}$ pound of bananas weighs than $\frac{4}{5}$ pound of bananas?

Ⓐ $\frac{4}{5} - \frac{9}{10}$ Ⓑ $\frac{9}{10} - \frac{4}{5}$ Ⓒ $\frac{9}{10} + \frac{4}{5}$ Ⓓ $\frac{4}{5} \times \frac{9}{10}$

44. **OPEN-ENDED** Write three fractions greater than 0 and less than 1 with different denominators whose sum is *greater* than 1. Write three fractions greater than 0 and less than 1 with different denominators whose sum is *less* than 1.

45. **MULTI-STEP PROBLEM** Chris, Ted, and Leroy are practicing for a swimming event. In 10 minutes, they swim a total of $\frac{7}{8}$ mile. Chris and Ted swim the distances shown below.
    a. **Calculate** How far does Leroy swim? *Explain* your choice of operations.
    b. **Calculate** How much farther does Leroy swim than either Chris or Ted? *Explain* your reasoning.

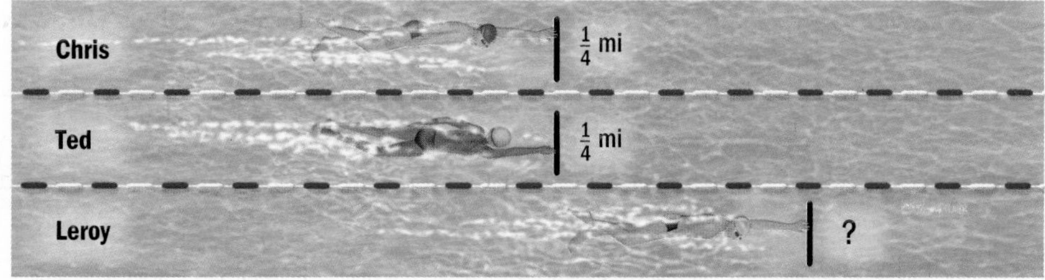

46. **SHORT RESPONSE** From the time you wake up, you need $\frac{3}{4}$ hour to get ready for school and $\frac{5}{12}$ hour to travel from home to school.
    a. Find the time (in hours) it takes for you to get to school from the time you wake up.
    b. If you wake up at 6:30 A.M., can you get to school by 7:30 A.M.? *Justify* your answer.

READING IN MATH **Read the information below for Exercises 47–50.**

Music In music, a $\frac{4}{4}$ time signature means that there are 4 beats per measure and that a quarter note (♩) gets 1 beat. The beats for seven musical notes with this time signature are shown in the table.

Note	𝅝	𝅗𝅥	♩	♪.	♪	𝅘𝅥𝅯.	𝅘𝅥𝅯
Beats	4	2	1	$\frac{3}{4}$	$\frac{1}{2}$	$\frac{3}{8}$	$\frac{1}{4}$

47. **Reading Music** Does this measure contain 4 beats? *Explain.*

48. **Reading Music** Does this measure contain 4 beats? *Explain.*

49. **Open-Ended** Give three other measures with exactly 4 different notes that contain 4 beats.

50. **Writing** The note 𝅘𝅥𝅯 is called a sixteenth note. *Explain* why this name makes sense using the information given above.

51. **CHALLENGE** Consider the difference $\frac{1}{2} - \frac{1}{4} - \frac{1}{8} - \frac{1}{16} - \cdots$. Find the difference of the first 4 fractions shown. Extend the pattern and find the difference of the first 6 fractions. If the pattern continues, will the difference ever reach 0? *Explain* your reasoning.

52. **CHALLENGE** A *unit fraction* is of the form $\frac{1}{a}$ where $a \neq 0$. Rewrite $\frac{7}{10}$ and $\frac{4}{15}$ as a sum of two unit fractions, where $a \neq 10$ and $a \neq 15$.

◆ CALIFORNIA STANDARDS SPIRAL REVIEW

Gr. 5 NS 1.4

53. What is the prime factorization of 44? ***(p. 6)***

Ⓐ 2×11 Ⓑ 4×11 Ⓒ $2^2 \times 11$ Ⓓ 2×22

Gr. 4 NS 3.2

54. What is the value of 138×62? ***(p. 662)***

Ⓐ 894 Ⓑ 1104 Ⓒ 6546 Ⓓ 8556

NS 2.1

55. Mark spends $\frac{9}{10}$ hour working on one part of a history project. Later, Jeremy spends $\frac{7}{10}$ hour working on another part of the project. What is the total time they spend working on the history project? ***(p. 69)***

Ⓐ $\frac{1}{5}$ hour Ⓑ $\frac{4}{5}$ hour Ⓒ $1\frac{3}{10}$ hours Ⓓ $1\frac{3}{5}$ hours

2.3 Adding and Subtracting Mixed Numbers

Standards NS 2.1 **Solve problems involving addition, subtraction,** multiplication, and division **of positive fractions and explain why a particular operation was used for a given situation.**

Connect ***Before*** you added and subtracted fractions. ***Now*** you will add and subtract mixed numbers to solve problems.

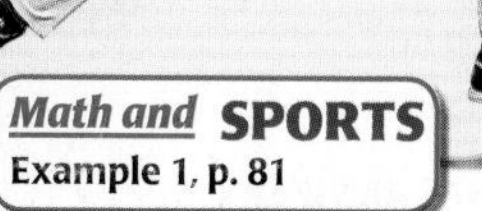

KEY VOCABULARY

- **least common denominator,** *p. 29*
- **mixed number, improper fraction,** *p. 35*

WORLD SERIES In 2004, the Boston Red Sox won the World Series for the first time in 86 years. In the American League Championship Series preceding the 2004 World Series, Tim Wakefield pitched $7\frac{1}{3}$ innings and Derek Lowe pitched $11\frac{1}{3}$ innings. What is the total number of innings they pitched?

To find the total number of innings, you need to add two mixed numbers. To add mixed numbers, first add the fraction parts as in Lesson 2.2. Then add the whole number parts. These steps are summarized below.

KEY CONCEPT *For Your Notebook*

Adding and Subtracting Mixed Numbers

1. Find the LCD of the fractions, if necessary.
2. Rename the fractions, if necessary. Then add or subtract the fractions.
3. Add or subtract the whole numbers.
4. Simplify if possible.

EXAMPLE 1 Adding with a Common Denominator

ANOTHER WAY

Rewrite the mixed numbers as improper fractions and then add.

$$7\frac{1}{3} + 11\frac{1}{3} = \frac{22}{3} + \frac{34}{3} = \frac{56}{3} = 18\frac{2}{3}$$

To solve the real-world problem above, find the sum of $7\frac{1}{3}$ and $11\frac{1}{3}$.

$$\begin{array}{r} 7\frac{1}{3} \\ +\ 11\frac{1}{3} \\ \hline 18\frac{2}{3} \end{array}$$

Add the whole numbers.

Add the fractions.

▶ **Answer** Tim Wakefield and Derek Lowe pitched a total of $18\frac{2}{3}$ innings.

CHECK Estimate the sum by rounding each mixed number to the nearest whole number.

$7\frac{1}{3} + 11\frac{1}{3} \approx 7 + 11 = 18.$ The answer is reasonable.

EXAMPLE 2 Subtracting with a Common Denominator

$6\frac{7}{9} - 4\frac{1}{9} = 2\frac{6}{9}$ **Subtract fractions and then subtract whole numbers.**

$= 2\frac{2}{3}$ **Simplify.**

EXAMPLE 3 Adding with Different Denominators

ESTIMATE ANSWERS

You can estimate the answer by rounding each mixed number to the nearest whole number. Because 5 + 4 = 9, the answer is reasonable.

$4\frac{5}{6} + 3\frac{3}{4} = 4\frac{10}{12} + 3\frac{9}{12}$ **Rewrite fractions using LCD of $\frac{5}{6}$ and $\frac{3}{4}$, 12.**

$= 7\frac{19}{12}$ **Add fractions and then add whole numbers.**

$= 7 + 1\frac{7}{12}$ **Write improper fraction as a mixed number.**

$= 8\frac{7}{12}$ **Add whole numbers.**

RENAMING When subtracting mixed numbers, sometimes the fractional part of the second mixed number is greater. If so, you have to *rename* the first mixed number to subtract the fractional parts. For example:

$$6\frac{1}{6} = 5 + 1 + \frac{1}{6}$$

$$= 5 + \frac{6}{6} + \frac{1}{6}$$

$$= 5 + \frac{7}{6}, \text{ or } 5\frac{7}{6}$$

EXAMPLE 4 Renaming to Subtract Mixed Numbers

AnimatedMath

For an interactive example of adding and subtracting mixed numbers go to **classzone.com.**

a. $6\frac{1}{6} - 3\frac{1}{3} = 6\frac{1}{6} - 3\frac{2}{6}$ **Rewrite fractions using LCD of $\frac{1}{6}$ and $\frac{1}{3}$.**

$= 5\frac{7}{6} - 3\frac{2}{6}$ **Rename $6\frac{1}{6}$ as $5\frac{7}{6}$.**

$= 2\frac{5}{6}$ **Subtract fractions and then subtract whole numbers.**

b. $7 - 5\frac{5}{8} = 6\frac{8}{8} - 5\frac{5}{8}$ **Rename 7 as $6\frac{8}{8}$.**

$= 1\frac{3}{8}$ **Subtract fractions and then subtract whole numbers.**

✓ GUIDED PRACTICE for Examples 1, 2, 3, and 4

Find the sum or difference. Simplify if possible.

1. $3\frac{1}{8} + 2\frac{5}{8}$ **2.** $1\frac{3}{4} + 4\frac{3}{8}$ **3.** $8\frac{5}{7} - 4\frac{1}{7}$ **4.** $8 - 5\frac{1}{10}$

2.3 EXERCISES

HOMEWORK KEY ◆ = **MULTIPLE CHOICE PRACTICE** Exs. 25, 26, 45, 53–55
○ = **HINTS AND HOMEWORK HELP** for Exs. 13, 19, 45 at classzone.com

SKILLS • PROBLEM SOLVING • REASONING

1. **VOCABULARY** When subtracting, when is it necessary to rename a mixed number?

2. **WRITING** *Describe* how to rename the mixed number $7\frac{3}{8}$ so that the whole part is 6.

SEE EXAMPLES 1 AND 2 on pp. 81–82 for Exs. 3–12

USING COMMON DENOMINATORS Find the sum or difference. Simplify if possible. Then estimate to check the answer.

3. $12\frac{3}{5} + 5\frac{1}{5}$
4. $22\frac{2}{7} + 17\frac{4}{7}$
5. $8\frac{7}{12} + 4\frac{5}{12}$
6. $8\frac{3}{4} + 2\frac{3}{4}$
7. $3\frac{2}{3} - 2\frac{1}{3}$
8. $7\frac{3}{5} - 3\frac{1}{5}$
9. $8\frac{4}{9} - 5\frac{2}{9}$
10. $13\frac{5}{6} - 9\frac{1}{6}$

ERROR ANALYSIS ***Describe*** **and correct the error made in finding the difference.**

11. $3\frac{1}{6} - 1\frac{5}{6} = 2\frac{4}{6} = 2\frac{2}{3}$ ✗

12. $4\frac{3}{7} - 2\frac{6}{7} = 4\frac{10}{7} - 2\frac{6}{7} = 2\frac{4}{7}$ ✗

SEE EXAMPLES 3 AND 4 on p. 82 for Exs. 13–25

FINDING SUMS AND DIFFERENCES Find the sum or difference. Simplify if possible. Then estimate to check the answer.

13. $4\frac{1}{4} + 3\frac{3}{8}$
14. $3\frac{2}{3} + 8\frac{1}{6}$
15. $4\frac{3}{4} + 6\frac{2}{3}$
16. $5\frac{1}{4} + 2\frac{5}{6}$
17. $6\frac{2}{5} + 11\frac{1}{6}$
18. $8\frac{1}{6} + 5\frac{7}{20}$
19. $8\frac{1}{8} - 1\frac{5}{8}$
20. $12\frac{3}{4} - 9\frac{1}{6}$
21. $5\frac{5}{8} - 2\frac{1}{4}$
22. $8\frac{4}{9} - 5\frac{2}{3}$
23. $7 - 3\frac{3}{10}$
24. $9 - 7\frac{4}{9}$

25. ◆ **MULTIPLE CHOICE** What is the value of $8\frac{1}{4} - 3\frac{5}{6}$?

Ⓐ 4 Ⓑ $4\frac{5}{12}$ Ⓒ $5\frac{2}{3}$ Ⓓ 6

26. ◆ **MULTIPLE CHOICE** Which expression has the sum $3\frac{2}{3}$?

Ⓐ $1\frac{1}{8} + 2\frac{7}{16}$ Ⓑ $2\frac{5}{12} + 1\frac{1}{4}$ Ⓒ $1\frac{17}{18} + 1\frac{7}{9}$ Ⓓ $1\frac{13}{15} + 1\frac{9}{10}$

ALGEBRA Evaluate the expression when $x = 7\frac{2}{5}$ and $y = 5\frac{1}{3}$.

27. $x + 1\frac{4}{5}$
28. $11\frac{1}{6} - x$
29. $y - 3\frac{2}{3}$
30. $y + 2\frac{7}{12}$
31. $9\frac{7}{9} + x$
32. $y - 3\frac{3}{7}$
33. $x - 3\frac{1}{4} - 2\frac{7}{10}$
34. $7\frac{1}{18} + y + 1\frac{3}{14}$

CHOOSE A METHOD **Copy and complete the statement using $<$, $>$, or $=$. Tell whether you used *mental math, estimation,* or *pencil and paper.***

35. $3\frac{1}{4} + 4\frac{1}{4} \ \underline{?}\ 7\frac{1}{2}$

36. $8\frac{1}{4} - 2\frac{1}{8} \ \underline{?}\ 6\frac{1}{2}$

37. $10\frac{1}{10} + 16\frac{1}{2} \ \underline{?}\ 27\frac{1}{2}$

38. $12\frac{2}{3} - 2\frac{7}{9} \ \underline{?}\ 10\frac{2}{3}$

39. $9\frac{4}{7} - 3\frac{11}{14} \ \underline{?}\ 5\frac{11}{14}$

40. $7\frac{3}{4} + 4\frac{5}{12} \ \underline{?}\ 12\frac{1}{6}$

CONNECT SKILLS TO PROBLEM SOLVING **Exercises 41–43 will help you prepare for problem solving.**

Which operation would you use to solve the problem? *Explain* why.

41. For a barbeque, you buy $2\frac{3}{4}$ pounds of ground beef and $7\frac{1}{4}$ pounds of chicken. What is the total weight of the meat?

42. Anna was $19\frac{1}{2}$ inches long at birth. At her 3 month checkup, she was $23\frac{1}{4}$ inches long. How much did she grow during that time?

43. You have $5\frac{5}{8}$ cups of cornmeal. You need $1\frac{3}{8}$ cups for a recipe. After you make the recipe, how much cornmeal do you have left?

SEE EXAMPLES 3 AND 4 on p. 82 for Exs. 44–47

44. RUNNING At track practice, you walk $\frac{1}{4}$ mile, run $5\frac{1}{2}$ miles, and then walk $1\frac{1}{4}$ miles. What is your total distance?

California @HomeTutor for problem solving help at classzone.com

Four laps around the track is 1 mile.

45. ◆ **MULTIPLE CHOICE** A boat begins a trip with $22\frac{7}{8}$ gallons of fuel in its tank. When the boat reaches its destination, the tank contains $14\frac{1}{4}$ gallons of fuel. On the return trip, the boat uses $2\frac{5}{12}$ gallons more fuel than it used to get to its original destination. How many total gallons of fuel does the boat use?

Ⓐ $3\frac{5}{24}$ gal Ⓑ $11\frac{1}{24}$ gal Ⓒ $19\frac{2}{3}$ gal Ⓓ $48\frac{1}{6}$ gal

California @HomeTutor for problem solving help at classzone.com

46. SHORT RESPONSE A car is $14\frac{4}{5}$ feet long. Another car is $1\frac{1}{10}$ feet longer. Can the two cars fit end to end in a driveway that is $31\frac{1}{2}$ feet long? If so, how much space is left? If not, how much more space is needed? *Explain* how you solved the problem.

47. CRAFTS You construct a rectangular picture frame out of strips of wood that are $\frac{3}{4}$ inch wide. The dimensions of the outside of the frame are $6\frac{1}{2}$ inches wide by $8\frac{1}{4}$ inches long. Can you fit a picture that is 5 inches wide and 7 inches long in your frame? *Justify* your answer.

48. **OPEN-ENDED** Give an example of a real-world situation where you need to *add* two mixed numbers. Give an example of a real-world situation where you need to *subtract* two mixed numbers. Write and evaluate an expression to solve each problem.

49. **WRITING** *Explain* how you can use mental math to find $7 - 3\frac{2}{5}$.

50. **REASONING** Can you subtract two mixed numbers and get an answer less than 1? Can you subtract a proper fraction from a mixed number and get an answer less than 1? *Explain* your reasoning and provide two examples.

51. **CHALLENGE** Using each digit from 1 to 9 exactly once and only proper fractional parts, write an expression with the greatest value that has the form $a\frac{b}{c} + m\frac{n}{p} + x\frac{y}{z}$. What is its value?

52. **CHALLENGE** The perimeter of the figure shown is $9\frac{3}{5}$. Find the values of x, y, and z.

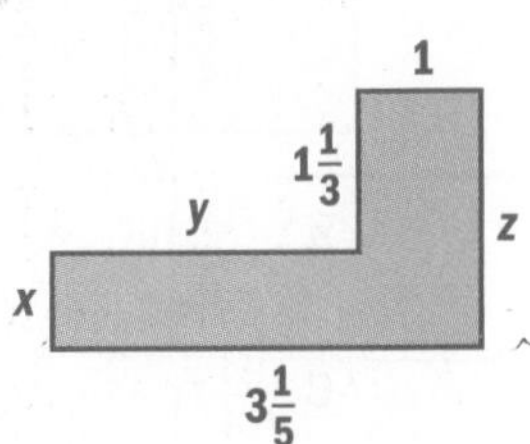

◆ CALIFORNIA STANDARDS SPIRAL REVIEW

Gr. 4 NS 3.2 53. What is the value of $1216 \div 8$? *(p. 664)*

Ⓐ 0.00152 Ⓑ 0.152 Ⓒ 152 Ⓓ 1527

Gr. 4 NS 1.3 54. What is 814,746 rounded to the nearest hundred? *(p. 665)*

Ⓐ 800,000 Ⓑ 814,000 Ⓒ 814,700 Ⓓ 814,750

NS 2.1 55. The height of a plant is $\frac{17}{28}$ inch. After one week, it is $\frac{29}{42}$ inch tall. How much did the plant grow in one week? *(p. 75)*

Ⓐ $\frac{1}{12}$ in. Ⓑ $\frac{3}{7}$ in. Ⓒ $1\frac{3}{14}$ in. Ⓓ $1\frac{25}{84}$ in.

QUIZ for Lessons 2.1–2.3

Find the sum or difference. Simplify if possible. ***(pp. 69, 75, 81)***

1. $\frac{7}{8} + \frac{5}{8}$
2. $\frac{7}{10} + \frac{1}{10}$
3. $\frac{8}{13} - \frac{3}{13}$
4. $\frac{11}{15} - \frac{2}{15}$
5. $\frac{5}{18} + \frac{4}{9}$
6. $\frac{2}{3} + \frac{3}{4}$
7. $\frac{1}{2} - \frac{2}{11}$
8. $1 - \frac{3}{10}$
9. $11\frac{7}{8} + 24\frac{5}{12}$
10. $6\frac{3}{16} + 9\frac{7}{12}$
11. $21\frac{3}{4} + 5\frac{9}{14}$
12. $19\frac{2}{7} + 7\frac{2}{3}$
13. $3\frac{7}{8} - 2\frac{5}{8}$
14. $15\frac{3}{16} - 7\frac{1}{2}$
15. $23\frac{7}{8} - 19\frac{15}{16}$
16. $7\frac{4}{9} - 6\frac{14}{15}$

17. **FUNDRAISING** A charity fundraising walk is 5 miles long. You stop for a break after walking $3\frac{1}{8}$ miles. How many more miles do you need to walk after the break? *Explain* your choice of operation. *(p. 81)*

MIXED REVIEW of Skills and Problem Solving

Multiple Choice Practice for Lessons 2.1–2.3

1. The table gives the lengths of 5 red pandas. What is the difference in the length of the longest panda and the shortest panda? **NS 2.1**

Panda	A	B	C	D	E
Length (feet)	$1\frac{2}{3}$	$2\frac{1}{8}$	$1\frac{3}{4}$	$2\frac{1}{2}$	$2\frac{1}{3}$

Ⓐ $\frac{11}{24}$ ft Ⓑ $\frac{2}{3}$ ft

Ⓒ $\frac{3}{4}$ ft Ⓓ $\frac{5}{6}$ ft

2. What is the value of $1\frac{7}{25} - w$ when $w = \frac{7}{15}$? **NS 2.1**

Ⓐ $\frac{16}{25}$ Ⓑ $\frac{61}{75}$

Ⓒ 1 Ⓓ $2\frac{1}{2}$

3. A "bookworm" eats its way through the three books of the same size shown below. It starts at the *last* page of Book I and continues until it comes to the *first* page of Book III. It always travels perpendicular to the pages and covers. Each cover is $\frac{1}{8}$ inch thick, and the pages of each book are $2\frac{1}{4}$ inches thick. How far does the "bookworm" eat? **NS 2.1**

Ⓐ $6\frac{3}{4}$ in. Ⓑ 7 in.

Ⓒ $7\frac{1}{4}$ in. Ⓓ $7\frac{1}{2}$ in.

4. What is the value of $\frac{7}{9} + \frac{1}{6} + \frac{11}{12}$? **NS 2.1**

Ⓐ $\frac{19}{27}$ Ⓑ $1\frac{3}{4}$

Ⓒ $1\frac{31}{36}$ Ⓓ $2\frac{1}{3}$

5. The storage area of an apartment complex is shared among three apartment units. The storage space is shown below. Which expression can you use to find the fraction of storage space allocated to Unit 3? **NS 2.1, MR 1.1**

Unit 1	Unit 2	Unit 3
$\frac{3}{10}$	$\frac{2}{5}$	?

Ⓐ $\frac{2}{5} + \frac{3}{10}$ Ⓑ $\frac{2}{5} - \frac{3}{10}$

Ⓒ $1 - \frac{3}{10} - \frac{2}{5}$ Ⓓ $1 + \frac{3}{10} + \frac{2}{5}$

6. What is the value of $x + 4\frac{7}{8}$ when $x = 4\frac{9}{20}$? **NS 2.1**

Ⓐ $1\frac{1}{14}$ Ⓑ $9\frac{13}{40}$

Ⓒ $10\frac{4}{7}$ Ⓓ $11\frac{13}{40}$

7. You have $\frac{3}{4}$ pound of roast beef and $\frac{1}{2}$ pound of turkey. You want to make 4 sandwiches, each with $\frac{1}{3}$ pound of meat. How can you determine if you have enough meat? **NS 2.1, MR 1.3**

Ⓐ Compare $\frac{3}{4} + \frac{1}{2}$ with $\frac{1}{3} + \frac{1}{3} + \frac{1}{3} + \frac{1}{3}$.

Ⓑ Compare $\frac{3}{4} - \frac{1}{2}$ with $\frac{1}{3} + \frac{1}{3} + \frac{1}{3} + \frac{1}{3}$.

Ⓒ Compare $\frac{3}{4} + \frac{1}{2}$ with $\frac{1}{3}$.

Ⓓ Compare $\frac{3}{4} - \frac{1}{2}$ with $\frac{1}{3}$.

2.4 Multiplication of Fractions

MATERIALS • colored pencils • paper

Standards

NS 2.2 Explain the meaning of multiplication and division of positive fractions and perform the calculations (e.g. $\frac{5}{8}$ divided by $\frac{15}{16} = \frac{5}{8} \times \frac{16}{15} = \frac{2}{3}$).

QUESTION How can you use models to multiply fractions?

You know that 4 groups of 8 can be written as 4×8. Similarly, $\frac{3}{4}$ of 8 can be written as $\frac{3}{4} \times 8$. To model $\frac{3}{4} \times \frac{1}{3}$, think of it as $\frac{3}{4}$ *of* $\frac{1}{3}$.

EXPLORE Use a model to find $\frac{3}{4} \times \frac{1}{3}$.

STEP 1 **Draw** a unit square and divide it into 3 equal horizontal sections. Shade one of the sections to model $\frac{1}{3}$.

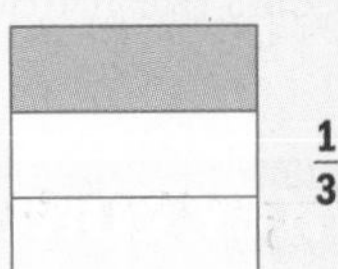

STEP 2 **Divide** the unit square into 4 equal vertical sections.

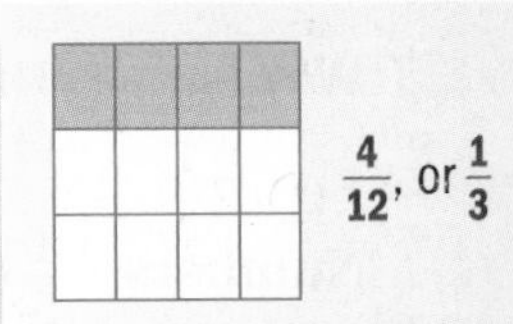

STEP 3 **Select** $\frac{3}{4}$ of $\frac{1}{3}$. The product of $\frac{3}{4}$ and $\frac{1}{3}$ is $\frac{3}{12}$, or $\frac{1}{4}$.

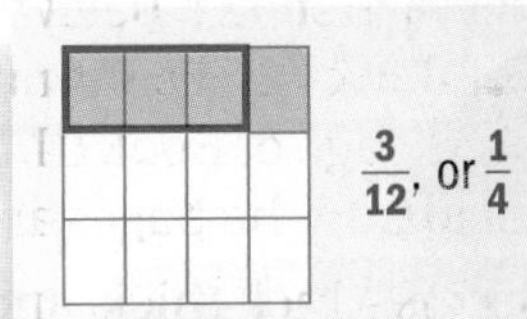

Notice that when you multiply $\frac{3}{4} \times \frac{1}{3}$, you divide $\frac{1}{3}$ into 4 equal sections and then select 3 of the sections.

DRAW CONCLUSIONS Use your observations to complete these exercises.

Use a model to find the product. Simplify if possible.

1. $\frac{1}{2} \times \frac{3}{4}$ **2.** $\frac{1}{6} \times \frac{2}{3}$ **3.** $\frac{3}{5} \times \frac{1}{3}$ **4.** $\frac{2}{3} \times \frac{2}{3}$

5. WRITING Suppose you are using a model to multiply two fractions.

a. How is the total number of sections in the model related to the product of the denominators of the fractions?

b. How is the number of sections selected in the model related to the product of the numerators of the fractions?

6. REASONING *Explain* how you can multiply fractions without using a model. Include two examples.

2.4 Multiplying Fractions and Mixed Numbers

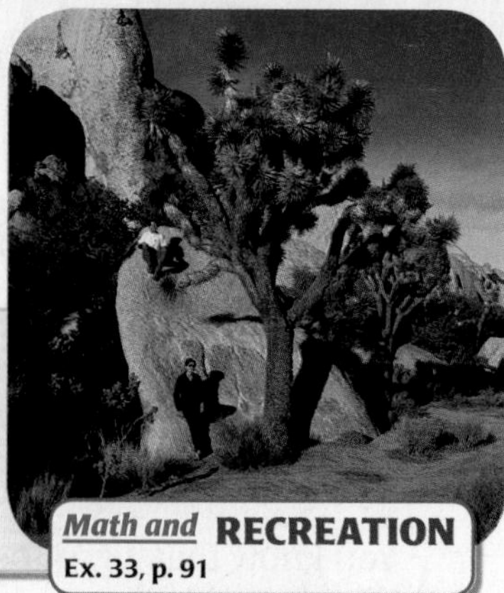

Standards **NS 2.1** **Solve problems involving** addition, subtraction, **multiplication,** and division **of positive fractions and explain why a particular operation was used for a given situation.**

Connect ***Before*** you added and subtracted fractions and mixed numbers. ***Now*** you will multiply fractions and mixed numbers.

Math and **RECREATION**
Ex. 33, p. 91

KEY VOCABULARY
- **greatest common factor,** *p. 10*
- **mixed number, improper fraction,** *p. 35*

PIZZA You and two friends share a pizza. The pizza is cut in half. One half is cut into three equal slices. What fraction of the whole pizza is each slice?

To find a fraction *of* an amount, you *multiply.* The activity on page 87 suggests the following method for finding the product of two fractions.

READING
A multiplication dot, as in $a \cdot c$, is sometimes used in place of an $\times$ to avoid confusion with the variable x.

KEY CONCEPT *For Your Notebook*

Multiplying Fractions

Words The product of two or more fractions is equal to the product of the numerators over the product of the denominators.

Numbers $\frac{1}{5} \cdot \frac{3}{8} = \frac{3}{40}$ **Algebra** $\frac{a}{b} \cdot \frac{c}{d} = \frac{a \cdot c}{b \cdot d}$

($b, d \neq 0$ because division by zero is undefined.)

EXAMPLE 1 Multiplying Fractions

To solve the problem above, you need to find $\frac{1}{3}$ *of* $\frac{1}{2}$ of the pizza by multiplying $\frac{1}{3} \times \frac{1}{2}$.

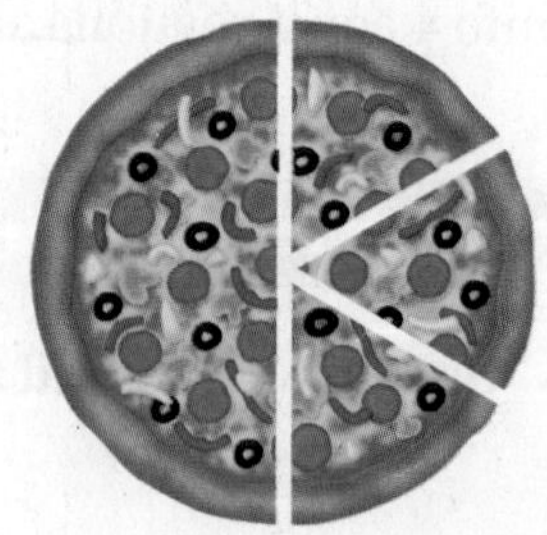

$\frac{1}{3} \times \frac{1}{2} = \frac{1 \times 1}{3 \times 2}$ **Use rule for multiplying fractions.**

$= \frac{1}{6}$ **Multiply.**

▸ **Answer** Each slice is $\frac{1}{6}$ of the whole pizza.

✓ **GUIDED PRACTICE for Example 1**

Find the product. Simplify if possible.

1. $\frac{1}{3} \times \frac{5}{6}$ **2.** $\frac{1}{4} \times \frac{7}{9}$ **3.** $\frac{5}{7} \times \frac{2}{3}$ **4.** $\frac{3}{5} \times \frac{3}{8}$

COMMON FACTORS Recall that to simplify a fraction, you divide the numerator and denominator by the greatest common factor. When multiplying fractions, you can divide out common factors *before* multiplying the numerators and denominators. If you divide out all common factors, your answer will automatically be in simplest form.

EXAMPLE 2 ◆ Multiple Choice Practice

What is the value of $\frac{7}{16} \times \frac{6}{7}$?

Ⓐ $\frac{13}{112}$ Ⓑ $\frac{3}{8}$ Ⓒ $\frac{2}{3}$ Ⓓ $2\frac{5}{8}$

ELIMINATE CHOICES
You are multiplying two numbers that are less than 1, so the product must be less than 1. You can eliminate choice D.

SOLUTION

$\frac{7}{16} \times \frac{6}{7} = \frac{7 \times 6}{16 \times 7}$ **Use rule for multiplying fractions.**

$= \frac{\overset{1}{\cancel{7}} \times \overset{3}{\cancel{6}}}{\underset{8}{\cancel{16}} \times \underset{1}{\cancel{7}}}$ **Divide out 7 and the GCF of 6 and 16, 2.**

$= \frac{3}{8}$ **Multiply.**

▶ **Answer** The correct answer is B. Ⓐ Ⓑ Ⓒ Ⓓ

WHOLE NUMBERS AND MIXED NUMBERS Any number divided by 1 is equal to itself. For example, $18 = \frac{18}{1}$. You have also learned that any mixed number can be rewritten as an improper fraction. You can use these facts to multiply fractions by whole numbers and mixed numbers.

EXAMPLE 3 Multiplying Whole Numbers and Fractions

Find the product of $\frac{2}{3}$ and 18.

$\frac{2}{3} \times 18 = \frac{2}{3} \times \frac{18}{1}$ **Write 18 as $\frac{18}{1}$.**

$= \frac{2 \times \overset{6}{\cancel{18}}}{\underset{1}{\cancel{3}} \times 1}$ **Use rule for multiplying fractions.**

$= \frac{12}{1}$, or 12 **Multiply.**

CHECK **Divide** 18 into 3 equal groups. Select 2 of the groups.

✓ GUIDED PRACTICE for Examples 2 and 3

Find the product. Simplify if possible.

5. $\frac{8}{11} \times \frac{11}{20}$ **6.** $\frac{4}{9} \times \frac{15}{22}$ **7.** $45 \times \frac{4}{5}$ **8.** $\frac{1}{6} \times 28$

EXAMPLE 4 Multiplying Mixed Numbers

FUNDRAISING For a fundraising breakfast, you use $2\frac{1}{3}$ large cartons of eggs. Each carton holds $1\frac{1}{2}$ dozen eggs. How many dozen eggs do you use in all?

$2\frac{1}{3} \times 1\frac{1}{2} = \frac{7}{3} \times \frac{3}{2}$ **Write $2\frac{1}{3}$ and $1\frac{1}{2}$ as improper fractions.**

$= \frac{7 \times \overset{1}{\cancel{3}}}{\underset{1}{\cancel{3}} \times 2}$ **Use rule for multiplying fractions. Divide out 3.**

$= \frac{7}{2}$, or $3\frac{1}{2}$ **Multiply.**

▸ **Answer** You use $3\frac{1}{2}$ dozen, or 42 eggs.

ANOTHER WAY

For an alternative method for solving the problem in Example 4, turn to page 93 for the **Problem Solving Workshop**.

✓ GUIDED PRACTICE for Example 4

9. $12\frac{1}{9} \times \frac{3}{8}$ **10.** $\frac{2}{3} \times 6\frac{1}{2}$ **11.** $2\frac{3}{4} \times 3\frac{1}{6}$ **12.** $4\frac{4}{5} \times 1\frac{1}{9}$

2.4 EXERCISES

HOMEWORK KEY

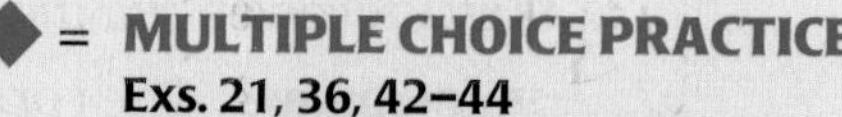
◆ = **MULTIPLE CHOICE PRACTICE** Exs. 21, 36, 42–44

○ = **HINTS AND HOMEWORK HELP** for Exs. 3, 13, 37 at classzone.com

SKILLS • PROBLEM SOLVING • REASONING

1. VOCABULARY Copy and complete: When multiplying fractions, you can divide out common factors so that the product will be in __?__.

2. WRITING *Describe* the steps in multiplying two mixed numbers.

SEE EXAMPLES 1, 2, 3, AND 4 on pp. 88–90 for Exs. 3–20

MULTIPLYING NUMBERS **Find the product. Simplify if possible.**

3. $\frac{3}{7} \times \frac{5}{6}$ **4.** $\frac{1}{10} \times \frac{1}{12}$ **5.** $\frac{2}{5} \times \frac{1}{9}$ **6.** $\frac{1}{8} \times \frac{3}{4}$

7. $\frac{5}{6} \times 12$ **8.** $8 \times \frac{3}{4}$ **9.** $\frac{1}{3} \times 6$ **10.** $5 \times \frac{1}{5}$

11. $3\frac{1}{6} \times 2$ **12.** $1\frac{1}{4} \times 50$ **13.** $4\frac{1}{8} \times \frac{2}{11}$ **14.** $\frac{4}{9} \times 1\frac{1}{8}$

15. $1\frac{2}{5} \times 4\frac{2}{7}$ **16.** $3\frac{1}{3} \times 2\frac{7}{10}$ **17.** $8\frac{4}{5} \times 5\frac{5}{11}$ **18.** $7\frac{1}{2} \times 4\frac{2}{5}$

ERROR ANALYSIS *Describe* **and correct the error made in multiplying.**

19. ✗ $\frac{2}{3} \times \frac{5}{9} = \frac{2 \times 5}{\underset{1}{\cancel{3}} \times \underset{3}{\cancel{9}}} = \frac{10}{3}$

20. ✗ $2\frac{1}{3} \times 3\frac{1}{2} = 2 \times 3 + \frac{1}{3} \times \frac{1}{2}$
$= 6\frac{1}{6}$

SEE EXAMPLE 4 on p. 90 for Ex. 21

21. ◆ **MULTIPLE CHOICE** Which of the following numbers, when multiplied by $4\frac{1}{3}$, results in a number greater than $4\frac{1}{3}$?

Ⓐ $\frac{1}{4}$ Ⓑ $\frac{7}{10}$ Ⓒ 1 Ⓓ $1\frac{1}{3}$

ESTIMATION Use estimation to copy and complete the statement with < or >. *Explain* your reasoning. Then find the exact product.

22. $\frac{9}{10} \times 1\frac{7}{9}$ _?_ 2

23. $\frac{1}{5} \times 5\frac{3}{5}$ _?_ 1

24. $1\frac{7}{8} \times 2\frac{2}{5}$ _?_ 2

25. $5\frac{1}{4} \times 1\frac{2}{7}$ _?_ $9\frac{3}{4}$

26. $4\frac{5}{6} \times 7\frac{1}{9}$ _?_ $35\frac{1}{5}$

27. $2\frac{2}{5} \times 5\frac{2}{9}$ _?_ 11

REASONING Copy and complete the statement using *always, sometimes,* or *never.* *Explain* your reasoning.

28. The product of a mixed number and a proper fraction is _?_ less than 1.

29. The product of two proper fractions is _?_ equal to 1.

30. The product of two mixed numbers is _?_ greater than 1.

CONNECT SKILLS TO PROBLEM SOLVING Exercises 31–34 will help you prepare for problem solving.

31. Katie receives $\frac{3}{5}$ of the 200 votes cast for class president. How many votes is this?

32. What is the height of a stack of 12 books that are each $2\frac{5}{8}$ inches thick?

33. The Ryan Mountain Trail in Joshua Tree National Park is $2\frac{2}{5}$ kilometers long. How far is it to the end of the trail and back?

34. A recipe calls for $3\frac{1}{2}$ cups of milk. You are making twice the recipe. How much milk should you use?

35. **HORSE HEIGHT** Horses are measured in *hands,* the distance across a typical adult palm. A hand is about $\frac{1}{3}$ foot. The average height of a horse is $15\frac{1}{2}$ hands. About how tall is an average horse in feet?

California @HomeTutor for problem solving help at classzone.com

A horse's height is measured to the highest point of its back.

36. ◆ **MULTIPLE CHOICE** You have 50 bricks that are each $7\frac{5}{8}$ inches long. Which expression can you use to find how far (in inches) the 50 bricks will extend if they are placed end to end?

Ⓐ $50 + 7\frac{5}{8}$ Ⓑ $50 - 7\frac{5}{8}$

Ⓒ $50 \times 7\frac{5}{8}$ Ⓓ $50 \div 7\frac{5}{8}$

California @HomeTutor for problem solving help at classzone.com

37. **SHORT RESPONSE** You plan to make lemonade for 15 to 20 people at your drama club meeting. Each glass requires $1\frac{1}{2}$ tablespoons of mix.

a. Find a high and a low estimate for the amount of lemonade mix you will need for the meeting.

b. You have a jar of lemonade mix that contains 20 tablespoons. Is this a reasonable amount for the meeting? *Justify* your answer.

38. **MULTI-STEP PROBLEM** Jen writes a 4-page book report. Each page takes $\frac{3}{4}$ hour to write. She also spends 1 hour proofreading.

a. Write and evaluate an expression to describe the total amount of time Jen spends *writing* the report. Then find the total time she spends working on the report, including proofreading.

b. Including proofreading, Anita completes her 4-page report at a rate of $1\frac{1}{4}$ hours per page. Write and evaluate an expression for the total time Anita spends on the report.

c. Who spends more time on the book report? How much more? *Explain* how you solved the problem.

39. **RECIPES** A recipe that makes 24 apple muffins is shown. How should you change the recipe to make 32 muffins? Write the new recipe. *Explain* how you solved the problem.

Recipe: APPLE MUFFINS

2 c baking mix
2 apples (peeled, cored, and grated)
3 eggs
1/2 c sugar
1 c milk
2 tsp cinnamon

40. **CHALLENGE** You conduct a survey of 210 students to find out what types of pets they have. One third of the students have a dog. Two fifths of those students also have a cat. How many students have a dog but *not* a cat? *Explain* how you solved the problem.

41. **CHALLENGE** *Explain* why $\frac{a \cdot c}{b \cdot c} = \frac{a}{b} \cdot 1$. Then explain how this justifies the method for finding equivalent fractions.

◆ CALIFORNIA STANDARDS SPIRAL REVIEW

NS 1.1 **42.** Which list of numbers is ordered from least to greatest? *(p. 40)*

Ⓐ 0.35, 0.8, 1.2, $1\frac{5}{16}$ Ⓑ 0.8, 0.35, 1.2, $1\frac{5}{16}$

Ⓒ 0.35, 0.8, $1\frac{5}{16}$, 1.2 Ⓓ 0.8, 0.35, $1\frac{5}{16}$, 1.2

Gr. 4 NS 2.2 **43.** What is the value of 12.16 rounded to the nearest tenth? *(p. 674)*

Ⓐ 10 Ⓑ 12 Ⓒ 12.1 Ⓓ 12.2

Gr. 5 NS 2.2 **44.** A company is making 1885 watches and will pack 65 watches in each box for shipping. How many boxes are needed? *(p. 671)*

Ⓐ 23 Ⓑ 27 Ⓒ 29 Ⓓ 31

Using ALTERNATIVE METHODS

Another Way to Solve Example 4, page 90

Standards
NS 2.2

In Example 4 on page 90, you found the total number of eggs by using a rule to multiply mixed numbers. You can also solve the problem by using models.

PROBLEM

FUNDRAISING For a fundraising breakfast, you use $2\frac{1}{3}$ large cartons of eggs. Each carton holds $1\frac{1}{2}$ dozen eggs. How many dozen eggs do you use in all?

METHOD

Using Area Models An alternate approach is to use a model to find $2\frac{1}{3}$ groups of $1\frac{1}{2}$.

STEP 1 **Draw** two unit squares. Each unit square represents 1 dozen eggs. Divide each unit square in half horizontally. Shade three halves to represent $1\frac{1}{2}$ dozen eggs.

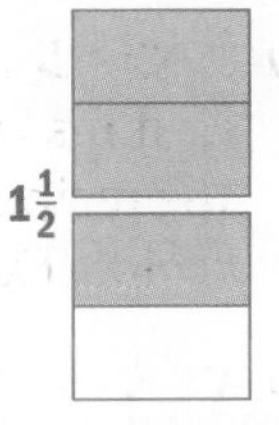

STEP 2 **Draw** two more copies of $1\frac{1}{2}$. Divide the last copy into thirds vertically. Select $2\frac{1}{3}$ of the copies of $1\frac{1}{2}$.

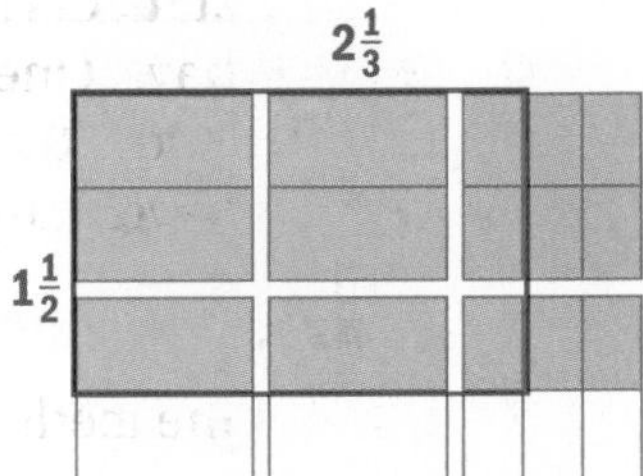

STEP 3 **Divide** all of the unit squares into the same number of sections. Each section represents $\frac{1}{6}$. Count the number of sixths selected.

$$\frac{21}{6} = 3\frac{3}{6} = 3\frac{1}{2}$$

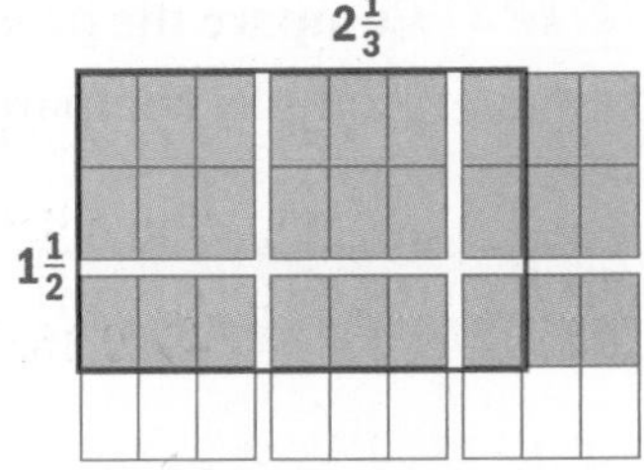

▶ **Answer** You use $3\frac{1}{2}$ dozen, or 42 eggs.

PRACTICE

1. **POSTER BOARD** You need $2\frac{3}{4}$ pieces of poster board. Each piece is $1\frac{1}{2}$ feet long. Find the total length of the pieces of poster board when they are placed end to end. Use a model to solve the problem.

2. **WALKING** You walk $3\frac{1}{2}$ times around your neighborhood. The route you take is $1\frac{1}{8}$ miles long. How many miles do you walk? Solve the problem by multiplying mixed numbers. Then use a model to check your answer.

Investigating Math ACTIVITY Use before Lesson 2.5

2.5 Modeling Fraction Division

MATERIALS • ruler

Standards
NS 2.2 Explain the meaning of multiplication and division of positive fractions and perform the calculations (e.g. $\frac{5}{8}$ divided by $\frac{15}{16} = \frac{5}{8} \times \frac{16}{15} = \frac{2}{3}$).

QUESTION **How can you divide by a fraction?**

You can use a ruler and patterns to model fraction division.

EXPLORE **Model division by $\frac{3}{8}$. Use a table to look for a pattern.**

STEP 1 **Use** a ruler divided into eighths of an inch. Find the quotient $3 \div \frac{3}{8}$.

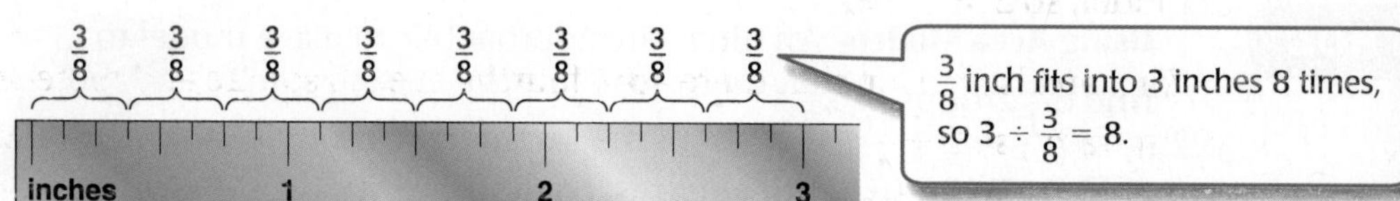

STEP 2 **Copy** and complete the table. Use a ruler to complete the left side.

Dividend		Divisor		Quotient	Dividend		Multiplier		Product
3	$\div$	$\frac{3}{8}$	$=$	8	3	$\times$	$\frac{8}{3}$	$=$	8
$\frac{3}{4}$	$\div$	$\frac{3}{8}$	$=$	?	$\frac{3}{4}$	$\times$	$\frac{8}{3}$	$=$	?
$\frac{3}{8}$	$\div$	$\frac{3}{8}$	$=$	?	$\frac{3}{8}$	$\times$	$\frac{8}{3}$	$=$	?

STEP 3 **Compare** the product to the quotient for each dividend. For example, compare $3 \div \frac{3}{8} = 8$ and $3 \times \frac{8}{3} = 8$.

DRAW CONCLUSIONS **Use a ruler to find the quotient. Then find the product.**

1. $3 \div \frac{3}{4}; 3 \times \frac{4}{3}$

2. $\frac{3}{4} \div \frac{1}{8}; \frac{3}{4} \times 8$

3. $\frac{3}{8} \div \frac{3}{16}; \frac{3}{8} \times \frac{16}{3}$

4. **REASONING** *Describe* how the divisor and the multiplier are related in the table shown above and in Exercises 1–3.

5. **REASONING** How can you find the number of sixteenths in 15 in.? in 30 in.? in $\frac{5}{8}$ in.? How can you use the results to find the number of groups of 15 sixteenths in 15 in.? in 30 in.? in $\frac{5}{8}$ in.? Use your results to explain why $\frac{5}{8} \div \frac{15}{16} = \frac{5}{8} \times \frac{16}{15}$.

2.5 Dividing Fractions and Mixed Numbers

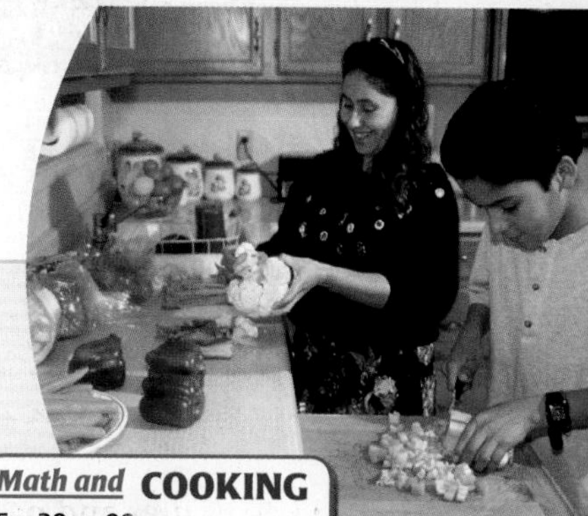

Standards **NS 2.1 Solve problems involving** addition, subtraction, multiplication, and **division of positive fractions and explain why a particular operation was used for a given situation.**

Connect ***Before*** you multiplied fractions and mixed numbers. ***Now*** you will divide fractions and mixed numbers to solve problems.

KEY VOCABULARY
- **reciprocal**

You can use a model to find the quotient $2 \div \frac{1}{4}$. First draw two unit squares. Then divide each square into fourths. There are 8 fourths in the model, so $2 \div \frac{1}{4} = 8$.

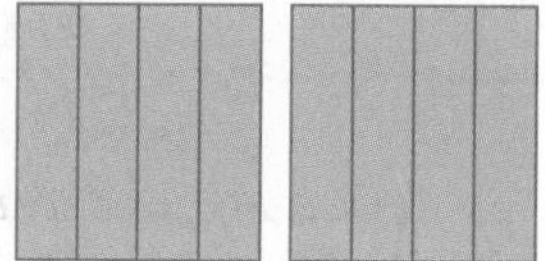

You can also reason that there are 4 fourths in each square and there are 2 squares, so $2 \div \frac{1}{4} = 2 \times 4 = 8$. The numbers $\frac{1}{4}$ and 4 are *reciprocals.* Two nonzero numbers whose product is 1 are **reciprocals**.

Animated Math For an interactive example of finding reciprocals go to **classzone.com**.

$\frac{2}{3}$ and $\frac{3}{2}$ are reciprocals, because $\frac{2}{3} \times \frac{3}{2} = 1$.

5 and $\frac{1}{5}$ are reciprocals, because $5 \times \frac{1}{5} = 1$.

Notice that two numbers are reciprocals if the numerator and denominator of their fraction forms are swapped. In the model above and in the activity on page 94, you used reciprocals to rewrite division problems as equivalent multiplication problems.

KEY CONCEPT *For Your Notebook*

Using Reciprocals to Divide

Words To divide by any nonzero number, multiply by its reciprocal.

Numbers $\frac{3}{4} \div \frac{2}{3} = \frac{3}{4} \times \frac{3}{2} = \frac{9}{8}$ **Algebra** $\frac{a}{b} \div \frac{c}{d} = \frac{a}{b} \cdot \frac{d}{c} = \frac{ad}{bc}$ $(b, c, d \neq 0)$

EXAMPLE 1 Dividing a Fraction by a Fraction

$\frac{1}{5} \div \frac{2}{3} = \frac{1}{5} \times \frac{3}{2}$ **Multiply by reciprocal.**

$= \frac{1 \times 3}{5 \times 2}$ **Use rule for multiplying fractions.**

$= \frac{3}{10}$ **Multiply.**

EXAMPLE 2 Dividing a Fraction by a Whole Number

CHECK SOLUTION

You can check your answer by multiplying the quotient and divisor. The result should equal the dividend.

$\frac{2}{5} \times 2 = \frac{2}{5} \times \frac{2}{1} = \frac{4}{5}$ ✓

$\frac{4}{5} \div 2 = \frac{4}{5} \times \frac{1}{2}$ **Multiply by reciprocal.**

$= \frac{\overset{2}{\cancel{4}} \times 1}{5 \times \underset{1}{\cancel{2}}}$ **Use rule for multiplying fractions. Divide out common factor.**

$= \frac{2}{5}$ **Multiply.**

EXAMPLE 3 Drawing a Diagram to Solve a Problem

IN-LINE SKATING You are setting up an in-line skating course that is 21 feet long to practice weaving around cones. You want a cone every $3\frac{1}{2}$ feet, but not at the start or end of the course. How many cones do you need?

SOLUTION

METHOD 1 Draw a diagram on graph paper. Make the course 21 grid boxes long. Draw a point to mark the location of a cone every $3\frac{1}{2}$ grid boxes but not at the start or end.

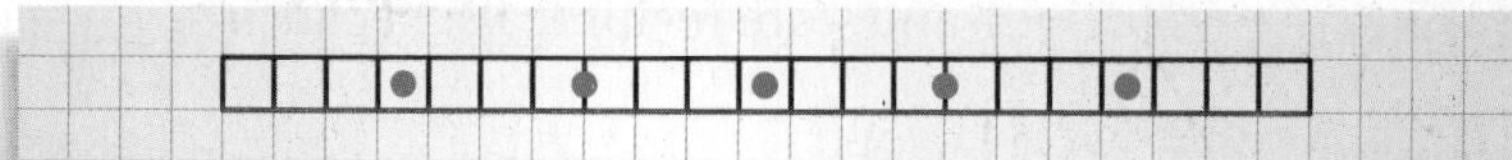

METHOD 2 Use division.

$21 \div 3\frac{1}{2} = 21 \div \frac{7}{2}$ **Write $3\frac{1}{2}$ as an improper fraction.**

$= \frac{21}{1} \times \frac{2}{7}$ **Multiply by reciprocal.**

$= \frac{\overset{3}{\cancel{21}} \times 2}{1 \times \underset{1}{\cancel{7}}}$ **Use rule for multiplying fractions. Divide out common factors.**

$= 6$ **Multiply.**

▸ **Answer** 6 is the number of $3\frac{1}{2}$-foot spaces separated by cones. Because you only want cones between these spaces, you need to subtract 1 to get the number of cones. You need 5 cones.

About the Standards

Grade 6 Standard MR 2.7 asks you to check that an answer is valid. You want to divide 21 feet into spaces of about 3 feet, which is about 7 spaces. The answer is valid.

✓ GUIDED PRACTICE for Examples 1, 2, and 3

Find the quotient. Simplify if possible.

1. $\frac{5}{6} \div \frac{7}{9}$ **2.** $\frac{9}{2} \div \frac{3}{2}$ **3.** $\frac{1}{6} \div 3$ **4.** $4 \div 2\frac{2}{3}$

5. WHAT IF? In Example 3, suppose you want the course to be 28 feet long. You want a cone at the start and end of the course and every $3\frac{1}{2}$ feet in between. How many cones do you need? *Explain.*

EXAMPLE 4 ◆ Multiple Choice Practice

What is the value of $8\frac{3}{4} \div 2\frac{5}{8}$?

Ⓐ $\frac{3}{10}$ Ⓑ $3\frac{1}{3}$ Ⓒ $22\frac{31}{32}$ Ⓓ $31\frac{1}{2}$

ELIMINATE CHOICES
Because you are dividing $8\frac{3}{4}$ by a number greater than 1, the answer will be less than $8\frac{3}{4}$. You can eliminate choices C and D.

SOLUTION

$8\frac{3}{4} \div 2\frac{5}{8} = \frac{35}{4} \div \frac{21}{8}$ **Write $8\frac{3}{4}$ and $2\frac{5}{8}$ as improper fractions.**

$= \frac{35}{4} \times \frac{8}{21}$ **Multiply by reciprocal.**

$= \frac{\overset{5}{\cancel{35}} \times \overset{2}{\cancel{8}}}{\underset{1}{\cancel{4}} \times \underset{3}{\cancel{21}}}$ **Use rule for multiplying fractions. Divide out common factors.**

$= \frac{10}{3}$, or $3\frac{1}{3}$ **Multiply.**

▶ **Answer** The correct answer is B. Ⓐ Ⓑ Ⓒ Ⓓ

 **GUIDED PRACTICE** for Example 4

6. $3\frac{1}{8} \div 2\frac{1}{4}$ **7.** $2\frac{2}{5} \div 12\frac{2}{5}$ **8.** $5\frac{2}{3} \div 6\frac{3}{5}$ **9.** $4\frac{1}{2} \div 1\frac{1}{4}$

2.5 EXERCISES

HOMEWORK KEY
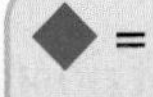 = **MULTIPLE CHOICE PRACTICE** Exs. 24, 25, 39, 48–50
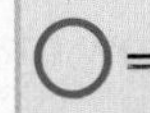 = **HINTS AND HOMEWORK HELP** for Exs. 7, 13, 39 at classzone.com

SKILLS • PROBLEM SOLVING • REASONING

VOCABULARY Write the reciprocal of the number.

1. $\frac{5}{6}$ **2.** 8 **3.** 1 **4.** $5\frac{2}{5}$

5. WRITING *Explain* how reciprocals are used in fraction division.

SEE EXAMPLES 1, 2, 3, AND 4 on pp. 95–97 for Exs. 6–21

FINDING QUOTIENTS Find the quotient. Then check the answer.

6. $\frac{3}{8} \div \frac{1}{4}$ **7.** $\frac{6}{7} \div \frac{5}{14}$ **8.** $\frac{5}{8} \div \frac{15}{16}$ **9.** $\frac{7}{12} \div \frac{14}{15}$

10. $\frac{9}{10} \div 6$ **11.** $4 \div \frac{3}{10}$ **12.** $2\frac{5}{6} \div 7$ **13.** $10 \div 4\frac{1}{6}$

14. $5 \div 3\frac{2}{3}$ **15.** $\frac{8}{9} \div 1\frac{2}{15}$ **16.** $7\frac{1}{6} \div \frac{7}{12}$ **17.** $3\frac{3}{5} \div \frac{12}{25}$

18. $10\frac{2}{7} \div 4\frac{4}{11}$ **19.** $4\frac{3}{8} \div 3\frac{1}{3}$ **20.** $6\frac{1}{5} \div 3\frac{4}{9}$ **21.** $15\frac{3}{4} \div 7\frac{5}{7}$

SEE EXAMPLES 1 AND 4 on pp. 95 and 97 for Exs. 22–24

ERROR ANALYSIS ***Describe*** **and correct the error made in dividing.**

22. $\frac{7}{9} \div \frac{2}{3} = \frac{9}{7} \cdot \frac{2}{3} = \frac{18}{21} = \frac{6}{7}$ ✗

23. $2\frac{2}{5} \div 2\frac{2}{3} = \frac{12}{5} \div \frac{8}{3} = \frac{5}{12} \cdot \frac{3}{8} = \frac{5}{32}$ ✗

24. ◆ **MULTIPLE CHOICE** Which multiplication expression is equivalent to the division expression $\frac{3}{20} \div \frac{4}{9}$?

Ⓐ $\frac{3}{20} \times \frac{4}{9}$ Ⓑ $\frac{3}{20} \times \frac{9}{4}$ Ⓒ $\frac{20}{3} \times \frac{4}{9}$ Ⓓ $\frac{20}{3} \times \frac{9}{4}$

25. ◆ **MULTIPLE CHOICE** What is the value of $x \div 2\frac{2}{5}$ when $x = 1\frac{1}{2}$?

Ⓐ $\frac{5}{8}$ Ⓑ $1\frac{3}{5}$ Ⓒ $2\frac{1}{5}$ Ⓓ $3\frac{3}{5}$

ALGEBRA Evaluate the expression when $x = \frac{5}{8}$, $y = 3$, and $z = 2\frac{3}{16}$.

26. $x \div 6$ **27.** $x \div 10$ **28.** $4\frac{1}{6} \div y$ **29.** $y \div \frac{4}{7}$

30. $z \div 1\frac{1}{4}$ **31.** $\frac{5}{9} \div z$ **32.** $3\frac{3}{5} \div x$ **33.** $y \div 7\frac{1}{8}$

CONNECT SKILLS TO PROBLEM SOLVING Exercises 34–36 will help you prepare for problem solving.

Which operation would you use to solve the problem? *Explain* why.

34. A punch recipe calls for $4\frac{1}{2}$ liters of orange juice and $2\frac{1}{4}$ liters of sparkling water. How many liters of punch does the recipe make?

35. You have a sheet of poster board that is $2\frac{1}{3}$ feet long. You divide it into 5 equal sections. How many feet long is each section?

36. Your dog eats $2\frac{2}{3}$ cups of dog food each day. How many cups of food will the dog eat in 30 days?

SEE EXAMPLES 2 AND 3 on p. 96 for Exs. 37 and 38

37. SERVINGS You prepare a long submarine sandwich for a party. The sandwich is cut into equal pieces as shown. How long is each piece?

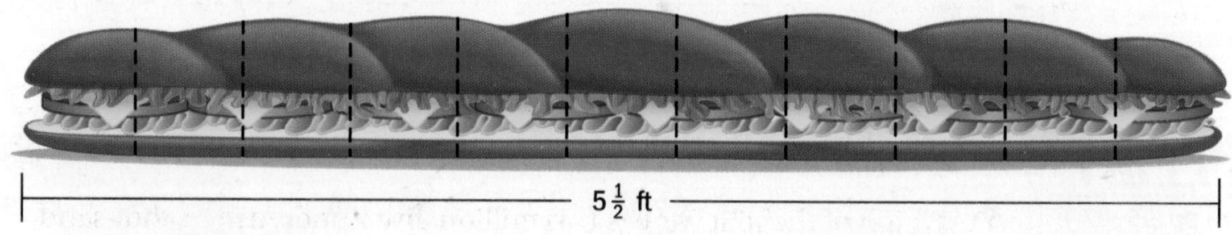

$5\frac{1}{2}$ ft

California @HomeTutor for problem solving help at classzone.com

38. SHELF SPACE A best-selling book is $2\frac{11}{16}$ inches thick. How many copies of the book will fit on a bookstore shelf that is 30 inches long? *Explain.*

California @HomeTutor for problem solving help at classzone.com

SEE EXAMPLE 3 on p. 96 for Exs. 39–41

39. ◆ **MULTIPLE CHOICE** Making pasta requires boiling 6 cups of water. Your measuring glass holds $1\frac{1}{2}$ cups. How many glassfuls do you need?

Ⓐ 4 Ⓑ $4\frac{1}{2}$ Ⓒ $6\frac{1}{2}$ Ⓓ 9

40. **SHORT RESPONSE** On a slalom skiing course, the distance from the start to the first gate is 15 meters. The distance from the last gate to the finish is 20 meters. The slalom course is 635 meters long and the distance between gates is $1\frac{1}{2}$ meters. How many gates are needed for the course? *Explain* your answer.

A slalom skiing course

41. **MULTI-STEP PROBLEM** You are an editor for your school yearbook. Each row of student photos is $8\frac{5}{8}$ inches wide, including $\frac{1}{4}$ inch margins on each side of the page. The photos are $1\frac{1}{4}$ inches wide and $\frac{1}{8}$ inch apart.

   a. Find a high and a low estimate of the number of photos per row.

   b. How many photos will fit in each row? *Explain* your reasoning.

42. **STORAGE** A CD case is about $\frac{7}{16}$ inch wide. A DVD case is about $\frac{1}{8}$ inch wider than a CD case. You put 8 DVDs on a shelf that is 20 inches wide. How much space is left on the shelf? How many CDs will fit in the remaining space? *Explain* how you solved the problem.

xy CHALLENGE ***Describe*** **the whole number value(s) of x that make the statement true.**

43. $x \div \frac{2}{3} = x$ 44. $4\frac{1}{2} \div x = 9$ 45. $1\frac{2}{5} \div x < 1\frac{2}{5}$ 46. $x \div \frac{7}{8} > x$

47. **xy CHALLENGE** *Describe* what happens to the value of the expression $y \div 100$ as y gets closer to zero. *Describe* what happens to the value of the expression $100 \div x$ as x gets closer to zero. *Justify* your answers.

◆ CALIFORNIA STANDARDS SPIRAL REVIEW

NS 2.2 48. What is the product of $\frac{5}{12}$ and $7\frac{3}{5}$? ***(p. 88)***

Ⓐ $\frac{25}{456}$ Ⓑ $3\frac{1}{6}$ Ⓒ $6\frac{5}{6}$ Ⓓ $8\frac{1}{60}$

Gr. 4 NS 1.1 49. Which of the following is two million, five hundred forty thousand, seven hundred twelve? ***(p. 665)***

Ⓐ 254,712 Ⓑ 2,504,712 Ⓒ 2,540,712 Ⓓ 2,500,040,712

Gr. 4 NS 3.3 50. Music lessons cost \$35 per week. What is the cost of taking music lessons for 36 weeks? ***(p. 671)***

Ⓐ \$315 Ⓑ \$1030 Ⓒ \$1260 Ⓓ \$3150

2.5 Fraction Operations

Standards

NS 2.2 Explain the meaning of multiplication and division of positive fractions and **perform the calculations** (e.g. $\frac{5}{8}$ divided by $\frac{15}{16} = \frac{5}{8} \times \frac{16}{15} = \frac{2}{3}$).

QUESTION How can you use a calculator to perform operations with fractions and mixed numbers?

Some calculators allow you to perform operations with fractions and mixed numbers. If you have such a calculator, be sure it is set to display answers as mixed numbers in simplest form.

EXAMPLE How many $\frac{1}{2}$ minute commercials can a television station run during a $2\frac{1}{2}$ minute break?

SOLUTION

To find the number of commercials that can be run, you need to find the quotient $2\frac{1}{2} \div \frac{1}{2}$.

Keystrokes	**Display**
2 [UNIT] 1 [/] 2 [÷] 1 [/] 2 [=]	5

The [UNIT] key is used to write a mixed number. The display for the key is ⌴.

▸ **Answer** The television station can run 5 commercials during the break.

PRACTICE

Use a calculator to evaluate the expression.

1. $\frac{5}{11} + \frac{7}{9}$
2. $\frac{2}{5} + \frac{5}{7}$
3. $\frac{19}{20} - \frac{3}{4}$
4. $\frac{2}{3} - \frac{2}{5}$
5. $5\frac{4}{7} \times \frac{1}{2}$
6. $\frac{3}{4} \times 10\frac{1}{15}$
7. $5\frac{11}{12} \div \frac{1}{4}$
8. $\frac{13}{20} \div \frac{7}{10}$
9. **UNIT COST** You buy $3\frac{1}{2}$ pounds of apples for \$5.95. What is the cost per pound of apples?
10. **POSTERS** A standard movie poster is $2\frac{1}{4}$ feet wide. The width of a wall is $13\frac{1}{2}$ feet. If each poster sells for \$12.95, how much will it cost to put one row of posters across the entire wall?

2.6 Adding and Subtracting Decimals

MATERIALS • base-ten pieces

Standards Preparation

Gr. 5 NS 2.1 Add, subtract, multiply, and divide **with decimals;** add with negative integers; subtract positive integers from negative integers; and verify the reasonableness of the results.

QUESTION How can you use models to add and subtract decimals?

You can add and subtract decimals using base-ten pieces. These models can help you understand the rules for adding and subtracting decimals.

EXPLORE Find 0.76 + 0.58.

STEP 1 **Model** the sum of 0.76 and 0.58 using base-ten pieces. Let each small square represent 1 hundredth.

STEP 2 **Combine** and group the pieces.

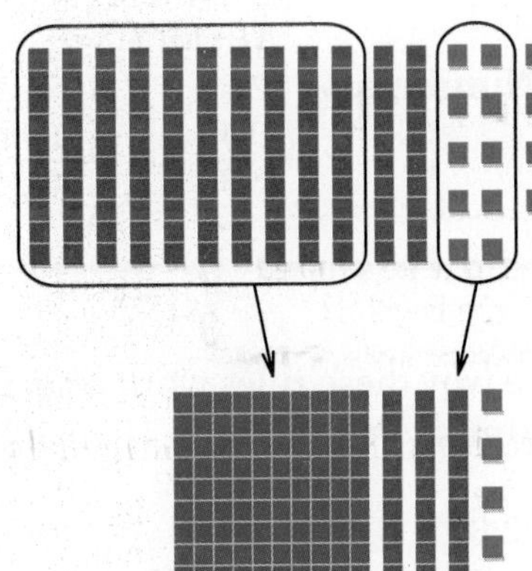

STEP 3 **Trade 10 tenths** for **1 one** and **10 hundredths** for **1 tenth**. The sum of 0.76 and 0.58 is 1.34.

DRAW CONCLUSIONS Use your observations to complete these exercises.

Use base-ten pieces to find the sum or difference.

1. 8.19 + 3.23 **2.** 6.13 + 2.11 **3.** 4.21 + 1.83 **4.** 7.80 + 3.93

5. 9.24 − 3.17 **6.** 1.85 − 0.96 **7.** 5.07 − 1.9 **8.** 8.6 − 4.75

Animated Math at classzone.com

9. WRITING When working with base-ten pieces, how is adding decimals similar to adding whole numbers? How is adding the two types of numbers different?

2.6 Adding and Subtracting Decimals

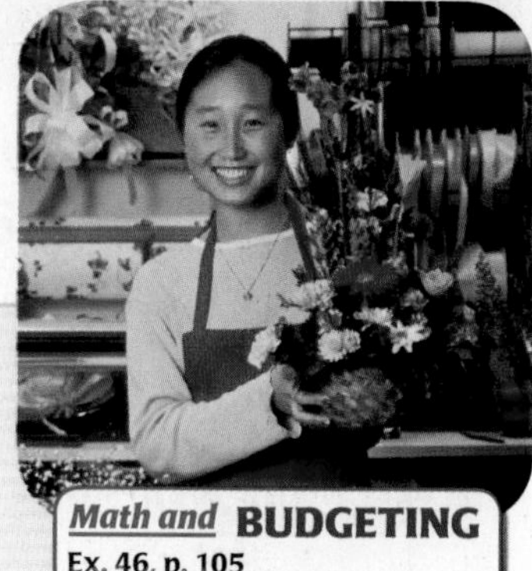

Math and BUDGETING
Ex. 46, p. 105

Standards Preparation **Gr. 5 NS 2.1** **Add, subtract,** multiply, and divide **with decimals;** add with negative integers; subtract positive integers from negative integers; **and verify the reasonableness of the results.**

Connect ***Before*** you added and subtracted fractions. ***Now*** you will add and subtract decimals to prepare for Grade 6 Standard NS 1.4.

KEY VOCABULARY
- **front-end estimation**

As the activity on page 101 suggests, adding or subtracting decimals is similar to adding or subtracting whole numbers. You add digits with the same place value, renaming as appropriate.

KEY CONCEPT *For Your Notebook*

Add or Subtract Decimals

Words To add or subtract two decimals, add or subtract as you would whole numbers, lining up decimal points. In the answer, place the decimal point in the same column as in the numbers above it.

Numbers

$$\begin{array}{r} 2.87 \\ +\ 0.49 \\ \hline 3.36 \end{array} \qquad \begin{array}{r} 7.214 \\ -\ 6.401 \\ \hline 0.813 \end{array}$$

To see why these rules work, you can write the decimals as fractions with a common denominator. Then add or subtract.

$$2.87 + 0.49 = \frac{287}{100} + \frac{49}{100} = \frac{336}{100} = 3.36$$

$$7.214 - 6.401 = \frac{7214}{1000} - \frac{6401}{1000} = \frac{813}{1000} = 0.813$$

EXAMPLE 1 Adding and Subtracting Decimals

Find the sum or difference.

a. 6.047 + 13.46

b. 9 − 5.28

SOLUTION

a. $\begin{array}{r} 6.047 \\ +\ 13.460 \\ \hline 19.507 \end{array}$ ← **Write a zero as a placeholder.**

b. $\begin{array}{r} 9.00 \\ -\ 5.28 \\ \hline 3.72 \end{array}$ ← **Write zeros as placeholders.**

EQUIVALENT DECIMALS
In part (a) of Example 1, 13.46 and 13.460 are equivalent because $\frac{46}{100}$ and $\frac{460}{1000}$ are equivalent.

EXAMPLE 2 Evaluating an Expression

Evaluate $6.7 + r + 5.2$ when $r = 2.14$.

CHECK REASONABLENESS

Round each decimal to the nearest whole number and add.

$7 + 2 + 5 = 14$ ✓

SOLUTION

$6.7 + r + 5.2 = 6.7 + 2.14 + 5.2$	**Substitute 2.14 for *r*.**
$= 8.84 + 5.2$	**Add the first two decimals.**
$= 14.04$	**Add.**

ESTIMATION One type of estimation is *front-end estimation.* To use **front-end estimation** to estimate a sum, add the first digits in the decimals, the *front-end digits.* Then estimate the sum of the remaining digits and add the results.

EXAMPLE 3 Estimating a Sum

VIDEO GAMES You want to buy three used video games with the prices shown. About how much will it cost to buy all three games?

Game A	\$8.79
Game B	\$7.29
Game C	\$7.89

ANOTHER WAY

Round to the nearest dollar. Then add.

\$8.79		\$9
\$7.29	→	\$7
+ \$7.89		+ \$8
		\$24

SOLUTION

STEP 1 **Add** the front-end digits, the dollars.

\$8.79
\$7.29
+ \$7.89
\$22

STEP 2 **Estimate** the sum of the remaining digits, the cents.

\$8.79 → \$1
\$7.29 →
+ \$7.89 → \$1
\$2

STEP 3 **Add** the results.

\$22
+ \$2
\$24

▶ **Answer** The estimated cost is about \$24.

✓ GUIDED PRACTICE for Examples 1, 2, and 3

Find the sum or difference.

1. $8.41 + 2.6$
2. $1.937 + 2.28$
3. $6 - 3.74$
4. $4.59 - 3.17$

Evaluate the expression when $a = 4.2$ and $b = 6.27$.

5. $a + 9.38$
6. $7.8 + b$
7. $10.03 - a$
8. $b - 1.84$

Use front-end estimation to estimate the sum or rounding to estimate the difference.

9. $3.85 + 5.21$
10. $5.78 - 2.63$
11. $8.26 - 3.82 - 1.92$
12. $6.41 + 3.27 + 1.96$

2.6 EXERCISES

HOMEWORK KEY

◆ = **MULTIPLE CHOICE PRACTICE** Exs. 32, 33, 49, 56–58

○ = **HINTS AND HOMEWORK HELP** for Exs. 3, 21, 45 at classzone.com

SKILLS • PROBLEM SOLVING • REASONING

1. **VOCABULARY** Copy and complete: To add or subtract decimals, begin by lining up the _?_.

2. **WRITING** *Explain* how to use front-end estimation to add decimals.

SEE EXAMPLE 1 on p. 102 for Exs. 3–16

USING OPERATIONS Find the sum or difference. Check the reasonableness of your answer.

3. $15.8 + 7.6$ 4. $124.6 + 47.01$ 5. $53.24 + 14.023$

6. $4 - 3.456$ 7. $90 - 7.5$ 8. $24.98 - 3.3$

9. $467.2 + 5.63 + 11$ 10. $27 - 3.204 - 10.8$ 11. $8.55 + 20.4 + 15$

12. $0.032 + 0.29 + 1$ 13. $26.17 - 9.002 - 1.9$ 14. $13.876 - 0.2 - 4.10$

ERROR ANALYSIS *Describe* and correct the error made in the calculation.

15.

$$\begin{array}{r} 3.48 \\ +\ 13 \\ \hline 3.61 \end{array}$$

16.

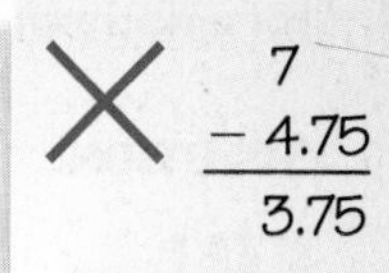

$$\begin{array}{r} 7 \\ -\ 4.75 \\ \hline 3.75 \end{array}$$

SEE EXAMPLE 2 on p. 103 for Exs. 17–22

EVALUATING EXPRESSIONS Evaluate the expression when $k = 5.874$, $m = 123.1$, $y = 26.3$, and $z = 12.28$.

17. $34 + z$ 18. $y - 19.46$ 19. $0.302 + z$

20. $k + 6.401 + 0.04$ 21. $140 - m - 1.078$ 22. $m - 6.78 - 28.3$

SEE EXAMPLE 3 on p. 103 for Exs. 23–32

ESTIMATION Use front-end estimation to estimate the sum or rounding to estimate the difference.

23. $5.24 + 9.79$ 24. $3.44 + 8.38$ 25. $6.6 - 4.45$

26. $8.75 - 5.67$ 27. $5.78 + 9 + 2.2$ 28. $4.11 + 5.90 + 8.02$

29. $9.7 - 5.45 - 2.12$ 30. $6.53 - 0.98 - 2.1$ 31. $5.72 + 6.15 + 1.05$

32. ◆ **MULTIPLE CHOICE** Using front-end estimation, which number added to 8.43 results in an estimated sum of 15?

Ⓐ 6.59   Ⓑ 7.59   Ⓒ 8.04   Ⓓ 8.45

33. ◆ **MULTIPLE CHOICE** The pattern on the number line starts with 0.14 and continues to increase. What is the next number in the pattern?

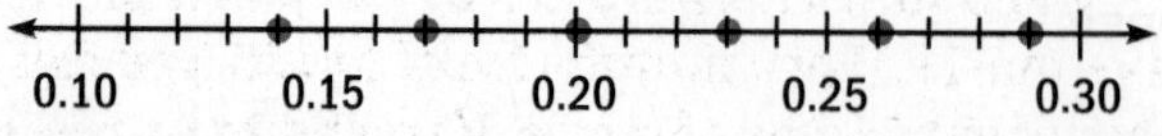

Ⓐ 0.11   Ⓑ 0.19   Ⓒ 0.32   Ⓓ 0.34

ESTIMATION **Use estimation to copy and complete the statement using < or >.**

34. 8.79 − 4.06 − 3.905 ? 3.9 − 1.81

35. 6.91 + 2.08 + 3.83 ? 2.748 + 9.1

36. 3.72 + 9.15 + 7.38 ? 41.14 − 22.045

37. 10.19 − 4.2 − 1.853 ? 18.2 − 12.311

38. 11.81 + 9.45 + 2.61 ? 12.91 + 12.028

39. 73.91 − 2.058 − 8.9 ? 42.15 + 22.045

CONNECT SKILLS TO PROBLEM SOLVING **Exercises 40–42 will help you prepare for problem solving.**

Write the expression you would use to solve the problem.

40. The price of a pair of jeans is $27. The price of a shirt is $16.95. What is the total cost of a pair of jeans and a shirt?

41. The high temperature was 74.35°F today and 68.72°F yesterday. How much warmer is today's high temperature than yesterday's?

42. A glass of juice costs $2.79. A bottle of water costs $1.85. How much more does the juice cost than the water?

SEE EXAMPLE 1 on p. 102 for Exs. 43–44

43. MAZES A cornfield maze grown in Annville, Pennsylvania, covered 3.3 acres. Another cornfield maze grown in Lindon, Utah, covered 12.6 acres. How many more acres did the maze in Lindon cover?

California @HomeTutor for problem solving help at classzone.com

A bird's eye view of a cornfield maze

44. CAPACITY You mix a cleaning solution using 1.18 liters water, 0.15 liter vinegar, and 0.02 liter liquid soap. At least how many liters must the container for this solution hold?

California @HomeTutor for problem solving help at classzone.com

SEE EXAMPLE 3 on p. 103 for Exs. 45–46

45. ART SUPPLIES Watercolor paints cost $8.69, a paint brush costs $3.78, and a canvas costs $6.32. Use front-end estimation to estimate the cost to buy all of the art supplies. How much higher or lower is your estimate than the exact total cost of the supplies?

46. SHORT RESPONSE A bouquet of tulips costs $6.49 and a bouquet of assorted flowers costs $8.53. You have $15. Is front-end estimation a reliable method to determine if you can buy both bouquets? *Justify* your answer.

47. SCAVENGER HUNT You are in a 3-part scavenger hunt. Your friend's team completes the game in 80.65 minutes. Your team's times for each part of the game are 22.35 minutes, 25.8 minutes, and 30.15 minutes. Which team has the faster time? How much faster? *Explain.*

48. VIDEO RENTAL A video store charges $4.75 to rent a new movie and $3.95 to rent other movies. For a monthy fee of $19.95, you can rent an unlimited number of either type of movie. If you rent two new movies and three others each month, is the monthly fee a better deal? *Explain.*

49. ◆ **MULTIPLE CHOICE** A city had 3.57 inches of rain in April, 7.30 inches of rain in May, and 5.14 inches of rain in June. Which is the *best* estimate for the amount of rainfall the city had during the three month period?

Ⓐ Less than 14 inches　　Ⓑ About 15 inches

Ⓒ About 16 inches　　Ⓓ More than 17 inches

50. **DIRECTIONS** The Internet driving directions below show directions from the entrance of the San Diego Zoo to the Visitor's Center in Balboa Park. How much shorter is the shortest route than the fastest route?

Driving Directions

http://mapit.geo

Shortest Route	Distance	Fastest Route	Distance
START 1: Go N on ZOO DR.	0.1 mile	START 1: Go NE on ZOO DR.	0.3 mile
→ 2: Turn RIGHT onto BALBOA PARK RD.	0.3 mile	→ 2: Turn RIGHT onto PARK BLVD.	1.1 mile
← 3: Turn LEFT onto ZOO PL.	0.1 mile	→ 3: Turn RIGHT onto PRESIDENTS WAY	0.2 mile
→ 4: Turn RIGHT onto PARK BLVD.	0.8 mile	→ 4: Turn RIGHT onto PAN AMERICAN RD. E	0.3 mile
→ 5: Turn RIGHT onto PRESIDENTS WAY	0.2 mile		
→ 6: Turn RIGHT onto PAN AMERICAN RD. E	0.3 mile		

51. **WRITING** When is the sum of two decimals a whole number? When is the difference of two decimals a whole number? *Explain* and give examples.

xy **CHALLENGE Find the unknown value.**

52. $6 + 2.4 + \underline{\ ?\ } = 8.8$　　53. $28 - 0.72 - \underline{\ ?\ } = 0.7$　　54. $9 - 4.2 - \underline{\ ?\ } = 3.7$

55. **CHALLENGE** The following snacks are available: water for $1.09, juice for $1.39, popcorn for $2.75, and trail mix for $1.99. List all of the possible combinations of different snacks that you can buy with $5.

◆ CALIFORNIA STANDARDS SPIRAL REVIEW

Gr. 4 NS 3.1　56. What is the value of 317,650 + 92,819? *(p. 661)*

Ⓐ 124,584　Ⓑ 309,469　Ⓒ 410,469　Ⓓ 1,245,840

NS 2.4　57. What is the greatest common factor of 36, 48, and 96? *(p. 10)*

Ⓐ 2　Ⓑ 12　Ⓒ 96　Ⓓ 288

NS 2.1　58. You are stacking computer games in a shipping box that is $16\frac{1}{2}$ inches high. Each game is $1\frac{3}{8}$ inches thick. How many games can you fit in the box in a single stack? *(p. 95)*

Ⓐ 12　Ⓑ 15　Ⓒ 17　Ⓓ 22

2.7 Multiplying and Dividing Decimals

Standards Preparation **Gr. 5 NS 2.1** Add, subtract, **multiply, and divide with decimals;** add with negative integers; subtract positive integers from negative integers, **and verify the reasonableness of the results.**

Connect ***Before*** you multipled and divided fractions. ***Now*** you will multiply and divide decimals to prepare for Grade 6 Standard NS 1.4.

KEY VOCABULARY
- **leading digit**
- **compatible numbers**

You can represent 1 whole with a 10×10 grid. The width of each row or column is 0.1. Each small square represents 0.01.

The area selected at the right represents seven tenths of 1.3, or 0.7×1.3. There are 91 squares selected, so $0.7 \times 1.3 = 0.91$.

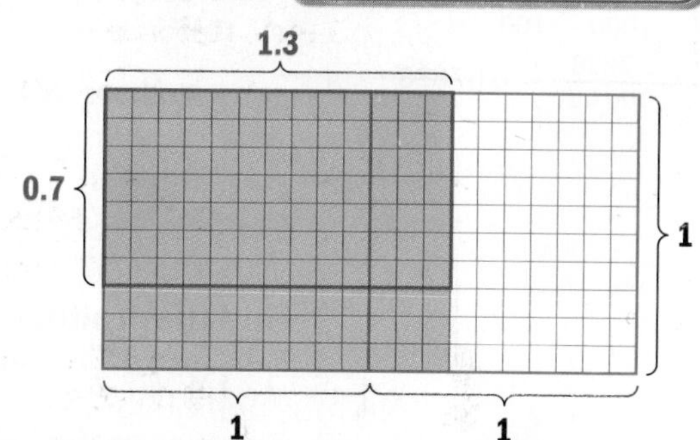

KEY CONCEPT *For Your Notebook*

Multiplying Decimals

Words Multiply decimals as you would whole numbers. Then place the decimal point in the product. The number of decimal places in the product is equal to the sum of the number of decimal places in the factors.

Numbers $0.7 \times 1.3 = 0.91$

EXAMPLE 1 Multiplying Decimals

Animated Math For an interactive example of multiplying decimals go to **classzone.com.**

$$\begin{array}{r} 5.82 \\ \times\, 0.41 \\ \hline 582 \\ 2328 \\ \hline 2.3862 \end{array}$$

2 decimal places
+ 2 decimal places
4 decimal places

CHECK REASONABLENESS To check that the product in Example 1 is reasonable, round each factor to the place value of the *leading digit,* and then multiply. The **leading digit** of a number is the first nonzero digit.

5.82 → 6 **Round to the nearest whole number.**

0.41 → 0.4 **Round to the nearest tenth.**

Because $6 \times 0.4 = 2.4$, the product in Example 1 is reasonable.

EXAMPLE 2 Multiplying Decimals

a.

$$\begin{array}{r} 6.45 \\ \times\ 18 \\ \hline 5160 \\ 645\ \\ \hline 116.10 \end{array}$$

2 decimal places
+ 0 decimal places

2 decimal places

After you place the decimal point, you can drop any zeros at the end of an answer.

▶**Answer** $6.45 \times 18 = 116.1$

b.

$$\begin{array}{r} 1.273 \\ \times\ 0.06 \\ \hline 0.07638 \end{array}$$

3 decimal places
+ 2 decimal places
5 decimal places

Write a zero before the 7 as a placeholder so that the number has five decimal places.

▶**Answer** $1.273 \times 0.06 = 0.07638$

ANOTHER WAY

You can also multiply decimals by rewriting them as fractions:

$1.273 \times 0.06 =$

$\frac{1273}{1000} \times \frac{6}{100} =$

$\frac{7638}{100,000} = 0.07638$

✓ GUIDED PRACTICE for Examples 1 and 2

Find the product. Then check that your answer is reasonable.

1. 1.4×7.2 **2.** 0.98×0.21 **3.** 6.89×0.07

4. 4.63×9 **5.** 12×0.05 **6.** 2.351×1.6

DIVIDING DECIMALS To divide decimals by whole numbers, you can use long division. Line up the decimal points in the quotient and the dividend.

EXAMPLE 3 Dividing a Decimal by a Whole Number

TEAM PHOTOS Your baseball team is ordering photo trading cards of each player on your team. A set of 25 cards costs $15.95. Find the price of each card. Round to the nearest cent.

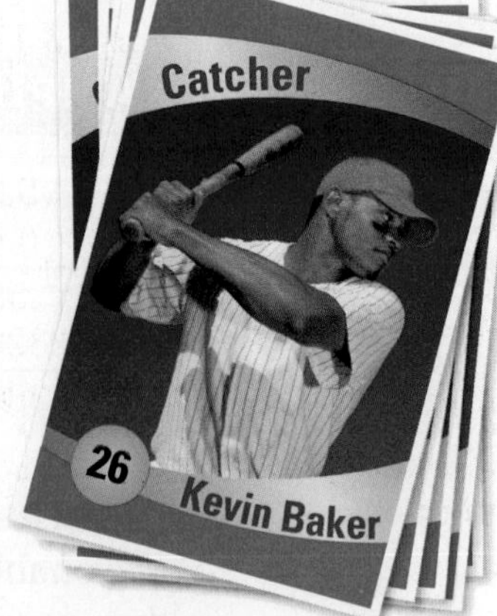

SOLUTION

To find the cost per card, you need to divide.

STEP 1 **Divide** $15.95 by 25.

$$\begin{array}{r} 0.638 \\ 25\overline{)15.950} \\ 15\ 0\ \ \\ \hline 95\ \\ 75\ \\ \hline 200 \\ 200 \\ \hline 0 \end{array}$$

Line up decimal point in quotient with decimal point in dividend.

Divide as you would with whole numbers.

STEP 2 **Round** to the nearest cent.

$.638 ⟶ $.64

▶**Answer** The price of each card is about $.64.

About the Standards

Note that Grade 6 Standard MR 2.6 expects you to round as specified. With money, round to the nearest hundredth to find the nearest cent.

About the Standards

Note that Grade 6 Standard MR 2.1 asks you to verify the reasonableness of results.

To check that the quotient in Example 3 is reasonable, you can use leading digits and *compatible numbers*. **Compatible numbers** are numbers that make a calculation easier.

Round divisor to place value of leading digit.

$25\overline{)15.95} \longrightarrow 30\overline{)15.00}$

Round dividend to a compatible number.

Because $15 \div 30 = 0.5$, the quotient in Example 3 is reasonable.

DIVIDING BY A DECIMAL Notice the pattern in the equations below.

$6 \div 3 = 2 \qquad 60 \div 30 = 2 \qquad 600 \div 300 = 2 \qquad 6000 \div 3000 = 2$

The quotient remains the same when the divisor and the dividend are multiplied by the same power of 10. This is because the quotients can be written as equivalent fractions multiplied by $\frac{10}{10}$, or 1. This fact can help you to divide decimals.

KEY CONCEPT — *For Your Notebook*

Dividing by a Decimal

Words When you divide by a decimal, multiply both the divisor and the dividend by a power of ten that will make the divisor a whole number.

Numbers $12.5\overline{)8.75} \longrightarrow 125\overline{)87.5}$ with quotient 0.7

EXAMPLE 4 Dividing Decimals

a. $3.17\overline{)3.804} \longrightarrow 317\overline{)380.4}$

$$\begin{array}{r} 1.2 \\ 317\overline{)380.4} \\ \underline{317} \\ 63\ 4 \\ \underline{63\ 4} \\ 0 \end{array}$$

Multiply the divisor and dividend by 100 by moving both decimal points two places to the right.

Line up decimal points in dividend and quotient.

b. $1.9\overline{)0.114} \longrightarrow 19\overline{)1.14}$

$$\begin{array}{r} 0.06 \\ 19\overline{)1.14} \\ \underline{1\ 14} \\ 0 \end{array}$$

Multiply the divisor and dividend by 10 by moving both decimal points one place to the right.

AVOID ERRORS

Don't forget to write zeros as placeholders and line up the decimal point in the quotient with the decimal point in the dividend.

✓ GUIDED PRACTICE for Examples 3 and 4

Find the quotient. Round to the nearest hundredth if necessary.

7. $110.85 \div 3$ **8.** $2.234 \div 1.3$ **9.** $9.5 \div 0.3$ **10.** $0.208 \div 5.2$

2.7 EXERCISES

HOMEWORK KEY ◆ = **MULTIPLE CHOICE PRACTICE** Exs. 23, 42, 76, 78, 89–91
○ = **HINTS AND HOMEWORK HELP** for Exs. 7, 25, 79 at classzone.com

SKILLS • PROBLEM SOLVING • REASONING

VOCABULARY **Round to the place value of the leading digit.**

1. 3.5 **2.** 9.15 **3.** 22.38 **4.** 18.06

5. **VOCABULARY** Using compatible numbers, what dividend and divisor would you use to estimate the quotient 54.2 ÷ 6.7?

6. **WRITING** *Explain* how you can use fractions to multiply decimals. Give an example.

SEE EXAMPLES 1 AND 2 on pp. 107–108 for Exs. 7–23

FINDING PRODUCTS **Find the product. Check that it is reasonable.**

7. 0.4 × 0.03 **8.** 0.06 × 0.6 **9.** 0.8 × 3 **10.** 0.05 × 8

11. 3.4 × 6.5 **12.** 9.3 × 8.1 **13.** 3.9 × 0.91 **14.** 0.7 × 0.01

15. 0.14 × 0.09 **16.** 6.08 × 0.2 **17.** 0.045 × 1.20 **18.** 25 × 0.052

19. 0.086 × 0.007 **20.** 33.501 × 3 **21.** 19.73 × 5.01 **22.** 40.21 × 1.03

23. ◆ **MULTIPLE CHOICE** What is the value of the expression 54.3 × 4.2?

Ⓐ 32.58 Ⓑ 228.06 Ⓒ 325.8 Ⓓ 2280.6

SEE EXAMPLES 3 AND 4 on pp. 108–109 for Exs. 24–39

FINDING QUOTIENTS **Find the quotient. Round your answer to the nearest hundredth if necessary.**

24. 0.245 ÷ 6 **25.** 3.65 ÷ 8 **26.** 3.45 ÷ 15 **27.** 9 ÷ 7.2

28. 7 ÷ 1.4 **29.** 12 ÷ 6.4 **30.** 68 ÷ 3.1 **31.** 9.97 ÷ 2.9

32. 75.4 ÷ 5.2 **33.** 0.3445 ÷ 6.5 **34.** 172.2 ÷ 82 **35.** 1500.96 ÷ 16

36. 2199.24 ÷ 41 **37.** 37.857 ÷ 7.5 **38.** 18.01 ÷ 3.28 **39.** 8.7822 ÷ 3.57

ERROR ANALYSIS ***Describe*** **and correct the error made in finding the product or quotient.**

40.

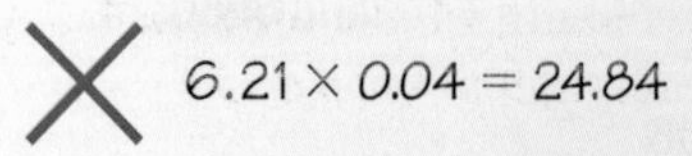

41.

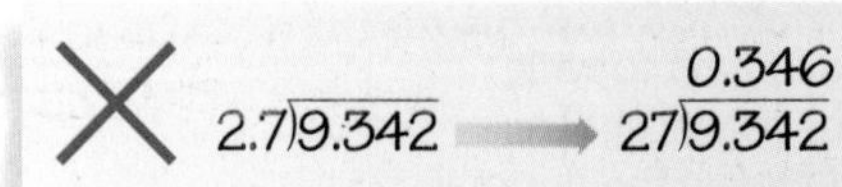

42. ◆ **MULTIPLE CHOICE** Which quotient is not equal to the others?

Ⓐ 225 ÷ 180 Ⓑ 22.5 ÷ 1.8 Ⓒ 225 ÷ 18 Ⓓ 2.25 ÷ 0.18

ESTIMATING PRODUCTS **Round to the place value of the leading digit to estimate the product.**

43. 3.45 × 90.2 **44.** 0.32 × 2.8 **45.** 4.57 × 199.4 **46.** 18.23 × 4.7

47. 6.92 × 0.08 **48.** 561 × 0.7 **49.** 15.75 × 0.013 **50.** 0.35 × 42.82

ESTIMATING QUOTIENTS **Use compatible numbers to estimate the quotient.**

51. 104.26 ÷ 4.98 **52.** 1206.47 ÷ 29.2 **53.** 1.90 ÷ 2.007 **54.** 32.158 ÷ 4.374

55. 143.865 ÷ 3.99 **56.** 15.4 ÷ 2.861 **57.** 36.794 ÷ 9.018 **58.** 358.1 ÷ 49.86

59. MODELING Copy the number line below. Use your copy to show how to represent 0.8 ÷ 0.2. Use the fact that division is repeated subtraction.

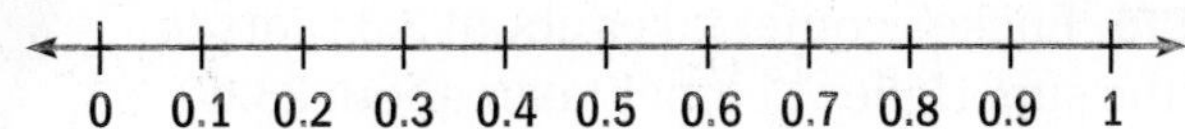

ALGEBRA **Evaluate the expression when $p = 2.64$ and $q = 0.9$.**

60. $7.654 \cdot p$ **61.** $1.12 \cdot q$ **62.** $p \cdot 5.08 \cdot p$ **63.** $q \cdot 1.12 \cdot p$

64. $3.6 \div q$ **65.** $p \div 0.275$ **66.** $p \div 0.03 \div 2.5$ **67.** $q \div 0.1 \div q$

68. OPEN-ENDED *Describe* the pattern used to relate the value of a term to its position n in the list. Create and describe your own pattern.

Position n	1	2	3	4	n
Value of term	1.5	3	4.5	6	?

DESCRIBING PATTERNS **Describe the pattern. Write the next three numbers.**

69. 0.12, 0.6, 3, 15, . . . **70.** 1, 0.5, 0.25, 0.125, . . . **71.** 2, 3, 4.5, 6.75, . . .

CONNECT SKILLS TO PROBLEM SOLVING **Exercises 72–75 will help you prepare for problem solving.**

Write the expression you would use to solve the problem.

72. Grapes are on sale for $1.25 per pound. You buy 1.8 pounds. How much do you pay for the grapes?

73. Your class holds a car wash to raise money for a field trip. You charge $4.75 per car and earn $779. How many cars does your class wash?

74. You have a wooden board that is 30 inches long. You cut it into pieces that are 3.75 inches long. How many pieces of wood do you have?

75. Wanda buys 3 CDs. With tax, each CD costs $14.69. How much does she spend?

SEE EXAMPLE 3 on p. 108 for Exs. 76–77

76. ◆ **MULTIPLE CHOICE** You knit a scarf using 4 balls of yarn. The yarn costs a total of $24.88. How much does each ball of yarn cost?

Ⓐ $.16 Ⓑ $6.22 Ⓒ $20.88 Ⓓ $99.52

California @HomeTutor for problem solving help at classzone.com

77. READING RATE Tyler can read about 1.25 pages per minute. Can he finish reading a 65-page book in one hour? About how long would it take him to finish? How many pages would he have left after reading a 120-page book for one hour? How much more time would he need? *Explain.*

California @HomeTutor for problem solving help at classzone.com

78. ◆ **MULTIPLE CHOICE** A wheelchair racer takes about 5.95 minutes to travel 1 mile. Which expression shows how long it would take the racer to finish a 26.2-mile marathon?

(A) $5.95 \div 26.2$ (B) $26.2 \div 5.95$

(C) $26.2 - 5.95$ (D) 5.95×26.2

Athletes use racing chairs.

79. **COMETS** Encke's comet takes about 3.3 years to orbit the sun. Halley's comet takes about 23.06 times as long. About how long does Halley's comet take to orbit the Sun? Round to the nearest tenth.

80. **SHORT RESPONSE** Copy the division problem below. *Explain* how to use estimation to place the decimal point in the quotient.

$$9.76\overline{)31.232}\quad 32$$

81. **WRITING** *Explain* how to use a number line model to find $1.5 \div 0.2$. Then explain how to use dollars and dimes to model $\$1.50 \div 0.2$.

82. **MULTI-STEP PROBLEM** It costs \$4.75 for a 25 ounce box of cereal and \$3.45 for a 15 ounce box.

a. What is the cost per ounce of each box of cereal?

b. How many times the cost per ounce of the smaller box is the cost per ounce of the larger box? *Explain.*

83. **GASOLINE** At one time, the price of gasoline ranged from \$3.19 to \$3.59 per gallon. A car needs 8.7 more gallons of gasoline to have a full tank. Is it possible that the cost to fill the tank is \$30.45? What is the *least* possible cost to fill the tank? *Explain* how you solved the problem.

84. **MEASUREMENT** The objects below have been magnified. Their actual width w is much smaller. Measure each object in millimeters.

Pollen

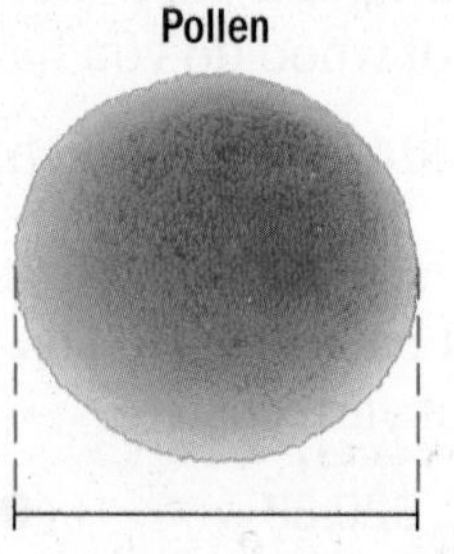

$w = 0.0013 \times$ width shown

Algae

$w = 0.0037 \times$ width shown

Blood cell

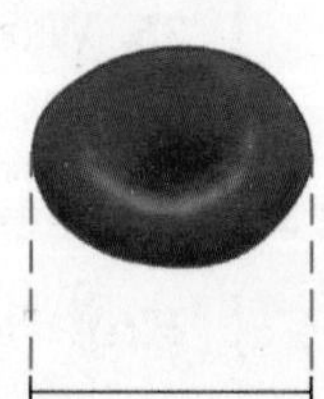

$w = 0.0006 \times$ width shown

a. Use your measurements to find the actual width w of each object.

b. List the actual objects in order from least to greatest width.

85. *xy* **REASONING** The quotient of a and b is a whole number. Can a be a decimal number if b is a whole number? Can b be a decimal number if a is a whole number? Can both a and b be decimal numbers? Can the quotient be greater than a? *Justify* your answers and give examples.

86. **REASONING** Which decimal number(s) can you divide by 2.3 to make the quotient *less* than 2.3? *greater* than 2.3? *equal* to 2.3? *Explain* your reasoning.

87. **CHALLENGE** Runner A runs at a pace of 6.54 miles per hour for 1.3 hours. Runner B runs at a pace of 7.08 miles per hour for 1.1 hours. Who runs farther? How much longer must the other runner continue to run to match the distance of the first runner? Round to the nearest hundredth of an hour. *Explain* how you solved the problem.

88. **CHALLENGE** A store sells crafts. The first week it prices 5 baskets at $20 each. After each week, the price of each unsold basket drops to 0.9 times the previous week's price. All 5 baskets sell in the same week for a total of at least $53. In what week(s) could they have been sold?

◆ CALIFORNIA STANDARDS SPIRAL REVIEW

NS 2.1 89. What is the value of $\frac{5}{6} + \frac{7}{10}$? *(p. 75)*

Ⓐ $\frac{3}{4}$ Ⓑ $\frac{6}{5}$ Ⓒ $\frac{23}{15}$ Ⓓ $\frac{49}{30}$

Gr. 5 NS 1.2 90. Which number is $6\frac{1}{8}$ written as a decimal? *(p. 40)*

Ⓐ 6.125 Ⓑ 6.18 Ⓒ 6.81 Ⓓ 61.8

Gr. 4 NS 3.4 91. During 4 days of basketball practice, you shoot a total of 140 free throws. You shoot the same number of free throws each day. How many free throws do you shoot per day? *(p. 671)*

Ⓐ 25 Ⓑ 30 Ⓒ 35 Ⓓ 40

QUIZ *for Lessons 2.4–2.7*

Find the product or quotient. *(p. 88, 94)*

1. $\frac{7}{15} \times \frac{3}{5}$ 2. $2\frac{5}{8} \times 1\frac{5}{9}$ 3. $17 \times \frac{15}{34}$ 4. $1\frac{1}{3} \times 4\frac{2}{9}$

5. $\frac{16}{21} \div \frac{7}{8}$ 6. $5\frac{5}{11} \div \frac{1}{15}$ 7. $5\frac{1}{2} \div 1\frac{3}{4}$ 8. $3\frac{3}{4} \div 6$

Find the sum or difference. Then check your answer. *(p. 102)*

9. 6.67 + 14.2 10. 13.1 + 0.137 11. 24.194 − 5.08 12. 7.2 − 0.006

Find the product or quotient. Round quotients to the nearest hundredth if necessary. Then check your answer. *(p. 107)*

13. 9.58 × 6.19 14. 4.01 × 12.8 15. 52 ÷ 0.079 16. 3.374 ÷ 0.35

17. **BOOKS** Ryan had 180 books. He gave away $\frac{1}{3}$ of his books and sold $\frac{3}{4}$ of the rest. How many books did he sell? *Explain* your reasoning. *(p. 88)*

MIXED REVIEW of Skills and Problem Solving

Multiple Choice Practice for Lessons 2.4–2.7

1. You have a piece of wood that is 51 inches long. For a craft project, you need pieces that are each $4\frac{1}{2}$ inches long.

51 in.

How many pieces that are $4\frac{1}{2}$ inches long can you cut from the wood? **NS 2.1**

Ⓐ 11 Ⓑ 12

Ⓒ 229 Ⓓ 230

2. What is the value of the expression $x \cdot 16.83$ when $x = 0.14$? **Gr. 5 NS 2.1**

Ⓐ 0.8415 Ⓑ 2.3562

Ⓒ 84.15 Ⓓ 235.62

3. What is $0.23 \div 6.18$ rounded to the nearest hundredth? **Gr. 5 NS 2.1**

Ⓐ 0.004 Ⓑ 0.03

Ⓒ 0.037 Ⓓ 0.04

4. In the table below, which description relates a position n to its value? **NS 2.2, MR 1.2**

Position n	*Value*
1	$2\frac{1}{2}$
2	5
3	$7\frac{1}{2}$
4	10
n	?

Ⓐ Multiply n by $1\frac{1}{2}$.

Ⓑ Divide n by $1\frac{1}{2}$.

Ⓒ Multiply n by $2\frac{1}{2}$.

Ⓓ Divide n by $2\frac{1}{2}$.

5. The table shows the amount of money raised by 3 homerooms at a school fair. How much more was the total raised by homerooms 6A and 6C than by homeroom 6B? **Gr. 5 NS 2.1**

Homeroom	6A	6B	6C
Money raised	\$133.88	\$148.59	\$122.77

Ⓐ \$14.71 Ⓑ \$108.06

Ⓒ \$137.48 Ⓓ \$159.70

6. What is the value of 13.57×2.8? **Gr. 5 NS 2.1**

Ⓐ 13.570 Ⓑ 37.996

Ⓒ 135.70 Ⓓ 379.96

7. The recipe shown makes enough garlic mashed potatoes for 5 servings. You want to make 150 servings for a garlic festival. How many cups of water and cups of milk do you need? **NS 2.1, MR 3.1**

Ⓐ $67\frac{2}{3}$ cups water and $9\frac{2}{3}$ cups milk

Ⓑ 70 cups water and 10 cups milk

Ⓒ $116\frac{2}{3}$ cups water and $16\frac{2}{3}$ cups milk

Ⓓ 350 cups water and 50 cups milk

8. What is the value of $2\frac{3}{16} \div 2\frac{1}{12}$? **NS 2.2**

Ⓐ $\frac{192}{875}$ Ⓑ $\frac{20}{21}$

Ⓒ $1\frac{1}{20}$ Ⓓ $52\frac{1}{2}$

2 CHAPTER SUMMARY

Standards
NS 2.1, NS 2.2, NS 2.4, Gr. 5 NS 2.1

BIG IDEAS

For Your Notebook

Big Idea 1

Solving Problems Using Addition and Subtraction of Fractions

You can use least common multiples to find common denominators in order to solve problems involving addition and subtraction of fractions.

Problem: A pear weighs $\frac{3}{4}$ pound and an apple weighs $\frac{9}{20}$ pound.

Question	*Expression*	*Rewrite using the LCD.*	*Answer*
How much more does the pear weigh than the apple?	$\frac{3}{4} - \frac{9}{20}$	$\frac{15}{20} - \frac{9}{20}$	$\frac{6}{20}$, or $\frac{3}{10}$ pound
What is the total weight of the pear and the apple?	$\frac{3}{4} + \frac{9}{20}$	$\frac{15}{20} + \frac{9}{20}$	$\frac{24}{20}$, or $1\frac{1}{5}$ pounds

Big Idea 2

Multiplying and Dividing Fractions

The product of two or more fractions is equal to the product of the numerators over the product of the denominators. To divide a fraction by any nonzero number, multiply by its reciprocal.

a. $\frac{2}{3} \times \frac{1}{2} = \frac{2 \times 1}{3 \times 2}$

$= \frac{\overset{1}{\cancel{2}} \times 1}{3 \times \underset{1}{\cancel{2}}}$ **Divide out common factor.**

$= \frac{1}{3}$

b. $\frac{3}{4} \div \frac{2}{3} = \frac{3}{4} \times \frac{3}{2}$ **Multiply by reciprocal.**

$= \frac{3 \times 3}{4 \times 2}$

$= \frac{9}{8}$, or $1\frac{1}{8}$

Big Idea 3

Adding, Subtracting, Multiplying, and Dividing Decimals

Operation	*Place the decimal point in the answer.*	*Examples*
Addition or subtraction	Line up the decimal points vertically in the numbers you are adding or subtracting. The decimal point in the answer is in the same column.	$7.34 + 6.51 = 13.85$; $7.34 - 6.51 = 0.83$
Multiplication	The number of decimal places in the product is equal to the sum of the number of decimal places in the factors.	1.43 ← 2 places × 0.8 ← 1 place 1.144 — 3 places
Division	Multiply both the divisor and the dividend by a power of ten that will make the divisor a whole number. Line up the decimal points in the quotient and the dividend.	$0.5\overline{)0.65}$ → $5\overline{)6.5}$ = 1.3 5 15 15 0

CHAPTER PROBLEM

Standards
NS 2.1, NS 2.2
Gr. 5 NS 2.1

APPLYING THE BIG IDEAS

Big Idea 1
You add and subtract fractions in **Step 1.**

Big Idea 2
You multiply and divide fractions in **Step 1, Step 2, and Step 3.**

Big Idea 3
You add, subtract, multiply, and divide decimals in **Step 2 and Step 3.**

PROBLEM How can you use decimals and fractions to revise a recipe to make a different number of servings and to find total costs?

STEP 1 **Revise the recipe.**

A recipe for Mango Peach Salsa is shown. You are making a greater number of servings for a picnic.

- What fraction or mixed number do you need to multiply the amounts by to make 1 serving? 10 servings? 20 servings? 30 servings?
- Revise the recipe to make your choice of 10, 20, or 30 servings.
- How much more of each item will you need?

Mango Peach Salsa
Serves 8

$1\frac{1}{3}$ c mangoes

$1\frac{1}{4}$ c peaches

$\frac{3}{4}$ of a chili pepper

$2\frac{1}{2}$ tbsp lime juice

STEP 2 **Estimate amounts.**

You shop for the ingredients at a farmer's market. One mango provides about 1.5 cups, one lime provides about 2 tablespoons, and one peach provides about 0.5 cup. Using the revised recipe from Step 1, find the number of mangoes, limes, peaches, and chili peppers you need.

STEP 3 **Calculate costs.**

Peaches cost \$1.25 per pound, chili peppers cost \$.75 per pound, mangoes cost \$1 each, and limes cost \$.49 each. A typical peach weighs $\frac{1}{4}$ pound and a typical pepper weighs $\frac{1}{8}$ pound. Use this information and the results from Step 2 to find the cost of each ingredient. Then find the total cost to make the recipe.

Extending the Problem

Use your results above to complete the exercises.

1. You buy three bags of tortilla chips to dip in the salsa for \$1.95 each. Using your answers from Step 3, what is the total cost to make your Mango Peach Salsa and to buy the tortilla chips?
2. Find a recipe for a different type of salsa. Copy the recipe and number of servings it makes. Revise the recipe to make 10 servings.
3. Find the cost of each ingredient in your revised recipe from Exercise 2. If you also buy three bags of tortilla chips for \$1.95 each, what is the total cost to make 10 servings of your recipe?
4. Estimate whether your recipe or an equal number of servings of Mango Peach Salsa is less expensive to make. About how much less? *Explain.*

2 CHAPTER REVIEW

California @HomeTutor
classzone.com
• Multi-Language Visual Glossary
• Vocabulary practice

REVIEW KEY VOCABULARY

- variable, *p. 70*
- algebraic expression, *p. 70*
- evaluate, *p. 70*
- reciprocal, *p. 95*
- front-end estimation, *p. 103*
- leading digit, *p. 107*
- compatible numbers, *p. 109*

VOCABULARY EXERCISES

Copy and complete the statement.

1. One method for estimating the sum of two or more numbers is __?__.
2. A letter used to represent one or more numbers is a(n) __?__.
3. Numbers that make a calculation easier are called __?__.
4. Two nonzero numbers whose product is 1 are __?__.
5. **NOTETAKING SKILLS** Make a *concept map* like the one shown on page 68 for *estimation*. Include all of the methods of estimation that you know.

REVIEW EXAMPLES AND EXERCISES

2.1 Adding and Subtracting Fractions *pp. 69–73*

NS 2.1

EXAMPLE

$$\frac{9}{10} + \frac{3}{10} = \frac{12}{10} \quad \textbf{Add numerators.}$$

$$= 1\frac{2}{10} \quad \textbf{Write as a mixed number.}$$

$$= 1\frac{1}{5} \quad \textbf{Simplify.}$$

EXERCISES

SEE EXAMPLES 1, 2, AND 3 on pp. 69–70 for Exs. 6–17

Find the sum or difference.

6. $\frac{3}{11} + \frac{5}{11}$
7. $\frac{7}{15} - \frac{4}{15}$
8. $\frac{6}{7} - \frac{4}{7}$
9. $\frac{11}{15} + \frac{1}{15}$
10. $\frac{8}{11} - \frac{5}{11}$
11. $\frac{11}{13} + \frac{2}{13}$
12. $\frac{2}{9} + \frac{8}{9}$
13. $\frac{11}{16} - \frac{7}{16}$

Evaluate the expression when $a = \frac{13}{24}$ and $b = \frac{7}{8}$.

14. $a + \frac{1}{24}$
15. $b + \frac{5}{8}$
16. $b - \frac{1}{8}$
17. $\frac{17}{24} - a$

2.2 Using a Common Denominator

pp. 75–80

NS 2.4

EXAMPLE

Find the sum or difference.

Rewrite the fractions using the LCD. Then add or subtract.

a. $\frac{1}{14} + \frac{2}{7} = \frac{1}{14} + \frac{2 \times 2}{7 \times 2}$

$= \frac{1}{14} + \frac{4}{14}$

$= \frac{5}{14}$

b. $\frac{3}{5} - \frac{1}{3} = \frac{3 \times 3}{5 \times 3} - \frac{1 \times 5}{3 \times 5}$

$= \frac{9}{15} - \frac{5}{15}$

$= \frac{4}{15}$

EXERCISES

SEE EXAMPLES 1, 2, 3, AND 4 on pp. 75–77 for Exs. 18–26

Find the sum or difference.

18. $\frac{1}{10} + \frac{4}{5}$ **19.** $\frac{5}{8} + \frac{1}{2}$ **20.** $\frac{3}{4} + \frac{2}{7}$ **21.** $\frac{8}{9} + \frac{5}{6}$

22. $\frac{3}{4} - \frac{2}{5}$ **23.** $\frac{2}{3} - \frac{1}{6}$ **24.** $\frac{9}{10} - \frac{1}{2}$ **25.** $1 - \frac{5}{12}$

26. CANDLES You light a candle that is $\frac{5}{6}$ inch tall. The candle melts to a height of $\frac{3}{4}$ inch. How much shorter is the candle? *Explain.*

2.3 Adding and Subtracting Mixed Numbers

pp. 81–85

NS 2.1

EXAMPLE

$10\frac{1}{4} - 4\frac{5}{6} = 10\frac{3}{12} - 4\frac{10}{12}$ **Rewrite fractions using LCD of $\frac{1}{4}$ and $\frac{5}{6}$, 12.**

$= 9\frac{15}{12} - 4\frac{10}{12}$ **Rename $10\frac{3}{12}$ as $9\frac{15}{12}$.**

$= 5\frac{5}{12}$ **Subtract fractions and then subtract whole numbers.**

EXERCISES

SEE EXAMPLES 1, 2, 3, AND 4 on pp. 81–82 for Exs. 27–31

Find the sum or difference.

27. $2\frac{1}{5} + 3\frac{3}{5}$ **28.** $10\frac{5}{8} - 8\frac{7}{8}$ **29.** $9\frac{13}{14} - 8\frac{3}{7}$ **30.** $6\frac{4}{21} + 16\frac{1}{6}$

31. KNITTING Carly is knitting a $36\frac{5}{8}$ inch long scarf. She has already knit $28\frac{3}{4}$ inches. How many more inches does Carly need to knit? *Explain.*

2.4 Multiplying Fractions and Mixed Numbers

pp. 88–92

NS 2.1, NS 2.2

EXAMPLE

$3\frac{3}{4} \times 4\frac{2}{5} = \frac{15}{4} \times \frac{22}{5}$ **Write $3\frac{3}{4}$ and $4\frac{2}{5}$ as improper fractions.**

$= \frac{\overset{3}{\cancel{15}} \times \overset{11}{\cancel{22}}}{\underset{2}{\cancel{4}} \times \underset{1}{\cancel{5}}}$ **Use rule for multiplying fractions. Divide out common factors.**

$= \frac{33}{2}$, or $16\frac{1}{2}$ **Multiply.**

EXERCISES

SEE EXAMPLES 1, 2, 3, AND 4 on pp. 88–90 for Exs. 32–36

Find the product.

32. $\frac{3}{10} \times \frac{5}{8}$ **33.** $\frac{7}{12} \times 18$ **34.** $5\frac{5}{6} \times \frac{2}{7}$ **35.** $4\frac{7}{8} \times 2\frac{4}{9}$

36. ORCHESTRA One half of an orchestra plays brass instruments. The horn section makes up $\frac{1}{7}$ of the brass instruments. What fraction of the whole orchestra is the horn section?

2.5 Dividing Fractions and Mixed Numbers

pp. 95–99

NS 2.1, NS 2.2

EXAMPLE

$\frac{5}{6} \div \frac{4}{9} = \frac{5}{6} \times \frac{9}{4}$ **Multiply by reciprocal.**

$= \frac{5 \times \overset{3}{\cancel{9}}}{\underset{2}{\cancel{6}} \times 4}$ **Use rule for multiplying fractions. Divide out common factor.**

$= \frac{15}{8}$, or $1\frac{7}{8}$ **Multiply.**

EXERCISES

SEE EXAMPLES 1, 2, 3, AND 4 on pp. 95–97 for Exs. 37–41

Find the quotient.

37. $\frac{7}{8} \div \frac{1}{12}$ **38.** $\frac{3}{5} \div 6$ **39.** $36 \div 6\frac{3}{4}$ **40.** $10\frac{1}{8} \div 1\frac{7}{20}$

41. STORAGE A DVD rack is $21\frac{1}{4}$ inches wide, including $\frac{1}{2}$ inch of wood on each side of the rack. A DVD case is about $\frac{9}{16}$ inch wide. How many DVD cases can fit on one shelf of the rack? *Explain* your answer.

2.6 Adding and Subtracting Decimals

pp.102–106

Gr. 5 NS 2.1

EXAMPLE

a. 9.325 + 17.38

```
   9.325
+ 17.380  <--- Write a zero as a placeholder.
  26.705
```

b. 8 − 3.74

```
   8.00  <--- Write zeros as placeholders.
 − 3.74
   4.26
```

EXERCISES

SEE EXAMPLES 1, 2, AND 3 on pp. 102–103 for Exs. 42–50

Find the sum or difference. Then check that your answer is reasonable.

42. 54.2 + 19.25 **43.** 1.295 + 24.6 **44.** 100 − 16.574 **45.** 35.002 − 0.18

Evaluate the expression when $x = 2.75$ and $y = 16.2$.

46. $x + 10.32$ **47.** $5 + y$ **48.** $y - 3.909$ **49.** $22.02 - x$

50. PERIMETER A rectangular garden is 9.2 feet long and 5.9 feet wide. *Estimate* the distance around the garden.

2.7 Multiplying and Dividing Decimals

pp. 107–113

Gr. 5 NS 2.1

EXAMPLE

a.

```
   2.354     3 decimal places
×   0.03   + 2 decimal places
 0.07062     5 decimal places
```

b. $1.2\overline{)6.0} \longrightarrow 12\overline{)60}$, quotient 5; 60; 0

Multiply divisor and dividend by 10.

Write a zero as a placeholder.

EXERCISES

SEE EXAMPLES 1, 2, 3, AND 4 on pp. 107–109 for Exs. 51–66

Find the product or quotient. Then check that your answer is reasonable.

51. 54 × 18.4 **52.** 2.5 × 34.6 **53.** 10.21 × 6.4 **54.** 0.002 × 9.009

55. 9.156 × 2.007 **56.** 195 × 0.084 **57.** 3.5 ÷ 14 **58.** 45.35 ÷ 9.07

59. 28.2 ÷ 3 **60.** 71 ÷ 0.5 **61.** 6363.14 ÷ 8.6 **62.** 0.2368 ÷ 0.74

Find the quotient. Round to the nearest cent.

63. \$4.68 ÷ 5 **64.** \$60.05 ÷ 2 **65.** \$16.95 ÷ 6 **66.** \$22.90 ÷ 50

2 CHAPTER TEST

1. **VOCABULARY** Write the reciprocal of each number: $\frac{3}{10}$, $7\frac{5}{8}$, 22.

2. **VOCABULARY** The first nonzero digit of a number is the __?__.

Find the sum or difference.

3. $\frac{4}{15} + \frac{2}{15}$
4. $\frac{1}{2} + \frac{8}{9}$
5. $\frac{2}{3} - \frac{4}{7}$
6. $1 - \frac{3}{10}$
7. $9\frac{3}{8} - 5\frac{1}{8}$
8. $14\frac{1}{6} + 12\frac{5}{6}$
9. $6\frac{2}{3} + 4\frac{3}{8}$
10. $7\frac{3}{4} - 5\frac{4}{5}$

Find the product or quotient.

11. $\frac{1}{5} \times \frac{1}{8}$
12. $\frac{4}{9} \times \frac{3}{16}$
13. $10 \times \frac{3}{4}$
14. $5\frac{1}{2} \times 2\frac{7}{9}$
15. $\frac{9}{17} \div \frac{3}{34}$
16. $\frac{7}{8} \div \frac{7}{12}$
17. $8\frac{2}{3} \div 5\frac{1}{6}$
18. $3\frac{6}{7} \div 1\frac{2}{7}$

Find the sum or difference. Then check that your answer is reasonable.

19. 28.07 + 10.89
20. 34.77 − 14.19
21. 6.67 + 2.36
22. 8.32 − 0.84
23. 6 − 2.65
24. 4.88 + 219.405
25. 30.105 − 9.9
26. 9.4 + 9.073

Find the product or quotient. Then check that your answer is reasonable.

27. 0.16×8
28. $60.25 \div 5$
29. $0.291 \div 9.7$
30. 0.94×0.63
31. $0.084 \div 0.2$
32. 0.009×0.9
33. 0.72×0.146
34. $12.75 \div 0.3$

35. **RAINFALL** A rain gauge is used to collect rainfall data. During a rainstorm, a gauge reads $1\frac{3}{8}$ inches after the first three hours and $2\frac{1}{3}$ inches two hours later. How much rain fell in those two hours?

36. **SURVEYS** At a middle school, two fifths of the students in each grade are chosen for a survey. Evaluate the expression $\frac{2}{5}x$ when $x = 265$, $x = 260$, and $x = 285$ to find the number of sixth, seventh, and eighth grade students chosen for the survey.

37. **ORIENTEERS** In the sport of orienteering, people use maps and compasses to find their way along an unfamiliar outdoor course. The table at the right shows the top finishing times of five women in a competition.

Results	*Time (min.)*
First place	25.4
Second place	27.75
Third place	28.7
Fourth place	29.05
Fifth place	29.32

   a. How much sooner did the winner of the competition finish before the fifth place finisher?

   b. Which two times are the closest?

   c. What is the greatest difference between two consecutive times in the list?

2 ◆ MULTIPLE CHOICE STRATEGIES

STRATEGIES YOU'LL USE:
- **SOLVE DIRECTLY**
- **ELIMINATE CHOICES**

Standards
NS 2.2, AF 1.1

If you have trouble solving a multiple choice problem directly, you may be able to use another approach to eliminate incorrect answer choices and obtain the correct answer.

PROBLEM 1

What value of k makes the expression $k \div 2\frac{3}{4}$ equal to $6\frac{8}{9}$?

Ⓐ $\frac{99}{248}$ Ⓑ $2\frac{50}{99}$ Ⓒ $9\frac{23}{36}$ Ⓓ $18\frac{17}{18}$

Strategy 1 SOLVE DIRECTLY

You know that to check a division problem, you can multiply the quotient and the divisor. The product should equal the dividend.

STEP 1 **Write** the related product.

quotient • divisor = dividend

$$6\frac{8}{9} \times 2\frac{3}{4} = k$$

STEP 2 **Multiply** to find the value of k.

$$6\frac{8}{9} \times 2\frac{3}{4} = \frac{62}{9} \times \frac{11}{4}$$

$$= \frac{\overset{31}{\cancel{62}} \times 11}{9 \times \underset{2}{\cancel{4}}}$$

$$= \frac{341}{18}, \text{ or } 18\frac{17}{18}$$

The correct answer is D. Ⓐ Ⓑ Ⓒ Ⓓ

Strategy 2 ELIMINATE CHOICES

In some cases, you can eliminate choices of a multiple choice question with reasoning and estimation.

Because you are dividing k by a number *greater* than 1, you can reason that the quotient, $6\frac{8}{9}$, must be *less* than k.

You can eliminate choices A and B.

Find a high and a low estimate using the remaining choices for k. (See page 669 for help with estimation.)

Choice C: $9\frac{23}{36} \div 2\frac{3}{4} \stackrel{?}{=} 6\frac{8}{9}$

A low estimate is $9 \div 3 = 3$. A high estimate is $10 \div 2 = 5$.

Because $6\frac{8}{9}$ is not between 3 and 5, you can eliminate choice C.

The correct answer is D. Ⓐ Ⓑ Ⓒ Ⓓ

PROBLEM 2

The dimensions of a photo of a painting are $\frac{1}{3}$ of the dimensions of the actual painting. Which expression shows the length of the photo if the actual length is $12\frac{1}{2}$ inches?

Ⓐ $\frac{1}{3} \div 12\frac{1}{2}$ Ⓑ $\frac{1}{3} \times 12\frac{1}{2}$ Ⓒ $12\frac{1}{2} \times 3$ Ⓓ $12\frac{1}{2} \div \frac{1}{3}$

Strategy 1 SOLVE DIRECTLY

Decide which operation to use and then write an expression.

To find the dimensions of the photo, you need to find $\frac{1}{3}$ *of* the dimensions of the actual painting. You need to multiply.

$$\frac{1}{3} \text{ of } 12\frac{1}{2} = \frac{1}{3} \times 12\frac{1}{2}$$

The correct answer is B. Ⓐ Ⓑ Ⓒ Ⓓ

Strategy 2 ELIMINATE CHOICES

You can use mathematical reasoning.

The length of the photo is *less* than the length of the actual painting, $12\frac{1}{2}$ inches.

$12\frac{1}{2} \div \frac{1}{3} = 12\frac{1}{2} \times 3$ is *greater* than $12\frac{1}{2}$.

You can eliminate choices C and D.

The length of the actual painting is *greater* than 12 inches long, so the length of the photo must be *greater* than $\frac{1}{3}$ of 12, or 4.

$\frac{1}{3} \div 12\frac{1}{2}$ is less than 4.

You can eliminate choice A.

The correct answer is B. Ⓐ Ⓑ Ⓒ Ⓓ

STRATEGY PRACTICE

Explain why you can eliminate the highlighted answer choice.

1. What is the value of $24\frac{3}{8} \div a$ when $a = 2\frac{1}{6}$?

   Ⓐ $11\frac{1}{4}$ Ⓑ $14\frac{1}{4}$ Ⓒ $22\frac{5}{24}$ Ⓓ ✗ $\mathbf{26\frac{13}{14}}$

2. One board has a length of $\frac{7}{12}$ foot. A longer board has a length of $1\frac{1}{2}$ feet. Which expression describes the difference in the lengths of the boards?

   Ⓐ $1\frac{1}{2} - \frac{7}{12}$ Ⓑ ✗ $\mathbf{\frac{7}{12} \times 1\frac{1}{2}}$ Ⓒ $\frac{7}{12} - 1\frac{1}{2}$ Ⓓ $\frac{7}{12} + 1\frac{1}{2}$

3. You divide $2\frac{1}{2}$ pizzas into slices that are each $\frac{1}{8}$ of a pizza. Which expression describes the total number of slices?

   Ⓐ $\frac{1}{8} - 2\frac{1}{2}$ Ⓑ ✗ $\mathbf{2\frac{1}{2} - \frac{1}{8}}$ Ⓒ $\frac{1}{8} \div 2\frac{1}{2}$ Ⓓ $2\frac{1}{2} \div \frac{1}{8}$

2 ◆ MULTIPLE CHOICE PRACTICE

1. A recipe for lemonade is shown. You need to make $1\frac{1}{2}$ times the recipe. How many cups of lemon juice do you need? **NS 2.1**

Recipe: LEMONADE

1 1/2 cups water

2/3 cup sugar

2/3 cup lemon juice

Ⓐ $\frac{4}{9}$ cup

Ⓑ 1 cup

Ⓒ 2 cups

Ⓓ $2\frac{1}{4}$ cups

2. Tina and Tim each have a kite. The string on Tina's kite is $75\frac{1}{2}$ feet long. Tim's kite string is $1\frac{3}{4}$ feet shorter than Tina's. Which expression can be used to find the length of Tim's kite string? **NS 2.1**

Ⓐ $75\frac{1}{2} \times 1\frac{3}{4}$

Ⓑ $75\frac{1}{2} \div 1\frac{3}{4}$

Ⓒ $75\frac{1}{2} + 1\frac{3}{4}$

Ⓓ $75\frac{1}{2} - 1\frac{3}{4}$

3. The pattern on the number line starts with 0.64. It continues to decrease as shown. What is the next number in the pattern? **MR 2.3, Gr. 5 NS 2.1**

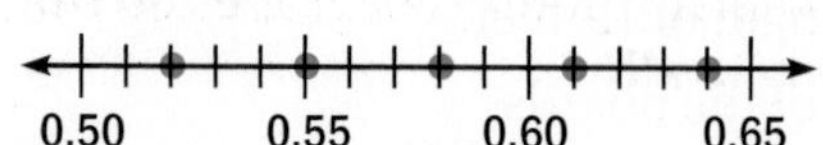

Ⓐ 0.47

Ⓑ 0.49

Ⓒ 0.50

Ⓓ 0.67

4. Using front-end estimation, the sum of 5.27 and another number is 13. Which could be the other number? **MR 2.1, Gr. 5 NS 2.1**

Ⓐ 6.82

Ⓑ 7.84

Ⓒ 8.56

Ⓓ 9.13

5. Bananas are on sale for \$.39 per pound. About how much does it cost to buy the bananas shown below? **MR 2.1, Gr. 5 NS 2.1**

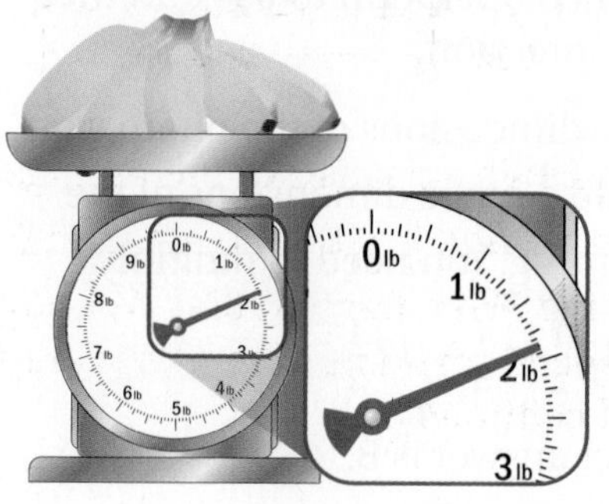

Ⓐ Less than \$.50

Ⓑ Greater than \$.50 and less than \$1.00

Ⓒ Greater than \$1.00 and less than \$1.50

Ⓓ More than \$1.50

6. What is the value of $w \cdot 3\frac{4}{7}$ when $w = 2\frac{8}{15}$? **NS 2.2**

Ⓐ $2\frac{2}{35}$

Ⓑ $6\frac{32}{105}$

Ⓒ $9\frac{1}{21}$

Ⓓ $9\frac{1}{15}$

7. What is $0.176 \div 0.62$ rounded to the nearest thousandth? **Gr. 5 NS 2.1**

Ⓐ 0.28

Ⓑ 0.283

Ⓒ 0.284

Ⓓ 0.3

8. What is the *greatest* number of compact disc cases the bottom shelf below can hold upright if each case is $\frac{7}{16}$ inch wide? **NS 2.1**

Ⓐ 4

Ⓑ 5

Ⓒ 22

Ⓓ 23

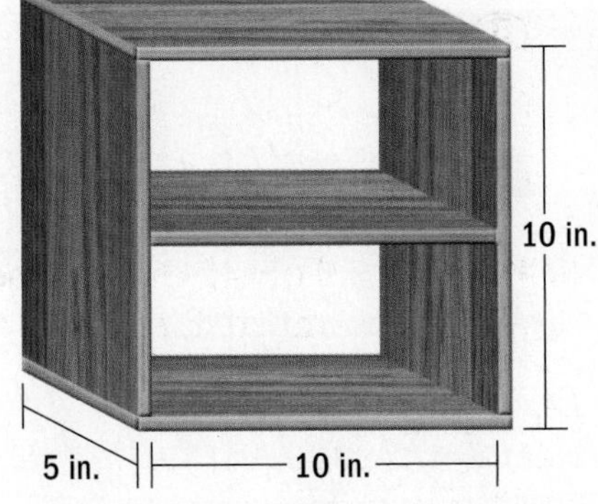

9. The Chen family spends $\frac{1}{3}$ of their budget on housing costs and $\frac{2}{5}$ of their budget on food and clothing. What fraction of their budget is left to spend on items other than housing, food, and clothing? **NS 2.1**

Ⓐ $\frac{1}{15}$

Ⓑ $\frac{2}{15}$

Ⓒ $\frac{4}{15}$

Ⓓ $\frac{11}{15}$

10. The prices for making copies at a self-service copy center are listed in the table below. How much will it cost you to make 7 copies of a 30 page report? **Gr. 5 NS 2.1**

Total number of pages	*Price per page*
1–100	$.08
101–200	$.06
over 200	$.05

Ⓐ $2.40

Ⓑ $10.50

Ⓒ $12.60

Ⓓ $16.80

11. What is the value of $b + \frac{7}{15} + \frac{5}{6}$ when $b = \frac{13}{20}$? **NS 2.1**

Ⓐ $\frac{5}{24}$

Ⓑ $1\frac{1}{4}$

Ⓒ $1\frac{1}{2}$

Ⓓ $1\frac{19}{20}$

12. You and a friend do yardwork for a neighbor. The neighbor pays $13.00 per hour for the two of you to split. How much do you each get paid if you work together for $2\frac{1}{2}$ hours? **NS 2.1**

Ⓐ $10.40

Ⓑ $16.25

Ⓒ $32.50

Ⓓ $65.00

13.

> You cook 6 cups of pasta. One serving is $\frac{3}{4}$ cup. How many servings do you cook?

Which of the following problems can be solved using the same arithmetic operation used to solve the problem above? **NS 2.1, MR 3.2**

Ⓐ Kim runs 2 miles in $\frac{1}{5}$ hour. What is Kim's speed in miles per hour?

Ⓑ Jan brings $1\frac{1}{3}$ pounds of grapes to a picnic. Ron brings $\frac{3}{4}$ pound of grapes. How many pounds of grapes do they bring in all?

Ⓒ A recipe for bread calls for $1\frac{1}{3}$ cups milk for each loaf. How much milk is needed for 3 loaves?

Ⓓ You can read 48 pages every hour. How many pages can you read in $2\frac{1}{2}$ hours?

3 Integers

Before

In previous chapters, you learned the following skills, which you'll use in Chapter 3:

- Ordering whole numbers, fractions, and decimals
- Performing operations with whole numbers
- Performing operations with fractions

Now

In Chapter 3 you'll study these

Big Ideas:

1. Comparing and ordering positive and negative numbers
2. Adding, subtracting, multiplying, and dividing integers
3. Using properties to evaluate expressions

Why?

So you can solve real-world problems about . . .

- Miniature golf, p. 132
- Scuba diving, p. 139
- Monkeys, p. 157
- Weightlifting, p. 164
- Rainfall, p. 171
- Trading cards, p. 177

at classzone.com

Get-Ready Games

Mixed Number Race

California Standards

Review ordering mixed numbers. *Gr. 6 NS 1.1*

Prepare for ordering negative fractions. *Gr. 6 NS 1.1*

A	T	N	R	O	M	H	A
$\frac{44}{7}$	$\frac{49}{6}$	$\frac{28}{3}$	$\frac{34}{5}$	$\frac{17}{2}$	$\frac{23}{4}$	$\frac{67}{8}$	$\frac{71}{9}$

How to Play

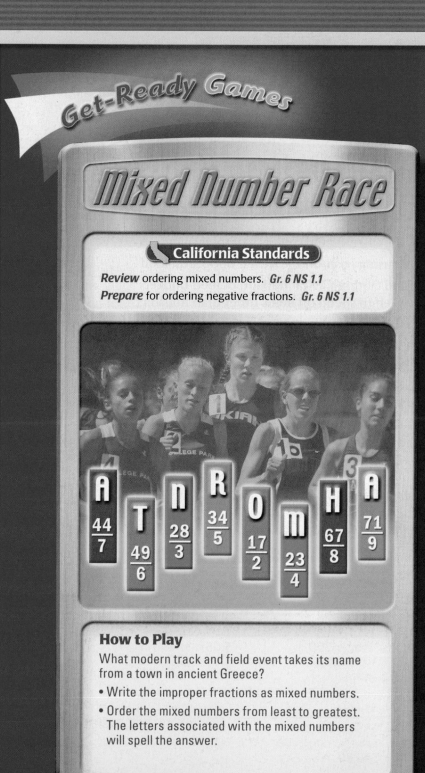

What modern track and field event takes its name from a town in ancient Greece?

- Write the improper fractions as mixed numbers.
- Order the mixed numbers from least to greatest. The letters associated with the mixed numbers will spell the answer.

California Standards

- **Gr. 6 NS 2.3 Solve addition, subtraction, multiplication, and division problems, including those arising in concrete situations, that use positive** and negative **integers and combinations of these operations.** *(Lessons 3.2, 3.3, 3.4, 3.5)*
- **Gr. 6 AF 1.3 Apply algebraic order of operations and the commutative, associative, and distributive properties to evaluate expressions; and justify each step in the process.** *(Lessons 3.6, 3.7, 3.8)*

TRIPLE JUMP

California Standards

Review multiplying positive fractions. ***Gr. 6 NS 2.2***
Prepare for multiplying integers. ***Gr. 6 NS 2.3***

How to Play

In the triple jump, athletes perform a *hop*, a *step*, and a *jump*.

- Use the numbers 24, 36, and 48. Choose one of the numbers for your hop, one for your step, and one for your jump.
- Use the formula above to find your total distance.
- Find the longest possible total distance.

Games Wrap-Up

Draw Conclusions

Complete these exercises after playing the games.

1. **WRITING** For *Mixed Number Race*, a student claims that $\frac{71}{9}$ is greater than $\frac{67}{8}$ because 71 is greater than 67 and 9 is greater than 8. *Describe* and correct the student's error.
2. **REASONING** *Explain* how you can be certain that the distance you found in *Triple Jump* is the longest possible distance.

3 Getting Ready

Prerequisite Skills

California @HomeTutor
Prerequisite skills practice at classzone.com

REVIEW VOCABULARY
- **reciprocal,** *p. 95*
- **power,** *p. 663*
- **base,** *p. 663*
- **exponent,** *p. 663*

VOCABULARY CHECK

Copy and complete using a review term from the list at the left.

1. The __?__ of 5 is $\frac{1}{5}$.
2. When a power is expressed as a product, the __?__ is the repeated factor and the __?__ is the number of times the factor is used.

SKILL CHECK

Evaluate the expression. Simplify if possible. *(p. 69)*

3. $\frac{3}{7}+\frac{2}{7}$
4. $\frac{6}{11}-\frac{2}{11}$
5. $\frac{4}{15}+\frac{2}{15}$
6. $\frac{5}{8}-\frac{3}{8}$
7. $\frac{2}{5}+\frac{7}{10}$
8. $\frac{2}{3}-\frac{5}{9}$
9. $\frac{11}{14}-\frac{1}{2}$
10. $\frac{5}{12}+\frac{17}{36}$

Write the decimal as a fraction or mixed number. *(p. 40)*

11. 0.35
12. 4.5
13. 2.85
14. 0.745

Order the numbers from least to greatest. *(p. 40)*

15. 9, $7\frac{1}{3}$, 8.9, 7.5, 0, 0.4
16. $\frac{5}{6}$, $\frac{3}{4}$, 0.25, 0.5, 1.23, 0
17. 0.45, 4.5, $\frac{4}{5}$, $\frac{5}{9}$, $\frac{9}{5}$, 3.50
18. 1, $\frac{8}{9}$, 1.123, $\frac{9}{8}$, 0.98, 1.12

Notetaking Skills

NOW YOU TRY
Make a *process diagram* for multiplying fractions. You may want to use colored pencils.

Focus on Graphic Organizers

Use a *process diagram* to organize the steps of a process, such as adding fractions. Write the steps in ovals.

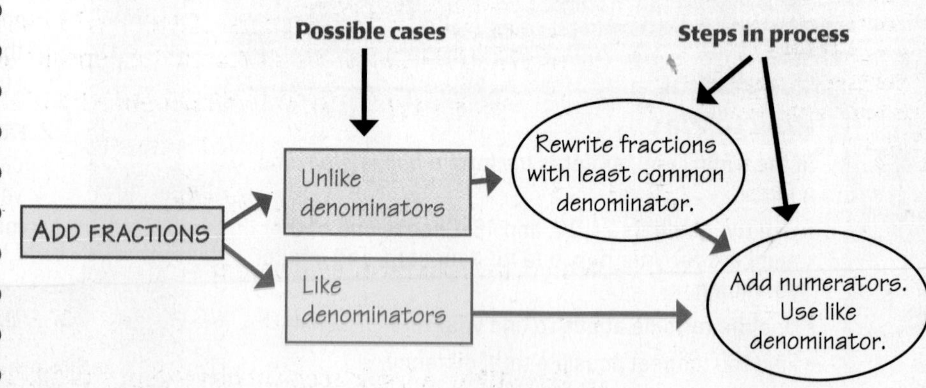

3.1 Ordering Integers on a Number Line

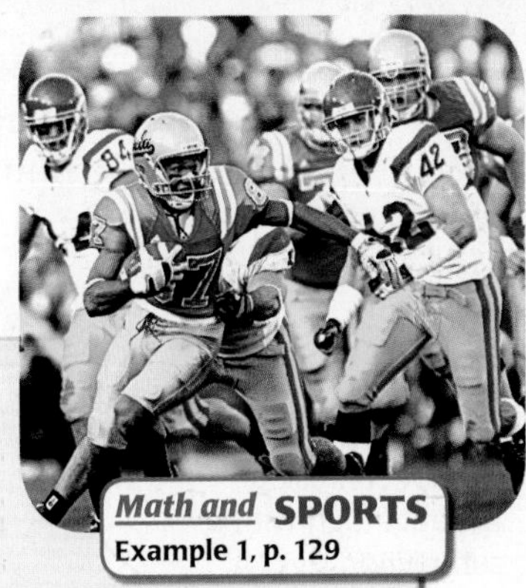

Standards Preparation Gr. 5 NS 1.5 **Identify and represent on a number line** decimals, fractions, mixed numbers, and **positive and negative integers.**

Connect *Before* you represented positive numbers on a number line. *Now* you will order integers using a number line to prepare for Grade 6 Standard NS 1.1.

KEY VOCABULARY
- integer
- negative integer
- positive integer
- opposite

The following numbers are **integers**:

$$\ldots, -4, -3, -2, -1, 0, 1, 2, 3, 4, \ldots$$

Negative integers are integers that are less than zero. **Positive integers** are integers that are greater than 0. Zero is neither positive nor negative.

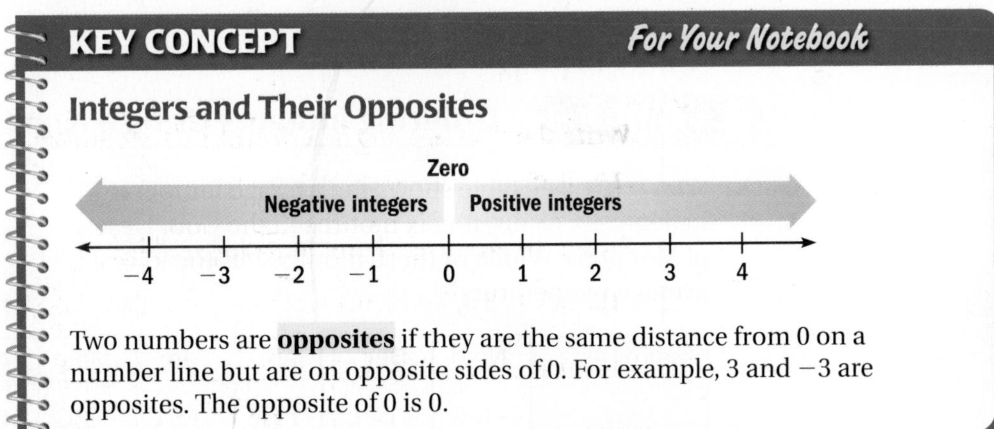

KEY CONCEPT
For Your Notebook
Integers and Their Opposites
Zero
Negative integers
Positive integers
−4
−3
−2
−1
0
1
2
3
4
Two numbers are opposites if they are the same distance from 0 on a number line but are on opposite sides of 0. For example, 3 and −3 are opposites. The opposite of 0 is 0.

EXAMPLE 1 Writing Integers

READING The integer −10 is read "negative ten." A number other than 0 that doesn't have a negative sign is considered to be positive. The integer 9 is read "positive nine" or "nine."

a. In three plays of a football game, a team gains 7 yards, loses 10 yards, and gains 9 yards. Use integers to represent the gains and losses.

7 yard gain: 7   10 yard loss: −10   9 yard gain: 9

b. A bank account has deposits of \$100 and \$150. It also has a withdrawal of \$75. Use integers to represent the deposits and withdrawals.

\$100 deposit: \$100   \$150 deposit: \$150   \$75 withdrawal: −\$75

✓ GUIDED PRACTICE for Example 1

Write the opposite of the integer.

1. 15   **2.** −8   **3.** −35   **4.** 100

5. BANKING A bank account has a deposit of \$200, and withdrawals of \$100 and \$250. Use integers to represent the deposits and withdrawals.

COMPARING INTEGERS You can use a number line to compare and order integers. Remember that numbers decrease as you move to the left on a number line and increase as you move to the right.

EXAMPLE 2 Comparing Integers Using a Number Line

AVOID ERRORS
Do not confuse a negative sign with a subtraction sign. A negative sign indicates a direction on a number line, not an operation.

a. Compare −2 and −5.

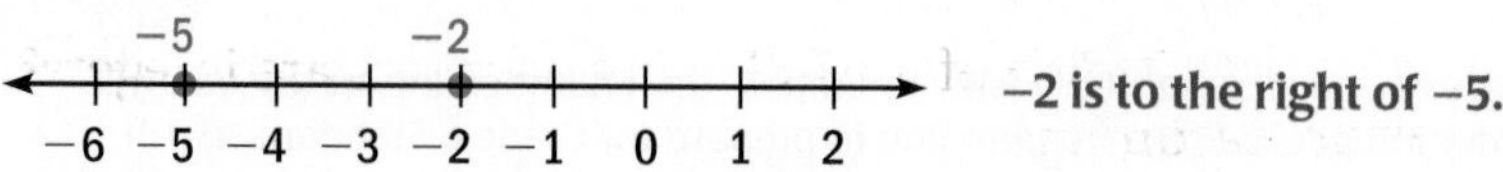

−2 is to the right of −5.

▶ **Answer** −2 > −5. You can also write −5 < −2.

b. Compare −6 and 1.

−6 1
−6 −5 −4 −3 −2 −1 0 1 2

−6 is to the left of 1.

▶ **Answer** −6 < 1. You can also write 1 > −6.

EXAMPLE 3 Ordering Integers Using a Number Line

WEATHER The table shows the average temperatures, in degrees Celsius, for six months in the Gobi Desert of Mongolia. Which of these months has the lowest average temperature?

Month	Nov.	Dec.	Jan.	Feb.	Mar.	Apr.
Average Temperature	−6°C	−14°C	−15°C	−12°C	−3°C	6°C

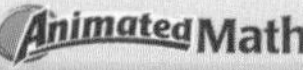

For an interactive example of ordering integers using a number line go to **classzone.com.**

SOLUTION

You can graph each integer on a number line to order the temperatures.

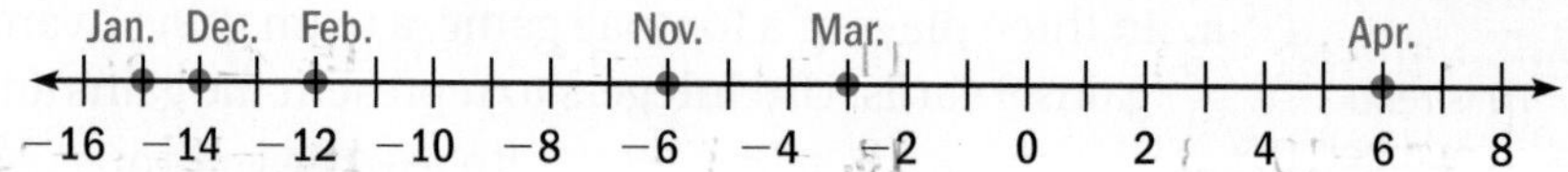

The temperatures from least to greatest are: −15, −14, −12, −6, −3, 6.

▶ **Answer** January has the lowest average temperature of −15°C.

GUIDED PRACTICE for Examples 2 and 3

Copy and complete the statement using < or >.

6. 0 _?_ −7 **7.** −9 _?_ 4 **8.** −5 _?_ −4 **9.** −3 _?_ −13

Order the integers from least to greatest.

10. 8, −4, −6, 4, −3, 1 **11.** −7, −12, −16, −10, −8

3.1 EXERCISES

HOMEWORK KEY ◆ = **MULTIPLE CHOICE PRACTICE** Exs. 11, 12, 55, 60–62

○ = **HINTS AND HOMEWORK HELP** for Exs. 9, 11, 57 at classzone.com

SKILLS • PROBLEM SOLVING • REASONING

1. **VOCABULARY** What is the opposite of 12?

2. **WRITING** Which of the following numbers are integers? *Justify* your reasoning.

$$2675, 0, -56, \frac{3}{4}, 75, 0.65$$

SEE EXAMPLE 1 on p. 129 for Exs. 3–6

WRITING INTEGERS AND OPPOSITES Write the integer that represents the situation. Then write the opposite of the integer.

3. 1333 feet above sea level
4. Sixteen degrees below zero
5. Nine million dollar loss
6. \$15 account withdrawal

SEE EXAMPLE 2 on p. 130 for Exs. 7–24

GRAPHING INTEGERS Graph the integer on a number line.

7. -9
8. 4
9. -6
10. opposite of 3

11. ◆ **MULTIPLE CHOICE** Which letter on the number line best identifies the location of -2?

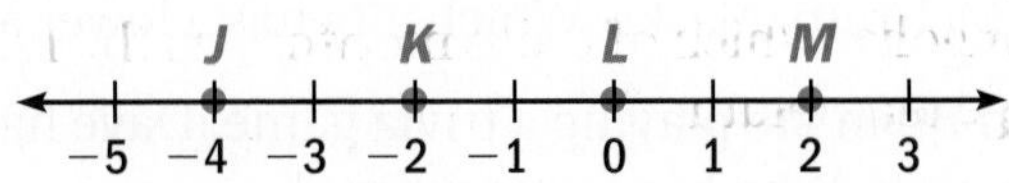

Ⓐ Point J　Ⓑ Point K　Ⓒ Point L　Ⓓ Point M

12. ◆ **MULTIPLE CHOICE** Which statement is true?

Ⓐ $-56 < -58$　Ⓑ $1 < -112$　Ⓒ $-7 > -5$　Ⓓ $-9 > -11$

COMPARING INTEGERS Copy and complete the statement using < or >.

13. 34 _?_ −43
14. −17 _?_ −13
15. 42 _?_ 37
16. 26 _?_ −267
17. −18 _?_ 3
18. −7 _?_ 4
19. −121 _?_ −125
20. 92 _?_ 96
21. 31 _?_ −15
22. −55 _?_ −58
23. 63 _?_ 54
24. −82 _?_ −74

SEE EXAMPLE 3 on p. 130 for Exs. 25–31

ORDERING INTEGERS Order the integers from least to greatest.

25. −28, 18, 7, −17, 0, −12
26. 99, −42, 13, −2, 11, −49
27. −150, 235, −435, 345, −75
28. −66, 21, 9, −10, −22, 44
29. 320, −250, −19, 15, 2
30. −11, −93, −84, 0, 9, −3

31. **ERROR ANALYSIS** *Describe* and correct the error in ordering the integers from least to greatest.

−1, −3, −7, −12 ✗

OPEN-ENDED Give a real-world quantity that the integer could represent.

32. -5 **33.** 0 **34.** 8 **35.** opposite of -7

36. ERROR ANALYSIS A student says that any integer is always greater than its opposite. *Describe* and correct the error in the student's reasoning.

37. REASONING Are 4 and -4 the same distance from 1 on a number line? *Justify* your answer using a number line.

xy ALGEBRA The statement $a < x < b$ means that on a number line, x is between a and b, but not equal to a or b. Give two integer values of the variable that make the statement true.

38. $0 < d$ **39.** $c < 23$ **40.** $-10 > k$ **41.** $b > -9$

42. $-4 < m < 1$ **43.** $2 < p < 7$ **44.** $-3 > r > -11$ **45.** $9 > t > -2$

46. $-1 < k < 4$ **47.** $-22 < g < -12$ **48.** $7 > s > 4$ **49.** $52 < x < 60$

CONNECT SKILLS TO PROBLEM SOLVING Exercises 50–53 will help you prepare for problem solving.

50. The elevation of Mount Kilimanjaro, in Africa, is 5895 meters. The surface elevation of Lake Assal is 512 meters below sea level. Use integers to represent these elevations.

51. The average December temperature in Fairbanks, Alaska, is -6°F. It is -4°F in McGrath, Alaska. Which city has a lower average temperature?

52. Dave and Brian are playing a trivia game. Dave has -2 points and Brian has -4 points. Who has fewer points?

53. In January, a bakery earns a profit of $75. The bakery earns the opposite profit in February. Use an integer to represent February's profit.

SEE EXAMPLE 3 on p. 130 for Exs. 54–55

54. MINIATURE GOLF In miniature golf, the player with the least score wins. Order the scores given in the table from least to greatest. Who was the winner?

Player	Andrew	Mandy	Lisa	Trina
Score	-5	$+3$	0	-4

California @HomeTutor for problem solving help at classzone.com

55. ◆ MULTIPLE CHOICE The table below lists the freezing temperatures of five liquids to the nearest degree Celsius. Which liquid has a freezing temperature closest to 0°C?

Liquid	Benzene	Butane	Cesium	Mercury
Freezing Temperature	6°C	-138°C	28°C	-39°C

Ⓐ Benzene Ⓑ Butane Ⓒ Cesium Ⓓ Mercury

California @HomeTutor for problem solving help at classzone.com

56. **FOOTBALL** The diagram below shows 4 plays in a football game. Each tick mark represents 1 yard. Represent the progress made on each play with an integer. How many total yards did the team gain or lose during these 4 plays if they were headed for the goal line shown?

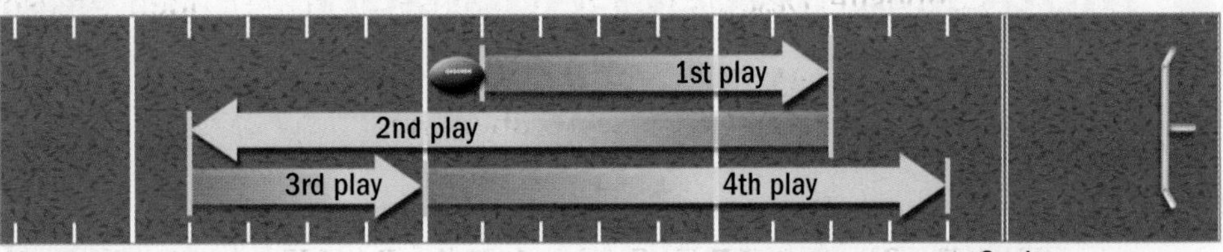

(57.) **MULTI-STEP PROBLEM** The table shows the highest and lowest elevations on the seven continents.

a. Order the continents by their highest elevations from least to greatest.

b. Order the continents by their lowest elevations from least to greatest.

c. North America's lowest elevation is in Death Valley, California. Which continent's lowest elevation is closest to Death Valley's lowest elevation?

Continent	*Highest Elevation (ft)*	*Lowest Elevation (ft)*
Africa	19,340	−512
Asia	29,035	−1349
Australia	7,310	−52
Europe	18,510	−92
North America	20,320	−282
South America	22,834	−131
Antarctica	16,066	−8383

58. **CHALLENGE** When a list of numbers is written in numerical order, the median of the numbers is the middle number or the average of the two middle numbers. The missing integer in the list of numbers below is the median of the numbers. What could the missing integer be?

$-44, 23, -11, 12, -27, \underline{\ ?\ }, -4, 0, 1$

59. **CHALLENGE** The numbers a, b, and c are integers from -3 to 3. Two of the integers are negative and the other is positive. Use the clues to find the values of a, b, and c.

Clues: $a < b$, $a > c$, $a < -1$, and $b < 2$

◆ CALIFORNIA STANDARDS SPIRAL REVIEW

NS 2.2 60. What is the value of $\frac{4}{7} \times \frac{3}{8}$? *(p. 88)*

Ⓐ $\frac{3}{14}$ Ⓑ $\frac{7}{15}$ Ⓒ $\frac{53}{56}$ Ⓓ $1\frac{11}{21}$

NS 2.4 61. What is $\frac{21}{63}$ in simplest form? *(p. 16)*

Ⓐ $\frac{1}{9}$ Ⓑ $\frac{1}{3}$ Ⓒ $\frac{7}{21}$ Ⓓ $\frac{21}{63}$

Gr. 5 NS 2.1 62. Vanessa has \$13.26 and buys a lunch which costs \$4.89. How much money does she have after buying lunch? *(p. 102)*

Ⓐ \$6.37 Ⓑ \$8.37 Ⓒ \$9.37 Ⓓ \$18.15

3.2 Modeling Integer Addition

MATERIALS • paper and pencil

Standards

NS 2.3 Solve addition, subtraction, multiplication, and division **problems,** including those arising in concrete situations, **that use positive and negative integers** and combinations of these operations.

QUESTION How can you model integer addition using a number line?

You know from your earlier work that you can use a number line to model the addition of two positive numbers. You can use a similar approach when adding integers. Move right to add a positive number. Move left to add a negative number.

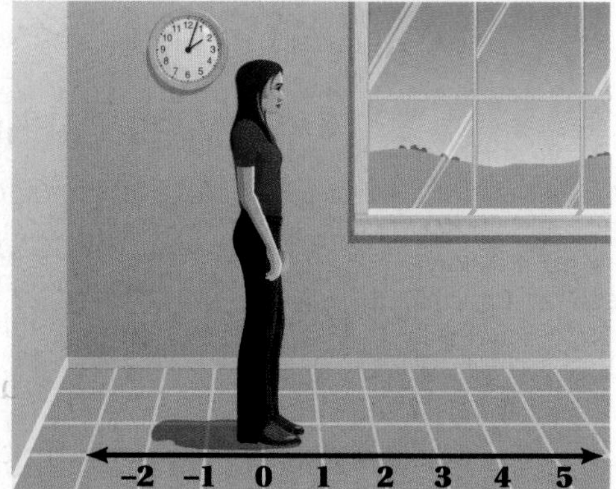

EXPLORE Find the sum $3 + (-2)$.

STEP 1 **Draw** a number line on a sheet of paper, or use a row of tiles on the classroom floor to represent a number line. Choose the edge of one tile to represent 0.

STEP 2 **Start** at 0. Move 3 units to the right.

STEP 3 **Move** 2 units to the left.

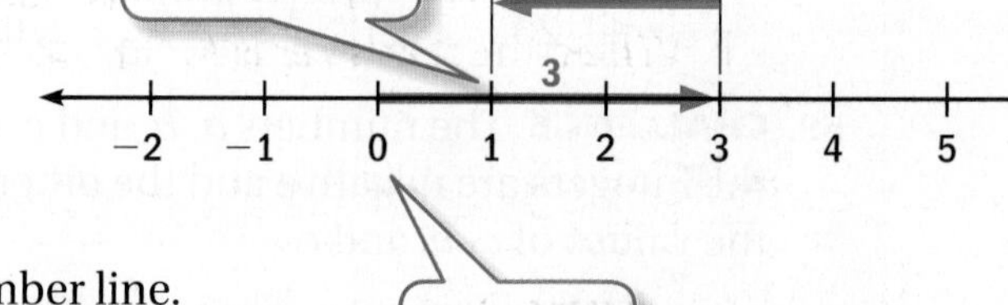

STEP 4 **Find** your final position on the number line. You are at 1, 1 unit to the right of 0. So, $3 + (-2) = 1$.

DRAW CONCLUSIONS Use your observations to complete these exercises.

Use a number line to find the sum.

1. $1 + 6$ **2.** $2 + 5$ **3.** $-3 + (-3)$ **4.** $-2 + (-3)$

5. $-7 + 3$ **6.** $-5 + 8$ **7.** $2 + (-5)$ **8.** $6 + (-2)$

9. REASONING *Describe* how to add $-8 + (-2)$ without using a number line.

10. REASONING *Describe* how to add $7 + (-4)$ without using a number line.

11. REASONING What is the sum of two integers that are opposites? *Justify* your answer using a number line.

3.2 Adding Integers

Math and DIVING
Ex. 61, p. 139

Standards NS 2.3 **Solve addition**, subtraction, multiplication, and division **problems, including those arising in concrete situations, that use positive and negative integers** and combinations of these operations.

Connect ***Before*** you compared and ordered integers. ***Now*** you will add integers.

KEY VOCABULARY
- **absolute value**

You can use a number line to add integers. Always start at 0. Move right to add a positive integer. Move left to add a negative integer.

EXAMPLE 1 ◆ Multiple Choice Practice

What is the value of $-5 + (-3)$?

Ⓐ -8 Ⓑ -2 Ⓒ 2 Ⓓ 8

ELIMINATE CHOICES
The sum of two negative integers is always negative. Choices C and D can be eliminated.

SOLUTION

Start at 0 on a number line.

Move **5** units to the **left**.

Then move **3** more units to the **left**.

−3
−5
−10 −8 −6 −4 −2 0 2

▸ **Answer** The final position is -8, so $-5 + (-3) = -8$.
The correct answer is A. Ⓐ Ⓑ Ⓒ Ⓓ

EXAMPLE 2 Using a Number Line to Add Integers

SCIENCE Atoms are made up of protons that have a charge of 1, neutrons that have a charge of 0, and electrons that have a charge of -1. One atom has 11 protons and 10 electrons. What is its total charge?

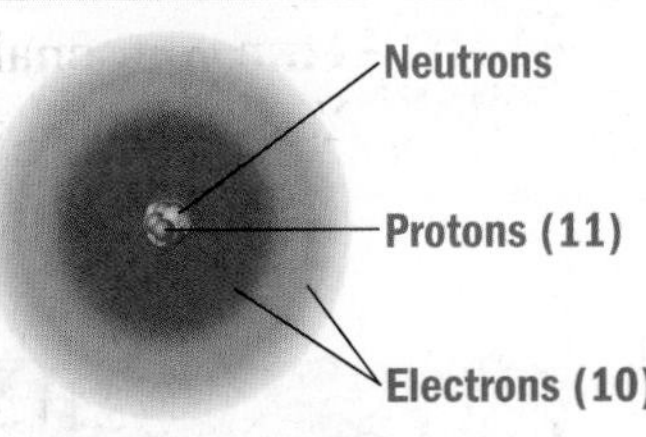

SOLUTION

The model represents moving **11** units to the **right**, and then **10** units to the **left**, or $11 + (-10) = 1$.

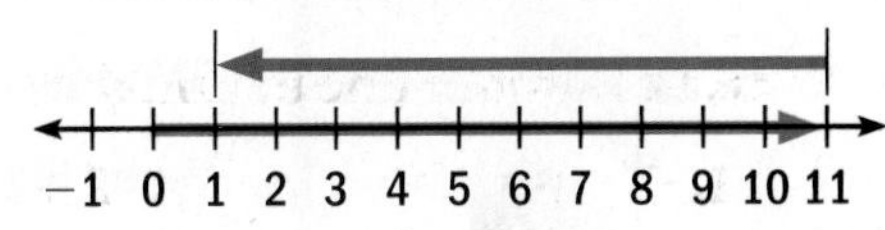

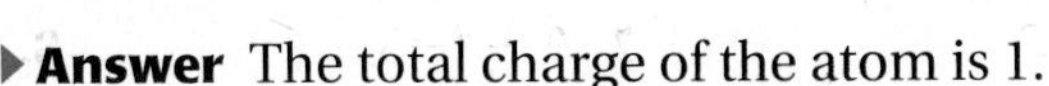

READING
The total charge of an atom is the sum of the charges of the protons, neutrons, and electrons.

▸ **Answer** The total charge of the atom is 1.

✓ GUIDED PRACTICE for Examples 1 and 2

Use a number line to find the sum.

1. $-9 + (-5)$ **2.** $-7 + 4$ **3.** $6 + (-13)$ **4.** $12 + (-9)$

VOCABULARY

Because distance cannot be negative, the absolute value of a number cannot be negative.

ABSOLUTE VALUE The **absolute value** of a number is the distance between the number and 0 on a number line. The absolute value of a number a is written $|a|$.

EXAMPLE 3 Finding Absolute Value

Find the absolute value of the number.

a. 8 **b.** −7 **c.** 0

SOLUTION

a. The distance between 8 and 0 is 8. So, $|8| = 8$.

b. The distance between −7 and 0 is 7. So $|-7| = 7$.

c. The distance between 0 and 0 is 0. So, $|0| = 0$.

GUIDED PRACTICE for Example 3

Find the absolute value of the number.

5. 100 **6.** −9 **7.** −45 **8.** 22

ADDING INTEGERS You can add integers without using a number line by representing the length of each arrow using absolute value.

When the numbers being added have the same sign, you add the lengths of the arrows. When the numbers being added have opposite signs, you need to find the difference in their lengths. The longer arrow determines the sign of the sum. These observations are summarized below.

KEY CONCEPT *For Your Notebook*

Adding Integers with Absolute Value

Words	Numbers
Same Signs Add the absolute values and use the common sign.	$10 + 14 = 24$ $-7 + (-5) = -12$
Different Signs Subtract the lesser absolute value from the greater absolute value and use the sign of the integer with the greater absolute value.	$13 + (-9) = 4$ $-11 + 6 = -5$
Opposites The sum of an integer and its opposite is 0.	$-4 + 4 = 0$

EXAMPLE 4 Adding Two Integers Using Absolute Value

a. Find the sum $-3 + (-12)$.

These integers have the same sign.

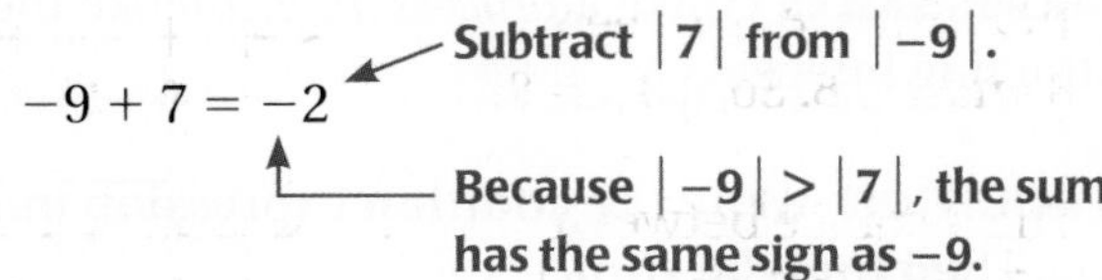
Add $|-3|$ and $|-12|$.
$-3 + (-12) = -15$
Both integers are negative, so the sum is negative.

b. Find the sum $-9 + 7$.

These integers have different signs.

$$-9 + 7 = -2$$

Subtract $|7|$ from $|-9|$.

Because $|-9| > |7|$, the sum has the same sign as -9.

AVOID ERRORS

Make sure your answer includes the sign of the integer with the greater absolute value.

✓ GUIDED PRACTICE for Example 4

Find the sum.

9. $-5 + (-11)$ **10.** $-9 + 6$ **11.** $0 + (-7)$

12. $-13 + 15$ **13.** $15 + (-8)$ **14.** $-12 + 12$

EXAMPLE 5 Adding Three or More Integers

PERSONAL FINANCE Aaron has kept track of his earnings and expenses for one week. Find the sum of his earnings and expenses.

Allowance: \$12
School field trip: −\$3
Pay from mowing lawns: \$13
Repaid sister: −\$5

AnimatedMath For an interactive example of adding integers go to **classzone.com.**

SOLUTION

You can find the sum by adding the integers two at a time.

$12 + (-3) + 13 + (-5) = 9 + 13 + (-5)$ **Add 12 and −3.**

$= 22 + (-5)$ **Add 9 and 13.**

$= 17$ **Add 22 and −5.**

▸**Answer** The sum of Aaron's earnings and expenses is \$17.

✓ GUIDED PRACTICE for Example 5

15. WHAT IF? In Example 5, suppose Aaron records these earnings and expenses for a week:

\$15, −\$13, −\$9, \$3, \$6

Find the sum of his earnings and expenses for the week.

3.2 EXERCISES

HOMEWORK KEY

◆ = **MULTIPLE CHOICE PRACTICE** Exs. 27, 36, 37, 64, 67–69

○ = **HINTS AND HOMEWORK HELP** for Exs. 15, 25, 63 at classzone.com

SKILLS • PROBLEM SOLVING • REASONING

VOCABULARY **Tell whether the statement is *true* or *false*. Explain.**

1. The absolute value of an integer is *always* its opposite.
2. The sum of an integer and its opposite is *always* 0.
3. **NOTETAKING SKILLS** Make a *process diagram* like the one on page 128 for subtracting integers.

SEE EXAMPLES 1 AND 2 on p. 135 for Exs. 4–6

MODELING ADDITION **Write the addition expression modeled on the number line. Then find the sum.**

4. 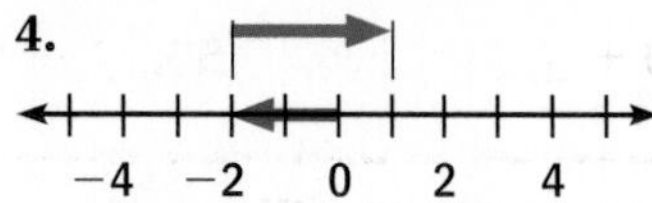

5. 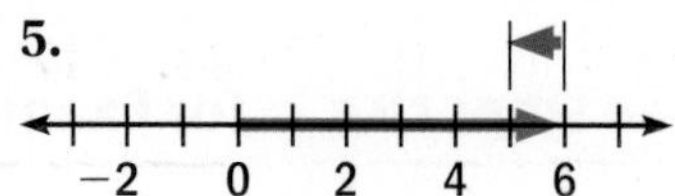

6. 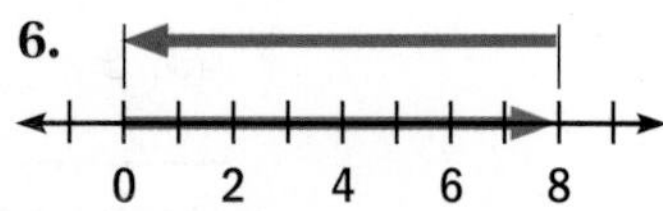

SEE EXAMPLE 3 on p. 136 for Exs. 7–14

FINDING ABSOLUTE VALUE **Find the absolute value of the number.**

7. −12
8. 0
9. 54
10. −3
11. −37
12. −567
13. 47
14. 19

SEE EXAMPLES 4 AND 5 on p. 137 for Exs. 15–29

ADDING INTEGERS **Tell whether the sum will be *positive*, *negative*, or *zero*. Then find the sum.**

15. $-3 + 6$
16. $9 + (-9)$
17. $-13 + (-1)$
18. $-20 + 5$
19. $0 + (-145)$
20. $-4 + (-15)$
21. $-27 + 27$
22. $25 + (-5)$
23. $-18 + (-7)$
24. $-37 + (-43)$
25. $4 + (-1) + (-5)$
26. $-7 + 2 + (-1)$

27. ◆ **MULTIPLE CHOICE** What is the value of $-31 + 12$?

Ⓐ −43 Ⓑ −19 Ⓒ 19 Ⓓ 43

ERROR ANALYSIS ***Describe*** **and correct the error made in finding the sum.**

28. ✗ $10 + (-15) = -25$

29. ✗ $-36 + 15 = 21$

COMPARING INTEGERS **Copy and complete the statement using <, >, or =.**

30. $|-5| \underline{?} 4$
31. $0 \underline{?} |-1|$
32. $|7| \underline{?} |-7|$
33. $-6 \underline{?} |2|$
34. $|-9| \underline{?} |-2|$
35. $|-12| \underline{?} 12$

36. ◆ **MULTIPLE CHOICE** Which expression has a value greater than −3?

Ⓐ $4 + (-9)$ Ⓑ $3 + (-8) + 1$ Ⓒ $-10 + 8$ Ⓓ $-1 + (-5) + 2$

37. ◆ **MULTIPLE CHOICE** Which statement is true when $x = -3$ and $y = |-3|$?

Ⓐ $y < x$ Ⓑ $0 > y$ Ⓒ $x < y$ Ⓓ $x > 0$

ALGEBRA Evaluate the expression when $a = 6$ and $b = -3$.

38. $-2 + a$
39. $b + (-6)$
40. $a + (-1)$
41. $7 + b$
42. $5 + b + (-4)$
43. $3 + (-3) + b$
44. $-8 + (-1) + a$
45. $4 + b + (-5)$

COMPARING SUMS Copy and complete the statement using <, >, or =.

46. $-2 + 3 + (-10)$ _?_ $(-6) + 12$
47. $-9 + 13$ _?_ $11 + (-7) + (-10)$
48. $5 + (-8) + (-4)$ _?_ $2 + (-9)$
49. $-5 + (-10)$ _?_ $-4 + (-5) + (-6)$

MENTAL MATH Copy and complete the statement using mental math.

50. $-2 +$ _?_ $= 2$
51. $-7 =$ _?_ $+ 10$
52. _?_ $+ (-5) = 0$
53. $8 = -8 +$ _?_
54. $-17 = -9 +$ _?_
55. _?_ $+ (-2) = -12$

CONNECT SKILLS TO PROBLEM SOLVING Exercises 56–59 will help you prepare for problem solving.

Write and evaluate an addition expression to find the value.

56. One atom has 16 protons and 18 electrons. The total charge is _?_.
57. A bird flies to a branch that is 40 feet above the ground. Then the bird descends 14 feet to a branch below. The height of the bird above the ground is _?_ feet.
58. A seal is 10 feet below sea level and dives an additional 30 feet below sea level. The position of the seal relative to sea level is _?_ feet.
59. You make deposits of \$30 and \$25 into your bank account. You make a withdrawal of \$20. Your account balance is \$_?_.

SEE EXAMPLE 5 on p. 137 for Exs. 60–61

60. **BOARD GAMES** You are playing a board game with a friend. You take one card each turn. If you get a positive integer, you move forward. If you get a negative integer, you move backward. You get the five cards shown on your first five turns. How far and in what direction have you moved along the board after these five turns?

California @HomeTutor for problem solving help at classzone.com

61. **SCUBA DIVING** A scuba diver dives to a depth of 60 feet, rises 25 feet, sinks 10 feet, and then rises 25 feet. Write and evaluate an addition expression that gives the diver's final position relative to sea level.

California @HomeTutor for problem solving help at classzone.com

62. **WRITING** *Explain* why the absolute value of a number is never negative.

63. **MULTI-STEP PROBLEM** Disc golf is a version of golf played with discs that are thrown at a target on each hole. *Par* is the expected number of throws needed to hit the target. Your score for each hole is the number of throws you make above or below par. The table gives the scores of two players for the first 7 holes of a 9-hole disc golf course.

Hole	Par	Ann	Leah
1	2	+3	+1
2	4	−1	0
3	4	+1	−1
4	3	−1	+2
5	2	0	+1
6	2	+1	+1
7	3	−1	−1
8	2	+2	?
9	4	?	?

a. **Calculate** What is each player's total score after Hole 7?

b. **Calculate** What does Leah need to score to be tied with Ann after Hole 8?

c. **Predict** Suppose the game is tied after Hole 8. Both players usually need one more throw on Hole 9 than on Hole 8. *Predict* who will win the game. *Explain* your reasoning.

64. ◆ **MULTIPLE CHOICE** Which statement is correct?

(A) The sum of a positive integer and a negative integer is always positive.

(B) The sum of a positive integer and a negative integer is never positive.

(C) The sum of three negative integers is always negative.

(D) The sum of three positive integers is sometimes negative.

65. **CHALLENGE** A bike shop owner records income and expenses by hand. The sum of all transactions for one day was \$20. What amount should be recorded for the new wrench set?

Bikes by the Beach

bicycle sold	\$95
flat tire repaired	\$5
new wrench set	?
cycling jersey sold	\$35
newspaper ad	−\$40

66. **CHALLENGE** You and two friends are playing a trivia game. A correct answer is worth 1 point. An incorrect answer is worth −1 point. You all respond to the ten questions. Beth's score is −2. Eduardo has six correct answers. What is your score if you are in second place? How many of your answers are correct?

◆ CALIFORNIA STANDARDS SPIRAL REVIEW

NS 2.4 67. What is the GCF of 28 and 42? *(p. 10)*

(A) 4 (B) 6 (C) 7 (D) 14

NS 2.1 68. What is the value of $\frac{3}{5} \div \frac{8}{9}$? *(p. 95)*

(A) $\frac{27}{40}$ (B) $\frac{8}{9}$ (C) $1\frac{13}{27}$ (D) $2\frac{2}{3}$

Gr. 5 NS 1.5 69. A 15°F drop in temperature can be represented by which integer? *(p. 129)*

(A) −150 (B) −15 (C) 15 (D) 150

3.3 Modeling Integer Subtraction

MATERIALS • paper and pencil

Standards

NS 2.3 Solve addition, **subtraction**, multiplication, and division **problems**, including those arising in concrete situations, **that use positive and negative integers** and combinations of these operations.

QUESTION How can you model subtracting a positive integer using a number line?

You have used a number line to add integers. You can also use a number line to model subtracting a positive integer. Start at 0. Then move left for a negative integer and right for a positive integer. Finally, move left to subtract a positive integer.

EXPLORE 1 What is the value of 2 − 4?

STEP 1 **Draw** a number line on a piece of paper, or use a row of tiles on the classroom floor to represent a number line. Choose the edge of one tile to represent 0.

STEP 2 **Start** at 0. Move 2 units to the **right**.

STEP 3 **Move** 4 units to the **left**.

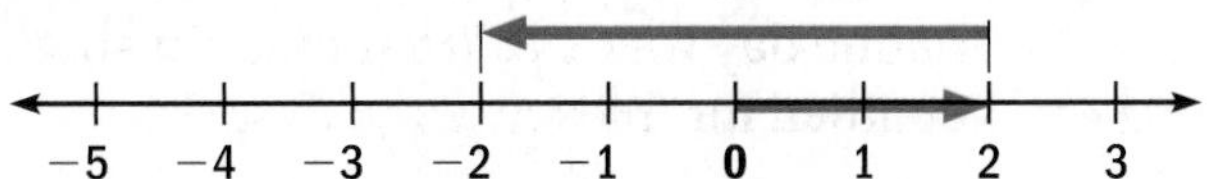

STEP 4 **Find** your final position on the number line. You are at −2, or 2 units to the left of 0. So, 2 − 4 = −2.

EXPLORE 2 What is the value of −3 − 4?

STEP 1 **Draw** a number line on a piece of paper, or use a row of tiles on the classroom floor to represent a number line. Choose the edge of one tile to represent 0.

STEP 2 **Start** at 0. Move 3 units to the **left**.

STEP 3 **Move** 4 units to the **left**.

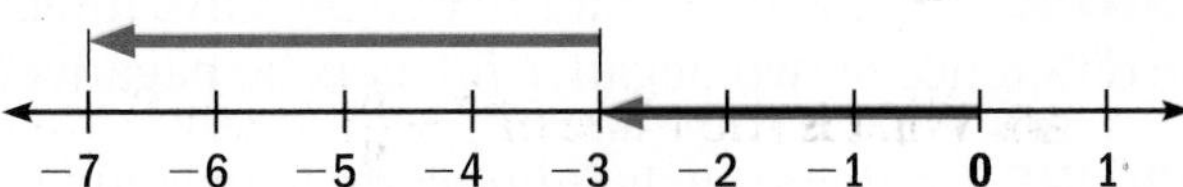

STEP 4 **Find** your final position on the number line. You are at −7, or 7 units to the left of 0. So, −3 − 4 = −7.

Continued on next page

Continued from the previous page

EXPLORE 3 How can you use patterns to subtract integers?

STEP 1 **Copy** the table at the right.

STEP 2 **Describe** the pattern in the *difference* column of the table.

STEP 3 **Complete** the table using the pattern described in Step 2.

Animated Math at classzone.com

Subtraction Expression	Difference	Equivalent Addition Expression
2 − 3	−1	2 + ?
2 − 2	0	2 + ?
2 − 1	1	2 + ?
2 − 0	2	2 + ?
2 − (−1)	?	2 + ?
2 − (−2)	?	2 + ?
2 − (−3)	?	2 + ?

DRAW CONCLUSIONS Use your observations to complete these exercises.

Find the difference using a number line.

1. 3 − 5 **2.** 4 − 7 **3.** 3 − 6 **4.** 1 − 4

5. −2 − 4 **6.** −4 − 2 **7.** −3 − 7 **8.** −1 − 3

9. Copy and complete the table.

Subtraction Expression	Difference	Equivalent Addition Expression
−3 − 3	−6	−3 + ?
−3 − 2	−5	−3 + ?
−3 − 1	−4	−3 + ?
−3 − 0	−3	−3 + ?
−3 − (−1)	?	−3 + ?
−3 − (−2)	?	−3 + ?
−3 − (−3)	?	−3 + ?

10. WRITING Can the difference of two negative integers be positive? Can the difference of two negative integers be negative? *Explain.*

11. WRITING Compare each *Subtraction Expression* in the completed tables to the *Equivalent Addition Expression*. How are they alike? How are they different?

12. REASONING Generalize your results above to suggest a rule for subtracting integers.

3.3 Subtracting Integers

Standards NS 2.3 **Solve** addition, **subtraction,** multiplication, and division **problems, including those arising in concrete situations, that use positive and negative integers** and combinations of these operations.

Connect ***Before*** you added integers. ***Now*** you will subtract integers.

KEY VOCABULARY

• **opposite,** *p. 129*

Number line models of the subtraction expression $5 - 2$ and the addition expression $5 + (-2)$ are shown below.

Subtraction Model: $5 - 2$

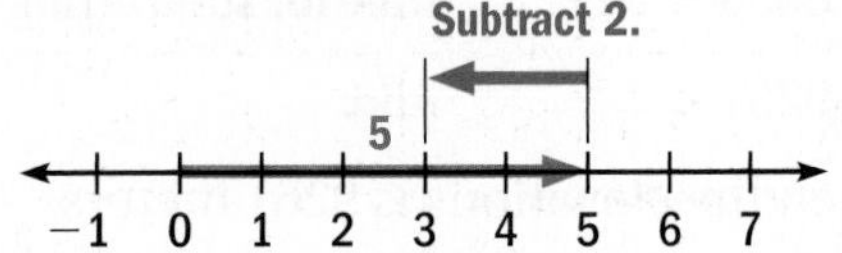

Addition Model: $5 + (-2)$

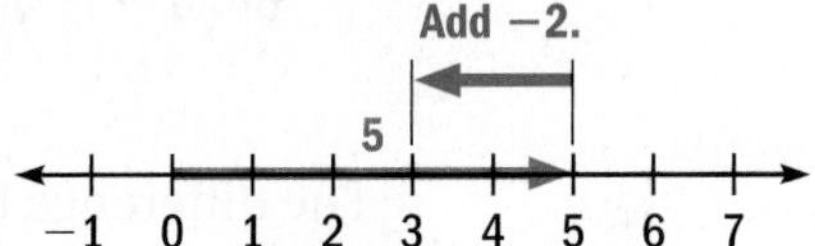

Notice that the model for $5 - 2 = 3$ is identical to the model for $5 + (-2) = 3$. This suggests the following rule for subtracting integers.

About the Standards

As part of Grade 6 Standard MR 3.3, you make generalizations and apply them. The key concept at the right is developed on p. 142 and will be applied throughout this lesson.

KEY CONCEPT *For Your Notebook*

Subtracting Integers

Words To subtract an integer, add its opposite.

Numbers $5 - 7 = 5 + (-7)$ **Algebra** $a - b = a + (-b)$

EXAMPLE 1 Subtracting Integers

a. $2 - 7 = 2 + (-7)$ **To subtract 7, add its opposite, −7.**

$= -5$ **Use rule for adding integers.**

b. $12 - (-9) = 12 + 9$ **To subtract −9, add its opposite, 9.**

$= 21$ **Use rule for adding integers.**

c. $-3 - (-5) = -3 + 5$ **To subtract −5, add its opposite, 5.**

$= 2$ **Use rule for adding integers.**

✓ **GUIDED PRACTICE for Example 1**

Find the difference.

1. $4 - 6$ **2.** $-7 - (-8)$ **3.** $-2 - 1$ **4.** $15 - (-3)$

EXAMPLE 2 ◆ Multiple Choice Practice

The elevation of the Dead Sea is -411 meters.

ELEVATION The highest point in Asia is Mount Everest at 8850 meters. The lowest point in Asia is the shore of the Dead Sea at 411 meters below sea level. What is the difference in elevation between Mount Everest and the Dead Sea?

Ⓐ 8439 meters Ⓑ 8441 meters

Ⓒ 9161 meters Ⓓ 9261 meters

ELIMINATE CHOICES
Mount Everest is above sea level. So, the difference must be greater than 8850 meters. Choices A and B can be eliminated.

SOLUTION

Find the difference of 8850 and -411 meters.

$8850 - (-411) = 8850 + 411$ **Rule for subtracting integers**

$= 9261$ **Add.**

The difference between the elevations is 9261 meters.

▶ **Answer** The correct answer is D. Ⓐ Ⓑ Ⓒ Ⓓ

AMOUNT OF CHANGE You can subtract to find a change in a variable such as temperature. To find the change, subtract the old or start value of the variable from the new or end value of the variable.

A change in a variable is positive when the value increases from start to end. The change is negative when the value decreases from start to end.

EXAMPLE 3 Finding a Change in Temperature

WEATHER In Fairfield, Montana, on December 24, 1924, the air temperature dropped a record amount. The temperature dropped from 63°F to -21°F in twelve hours. What was the change in temperature?

About the Standards
You should check your solution in the context of the original situation as part of Grade 6 Standard MR 2.7.

SOLUTION

Change in temperature = **end temperature** − **start temperature**

$= \mathbf{-21} - \mathbf{63}$ **Substitute values.**

$= -21 + (-63)$ **Rule for subtracting integers**

$= -84$ **Add.**

▶ **Answer** The change in temperature was -84°F. The temperature dropped 84°F.

CHECK Look back at the problem. The temperature dropped more than 63°F, from 63°F to -21°F, so the answer must be negative and greater than 63°F.

✓ GUIDED PRACTICE for Examples 2 and 3

5. **ELEVATION** Find the difference between an elevation of 535 feet above sea level and an elevation of 8 feet below sea level.

6. **TEMPERATURE** The temperature at 6 A.M. was $-12°F$. At 3 P.M. the temperature was $32°F$. What was the change in temperature?

3.3 EXERCISES

HOMEWORK KEY

◆ = **MULTIPLE CHOICE PRACTICE** Exs. 21, 34, 43, 56–58

○ = **HINTS AND HOMEWORK HELP** for Exs. 7, 13, 45 at classzone.com

SKILLS • PROBLEM SOLVING • REASONING

1. **VOCABULARY** Copy and complete: To simplify the expression $8 - (-9)$, you can add the _?_ of -9 to 8.

2. **WRITING** A negative integer is subtracted from a positive integer. Is the result *positive* or *negative*? *Explain* your reasoning.

SEE EXAMPLE 1 on p. 143 for Exs. 3–21

MATCHING EXPRESSIONS Match the subtraction expression with the equivalent addition expression.

3. $-7 - 3$
4. $7 - (-3)$
5. $-7 - (-3)$
6. $7 - 3$

A. $-7 + 3$
B. $7 + (-3)$
C. $-7 + (-3)$
D. $7 + 3$

SUBTRACTING INTEGERS Find the difference.

7. $13 - (-4)$
8. $-9 - 3$
9. $10 - 12$
10. $-17 - 9$
11. $15 - (-18)$
12. $13 - 24$
13. $25 - 5$
14. $7 - (-7)$
15. $-5 - (-25)$
16. $-54 - (-7)$
17. $-56 - 28$
18. $33 - (-27)$

ERROR ANALYSIS ***Describe*** **and correct the subtraction error made.**

19. ✗ $3 - (-6) = 3 - 6 = -3$

20. ✗ $-8 - (-4) = 8 + 4 = 12$

21. ◆ **MULTIPLE CHOICE** What is the value of $-14 - (-7)$?

Ⓐ -21 Ⓑ -7 Ⓒ -2 Ⓓ 7

ALGEBRA Evaluate the expression for the given value of the variable.

22. $m - 5$ when $m = 4$
23. $9 - y$ when $y = -11$
24. $-22 - x$ when $x = -16$
25. $t - (-63)$ when $t = -17$
26. $-16 - r$ when $r = -12$
27. $-42 - z$ when $z = 23$

MENTAL MATH **Copy and complete using <, >, or =.**

28. $-4 - (-5) \underline{?} 0$ **29.** $5 - (-8) \underline{?} 0$ **30.** $-8 - 9 \underline{?} 0$

31. $6 - (-2) \underline{?} 4$ **32.** $3 - 5 \underline{?} 2$ **33.** $-4 - 5 \underline{?} -9$

34. ◆ **MULTIPLE CHOICE** Which expression has the greatest value?

Ⓐ $-3 - (-4)$ Ⓑ $2 - (-5)$ Ⓒ $-6 - 4$ Ⓓ $-2 - (-8)$

COMPARING DIFFERENCES **Copy and complete the statement using <, >, or =.**

35. $4 - (-1) \underline{?} 7 - 4$ **36.** $-3 - (-9) \underline{?} 5 - (-2)$

37. $-6 - 8 - (-5) \underline{?} 2 - (-10)$ **38.** $2 - 9 \underline{?} -4 - (-3) - 6$

CONNECT SKILLS TO PROBLEM SOLVING **Exercises 39–42 will help you prepare for problem solving.**

Write a subtraction expression to represent each value.

39. Your score in a game is 300 points and your friend's score is −100 points. The difference between your score and your friend's score is ?.

40. The high temperature for the day was 12°C and the low temperature was −3°C. The difference between the high and low temperature was ?.

41. An elevator is 75 feet above ground and descends to a level that is 35 feet below ground. The change in elevation of the elevator is ?.

42. On Monday, the price of a stock was $14 per share. On Tuesday, the price of the same stock was $8 per share. The change in the stock price was ?.

SEE EXAMPLE 2 on p. 144 for Ex. 43

43. ◆ **MULTIPLE CHOICE** The highest and lowest points in South America are Mount Aconcagua at 22,834 feet above sea level and the Valdes Peninsula at 131 feet below sea level. What is the difference between these highest and lowest elevations?

Ⓐ 22,703 ft Ⓑ 22,819 ft Ⓒ 22,965 ft Ⓓ 24,144 ft

California @HomeTutor for problem solving help at classzone.com

SEE EXAMPLE 3 on p. 144 for Ex. 44

44. **MULTI-STEP PROBLEM** A professional cliff diver dives from a ledge 65 feet above the surface of the water. The diver reaches an underwater depth of 15 feet before returning to the surface.

a. What operation do you use to find a change in elevation?

b. Which integers represent the highest and lowest elevations of the dive?

c. Write and evaluate an expression to find the change in elevations from the highest to the lowest points of the dive.

California @HomeTutor for problem solving help at classzone.com

Initial Height: 65 feet

SEE EXAMPLE 3 on p. 144 for Ex. 45

45. **DEATH VALLEY** The lowest point in Death Valley, California, is 282 feet below sea level and the highest point is 11,049 feet above sea level. What is the change in elevation from the highest point to the lowest point?

46. **PLANET TEMPERATURES** A temperature expressed using the Kelvin (K) unit can be converted to degrees Celsius (°C) by using the formula $C = K - 273$. Convert the temperatures given in the table to degrees Celsius.

Planet	Mean Surface Temperature
Mercury	452 K
Earth	281 K
Jupiter	120 K
Saturn	88 K
Pluto	37 K

47. **SHORT RESPONSE** *Describe* the following pattern in two ways: 2, −1, −4, −7, ... Write the next three integers. *Explain* how this shows the relationship between integer addition and integer subtraction.

48. **REASONING** When you subtract an integer from its opposite, is the result always positive? *Justify* your answer using examples of both positive and negative integers.

49. **HISTORY** The illustration shows the beginning construction dates of significant landmarks. The positive integers represent the years A.D. and the negative integers represent the years B.C. Find the difference between each pair of events listed.

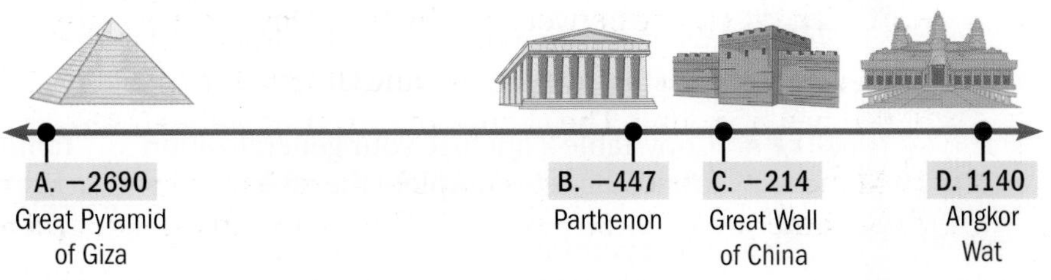

a. D and A b. D and B c. A and C d. B and C

CHALLENGE For what values of *a* and *b* is the statement true?

50. $|a - b| = |a| - |b|$

51. $-|a - b| = |b - a|$

52. $|a - b| = |b - a|$

53. $|a + b| = |a| + |b|$

54. $|a + b| = |a| - |b|$

55. $|a + b| = -|a - b|$

◆ CALIFORNIA STANDARDS SPIRAL REVIEW

NS 2.3

56. What is the value of 221 + (−460)? ***(p. 135)***

(A) −681 (B) −239 (C) 239 (D) 681

Gr. 5 NS 2.1

57. What is the value of 3.45 × 0.62? ***(p. 107)***

(A) 0.2139 (B) 2.139 (C) 21.39 (D) 213.9

NS 2.1

58. Bill ate $\frac{5}{12}$ of a salad for lunch and $\frac{1}{3}$ of the same salad for dinner. What fraction represents the amount of salad that is uneaten? ***(p. 69)***

(A) $\frac{1}{12}$ (B) $\frac{1}{4}$ (C) $\frac{1}{3}$ (D) $\frac{3}{4}$

3.4 Multiplying Integers

Math and SHIPPING
Ex. 59, p. 152

Standards **NS 2.3** **Solve** addition, subtraction, **multiplication**, and division **problems, including those arising in concrete situations, that use positive and negative integers** and combinations of these operations.

Connect ***Before*** you multiplied whole numbers, decimals, and fractions. ***Now*** you will multiply integers.

KEY VOCABULARY
- **opposite**, *p. 129*

About the Standards

In the activity, you analyze patterns to generalize a rule for multiplying integers as part of Grade 6 Standards MR 1.1 and MR 1.2.

ACTIVITY

You can use patterns to find rules for multiplying numbers.

STEP 1 Copy and complete Table 1.

STEP 2 What pattern do you see in each column in Table 1? Extend Table 1 using these patterns to find the next two products, $3 \cdot (-1)$ and $3 \cdot (-2)$.

STEP 3 What do you notice about the product of a positive integer and a negative integer?

STEP 4 Copy Table 2 and use your generalization from Step 3 to complete the table.

STEP 5 What pattern do you see in each column in Table 2? Extend Table 2 using these patterns to find the next two products, $-3 \cdot (-1)$ and $-3 \cdot (-2)$.

STEP 6 What do you notice about the product of two negative integers?

Table 1

Expression	Product
$3 \cdot 3$	9
$3 \cdot 2$	?
$3 \cdot 1$	?
$3 \cdot 0$	?

Table 2

Expression	Product
$-3 \cdot 3$	?
$-3 \cdot 2$	?
$-3 \cdot 1$	?
$-3 \cdot 0$	?

The activity suggests that there are three rules for multiplying integers.

KEY CONCEPT *For Your Notebook*

Multiplying Integers

Words	Numbers
Same Signs The product of two integers with the same sign is positive.	$4 \cdot 2 = 8$ $-4 \cdot (-2) = 8$
Different Signs The product of two integers with different signs is negative.	$4 \cdot (-2) = -8$ $-4 \cdot 2 = -8$
Zero The product of an integer and 0 is 0.	$4 \cdot 0 = 0$ $-4 \cdot 0 = 0$

EXAMPLE 1 Multiplying Integers

READING
You can also represent multiplication using parentheses.
$4(6) = 4 \cdot 6 = 4 \times 6$

a. $-5(-7) = 35$ **The product of two integers with the same sign is positive.**

b. $-8(2) = -16$ **The product of two integers with different signs is negative.**

c. $-12(0) = 0$ **The product of an integer and 0 is 0.**

OPPOSITES The activity suggests that multiplying a number by -1 produces its opposite. For example, $-1 \cdot 3 = -3$ and $(-1)(-3) = 3$. This suggests that the opposite of a, $(-a)$, can be written as $(-1) \cdot a$.

EXAMPLE 2 Evaluating Variable Expressions

Evaluate $-5 \cdot (-a)$ when $a = -3$.

SOLUTION

$-5 \cdot (-a) = -5 \cdot [(-1) \cdot a]$	**Rewrite $-a$ as $(-1) \cdot a$.**
$= -5[(-1)(-3)]$	**Substitute -3 for a.**
$= -5(3)$	**Multiply -1 and -3.**
$= -15$	**Multiply -5 and 3.**

EXAMPLE 3 Using Integer Multiplication

GREENLAND Most of Greenland is covered with ice that can reach a thickness of up to 2 miles. Scientists estimate that 3 feet of this ice melts each year. Find the change in the thickness of the ice after 10 years.

Ice melts 3 feet per year.

ANOTHER WAY
For an alternative method for solving the problem in Example 3, turn to page 153 for the **Problem Solving Workshop**.

SOLUTION

You can find the total change in the ice thickness by multiplying the yearly change by the number of years. Use -3 for the yearly change because the thickness of the ice decreases by 3 feet each year.

Change in ice thickness $= -3(10) = -30$

▶ **Answer** The thickness of the ice will decrease 30 feet in 10 years.

✓ GUIDED PRACTICE for Examples 1, 2, and 3

Find the product.

1. $-9(2)$ **2.** $-3(-4)$ **3.** $5(-5)$ **4.** $0(-14)$

5. Evaluate $5 \cdot (-b)$ when $b = -2$. **6.** Evaluate $-a \cdot (8)$ when $a = -6$.

7. WHAT IF? In Example 3, what is the change in thickness of the ice after 8 years?

3.4 EXERCISES

HOMEWORK KEY ◆ = **MULTIPLE CHOICE PRACTICE** Exs. 26, 27, 54, 62–64

○ = **HINTS AND HOMEWORK HELP** for Exs. 5, 15, 55 at classzone.com

SKILLS • PROBLEM SOLVING • REASONING

VOCABULARY **Copy and complete using *positive* or *negative*.**

1. The product of two negative integers is _?_.
2. The product of a negative integer and its opposite is _?_.
3. **WRITING** *Explain* how to find the product of three negative integers.

SEE EXAMPLE 1 on p. 149 for Exs. 4–26

MULTIPLYING INTEGERS **Find the product.**

4. $4(8)$ 5. $-3(11)$ 6. $5(-6)$ 7. $-2(-12)$

8. $11(10)$ 9. $0(-15)$ 10. $-9(-7)$ 11. $-8(5)$

12. $-13(0)$ 13. $15(-2)$ 14. $-5(7)$ 15. $-4(-7)$

16. $6(-6)(2)$ 17. $-4(-4)(-2)$ 18. $10(0)(-7)$ 19. $5(-1)(9)$

20. $2(1)(-11)(6)$ 21. $8(-3)(2)(-6)$ 22. $7(3)(-4)(0)$ 23. $-5(-5)(3)(-2)$

ERROR ANALYSIS ***Describe*** **and correct the error made in multiplying.**

24. ✗ $(-3)(-6) = -18$

25. ✗ $5(-3) = 5(-1)(-3) = 15$

26. ◆ **MULTIPLE CHOICE** What is the product of -9 and -11?

(A) -99 (B) -20 (C) 2 (D) 99

SEE EXAMPLE 2 on p. 149 for Exs. 27–35

27. ◆ **MULTIPLE CHOICE** What is the value of $11 \cdot (-a)$ when $a = -3$?

(A) -33 (B) 8 (C) 14 (D) 33

xy EVALUATING EXPRESSIONS **Evaluate the expression when $a = -5$, $b = -2$, and $c = -7$.**

28. $7 \cdot c$ 29. $-4 \cdot b$ 30. $-5 \cdot a$ 31. $3 \cdot b$

32. $-8 \cdot (-c)$ 33. $-a \cdot 4$ 34. $2 \cdot (-4) \cdot (-b)$ 35. $5 \cdot (-c) \cdot (-4)$

MENTAL MATH **Copy and complete the statement using mental math.**

36. $-25 \cdot$ _?_ $= -100$ 37. $2 \cdot$ _?_ $= -10$ 38. $-6 \cdot$ _?_ $= -60$

39. $-9 \cdot$ _?_ $= 36$ 40. $4 \cdot$ _?_ $= -32$ 41. $-5 \cdot$ _?_ $= 65$

42. $-4 \cdot$ _?_ $= -48$ 43. $3 \cdot$ _?_ $= -3$ 44. $-3 \cdot$ _?_ $= -27$

NUMBER SENSE **Find the missing numbers in the multiplication pattern.**

45. __, -63, 189, __, 1701 46. 7, -28, __, __, 1792 47. -5, __, __, 625, -3125

CONNECT SKILLS TO PROBLEM SOLVING **Exercises 48–51 will help you prepare for problem solving.**

48. The change, in dollars, of the price of a stock can be given by the expression $(-3)(5)$. What is the change in price of the stock?

49. The change, in feet, of the altitude of a hot air balloon can be given by the expression $(-9)(20)$. What is the change in the altitude?

50. Mary withdraws \$20 from her bank account each day for 4 days. Write a multiplication expression to find the change in Mary's bank account.

51. The water level of an ocean bay falls 2 feet per hour from high tide until low tide 5 hours later. Write a multiplication expression to find the change in the water level during this time.

SEE EXAMPLE 3 on p. 149 for Exs. 52–56

52. ANTARCTICA At McMurdo Station, Antarctica, the average low temperature for May is 16°F below 0°F. The lowest recorded temperature is 3 times the average low temperature for May.

a. What integer represents the average low temperature for May?

b. What operation is needed to find the lowest recorded temperature for May?

c. Write and evaluate an expression to find the lowest temperature recorded in May at McMurdo Station.

California @HomeTutor for problem solving help at classzone.com

53. DIVING SEALS A seal dives at a speed of 2 meters per second. What is the change in the seal's position after 30 seconds?

California @HomeTutor for problem solving help at classzone.com

Seal diving in a kelp forest

54. ◆ MULTIPLE CHOICE A whale dives at a speed of 3 feet per second. What value represents the whale's change in position after 15 seconds?

Ⓐ -45 feet Ⓑ -15 feet

Ⓒ 18 feet Ⓓ 45 feet

55. MULTI-STEP PROBLEM The temperature at 11:00 P.M. is -9°F. The temperature has been falling 3°F per hour for 7 hours.

a. Write an integer to represent the hourly change in temperature.

b. Write a multiplication expression to find how much warmer the temperature was 7 hours earlier.

c. What was the temperature at 4:00 P.M.?

56. AIRPLANE LANDING An airplane descends 4 feet every second prior to landing. What is the airplane's altitude 10 seconds prior to landing?

57. PUZZLE PROBLEM What is the least possible sum of two integers whose product is 36? *Justify* your answer.

58. **GAMES** Peter is playing a card game in which he gains points for playing cards and loses points for cards left in his hand. Each jack, queen, and king is worth 10 points. Each ace and the numbers 2 through 10 are worth 5 points. Peter has gained 30 points, but he still has 2 jacks, a 3, a 7, and an 8 left in his hand.

a. Multiply to find the value of the jacks left in Peter's hand.

b. Multiply to find the values of the 3, 7, and 8 left in his hand.

c. What is Peter's score for the game?

59. **PANAMA CANAL** In the Panama Canal, a system of locks releases water from upper chambers into lower chambers so that ships can move through the canal. The water level in an upper chamber begins at 72 feet and falls about 3 feet every minute for 9 minutes.

Write and evaluate an expression that represents the change in the water depth after 9 minutes. Then find the depth of the water after 9 minutes.

Panama Canal

60. **CHALLENGE** The first four numbers in a pattern are -1, 2, -3, and 4. What is the 25th number in the pattern?

61. **CHALLENGE** Imagine creating a three-digit integer and a two-digit integer using each of the digits 1, 3, 5, 7, and 9 exactly once. The integers may be either positive or negative. What two integers give the greatest possible product? the least possible product? What are these products?

◆ CALIFORNIA STANDARDS SPIRAL REVIEW

Gr. 5 NS 2.1 62. What is the value of $10.24 \div 6.4$? *(p. 107)*

Ⓐ 0.16 Ⓑ 1.6 Ⓒ 16 Ⓓ 160

NS 2.3 63. What is the value of $32 - (-46)$? *(p. 143)*

Ⓐ -78 Ⓑ -14 Ⓒ 14 Ⓓ 78

NS 2.3 64. Mary makes a deposit of \$425 into her bank account and withdraws \$230 and \$145. What is the change in her bank account balance? *(p. 135)*

Ⓐ $-\$800$ Ⓑ $-\$50$ Ⓒ \$50 Ⓓ \$800

PROBLEM SOLVING WORKSHOP
LESSON 3.4

Using ALTERNATIVE METHODS

Another Way to Solve Example 3, page 149

Standards
NS 2.3

In Example 3 on page 149, you saw how to solve the problem about the change in ice thickness by using integer multiplication. You can also solve the problem by using repeated addition on a number line.

PROBLEM

GREENLAND Most of Greenland is covered with ice that can reach a thickness of up to 2 miles. Scientists estimate that 3 feet of this ice melts each year. Find the change in the thickness of the ice after 10 years.

METHOD

Using a Number Line An alternate approach is to use addition on a number line.

STEP 1 **Write** the yearly change as an integer.

Use -3 for the yearly change because the thickness of the ice decreases by 3 feet each year.

STEP 2 **Write** an addition expression to represent the change in thickness after 10 years.

$$-3 + (-3) + (-3) + (-3) + (-3) + (-3) + (-3) + (-3) + (-3) + (-3)$$

STEP 3 **Use** a number line to find the sum of the addition expression.

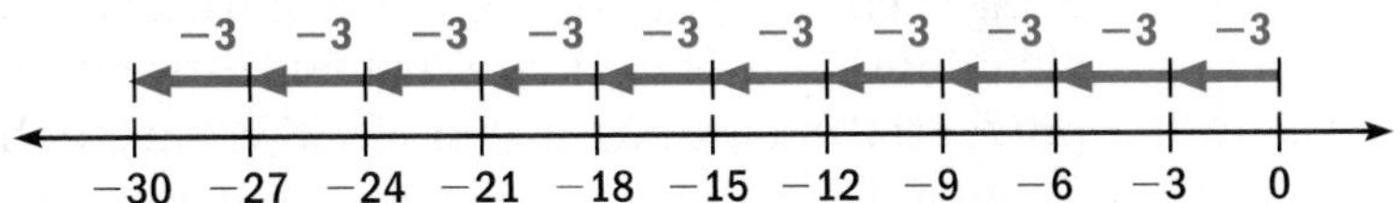

▶ **Answer** The thickness of the ice will decrease 30 feet in 10 years.

PRACTICE

1. **DOLPHINS** The northern bottle-nosed dolphin can dive at a speed of 3 feet per second. Suppose a northern bottle-nosed dolphin descends at 3 feet per second for 12 seconds. Use a number line to find the change in the depth of the dolphin after 12 seconds.

2. **GAME SHOWS** On a game show, a player gains 10 points for every correct answer and loses 5 points for every incorrect answer. Sarah answers the first 4 questions correctly, and then answers the next 7 questions incorrectly. Find her score using a number line. Find her score without using a number line.

3.5 Dividing Integers

Standards **NS 2.3** **Solve** addition, subtraction, multiplication, and **division problems, including those arising in concrete situations, that use positive and negative integers and combinations of these operations.**

Connect ***Before*** you multiplied integers. ***Now*** you will divide integers.

Math and **SCIENCE**
Ex. 42, p. 157

KEY VOCABULARY
- **mean**

ACTIVITY

You can evaluate a division problem by using related multiplication.

STEP 1 **Copy** and complete the table.

Division Problem	*Related Multiplication Sentence*	*Quotient*
$18 \div 9 = ?$	$? \cdot 9 = 18$	2
$-15 \div 5 = ?$	?	?
$-14 \div 7 = ?$	?	?
$10 \div (-2) = ?$	?	?
$-12 \div (-4) = ?$	?	?

STEP 2 **Copy** and complete the statement using *positive* or *negative*.

a. A negative integer divided by a positive integer is __?__.

b. A positive integer divided by a negative integer is __?__.

c. A negative integer divided by a negative integer is __?__.

Rules for dividing integers are similar to rules for multiplying integers.

KEY CONCEPT *For Your Notebook*

Dividing Integers

Words	**Numbers**
Same Signs The quotient of two integers with the same sign is positive.	$10 \div 2 = 5, \frac{-24}{-3} = 8$
Different Signs The quotient of two integers with different signs is negative.	$15 \div (-3) = -5, \frac{-18}{6} = -3$
Zero The quotient of 0 and any nonzero integer is 0.	$0 \div 17 = 0, \frac{0}{-9} = 0$

EXAMPLE 1 ◆ Multiple Choice Practice

What is the value of $28 \div (-4)$?

Ⓐ -32 Ⓑ -7 Ⓒ 7 Ⓓ 32

ELIMINATE CHOICES

The quotient of two integers with different signs is negative, so choices C and D can be eliminated.

SOLUTION

$28 \div (-4) = -7$ ← **Divide 28 by 4.**

The quotient of two integers with different signs is negative.

▶ **Answer** The correct answer is B. Ⓐ Ⓑ Ⓒ Ⓓ

DIVIDING BY ZERO You cannot divide by 0. The quotient is *undefined*. To see why, rewrite $8 \div 0 = \underline{?}$ as $\underline{?} \cdot 0 = 8$. This statement, $\underline{?} \cdot 0 = 8$, is never true because any number multiplied by 0 is 0.

EXAMPLE 2 Dividing Integers

Find the quotient.

a. $-10 \div (-5) = 2$ ← **Divide 10 by 5.**

The quotient of two integers with the same sign is positive.

CHECK Use multiplication to check the answer. Because $2 \times (-5) = -10$, the answer is correct.

b. $\frac{-12}{3} = -4$ ← **Divide 12 by 3.**

The quotient of two integers with different signs is negative.

CHECK Because $-4 \times 3 = -12$, the answer is correct.

c. $\frac{0}{-5} = 0$ ← **The quotient of 0 and any nonzero integer is 0.**

CHECK Because $0 \times (-5) = 0$, the answer is correct.

✓ GUIDED PRACTICE for Examples 1 and 2

Find the quotient.

1. $-24 \div (-6)$ **2.** $-15 \div 3$ **3.** $72 \div (-2)$ **4.** $0 \div (-9)$

5. $\frac{0}{-12}$ **6.** $\frac{36}{-6}$ **7.** $\frac{-81}{9}$ **8.** $\frac{-39}{3}$

MEAN The **mean** of a data set is the sum of the values divided by the number of values.

EXAMPLE 3 Finding a Mean

COLD TEMPERATURES The table shows the high temperatures in Bangor, Maine, for five days in January. Find the mean daily high temperature.

Day	*Temperature*
Monday	3°C
Tuesday	–3°C
Wednesday	–5°C
Thursday	2°C
Friday	–7°C

About the Standards

This lesson introduces *mean*. You will learn more about *mean* in Chapter 7 as part of Grade 6 Standard SDAP 1.1.

SOLUTION

The mean is calculated by finding the sum of the high temperatures and then dividing by the number of days.

$$\text{Mean} = \frac{3 + (-3) + (-5) + 2 + (-7)}{5} = \frac{-10}{5} = -2$$

Answer The mean daily high temperature was -2°C.

✓ GUIDED PRACTICE for Example 3

9. Find the mean of the elevations below.
-284 ft, -245 ft, -372 ft, -356 ft, and -343 ft

3.5 EXERCISES

HOMEWORK KEY

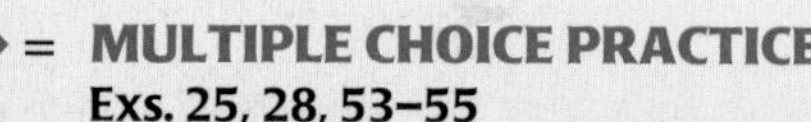

◆ = **MULTIPLE CHOICE PRACTICE** Exs. 25, 28, 53–55

○ = **HINTS AND HOMEWORK HELP** for Exs. 9, 19, 45 at classzone.com

SKILLS • PROBLEM SOLVING • REASONING

VOCABULARY **Copy and complete the statement.**

1. The quotient of a negative integer and a positive integer is _?_.
2. The quotient of two negative integers is _?_.
3. The quotient of any positive or negative number and zero is _?_.
4. **WRITING** What can you tell about two integers when their quotient is positive? negative? zero? *Explain* your reasoning.

SEE EXAMPLES 1 AND 2 on p. 155 for Exs. 5–24

DIVIDING INTEGERS **Find the quotient.**

5. $-44 \div 11$	**6.** $-64 \div 32$	**7.** $70 \div (-10)$	**8.** $34 \div (-17)$
(9.) $-76 \div (-19)$	**10.** $-84 \div (-7)$	**11.** $-63 \div (-9)$	**12.** $-52 \div 13$
13. $-24 \div 8$	**14.** $72 \div (-9)$	**15.** $0 \div (-121)$	**16.** $-96 \div (-12)$
17. $6 \div (-2)$	**18.** $0 \div (-12)$	**(19.)** $-26 \div 13$	**20.** $-42 \div (-7)$
21. $-32 \div 0$	**22.** $0 \div (-3)$	**23.** $-48 \div 12$	**24.** $-42 \div 0$

25. ◆ **MULTIPLE CHOICE** What is the value of $68 \div (-2)$?

Ⓐ -66 Ⓑ -34 Ⓒ 34 Ⓓ 66

ERROR ANALYSIS ***Describe*** **and correct the division error made.**

26. ✗ $-20 \div (-5) = -4$

27. ✗ $\frac{-24}{12} = 2$

28. ◆ **MULTIPLE CHOICE** Which expression has a value of -6?

Ⓐ $-24 \div (-4)$ Ⓑ $42 \div 7$ Ⓒ $48 \div (-8)$ Ⓓ $-42 \div (-7)$

SEE EXAMPLE 3 on p. 156 for Exs. 29–34

FINDING MEANS **Find the mean of the integers.**

29. $-10, -6, 3, 9$
30. $7, -9, 9, -7, 0$
31. $-46, -33, 0, 11$
32. $10, -27, 6, -9$
33. $-17, -4, 5, 21, 30$
34. $8, -11, 18, -8, -2$

COMPARING QUOTIENTS **Copy and complete the statement using <, >, or =.**

35. $-4 \div 2$? $-4 \div (-2)$
36. $46 \div (-23)$? $-46 \div 23$
37. $0 \div 4$? $0 \div 7$
38. $-25 \div (-5)$? $5 \div (-1)$

CONNECT SKILLS TO PROBLEM SOLVING **Exercises 39–41 will help you prepare for problem solving.**

Use the following information: A bowling alley's gains and losses over several weeks are \$450, −\$675, \$1230, −\$776, and −\$95.

39. Find the sum of the gains and losses for the bowling alley.
40. How many weeks of data are included in the list?
41. Use your answers to Exercises 39 and 40 to find the mean.

SEE EXAMPLE 3 on p. 156 for Exs. 42–43

42. **MACAQUE MONKEYS** During the winter in Japan, macaque monkeys find warmth in a hot spring that is fed by the Shirane Volcano. The water temperatures at noon for 5 days were 35°C, 39°C, 38°C, 35°C, and 38°C. Find the mean water temperature. The mean air temperature is −5°C. What is the difference between the mean water temperature and the mean air temperature?

California @HomeTutor for problem solving help at classzone.com

Macaque monkey in hot spring where the air temperature is −5°C

43. **WEATHER** During a storm, the temperature drops 28°F in 4 hours. What is the mean change in temperature per hour?

California @HomeTutor for problem solving help at classzone.com

44. **REASONING** Is a nonzero integer divided by its opposite always equal to -1? *Explain* and include examples.

45. **SHORT RESPONSE** Use a number line to explain why a negative integer divided by a negative integer must be a positive integer.

CHALLENGE Use the number line to complete the statement using <, >, or =.

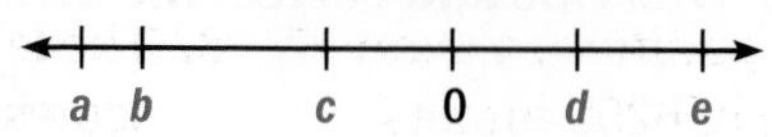

46. $a \div c \underline{?} 0$ **47.** $d \div c \underline{?} 0$ **48.** $e \div d \underline{?} a$

49. $0 \div a \underline{?} 0 \div e$ **50.** $e \div a \underline{?} e \div d$ **51.** $c \div d \underline{?} a \div b$

52. CHALLENGE The mean of five daily high temperatures is −3°C. Four of the temperatures are shown. Find the fifth temperature.

−2°C −7°C 1°C −4°C

◆ CALIFORNIA STANDARDS SPIRAL REVIEW

NS 2.2 **53.** What is the value of $5 \div \frac{3}{4}$? *(p. 95)*

Ⓐ $3\frac{3}{4}$ Ⓑ $4\frac{1}{4}$ Ⓒ $5\frac{4}{3}$ Ⓓ $6\frac{2}{3}$

Gr. 5 NS 1.3 **54.** What is the value of 6^3? *(p. 663)*

Ⓐ 2 Ⓑ 18 Ⓒ 216 Ⓓ 729

MR 2.0 **55.** The sum of the digits of a two digit number is 9. The tens' digit is 3 more than twice the ones' digit. What is the number? *(p. 47)*

Ⓐ 27 Ⓑ 36 Ⓒ 63 Ⓓ 72

QUIZ *for Lessons 3.1–3.5*

Write the integer that represents the situation. *(p. 129)*

1. profit of $85 **2.** loss of 7 yards **3.** 12 degrees below 0

Order the integers from least to greatest. *(p. 129)*

4. −1, 3, −3, 0, −5 **5.** 0, −7, 6, −3, 2 **6.** 11, −11, 3, −3, −7

7. Name two different integers that have an absolute value of 25. *(p. 135)*

Evaluate the expression.

8. $-7 + (-4)$ *(p. 135)* **9.** $21 + (-15)$ *(p. 135)* **10.** $17 - (-17)$ *(p. 143)*

11. $-6(13)$ *(p. 148)* **12.** $56 \div (-7)$ *(p. 154)* **13.** $-15 \div (-3)$ *(p. 154)*

14. STOCK MARKET A newspaper reports these changes in the price of a stock over five days: −2, −3, 6, −8, 2. Find the mean daily change. *(p.154)*

15. TEMPERATURE At dawn this morning, the temperature was −3°F. By noon, the temperature was 25°F. What was the change in temperature? *(p. 143)*

MIXED REVIEW *of Skills and Problem Solving*

Multiple Choice Practice for Lessons 3.1–3.5

1. On a mountain climbing expedition, a team descends from an elevation of 6250 meters at Camp B to an elevation of 4595 meters at Camp A. Which statement describes how to find the team's change in elevation? **NS 2.3**

   Ⓐ Add 4595 and 6250.

   Ⓑ Add −4595 and −6250.

   Ⓒ Subtract 4595 from 6250.

   Ⓓ Subtract 6250 from 4595.

2. What is the value of $-16 + (-37)$? **NS 2.3**

   Ⓐ −53 Ⓑ −21

   Ⓒ 21 Ⓓ 53

3. **NUMBER CLUES** The clues below give information about the location of integers represented by the letters *a*, *b*, *c*, *d*, and *e* on a number line. How many of the integers are negative? **Gr. 5 NS 1.5**

   - *c* lies halfway between *e* and *a*.
   - *a* is a positive integer.
   - *b* lies 6 units to the right of *a*.
   - *e* lies halfway between *d* and *c*.
   - *c* is a negative integer.

   Ⓐ 1 Ⓑ 2

   Ⓒ 3 Ⓓ more than 3

4. What are the next three numbers in the pattern below? **NS 2.3**

   2, −4, 8, −16, . . .

   Ⓐ 18, −20, 22 Ⓑ −18, 20, −22

   Ⓒ 32, −64, 128 Ⓓ −32, 64, −128

5. What is the value of $-13(-7)$? **NS 2.3**

   Ⓐ −91 Ⓑ −6

   Ⓒ 20 Ⓓ 91

6. The table gives the scores of two players for a 9 hole game of golf. The least total score wins. Noah won the game by two strokes. What was Collin's score on the 9th hole? **NS 2.3, MR 1.3**

Hole	Collin	Noah
1	−1	0
2	+1	−1
3	+1	+1
4	0	−1
5	+2	+1
6	+1	+2
7	−2	−1
8	−1	0
9	?	−1

   Ⓐ −2

   Ⓑ −1

   Ⓒ +1

   Ⓓ +2

7. A brown pelican is flying 20 feet above the surface of the water. The pelican dives down and catches a fish swimming 5 feet below the surface. What is the pelican's change in elevation for the dive? **NS 2.3, MR 1.1**

   Ⓐ −25 feet Ⓑ −15 feet

   Ⓒ 15 feet Ⓓ 25 feet

8. What is the mean of 19, −22, −34, 21, −8, and 12? **NS 2.3**

   Ⓐ −12 Ⓑ −2

   Ⓒ $19\frac{1}{3}$ Ⓓ 116

3.6 Order of Operations

Math and MUSIC
Example 1, p. 160

Standards **AF 1.4 Solve problems manually by using the correct order of operations** or by using a scientific calculator.

NS 2.3 Solve addition, subtraction, multiplication and division problems, including those arising in concrete situations, that use positive and negative integers and combinations of these operations.

Connect ***Before*** you evaluated expressions involving one operation. ***Now*** you will evaluate expressions involving two or more operations.

KEY VOCABULARY
- **order of operations**

MUSIC You buy a used guitar for \$50. You then pay \$10 for each of five guitar lessons. The total cost can be found by evaluating the expression $50 + 10 \times 5$. Is the total cost \$100 or \$300?

To make sure everyone gets the same result when evaluating an expression, mathematicians always use a set of rules called the **order of operations**.

KEY CONCEPT *For Your Notebook*

Order of Operations

1. Evaluate expressions inside grouping symbols.
2. Evaluate powers.
3. Multiply and divide from left to right.
4. Add and subtract from left to right.

EXAMPLE 1 Following Order of Operations

To find the guitar costs described above, evaluate $50 + 10 \times 5$.

$50 + 10 \times 5 = 50 + 50$	**First multiply 10 and 5.**
$= 100$	**Then add 50 and 50.**

▸ **Answer** The total cost is \$100.

GUIDED PRACTICE for Example 1

Evaluate the expression.

1. $5 + 6 \times 5$
2. $20 - 4^2 \div 2$
3. $10 \times 3 + 3^3$
4. **WHAT IF?** In Example 1, suppose each guitar lesson costs \$8. What is the total cost of buying the guitar and taking five guitar lessons?

LEFT-TO-RIGHT RULE When an expression has a string of additions and subtractions or a string of multiplications and divisions, you need to perform the operations in order from left to right.

EXAMPLE 2 Using the Left-to-Right Rule

a. $12 - 7 + 3 - 6 = 5 + 3 - 6$ **Subtract 7 from 12.**

$= 8 - 6$ **Add 5 and 3.**

$= 2$ **Subtract 6 from 8.**

b. $54 \div \frac{9}{11} \times 0.3 = 54 \times \frac{11}{9} \times 0.3$ **Multiply by reciprocal.**

$= 66 \times 0.3$ **Multiply 54 and $\frac{11}{9}$.**

$= 19.8$ **Multiply 66 and 0.3.**

EXAMPLE 3 ◆ Multiple Choice Practice

What is the value of $9 + 6 \times 4 - 7$?

Ⓐ -45 Ⓑ -9 Ⓒ 26 Ⓓ 53

SOLUTION

$9 + 6 \times 4 - 7 = 9 + 24 - 7$ **Multiply 6 and 4.**

$= 33 - 7$ **Add 9 and 24.**

$= 26$ **Subtract 7 from 33.**

▶ **Answer** The correct answer is C. Ⓐ Ⓑ Ⓒ Ⓓ

✓ GUIDED PRACTICE for Examples 2 and 3

Evaluate the expression.

5. $25 - 6 - 14 + 3$

6. $18 - 10.65 + 5 - 1.16$

7. $16 \div 2 \cdot \frac{1}{3}$

8. $\frac{8}{9} \div 4 \times 45$

9. $8 + 12 \div (-2) - 3$

10. $-5 + 9 \div 3 - 2$

GROUPING SYMBOLS Grouping symbols indicate operations that should be performed first. The most common grouping symbols are parentheses ( ) and brackets [ ]. A fraction bar groups the numerator separate from the denominator. You will use grouping symbols in Example 4.

A way to help you remember the order of operations is **PEMDAS**.

Parentheses **E**xponents **M**ultiplication **D**ivision **A**ddition **S**ubtraction

EXAMPLE 4 Using Grouping Symbols

AnimatedMath

For an interactive example of order of operations go to **classzone.com.**

a. $4(-8 - 5) = 4(-13)$ **Subtract inside parentheses.**

$= -52$ **Multiply 4 and −13.**

b. $\frac{13 + 7}{2 \cdot 5} = \frac{20}{10}$ **Evaluate expressions grouped by fraction bar.**

$= 2$ **Divide 20 by 10.**

c. $(4 + 1)^2 \cdot (-3) = 5^2 \cdot (-3)$ **Add inside parentheses.**

$= 25 \cdot (-3)$ **Evaluate the power.**

$= -75$ **Multiply 25 and −3.**

✓ GUIDED PRACTICE for Example 4

Evaluate the expression.

11. $(3 + 7)(6 - 3)^2$
12. $\frac{8 \cdot 3}{4 + 2}$
13. $16(9 + 1) - 30$

3.6 EXERCISES

HOMEWORK KEY

◆ = **MULTIPLE CHOICE PRACTICE** Exs. 34, 35, 53, 60, 69–71

○ = **HINTS AND HOMEWORK HELP** for Exs. 9, 21, 53 at classzone.com

SKILLS • PROBLEM SOLVING • REASONING

VOCABULARY Copy and complete the statement using *before* or *after*.

1. To evaluate $7 + 8^2$, evaluate the power __?__ adding.
2. To evaluate $20 - 5 \div 5$, do the subtraction __?__ dividing.
3. **WRITING** *Describe* the steps you use to evaluate the expression $14 + 6^2 - 15 \div 3 + 1$.

SEE EXAMPLES 1, 2, AND 3 on pp. 160–161 for Exs. 4–19

EVALUATING EXPRESSIONS Evaluate the expression.

4. $6 + 7 \cdot 4$
5. $14 - 8 \div 3$
6. $36 \div 3 - 2^3$
7. $40 - 36 \div 3^2$
8. $17 + 4 - 16$
9. (circled) $64 \div 8 \times 5$
10. $42 \div 7 \times 5 \div 5$
11. $12 - 28 - (-5)$
12. $21 - 16 + 4 \cdot 4$
13. $9 \div 3 \times \left(\frac{1}{3}\right)^4$
14. $16 \div 2^2 - 1 \times 3$
15. $8 - 2^2 + 12 \div 6$
16. $25 + 7 \cdot 3 - 17$
17. $6 \times 4 \div 12 - 3$
18. $49 \div 7 \cdot 3^3 \div 9$
19. $4 - 12 \div 4 \times 3^2$

SEE EXAMPLE 4 on p. 162 for Exs. 20–31

20. $\frac{1}{6}(16 - 7)$
21. (circled) $\frac{3}{4}(25 \div 5)$
22. $-7(32 - 24)$
23. $(5 - 3)^2$
24. $\frac{-12 + 6}{3 - 1}$
25. $\frac{20 + 8}{(-4)}$
26. $\frac{13 - 17}{2}$
27. $\frac{24 - 32 - 8}{21 - 29}$
28. $14 \div (8 - 15)$
29. $6 \times (14 - 24)^2$
30. $16 \div (3^2 - 1)$
31. $(0.75 + 6)(5 - 2)^2$

SEE EXAMPLES 1, 2, AND 3 on pp. 160–161 for Exs. 32–33

ERROR ANALYSIS ***Describe*** **and correct the error made in evaluating.**

32. ✗ $8 - 4 + 3 = 8 - 7$
$= 1$

33. ✗ $27 \div 3^2 = 9^2$
$= 81$

34. ◆ **MULTIPLE CHOICE** What is the first step in evaluating $4 + 3 \times 7^2 - 7$?

Ⓐ Add 4 and 3. Ⓑ Multiply 3 and 7.

Ⓒ Subtract 7 from 7. Ⓓ Evaluate 7^2.

35. ◆ **MULTIPLE CHOICE** What is the value of $6 \times 3 + 16 \div (-2)$?

Ⓐ −54 Ⓑ −17 Ⓒ 10 Ⓓ 17

MENTAL MATH **Copy and complete. Use +, −, ×, or ÷ to make the statement true.**

36. $12 \div 4 \underline{?} 3 = 9$
37. $16 \underline{?} 4 \times 2 = 24$
38. $9 \underline{?} 18 \div 3 = 3$
39. $8 + 14 \underline{?} 2 = 36$
40. $6 \underline{?} 2 + 8 \div 4 = 6$
41. $9 + 8 \times 2 = 30 \div 6 \underline{?} 5$
42. $2^3 - 5 \times 6 \underline{?} 10 = 5$
43. $10 \underline{?} 32 \div 8 = 6$
44. $14 \underline{?} 7 \times 5 = 20 \div 4 \times 2$

PUZZLE PROBLEM **Copy and complete the statement by placing parentheses to make the statement true.**

45. $20 - 3^2 \times 2 + 8 \stackrel{?}{=} 110$
46. $2 \times 9 - 4 + 3 \stackrel{?}{=} 13$
47. $8 - 2 \times 6 \div 3^2 \stackrel{?}{=} 4$

CONNECT SKILLS TO PROBLEM SOLVING **Exercises 48–50 will help you prepare for problem solving.**

Copy and complete the expression to represent the unknown value.

48. You wash 7 cars. You earn \$5 per car and receive \$4 in tips. The total amount of money you earn is $7 \times \underline{?} + \underline{?}$.

49. The French club is selling soups and salads to raise money for a class trip. The cost of paper plates and napkins is \$240. The club sells 86 soups for \$4 each and 98 salads for \$5 each. The amount of money the French club raises is $4 \times \underline{?} + 5 \times \underline{?} - \underline{?}$.

50. A submarine starts at sea level. It dives 130 feet, rises 90 feet, and then dives by an amount equal to 3 times the previous dive. The depth of the submarine is $-130 + \underline{?} + \underline{?} \times \underline{?}$.

SEE EXAMPLE 1 on p. 160 for Ex. 51

51. **MULTI-STEP PROBLEM** A whale watching trip costs \$32 for adults and \$23 for students.

a. Write an expression for the cost of 40 adults.

b. Write an expression for the cost of 20 students.

c. Write and evaluate an expression to find the total cost of the trip.

Whale watching: Adults \$32

California @HomeTutor for problem solving help at classzone.com

52. **DECORATING** Juan buys 368 square feet of wallpaper for $1.10 per square foot to decorate his bedroom. Leah buys 320 square feet of wallpaper for $1.25 per square foot to decorate her bedroom. Write and evaluate an expression to show how much more money Juan spends than Leah.

California @HomeTutor for problem solving help at classzone.com

(53.) ◆ **MULTIPLE CHOICE** You buy 3 notebooks that cost $2 each, 5 pens that cost a total of $4, and 2 erasers that cost $1 each. You give the cashier $20. How much change do you receive?

Ⓐ $6 Ⓑ $8 Ⓒ $9 Ⓓ $13

54. **PUZZLE PROBLEM** Using only the number 4 exactly three times, write an expression with a value of 2. Then repeat this exercise to write expressions with values of 3, 4, and 5.

55. **WEIGHTLIFTING** In an Olympic weightlifting event, Cheryl Haworth lifted one 15 kilogram bar, four plates that each weighed 25 kilograms, and 2 plates that each weighed 20 kilograms. Write and evaluate an expression to find the total weight she lifted.

Cheryl Haworth

56. **SHORT RESPONSE** Write an expression with 4 terms and 3 different operations in which you work from left to right to evaluate. Write another expression that you cannot evaluate from left to right. *Explain* your process.

57. **GOLF** On an 18 hole golf course, Juan scores -1 on 7 holes, $+2$ on 1 hole, -2 on 1 hole, $+1$ on 6 holes, and 0 on 3 holes. Find Juan's total score for 18 holes.

58. **MULTI-STEP PROBLEM** You want to buy a gift for each of 6 friends. Use the pricing information for Joe's Joke Shop given in the table.

Joe's Joke Shop	
Chattering teeth	$3.25
Hand buzzer	$4.50

a. **Calculate** You have $23. Can you buy 6 chattering teeth? 6 hand buzzers?

b. **Make a List** You want to buy at least one of each item. Make a list of all the possible ways you can buy 6 gifts regardless of the total cost.

c. **Interpret** Find the total cost of each combination you listed in part (b). Which combinations of gifts could you buy with $23?

59. **OPEN-ENDED** Pick a phone number without the area code. Replace the hyphen with an equal sign. Then insert symbols to try and make a true statement. (Not all phone numbers will work.)

60. ◆ **MULTIPLE CHOICE** You deposit two checks for $42.38 and one check for $65.83. You then withdraw $32.48 to pay your phone bill and $42 to buy a game. What is the change in your account balance?

Ⓐ $9.41 Ⓑ $76.11 Ⓒ $182.69 Ⓓ $225.07

READING IN MATH **Read the information below for Exercises 61–63.**

For inexpensive fun for the whole family, come to **Strike Lanes**.

- 30 automated lanes
- Video arcade with games for all ages
- Friendly, helpful staff

cake $2.00 per person

beverages $1.00 per person

Planning a birthday party? Try our Deluxe Birthday Package for 12–20 people. Only $125 for 3 games of bowling, cake, balloons, and unlimited beverages. **Strike Lanes** has friendly, helpful staff who will provide your child with a memorable party.

61. Calculate You are planning a party at Strike Lanes for 10 people. Write and evaluate an expression for the total cost including 3 games of bowling, cake, and beverages.

62. Calculate You are considering the Deluxe Birthday Package for 20 children. Write and evaluate an expression for the cost per person.

63. Reasoning Would the Deluxe Birthday Package cost less than paying the rate per person if 17 people attend? *Explain* your reasoning.

64. CHALLENGE At an amusement park, a 2 day pass costs $55 per person. A hotel costs $50 per night. A family of 4 plans to go to this park for 2 days and spend 2 nights in 1 room at the hotel. Write an expression that represents how much the family will pay for the 2 day passes and the hotel.

CHALLENGE Evaluate the expression. Then rewrite the expression with parentheses so that its value is increased, and so that its value is decreased.

65. $8 \times 3 + 12 \div 3$

66. $36 \div 2 \times 6 + 7$

67. $4^2 + 5 \times 4 \div 2 + 8$

68. $28 + 2^5 - 36 \div 4 \times 2$

◆ CALIFORNIA STANDARDS SPIRAL REVIEW

NS 1.1 **69.** Which list shows $\frac{13}{16}, \frac{7}{10}, \frac{8}{11},$ and $\frac{77}{100}$ in order from least to greatest? *(p. 29)*

Ⓐ $\frac{13}{16}, \frac{7}{10}, \frac{8}{11}, \frac{77}{100}$ Ⓑ $\frac{7}{10}, \frac{8}{11}, \frac{77}{100}, \frac{13}{16}$ Ⓒ $\frac{7}{10}, \frac{77}{100}, \frac{8}{11}, \frac{13}{16}$ Ⓓ $\frac{77}{100}, \frac{7}{10}, \frac{8}{11}, \frac{13}{16}$

NS 2.3 **70.** What is the mean of −19, −10, −16, and 13? *(p. 154)*

Ⓐ −58 Ⓑ −8 Ⓒ 8 Ⓓ 58

NS 2.3 **71.** You have $60 in your savings account. Each week you withdraw $5 without making additional deposits. Which integer represents the change in the number of dollars in your account over 6 weeks? *(p. 148)*

Ⓐ −$60 Ⓑ −$30 Ⓒ $30 Ⓓ $60

Technology **ACTIVITY** *Use after Lesson 3.6*

3.6 Using Order of Operations

Standards

AF 1.4 Solve problems manually by using the correct order of operations or **by using a scientific calculator.**

You can use the [( ], [ )], and [^] keys to evaluate expressions.

QUESTION How can you use a calculator to evaluate expressions using the order of operations?

EXAMPLE 1 **You buy 7 quarts of strawberries and 6 quarts of raspberries at a fruit stand. Each quart of fruit costs $3. What is the total cost?**

SOLUTION

To find the total cost, evaluate the expression $3(7 + 6)$.

Keystrokes	Display
3 [( ] 7 [+] 6 [ )] [=]	39

▶ **Answer** The total cost is $39.

EXAMPLE 2 **You can estimate the number of strawberries in one quart by evaluating 3^3. About how many strawberries are in 7 quarts?**

SOLUTION

Estimate the number of strawberries in 7 quarts by evaluating 7×3^3.

Keystrokes	Display
7 [×] 3 [^] 3 [=]	189

▶ **Answer** There are about 189 strawberries in 7 quarts.

PRACTICE

Use a calculator to evaluate the expression.

1. $3 + 4 \cdot 5$
2. $9^2 - 3^2$
3. $\frac{14 + 6}{4 + 1}$
4. $(4 + 2)^2 + 5^2$
5. $\frac{26 + 9}{4^2 - 9}$
6. $314 - (3 + 3)^3$
7. $5 + \frac{8^3}{64}$
8. $6 \cdot 4^4 + 20$
9. **BLUEBERRIES** You can estimate the number of blueberries in one pint by evaluating 6^3. About how many blueberries are in 5 pints?
10. **MEASUREMENT** You can find the number of cubic inches in a cubic yard by evaluating 36^3. How many cubic inches are in 6 cubic yards?

3.7 Rational Numbers and their Properties

Math and SPORTS
Ex. 46, p. 171

Standards **NS 1.1 Compare and order positive and negative fractions, decimals, and mixed numbers and place them on a number line.**

AF 1.3 Apply algebraic order of operations and the commutative, associative, and distributive **properties to evaluate expressions; and justify each step in the process.**

Connect ***Before*** you ordered integers and used the order of operations. ***Now*** you will order rational numbers and apply their properties.

KEY VOCABULARY
- **rational number**
- **additive inverse**
- **additive identity**
- **multiplicative inverse**
- **multiplicative identity**

A **rational number** is a number that can be written as $\frac{a}{b}$ where a and b are integers and $b \neq 0$.

The Venn diagram shows the relationships among rational numbers, integers, and whole numbers. A few examples of each type are included. Notice that integers include whole numbers and rational numbers include integers.

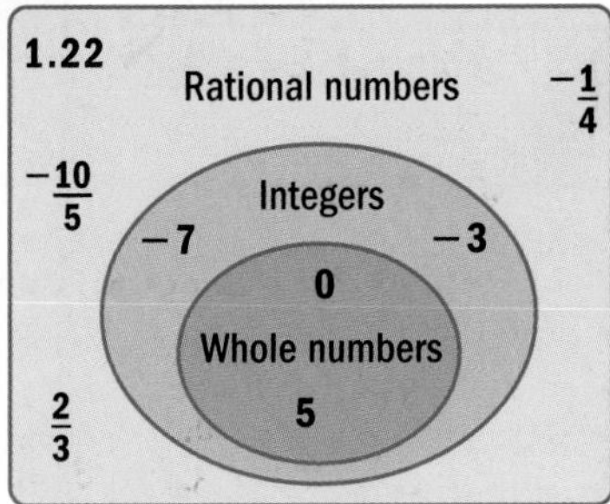

EXAMPLE 1 Identifying Rational Numbers

Show that the number is rational by writing it in $\frac{a}{b}$ form.

a. $6 = \frac{6}{1}$ **b.** $-\frac{3}{5} = \frac{3}{-5}$ **c.** $0.75 = \frac{3}{4}$ **d.** $-2\frac{1}{3} = \frac{-7}{3}$

PLACING SIGNS
Fractions can be negative. The negative sign in a negative fraction can appear in front of the fraction bar, in the numerator, or in the denominator.

EXAMPLE 2 Ordering Rational Numbers

Order $-1, -1.625, \frac{1}{2}, -1\frac{1}{4}$, and $-\frac{3}{8}$ from least to greatest.

Write each number using a common denominator: $-1, -1\frac{5}{8}, \frac{4}{8}, -1\frac{2}{8}, -\frac{3}{8}$.

Then graph each number on a number line, using tick marks at every eighth.

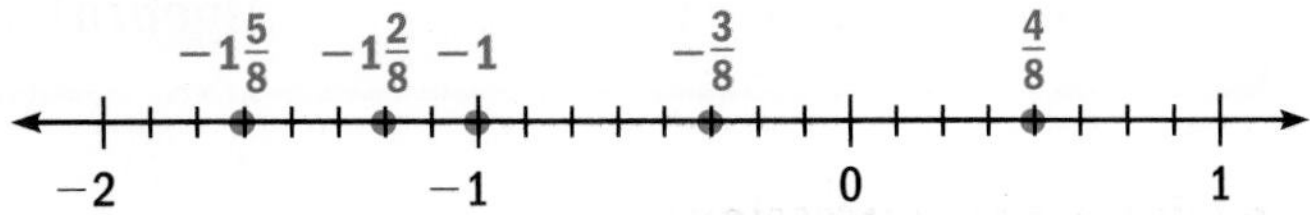

▶ **Answer** From least to greatest, the numbers are: $-1.625, -1\frac{1}{4}, -1, -\frac{3}{8}, \frac{1}{2}$.

✓ GUIDED PRACTICE for Examples 1 and 2

Show that each number is rational by writing it in $\frac{a}{b}$ form. Then order the numbers from least to greatest.

1. $2.5, -1, -\frac{5}{8}, -0.8$

2. $4\frac{1}{5}, -3.6, -3\frac{8}{9}, 0$

FAMILIAR PROPERTIES You can perform operations with rational numbers as you did with decimals, fractions, and integers. You may recall the commutative and associative properties listed below. They can help you add and multiply rational numbers.

VOCABULARY
To help you remember the properties, recall that *commuters* are people who *move* or travel, and people you *associate* with are the friends in your *group*.

Commutative property of addition	$5 + 6 = 6 + 5$
Commutative property of multiplication	$5 \times 6 = 6 \times 5$
Associative property of addition	$(5 + 6) + 7 = 5 + (6 + 7)$
Associative property of multiplication	$(5 \times 6) \times 7 = 5 \times (6 \times 7)$

Four other number properties are shown below. You may have seen the identity properties called the properties of 0 and 1 in other courses.

KEY CONCEPT — *For Your Notebook*

Inverse Property of Addition

Words The sum of a number and its **additive inverse**, or opposite, is 0.

Numbers $5 + (-5) = 0$ **Algebra** $a + (-a) = 0$

Identity Property of Addition

Words The sum of a number and the **additive identity**, 0, is the number.

Numbers $-7 + 0 = -7$ **Algebra** $a + 0 = a$

Inverse Property of Multiplication

Words The product of a nonzero number and its **multiplicative inverse**, or reciprocal, is 1.

Numbers $\frac{3}{4} \cdot \frac{4}{3} = 1$ **Algebra** For nonzero integers a and b, $\frac{a}{b} \cdot \frac{b}{a} = 1$

Identity Property of Multiplication

Words The product of a number and the **multiplicative identity**, 1, is the number.

Numbers $9 \cdot 1 = 9$ **Algebra** $a \cdot 1 = a$

EXAMPLE 3 Identifying Properties

REVIEW PROPERTIES
For help with the commutative and associative properties, see pp. 676–677.

Tell which property is being illustrated.

a. $\frac{4}{5} \cdot \left(\frac{5}{4}\right) = 1$ **Inverse property of multiplication**

b. $-35 + 35 = 0$ **Inverse property of addition**

c. $-4 + 8 = 8 + (-4)$ **Commutative property of addition**

d. $(-79)(1) = -79$ **Identity property of multiplication**

EXAMPLE 4 Using Familiar Properties

Evaluate the expression. *Justify* each step.

RECALL THE ORDER OF OPERATIONS

Using the order of operations, you would normally add $-7 + 4$ first. Using properties to reorder and regroup can make the calculations easier.

a. $-7 + 4 + (-3) = [-7 + 4] + (-3)$ Order of operations

$= [4 + (-7)] + (-3)$ Commutative property of addition

$= 4 + [(-7) + (-3)]$ Associative property of addition

$= 4 + (-10)$ Add -7 and -3.

$= -6$ Add 4 and -10.

b. $-25(7)(-4) = [-25(7)](-4)$ Order of operations

$= [7(-25)](-4)$ Commutative property of multiplication

$= 7[(-25)(-4)]$ Associative property of multiplication

$= 7(100)$ Multiply -25 and -4.

$= 700$ Multiply 7 and 100.

EXAMPLE 5 Using Properties

Evaluate the expression. *Justify* each step.

a. $7 + 8 + (-7) = [7 + 8] + (-7)$ Order of operations

$= [8 + 7] + (-7)$ Commutative property of addition

$= 8 + [7 + (-7)]$ Associative property of addition

$= 8 + 0$ Inverse property of addition

$= 8$ Identity property of addition

b. $\frac{5}{3} \cdot \frac{7}{4} \cdot \frac{4}{7} = \left(\frac{5}{3} \cdot \frac{7}{4}\right) \cdot \frac{4}{7}$ Order of operations

$= \frac{5}{3} \cdot \left(\frac{7}{4} \cdot \frac{4}{7}\right)$ Associative property of multiplication

$= \frac{5}{3} \cdot 1$ Inverse property of multiplication

$= \frac{5}{3}$ Identity property of multiplication

✓ GUIDED PRACTICE for Examples 3, 4, and 5

Tell which property is being illustrated.

3. $-3 + 0 = -3$

4. $15 \times 8 = 8 \times 15$

5. $(5 + 4) + 6 = 5 + (4 + 6)$

Evaluate the expression. *Justify* each step.

6. $3.5 + [(-3) + 6.5]$

7. $-6(3)(-5)$

8. $\frac{1}{3} \cdot \frac{5}{6} \cdot 3$

3.7 EXERCISES

HOMEWORK KEY ◆ = **MULTIPLE CHOICE PRACTICE** Exs. 30, 37, 46, 58–60
○ = **HINTS AND HOMEWORK HELP** for Exs. 17, 25, 45 at classzone.com

SKILLS • PROBLEM SOLVING • REASONING

1. **VOCABULARY** Copy and complete: The additive identity is the number __?__. The multiplicative identity is the number __?__.

2. **WRITING** You are given two rational numbers. *Describe* how to find a rational number that is between the two numbers.

SEE EXAMPLE 1 on p. 167 for Exs. 3–10

WRITING RATIONALS **Write the number in its rational form $\frac{a}{b}$.**

3. 0.4
4. $-3\frac{5}{8}$
5. 3
6. -12
7. $2\frac{1}{5}$
8. $-\frac{7}{9}$
9. -5.8
10. 0.98

Animated Math at classzone.com

SEE EXAMPLE 2 on p. 167 for Exs. 11–23

GRAPHING AND COMPARING **Graph the numbers on a number line. Then compare them using <, >, or =.**

11. $-0.8, -\frac{4}{5}$
12. $-0.75, -\frac{5}{8}$
13. $-\frac{6}{7}, -\frac{7}{6}$
14. $-2\frac{1}{2}, -2.625$
15. $-1.25, -1\frac{1}{5}$
16. $-3\frac{1}{5}, -3\frac{3}{10}$

ORDERING RATIONAL NUMBERS **Order the numbers from least to greatest.**

17. $3, -4, -1.25, 4.31, -3.7$
18. $\frac{2}{5}, 0.25, -0.85, \frac{-3}{5}$
19. $-3.1, -4, -\frac{10}{3}, -3\frac{3}{4}, -3.7$
20. $3, -2\frac{2}{3}, 0, -\frac{5}{4}, -0.85$
21. $\frac{3}{10}, -1\frac{1}{3}, 0.02, 1, -0.5$
22. $-4.25, 1, -\frac{22}{5}, -4\frac{7}{8}, -3$

23. **ERROR ANALYSIS** *Describe* and correct the error made in ordering the rational numbers from least to greatest.

✗ $\frac{1}{6}, \frac{1}{3}, -0.\overline{6}, -\frac{5}{6}, -1\frac{1}{3}$

SEE EXAMPLE 3 on p. 168 for Exs. 24–30

IDENTIFYING PROPERTIES **Tell which property is being illustrated.**

24. $-24 + 24 = 0$
25. $2.3 + 11.4 = 11.4 + 2.3$
26. $7 \times (12 \times 3) = (7 \times 12) \times 3$
27. $8 + 0 = 8$
28. $\frac{3}{5} \cdot \frac{5}{3} = 1$
29. $5 \times (6 \times 19) = 5 \times (19 \times 6)$

30. ◆ **MULTIPLE CHOICE** Which equation illustrates the associative property of addition?

Ⓐ $5 + 22 = 22 + 5$
Ⓑ $(15 + 3) + 67 = 15 + (3 + 67)$
Ⓒ $5(-17) = -17(5)$
Ⓓ $(6 \cdot 8) \cdot 10 = 6 \cdot (8 \cdot 10)$

SEE EXAMPLES 4 AND 5 on p. 169 for Exs. 31–37

REASONING **Evaluate the expression. *Justify* each step.**

31. $4 + 17 + (-4)$ **32.** $43 + 68 + 57$ **33.** $7(-8)(5)$

34. $-4 + [7 + (-6)]$ **35.** $14 \cdot \frac{2}{3} \cdot \frac{1}{14}$ **36.** $2(3)(35)$

37. ◆ **MULTIPLE CHOICE** Which expression is *not* equivalent to $2(-4)(5)$?

Ⓐ $[2(-4)](5)$ Ⓑ $(-4)[(2)(5)]$ Ⓒ $[(-4)(5)](2)$ Ⓓ $(2 - 4)(5)$

38. **REASONING** What numbers are their own multiplicative inverse? What number is its own additive inverse? *Explain* your reasoning.

WRITING EQUIVALENT FRACTIONS **Tell which rational form of 1 is used to write the equivalent fraction.**

39. $\frac{2}{3} \cdot \underline{\ ?\ } = \frac{24}{36}$ **40.** $\frac{3}{4} \cdot \underline{\ ?\ } = \frac{45}{60}$ **41.** $2\frac{7}{8} \cdot \underline{\ ?\ } = 2\frac{175}{200}$

CONNECT SKILLS TO PROBLEM SOLVING **Exercises 42–44 will help you prepare for problem solving.**

42. The freezing point of oxygen is −218.4°C, and the freezing point of nitrogen is −209.86°C. Which of the elements has a lower freezing point?

43. A submarine dives to a depth of −28.5 feet. On the submarine's next dive, it dives to a depth of −28.57 feet. Which of the dives is closer to sea level?

44. Today stock A fell 32.65 points per share, and stock B fell 32.658 points per share. Which stock lost more points per share?

SEE EXAMPLE 2 on p. 167 for Ex. 45

45. **RAINFALL** The table shows the amount of rainfall, in inches, above or below the mean for four regions of Oklahoma during a recent drought. Order the numbers from least to greatest. Which region's rainfall was the most above the mean?

Region	Panhandle	Northeast	Southwest	Southeast
Departure from Mean	−5.87	$-\frac{631}{100}$	$-8\frac{4}{25}$	1.97

Crop affected by drought

California @HomeTutor for problem solving help at classzone.com

SEE EXAMPLE 4 on p. 169 for Ex. 46

46. ◆ **MULTIPLE CHOICE** Your team needs a total of 21 points to win a volleyball game. Your team has 15 points. You score 3 points on your serve. Which expression *cannot* be used to find the number of points your team needs to reach 21?

Ⓐ $21 - 15 - 3$ Ⓑ $15 - 21 - 3$ Ⓒ $-15 + 21 - 3$ Ⓓ $-15 - 3 + 21$

California @HomeTutor for problem solving help at classzone.com

47. **OPEN-ENDED** Give an example of a rational number that is not an integer. Give an example of an integer that is not a whole number.

READING IN MATH **Read the information below for Exercises 48–50.**

Stocks Shares of stock represent partial ownership in public companies. These shares are sold on the stock market. As the value of a company rises and falls, the value of each individual share in that company will vary.

You own shares of stock in seven companies. The change in price (in dollars) of one share of each company for one day are shown below.

Stock A	Stock B	Stock C	Stock D	Stock E	Stock F	Stock G
0.13	−0.54	0.05	0.05	−0.1	−0.03	−0.56

48. **Interpreting** Which stock price rose the most? Which stock price fell the least?

49. **Loss or Gain** You own 100 shares of stock B. How much did you lose or gain on that day?

50. **Predicting Gain** If the price of stock A continues to change at the same rate, how many days will it take to gain over $1 per share?

Stock B fell 0.54.

51. **REASONING** Use the properties of addition to show that the expression $5 + 7 + (-5) + (-7)$ is equal to 0. *Justify* each step.

ALGEBRA **Evaluate the expression when *a, b, m, n* ≠ 0.**

52. $(-x + x) \cdot y$

53. $\left(\frac{m}{n} \cdot \frac{n}{m}\right) + (-1)$

54. $\left(\frac{a}{b} \cdot \frac{b}{a}\right) \cdot [b + (-b)]$

CHALLENGE **Tell whether or not the expressions are equal. Do exponents have associative and commutative properties? *Explain* your answer.**

55. $2^3 \stackrel{?}{=} 3^2$

56. $(3^2)^3 \stackrel{?}{=} (3^3)^2$

57. $(2^2)^3 \stackrel{?}{=} 2^{(2^3)}$

◆ CALIFORNIA STANDARDS SPIRAL REVIEW

Gr. 5 NS 1.5

58. Which list is in order from least to greatest? *(p. 129)*

Ⓐ 2, −3, 6, −8 Ⓑ −8, −3, 2, 6 Ⓒ −8, 6, −3, 2 Ⓓ −3, −8, 6, 2

NS 2.1

59. What is the value of $1\frac{3}{8} + \frac{2}{5} + \frac{9}{16}$? *(p. 81)*

Ⓐ $1\frac{13}{20}$ Ⓑ $2\frac{27}{80}$ Ⓒ $2\frac{21}{40}$ Ⓓ $3\frac{11}{40}$

AF 1.4

60. You buy 3 shirts for $10 each, 1 pair of jeans for $25, and 2 hats for $15 each. You give the cashier $100. How much change do you receive? *(p. 160)*

Ⓐ $15 Ⓑ $28 Ⓒ $33 Ⓓ $45

3.8 The Distributive Property

Math and THEATER
Example 1, p. 173

Standards **AF 1.3 Apply algebraic order of operations and the commutative, associative, and distributive properties to evaluate expressions; and justify each step in the process.**

Connect ***Before*** you applied the order of operations and other properties. ***Now*** you will also apply the distributive property.

KEY VOCABULARY
- **equivalent expressions**

THEATER A set designer is building a backdrop for a scene in the play *The Miracle Worker*. The plywood pieces used for the backdrop are made from a 4 foot by 6 foot rectangle joined to a 4 foot by 3 foot rectangle. What two expressions could you use to find the area of wallpaper needed to cover both pieces?

EXAMPLE 1 Writing Equivalent Expressions

To find the total area described above, find the sum of the areas of the separate pieces or find the area of the joined pieces.

REVIEW AREA
For help with area, see p. 685.

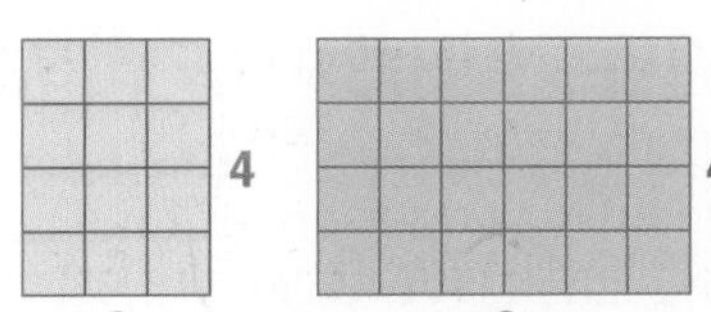

Area $= 4(3) + 4(6)$

$= 12 + 24 = 36 \text{ ft}^2$

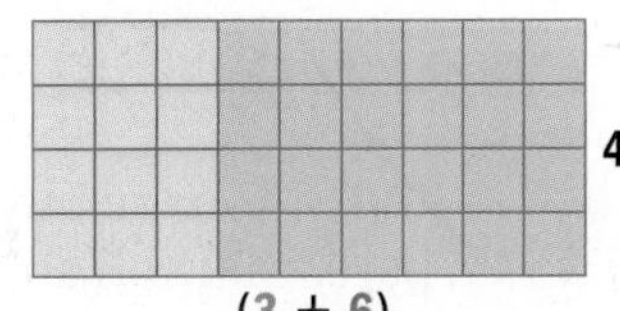

Area $= 4(3 + 6)$

$= 4(9) = 36 \text{ ft}^2$

✓ GUIDED PRACTICE for Example 1

1. **WHAT IF?** Write two expressions for the total area if a set designer joins a 2 foot by 7 foot rectangle of plywood to a piece that is 2 feet by 4 feet.

EXPRESSIONS Both expressions in Example 1 are equal to 36. They are called **equivalent expressions** because they have the same value. These expressions are an example of the *distributive property*.

KEY CONCEPT *For Your Notebook*

The Distributive Property

Algebra For all numbers a, b, and c, $a(b + c) = ab + ac$ and $a(b - c) = ab - ac$.

Numbers $8(10 + 4) = 8(10) + 8(4)$ and $3(4 - 2) = 3(4) - 3(2)$

EXAMPLE 2 Writing Equivalent Expressions

AVOID ERRORS

Don't forget when using the distributive property to multiply the outside number by *both* numbers inside the parentheses.

Use the distributive property to write an equivalent expression. Check your answer.

a. $-4(5 + 8)$ **b.** $4(50 - 3)$ **c.** $7(9) + 7(5)$

SOLUTION

a. Expression: $-4(5 + 8) = -4(5) + (-4)(8)$ **Distributive property**

CHECK $-4(13) \stackrel{?}{=} -20 + (-32)$ **Simplify.**

$-52 = -52$ ✓ **Answer checks.**

b. Expression: $4(50 - 3) = 4(50) - 4(3)$ **Distributive property**

CHECK $4(47) \stackrel{?}{=} 200 - 12$ **Simplify.**

$188 = 188$ ✓ **Answer checks.**

c. Expression: $7(9) + 7(5) = 7(9 + 5)$ **Distributive property**

CHECK $63 + 35 \stackrel{?}{=} 7(14)$ **Simplify.**

$98 = 98$ ✓ **Answer checks.**

EXAMPLE 3 Using the Distributive Property

DVDs You are buying 8 DVDs as door prizes for a party that you are having. Each DVD costs \$15.95. Use the distributive property to find the total cost of the DVDs.

DVDs cost \$15.95.

Animated Math

For an interactive example of the distributive property go to **classzone.com**.

SOLUTION

$8(15.95) = 8(16.00 - 0.05)$ **Write 15.95 as a difference of a whole number and a decimal.**

$= 8(16.00) - 8(0.05)$ **Distributive property**

$= 128.00 - 0.40$ **Multiply.**

$= 127.60$ **Subtract.**

▶ **Answer** The total cost of the DVDs is \$127.60.

✓ **GUIDED PRACTICE** for Examples 2 and 3

Use the distributive property to write an equivalent expression. Check your answer.

2. $6\left(\frac{1}{7}\right) + 6\left(\frac{6}{7}\right)$ **3.** $-6(12 + 3)$ **4.** $8(12 - 5)$ **5.** $3(11) - 3(4)$

6. WHAT IF? Suppose in Example 3 that each DVD costs \$17.90. Find the total cost of buying 6 DVDs.

EXAMPLE 4 Justifying Steps Using Properties

Evaluate the expression 27(−3) + 27(4) − 6 and justify your steps.

About the Standards

In Example 4, you express the solution using appropriate notation and terms as required by Grade 6 Standard MR 2.5.

SOLUTION

$27(-3) + 27(4) - 6 = 27(-3 + 4) - 6$	**Distributive property**
$= 27(1) - 6$	**Order of operations**
$= 27 - 6$	**Identity property of multiplication**
$= 21$	**Subtract 6 from 27.**

✓ GUIDED PRACTICE for Example 4

Evaluate the expression and justify your steps.

7. $5\left(\frac{1}{3}\right) + 5\left(\frac{2}{3}\right) + (-2)$
8. $3 + 7(6) + 7(-6)$
9. $12 + 18(-8) + 18(9)$

3.8 EXERCISES

HOMEWORK KEY

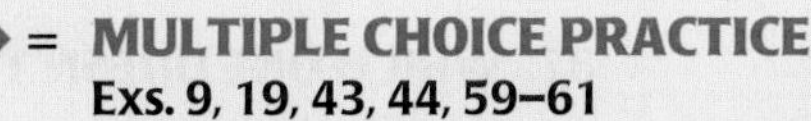

◆ = **MULTIPLE CHOICE PRACTICE** Exs. 9, 19, 43, 44, 59–61

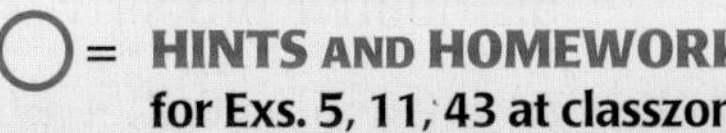

○ = **HINTS AND HOMEWORK HELP** for Exs. 5, 11, 43 at classzone.com

SKILLS • PROBLEM SOLVING • REASONING

1. **VOCABULARY** Copy and complete: You can use the distributive property to write _?_ expressions.

2. **WRITING** One meaning of the word *distribute* is to supply or deliver to each individual in a group. How can this meaning help you remember the distributive property?

SEE EXAMPLES 1 AND 2 on pp. 173–174 for Exs. 3–9

WRITING EQUIVALENT EXPRESSIONS Use the distributive property to write an equivalent expression. Check your answer.

3. $5(3 + 7)$
4. $4(4 + 5)$
5. $7(3) + 7(4)$
6. $8(100 - 4)$
7. $6\left(\frac{5}{12}\right) - 6\left(\frac{1}{12}\right)$
8. $4\left(\frac{3}{5}\right) + 4\left(\frac{2}{5}\right)$

9. ◆ **MULTIPLE CHOICE** Which expression is equivalent to $3(-4 + 3)$?

   Ⓐ $4(3) + 4(3)$ Ⓑ $3(-4) + 3(3)$ Ⓒ $4(3) - 4(3)$ Ⓓ $3(4) + 3(3)$

SEE EXAMPLE 3 on p. 174 for Exs. 10–18

DISTRIBUTIVE PROPERTY Use the distributive property to evaluate.

10. $7(8.2)$
11. $6(16.85)$
12. $8(19.97)$
13. $11\left(\frac{5}{8}\right) + 11\left(\frac{3}{8}\right)$
14. $13\left(\frac{3}{7}\right) - 13\left(-\frac{4}{7}\right)$
15. $3\left(\frac{2}{5}\right) - 3\left(\frac{-1}{5}\right)$
16. $3(7.3) + 3(2.7)$
17. $4(8.1) + 4(2.9)$
18. $9(13.2) + 9(6.8)$

SEE EXAMPLE 3 on p. 174 for Exs. 19–21

19. ◆ **MULTIPLE CHOICE** What is the value of the expression 9(8.5)?

Ⓐ 36 Ⓑ 72.5 Ⓒ 76.5 Ⓓ 81

ERROR ANALYSIS ***Describe*** **and correct the error made in evaluating.**

20. ✗ $-8(5 + 4) = -40 + 32$
$= -8$

21. ✗ $3(9) + 3(7) = (3 + 3)(9 + 7)$
$= (6)(16) = 96$

SEE EXAMPLE 4 on p. 175 for Exs. 22–36

IDENTIFYING PROPERTIES **Tell which property is being illustrated.**

22. $-2 + 19 = 19 + (-2)$
23. $11 + (-11) = 0$
24. $\frac{3}{8} \cdot \frac{1}{8} = \frac{1}{8} \cdot \frac{3}{8}$
25. $3(11 \cdot 8) = (3 \cdot 11)8$
26. $\frac{2}{3} \times \frac{3}{2} = 1$
27. $3(11 + 8) = 3 \cdot 11 + 3 \cdot 8$
28. $5 \cdot 7 - 5 \cdot 15 = 5(7 - 15)$
29. $(-17)(1) = -17$
30. $2 + (9 + 3) = (3 + 9) + 2$

EVALUATING EXPRESSIONS **Evaluate the expression and justify your steps.**

31. $4\left(\frac{4}{5}\right) + 4\left(\frac{1}{5}\right) + (-4)$
32. $8(0.95) + 8(0.05) + 2$
33. $4(8) - 20 + 4(-8)$
34. $17(2) + 17(-2) - 13$
35. $-15 + 15(7) + 15(-6)$
36. $2 + 39(8) + 39(-8) - 2$

37. **WHICH ONE DOESN'T BELONG?** Which of the following does *not* use the distributive property correctly?

A. $6(2 + 5) = 6(2) + 6(5)$
B. $-3(8) + (-3)(2) = -3(8 - 2)$
C. $5(3) + 5(5) = 5(3 + 5)$
D. $4(12 - 7) = 4(12) - 4(7)$

CONNECT SKILLS TO PROBLEM SOLVING **Exercises 38–40 will help you prepare for problem solving.**

Use the distributive property to copy and complete the statement.

38. Mark buys 3 steaks that cost \$6 each and 3 potatoes that cost \$.50 each.
Total cost = 3(_?_ + _?_) = 3 × _?_ + 3 × _?_.

39. You would like to buy 4 shirts that cost \$20.30 each.
Total cost = 4(_?_ + _?_) = 4 × _?_ + 4 × _?_.

40. You buy 2 loaves of bread for \$2.15 each.
Total cost = 2(_?_ + _?_) = 2 × _?_ + 2 × _?_.

SEE EXAMPLE 2 on p. 174 for Exs. 41–42

41. **PUMPKINS** You buy 2 pumpkins to carve. The pumpkins weigh 10 pounds and 6 pounds and cost \$.70 per pound. Use the distributive property to write two equivalent expressions to represent the total cost of the pumpkins.

California @HomeTutor for problem solving help at classzone.com

42. **MOVIE TICKETS** You buy 4 adult and 6 children's tickets to a movie. The price of each ticket is \$6.75. Use the distributive property to write two equivalent expressions to represent the total cost of the tickets.

California @HomeTutor for problem solving help at classzone.com

SEE EXAMPLE 3
on p. 174
for Exs. 43–47

43. ◆ **MULTIPLE CHOICE** A recorded song lasts 4.25 minutes. Which expression does *not* represent the amount of time it takes to play the song 3 times?

Ⓐ $3(4 + 0.25)$ Ⓑ $3(4) + 3(0.25)$ Ⓒ $3(5 - 0.75)$ Ⓓ $3(5) - 3(0.25)$

44. ◆ **MULTIPLE CHOICE** You buy 5 CDs for $9.95 each. Which expression represents the total cost of the CDs?

Ⓐ $5(10) - 5(0.05)$ Ⓑ $5(10 + 0.05)$ Ⓒ $5(10) - 0.05$ Ⓓ $10(5 - 0.05)$

Animated **Math** at classzone.com

45. **TALENT SHOW** At a talent show, each group has 2 minutes to set up, $\frac{1}{2}$ minute for an introduction, and 5 minutes for the act. There are 20 groups performing. Use the distributive property to find how long, in minutes, the talent show will be.

Total groups = 20

46. **TRADING CARDS** A friend is selling his collection of trading cards. He is selling each card for $.95, and you want to purchase 20 cards. Use the distributive property to write and evaluate an expression to find the total cost of 20 cards.

47. **GEOMETRY** The expression $2l + 2w$ is used to find the perimeter of a rectangle. Use the distributive property to write an equivalent expression for the perimeter. Show that both formulas give the same result for the perimeter of a rectangle that is 14 meters by 12 meters.

48. **SHORT RESPONSE** You want to find the product 25×115. How can you use the distributive property to find the product? *Explain.*

49. **BANK** A scale drawing of the layout of a bank is shown. Write two expressions for the actual perimeter of the bank, if the actual bank is x times as large as this drawing. Evaluate each expression when $x = 400$ and when $x = 282.8$.

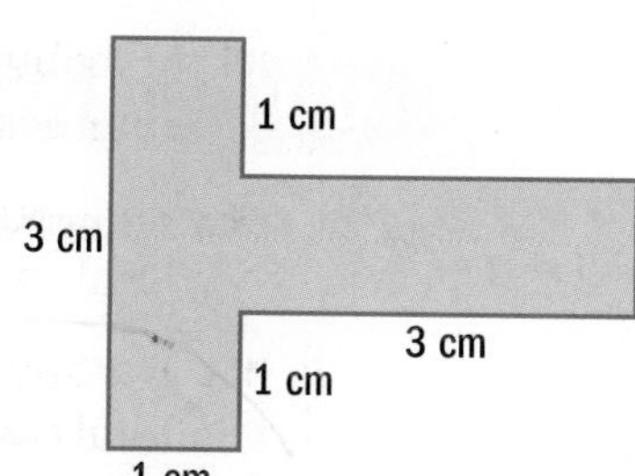

50. **OPEN-ENDED** *Describe* a real-world situation that can be modeled by the expression $4(1 - 0.05)$. Then solve the problem and interpret the solution.

51. **MULTI-STEP PROBLEM** A rectangular table is 3 feet wide and 6 feet long. The table is extended by adding another rectangular table that is 2 feet wide and 3 feet long.

  a. Draw the above scenario using graph paper.

  b. Write two different expressions for the combined area.

  c. Evaluate both expressions from part (b).

52. **REASONING** Use the distributive property and the fact that $-a = -1(a)$ to show that $-x + (-y) = -(x + y)$ when x and y are positive.

53. **FUNDRAISING** A club is selling sandwiches and pizzas to raise money. The club charges \$4.75 for each sandwich and \$5.75 for each pizza. It costs the club \$2.25 for each sandwich and \$2.50 for each pizza. The club sells 30 sandwiches and 20 pizzas. Write an expression to represent the total profit made. How much profit does the club make?

CHALLENGE Show how you can use the distributive property twice to simplify the expression. Then evaluate the expression.

54. (0.98)(7.03) **55.** (1.1)(6.89) **56.** (0.99)(9.98) **57.** (3.01)(6.05)

58. **CHALLENGE** You and two friends go to a baseball game. Together you have \$50. Each ticket costs \$10. Each of you buys a hot dog that costs \$2 and a large drink. When you leave the stadium, all together you have \$2 left. How much did each drink cost?

◆ CALIFORNIA STANDARDS SPIRAL REVIEW

NS 1.1 59. Which number is less than $\frac{7}{20}$? *(p. 167)*

Ⓐ $\frac{3}{5}$ Ⓑ $\frac{3}{10}$ Ⓒ 0.35 Ⓓ 0.4

AF 1.4 60. What is the value of $-7 + 9 + (-3) + 11$? *(p. 160)*

Ⓐ -10 Ⓑ 1 Ⓒ 10 Ⓓ 30

Gr. 5 NS 2.1 61. Steve buys a DVD that costs \$17.25, a CD that costs \$11.99, and a book that costs \$21.85. What is the most reasonable estimate of the total cost? *(p. 102)*

Ⓐ \$48 Ⓑ \$51 Ⓒ \$54 Ⓓ \$60

QUIZ *for Lessons 3.6–3.8*

Evaluate the expression. *(p. 160)*

1. $2 \cdot 6 + 4 - 3 \cdot 12$ **2.** $(3 + 7) + 2^3 \div 6$ **3.** $3 + 2(10 - 8)^2 + 12$

Evaluate the expression. *Justify* each step. *(p. 167)*

4. $5.1 + (-3) + 6.9$ **5.** $\frac{1}{5}(-12)(5)$ **6.** $7 + 16.3 + (-7)$

Use the distributive property to evaluate the expression. *(p. 174)*

7. $12(9) - 12(3)$ **8.** $4(6.9)$ **9.** $8(5.4)$

10. **CAR WASH** The members of a club hold a car wash and earn \$4.25 for each car they wash and \$3.75 for each car they wax. The club washes and waxes 16 cars. Use the distributive property to write and evaluate two different expressions for the total amount of money the club earned. *(p. 174)*

MIXED REVIEW of Skills and Problem Solving

Multiple Choice Practice for Lessons 3.6–3.8

1. Your class held a two-day car wash for a fundraiser. Your class washed 20 cars on the first day and 40 cars on the second day. The class charged \$7 for each car. Which expression gives the total amount of money raised by the class? **AF 1.3**

   (A) $7(20) + 40$

   (B) $7(20 + 40)$

   (C) $7(40) + 20$

   (D) $7 + 40 + 20$

2. You buy 2 pairs of shorts, 4 shirts, and 2 bottles of water for the prices shown below. What is the total cost? **AF 1.4**

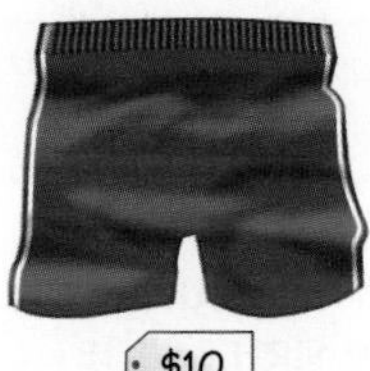

   (A) \$32 (B) \$34

   (C) \$42 (D) \$52

3. Which of the following is true? **AF 1.4**

   (A) $2 + 4 \times 7 - 9 \div 3 = 3$

   (B) $12 \div 3 + 1 \times 5 - 4 = 21$

   (C) $3 \times (6 + 2) - 10 \div 5 = 3$

   (D) $15 - 3 \times 2 + 12 \div 6 = 11$

4. Which list shows $-2\frac{5}{6}$, -3.18, $-\frac{79}{25}$, $-3\frac{1}{8}$, and -2.68 in order from least to greatest? **NS 1.1**

   (A) $-2\frac{5}{6}, -3.18, -\frac{79}{25}, -3\frac{1}{8}, -2.68$

   (B) $-3.18, -\frac{79}{25}, -3\frac{1}{8}, -2\frac{5}{6}, -2.68$

   (C) $-2.68, -2\frac{5}{6}, -3\frac{1}{8}, -\frac{79}{25}, -3.18$

   (D) $-\frac{79}{25}, -3.18, -3\frac{1}{8}, -2\frac{5}{6}, -2.68$

5. You buy the ham and cheese shown below for the amounts shown. Which expression *cannot* be used to find the total cost? **AF 1.3, MR 2.7**

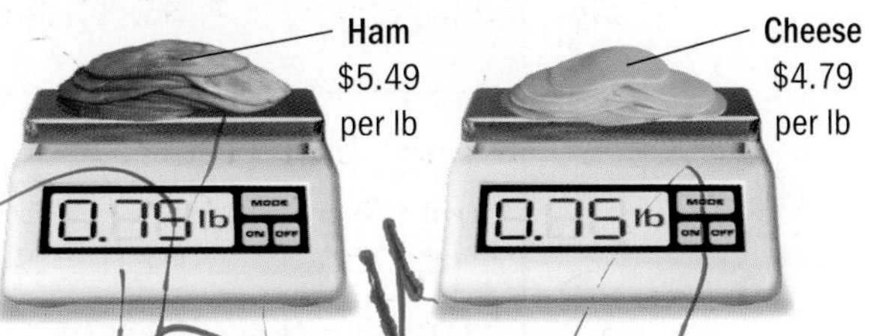

   (A) $0.75(5.49) + 0.75(4.79)$

   (B) $0.75(5.49 + 4.79)$

   (C) $0.75(10) + 0.75(0.28)$

   (D) $1.50(5.49 + 4.79)$

6. Which property is illustrated by the statement $4 \cdot 32 \cdot \frac{1}{4} = 32 \cdot 4 \cdot \frac{1}{4}$? **AF 1.3**

   (A) Commutative property of multiplication

   (B) Identity property of multiplication

   (C) Associative property of multiplication

   (D) Distributive property

7. The table shows the change in the price, in dollars, of one share of four stocks for one day. Which stock's price decreased the most? **NS 1.1, MR 1.1**

Stock P	Stock Q	Stock R	Stock S
0.15	−0.25	$-\frac{1}{5}$	$\frac{1}{25}$

   (A) Stock P (B) Stock Q

   (C) Stock R (D) Stock S

8. What is the value of $\frac{3}{8} \cdot 7 \cdot 8 - 5^3 - 25$? **AF 1.4**

   (A) −729 (B) −129

   (C) −79 (D) −9

3 CHAPTER SUMMARY

Standards
NS 1.1, NS 2.3, AF 1.3, AF 1.4; Gr. 5 NS 1.5

BIG IDEAS *For Your Notebook*

Big Idea 1

Comparing and Ordering Positive and Negative Numbers

You can graph rational numbers on a number line to help compare them.

Numbers	Numbers placed on a number line	Order least to greatest
−5, 2, −3, 4, −6	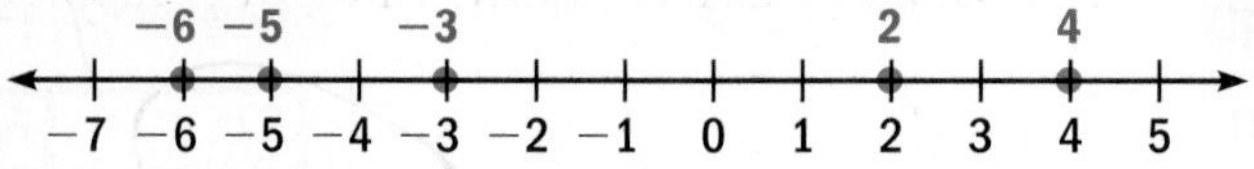	−6, −5, −3, 2, 4
−1.5, 0.5, $\frac{3}{4}$, $-1\frac{1}{4}$, −0.75	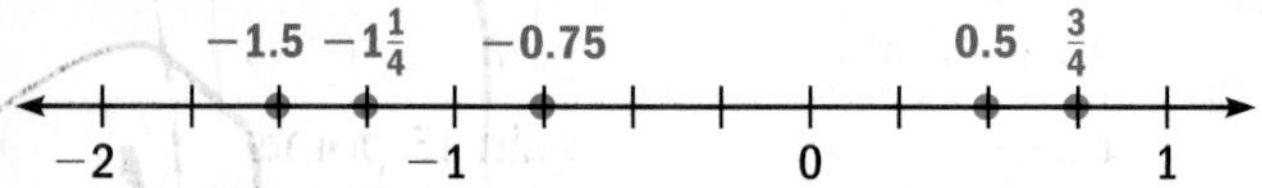	−1.5, $-1\frac{1}{4}$, −0.75, 0.5, $\frac{3}{4}$

Big Idea 2

Adding, Subtracting, Multiplying, and Dividing Integers

Expression	Rule when a and b have the same sign	Rule when a and b have different signs
$a + b$	Add $\lvert a\rvert$ and $\lvert b\rvert$. The sum has the same sign as *a* and *b*.	Subtract the lesser absolute value from the greater absolute value. The sum has the same sign as the number with the greater absolute value.
$a - b$	To subtract *b* from *a*, add the opposite of *b* to *a*: $a - b = a + (-b)$. Then use the addition rules.	
$a \times b$	Multiply $\lvert a\rvert$ by $\lvert b\rvert$. The product is positive.	Multiply $\lvert a\rvert$ by $\lvert b\rvert$. The product is negative.
$\frac{a}{b}$	Divide $\lvert a\rvert$ by $\lvert b\rvert$. The quotient is positive.	Divide $\lvert a\rvert$ by $\lvert b\rvert$. The quotient is negative.

Big Idea 3

Using Properties to Evaluate Expressions

The correct order of operations is **P**arentheses, **E**xponents, **M**ultiplication, or **D**ivision (left to right), then **A**ddition or **S**ubtraction (left to right).

Property	Addition	Multiplication
Commutative Property	$2 + 3 = 3 + 2$	$2 \times 3 = 3 \times 2$
Associative Property	$(2 + 3) + 4 = 2 + (3 + 4)$	$(2 \times 3) \times 4 = 2 \times (3 \times 4)$
Inverse Property	$7 + (-7) = 0$	$\frac{2}{5} \cdot \frac{5}{2} = 1$
Identity Property	$9 + 0 = 9$	$4 \cdot 1 = 4$
Distributive Property	$6(8 + 3) = 6(8) + 6(3)$ and $6(8 - 3) = 6(8) - 6(3)$	

CHAPTER PROBLEM

Standards
NS 1.1, NS 2.3, AF 1.4, AF 1.3

APPLYING THE
BIG IDEAS

Big Idea 1
You order integers in **Step 1** and **Step 4.**

Big Idea 2
You use integer operations in **Step 2, Step 3, Ex. 1** and **Ex. 2.**

Big Idea 3
You use properties to evaluate expressions in **Step 2, Step 3,** and **Ex. 2.**

PROBLEM How can you use integers and the properties of integers to find your score in a video game?

STEP 1 **Write and order integers.**

The table below shows the different actions in a video game and their point values. Rewrite the table using integers for the point values. Order the actions from least point value to greatest point value.

Action	*Points*
break a box	gain 10 points
collect a coin	gain 15 points
fall in a pit	lose 40 points
find a key	gain 150 points
finish stage	gain 500 points
run into an obstacle	lose 60 points

STEP 2 **Write and evaluate an expression.**

Suppose in one stage of the game you fall into 2 pits, collect 5 coins, run into 2 obstacles, and finish the stage. Write and evaluate an addition expression to find your total score for the stage.

STEP 3 **List a set of actions.**

List two sets of actions for one stage of the game. Choose actions so that one set finishes with a positive score and the other set finishes with a negative score. Exchange your lists of actions with a classmate. Write and evaluate addition expressions to find the total points scored in your classmate's series of actions. Check each other's work.

STEP 4 **Order point totals.**

Ask your teacher to write the point totals for each list of actions in Step 3 on the board. Order the point totals from least to greatest. Which list of actions in Step 3 gives the greatest total score? the least total score?

Extending the Problem

Use your results from the problem to complete the exercises.

1. Find the mean of the point totals from Step 4.
2. List a set of actions for a whole game of 3 stages. Write and evaluate an addition expression to find your total score in the game.

3 CHAPTER REVIEW

California @HomeTutor
classzone.com
• Multi-Language Visual Glossary
• Vocabulary practice

REVIEW KEY VOCABULARY

- integer, *p. 129*
- negative integer, *p. 129*
- positive integer, *p. 129*
- opposite, *p. 129*
- absolute value, *p. 136*
- mean, *p. 156*
- order of operations, *p. 160*
- rational number, *p. 167*
- additive inverse, *p. 168*
- additive identity, *p. 168*
- multiplicative inverse, *p. 168*
- multiplicative identity, *p. 168*
- equivalent expressions, *p. 173*
- distributive property, *p. 173*

VOCABULARY EXERCISES

1. Identify all integers and all pairs of opposites among the numbers 2.3, −4, 5, −2.3, −2, and 4.
2. How is the multiplicative inverse of a number different from the additive inverse of a number? *Explain.*
3. Expressions that have the same value are called __?__.
4. Identify and describe the properties of the additive identity and the multiplicative identity.
5. **NOTETAKING SKILLS** Make a *process diagram* similar to the one on page 128 for multiplying integers.

REVIEW EXAMPLES AND EXERCISES

3.1 Ordering Integers on a Number Line *pp. 129–133*

Gr. NS 1.5

EXAMPLE

Graph and compare −2 and 3.

▸ **Answer** Because −2 is to the left of 3, $-2 < 3$ or $3 > -2$.

EXERCISES

SEE EXAMPLES 1, 2, AND 3 on pp. 129–130 for Exs. 6–11

Copy and complete the statement using < or >.

6. 12 _?_ −23
7. −44 _?_ 7
8. −21 _?_ −19
9. −4 _?_ −7
10. Graph and order the integers from least to greatest: 7, 9, 8, −8, −10, 11.
11. **FINANCE** Write the integer that corresponds to a bank withdrawal of $350.

3.2 Adding Integers

pp. 135–140

NS 2.3

EXAMPLE

Find the sum −2 + (−4) using a number line.

Start at 0. Move 2 units to the **left**.

Then move 4 more units to the **left**.

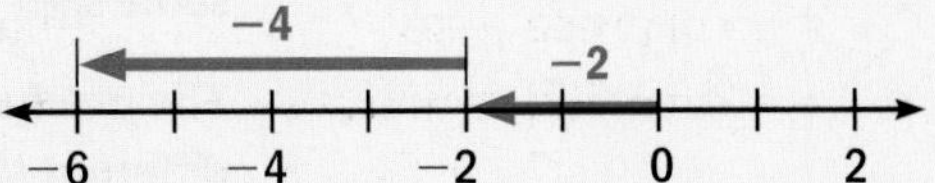

▸ **Answer** The final position is −6, so −2 + (−4) = −6.

EXERCISES

SEE EXAMPLES 1 AND 4 on pp. 135–137 for Exs. 12–22

Find the sum.

12. −14 + 29

13. 31 + (−73)

14. −47 + (−13)

15. −16 + (−22)

16. 52 + (−11)

17. −94 + 71

18. −36 + (−19)

19. −27 + (−68)

20. −32 + (−11) + 12

21. −20 + (−64) + (−42)

22. **CHEMISTRY** An atom has 19 protons and 18 electrons. Write and evaluate an addition expression to find the total charge of the atom.

3.3 Subtracting Integers

pp. 143–147

NS 2.3

EXAMPLE

Find the difference 5 − 8.

5 − 8 = 5 + (− 8) **Write as an addition expression.**

= −3 **Use rule for adding integers.**

EXERCISES

SEE EXAMPLES 1, 2, AND 3 on pp. 143–144 for Exs. 23–31

Find the difference.

23. 1 − 8

24. 11 − (−2)

25. −7 − 3

26. 34 − (−41)

27. −15 − 7

28. 19 − (−28)

29. 12 − 35

30. −48 − (−48)

31. **WEATHER** The high temperature today was 13°F, and the low temperature was −5°F. What was the change in temperature today?

3.4 Multiplying Integers

pp. 148–153

NS 2.3

EXAMPLE

a. $-3(-8) = 24$ **The product of two integers with the same sign is positive.**

b. $-6(7) = -42$ **The product of two integers with different signs is negative.**

EXERCISES

SEE EXAMPLES 1, 2, AND 3 on p. 149 for Exs. 32–44

Find the product.

32. $-10(10)$ **33.** $-27(0)$ **34.** $-6(-3)$ **35.** $-9(-2)(-3)$

36. $-5(-7)$ **37.** $-19(6)$ **38.** $-8(-4)(-2)$ **39.** $-15(0)(-3)$

Evaluate the expression when $a = -3$.

40. $a \cdot 4$ **41.** $-a \cdot 12$ **42.** $3 \cdot (-a)$ **43.** $-7 \cdot (-a)$

44. POPULATION Suppose the average population of a town has been decreasing by 115 people per year. How has the population changed over the last six years?

3.5 Dividing Integers

pp. 154–158

NS 2.3

EXAMPLE

a. $36 \div (-9) = -4$ **The quotient of two integers with different signs is negative.**

b. $\frac{-56}{-8} = 7$ **The quotient of two integers with the same sign is positive.**

EXERCISES

SEE EXAMPLES 1, 2, AND 3 on pp. 155–156 for Exs. 45–53

Find the quotient.

45. $-88 \div 22$ **46.** $96 \div (-32)$ **47.** $0 \div (-37)$ **48.** $-87 \div (-29)$

49. $-56 \div (-28)$ **50.** $19 \div (-1)$ **51.** $-84 \div 21$ **52.** $0 \div (-52)$

53. TEMPERATURES The high temperatures for five days in Dzalinda, Siberia, were −11°C, −5°C, −4°C, 1°C, and 4°C. What is the mean of these temperatures?

3.6 Order of Operations

pp. 160–165

AF 1.4

EXAMPLE

$2 \times 3^3 + (20 - 6) \div 7 = 2 \times 3^3 + \mathbf{14} \div 7$ **Evaluate inside grouping symbols.**

$= 2 \times \mathbf{27} + 14 \div 7$ **Evaluate powers.**

$= \mathbf{54} + \mathbf{2}$ **Multiply and divide from left to right.**

$= 56$ **Add.**

EXERCISES

SEE EXAMPLES 1, 2, 3, AND 4 on pp. 160–162 for Exs. 54–65

Evaluate the expression.

54. $50 - 2 \cdot (-10) + 4$

55. $-4 + 3(7 + 5)$

56. $(15 \div 3)^2$

57. $39 + (1 + 5)^2$

58. $6 - 27 \div 3 + 14$

59. $2(4^2 - 35) - 10$

60. $\frac{5 \cdot 6}{6 + 9}$

61. $\frac{(1 + 4)^3}{10 \div 2}$

62. $\frac{6^2 + 4}{9 - 1}$

63. $12 + 1 - 3 \times 4$

64. $8[2 \times 3 \div (-3)]$

65. $1 + 6(2 + 8)$

3.7 Rational Numbers and their Properties

pp. 167–172

NS 1.1
AF 1.3

EXAMPLE

a. $-15(3)(-6) = [-\mathbf{15(3)}](-6)$ **Order of operations**

$= [3(-\mathbf{15})](-6)$ **Commutative property of multiplication**

$= 3[(-15)(-6)]$ **Associative property of multiplication**

$= 3(90)$ **Multiply –15 and –6.**

$= 270$ **Multiply 3 and 90.**

b. Order $-\frac{2}{3}$, 1, $-1\frac{5}{6}$, $1.\overline{6}$, and $-1.\overline{3}$ from least to greatest.

▸ **Answer** From least to greatest, the numbers are $-1\frac{5}{6}$, $-1.\overline{3}$, $-\frac{2}{3}$, 1, $1.\overline{6}$.

EXERCISES

SEE EXAMPLES 1, 2, 3, 4, AND 5 on pp. 167–169 for Exs. 66–74

Show that the numbers are rational by writing each number in $\frac{a}{b}$ form. Use a number line to order the numbers from least to greatest.

66. $-3.7, 3\frac{5}{8}, -3.1, -\frac{16}{5}, 3$

67. $2.4, -2.1, -2\frac{4}{5}, 2, 2\frac{1}{9}$

68. $-6.2, 6\frac{1}{4}, 6.34, 6, -\frac{19}{3}$

Evaluate the expression. *Justify* each step.

69. $-2 + 17 + 2$

70. $12 \cdot (-27) \cdot \frac{1}{12}$

71. $\frac{3}{7} \cdot (-1) \cdot \frac{7}{3}$

72. $-7 + (-7) + 7$

73. $25(-9)(-4)$

74. $\frac{1}{6} \cdot (-15) \cdot 6$

3.8 The Distributive Property

pp. 173–178

AF 1.3

EXAMPLE

Use the distributive property to write an equivalent expression for 3(18 − 7). Check your answer.

Expression: $3(18 - 7) = 3(18) - 3(7)$ **Distributive property**

CHECK $3(11) \stackrel{?}{=} 54 - 21$ **Simplify.**

$33 = 33$ ✓ **Answer checks.**

EXAMPLE

SWEATERS You buy 4 sweaters that cost \$25.15 each. Use the distributive property to find the total cost of the sweaters.

$4(25.15) = 4(25 + 0.15)$ **Write 25.15 as a sum of a whole number and a decimal.**

$= 4(25) + 4(0.15)$ **Distributive property**

$= 100 + 0.60$ **Multiply.**

$= 100.60$ **Add.**

▶ **Answer** The total cost of the sweaters is \$100.60.

EXERCISES

SEE EXAMPLES 2 AND 3 on pp. 174 for Exs. 75–79

Use the distributive property to write an equivalent expression. Then evaluate the expression.

75. $9\left(\frac{5}{12}\right) + 9\left(\frac{7}{12}\right)$

76. $4(0.98)$

77. $6(1.03)$

78. $9(2.6) + 9(5.4)$

79. LAWN MOWING You mow lawns for 9 hours at \$8.90 an hour. Use the distributive property to write two expressions for the amount you earn.

3 CHAPTER TEST

1. **VOCABULARY** Copy and complete: The _?_ of a data set is the sum of the values divided by the number of values.

2. **VOCABULARY** Copy and complete: The sum of a number and its _?_ or _?_ is always 0.

Order the integers from least to greatest.

3. 16, −17, 32, 7, −15
4. 38, −120, 201, −12, −422
5. −72, −54, 102, 33, 16

Find the sum, difference, product, or quotient.

6. $-12 + 10$
7. $11 + (-8)$
8. $-9 + (-9)$
9. $-4 + (-6)$
10. $7 - (-27)$
11. $36 - 56$
12. $-12(-3)$
13. $15(-3)$
14. $-46 \div (-23)$

Evaluate the expression.

15. $20 + 16 \div 4$
16. $15 - \frac{7}{4}(5 - 3)^2$
17. $(-4) \cdot 8 + 8 \div (-4)$
18. $9 \cdot (2 + 14 \div 7)$
19. $(28 \div 2^2 - 6) + 10$
20. $3^3 + 7 - 5$

Show that the numbers are rational by writing each number in $\frac{a}{b}$ form. Use a number line to order the numbers from least to greatest.

21. $9.6, -\frac{7}{9}, -5, -4\frac{5}{6}, 9\frac{1}{2}$
22. $2\frac{5}{6}, 0, -2.3, -3\frac{3}{4}, 2.4$

Evaluate the expression. *Justify* each step.

23. $16 + (-21) + (-16)$
24. $9 \cdot 16 \cdot \frac{1}{9}$
25. $5\left(\frac{5}{6}\right) + 5\left(\frac{1}{6}\right)$
26. $4(8.5)$

27. **DIVING** After entering the water, a diver descends 6 feet per second for 5 seconds, rises 2 feet per second for 10 seconds, and then descends 10 feet. Express the diver's new position as an integer.

28. **COLDEST TEMPERATURE** The coldest recorded temperature in South Carolina is −28°C, and the coldest recorded temperature in North Carolina is −37°C. Which state has the lower coldest recorded temperature?

29. **ALTITUDE** A hot air balloon descends 210 feet each minute when landing. What is the change in the altitude of the balloon during 3 minutes of descent?

30. **COLORED PENS** You buy three colored pens. Each pen costs $.95. Use the distributive property to write and evaluate two expressions to find the total cost of the colored pens.

3 ◆ MULTIPLE CHOICE STRATEGIES

STRATEGIES YOU'LL USE:
- **SOLVE DIRECTLY**
- **ELIMINATE CHOICES**

Standards
AF 1.3, NS 2.3

If you have trouble solving a multiple choice problem directly, you may be able to use another approach to eliminate incorrect answer choices.

PROBLEM 1

The cost of one game of bowling at a bowling alley is \$2.75. Renting a pair of bowling shoes costs \$3.50, and a slice of pizza costs \$1.25. You bowl 2 games, rent a pair of bowling shoes, and buy 2 slices of pizza. What is the total cost of your trip to the bowling alley?

Ⓐ \$5.50 Ⓑ \$7.50 Ⓒ \$11.50 Ⓓ \$15.00

Strategy 1 SOLVE DIRECTLY

Identify what you know, then write and evaluate an expression for the total cost.

STEP 1 **Identify** what you know.
- You bowl 2 games for \$2.75 each.
- You rent 1 pair of shoes for \$3.50.
- You buy 2 slices of pizza for \$1.25 per slice.

STEP 2 **Write** an expression for the total cost of your trip.

Total cost = 2(2.75) + 3.50 + 2(1.25)

STEP 3 **Evaluate** the expression in Step 2.

$$\begin{aligned}\text{Total cost} &= 2(2.75) + 3.50 + 2(1.25)\\ &= 2(2.75 + 1.25) + 3.50\\ &= 2(4) + 3.5\\ &= 8 + 3.5\\ &= 11.5\end{aligned}$$

The total cost of your trip to the bowling alley is \$11.50.

The correct answer is C. Ⓐ Ⓑ Ⓒ Ⓓ

Strategy 2 ELIMINATE CHOICES

By rounding to the nearest dollar, you can use estimates to identify answer choices that can be eliminated.

Find an underestimate by rounding each price down.

$$2.75 + 2.75 + 3.5 + 1.25 + 1.25 \approx 2 + 2 + 3 + 1 + 1 = 9$$

The cost must be greater than \$9, so you can eliminate choices A and B.

Find an overestimate by rounding each price up.

$$2.75 + 2.75 + 3.5 + 1.25 + 1.25 \approx 3 + 3 + 4 + 2 + 2 = 14$$

The most the total cost can be is \$14, so you can eliminate choice D.

The correct answer is C. Ⓐ Ⓑ Ⓒ Ⓓ

PROBLEM 2

A mine shaft is being drilled from the surface using a method that progresses downward through the rock the same distance each day. In a 6 day period, the drill went from −16 feet to −64 feet. What integer represents the drill's position relative to the surface after 26 days?

Ⓐ −1248 feet Ⓑ −208 feet Ⓒ 208 feet Ⓓ 1248 feet

Strategy 1 SOLVE DIRECTLY

Find the daily change in the drill's position relative to the surface and multiply by 26.

STEP 1 **Subtract** to find the change in the drill's position in 6 days.

$$-64 - (-16) = -48 \text{ feet}$$

STEP 2 **Divide** by 6 days to find the daily change in the drill's position.

$$-48 \div 6 = -8 \text{ feet}$$

STEP 3 **Multiply** by 26 to find the drill's position relative to the surface after 26 days.

$$-8 \times 26 = -208 \text{ feet}$$

The correct answer is B. Ⓐ Ⓑ Ⓒ Ⓓ

Strategy 2 ELIMINATE CHOICES

You can often use reasoning to identify answer choices that can be eliminated.

The drill's position relative to the surface must be a negative number because each day it progresses farther *below* the surface. So, you can eliminate choices C and D.

Because the drill descends −48 ft in 6 days, you know that in 26 days its position will change between 4 and 5 times as much.

$$4(-48) = -192$$

$$5(-48) = -240$$

You can eliminate choice A because it is not between −192 feet and −240 feet.

The correct answer is B. Ⓐ Ⓑ Ⓒ Ⓓ

STRATEGY PRACTICE

Explain why you can eliminate the highlighted answer choice.

1. You have 45 video game tokens. You use 6 tokens at the arcade every week for 3 weeks in a row. What integer represents the change in your number of tokens over 3 weeks?

   Ⓐ −18 Ⓑ −9 Ⓒ ✕ **27** Ⓓ 36

2. What is the value of 3(2.25) + 2(4) + 7?

   Ⓐ ✕ **6** Ⓑ 14.75 Ⓒ 21.75 Ⓓ 47.25

3. What is the value of 7(3 − 7)?

   Ⓐ −28 Ⓑ ✕ **3** Ⓒ 7 Ⓓ 28

3 ◆ MULTIPLE CHOICE PRACTICE

1. Liam used the following process to find the sum $3 + (-5)$.

STEP 1 Find absolute value of 3 and −5.

$|3| = 3 \qquad |-5| = 5$

STEP 2 Find difference between absolute values.

$5 - 3 = 2$

STEP 3 Use sign of number farther from 0.

$3 + (-5) = -2$

Using this method, which expression is equal to the sum $a + b$, when $a > 0$, $b < 0$, and b is farther from 0 than a? **NS 2.3, MR 3.3**

Ⓐ $-b - a$

Ⓑ $-(-b - a)$

Ⓒ $-(b - a)$

Ⓓ $-(a - b)$

2. What is the value of $64 - 8 \times 2^2$? **AF 1.4**

Ⓐ −192

Ⓑ 32

Ⓒ 48

Ⓓ 12,544

3. Which property can be used to show that the expression $-8 + (8 + 4)$ is equivalent to the expression $(-8 + 8) + 4$? **AF 1.3**

Ⓐ Associative property of addition

Ⓑ Commutative property of addition

Ⓒ Identity property of multiplication

Ⓓ Distributive property

4. Which expression has a value of −24? **NS 2.3**

Ⓐ (−6)(−4)

Ⓑ (6)(4)

Ⓒ (−8)(−3)

Ⓓ (−8)(3)

5. The altitude of a hot-air balloon is shown. It rises for 3 minutes at a rate of 15 feet per minute. It then drops 12 feet per minute for 5 minutes. What is the new altitude of the hot-air balloon? **AF 1.4**

Ⓐ −15 feet

Ⓑ 200 feet

Ⓒ 230 feet

Ⓓ 320 feet

6. The product of five integers is negative. Which of the following *cannot* be true about the integers? **NS 2.3, MR 1.2**

Ⓐ 3 are negative, 2 are positive

Ⓑ 2 are negative, 3 are positive

Ⓒ 4 are positive, 1 is negative

Ⓓ 5 are negative

7. The clues below give information about the location of four integers, a, b, c, and d, on a number line. What is the value of d when $a = -4$? **Gr. 5 NS 1.5**

- *a is 2 greater than c.*
- *c is half of b.*
- *d is 5 less than b.*

Ⓐ −17

Ⓑ −9

Ⓒ −7

Ⓓ 2

8. The temperature this morning was 23°F below the high temperature for the day. It is now 8°F warmer than this morning. What is the difference between the high temperature for the day and the temperature it is now? **NS 2.3**

Ⓐ 11°F

Ⓑ 15°F

Ⓒ 16°F

Ⓓ 31°F

9. Which list shows $-0.\overline{6}$, $-1\frac{2}{3}$, 1, $-\frac{5}{8}$ and $1\frac{1}{3}$ in order from least to greatest? **NS 1.1**

Ⓐ $-0.\overline{6}, -1\frac{2}{3}, 1, -\frac{5}{8}, 1\frac{1}{3}$

Ⓑ $-1\frac{2}{3}, -0.\overline{6}, -\frac{5}{8}, 1, 1\frac{1}{3}$

Ⓒ $-\frac{5}{8}, -0.\overline{6}, 1, 1\frac{1}{3}, -1\frac{2}{3}$

Ⓓ $-1\frac{2}{3}, -\frac{5}{8}, -0.\overline{6}, 1, 1\frac{1}{3}$

10. You have \$1295 in a bank account. After paying bills, you have a balance of \$970. What is the change in the balance of the account? **NS 2.3**

Ⓐ −\$970

Ⓑ −\$325

Ⓒ \$325

Ⓓ \$2265

11. Which expression *cannot* be used to find the cost of buying 4 DVDs at the price shown? **AF 1.3, MR 2.5**

Ⓐ 4(14 − 0.15)

Ⓑ 4(13) + 4(0.85)

Ⓒ 4(14 + 0.15)

Ⓓ 4(14) − 4(0.15)

12. What is the value of −18 + (−16)? **NS 2.3**

Ⓐ −34

Ⓑ −2

Ⓒ 2

Ⓓ 34

13. Which expression is *not* equivalent to the expression $(5 - 3)^2 + 6 \div 2$? **AF 1.4**

Ⓐ $2^2 + 6 \div 2$

Ⓑ $(5 - 3)^2 + (6 \div 2)$

Ⓒ $(2^2 + 6) \div 2$

Ⓓ $(5 - 3)^2 + 3$

14. The table shows the daily high temperatures for five days in February in Barrow, Alaska. What is the mean daily high temperature? **NS 2.3**

Day	*Temperature*
Tuesday	4°F
Wednesday	−3°F
Thursday	−13°F
Friday	−20°F
Saturday	2°F

Ⓐ −31.6°F

Ⓑ −6°F

Ⓒ −5°F

Ⓓ 8.4°F

15. One morning, the temperature was 9°F below zero. The temperature rose 13°F by noon and then dropped 6°F by evening. What was the evening temperature? **NS 2.3**

Ⓐ −16°F

Ⓑ −2°F

Ⓒ 7°F

Ⓓ 16°F

3 CUMULATIVE REVIEW Chapters 1–3

Use a factor tree to write the prime factorization of the number. *(p. 5)*

1. 48 **2.** 90 **3.** 351 **4.** 495

Find the GCF and the LCM of the numbers. *(pp. 10, 21)*

5. 8, 14 **6.** 15, 54 **7.** 64, 144 **8.** 42, 70, 105

Write two fractions that are equivalent to the given fraction. *(p. 16)*

9. $\frac{1}{5}$ **10.** $\frac{1}{10}$ **11.** $\frac{3}{7}$ **12.** $\frac{3}{5}$

13. $\frac{3}{11}$ **14.** $\frac{9}{20}$ **15.** $\frac{4}{25}$ **16.** $\frac{3}{100}$

Find the sum or difference.

17. $\frac{1}{8}+\frac{1}{2}$ *(p. 75)* **18.** $\frac{2}{3}+\frac{3}{4}$ *(p. 75)* **19.** $\frac{8}{9}-\frac{5}{6}$ *(p. 75)*

20. $\frac{7}{12}-\frac{2}{5}$ *(p. 75)* **21.** $3\frac{3}{8}+1\frac{7}{8}$ *(p. 81)* **22.** $8\frac{3}{16}-4\frac{9}{16}$ *(p. 81)*

23. $7+(-3)$ *(p. 135)* **24.** $-16-12$ *(p. 143)* **25.** $24-(-15)$ *(p.143)*

Find the product or quotient.

26. $\frac{1}{6}\times\frac{1}{9}$ *(p. 88)* **27.** $\frac{4}{7}\times\frac{5}{12}$ *(p. 88)* **28.** $3\frac{3}{4}\times7\frac{7}{10}$ *(p. 88)*

29. $9\frac{3}{8}\times6\frac{11}{15}$ *(p. 88)* **30.** $\frac{7}{8}\div\frac{3}{4}$ *(p. 95)* **31.** $\frac{7}{12}\div\frac{4}{5}$ *(p. 95)*

32. $5\frac{5}{9}\div3\frac{1}{3}$ *(p. 95)* **33.** $8\frac{2}{5}\div2\frac{7}{10}$ *(p. 95)* **34.** $8(-6)$ *(p. 148)*

35. $-16(-5)$ *(p. 148)* **36.** $-36\div(-6)$ *(p. 154)* **37.** $-56\div14$ *(p. 154)*

Use a number line to order the numbers from least to greatest. *(p. 167)*

38. $-2, 5, -8, 10, -6,$ **39.** $-19, -30, -23, 28, 0$

40. $2.6, \frac{1}{6}, 2\frac{2}{3}, 0$ **41.** $-1.26, -1\frac{1}{4}, 1\frac{1}{4}, 1.40$

42. $-\frac{7}{4}, -1\frac{5}{8}, -2.3, -1\frac{7}{16}, -2$ **43.** $-0.8, 1\frac{1}{4}, \frac{5}{12}, 1.4, -\frac{3}{4}$

Evaluate the expression. *(p. 160, 173)*

44. $3+8\times2$ **45.** $\frac{1}{5}(23-8)$ **46.** $45-3\times4^2$

47. $18\div6\times11$ **48.** $\frac{7+18}{-5}$ **49.** $13(6-8)$

50. $12-42\div6$ **51.** $(8-6)^3(-4+2)$ **52.** $0.25\times20-6$

53. $12(6.75)$ **54.** $3\left(\frac{4}{7}\right)-3\left(\frac{2}{7}\right)$ **55.** $(9-7)^4(8-3)^2$

Evaluate the expression. ***Justify*** **each step.** ***(p. 167)***

56. $6.4 + [3.6 + (-6)]$

57. $8 \cdot \frac{7}{9} \cdot \frac{1}{8}$

58. $13 + (-9) + 7$

59. $(-12)(6)(-5)$

60. $6 + 18 + (-6)$

61. $\frac{5}{8} \times \frac{7}{11} \times \frac{11}{7}$

62. GIFT BAGS You are filling bags with marbles to give as gifts. You are using 80 blue marbles, 112 green marbles, 144 yellow marbles, and 192 red marbles. You want the bags of marbles to be identical and have no leftover marbles. What is the greatest number of bags that you can fill? How many marbles of each color are in each bag? ***(p. 10)***

63. ELECTRONIC MESSAGES Three computers check for electronic messages at 8:00 A.M. The first computer is set up to check for messages every 7 minutes, the second computer checks every 15 minutes, and the third computer checks every 20 minutes. What is the next time that all three computers check for messages at the same time? ***(p. 21)***

64. SURVEYS The table shows the results of a survey of 12 to 14 year olds asking what their favorite breakfast food is. Order the results from least to greatest. What is the favorite breakfast food? ***(p. 30)***

Food	***Cereal***	***Eggs***	***Oatmeal***	***Fruit***
Number of 12 to 14 year olds	$\frac{2}{5}$	0.26	0.08	$\frac{3}{20}$

65. DIAMONDS A diamond's weight is measured in carats. A ring has one $\frac{1}{4}$ carat diamond and two $\frac{1}{8}$ carat diamonds. What is the total weight of the diamonds on the ring? ***(p. 75)***

66. WOOD BEAMS You have a beam of wood that is $16\frac{5}{8}$ feet long. You want to cut the beam of wood into pieces that are $\frac{7}{8}$ foot long. How many $\frac{7}{8}$ foot pieces can you cut? ***(p. 95)***

67. DELI PRICES At a deli, ham costs $4.99 per pound. Turkey costs $5.29 per pound. You buy 1.5 pounds of turkey and 1.75 pounds of ham. Which costs you more, the ham or the turkey? How much more? ***(p. 107)***

68. WIND CHILL FACTOR The wind chill factor tells how cold it feels outside based on the temperature and wind speed. The wind chill factor was 18°F at 8:00 A.M. but dropped to −14°F by 1:00 P.M. What was the change in wind chill factor? ***(p. 143)***

69. PARTY STORE At a party supply store, you buy 2 hats that cost $2 each, 4 flashing wands that cost $3 each, and 2 gift boxes that cost $1 each. You give the cashier $20. How much change do you receive? ***(p. 173)***

4 Expressions and Equations

Before

In previous chapters, you learned the following skills, which you'll use in Chapter 4:

- Performing operations with fractions
- Evaluating expressions with one variable
- Using the order of operations

Now

In Chapter 4 you'll study these ***Big Ideas:***

1. Writing and evaluating expressions using up to three variables
2. Using familiar formulas
3. Writing and solving one-step equations

Why?

So you can solve real-world problems about . . .

- School dances, p. 200
- Photographs, p. 210
- Amusement parks, p. 223
- Swimming, p. 224
- Jump rope, p. 238
- Baseball, p. 238

at classzone.com

Operation Scramble

California Standards

Review using operations. ***Gr. 6 NS 2.0***

Prepare for evaluating algebraic expressions. ***Gr. 6 AF 1.2***

Materials

- One deck of *Operation Scramble* cards
- A pencil and piece of paper for each player

How to Play Play in pairs. Shuffle the deck of cards and deal four cards to each player. Players should not show each other their cards. Turn over the next card in the deck and place it face up where both players can see it. The number on this card is the *target number*. Both players should follow the steps on the next page.

Expression Cards **Target Card**

CALIFORNIA STANDARDS

- **Gr. 6 AF 1.1 Write and solve one-step linear equations in one variable.** *(Lessons 4.5, 4.6, 4.7)*
- **Gr. 6 AF 1.2 Write and evaluate an algebraic expression for a given situation, using up to three variables.** *(Lessons 4.1, 4.2)*
- **Gr. 6 AF 3.2 Express in symbolic form simple relationships arising from geometry.** *(Lesson 4.4)*

1 **Use** the numbers on all four of the cards in your hand and any of the operations $+$, $-$, $\times$, and $\div$ to write an expression that equals the target number. Do not use parentheses.

2 **Tell** your opponent when you have finished writing your expression. Both players must stop working.

3 **Check** the work of the player who finished writing first. If the expression is correct, that player earns one point.

How to Win Be the first player to earn three points.

Games Wrap-Up

Draw Conclusions

Complete these exercises after playing the game.

1. WRITING A student playing *Operation Scramble* claims that $4 - 2 \times 3 \times 1$ is equal to the target number 6. *Describe* and correct the student's error.

2. REASONING Suppose you have only even numbers on the cards in your hand, and the target number is odd. Give an example of a correct expression and target number that fits this description. *Explain* how you chose the correct operations to use.

4 Getting Ready

Prerequisite Skills

California @HomeTutor
Prerequisite skills practice at classzone.com

REVIEW VOCABULARY

- **variable,** *p. 70*
- **algebraic expression,** *p. 70*
- **evaluate,** *p. 70*
- **perimeter,** *p. 684*
- **area,** *p. 685*

VOCABULARY CHECK

Copy and complete using a review term from the list at the left.

1. The distance around a figure is the __?__ of the figure. The number of square units needed to cover a figure is the __?__ of the figure.
2. A letter used to represent one or more numbers is called a(n) __?__.
3. To evaluate a(n) __?__, substitute values for the variables and then simplify the resulting numerical expression.

SKILL CHECK

Evaluate the expression. ***(p. 160)***

4. $18 - 3 \cdot 7 + 4$
5. $(6 - 2)^3 + 3 \cdot 5$
6. $4 \cdot 3.1 + 5 \cdot 1.2$
7. $6(8.2 - 5.2)^2$
8. $\frac{2}{3} \cdot \frac{3}{4} - \frac{1}{8}$
9. $\frac{15 - 27}{4 - 8}$

Evaluate the expression when $x = 4$, $y = 2$, and $z = -3$.
(pp. 135, 143, 148, 154)

10. $-5 + x$
11. $y - 9$
12. $3 \cdot z$
13. $\frac{x}{-2}$
14. $z + 7$
15. $\frac{-10}{y}$

Notetaking Skills

NOW YOU TRY
Make an *information frame* for the associative property of addition. You may want to use colored pencils.

Focus on Graphic Organizers

Use an *information frame* to organize information about a property or idea, such as the identity property of multiplication.

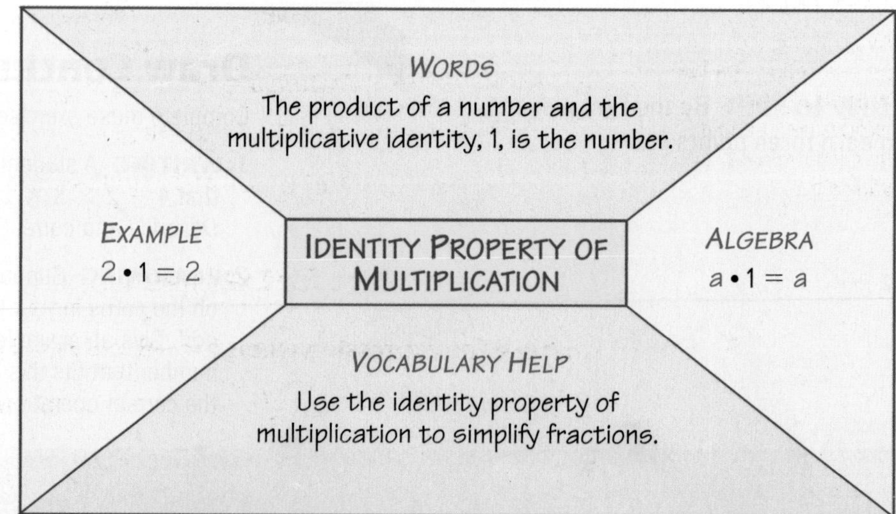

WORDS
The product of a number and the multiplicative identity, 1, is the number.
EXAMPLE
2 • 1 = 2
IDENTITY PROPERTY OF MULTIPLICATION
ALGEBRA
a • 1 = a
VOCABULARY HELP
Use the identity property of multiplication to simplify fractions.

4.1 Evaluating Expressions

Math and SPORTS
Ex. 34, p. 199

Standards **AF 1.2** Write and **evaluate an algebraic expression for a given situation, using up to three variables.**

Connect ***Before*** you used the order of operations. ***Now*** you will apply it to evaluating algebraic expressions.

KEY VOCABULARY
- **variable,** *p. 70*
- **algebraic expression,** *p. 70*
- **evaluate,** *p. 70*

Recall that an algebraic expression consists of numbers, variables, and operations. You can represent multiplication and division within expressions in more than one way.

Multiplication	**Division**
multiplication dot: $5 \cdot x$	division symbol: $x \div 8$
parentheses: $5(x)$	fraction bar: $\frac{x}{8}$
no symbol: $5x$	

When evaluating an algebraic expression, remember to use the order of operations after substituting for the variable(s).

EXAMPLE 1 Evaluating Algebraic Expressions

a. Evaluate $\frac{y}{2}$ when $y = 0.8$.

$\frac{y}{2} = \frac{0.8}{2}$ **Substitute 0.8 for *y*.**

$= 0.4$ **Divide.**

b. Evaluate $x^2 + 2$ when $x = 4$.

$x^2 + 2 = (4)^2 + 2$ **Substitute 4 for *x*.**

$= 16 + 2$ **Evaluate the power.**

$= 18$ **Add.**

c. Evaluate $-4b - 7$ when $b = -3$.

$-4b - 7 = -4(-3) - 7$ **Substitute −3 for *b*.**

$= 12 - 7$, or 5 **Multiply. Then subtract.**

AVOID ERRORS
Avoid using the multiplication symbol × in an algebraic expression. It could be confused with the variable *x*.

✓ GUIDED PRACTICE for Example 1

Evaluate the expression when $a = -6$ and $m = 1.3$.

1. $m - 0.5$ **2.** $\frac{2a}{3}$ **3.** $3m + 3.6$ **4.** $4 - a^2 + 10$

EXAMPLE 2 Evaluating with Two or More Variables

a. Evaluate $x^2 + y^2$ when $x = -3$ and $y = -6$.

$x^2 + y^2 = (-3)^2 + (-6)^2$ **Substitute −3 for *x* and −6 for *y*.**

$= 9 + 36$ **Evaluate the powers.**

$= 45$ **Add.**

b. Evaluate $\frac{2a + b}{c}$ when $a = -1$, $b = 7$, and $c = 5$.

$\frac{2a + b}{c} = \frac{2(-1) + 7}{5}$ **Substitute −1 for *a*, 7 for *b*, and 5 for *c*.**

$= \frac{-2 + 7}{5}$ **Multiply.**

$= \frac{5}{5}$ **Add.**

$= 1$ **Divide.**

EXAMPLE 3 Evaluating a Real-World Expression

JOB EARNINGS You earn \$8.50 per hour walking dogs and \$5.75 per hour mowing lawns. The total amount you earn is given by the expression $8.5x + 5.75y$ where x is the amount of time (in hours) you walk dogs and y is the amount of time (in hours) you mow lawns.

Find the amount you earn if you walk dogs for 6 hours and mow lawns for 10 hours.

Walking dogs: \$8.50 per hour

About the Standards

In Example 3, you can use estimation to verify the reasonableness of calculated results, as mentioned in Grade 6 Standard MR 2.1.

$8.5(6) + 5.75(10)$

$\approx 9(6) + 6(10)$

$= 114$

SOLUTION

Identify the values of the variables: $x = 6$ and $y = 10$.

$8.5x + 5.75y = 8.5(6) + 5.75(10)$ **Substitute.**

$= 51 + 57.5$ **Multiply.**

$= 108.5$ **Add.**

▶ **Answer** You earn \$108.50.

✓ GUIDED PRACTICE for Examples 2 and 3

Evaluate the expression when $q = \frac{2}{5}$, $r = -6$, $s = 4$, and $t = 8.6$.

5. $r \cdot s$ **6.** $10q + r$ **7.** $r^2 - 5t$ **8.** $3s + 5q$

9. $\frac{s + 0.3}{t}$ **10.** $\frac{r + s}{t - 3.6}$ **11.** $6s - 2r + t$ **12.** $15q + r^2 - t$

13. WHAT IF? In Example 3, suppose that you walk dogs for 12 hours and mow lawns for 3 hours. Find the total amount you earn.

4.1 EXERCISES

HOMEWORK KEY

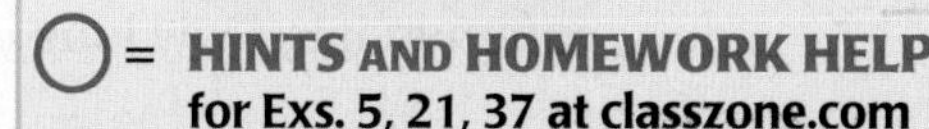

◆ = MULTIPLE CHOICE PRACTICE Exs. 25, 35, 44–46

○ = HINTS AND HOMEWORK HELP for Exs. 5, 21, 37 at classzone.com

SKILLS • PROBLEM SOLVING • REASONING

1. **VOCABULARY** Identify the variable in the expression $9 - 7c + 5^2$.

2. **WRITING** *Explain* how to evaluate an algebraic expression with more than one operation.

SEE EXAMPLES 1 AND 2 on pp. 197–198 for Exs. 3–25

EVALUATING Evaluate the expression when $x = 5$, $y = -3$, $r = \frac{1}{2}$, and $s = 0.75$.

3. $0.5x$
4. $8r - 12$
5. $8 - 6y$
6. $2 + 3s$
7. $7(s - 0.25)$
8. $-3y - 11$
9. $7(4s + x)$
10. $8r - y + 2$
11. $3xy$
12. $3x - 6(s + 0.5)$
13. $-4y - 2s$
14. $1.3x - 6s + y$
15. $3 + 4x^2$
16. $x^2 + 10r$
17. $xy^2 + 4r$
18. $y^3 - 8x$
19. $\frac{4s}{2}$
20. $\frac{x - y}{4}$
21. $\frac{5x + y}{2}$
22. $\frac{8s}{xy}$

ERROR ANALYSIS *Describe* and correct the error made in evaluating the expression when $a = 3$ and $b = -8$.

23. ✗ $2a = 23$

24. ✗ $b - a = 3 - (-8)$
$= 3 + 8$
$= 11$

25. ◆ **MULTIPLE CHOICE** Evaluate $2a + 4 \div b^2$ when $a = 6$ and $b = 2$.

Ⓐ 4 Ⓑ 5 Ⓒ 13 Ⓓ 16

COMPARING VALUES Copy and complete the statement using <, >, or = when $x = -7$ and $y = 15$.

26. $y + 9$? $4x + 3y$
27. $x + y - 4$? $\frac{y}{5}$
28. $20 - y$? $\frac{14}{x} + \frac{30}{y}$
29. $x^2 + 12y$? $40 + y$
30. $3xy$? $y(x + 6)$
31. $4(x + y)$? $52 + x$

CONNECT SKILLS TO PROBLEM SOLVING Exercises 32–34 will help you prepare for problem solving.

32. The expression $\frac{w}{17}$, where w is weight (in pounds) on Earth, can be used to approximate a weight (in pounds) on Pluto. Evaluate $\frac{w}{17}$ when $w = 85$.

33. The total earnings of a person who earns d dollars per week for w weeks is given by the expression dw. Evaluate dw when $d = 120$ and $w = 9$.

34. The points earned by a basketball player who makes a free throws, b two point shots, and c three point shots is given by the expression $a + 2b + 3c$. Evaluate $a + 2b + 3c$ when $a = 11$, $b = 12$ and $c = 3$.

SEE EXAMPLE 3 on p. 198 for Exs. 35–37

35. ◆ **MULTIPLE CHOICE** The actual length of a TV show that airs in a 1 hour time slot is given by $60 - c$ where c is the amount of time (in minutes) of commercials. How long is a show with $\frac{3}{10}$ hour of commercials?

Ⓐ 18 min Ⓑ 32 min Ⓒ 42 min Ⓓ 52 min

California @HomeTutor for problem solving help at classzone.com

36. **BAMBOO GROWTH** Bamboo makes up most of a panda's diet. You can predict the amount of growth for a stem of bamboo by evaluating the expression gn where g is the average amount (in inches) grown each day and n is the number of days. Predict the amount of growth in one week for bamboo that grows an average of 12 inches each day.

California @HomeTutor for problem solving help at classzone.com

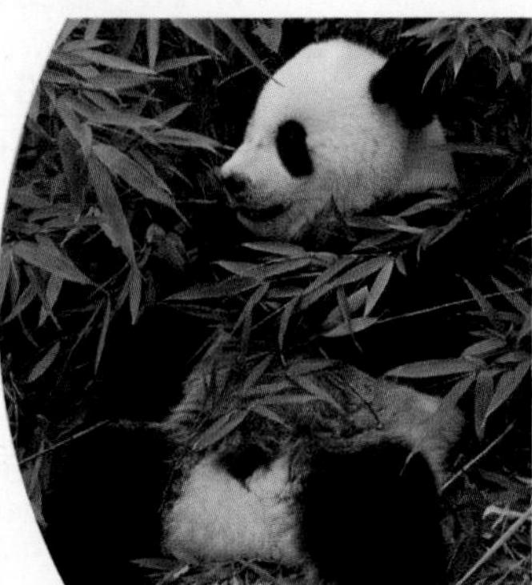
Daily average bamboo growth: 12 inches

37. **DANCE** Tickets to a school dance cost \$3.50 each, and refreshments cost \$1.75 each. The total revenue is given by the expression $3.5x + 1.75y$ where x is the number of tickets sold and y is the number of refreshments sold. Find the total revenue if 245 tickets and 310 refreshments are sold.

38. **SHORT RESPONSE** If the expression $\frac{x}{y}$ has a value of 3, what are some possible values of x and y? *Describe* the relationship of x to y.

CHALLENGE Tell whether the given expressions are *always, sometimes,* or *never* equal. *Explain* your reasoning.

39. $x + x; 2x$ 40. $x + 4; x - 4$ 41. $x + 4; x$ 42. $\frac{x}{4}; 4x$

43. **CHALLENGE** Use $xy = 32$. Make a table of the possible whole number values of x and y, with the x-values in numerical order. *Describe* the pattern of the y-values. As the value of x increases, how does y change? *Explain.*

◆ California Standards Spiral Review

NS 2.2 44. What is the quotient of $\frac{5}{12}$ and $\frac{10}{3}$? ***(p. 95)***

Ⓐ $3\frac{3}{4}$ Ⓑ $1\frac{7}{18}$ Ⓒ $\frac{1}{2}$ Ⓓ $\frac{1}{8}$

AF 1.3 45. Which expression is equivalent to $-2(10 - 7)$? ***(p. 173)***

Ⓐ $-2(10) + (-2)(-7)$ Ⓑ $-2(-10) - (-2)(7)$

Ⓒ $-2(10) - (2)(7)$ Ⓓ $-2(10) + (-2)(7)$

NS 2.3 46. The highest point on an iceberg is 75 feet above sea level. The lowest point on the iceberg is 128 feet below sea level. What is the difference between the highest and lowest points on the iceberg? ***(p. 143)***

Ⓐ 53 ft Ⓑ 150 ft Ⓒ 203 ft Ⓓ 256 ft

4.1 Evaluating Expressions

Standards
AF 1.2 Write and **evaluate** an algebraic expression for a given situation, using up to three variables.

QUESTION How can you use spreadsheet software to evaluate an expression?

A spreadsheet has rows and columns for organizing data. The rows are labeled with numbers. The columns are labeled with letters. The intersection of a row and a column forms a *cell*. Cells are named according to the column and row in which they are located. For instance, the cell in column A and row 1 is named A1.

	A	B	C
1			
2			
3			
4			

EXAMPLE Evaluate an expression.

Evaluate the expression $-2x - 48$.

STEP 1 **Label** cells A1 and B1 as shown. Then enter the value "-2" to substitute for x and the formula for the expression, as shown. In the formula "-2*A2 $-$ 48," cell A2 stands for x.

	A	B
1	Value of x	Value of expression
2	−2	=−2*A2−48

STEP 2 **Enter** more values to substitute for x as shown. Then use the *fill down* feature to have the spreadsheet calculate the values of the expression for these new x-values.

	A	B
1	Value of x	Value of expression
2	−2	−44
3	−1	−46
4	0	−48
5	1	−50
6	2	−52
7	3	−54

PRACTICE

Use a spreadsheet to evaluate the expression when $x = -2, -1, 0, 1,$ 2, and 3.

1. $3x + 8$ **2.** $5x - 2$ **3.** $-9x - 1$ **4.** $-7x + 4$

5. **REASONING** The total value (in dollars) of n nickels, d dimes, and q quarters is $0.05n + 0.1d + 0.25q$. *Explain* how you would use a spreadsheet to evaluate this expression. Then evaluate the expression to find the total value of 6 nickels, 8 dimes, and 3 quarters.

4.2 Writing Expressions

Math and GEOLOGY
Ex. 40, p. 206

Standards **AF 1.2** **Write and evaluate an algebraic expression for a given situation, using up to three variables.**

Connect ***Before*** you evaluated algebraic expressions. ***Now*** you will write algebraic expressions.

KEY VOCABULARY
- **verbal model**

To solve real-world problems, you need to translate verbal phrases and sentences into algebraic expressions and *equations*. Look for key words that indicate addition, subtraction, multiplication, and division.

Addition	Subtraction	Multiplication	Division
plus	minus	times	divided by
the sum of	the difference of	the product of	the quotient of
increased by	decreased by	multiplied by	separate into equal parts
total	fewer than	of	
more than	less than	twice	
added to	subtracted from		

Order is important in subtraction and division expressions. For example, the phrase "2 less than a number" is written as $x - 2$, not $2 - x$. Similarly, the phrase "a number divided by 5" is written as $x \div 5$, not $5 \div x$.

EXAMPLE 1 Translating Verbal Phrases

READING
The phrase "the difference of a and b" is written as $a - b$, not $b - a$. The phrase "the quotient of a and b" is written as $a \div b$.

Verbal phrase	Expression
a. 5 more than twice a number	$2x + 5$
b. The sum of 2 and a number to the fourth power	$2 + x^4$
c. 3 times the difference of a number and 2	$3(x - 2)$
d. 4 decreased by the quotient of a number and 7	$4 - \frac{x}{7}$

✓ GUIDED PRACTICE for Example 1

Write the verbal phrase as an algebraic expression. Let *n* represent the number.

1. 3 less than a number

2. 8 more than twice a number

3. A number squared divided by 4

4. 5 less the product of 3 and 6 less than a number

EXAMPLE 2 ◆ Multiple Choice Practice

A jeweler sold x necklaces for \$8.50 each and y bracelets for \$3.40 each. Which expression gives the difference between the amount earned from selling necklaces and the amount earned from selling bracelets?

Ⓐ $3.4x + 8.5y$ Ⓑ $11.9(x - y)$ Ⓒ $3.4x - 8.5y$ Ⓓ $8.5x - 3.4y$

ELIMINATE CHOICES
In Example 2, you can eliminate choice A because the key word "difference" indicates subtraction.

SOLUTION

The amount earned from selling x necklaces is $8.5x$. The amount earned from selling y bracelets is $3.4y$. The difference is $8.5x - 3.4y$.

▶ **Answer** The correct answer is D. Ⓐ Ⓑ Ⓒ Ⓓ

VERBAL MODELS A **verbal model** uses words as labels and uses math symbols to relate the words. You can use verbal models to solve problems.

EXAMPLE 3 Using a Verbal Model

TICKET PRICES The diagram shows the prices of tickets for different sections of a theater. For one show, 203 first-level tickets, 150 second-level tickets, and 22 third-level tickets are sold. Write and evaluate an expression to find the total ticket sales.

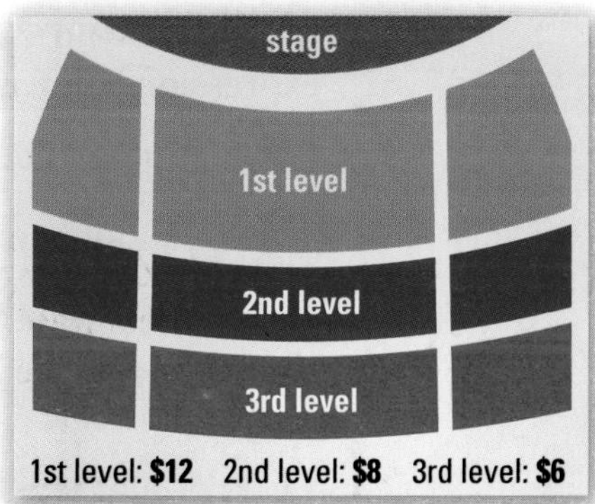

ASSIGN VARIABLES
Use easy-to-remember variables to represent values. For instance, in Example 3, f represents first-level tickets.

SOLUTION

Write a verbal model. Let f be the number of first-level tickets, s be the number of second-level tickets, and t be the number of third-level tickets.

Price of first-level ticket • Number of first-level tickets + Price of second-level ticket • Number of second-level tickets + Price of third-level ticket • Number of third-level tickets

$12f + 8s + 6t = 12(203) + 8(150) + 6(22)$ **Substitute values.**

$= 3768$ **Simplify.**

▶ **Answer** The total ticket sales are \$3768.

✓ GUIDED PRACTICE for Examples 2 and 3

5. **WHAT IF?** In Example 2, suppose that the jeweler sold each necklace for \$9.25 and each bracelet for \$5.75. Write an expression for the difference.

6. **WHAT IF?** In Example 3, suppose 215 first-level tickets, 160 second-level tickets, and 43 third-level tickets are sold. Find the total ticket sales.

4.2 EXERCISES

HOMEWORK KEY

◆ = **MULTIPLE CHOICE PRACTICE** Exs. 13, 20, 37, 48–50

○ = **HINTS AND HOMEWORK HELP** for Exs. 9, 15, 37 at classzone.com

SKILLS • PROBLEM SOLVING • REASONING

1. **VOCABULARY** Copy and complete: A model that uses words as labels and uses math symbols to relate the words is a(n) __?__.

2. **WRITING** Write the phrase "two less than a number n" as an algebraic expression. *Explain* how to evaluate the expression when $n = 5$.

SEE EXAMPLE 1 on p. 202 for Exs. 3–13

MATCHING Match the verbal phrase with its algebraic expression.

3. 4 more than a number — **A.** $4 - x$
4. The quotient of a number and 4 — **B.** $x + 4$
5. The difference of 4 and a number — **C.** $\frac{x}{4}$
6. 4 less than a number — **D.** $x - 4$

WRITING EXPRESSIONS Write the verbal phrase as an algebraic expression. Let n represent the number.

7. A number added to -7
8. $\frac{1}{3}$ of a number
9. The quotient of a number plus 6 and 3
10. 0.35 less than twice a number
11. The sum of a number divided by 6 and 2
12. 4 fewer than the cube of a number

Animated Math at classzone.com

13. ◆ **MULTIPLE CHOICE** Which expression represents the phrase "two times the difference of x and 3"?

    (A) $2x - 3$ (B) $2(x - 3)$ (C) $2(3 - x)$ (D) $2(x + 3)$

SEE EXAMPLES 2 AND 3 on p. 203 for Exs. 14–28

WRITING EXPRESSIONS Write the phrase as an algebraic expression.

14. y plus the product of -5 and x
15. The quotient of a cubed and b
16. The difference of c squared and d
17. The product of 1.2 minus r and s
18. The sum of m and $\frac{1}{2}$ and n and p
19. f to the ninth power plus g plus h

20. ◆ **MULTIPLE CHOICE** Which expression represents the phrase "the sum of x cubed and y"?

    (A) $(x + y)^3$ (B) $x^3 + y^3$ (C) $x^3 + y$ (D) $x + y^3$

WRITING PHRASES Write a verbal phrase for the algebraic expression.

21. $3 + a$
22. $13b$
23. $5x + 1$
24. $w - 2y$
25. $n^2 + p$
26. $\frac{c + d}{9}$
27. $2(a + b + c)$
28. $\frac{m - n}{c}$

29. **ERROR ANALYSIS** Andrea says that "7 less than a number" is written as $7 - x$. *Describe* and correct the error.

30. **ERROR ANALYSIS** Derrick says that "a number squared plus the product of another number and 4" can be translated as $n^2 + 4n$. *Describe* and correct the error.

CONNECT SKILLS TO PROBLEM SOLVING Exercises 31–34 will help you prepare for problem solving.

Write the real-world phrase as an algebraic expression. Identify what the variable represents.

31. 3 years older than Theo
32. 5 inches shorter than Ann
33. Half of your class
34. Twice a team's score

SEE EXAMPLE 3 on p. 203 for Exs. 35–39

35. **MULTI-STEP PROBLEM** The Rio Grande River is 450 miles longer than the Colorado River.
   a. Write a verbal model that represents the length of the Rio Grande River.
   b. Use the model to write an expression in terms of the length c (in miles) of the Colorado River.
   c. The Colorado River is 1450 miles long. Evaluate the expression to find the length of the Rio Grande River.

California @HomeTutor for problem solving help at classzone.com

Length of Colorado River: 1450 miles

36. **BUSINESS** A vehicle rental company charges \$25 to rent a moving van plus \$.50 for each mile traveled. Write an expression that represents the total cost of renting a van and driving d miles. What is the total cost of renting a van and driving 20 miles?

California @HomeTutor for problem solving help at classzone.com

37. ◆ **MULTIPLE CHOICE** You buy a digital video recorder for \$99, and the cost per month for the recorder's data service is d dollars. What is your total cost for 1 year?

   (A) $12d$ (B) $(99 + 12)d$ (C) $99 + 12d$ (D) $99d$

38. **SAVINGS** You already have x dollars saved, and you plan to save an additional \$10.50 per week. Write an expression to represent the total amount of money you will have after w weeks. How much money will you have after 12 weeks if you already have \$42.75 saved?

39. **DONATIONS** Carmela is donating a total of b books. She plans to donate c books to a library and d books to a daycare center. She will divide the rest evenly between two schools. Write an expression to represent the number of books that she will donate to each school. How many books will she donate to each school if she has 150 books to donate and she donates 30 to the library and 10 to the daycare center?

40. CAVES You are exploring a cave in which rock formations called stalagmites grow up from the cave floor. The stalagmites in the cave are underwater in a pool 55 feet deep.

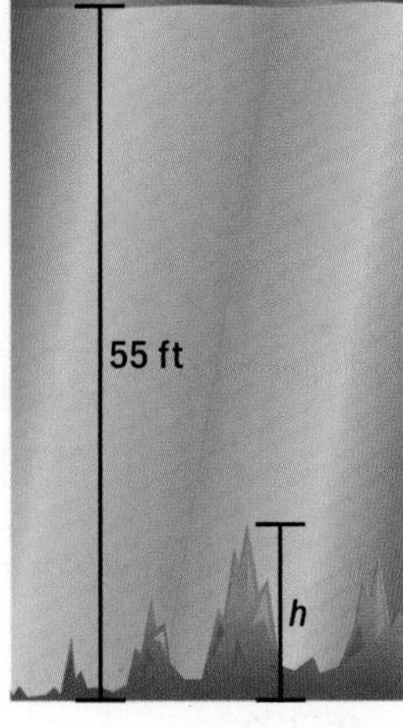

a. Let h represent the height (in feet) of a stalagmite. Write an expression to represent the distance between the tip of a stalagmite and the water surface.

b. What is the distance between the tip of a stalagmite and the water surface for a stalagmite with a height of 10 feet? 15 feet? 20 feet?

c. How does the distance between the tip of a stalagmite and the water surface change as the height of the stalagmite increases?

41. WRITING Is "three less than a number" equivalent to "the difference of three and a number"? *Explain* your reasoning.

42. PUZZLE PROBLEM You are x years old. Your brother is 3 years older than you. Your sister is 4 years younger than your brother. Write expressions that represent your brother's age and your sister's age. If you are 13 years old, how old are your brother and sister?

43. OPEN-ENDED *Describe* a real-world situation that can be modeled by the expression $x - 2(5) + 8$. Evaluate the expression when $x = 30$. *Explain* what the value of the expression means in this situation.

CHALLENGE Write a verbal phrase for the algebraic expression.

44. $\frac{x^3}{y - 8}$ **45.** $(3q)(9 - r)$ **46.** $\frac{a + 12}{b^2}$

47. CHALLENGE Juan and Micah are asked to write the phrase "4 times a number plus 8" as an expression and then find the value of the expression when $n = 8$. Juan writes $4n + 8$ and gets 40. Micah writes $4(n + 8)$ and gets 64. Are they both right? *Explain* your reasoning.

◆ CALIFORNIA STANDARDS SPIRAL REVIEW

NS 2.3 **48.** What is the product of -12 and -34? *(p. 148)*

Ⓐ -408 Ⓑ -46 Ⓒ 46 Ⓓ 408

NS 2.4 **49.** What is the greatest common factor of 45 and 56? *(p. 10)*

Ⓐ 1 Ⓑ 3 Ⓒ 8 Ⓓ 15

AF 1.2 **50.** You have a coupon for \$3 off a meal at a new restaurant. The expression $c - 3$ represents the price (in dollars) of a meal that costs c dollars when you use the coupon. How much will you pay for a \$12 meal with the coupon? *(p. 197)*

Ⓐ \$4 Ⓑ \$9 Ⓒ \$10 Ⓓ \$15

4.3 Simplifying Expressions

Math and MUSIC
Ex. 38, p. 210

Standards Preparation Gr. 5 AF 1.3 **Know and use the distributive property in** equations and **expressions with variables.**

Connect ***Before*** you wrote algebraic expressions. ***Now*** you will use properties to simplify expressions to prepare for Grade 6 Standard AF 3.1.

KEY VOCABULARY
- **terms**
- **coefficient**
- **like terms**
- **constant term**

The parts of an algebraic expression that are added together are called **terms**. In a term that is the product of a number and a variable part, the number is called the **coefficient** of the term.

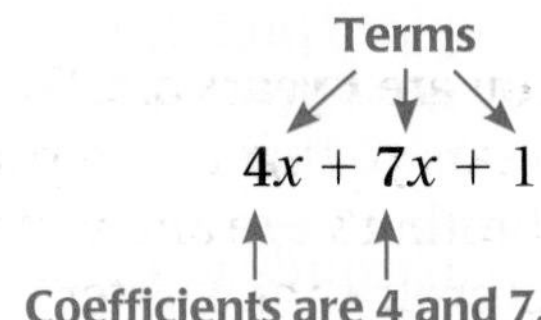

Terms
$4x + 7x + 1$
Coefficients are 4 and 7.

Like terms have identical variable parts with corresponding variables raised to the same power. A term that has no variable is a **constant term**. Two or more constant terms in an expression are also like terms. In the expression above, $4x$ and $7x$ are like terms, and 1 is a constant term.

EXAMPLE 1 Coefficients, Like Terms, and Constant Terms

READING
The coefficient of x is 1. The coefficient of $-x$ is -1. So, the expression $3x - x$ can be written as $3x - 1x$, or $3x + (-1x)$.

Identify the coefficients, like terms, and constant terms of the expression $x + 4 - 2x - 10$.

Write the expression as a sum: $x + 4 + (-2x) + (-10)$.

Coefficients: $1, -2$ **Like terms:** x and $-2x$, 4 and -10 **Constant terms:** $4, -10$

DISTRIBUTIVE PROPERTY The distributive property allows you to *combine like terms* so you can simplify an algebraic expression. For example, $2x + 3x = (2 + 3)x = 5x$. An expression is *simplified* if it does not contain grouping symbols and if all like terms are combined.

EXAMPLE 2 Combining Like Terms

READING
The commutative and associative properties of addition allow you to group like terms after writing the expression as a sum.

Simplify the expression $7c + 9 - 3c$.

$7c + 9 - 3c = 7c + 9 + (-3c)$	**Write expression as a sum.**
$= 9 + 7c + (-3c)$	**Group like terms.**
$= 9 + [7 + (-3)]c$	**Distributive property**
$= 9 + 4c$	**Simplify.**

EXAMPLE 3 Simplifying an Expression

Simplify the expression $5(w-4)+w+8$.

SIMPLIFYING

As Example 3 shows, you use the distributive property before you combine like terms to simplify an expression.

$5(w-4)+w+8 = 5w-20+w+8$		**Distributive property**
	$= 5w+(-20)+w+8$	**Write as a sum.**
	$= 5w+w+(-20)+8$	**Group like terms.**
	$= 6w+(-12)$	**Combine like terms.**
	$= 6w-12$	**Rewrite without parentheses.**

EXAMPLE 4 Writing and Simplifying an Expression

BUSINESS A bicycle mechanic charges \$11 to adjust brakes and \$20 to replace tires. Last month, twice as many customers wanted tires replaced as wanted brakes adjusted.

Write and simplify an expression for the amount the mechanic earned for these services last month. How much did the mechanic earn if 15 customers wanted brakes adjusted?

Cost to adjust brakes: \$11

SOLUTION

Write a verbal model. Let n represent the number of customers who wanted brakes adjusted.

Charge to adjust brakes · Customers wanting brakes adjusted + Charge to replace tires · Customers wanting tires replaced

$11n+20(2n) = 11n+40n$	**Multiply.**
$= 51n$	**Combine like terms.**
$= 51(15)$	**Substitute 15 for n.**
$= 765$	**Multiply.**

▶ **Answer** The mechanic earned \$765 last month.

✓ GUIDED PRACTICE for Examples 1, 2, 3, and 4

Identify the coefficients, like terms, and constant terms of the expression.

1. $-3z+1+4z$ **2.** $15-9r+7r-6$ **3.** $2y+8-2y-4$

Simplify the expression.

4. $16+8(k+9)$ **5.** $6(a-18)-1-6a$ **6.** $-7(m+5)+2m$

7. WHAT IF? In Example 4, suppose that 26 customers wanted tires replaced. How much did the mechanic earn?

4.3 EXERCISES

HOMEWORK KEY

◆ = **MULTIPLE CHOICE PRACTICE** Exs. 7, 30, 38, 44–46

○ = **HINTS AND HOMEWORK HELP** for Exs. 5, 29, 39 at classzone.com

SKILLS • PROBLEM SOLVING • REASONING

1. VOCABULARY Identify the coefficients in the expression $5z - 7 + 2z$.

2. WRITING *Explain* how you know whether two terms are like terms.

SEE EXAMPLE 1 on p. 207 for Exs. 3–7

COEFFICIENTS AND TERMS Identify the coefficients, like terms, and constant terms of the expression.

3. $3x + 4 - x$ **4.** $7z - 9z + 2 + z$ **(5.)** $10 - 4y + 5y - 8$

6. ERROR ANALYSIS Sydney says that the coefficient of the last term in the expression $6y + 5 - 3y$ is 3. *Describe* and correct the error.

7. ◆ MULTIPLE CHOICE Which are like terms in the expression $3 + 3x - 5x$?

Ⓐ 3 and $3x$ Ⓑ $3x$ and $-5x$ Ⓒ 3 and $-5x$ Ⓓ 3 and -5

SEE EXAMPLE 2 on p. 207 for Exs. 8–17

COMBINING LIKE TERMS Combine like terms to simplify the expression.

8. $3a + 9 - a$ **9.** $18 + 4b + 6$ **10.** $-8c + 4 - 5$

11. $14t + 15 - 2t$ **12.** $4k - 10 + 7 - 7k$ **13.** $6 - 2m - 7 + 3m$

14. $10x + 4.5 + x - 4$ **15.** $14.9 - y + y + 5.78$ **16.** $5.7p + 3 - 2.4p - 2p$

17. ERROR ANALYSIS *Describe* and correct the error made in simplifying the expression.

$$1 + 4x + 3x = (1 + 4 + 3)x$$
$$= 8x$$

SEE EXAMPLE 3 on p. 208 for Exs. 18–30

SIMPLIFYING EXPRESSIONS Simplify the expression.

18. $6(1 - j) + 2j$ **19.** $5(z + 2) - 8$ **20.** $4w - 2 + 2(w + 1)$

21. $-s(4 - 7) + 5 + 3s$ **22.** $5 + 2(n - 3) + 2n - 4$ **23.** $-2(2 + b) + 5b + 3b$

24. $6(d - 4) + 2(d - 9)$ **25.** $7(m - 2) - 2m + 1$ **26.** $4(1.5x - 2 + 2x) - 2x$

27. $1.6r + 4(2 + 3.6r) - 5r$ **28.** $3(2 + 4v) + \frac{2}{3}v + \frac{1}{3}v$ **(29.)** $2\left(2t + \frac{2}{7} - 2t\right) + 8t$

30. ◆ MULTIPLE CHOICE Which expression shows $-4(n - 3) + 2n$ in simplified form?

Ⓐ $-2n - 12$ Ⓑ $-6n - 12$ Ⓒ $-2n + 12$ Ⓓ $-4n + 12 + 2n$

COMPARING EXPRESSIONS Tell whether the expressions are equivalent.

31. $7x + 2x^2$; $9x^2$ **32.** $6x \cdot x + 3x$; $2x^2 + 3x + 4x^2$ **33.** $3x^3 - 2x^3$; $-4x^3 + 5x^3$

34. WRITING *Explain* how you can use the distributive property to combine like terms. Include two examples.

CONNECT SKILLS TO PROBLEM SOLVING **Exercises 35–37 will help you prepare for problem solving.**

35. You have an equal number of nickels, dimes, and quarters. Write and simplify an expression for the total value (in dollars) of the coins.

36. Jen has three times the number of CDs that you have. Write and simplify an expression for the total number of CDs that you and Jen have.

37. You worked half as many hours this week as you did last week. Write and simplify an expression for the total hours you worked both weeks.

SEE EXAMPLE 4 on p. 208 for Exs. 38–39

38. ◆ **MULTIPLE CHOICE** You practiced piano for three weeks. In the first week, you practiced n hours. In the second week, you practiced 1.2 times as many hours as in the first week. In the third week, you practiced 1.5 times as many hours as in the first week. Which expression gives the total hours you practiced during the three weeks?

Ⓐ $1.8n$ Ⓑ $2.7n$ Ⓒ $n + 2.7$ Ⓓ $3.7n$

California @HomeTutor for problem solving help at classzone.com

39. PHOTOGRAPHS You have just returned from a 3 day trip. On day 1 of your trip, you took 10 photos. On day 3 of the trip, you took twice as many photos as you did on day 2.

a. Write and simplify an expression for the total number of photos you took on the trip.

b. If you took 12 photos on day 2, how many photos did you take in all?

California @HomeTutor for problem solving help at classzone.com

You took 10 photos on day 1.

CHALLENGE **Copy and complete the statement using <, >, or = (for $x \geq 1$).**

40. $3x^2 + 6x$ __?__ $3(x^2 + 2x)$ **41.** $5 + 2(x - 3)$ __?__ $2x + 2$ **42.** $4(x^2 + 1)$ __?__ $2x^2 + 4$

43. CHALLENGE In Example 2 on page 207, explain how you can use the commutative and associative properties of addition to show that $7c + 9 + (-3c)$ is equivalent to $9 + [7c + (-3c)]$.

◆ CALIFORNIA STANDARDS SPIRAL REVIEW

Gr. 4 NS 1.2 **44.** Which of the following is *not* a true statement? ***(p. 675)***

Ⓐ $2.3 > 2.033$ Ⓑ $0.8 < 0.83$ Ⓒ $1.14 < 1.125$ Ⓓ $0.44 > 0.429$

Gr. 5 NS 2.1 **45.** What is the product of 1.2 and 1.1? ***(p. 107)***

Ⓐ 0.132 Ⓑ 1.32 Ⓒ 2.3 Ⓓ 13.2

AF 1.2 **46.** You have d dollars and then buy a souvenir for \$12. Which expression represents the amount of money you have left? ***(p. 202)***

Ⓐ $d + 12$ Ⓑ $d - 12$ Ⓒ $12 - d$ Ⓓ $12d$

4.4 Investigating Formulas

MATERIALS • graph paper

Standards
AF 3.2 Express in symbolic form simple relationships arising from geometry.

QUESTION **How can you develop formulas for finding perimeter and area?**

You can use graph paper to develop formulas for the perimeters and areas of rectangles and squares.

EXPLORE **Find the perimeter and area of a rectangle with a length of 10 units and a width of 4 units.**

STEP 1 **Draw** a rectangle that has a length of 10 units and a width of 4 units.

This square represents 1 square unit.

4 units

10 units

STEP 2 **Find** the total length of all four sides. The perimeter is 28 units.

STEP 3 **Count** the number of square units that cover the rectangle. The area is 40 square units.

DRAW CONCLUSIONS **Use your observations to complete these exercises.**

Draw a rectangle or square with the dimensions given in the table. Then copy and complete the table.

1.

Rectangle

Length	Width	Perimeter	Area
4	3	?	?
5	4	?	?
9	5	?	?

2.

Square

Side length	Perimeter	Area
4	?	?
6	?	?
7	?	?

3. **WRITING** How can you use the length and the width of a rectangle to find its perimeter? to find its area? How can you use the side length of a square to find its perimeter? to find its area?

4. **REASONING** Write expressions for the perimeter and area of a rectangle with length l and width w. Write expressions for the perimeter and area of a square with side length s.

4.4 Using Familiar Formulas

Math and **SPORTS**
Ex. 38, p. 216

Standards **AF 3.1 Use variables in expressions describing geometric quantities** (e.g. $P = 2w + 2l$, $A = \frac{1}{2}bh$, $C = \pi d$ – **the formulas for the perimeter of a rectangle,** the area of a triangle, and the circumference of a circle, respectively).

AF 3.2 Express in symbolic form simple relationships arising from geometry.

Connect ***Before*** you wrote algebraic expressions. ***Now*** you will use variables to express formulas.

KEY VOCABULARY
- **equation**
- **formula**
- **perimeter,** *p. 684*
- **area,** *p. 685*

An **equation** is a mathematical sentence formed by setting two expressions equal. A **formula** is an equation that relates two or more quantities such as perimeter, length, and width.

The perimeter of a figure is the distance around the figure. The area is the amount of surface the figure covers. The activity on page 211 suggests that you can use formulas to find the perimeters and areas of rectangles and squares.

KEY CONCEPT *For Your Notebook*

Perimeter and Area Formulas

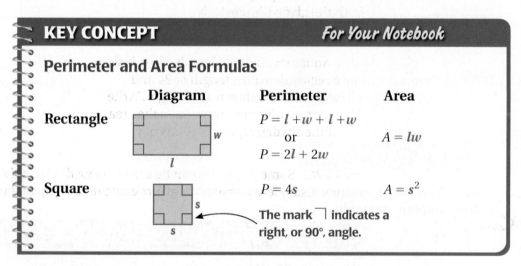

	Diagram	Perimeter	Area
Rectangle		$P = l + w + l + w$ or $P = 2l + 2w$	$A = lw$
Square	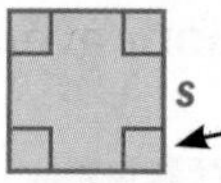	$P = 4s$	$A = s^2$

The mark ⌉ indicates a right, or 90°, angle.

EXAMPLE 1 Expressing Perimeter and Area

Write and simplify expressions for the perimeter and area of the rectangle.

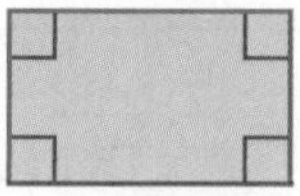

Perimeter of rectangle

$P = 2l + 2w$ **Write formula.**

$= 2(1.6n) + 2(n)$ **Substitute.**

$= 5.2n$ **Simplify.**

Area of rectangle

$A = lw$ **Write formula.**

$= (1.6n)(n)$ **Substitute.**

$= 1.6n^2$ **Simplify.**

VOCABULARY
Perimeter is measured in linear units such as feet. Area is measured in square units such as square feet, written as ft^2.

EXAMPLE 2 ◆ Multiple Choice Practice

A square with a side of x is inside a square with a side of 10, as pictured at the right. Which expression represents the area of the shaded region in terms of x?

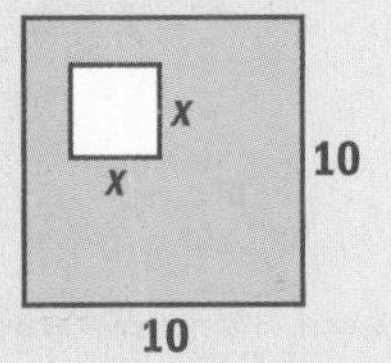

ELIMINATE CHOICES
In Example 2, you need to subtract the area of the smaller square from the area of the larger square. You can eliminate choice A.

Ⓐ $100 + x^2$ Ⓑ $100 - x^2$

Ⓒ $100 - 2x$ Ⓓ $100 - 4x$

SOLUTION

The area of the shaded region is equal to the area of the large square minus the area of the small square. The area of the large square is $10(10) = 100$. The area of the small square is $x(x) = x^2$. So, the area of the shaded region is $100 - x^2$.

▶ **Answer** The correct answer is B. Ⓐ Ⓑ Ⓒ Ⓓ

GUIDED PRACTICE for Examples 1 and 2

Write and simplify expressions for the perimeter and area of a rectangle with the given dimensions.

1. $l = 6, w = x + 5$
2. $l = 4x, w = x$
3. A square with a side length of y is inside a rectangle with a length of 24 and a width of 8, as shown at the right. Write an expression that represents the area of the shaded region in terms of y.

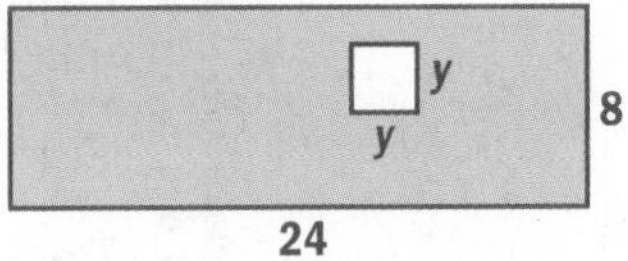

DISTANCE Some problems can be solved using the formula below that relates distance, a constant or average rate (or speed), and time.

KEY CONCEPT *For Your Notebook*

Formula Relating Distance, Rate, and Time

Words The distance traveled d is the product of the constant or average rate r and the time t.

Algebra $d = r \cdot t$, or $d = rt$

Numbers $d = 45\ \frac{\text{miles}}{\cancel{\text{hour}}} \cdot 3\ \cancel{\text{hours}} = 135$ miles

Abbreviations are often used when referring to rates, such as speed. For example, miles per hour may be written as mi/h, feet per minute as ft/min, and meters per second as m/sec.

EXAMPLE 3 Using Formula for Distance

Kimi runs at 0.09 mi/min.

RUNNING Kimi runs at a steady rate of 0.09 mile per minute for n minutes and then takes a break. After the break, she runs 3 more miles. Write an expression for the total distance she runs.

About the Standards

Notice that in order to find the total distance in Example 3, you can break the problem into simpler parts, as called for in Grade 6 Standard MR 1.3.

SOLUTION

STEP 1 **Use** the formula for distance to find the distance Kimi runs before the break.

$d = rt$ **Write formula for distance.**

$= 0.09n$ **Substitute 0.09 for r and n for t.**

STEP 2 **Add** the distance run after the break: $0.09n + 3$.

▶ **Answer** The total distance Kimi runs is $(0.09n + 3)$ miles.

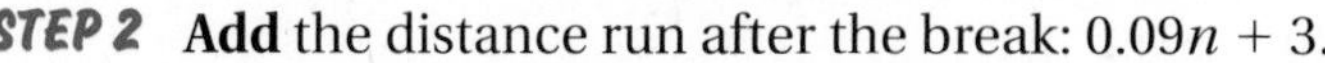

KEY CONCEPT — *For Your Notebook*

Temperature Conversions

Words	Formulas	Numbers
Convert Celsius to Fahrenheit	$F = \frac{9}{5}C + 32$	$71.6 = \frac{9}{5}(22) + 32$
Convert Fahrenheit to Celsius	$C = \frac{5}{9}(F - 32)$	$22 = \frac{5}{9}(71.6 - 32)$

EXAMPLE 4 Converting a Temperature

Convert 30°C to degrees Fahrenheit.

$F = \frac{9}{5}C + 32$ **Write formula for degrees Fahrenheit.**

$= \frac{9}{5}(30) + 32$ **Substitute 30 for C.**

$= 54 + 32$ **Multiply.**

$= 86$ **Add.**

▶ **Answer** The temperature 30°C is equal to 86°F.

CHECK ANSWER

You can check your answer to Example 4 by substituting 86 for F in the formula $C = \frac{5}{9}(F - 32)$ and showing that $C = 30$.

✓ GUIDED PRACTICE for Examples 3 and 4

4. **DISTANCE** How far does a car travel in 2 hours at a rate of 40 mi/h?
5. Convert **(a)** 45°C to degrees Fahrenheit and **(b)** 77°F to degrees Celsius.

4.4 EXERCISES

HOMEWORK KEY

◆ = **MULTIPLE CHOICE PRACTICE** Exs. 14, 23, 32, 40, 44–46

○ = **HINTS AND HOMEWORK HELP** for Exs. 11, 15, 41 at classzone.com

SKILLS • PROBLEM SOLVING • REASONING

1. **VOCABULARY** Copy and complete: An equation that relates two or more quantities is a(n) __?__.

2. **WRITING** *Describe* the difference between area and perimeter.

SEE EXAMPLE 1 on p. 212 for Exs. 3–13

PERIMETER **Write and simplify an expression for the figure's perimeter.**

3. 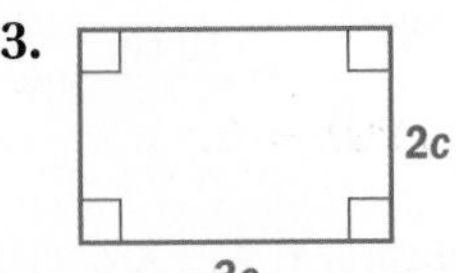

4. 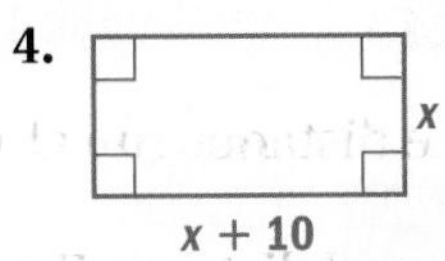

5. 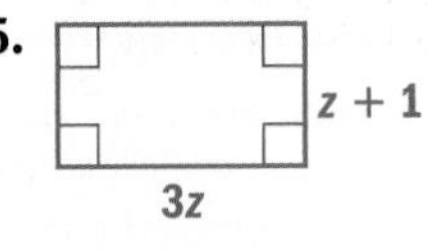

ERROR ANALYSIS ***Describe*** **and correct the error made in finding the perimeter or area of the figure shown.**

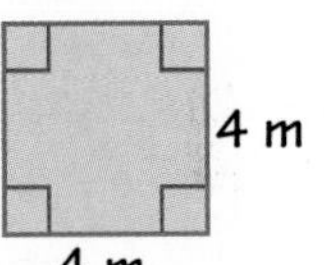

6. ✗ $A = s^2$
$= 4^2$
$= 16$ meters

7. ✗ $P = l + w$
$= 4 + 4$
$= 8$ meters

PERIMETER AND AREA **Write and simplify expressions for the perimeter and area of the rectangle with the given dimensions.**

8. $l = 6y, w = y$

9. $l = 2.7a, w = 12a$

10. $l = p + 3, w = 5$

11. $l = d + 7, w = 6$

12. $l = 2, w = x - 4$

13. $l = 2g - 3, w = 8$

SEE EXAMPLE 2 on p. 213 for Ex. 14

14. ◆ **MULTIPLE CHOICE** A square with a side of x is inside a square with a side of 12, as pictured at the right. Which expression represents the area of the shaded region in terms of x?

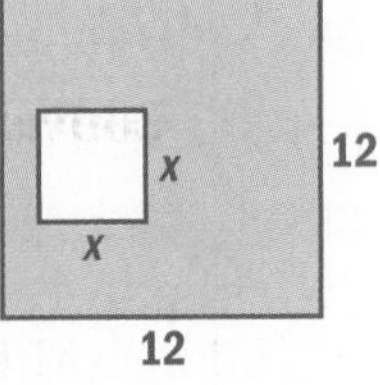

Ⓐ $144 - x^2$ Ⓑ $x^2 - 144$

Ⓒ $48 - x^2$ Ⓓ $x^2 - 48$

SEE EXAMPLE 3 on p. 214 for Exs. 15–23

DISTANCE **Find the distance for the given rate and time.**

15. $r = 7$ in./min, $t = 9$ minutes

16. $r = 14$ m/sec, $t = 18$ seconds

17. $r = 58$ mi/h, $t = 2.5$ hours

18. $r = 60$ yd/sec, $t = 25$ seconds

19. $r = 118$ ft/min, $t = (x - 2)$ minutes

20. $r = x$ km/h, $t = 1.5$ hours

21. $r = 3x$ cm/sec, $t = 35$ seconds

22. $r = 40$ mi/h, $t = (x + 8)$ hours

23. ◆ **MULTIPLE CHOICE** Bill drives s miles per hour for 1 hour 30 minutes. Which expression can be used to find how many miles Bill drives?

Ⓐ $130s$ Ⓑ $90s$ Ⓒ $1.5s$ Ⓓ $1.3s$

SEE EXAMPLE 4 on p. 214 for Exs. 24–31

CONVERTING TEMPERATURES Convert the temperature to degrees Celsius or to degrees Fahrenheit.

24. 5°C **25.** 32°F **26.** 86°F **27.** 20°C

28. 65.3°F **29.** 18°C **30.** 34°C **31.** 112.1°F

32. ◆ **MULTIPLE CHOICE** The low temperature on Friday was x°C. The high temperature on Friday was 15°C higher than the low temperature. Which expression represents the high temperature in degrees Fahrenheit?

Ⓐ $\frac{9}{5}x + 35$ Ⓑ $\frac{9}{5}x + 59$ Ⓒ $\frac{5}{9}(x - 17)$ Ⓓ $\frac{5}{9}(x - 47)$

COMPOSITE FIGURES Find the perimeter and area of the figure.

33.

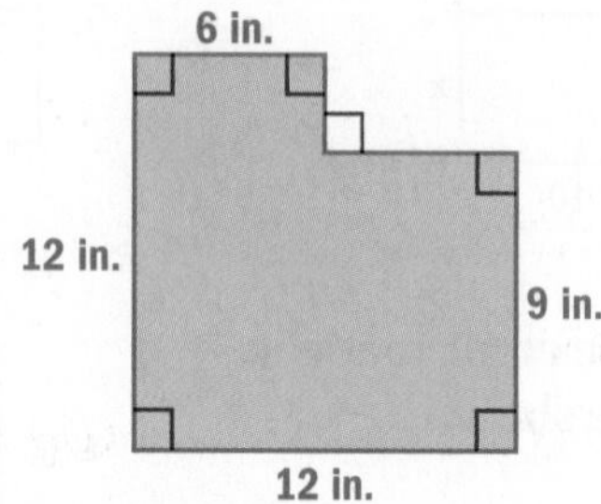

34.

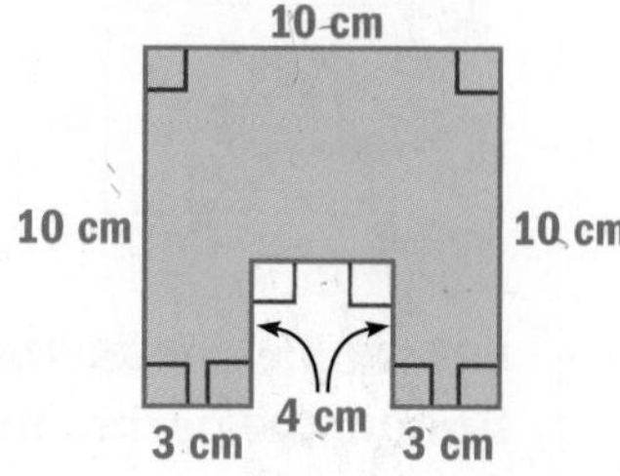

Animated Math at classzone.com

CONNECT SKILLS TO PROBLEM SOLVING Exercises 35–38 will help you prepare for problem solving.

35. A rabbit ran 22 feet per second for 12 seconds. How many feet did it run?

36. Yesterday's low temperature was 10°C. What was yesterday's low temperature in degrees Fahrenheit?

37. A square rug has a side length of 30 inches. What is the area of the rug?

38. A rectangular soccer field is 100 yards long and 70 yards wide. What is the perimeter of the soccer field?

SEE EXAMPLE 1 on p. 212 for Ex. 39

39. **GEOMETRY** A rectangle is four times as long as it is wide. Write and simplify expressions for the perimeter and area of the rectangle in terms of the width c.

California @HomeTutor for problem solving help at classzone.com

SEE EXAMPLE 3 on p. 214 for Ex. 40

40. ◆ **MULTIPLE CHOICE** A tiger beetle ran 53 centimeters per second for n seconds and then ran an additional 135 centimeters. How many centimeters did the beetle run?

Ⓐ $135n + 53$ Ⓑ $53n + 135$ Ⓒ $188n$ Ⓓ $n + 188$

California @HomeTutor for problem solving help at classzone.com

41. **CHEMISTRY** The boiling point of iron is 2750°C, and its melting point is 1535°C. What is the difference (in degrees Fahrenheit) between the boiling point and melting point of iron?

42. **CHARITY WALK** Each year, you enter a walk for charity. The table shows the times and rates you walked last year and this year. How much farther did you walk this year than last year?

	Time	*Rate*
Last year	2 hours 40 minutes	3.9 mi/h
This year	2 hours 30 minutes	4.5 mi/h

43. **CHALLENGE** Your rectangular yard is twice as long as it is wide. You fenced in the yard using 240 feet of fencing. You want to fertilize your yard. Each bag of fertilizer covers 2000 square feet. How many bags should you buy? *Explain* how you solved the problem.

◆ CALIFORNIA STANDARDS SPIRAL REVIEW

NS 2.4 44. What is the least common multiple of 25, 40, and 60? ***(p. 21)***

Ⓐ 5 Ⓑ 25 Ⓒ 120 Ⓓ 600

AF 1.4 45. What is the value of $-32 - (13 - 16)$? ***(p. 160)***

Ⓐ -35 Ⓑ -29 Ⓒ 29 Ⓓ 35

AF 1.2 46. You made 8 shots in your first basketball game and x shots in your second game. In your third game, you made twice as many shots as in your second game. Which expression gives the total number of shots you made in the three games? ***(p. 207)***

Ⓐ $8 + 2x$ Ⓑ $\frac{8 + 2x}{3}$ Ⓒ $8 + 3x$ Ⓓ $16x^2$

QUIZ *for Lessons 4.1–4.4*

Evaluate the expression when $x = -4$, $y = 0.6$, and $z = 2$. ***(p. 197)***

1. $4x - 10y$
2. $x^2 + 3z$
3. $\frac{2x + 7z}{6}$
4. $x^3 + 20y$

Write the real-world phrase as an algebraic expression. Identify what the variable represents. ***(p. 202)***

5. 4 years less than Sam's age
6. \$3 more than twice the cost of a ticket

Simplify the expression. ***(p. 207)***

7. $b - 8 - 6b + 10$
8. $10a + 15(a - 7)$
9. $-6 + 6(-c + 5) - 4c$

10. A rectangle has a length of 9 feet and a width of $(x + 3)$ feet. Write and simplify expressions for the perimeter and area of the rectangle. ***(p. 212)***

11. **TRAINS** A train travels at a constant rate of 50 miles per hour for 2 hours and then travels 35 miles more. Find the total distance traveled. ***(p. 212)***

MIXED REVIEW of Skills and Problem Solving

Multiple Choice Practice for Lessons 4.1–4.4

1. Water enters a storage tank through two pipes and drains out of the tank from a third pipe, as shown. Let x be the amount of time (in seconds) after the pipes start filling an empty tank. What does the expression $8x + 5x - 3x$ represent? **AF 1.2**

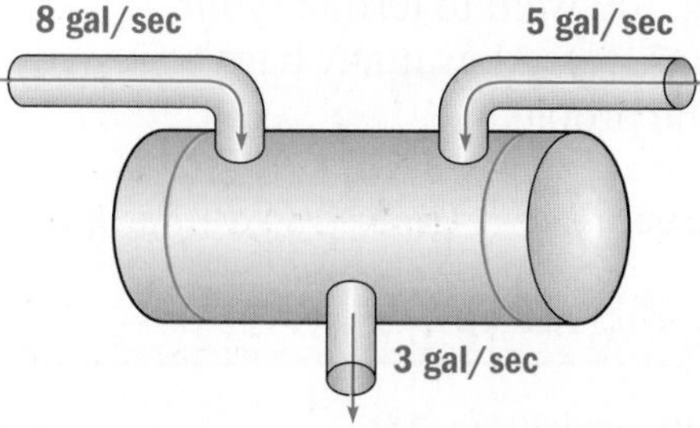

   Ⓐ The number of gallons that will pour into the tank

   Ⓑ The number of gallons that will drain out of the tank

   Ⓒ The number of gallons that will be in the tank if the drain is left closed

   Ⓓ The number of gallons that will be in the tank if the drain is left open

2. Which expression represents the perimeter of the rectangle below? **AF 3.1, MR 1.1**

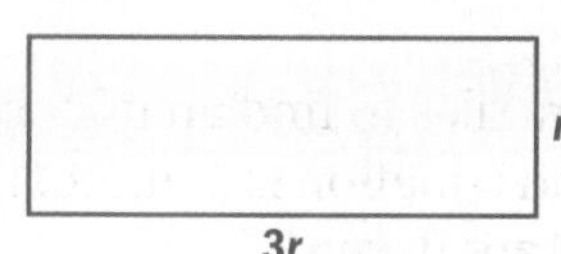

   Ⓐ $4r$ Ⓑ $6r$

   Ⓒ $8r$ Ⓓ $3r^2$

3. Vicky drove for 60 miles and then stopped at a rest stop. Then Vicky drove at a constant rate of 55 miles per hour for n hours. Which expression describes the total distance that Vicky drove? **AF 1.2**

   Ⓐ $115n$ Ⓑ $60 + 55n$

   Ⓒ $55 + 60n$ Ⓓ $15n$

4. Suppose that the temperature in Montreal, Quebec, in Canada is 21°C. What is the temperature in degrees Fahrenheit? **AF 1.2**

   Ⓐ −6.1°F Ⓑ 37.8°F

   Ⓒ 43.7°F Ⓓ 69.8°F

5. A rectangle is inside another rectangle, as shown below. Which expression represents the area of the shaded region? **AF 3.2**

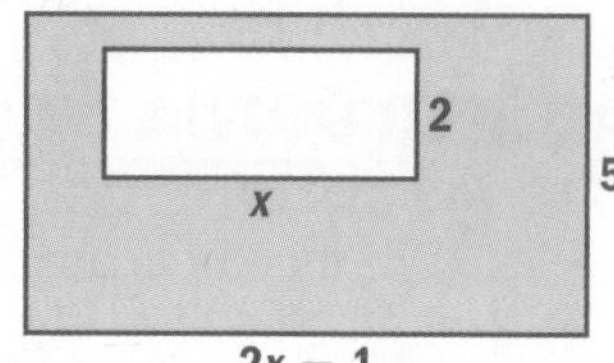

   Ⓐ $8x - 5$ Ⓑ $3x - 3$

   Ⓒ $2x + 4$ Ⓓ $12x - 5$

6. What is the simplified form of the expression $-2(-6x + 8) + 5x$? **Gr. 5 AF 1.3**

   Ⓐ $-x - 16$ Ⓑ $5x + 20$

   Ⓒ $17x - 16$ Ⓓ $17x + 16$

7. What is the value of the expression $3x + 7y$ when $x = -8$ and $y = 6$? **AF 1.2**

   Ⓐ 66 Ⓑ 18

   Ⓒ −18 Ⓓ −38

8. Terry has p posters. Glen has 4 times the number of posters Terry has. Which expression describes the number of posters Terry and Glen have altogether? **AF 1.2, MR 3.3**

   Ⓐ $3p$ Ⓑ $4p$

   Ⓒ $5p$ Ⓓ $4 - p$

9. Which expression represents the phrase "3.5 times the difference of x squared and y"? **AF 1.2**

   Ⓐ $3.5(x^2 - y)$ Ⓑ $3.5(x - y)^2$

   Ⓒ $3.5(x - y)$ Ⓓ $3.5x^2 - y$

4.5 Equations and Mental Math

AF 1.1 **Write and solve one-step linear equations in one variable.**

Connect

Before you used mental math to add, subtract, multiply, and divide.
Now you will use mental math to solve an equation.

KEY VOCABULARY
- **solution**
- **solving an equation**
- **equation,** *p. 212*

ACTIVITY

You can use algebra tiles to find the value of a variable in an equation.

STEP 1 Use tiles to model the statement $n + 3 = 5$. Let each tile represent 1.

STEP 2 Replace n with tiles until you have the same number of tiles on each side of the equal sign.

STEP 3 Replacing n with 2 tiles gives a total of 5 tiles on each side, so $n = 2$.

Model with algebra tiles to help you find the value of the variable.

1. $6 + x = 10$ **2.** $y + 2 = 9$ **3.** $8 = m + 3$

SOLUTIONS In the activity, you used algebra tiles to find an unknown value of a variable in an equation. A **solution** of an equation is a number that you can substitute for a variable to make the equation true.

EXAMPLE 1 Checking Possible Solutions

Tell whether the number is a solution of $n + 5 = 14$.

a. 9 **b.** 7

SOLUTION

a. $n + 5 = 14$ **Write equation.**
$9 + 5 \stackrel{?}{=} 14$ **Substitute 9 for n.**
$14 = 14$ **14 = 14, so 9 is a solution.**

b. $n + 5 = 14$ **Write equation.**
$7 + 5 \stackrel{?}{=} 14$ **Substitute 7 for n.**
$12 \neq 14$ **12 ≠ 14, so 7 is *not* a solution.**

READING

Symbol	Meaning
$=$	is equal to
$\stackrel{?}{=}$	is equal to?
$\neq$	is not equal to

EXAMPLE 2 Translating Verbal Sentences

READING
When translating verbal sentences into equations, look for key words like "is" and "equals," which can be represented by the symbol =.

	Verbal sentence	Equation
a.	The difference of twice a number and 3 equals −4.	$2y - 3 = -4$
b.	The product of 9 and a number is 36.	$9y = 36$
c.	−3 is equal to twice the sum of a number and 2.	$-3 = 2(y + 2)$

SOLVING AN EQUATION Finding all solutions of an equation is called **solving the equation**. You can use mental math to solve simple equations by thinking of the equation as a question.

EXAMPLE 3 Using Mental Math to Solve Equations

Animated Math
For an interactive example of using mental math to solve equations go to **classzone.com**.

	Equation	Question	Solution	Check
a.	$9 + x = 12$	Nine plus what number equals 12?	3	$9 + \mathbf{3} = 12$
b.	$n - 5 = 10$	What number minus 5 equals 10?	15	$\mathbf{15} - 5 = 10$
c.	$4t = 20$	Four times what number equals 20?	5	$4(\mathbf{5}) = 20$
d.	$\frac{m}{3} = 12$	What number divided by 3 equals 12?	36	$\frac{\mathbf{36}}{3} = 12$

✓ GUIDED PRACTICE for Examples 1, 2, and 3

Tell whether the number is a solution of the equation.

1. $3x = 12; 4$ **2.** $7 = 13 - n; 5$ **3.** $\frac{6}{y} = 3; 2$

4. Write as an equation: The difference of 5 and twice a number is 17.

Solve the equation using mental math.

5. $7x = 35$ **6.** $15 = m - 6$ **7.** $12 + a = 32$ **8.** $\frac{24}{n} = 6$

EXAMPLE 4 Using an Area Formula

What is the width of a rectangle that has a length of 7 feet and an area of 42 square feet?

$A = lw$ **Write formula for area of a rectangle.**

$42 = 7w$ **Substitute 42 for *A* and 7 for *l*.**

$42 = 7 \cdot 6$ **Use mental math to solve equation.**

▶ **Answer** The width of the rectangle is 6 feet.

EXAMPLE 5 Using Formula for Distance

HOMING PIGEONS A homing pigeon is a bird trained to fly back to its home. Homing pigeons can fly at a speed of about 50 miles per hour. About how long would a homing pigeon take to fly 300 miles?

Flying speed of homing pigeon: 50 mi/h

SOLUTION

$d = rt$	Write formula for distance.
$300 = 50t$	Substitute 300 for d and 50 for r.
$300 = 50 \cdot 6$	Use mental math to solve equation.

▸ **Answer** A homing pigeon would take about 6 hours to fly 300 miles.

✓ GUIDED PRACTICE for Examples 4 and 5

9. **WHAT IF?** In Example 4, suppose that the rectangle has a length of 8 inches and an area of 48 square inches. What is the width?

10. **TRAVEL** A car travels on a highway at a constant speed of 60 miles per hour. About how long does it take the car to travel 120 miles?

4.5 EXERCISES

HOMEWORK KEY

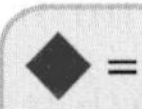 = **MULTIPLE CHOICE PRACTICE** Exs. 27, 48, 51, 63–65

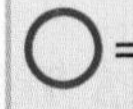 = **HINTS AND HOMEWORK HELP** for Exs. 5, 19, 49 at classzone.com

SKILLS • PROBLEM SOLVING • REASONING

1. **VOCABULARY** Copy and complete: A number that you can substitute for a variable to make an equation true is a(n) __?__ of the equation.

2. **WRITING** *Explain* the difference between an expression and an equation. Give an example of each.

SEE EXAMPLE 1 on p. 219 for Exs. 3–8

CHECKING SOLUTIONS Tell whether the number is a solution of the equation.

3. $5x = 35; 7$
4. $16 + y = 22; 8$
5. $9 = z - 12; 20$
6. $40 = 8r; 5$
7. $s + 5 = 11; 7$
8. $24 - a = 13; 9$

SEE EXAMPLE 2 on p. 220 for Exs. 9–12

WRITING EQUATIONS Write the verbal sentence as an equation. Let n represent the number.

9. The sum of a number and −9 equals 24.
10. A number times −5 is 10.
11. The quotient of 3 and a number is twice 23.
12. The difference of −4 times a number and 3 is 27.

SEE EXAMPLE 2
on p. 220
for Exs. 13–14

ERROR ANALYSIS ***Describe* and correct the error in writing the equation.**

13. What number divided by 7 is 28?
$\frac{7}{x} = 28$ ✗

14. What number added to 5 is 23?
$5 + 23 = x$ ✗

SEE EXAMPLE 3
on p. 220
for Exs. 15–27

MENTAL MATH Solve the equation using mental math.

15. $4m = 24$ **16.** $r - 6 = 7$ **17.** $18 = 9 + s$

18. $20 - b = 3$ **19.** $8 = 25 - t$ **20.** $10x = 120$

21. $10 = c + 7$ **22.** $d + 8 = 15$ **23.** $44 = 11p$

24. $\frac{z}{3} = 7$ **25.** $\frac{a}{6} = 8$ **26.** $\frac{36}{y} = 6$

27. ◆ **MULTIPLE CHOICE** What is the solution of the equation $\frac{21}{a} = 3$?

Ⓐ 3 Ⓑ 7 Ⓒ 18 Ⓓ 63

SEE EXAMPLE 4
on p. 220
for Exs. 28–31

AREA FORMULA Use the formula for the area of a rectangle to find the unknown value.

28. $A = 66 \text{ m}^2$, $l = 11$ m, $w =$ _?_ m **29.** $A = 100 \text{ yd}^2$, $l =$ _?_ yd, $w = 4$ yd

30. $A = 81 \text{ in.}^2$, $l = 9$ in., $w =$ _?_ in. **31.** $A = 28 \text{ ft}^2$, $l = 7$ ft, $w =$ _?_ ft

SEE EXAMPLE 5
on p. 221
for Exs. 32–35

TRAVEL TIME Use the formula for distance to find the unknown time.

32. $d = 100$ mi, $r = 25$ mi/h, $t =$ _?_ h **33.** $d = 16$ km, $r = 8$ km/h, $t =$ _?_ h

34. $d = 72$ mi, $r = 9$ mi/h, $t =$ _?_ h **35.** $d = 240$ yd, $r = 60$ yd/sec, $t =$ _?_ sec

COMPARING SOLUTIONS Tell whether the equations have the same solution.

36. $x + 4 = 5$ and $x + 2 = 3$ **37.** $5y = 45$ and $6y = 48$

38. $12 - p = 11$ and $5 - p = 4$ **39.** $\frac{18}{b} = 6$ and $\frac{12}{b} = 3$

REASONING Tell whether the equation is *always, sometimes,* or *never* true.

40. $1 \cdot x = x$ **41.** $x + 3 = x + 4$ **42.** $0 \cdot x = 5$ **43.** $3x = 6x$

CONNECT SKILLS TO PROBLEM SOLVING Exercises 44–46 will help you prepare for problem solving.

Copy and complete the equation with an algebraic expression to represent the situation. Identify what the variable represents.

44. Scott is 65 inches tall. Scott is 4 inches taller than you. Equation: 65 = _?_.

45. You have 24 CDs in your collection. You have 12 fewer CDs than Lily. Equation: 24 = _?_.

46. You bike at a steady rate of 12 miles per hour. You travel 24 miles. Equation: 24 = _?_.

SEE EXAMPLES 2 AND 3 on p. 220 for Exs. 47–50

Capacity of St. Louis Arch elevator train: 40 people

47. **ST. LOUIS ARCH** The elevator train inside the St. Louis Arch can carry a total of 40 people, with 5 people in each car. Write and solve a multiplication equation to find the number of cars in the train.

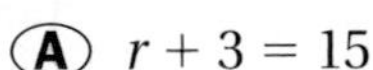
California @HomeTutor for problem solving help at classzone.com

48. ◆ **MULTIPLE CHOICE** You are decorating a cake with 15 roses. You want an equal number of roses in each of the 3 rows on the cake. Which equation would you use to find the number r of roses in each row?

(A) $r + 3 = 15$ (B) $15 - r = 3$

(C) $3r = 15$ (D) $\frac{3}{r} = 15$

California @HomeTutor for problem solving help at classzone.com

49. **AMUSEMENT PARKS** A water ride at an amusement park has a total of 64 seats. Suppose that 48 seats are occupied. Write and solve an addition equation to find the number of empty seats.

50. **SHORT RESPONSE** A skier on a ski lift travels 3000 feet to the top of a mountain at a constant rate of 600 feet per minute. How long does it take the skier to reach the top of the mountain? How long does it take to travel 1000 feet? *Explain.*

51. ◆ **MULTIPLE CHOICE** The amount in a jar for tips is divided equally among 6 workers. Each worker receives \$12. How much money was in the jar?

(A) \$2 (B) \$8 (C) \$18 (D) \$72

52. **MULTI-STEP PROBLEM** The school treasurer has \$40 to spend on a party for the students in band class. The party for the band class will cost \$120.
 a. Solve the equation $x + 40 = 120$ to find how much more money the treasurer will need for the party.
 b. The class has 40 students. Each student will pay the same amount for the party. Write and solve a multiplication equation to find the amount that each student will pay.
 c. If the number of students in the band class is greater than 40, what happens to the cost per student? *Explain.*

53. **HOT AIR BALLOON** A hot air balloon travels downward at a constant speed of 240 feet per minute, as shown.
 a. Write an equation to represent the situation. Then use mental math to find the balloon's original altitude.
 b. How long does it take the balloon to reach the ground from its original altitude? *Explain* your reasoning.

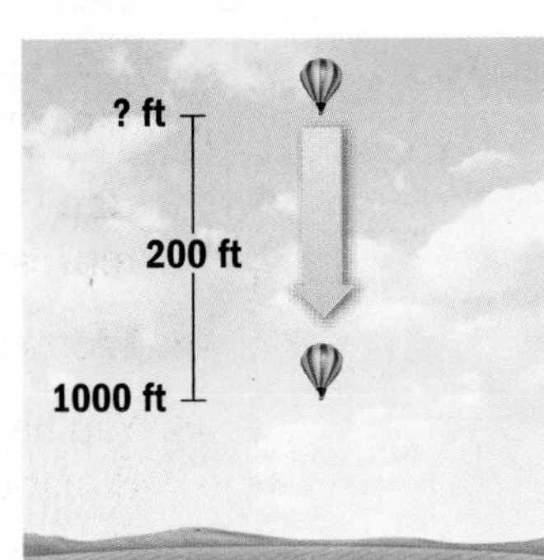

54. **OPEN-ENDED** *Describe* a situation that could be modeled using the equation $x - 49 = 8$. Solve the equation. *Explain* what the solution represents in the situation.

55. SWIMMING Tammy and John van Wisse were the first brother and sister to swim across the English Channel. Tammy's crossing time of 512 minutes was 15 minutes longer than John's crossing time.

a. Write an addition equation to represent the situation.

b. Use mental math to solve the equation. Then find how long (in hours and minutes) John took to swim across the English Channel.

Tammy van Wisse's crossing time: 512 min

56. WRITING *Explain* why the equations $x + 3 = 5$ and $3 + x = 5$ have the same solution, but $x - 5 = 3$ and $5 - x = 3$ do not.

CHALLENGE Solve the equation using mental math.

57. $2p + 0 = 6$ **58.** $4 - 2a = 0$ **59.** $10 - 3y = 1$ **60.** $2x + 1 = 5$

61. CHALLENGE You take 5 less than three times a number and add 7. The result is 14. Find the number. *Explain* how you found your answer.

62. CHALLENGE You spend half your money on a pair of shoes. You spend half of what you have left on a pair of pants. Then you spend half of what you have left on lunch. You have $10 left. How much money did you start with?

a. Work Backward Use the strategy *work backward* to solve.

b. Write an Equation Write and solve an equation to represent the situation.

c. Compare *Describe* how the method in part (a) can help you write and solve the equation in part (b).

◆ CALIFORNIA STANDARDS SPIRAL REVIEW

AF. 3.1 **63.** Which expression represents the perimeter of the rectangle at the right? *(p. 212)*

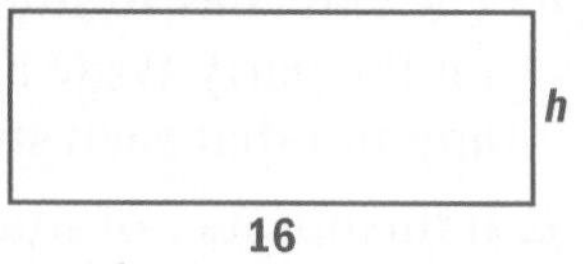

Ⓐ $16h$ Ⓑ $32 + 2h$ Ⓒ $16 - h$ Ⓓ $16 + h$

GR. 5 NS. 1.5 **64.** Which number does the point represent on the number line? *(p. 673)*

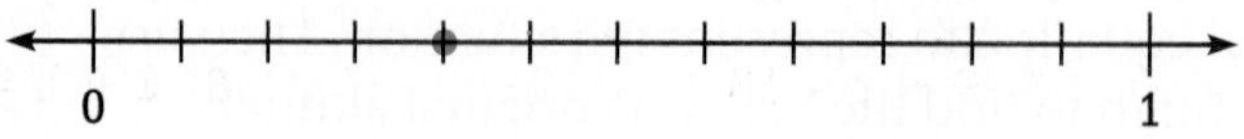

Ⓐ $\frac{1}{3}$ Ⓑ $\frac{4}{11}$ Ⓒ $\frac{2}{5}$ Ⓓ 4

NS. 2.3 **65.** A fish is 6 meters below sea level. The fish dives 19 meters. What is the position of the fish relative to sea level? *(p. 143)*

Ⓐ −25 m Ⓑ −13 m Ⓒ 3 m Ⓓ 13 m

4.6 Modeling Addition Equations

MATERIALS • algebra tiles

Standards
AF 1.1 Write and **solve one-step linear equations in one variable.**

QUESTION How can you model and solve addition equations?

You can use algebra tiles to model and solve simple addition equations.

x-tile	1-tile
An *x*-tile represents the variable *x*.	A 1-tile represents positive 1.

EXPLORE Solve $x + 2 = 5$.

STEP 1 **Model** $x + 2 = 5$ using algebra tiles.

STEP 2 **Take** away two 1-tiles from each side.

STEP 3 **Identify** the solution. The x-tile is equal to three 1-tiles. So, the solution of the equation $x + 2 = 5$ is 3.

CHECK $3 + 2 = 5$ ✓

DRAW CONCLUSIONS Use your observations to complete these exercises.

Use algebra tiles to model and solve the equation.

1. $x + 3 = 8$ **2.** $x + 4 = 5$ **3.** $x + 1 = 7$

4. $6 + x = 11$ **5.** $9 + x = 13$ **6.** $2 + x = 10$

7. **WRITING** In the Explore, explain why you took away two 1-tiles from each side of the equation and not just from the left side.

8. **REASONING** *Describe* how you would use algebra tiles to solve the equation $4 + x + 2 = 10$. Then solve the equation.

4.6 Solving Addition and Subtraction Equations

Math and SPACE SCIENCE
Example 4, p. 228

Standards AF 1.1 **Write and solve one-step linear equations in one variable.**

Connect ***Before*** you solved equations using mental math. ***Now*** you will solve addition and subtraction equations using properties.

KEY VOCABULARY
- **inverse operations**
- **equivalent equations**

The activity on page 225 shows how to solve an *addition* equation using algebra tiles by *taking away* tiles from each side. An operation that "undoes" another operation is an **inverse operation**. Addition and subtraction are inverse operations.

Performing the same operation with the same number on each side of an equation results in a new equation that has the same solution as the original equation. **Equivalent equations** have the same solution. Forming equivalent equations can help you find the solution of an equation.

KEY CONCEPT *For Your Notebook*

Subtraction Property of Equality

Words Subtracting the same number from each side of an equation produces an equivalent equation.

Algebra $x + a = b \longrightarrow x + a - a = b - a$

EXAMPLE 1 Solving an Addition Equation

Solve the equation $x + 7 = -10$.

$x + 7 = -10$	**Write original equation.**
$\underline{-7 \quad\; -7}$	**Subtract 7 from each side.**
$x = -17$	**Simplify.**

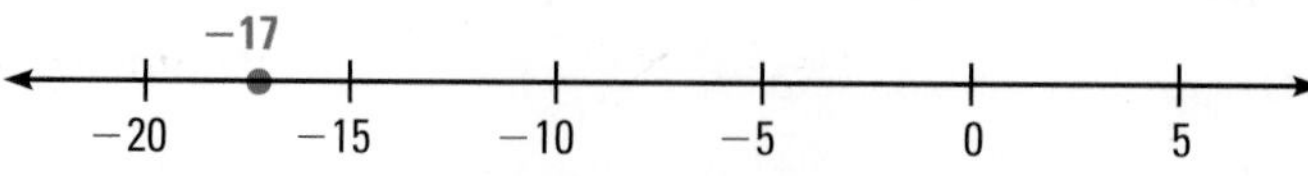

CHECK

$x + 7 = -10$	**Write original equation.**
$-17 + 7 \stackrel{?}{=} -10$	**Substitute −17 for *x*.**
$-10 = -10$ ✓	**Solution checks.**

KEY CONCEPT — For Your Notebook

Addition Property of Equality

Words Adding the same number to each side of an equation produces an equivalent equation.

Algebra $x - a = b \longrightarrow x - a + a = b + a$

EXAMPLE 2 Solving a Subtraction Equation

Solve the equation $-9 = y - 12$.

$-9 = y - 12$	Write original equation.
$-9 + \mathbf{12} = y - 12 + \mathbf{12}$	Add 12 to each side.
$3 = y$	Simplify.

CHECK

$-9 = y - 12$	Write original equation.
$-9 \stackrel{?}{=} 3 - 12$	Substitute 3 for y.
$-9 = -9$ ✓	Solution checks.

Animated Math
For an interactive example of solving equations go to **classzone.com**.

EXAMPLE 3 Combining Like Terms

Solve the equation $2 = 1.3 + a + 4.7$.

$2 = 1.3 + a + 4.7$	Write original equation.
$2 = 1.3 + 4.7 + a$	Group like terms.
$2 = 6 + a$	Combine like terms.
$2 - \mathbf{6} = 6 - \mathbf{6} + a$	Subtract 6 from each side.
$-4 = a$	Simplify.

CHECK

$2 = 1.3 + a + 4.7$	Write original equation.
$2 \stackrel{?}{=} 1.3 + (-4) + 4.7$	Substitute −4 for a.
$2 \stackrel{?}{=} 6 + (-4)$	Add 1.3 and 4.7.
$2 = 2$ ✓	Solution checks.

AVOID ERRORS
Whether you add or subtract vertically or horizontally to solve equations, remember to perform the same operation on each side of the equation.

✓ GUIDED PRACTICE for Examples 1, 2, and 3

Solve the equation. Graph and check your solution.

1. $t + 8 = 15$
2. $8 + x = -4$
3. $8 = m - 6$
4. $p - 2 = -5$
5. $5 = 4 + c - 2$
6. $3.4 + s - 1.3 = 6.8$

EXAMPLE 4 Writing and Solving an Equation

Flight to moon: 103 hours

SPACE SCIENCE The *Apollo 11* mission lasted about 195.5 hours. The flight from Earth to the moon lasted about 103 hours. The flight from the moon back to Earth lasted about 71 hours. About how many hours did the *Apollo 11* astronauts spend on the moon?

ANOTHER WAY

For an alternative method for solving the problem in Example 4, turn to p. 232 for the **Problem Solving Workshop**.

SOLUTION

Write a verbal model. Let t represent the amount of time (in hours) the astronauts spent on the moon.

Length of Mission	=	Length of flight to moon	+	Time spent on moon	+	Length of flight to Earth

$195.5 = 103 + t + 71$	**Write equation.**
$195.5 = 174 + t$	**Combine like terms.**
$195.5 - \mathbf{174} = 174 - \mathbf{174} + t$	**Subtract 174 from each side.**
$21.5 = t$	**Simplify.**

▶ **Answer** The *Apollo 11* astronauts spent about 21.5 hours on the moon.

GUIDED PRACTICE for Example 4

7. **PARTY PLANNING** You spent \$50 for streamers, balloons, and flowers. You spent \$12.50 on streamers and \$15 on balloons. Write and solve an equation to find how much you spent on flowers.

4.6 EXERCISES

HOMEWORK KEY

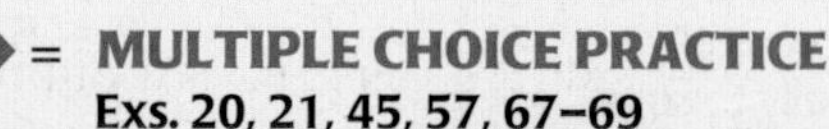

◆ = **MULTIPLE CHOICE PRACTICE** Exs. 20, 21, 45, 57, 67–69

○ = **HINTS AND HOMEWORK HELP** for Exs. 7, 25, 57 at classzone.com

SKILLS • PROBLEM SOLVING • REASONING

1. **VOCABULARY** Name a pair of inverse operations.

2. **WRITING** *Explain* why $x + 3 = 5$ and $x = 2$ are equivalent equations.

SEE EXAMPLES 1 AND 2 on pp. 226–227 for Exs. 3–21

SOLVING EQUATIONS **Solve the equation. Graph and check your solution.**

3. $c + 5 = 8$
4. $n + 7 = 10$
5. $6 + p = -11$
6. $m + 9 = 18$
7. $y + 13 = -17$
8. $14 = v + 10$
9. $13 + w = -7$
10. $t - 3 = 2$
11. $-7 = b + 7$
12. $h - 9.3 = 28$
13. $z - 6.8 = 13.9$
14. $14.2 = d + 5.1$
15. $r - 10 = 10.2$
16. $s - \frac{3}{7} = \frac{6}{7}$
17. $\frac{3}{8} = \frac{5}{16} + x$

ERROR ANALYSIS ***Describe*** **and correct the error made in solving the equation.**

18.

$$\begin{array}{r} x - 5 = 22 \\ -5 \quad -5 \\ \hline x = 17 \end{array}$$

19.

$$\begin{array}{r} x + 8 = 14 \\ -8 \quad +8 \\ \hline x = 22 \end{array}$$

20. ◆ **MULTIPLE CHOICE** Which equation has a solution of 5?

(A) $x - 5 = 10$ (B) $5 + x = 10$ (C) $10 + x = 5$ (D) $10 = 5 - x$

21. ◆ **MULTIPLE CHOICE** What value of m makes the equation $m + 14 = 9$ true?

(A) -23 (B) -5 (C) 5 (D) 23

SEE EXAMPLE 3 on p. 227 for Exs. 22–36

COMBINING LIKE TERMS **Solve the equation.**

22. $3 + r + 3 = -8$ **23.** $5 = m - 6 + 3$ **24.** $9 = c - 10 - 14$

25. $2 + n - 3 = 6$ **26.** $3 = 5 + x - 1$ **27.** $k + 6 - 10 = 17$

28. $3 + g + 4 = -18$ **29.** $5 = -9 + 14 + v$ **30.** $-9 = w - 11 + 12$

31. $15.7 = 9 + p - 1$ **32.** $2.3 + h + 3.1 = 27$ **33.** $8.6 = d + 4 - 2.4$

34. $3y - 2y + 8 = 4$ **35.** $7.2 = 4z + 3 - 3z$ **36.** $14 - s + 2s = 6$

SEE EXAMPLE 4 on p. 228 for Exs. 37–45

TRANSLATING SENTENCES **Write the verbal sentence as an equation. Then solve the equation.**

37. 5 less than a number p is -17.

38. The sum of 6 and a number x is 3.

39. 6 more than a number m is 13.

40. A number t decreased by 1 is -3.

41. A number y minus 11 is -16.

42. A number r added to -4 is 8.

43. $2\frac{1}{3}$ more than a number n is $4\frac{1}{2}$.

44. A number z decreased by 7.2 is 12.9.

45. ◆ **MULTIPLE CHOICE** The difference of a number x and 3 equals 2. What is the value of x?

(A) -5 (B) -1 (C) 1 (D) 5

REASONING ***Justify*** **each step in solving the equation.**

46.

$(24 + x) - 14 = 2$	
$(24 + x) + (-14) = 2$	?
$(x + 24) + (-14) = 2$	?
$x + [24 + (-14)] = 2$	?
$x + 10 = 2$	?
$x + 10 - 10 = 2 - 10$	?
$x = -8$	?

47.

$1 = -6 + x + 9$	
$1 = (-6 + x) + 9$	?
$1 = [x + (-6)] + 9$	?
$1 = x + (-6 + 9)$	?
$1 = x + 3$	?
$1 - 3 = x + 3 - 3$	?
$-2 = x$	?

48. **OPEN-ENDED** Write 3 different addition equations that each have a solution of -5.

GEOMETRY Write and solve an equation to find the unknown value of the variable.

49. Perimeter: 13 ft

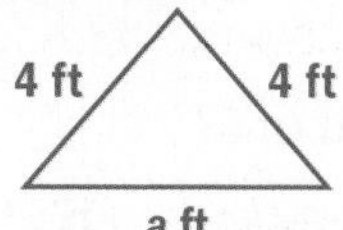

50. Perimeter: 21.5 in.

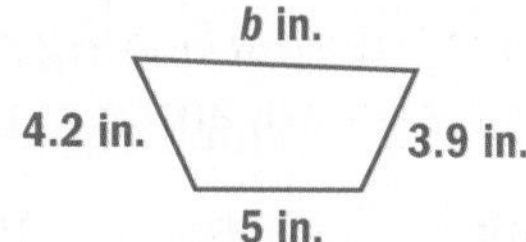

51. Perimeter: 42.5 m

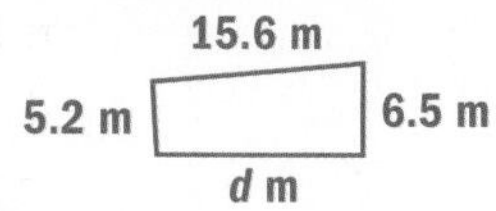

CONNECT SKILLS TO PROBLEM SOLVING Exercises 52–55 will help you prepare for problem solving.

Write an equation that can be used to solve the problem.

52. After Marie deposits a check for \$55, the new balance of her account is \$280. What was the balance b before she deposited the check?

53. Locker mirrors are on sale for \$5.75. This price is \$1.50 less than the regular price. What is the regular price r?

54. While holding his cat, Bill steps on a scale. The scale reads 127 pounds. Alone, Bill weighs 112 pounds. What is the weight w of Bill's cat?

55. The difference between the high and low temperatures one day was 23°F. The low temperature was 45°F. What was the high temperature t?

SEE EXAMPLE 4 on p. 228 for Exs. 56–58

56. **MULTI-STEP PROBLEM** You and your friend are going on a boat tour as shown at the right. The tour takes you from the dock to a coral reef, then to an island, and back to the dock. The tour is 5 miles long.

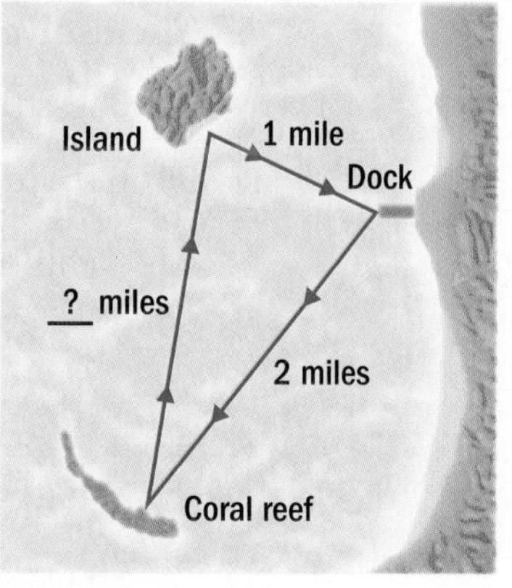

 a. Write a verbal model that represents the situation.
 b. Let x represent the distance (in miles) between the reef and the island. Use the model to write an equation.
 c. Solve the equation.

California @HomeTutor for problem solving help at classzone.com

57. ◆ **MULTIPLE CHOICE** Judy is 7 years younger than Lily. Which equation can be used to find Lily's age L (in years) if Judy is 14 years old?

Ⓐ $14 = L + 7$ Ⓑ $14 = L - 7$ Ⓒ $14 = 7L$ Ⓓ $14 = 7 - L$

California @HomeTutor for problem solving help at classzone.com

58. **SCIENCE** The atomic mass of an atom is about equal to the sum of the numbers of protons and neutrons it contains. Write and solve equations to find the number n of neutrons in an atom of each element in the table.

Element	Gold	Silver	Mercury
Atomic mass	197	108	201
Protons	79	47	80

59. **WRITING** Jared solves the equation $-5 + x = 2$ by subtracting -5 from each side. Carlos solves the same equation by adding 5 to each side. Are they both correct? *Explain* your reasoning.

60. **COSTUME PARTY** You need to make a costume to wear to your friend's costume party. You have \$25 to spend. Write and solve an addition equation to find how much money you have left after buying 2.5 yards of fabric, a wig, 2 sheets of poster board, and a mask.

Item	Fabric	Wig	Poster board	Mask
Cost	\$3.50 per yard	\$5.39	\$1.99 per sheet	\$4.25

61. **SHORT RESPONSE** *Describe* a real-world situation that can be represented by the equation $d + 12 = 20$. *Explain* what d represents.

62. **MULTI-STEP PROBLEM** At a store, you can buy used CDs for \$3.49, used DVDs for \$8.99, or used video games for \$12.50. You have \$25, but you have to buy a package of CD holders that costs \$4.75.
   a. Write and solve an equation to find out how much money you can spend on other items.
   b. Use your answer to part (a) to write and solve an equation to find how much money you will have left if you buy a video game.
   c. After buying a package of CD holders and a video game, what else can you buy? *Explain* your reasoning.

CHALLENGE ***Describe*** **the values of** x **that make each statement true.**

63. $5x + 5 = 5(x + 1)$

64. $x - 7 - x = 0$

65. $3x - x + 16 = 2(x + 8)$

66. **CHALLENGE** Ricardo is x years old. Natalie's age is 4 more than triple Ricardo's age. Keisha is 2 years older than Natalie. Find each person's age if 7 times Ricardo's age equals the sum of Natalie's and Keisha's ages.

◆ California Standards Spiral Review

AF 1.1 67. What is the solution of the equation $\frac{a}{7} = 8$? *(p. 219)*

Ⓐ 1 Ⓑ 15 Ⓒ 49 Ⓓ 56

NS 2.2 68. What is the value of $\frac{5}{8} \div \frac{25}{52}$? *(p. 95)*

Ⓐ $\frac{5}{7}$ Ⓑ $\frac{10}{13}$ Ⓒ $1\frac{3}{10}$ Ⓓ $1\frac{2}{5}$

Gr. 5 NS 2.1 69. Tom has \$13.25. He wants to buy packs of baseball cards that cost \$2.75 each. How many packs of baseball cards can he buy? *(p. 107)*

Ⓐ 1 Ⓑ 4 Ⓒ 5 Ⓓ 10

PROBLEM SOLVING WORKSHOP
LESSON 4.6

Using ALTERNATIVE METHODS

Another Way to Solve Example 4, page 228

Standards
AF 1.1

In Example 4 on page 228, you saw how to solve the problem about time spent on the moon by writing an addition equation. You can also solve the problem by using number sense.

PROBLEM

SPACE SCIENCE The *Apollo 11* mission lasted about 195.5 hours. The flight from Earth to the moon lasted about 103 hours. The flight from the moon back to Earth lasted about 71 hours. About how many hours did the *Apollo 11* astronauts spend on the moon?

METHOD

Using Number Sense An alternative approach is to use number sense to interpret the relationships among the numbers in the problem.

STEP 1 **Understand** the problem. The time spent on the moon is equal to the total time of the mission less the time traveling to the moon and back.

STEP 2 **Find** the time spent traveling to the moon and back.

$$\begin{aligned}\text{Travel time} &= 103 + 71\\ &= 174\end{aligned}$$

STEP 3 **Subtract** the travel time from the total time of the mission to find the time spent on the moon.

$$\begin{aligned}\text{Time on moon} &= 195.5 - 174\\ &= 21.5\end{aligned}$$

▶ **Answer** The *Apollo 11* astronauts spent about 21.5 hours on the moon.

PRACTICE

1. **FOOTBALL** A football team needs to gain 10 yards in four downs to keep possession of the ball. In the first three downs, the team gains 3 yards, 1 yard, and 2 yards. How many yards does the team need to gain on the fourth down to keep possession of the ball? Solve this problem using two different methods.

2. **FUNDRAISING** John and Elizabeth sold flowers to raise money for their French club. They raised $113, which was $187 less than the club's fundraising goal. What was the club's fundraising goal? Solve this problem using two different methods.

Investigating Math ACTIVITY *Use before Lesson 4.7*

4.7 Modeling Multiplication Equations

MATERIALS • algebra tiles

Standards

AF 1.1 Write and **solve one-step linear equations in one variable.**

QUESTION How can you model and solve multiplication equations?

You can use algebra tiles to model and solve simple multiplication equations.

EXPLORE Solve $3x = 12$.

STEP 1 **Model** $3x = 12$ using algebra tiles.

STEP 2 **Divide** the x-tiles and 1-tiles into 3 equal groups.

STEP 3 **Identify** the solution. One x-tile is equal to four 1-tiles. So, the solution of the equation $3x = 12$ is 4.

CHECK $3(4) = 12$ ✓

DRAW CONCLUSIONS Use your observations to complete these exercises.

Use algebra tiles to model and solve the equation.

1. $5x = 15$ **2.** $2x = 4$ **3.** $4x = 8$ **4.** $4x = 20$

5. $3x = 18$ **6.** $7x = 21$ **7.** $2x + 3x = 5$ **8.** $2x + 4x = 12$

9. WRITING The example above uses a property called the *division property of equality,* which is similar to the addition and subtraction properties of equality. *Explain* what the division property of equality allows you to do.

4.7 Solving Multiplication and Division Equations

Standards **AF 1.1** **Write and solve one-step linear equations in one variable.**

Connect ***Before*** you solved addition and subtraction equations. ***Now*** you will solve multiplication and division equations.

Math and **AVIATION**
Example 4, p. 236

KEY VOCABULARY

- **inverse operations,** *p. 226*

Recall that inverse operations "undo" each other. Multiplication and division are inverse operations. The activity on page 233 suggests that you can use division to solve a multiplication equation. Similarly, you can use multiplication to solve a division equation.

KEY CONCEPT *For Your Notebook*

Division Property of Equality

Words Dividing each side of an equation by the same nonzero number produces an equivalent equation.

Algebra $ax = b\ (a \neq 0) \rightarrow \frac{ax}{a} = \frac{b}{a}$

EXAMPLE 1 Solving a Multiplication Equation

Solve the equation (a) $-3x = 45$ and (b) $-x = -8$.

a.

$-3x = 45$	Write original equation.	**CHECK**	$-3x = 45$
$\frac{-3x}{-3} = \frac{45}{-3}$	Divide each side by -3.		$-3(-15) \stackrel{?}{=} 45$
$x = -15$	Simplify.		$45 = 45$ ✓

b.

$-x = -8$	Write original equation.	**CHECK**	$-x = -8$
$-1x = -8$	Rewrite $-x$ as $-1x$.		$-(8) \stackrel{?}{=} -8$
$\frac{-1x}{-1} = \frac{-8}{-1}$	Divide each side by -1.		$-8 = -8$ ✓
$x = 8$	Simplify.		

GUIDED PRACTICE for Example 1

Solve the equation. Graph and check your solution.

1. $6a = 54$ **2.** $-13v = 65$ **3.** $16 = -s$

4. $-17 = -b$ **5.** $8g = 88$ **6.** $-12n = 108$

KEY CONCEPT — For Your Notebook

Multiplication Property of Equality

Words Multiplying each side of an equation by the same nonzero number produces an equivalent equation.

Algebra $\frac{x}{a} = b \ (a \neq 0) \longrightarrow a \cdot \frac{x}{a} = a \cdot b$

EXAMPLE 2 Solving a Division Equation

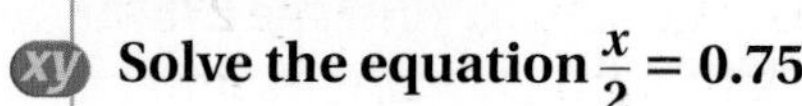

Solve the equation $\frac{x}{2} = 0.75$.

$\frac{x}{2} = 0.75$	**Write original equation.**
$2 \cdot \frac{x}{2} = 2 \cdot 0.75$	**Multiply each side by 2.**
$x = 1.5$	**Simplify.**

✓ GUIDED PRACTICE for Example 2

Solve the equation. Graph and check your solution.

7. $\frac{c}{2} = 13$ **8.** $3.4 = \frac{d}{5}$ **9.** $\frac{s}{-4} = -3$

RECIPROCALS Recall that two numbers whose product is 1 are reciprocals, or multiplicative inverses. For example, $\frac{3}{4}$ and $\frac{4}{3}$ are reciprocals because $\frac{3}{4}\left(\frac{4}{3}\right) = 1$. To solve an equation containing a fractional coefficient, multiply each side of the equation by the reciprocal of the coefficient. This will result in a coefficient of 1.

EXAMPLE 3 Solving an Equation Using a Reciprocal

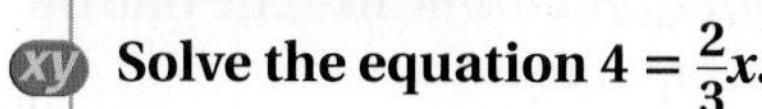

Solve the equation $4 = \frac{2}{3}x$.

$4 = \frac{2}{3}x$	**Write original equation.**
$\left(\frac{3}{2}\right)(4) = \left(\frac{3}{2}\right)\frac{2}{3}x$	**Multiply each side by $\frac{3}{2}$, the reciprocal of $\frac{2}{3}$.**
$6 = x$	**Simplify.**

USE RECIPROCALS
For help with finding a reciprocal, see p. 95.

✓ GUIDED PRACTICE for Example 3

Solve the equation. Graph and check your solution.

10. $\frac{4}{5}r = 1$ **11.** $2 = \frac{2}{5}t$ **12.** $\frac{1}{2}p = 10$

EXAMPLE 4 ◆ Multiple Choice Practice

A blimp travels 300 miles at a constant speed of 40 miles per hour. Which equation can you use to find the time t (in hours) that the blimp travels?

Ⓐ $40 = 300t$ Ⓑ $300 = 40t$ Ⓒ $300 = t + 40$ Ⓓ $40 = \frac{t}{300}$

ELIMINATE CHOICES
There is no addition in the formula for distance. You can eliminate choice C.

SOLUTION

$d = rt$	**Write formula for distance.**
$300 = 40t$	**Substitute 300 for *d* and 40 for *r*.**
$\frac{300}{40} = \frac{40t}{40}$	**Divide each side by 40.**
$7.5 = t$	**Simplify.**

▸ **Answer** The blimp travels for 7.5 hours. The equation used to find the time is $300 = 40t$. The correct answer is B. Ⓐ Ⓑ Ⓒ Ⓓ

GUIDED PRACTICE for Example 4

13. **MOVIE LENGTHS** A movie is sold as a DVD set that includes 7.5 hours of bonus material. This is 3 times as long as the movie itself. Write and solve an equation to find the length m (in hours) of the movie.

4.7 EXERCISES

HOMEWORK KEY

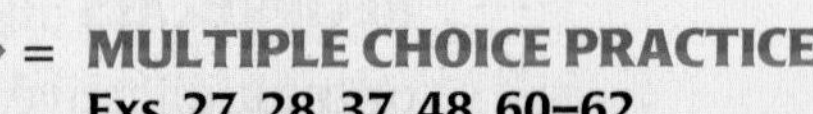

◆ = **MULTIPLE CHOICE PRACTICE** Exs. 27, 28, 37, 48, 60–62

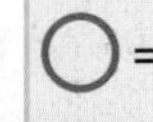

○ = **HINTS AND HOMEWORK HELP** for Exs. 5, 19, 53 at classzone.com

SKILLS • PROBLEM SOLVING • REASONING

1. **VOCABULARY** Copy and complete: Multiplication and division are _?_.

2. **NOTETAKING SKILLS** Make an *information frame* like the one on page 196 for the division property of equality.

SEE EXAMPLES 1, 2, AND 3 on pp. 234–235 for Exs. 3–22

SOLVING EQUATIONS **Solve the equation. Graph and check your solution.**

3. $14q = 42$
4. $-20v = 100$
5. $-t = -9$
6. $9s = -27$
7. $\frac{w}{2} = 8$
8. $-7 = \frac{z}{-3}$
9. $\frac{c}{14} = -11$
10. $\frac{r}{-2} = 10$
11. $1.5h = 10.5$
12. $3.5f = 24.5$
13. $3 = 1.2g$
14. $\frac{a}{2.8} = 4$
15. $\frac{b}{1.2} = 1.8$
16. $3.6 = \frac{k}{5.5}$
17. $\frac{3}{4}y = 12$
18. $\frac{3}{10}p = 6$
19. $\frac{4}{3}m = 12$
20. $\frac{5}{7}n = 5$
21. $\frac{1}{2}c = 12$
22. $9 = \frac{3}{4}x$

SEE EXAMPLES 1 AND 2 on pp. 234–235 for Exs. 23–28

CHOOSE A STRATEGY ***Explain*** **how to solve the equation. Then solve.**

23. $3x = 15$ **24.** $-4x = 16$ **25.** $\frac{x}{9} = -2$ **26.** $\frac{x}{15} = -7$

27. ◆ **MULTIPLE CHOICE** Which describes how to solve $-8y = 40$ in one step?

Ⓐ Divide each side by 40. Ⓑ Multiply each side by -8.

Ⓒ Divide each side by -8. Ⓓ Divide each side by 8.

28. ◆ **MULTIPLE CHOICE** Which equation has a solution of -2?

Ⓐ $4y = 8$ Ⓑ $-4y = 8$ Ⓒ $8y = 4$ Ⓓ $-8y = 4$

SEE EXAMPLES 1 AND 3 on pp. 234–235 for Exs. 29–30

ERROR ANALYSIS ***Describe*** **and correct the error made in solving the equation.**

29.

✗
$$-3x = 48$$
$$\frac{-3x}{3} = \frac{48}{3}$$
$$x = 16$$

30.

✗
$$\frac{4}{5}x = 20$$
$$\frac{4}{5} \cdot \frac{4}{5}x = \frac{4}{5} \cdot 20$$
$$x = 16$$

SEE EXAMPLE 4 on p. 236 for Exs. 31–36

TRANSLATING SENTENCES **Write the verbal sentence as an equation. Then solve. Let n represent the number.**

31. The product of 11 and a number is -22.

32. The quotient of a number and 3 is 6.6.

33. A number divided by -11 is -7.

34. The product of $\frac{2}{3}$ and a number is 18.

35. A number multiplied by $\frac{4}{13}$ is 2.

36. The quotient of a number and 5 is 11.3.

37. ◆ **MULTIPLE CHOICE** The quotient of x and 9 is y. Which equation can be used to find the value of x?

Ⓐ $x = \frac{9}{y}$ Ⓑ $x = 9y$ Ⓒ $x = \frac{y}{9}$ Ⓓ $xy = 9$

COMBINING LIKE TERMS **Solve the equation. Check your solution.**

38. $2x + 3x = 12$ **39.** $7a - 5a = 15$ **40.** $10 = b + 8b$

41. $9z + 3z = 6$ **42.** $3 = m + 3m$ **43.** $6p - 2p = 9$

CONNECT SKILLS TO PROBLEM SOLVING **Exercises 44–46 will help you prepare for problem solving.**

Write an equation that can be used to solve the problem.

44. You throw a disc 30 feet to your dog. The average speed of the disc is 12 feet per second. How long is the disc in the air?

45. A rectangle has a length of 7.5 meters and an area of 45 square meters. Find the width of the rectangle.

46. Five friends plan to equally share the total cost of dinner at a restaurant. Each friend will pay $12.50. Find the total cost of dinner.

SEE EXAMPLE 4 on p. 236 for Exs. 47–48

47. MIGRATION Use the diagram at the right. Write and solve an equation to find the time it takes the plover to migrate.

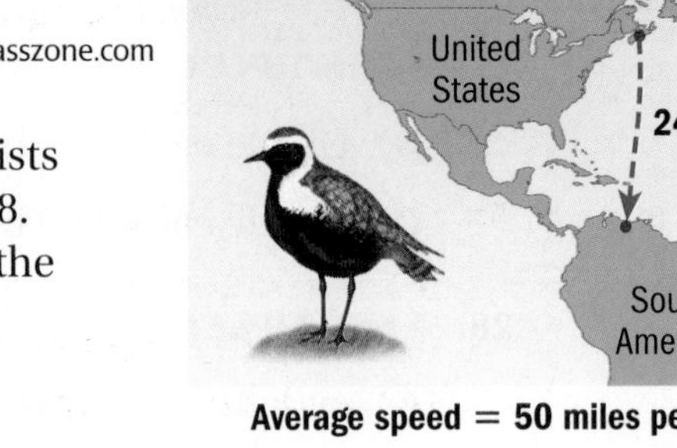

California @HomeTutor for problem solving help at classzone.com

48. ◆ MULTIPLE CHOICE Your telephone bill lists a call that lasted m minutes and cost $1.08. Which algebraic equation best describes the cost C (in dollars) per minute?

Ⓐ $C = \frac{1.08}{m}$ Ⓑ $C = \frac{m}{1.08}$

Ⓒ $C = m + 1.08$ Ⓓ $C = m - 1.08$

California @HomeTutor for problem solving help at classzone.com

49. OPEN-ENDED *Describe* a real-world situation that could be solved using the equation $\frac{t}{5} = 20$.

READING *IN* MATH **Read the information below for Exercises 50–52.**

Jump Rope USA Jump Rope holds many single and double jump rope competitions in the United States. Competitors are split up into age divisions and can compete individually, in pairs, or as a team.

Suppose that in the 3 minute speed event, a jumper's right foot strikes the ground 309 times. Assume that the jumper keeps a steady pace.

Right foot strikes ground 309 times in 3 minutes.

50. Model Write a multiplication equation that can be used to find the number of times the jumper's right foot strikes the ground in 1 minute.

51. Solve Write an equivalent division equation for the situation. Then use the division equation to solve the problem.

52. Calculate How many times does the jumper's right foot strike the ground in 1 second? Round your answer to the nearest tenth.

53. SHORT RESPONSE In one day, a ski lift can carry 11,200 people. The lift runs from 9:00 A.M. to 4:00 P.M. Write and solve an equation to find the average number of people the lift carries in 1 hour. Estimate the number of people who could ride the lift by noon. *Explain* your reasoning.

54. BASEBALL In 1931, Ernest Swanson set a record by circling the 4 bases of a baseball diamond at an average speed of 27 feet per second. Consecutive bases are 90 feet apart. How long did it take him to circle the bases? Round your answer to the nearest tenth.

55. **REASONING** Is it possible to solve the equation $5x = 29$ by *multiplying* each side of the equation by the same number? *Explain* your reasoning.

CHALLENGE Solve the equation.

56. $-4x - 7 = -9$

57. $\frac{y + 6}{4} = -3$

58. $13 - 5w = -19$

59. **CHALLENGE** Maura exchanged U.S. dollars for 1284 Mexican pesos at an exchange rate of about $10\frac{7}{10}$ pesos for each U.S. dollar. Write an equation that models the situation and can be solved by multiplying both sides by a reciprocal. How many U.S. dollars did Maura exchange?

◆ CALIFORNIA STANDARDS SPIRAL REVIEW

AF 1.1 60. What is the value of x in the equation $15 = 5x$? *(p. 219)*

Ⓐ 3 Ⓑ 5 Ⓒ 10 Ⓓ 75

NS 1.1 61. Which rational number is the greatest? *(p. 167)*

Ⓐ $-\frac{4}{6}$ Ⓑ $-0.\overline{7}$ Ⓒ -0.68 Ⓓ $-\frac{7}{10}$

NS 2.1 62. Two books are stacked on top of each other. One book has a height of $\frac{7}{8}$ inch and the other book has a height of $\frac{5}{16}$ inch. What is the height of the stack of books? *(p. 75)*

Ⓐ $\frac{1}{2}$ in. Ⓑ $\frac{3}{4}$ in. Ⓒ $1\frac{3}{16}$ in. Ⓓ $1\frac{1}{2}$ in.

QUIZ *for Lessons 4.5–4.7*

Write the verbal sentence as an equation. Let *n* represent the number. *(p. 219)*

1. 5 increased by twice a number is 13.
2. 12 is equal to four times the difference of a number and 8.

Solve the equation. Graph and check your solution.

3. $14 + x = 45$ *(p. 226)*
4. $0.2 + y + 4.3 = 5$ *(p. 226)*
5. $t - 37 = 51$ *(p. 226)*
6. $11 = \frac{a}{8}$ *(p. 234)*
7. $55 = 2.5p$ *(p. 234)*
8. $\frac{2}{9}c = 12$ *(p. 234)*

9. **MUSIC** You want to buy a clarinet that costs $250. You have saved $145, and your aunt loans you $70. Write and solve an equation to find the amount you still need to save to buy the clarinet. *(p. 226)*

10. **MUSEUM ADMISSION** The cost of admission to a museum is $32 for 4 adults. Write and solve an equation to find the cost of admission for 1 adult. *(p. 234)*

MIXED REVIEW of Skills and Problem Solving

Multiple Choice Practice for Lessons 4.5–4.7

1. The Empire State Building is in New York City. The U.S. Bank Tower is in Los Angeles. Using the diagram, what is the height h of the U.S. Bank Tower? **AF 1.1**

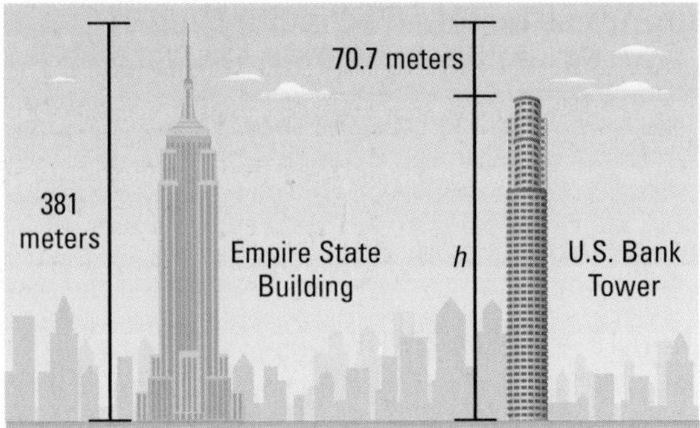

   Ⓐ 310.3 m　Ⓑ 311.3 m
   Ⓒ 381 m　Ⓓ 451.7 m

2. What is the value of x that makes the equation $\frac{x}{9} = -5$ true? **AF 1.1**

   Ⓐ -45　Ⓑ -4
   Ⓒ 4　Ⓓ 45

3. Jill spent \$21.75 on admission, lunch, and souvenirs during a trip to the zoo. The table shows the amounts spent on lunch and souvenirs. Which equation can you use to find the amount a (in dollars) spent on admission? **AF 1.1, MR 1.2**

Purchase	lunch	souvenirs
Amount spent	\$7.25	\$9.00

   Ⓐ $7.25 + a = 21.75 + 9$
   Ⓑ $7.25 + 9 = a + 21.75$
   Ⓒ $7.25 + 9 + a = 21.75$
   Ⓓ $a = 7.25 + 9 + 21.75$

4. Which equation has a solution of 23? **AF 1.1**

   Ⓐ $18 + x = 5$　Ⓑ $x - 40 = -17$
   Ⓒ $\frac{x}{5} = 3.6$　Ⓓ $7x = 168$

5. The sum of 8 and w is -19. What is the value of w? **AF 1.1**

   Ⓐ 27　Ⓑ 11
   Ⓒ -11　Ⓓ -27

6. Jacob is playing a board game with a friend. In the first round, Jacob loses 12 counters, which is $\frac{2}{3}$ of his starting amount. How many counters did Jacob have at the start of the game? **AF 1.1**

   Ⓐ 6　Ⓑ 8
   Ⓒ 12　Ⓓ 18

7. The table shows the prices of a daily bike pass and a season pass at a mountain bike resort. You want to find the number n of daily bike passes that would cost the same amount as one season pass. Which equation can be used to solve the problem? **AF 1.1**

Item	*Price*
daily bike pass	\$20
season pass	\$260

   Ⓐ $260 - n = 20$　Ⓑ $20n = 260$
   Ⓒ $\frac{n}{20} = 260$　Ⓓ $260n = 20$

8. What is the solution of the equation $\frac{2}{3}x = \frac{1}{3}$? **AF 1.1, MR 2.7**

   Ⓐ $4\frac{1}{2}$　Ⓑ $\frac{1}{2}$
   Ⓒ $\frac{1}{3}$　Ⓓ $\frac{2}{9}$

9. The rectangle below has an area of 50 square inches. What is the width? **AF 1.1**

   12.5 in.

   Ⓐ 4 in.　Ⓑ 6.25 in.
   Ⓒ 12.5 in.　Ⓓ 37.5 in.

4 CHAPTER SUMMARY

Standards
AF 1.1, AF 1.2, AF 3.1, AF 3.2, Gr. 5 AF 1.3

BIG IDEAS

For Your Notebook

Big Idea 1

Writing and Evaluating Expressions Using up to Three Variables

You can write a verbal phrase as an algebraic expression. To evaluate an algebraic expression, substitute the value of the variable(s) into the expression and then simplify.

Verbal phrase	Expression	Evaluate when $x = -2$, $y = 7$, and $z = -3$
4 times the difference of x and 3	$4(x - 3)$	$4(-2 - 3) = 4(-5) = -20$
The sum of y and the product of x and z	$y + xz$	$7 + (-2)(-3) = 7 + 6 = 13$

Big Idea 2

Using Familiar Formulas

The formulas for perimeter and area of a rectangle and square, for distance, and for temperature conversions have many applications. You may need to combine like terms to simplify the expressions formed using these formulas.

	Formula	Variables
Perimeter	$P = 2l + 2w$ (rectangle) $P = 4s$ (square)	l = length, w = width, s = side length
Area	$A = lw$ (rectangle) $A = s^2$ (square)	l = length, w = width, s = side length
Distance	$d = rt$	d = distance, r = rate, t = time
Celsius to Fahrenheit	$F = \frac{9}{5}C + 32$	F = degrees Fahrenheit, C = degrees Celsius
Fahrenheit to Celsius	$C = \frac{5}{9}(F - 32)$	C = degrees Celsius, F = degrees Fahrenheit

Big Idea 3

Writing and Solving One-Step Equations

You can solve a one-step equation by adding, subtracting, multiplying by, or dividing by the same number on each side of the equation.

Property	Example
Subtraction Property of Equality	$a + 6 = 8 \rightarrow a + 6 - 6 = 8 - 6 \rightarrow a = 2$
Addition Property of Equality	$b - 3 = 2 \rightarrow b - 3 + 3 = 2 + 3 \rightarrow b = 5$
Division Property of Equality	$7c = 35 \rightarrow \frac{7c}{7} = \frac{35}{7} \rightarrow c = 5$
Multiplication Property of Equality	$\frac{d}{3} = 9 \rightarrow 3 \cdot \frac{d}{3} = 3 \cdot 9 \rightarrow d = 27$

CHAPTER PROBLEM

Standards
AF 1.1, AF 1.2, AF 3.1, AF 3.2, Gr. 5 AF 1.3

APPLYING THE
BIG IDEAS

Big Idea 1
You write and evaluate expressions in **Steps 3 and 4.**

Big Idea 2
You use familiar perimeter formulas in **Ex. 3.**

Big Idea 3
You write and solve one-step equations in **Step 4 and Ex. 3.**

PROBLEM How can you use expressions and equations to write algebraic puzzles about triangles?

STEP 1 **Draw and measure a triangle.**

Draw a triangle with three different side lengths on a sheet of paper. Measure the length of each side in centimeters. Then find the perimeter of the triangle.

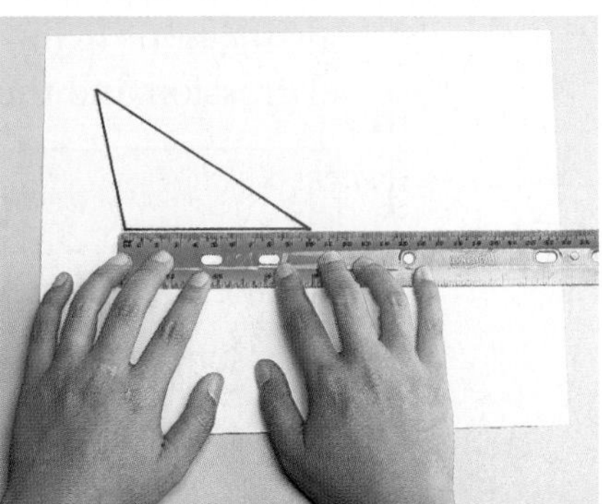

STEP 2 **Create a puzzle.**

On another sheet of paper, copy and complete the sentences below.

- My triangle has a perimeter of ___?___ centimeters.
- The longest side is ___?___ times as long as the shortest side.
- The next longest side is ___?___ times as long as the shortest side.

STEP 3 **Write an equation.**

Exchange puzzles with a classmate. Let s represent the length (in centimeters) of the shortest side. Write multiplication expressions for the lengths of the other two sides in terms of s. Then write an equation that relates the side lengths and the perimeter.

STEP 4 **Solve an equation.**

Solve the equation to find the length of the shortest side. Then find the length of each side of your classmate's triangle. Summarize the steps you took to solve the problem.

Extending the Problem

Use your results from the problem to complete the exercises.

1. Draw a rectangle that is not a square. Measure the length and width of each side in centimeters and calculate the area.
2. Use the rectangle in Exercise 1 to copy and complete the sentences below.
   - My rectangle has an area of ___?___ square centimeters.
   - The width of the rectangle is ___?___ centimeters.
   - The length is ___?___ times as long as the width.
3. *Explain* how a classmate could use these sentences to find the length and perimeter of the rectangle.

4 CHAPTER REVIEW

California @HomeTutor
classzone.com
• Multi-Language Visual Glossary
• Vocabulary practice

REVIEW KEY VOCABULARY

- verbal model, *p. 203*
- terms, *p. 207*
- coefficient, *p. 207*
- like terms, *p. 207*
- constant term, *p. 207*
- equation, *p. 212*
- formula, *p. 212*
- solution, *p. 219*
- solving an equation, *p. 220*
- inverse operations, *p. 226*
- equivalent equations, *p. 226*

VOCABULARY EXERCISES

In Exercises 1–6, copy and complete the statement.

1. Two equations that have the same solution are ___?___.
2. Operations that "undo" each other are ___?___.
3. The number 3 in the term $3x$ is called the ___?___ of the term.
4. A mathematical sentence formed by setting two expressions equal is a(n) ___?___.
5. The number 8 is the ___?___ of the equation $9x = 72$.
6. The equation $P = 4s$ is the ___?___ for the perimeter of a square.
7. **NOTETAKING SKILLS** Make an *information frame* like the one on page 196 for the subtraction property of equality.

REVIEW EXAMPLES AND EXERCISES

4.1 Evaluating Expressions *pp. 197–200*

AF 1.2

EXAMPLE

Evaluate $7x + 2yz$ when $x = -3$, $y = 5$, and $z = 6$.

$7x + 2yz = 7(-3) + 2(5)(6)$	**Substitute −3 for *x*, 5 for *y*, and 6 for *z*.**
$= -21 + 2(5)(6)$	**Multiply.**
$= -21 + 60$	**Multiply.**
$= 39$	**Add.**

EXERCISES

SEE EXAMPLES 1 AND 2 on pp. 197–198 for Exs. 8–15

Evaluate the expression when $r = 4$, $s = \frac{3}{8}$, and $t = -3$.

8. $7 + 8r$
9. $s \div \frac{9}{16}$
10. $4(t - 7)$
11. $\frac{3r - 7t}{3}$
12. $2rs$
13. $2t^2 - 8s$
14. $\frac{-6r}{t}$
15. $4rs + 3t$

4.2 Writing Expressions

pp. 202–206

AF 1.2

EXAMPLE

Write the verbal phrase as an algebraic expression.

	Verbal phrase	**Expression**
a.	6 less than triple a number	$3n - 6$
b.	7 minus a number squared	$7 - x^2$

EXERCISES

SEE EXAMPLES 1, 2, AND 3 on pp. 202–203 for Exs. 16–20

Write the verbal phrase as an algebraic expression. Let w represent the number.

16. 2 more than a number

17. Twice the sum of a number and 4

18. $\frac{1}{4}$ the difference of a number and 7

19. The quotient of 6 and the sum of 5 and a number

20. **SCHOOL SUPPLIES** You are buying school supplies. Notebooks cost $3 each, folders cost $1.50 each, and glue sticks cost $.65 each. Write an expression for the total cost of n notebooks, f folders, and g glue sticks.

4.3 Simplifying Expressions

pp. 207–210

Gr.5 AF 1.3

EXAMPLE

Simplify the expression $4(2z + 1) - 3z$.

$4(2z + 1) - 3z = 8z + 4 - 3z$	**Distributive property**
$= 8z + 4 + (-3z)$	**Write as a sum.**
$= 8z + (-3z) + 4$	**Group like terms.**
$= 5z + 4$	**Combine like terms.**

EXERCISES

SEE EXAMPLES 2, 3, AND 4 on pp. 207–208 for Exs. 21–27

Simplify the expression.

21. $9x + 4 - x - 8$

22. $14 + 2y + 3 - 6y$

23. $5z + 9 - 4z - 15$

24. $-11 + 5b + 6 - 2b$

25. $10 + 7(d - 4)$

26. $-3(g + 2) + 8g$

27. **FLOWERS** A florist has r roses. The number of tulips that the florist has is 3 more than twice the number of roses. Write and simplify an expression for the total number of roses and tulips.

4.4 Using Familiar Formulas

pp. 212–217

AF 3.1, AF 3.2

EXAMPLE

Write and simplify expressions for the area and perimeter of the rectangle.

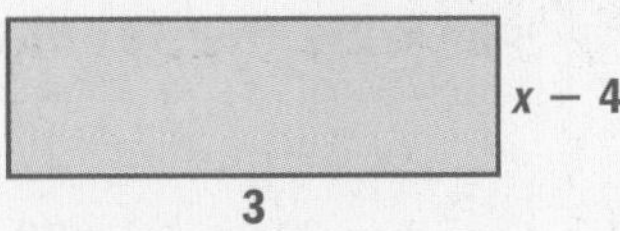

Perimeter of rectangle		**Area of rectangle**	
$P = 2l + 2w$	**Write formula.**	$A = lw$	**Write formula.**
$= 2(3) + 2(x - 4)$	**Substitute.**	$= (3)(x - 4)$	**Substitute.**
$= 2x - 2$	**Simplify.**	$= 3x - 12$	**Distributive property**

EXERCISES

SEE EXAMPLES 1, 3, AND 4 on pp. 212–214 for Exs. 28–31

Write and simplify expressions for the perimeter and area of a rectangle with the given dimensions.

28. $l = 7z, w = z$

29. $l = n + 3, w = 0.5$

30. Find the distance traveled at a constant speed of 4 mi/h for 0.5 hour.

31. **TEMPERATURE** The body temperature of a dog is about 39°C. What is the body temperature in degrees Fahrenheit?

4.5 Equations and Mental Math

pp. 219–224

AF 1.1

EXAMPLE

Write the verbal sentence as an equation.

Verbal sentence	**Equation**
a. A number increased by 7 is 13.	$x + 7 = 13$
b. The difference of 3 times a number and 4 is 8.	$3y - 4 = 8$

EXERCISES

SEE EXAMPLES 2 AND 3 on p. 220 for Exs. 32–38

Write the verbal sentence as an equation. Let *n* represent the number.

32. 8 less than a number is −25.

33. A number divided by 7 is 3.

34. The quotient of a number and 9 is 26.

35. The sum of a number squared and 3 is 7.

Solve the equation using mental math.

36. $x - 13 = 8$

37. $y + 3 = -9$

38. $-8z = -40$

4.6 Solving Addition and Subtraction Equations

pp. 226–231

AF 1.1

EXAMPLE

a. Solve the equation $n + 31 = 50$.

$n + 31 = 50$	Write original equation.
$n + 31 - 31 = 50 - 31$	Subtract 31 from each side.
$n = 19$	Simplify.

b. Solve the equation $-15 = y - 10$.

$-15 = y - 10$	Write original equation.
$-15 + 10 = y - 10 + 10$	Add 10 to each side.
$-5 = y$	Simplify.

EXERCISES

SEE EXAMPLES 1, 2, 3, AND 4 on pp. 226–228 for Exs. 39–45

Solve the equation. Graph and check your solution.

39. $x - 3 = 13$
40. $-5 = z - 19$
41. $9.6 + g = 11.4$
42. $a + 4 = 9$
43. $7.4 + y - 5.6 = 19.2$
44. $-11 = m - 7 + 9$
45. **CARD COLLECTING** Kerry has 55 baseball cards, which is 18 less than the number of cards Timothy has. How many cards does Timothy have?

4.7 Solving Multiplication and Division Equations

pp. 234–239

AF 1.1

EXAMPLE

a. Solve the equation $6m = -78$.

$6m = -78$	Write equation.
$\frac{6m}{6} = \frac{-78}{6}$	Divide each side by 6.
$m = -13$	Simplify.

b. Solve the equation $\frac{x}{2} = 3.5$.

$\frac{x}{2} = 3.5$	Write equation.
$2 \cdot \frac{x}{2} = 2 \cdot 3.5$	Multiply each side by 2.
$x = 7$	Simplify.

EXERCISES

SEE EXAMPLES 1, 2, AND 3 on pp. 234–235 for Exs. 46–51

Solve the equation. Graph and check your solution.

46. $-k = 12$
47. $-11z = -33$
48. $90 = -5b$
49. $\frac{p}{-8} = 5$
50. $2.25 = \frac{t}{16}$
51. $\frac{2}{5}y = 6$

4 CHAPTER TEST

1. **VOCABULARY** Identify the coefficients, like terms, and constant terms of the expression $8x - 5 - x$.

2. **VOCABULARY** Copy and complete: Addition and _?_ are inverse operations. Multiplication and _?_ are inverse operations.

Evaluate the expression when $a = -6$, $b = 0.75$, and $c = 2$.

3. $a^2 + 3c$

4. $\frac{8 - 3c}{b}$

5. $cb - 3a$

6. $(4b)^3 + ac$

Write the verbal phrase or sentence as an algebraic expression or equation. Let x represent the number.

7. 5 more than twice a number

8. 12 less than a number is -19.

9. 18 more than a number is 2.

10. 7 less than triple a number

Simplify the expression.

11. $3b - 2 + 4b$

12. $10(h - 1) + h + 9$

Find the perimeter and area of the rectangle with the given dimensions.

13. $l = 7$ in., $w = 5$ in.

14. $l = 6$ m, $w = 14$ m

15. $l = 5x$ cm, $w = 7$ cm

16. $l = 8$ ft, $w = (x - 4)$ ft

Find the distance for the given rate and time.

17. $r = 44$ mi/h, $t = 0.75$ hour

18. $r = 38$ ft/sec, $t = 15$ seconds

19. $r = 7.5$ cm/min, $t = 8$ minutes

20. $r = 8$ km/h, $t = 3$ hours

Convert the temperature to degrees Celsius or to degrees Fahrenheit.

21. 77°F

22. 18°C

23. 41°F

24. 24°C

Solve the equation. Graph and check your solution.

25. $-3 = x + 4$

26. $12 = n + 7$

27. $c - 10.7 = 14.3$

28. $20k = -320$

29. $\frac{m}{6} = -13$

30. $\frac{2}{7}y = 10$

31. $8 = 5r$

32. $s - 4 = -6$

33. **GEOMETRY** Write and simplify an expression for the perimeter of the rectangle shown.

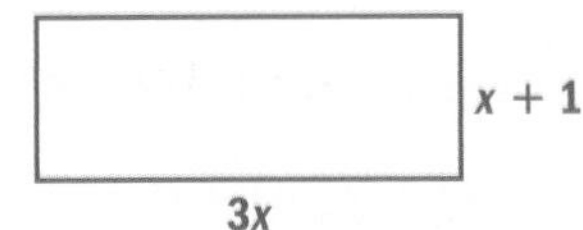

34. **BASKETBALL** In 1993, Bobby Hurley broke the NCAA all-time assist record for Division I men's basketball. Hurley had 1076 assists, which was 38 more than the previous record. Write and solve an equation to find the previous assist record.

4 ◆ MULTIPLE CHOICE STRATEGIES

STRATEGIES YOU'LL USE:
- **SOLVE DIRECTLY**
- **ELIMINATE CHOICES**

Standards
AF 1.1, AF 1.2, AF 1.3

If you have difficulty solving a multiple choice problem directly, you may be able to use another approach to eliminate incorrect answer choices and obtain the correct answer.

PROBLEM 1

You are recording a talent show for a friend. The tape can hold 2 hours of recordings, and each skit lasts 3.5 minutes. Which expression represents the amount of time (in minutes) left on the tape after recording s skits?

Ⓐ $120 - s$ Ⓑ $120 + s$ Ⓒ $120 - 3.5s$ Ⓓ $120 + 3.5s$

Strategy 1 SOLVE DIRECTLY

First, convert all times to minutes. Then find the amount of time needed for s skits and use this information to write an expression.

STEP 1 **Convert** 2 hours to minutes to find the length of the tape in minutes.

$$2 \text{ hours} \cdot \frac{60 \text{ minutes}}{1 \text{ hour}} = 120 \text{ minutes}$$

STEP 2 **Find** the amount of time for s skits.

Each skit lasts 3.5 minutes. So, the total time for s skits is $3.5s$ minutes.

STEP 3 **Write** an expression using a verbal model.

Total time of tape	−	Time for s skits

$$120 - 3.5s$$

The correct answer is C. Ⓐ Ⓑ Ⓒ Ⓓ

Strategy 2 ELIMINATE CHOICES

Evaluate the reasonableness of the solution in the context of the original situation.

First, find the length (in minutes) of the tape.

$$2 \text{ hours} \cdot \frac{60 \text{ minutes}}{1 \text{ hour}} = 120 \text{ minutes}$$

Choice A: $120 - s$
This choice does not account for each skit being 3.5 minutes long. So, you can eliminate choice A.

Choices B and D: $120 + s$ and $120 + 3.5s$
The values of the expressions will always be greater than 120 for any positive value of s. So, you can eliminate choices B and D.

The correct answer is C. Ⓐ Ⓑ Ⓒ Ⓓ

PROBLEM 2

The steps Mary took to evaluate the expression $4r + 12 \div 4$ when $r = 5$ are shown at the right. What should Mary have done differently in order to evaluate the expression?

Ⓐ Divided (20 + 4) by (12 + 4) Ⓑ Added (12 ÷ 4) to 20

Ⓒ Divided (20 + 4) by (20 ÷ 4) Ⓓ Added 12 to (20 ÷ 4)

$4r + 12 \div 4$ when $r = 5$
$4 \times 5 = 20$
$20 + 12 = 32$
$32 \div 4 = 8$

Strategy 1 SOLVE DIRECTLY

Identify each step you would use in the order of operations to evaluate the expression.

STEP 1 **Substitute** 5 for r in the expression.

$4r + 12 \div 4 = 4(5) + 12 \div 4$

STEP 2 **Choose** the first step in evaluating the expression. Multiply and divide from left to right. The first step is 4(5).

STEP 3 **Choose** the next step. Divide before you add. The next step is (12 ÷ 4).

STEP 4 **Choose** the next step. Add (12 ÷ 4) to 4(5), or 20.

The correct answer is B. Ⓐ Ⓑ Ⓒ Ⓓ

Strategy 2 ELIMINATE CHOICES

Compare the value of each answer choice to the value of the expression.

First, evaluate the expression when $r = 5$.

$$4r + 12 \div 4 = 4(5) + 12 \div 4$$
$$= 20 + 3$$
$$= 23$$

Choice A: (20 + 4) ÷ (12 + 4) = 1.5 ✗

Choice B: 20 + (12 ÷ 4) = 23 ✓

Choice C: (20 + 4) ÷ (20 ÷ 4) = 4.8 ✗

Choice D: (20 ÷ 4) + 12 = 17 ✗

The correct answer is B. Ⓐ Ⓑ Ⓒ Ⓓ

STRATEGY PRACTICE

Explain why you can eliminate the highlighted answer choice.

1. You scored 8 fewer goals than your friend this past soccer season. You scored 16 goals. How many goals did your friend score?

   Ⓐ 2 Ⓑ ✗ **8** Ⓒ 24 Ⓓ 138

2. You walk 4 miles per hour. How long do you take to walk 3 miles?

   Ⓐ $\frac{1}{2}$ h Ⓑ $\frac{3}{4}$ h Ⓒ ✗ **1 h** Ⓓ 12 h

3. What is the area of a rectangle with length 6 and width $(x - 7)$?

   Ⓐ $6x - 7$ Ⓑ $x - 1$ Ⓒ $6x - 42$ Ⓓ ✗ $\mathbf{2x - 2}$

4 ◆ MULTIPLE CHOICE PRACTICE

1. Jaime is 61.5 inches tall. Jaime is 3 inches taller than Kyle. Which equation can be used to find Kyle's height k (in inches)? **AF 1.1**

   Ⓐ $61.5 = k + 3$

   Ⓑ $61.5 = k - 3$

   Ⓒ $61.5 = 3k$

   Ⓓ $61.5 = 3 - k$

2. The rectangle shown has a perimeter of 450 feet. Which equation can be used to find the width p? **AF 3.2**

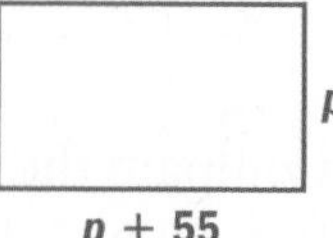

   Ⓐ $2p + 55 = 450$

   Ⓑ $4p + 110 = 450$

   Ⓒ $112p = 450$

   Ⓓ $p(p + 55) = 450$

3. What is the solution of $5 = \frac{4}{5}x$? **AF 1.1**

   Ⓐ $\frac{4}{25}$

   Ⓑ 4

   Ⓒ $6\frac{1}{4}$

   Ⓓ $6\frac{1}{2}$

4. What is the solution of $-5c = -125$? **AF 1.1**

   Ⓐ -120

   Ⓑ -25

   Ⓒ 25

   Ⓓ 625

5. Which equation has a solution of -20? **AF 1.1**

   Ⓐ $5w = 100$

   Ⓑ $\frac{w}{-5} = -4$

   Ⓒ $\frac{w}{10} = -2$

   Ⓓ $w - 70 = 50$

6. What is the area of a rectangle with length 7 and width $(h + 8)$? **AF 3.1**

   Ⓐ $7h + 8$

   Ⓑ $7h + 56$

   Ⓒ $h + 15$

   Ⓓ $2h + 30$

7. The equation $x + 4 = 6$ is modeled below. What is the value of x? **AF 1.1, MR 2.4**

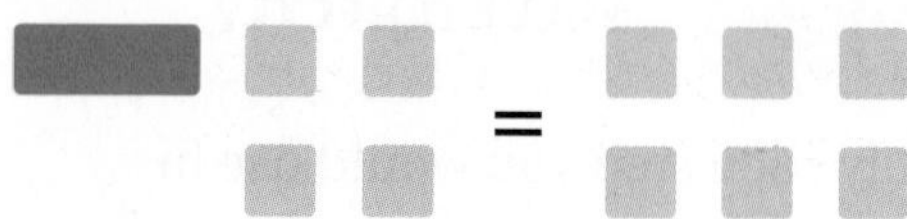

   Ⓐ -10

   Ⓑ -2

   Ⓒ 2

   Ⓓ 10

8. A beach volleyball court has a perimeter of 48 meters. The width is 8 meters. Which equation can be used to find the value of r? **AF 3.2, MR 3.2**

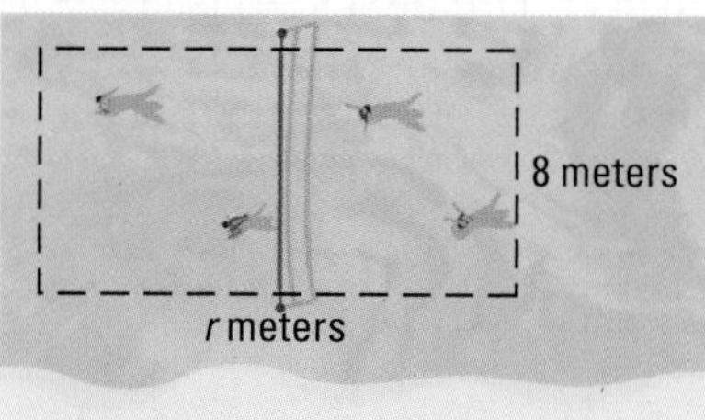

   Ⓐ $48 = r + 8$

   Ⓑ $48 = 2r + 8$

   Ⓒ $48 = 2r + 16$

   Ⓓ $48 = 2r - 16$

9. Which algebraic equation best describes the total cost C (in dollars) of j juice cans that cost \$1.39 each? **AF 1.2**

   Ⓐ $C = j + 1.39$

   Ⓑ $C = 1.39j$

   Ⓒ $C = j - 1.39$

   Ⓓ $C = 1.39 - j$

10. A school club rents a bus for \$200 for a field trip to a museum. A museum ticket costs \$4.50 per person. Which expression represents the total cost of the trip for n people? **AF 1.2**

Ⓐ $200 \div (4.5n)$

Ⓑ $200(4.5n)$

Ⓒ $200 - 4.5n$

Ⓓ $200 + 4.5n$

11. Water boils at 100°C. What is this temperature in degrees Fahrenheit? **AF 2.1**

Ⓐ 87.6°F

Ⓑ 148°F

Ⓒ 212°F

Ⓓ 237.6°F

12. You buy p pairs of shorts, s shirts, and b bottles of water for the prices shown below. Your friend buys $2p$ pairs of shorts. Which expression represents the total cost of you and your friend's purchases? **AF 1.2, MR 2.2**

Item	Price
pair of shorts	\$12
shirt	\$6
bottle of water	\$1

Ⓐ $12p + 6s + b$

Ⓑ $14p + 6s + b$

Ⓒ $19(3p + s + b)$

Ⓓ $36p + 6s + b$

13. Which expression gives the total value (in dollars) of n nickels, d dimes, and q quarters? **AF 1.2**

Ⓐ $n + d + q$

Ⓑ $0.4(n + d + q)$

Ⓒ $0.05n + 0.1d + 0.25q$

Ⓓ $5n + 10d + 25q$

14. How long will a car take to travel 25 miles at the speed limit shown below? **AF 1.1**

Ⓐ 0.5 h

Ⓑ 2 h

Ⓒ 50 h

Ⓓ 75 h

15. What is the perimeter of a rectangle with length $7x$ and width x? **AF 3.1**

Ⓐ $7x^2$

Ⓑ $6x$

Ⓒ $8x$

Ⓓ $16x$

16. The steps Jason took to evaluate the expression are shown below. What should Jason have done differently in order to evaluate the expression? **AF 1.3**

$5r - 5 \div 5$ when $r = 2$
$5 \times 2 = 10$
$10 - 5 = 5$
$5 \div 5 = 1$

Ⓐ Subtracted $(5 \div 5)$ from 10

Ⓑ Subtracted 5 from $(10 \div 5)$

Ⓒ Divided $(10 - 5)$ by (10×5)

Ⓓ Divided $(10 - 5)$ by $(10 - 5)$

17. If n is a multiple of 3, which of the following statements is true about the sum $(n - 1) + (n + 1)$? **AF 1.3, MR 1.2**

Ⓐ The sum is 0.

Ⓑ The sum is odd.

Ⓒ The sum is a prime number.

Ⓓ The sum is a multiple of 6.

5 Ratios and Proportions

Before

In previous chapters, you learned the following skills, which you'll use in Chapter 5:

- Writing fractions in simplest form
- Writing fractions as decimals to compare numbers
- Solving multiplication and division equations

Now

In Chapter 5 you'll study these ***Big Ideas:***

1. Interpreting and using ratios
2. Solving rate problems
3. Using proportions to solve problems

Why?

So you can solve real-world problems about . . .

- Batting averages, p. 259
- Hovercraft speeds, p. 263
- Nutrition, p. 269
- Sports, p. 279
- Sculpture, p. 284
- Art, p. 285

at classzone.com

Get-Ready Games

Fraction Action

California Standards

Review comparing fractions. ***Gr. 6 NS 1.1***

Prepare for understanding rates. ***Gr. 6 AF 2.2***

Materials

- One *Fraction Action* game board

- Two number cubes

- Markers of two colors

How to Play Play in pairs. Players should take turns following the steps on the next page.

CALIFORNIA STANDARDS

- **Gr. 6 NS 1.3 Use proportions to solve problems (e.g., determine the value of N if $\frac{4}{7} = \frac{N}{21}$,** find the length of a side of a polygon similar to a known polygon). **Use cross-multiplication as a method for solving such problems, understanding it as the multiplication of both sides of an equation by a multiplicative inverse.** ***(Lessons 5.3, 5.4, 5.5)***
- **Gr. 6 AF 2.2 Demonstrate an understanding that *rate* is a measure of one quantity per unit value of another quantity.** ***(Lessons 5.2, 5.4)***

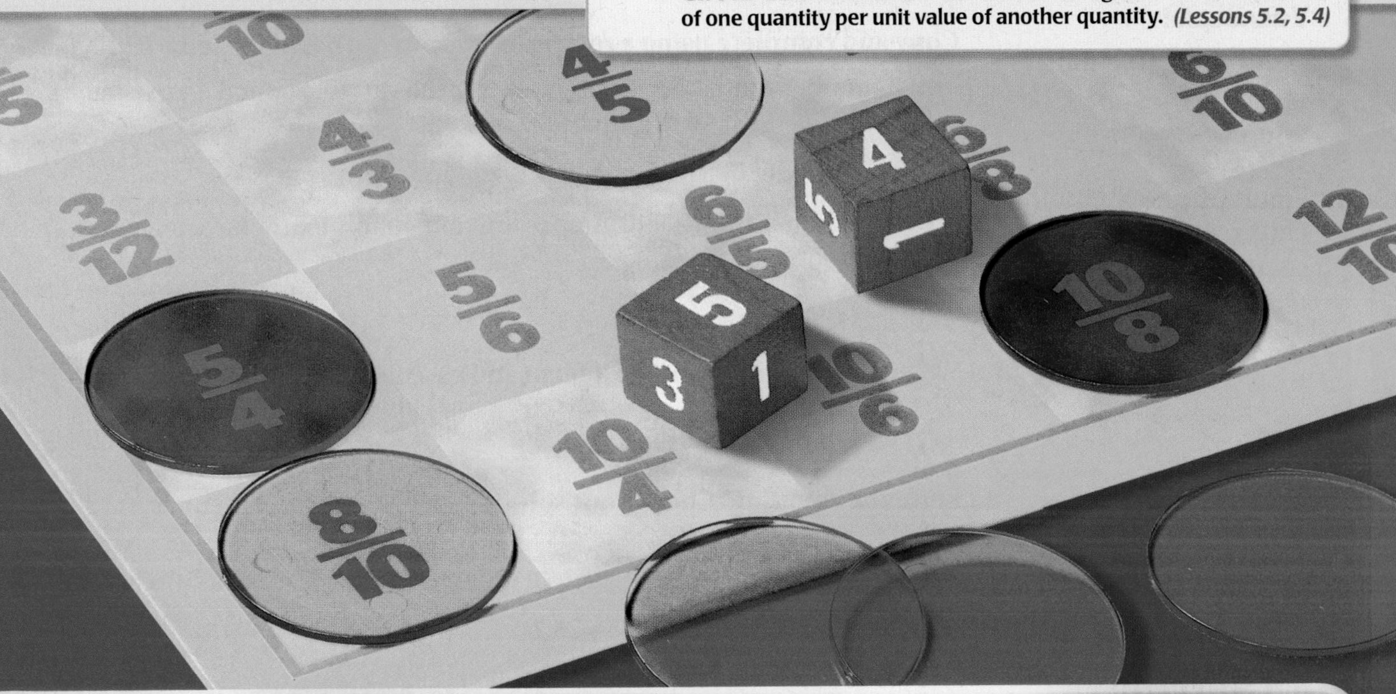

1 Roll both number cubes.

2 Form a fraction using the numbers rolled. One number is the numerator and the other number is the denominator.

3 Cover the fractions on the board that are equivalent to the fraction formed, using markers of your color. A fraction should not be covered more than once.

How To Win Be the first player to cover three spaces in a row (either horizontally, vertically, or diagonally). Or be the first player to use all of your markers.

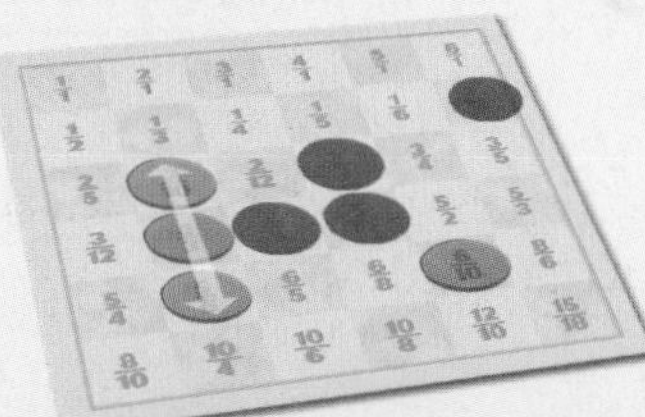

Games Wrap-Up

Draw Conclusions

Complete these exercises after playing the game.

1. **WRITING** After rolling the number cubes, how did you decide which of the numbers to use as the numerator and which to use as the denominator? *Explain.*
2. **REASONING** How many spaces can you cover on the game board if you roll the same number on both cubes? *Explain* your reasoning.

5 Getting Ready

Prerequisite Skills

California @HomeTutor
Prerequisite skills practice at classzone.com

REVIEW VOCABULARY

- **equivalent fractions,** *p. 16*
- **simplest form,** *p. 17*
- **multiplicative inverse,** *p. 168*
- **equation,** *p. 212*
- **solution,** *p. 219*

VOCABULARY CHECK

Copy and complete using a review term from the list at the left.

1. A number that you can substitute for the variable to make an equation true is a(n) _?_ of the equation.
2. The product of a number and its _?_, or reciprocal, is 1.
3. A fraction is in _?_ if its numerator and denominator have a greatest common factor of 1.

SKILL CHECK

Write the fraction in simplest form and as a decimal. ***(pp. 16, 40)***

4. $\frac{38}{40}$
5. $\frac{15}{48}$
6. $\frac{12}{96}$
7. $\frac{9}{54}$

Solve the equation. Check your solution. ***(p. 234)***

8. $12p = 72$
9. $\frac{w}{4} = 5$
10. $\frac{2}{5}t = 14$
11. $\frac{x}{3} = 10$
12. $\frac{3}{2}k = 6$
13. $6.3y = 25.2$
14. $\frac{z}{8} = 36$
15. $\frac{m}{9.9} = 2$

Notetaking Skills

NOW YOU TRY
Make a *word magnet* for *equation.*

Focus on Graphic Organizers

Use a *word magnet* to organize words and ideas that are related to a new vocabulary word, such as *expression.*

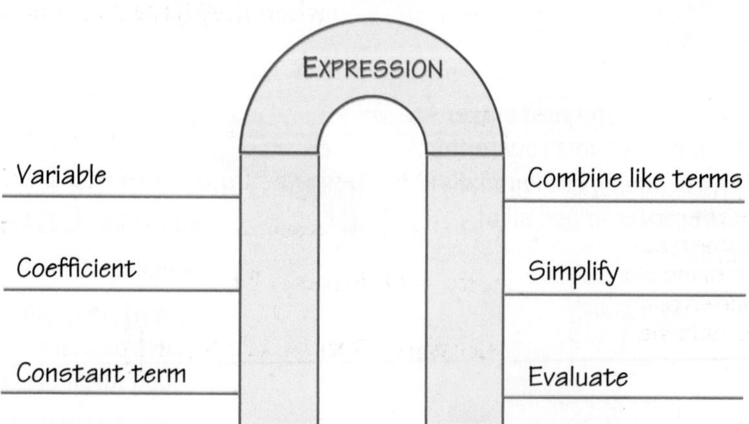

5.1 Ratios

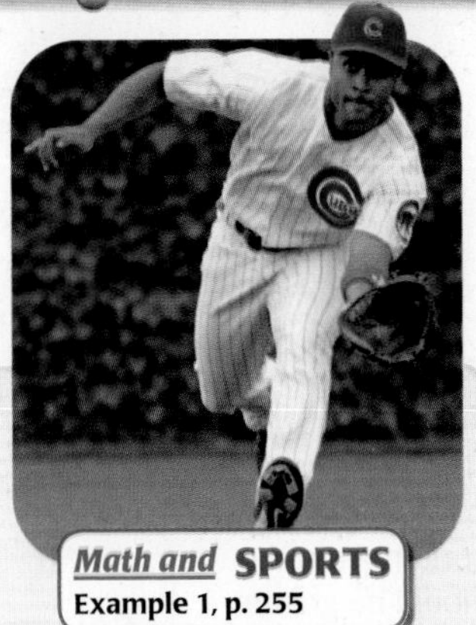

Math and SPORTS
Example 1, p. 255

Standards NS 1.2 **Interpret and use ratios in different contexts (e.g., batting averages,** miles per hour) **to show the relative sizes of two quantities, using appropriate notations (*a*/*b*, *a* to *b*, *a* : *b*).**

Connect ***Before*** you wrote and compared fractions. ***Now*** you will write and compare ratios.

KEY VOCABULARY
- **ratio**
- **equivalent ratios**

BASEBALL How can you compare a baseball team's wins to its losses during spring training?

A **ratio** uses division to compare two numbers. There are three ways to write a ratio of two numbers.

Spring Training

Team	Wins	Losses
San Diego Padres	16	11
L.A. Dodgers	18	13
Chicago Cubs	17	14

KEY CONCEPT *For Your Notebook*

Writing a Ratio

Words	Numbers	Algebra
wins to losses	18 to 13	a to b, where b is nonzero
$\frac{\text{wins}}{\text{losses}}$	$\frac{18}{13}$	$\frac{a}{b}$, where b is nonzero
wins : losses	18 : 13	$a : b$, where b is nonzero

All three ways of writing the ratio of two numbers are read "the ratio of a to b," so 18 : 13 is read "the ratio of eighteen to thirteen." Two ratios are **equivalent ratios** when they have the same value.

EXAMPLE 1 Writing a Ratio

AVOID ERRORS
Be sure that the first quantity in the ratio goes in the numerator and that the second quantity goes in the denominator.

Use the table above to make comparisons about games played.

a. Cubs' wins to losses

wins = 17; losses = 14

▶ **Answer** 17 to 14, 17 : 14, or $\frac{17}{14}$

b. Cubs' wins to games played

wins = 17; games = 17 + 14 = 31

▶ **Answer** 17 to 31, 17 : 31, or $\frac{17}{31}$

GUIDED PRACTICE for Example 1

1. Write the ratio of wins to games played for the Padres.

EXAMPLE 2 ◆ Multiple Choice Practice

Wait time is 90 minutes.

You wait in line for 90 minutes to ride a roller coaster. The ride lasts 2 minutes. What is the ratio of time spent in line to time spent on the ride?

Ⓐ 1 : 88 Ⓑ 1 : 45

Ⓒ 45 : 1 Ⓓ 88 : 1

ELIMINATE CHOICES

Because the time spent in line is greater than the time spent on the ride, the first number in the ratio should be greater than the second. You can eliminate choices A and B.

SOLUTION

Write the ratio, with time spent in line in the numerator.

$$\frac{\text{Time in line}}{\text{Time on ride}} = \frac{90}{2}$$ **Write ratio.**

$$= \frac{45}{1}$$ **Simplify ratio.**

▶ **Answer** The ratio of time spent in line to time spent on the ride is 45 : 1. The correct answer is C. Ⓐ Ⓑ Ⓒ Ⓓ

COMPARING RATIOS To compare ratios, you can write them in fraction form and compare the fractions. You can also compare ratios in decimal form.

EXAMPLE 3 Comparing Ratios

MUSIC According to the table, who has the greater ratio of rock CDs to pop CDs, Luis or Ana?

	Rock	*Pop*	*Hip-hop*
Luis	9	24	16
Ana	28	70	40

SOLUTION

REWRITE FRACTIONS

For help with writing fractions as decimals, see p. 40.

	Luis	Ana
STEP 1 **Write** the ratios in fraction form.	$\frac{\text{Rock}}{\text{Pop}} = \frac{9}{24}$	$\frac{\text{Rock}}{\text{Pop}} = \frac{28}{70}$
STEP 2 **Write** the ratios as decimals.	$= 0.375$	$= 0.4$

▶ **Answer** Because 0.4 > 0.375, Ana has a greater ratio of rock to pop CDs.

✓ GUIDED PRACTICE for Examples 2 and 3

2. **WHAT IF?** In Example 2, suppose you wait in line for 80 minutes. What is the ratio of time spent in line to time spent on the ride?

3. **WHAT IF?** In Example 3, who has a greater ratio of pop CDs to hip-hop CDs?

4. **WHAT IF?** In Example 3, who has a greater ratio of hip-hop CDs to rock CDs?

5.1 EXERCISES

HOMEWORK KEY
◆ = **MULTIPLE CHOICE PRACTICE** Exs. 30, 37, 45, 58–60
○ = **HINTS AND HOMEWORK HELP** for Exs. 13, 25, 45 at classzone.com

SKILLS • PROBLEM SOLVING • REASONING

1. **VOCABULARY** Copy and complete: If the ratio of dogs to cats is 5 : 2, then for every 5 dogs there are _?_.

2. **WRITING** *Describe* two ways to compare two ratios.

SEE EXAMPLE 1 on p. 255 for Exs. 3–6

WRITING RATIOS Write the ratio of the first number to the second number in three ways.

3. 1, 7
4. 1, 1
5. 3, 10
6. 15, 2

SEE EXAMPLE 2 on p. 256 for Exs. 7–23

SIMPLIFYING RATIOS Write the ratio as a fraction in simplest form.

7. $\frac{7}{14}$
8. $\frac{12}{15}$
9. 8 : 14
10. 9 : 30
11. 9 to 5
12. 20 to 35
13. 32 : 48
14. 30 : 75
15. 10 to 64
16. 65 to 130
17. $\frac{54}{72}$
18. $\frac{6}{33}$
19. $\frac{26}{91}$
20. $\frac{18}{63}$
21. 12 to 35
22. 56 to 119

Animated Math at classzone.com

23. **ERROR ANALYSIS** *Describe* and correct the error made in writing the ratio of 16 to 18.

$$\times \quad \frac{16}{18+16} = \frac{16}{34} = \frac{8}{17}$$

SEE EXAMPLE 3 on p. 256 for Exs. 24–30

COMPARING RATIOS Copy and complete the statement using <, >, or =.

24. 9 : 15 _?_ 8 : 20
25. 18 : 12 _?_ 54 : 36
26. 72 : 96 _?_ 56 : 80
27. 10 : 12 _?_ 48 : 72
28. 81 : 63 _?_ 60 : 35
29. 12 : 51 _?_ 20 : 85

30. ◆ **MULTIPLE CHOICE** Which ratio is *not* equivalent to 6 to 10?

Ⓐ 6 : 10 Ⓑ 3 : 5 Ⓒ $\frac{18}{30}$ Ⓓ $\frac{5}{3}$

ORDERING RATIOS Write the ratios in order from least to greatest.

31. 5 : 8, 3 : 6, 15 : 5
32. 4 : 3, 6 : 5, 11 : 9
33. 3 : 8, 1 : 7, 2 : 9
34. 12 : 16, 18 : 28, 12 : 14
35. 18 : 72, 20 : 75, 10 : 36
36. 33 : 24, 51 : 39, 36 : 27

37. ◆ **MULTIPLE CHOICE** Which ratio is greatest?

Ⓐ 24 : 36 Ⓑ 60 : 32 Ⓒ 7 : 12 Ⓓ 43 : 24

38. **ERROR ANALYSIS** Zach wants to find the ratio of his T-shirts to jeans. He has 14 T-shirts and 9 pairs of jeans. *Describe* and correct his error.

$$\times \quad \frac{\text{T-shirts}}{\text{Jeans}} = \frac{9}{14}$$

CONNECT SKILLS TO PROBLEM SOLVING **Exercises 39–42 will help you prepare for problem solving.**

39. Jean has 11 trees in her yard and Anita has 8 trees in her yard. Write the ratio of trees in Jean's yard to trees in Anita's yard.

40. In a survey of 100 dentists, 61 of the dentists prefer toothpaste A to toothpaste B. Write the ratio of the number of dentists who prefer toothpaste A to the number of dentists surveyed.

41. The total cost of an appetizer and a main course is $18. The cost of the appetizer is $5. Write the ratio of the cost of the appetizer to the total cost.

42. A bag has 20 blue marbles and 7 red marbles. Find the total number of marbles. Then write the ratio of red marbles to total marbles.

SEE EXAMPLES 1 AND 2 on pp. 255–256 for Exs. 43–49

43. SCIENCE A chameleon is a kind of lizard. There are about 3000 known kinds of lizards and 2900 known kinds of snakes. Write the ratio of known kinds of lizards to known kinds of snakes.

California @HomeTutor for problem solving help at classzone.com

Jackson's chameleon, from Madagascar, is one of 3000 known kinds of lizards.

44. TIME RATIOS You spend a total of $1\frac{3}{4}$ hours at a restaurant. You spend 20 minutes eating. What is the ratio of your time spent at the restaurant to your time spent eating?

California @HomeTutor for problem solving help at classzone.com

45. ◆ **MULTIPLE CHOICE** You used 12 feet of fleece to make a blanket and 2 feet of fleece to make a vest. What is the ratio of fleece for the blanket to fleece for the vest?

Ⓐ $\frac{1}{10}$ Ⓑ $\frac{1}{6}$ Ⓒ $\frac{6}{1}$ Ⓓ $\frac{10}{1}$

46. AWARDS Count the number of ribbons and the number of trophies. Write the ratio of ribbons to trophies.

STUDENT RATIOS **The table shows the numbers of boys and girls in the 7th and 8th grades at a school. Use the table to write the specified ratio.**

47. 8th grade girls to 8th grade boys

48. 7th grade girls to all 7th graders

49. 8th grade boys to all 8th graders

	Boys	*Girls*
7th	48	42
8th	36	44

50. WRITING For a fundraiser, the ratio of raffle tickets you sold to raffle tickets your friend sold was 11 to 5. Does this mean that you sold 11 raffle tickets and your friend sold 5 raffle tickets? *Explain.*

SEE EXAMPLE 3 on p. 256 for Ex. 51

51. SHORT RESPONSE In a basketball game, Albert made 11 out of 15 free throws and Jake made 10 out of 13 free throws. Who had the greater ratio of free throws made to free throws attempted? *Explain* your reasoning.

SEE EXAMPLES 2 AND 3 on p. 256 for Ex. 52

52. **BATTING AVERAGES** The table shows the number of hits and the number of at bats for three players on a baseball team.

Player	Hits	At bats
Chris	74	250
Jason	57	200
Sean	48	160

a. Write the ratio of the number of hits to the number of at bats for each player.

b. A batting average is found by writing the ratio from part (a) as a decimal rounded to the nearest thousandth. Find each player's batting average.

c. *Compare* the batting averages. Who has the highest average?

53. **OPEN-ENDED** Eve has 10 CDs in her collection and Mieko has 16 CDs. Eve adds x CDs to her collection and Mieko adds y CDs. Find two possible values for x and y so that the ratio of Eve's CDs to Mieko's CDs remains the same. *Explain* how you found your answer.

54. **CHECKING REASONABLENESS** Use the diagram to write the ratio of the distance the person ran to the distance the dog ran. Write your answer as a decimal rounded to the nearest hundredth. *Describe* how the diagram can help you check that your answer is reasonable.

55. **REASONING** One square has side length s and another square has side length $2s$. What is the ratio of the area of the larger square to the area of the smaller square? *Justify* your reasoning.

56. **CHALLENGE** The ratio of a to b is 3 to 8, and the ratio of b to c is 4 to 5. What is the ratio of a to the sum of a, b, and c?

57. **CHALLENGE** A fruit basket contains apples, oranges, and pears. The apples weigh twice as much as the oranges and three times as much as the pears. What is the ratio of the weight of the apples to the total weight of the fruit in the basket?

◆ CALIFORNIA STANDARDS SPIRAL REVIEW

AF 1.1 58. What is the value of a in the equation $-12a = 72$? ***(p. 234)***

Ⓐ -864 Ⓑ -6 Ⓒ 6 Ⓓ 864

AF 1.1 59. Which equation has a solution of -2? ***(p. 226)***

Ⓐ $y - 2 = 4$ Ⓑ $y - 4 = -6$ Ⓒ $y + 4 = -2$ Ⓓ $y + 2 = 4$

NS 2.3 60. The temperature drops 2°F every hour. What is the change in temperature after 4 hours? ***(p. 148)***

Ⓐ -8°F Ⓑ -6°F Ⓒ 6°F Ⓓ 8°F

5.2 Rates

Math and SPACE
Ex. 45, p. 264

Standards

AF 2.2 Demonstrate an understanding that *rate* is a measure of one quantity per unit value of another quantity.

AF 2.3 Solve problems involving rates, average speed, distance, and time.

NS 1.2 Interpret and use ratios in different contexts (e.g., batting averages, **miles per hour**) to show the relative sizes of two quantities, using appropriate notations (*a*/*b*, *a* to *b*, *a* : *b*).

Connect

Before you used ratios to compare two quantities. ***Now*** you will use rates to compare two quantities with different units.

KEY VOCABULARY

- **rate**
- **unit rate**

ACTIVITY

You can rewrite ratios to compare two rates.

STEP 1 **Count** the number of times your heart beats in 10 seconds. Use a watch or clock. Record the ratio in fraction form.

STEP 2 **Ask** your partner to count his or her pulse for 15 seconds. Record the ratio in fraction form.

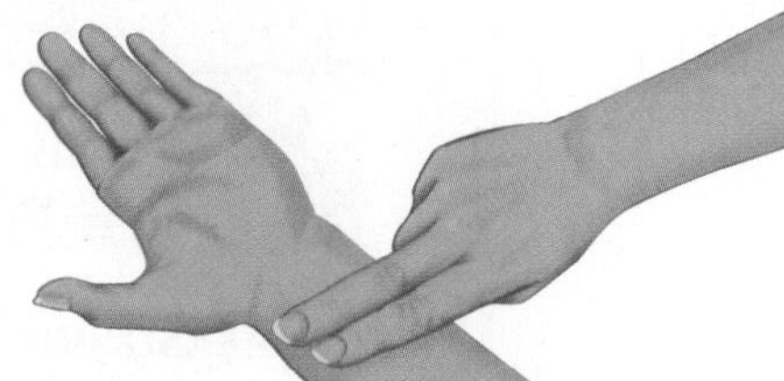

STEP 3 **Decide** whose pulse is faster. Explain how you decided.

READING

The fraction bar, the slash, and the word "per" mean "for every."

A **rate** is a ratio of two quantities measured in different units. A **unit rate** has a denominator of 1 unit. The three unit rates below are equivalent.

$$\frac{15 \text{ mi}}{1 \text{ h}} \qquad 15 \text{ mi/h} \qquad 15 \text{ miles per hour}$$

EXAMPLE 1 Finding a Unit Rate

KUDZU During peak growing season, the kudzu vine can grow 6 inches in 12 hours. What is the peak growth rate of kudzu in inches per hour?

Animated Math

For an interactive example on finding unit rates go to **classzone.com.**

SOLUTION

First, write a rate comparing the inches grown to the hours it took to grow. Then rewrite the rate so that the denominator is 1.

$\frac{6 \text{ in.}}{12 \text{ h}} = \frac{6 \text{ in.} \div 12}{12 \text{ h} \div 12}$ **Divide numerator and denominator by 12.**

$= \frac{0.5 \text{ in.}}{1 \text{ h}}$ **Simplify.**

▶ **Answer** The peak growth rate of kudzu is about 0.5 inch per hour.

AVERAGE SPEED If you know the distance traveled and the travel time for a moving object, you can find the average rate, or average speed, by dividing the distance by the time.

$$\text{Average rate} = \frac{\text{Distance}}{\text{Time}}$$

Average rate is usually written as a unit rate.

EXAMPLE 2 Finding Average Speed

Race time: 2 min 30 sec

SPEED SKATING A skater took 2 minutes 30 seconds to complete a 1500 meter race. What was the skater's average speed?

SOLUTION

STEP 1 **Rewrite** the time so that the units are the same.

$2 \text{ min} + 30 \text{ sec} = 120 \text{ sec} + 30 \text{ sec} = 150 \text{ sec}$

STEP 2 **Find** the average speed by dividing the distance by the time.

$$\frac{1500 \text{ m}}{150 \text{ sec}} = \frac{1500 \text{ m} \div 150}{150 \text{ sec} \div 150}$$ Divide numerator and denominator by 150.

$$= \frac{10 \text{ m}}{1 \text{ sec}}$$ Simplify.

▶ **Answer** The skater's average speed was 10 meters per second.

About the Standards

Grade 6 Standard AF 2.1 asks you to convert one unit of measurement to another. In Example 2, you convert measures of time. You will do more conversions in Chapter 10.

EXAMPLE 3 Comparing Unit Rates

PASTA PRICES A store sells the same pasta in two ways: 10 pounds of bulk pasta for $15.00 or 2 pounds of packaged pasta for $3.98. Which is the better buy?

SOLUTION

To find the better buy, compare the unit prices.

Bulk pasta: $\frac{\$15.00}{10 \text{ lb}} = \frac{\$1.50}{1 \text{ lb}}$ Write as a unit rate.

Packaged pasta: $\frac{\$3.98}{2 \text{ lb}} = \frac{\$1.99}{1 \text{ lb}}$ Write as a unit rate.

▶ **Answer** The bulk pasta is the better buy because it costs less per pound.

FIND UNIT PRICE

A unit price is a type of unit rate.

✓ GUIDED PRACTICE for Examples 1, 2, and 3

1. **BIKING** You biked 68 miles in 4 days. Find the unit rate.

2. **AVERAGE SPEED** It takes you 1 minute 40 seconds to walk 550 feet. What is your average speed?

3. **COSTS** Which of the following is the better buy: 2 batteries for $1.50 or 6 batteries for $4.80?

5.2 EXERCISES

HOMEWORK KEY

◆ = **MULTIPLE CHOICE PRACTICE** Exs. 19, 20, 44, 49–51

○ = **HINTS AND HOMEWORK HELP** for Exs. 13, 23, 41 at classzone.com

SKILLS • PROBLEM SOLVING • REASONING

VOCABULARY **Copy and complete.**

1. A ratio of two quantities measured in different units is a(n) _?_.

2. Dollars per pound and miles per hour are real-world examples of _?_.

3. **WRITING** Is every ratio a rate? Is every rate a ratio? *Explain.*

SEE EXAMPLE 1 on p. 260 for Exs. 4–19

FINDING UNIT RATES **Find the unit rate.**

4. $\frac{12\text{ L}}{2\text{ days}}$

5. $\frac{\$56}{8\text{ lb}}$

6. $\frac{\$16}{5\text{ people}}$

7. $\frac{\$21}{6\text{ oz}}$

8. $\frac{153\text{ m}}{5\text{ sec}}$

9. $\frac{48\text{ students}}{3\text{ teachers}}$

10. $\frac{24\text{ servings}}{9\text{ packages}}$

11. $\frac{\$124.50}{6\text{ tickets}}$

12. $\frac{468\text{ visitors}}{4\text{ days}}$

13. $15 for 2 plants

14. 5 pints in 9 salads

15. 14 cups for 8 servings

16. 7 phone calls in 2 hours

17. 12 inches in 4 years

18. 45 e-mails in 5 days

19. ◆ **MULTIPLE CHOICE** You spend $36 for 8 hats. What is the unit rate?

   (A) $\frac{\$.22}{1\text{ hat}}$ (B) $\frac{\$4.50}{1\text{ hat}}$ (C) $\frac{\$9}{1\text{ hat}}$ (D) $\frac{\$36}{1\text{ hat}}$

SEE EXAMPLE 2 on p. 261 for Exs. 20–30

20. ◆ **MULTIPLE CHOICE** Which speed is *not* equivalent to 55 mi/h?

   (A) $\frac{110\text{ mi}}{2\text{ h}}$ (B) $\frac{265\text{ mi}}{6\text{ h}}$ (C) $\frac{385\text{ mi}}{7\text{ h}}$ (D) $\frac{550\text{ mi}}{10\text{ h}}$

FINDING AVERAGE SPEEDS **Find the average speed.**

21. 120 miles in 2 hours

22. 27 meters in 18 seconds

23. 51 meters in 4 minutes 15 seconds

24. 10 kilometers in 40 minutes 5 seconds

25. 160 feet in 5 minutes 20 seconds

26. 700 feet in 1 minute 10 seconds

27. 240 kilometers in 3 hours 20 minutes

28. 90 miles in 2 hours 40 minutes

29. 390 yards in 2 minutes 10 seconds

30. 138 miles in 3 hours 4 minutes

31. **ERROR ANALYSIS** You spend $19.50 for 3 bottles of shampoo. *Describe* and correct the error made in finding the unit rate for a bottle of shampoo.

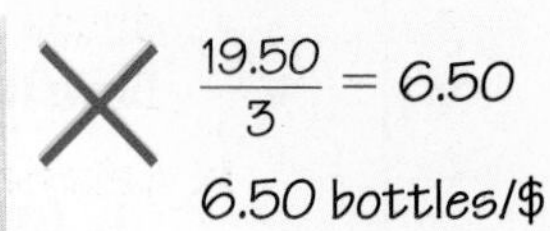

32. **ERROR ANALYSIS** You spend $20 for 2 CDs. *Describe* and correct the error made in finding the unit rate for the CDs.

   ✗ $\frac{2}{20} = \frac{1}{10}$

   1 CD/$10

CONNECT SKILLS TO PROBLEM SOLVING **Exercises 33–37 will help you prepare for problem solving.**

33. You pick 15 tomatoes from your garden in 3 days. Find the average number of tomatoes picked per day.

34. Find the average speed of a butterfly that flies 24 miles in 4 hours.

35. A football team scores 90 points in 4 games. Find the average points per game for the team.

36. You buy 6 note cards for $8.94. Write the unit price.

37. You buy 3 pens for $2.67. Write the unit price.

SEE EXAMPLE 2 on p. 261 for Exs. 38, 42

38. SHORT RESPONSE It takes you 2 hours 30 minutes to travel 155 miles by car. *Explain* how to find the car's average speed in miles per hour.

California @HomeTutor for problem solving help at classzone.com

SEE EXAMPLE 3 on p. 261 for Exs. 39–41

39. MULTI-STEP PROBLEM To be considered a "fast talker," you should be able to clearly speak at least 350 words in 60 seconds. Sean can speak 60 words in 15 seconds.

a. Write the "fast talker" rate as a unit rate.

b. Write Sean's rate of talking as a unit rate.

c. *Compare* the unit rates. Is Sean a "fast talker"?

California @HomeTutor for problem solving help at classzone.com

BETTER BUY **Find the better buy for each pair of foods.**

40.

2 qt
$2.78

1.5 qt
$2.25

41.

17 oz
$3.40

14 oz
$3.08

42. HOVERCRAFT SPEEDS A hovercraft scooter travels 9 miles in 45 minutes. Find its average speed in miles per hour.

43. MULTI-STEP PROBLEM The *density* of a substance is the ratio of its mass to its volume, written as a unit rate.

a. **Calculate** A 500 cubic centimeter sample of sea water has a mass of 514 grams. Find its density.

b. **Calculate** A 300 cubic centimeter sample of an iceberg has a mass of 267 grams. Find its density.

c. **Compare** Which is denser, sea water or an iceberg? *Explain* why your answer is reasonable.

Only about 10% of an iceberg is visible above the water line.

44. ◆ **MULTIPLE CHOICE** There are 275 students going on a field trip. The school wants a student-teacher ratio less than or equal to 15 students to 1 teacher. What is the least number of teachers needed?

Ⓐ 16 Ⓑ 17 Ⓒ 18 Ⓓ 19

45. **MULTI-STEP PROBLEM** The diagram below shows the longest distance a NASA Mars rover can travel in the given amount of time.

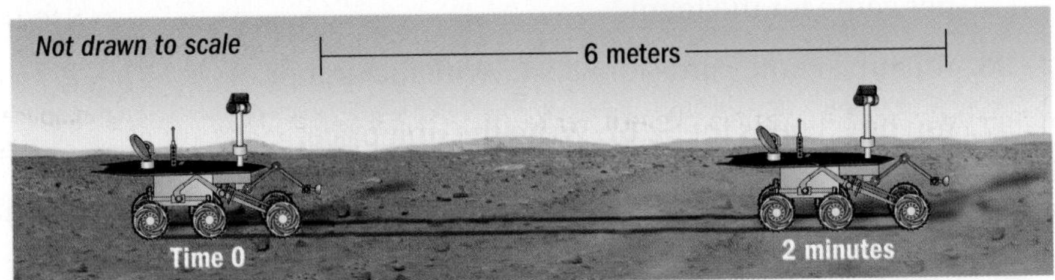

a. **Write a Ratio** Write the greatest speed of a rover as a unit rate in meters per minute.

b. **Make a Table** Make a table that shows the number of meters a rover can move at its greatest speed in 5, 6, and 7 minutes.

c. **xy Write an Equation** Write an equation relating the number of meters d a rover can move at its greatest speed in t minutes.

46. **RECIPES** A recipe for rice pudding uses $\frac{1}{2}$ cup of rice and serves 6 people. Write the cups of rice per person as a unit rate. How many cups of rice do you need to serve 75 people?

47. **CHALLENGE** Ron runs 96 miles in 30 days, Sarah runs 25 miles in 7 days, and Cho runs 46 miles in two weeks. On average, who runs the farthest per day? *Explain* how you found your answer.

48. **CHALLENGE** You run the first 2 miles of a 5 mile race at a rate of 300 yards per minute. Then you run the last 3 miles at a rate of 220 yards per minute. Is your average rate for the race 260 yards per minute? *Explain* your reasoning. (1760 yards = 1 mile)

◆ CALIFORNIA STANDARDS SPIRAL REVIEW

NS 2.1 49. What is the value of $12\frac{5}{8} - 3\frac{7}{12}$? *(p. 81)*

Ⓐ $8\frac{23}{24}$ Ⓑ $9\frac{1}{24}$ Ⓒ $9\frac{1}{12}$ Ⓓ $16\frac{5}{24}$

AF 3.1 50. A rectangle is 28 inches long and w inches wide. Which expression represents the area of the rectangle in square inches? *(p. 212)*

Ⓐ $28 + w$ Ⓑ $\frac{28}{w}$ Ⓒ $56 + 2w$ Ⓓ $28w$

NS 1.2 51. A basketball team scored 80 points in one game. Emma scored 25 of those points. What is the ratio of Emma's points to the team's points? *(p. 255)*

Ⓐ $\frac{5}{21}$ Ⓑ $\frac{5}{16}$ Ⓒ $\frac{16}{5}$ Ⓓ $\frac{21}{5}$

Standards

NS 1.3 Use proportions to solve problems (e.g., determine the value of *N* if $\frac{4}{7} = \frac{N}{21}$, find the length of a side of a polygon similar to a known polygon). Use cross-multiplication as a method for solving such problems, understanding it as the multiplication of both sides of an equation by a multiplicative inverse.

5.3 Modeling Proportions

MATERIALS • chips of two colors (or pennies and dimes)

QUESTION How can you model and solve a proportion?

An equation stating that two ratios are equivalent, such as $\frac{2}{4} = \frac{1}{2}$, is called a *proportion*. You can use a chip model to solve a proportion with a variable.

EXPLORE Use a chip model to find the unknown value in the proportion $\frac{2}{3} = \frac{n}{6}$.

STEP 1 **Model** the proportion using red and yellow chips.

The ratio tells you to use 2 red chips for every 3 yellow chips.

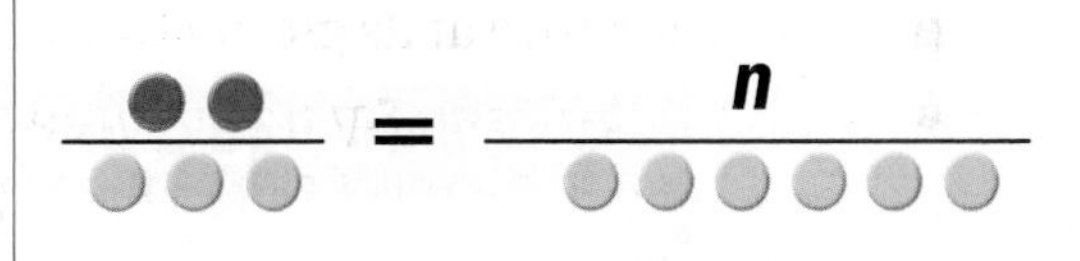

STEP 2 **Notice** that the first ratio has a denominator of 3. Separate the 6 yellow chips in the second ratio into groups of 3.

STEP 3 **Place** 2 red chips in the numerator of the second ratio for every 3 yellow chips in the denominator. Four red chips are placed, so $n = 4$.

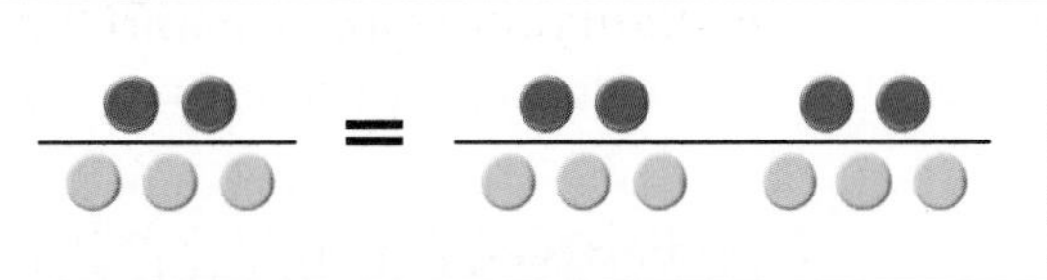

DRAW CONCLUSIONS Use your observations to complete these exercises.

Use a chip model to find the unknown value. Animated Math at classzone.com

1. $\frac{1}{3} = \frac{x}{15}$ 2. $\frac{n}{6} = \frac{5}{2}$ 3. $\frac{z}{8} = \frac{3}{2}$ 4. $\frac{3}{4} = \frac{s}{16}$

5. **WRITING** In Step 2, the second ratio has how many times as many chips as the first ratio? How could you use this relationship to find *n*?

6. **OPEN-ENDED** Find two more ratios that are equivalent to $\frac{2}{3}$. *Explain* how to find ratios that are equivalent to any ratio you are given.

5.3 Writing and Solving Proportions

Standards **NS 1.3** **Use proportions to solve problems (e.g., determine the value of N if $\frac{4}{7} = \frac{N}{21}$,** find the length of a side of a polygon similar to a known polygon). Use cross-multiplication as a method for solving such problems, understanding it as the multiplication of both sides of an equation by a multiplicative inverse.

AF 2.3 **Solve problems involving rates,** average speed, distance, and time.

Connect ***Before*** you wrote ratios. ***Now*** you will solve proportions using equivalent ratios and algebra.

Math and **FITNESS**
Example 1, p. 266

KEY VOCABULARY
- **proportion**
- **multiplicative inverse,** *p. 168*

SPORTS A person burned about 70 calories while in-line skating for 10 minutes. About how many calories would the skater burn in 60 minutes? In Example 1, you will use a *proportion* to answer this question.

KEY CONCEPT *For Your Notebook*

Proportion

Words A **proportion** is an equation that states that two ratios are equivalent.

Numbers $\frac{3}{5} = \frac{6}{10}$ **The proportion is read "3 is to 5 as 6 is to 10."**

Algebra $\frac{a}{b} = \frac{c}{d}$, where b and d are nonzero numbers.

USING EQUIVALENT RATIOS When one of the numbers in a proportion is unknown, you can find the number by *solving the proportion.* One way to solve a proportion is to use mental math to find an equivalent ratio.

EXAMPLE 1 Solving Proportions Using Equivalent Ratios

ANOTHER WAY
For an alternative method for finding the number of calories burned in Example 1, turn to p. 272 for the **Problem Solving Workshop**.

Find the number C of calories the skater above would burn in 60 minutes by solving the proportion $\frac{70}{10} = \frac{C}{60}$.

STEP 1 Ask yourself: What number can you multiply 10 by to get 60?

$$\frac{70}{10} = \frac{C}{60} \quad (10 \times ?)$$

STEP 2 Because $10 \times 6 = 60$, multiply the numerator by 6 to find C.

$$\frac{70}{10} = \frac{C}{60} \quad (\times 6 \text{ top and bottom})$$

▶ **Answer** Because $70 \times 6 = 420$, $C = 420$. So, the person would burn about 420 calories while in-line skating for 60 minutes.

✓ GUIDED PRACTICE for Example 1

Use equivalent ratios to solve the proportion.

1. $\frac{1}{5} = \frac{z}{20}$ **2.** $\frac{8}{3} = \frac{k}{18}$ **3.** $\frac{27}{c} = \frac{9}{12}$ **4.** $\frac{9}{n} = \frac{99}{22}$

USING ALGEBRA The same method you used to solve division equations in Lesson 4.7 can be used to solve proportions that have the variable in the numerator.

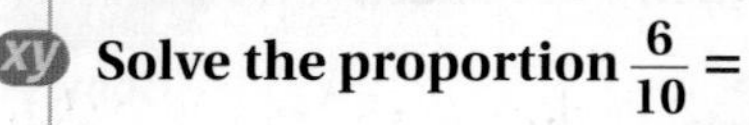

EXAMPLE 2 Solving Proportions Using Algebra

Solve the proportion $\frac{6}{10} = \frac{x}{25}$.

$\frac{6}{10} = \frac{x}{25}$	Write original proportion.
$25 \cdot \frac{6}{10} = 25 \cdot \frac{x}{25}$	Multiply each side by 25.
$\frac{150}{10} = x$	Simplify.
$15 = x$	Simplify fraction.

▶ **Answer** The solution is 15.

ANOTHER WAY

You can think of $\frac{x}{25}$ as $\frac{1}{25} \cdot x$ and use a multiplicative inverse to solve the proportion.

$\frac{25}{1} \cdot \frac{6}{10} = \frac{25}{1} \cdot \frac{1}{25} \cdot x$

$15 = x$

✓ GUIDED PRACTICE for Example 2

Use algebra to solve the proportion.

5. $\frac{4}{14} = \frac{m}{49}$ **6.** $\frac{25}{30} = \frac{x}{12}$ **7.** $\frac{h}{33} = \frac{2}{6}$ **8.** $\frac{b}{8} = \frac{7}{28}$

About the Standards

Grade 6 Standard MR 1.1 asks you to identify relationships in problems. Here you must identify relationships to set up proportions.

SETTING UP A PROPORTION A proportion may be set up several ways. Consider the following problem.

Yesterday you bought 8 folders for $4. Today you need to buy 5 more folders. How much will 5 folders cost?

The information is arranged in the two tables below, in which x represents the cost of 5 folders. Either of the proportions that follow from the tables can be used to solve the problem.

	Yesterday	*Today*
Cost	4	x
Folders	8	5

Proportion: $\frac{4}{8} = \frac{x}{5}$

	Folders	*Cost*
Today	5	x
Yesterday	8	4

Proportion: $\frac{5}{8} = \frac{x}{4}$

In other words, you may use either the ratios formed by comparing yesterday's data to today's data or folders to cost.

EXAMPLE 3 ◆ Multiple Choice Practice

The elevators in some skyscrapers can pass 80 floors in 45 seconds. How many floors can the elevators pass in 9 seconds?

Ⓐ 2　　Ⓑ 5

Ⓒ 16　　Ⓓ 107

Some elevators can pass 80 floors in 45 seconds.

SOLUTION

AVOID ERRORS

Don't confuse numerators and denominators in a proportion. For example:

$\frac{80 \text{ floors}}{45 \text{ sec}} \neq \frac{9 \text{ sec}}{x \text{ floors}}$

STEP 1 **Write** a proportion. Let x represent the number of floors passed in 9 seconds.

$\frac{80}{45} = \frac{x}{9}$ ← **Floors** / ← **Seconds**

STEP 2 **Solve** the proportion.

$\frac{80}{45} = \frac{x}{9}$　　**Write original proportion.**

$9 \cdot \frac{80}{45} = 9 \cdot \frac{x}{9}$　　**Multiply each side by 9.**

$16 = x$　　**Simplify.**

▸ **Answer** The elevators can pass 16 floors in 9 seconds.
The correct answer is C. Ⓐ Ⓑ Ⓒ Ⓓ

GUIDED PRACTICE for Example 3

9. **WHAT IF?** Suppose the elevators in Example 3 could pass 70 floors in 63 seconds. How many floors could the elevators pass in 9 seconds?

5.3 EXERCISES

HOMEWORK KEY
◆ = **MULTIPLE CHOICE PRACTICE** Exs. 11, 20, 31, 46–48
○ = **HINTS AND HOMEWORK HELP** for Exs. 9, 17, 31 at classzone.com

SKILLS • PROBLEM SOLVING • REASONING

1. **VOCABULARY** Copy and complete: An equation that states that two ratios are equivalent is a(n) _?_.

2. **WRITING** *Express* the proportion in Step 1 of Example 3 using words.

SEE EXAMPLE 1 on p. 266 for Exs. 3–11

USING EQUIVALENT RATIOS **Use equivalent ratios to solve the proportion.**

3. $\frac{3}{7} = \frac{a}{21}$
4. $\frac{4}{36} = \frac{w}{9}$
5. $\frac{2}{s} = \frac{18}{45}$
6. $\frac{4}{c} = \frac{2}{10}$
7. $\frac{14}{8} = \frac{42}{m}$
8. $\frac{51}{z} = \frac{3}{2}$
9. $\frac{11}{4} = \frac{121}{x}$
10. $\frac{65}{s} = \frac{13}{6}$

11. ◆ **MULTIPLE CHOICE** What is the value of n in the proportion $\frac{4}{7} = \frac{n}{21}$?

Ⓐ 12 Ⓑ 18 Ⓒ 28 Ⓓ 37

SEE EXAMPLE 2 on p. 267 for Exs. 12–20

USING ALGEBRA **Use algebra to solve the proportion.**

12. $\frac{h}{8} = \frac{3}{12}$
13. $\frac{k}{27} = \frac{4}{6}$
14. $\frac{6}{14} = \frac{m}{21}$
15. $\frac{20}{16} = \frac{n}{12}$
16. $\frac{m}{20} = \frac{5}{16}$
17. $\frac{h}{8} = \frac{7}{10}$
18. $\frac{30}{6} = \frac{b}{7}$
19. $\frac{z}{8} = \frac{5}{7}$

20. ◆ **MULTIPLE CHOICE** What is the value of d in the proportion $\frac{36}{42} = \frac{d}{28}$?

Ⓐ 22 Ⓑ 24 Ⓒ 33 Ⓓ 50

SEE EXAMPLE 3 on p. 268 for Exs. 21–24

WRITING PROPORTIONS **Write and solve the proportion.**

21. 8 is to 3 as w is to 12.
22. m is to 32 as 3 is to 4.
23. p is to 30 as 10 is to 12.
24. 6 is to 16 as z is to 40.

CONNECT SKILLS TO PROBLEM SOLVING **Exercises 25–27 will help you prepare for problem solving.**

Write a proportion that could be used to solve the problem.

25. It takes 4 quarts of paint to cover 560 square feet. How many quarts of this paint are needed to cover 140 square feet?

26. Kate is reading a 168 page book. Kate reads the first 15 pages of the book in 20 minutes. How many minutes will it take her to read the entire book?

27. An office with 280 square feet of floor space rents for $1400 a month. A larger office rents for $1700 a month. The cost per square foot for each office is the same. How much floor space is in the larger office?

SEE EXAMPLE 3 on p. 268 for Exs. 28–30

28. **SHOPPING** You can buy 3 CDs for $27 from a music store. How many CDs can you buy for $63?

California @HomeTutor for problem solving help at classzone.com

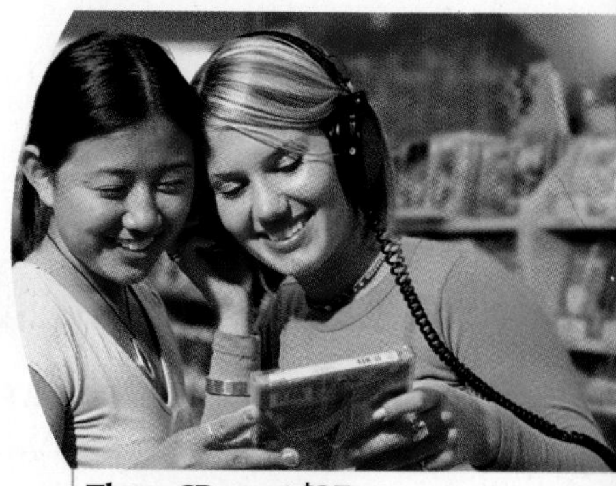

Three CDs cost $27.

29. **NUTRITION** The average American eats 57 pounds of apples over 3 years. At this rate, how many pounds of apples does the average American eat in 15 years?

California @HomeTutor for problem solving help at classzone.com

30. **ERROR ANALYSIS** To make orange food coloring, 2 drops of red are mixed with 3 drops of yellow. *Describe* and correct the error in the proportion used to find the number r of drops of red to add to 12 drops of yellow.

✗ $\frac{3}{2} = \frac{r}{12}$

31. ◆ **MULTIPLE CHOICE** A recipe that makes 12 pints of salsa uses 35 tomatoes. Which proportion can *not* be used to find the number t of tomatoes needed to make 2 pints of salsa?

(A) $\frac{1}{6} = \frac{t}{35}$ (B) $\frac{t}{35} = \frac{12}{2}$ (C) $\frac{35}{12} = \frac{t}{2}$ (D) $\frac{t}{35} = \frac{2}{12}$

32. **REASONING** Is it possible to write a proportion using $\frac{11}{13}$ and $\frac{55}{65}$? *Explain* your reasoning.

33. **PET CARE** The table lists the number of cups of flour needed to make dough for a given number of dog biscuits. Copy and complete the table.

Biscuits	32	48	?
Flour (cups)	2	?	5

READING IN MATH **Read the information below for Exercises 34–36.**

34. **Analyze** How long would a 150 pound person have to ballroom dance to burn as many calories as he or she would burn while high energy dancing during 45 minutes? *Explain* your reasoning.

35. **Calculate** How many calories would a 150 pound person burn during 45 minutes of ballroom dancing?

36. **Compare** To the nearest minute, how much longer would a 150 pound person have to spend ballroom dancing than doing Latin dance to burn 500 calories?

Dancing and Calories

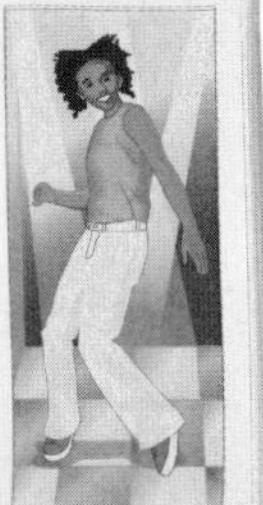

Dancing is not only fun, it's also healthy, because it's an effective means of burning calories. Recent research shows that during 30 minutes of high energy dancing, like hip-hop or Latin dance, a 150 pound person burns approximately 212 calories. The same person burns roughly 106 calories while ballroom dancing for 30 minutes. So, whatever style of dance you prefer, dancing is a healthy exercise alternative.

37. **HISTORY** The length of a Viking ship is given below. What is its width?

The ratio of width to length is 3:20.
70 ft

38. **POPULATION** In the United States, 21 out of every 100 people are under the age of 15. In a town of 20,000 people, how many people would you expect to be under the age of 15? 15 and over? *Explain* your reasoning.

CHALLENGE **Solve the proportion.**

39. $\frac{30}{v} = \frac{12}{16}$ 40. $\frac{8}{x} = \frac{6}{15}$ 41. $\frac{22}{33} = \frac{16}{y}$ 42. $\frac{4}{24} = \frac{6}{z}$

43. **CHALLENGE** A car travels at a constant speed of 56 miles per hour. How far will it travel in 45 minutes 45 seconds?

In Exercises 44–45, solve the problem without using a proportion.

EXTENSION **Solving Rate Problems Without a Proportion**

You spend \$12 to purchase 3 pounds of ham. How much will it cost to purchase 8 pounds of ham?

SOLUTION

The price per pound of ham is $\frac{\$12}{3} = \$4$. To buy 8 pounds of ham, it will cost $8 \times \$4 = \$32$.

▶ **Answer** The cost for 8 pounds of ham is \$32.

44. You spend \$9 to purchase 3 gallons of iced tea. How much will it cost to purchase 5 gallons of iced tea?

45. Mark runs 3 miles in 24 minutes at a constant speed. How many minutes will it take him to run 7 miles?

◆ CALIFORNIA STANDARDS SPIRAL REVIEW

NS 2.4 **46.** What is the least common multiple of 42 and 56? *(p. 22)*

Ⓐ 7 Ⓑ 14 Ⓒ 168 Ⓓ 2352

AF 1.2 **47.** What is the value of $3x^2 - 27$ when $x = -4$? *(p. 197)*

Ⓐ −75 Ⓑ −39 Ⓒ −3 Ⓓ 21

AF 2.2 **48.** A painter can paint 120 square feet in 5 minutes. How many square feet can the painter paint in one minute? *(p. 260)*

Ⓐ $\frac{1}{24}$ Ⓑ 24 Ⓒ 48 Ⓓ 600

QUIZ for Lessons 5.1–5.3

Write the ratio as a fraction in simplest form. *(p. 255)*

1. $\frac{12}{16}$ **2.** 5 to 6 **3.** 18 to 4 **4.** 20 : 5

5. ZOOLOGY The number of teeth in the upper and lower jaws for each of two animals is shown in the table. Which animal has the greater ratio of teeth in the upper jaw to teeth in the lower jaw? *(p. 255)*

Animal	Upper teeth	Lower teeth
Elk	14	20
Bear	20	22

Find the unit rate. *(p. 260)*

6. \$2.25 for 5 lb **7.** \$6 for 5 pens **8.** 900 mi in 3 h **9.** 2 ft in 8 days

Use equivalent ratios or algebra to solve the proportion. *(p. 266)*

10. $\frac{a}{20} = \frac{7}{4}$ **11.** $\frac{24}{30} = \frac{n}{40}$ **12.** $\frac{9}{27} = \frac{d}{15}$ **13.** $\frac{27}{x} = \frac{3}{11}$

PROBLEM SOLVING WORKSHOP
LESSON 5.3

Using ALTERNATIVE METHODS

Another Way to Solve Example 1, page 266

Standards
AF 2.0, AF 2.3

In Example 1 on page 266, you saw how to solve the problem about the number of calories burned from in-line skating by using a proportion. You can also solve the problem by making a table.

PROBLEM

SPORTS A person burned about 70 calories while in-line skating for 10 minutes. About how many calories would the skater burn in 60 minutes?

METHOD

Making a Table An alternate approach is to make a table.

STEP 1 **Choose** an increment for the table. You know that for every 10 minutes of in-line skating, about 70 calories are burned. So, use an increment of 10 minutes.

STEP 2 **Make** a table for the amount of time the person spends in-line skating and the calories burned. End the table at 60 minutes.

In-line skating (minutes)	*Calories burned*
10	70
20	140
30	210
40	280
50	350
60	420

▶ **Answer** The person would burn about 420 calories while in-line skating for 60 minutes.

PRACTICE

1. **SWIMMING** A person burned about 120 calories while swimming for 15 minutes. Use a table to find about how many calories the swimmer would burn in 60 minutes.

2. **WHAT IF?** In Exercise 1, how many calories would the person burn while swimming for 45 minutes? Use your table.

3. **FERTILIZER** The weight of 3 bags of fertilizer is 45 pounds. What is the weight of 5 bags of fertilizer? Solve this problem using two methods.

4. **FUNDRAISER** The softball team washes 4 cars in 18 minutes. How many cars can they wash in 45 minutes? Solve this problem using two methods.

MIXED REVIEW of Skills and Problem Solving

Multiple Choice Practice for Lessons 5.1–5.3

1. The table shows the number of boys and girls in grades 9–12 at a school. How can you find the ratio of girls in 9th grade to girls in the whole school? **NS 1.2, MR 1.1**

Grade	Boys	Girls
9	110	88
10	75	90
11	70	80
12	84	63

Ⓐ Divide the number of 9th grade girls by the number of 9th grade boys.

Ⓑ Divide the number of 9th grade girls by the total number of high school boys.

Ⓒ Divide the total number of high school girls by the number of 9th grade girls.

Ⓓ Divide the number of 9th grade girls by the total number of high school girls.

2. What is the unit rate for $\frac{\$42}{14 \text{ gallons}}$? **AF 2.2**

Ⓐ $\$\frac{1}{3}$ per gallon

Ⓑ 3 gallons per dollar

Ⓒ $3 per gallon

Ⓓ $28 per gallon

3. All of the cashiers at a restaurant make the same hourly wage. The table shows the total hours worked by the cashiers and their total wages for two months. Which proportion can you use to find the wages w paid to the cashiers in February? **NS 1.3**

Month	Wages paid	Hours worked
January	$2520	320
February	?	360

Ⓐ $\frac{w}{360} = \frac{2520}{320}$ Ⓑ $\frac{320}{2520} = \frac{w}{360}$

Ⓒ $\frac{w}{2520} = \frac{320}{360}$ Ⓓ $\frac{360}{2520} = \frac{w}{320}$

4. Cans of soup come in three sizes. An 8 ounce can costs $1.28, a 12 ounce can costs $1.80, and a 16 ounce can costs $2.48. What can you conclude? **AF 2.2**

Ⓐ The 8 ounce can is the best buy.

Ⓑ The 12 ounce can is the best buy.

Ⓒ The 16 ounce can is the best buy.

Ⓓ Two 8 ounce cans cost the same as one 16 ounce can.

5. The female Angonoka tortoise lays eggs in groups called clutches. The table shows the total number of eggs one female tortoise lays in 5 clutches. How many eggs would a female tortoise lay if she lays 8 clutches of the same size? **NS 1.3, MR 2.5**

Clutches	Eggs
5	30
8	?

Ⓐ 19 Ⓑ 33

Ⓒ 48 Ⓓ 78

6. A car travels 9 miles in 15 minutes. What is the car's average speed in miles per hour? **AF 2.3**

Ⓐ 0.6 mi/h

Ⓑ 2.25 mi/h

Ⓒ 36 mi/h

Ⓓ 60 mi/h

7. Evan collects 24 shells at the beach. Kyla collects 12 more shells than Evan does. What is the ratio of Evan's shells to Kyla's shells? **NS 1.2**

Ⓐ 1 : 2 Ⓑ 2 : 3

Ⓒ 3 : 2 Ⓓ 2 : 1

5.4 Solving Proportions Using Cross Products

Math and NATURE
Example 4, p. 276

Standards **NS 1.3** **Use proportions to solve problems (e.g., determine the value of N if $\frac{4}{7} = \frac{N}{21}$, find** the length of a side of a polygon similar to a known polygon). **Use cross-multiplication as a method for solving such problems, understanding it as the multiplication of both sides of an equation by a multiplicative inverse.**

AF 2.2 **Demonstrate an understanding that *rate* is a measure of one quantity per unit value of another quantity.**

Connect ***Before*** you solved proportions using equivalent ratios and algebra. ***Now*** you will solve proportions using cross products.

KEY VOCABULARY
- **cross products**
- **multiplicative inverse,** *p. 168*

The **cross products** in the proportion $\frac{2}{3} = \frac{4}{6}$ are $2 \cdot 6$ and $3 \cdot 4$. You can use multiplicative inverses to understand why the cross products are equal.

$\frac{2}{3} = \frac{4}{6}$ **Write proportion.**

$\frac{\cancel{3}}{1} \cdot \frac{2}{\cancel{3}} \cdot \frac{6}{1} = \frac{3}{1} \cdot \frac{4}{\cancel{6}} \cdot \frac{\cancel{6}}{1}$ **Multiply each side by $\frac{3}{1}$ and $\frac{6}{1}$.**

$2 \cdot 6 = 3 \cdot 4$ **Simplify.**

KEY CONCEPT *For Your Notebook*

Cross Products Property

Words The cross products of a proportion are equal.

Numbers $\frac{3}{4} = \frac{15}{20}$ $4 \cdot 15 = 60$ $3 \cdot 20 = 60$

Algebra If $\frac{a}{b} = \frac{c}{d}$ where b and d are nonzero numbers, then $ad = bc$.

LOOKING AHEAD
You will justify the cross products property in Exercise 56 on p. 279.

EXAMPLE 1 Solving a Proportion Using Cross Products

Use the cross products property to solve $\frac{2}{9} = \frac{3}{d}$.

$\frac{2}{9} = \frac{3}{d}$ **Write original proportion.**

$2 \cdot d = 9 \cdot 3$ **Use cross products property.**

$\frac{2d}{2} = \frac{9 \cdot 3}{2}$ **Divide each side by 2.**

$d = 13.5$ **Simplify.**

VOCABULARY
Finding cross products is sometimes called *cross-multiplication* because of the "X" shape formed by the diagonal numbers in a proportion.

✓ GUIDED PRACTICE for Example 1

1. Solve $\frac{b}{10} = \frac{3}{4}$.
2. Solve $\frac{a}{15} = \frac{5}{6}$.
3. Solve $\frac{4}{5} = \frac{28}{c}$.

EXAMPLE 2 Writing and Solving a Proportion

 **SCIENCE** A person who weighs 105 pounds on Earth would weigh about 17.5 pounds on the moon. About how much would a 60 pound dog weigh on the moon?

SOLUTION

ANOTHER WAY
You can also find the dog's weight by using an equivalent proportion such as:

$\frac{17.5}{105} = \frac{w}{60}$

To find the weight w (in pounds) of a 60 pound dog on the moon, write and solve a proportion using the weight of the person.

Person Dog

$\frac{105}{17.5} = \frac{60}{w}$ ← **Weight on Earth** / ← **Weight on moon**

$105w = 17.5 \cdot 60$ **Use cross products property.**

$w = 10$ **Divide each side by 105.**

▶ **Answer** A 60 pound dog would weigh about 10 pounds on the moon.

EXAMPLE 3 ◆ Multiple Choice Practice

Rosa spent a total of \$.75 to dry one load of her clothes at a laundromat. One quarter operates the dryer for 15 minutes. At most, how many minutes were her clothes in the dryer?

Ⓐ 0.75 min Ⓑ 20 min Ⓒ 45 min Ⓓ 90 min

ELIMINATE CHOICES
One quarter, or \$.25, operates the dryer for 15 minutes. So, 3 quarters will operate the dryer for more than 15 minutes. Choice A can be eliminated.

SOLUTION

STEP 1 **Convert** the money spent into quarters. Because 1 quarter equals \$.25, Rosa used $0.75 \div 0.25$, or 3 quarters, to dry her clothes.

STEP 2 **Write** a proportion to find the greatest amount of time t (in minutes) her clothes were in the dryer.

$\frac{1}{15} = \frac{3}{t}$ ← **Quarters** / ← **Time**

$1 \cdot t = 15 \cdot 3$ **Use cross products property.**

$t = 45$ **Simplify.**

▶ **Answer** At most, her clothes were in the dryer for 45 minutes. The correct answer is C. Ⓐ Ⓑ Ⓒ Ⓓ

✓ GUIDED PRACTICE for Examples 2 and 3

4. **WHAT IF?** In Example 2, suppose that a 150 pound astronaut stood on the moon. How much would the astronaut weigh?

5. **WHAT IF?** In Example 3, suppose one quarter operates the dryer for 20 minutes. At most, how many minutes were her clothes in the dryer?

EXAMPLE 4 Solve a Multi-Step Problem

PENGUINS The ratio of rockhopper penguins to African penguins at a zoo is 3 to 7. There are 50 of these penguins in all. How many are rockhoppers?

SOLUTION

STEP 1 **Determine** the ratio of rockhoppers to total penguins.

$\frac{3}{3+7} = \frac{3}{10}$ **For every 10 penguins, 3 are rockhoppers.**

ANOTHER WAY

In Example 4, you can also solve the proportion using the methods you learned in Lesson 5.3.

STEP 2 **Write** and solve a proportion to find the number r of rockhoppers.

$\frac{3}{10} = \frac{r}{50}$ ← **Rockhoppers** / ← **Total penguins**

$3 \cdot 50 = 10r$ **Use cross products property.**

$\frac{3 \cdot 50}{10} = \frac{10r}{10}$ **Divide each side by 10.**

$15 = r$ **Simplify.**

Rockhopper penguin

▶**Answer** There are 15 rockhoppers at the zoo.

GUIDED PRACTICE for Example 4

6. **ART SUPPLIES** The ratio of tubes of acrylic paint to tubes of oil paint is 3 : 2. There are 65 tubes of these paints in all. How many are acrylic?

5.4 EXERCISES

HOMEWORK KEY

◆ = **MULTIPLE CHOICE PRACTICE** Exs. 19, 35, 47, 50, 61–63

○ = **HINTS AND HOMEWORK HELP** for Exs. 5, 25, 49 at classzone.com

SKILLS • PROBLEM SOLVING • REASONING

1. **VOCABULARY** What are the cross products of the proportion $\frac{2}{7} = \frac{10}{35}$?

2. **NOTETAKING SKILLS** Make a *word magnet* like the one on page 254 for *proportion.*

SEE EXAMPLE 1 on p. 274 for Exs. 3–18

SOLVING PROPORTIONS **Use cross products to solve the proportion.**

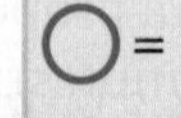

3. $\frac{5}{2} = \frac{y}{10}$	4. $\frac{n}{8} = \frac{3}{12}$	5. $\frac{5}{20} = \frac{3}{d}$	6. $\frac{8}{6} = \frac{12}{s}$
7. $\frac{9}{2} = \frac{36}{n}$	8. $\frac{a}{24} = \frac{7}{8}$	9. $\frac{30}{6} = \frac{b}{7}$	10. $\frac{3}{x} = \frac{4}{28}$
11. $\frac{4}{p} = \frac{14}{28}$	12. $\frac{6.8}{z} = \frac{2}{5}$	13. $\frac{a}{4} = \frac{3.5}{2}$	14. $\frac{7}{10} = \frac{k}{8}$
15. $\frac{20}{m} = \frac{16}{5}$	16. $\frac{6}{9.6} = \frac{9}{d}$	17. $\frac{22}{c} = \frac{5.5}{11}$	18. $\frac{3.6}{3} = \frac{y}{14.4}$

SEE EXAMPLE 1
on p. 274
for Exs. 19–21

19. ◆ **MULTIPLE CHOICE** Which proportion does not have a solution of 4?

Ⓐ $\frac{a}{6} = \frac{22}{33}$ Ⓑ $\frac{20}{35} = \frac{c}{7}$ Ⓒ $\frac{12}{3} = \frac{4}{n}$ Ⓓ $\frac{8}{w} = \frac{34}{17}$

ERROR ANALYSIS ***Describe*** **and correct the error in solving the proportion.**

20.

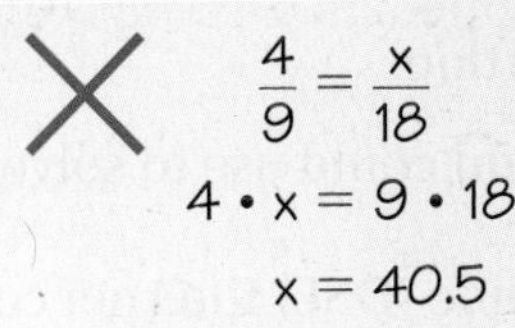

21.

$$\frac{y}{8} = \frac{28}{32}$$

$$y + 32 = 8 + 28$$

$$y = 4$$

SEE EXAMPLE 2
on p. 275
for Exs. 22–26

APPLYING PROPORTIONS **The ratio of an animal's weight on Earth to its weight on the moon is 21 pounds to 3.5 pounds. Find the unknown weight.**

22. Elephant: 9000 pounds on Earth
23. Rabbit: 0.8 pound on the moon
24. Koala: 4 pounds on the moon
25. Giraffe: 3000 pounds on Earth

26. **ESTIMATION** There are about 18.3 meters in 20 yards. *Estimate* the fraction of a meter in one yard.

SEE EXAMPLE 4
on p. 276
for Exs. 27–35

USING PROPORTIONS **Use the ratio of boys to girls and the class size to find the number of boys and the number of girls in each class.**

27. 3 : 5, 80
28. 5 : 4, 45
29. 4 : 3, 35
30. 3 : 4, 84
31. 7 : 3, 70
32. 5 : 7, 60
33. 2 : 3, 65
34. 6 : 7, 52

35. ◆ **MULTIPLE CHOICE** The ratio of two amounts *a* and *b* is 2 : 1. The total of the two amounts is 24. Which proportion can you use to find the amount *a*?

Ⓐ $\frac{2}{3} = \frac{24}{a}$ Ⓑ $\frac{2}{1} = \frac{a}{24}$ Ⓒ $\frac{24}{a} = \frac{2}{1}$ Ⓓ $\frac{a}{24} = \frac{2}{3}$

xy ALGEBRA **Solve the proportion.**

36. $\frac{15}{4} = \frac{9}{2n}$
37. $\frac{5b}{16} = \frac{5}{8}$
38. $\frac{18}{3w} = \frac{12}{30}$
39. $\frac{7}{8} = \frac{3d}{28}$

In Exercises 40–43, tell whether the ratios form a proportion.

EXTENSION **Deciding Whether Ratios Form a Proportion**

Only ratios that form a proportion are equal.

$\frac{2}{9} \stackrel{?}{=} \frac{5}{16}$ **Write the possible proportion.**

$2 \cdot 16 \stackrel{?}{=} 9 \cdot 5$ **Find cross products.**

$32 \neq 45$ **Multiply. The cross products are not equal.**

▶ **Answer** The ratios do not form a proportion.

40. $\frac{24}{104}, \frac{3}{13}$
41. $\frac{6}{7}, \frac{21}{18}$
42. $\frac{3.4}{4.3}, \frac{5.6}{6.5}$
43. $\frac{9}{4.3}, \frac{54}{25.8}$

CONNECT SKILLS TO PROBLEM SOLVING **Exercises 44–46 will help you prepare for problem solving.**

Use the following information: There are 5 grams of protein in 3 teaspoons of peanut butter.

44. Write a proportion you could use to find the amount of protein p (in grams) in 9 teaspoons of peanut butter.

45. Identify the cross products in your proportion.

46. Use cross products to write an equation you could use to solve for p.

SEE EXAMPLE 2
on p. 275
for Exs. 47–49

47. ◆ **MULTIPLE CHOICE** A digital subscriber line (DSL) Internet connection can transfer 42 megabits of information in 5 minutes. How long would it take to transfer 75.6 megabits of information?

Ⓐ 1 min 48 sec Ⓑ 6 min 35 sec Ⓒ 9 min Ⓓ 15 min

California @HomeTutor for problem solving help at classzone.com

48. **OPEN-ENDED** During the Gold Rush, one pioneer tried to travel west in a wagon with a sail. An advertisement for this *wind wagon* claimed that it could travel 15 miles per hour. How far could the advertisement say the wagon traveled in 30 minutes? Give another equivalent speed that the advertisement could use.

California @HomeTutor for problem solving help at classzone.com

49. **MULTI-STEP PROBLEM** Use the dimensions of two ocean waves shown in the table.

Ocean Wave Dimensions

	Height (meters)	Wavelength (meters)
Wave 1	10.2	71.4
Wave 2	12.7	88.9

wavelength
height
Not drawn to scale

a. Compare Is the ratio of height to wavelength the same for both waves? *Explain* your reasoning.

b. Interpret The ratio of height to the wavelength of a wave when it breaks is 1 to 7. Were the measures of the waves in the table taken just as the waves broke? *Explain* your reasoning.

SEE EXAMPLE 3
on p. 275
for Exs. 50–52

50. ◆ **MULTIPLE CHOICE** Lia puts \$3.75 in a parking meter. One quarter operates the meter for 15 minutes. Which proportion can you use to find the maximum time t (in minutes) Lia can legally park at the meter?

Ⓐ $\frac{1}{15} = \frac{15}{t}$ Ⓑ $\frac{1}{15} = \frac{3.75}{t}$ Ⓒ $\frac{1}{15} = \frac{t}{15}$ Ⓓ $\frac{1}{15} = \frac{3.75}{t}$

51. **MUSIC** The ratio of the number of Abby's CDs to the number of Chen's CDs is 7 to 8. Abby has 84 CDs. Together how many CDs do they have?

52. **SPORTS** At a typical National Football League game, the ratio of males to females in attendance is 3 : 2. If there are 27,000 female spectators at a typical game, what is the number of total spectators?

53. **MEASUREMENT** On a sunny day, go outside and have a classmate measure your height and the length of your shadow. Then measure the length of the shadow of a tall object, such as a tree or flagpole. The height to shadow ratio is the same for both you and the object. Use this fact to find the height of the tall object.

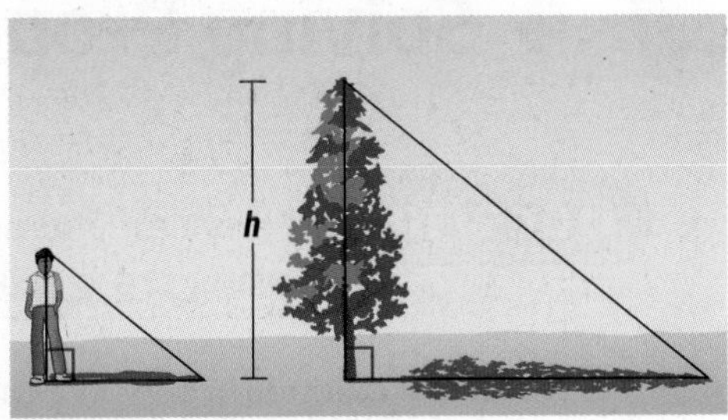

SEE EXAMPLE 4 on p. 276 for Exs. 54–55

54. **SURVEYS** A survey of sixth graders found that the ratio of students who use a pen to do their math homework to students who use a pencil is 2 to 7. The total number of sixth graders surveyed was 81. How many of the students surveyed use a pen to do their math homework?

55. **NATIONAL ZOO** The total number of vertebrate and invertebrate animals at the National Zoo in Washington, D.C., at one time was 2492 animals. The ratio of vertebrates to invertebrates was about 10.6 to 1. About how many of the animals were invertebrates?

The total number of animals was 2492.

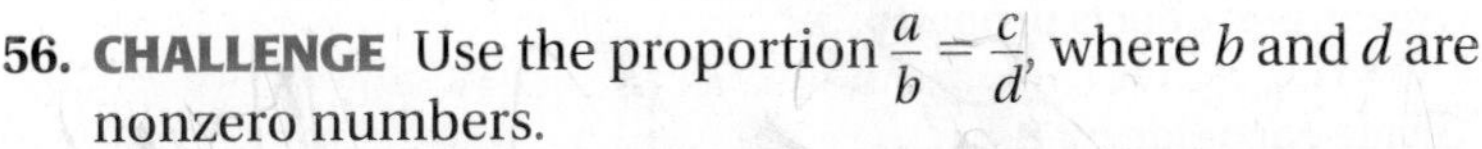

56. **CHALLENGE** Use the proportion $\frac{a}{b} = \frac{c}{d}$, where b and d are nonzero numbers.
   a. Use the multiplication property of equality to rewrite the proportion so the denominators are equal to 1.
   b. *Describe* your process.
   c. What do you notice about your resulting equation? *Explain* the meaning of your result for any proportion.

CHALLENGE Solve the proportion.

57. $\frac{5}{t+6} = \frac{1}{2}$ 58. $\frac{9}{16} = \frac{a+12}{64}$ 59. $\frac{3}{4} = \frac{9}{x+3}$ 60. $\frac{x+51}{54} = \frac{10}{6}$

◆ CALIFORNIA STANDARDS SPIRAL REVIEW

AF 1.1 61. The difference of x and 3 is 6. What is the value of x? ***(p. 226)***

Ⓐ −9 Ⓑ −3 Ⓒ 3 Ⓓ 9

AF 1.4 62. What is the value of $7^2 + 8 \times (-4) + 3$? ***(p. 160)***

Ⓐ −57 Ⓑ 20 Ⓒ 41 Ⓓ 84

NS 1.3 63. A bag of trail mix weighing 9 pounds costs $27. Which proportion could you use to find the pounds of trail mix you could get for $2? ***(p. 266)***

Ⓐ $\frac{2}{9} = \frac{x}{27}$ Ⓑ $\frac{9}{2} = \frac{27}{x}$ Ⓒ $\frac{2}{x} = \frac{9}{27}$ Ⓓ $\frac{x}{9} = \frac{2}{27}$

5.4 Solving Proportions

Standards

NS 1.3 Use proportions to solve problems (e.g., determine the value of *N* if $\frac{4}{7} = \frac{N}{21}$, find the length of a side of a polygon similar to a known polygon). **Use cross-multiplication as a method for solving such problems**, understanding it as the multiplication of both sides of an equation by a multiplicative inverse.

QUESTION **How can you use a calculator to solve proportions using cross products?**

You can use a calculator to solve proportions by using cross products. Calculator keystrokes allow you to perform the multiplication and the division in a single step.

EXAMPLE **Solve $\frac{5}{8} = \frac{x}{16}$.**

Method 1

Solve the proportion on paper using the cross products property.

$\frac{5}{8} = \frac{x}{16}$	**Write proportion.**
$5 \cdot 16 = 8x$	**Use cross products property.**
$\frac{5 \cdot 16}{8} = \frac{8x}{8}$	**Divide each side by 8.**
$10 = x$	**Simplify.**

Method 2

Solve the proportion using a calculator. Use keystrokes that correspond to the process used above in Method 1.

Keystrokes	Display
5 [×] 16 [÷] 8 [=]	10

▶ **Answer** The value of x is 10.

PRACTICE

Solve the proportion using a calculator.

1. $\frac{8}{13} = \frac{c}{52}$ **2.** $\frac{w}{5} = \frac{18}{15}$ **3.** $\frac{7}{11} = \frac{k}{44}$ **4.** $\frac{4}{10} = \frac{p}{25}$

5. $\frac{18}{39} = \frac{a}{26}$ **6.** $\frac{24}{42} = \frac{s}{28}$ **7.** $\frac{y}{6} = \frac{40}{16}$ **8.** $\frac{b}{71} = \frac{3}{4}$

9. ENROLLMENT The ratio of girls to boys at a middle school is 7 to 8. There are 248 boys at the school. How many girls are at the school?

10. WRITING *Describe* the process for solving a proportion using a calculator.

5.5 Scale Drawings and Models

Math and MODELS
Example 3, p. 283

Standards **NS 1.3 Use proportions to solve problems** (e.g., determine the value of N if $\frac{4}{7} = \frac{N}{21}$, find the length of a side of a polygon similar to a known polygon). **Use cross-multiplication as a method for solving such problems**, understanding it as the multiplication of both sides of an equation by a multiplicative inverse.

Connect ***Before*** you learned how to solve proportions. ***Now*** you will use proportions to solve problems involving scale drawings and models.

KEY VOCABULARY
- scale drawing
- scale
- scale model

Maps and floor plans are examples of *scale drawings.* A **scale drawing** is a diagram of an object in which the dimensions are in proportion to the actual dimensions of the object.

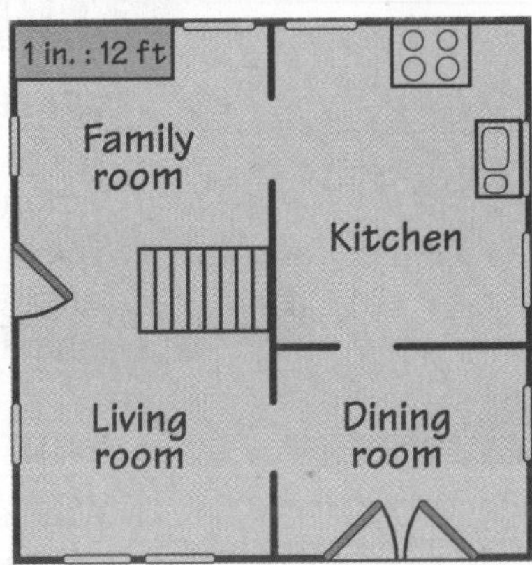

The **scale** on a scale drawing tells how the drawing's dimensions and the actual dimensions are related. The scale "1 in. : 12 ft" means that 1 inch in the floor plan represents an actual distance of 12 feet.

EXAMPLE 1 ◆ Multiple Choice Practice

A floor plan uses a scale of 1 inch equals 12 feet. How many feet are represented by 8 inches on this floor plan?

Ⓐ 0.67 ft Ⓑ 12 ft Ⓒ 19 ft Ⓓ 96 ft

About the Standards
You find unknown lengths using a scale drawing in Example 1. You will find unknown lengths in similar polygons in Chapter 9, as called for in Grade 6 Standard NS 1.3.

SOLUTION

Write and solve a proportion to find the actual distance d (in feet).

$$\frac{1}{12} = \frac{8}{d}$$ ← inches / ← feet

$1 \cdot d = 12 \cdot 8$ **Use cross products property.**

$d = 96$ **Simplify.**

▶ **Answer** The actual distance represented by 8 inches on this floor plan is 96 feet. The correct answer is D. Ⓐ Ⓑ Ⓒ Ⓓ

GUIDED PRACTICE for Example 1

1. **WHAT IF?** In Example 1, suppose the scale is 1 inch equals 9 feet. How many feet are represented by 8 inches on this floor plan?

About the Standards

One aspect of Grade 6 Standard NS 1.2 is interpreting ratios. When a scale is written as a ratio, it usually takes the form scale model : actual object.

SCALE MODELS A **scale model** is a model of an object in which the dimensions are in proportion to the actual dimensions of the object. The scale of a scale model is often given as a ratio, with or without units. In order for a scale to be given without units, the dimensions must be expressed in the same units.

Scale using same units	**Scale using different units**
1 ft : 4 ft or 1 : 4	1 in. : 2 ft

The scale 1 : 4 can also be written as $\frac{1}{4}$. A scale that is written as a fraction without units is called a *scale factor.*

EXAMPLE 2 Finding a Dimension on a Scale Model

WHITE HOUSE A scale model of the White House has been displayed at various museums across the country. The scale of the model is 1 : 12. The length of the White House is 168 feet. Find the length of the model.

Scale of model is 1 : 12.

AnimatedMath

For an interactive example of finding scale model dimensions, go to **classzone.com.**

SOLUTION

Write and solve a proportion to find the length x of the model of the White House.

$$\frac{1}{12} = \frac{x}{168}$$ ← Scale model (numerators), ← Full size (denominators)

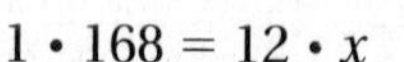

$1 \cdot 168 = 12 \cdot x$ **Use cross products property.**

$14 = x$ **Divide each side by 12.**

The length of the White House is given in feet. Since the scale is given *without* units, the length of the model must also be in feet.

▸ **Answer** The length of the model is 14 feet.

✓ GUIDED PRACTICE for Example 2

2. **WHAT IF?** In Example 2, suppose the height of the facade on the south side of the White House is 60 feet. What is this height on the model?

3. **EIFFEL TOWER** The model of the Eiffel Tower in Tobu World Square, Japan, is 12 meters high. Use the scale of 1 : 25 to estimate the height of the actual Eiffel Tower.

4. **MUSEUM MODELS** A museum of natural history is making a scale model of a carpenter ant. The scale used is 12.5 cm : 1 mm. If the actual length of the ant is 6.4 mm, what is the length of the model?

EXAMPLE 3 Finding a Scale

DINOSAURS A museum is creating a full-size Tyrannosaurus rex from a model. The model is 2.5 feet in length, from the nose to the tail. The resulting dinosaur will be 40 feet in length. What is the model's scale?

SOLUTION

Write a ratio. Then simplify.

Scale model → / **Full size** → $\frac{2.5 \text{ ft}}{40 \text{ ft}} = 2\frac{1}{2} \div 40 = \frac{5}{2} \cdot \frac{1}{40} = \frac{1}{16}$

▸ **Answer** The scale of the model is 1 : 16.

✓ GUIDED PRACTICE for Example 3

5. **WHAT IF?** Suppose the model of the Tyrannosaurus rex in Example 3 is $6\frac{2}{3}$ feet in length. What is the scale of the model?

5.5 EXERCISES

HOMEWORK KEY

◆ = **MULTIPLE CHOICE PRACTICE** Exs. 25, 26, 32, 33, 41–43

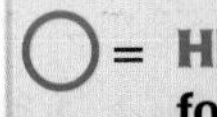

○ = **HINTS AND HOMEWORK HELP** for Exs. 9, 23, 33 at classzone.com

SKILLS • PROBLEM SOLVING • REASONING

1. **VOCABULARY** Copy and complete: A model of an object in which the dimensions are in proportion to the actual dimensions of the object is a(n) _?_.

2. **WRITING** *Explain* what it means if a drawing is "not to scale."

SEE EXAMPLE 1 on p. 281 for Exs. 3–10

MATCHING DISTANCES The scale on a floor plan is 1 in. : 15 ft. Match the distance on the floor plan with the actual distance.

3. 2 in. 4. 3.5 in. 5. 2.2 in. 6. 1.6 in.

A. 33 ft B. 30 ft C. 24 ft D. 52.5 ft

FINDING DISTANCES The scale on a map is 1 in. : 25 mi. Find the actual distance in miles for the given length on the map.

7. 3 in. 8. 10 in. 9. 5.2 in. 10. 8.7 in.

SEE EXAMPLE 2 on p. 282 for Exs. 11–14

FINDING LENGTHS The scale used to build the scale model of an airplane is 1 : 72. Find the wingspan of the model airplane to the nearest tenth of a meter. Check for reasonableness.

11. *Wright Flyer* wingspan: 12.3 m
12. *Spirit of St. Louis* wingspan: 14 m
13. Jumbo jet wingspan: 59.6 m
14. Jumbo jet wingspan: 79.8 m

SEE EXAMPLE 2 on p. 282 for Ex. 15

15. ERROR ANALYSIS The scale used in a scale drawing is 1 in. : 5 ft. The width of the actual object is 15 feet. *Describe* and correct the error made in finding the width of the drawing.

$\frac{1}{5} = \frac{x}{15}$

$1 \cdot 15 = 5 \cdot x$

$x = 3$

The width of the drawing is 3 feet.

SEE EXAMPLE 3 on p. 283 for Exs. 16–26

FINDING THE SCALE Write the ratio as a scale in simplest form.

16. $\frac{2\text{ m}}{16\text{ m}}$ **17.** $\frac{7\text{ cm}}{70\text{ cm}}$ **18.** $\frac{18\text{ mm}}{10\text{ mm}}$ **19.** $\frac{96\text{ ft}}{20\text{ ft}}$

20. $\frac{0.5\text{ in.}}{2\text{ in.}}$ **21.** $\frac{7.5\text{ km}}{5\text{ km}}$ **22.** $\frac{1\frac{4}{5}\text{ yd}}{27\text{ yd}}$ **23.** $\frac{6\frac{2}{5}\text{ in.}}{64\text{ in.}}$

24. ERROR ANALYSIS The length of an item is enlarged from 15.2 millimeters to 152 millimeters. *Describe* and correct the error made in finding the scale of the enlargement to the original.

$\frac{15.2}{152} = 15\frac{1}{5} \div 152$

$= \frac{76}{5} \cdot \frac{1}{152} = \frac{1}{10}$

The scale is 1 : 10.

25. ◆ **MULTIPLE CHOICE** A length of a scale model is 22 inches. The actual length is 33 inches. What is the scale factor?

Ⓐ $\frac{3}{2}$ Ⓑ $\frac{2}{3}$ Ⓒ $\frac{1}{11}$ Ⓓ $\frac{1}{15}$

26. ◆ **MULTIPLE CHOICE** A 24 inch by 30 inch scale drawing is created from an 8 inch by 10 inch photograph. Which of the following scales is *not* correct?

Ⓐ 12 in. : 4 in. Ⓑ 15 in. : 5 in. Ⓒ $\frac{3}{1}$ Ⓓ 2 : 6

27. REASONING A scale of a model is 1 : 0.2. Is the scale model larger or smaller than the actual object? *Explain* your reasoning.

CONNECT SKILLS TO PROBLEM SOLVING Exercises 28–30 will help you prepare for problem solving.

Use the following information: A carpenter makes miniature replicas of Victorian furniture. The scale model of a table that the carpenter made is 3 inches long. The full-size table is 36 inches long.

28. Express the model's scale with units. What is the model's *scale factor*?

29. Suppose the width of the full-size table is 24 inches. Write a proportion you could use to find the width of the model.

30. Suppose the width of the model is 1.5 inches. Write a proportion you could use to find the width of the full-size table.

SEE EXAMPLE 2 on p. 282 for Ex. 31

31. SCULPTURE Each bowling pin in a sculpture is a scale model of an actual bowling pin that is 38 centimeters tall. The model's scale is 1 : 0.05. Find the height of a bowling pin in the sculpture.

California @HomeTutor for problem solving help at classzone.com

SEE EXAMPLE 1
on p. 281
for Ex. 32

32. ◆ **MULTIPLE CHOICE** The distance on the map between Ukiah and Redding is 2 centimeters. How many kilometers are represented by this distance on the map?

Ⓐ 21.75 km　　Ⓑ 43.5 km

Ⓒ 87 km　　Ⓓ 174 km

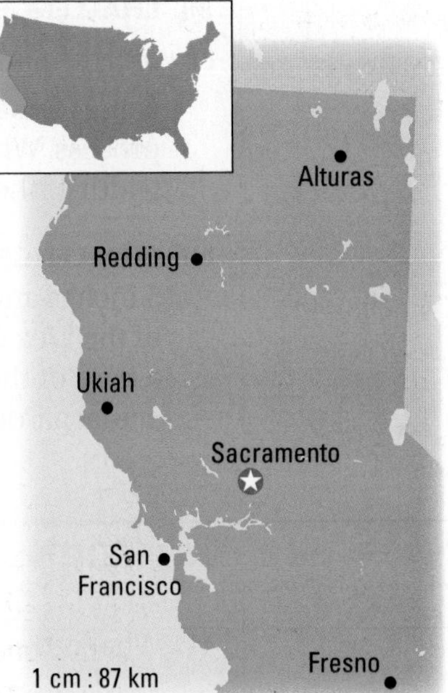

California @HomeTutor for problem solving help at classzone.com

33. ◆ **MULTIPLE CHOICE** You use a scale of 1 in. : 8 ft to make a scale drawing of your classroom. The actual length of your classroom is 36 feet. What should be the length of the classroom in the drawing?

Ⓐ 1 in.　　Ⓑ 4.5 in.

Ⓒ 36 in.　　Ⓓ 288 in.

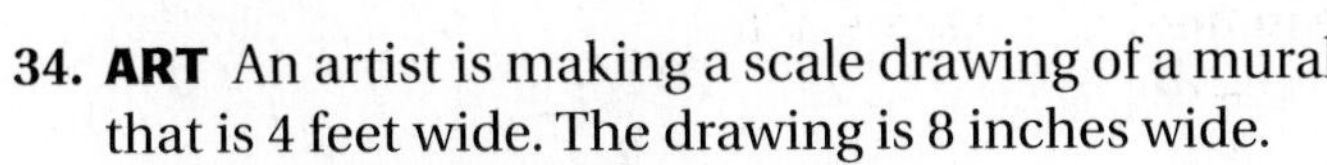

SEE EXAMPLES 2 AND 3
on pp. 282–283
for Ex. 34

34. **ART** An artist is making a scale drawing of a mural that is 4 feet wide. The drawing is 8 inches wide.

    a. What is the scale of the drawing?

    b. The length of the mural is 5 feet. What is the length of the scale drawing?

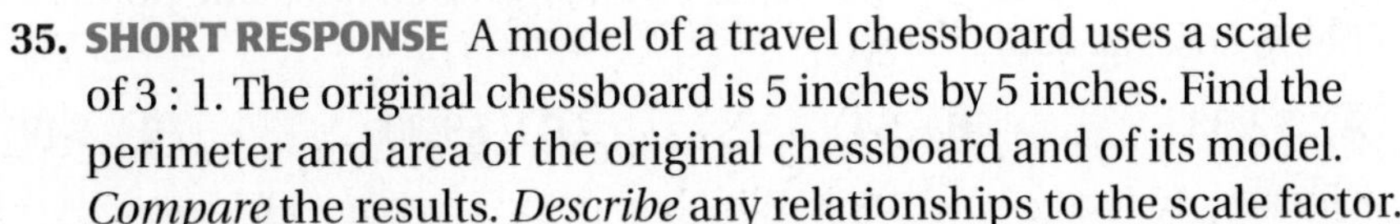

35. **SHORT RESPONSE** A model of a travel chessboard uses a scale of 3 : 1. The original chessboard is 5 inches by 5 inches. Find the perimeter and area of the original chessboard and of its model. *Compare* the results. *Describe* any relationships to the scale factor.

36. **MEASUREMENT** Use a metric ruler to measure the sides of the hexagon. Create a scale drawing of it with a scale of 5 cm : 1 cm.

37. **TIMELINE** The table lists six U.S. Presidents who served late in the twentieth century and the year each took office. Make a timeline showing the length of the term of each President listed. Use the scale 0.5 centimeters : 2 years.

President	Nixon	Ford	Carter	Reagan	G. Bush	Clinton
Year took office	1969	1974	1977	1981	1989	1993

38. **MULTI-STEP PROBLEM** The picture of a maple leaf is on a 5 centimeter by 5 centimeter grid. The scale shown is of the form scale model : actual object.

    a. **Draw at Actual Size** Make a drawing of the leaf at its actual size.

    b. **Draw a Smaller Model** Use your drawing to make a scale drawing using the scale 0.5 cm : 2 cm.

    c. **Compare** *Estimate* the area of the leaf in the picture and in your two drawings. *Compare* the areas.

39. **CHALLENGE** The width of an object is 8 feet. You make a model of the object using a scale factor of $\frac{1}{2}$. Then you make a model of the model using the same scale factor. In total, you make four models by this process. What is the value of x in the scale x feet : 8 feet, where x is the width of the fourth model?

40. **CHALLENGE** A scale drawing of a rectangular garden has a length of 5 inches and a width of 3.5 inches. The scale is 1 : $12x$. Write a ratio of the area of the scale drawing to the area of the actual garden. Write a ratio of the perimeter of the scale drawing to the perimeter of the actual garden. *Compare* each ratio to the scale.

◆ California Standards Spiral Review

NS 2.2 41. What is the value of $\frac{7}{12} \cdot \frac{14}{18}$? *(p. 88)*

Ⓐ $\frac{49}{108}$ Ⓑ $\frac{2}{3}$ Ⓒ $\frac{3}{4}$ Ⓓ $\frac{4}{3}$

NS 2.3 42. What is the value of $-42 - 17$? *(p. 143)*

Ⓐ -59 Ⓑ -25 Ⓒ 25 Ⓓ 59

AF 2.2 43. Jake buys 3.5 pounds of cheese for $14. How much does one pound of cheese cost? *(p. 260)*

Ⓐ $2.33 Ⓑ $4 Ⓒ $9.33 Ⓓ $49

Quiz for Lessons 5.4–5.5

Use cross products to solve the proportion. *(p. 274)*

1. $\frac{a}{15} = \frac{2}{6}$ 2. $\frac{9}{b} = \frac{2}{8}$ 3. $\frac{2}{3} = \frac{7}{y}$ 4. $\frac{10}{8} = \frac{x}{5.6}$

5. **ADVERTISING** In a magazine, the ratio of pages with advertisements to pages without advertisements is 6 : 5. The magazine has 143 pages. How many pages have advertisements? *(p. 274)*

6. **RECIPES** You need 2.5 pounds of ground beef to make tacos for 16 people. How many pounds of ground beef do you need to make tacos for 24 people? *(p. 274)*

7. **MAPS** The scale on a map is 1 cm : 65 km. The distance between two cities on the map is 5.5 centimeters. What is the actual distance? *(p. 281)*

8. **SWIMMING POOL** The scale drawing of a swimming pool has a scale of 1 in. : 2.5 ft. The length of the actual pool is 20 feet. What is the length of the swimming pool in the scale drawing? *(p. 281)*

9. **BASKETBALL** A model of a basketball court has a length of 2.35 feet. The length of an actual basketball court is 94 feet. What is the scale of the model? *(p. 281)*

Multiple Choice Practice for Lessons 5.4–5.5

1. Mr. Lavin is using the scale drawing below to build a playroom for his children. What width in the scale drawing would represent a door 4 feet wide? **NS 1.3**

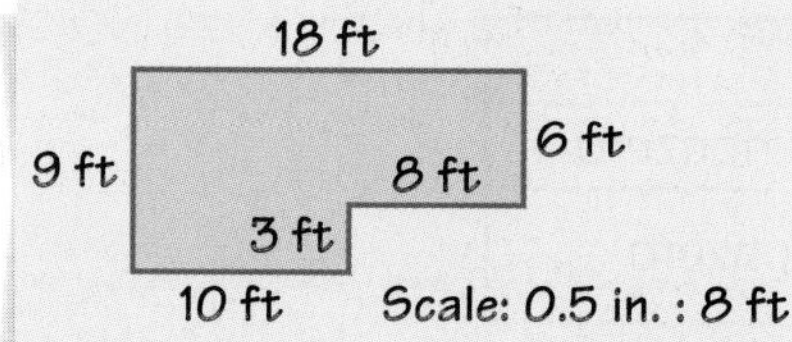

   Ⓐ 0.25 in. Ⓑ 1 in.
   Ⓒ 2 in. Ⓓ 4 in.

2. At a camp, the ratio of campers who want to canoe to campers who do not want to canoe is 7 : 2. The cost of canoe rentals is $5 per person. What other information is needed to find the cost of canoeing for all the canoers? **NS 1.3, MR 1.1**

   Ⓐ How long the canoes will be rented
   Ⓑ The total number of campers
   Ⓒ The number of canoes available
   Ⓓ The cost of snacks

3. What is the value of x in the proportion $\frac{9}{x} = \frac{6}{4}$? **NS 1.3**

   Ⓐ 1.5 Ⓑ 3
   Ⓒ 6 Ⓓ 13.5

4. Johanne recently read 4 books of various lengths. The numbers of pages in each book and the amount of time it took Johanne to read each book are listed below. At this rate, how many hours will it take her to read a 180 page book? **AF 2.0, MR 1.2**

Pages	90	120	180	190	240
Hours	4.5	6	?	9.5	12

   Ⓐ 7 h Ⓑ 8 h
   Ⓒ 8.5 h Ⓓ 9 h

5. Which proportion has a solution of 6? **NS 1.3**

   Ⓐ $\frac{6}{16} = \frac{c}{24}$ Ⓑ $\frac{b}{32} = \frac{27}{48}$
   Ⓒ $\frac{4}{28} = \frac{w}{42}$ Ⓓ $\frac{15}{18} = \frac{5}{2x}$

6. Outside of the Louisville Slugger Museum in Louisville, Kentucky, there is a scale model of Babe Ruth's bat. The model's scale is 1 : 0.0236. If the model is 120 feet tall, how long is the actual bat? **NS 1.3**

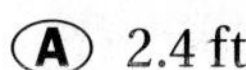

   Ⓐ 2.4 ft
   Ⓑ 2.832 ft
   Ⓒ 5 ft
   Ⓓ 5085 ft

7. The distance from your home to the beach parking lot measures 1.25 inches on the map. How many miles will Jenna need to drive when she leaves your home and goes to the beach? **NS 1.3**

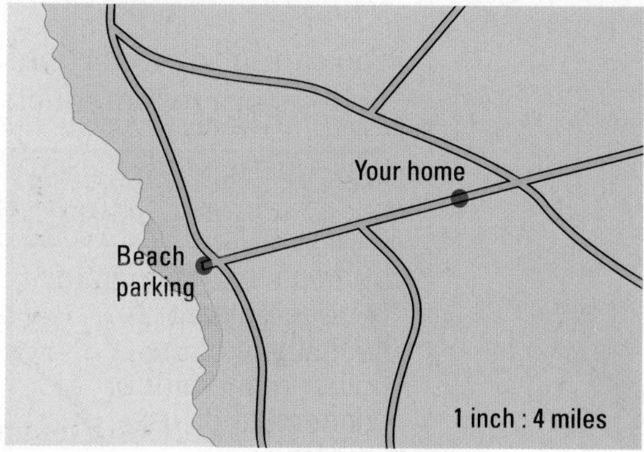

   Ⓐ 3.2 mi
   Ⓑ 4 mi
   Ⓒ 5 mi
   Ⓓ 5.25 mi

5 CHAPTER SUMMARY

Standards
NS 1.2, NS 1.3, AF 2.2, AF 2.3

BIG IDEAS

For Your Notebook

Big Idea 1

Interpreting and Using Ratios

A ratio uses division to compare two numbers. For example, you can compare a baseball player's 32 hits to 77 at bats using a ratio as shown.

Words	*Numbers*	*Algebra*
hits to at bats	32 to 77	a to b, where b is nonzero
$\frac{\text{hits}}{\text{at bats}}$	$\frac{32}{77}$	$\frac{a}{b}$, where b is nonzero
hits : at bats	32 : 77	$a : b$, where b is nonzero

The ratio of hits to at bats is a batting average, which is often written as a decimal rounded to the nearest thousandth, such as 0.416.

Big Idea 2

Solving Rate Problems

A rate, such as average speed, is a ratio of two quantities measured in different units. A unit rate has a denominator of 1 unit.

For example, the average speed of a runner who completes a 200-meter race in 25 seconds is 8 meters per second, as shown below.

$$\frac{200 \text{ m}}{25 \text{ sec}} = \frac{200 \text{ m} \div 25}{25 \text{ sec} \div 25}$$ **Divide numerator and denominator by 25.**

$$= \frac{8 \text{ m}}{1 \text{ sec}}$$ **Simplify.**

Big Idea 3

Using Proportions to Solve Problems

You can solve proportions by using equivalent ratios, by using algebra, or by using cross products.

Solving proportions using equivalent ratios	*Solving proportions using algebra*	*Solving proportions using cross products*
When either numerator or denominator is a multiple of the other numerator or denominator, use mental math.	When the variable is in the numerator, use the multiplication property of equality. This is the same as multiplying by the multiplicative inverse.	Cross products can be used to solve any proportion. They are especially useful when the variable is in the denominator.
$\frac{x}{16} = \frac{15}{48}$ (× 3, × 3) What number times 3 equals 15? $x = 5$	$\frac{y}{21} = \frac{15}{35}$ $21 \cdot \frac{y}{21} = 21 \cdot \frac{15}{35}$ $y = 9$	$\frac{15}{24} = \frac{10}{z}$ $15z = 24 \cdot 10$ $z = 16$

CHAPTER PROBLEM

Standards
NS 1.2, NS 1.3, AF 2.2, AF 2.3

APPLYING THE
BIG IDEAS

Big Idea 1
You interpret and use ratios in **Step 2** and **Ex. 1.**

Big Idea 2
You solve a rate problem in **Ex. 2.**

Big Idea 3
You use proportions in **Step 4.**

PROBLEM How can you use ratios, proportions, and scales to find the dimensions for a scale drawing?

STEP 1 **Choose a location.**

Choose a familiar location that you can measure, such as a classroom, a room in your home, or a recreational area.

U.S. Olympic Training Center

STEP 2 **Choose a scale.**

Choose an appropriate scale, in inches to feet, for a scale drawing of your chosen location. For example, the scale drawing of a tennis court at the U.S. Olympic Training Center in Chula Vista, California, uses a scale of 1 inch to 31 feet. The actual dimensions of the tennis court are 78 feet by 36 feet.

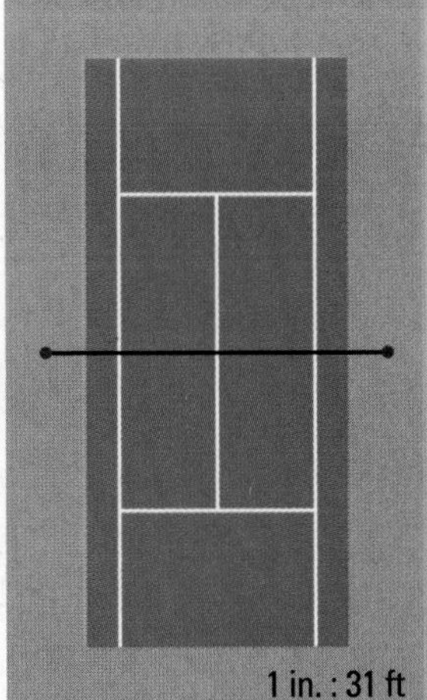

STEP 3 **Measure dimensions.**

Measure the outer dimensions of your location. Also measure key features, such as doors and windows, top surfaces of pieces of furniture, or any special lines and boundaries.

STEP 4 **Write and solve proportions.**

Using the scale you chose in Step 2, write and solve proportions to find all the dimensions you will need to make a scale drawing of your location.

STEP 5 **Make a scale drawing.**

Make a scale drawing of your location using the dimensions you found in Step 4.

Extending the Problem

Use your results from the problem to complete the exercises.

1. Find the perimeter and area of your location and of your scale drawing. Then find the ratio of the perimeters and the ratio of the areas. Compare your ratios to your scale. *Describe* any relationships.

2. You plan to make an improvement to your chosen location. Perhaps you plan to put carpet in your room, plant grass seed on the ground, or paint the floor. Decide on an improvement and do research to find the cost per square foot. For example, it might cost about $.08 per square foot to paint. Then find how much it will cost to cover the entire floor or ground space of your location.

5 CHAPTER REVIEW

California @HomeTutor
classzone.com
- Multi-Language Visual Glossary
- Vocabulary practice

REVIEW KEY VOCABULARY

- ratio, *p. 255*
- equivalent ratios, *p. 255*
- rate, *p.260*
- unit rate, *p. 260*
- proportion, *p. 266*
- cross products, *p. 274*
- scale drawing, *p. 281*
- scale, *p. 281*
- scale model, *p. 282*

VOCABULARY EXERCISES

Copy and complete the statement.

1. The ratio of plays to novels on a bookshelf is 10 to 24. This means that for every 5 plays there are _?_ novels.
2. A ratio of two quantities measured in different units is a(n) _?_.
3. An equation stating that two ratios are equivalent is a(n) _?_.
4. **NOTETAKING SKILLS** Make a *word magnet* like the one on page 254 for *scale*.

REVIEW EXAMPLES AND EXERCISES

5.1 Ratios

pp. 255–259

NS 1.2

EXAMPLE

ANIMAL KENNEL Use the table to find the ratios of pets at a boarding kennel.

	Friday	Saturday
Cats	3	10
Dogs	15	25

a. Cats to dogs on Friday

$\frac{\text{Cats}}{\text{Dogs}} = \frac{3}{15} = \frac{1}{5}$, 1 to 5, or 1 : 5

b. Dogs to total cats and dogs on Saturday

$\frac{\text{Dogs}}{\text{Cats and dogs}} = \frac{25}{35} = \frac{5}{7}$, 5 to 7, or 5 : 7

EXERCISES

SEE EXAMPLES 1, 2, AND 3 on pp. 255–256 for Exs. 5–11

Write the ratio in two other ways, including as a fraction in simplest form.

5. 9 to 81
6. 63 to 7
7. 20 : 35

Copy and complete the statement using <, >, or =.

8. 5 : 10 _?_ 1 : 5
9. 6 : 14 _?_ 6 : 10
10. 1 : 4 _?_ 13 : 52
11. **GARDENING** A dogwood tree has a height of 10 feet and a width of 4 feet. Write the ratio of the height to the width in simplest form.

5.2 Rates

pp. 260–264

AF 2.2
AF 2.3
NS 1.2

EXAMPLE

PENCIL COSTS A stationery store sells mechanical pencils in packages of 2 pencils for $1.98. Find the unit price.

$$\text{unit price} = \frac{\$1.98}{2} = \frac{\$1.98 \div 2}{2 \div 2} = \frac{\$.99}{1}$$ **Divide numerator and denominator by 2.**

EXERCISES

SEE EXAMPLES 1, 2, AND 3 on pp. 260–261 for Exs. 12–18

Find the unit rate.

12. $20 for 4 persons
13. 22 ounces for 4 servings
14. $17.50 for 10 pens
15. **KAYAKING** Ben traveled 560 feet in a kayak in 112 seconds. What was Ben's average speed?

Find the better buy for each pair of foods.

16. 6 ounce can of tuna for $1.25; 9 ounce can of tuna for $1.99
17. 16 ounce bottle of salad dressing for $3.89; 20 ounce bottle of salad dressing for $5.59
18. 5.5 ounce bag of popcorn for $2.49; 9 ounce bag of popcorn for $2.99

5.3 Writing and Solving Proportions

pp. 266–271

NS 1.3
AF 2.3

EXAMPLE

Solve the proportion $\frac{10}{8} = \frac{a}{20}$.

$\frac{10}{8} = \frac{a}{20}$ **Write original proportion.**

$20 \cdot \frac{10}{8} = 20 \cdot \frac{a}{20}$ **Multiply each side by 20.**

$\frac{200}{8} = a$ **Simplify.**

$25 = a$ **Simplify fraction.**

EXERCISES

SEE EXAMPLES 1 AND 2 on pp. 266–267 for Exs. 19–22

Solve the proportion using equivalent ratios or algebra.

19. $\frac{16}{20} = \frac{24}{s}$
20. $\frac{6}{w} = \frac{12}{18}$
21. $\frac{10}{25} = \frac{m}{5}$
22. $\frac{7}{21} = \frac{x}{6}$

5.4 Solving Proportions Using Cross Products

pp. 274–279

NS 1.3
AF 2.2

EXAMPLE

CAR WASH A group of students washes 3 cars in 12 minutes. Write and solve a proportion to find how long it will take to wash 7 cars.

$\frac{3}{12} = \frac{7}{x}$ ← **Cars** ← **Minutes**

$3 \cdot x = 12 \cdot 7$ **Use cross products property.**

$x = 28$ **Divide each side by 10.**

▶ **Answer** The group of students can wash 7 cars in 28 minutes.

EXERCISES

SEE EXAMPLES 1, 2, AND 3 on pp. 274–275 for Exs. 23–27

Solve the proportion using cross products.

23. $\frac{k}{16} = \frac{5}{10}$ **24.** $\frac{y}{12} = \frac{4}{16}$ **25.** $\frac{8}{18} = \frac{6}{n}$ **26.** $\frac{7.5}{b} = \frac{9}{24}$

27. CARNIVALS Ravi spends $18 for 24 tickets to use on rides at a carnival. Each ride requires 3 tickets. How much money do 3 rides cost?

5.5 Scale Drawings and Models

pp. 281–286

NS 1.3

EXAMPLE

SUBMARINES The scale used to make a scale model of a submarine is 1 : 35. The length of the actual submarine is 98 meters. Find the length of the model.

$\frac{1}{35} = \frac{m}{98}$ ← **Scale model** ← **Submarine**

$1 \cdot 98 = 35 \cdot m$ **Use cross products property.**

$2.8 = m$ **Divide each side by 35.**

▶ **Answer** The length of the model is 2.8 meters.

EXERCISES

SEE EXAMPLES 1 AND 3 on pp. 281–283 for Exs. 28–29

28. WHAT IF? A model of a submarine has a length of 6.6 meters. Use the scale in the example above to find the length of the actual submarine.

29. DOLL HOUSE A bed is 78 inches long. A scale model of the bed found in a doll house is 6.5 inches long. What is the scale of the model?

5 CHAPTER TEST

1. **VOCABULARY** Two ratios are __?__ when they have the same value.

2. **VOCABULARY** A(n) __?__ is a diagram of an object in which the dimensions are in proportion to the actual dimensions of the object.

Write the ratio in two other ways, including as a fraction in simplest form.

3. $\frac{168}{28}$ 4. 76 to 19 5. 23 : 184 6. 46 : 1012

Copy and complete the statement using <, >, or =.

7. 9 : 2 _?_ 25 : 2 8. 20 : 8 _?_ 50 : 20 9. 11 : 12 _?_ 96 : 144 10. 440 : 5 _?_ 510 : 6

Find the unit rate.

11. 80 students for 4 teachers
12. $16.68 for 12 juice bottles
13. 24 ounces for 3 people

Solve the proportion. Tell which method you used.

14. $\frac{5}{8} = \frac{75}{a}$ 15. $\frac{8}{b} = \frac{2}{3}$ 16. $\frac{8}{10} = \frac{n}{60}$ 17. $\frac{s}{18} = \frac{21}{54}$

18. $\frac{c}{9} = \frac{4}{16}$ 19. $\frac{12}{5} = \frac{d}{8}$ 20. $\frac{w}{52} = \frac{12}{16}$ 21. $\frac{55}{6} = \frac{11}{t}$

22. $\frac{1.25}{5} = \frac{x}{18}$ 23. $\frac{y}{3} = \frac{24.8}{8}$ 24. $\frac{9}{10} = \frac{3.6}{z}$ 25. $\frac{5}{r} = \frac{6}{8.4}$

26. **AVERAGE SPEED** A car travels 315 miles in 6 hours. Write the average speed of the car as a unit rate in miles per hour.

27. **FLOWERS** Which is the better buy: 6 cut flowers for $5.94 or 9 cut flowers for $8.99?

28. **WOOD STAIN** Three gallons of oil based stain cover about 1050 square feet of a flat surface. Use a table or a proportion to find how many gallons of stain are needed to cover 3150 square feet.

29. **RAFFLE** The student council sold raffle tickets at the winter dance. Each raffle ticket cost $2. Admission to the dance was $5. Wayne spent a total of $27 at the dance. How many raffle tickets did he buy?

FLOOR PLANS In Exercises 30–32, use the following information.

The floor plan of the first floor of a house uses the scale 1 cm : 1.5 m. Find the actual length and width of the room given its length and width on the floor plan.

30. Living room
length: 5 cm
width: 4 cm

31. Kitchen
length: 4 cm
width: 3.5 cm

32. Family room
length: 5.25 cm
width: 4.5 cm

5 ◆ MULTIPLE CHOICE STRATEGIES

STRATEGIES YOU'LL USE:
- **SOLVE DIRECTLY**
- **ELIMINATE CHOICES**

Standards
NS 1.3

If you have trouble solving a multiple choice problem directly, you may be able to use another approach to eliminate incorrect answer choices and obtain the correct answer.

PROBLEM 1

A revolution is one complete turn. When gear A turns 2 revolutions, gear B turns 7 revolutions. How many revolutions does gear B turn when gear A turns 42 revolutions?

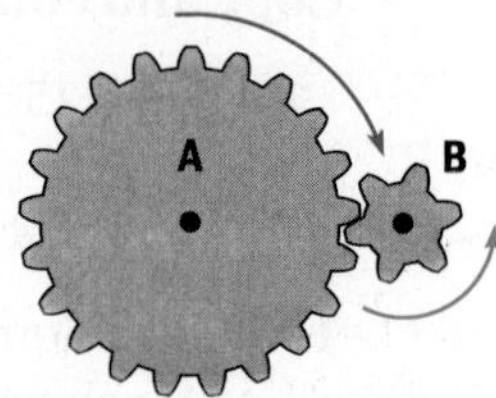

Ⓐ 12 Ⓑ 47 Ⓒ 147 Ⓓ 154

Strategy 1 SOLVE DIRECTLY

First, write a proportion that can be used to solve the problem. Then solve the problem.

STEP 1 **Write** a proportion. The ratio of revolutions of gear A to revolutions of gear B is 2 : 7. Let x be the number of revolutions of gear B when gear A turns 42 revolutions.

$$\frac{2}{7} = \frac{42}{x} \quad \begin{array}{l}\leftarrow \textbf{Gear A} \\ \leftarrow \textbf{Gear B}\end{array}$$

STEP 2 **Solve** the proportion.

$$\frac{2}{7} = \frac{42}{x}$$

$$2x = 7 \cdot 42$$

$$\frac{2x}{2} = \frac{7 \cdot 42}{2}$$

$$x = 147$$

Gear B turns 147 revolutions when gear A turns 42 revolutions.

The correct answer is C. Ⓐ Ⓑ Ⓒ Ⓓ

Strategy 2 ELIMINATE CHOICES

You can form ratios and use number sense to see which ratio is equivalent to $\frac{2}{7}$.

Choice A: $\frac{42}{12} \stackrel{?}{=} \frac{2}{7}$

These ratios are not equal, because $\frac{42}{12} > 1$ and $\frac{2}{7} < 1$.

You can eliminate choice A.

Choice B: $\frac{42}{47} \stackrel{?}{=} \frac{2}{7}$

These ratios are not equal, because $\frac{42}{47} > \frac{1}{2}$ and $\frac{2}{7} < \frac{1}{2}$.

You can eliminate choice B.

Choice C: $\frac{42}{147} \stackrel{?}{=} \frac{2}{7}$

These ratios are equal, because $\frac{42 \div 21}{147 \div 21} = \frac{2}{7}$.

The correct answer is C. Ⓐ Ⓑ Ⓒ Ⓓ

PROBLEM 2

A farmer harvested 64,000 pounds of apples from a 4 acre orchard. Which proportion can be used the find the expected harvest of apples a (in pounds) from a 14 acre orchard?

Ⓐ $\frac{14}{64,000} = \frac{4}{a}$ Ⓑ $\frac{14}{64,000} = \frac{a}{4}$ Ⓒ $\frac{4}{64,000} = \frac{a}{14}$ Ⓓ $\frac{4}{64,000} = \frac{14}{a}$

Strategy 1 SOLVE DIRECTLY

Write two ratios and then use the ratios to write a proportion.

STEP 1 **Write** the ratio of the number of acres to the pounds of apples harvested for the 4 acre orchard.

$\frac{4}{64,000}$ ← **Acres** / ← **Pounds of apples**

STEP 2 **Write** another ratio for the number of acres to the expected harvest a from the 14 acre orchard.

$\frac{14}{a}$ ← **Acres** / ← **Pounds of apples**

STEP 3 **Set** the ratios equal to each other to form a proportion.

$$\frac{4}{64,000} = \frac{14}{a}$$

The correct answer is D. Ⓐ Ⓑ Ⓒ Ⓓ

Strategy 2 ELIMINATE CHOICES

Look at the forms of the ratios in the answer choices. The ratios on the left side of each proportion are all of the form $\frac{\text{Acres}}{\text{Apples harvested}}$.

In choices A and B, the ratio on the left doesn't match this form correctly, because the number of acres in the numerator, 14, doesn't correspond to the amount of apples harvested in the denominator, 64,000 pounds. You can eliminate choices A and B.

In choice C, the ratio on the right has the form $\frac{\text{Apples harvested}}{\text{Acres}}$. You can eliminate choice C.

The correct answer is D. Ⓐ Ⓑ Ⓒ Ⓓ

STRATEGY PRACTICE

Explain why you can eliminate the highlighted answer choice.

1. The ship in the scale drawing is 5.2 centimeters long. How long is the actual ship?

Ⓐ ✗ **17.2 m** Ⓑ 60 m

Ⓒ 62.4 m Ⓓ 1200 m

2. A car travels 190 miles in 5 hours. What is the average speed of the car?

Ⓐ 3.8 mi/h Ⓑ 38 mi/h Ⓒ 40 mi/h Ⓓ ✗ **950 mi/h**

5 ◆ MULTIPLE CHOICE PRACTICE

1. A scale drawing of a stained glass panel is shown below. The actual panel is 56 centimeters wide. How tall is the panel? **NS 1.3**

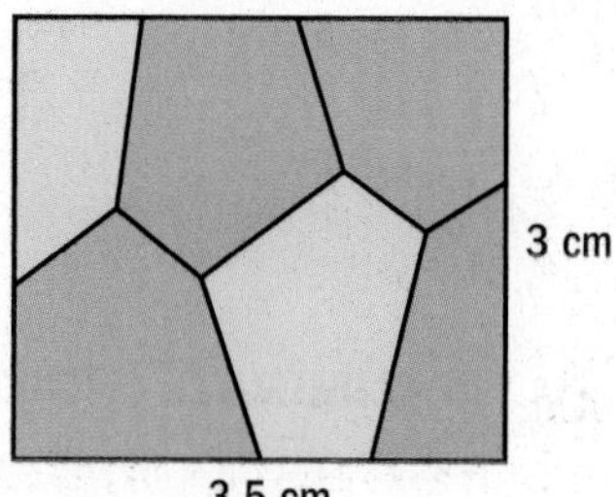

Ⓐ 6 cm

Ⓑ 48 cm

Ⓒ 50 cm

Ⓓ 65 cm

2. A car gets 21 miles per gallon of gasoline. How many gallons of gasoline does the car need to travel 252 miles? **AF 2.2**

Ⓐ 7 gal

Ⓑ 11 gal

Ⓒ 12 gal

Ⓓ 13 gal

3. The table shows the prices of four different boxes of cereal.

Cereal Prices	
Box size (ounces)	***Price***
16.75	$2.98
18	$3.15
19.25	$3.99
27	$4.89

Which box has the lowest price per ounce? **AF 2.2, MR 1.2**

Ⓐ 16.75 oz box

Ⓑ 18 oz box

Ⓒ 19.25 oz box

Ⓓ 27 oz box

4. What is the value of x in the proportion $\frac{x}{35} = \frac{21}{49}$? **NS 1.3**

Ⓐ 2.1

Ⓑ 7

Ⓒ 15

Ⓓ 29.4

5. On the map of an amusement park, the distance from the roller coaster to the bumper cars is 1.25 inches. What is the actual distance? **NS 1.3**

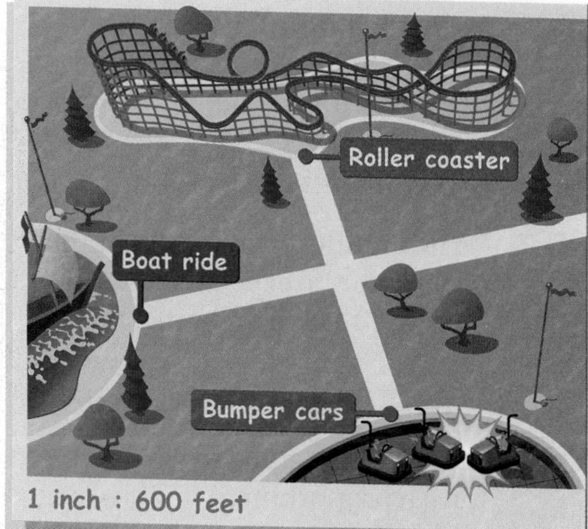

Ⓐ 150 ft

Ⓑ 480 ft

Ⓒ 750 ft

Ⓓ 3000 ft

6. You buy 6 pairs of socks for $4.50. Which proportion can be used to find the cost of 9 pairs of socks? **NS 1.3**

Ⓐ $\frac{6}{4.5} = \frac{x}{9}$

Ⓑ $\frac{4.5}{6} = \frac{x}{9}$

Ⓒ $\frac{9}{6} = \frac{4.5}{x}$

Ⓓ $\frac{4.5}{9} = \frac{6}{x}$

7. An advertisement for furniture includes a scale drawing of a dresser. The dimensions for the dresser in the advertisement are shown below. The actual width of the dresser is 35 inches. What is the actual height of the dresser? **NS 1.3**

Ⓐ 25.455 in.

Ⓑ 35 in.

Ⓒ 48.125 in.

Ⓓ 72.875 in.

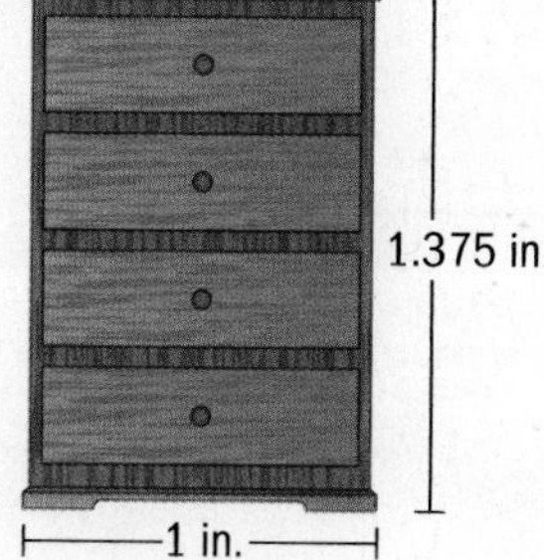

8. A jar contains 15 red marbles, 3 green marbles, 2 white marbles, and 10 blue marbles. What is the ratio of red marbles to all marbles? **NS 1.2**

Ⓐ $\frac{1}{4}$

Ⓑ $\frac{1}{2}$

Ⓒ $\frac{1}{1}$

Ⓓ $\frac{2}{1}$

9. You made \$30 for babysitting for 4 hours, including a \$4 tip. How much money could you expect to make in 6 hours without a tip? **AF 2.2**

Ⓐ \$30

Ⓑ \$36

Ⓒ \$39

Ⓓ \$48

10. A car travels 84 miles in 1 hour 30 minutes. What is the car's average speed? **AF 2.3**

Ⓐ 42 mi/h

Ⓑ 56 mi/h

Ⓒ 65 mi/h

Ⓓ 84 mi/h

11. There are 180 calories in a 30 gram serving of walnuts. How many calories are there in a 120 gram serving of walnuts? **AF 2.2**

Ⓐ 20 calories

Ⓑ 30 calories

Ⓒ 360 calories

Ⓓ 720 calories

12. The ratio of a baseball player's hits to at bats, or batting average, is 56 to 232. Which ratio is *not* equivalent to this? **NS 1.2**

Ⓐ 7 to 36

Ⓑ 7 to 29

Ⓒ 28 : 116

Ⓓ $\frac{14}{58}$

13. The table shows the wins and losses for teams in the NBA during the 2004–2005 season. Which team has a ratio of wins to games played closest to 0.5? **NS 1.2, MR 1.3**

Team	*Wins*	*Losses*
Dallas Mavericks	58	24
Detroit Pistons	54	28
Washington Wizards	45	37
L.A. Lakers	34	48

Ⓐ Mavericks

Ⓑ Pistons

Ⓒ Wizards

Ⓓ Lakers

14. James can read 25 pages in 35 minutes. At that rate, how long will it take for James to read 70 pages? **AF 2.3**

Ⓐ 50 min

Ⓑ 80 min

Ⓒ 85 min

Ⓓ 98 min

6 Percents

Before

In previous chapters, you learned the following skills, which you'll use in Chapter 6:

- Writing fractions as decimals
- Writing decimals as fractions
- Solving proportions

Now

In Chapter 6 you'll study these

Big Ideas:

1. Writing equivalent fractions, decimals, and percents
2. Calculating with percents
3. Solving problems involving percents

Why?

So you can solve real-world problems about . . .

- Racing, p. 310
- Orangutans, p. 311
- Volcanoes, p. 311
- Movie sequels, p. 316
- Basketball, p. 322
- Sales tax, p. 328

Get-Ready Games

NUMBER CHALLENGE

California Standards

Review comparing fractions and decimals. ***Gr. 6 NS 1.1***

Prepare for calculating percentages. ***Gr. 6 NS 1.4***

Materials

- One deck of *Number Challenge* cards

How to Play Play in pairs. Deal half of the cards to each player. Place your cards face down in a pile in front of you. On each turn, both players should follow the steps on the next page.

California Standards

- **Gr. 6 NS 1.4** Calculate given percentages of quantities and solve problems involving discounts at sales, interest earned, and tips. *(Lessons 6.2, 6.3, 6.4, 6.5, 6.6)*
- **Gr. 5 NS 1.2** Interpret percents as a part of a hundred; find decimal and percent equivalents for common fractions and explain why they represent the same value; compute a given percent of a whole number. *(Lesson 6.1)*

1 **Flip** over the top card in your pile. The player whose card has the greater number collects both cards and adds them to the bottom of his or her pile.

2 **Challenge** your opponent to a rematch if the numbers flipped are equal. Place two cards face down. Then repeat Step 1. The player who wins this round collects all of the cards played.

How To Win Collect all of the cards. Or be the player to have the greater number of cards after all of the cards have been played.

Games Wrap-Up

Draw Conclusions

Complete these exercises after playing the game.

1. **WRITING** Which six cards have the greatest numbers? If you have all of these cards, can you lose the game? *Explain* your reasoning.
2. **REASONING** Suppose you turn over the card with the number 0.8. Is your opponent likely to have a higher number or a lower number? *Explain* your reasoning.

6 Getting Ready

Prerequisite Skills

California @HomeTutor
Prerequisite skills practice at classzone.com

REVIEW VOCABULARY

- **ratio,** *p. 255*
- **proportion,** *p. 266*
- **decimal,** *p. 672*

VOCABULARY CHECK

Copy and complete using a review term from the list at the left.

1. A(n) __?__ is an equation that states that two ratios are equivalent.
2. A(n) __?__ uses division to compare two numbers.

SKILL CHECK

Write the fraction as a decimal. *(p. 40)*

3. $\frac{1}{2}$ 4. $\frac{3}{4}$ 5. $\frac{4}{5}$ 6. $\frac{7}{10}$

Write the decimal as a fraction in simplest form. *(p. 40)*

7. 0.6 8. 0.1 9. 0.95 10. 0.45

Find the product or quotient. *(p. 107)*

11. 82×0.64 12. 0.78×105 13. 0.5×120 14. 0.8×76

Use the cross products property to solve the proportion. *(p. 274)*

15. $\frac{11}{4} = \frac{33}{n}$ 16. $\frac{a}{28} = \frac{6}{7}$ 17. $\frac{25}{5} = \frac{b}{6}$ 18. $\frac{3}{x} = \frac{5}{45}$

Notetaking Skills

NOW YOU TRY

Write the formula for the area of a rectangle in a *formula triangle.*

Focus on Graphic Organizers

Use a *formula triangle* to organize the variables and operations of a new formula, such as $d = rt$.

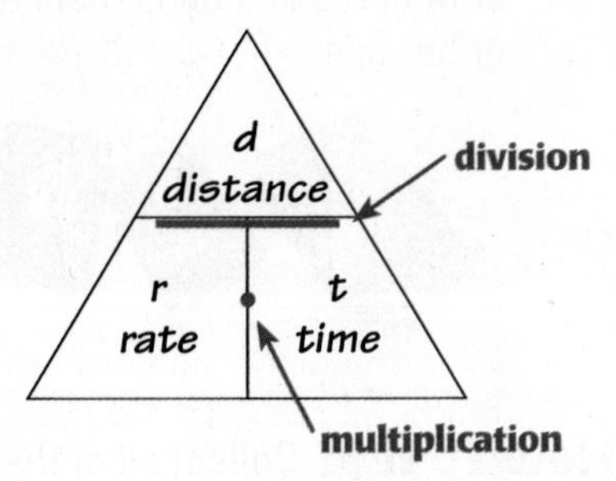

Cover the variable that you want to find. Use the remaining variables and the operation between them to find the unknown variable.

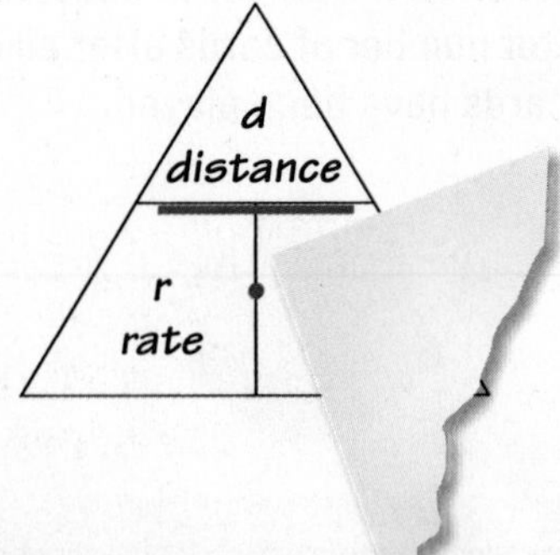

6.1 Percents and Fractions

Math and SPORTS
Example 4, p. 302

Standards Gr. 5 NS 1.2 **Interpret percents as part of a hundred; find** decimal and **percent equivalents for common fractions and explain why they represent the same value; compute a given percent of a whole number.**

Connect ***Before*** you multiplied fractions and whole numbers. ***Now*** you will multiply to find a percent of a number in preparation for Grade 6 Standard NS 1.4.

KEY VOCABULARY
- **percent**

The word *percent* means "per hundred." A **percent** is a ratio whose denominator is 100. The symbol for percent is %. Percents are useful for comparing ratios with different denominators. For example, sales tax rates are easier to compare as percents than as fractions.

VOCABULARY
You can remember that percent means "per hundred" by thinking of how many cents are in a dollar.

KEY CONCEPT — *For Your Notebook*

Understanding Percent

The model at the right has 16 out of 100 squares shaded. You can say that 16 percent of the squares are shaded.

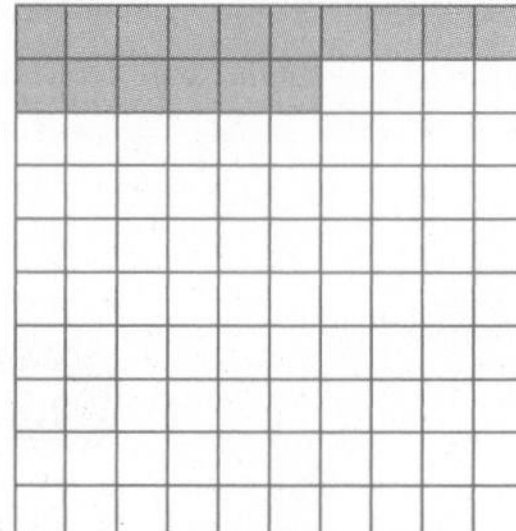

Numbers You can write 16 percent as $\frac{16}{100}$ or as 16%.

Algebra You can write p percent as $\frac{p}{100}$ or as p%.

EXAMPLE 1 Writing Percents as Fractions

Write the percent as a fraction.

a. $37\% = \frac{37}{100}$

b. $50\% = \frac{50}{100} = \frac{1}{2}$

EXAMPLE 2 Writing Fractions as Percents

Rewrite the fraction with a denominator of 100 to write a fraction as a percent.

a. $\frac{4}{5} = \frac{4 \times 20}{5 \times 20} = \frac{80}{100} = 80\%$

b. $\frac{3}{4} = \frac{3 \times 25}{4 \times 25} = \frac{75}{100} = 75\%$

✓ GUIDED PRACTICE for Examples 1 and 2

Write the percent as a fraction or the fraction as a percent. Draw a model of the percent.

1. 24%

2. 55%

3. $\frac{7}{10}$

4. $\frac{1}{50}$

Below are some common percents that you should remember.

Common Percents					
$10\% = \frac{1}{10}$	$20\% = \frac{1}{5}$	$25\% = \frac{1}{4}$	$30\% = \frac{3}{10}$	$40\% = \frac{2}{5}$	$50\% = \frac{1}{2}$
$60\% = \frac{3}{5}$	$70\% = \frac{7}{10}$	$75\% = \frac{3}{4}$	$80\% = \frac{4}{5}$	$90\% = \frac{9}{10}$	$100\% = 1$

PERCENT OF A NUMBER You can find a percent of a number the way you found a fraction of a number on page 88 of Lesson 2.4. You write the percent as a fraction and then multiply.

EXAMPLE 3 Finding a Percent of a Number

Find 60% of 75.

$60\% \text{ of } 75 = \frac{3}{5} \cdot 75$ **Write percent as a fraction and multiply.**

$= \frac{3 \cdot \overset{15}{\cancel{75}}}{\underset{1}{\cancel{5}} \cdot 1}$ **Use rule for multiplying fractions. Divide out common factor.**

$= 45$ **Multiply.**

EXAMPLE 4 Using Percents

TENNIS In March of 2005, 14 of the top 100 women's tennis players were from the United States. What percent of the top 100 women's tennis players were *not* from the United States?

Animated Math

For an interactive example of using percents go to **classzone.com.**

SOLUTION

You know that $\frac{14}{100} = 14\%$ of the players were from the United States. To find the percent of tennis players who were *not* from the United States, use the fact that 100% represents the entire group of players.

$$100\% - 14\% = 86\%$$

▶ **Answer** In March of 2005, 86% of the top 100 women's tennis players were *not* from the United States.

✓ GUIDED PRACTICE for Examples 3 and 4

5. Find 70% of 900.

6. Find 25% of 200.

7. Find 80% of 250.

8. **WHAT IF?** Suppose 12 of the top 100 men's tennis players are from the Unites States. What percent of the top 100 men's tennis players are *not* from the United States?

6.1 EXERCISES

HOMEWORK KEY
◆ = **MULTIPLE CHOICE PRACTICE** Exs. 43, 62, 67–69
○ = **HINTS AND HOMEWORK HELP** for Exs. 31, 35, 63 at classzone.com

SKILLS • PROBLEM SOLVING • REASONING

1. **VOCABULARY** What does *percent* mean?

2. **WRITING** What does 100% of a set represent? For example, what part of your class is 100% of it? *Explain.*

SEE EXAMPLE 1 on p. 301 for Exs. 3–17, 33

REWRITING PERCENTS Write the percent as a fraction in simplest form.

3. 11% 4. 23% 5. 82% 6. 20% 7. 8%
8. 67% 9. 34% 10. 92% 11. 14% 12. 25%
13. 22% 14. 42% 15. 36% 16. 13% 17. 32%

SEE EXAMPLE 2 on p. 301 for Exs. 18–32, 34

REWRITING FRACTIONS Write the fraction as a percent.

18. $\frac{3}{10}$ 19. $\frac{13}{25}$ 20. $\frac{77}{100}$ 21. $\frac{3}{5}$ 22. $\frac{3}{20}$
23. $\frac{11}{25}$ 24. $\frac{13}{50}$ 25. $\frac{14}{25}$ 26. $\frac{1}{10}$ 27. $\frac{7}{20}$
28. $\frac{23}{50}$ 29. $\frac{19}{20}$ 30. $\frac{7}{10}$ (31.) $\frac{36}{200}$ 32. $\frac{60}{300}$

ERROR ANALYSIS ***Describe*** **and correct the error made below.**

33. ✗ $80\% = \frac{8}{100} = \frac{2}{25}$

34. ✗ $\frac{23}{25} = \frac{92}{100} = 0.92\%$

SEE EXAMPLE 3 on p. 302 for Exs. 35–43

FINDING PERCENTS Find the percent of the number.

(35.) 80% of 55 36. 30% of 90 37. 50% of 250 38. 60% of 85
39. 20% of 75 40. 50% of 32 41. 45% of 180 42. 90% of 200

43. ◆ **MULTIPLE CHOICE** What is 40% of 120?

Ⓐ 3 Ⓑ 48 Ⓒ 300 Ⓓ 4800

MENTAL MATH Use mental math to find the percent of the number.

44. 10% of 60 45. 25% of 40 46. 20% of 80 47. 75% of 36
48. 50% of 68 49. 30% of 200 50. 40% of 20 51. 60% of 90

ORDERING RATIOS Order the ratios from least to greatest.

52. 6 : 25, 23%, $\frac{1}{4}$ 53. 81%, $\frac{41}{50}$, 4 : 5 54. 73%, $\frac{7}{10}$, 18 : 25
55. $\frac{9}{10}$, 23 : 25, 89% 56. $\frac{13}{20}$, 66%, 16 : 25 57. 3 : 20, $\frac{7}{50}$, 12%

CONNECT SKILLS TO PROBLEM SOLVING **Exercises 58–60 will help you prepare for problem solving.**

Use the following question: On a street, 18 out of 20 houses have attached garages. What percent of houses have attached garages?

58. Write 18 out of 20 as a fraction.

59. Write the fraction using a denominator of 100.

60. Write the fraction as a percent.

SEE EXAMPLE 4 on p. 302 for Ex. 61

61. RECYCLING Eleven states refund money for the return of bottles. What percent of the 50 states do *not* refund money for returning bottles?

California @HomeTutor for problem solving help at classzone.com

62. ◆ **MULTIPLE CHOICE** A bake sale for a school trip raised \$300. If 20% of the money was for bake sale expenses, how much went toward the trip?

(A) \$20 (B) \$60 (C) \$240 (D) \$280

California @HomeTutor for problem solving help at classzone.com

63. SHORT RESPONSE The sales tax rate in New Mexico is $\frac{1}{20}$. The sales tax rate in Nevada is $\frac{13}{200}$. Write each of these sales tax rates as a percent. Which state has the greater sales tax rate? *Explain.*

64. TRANSPORTATION A recent survey found that 88% of people drive to work, 2% take the subway, and 3% take the bus. Write these percents as fractions. What percent of people surveyed use a different form of transportation to get to work?

2% of people take the subway to work.

65. CHALLENGE Is 80% of 80% of 125 the same as 64% of 125? *Justify* your reasoning.

66. CHALLENGE Aaron received 320 points out of a possible 400 in his history class. What percent of the possible points did Aaron receive? How many more points did he need to receive a 93% in history?

◆ CALIFORNIA STANDARDS SPIRAL REVIEW

NS 1.3 **67.** Solve the proportion $\frac{4}{12} = \frac{x}{15}$ for x. ***(p. 266)***

(A) 3.2 (B) 5 (C) 45 (D) 60

AF 2.2 **68.** You spend \$4.80 on 12 cans of juice. What is the unit rate? ***(p. 260)***

(A) $\frac{\$.40}{1 \text{ can}}$ (B) $\frac{\$.52}{1 \text{ can}}$ (C) $\frac{\$2.50}{1 \text{ can}}$ (D) $\frac{\$4.80}{1 \text{ can}}$

NS 1.3 **69.** The actual length of a parking lot is 1260 inches. What is the length of the parking lot in a scale drawing using a scale of 1 in. : 144 in.? ***(p. 281)***

(A) 8.75 in. (B) 11.67 in. (C) 144 in. (D) 1260 in.

6.2 Using Percent Bar Models

MATERIALS • paper and pencil

Standards

NS 1.4 Calculate given percentages of quantities and solve problems involving discounts at sales, interest earned, and tips.

QUESTION How can you use a percent bar model to find a percent?

You can use a percent bar model to write a part-to-whole ratio, such as 4 out of 9 students, as a percent.

EXPLORE What percent of 9 is 4?

STEP 1 **Draw** a percent bar model and label it as shown.

Label the left side of the bar from 0 to the whole amount, 9. Then shade the bar to the part of the whole, 4.

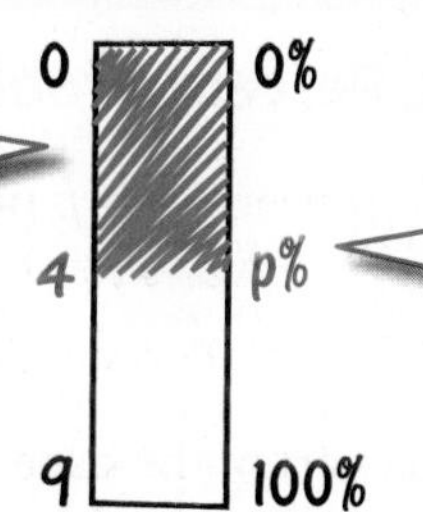

Label the right side of the bar from 0% to 100%. Use p% to represent the unknown percent.

STEP 2 **Use** the percent bar model to write and solve a proportion.

The arrangement of the numbers in the percent bar model tells you how to set up the proportion.

$\frac{4}{9} = \frac{p}{100}$ **Write proportion.**

$100 \cdot \frac{4}{9} = 100 \cdot \frac{p}{100}$ **Multiply each side by 100.**

$\frac{400}{9}$, or $44\frac{4}{9} = p$ **Simplify.**

▶ **Answer** The number 4 is $44\frac{4}{9}$% of 9.

DRAW CONCLUSIONS Use your observations to complete these exercises.

Use a percent bar model to find the percent.

1. What percent of 48 is 6?
2. What percent of 135 is 90?
3. **REASONING** *Describe* how to use a percent bar model to find what percent one number is of another.
4. **REASONING** Use a percent bar model to find what number is 72% of 200. *Describe* how to use a percent bar model to find a percent of any number.

6.2 Percents and Proportions

Standards **NS 1.4 Calculate given percentages of quantities** and solve problems involving discounts at sales, interest earned, and tips.

Connect ***Before*** you used a fraction to find a percent of a number. ***Now*** you will use proportions to solve percent problems.

Math and **SPORTS**
Example 2, p. 307

KEY VOCABULARY
- **proportion,** *p. 266*
- **percent,** *p. 301*

The activity on page 305 suggests how you can use a percent bar model to help you set up a proportion. This proportion relates a percent ratio to a *part-to-whole* or *part-to-base ratio.* You can solve this proportion to find an unknown *percent, part,* or *base.*

KEY CONCEPT *For Your Notebook*

Solving Percent Problems

You can represent "a is p percent of b" with the proportion

$$\frac{a}{b} = \frac{p}{100}$$

where a is part of the base b and p%, or $\frac{p}{100}$, is the percent.

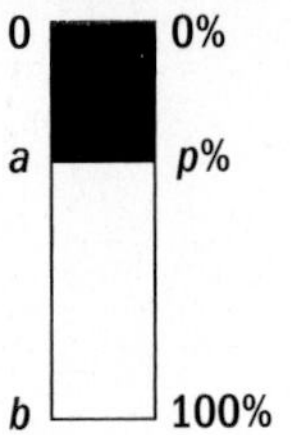

EXAMPLE 1 Finding a Percent

READING
In a percent problem, the word that follows "of" is usually the base b. In Example 1, "of 3" means that the base is 3.

What percent of 3 is 1?

$\frac{a}{b} = \frac{p}{100}$ **Write proportion.**

$\frac{1}{3} = \frac{p}{100}$ **Substitute 1 for a and 3 for b.**

$100 \cdot \frac{1}{3} = 100 \cdot \frac{p}{100}$ **Multiply each side by 100.**

$33\frac{1}{3} = p$ **Simplify.**

▶ **Answer** 1 is $33\frac{1}{3}$% of 3.

✓ GUIDED PRACTICE for Example 1

Use a proportion to answer the question.

1. What percent of 40 is 16?
2. What percent of 400 is 52?
3. **SANDALS** In a classroom of 25 students, 16 students are wearing sandals. What percent of the students are wearing sandals?

Below are some other common percents that you should learn. By using a proportion, you can write *any* fraction as a percent.

Common Percents					
$12\frac{1}{2}\% = \frac{1}{8}$	$33\frac{1}{3}\% = \frac{1}{3}$	$37\frac{1}{2}\% = \frac{3}{8}$	$62\frac{1}{2}\% = \frac{5}{8}$	$66\frac{2}{3}\% = \frac{2}{3}$	$87\frac{1}{2}\% = \frac{7}{8}$

PERCENT OF A NUMBER In Lesson 6.1, you found a common percent of a number using a fraction. Now you can use a proportion to find any percent of a number.

EXAMPLE 2 Finding a Part of a Base

SURFING In a survey, 525 teenagers were asked to name the water sport that they would most like to try. Of the teenagers surveyed, 20% said "surfing." How many teenagers said "surfing?"

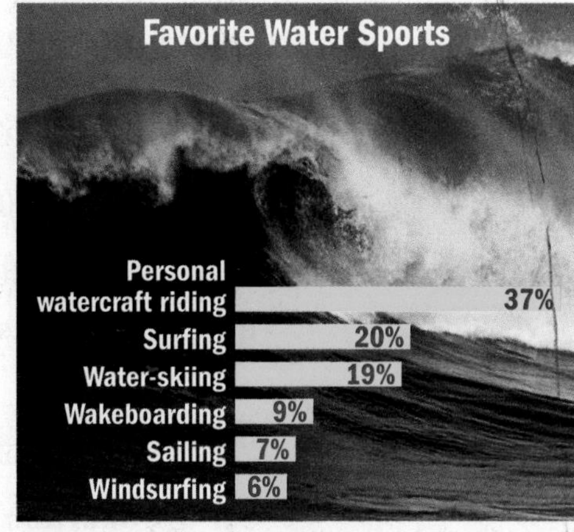

SOLUTION

To find the number of teenagers who said "surfing," use a proportion.

$\frac{a}{b} = \frac{p}{100}$ **Write proportion.**

$\frac{a}{525} = \frac{20}{100}$ **Substitute 525 for *b* and 20 for *p*.**

$525 \cdot \frac{a}{525} = 525 \cdot \frac{20}{100}$ **Multiply each side by 525.**

$a = \frac{\overset{105}{\cancel{525}} \cdot \overset{1}{\cancel{20}}}{\underset{1}{\cancel{\underset{\cancel{20}}{100}}}}$ **Use rule for multiplying fractions. Divide out common factors.**

$a = 105$ **Multiply.**

▸ **Answer** In the survey, 105 out of 525 teenagers said "surfing."

CHECK 20% of 525 is about $\frac{1}{5}$ of 500, or about 100, so 105 is reasonable.

About the Standards

In Example 2, you can use estimation to check the reasonableness of calculations, as part of Standard MR 2.1.

✓ GUIDED PRACTICE for Example 2

Use a proportion to answer the question.

4. What number is 76% of 25?

5. What number is 5% of 400?

6. What number is 12% of 50?

7. What number is 37% of 200?

FINDING A BASE When you are asked to find the base in a percent problem, you solve for b in the proportion $\frac{a}{b} = \frac{p}{100}$. In this case, you may want to use the cross products property, as shown in Example 3.

EXAMPLE 3 Finding a Base

42 is 30% of what number?

$\frac{a}{b} = \frac{p}{100}$ Write proportion.

$\frac{42}{b} = \frac{30}{100}$ Substitute 42 for a and 30 for p.

$42 \cdot 100 = b \cdot 30$ Cross products property

$\frac{42 \cdot 100}{30} = \frac{b \cdot 30}{30}$ Divide each side by 30.

$140 = b$ Simplify.

▶ **Answer** 42 is 30% of 140.

CHECK 30% of 140 is about $\frac{1}{3}$ of 150, which is 50. Since 50 is close to 42, the answer is reasonable.

✓ GUIDED PRACTICE for Example 3

Use a proportion to answer the question.

8. 14 is 56% of what number?

9. 9 is 45% of what number?

10. 16 is 17% of what number?

11. 24 is 96% of what number?

6.2 EXERCISES

HOMEWORK KEY

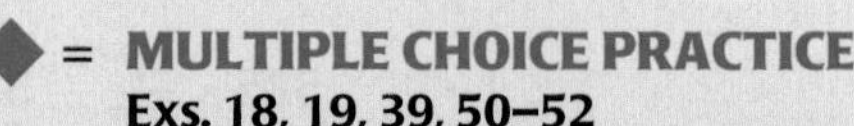
◆ = **MULTIPLE CHOICE PRACTICE** Exs. 18, 19, 39, 50–52

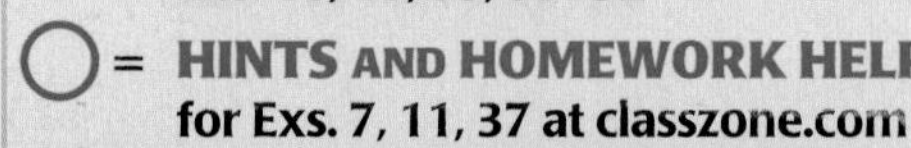
○ = **HINTS AND HOMEWORK HELP** for Exs. 7, 11, 37 at classzone.com

SKILLS • PROBLEM SOLVING • REASONING

1. VOCABULARY Write 72% as a fraction.

2. WRITING *Describe* how you can identify the base in a percent problem. Include three examples.

SEE EXAMPLES 1, 2, AND 3 on pp. 306–308 for Exs. 3–5

MATCHING **Match the question with the correct proportion.**

3. 60 is 25% of what number? **A.** $\frac{a}{60} = \frac{25}{100}$

4. What percent of 60 is 25? **B.** $\frac{25}{60} = \frac{p}{100}$

5. What is 25% of 60? **C.** $\frac{60}{b} = \frac{25}{100}$

SEE EXAMPLES 1, 2, AND 3 on pp. 306–308 for Exs. 6–19

USING PROPORTIONS Use a proportion to answer the question. Check your answer for reasonableness.

6. What percent of 30 is 3?
7. What percent of 50 is 47?
8. 51 is 17% of what number?
9. 16 is 80% of what number?
10. What number is 14% of 350?
11. 12 is 8% of what number?
12. 18 is 45% of what number?
13. What percent of 20 is 6?
14. What number is $12\frac{1}{2}$% of 64?
15. What number is $66\frac{2}{3}$% of 81?

at classzone.com

ERROR ANALYSIS ***Describe*** **and correct the error made.**

16. What number is 30% of 62?

$$\frac{62}{b} = \frac{30}{100}$$

$$62 \cdot 100 = b \cdot 30$$

$$\frac{62 \cdot 100}{30} = \frac{b \cdot 30}{30}$$

$$206\frac{2}{3} = b$$

17. 18 is 24% of what number?

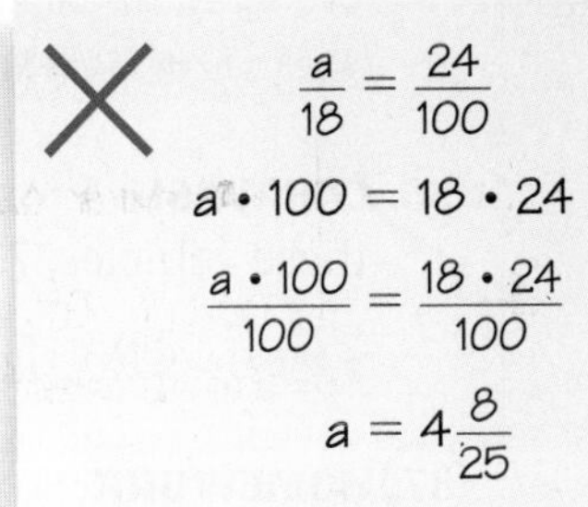

$$\frac{a}{18} = \frac{24}{100}$$

$$a \cdot 100 = 18 \cdot 24$$

$$\frac{a \cdot 100}{100} = \frac{18 \cdot 24}{100}$$

$$a = 4\frac{8}{25}$$

18. ◆ **MULTIPLE CHOICE** What number is 75% of 44?

Ⓐ $3\frac{3}{10}$ Ⓑ $17\frac{31}{44}$ Ⓒ 33 Ⓓ $58\frac{2}{3}$

19. ◆ **MULTIPLE CHOICE** What percent of 155 is 62?

Ⓐ $2\frac{1}{2}$% Ⓑ 4% Ⓒ 25% Ⓓ 40%

INTERPRETING MODELS Write the fraction represented by the model as a percent. Round your answer to the nearest whole percent.

20. 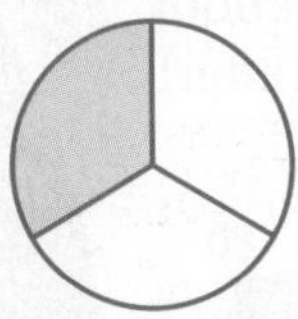

21. 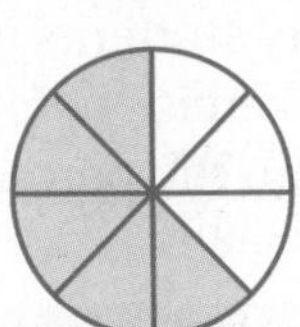

22. 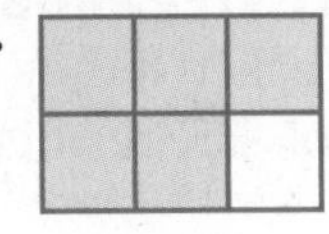

23. 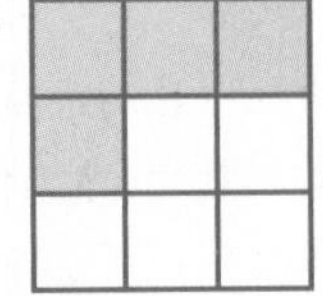

ESTIMATION Estimate the answer using common percents.

24. What percent of 256 is 52?
25. 88 is what percent of 359?
26. 25 is 64% of what number?
27. What is 35% of 313?
28. What is 73% of 195?
29. What is 39% of 78?

30. **MENTAL MATH** If 1% of a number is 6, what is the number?

31. **REASONING** If 5% of a number is y, then what is 100% of the number? *Explain* your reasoning.

CONNECT SKILLS TO PROBLEM SOLVING **Exercises 32–34 will help you prepare for problem solving.**

Use the following question: You know 25% of the students in your sixth grade class will audition for the school play. There are 72 sixth graders in your school. How many students will audition for the play?

32. Which numbers in the situation above represent the base and the part of the base?

33. Write a proportion to determine how many sixth graders will audition for the school play.

34. Solve the proportion you wrote in Exercise 33.

SEE EXAMPLES 1, 2, AND 3 on pp. 306–308 for Exs. 35–39

35. SURVEYS In a survey, 30 people said that turkey is their favorite meat. This was 24% of the total people surveyed. How many people were surveyed?

California @HomeTutor for problem solving help at classzone.com

36. CAR WASH A total of 148 vehicles were washed at a car wash today. Of these vehicles, 75% were cars. How many cars were washed today?

California @HomeTutor for problem solving help at classzone.com

37. HOMEWORK So far you have completed 80% of the problems for your math homework. Your assignment has 45 problems. How many problems do you have left to do?

38. RACING The first lap of an auto race is 2500 meters. This is 10% of the total race distance. What is the total race distance?

39. ◆ **MULTIPLE CHOICE** A business made a \$5650 profit in May. In June, the business made about 92% of the profit for May. About how much was the profit for June?

Ⓐ \$1628 Ⓑ \$5198 Ⓒ \$5558 Ⓓ \$6141

40. MULTI-STEP PROBLEM Eighty students at a middle school were asked if they prefer to exercise before school or after school. The results are given in the percent bar model.

a. Interpret the Diagram How many students surveyed prefer to exercise after school?

b. Write a Proportion Solve a proportion to find the percent of students that prefer to exercise after school.

c. Make a Prediction The school enrolls a total of 400 students. Predict how many of these students would prefer to exercise after school. *Explain.*

41. **ORANGUTANS** Borneo and Sumatra were home to about 35,900 orangutans in 1997. By 1998, the population had fallen about 43%. About how many orangutans were left in Borneo and Sumatra in 1998?

Orangutans in 1997: 35,900

42. **RAKING LEAVES** You rake leaves to earn extra money, charging $25 per lawn. On Saturday, you rake 6 lawns. On Sunday you rake 2 lawns. You want to save 60% of your earnings and spend the rest. How much money do you spend? How much money do you save?

43. **VOLCANOES** The 65 active volcanoes in the United States are about $4\frac{1}{3}\%$ of all volcanoes on Earth. Estimate the number of volcanoes on earth.

44. **REASONING** The table shows the amounts of time your friend spends doing different activities. Your friend claims that this leaves about 10% of each year, or about 36 days, to go to school. *Describe* the error in this reasoning.

Activity	*Amount per year*
Sleeping	35%
Eating	10%
Summer vacation	25%
Weekends	15%
Grooming	5%

xy **CHALLENGE Use a proportion to answer the question in terms of x.**

45. What number is 25% of $8x$?

46. $25x$ is 10% of what number?

47. 5% of what number is x?

48. What percent of $40x$ is $15x$?

49. **CHALLENGE** You took a science test made up of 30 multiple choice questions and 15 true-or-false questions. Each question was worth the same number of points. You answered 12 true-or-false questions correctly, and you answered 90% of the multiple choice questions correctly. What percent of the entire test did you answer correctly?

◆ CALIFORNIA STANDARDS SPIRAL REVIEW

AF 3.1 50. A rectangle has width w. Its length is 8 times its width. Which expression can you use to find the area of the rectangle? *(p. 212)*

Ⓐ $8w$ Ⓑ $18w$ Ⓒ $8w^2$ Ⓓ $w^2 + 8w$

AF 1.1 51. What is the value of y in the equation $3.25y = 78$? *(p. 234)*

Ⓐ 24 Ⓑ 45.5 Ⓒ 104 Ⓓ 253.5

AF 2.3 52. A scooter travels 2.4 miles in 18 minutes. What is the average speed of the scooter in miles per hour? *(p. 260)*

Ⓐ 0.13 mi/h Ⓑ 7.5 mi/h Ⓒ 8 mi/h Ⓓ 13.33 mi/h

6.3 Percents and Decimals

Standards **NS 1.4** **Calculate given percentages of quantities** and solve problems involving discounts at sales, interest earned, and tips.

Connect ***Before*** you solved percent problems involving fractions. ***Now*** you will solve percent problems involving decimals.

Math and **SUMMER JOBS**
Ex. 82, p. 316

KEY VOCABULARY
- **percent,** *p. 301*
- **decimal,** *p. 672*

You can write a percent as a decimal and a decimal as a percent by first writing it as a fraction with a denominator of 100. For example:

$$37\% = \frac{37}{100} = 0.37 \qquad 0.63 = \frac{63}{100} = 63\%$$

The Examples suggest that to write a percent as a decimal, you drop the percent sign and move the decimal point two places to the left.

To write a decimal as a percent, you move the decimal point two places to the right and insert a percent sign.

EXAMPLE 1 Writing Percents as Decimals

a. $48\% = 48\%$ $= 0.48$

b. $9\% = 09\%$ $= 0.09$

c. $75.5\% = 75.5\%$ $= 0.755$

EXAMPLE 2 Writing Decimals as Percents

a. $0.13 = 0.13$ $= 13\%$

b. $0.04 = 0.04$ $= 4\%$

c. $0.027 = 0.027$ $= 2.7\%$

You can approximate a fraction as a percent by writing the fraction as a decimal to the nearest thousandth. Then, write the decimal as a percent.

EXAMPLE 3 Approximating Percents

Joe saves $\frac{5}{6}$ of his allowance. What percent of his allowance does he save?

SOLUTION

$\frac{5}{6} \approx 0.833$ **Divide 5 by 6. Round to the nearest thousandth.**

$= 83.3\%$ **Write as a percent.**

▶ **Answer** Joe saves about 83.3% of his allowance.

Animated **Math**
For an interactive example of approximating percents go to **classzone.com.**

✓ GUIDED PRACTICE for Examples 1, 2, and 3

Write the percent as a decimal or the decimal as a percent.

1. 25% **2.** 34% **3.** 0.06 **4.** 0.09

5. 5.2% **6.** 6.3% **7.** 0.578 **8.** 0.457

9. WHAT IF? In Example 3, suppose Joe saves $\frac{5}{7}$ of his allowance. What percent of his allowance does he now save?

SMALL AND LARGE PERCENTS Percents less than 1% represent numbers less than 0.01, or $\frac{1}{100}$. Percents greater than 100% represent numbers greater than 1. For example, the models below represent **0.5%** and **150%**.

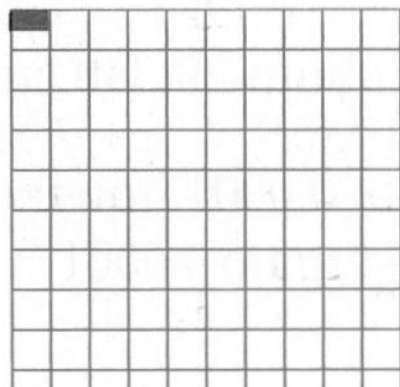

0.5%

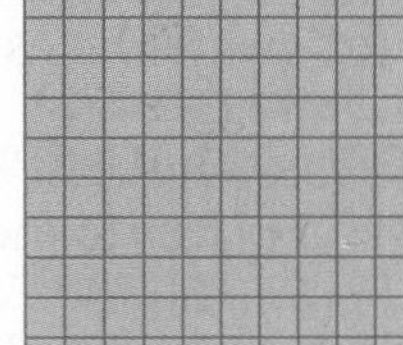
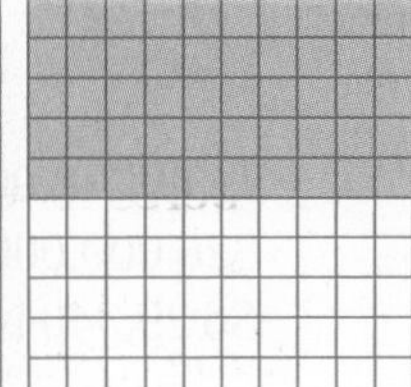

150%

EXAMPLE 4 Rewriting Small and Large Percents

GEOGRAPHY The surface area of Lake Englebright is 0.7% of the surface area of Lake Tahoe. The surface area of Lake Tahoe is 282% of the surface area of Clear Lake. Write these percents as decimals.

ANOTHER WAY

You can also use equivalent fractions to write 0.7% as a decimal.

$0.7\% = \frac{0.7}{100} = \frac{7}{1000}$
$= 0.007$

SOLUTION

To write the percents as decimals, follow the same rules as for percents between 1% and 100%.

Lake Engelbright: $0.7\% = 00.7\%$
$= 0.007$

Lake Tahoe: $282\% = 282\%$
$= 2.82$

✓ GUIDED PRACTICE for Example 4

Write the percent as a decimal.

10. 0.25% **11.** 0.13% **12.** 0.06% **13.** 0.0014%

14. 250% **15.** 375% **16.** 436% **17.** 178%

PERCENT OF A NUMBER You can multiply to find a percent of a number as you did in Lesson 6.1. First write the percent as a decimal.

EXAMPLE 5 Using Percents

EARTH SCIENCE The total amount of water on Earth, including salt water and fresh water, is about 326,000,000 cubic miles. Of this amount, 0.009% is in fresh water lakes. What is the amount of water in fresh water lakes?

AVOID ERRORS
Multiplying a number by a percent less than 100% results in a number less than the original number. Multiplying by a percent *greater* than 100% results in a number greater than the original.

SOLUTION

0.009% of 326,000,000 = **0.00009** × 326,000,000 **Write percent as a decimal.**

= 29,340 **Multiply.**

▸ **Answer** Fresh water lakes contain about 29,340 cubic miles of fresh water.

CHECK 0.009% is about 0.01%, or about 0.0001. You move the decimal point in 326,000,000 four places to the left to estimate 0.0001 × 326,000,000 = 32,600. So 29,340 is reasonable. ✓

 **GUIDED PRACTICE** for Example 5

18. **GREAT LAKES** Of the amount of water in fresh water lakes, about 10.2% is in Lake Superior. What is the amount of fresh water in Lake Superior?

6.3 EXERCISES

HOMEWORK KEY
◆ = **MULTIPLE CHOICE PRACTICE** Exs. 23, 58, 75, 83, 92–94
○ = **HINTS AND HOMEWORK HELP** for Exs. 25, 47, 87 at classzone.com

SKILLS • PROBLEM SOLVING • REASONING

1. **VOCABULARY** Write a decimal that is greater than 100%. Write a decimal that is less than 1%.

2. **WRITING** *Describe* the steps you would use to write 52% as a decimal.

SEE EXAMPLE 1 on p. 312 for Exs. 3–10

REWRITING PERCENTS **Write the percent as a decimal.**

3. 47%
4. 3%
5. 8%
6. 11%
7. 42.5%
8. 23.8%
9. 1.65%
10. 3.01%

SEE EXAMPLE 2 on p. 312 for Exs. 11–23, 45

REWRITING DECIMALS **Write the decimal as a percent.**

11. 0.26
12. 0.07
13. 0.205
14. 0.23
15. 0.15
16. 0.01
17. 0.85
18. 0.17
19. 0.586
20. 0.35
21. 0.0995
22. 0.61

23. ◆ **MULTIPLE CHOICE** What is 0.5378 written as a percent?

(A) 0.5378% (B) 53.78% (C) 537.8% (D) 5378%

SEE EXAMPLE 3 on p. 312 for Exs. 24–31

APPROXIMATING PERCENTS **Approximate the fraction as a percent. Round to the nearest tenth of a percent.**

24. $\frac{11}{15}$ 25. $\frac{13}{21}$ 26. $\frac{17}{18}$ 27. $\frac{23}{30}$

28. $\frac{14}{39}$ 29. $\frac{5}{26}$ 30. $\frac{5}{1000}$ 31. $\frac{52}{10,000}$

SEE EXAMPLE 4 on p. 313 for Exs. 32–44

SMALL AND LARGE PERCENTS **Write the percent as a decimal and as a fraction or mixed number.**

32. 0.15% 33. 0.02% 34. 0.89% 35. 0.71%

36. 0.036% 37. 0.78% 38. 450% 39. 252%

40. 465% 41. 1275% 42. 1000% 43. 615%

44. **ERROR ANALYSIS** *Describe* and correct the error made in writing the percent as a decimal.

0.002% = 0.002% = 0.2

45. **ERROR ANALYSIS** *Describe* and correct the error made in writing the decimal as a percent.

15.78 = 0.1578 = 0.1578%

SEE EXAMPLE 5 on p. 314 for Exs. 46–58

USING PERCENTS **Find the percent of the number.**

46. 0.8% of 200 47. 0.003% of 550 48. 350% of 12 49. 465% of 30

50. 185% of 78 51. 0.16% of 135 52. 0.0005% of 1222 53. 1235% of 34

54. 230% of 62 55. 1455% of 23 56. 0.006% of 1750 57. 0.24% of 850

58. ◆ **MULTIPLE CHOICE** What is 0.007% of 260?

(A) 0.0182 (B) 0.182 (C) 1.82 (D) 182

MIXED NUMBERS **Write the mixed number as a decimal and as a percent.**

59. $3\frac{1}{4}$ 60. $6\frac{4}{5}$ 61. $9\frac{2}{3}$ 62. $12\frac{3}{8}$

63. $13\frac{7}{10}$ 64. $15\frac{11}{20}$ 65. $25\frac{3}{5}$ 66. $35\frac{8}{9}$

NUMBER SENSE **Copy and complete the statement using $<$, $>$, or $=$.**

67. 0.14% _?_ 0.014 68. 3.4 _?_ 34% 69. 0.59 _?_ 59% 70. 44.80% _?_ $\frac{6}{7}$

71. $\frac{4}{9}$ _?_ 51% 72. 85% _?_ $\frac{21}{25}$ 73. 0.62 _?_ $\frac{16}{25}$ 74. 0.52 _?_ $\frac{13}{25}$

75. ◆ **MULTIPLE CHOICE** Which list of values is in order from least to greatest?

(A) 1018%, 10.2, 102, 1016 (B) 10.2, 1018%, 102, 1016

(C) 10.2, 102, 1018%, 1016 (D) 10.2, 102, 1016, 1018%

CONNECT SKILLS TO PROBLEM SOLVING **Exercises 76–79 will help you prepare for problem solving.**

76. Mary answered 84% of the questions on a test correctly. Write the percent as a decimal.

77. For a sixth grade play, 0.65 of the students who tried out were selected to be in the play. Write the decimal as a percent.

78. In a survey, $\frac{18}{51}$ of the people surveyed said that their favorite type of movie is action. Write the fraction as a percent. Round to the nearest tenth of a percent.

79. At a factory, 0.0002 of the cars produced have a defect. What percent of cars produced have a defect?

SEE EXAMPLE 5 on p. 314 for Exs. 80–81

80. TOY CARS The price of a miniature toy car in 1968 was 0.295% of its current price. Later the car became a collector's item valued at \$200. What was the price of the toy car in 1968?

Vintage toy car worth \$200

California @HomeTutor for problem solving help at classzone.com

81. MOVIE SEQUELS A movie made \$1,582,000. Its sequel made 104% of the original. How much money did the sequel make?

California @HomeTutor for problem solving help at classzone.com

82. SUMMER JOBS The money Anita earned working for a landscaper this summer is 120% of the money she earned last summer. Did Anita earn more or less money this summer than last summer? *Explain.*

83. ◆ **MULTIPLE CHOICE** LCD TV sales represented about 0.676% of the total sales of electronics in 2003. Which value is *not* equal to 0.676%?

Ⓐ 0.00676 Ⓑ $\frac{676}{1000}$ Ⓒ $\frac{676}{100,000}$ Ⓓ $\frac{169}{25,000}$

REASONING **Tell whether the statement is reasonable. *Explain.***

84. "Work" was listed as an after school activity by 110% of your classmates.

85. Of the 100 people surveyed, 0.05% said that they drive mopeds.

86. Your math test score is 125% of your last test score.

87. HOUSING COSTS Typical sale prices of single-family houses in San Bernardino County are shown at the right. Write the ratio of the price for 2005 to the price for 2002 as a percent. Does your answer suggest that the typical price about doubled in 3 years? *Explain.*

Year	Typical Sale Price
2002	\$176,500
2003	\$221,000
2004	\$296,400
2005	\$343,400

88. POPULATION In 2005, Argentina's population was about 0.613% of the world population of about 6,446,000,000 people. Find a high and a low estimate of the population of Argentina in 2005.

89. **MENTAL MATH** What is 200% of 8? What is 300% of 8? What is 400% of 8? *Describe* how you can find these answers using mental math.

90. **CHALLENGE** In 2001, 229 million cartons of apples were produced in the United States. Of these apples, 61% were eaten as fresh fruit. Of the apples used for other apple products, 21% were used for cider and juice. Estimate how many of the total cartons of apples were *not* used for cider and juice. *Justify* your answer.

229 million cartons

91. **CHALLENGE** You enlarge a 4 inch by 4 inch graph on a photo copier to 150%. You enlarge the enlargement to 150%. Are the dimensions of your graph now 200%, 225%, or 300% of the original dimensions? *Explain.*

◆ CALIFORNIA STANDARDS SPIRAL REVIEW

NS 1.1 92. Which of the following is *not* a true statement? *(p. 167)*

Ⓐ $\frac{11}{7} < 1.58$ Ⓑ $0.4 > \frac{4}{9}$ Ⓒ $\frac{17}{4} > 4.21$ Ⓓ $0.61 < \frac{5}{8}$

NS 1.2 93. Which ratio is *not* equivalent to the ratio 30 to 45? *(p. 255)*

Ⓐ 2:3 Ⓑ 9:12 Ⓒ 6:9 Ⓓ 30:45

NS 1.4 94. A business made $7495 in sales this month. Last month, the business made about 94% of this month's sales. About how much money did the business make in sales last month? *(p. 306)*

Ⓐ $6834 Ⓑ $7045 Ⓒ $7973 Ⓓ $9400

QUIZ *for Lessons 6.1–6.3*

Write the percent as a fraction or the fraction as a percent. *(p. 301)*

1. 18% 2. 74% 3. $\frac{17}{20}$ 4. $\frac{12}{25}$

Use a proportion to answer the question. *(p. 306)*

5. What number is 82% of 50? 6. 11 is 22% of what number?

7. What percent of 75 is 12? 8. 42 is 60% of what number?

Write the percent as a decimal or the decimal as a percent. *(p. 312)*

9. 5.4% 10. 79% 11. 0.712 12. 11.75

13. **COLOR PERCENTAGES** In a bag of 40 marbles, 18 are blue. What percent of the marbles in the bag are blue? *(p. 301)*

14. **FOOD DONATIONS** Your school is having a canned food drive. The school goal is to collect 250 cans. So far students have reached 20% of their goal. How many cans have students collected so far? *(p. 306)*

MIXED REVIEW of Skills and Problem Solving

Multiple Choice Practice for Lessons 6.1–6.3

1. A survey asked 1600 people to name their favorite outdoor activities. The top four answers are shown. Which statement best supports the information? **NS 1.4, MR 1.1**

Favorite Activity	*Responses*
Hiking	200
Swimming	120
Camping	10%
Biking	20%
Other	?

   Ⓐ 20% of the people chose an activity other than the four listed.

   Ⓑ 0.125 of the people chose hiking.

   Ⓒ 160 more people chose biking than camping.

   Ⓓ 12% of the people chose swimming.

2. 45 is 36% of what number? **NS 1.4**

   Ⓐ 16.2 Ⓑ 80

   Ⓒ 125 Ⓓ 140

3. The percent bar model below shows the contents of ocean water by weight. What fraction of ocean water is *not* oxygen, hydrogen, or chlorine? **Gr. 5 NS 1.2**

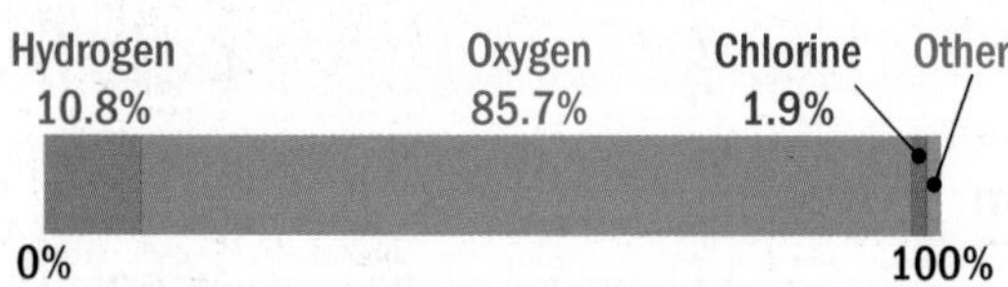

   Ⓐ $\frac{1}{100}$ Ⓑ $\frac{2}{125}$

   Ⓒ $\frac{1}{5}$ Ⓓ $\frac{99}{100}$

4. In a classroom of 32 students, 8 students have blue eyes. What percent of students in the classroom have blue eyes. **NS 1.4**

   Ⓐ 0.25% Ⓑ 2.5%

   Ⓒ 4% Ⓓ 25%

5. A survey asked people to answer a question with *yes, no,* or *maybe.* Of the 576 people who responded to the survey, 62.5% answered *yes* and 25% answered *no.* Which equation can be used to find x, the number of people who answered *maybe?* **NS 1.4**

   Ⓐ $x = 0.125 \cdot 576$ Ⓑ $x = 0.25 \cdot 576$

   Ⓒ $x = 0.625 \cdot 576$ Ⓓ $x = 0.875 \cdot 576$

6. The table shows the number of students in your science class who received each grade on a test. What percent of the students received an A on the test? **NS 1.4**

Grade	A	B	C	D	F
Number of students	3	10	9	2	1

   Ⓐ 3% Ⓑ 12%

   Ⓒ 15% Ⓓ 40%

7. Which list shows $\frac{2}{3}$, 71%, $\frac{3}{5}$, and 6.7% ordered from least to greatest? **Gr. 5 NS 1.2**

   Ⓐ $\frac{2}{3}$, 71%, $\frac{3}{5}$, 6.7%

   Ⓑ 6.7%, $\frac{2}{3}$, $\frac{3}{5}$, 71%

   Ⓒ $\frac{2}{3}$, 6.7%, $\frac{3}{5}$, 71%

   Ⓓ 6.7%, $\frac{3}{5}$, $\frac{2}{3}$, 71%

8. What number is 15% of 400? **NS 1.4**

   Ⓐ 6 Ⓑ 60

   Ⓒ 600 Ⓓ 6000

9. Ron spent $\frac{11}{12}$ of his allowance one week to fix his bike. What percent of his allowance did Ron spend? Round to the nearest hundredth of a percent. **MR 2.1, Gr. 5 NS 1.2**

   Ⓐ 1.09% Ⓑ 9.17%

   Ⓒ 91.67% Ⓓ 91.70%

6.4 The Percent Equation

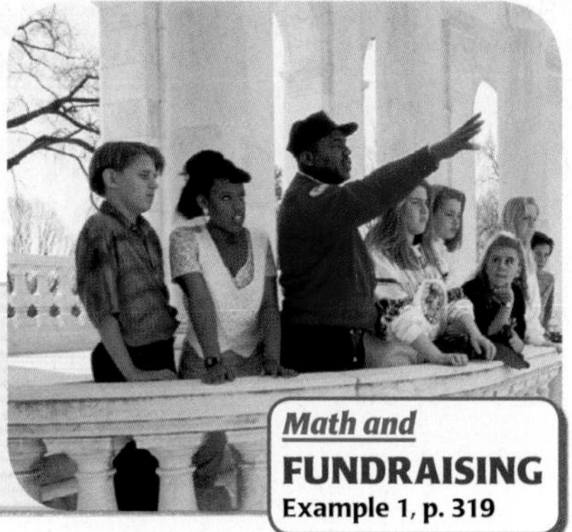

Math and FUNDRAISING
Example 1, p. 319

Standards **NS 1.4 Calculate given percentages of quantities and solve problems** involving discounts at sales, interest earned, and tips.

Connect ***Before*** you used proportions to solve percent problems. ***Now*** you will use equations to solve percent problems.

KEY VOCABULARY
- **percent equation**
- **percent,** *p. 301*

In Lesson 6.2, you solved percent problems using the proportion $\frac{a}{b} = \frac{p}{100}$, where a is part of the base b and $\frac{p}{100}$ is the percent. By solving this proportion for a, you obtain the *percent equation* described below, as you will see in Exercise 43.

KEY CONCEPT *For Your Notebook*

The Percent Equation

You can represent "a is p percent of b" with the **percent equation**

$$a = p\% \cdot b$$

where a is part of the base b and $p\%$ is the percent.

EXAMPLE 1 Finding a Part of a Base

 **FUNDRAISING** Your class has raised 80% of its $8000 goal for a trip to Washington, D.C. How much money has your class raised for the trip?

Lincoln Memorial, Washington Monument, and U.S. Capitol

SOLUTION

$a = p\% \cdot b$	**Write percent equation.**
$= 80\% \cdot 8000$	**Substitute 80 for p and 8000 for b.**
$= 0.8 \cdot 8000$	**Write percent as a decimal.**
$= 6400$	**Multiply.**

▶ **Answer** Your class has raised $6400 for the trip to Washington, D.C.

READING
In Example 1, as in fraction problems, **of** means to multiply. So 80% **of** $8000 means 0.80 × 8000.

✓ **GUIDED PRACTICE** for Example 1

1. What number is 20% of 110?
2. What number is 25% of 88?
3. What number is 40% of 150?
4. What number is 75% of 800?

EXAMPLE 2 Finding a Base

The number 117 is 45% of what number?

$a = p\% \cdot b$	**Write percent equation.**
$117 = 45\% \cdot b$	**Substitute 117 for *a* and 45 for *p*.**
$\frac{117}{0.45} = \frac{0.45 \cdot b}{0.45}$	**Write percent as a decimal. Then divide each side by 0.45.**
$260 = b$	**Simplify.**

▶ **Answer** The number 117 is 45% of 260.

EXAMPLE 3 Finding a Percent

90 is what percent of 150?

About the Standards

You can use common percents to check the reasonableness of the answer, as called for in MR 2.1. You know that 50%, or $\frac{1}{2}$, of 150 is 75. Because 90 is greater than 75, 60% is reasonable.

$a = p\% \cdot b$	**Write percent equation.**
$90 = p\% \cdot 150$	**Substitute 90 for *a* and 150 for *b*.**
$\frac{90}{150} = \frac{p\% \cdot 150}{150}$	**Divide each side by 150.**
$\frac{3}{5} = p\%$	**Simplify fraction.**
$60\% = p\%$	**Write as a percent.**

▶ **Answer** The number 90 is 60% of 150.

EXAMPLE 4 Finding a Commission

VOCABULARY

A *commission* is money earned by many sales people. It is usually a percent of each sale.

SHOE SALES A shoe salesperson sells a pair of shoes for $60. The salesperson receives a 9% commission on the sale. How much is the commission?

SOLUTION

$a = p\% \cdot b$	**Write percent equation.**
$= 9\% \cdot 60$	**Substitute 9 for *p* and 60 for *b*.**
$= 0.09 \cdot 60$	**Write percent as a decimal.**
$= 5.4$	**Multiply.**

▶ **Answer** The commission is $5.40.

✓ GUIDED PRACTICE for Examples 2, 3, and 4

5. 130 is 65% of what number?

6. 50 is what percent of 250?

7. COMMISSION A clothing salesperson sells a suit for $350. The salesperson receives an 8% commission on the sale. How much is the commission?

6.4 EXERCISES

HOMEWORK KEY

◆ = MULTIPLE CHOICE PRACTICE Exs. 21, 22, 38, 51–53

○ = HINTS AND HOMEWORK HELP for Exs. 5, 17, 39 at classzone.com

SKILLS • PROBLEM SOLVING • REASONING

1. **VOCABULARY** Does the answer to the following question represent the *part of the base*, the *base*, or the *percent*: Ten is 25% of what number?

2. **WRITING** State the percent equation in words.

SEE EXAMPLES 1 AND 2 on pp. 319–320 for Exs. 3–12

USING THE PERCENT EQUATION Find the unknown number.

3. What number is 20% of 200?
4. What number is 40% of 500?
5. 45 is 25% of what number?
6. 93 is 75% of what number?
7. What number is 35% of 300?
8. What number is 15% of 200?
9. 65 is 65% of what number?
10. 8 is 32% of what number?
11. What number is 48% of 150?
12. 246 is 82% of what number?

SEE EXAMPLE 3 on p. 320 for Exs. 13–21

FINDING THE PERCENT Use the percent equation to find the percent. Round to the nearest whole percent if necessary.

13. 35 is what percent of 50?
14. 54 is what percent of 60?
15. What percent of 300 is 51?
16. 42 is what percent of 62?
17. What percent of 111 is 80?
18. What percent of 65 is 39?
19. 46 is what percent of 184?
20. What percent of 114 is 19?

21. ◆ **MULTIPLE CHOICE** To the nearest whole percent, what percent of 75 is 33?

   Ⓐ 23% Ⓑ 44% Ⓒ 228% Ⓓ 440%

SEE EXAMPLES 1 AND 2 on pp. 319–320 for Exs. 22–24

22. ◆ **MULTIPLE CHOICE** The number 91 is 65% of what number?

   Ⓐ 8 Ⓑ 80 Ⓒ 140 Ⓓ 800

ERROR ANALYSIS *Describe* and correct the error made in using the percent equation.

23.

What number is 30% of 180?
$a = p\% \cdot b$
$a = 30\% \cdot 180$
$= 5400$

24.

84 is 21% of what number?
$a = p\% \cdot b$
$a = 0.21 \cdot 84$
$= 17.64$

NUMBER SENSE Copy and complete the statement using <, >, or =.

25. 40% of 120 _?_ 120% of 40
26. 20% of 60 _?_ 30% of 50
27. 160% of 15 _?_ 1% of 240
28. 25% of 100 _?_ 50% of 50
29. 30% of 140 _?_ 140% of 30
30. 15% of 30 _?_ 25% of 160

SEE EXAMPLE 2 on p. 320 for Exs. 31–32

PATTERNS Copy and complete the pattern.

31. 15% of __?__ is 3

15% of __?__ is 6

15% of __?__ is 9

15% of __?__ is 12

15% of __?__ is $3n$

32. __?__ % of 80 = 2

__?__ % of 80 = 4

__?__ % of 80 = 6

__?__ % of 80 = 8

__?__ % of 80 = $2n$

CONNECT SKILLS TO PROBLEM SOLVING Exercises 33–35 will help you prepare for problem solving.

Use the following information: An art gallery sells a painting for $575 and receives a 40% commission.

33. In this situation, are you given the *base* or the *part of the base*?

34. Write an equation to find the amount of money the art gallery receives.

35. Solve the equation.

SEE EXAMPLE 3 on p. 320 for Exs. 36, 39

36. BASEBALL Your baseball team won 15 out of 21 games. What percent of the games did your team win?

California @HomeTutor for problem solving help at classzone.com

37. BASKETBALL The Los Angeles Sparks won 87.5% of 32 regular season games before winning the WNBA championship in 2001. How many games did they win?

California @HomeTutor for problem solving help at classzone.com

Lisa Leslie was a WNBA champion.

38. ◆ **MULTIPLE CHOICE** In Phoenix, Arizona, the average temperature is 85°F or higher for 25% of the year. During how many *weeks* of the year is the average temperature 85°F or higher?

Ⓐ 13 Ⓑ 21

Ⓒ 39 Ⓓ 91

(39.) PRECIPITATION In Eureka, California, it rains an average of 119 days per year. About what percent of the year does it rain?

SEE EXAMPLE 4 on p. 320 for Exs. 40–41

40. COMMISSIONS Which earns more money: a 10% commission on $630 or a 15% commission on $480?

41. ELECTRONICS Jon receives a 15% commission for selling stereos. Today he sells one stereo and receives $37.50. What is the price of the stereo?

42. GEOMETRY The length of a rectangle is 150% of its width, w. Use the percent equation to find the length of the rectangle in terms of w. Then write a formula for the area of the rectangle in terms of w.

43. REASONING Solve the proportion $\frac{a}{b} = \frac{p}{100}$ for a. Show your reasoning. Compare your result with the percent equation.

READING *IN* MATH **Read the information below for Exercises 44–45.**

Winter Sports Skiing and ice skating were once the most popular winter sports. Since the first snowboard was created in 1965, the sport of snowboarding has steadily grown in popularity. Meanwhile, skiing has dropped in popularity in the United States from its peak of about 12 million skiers in 1988.

Winter Sports Participation in the U.S. (in millions)			
Year	***Skiing***	***Snowboarding***	***Ice Skating***
1998	7.7	3.6	7.8
2003	6.8	6.3	5.1

44. **Calculate** The number of skiers in 2003 is what percent of the number of skiers in 1988?

45. **Predict** *Predict* the number of participants in each sport in 2008. Round to the nearest tenth of a million. *Explain* your reasoning.

CHALLENGE **Tell if the statement is *true* or *false*. *Justify* your answer.**

46. 25% of 25% of x is 50% of x

47. 5% of $(x + 5)$ is $5 + 5\%$ of x

48. 10% more than x is $1.1x$

49. 10% less than x is $0.9x$

50. **CHALLENGE** You have \$200, and you would like to rent a sailboat for 4 hours. It costs \$45 per hour or \$130 per day. What percent of your total money will you save by choosing the better rate? *Explain* how you found your answer.

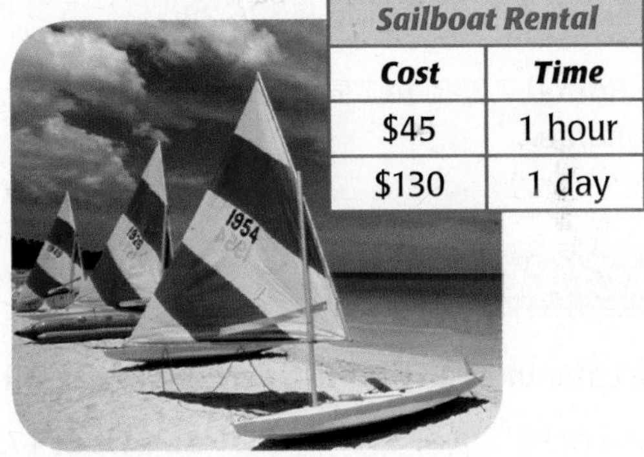

Sailboat Rental	
Cost	***Time***
\$45	1 hour
\$130	1 day

◆ CALIFORNIA STANDARDS SPIRAL REVIEW

AF 1.4 51. What is the value of $-8(2) + 3^2 - 14$? ***(p. 160)***

Ⓐ −137 Ⓑ −21 Ⓒ 39 Ⓓ 155

NS 2.4 52. What is the greatest common factor of 30 and 75? ***(p. 10)***

Ⓐ 1 Ⓑ 3 Ⓒ 10 Ⓓ 15

AF 1.2 53. You have a box of crackers that contains c crackers. You divide the crackers evenly among you and two friends. Which expression represents the number of crackers that you now have? ***(p. 202)***

Ⓐ $c - 2$ Ⓑ $c - 3$ Ⓒ $\frac{c}{2}$ Ⓓ $\frac{c}{3}$

6.4 Finding a Percent of a Number

Standards

NS 1.4 Calculate given percentages of quantities and solve problems involving discounts at sales, interest earned, and tips.

QUESTION How can you use a calculator to find a percent of a number?

EXAMPLE **A computer salesperson sells a computer for $500. The salesperson receives a 7.25% commission on the sale. How much is the commission?**

You can use the percent feature, [2nd] [%], to find a percent of a number. The percent feature can often be found above the left parenthesis key, [(].

SOLUTION

Use the percent equation $a = p\% \cdot b$ with $p\% = 7.25\%$ and $b = 500$.

Keystrokes	Display
7.25 [2nd] [%] [×] 500 [=]	36.25

▸**Answer** The commission is $36.25.

CHECK Round 7.25% to 7%. Because $7\% \cdot 500 = 35$, the answer is reasonable.

PRACTICE

Use a calculator to find the percent of the number.

1. 8% of 90 **2.** 14% of 173 **3.** 57% of 13.7

4. 350.6% of 8 **5.** 24.3% of 99 **6.** 7.28% of 205

7. 72% of 12 **8.** 147% of 20 **9.** 93% of 65

10. 49.1% of 11 **11.** 268.4% of 5 **12.** 942% of 60

13. **COMMISSIONS** A salesperson sells a television for $300. The salesperson receives a 5.5% commission on the sale. How much is the commission?

14. **TESTING** You answered 85% of the 20 questions correctly on your history test. How many questions did you answer correctly?

15. **HOCKEY** A hockey team has 36 wins. The team has won 45% of its games. How many games has the team played?

16. **GAMES** You have completed 25% of the stages of a video game. You are on stage 19. How many total stages make up the video game?

6.5 Discounts, Markups, Tips, and Sales Tax

Math and RETAIL
Example 1, p. 325

Standards **NS 1.4 Calculate given percentages of quantities and solve problems involving discounts at sales,** interest earned, **and tips.**

Connect ***Before*** you solved percent problems. ***Now*** you will use percents to find discounts, markups, tips, and sales tax.

KEY VOCABULARY
- **percent,** *p. 301*

DISCOUNTS A decrease in the price of an item is a *discount.* To find the sale price of an item, do the following:

STEP 1 **Find** the amount of the discount.

STEP 2 **Subtract** the discount from the original price.

EXAMPLE 1 Finding a Discounted Sale Price

CLOTHING You buy a pair of jeans that is 30% off the original price of \$29. What is the sale price?

SOLUTION

STEP 1 **Find** the amount of the discount.

$$\text{Discount} = \mathbf{30\%} \text{ of } \$29$$
$$= \mathbf{0.3} \times 29 \quad \textbf{Write 30\% as a decimal.}$$
$$= 8.7 \quad \textbf{Multiply.}$$

STEP 2 **Subtract** the discount from the original price.

$$\text{Sale price} = \text{original price} - \text{discount}$$
$$= 29 - 8.70 = 20.30$$

▶ **Answer** The sale price is \$20.30.

✓ **GUIDED PRACTICE** for Example 1

1. **SALE ITEMS** A store is selling sandals at 20% off their original price. What is the sale price of a pair of sandals originally priced at \$20?

MARKUPS A retail store buys items from manufacturers at *wholesale prices.* The store then sells the items to customers at higher *retail prices.* The increase from the wholesale price to the retail price is the *markup.* To find the retail price of an item, use the following steps.

STEP 1 **Find** the amount of the markup.

STEP 2 **Add** the markup to the wholesale price.

EXAMPLE 2 Finding a Markup and Retail Price

SKATEBOARDS A store that sells skateboards buys them from a manufacturer at a wholesale price of \$57. The store's markup is 150%. What is the retail price?

AVOID ERRORS
In Example 2, do not stop after multiplying 1.5×57. You have to add the result, \$85.50, to the wholesale price to get the retail price.

SOLUTION

STEP 1 **Find** the amount of the markup.

Markup = **150%** of \$57

$= \mathbf{1.5} \times 57$ **Write 150% as a decimal.**

$= 85.50$ **Multiply.**

STEP 2 **Add** the markup to the wholesale price.

Retail price = wholesale price + markup

$= 57.00 + 85.50 = 142.50$

▶ **Answer** The retail price is \$142.50.

TIPS AND SALES TAX Tips and sales tax are amounts that are added to the price of a purchase. Sales tax and tips are usually calculated using a percent of the purchase price. The tip at a restaurant is based on the food bill only. Do not include the sales tax when finding a tip.

EXAMPLE 3 ◆ Multiple Choice Practice

RESTAURANTS At a restaurant, you order a meal that costs \$12. You leave a 20% tip. What is the total cost of the meal?

Ⓐ \$2.40 Ⓑ \$9.60

Ⓒ \$12.20 Ⓓ \$14.40

ELIMINATE CHOICES
Because your meal costs \$12, the total cost including a tip will be more than \$12. You can eliminate Choices A and B.

SOLUTION

STEP 1 **Find** the tip: **20%** of \$12 = $\mathbf{0.20} \times 12 = 2.40$

STEP 2 **Add** the food bill and tip: $12 + 2.40 = 14.40$

▶ **Answer** The total cost is \$14.40. The correct answer is D. Ⓐ Ⓑ Ⓒ Ⓓ

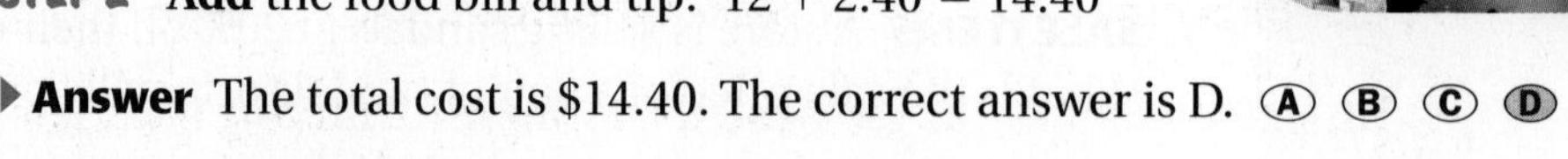

GUIDED PRACTICE for Examples 2 and 3

2. **GUITARS** A store buys toy guitars from a manufacturer at a wholesale price of \$38. The store's markup is 85%. What is the retail price?

3. **WHAT IF?** Suppose the bill in Example 3 is \$15. Find the total cost of the meal if you want to leave a 20% tip.

EXAMPLE 4 Solve a Multi-Step Problem

SALES TAX A jacket that originally cost \$50 is on sale for 20% off. Find the total cost of the jacket if it has a 5% sales tax.

ANOTHER WAY

For an alternative method for solving the problem in Example 4, turn to page 330 for the Problem Solving Workshop.

SOLUTION

STEP 1 **Find** the amount of the discount.

Discount = 20% of \$50 = $0.20 \times 50 = 10$

STEP 2 **Subtract** the discount from the original price to find the sale price.

Sale price = $50 - 10 = 40$

STEP 3 **Find** the sales tax on the sale price.

Sales tax = 5% of \$40 = $0.05 \times 40 = 2$

STEP 4 **Add** the sales tax to the sale price to find the total cost.

Total cost = $40 + 2 = 42$

▶ **Answer** The total cost of the jacket is \$42.

✓ GUIDED PRACTICE for Example 4

4. **WHAT IF?** Suppose the original price of the jacket in Example 4 is \$60. Find the total cost of the jacket with a 20% discount and a 5% sales tax.

6.5 EXERCISES

HOMEWORK KEY

◆ = **MULTIPLE CHOICE PRACTICE** Exs. 19, 26, 27, 35–37

○ = **HINTS AND HOMEWORK HELP** for Exs. 7, 17, 27 at classzone.com

SKILLS • PROBLEM SOLVING • REASONING

VOCABULARY **Based on the calculations shown, identify the dollar value or percent that matches the description.**

$0.05 \times 15 = 0.75$
$15 + 0.75 = 15.75$

1. Original price
2. Amount of sales tax
3. Total cost
4. Sales tax percent
5. **NOTETAKING SKILLS** Write the formula for finding the amount of sales tax on an item using a *formula triangle* similar to the one on page 300.

SEE EXAMPLE 1 on p. 325 for Exs. 6–9

APPLYING DISCOUNTS **Find the sale price with the given discount.**

6. Original price: \$40
   Discount: 10%
7. Original price: \$70
   Discount: 20%
8. Original price: \$36
   Discount: 30%
9. Original price: \$24
   Discount: 20%

SEE EXAMPLE 2
on p. 326
for Ex. 10–14

FINDING RETAIL PRICES Find the retail price with the given markup. Check that your answer is reasonable.

10. Wholesale price: $40
Markup: 60%

11. Wholesale price: $55
Markup: 50%

12. Wholesale price: $25
Markup: 125%

13. Wholesale price: $45
Markup: 105%

14. ERROR ANALYSIS A friend says that the retail price of an item with a wholesale price of $80 is $100 after a markup of 125%. *Describe* and correct the error in the person's statement.

SEE EXAMPLE 3
on p. 326
for Exs. 15–18

FINDING TOTAL COSTS Find the total cost with the given tip or sales tax. Check that your answer is reasonable.

15. Food bill before tax: $25
Sales tax: 6%

16. Food bill before tax: $32
Sales tax: 7%

17. Food bill before tax: $45
Tip: 20%

18. Food bill before tax: $65
Tip: 15%

19. ◆ **MULTIPLE CHOICE** Which expression represents the price of an item with an original price p after a discount of 25%?

(A) $0.25p$ (B) $p - 0.25p$ (C) $p + 0.25p$ (D) $p + 0.75p$

ESTIMATION Use the information to estimate the total cost of the meal.

20. Cost of meal: $35.27
Tax: 6%; tip: 18%

21. Cost of meal: $23.18
Tax: 4.5%; tip: 17%

CONNECT SKILLS TO PROBLEM SOLVING Exercises 22–24 will help you prepare for problem solving.

Use the following information: At a restaurant, you order a meal that costs $16. The sales tax is 5%. You leave a 15% tip.

22. Find the amount of the tip you leave.

23. Find the amount of the tax you pay.

24. Find the total cost of the meal.

SEE EXAMPLE 2
on p. 326
for Ex. 25

25. SPORTING GOODS A sporting goods store purchases in-line skates, skateboards, and sneakers for the wholesale prices listed in the table. Find the retail price of each item.

Item	Wholesale Price	Markup
In-line skates	$80	105%
Skateboards	$100	125%
Sneakers	$30	130%

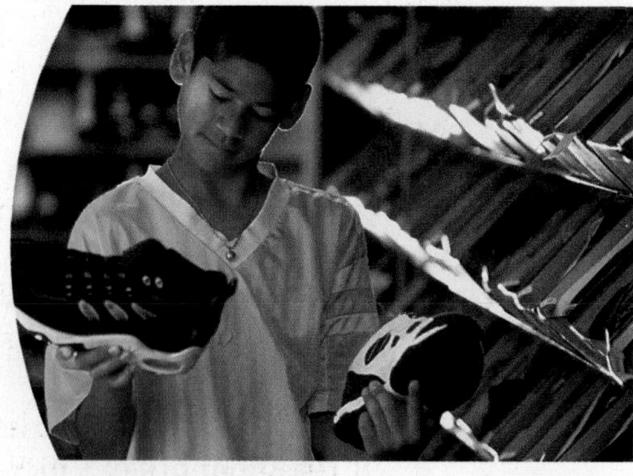

California @HomeTutor for problem solving help at classzone.com

SEE EXAMPLES 1 AND 4
on pp. 325, 327 for Ex. 26

26. ◆ **MULTIPLE CHOICE** A pair of shoes costs \$50. You have a coupon for 20% off. What is the total cost of the shoes after 7.25% sales tax is included?

Ⓐ \$40 Ⓑ \$42.90 Ⓒ \$53.63 Ⓓ \$61.69

California @HomeTutor for problem solving help at classzone.com

SEE EXAMPLES 3 AND 4
on pp. 326–327 for Ex. 27

27. ◆ **MULTIPLE CHOICE** At a restaurant, the cost of your meal is \$18. You leave a 15% tip. The sales tax is 7%. What is the total amount of the bill?

Ⓐ \$20.70 Ⓑ \$21.96 Ⓒ \$22.15 Ⓓ \$35.19

28. **COMPARE** Your dinner bill for Monday is \$22.79. The sales tax is 7% and you leave a 20% tip. Your dinner bill for Tuesday is \$23.84. The sales tax is 6% and you leave a 15% tip. For which meal do you pay more? *Explain.*

29. **REASONING** An \$80 tennis racket is marked up 50% then discounted 50%. Will the final price of the tennis racket be \$80? *Explain.*

30. **SHORT RESPONSE** You have the two coupons shown below. If you spend \$60, in which order do you want the coupons used? *Explain.*

31. **SHOPPING** You have a coupon for 10% off the price of a CD. You pay \$18 for a CD. How much would you pay if you did *not* have a coupon?

CHALLENGE Let x represent the original price. Match the given discount and markup with the correct expression for the new price.

32. 80% markup, then 20% discount — **A.** New price $= 0.2 \times 2.2x$

33. 120% markup, then 80% discount — **B.** New price $= 0.8 \times 1.8x$

34. 20% markup, then 20% discount — **C.** New price $= 0.8 \times 1.2x$

◆ CALIFORNIA STANDARDS SPIRAL REVIEW

NS 2.1 35. What is the value of $2\frac{3}{8} \times 4\frac{4}{7}$? *(p. 88)*

Ⓐ $9\frac{3}{7}$ Ⓑ $9\frac{6}{7}$ Ⓒ $10\frac{3}{7}$ Ⓓ $10\frac{6}{7}$

AF 1.1 36. What is the value of a in the equation $45 \div a = 3$? *(p. 234)*

Ⓐ 5 Ⓑ 9 Ⓒ 12 Ⓓ 15

AF 2.3 37. Matt can run 1 mile in 8 minutes. At this rate, how many miles can he run in 1 hour? *(p. 260)*

Ⓐ 7 miles Ⓑ 7.5 miles Ⓒ 8 miles Ⓓ 8.5 miles

PROBLEM SOLVING WORKSHOP
LESSON 6.5

Using ALTERNATIVE METHODS

Another Way to Solve Example 4, page 327

Standards
NS 1.4

In Example 4 on page 327, you saw how to solve the problem about the total price of a jacket. In Example 4, you found and subtracted the discount from the original price. Then you found and added the sales tax. You can also use number sense to solve the problem.

PROBLEM

SALES TAX A jacket that originally cost \$50 is on sale for 20% off. Find the total cost of the jacket if it has a 5% sales tax.

METHOD

Using Number Sense An alternate approach is to use number sense and multiplication to first find the sale price and then the total cost with tax.

STEP 1 **Find** the sale price.

Notice that for a 20% discount, you actually pay 80% of the original price.

Sale price $= 80\%$ of \$50	**Write equation.**
$= 0.80 \times 50$	**Write 80% as a decimal.**
$= 40$	**Multiply.**

STEP 2 **Find** the total cost with tax.

Notice that the total cost is 100% of the sale price plus an extra 5% of the sale price, which is the same as 105% of the sale price.

Total cost $= 105\%$ of \$40	**Write equation.**
$= 1.05 \times 40$	**Write 105% as a decimal.**
$= 42$	**Multiply.**

▶ **Answer** The total cost of the jacket is \$42.

PRACTICE

1. **FOOTWEAR** A store is selling sneakers at 25% off the original price. What is the sale price of a pair of sneakers originally priced at \$55? Solve the problem in two ways.

2. **CLOTHING** You buy a sweater that is 15% off the original price of \$40. What is the sale price?

3. **WHAT IF?** Suppose the jacket in the Example above is on sale for 30% off the original price. What is the total cost of the jacket?

4. **JEWELRY** A store is discounting all jewelry by 20%. What is the total cost of a bracelet originally priced at \$65 that has a sales tax of 6%?

6.6 Simple Interest

Math and FINANCE
Ex. 37, p. 334

Standards **NS 1.4 Calculate given percentages of quantities and solve problems involving** discounts at sales, **interest earned,** and tips.

Connect ***Before*** you calculated discounts, markups, tips, and sales tax. ***Now*** you will calculate simple interest.

KEY VOCABULARY
- interest
- principal
- simple interest
- annual interest rate
- balance

The amount earned or paid for the use of money is called **interest**. The amount of money deposited or borrowed is the **principal**. When interest is earned or paid only on the principal, it is **simple interest**. The **annual interest rate** is the percent of the principal earned or paid per year. The sum of the interest and the principal is called the **balance**.

KEY CONCEPT *For Your Notebook*

Simple Interest

Words Simple interest I is the product of the principal P, the annual interest rate r written as a decimal, and the time t in years.

Algebra $I = Prt$

Numbers A \$500 deposit earns 6% simple annual interest for 4 years.
$I = (\$500)(0.06)(4) = \$120$

EXAMPLE 1 ◆ Multiple Choice Practice

LOANS Tim's parents lend Tim \$100 so he can buy a radio-controlled airplane. They charge Tim 5% simple annual interest. What will be the total amount that Tim will owe his parents in 1 year?

(A) \$5 (B) \$95 (C) \$105 (D) \$500

Animated Math
For an interactive example involving simple interest go to **classzone.com**.

SOLUTION

STEP 1 **Find** the interest due.

$I = Prt$ **Write simple interest formula.**

$= (100)(0.05)(1)$ **Substitute 100 for *P*, 0.05 for *r*, and 1 for *t*.**

$= 5$ **Multiply.**

STEP 2 **Add** the interest to the principal: \$100 + \$5 = \$105.

▶ **Answer** Tim will owe a balance of \$105.
The correct answer is C. (A) (B) (C) (D)

EXAMPLE 2 Finding an Interest Rate

INVESTMENT You buy savings bonds worth \$250. After 6 months the bonds are worth \$257.50. Find the simple annual interest rate.

STEP 1 **Find** the interest by subtracting the principal from the balance.

\$257.50 − \$250 = \$7.50

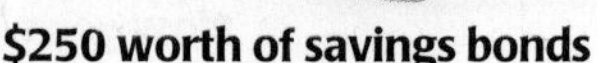

\$250 worth of savings bonds

STEP 2 **Use** the simple interest formula and solve for r.

$I = Prt$	**Write simple interest formula.**
$7.5 = (250)(r)\left(\frac{6}{12}\right)$	**Substitute 7.5 for I, 250 for P, and $\frac{6}{12}$ for t.**
$7.5 = 125r$	**Multiply.**
$\frac{7.5}{125} = \frac{125r}{125}$	**Divide each side by 125.**
$0.06 = r$	**Simplify.**
$6\% = r$	**Write decimal as a percent.**

▶ **Answer** The simple annual interest rate is 6%.

AVOID ERRORS

When using the simple interest formula, make sure you write the number of months as a fraction of a year. For example, 7 months should be written as $\frac{7}{12}$.

EXAMPLE 3 Finding an Amount of Time

INVESTMENT Tricia put \$750 into a certificate of deposit. Her simple annual interest rate is 4%. She receives a check for the interest at the end of each year. How long will it take to earn \$150 in interest?

$I = Prt$	**Write simple interest formula.**
$150 = (750)(0.04)t$	**Substitute 150 for I, 750 for P, and 0.04 for r.**
$150 = 30t$	**Multiply.**
$\frac{150}{30} = \frac{30t}{30}$	**Divide each side by 30.**
$5 = t$	**Simplify.**

▶ **Answer** It will take Tricia 5 years to earn \$150 in simple interest.

✓ GUIDED PRACTICE for Examples 1, 2, and 3

1. **SAVINGS** Miguel deposited \$500 into an account that earns 6% simple annual interest. What will his account balance be after 2 years?

2. **INTEREST RATES** You buy a savings bond worth \$300. After 4 months, the bond is worth \$305. Find the simple annual interest rate.

3. **WHAT IF?** Suppose the simple interest rate in Example 3 is 5%. How long will it take Tricia to earn \$150 in interest?

6.6 EXERCISES

HOMEWORK KEY

◆ = **MULTIPLE CHOICE PRACTICE** Exs. 13, 28, 34, 43–45

○ = **HINTS AND HOMEWORK HELP** for Exs. 7, 21, 37 at classzone.com

SKILLS • PROBLEM SOLVING • REASONING

1. **VOCABULARY** What is an amount of money earned on principal called?

2. **WRITING** Would you want a high or low interest rate when you borrow money? when you save money? *Explain* your choices.

SEE EXAMPLE 1 on p. 331 for Exs. 3–15

CALCULATING SIMPLE INTEREST For an account that earns simple annual interest, find the interest earned and the balance of the account.

3. \$30 at 1% for 10 years
4. \$100 at 8% for 3 years
5. \$50 at 10% for 4 years
6. \$200 at 4.5% for 8 years
7. \$252 at 8% for 2 months
8. \$450 at 4% for $\frac{1}{2}$ year
9. \$6240 at 10.4% for 9 months
10. \$2000 at 9.6% for 8 months
11. \$5000 at 4.5% for 4 months
12. \$400 at 3% for 1 month

13. ◆ **MULTIPLE CHOICE** What is the balance after 1.5 years of a savings account that begins with \$700 and earns 6% simple annual interest?

Ⓐ \$742 Ⓑ \$756 Ⓒ \$763 Ⓓ \$1456

ERROR ANALYSIS *Describe* **and correct the error made in finding the interest earned.**

14.

\$200 at 4% simple interest for 36 months

✗ $I = (200)(0.04)(36)$
$= \$288$

15.

\$300 at 6% simple interest for 6 months

✗ $I = (300)(6)\left(\frac{1}{2}\right)$
$= \$900$

SEE EXAMPLES 1, 2, AND 3 on pp. 331–332 for Exs. 16–27

ALGEBRA Find the unknown quantity.

16. I = ?, P = \$2000, r = 9.8%, t = 5 years
17. I = \$84, P = ?, r = 7%, t = 2 years
18. I = \$468, P = \$6240, r = ?, t = 9 months
19. I = \$9, P = \$450, r = 4%, t = ?
20. Balance = \$1530, I = \$30, r = 6%, t = ?
21. Balance = \$620, I = \$20, r = 5%, t = ?
22. Balance = ?, I = \$110, r = 5.5%, t = 1 year
23. Balance = ?, I = \$60, r = 4%, t = 5 years
24. Balance = \$1530, I = \$30, r = ?, t = 4 months
25. Balance = \$620, I = \$20, r = ?, t = 8 months
26. Balance = \$2055, I = \$55, r = 5.5%, t = ?
27. Balance = \$960, I = \$160, r = 4%, t = ?

28. ◆ **MULTIPLE CHOICE** After 9 months a savings account earned \$9 in interest at a simple interest rate of 5%. What was the amount deposited into the savings account?

Ⓐ \$20 Ⓑ \$24 Ⓒ \$135 Ⓓ \$240

29. **CHECKING REASONABLENESS** Use estimation and mental math to check the reasonableness of the amount of interest shown at the right. *Explain* your reasoning.

$P = \$98$
$r = 5\%$
$t = 1$
$I = \$4.90$

CONNECT SKILLS TO PROBLEM SOLVING Exercises 30–33 will help you prepare for problem solving.

Use the following information: You put \$700 into a certificate of deposit that earns 2.5% simple annual interest for 18 months.

30. Identify the principal.

31. Write the interest rate as a decimal.

32. Write the time as a fraction of a year.

33. Find the amount of interest earned.

SEE EXAMPLE 1 on p. 331 for Exs. 34–36

34. ◆ **MULTIPLE CHOICE** Jerome put \$350 into a 6 month certificate of deposit. The certificate earned 4.2% simple annual interest. What was the balance after 6 months?

Ⓐ \$7.35 Ⓑ \$342.65 Ⓒ \$357.35 Ⓓ \$700.25

California @HomeTutor for problem solving help at classzone.com

35. **CREDIT CARDS** A credit card company charges 9.6% simple annual interest on any unpaid balance each month. During the past month Javier had an unpaid balance of \$375. What is the interest charge?

California @HomeTutor for problem solving help at classzone.com

36. **SECURITY DEPOSIT** When signing a lease for an apartment, your sister pays a security deposit of \$600 that earns 4% simple annual interest. At the end of a year, how much interest has she earned?

Security deposit is \$600.

SEE EXAMPLE 2 on p. 332 for Exs. 37–38

37. **BANKING** Adam deposited \$250 into an account. At the end of 6 months his balance is \$255. What is the simple annual interest rate?

38. **INVESTMENT** You buy a savings bond worth \$500. After 18 months the bond is worth \$560. Find the simple annual interest rate.

SEE EXAMPLE 3 on p. 332 for Ex. 39

39. **INTEREST** Ann has \$300 in a savings account that earns 1.75% simple annual interest. In how many years will she have \$21 in interest?

40. SHORT RESPONSE Rick wants to borrow \$4500 to buy a car. His sister and uncle will both lend him the money at the rates shown at the right. To whom will Rick pay less money overall? *Explain* your reasoning.

	Interest Rate	Time (years)
Sister	9%	6
Uncle	11.5%	4

41. CHALLENGE You put \$500 in a savings account that earns 4.5% simple annual interest. Your friend puts \$400 in an account that earns 6% simple annual interest. Which of you will have a balance of \$600 in the fewest years? *Explain* your reasoning.

42. CHALLENGE Amanda has \$600 in a savings account that earns 4% simple annual interest. At the beginning of each month, she deposits \$200 into the savings account. How much is in the account at the beginning of the seventh month before she makes her seventh deposit? *Justify* your answer.

◆ CALIFORNIA STANDARDS SPIRAL REVIEW

AF 1.4 **43.** What is the value of $-4(7 - 3) + 4$? *(p. 160)*

Ⓐ −36 Ⓑ −16 Ⓒ −12 Ⓓ 20

NS 1.4 **44.** 36 is 20% of what number? *(p. 319)*

Ⓐ 7.2 Ⓑ 12.25 Ⓒ 60 Ⓓ 180

NS 1.4 **45.** At a restaurant, you order a meal that costs \$8. You leave a 15% tip. What is the total cost of the meal? *(p. 325)*

Ⓐ \$6.80 Ⓑ \$8.02 Ⓒ \$9.20 Ⓓ \$9.50

QUIZ *for Lessons 6.4–6.6*

Use the percent equation to answer the question. *(p. 319)*

1. 82 is 205% of what number?
2. What percent of 50 is 28?

Use the given information to find the new price. *(p. 325)*

3. Original price: \$75
   Discount: 26%
4. Wholesale price: \$44
   Markup: 48%
5. **CLASS PRESIDENT** Kathy and Joshua are running for class president. Joshua received 45% of the votes. If all 120 students in the class voted, how many votes did Kathy receive? *(p. 319)*
6. **TIPS** You and two friends go to dinner. The bill comes to \$36. You want to leave a 20% tip. What is the total cost of the meal? *(p. 325)*
7. **SAVINGS** Suppose you put \$800 into a savings account that earns 2.5% simple annual interest. How long will it take to earn \$60 in interest? *(p. 331)*

Multiple Choice Practice for Lessons 6.4–6.6

1. Marie deposits $125 in a savings account that earns 3% simple annual interest. What is the balance in the account after 3 years? **NS 1.4**

   Ⓐ $11.25 Ⓑ $112.50 Ⓒ $113.75 Ⓓ $136.25

2. What percent of 180 is 81? **NS 1.4**

   Ⓐ 35% Ⓑ 40% Ⓒ 45% Ⓓ 55%

3. The bar graph below shows the results of a survey that asked 240 students how they get to school. What percent of students walk to school? **NS 1.4**

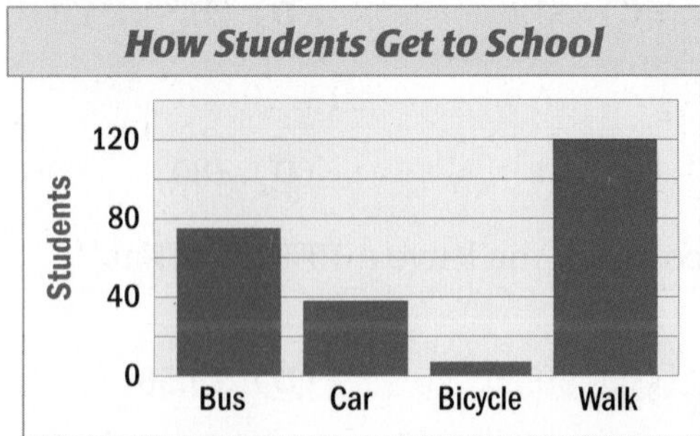

   Ⓐ 5% Ⓑ 25% Ⓒ 50% Ⓓ 120%

4. An item is on sale for 30% off the original price of $44. What is the sale price? **NS 1.4**

   Ⓐ $13.20 Ⓑ $30.80 Ⓒ $37.40 Ⓓ $57.20

5. You deposit $80 into a bank account that earns 2% simple annual interest. What is the amount of interest earned after 2 years? **NS 1.4**

   Ⓐ $3.20 Ⓑ $32.00 Ⓒ $38.40 Ⓓ $320.00

6. 16 is 32% of what number? **NS 1.4**

   Ⓐ 5 Ⓑ 50 Ⓒ 51.2 Ⓓ 512

7. You have $40. CDs are on sale as shown. The sales tax is 5%. What is the greatest number of CDs you can buy? **NS 1.4, MR 2.6**

   Ⓐ 2 Ⓑ 3 Ⓒ 4 Ⓓ 5

8. What number is 70% of 150? **NS 1.4**

   Ⓐ 98 Ⓑ 105 Ⓒ 112 Ⓓ 119

9. Kara once earned a 10% commission on all sales. Now, Kara earns a 15% commission. How much more will she now earn for selling a $175 item? **NS 1.4**

   Ⓐ $8.75 Ⓑ $12.25 Ⓒ $17.50 Ⓓ $21.00

10. The table shows the principal and balance after one year for 4 savings accounts. Which account has the highest interest rate? **NS 1.4, MR 2.2**

Account	Principal	Balance (after 1 yr)
A	$300	$330
B	$500	$545
C	$650	$718.25
D	$850	$930.75

   Ⓐ Account A Ⓑ Account B Ⓒ Account C Ⓓ Account D

6 CHAPTER SUMMARY

Standards
NS 1.4,
Gr. 5 NS 1.2

BIG IDEAS

For Your Notebook

Big Idea 1

Writing Equivalent Fractions, Decimals, and Percents

Denominator divides evenly into 100:

$\frac{4}{5} = \frac{80}{100} = 0.80 = 80\%$

Denominator does not divide evenly into 100:

$\frac{1}{120} = 1 \div 120 = 0.00833... \approx 0.83\%$

Big Idea 2

Calculating with Percents

You can represent "*a* is *p* percent of *b*" in the two ways shown below.

Proportion: $\frac{a}{b} = \frac{p}{100}$ **Equation:** $a = p\% \cdot b$

What is 5% of 60?	*What percent of 60 is 27?*	*60 is 40% of what number?*
$5\% \text{ of } 60 = \frac{1}{20} \cdot 60$ $= \frac{1 \cdot 60}{20 \cdot 1}$ $= 3$ 5% of 60 is 3.	$\frac{27}{60} = \frac{p}{100}$ $100 \cdot \frac{27}{60} = 100 \cdot \frac{p}{100}$ $45 = p$ 27 is 45% of 60.	$\frac{60}{b} = \frac{40}{100}$ $60 \cdot 100 = b \cdot 40$ $\frac{60 \cdot 100}{40} = \frac{b \cdot 40}{40}$ $150 = b$ 60 is 40% of 150.

Big Idea 3

Solving Problems Involving Percents

Problem Type	*How to Calculate*	*How to Apply*
Commission of 8% on a sale of a \$540 item	Find 8% of \$540. $0.08 \times 540 = 43.20$	Salesperson earns a commission of \$43.20.
Markup of 150% on a wholesale price of \$84	Find 150% of 84. $1.5 \times 84 = 126$	Add to find new price. $84 + 126 = \$210$
Discount of 33% on a purchase of \$45	Find 33% of \$45. $0.33 \times 45 = 14.85$	Subtract to find new price. $45.00 - 14.85 = \$30.15$
Sales tax of 8% on a purchase of \$45	Find 8% of \$45. $0.08 \times 45 = 3.60$	Add to find total cost. $45 + 3.60 = \$48.60$
Tip of 15% on a meal price of \$12	Find 15% of \$12. $0.15 \times 12 = 1.80$	Add to find total cost. $12 + 1.80 = \$13.80$
Simple annual interest of 4% on principal of \$450 for 2 years	Use formula $I = Prt$. $450 \times 0.04 \times 2 = 36$	Add to find new balance. $450 + 36 = \$486$

CHAPTER PROBLEM

Standards
NS 1.4,
Gr. 5 NS 1.2

APPLYING THE BIG IDEAS

Big Idea 1
You write equivalent fractions, decimals, and percents in **Step 3.**

Big Idea 2
You find a percent of a number in **Ex. 1.**

Big Idea 3
You solve problems involving discounts, sales tax, tips, and simple interest in **Exs. 2, 3, and 4.**

PROBLEM How can you use percents to compare how two people would spend money?

STEP 1 **Write fractions, decimals, and percents.**
Keith has budgeted \$200 that he expects to earn over the next 4 months. The table below shows how Keith will spend his money. Copy the table and add three more rows. Write each cost as a fraction, decimal, and percent of the total.

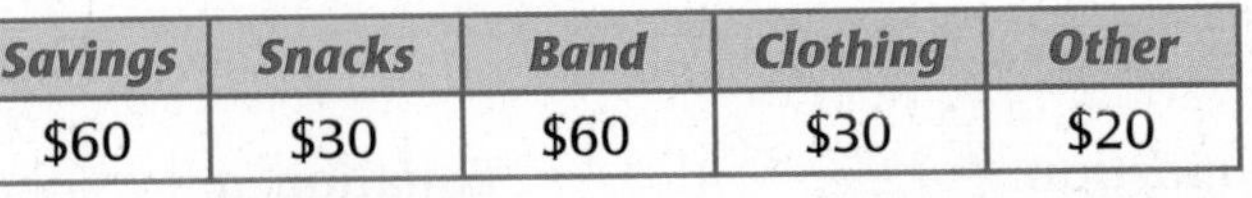

Savings	*Snacks*	*Band*	*Clothing*	*Other*
\$60	\$30	\$60	\$30	\$20

Keith pays part of his instrument rental.

STEP 2 **Decide how you would spend your money.**
Suppose you earn \$160 in four months, and you save at least 10% of it. How much money would you budget for each of the following: savings, snacks, music, clothing, and other? Record your budget in a table.

STEP 3 **Calculate percents.**
Write the portion of your money that you budgeted for each category as a fraction, decimal, and percent. Record the data in your table from Step 2.

STEP 4 **Compare results.**
Explain why you would use percents rather than dollar amounts to compare your budget to Keith's budget.

Extending the Problem

Use your results from the problem above to complete the exercises.

1. For which two categories did you budget the most money? Use two methods to calculate the total percent of your money that you budgeted for those two categories combined.
2. Add the amounts of money you budgeted for savings, snacks, clothing, music, and other. Suppose the sales tax is 7%. How much money in sales tax will you spend on these categories? How does this affect your budget?
3. Suppose you deposit your savings into a bank account that earns 2.5% simple annual interest. How much interest will you earn in 1 year?
4. Suppose that the stores where you buy your music, clothing, and snacks have a sale where everything is discounted 20%. If you put this extra money in your savings account, what will your balance be?

6 CHAPTER REVIEW

California @HomeTutor
classzone.com
• Multi-Language Visual Glossary
• Vocabulary practice

REVIEW KEY VOCABULARY

- percent, *p. 301*
- percent equation, *p. 319*
- interest, *p. 331*
- principal, *p. 331*
- simple interest, *p. 331*
- annual interest rate, *p. 331*
- balance, *p. 331*

VOCABULARY EXERCISES

Copy and complete the statement.

1. A ratio whose denominator is 100 is a(n) __?__.
2. The amount of money deposited or borrowed is called the __?__.
3. The amount earned or paid for the use of money is called __?__.
4. The sum of the interest and the principal is called the __?__.
5. **NOTETAKING SKILLS** Write the formula for simple interest in a *formula triangle* similar to the one on page 300.

REVIEW EXAMPLES AND EXERCISES

6.1 Percents and Fractions *pp. 301–304*

Gr. 5 NS 1.2

EXAMPLE

Write the percent as a fraction or the fraction as a percent.

a. $41\% = \frac{41}{100}$

b. $\frac{13}{25} = \frac{52}{100} = 52\%$

EXAMPLE

Find 75% of 116. Use the fact that $75\% = \frac{3}{4}$.

$$75\% \text{ of } 116 = \frac{3}{4} \cdot 116 = \frac{3 \cdot \overset{29}{\cancel{116}}}{\underset{1}{\cancel{4}}} = 87$$

▸ **Answer** 75% of 116 is 87.

CHECK You can use compatible numbers to check the reasonableness of the answer. Because $\frac{3}{4} \cdot 116 \approx \frac{3}{4} \cdot 120 = 90$, the answer is reasonable.

EXERCISES

SEE EXAMPLES 1, 2, 3, AND 4 on pp. 301–302 for Exs. 6–19

Write the percent as a fraction or the fraction as a percent.

6. 19% **7.** 65% **8.** 36% **9.** 98% **10.** 22%

11. $\frac{2}{25}$ **12.** $\frac{9}{20}$ **13.** $\frac{3}{5}$ **14.** $\frac{39}{50}$ **15.** $\frac{17}{20}$

Find the percent of the number. Check your answer for reasonableness.

16. 30% of 80 **17.** 25% of 130 **18.** 16% of 75

19. **CRIMINAL JUSTICE** Nine out of twelve members of a jury are over 35 years old. What percent of the jury is *not* over 35 years old?

6.2 Percents and Proportions

pp. 306–311

NS 1.4

EXAMPLE

What percent of 120 is 72?

$\frac{a}{b} = \frac{p}{100}$ **Write proportion.**

$\frac{72}{120} = \frac{p}{100}$ **Substitute 72 for *a* and 120 for *b*.**

$100 \cdot \frac{72}{120} = 100 \cdot \frac{p}{100}$ **Multiply each side by 100.**

$\frac{\overset{5}{\cancel{100}} \cdot \overset{12}{\cancel{72}}}{\underset{1}{\cancel{\underset{6}{\cancel{120}}}}} = p$ **Use rule for multiplying fractions. Divide out common factors.**

$60 = p$ **Multiply.**

▸ **Answer** 72 is 60% of 120.

EXERCISES

SEE EXAMPLES 1, 2, AND 3 on pp. 306–308 for Exs. 20–28

Use a proportion to answer the question.

20. What percent of 75 is 12? **21.** What percent of 70 is 42?

22. What percent of 240 is 192? **23.** What percent of 340 is 51?

24. What number is 35% of 200? **25.** 18 is 90% of what number?

26. 72 is 40% of what number? **27.** What number is 9% of 200?

28. **NUTRITION** A vitamin pill provides 14% of the magnesium that an adult needs per day. The pill contains 40 milligrams of magnesium. How many milligrams of magnesium does an adult need per day?

6.3 Percents and Decimals

pp. 312–317

NS 1.4

EXAMPLE

MANUFACTURING A company that makes paper plates has to throw away about 0.15% of the plates because they are defective. The company has just made 4000 plates. About how many of the plates must the company throw away?

SOLUTION

0.15% of $4000 = 0.0015 \times 4000$ **Write percent as a decimal.**

$= 6$ **Multiply.**

▶ **Answer** The company must throw away about 6 of the 4000 plates.

EXERCISES

SEE EXAMPLES 1, 2, 3, AND 4 on pp. 312–313 for Exs. 29–34

Write the percent as a decimal or the decimal as a percent.

29. 31% **30.** 135% **31.** 0.28% **32.** 0.0041 **33.** 1.24

34. TESTS John answered 85% of the 40 test questions correctly. How many questions did John answer correctly?

6.4 The Percent Equation

pp. 319–323

NS 1.4

EXAMPLE

12 is 40% of what number?

$a = p\% \cdot b$ **Write percent equation.**

$12 = 40\% \cdot b$ **Substitute 12 for *a* and 40 for *p*.**

$12 = 0.40 \cdot b$ **Write percent as a decimal.**

$\frac{12}{0.40} = \frac{0.40b}{0.40}$ **Divide each side by 0.40.**

$30 = b$ **Simplify.**

▶ **Answer** 12 is 40% of 30.

EXERCISES

SEE EXAMPLES 2, 3, AND 4 on p. 320 for Exs. 35–37

Use the percent equation to answer the question.

35. 60 is 125% of what number? **36.** What percent of 500 is 2?

37. COMMISSIONS Joe sells a television for $425. Joe earns a 15% commission on the sale. How much is the commision?

6.5 Discounts, Markups, Tips, and Sales Tax

pp. 325–329

NS 1.4

EXAMPLE

FURNITURE A \$750 sofa is now 30% off. What is the sale price?

Discount: 30% of \$750 = **0.3** × \$750 = \$225

Sale Price: \$750 − \$225 = \$525

▶ **Answer** The sale price is \$525.

EXERCISES

SEE EXAMPLES 1, 2, 3, AND 4 on pp. 325–327 for Exs. 38–42

Use the given information to find the new price.

38. Original price: \$72
Discount: 75%

39. Original price: \$60
Discount: 9%

40. Wholesale price: \$67
Markup: 115%

41. DINING You and your family are eating at a restaurant. The food bill is \$40. Your family leaves a 20% tip. The sales tax is 6%. What is the total cost of the meal?

42. CLOTHING You buy a pair of jeans that are on sale for 20% off the original price. You pay \$18 for the jeans. What was the original price?

6.6 Simple Interest

pp. 331–335

NS 1.4

EXAMPLE

INTEREST You have \$180 in an account that earns 5% simple annual interest. How much interest will the account earn in 6 months?

$$I = Prt = (180)(0.05)\left(\frac{6}{12}\right) = \$4.50$$

▶ **Answer** The account will earn \$4.50 in 6 months.

EXERCISES

SEE EXAMPLES 1, 2, AND 3 on pp. 331–332 for Exs. 43–47

Find the unknown quantity.

43. $I = \underline{\ ?\ }$
$P = \$550$
$r = 14.5\%$
$t = 4$ years

44. $I = \$590$
$P = \underline{\ ?\ }$
$r = 2.5\%$
$t = 10$ years

45. $I = \$7$
$P = \$175$
$r = 16\%$
$t = \underline{\ ?\ }$

46. $I = \$1210$
$P = \$15{,}000$
$r = \underline{\ ?\ }$
$t = 11$ months

47. BANKING Maggie had \$600 in a savings account. In 3 months she earned \$6 in interest. What was the simple annual interest rate?

6 CHAPTER TEST

1. **VOCABULARY** The percent equation is $a = p\% \cdot b$, where a is part of the __?__ b and $p\%$ is the percent.

2. **VOCABULARY** When interest is earned or paid only on the __?__, it is called simple interest.

Write the percent as a fraction or the fraction as a percent.

3. 65%
4. 40%
5. $\frac{12}{25}$
6. $\frac{4}{5}$

Use a proportion to answer the question.

7. What number is 15% of 30?
8. What number is 30% of 210?
9. 12 is 60% of what number?
10. What percent of 40 is 18?

Write the percent as a decimal or the decimal as a percent.

11. 0.037
12. 208%
13. 0.45%
14. 1.35

Use the percent equation to answer the question.

15. What number is 134% of 20,000?
16. 32 is 40% of what number?
17. What percent of 25 is 24?
18. What percent of 60 is 3?

Find the unknown quantity.

19. $I = \underline{\ ?\ }$
$P = \$500$
$r = 5\%$
$t = 3$ years
20. $I = \$600$
$P = \underline{\ ?\ }$
$r = 3\%$
$t = 10$ years
21. $I = \$39$
$P = \$800$
$r = 6.5\%$
$t = \underline{\ ?\ }$
22. $I = \$15.30$
$P = \$90$
$r = \underline{\ ?\ }$
$t = 5$ years

23. **ADVERTISING** An advertisement says that 5 out of 7 doctors prefer a certain product. What percent of doctors do *not* prefer the product?

24. **CLOTHING** You want to buy a shirt that costs \$20. The sales tax is 7.25%. What is the total cost of the shirt?

25. **BACKPACKS** Which backpack in the table costs less after the discounts are taken? *Justify* your reasoning.

26. **TIPS** You pay \$14 for dinner and want to leave a 15% tip. What is the total cost of the meal?

Backpack Sale		
Nylon	Original Price	\$40
	Discount	20% off
Canvas	Original Price	\$50
	Discount	40% off

27. **LOANS** You borrow \$240 from your parents. One year later you pay back \$270. How much interest did you pay your parents? What was the simple annual interest rate?

6 ◆ MULTIPLE CHOICE STRATEGIES

STRATEGIES YOU'LL USE:
- **SOLVE DIRECTLY**
- **ELIMINATE CHOICES**

Standards
NS 1.4

If you have trouble solving a multiple choice problem directly, you may be able to use another approach to eliminate incorrect answer choices and obtain the correct answer.

PROBLEM 1

If 40% of a number is 28, what is 50% of the number?

Ⓐ 5.6 Ⓑ 14 Ⓒ 35 Ⓓ 71

Strategy 1 SOLVE DIRECTLY

First, find the number such that 40% of it is 28. Then find 50% of the number.

STEP 1 **Find** the number such that 40% of it is 28.

$$\frac{a}{b} = \frac{p}{100}$$

$$\frac{28}{b} = \frac{40}{100}$$

$$28 \cdot 100 = b \cdot 40$$

$$\frac{28 \cdot 100}{40} = \frac{b \cdot 40}{40}$$

$$70 = b$$

40% of 70 is 28.

STEP 2 **Find** 50% of 70.

$$\frac{a}{b} = \frac{p}{100}$$

$$\frac{a}{70} = \frac{50}{100}$$

$$a \cdot 100 = 70 \cdot 50$$

$$\frac{a \cdot 100}{100} = \frac{70 \cdot 50}{100}$$

$$a = 35$$

50% of 70 is 35.

The correct answer is C. Ⓐ Ⓑ Ⓒ Ⓓ

Strategy 2 ELIMINATE CHOICES

In some cases, you can use number sense to identify incorrect answer choices.

- Because 40% of the number is 28, then 50% of the number must be greater than 28. You can eliminate choices A and B.
- Because 40% of a number is 28, then 80% of the number is 2 • 28, or 56. So, 50% of the number is between 28 and 56. You can eliminate choice D.

The correct answer is C. Ⓐ Ⓑ Ⓒ Ⓓ

PROBLEM 2

A store is selling all DVDs at 15% off the original price. What is the sale price of a DVD originally priced at $18?

Ⓐ $2.70 Ⓑ $15.30 Ⓒ $20.70 Ⓓ $27.00

Strategy 1 SOLVE DIRECTLY

Find the discount. Then subtract the discount from the original price.

STEP 1 **Find** the discount.

Discount = 15% of $18

= 0.15×18

= 2.7

STEP 2 **Subtract** the discount from the original price.

Sale price = Original price − Discount

= 18 − 2.7

= 15.30

The sale price is $15.30.

The correct answer is B. Ⓐ Ⓑ Ⓒ Ⓓ

Strategy 2 ELIMINATE CHOICES

In some cases, you can use number sense to identify incorrect answer choices.

- Because the store is selling all DVDs at 15% off the original price, the sale price of a DVD will be less than $18. You can eliminate choices C and D.
- With a 15% discount, you pay more than half price. Because $2.70 is less than half price, you can eliminate choice A.

The correct answer is B. Ⓐ Ⓑ Ⓒ Ⓓ

STRATEGY PRACTICE

Explain why you can eliminate the highlighted answer choice.

1. What number is 30% of 84?

   Ⓐ 25.2 Ⓑ 58.8 Ⓒ 120 Ⓓ ✗ **280**

2. A store that sells refrigerators buys them at a wholesale price of $180. The store's markup is 160%. What is the retail price?

   Ⓐ ✗ **$108** Ⓑ $278 Ⓒ $288 Ⓓ $468

3. You are buying a backpack for $24. The sales tax is 7%. What is the total cost of the backpack?

   Ⓐ $1.68 Ⓑ ✗ **$22.32** Ⓒ $25.68 Ⓓ $40.80

6 ◆ MULTIPLE CHOICE PRACTICE

1. A landscaper designed a plan for a flower bed in a rectangular front lawn, as shown in the shaded part of the grid below. What percent of the front lawn will be the flower bed? **Gr. 5 NS 1.2**

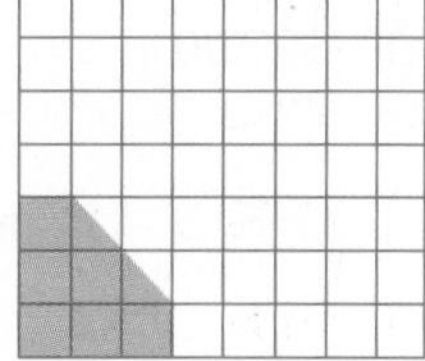

Ⓐ 7%

Ⓑ 8%

Ⓒ 12.5%

Ⓓ 20%

2. 51 is 5% of what number? **NS 1.4**

Ⓐ 10.2

Ⓑ 25.5

Ⓒ 102

Ⓓ 1020

3. The table shows the portion of votes cast for each of the 3 students in a recent school election. If 1200 votes were cast, how many students voted for Jimmy? **NS 1.4**

Student	*Votes*
Anna	$\frac{2}{5}$
Beth	30%
Jimmy	?

Ⓐ 360

Ⓑ 400

Ⓒ 480

Ⓓ 840

4. What is 45% of 80? **Gr. 5 NS 1.2**

Ⓐ 3.6

Ⓑ 32

Ⓒ 36

Ⓓ 360

5. Tela invests $1500 in a 1 year certificate of deposit. At the end of 1 year, her balance is $1530. What is the simple annual interest rate? **NS 1.4**

Ⓐ 0.02%

Ⓑ 1.02%

Ⓒ 1.9%

Ⓓ 2%

6. Ms. Shaffer advises the school yearbook staff. The percent bar model shows the grade levels of the staff members. What percent of the staff members are sixth graders? **NS 1.4**

0 12 26
Eighth Seventh Sixth
0% 30% 100%

Ⓐ 14%

Ⓑ 30%

Ⓒ 35%

Ⓓ 62%

7. What percent of 40 is 14? **NS 1.4**

Ⓐ 0.35%

Ⓑ 2.9%

Ⓒ 3.5%

Ⓓ 35%

8. After a meal at a restaurant, you are given the bill shown. You want to leave a 20% tip. Which of the following tips should you leave? **NS 1.4**

Ⓐ $.20

Ⓑ $2.00

Ⓒ $4.50

Ⓓ $5.00

GUEST CHECK
040326
1 salad
2 chicken sandwich
2 iced tea
$24.80
TAX
THANK YOU

9. A store is selling sweaters at 60% off the original price. Sales tax is 7%. Using estimation, which value for the final cost is most reasonable? **NS 1.4, MR 2.1**

Ⓐ $9.30

Ⓑ $10.07

Ⓒ $10.70

Ⓓ $16.05

10. A store is selling baseball gloves for 30% off the original price. The original price of a baseball glove is $60. The sales tax is 6%. What is the total cost of the baseball glove? **NS 1.4**

Ⓐ $42.00

Ⓑ $44.52

Ⓒ $63.60

Ⓓ $67.20

11. The dinner bill for you and two friends is $22.50. You leave an 18% tip. You and your friends split the cost evenly. How much money will each person pay? **NS 1.4, MR 1.3**

Ⓐ $6.64

Ⓑ $7.50

Ⓒ $8.85

Ⓓ $13.28

12. You invest $300 into a 2 year certificate of deposit that earns 6.5% simple annual interest. What is the balance at the end of 2 years? **NS 1.4**

Ⓐ $39

Ⓑ $339

Ⓒ $390

Ⓓ $500

13. Ethan worked a total of 30 hours this week, 16 of which he worked on the weekend. Which of the following best represents the percent of his hours that he did *not* work on the weekend? **Gr. 5 NS 1.2**

Ⓐ 14%

Ⓑ 47%

Ⓒ 53%

Ⓓ 67%

14. The bar graph represents the percent of students in sixth grade that participate in four after school activities. Of the 150 students in the sixth grade, how many participate in the drama club? **NS 1.4, MR 2.4**

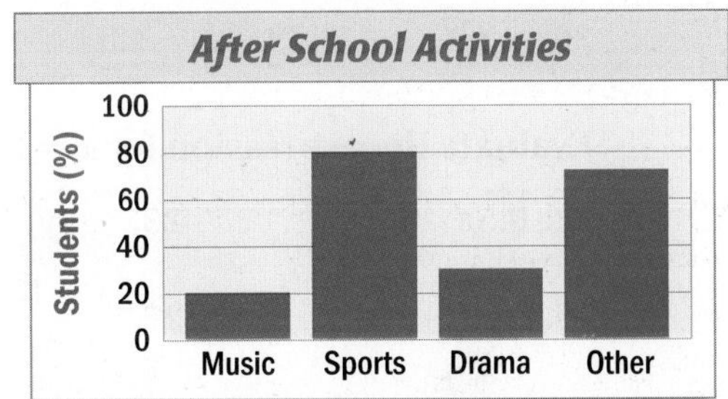

Ⓐ 30

Ⓑ 45

Ⓒ 105

Ⓓ 120

15. Students in a ski club made 5000 paper flowers for a parade float. The colors of the flowers are shown in the table. How many purple flowers did they make? **NS 1.4**

Ⓐ 750

Ⓑ 900

Ⓒ 1450

Ⓓ 1800

Color	*Amount*
Red	29%
White	20%
Yellow	15%
Purple	?
Blue	18%

6 CUMULATIVE REVIEW Chapters 1–6

Evaluate the expression. Simplify if possible.

1. $\frac{6}{11} + \frac{3}{11}$ *(p. 69)*
2. $\frac{7}{9} - \frac{4}{9}$ *(p. 69)*
3. $8\frac{1}{3} - 5\frac{3}{4}$ *(p. 81)*
4. $6\frac{5}{6} + 3\frac{3}{8}$ *(p. 81)*
5. $\frac{2}{5} \times \frac{10}{13}$ *(p. 88)*
6. $4\frac{8}{15} \times 9\frac{1}{2}$ *(p. 88)*
7. $7\frac{5}{7} \div 2\frac{9}{10}$ *(p. 95)*
8. $\frac{5}{8} \div \frac{3}{14}$ *(p. 95)*

Evaluate the expression.

9. $-4 + (-14)$ *(p. 135)*
10. $24 + (-36) + 16$ *(p. 135)*
11. $12 - (-18)$ *(p. 143)*
12. $3 - 6 - (-4)$ *(p. 143)*
13. $3(-12)$ *(p. 148)*
14. $-6(-4)(2)$ *(p. 148)*
15. $3(-2)(-1)(8)$ *(p. 148)*
16. $63 \div (-9)$ *(p. 154)*
17. $-36 \div (-2)$ *(p. 154)*

Order the numbers from least to greatest. *(p. 167)*

18. $-2\frac{1}{3}, -3\frac{3}{11}, 3, -2.5, -3\frac{1}{4}, 3.27$
19. $-1\frac{14}{25}, -2, -2.55, -4\frac{1}{3}, 4$
20. $-3\frac{3}{10}, -\frac{1}{3}, 3.33, 4\frac{1}{3}, -4.3$
21. $-0.53, -\frac{8}{15}, -1\frac{53}{100}, 1.53, \frac{8}{15}$

Evaluate the expression for $x = 2$, $y = -1$, and $z = 0.25$. *(p. 197)*

22. $0.5z$
23. $-4y^3 - 12$
24. $6(3y - x)$
25. $xy^2 + 4y$
26. yz
27. $\frac{x - 12y}{5}$
28. $\frac{x + 8y}{3} + 4z$
29. $(x + 8y)^2 - 3z$

Simplify the expression. *(p. 207)*

30. $6x + 9 - 2x - 14$
31. $5(y + 3) + 2y$
32. $8 + 4(z - 5) - 17z$
33. $18a - 4 + 6 - 7a$
34. $-6(3 - b) + 33 + 4b$
35. $12(2c - 4) - 8c$

Convert the temperature to degrees Celsius or degrees Fahrenheit. *(p. 212)*

36. 56°F
37. 15°C
38. 30°C

Solve the equation. Check your solution. *(pp. 226, 234)*

39. $n + 8 = -4$
40. $w - 7.6 = 3.1$
41. $35 + r - 2 = 12$
42. $-6p = 54$
43. $\frac{3}{10}x = 7.5$
44. $\frac{2}{5}t = 8$
45. $-36 + p - 40 = 54$
46. $\frac{1}{3}x = 8$
47. $42 - t - 16 = 3$

Solve the proportion. *(p. 274)*

48. $\frac{3}{8} = \frac{x}{40}$
49. $\frac{y}{12} = \frac{22}{8}$
50. $\frac{5}{7.5} = \frac{7}{z}$
51. $\frac{6.3}{w} = \frac{2.7}{9.9}$
52. $\frac{2}{5} = \frac{14}{x}$
53. $\frac{3}{7} = \frac{t}{42}$
54. $\frac{12}{3} = \frac{144}{s}$
55. $\frac{4}{16} = \frac{2}{y}$

Use the percent equation to answer the question. ***(p. 319)***

56. 48 is 60% of what number?

57. What number is 72% of 150?

58. What percent of 150 is 24?

59. 108 is 36% of what number?

Use the given information to find the unknown value. ***(p. 325)***

60. Wholesale price = \$49
Markup = 30%
Retail price = __?__

61. Retail price = \$24.50
Tax = 5%
Total cost = __?__

62. Original price = \$40
Discount = 30%
Sale price = __?__

63. Food bill before tax = \$15.48
Tip = 20%
Cost with tip = __?__

Find the unknown quantity. ***(p. 331)***

64. I = __?__
P = \$200
r = 4%
t = 5 years

65. I = \$60
P = __?__
r = 3%
t = 3 years

66. I = \$25
P = \$600
r = __?__
t = 10 months

67. I = \$12
P = \$450
r = 4%
t = __?__

68. SHOPPING You want to buy a shirt for \$16.30, a pair of jeans for \$32.99, and a pair of shoes for \$29.25. How much money will you spend? ***(p. 102)***

69. GASOLINE A gas station is selling gasoline for \$3.11 per gallon. A customer buys x gallons and pays a total of \$25. Write and solve an equation to find how many gallons of gasoline the customer buys. Round your answer to the nearest hundredth. ***(p. 234)***

70. AIR TRAVEL An airplane can travel 150 miles in 30 minutes. At this rate, how many hours will it take the airplane to travel 900 miles? ***(p. 260)***

71. STATUE OF LIBERTY The height of the Statue of Liberty from the base to the torch is approximately 151 feet. A book has a picture of the Statue of Liberty that has a height of $\frac{2}{3}$ foot from the base to the torch. What is the scale of the picture? ***(p. 281)***

72. BASEBALL CAPS A minor league baseball team is giving away a free baseball cap to each of the first 100 fans who attend the game. The total attendance for the game is 5250. What percent of the crowd receives a free cap? Round your answer to the nearest tenth of a percent. ***(p. 319)***

73. COMPACT DISCS A store has CDs priced at \$14 each. The store is discounting the price by 15%. You have \$25 to spend. Do you have enough money to pay for 2 CDs if the sales tax is 6%? *Explain.* ***(p. 325)***

7 Analyzing Data

Before

In previous chapters, you learned the following skills, which you'll use in Chapter 7:

- Reading a bar graph
- Performing operations with fractions, decimals, and percents
- Calculating a mean

Now

In Chapter 7 you'll study these ***Big Ideas:***

1. Evaluating sampling methods and validity of claims
2. Computing and analyzing statistics
3. Making and analyzing data displays

Why?

So you can solve real-world problems about . . .

- Vacation destinations, p. 363
- Sea turtles, p. 368
- Tree heights, p. 376
- Walking trails, p. 383
- Stamp prices, p. 396
- Advertising, p. 397

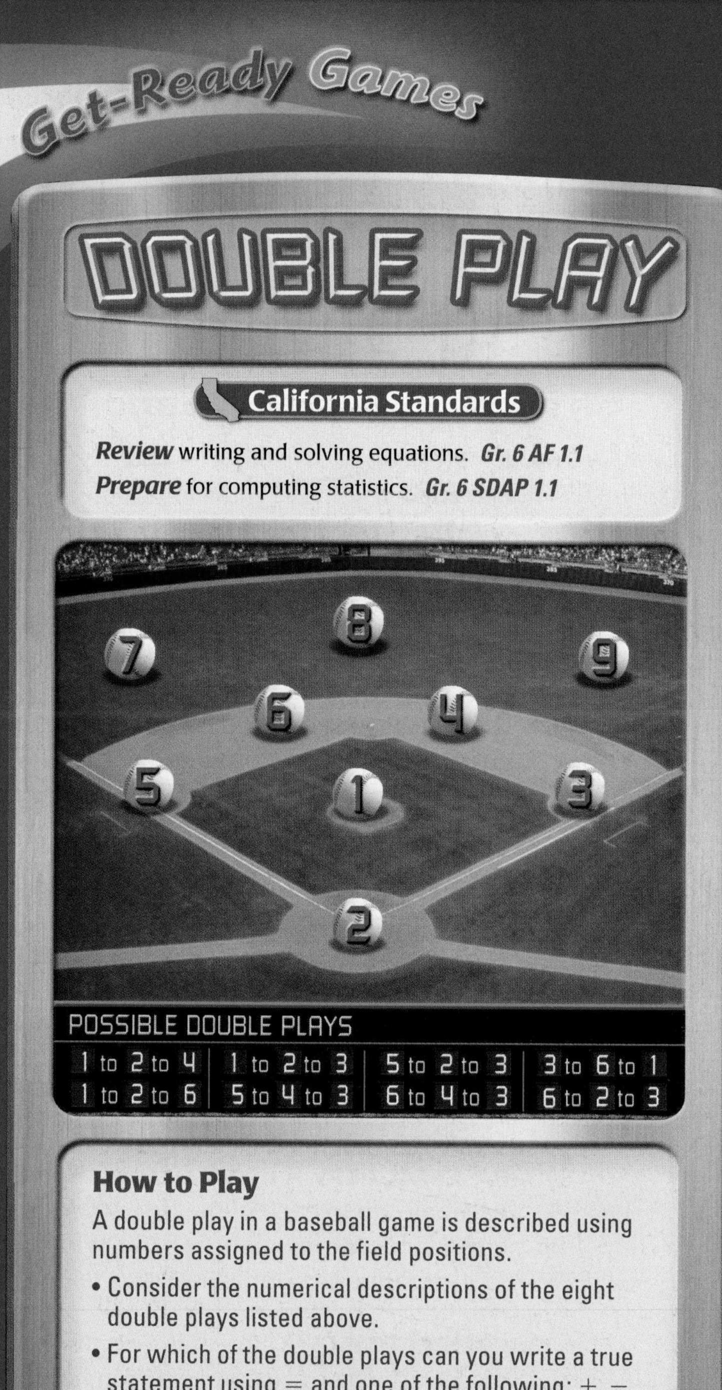

California Standards

Review writing and solving equations. ***Gr. 6 AF 1.1***
Prepare for computing statistics. ***Gr. 6 SDAP 1.1***

POSSIBLE DOUBLE PLAYS

1 to 2 to 4	1 to 2 to 3	5 to 2 to 3	3 to 6 to 1
1 to 2 to 6	5 to 4 to 3	6 to 4 to 3	6 to 2 to 3

How to Play

A double play in a baseball game is described using numbers assigned to the field positions.

- Consider the numerical descriptions of the eight double plays listed above.
- For which of the double plays can you write a true statement using = and one of the following: +, −, ×, or ÷? List all of the possible statements.

California Standards

- **Gr. 6 SDAP 1.0 Students compute and analyze statistical measurements for data sets.** ***(Lessons 7.3, 7.4, 7.5, 7.6)***
- **Gr. 6 SDAP 2.0 Students use data samples of population and describe the characteristics and limitations of the samples.** ***(Lessons 7.1, 7.2, 7.7)***

PITCHER SHUFFLE

California Standards

Review ordering decimals. ***Gr. 6 NS 1.1***

Prepare for computing median. ***Gr. 6 SDAP 1.1***

PLAYER	10	14	19	8	4	22
ERA	3.71	2.03	2.65	1.82	3.77	4.22

How to Play

A pitcher's earned run average (ERA) indicates the pitcher's success in preventing batters from scoring. A low ERA is desirable.

- Order the ERAs from least to greatest.
- Use the first letter of the name with the lowest ERA, the second letter of the name with the second lowest ERA, etc. The letters spell the last name of the pitcher with the lowest career ERA of active pitchers in 2005.

Games Wrap-Up

Draw Conclusions

Complete these exercises after playing the games.

1. WRITING Consider the pitcher whose name you found in *Pitcher Shuffle*. What percent of active pitchers had a career ERA less than his in 2005? *Explain* your reasoning.

2. REASONING For the field positions in *Double Play*, how many different true statements can you write for the *triple* play 7 to 2 to 5 to 4 using $=$ and $+$, $-$, $\times$, or $\div$? List all of the possible statements.

7 Getting Ready

Prerequisite Skills

California @HomeTutor
Prerequisite skills practice at classzone.com

REVIEW VOCABULARY

- **mean,** *p. 156*
- **line plot,** *p. 686*
- **bar graph,** *p. 687*

VOCABULARY CHECK

Copy and complete using a review term from the list at the left.

1. In a data set, the sum of the values divided by the number of values is the __?__ of the data set.

2. A(n) __?__ uses a number line to show how often data values occur.

SKILL CHECK

Find the mean of the integers. *(p. 154)*

3. 17, 22, 24, 28, 29, 36

4. 34, 37, 38, 42, 42, 45, 49

Make a line plot of the data. *(p. 686)*

5. 10, 9, 8, 8, 9, 7, 11, 10, 8, 9, 8

6. 6, 7, 9, 5, 7, 9, 6, 5, 5, 7, 9, 7, 7

The bar graph shows the average swimming speeds for some common fish. *(p. 687)*

7. What is the average swimming speed for carp?

8. What fish swims at an average speed of 8 kilometers per hour?

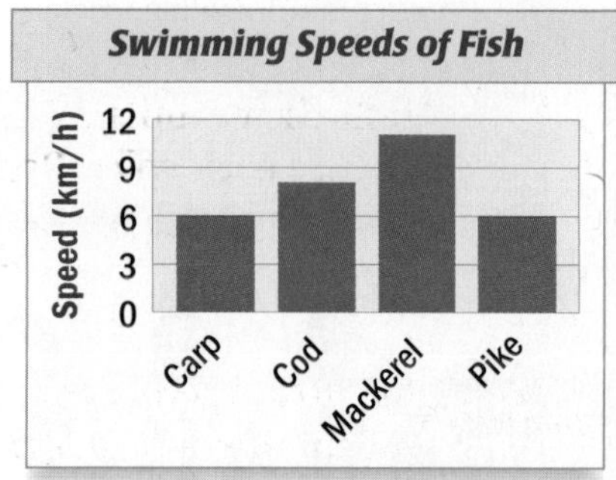

Notetaking Skills

NOW YOU TRY
Use a *notetaking organizer* to write your notes about the percent equation. You may want to use colored pencils.

Focus on Graphic Organizers

Use a *notetaking organizer* to write your notes, vocabulary, and questions about a topic, such as writing percents as fractions.

Write important vocabulary or formulas in the narrow column.

Write p percent as p% or $\frac{p}{100}$	Writing percents as fractions: $20\% = \frac{20}{100} = \frac{1}{5}$ Writing fractions as percent: $\frac{3}{5} = \frac{3 \times 20}{5 \times 20} = \frac{60}{100} = 60$
How can you write a decimal as a percent?	

Write your notes about percents and fractions in this space.

Write your questions about percents here.

7.1 Collecting Data

MATERIALS • pencil and paper

Standards

SDAP 2.1 Compare different samples of a population with the data from the entire population and identify a situation in which it makes sense to use a sample.

QUESTION **How do the data from some class members compare with the data from the entire class?**

When you survey only part of a group, or *population,* the part you survey is a *sample.* Your surveying method is a *sampling method.*

EXPLORE **Use different sampling methods and compare results.**

STEP 1 **Copy** the table at the right. Ask students sitting in the first seat of each row the question below.

Which is your favorite color: red, blue, green, or yellow?

Tally the number of students who choose each color. Record your results and the sample size in the column of your table labeled *Step 1.*

	Step 1	*Step 2*	*Step 3*
Number who said red	?	?	?
Number who said blue	?	?	?
Number who said green	?	?	?
Number who said yellow	?	?	?
Total students asked (Sample size)	?	10	?

STEP 2 **Ask** 10 randomly chosen students the question from Step 1. Tally the number of students who choose each color. Record your results in the column labeled *Step 2.*

STEP 3 **Write** your favorite of the four colors on a piece of paper and give it to your teacher. Tally the results for the entire class (population) and use the data for the column labeled *Step 3.*

DRAW CONCLUSIONS **Use your observations to complete these exercises.**

1. Write the percent of students who chose "blue" for each sampling method in Steps 1 and 2 above.
2. Compare the percent of students who chose "blue" in Step 1 and in Step 2 to the percent of students who chose "blue" in the entire class. Which sampling method has results closer to the results for the entire class?
3. **REASONING** Would you expect sample size to affect how closely the sample results agree with the population results? *Explain* your reasoning.
4. **REASONING** Does it make sense to use a sample in this situation? *Explain* your reasoning.

7.1 Sampling Methods

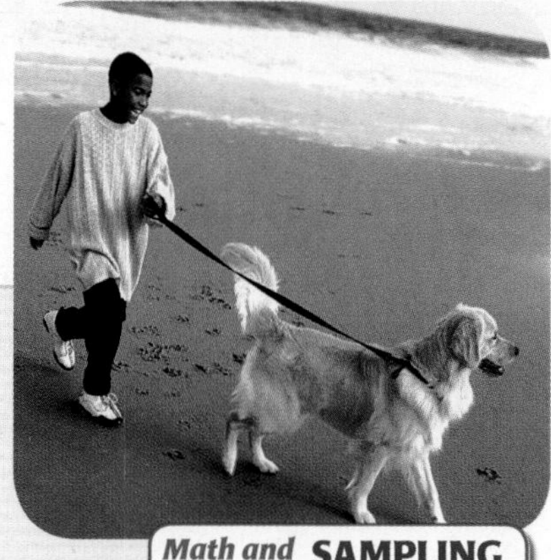

Math and SAMPLING
Exs. 14–16, p. 357

Standards SDAP 2.1 **Compare different samples of a population with the data from the entire population and identify a situation in which it makes sense to use a sample.**

SDAP 2.2 **Identify different ways of selecting a sample (e.g., convenience sampling, responses to a survey, random sampling) and which method makes a sample more representative for a population.**

Connect ***Before*** you used bar graphs to compare data. ***Now*** you will identify and compare sampling methods and recognize how a method may create a biased sample.

KEY VOCABULARY
- **population**
- **sample**
- **random sampling**
- **systematic sampling**
- **convenience sampling**
- **self-selected sampling**
- **biased sample**

One way to collect data about a group is by conducting a survey. A **population** is the entire group of people or objects that you want information about. When it is difficult to survey an entire population, such as all citizens, a **sample**, or a part of the entire group, is surveyed.

EXAMPLE 1 Comparing Samples

SLEEP SURVEY You want to find out how much sleep students at a large school got last night. You survey two first-period classes.

a. Identify the population and the samples.

b. Decide whether it makes sense to use samples.

c. Suppose all first-period classes are surveyed and the mean for the student population is 8 hours of sleep. Compare this mean with the means for the samples.

Hours of Sleep

Class A	Class B
6, 6	
6.5, 6.5	
7, 7, 7, 7	7, 7, 7
7.5, 7.5, 7.5	7.5, 7.5, 7.5
8, 8, 8	8, 8, 8
8.5, 8.5	8.5, 8.5, 8.5
9	9, 9, 9, 9, 9
9.5	9.5, 9.5, 9.5
10, 10	

SOLUTION

a. The population is all of the students at the school. There are two samples: the students in Class A and the students in Class B.

b. Yes, it makes sense to use class samples with a large school population.

c. The mean number of hours of sleep last night is 7.75 for Class A and 8.325 for Class B. Compared with a population mean of 8, students in Class A got less sleep and students in Class B got more sleep.

✓ GUIDED PRACTICE for Example 1

1. WHAT IF? Suppose you survey another class. Below are their hours of sleep. Compare the mean for Class C with the population mean.

Class C: 6.5, 8, 9, 7.5, 7, 9, 8.5, 9.5, 10, 6.5, 6, 8, 7.5, 7, 8.5

SAMPLES Four ways to collect samples of a population are listed below. Because a sample is meant to give you information about an entire population, a sample should be representative of the population.

KEY CONCEPT *For Your Notebook*

Sampling Methods

In **random sampling**, each person or object in a population has an equally likely chance of being selected.

In **systematic sampling**, a pattern is used to select members of a population.

In **convenience sampling**, easy to reach members of a population are selected.

In **self-selected sampling**, members of a population volunteer to be part of the sample.

Random samples are most likely to be representative of the population. Samples that are not representative of the population, such as most convenience samples and self-selected samples, are **biased samples**.

EXAMPLE 2 Identifying Sampling Methods

DANCE SURVEY A sample of students at a school is asked to choose movies, historical figures, or sports as a theme for a costume dance. Identify the sampling method. Tell whether the sample is likely to be biased.

a. Survey members of the movie club during a club meeting.

b. Survey every fourth student entering the school one morning.

c. Point to a name on a list of all students. Repeat 20 times.

SOLUTION

a. This is convenience sampling. The sample is biased, because the members of the movie club are more likely to favor a movie theme.

b. This is systematic sampling. The sample is probably not biased.

c. This is random sampling. The sample is probably not biased.

✓ **GUIDED PRACTICE** for Example 2

MUSIC SURVEY You survey musicians about their favorite types of music. Identify the sampling method. Tell whether the sample is likely to be biased.

2. Place an ad in a rock music magazine and have readers call to respond.

3. Survey every other person entering a music school.

EXAMPLE 3 ◆ Multiple Choice Practice

A newspaper reporter conducts a survey asking people who they plan to vote for as mayor. Which of the following methods is the *best* way for the reporter to choose a representative sample of the city's voters?

Ⓐ Survey people at a rally for one of the candidates.

Ⓑ Place a survey in a candidate's newsletter so that people can call in their choices for mayor.

Ⓒ Survey every twentieth person on the city's voter registration list.

Ⓓ Survey every second student entering a high school.

SOLUTION

Choices A and B are not representative samples because people connected to a candidate would tend to favor that candidate. Choice D includes people who cannot vote so it is not a representative sample of the voters.

▶**Answer** The reporter should survey every twentieth person on the city's voter registration list. The correct answer is C. Ⓐ Ⓑ Ⓒ Ⓓ

GUIDED PRACTICE for Example 3

4. **EVENING NEWS** *Describe* a sampling method that a television station can use to choose a representative sample of the people from the towns in its viewing area.

7.1 EXERCISES

HOMEWORK KEY

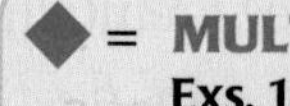

◆ = **MULTIPLE CHOICE PRACTICE** Exs. 10, 17, 21–23

○ = **HINTS AND HOMEWORK HELP** for Exs. 5, 9, 19 at classzone.com

SKILLS • PROBLEM SOLVING • REASONING

1. **VOCABULARY** The sampling method in which members of a population volunteer to be part of the sample is ___?___.

2. **WRITING** *Describe* the difference between a population and a sample.

SEE EXAMPLE 1 on p. 354 for Exs. 3–6

SAMPLE OR POPULATION Decide whether it makes sense to survey a sample to collect the data. *Explain* your reasoning.

3. The salaries of employees at a company of 40 employees

4. The most popular car colors among car owners in the United States

5. The favorite television shows of television watchers in the United States

6. The favorite types of books among students in a classroom of 25 students

SEE EXAMPLE 2
on p. 355
for Exs. 7–11

IDENTIFYING METHODS You survey voters about using tax money to expand the town library. Identify the sampling method. Tell whether the sample is likely to be biased.

7. Survey people as they leave the library.

8. Place a questionnaire in the town newspaper.

9. Survey every tenth person on the town's voter registration list.

10. ◆ **MULTIPLE CHOICE** A reporter is writing about Internet shopping. The reporter calls 10 friends and asks whether they purchased items online last month. Which sampling method did the reporter use?

Ⓐ convenience Ⓑ self-selected Ⓒ systematic Ⓓ random

11. **ERROR ANALYSIS** Lucius surveys every third student who enters the school. He claims that this sampling method is a self-selected sample. *Describe* and correct Lucius's error.

SEE EXAMPLES 1 AND 3
on pp. 354, 356
for Exs. 12–13

OPEN-ENDED Identify the population. *Describe* a sampling method that is likely to result in a representative sample.

12. A cafeteria manager wants to know the favorite school lunch among the students in a school district.

13. A city planner wants to know whether residents favor using public funds to pay for a new baseball stadium.

CONNECT SKILLS TO PROBLEM SOLVING Exercises 14–16 will help you prepare for problem solving.

Use the following information: You want to know the percent of students at your school that have a pet. You survey all the students in your apartment building who go to your school.

14. Identify the population, the sample, and the sampling method.

15. Tell whether the sample is likely to be biased. *Explain* your reasoning.

16. *Describe* another sampling method you could use.

SEE EXAMPLE 3
on p. 356
for Ex. 17

17. ◆ **MULTIPLE CHOICE** A principal plans to survey sixth grade students to find out where they want to go on a field trip. Which sampling method is *most* likely to produce a representative sample?

Ⓐ Survey students at a science club meeting.

Ⓑ Survey the person in the first seat of each row in each sixth grade homeroom.

Ⓒ Survey a group of students eating together.

Ⓓ Survey by calling on students who raise their hands at a sixth grade assembly.

Upper Newport Bay Ecological Reserve, Newport Beach, CA

California @HomeTutor for problem solving help at classzone.com

SEE EXAMPLES 2 AND 3 on pp. 355–356 for Ex. 18

18. **SCHOOL SPENDING** The athletic department at a school has been given a donation. A survey will be conducted to find how the student body wants the money to be spent, using the options listed at the right. Identify each sampling method. Then tell which sample is *least* likely to be biased. *Explain* your reasoning.
   - **A.** Survey girls as they leave gym class.
   - **B.** Survey every third student from a list of all students.
   - **C.** Survey the students on the baseball team.

How $hould we $pend the money?

$ $ $ $ $ $ $ $ $ $ $ $ $

Choose one:

- ❑ Buy new baseball team uniforms.
- ❑ Add more bleachers in the gym.
- ❑ Put new lockers in the girls' locker room.

California @HomeTutor for problem solving help at classzone.com

SEE EXAMPLES 1, 2, AND 3 on pp. 354–356 for Ex. 19

19. **MULTI-STEP PROBLEM** An educator wants to find the percent of sixth grade students in the state that have visited an art museum this year. The educator starts by surveying all sixth grade students in one county. Of the 735 sixth grade students in this county, 273 students have visited an art museum this year.
   - **a.** Identify the population, the sample, and the sampling method.
   - **b.** After surveying all of the sixth grade students in the state, the results show that about 42% have visited an art museum. *Compare* the county results to the state results.
   - **c.** Is the sampling method likely to produce a representative sample? *Explain* your reasoning.

20. **CHALLENGE** A youth center surveys its members to learn whether the dance studio should be remodeled. *Describe* three methods for conducting the survey: one with a sample biased for the remodeling, one with a sample biased against the remodeling, and one with a sample not likely to be biased.

◆ CALIFORNIA STANDARDS SPIRAL REVIEW

AF 3.1 21. A rectangle has a length of 8 inches and a width of $2x$ inches. Which expression represents the area of the rectangle? *(p. 212)*

Ⓐ $2x + 8$ Ⓑ $4x + 16$ Ⓒ $16x$ Ⓓ $16x^2$

NS 1.4 22. You deposit $800 into an account. After 6 months, the balance is $814. What is the simple annual interest rate? *(p. 331)*

Ⓐ 0.3% Ⓑ 3.5% Ⓒ 8.5% Ⓓ 10.5%

NS 1.2 23. The wins (W) and losses (L) for 4 basketball teams are shown below. Which team has the greatest ratio of wins to games played? *(p. 255)*

Ⓐ W: 28, L: 14 Ⓑ W: 21, L: 10 Ⓒ W: 19, L: 14 Ⓓ W: 17, L: 9

7.2 Sampling Errors

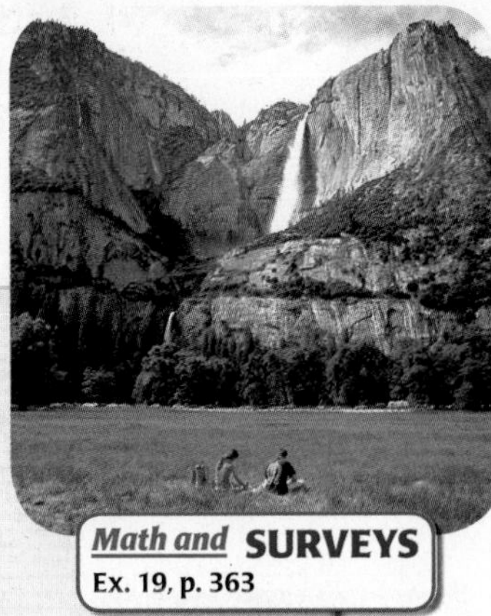

Math and SURVEYS
Ex. 19, p. 363

Standards SDAP 2.3 **Analyze data displays and explain why the way in which the question was asked might have influenced the results obtained** and why the way in which the results were displayed might have influenced the conclusions reached.

SDAP 2.4 **Identify data that represent sampling errors and explain why the sample (and the display) might be biased.**

Connect ***Before*** you identified sampling methods. ***Now*** you will identify sampling errors and bias and evaluate the validity of claims.

KEY VOCABULARY
- **population,** *p. 354*
- **sample,** *p. 354*
- **biased sample,** *p. 355*

Questions on a survey should be phrased so that the answers will accurately reflect the opinions or actions of the people surveyed. Otherwise, displays and claims based on the results might be biased or invalid.

EXAMPLE 1 Identifying Potentially Biased Questions

Tell whether the question could produce biased results. If so, explain why and rewrite the question so that it is not biased.

> *Do you, like most people your age, dislike listening to boring classical music?* ❑ *yes* ❑ *no*

SOLUTION

A response of "no" implies that a person disagrees with most people his or her age and likes listening to "boring" music. The question is biased because it encourages a response of "yes." You could rewrite the question as "Do you like listening to classical music?"

EXAMPLE 2 Claims Based on Biased Questions

SKATEBOARDING Randomly selected town residents are surveyed about a ban on skateboarding on public property. The survey question and the results are displayed below. Is the given claim valid? *Explain.*

Question: Do you agree with the town's unfair ban on skateboarding on public property?

Claim: Most residents oppose the ban.

Agree with Ban?	
Yes	20%
No	70%
Not sure	10%

SOLUTION

The claim may not be valid because the question is biased. The word "unfair" gives a negative opinion of the ban and encourages a response of "no."

SAMPLES AND SURVEY METHODS Claims based on survey results can be invalid for reasons other than a biased question. For example, the claim could be based on a biased sample or on other sampling errors.

EXAMPLE 3 Claims Based on Biased Samples

BASEBALL You want to know about baseball game attendance among U.S. residents. You survey people as they enter a ballpark for a game. The survey question and results are displayed below. Is the given claim valid? *Explain.*

Question: On average, how many baseball games do you attend per season?

Claim: Most U.S. residents attend at least 2 games per season.

Baseball Game Attendance	
0–1	15%
2–4	35%
5 or more	50%

About the Standards

Grade 6 Standard SDAP 2.5 asks you to evaluate the validity of claims. You will continue exploring validity of claims in Lesson 7.7.

SOLUTION

The claim may not be valid because the sample is biased. People entering a ballpark are more likely to attend games than U.S. residents in general.

EXAMPLE 4 Claims Based on Flawed Methods

ADVERTISING A toothpaste company employee surveys randomly chosen dentists while giving away free samples. The survey question and results are displayed below. Is the company's advertising claim valid? *Explain.*

Question: Would you recommend our toothpaste to your patients?

Claim: Eighty percent of dentists would recommend our brand of toothpaste.

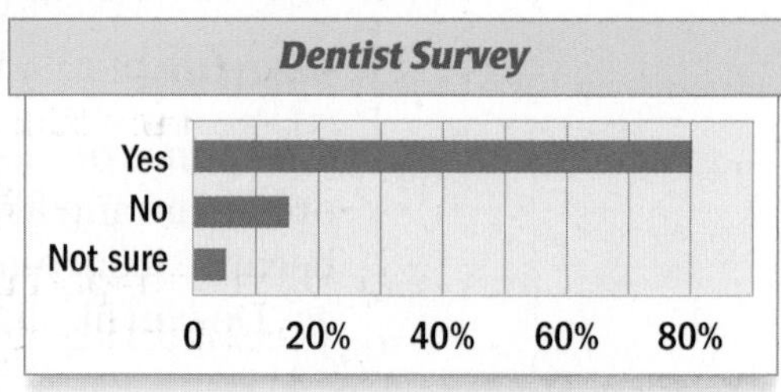

SOLUTION

The claim may not be valid. Dentists accepting free samples are unlikely to admit to the employee that they would not recommend the product.

✓ GUIDED PRACTICE for Examples 1, 2, 3, and 4

Tell whether the question could produce biased results. If so, explain why and rewrite the question so that it is not biased.

1. Do you prefer pears or delicious, juicy oranges?
2. How many times per month do you shop at a grocery store?
3. **WHAT IF?** In Example 3, suppose the survey is conducted at a mall rather than at a ballpark. Is this sample likely to be biased? *Explain.*
4. **WHAT IF?** In Example 4, describe a method for conducting the survey that might make the results and the claim *more* likely to be valid.

7.2 EXERCISES

HOMEWORK KEY ◆ = **MULTIPLE CHOICE PRACTICE** Exs. 8, 12, 18, 24–26
○ = **HINTS AND HOMEWORK HELP** for Exs. 7, 11, 19 at classzone.com

SKILLS • PROBLEM SOLVING • REASONING

1. **VOCABULARY** Copy and complete: A sample that is not representative of a population is a(n) __?__.

2. **WRITING** *Write* a biased survey question.

SEE EXAMPLE 1 on p. 359 for Exs. 3–8

ANALYZING QUESTIONS Tell whether the question could produce biased results. If so, explain why and rewrite the question so that it is not biased.

3. How often do you read the school newspaper?

4. Would you rather spend a Friday night watching an exciting movie with your friends or baby-sitting a crying baby?

5. Should the city spend more money on trash cans for our litter-filled city parks?

6. Do you support the state's process for getting a driver's license?

7. Would you rather relax at home or go to a noisy, crowded mall?

8. ◆ **MULTIPLE CHOICE** You survey the community to see if people support the construction of a convenience store on an unused parking lot. Which of the following questions is *least* likely to produce biased results?

   (A) Our community already has plenty of convenience stores. Do you support the construction of another convenience store?

   (B) Do you support the construction of a convenience store?

   (C) Do you support the construction of a convenience store or do you think the site should be used for something more desirable?

   (D) Do you support the construction of an unnecessary convenience store?

SEE EXAMPLES 2, 3, AND 4 on pp. 359–360 for Exs. 9–11

IDENTIFYING BIAS The given claim about students at one school is invalid. *Explain* why the survey described might have led to this invalid claim.

> **Claim:** Most students spend 45 minutes or more per night on math problems.

9. Students were surveyed in front of their math teachers.

10. Random students in the cafeteria were asked, "How long do you spend on math problems each night, keeping in mind that the teachers highly recommend at least 45 minutes per night?"

11. Students in the math club were asked, "How long do you spend on math problems each night?"

SEE EXAMPLE 3
on p. 360
for Ex. 12

12. ◆ **MULTIPLE CHOICE** You want to conduct a survey asking people to name their favorite sport. Which sample is *least* likely to be biased?

Ⓐ Ask every fifth person entering a baseball stadium.

Ⓑ Ask the members of a high school football team.

Ⓒ Ask every tenth person entering a sporting goods store.

Ⓓ Ask every other person leaving a golf course.

13. **ERROR ANALYSIS** Your friend is trying to conduct an unbiased survey to find out how often people in your town go to the movies each month. Your friend surveys 30 people standing in line at a local movie theater. *Describe* and correct your friend's error.

CONNECT SKILLS TO PROBLEM SOLVING Exercises 14–16 will help you prepare for problem solving.

Use the following information: You ask people entering a video store on a Friday night, "How many DVDs do you watch each weekend?" The results are displayed at the right.

DVDs Viewed on Weekends	
1 DVD	31%
2 DVDs	58%
3 DVDs	11%

14. Identify the sample. Is it biased? *Explain.*

15. Identify the question. Is it biased? *Explain.*

16. Is a claim that most people watch 2 DVDs per weekend valid? *Explain.*

SEE EXAMPLE 4
on p. 360
for Ex. 17

17. **TEAM NAME** A basketball team needs a name. Two names have been suggested. Just before the vote, one team member suggests a third name. Then the team members vote by saying aloud which name they prefer. The third name suggested gets the most votes. Do you think the result is valid? *Explain* your reasoning.

California @HomeTutor for problem solving help at classzone.com

18. ◆ **MULTIPLE CHOICE** You ask people at a campground to name their favorite camping activity. You claim, based on the survey, that having a campfire is the favorite activity. Which of the following would be the *most* likely reason for your claim to be invalid?

Ⓐ You asked, "Which activity is your favorite?"

Ⓑ You surveyed every fourth person arriving at the campground.

Ⓒ You asked, "Of all the camping activities available, including warm and inviting campfires, which is your favorite?"

Ⓓ You surveyed people at the campground lodge.

Campfires are a favorite activity of many campers.

California @HomeTutor for problem solving help at classzone.com

19. **VACATION DESTINATIONS** You survey California residents about their favorite in-state vacation destination. You randomly survey people at a mall. The results are displayed at the right. Is the given claim valid? *Explain* your reasoning.

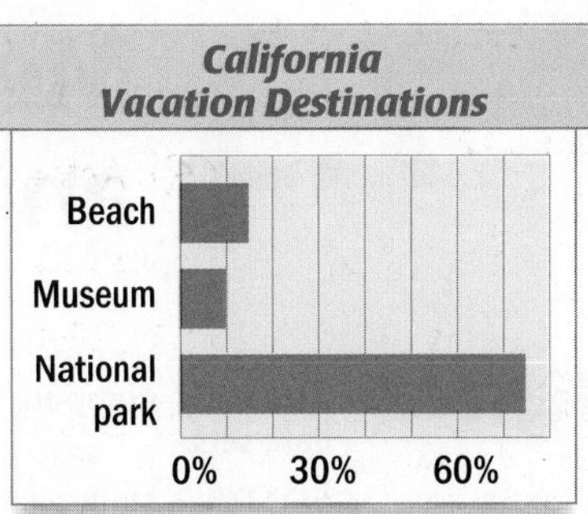

Question: Which do you like to visit most in California: the hot and crowded beaches, the boring museums, or the gorgeous national parks?

Claim: Most California residents choose national parks as their favorite in-state vacation destination.

20. **WRITING** *Identify* three reasons why a claim based on survey results may *not* be valid.

21. **REASONING** For a class project, you and your friend each conduct a survey asking students to name their favorite class. You survey all students in one sixth grade homeroom. Your friend surveys every fifth student on a list of all students in the school. Which sample is *least* likely to be biased? *Explain* your reasoning.

22. **CHALLENGE** In a survey conducted at your school, 90% of the students said that they support more funding for the school's track team. Give three possible reasons why the survey could have produced this result.

23. **CHALLENGE** As 1000 gears are produced at a factory, 50 of them are selected to be inspected. If no defective gears are found in the sample, then all of the gears are approved. List three possible ways for selecting the 50 gears to be inspected so that the results are likely to be valid.

◆ CALIFORNIA STANDARDS SPIRAL REVIEW

NS 1.3 24. What is the value of x in the proportion $\frac{3}{8} = \frac{x}{24}$? ***(p. 266)***

Ⓐ 1 Ⓑ 9 Ⓒ 64 Ⓓ 72

AF 3.2 25. The rectangle shown has a perimeter of 45 feet. Which equation can be used to find the width x? ***(p. 212)***

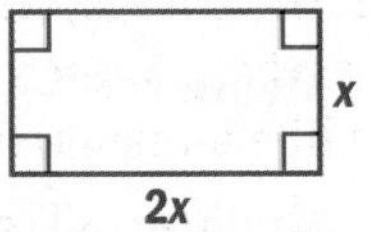

Ⓐ $2x^2 = 45$ Ⓑ $3x = 45$ Ⓒ $4x = 45$ Ⓓ $6x = 45$

NS 2.3 26. You have \$35 in your bank account. You deposit \$18 one day and withdraw \$40 the next day. Which expression would you use to calculate the final amount in your bank account? ***(p. 135)***

Ⓐ $35 + (-18) + (-40)$ Ⓑ $35 + 18 + (-40)$

Ⓒ $35 + (-18) + 40$ Ⓓ $35 + 18 + 40$

7.3 Mean, Median, and Mode

Math and **SURVEYS**
Ex. 31, p. 369

Standards **SDAP 1.1** Compute the range, mean, median, and mode of data sets.

SDAP 1.2 Understand how additional data added to data sets may affect these computations.

SDAP 1.4 Know why a specific measure of central tendency (mean, median) provides the most useful information in a given context.

Connect ***Before*** you compared data in samples and populations. ***Now*** you will describe data using mean, median, and mode.

KEY VOCABULARY
- **median**
- **mode**
- **mean,** *p. 156*

You found the mean of a set of data in Lesson 3.5. Two other measures that describe an average, or the *center* of a set of data, are the median and mode.

VOCABULARY
The mean, median, and mode are *measures of central tendency*, because they each represent the center of the data.

KEY CONCEPT *For Your Notebook*

Measures of Central Tendency

The **mean** of a data set is the sum of the values divided by the number of values.

The **median** of a data set is the middle value when the values are written in numerical order. If a data set has an even number of values, the median is the mean of the two middle values.

The **mode** of a data set is the value that occurs most often. A data set can have no mode, one mode, or more than one mode.

EXAMPLE 1 Finding Mean, Median, and Mode

Find the mean, median, and mode(s) of 2, 3, 3, 4, 8, 10, 11, and 15.

Mean: $\frac{2+3+3+4+8+10+11+15}{8} = \frac{56}{8} = 7$

Median: The median is the mean of the two middle values, 4 and 8.

$\text{Median} = \frac{4+8}{2} = \frac{12}{2} = 6$

Mode: The data value that occurs most often is 3.

✓ GUIDED PRACTICE for Example 1

1. Find the mean, median, and mode of the ages of players on a baseball team: 11, 11, 13, 13, 12, 13, 11, 12, 10, 13, and 13.

EXAMPLE 2 ◆ Multiple Choice Practice

Paul found the mean and median of the numbers 5, 5, and 8. If the number 2 were added to the list of numbers, then

Ⓐ the median would increase. Ⓑ the median would decrease.

Ⓒ the mean would increase. Ⓓ the mean would decrease.

SOLUTION

INCLUDING NEW DATA
In Example 2, the mode is not affected when you include the number 2 in the list, because 5 still occurs most often.

The new list of numbers is 2, **5**, **5**, and 8. The median is still 5 because the mean of the two middle numbers is 5.

The mean of 5, 5, and 8 is $18 \div 3 = 6$. If you were to add 6 to the list, the mean would still be 6, because $(18 + 6) \div 4 = 6$. However, if you were to add a number less than 6, such as 2, the mean would decrease.

▶ **Answer** The correct answer is D. Ⓐ Ⓑ Ⓒ Ⓓ

✓ GUIDED PRACTICE for Example 2

2. **WHAT IF?** In Example 2, suppose 8 were added to the list of numbers, instead of 2. What would happen to the mean, median, and mode(s)?

CHOOSING MEASURES
More than one measure of central tendency may be useful depending on the context.

USEFUL MEASURES One measure of central tendency might provide more useful information than another in a particular situation.

- The *mean* might be most useful when there is a large gap between low and high values, since the median could reflect only low or high values.
- The *median* might be most useful when a very high or very low value distorts the mean.
- The *mode* might be most useful when you want to identify the most common value or when the data are non-numerical.

EXAMPLE 3 Choosing a Useful Measure

DANCE-A-THON You receive nine pledges for your participation in a dance-a-thon. Which measure is most useful for describing a typical data value?

\$1 \$8 \$12 \$10 \$45 \$9 \$1 \$7 \$6

SOLUTION

AVOID ERRORS
If the data are not ordered, you need to order the data to find the median.

The mean, 11, is distorted by the \$45 pledge, so most data values are less than the mean. The mode, 1, is not typical because it is less than most of the data values. The median, 8, represents the data values more closely.

▶ **Answer** The median is most useful for describing a typical data value.

EXAMPLE 4 Analyzing a Claim

ANOTHER WAY
For an alternative method for solving the problem in Example 4, turn to page 370 for the **Problem Solving Workshop**.

CAMERAS The prices of 16 digital cameras in stock at a store are:

$180, $180, $180, $180, $190, $190, $190, $200, $200, $200, $210, $210, $230, $230, $240, and $260.

Does the average price shown in the advertisement describe the prices well? Why might this price be advertised?

SOLUTION

The advertised price of $180 is the most common price, or the mode. It does not describe the data well because it is less than most of the prices. This price might be advertised to suggest that the store sells inexpensive digital cameras.

✓ **GUIDED PRACTICE** for Examples 3 and 4

3. **FUNDRAISER** The following list of data shows donations received during a youth center fundraiser.

   $25 $30 $20 $150 $35 $40 $25 $20

   A potential donor wants to know what a typical donation is. Does the mean represent a typical donation? *Explain* why or why not. If not, which measure is most useful for describing a typical donation?

7.3 EXERCISES

HOMEWORK KEY
◆ = **MULTIPLE CHOICE PRACTICE** Exs. 10, 19, 24, 40–42
○ = **HINTS AND HOMEWORK HELP** for Exs. 5, 17, 25 at classzone.com

SKILLS • PROBLEM SOLVING • REASONING

VOCABULARY Tell whether the statement is *true* or *false*.

1. The value that occurs the most often in a data set is the mode.
2. Data values need to be written in numerical order to find the median.
3. **WRITING** *Explain* how additional data added to a data set could affect the mean.

SEE EXAMPLE 1
on p. 364 for Exs. 4–12

FINDING MEASURES Find the mean, median, and mode(s) of the data.

4. 4, 4, 8, 11, 12, 16, 22
5. 108, 490, 502, 502, 502, 518
6. 20, 26, 31, 42, 44, 47, 51, 75
7. 46, 23, 63, 23, 81, 75, 46
8. 1.1, 0, 3, 2.8, 4.6
9. 7.6, 7.6, 6.1, 6, 14.3

10. ◆ **MULTIPLE CHOICE** The amount of money you earned each week from baby-sitting is listed below. What is the mean of the data?

$15 $20 $10 $15 $20 $15 $15 $10

(A) $10 (B) $15 (C) $20 (D) $25

ERROR ANALYSIS ***Describe*** **and correct the error made in finding the given measure of central tendency of the data set.**

11.

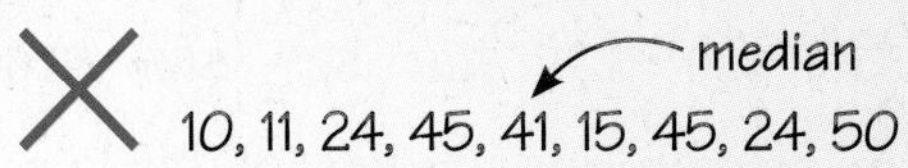

12.

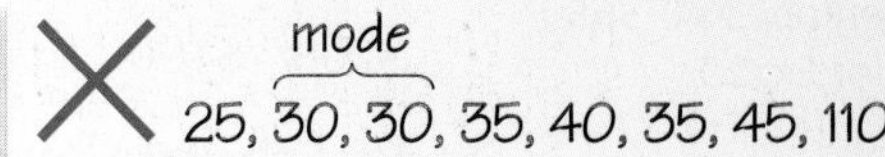

SEE EXAMPLE 2 on p. 365 for Exs. 13–19

INCLUDING VALUES ***Describe*** **how including the new value in the data set will affect the mean, median, and mode.**

13. 13, 13, 18, new value: 7

14. 2, 2, 2, 2, new value: 4

15. 7, 8, 7, 5, 7, new value: 2

16. 5, 4, 7, 6, new value: 5.5

17. 15, 10, 14, 9 new value: 8.5

18. 6, 8, 10, 8, 12, new value: 6

19. ◆ **MULTIPLE CHOICE** Charles found the mean and median of the numbers 7, 11, 15, and 23. If the number 14 were added to the list of numbers, then

(A) the median would increase.

(B) the median would decrease.

(C) the mean would increase.

(D) the mean would decrease.

CONNECT SKILLS TO PROBLEM SOLVING **Exercises 20–22 will help you prepare for problem solving.**

Tell which measure of central tendency is probably most useful for describing a typical data value in the given context.

20. The salaries of 10 company employees, including the president of the company.

21. The commuting times of 9 students, 5 who live within one mile of school and 4 who live more than eight miles from school

22. The sizes of 100 T-shirts sold at a store in one day

SEE EXAMPLES 1 AND 3 on pp. 364–365 for Ex. 23

23. **INDY 500** The table shows the speeds of the fastest qualifiers in the Indy 500 each year for 1999–2004. Find the mean and median rounded to the nearest thousandth. *Explain* why the median might be a useful measure to describe the data.

Year	Speed (mi/h)
1999	225.179
2000	223.471
2001	226.037
2002	231.342
2003	231.725
2004	222.024

California @HomeTutor for problem solving help at classzone.com

24. ◆ **MULTIPLE CHOICE** Your mean quiz score after 5 math quizzes was 85%. You scored 91% on today's math quiz. What is your new mean quiz score?

(A) 85% (B) 86% (C) 87% (D) 88%

California @HomeTutor for problem solving help at classzone.com

SEE EXAMPLES 1 AND 3 on pp. 364–365 for Ex. 25

(25.) **HOUSEHOLD BUDGETING** The monthly gas bill amounts last year for the Lopez family are listed below.

\$200 \$190 \$170 \$90 \$75 \$30 \$25 \$20 \$25 \$65 \$160 \$170

a. **Calculate** Find the mean, median, and mode(s) of the data.

b. **Interpret** The Lopez family is trying to budget for this year's gas bills. Which measure will give the Lopez family the most useful information so that they can decide how much money to set aside for monthly gas bills? *Explain* your reasoning.

SEE EXAMPLE 4 on p. 366 for Ex. 26

26. **MULTI-STEP PROBLEM** The list below shows the prices of several homes in an area.

\$145,000 \$115,000 \$150,000 \$115,000 \$198,000,
\$215,000 \$130,000 \$140,000 \$170,000 \$300,000

a. A real estate agent says that the average cost of a home in the area is \$115,000. Does \$115,000 describe the prices well? Why or why not?

b. Why might a real estate agent use \$115,000 as the average price?

c. Which measure(s) provides you with the information you would most want to know when buying a home? *Explain.*

READING *IN* MATH **Read the information below for Exercises 27–30.**

Sea Turtles Adult sea turtles come in many sizes. The adult Leatherback turtle, one of the longest sea turtles, can have a length of 96 inches. The table shows the measured lengths for a sample of 6 adult sea turtles.

Adult Sea Turtle Lengths (inches)			
Type of turtle	***Length***	***Type of turtle***	***Length***
Kemps Ridley	30	Loggerhead	48
Olive Ridley	30	Green	48
Hawksbill	30	Flatback	39

27. **Calculate** Find the mean, median, and mode of the data from the sample.

28. **Reasoning** Suppose you include the length of the Leatherback turtle, as described above, with the data. How does this value affect the mean length found in Exercise 27?

Green Sea Turtle

29. **Compare** Does the median or the mode change when these measures are computed for the 7 turtles including the Leatherback? *Explain.*

30. **Reasoning** Are the measures from these samples likely to describe a typical length of an adult sea turtle for the entire population? *Explain.*

31. **SHORT RESPONSE** In a survey asking students the number of hours spent on homework last night, the most frequent response was 0.5 hour. The typical response was 1 hour. Which response represents the mode? Does the other response represent the mean or the median? *Explain.*

32. **SHORT RESPONSE** A set of data does not need to involve numbers. Find the mode(s) of the baseball cap colors. *Explain* why the mode is the only appropriate measure.

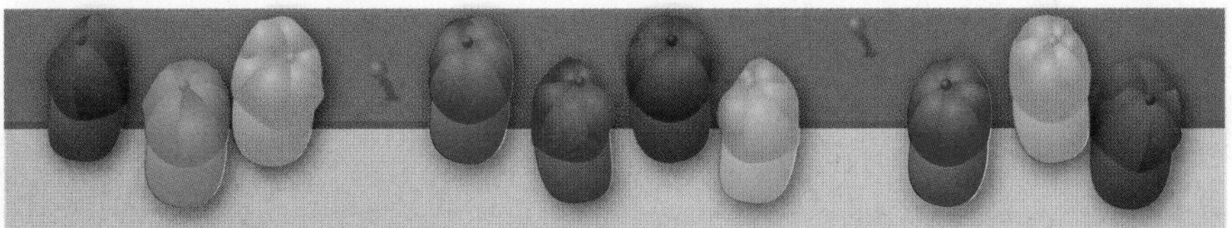

33. **STEM-AND-LEAF PLOT** A stem-and-leaf plot is a data display that helps you see how data are distributed. The stem-and-leaf plot at the right shows the ages of people at a family reunion.

    a. Find the mean, median, and mode(s).

    b. Suppose that a 98 year old family member arrives at the reunion. *Describe* the effect on the mean, median, and mode.

Ages of Relatives

Stem	Leaves
0	2 5 5 7 9
1	1 1 3 4 7 9
2	2 5 7 8
3	2 3 4 4 9
4	0 2
5	3 7
6	0 1

Key: 1 | 1 = 11 years old

34. **PUZZLE PROBLEM** Find five numbers with a mean of 16, a median of 15, and a mode of 21.

CHALLENGE Find the value of x that makes the mean the given number.

35. 5, 8, 9, 4, 1, x; mean = 5

36. 12, 7, 18, 15, 11, 9, x; mean = 12

37. 3.5, 1.5, 2.4, 4.6, 6.8, x; mean = 4.3

38. 3.0, 5.1, 9.8, 11.2, 12.5, 9.3, x; mean = 8.5

39. **CHALLENGE** Create a set of at least seven data values that has at least four different values and for which all three measures are equal.

CALIFORNIA STANDARDS SPIRAL REVIEW

AF 1.2 40. What is the value of $3x^2 + 16 \cdot 2y$ when $x = 4$ and $y = -2$? *(p. 197)*

Ⓐ −256 Ⓑ −52 Ⓒ −16 Ⓓ 112

SDAP 2.2 41. A survey asks teachers as they leave a faculty lounge about their class sizes. Which sampling method is used? *(p. 354)*

Ⓐ convenience Ⓑ self-selected Ⓒ systematic Ⓓ random

AF 2.2 42. Melissa works 3 hours and earns \$24. How much does Melissa earn when she works 8 hours? *(p. 274)*

Ⓐ \$16 Ⓑ \$48 Ⓒ \$64 Ⓓ \$128

Using ALTERNATIVE METHODS

Another Way to Solve Example 4, page 366

Standards
SDAP 1.4

In Example 4 on page 366, you saw how to solve the problem about digital camera prices by analyzing an ordered list of data. You can also solve the problem by using a line plot.

PROBLEM

CAMERAS The prices of 16 digital cameras in stock at a store are:

$180, $180, $180, $180, $190, $190, $190, $200, $200, $200, $210, $210, $230, $230, $240, and $260.

Does the average price shown in the advertisement describe the prices well? Why might this price be advertised?

METHOD

Using a Line Plot An alternative approach is to use a line plot.

STEP 1 **Make** a line plot of the data. Using equal intervals, draw a number line that includes all data values. Mark an X above the number line to show the frequency of each data value.

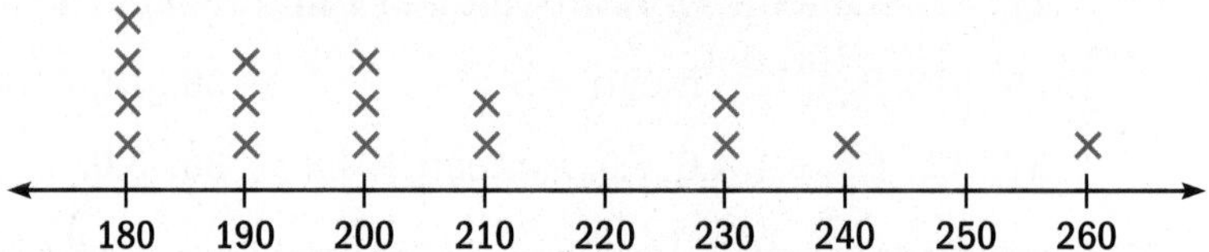

STEP 2 **Analyze** the line plot. You can see that $180 is the mode. It does not describe the data well because it is less than most of the prices. This price might be advertised to suggest that the store sells inexpensive digital cameras.

PRACTICE

1. **VIDEO GAMES** Jill says that her average score on a video game is 500. Jill's scores from playing the video game 8 times are shown below.

   350, 300, 200, 500, 250, 450, 550, 500

   Does 500 describe Jill's scores well? Why might Jill use 500 as her average score? Make a line plot to solve the problem.

2. **BASEBALL** A sports report states that the average number of wins by a baseball team is 77. The number of wins by a baseball team in 10 seasons are shown below.

   82, 94, 97, 88, 88, 71, 69, 55, 59, 72

   Does 77 describe the number of wins well? Why might a report use this number? Make a line plot to solve the problem.

7.4 Organizing Data Using the Median

MATERIALS • pencil and paper

Standards

SDAP 1.1 Compute the range, mean, **median**, and mode **of data sets.**

QUESTION How can you organize data using the median?

EXPLORE Use the median to divide your class into groups according to the number of letters in students' first and last names.

STEP 1 **Count** the number of letters in your first and last name. Write the total on a piece of paper.

STEP 2 **Form** a line with your classmates. Hold up your papers, arranging yourselves from least to greatest number of letters.

STEP 3 **Find** the median number of letters.

STEP 4 **Use** the median to divide the line into a lower half and an upper half. If there is an odd number of students, the median is not included in either the lower or upper half.

STEP 5 **Repeat** Steps 3 and 4 for each half. The original line should be divided into 4 parts.

DRAW CONCLUSIONS Use your observations to complete these exercises.

Answer the following questions about the data for your class.

1. What is the median of the data for your entire class?
2. What is the median of the data in the lower half?
3. What is the median of the data in the upper half?
4. What are the least and greatest data values?
5. **REASONING** About what fraction of the class should have numbers of letters that are greater than the median of the lower half and less than the median of the upper half? Count the number of students that fall in this interval. *Compare* this number to the total number of students.

7.4 Range and Outliers

Standards **SDAP 1.1** **Compute the range, mean, median, and mode of data sets.**

SDAP 1.3 **Understand how the inclusion or exclusion of outliers affects these computations.**

Connect ***Before*** you calculated measures of central tendency. ***Now*** you will analyze how the inclusion or exclusion of outliers affects these measures.

Math and **NATURE** Ex. 21, p. 376

KEY VOCABULARY

- **lower extreme, upper extreme**
- **lower quartile, upper quartile**
- **range**
- **interquartile range**
- **outlier**
- **box-and-whisker plot**

In Lesson 7.3, you computed measures of central tendency. Now you will describe the *spread* of a data set and tell how extreme data values can affect the mean, median, and mode.

KEY CONCEPT *For Your Notebook*

Describing the Spread of Data

The least data value in a data set is the **lower extreme**. The greatest data value is the **upper extreme**.

The median of the lower half of a data set is the **lower quartile**. The median of the upper half is the **upper quartile**.

The **range** of a data set is the difference between the upper and lower extremes. The **interquartile range** is the difference between the upper and lower quartiles. These measures describe how spread out the data are.

EXAMPLE 1 Computing Statistics

Find the median, extremes, quartiles, range, and interquartile range of the data set 60, 70, 42, 60, 40, 76, 78, 150, and 78.

STEP 1 **Order** the data and identify the median and the extremes.

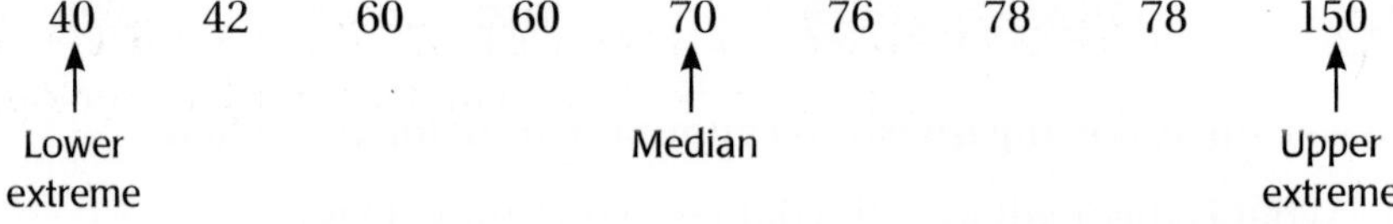

STEP 2 **Identify** the quartiles using the lower and upper halves of the data.

40 42 60 60 76 78 78 150

Lower quartile: $(42 + 60) \div 2 = 51$

Upper quartile: $(78 + 78) \div 2 = 78$

STEP 3 **Subtract** the extremes to find the range: $150 - 40 = 110$.

STEP 4 **Subtract** the quartiles to find the interquartile range: $78 - 51 = 27$.

AVOID ERRORS

If a data set has an odd number of values, the median is not included in either the lower half or the upper half.

OUTLIERS An **outlier** is a value in a data set that is much greater or much less than the other values. Outliers can affect statistical measures.

EXAMPLE 2 Describing Effects of Outliers

Use the data set 30, 90, 93, 99, 113, 113, and 141. The data value 30 is an outlier.

a. Calculate the mean, median, mode(s), and range of the data.

b. Calculate the mean, median, mode(s), and range of the data *excluding* the outlier 30.

c. How does the *exclusion* of the outlier affect the mean, median, mode(s), and range of the data? *Explain.*

SOLUTION

a. Mean: $\frac{30 + 90 + 93 + 99 + 113 + 113 + 141}{7} = \frac{679}{7} = 97$

Median: The median is the middle value, 99.

Mode: The number that occurs most often is 113.

Range: Subtract the extremes: $141 - 30 = 111$

b. Mean: $\frac{90 + 93 + 99 + 113 + 113 + 141}{6} = \frac{649}{6} \approx 108.2$

Median: The median is $\frac{99 + 113}{2} = 106$.

Mode: The number that occurs most often is 113.

Range: Subtract the extremes: $141 - 90 = 51$

c. The *exclusion* of the outlier affects these measures as follows:

- The mean increases by about 11.2 and the median increases by 7. The mean and median increase because the outlier is the least data value.
- The mode does not change because the outlier is not a mode.
- The range decreases by 60. The range decreases significantly because the remaining data values are much closer together on the number line.

✓ GUIDED PRACTICE for Examples 1 and 2

Find the median, extremes, quartiles, range, and interquartile range.

1. 48, 52, 59, 61, 64, 64, 86

2. 18, 16, 48, 6, 22, 17, 9, 5, 14, 15

How does the *exclusion* of the outlier affect the mean, median, mode, and range of the data from the given exercise. *Explain.*

3. Exercise 1; the outlier is 86.

4. Exercise 2; the outlier is 48.

A **box-and-whisker plot** is a data display that divides a data set into four parts using the lower extreme, lower quartile, median, upper quartile, and upper extreme.

EXAMPLE 3 Using a Box-and-Whisker Plot

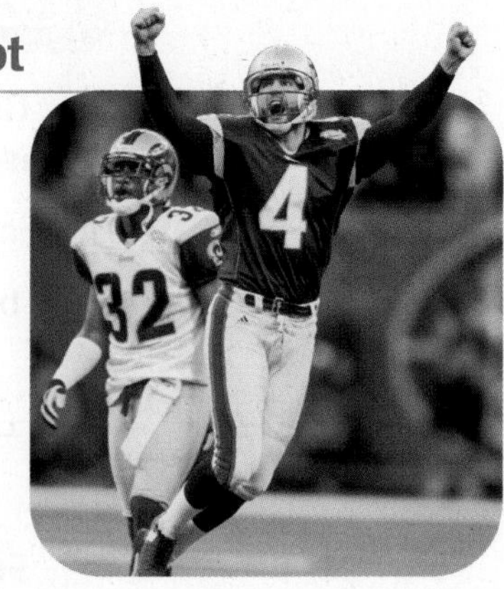

FOOTBALL The box-and-whisker plots below show the spread of the differences between the number of points scored by the winning and losing teams in forty Super Bowl games.

The data in the blue plot have an outlier of 45. The green plot displays the same data but does not include the outlier. How does *excluding* the outlier affect the median and the range of the data?

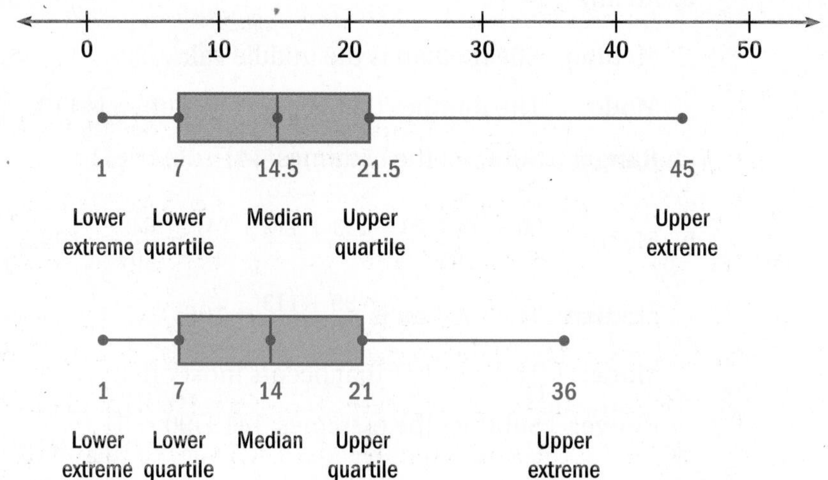

SOLUTION

When the outlier is *included,* the median is 14.5 and the range is 44. When the outlier is *excluded,* the median is 14 and range is 35. The median slightly decreases and the range greatly decreases when the outlier is excluded.

✓ GUIDED PRACTICE for Example 3

5. **FOOTBALL** The box-and-whisker plot shows the spread of the St. Louis Rams' game scores for a season. If the outlier 48 is *excluded,* the median is 31. *Compare* the medians. Then tell whether the range *excluding* the outlier is greater or less than the range *including* the outlier. *Explain.*

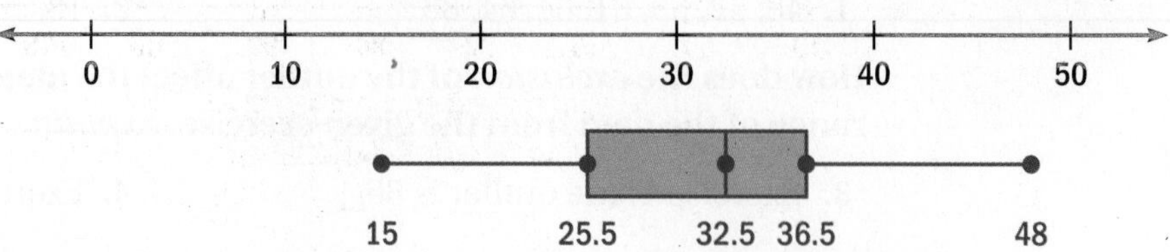

7.4 EXERCISES

HOMEWORK KEY
◆ = **MULTIPLE CHOICE PRACTICE** Exs. 7, 12, 20, 24–26
○ = **HINTS AND HOMEWORK HELP** for Exs. 5, 9, 21 at classzone.com

SKILLS • PROBLEM SOLVING • REASONING

1. **VOCABULARY** The range is the difference between the _?_ and the _?_.

2. **WRITING** *Describe* how outliers can affect measures of central tendency.

SEE EXAMPLE 1 on p. 372 for Exs. 3–7

COMPUTING STATISTICS Find the median, extremes, quartiles, range, and interquartile range of the data.

3. 55, 59, 62, 53, 57, 57, 62, 50, 60

4. 18, 24, 9, 33, 26, 17, 3, 22, 7, 38

5. 5.8, 3.4, 7.4, 8.5, 1.9, 6.5, 5.8, 9.2

6. 345, 416, 728, 396, 651, 524

7. ◆ **MULTIPLE CHOICE** What is the range of the data set 81, 72, 46, 68, 91, 54, 83, 94, and 41?

   (A) 29.5 (B) 37 (C) 40 (D) 53

SEE EXAMPLE 2 on p. 373 for Exs. 8–13

UNDERSTANDING OUTLIERS Compare the mean, median, mode(s) and range of the data set *with* and *without* the outlier in red.

8. 23, 27, 20, 5, 32, 31, 39, 32

9. 100, 84, 92, 89, 45, 72, 85, 91

10. 140, 180, 625, 215, 310, 190, 186

11. 64, 120, 33, 75, 81, 76, 69, 85, 89

12. ◆ **MULTIPLE CHOICE** What is the effect of excluding the outlier 17 on the median and range of these data: 45, 17, 52, 61, 48, 56, 54, 75, 60, and 49?

   (A) Median and range decrease
   (B) Median increases, range decreases
   (C) Median and range increase
   (D) Median and range stay the same

13. **ERROR ANALYSIS** A student says that an outlier in a data set affects the mode more than the mean or median. *Describe* and correct the student's error.

SEE EXAMPLES 1 AND 3 on pp. 372, 374 for Exs. 14–15

USING A BOX-AND-WHISKER PLOT Find the median, extremes, quartiles, range, and interquartile range of the data in the box-and-whisker plot.

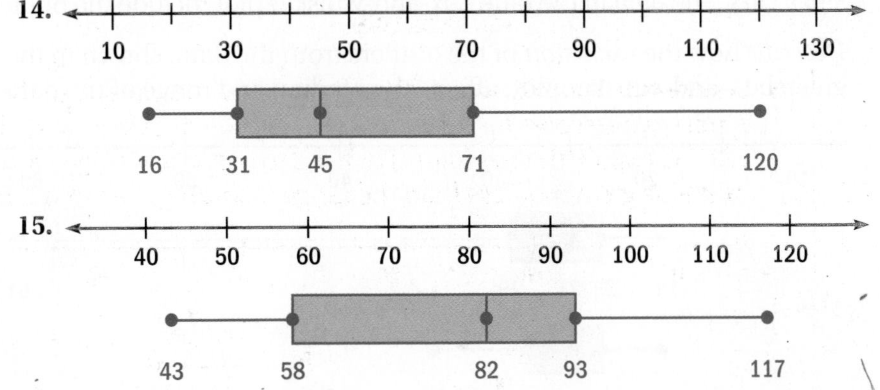

CONNECT SKILLS TO PROBLEM SOLVING **Exercises 16–18 will help you prepare for problem solving.**

The data show the number of DVDs rented each day over 14 days.

38, 42, 50, 65, 68, 52, 55, 40, 34, 41, 60, 60, 58, 51

16. Find the mean, median, mode(s), and range of the data.

17. The number of DVDs rented on the 15th day was an outlier of 106. Find the mean, median, mode(s), and range of the data *including* this outlier.

18. How does the *inclusion* of this outlier affect the mean, median, mode(s), and range of the data?

SEE EXAMPLE 2 on p. 373 for Exs. 19–21

19. WATCH PRICES The prices of watches at a store are listed.

$28 $170 $47 $72 $30 $95 $55 $68

Calculate the mean, median, mode(s) and range of the data. Identify the outlier. How does its *exclusion* affect the mean, median, mode(s), and range? *Explain.*

California @HomeTutor for problem solving help at classzone.com

Prices vary from $28 to $170.

20. ◆ **MULTIPLE CHOICE** One weekend, a theater sold the following numbers of tickets for a new movie. Which measure decreases when the outlier is *excluded*?

300, 325, 400, 425, 450, 475, 475, 500, 500, 500, 525, 750

Ⓐ Mean Ⓑ Median Ⓒ Mode Ⓓ Lower extreme

California @HomeTutor for problem solving help at classzone.com

(21.) **TREE HEIGHTS** The heights (to the nearest foot) of coastal redwood trees known to be over 340 feet tall are given below. Find the mean, median, mode(s), and range of the data. Suppose that the shortest tree is hit by lightning and its height is reduced to 345 feet. How does this affect the mean, median, mode(s), and range of the data?

358, 358, 358, 358, 359, 359, 360, 361, 361, 363, 363, 364, 366, 366, 368

SEE EXAMPLE 3 on p. 374 for Ex. 22

22. FUEL ECONOMY The box-and-whisker plots show the spread of the average miles per gallon of gasoline used in city driving for one year's models of small cars. The data in the blue box-and-whisker plot include the outliers.

Describe how the *exclusion* of the outliers from the data, shown in the green box-and-whisker plot, affects the median and range of the data.

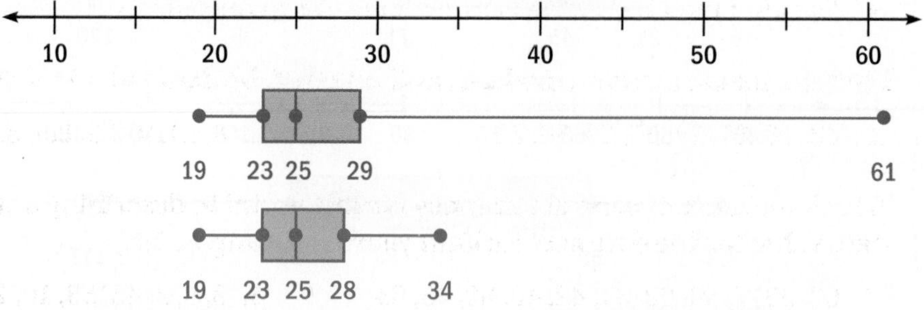

23. **CHALLENGE** The diagram below shows the distance (in yards) that Julia and Ty each hit 14 golf balls at a driving range. Make a box-and-whisker plot for each person using the same number line. Then make a conclusion about who can hit the ball farther. *Justify* your reasoning.

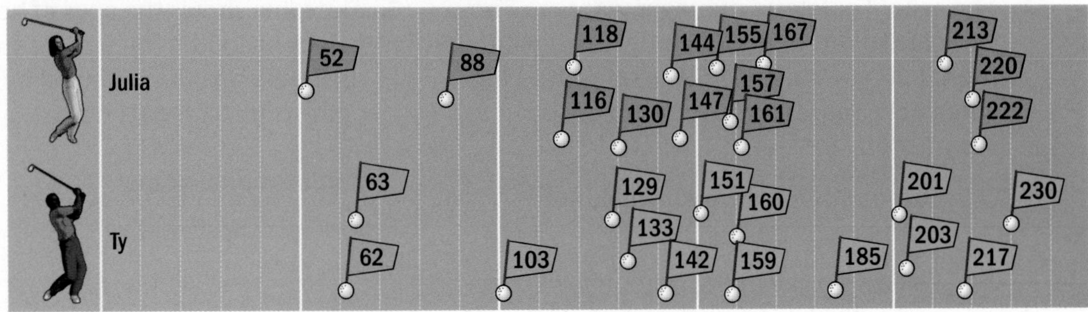

◆ CALIFORNIA STANDARDS SPIRAL REVIEW

SDAP 1.1 24. What is the mean of 48, 53, 66, 29, 18, and 44? ***(p. 154)***

Ⓐ 43 Ⓑ 46 Ⓒ 48 Ⓓ 53

AF 1.4 25. What is the value of $16 + 24 - (13 \times 6 + 5)$? ***(p. 160)***

Ⓐ −103 Ⓑ −43 Ⓒ 167 Ⓓ 297

NS 1.4 26. A salesperson receives a 7% commission on sales. How much commission does the salesperson receive for a sale of $285? ***(p. 319)***

Ⓐ $7 Ⓑ $19.95 Ⓒ $28.50 Ⓓ $199.50

QUIZ *for Lessons 7.1–7.4*

A news program wants to find out what city residents think about funding for space exploration. Identify the sampling method. Tell whether the sample is likely to be biased. *Explain* your reasoning. *(p. 354)*

1. Survey city residents attending a show at the planetarium.
2. Survey every fiftieth person from a list of city residents.

Tell whether the question is likely to produce biased results. If so, explain why and rewrite the question so that it is not biased. *(p. 359)*

3. Do you like wearing soft leather gloves or rough wool mittens?
4. Do you prefer heavy metal music or classical music?

Find the mean, median, mode(s), and range of the data. *(pp. 364, 372)*

5. 42, 16, 21, 34, 25, 28, 30, 20
6. 8.4, 8.9, 8.5, 8.5, 8, 7.9, 9.3

Which measure of central tendency is most useful in describing a typical data value for the data set? *Explain* your reasoning. *(p. 364)*

7. 62, 33, 7, 56, 52, 34, 42, 40, 68, 45, 63
8. 3, 9, 2, 45, 53, 10, 2, 48, 7, 9, 56, 52, 41

MIXED REVIEW of Skills and Problem Solving

Multiple Choice Practice for Lessons 7.1–7.4

1. The school cafeteria manager wants to know which foods students who buy lunch want at the salad bar. Which is the *best* method for choosing a representative sample? **SDAP 2.2, MR 3.1**

   (A) Survey students who bring lunch from home.

   (B) Place a survey in the school newspaper and collect responses.

   (C) Survey every third person in the lunch line.

   (D) Survey one classroom of students.

2. The range of screen sizes of televisions at a store is 45 inches. The smallest television is 15 inches. What is the largest television screen size at the store? **SDAP 1.1**

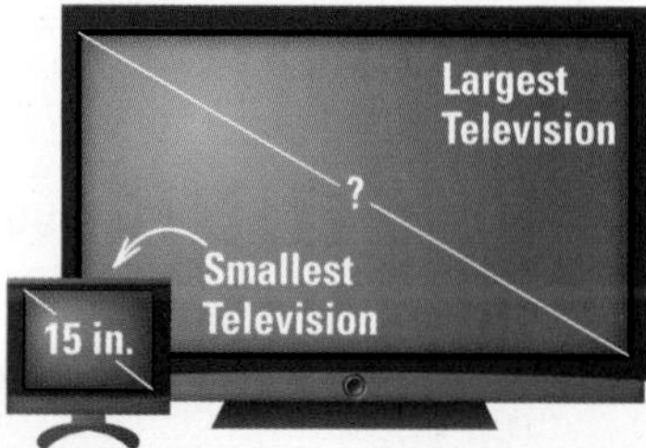

   (A) 15 in. (B) 30 in.

   (C) 45 in. (D) 60 in.

3. The prices of DVD players at a store are listed below. What is the median? **SDAP 1.1**

   \$58, \$70, \$150, \$95, \$140, \$68, \$56, \$130, \$130, \$66, \$60, \$95, \$150, \$142, \$85, \$125

   (A) \$95 (B) \$95.50

   (C) \$130 (D) \$150

4. A newspaper editor wants to know what readers think of recent changes to the paper. An ad is placed in the newspaper asking people to call in to give their opinions. What is this sampling method? **SDAP 2.2**

   (A) Convenience (B) Self-selected

   (C) Systematic (D) Random

5. The table shows the ages of houses in a neighborhood. Which measure of the age of the houses is *most* affected by the exclusion of the outlier? **SDAP 1.3**

Age of house (years)	5	13	14	42
Number of houses	8	2	1	1

   (A) Mean (B) Median

   (C) Mode (D) None are affected.

6. Mara found the mean and median of the numbers 1, 4, 6, and 16. If the number 5 were added to the list of numbers, then **SDAP 1.2, MR 1.2**

   (A) the median would increase.

   (B) the median would decrease.

   (C) the mean would increase.

   (D) the mean would decrease.

7. A television news team stands on a busy street with a camera and asks random people "Have you broken a promise in the past year?" The team claims, based on the results below, that most people keep their promises. What is the *most* likely reason for this claim to be invalid? **SDAP 2.4**

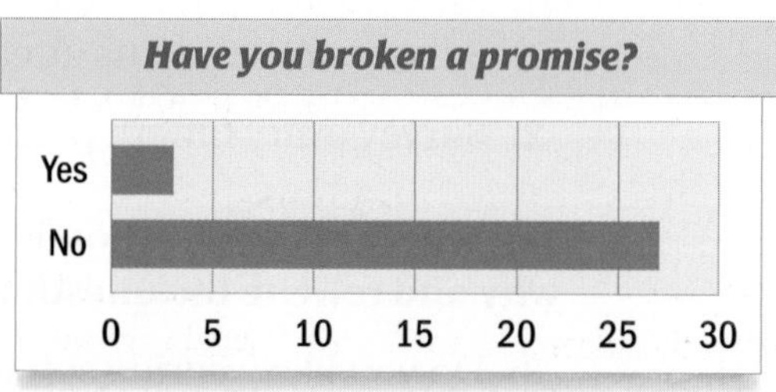

   (A) The survey was conducted by a news reporter.

   (B) The question is biased.

   (C) People who have broken a promise may be too embarrassed to say "yes" on camera.

   (D) The sample is self-selected.

7.5 Histograms

Math and NATURE
Example 3, p. 381

Standards Preparation Grade 5 SDAP 1.2 **Organize and display single-variable data in appropriate graphs and representations (e.g., histogram,** circle graphs) and explain which types of graphs are appropriate for various data sets.

Connect ***Before*** you made bar graphs. ***Now*** you will make and interpret histograms to prepare for Grade 6 SDAP 2.3.

KEY VOCABULARY
- **frequency table**
- **frequency**
- **histogram**

You can use a *frequency table* to help organize and interpret data. A **frequency table** is used to group data values into intervals. The **frequency** of an interval is the number of values that lie in the interval.

READING
A tally mark, |, represents one data value. The mark 𝍸 represents five data values.

Data Values

Calendars Sold in Mr. Moore's Homeroom

1, 7, 12, 2, 3, 22, 7, 5, 10, 1, 15, 9, 8, 2, 7, 17, 24, 14, 5, 4

Frequency Table

Interval	Tally	Frequency
1–5	𝍸 III	8
6–10	𝍸 I	6
11–15	III	3
16–20	I	1
21–25	II	2

EXAMPLE 1 Making a Frequency Table

SCIENCE The numbers of named stars in a group of 34 constellations are listed below. Make a frequency table of the data.

7, 5, 4, 10, 5, 7, 2, 6, 8, 1, 5, 1, 3, 1, 12, 11, 2, 11,
2, 5, 0, 6, 14, 8, 3, 1, 15, 10, 0, 2, 0, 15, 9, 1

SOLUTION

AVOID ERRORS
Notice that the second interval starts at 4, not 3, because 3 can be in only one interval.

STEP 1 **Choose** intervals of equal size that cover all the data values, which range from 0 to 15. Use from four to ten intervals. You can use four intervals of four numbers, beginning with 0–3, as in the table.

STEP 2 **Make** a tally mark next to the appropriate interval for each data value.

STEP 3 **Write** the frequency for each interval by totaling the number of tally marks for the interval.

Interval	Tally	Frequency
0–3	𝍸 𝍸 IIII	14
4–7	𝍸 IIII	9
8–11	𝍸 II	7
12–15	IIII	4

HISTOGRAMS A **histogram** is a graph that displays data from a frequency table. A histogram has one bar for each interval that contains data values. The length of the bar indicates the frequency for the interval.

EXAMPLE 2 Making a Histogram

MUSIC Every Sunday morning, a radio station plays a countdown of the top 30 requested songs from the previous week. The table shows the number of weeks that each of the songs on this week's top 30 have been on the countdown.

Make a histogram of the data.

Weeks	Tally	Frequency
1–5	||||	4
6–10	~~||||~~ ~~||||~~ |	11
11–15	~~||||~~ ||||	9
16–20	||||	4
21–25		0
26–30	||	2

SOLUTION

STEP 1 **Draw** and label the horizontal and vertical axes.

List each interval from the frequency table on the horizontal axis.

The greatest frequency is 11. Start the vertical axis at 0 and end it at 12, using increments of 2.

STEP 2 **Draw** a bar for each interval. The bars should have the same width.

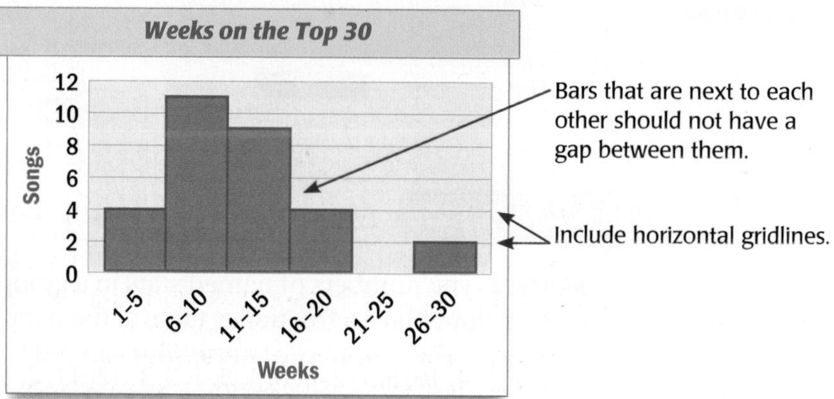

AVOID ERRORS

Make sure that your histogram includes all the intervals in the table, even the intervals that have a frequency of 0.

✓ GUIDED PRACTICE for Examples 1 and 2

1. **TYPING RATES** The numbers of words that students in a typing class type in a minute are given below. Make a frequency table and histogram of the data. Use the intervals 16–20, 21–25, 26–30, 31–35, and 36–40.

   25, 19, 23, 29, 34, 26, 30, 40, 33, 20, 35, 35, 25, 29, 36, 22, 31

2. **SCHOOL LUNCHES** The numbers of students in your class who brought lunch to school each day for two weeks are given below. Make a frequency table and histogram of the data. Use five intervals of five numbers.

   21, 15, 11, 8, 16, 18, 23, 27, 12, 12

EXAMPLE 3 ◆ Multiple Choice Practice

The histogram shows the numbers of butterflies spotted in a butterfly garden from 8:01 A.M. to 8 P.M.

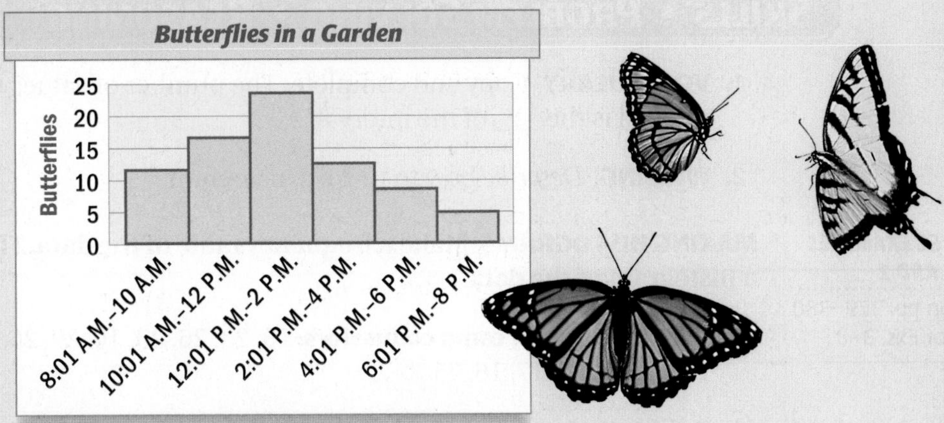

Which statement is valid about the number of butterflies spotted?

Ⓐ The number of butterflies spotted decreased during the morning.

Ⓑ More butterflies were spotted in the garden from 8:01 A.M. to 12 P.M. than from 12:01 P.M. to 4 P.M.

Ⓒ The number of butterflies spotted from 8:01 A.M. to 10 A.M. was about twice the number of butterflies spotted from 12:01 P.M. to 2 P.M.

Ⓓ The numbers of butterflies spotted from 8:01 A.M. to 10 A.M. and from 2:01 P.M. to 4 P.M. were about the same.

SOLUTION

The number of butterflies spotted from 8:01 A.M. to 10 A.M. was about 12. The number spotted from 2:01 P.M. to 4 P.M. was about 13.

▶ **Answer** The numbers of butterflies spotted from 8:01 A.M. to 10 A.M. and from 2:01 P.M. to 4 P.M. were about the same.
The correct answer is D. Ⓐ Ⓑ Ⓒ Ⓓ

GUIDED PRACTICE for Example 3

Use the histogram from Example 3.

3. Is the number of butterflies spotted from 8:01 A.M. to 2 P.M. greater than the number of butterflies spotted from 2:01 P.M.to 8 P.M.? *Explain* your reasoning.

4. Is the number of butterflies spotted from 12:01 P.M. to 4 P.M. greater than the number of butterflies spotted from 2:01 P.M. to 8 P.M.? *Explain* your reasoning.

5. Make another comparison supported by the data.

7.5 EXERCISES

HOMEWORK KEY

◆ = **MULTIPLE CHOICE PRACTICE** Exs. 8, 13, 14, 23–25

○ = **HINTS AND HOMEWORK HELP** for Exs. 3, 9, 17 at classzone.com

SKILLS • PROBLEM SOLVING • REASONING

1. **VOCABULARY** Copy and complete: The number of values that lie in an interval is the __?__ of the interval.

2. **WRITING** *Describe* how to make a histogram.

SEE EXAMPLES 1 AND 2 on pp. 379–380 for Exs. 3–8

MAKING HISTOGRAMS Make a frequency table of the data. Then make a histogram of the data.

3. **Ages (in years) of camp counselors:** 19, 23, 26, 23, 16, 20, 26, 19, 21, 24, 21, 17, 27, 25, 22, 17, 16, 25

4. **Heights (in feet) of trees:** 5, 21, 18, 16, 8, 10, 16, 12, 21, 11, 7, 21, 19, 12, 13, 15, 8, 17, 11, 5, 9, 7, 20, 19

5. **Math test scores (in percents) for a class:** 70, 78, 68, 82, 91, 98, 76, 97, 89, 79, 88, 90, 85, 77, 84, 82, 90, 86, 93, 64, 94, 68, 86, 87

6. **Prices (in dollars) of wicker furniture:** 199, 329, 79, 149, 179, 149, 99, 69, 69, 99, 279, 129, 279, 79, 129, 189, 199, 79, 109, 89, 119, 119, 149, 99

7. **ERROR ANALYSIS** The list below shows prices (in dollars) of televisions at a store. *Describe* and correct the error in the frequency table of the prices.

   170, 135, 120, 175, 200, 260, 275, 160, 230, 165, 280, 150, 180, 280, 125, 100

Interval	Tally	Frequency
100–150	~~||||~~	5
150–200	~~||||~~ ||	7
200–250	||	2
250–300	||||	4

8. ◆ **MULTIPLE CHOICE** Which intervals can be used to make a frequency table of the lengths (in inches) of alligators at an alligator farm?

   90, 127, 103, 125, 118, 100, 117, 101, 116, 129, 128, 105, 99, 123

   Ⓐ 90–99, 99–109, 109–119, 119–129 Ⓑ 90–99, 100–109, 110–119, 120–129

   Ⓒ 90–110, 111–120, 121–130, 131–140 Ⓓ 90–100, 100–110, 110–120, 120–130

SEE EXAMPLE 3 on p. 381 for Ex. 9

9. **ERROR ANALYSIS** The histogram at the right shows the number of cars sold each week at a car dealership. Your friend says that there were 12 weeks when the dealership sold from 1 to 15 cars. *Describe* and correct your friend's error.

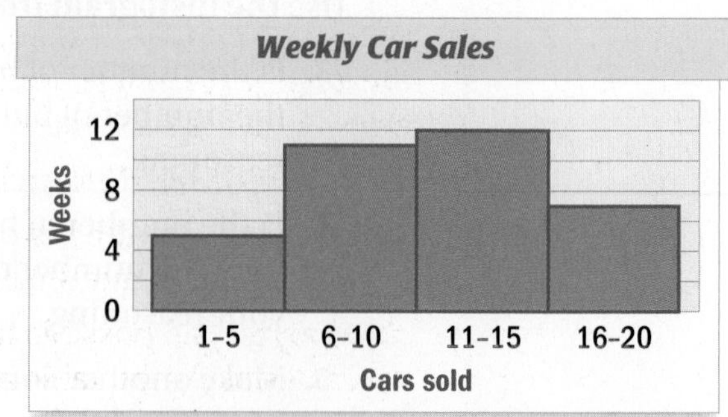

CONNECT SKILLS TO PROBLEM SOLVING **Exercises 10–12 will help you prepare for problem solving.**

Use the following information: The numbers of minutes spent online by students during one day are listed below.

15, 32, 8, 5, 0, 35, 19, 22, 60, 25, 38, 8, 7, 5, 2, 0, 30, 32, 45, 40, 25, 20, 23, 32, 44, 18, 26, 35, 20, 10, 37, 18, 30, 8, 5, 36, 10, 21, 28, 15

10. Choose intervals and make a frequency table of the data.

11. Make a histogram of the data.

12. Make a valid conclusion about the data displayed in the histogram.

SEE EXAMPLE 3 on p. 381 for Exs. 13–15

AMERICAN HISTORY **In Exercises 13–15, use the histogram showing the years that the 50 states were admitted to the Union.**

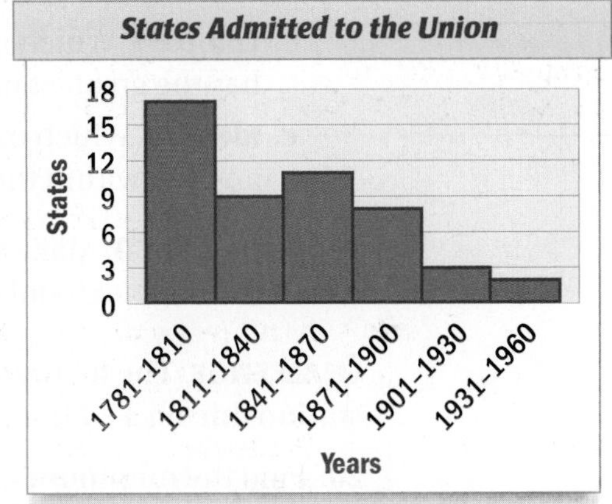

13. ◆ **MULTIPLE CHOICE** How many states were admitted from 1781 to 1810?

Ⓐ 15 Ⓑ 16

Ⓒ 17 Ⓓ 18

California @HomeTutor for problem solving help at classzone.com

14. ◆ **MULTIPLE CHOICE** California was admitted to the Union in 1850. Which statement is *not* valid based on this information?

Ⓐ At least 13 states were admitted to the Union after California.

Ⓑ At least 26 states were admitted to the Union before California.

Ⓒ More than 24 states were admitted to the Union after California.

Ⓓ Ten other states were admitted in the same 30 year interval as California.

California was admitted to the Union in 1850.

California @HomeTutor for problem solving help at classzone.com

15. **WRITING** *Write* a valid conclusion about the data in the histogram.

16. **WALKING TRAILS** The frequency table shows the lengths (in miles) of 35 historical walking trails in the United States.

a. **Draw a Graph** Make a histogram of the data.

b. **Interpret** Use the histogram to make a conclusion about the data.

c. **Analyze** Is it possible to list individual data values using the table or histogram? *Explain.*

Length (mi)	*Frequency*
3–4.9	4
5–6.9	5
7–8.9	17
9–10.9	2
11–12.9	6
13–14.9	1

17. **SHORT RESPONSE** Use the frequency table in Exercise 16 to make a new frequency table and histogram with the following intervals: 3–6.9, 7–10.9, 11–14.9. How does changing the intervals affect the histogram?

18. **MULTI-STEP PROBLEM** The point totals for each team in a Hawaiian canoe racing regatta are listed below. The team with the most points wins.

    72, 69, 65, 54, 45, 44, 37, 36, 34, 33, 32,
    32, 29, 27, 24, 21, 20, 18, 14, 14, 14, 13,
    12, 11, 10, 10, 9, 8, 7, 7, 4, 4, 1, 0

    a. **Draw a Graph** Make a histogram of the data. *Explain* how you chose the intervals.

    b. **Compare** Which interval in your histogram has the greatest number of data values?

    c. **Identify** Which measures of central tendency, if any, fall within the interval identified in part (b)?

Hawaiian canoe race

19. **OPEN-ENDED** Make a frequency table of the numbers of chapters in 10 different textbooks. What conclusions can you make?

CHALLENGE The histogram shows the number of departures from a bus station during a 24 hour period beginning at 12:01 A.M.

20. Find the minimum and maximum number of departures that could have taken place between 8:01 A.M. and 2 P.M.

21. From the histogram, can you list the number of departures that took place between 4:01 P.M. and 4 A.M.? If so, find this number. If not, explain why not.

22. Find the minimum and maximum number of departures that could have taken place between 10:01 A.M. and 2 P.M.

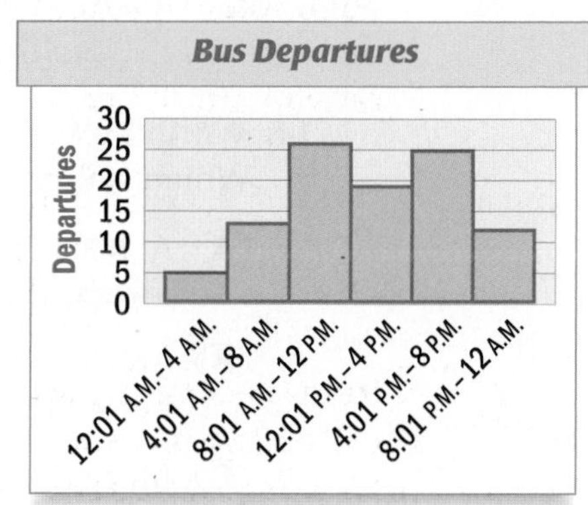

◆ CALIFORNIA STANDARDS SPIRAL REVIEW

NS 1.2 23. Which is the least ratio? *(p. 255)*

Ⓐ 1:2 Ⓑ 3:7 Ⓒ 4:9 Ⓓ 7:16

NS 2.2 24. What is the product of 14 and $\frac{5}{8}$? *(p. 88)*

Ⓐ $8\frac{3}{4}$ Ⓑ $9\frac{1}{4}$ Ⓒ $9\frac{3}{4}$ Ⓓ $10\frac{1}{4}$

AF 2.3 25. A runner completes a 21 mile race in 2 hours 24 minutes. What is the average speed of the runner in miles per hour? *(p. 260)*

Ⓐ 7.75 mi/h Ⓑ 8.25 mi/h Ⓒ 8.75 mi/h Ⓓ 9.25 mi/h

Standards Preparation

Grade 5 MG 2.1
Measure, identify, **and draw angles**, perpendicular and parallel lines, rectangles, and triangles **by using appropriate tools (e.g.,** straightedge, ruler, **compass, protractor**, drawing software).

7.6 Measuring Angles

MATERIALS • protractor • compass • tracing paper

QUESTION How can you measure and draw angles?

EXPLORE 1 Measure the angle.

An *angle* is formed by connecting two *rays*, as shown at the right. An angle is measured in units called *degrees* (°). The measure of an angle can be found by using a *protractor*, as shown below.

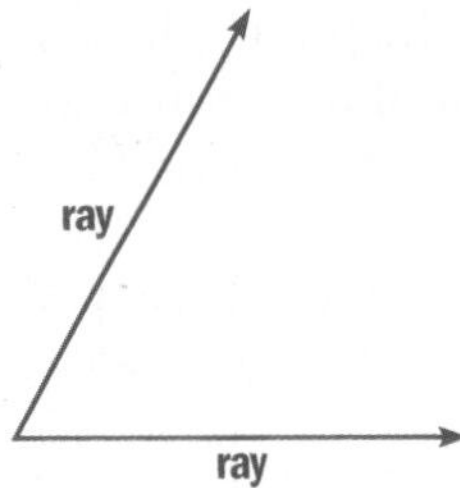

STEP 1 **Place** the protractor on the angle so the protractor's center point is on the point where the two rays meet, called the *vertex* of the angle. Line up one ray with the 0° line.

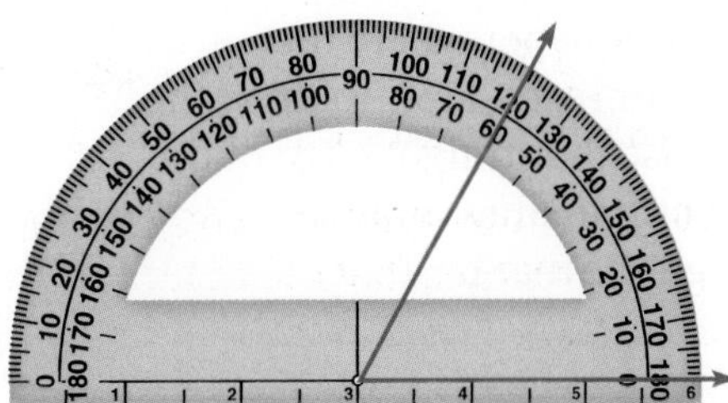

STEP 2 **Read** the angle measure. The measure of the angle is found by reading where the other ray crosses the curved portion of the protractor. The measure of the angle is 60°.

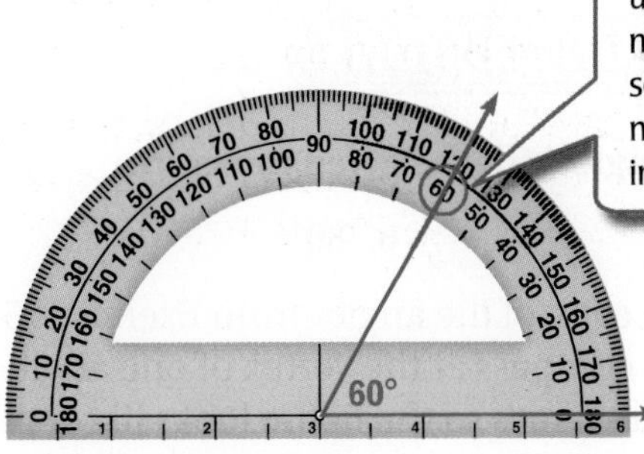

60°
The first ray lines up with the 0° mark on the inside scale, so read the measure from the inside scale.

Animated Math at classzone.com

DRAW CONCLUSIONS Use your observations to complete these exercises.

Use tracing paper to copy the angle. Then extend the rays and measure the angle using a protractor.

1.

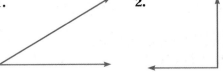

2.

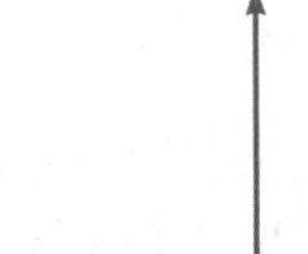

3.

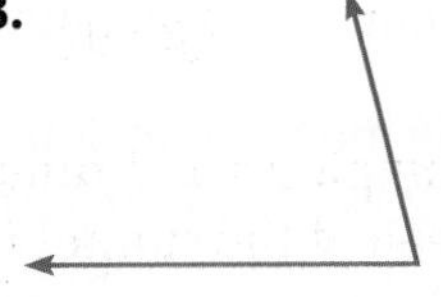

4.

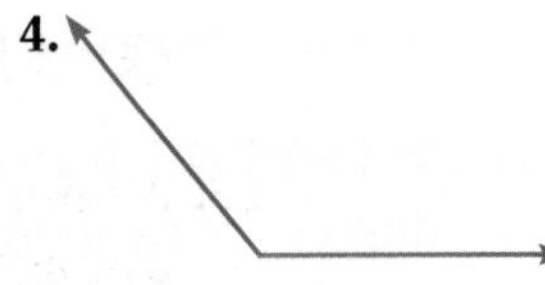

Continued on next page

Continued from the previous page

EXPLORE 2 Draw an angle that measures 115°.

STEP 1 **Draw** a ray using the straight edge of the protractor. Label the endpoint A.

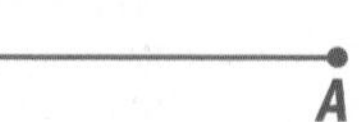
A

STEP 2 **Place** your protractor on the ray so that the point A lies on the center point of the protractor and the ray lines up with one of the 0° lines.

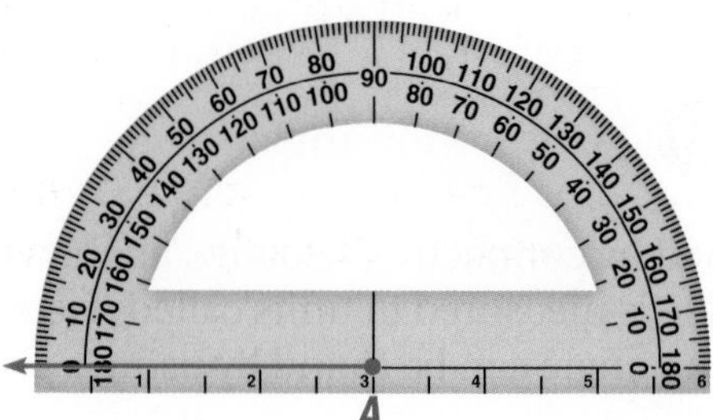
A

STEP 3 **Mark** your paper where the protractor reads 115°. To draw the angle, use the straight edge of the protractor to draw a ray from A through the mark.

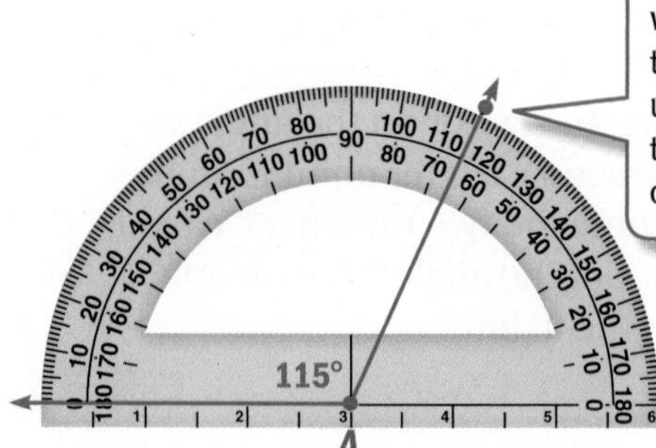
115°
A
The first ray lines up with the 0° mark on the outside scale, so use the outside scale to mark a measure of 115°.

DRAW CONCLUSIONS Use your observations to complete these exercises.

Draw an angle with the given measure.

5. 120° **6.** 80° **7.** 55° **8.** 105°

9. a. Use each of the angles from Exercises 5–8. Place the point of a compass at the vertex of one angle. Draw an *arc* across the two rays so the figure looks like a pie wedge. Repeat using the same compass setting for each angle.

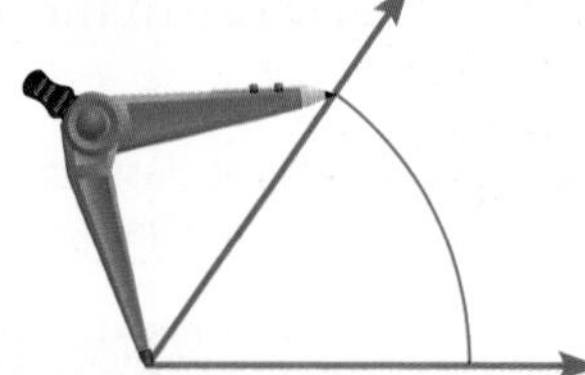

b. Cut out the four figures and put them together so that the vertices meet and there are no gaps or overlaps between the sides. What shape do these arcs form? What is the sum of the angle measures?

10. REASONING If an angle measure of 360° represents 100%, what percent does the measure of each angle in Exercises 5–8 represent? Round to the nearest tenth of a percent. *Explain* your reasoning.

11. REASONING If an angle measure of 360° represents 100%, how many degrees correspond to 25%? *Explain* your reasoning.

12. REASONING *Describe* one advantage of having two scales on a protractor.

7.6 Circle Graphs

Standards Preparation Grade 5 SDAP 1.2 **Organize and display single-variable data in appropriate graphs and representations (e.g.,** histogram, **circle graphs)** and explain which types of graphs are appropriate for various data sets.

Connect ***Before*** you found a percent of a number. ***Now*** you will use percents to make and interpret circle graphs to prepare for Grade 6 Standard SDAP 2.3.

Math and **TRANSPORTATION** Exs. 15–17, p. 390

KEY VOCABULARY
- **circle graph**
- **angle**
- **vertex**
- **degrees** (°)
- **ray,** *p. 683*

A **circle graph**, such as the one shown in Example 1 below, displays data as sections of a circle. The entire circle represents all the data. Each section is labeled using the actual data or using the data expressed as fractions, decimals, or percents of the sum of the data.

The sections of a circle graph can be described mathematically using *angles*. An **angle** consists of two rays that begin at a common point, called the **vertex**. The plural of vertex is *vertices.*

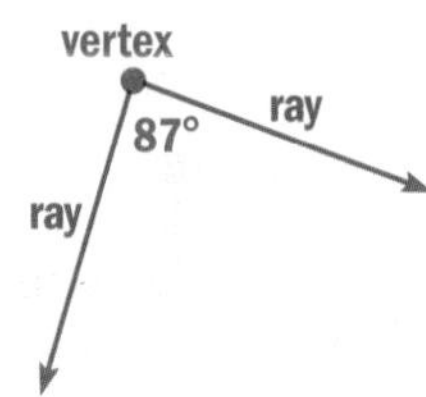

You can use a protractor to measure and draw angles, as shown in the activity on pages 385–386. Angles are measured in units called **degrees** (°).

EXAMPLE 1 Interpreting a Circle Graph

CLASS SURVEY The results of a survey are displayed in the circle graph below. What are three conclusions you can make about the data?

ADD THE DATA
When the data in a circle graph are expressed as fractions, decimals, or percents, the sum of the data must be 1, or 100%.

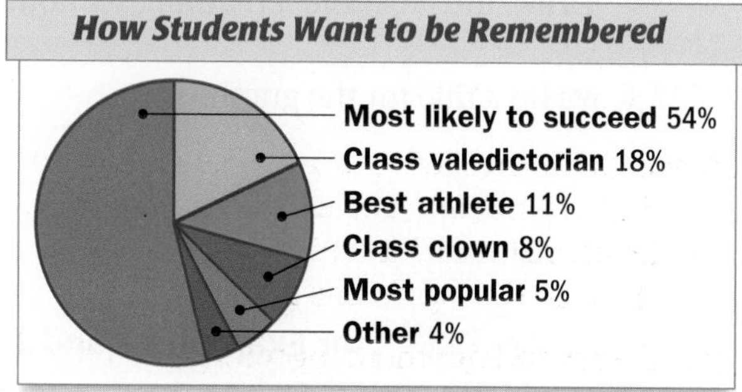

SOLUTION

- The largest section in the circle graph is labeled "most likely to succeed." This is how most students want to be remembered.
- More students want to be remembered as "class valedictorian" than as "class clown."
- Together, "class clown" and "best athlete" are more popular ways to be remembered than "class valedictorian."

MAKING CIRCLE GRAPHS To make a circle graph, you need to find the angle measure for each section. The sum of all the angle measures should equal 360°.

EXAMPLE 2 Making a Circle Graph Using Percents

SIBLINGS The table shows the results of a survey that asked students how many siblings (brothers and sisters) they have. Display the data in a circle graph.

Siblings	Percent
None	10%
One	40%
Two	25%
Three or more	25%

SOLUTION

STEP 1 **Find** the angle measure for each section.

Section	Angle Measure
None	10% of 360° = 0.10 • 360° = 36°
One sibling	40% of 360° = 0.40 • 360° = 144°
Two siblings	25% of 360° = 0.25 • 360° = 90°
Three or more	25% of 360° = 0.25 • 360° = 90°

USE A COMPASS
For help using a compass, see p. 682.

STEP 2 **Draw** a circle using a compass. Mark its center.

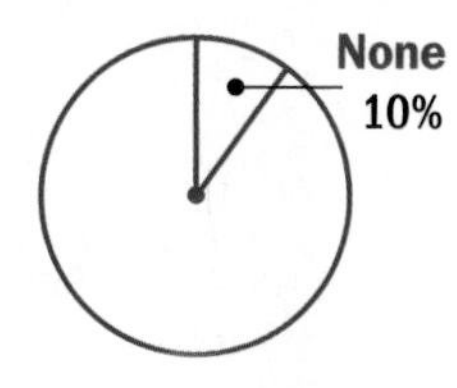

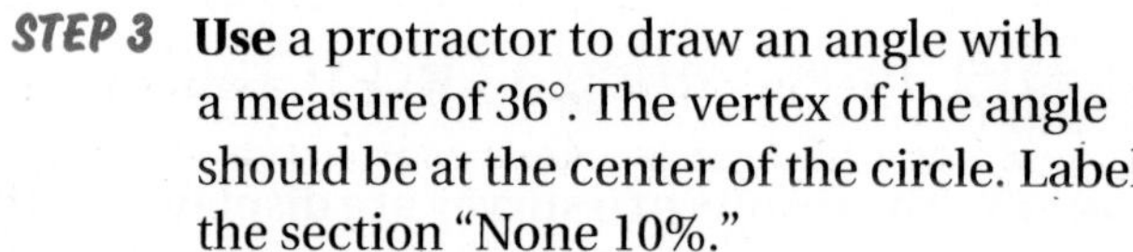

STEP 3 **Use** a protractor to draw an angle with a measure of 36°. The vertex of the angle should be at the center of the circle. Label the section "None 10%."

STEP 4 **Draw** and label the remaining sections.

STEP 5 **Write** a title for the graph.

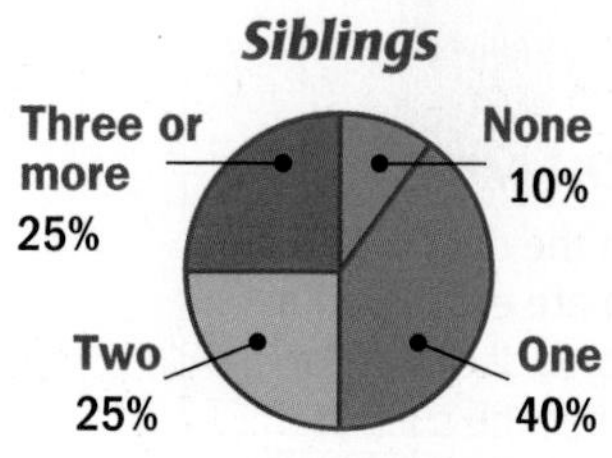

✓ GUIDED PRACTICE for Examples 1 and 2

1. **BEST ATHLETE** Use the circle graph on page 387. Can you tell from the graph how many people chose "Best athlete"? *Explain* your reasoning.

2. **CLOTHING** The table shows the results of a survey that asked students what they wear to school. Display the data in a circle graph.

Clothing	Percent
Jeans	55%
Other pants	30%
Skirts or dresses	15%

3. Make a conclusion about the data in the circle graph in Exercise 2.

EXAMPLE 3 Making a Circle Graph Using Data

EXERCISING The table shows the results of a survey that asked people their favorite type of exercise. Display the data in a circle graph.

Favorite Exercise	*People*
Jogging	22
Weightlifing	12
Aerobics	8
Other	6

SOLUTION

STEP 1 **Find** the total number of people surveyed: $22 + 12 + 8 + 6 = 48$.

STEP 2 **Find** the angle measure for each section. Write the data for each group as a fraction of all the people and multiply by 360°.

Jogging	**Weightlifing**	**Aerobics**	**Other**
$\frac{22}{48} \cdot 360° = 165°$	$\frac{12}{48} \cdot 360° = 90°$	$\frac{8}{48} \cdot 360° = 60°$	$\frac{6}{48} \cdot 360° = 45°$

STEP 3 **Draw** and label the circle graph.

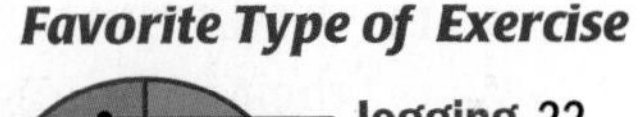

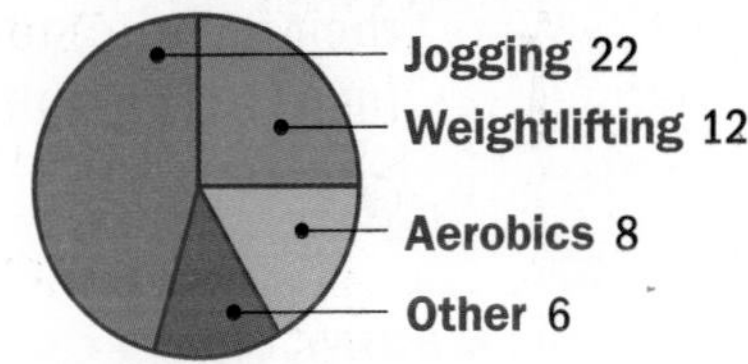

Animated Math
For an interactive example of making circle graphs go to **classzone.com.**

GUIDED PRACTICE for Example 3

4. **WHAT IF?** In Example 3, suppose that 12 people favored aerobics and 18 people favored jogging. Make a circle graph using the new data.

7.6 EXERCISES

HOMEWORK KEY
◆ = **MULTIPLE CHOICE PRACTICE** Exs. 4, 11, 19, 24–26
○ = **HINTS AND HOMEWORK HELP** for Exs. 7, 13, 21 at classzone.com

SKILLS • PROBLEM SOLVING • REASONING

1. **VOCABULARY** Angles are measured in units called _?_.

2. **WRITING** *Describe* the steps for making a circle graph when the data are given in percents.

SEE EXAMPLE 1 on p. 387 for Exs. 3–4

INTERPRETING GRAPHS The graph shows the types of hits made by Cal Ripken, Jr., in one season.

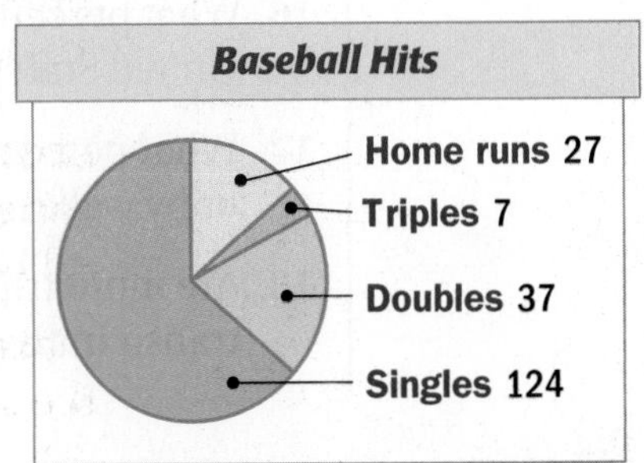

3. How many total hits did he have that season?

4. ◆ **MULTIPLE CHOICE** About what fraction of his hits were doubles or triples?

Ⓐ $\frac{1}{4}$ Ⓑ $\frac{1}{3}$ Ⓒ $\frac{3}{8}$ Ⓓ $\frac{5}{8}$

SEE EXAMPLE 2
on p. 388
for Exs. 5–8

FINDING ANGLE MEASURES **Find the angle measure that corresponds to the percent of a circle.**

5. 5%
6. 70%
7. 45%
8. 20%

SEE EXAMPLES 2 AND 3
on pp. 388–389
for Exs. 9–15

ERROR ANALYSIS **The table shows the results of a survey that asked students where they most often buy CDs. *Describe* and correct the error made in finding the angle of the circle graph for the given category.**

Buying CDs	Retail Store	Online	CD club
Percent	56%	24%	20%

9. Online

✗ $\frac{1}{24} \times 360° = \frac{360}{24}$, or 15°

10. CD Club

✗ 20% chose CD club, so the angle is 20°.

11. ◆ **MULTIPLE CHOICE** In a survey, 25 out of 75 students chose math as their favorite subject. What angle measure would you use to show this on a circle graph?

Ⓐ 3° Ⓑ 25° Ⓒ 100° Ⓓ 120°

MAKING CIRCLE GRAPHS **Display the survey data in a circle graph.**

12.

School Involvement	Students
Very involved	30%
Somewhat involved	50%
Not that involved	15%
Not involved at all	5%

13.

Favorite Fruit	Students
Apples	45%
Grapes	25%
Oranges	20%
Bananas	10%

14.

Favorite Movie Type	People
Action	18
Comedy	15
Horror	5
Science Fiction	2

15.

Favorite Drink	People
Juice	36
Milk	18
Water	16
Sports Drink	10

CONNECT SKILLS TO PROBLEM SOLVING **Exercises 16–18 will help you prepare for problem solving.**

16. What percent of trips are *not* by car in the United States?

17. What percent of trips are either by bicycle or by walking in the United States?

18. Are more trips made by walking or by public transit in the United States?

Transportation in the United States (% of trips)

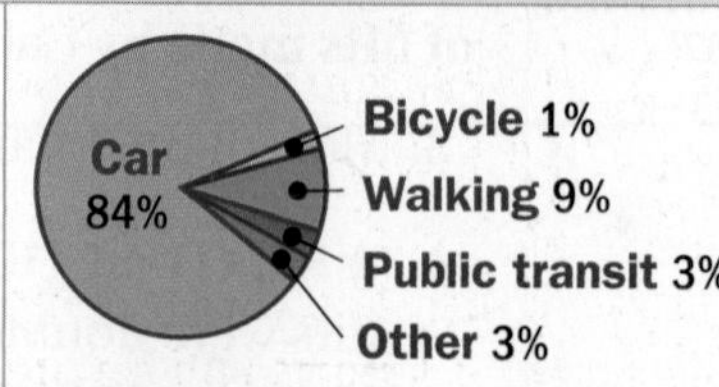

19. ◆ **MULTIPLE CHOICE** A survey asked 100 students chosen at random their favorite sport. The results are shown. Estimate how many students out of 500 would say that basketball is their favorite sport.

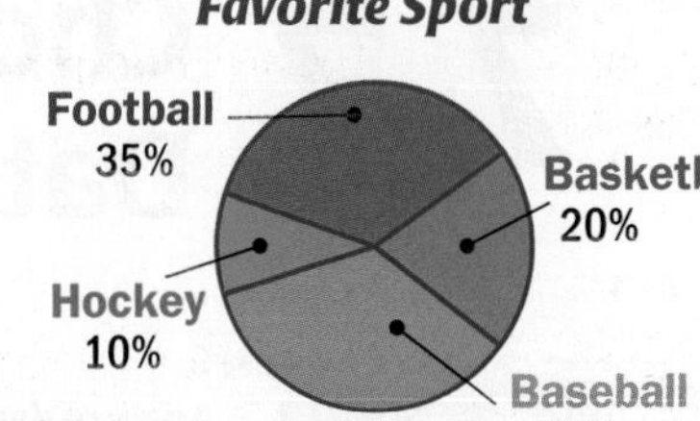

Ⓐ 20 Ⓑ 25 Ⓒ 100 Ⓓ 175

California @HomeTutor for problem solving help at classzone.com

20. **REASONING** Would your estimate in Exercise 19 be valid if the survey was only given to students at a basketball game? *Explain.*

California @HomeTutor for problem solving help at classzone.com

SEE EXAMPLES 1, 2, AND 3 on pp. 387–389 for Exs. 21–22

21. **UNITED STATES SYMBOL** The table shows the results of a survey that asked people to name the item among those listed that most symbolizes the United States. Display the data in a circle graph. Round the angle measures to the nearest degree. Make a conclusion about the data in your graph.

Item	Percent
American flag	67%
Statue of Liberty	17%
Bald eagle	8%
White House	5%
Liberty Bell	2%
Mount Rushmore	1%

22. **WRITING** Make a bar graph and a circle graph using the data of students' favorite vegetables. Which graph more clearly shows that over half of the students prefer potatoes or corn? *Justify* your answer.

Vegetables	Carrots	Potatoes	Corn	Broccoli	Other
Students	30	30	20	5	5

23. **CHALLENGE** The chemical composition of the layers of Earth by mass is shown. Copy and complete the table. Display the data in a circle graph.

Chemical	Iron	Oxygen	Silicon	Magnesium	Other
Fraction	$\frac{173}{500}$	?	$\frac{19}{125}$	$\frac{127}{1000}$	?
Percent	?	?	?	?	8%

◆ CALIFORNIA STANDARDS SPIRAL REVIEW

AF 1.1 24. What is the value of x in the equation $3x = 48$? ***(p. 234)***

Ⓐ 12 Ⓑ 15 Ⓒ 16 Ⓓ 18

AF 2.2 25. You buy a 5.5 pound ham for $8.25. What is the cost per pound? ***(p. 260)***

Ⓐ $1.25 Ⓑ $1.50 Ⓒ $1.75 Ⓓ $1.90

AF 2.3 26. At a factory, one plastic part is produced every 45 seconds. How many parts will be produced in 2 hours? ***(p. 266)***

Ⓐ 120 Ⓑ 140 Ⓒ 150 Ⓓ 160

7.7 Choosing and Analyzing Data Displays

Standards **SDAP 2.3 Analyze data displays and explain** why the way in which the question was asked might have influenced the results obtained and **why the way in which the results were displayed might have influenced the conclusions reached.**

SDAP 2.5 Identify claims based on statistical data and, in simple cases, evaluate the validity of the claims.

Connect ***Before*** you displayed data using several types of graphs. ***Now*** you will choose appropriate data displays and analyze the displays to make valid claims.

Math and **MENUS**
Exs. 13–18, p. 396

KEY VOCABULARY
- **ordered pair,** *p. 678*
- **line graph,** *p. 688*

You have seen and used many types of data displays earlier in this course and in previous courses. Data can often be displayed in more than one way. The table below suggests how you might use displays for different purposes.

KEY CONCEPT *For Your Notebook*

Appropriate Data Displays

- Use a *line plot* to show how often each number occurs.
- Use a *bar graph* to display data in distinct categories.
- Use a *line graph* to display data over time.
- Use a *circle graph* to represent data as parts of a whole.
- Use a *box-and-whisker plot* to display how the data are spread out.
- Use a *histogram* to compare the frequencies of data that fall in equal intervals.

EXAMPLE 1 Choosing Appropriate Data Displays

a. GOLF You want to display your golf scores for the year, without displaying all the individual data. Which data display(s) could you use?

▸**Answer** Either a *box-and-whisker plot* or a *histogram* will show how the data are distributed without showing all the individual data.

b. STAMPS You want to display the percent of people surveyed who prefer each stamp from a list of stamps. Which data display(s) could you use?

▸**Answer** A *bar graph* will display the percent who favor each stamp. A *circle graph* will display these percents as parts of a whole.

USING LINE GRAPHS Recall that a *line graph* uses points connected by line segments to represent ordered pairs of data. Line graphs are often used to show change over time. You can use a break at the beginning of the vertical scale to focus on the interval where the data fall.

EXAMPLE 2 Making and Analyzing Line Graphs

About the Standards

You can estimate unknown quantities from a line graph. You will apply this aspect of Grade 6 Standard MR 2.3 in Exercise 26 on p. 397.

BOWLING The table shows the number of bowling centers in the United States from 2000 to 2003. Make two line graphs of the data, one with a break in the scale. Then make a conclusion based on each graph.

Bowling Centers	
Year	**Number**
2000	6247
2001	6022
2002	5973
2003	5811

STEP 1 **Think** of each pair of numbers in the table as an *ordered pair*: (**year**, **number**).

STEP 2 **Choose** scales that include all the number values in the table.

STEP 3 **Plot** each point.

STEP 4 **Draw** line segments to connect the points.

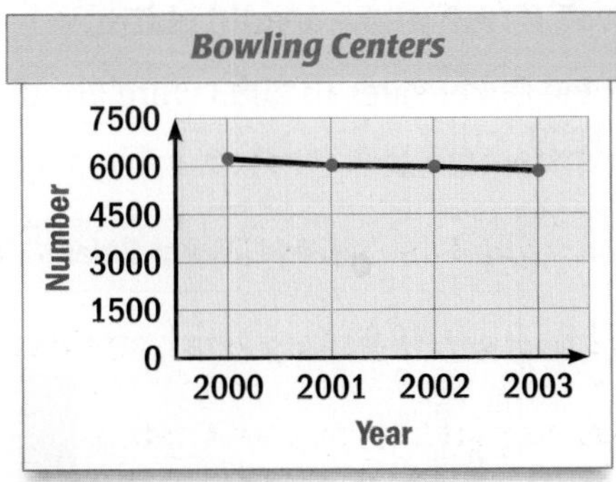

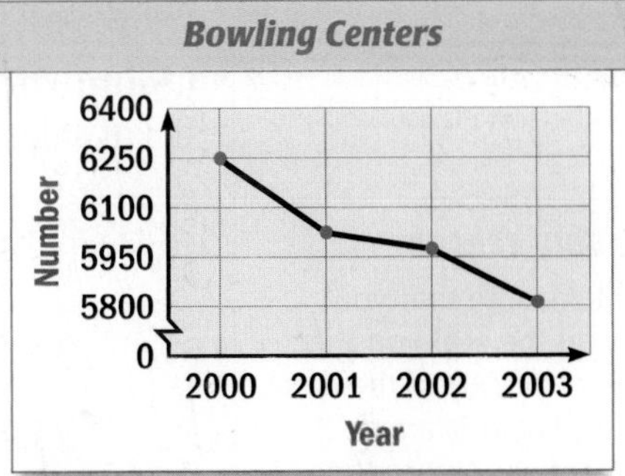

READING

The symbol ⌇ on the vertical axis indicates that there is a break in the scale.

STEP 5 **Analyze** each graph to make a conclusion. From the first graph, you can conclude that the number of bowling centers decreased slightly from 2000 to 2003. From the second graph, you can conclude that the number of bowling centers decreased more rapidly from 2000 to 2001 than from 2001 to 2002.

✓ GUIDED PRACTICE for Examples 1 and 2

1. **AGES** Which data display(s) could be used to show the age of each student at a student council meeting?

2. **PET CATS** The table below shows the number of pet cats in the United States from 1993 to 2003. Make two line graphs of the data, one with a break in the scale. Then make a conclusion based on each graph.

Pet Cats in the United States						
Year	1993	1995	1997	1999	2001	2003
Cats (millions)	64	66	70	73	76	78

ANALYZING DATA DISPLAYS You need to read and interpret data displays carefully so that you can identify valid claims. Examples of data displays that could potentially be misinterpreted are shown below.

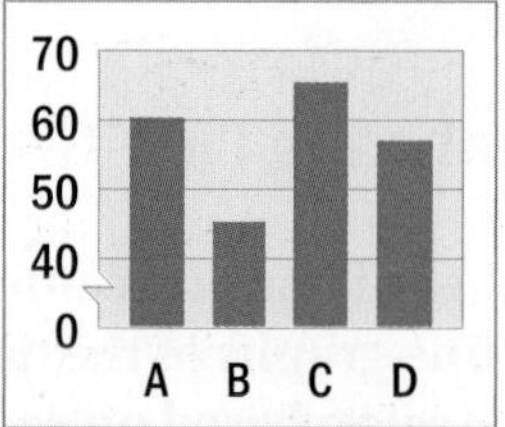

Break in the Scale
The break in the scale exaggerates differences in bar lengths.

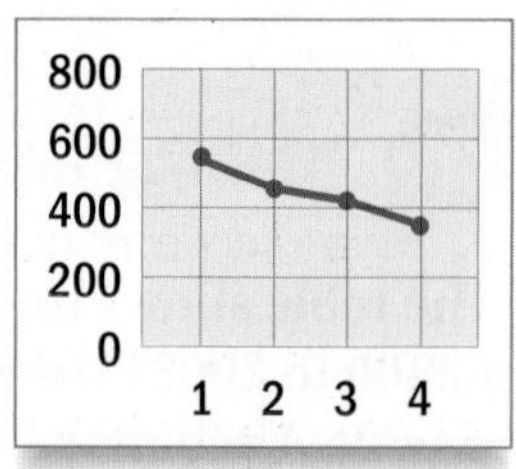

Large Increments
The large increments compress the graph vertically.

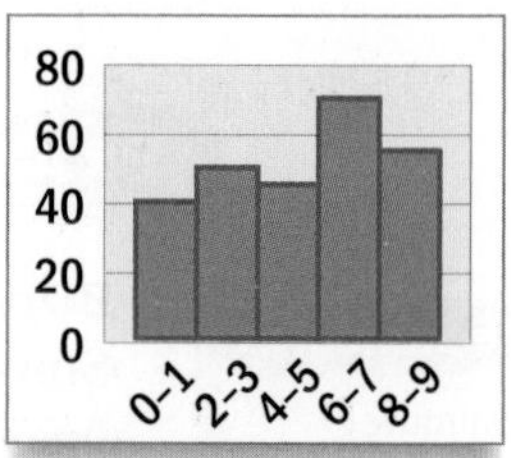

Small Intervals
The small intervals make it less clear how the data are clustered.

EXAMPLE 3 Evaluating Claims from Data Displays

MOVIE THEATERS Tell whether the following claim is valid based on the bar graph below. If not, make a valid claim.

Claim: The movie ticket sales in 2003 were about three times the movie ticket sales in 1999.

AVOID ERRORS
Make sure that you read the scale on the vertical axis of the data display in Example 3 carefully. Notice the break in the scale.

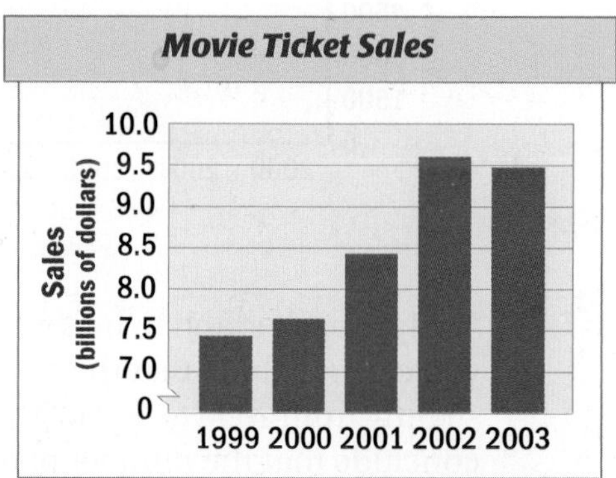

SOLUTION

This claim is not valid. There is a break in the scale on the vertical axis that makes it appear as though the data value for 2003 is about three times as high as the data value for 1999. However, the actual sales of about \$9.4 billion in 2003 are not even twice the sales of about \$7.4 billion in 1999. A valid claim is that the sales in 2003 were about \$2 billion more than the sales in 1999.

 **GUIDED PRACTICE** for Example 3

3. **WHAT IF?** In Example 3, suppose the claim is that the sales in 2001 were more than twice the sales in 1999. Is this claim valid based on the bar graph? If not, make a valid claim.

7.7 EXERCISES

HOMEWORK KEY

◆ = MULTIPLE CHOICE PRACTICE
Exs. 6, 7, 8, 32–34

○ = HINTS AND HOMEWORK HELP
for Exs. 3, 9, 27 at classzone.com

SKILLS • PROBLEM SOLVING • REASONING

1. **VOCABULARY** Copy and complete: Use a(n) _?_ to display data over time.

2. **NOTETAKING SKILLS** Use a *notetaking organizer* like the one on page 352 to organize your notes about types of data displays.

SEE EXAMPLE 1 on p. 392 for Exs. 3–8

CHOOSING DISPLAYS Choose one or more appropriate data displays for the data. *Explain* your choice(s).

3. The change in state population over the last 5 years

4. The results of a survey that asked people their favorite basketball team

5. The lengths of long distance phone calls, without displaying all the individual call lengths

6. ◆ **MULTIPLE CHOICE** A house was worth \$125,000 in 1990, \$133,000 in 1995, \$149,000 in 2000, and \$165,000 in 2005. Which data display could you use to show the change in the house's value over that time?

Ⓐ Line plot   Ⓑ Histogram   Ⓒ Line graph   Ⓓ Circle graph

7. ◆ **MULTIPLE CHOICE** Which data display would be most appropriate to represent data as parts of a whole?

Ⓐ Line plot   Ⓑ Line graph

Ⓒ Box-and-whisker plot   Ⓓ Circle graph

8. ◆ **MULTIPLE CHOICE** Which data display would be most appropriate for the data below?

Ages of Students in a CPR Class						
Interval	10–19	20–29	30–39	40–49	50–59	60–69
Frequency	5	11	9	7	7	5

Ⓐ Line graph   Ⓑ Line plot

Ⓒ Box-and-whisker plot   Ⓓ Histogram

SEE EXAMPLE 2 on p. 393 for Exs. 9–12

MAKING LINE GRAPHS Decide whether or not to use a broken scale to make a line graph of the data. Then make a line graph of the data.

9.

Hour (A.M.)	7	8	9	10
Cars in lot	1	4	15	17

10.

Hour (P.M.)	1	2	3	4
Tickets sold	81	90	103	120

11.

Year	1998	2000	2002
Students	1253	1425	1310

12.

Month	1	2	3	4
Members	8	12	24	20

SEE EXAMPLE 3 on p. 394 for Exs. 13–18

EVALUATING CLAIMS **The graph shows the results of a survey that asked students to choose their favorite meal. Tell whether the claim is *true* or *false*. *Explain* your reasoning.**

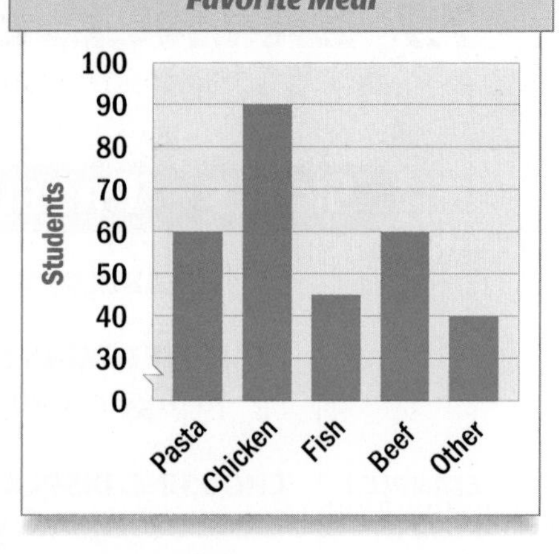

13. Pasta is as popular as beef.
14. Beef is twice as popular as *other*.
15. Pasta is twice as popular as *other*.
16. Fish is more popular than beef.
17. Chicken is twice as popular as fish.
18. Chicken is 1.5 times as popular as beef.
19. **ERROR ANALYSIS** A student wants to display the increasing value of a savings account over the past 10 months. The student chooses a circle graph to display the data. *Describe* and correct the error made in choosing that display for the data.

CONNECT SKILLS TO PROBLEM SOLVING **Exercises 20–22 will help you prepare for problem solving.**

Use the table which shows the number of endangered or threatened bird species in the United States.

Year	1992	1993	1994	1995	1996	1997	1998	1999	2000
Species	84	88	90	91	90	93	93	89	93

20. Choose a scale, with a break in it, that is appropriate for making a line graph of the data.
21. Make a line graph of the data.
22. Make a conclusion based on the line graph.

SEE EXAMPLES 1 AND 2 on pp. 392–393 for Exs. 23–24

23. **STAMP PRICES** The stamps below show the cost to mail a letter in the given years. Choose and make a display of the data. *Explain* your choice. Then use the display to make a conclusion about the data.

1961

1969

1980

1989

2000

2005

California @HomeTutor for problem solving help at classzone.com

24. **WRITING** Should a bar graph or a line graph be used to compare the number of restaurants of different types in a city? *Explain*.

California @HomeTutor for problem solving help at classzone.com

SEE EXAMPLE 3 on p. 394 for Exs. 25–28

25. **ADVERTISING** Tell whether the following claim is valid based on the advertisement below. If not, make a valid claim.

Claim: The January sales were more than double the November sales.

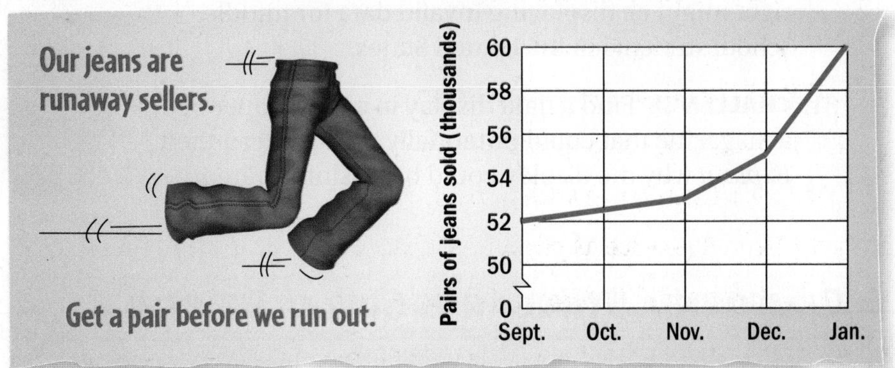

26. **RADIO STATIONS** The two graphs below both show the number of AM radio stations in the United States from 1995 to 2001. Which of the following estimates is valid based on the graphs? *Explain.*

A. There will be almost no AM radio stations in 2010.

B. The number of AM radio stations in 2010 will be less than the number of AM radio stations in 1995.

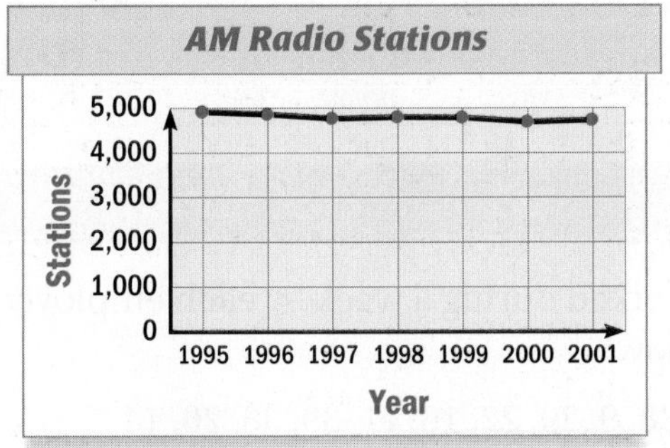

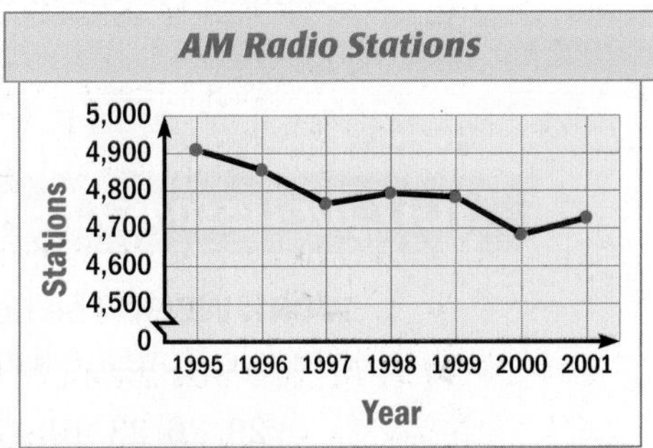

27. **TEST SCORES** Make a histogram for the test scores below. Use 76–81 as the first interval.

76, 79, 80, 81, 82, 82, 83, 84, 85, 86, 87, 88, 88, 92, 93, 95, 96, 96

Make a second histogram using 76–78 as the first interval. Which histogram more clearly shows how the test scores are clustered? *Explain* your reasoning.

28. **MULTI-STEP PROBLEM** The graph shows the amount of waste recycled in the United States in three different years.

a. **Interpret** About how many times as much waste was recycled in 2000 as in 1990?

b. **Analyze** About how many times the area of the recycle bin for 1990 is the area of the recycle bin for 2000?

c. **Make Conclusions** *Explain* why the graph might lead to invalid conclusions.

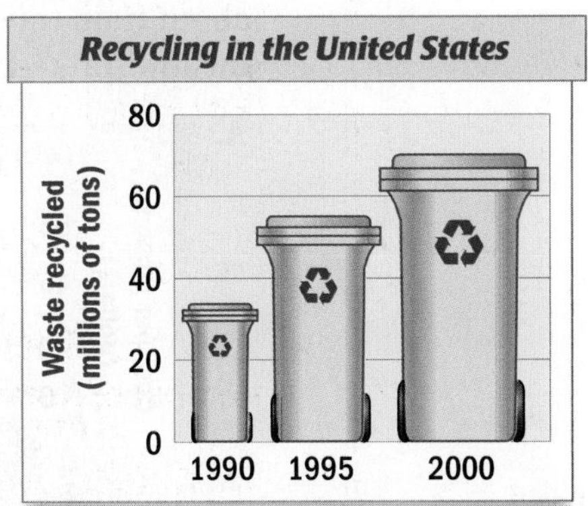

29. **OPEN-ENDED** Give an example of data that can be displayed in a histogram but not in a line graph. *Explain* your reasoning.

30. **CHALLENGE** *Explain* why the circle graph at the right might be displaying invalid data for middle school students in the United States.

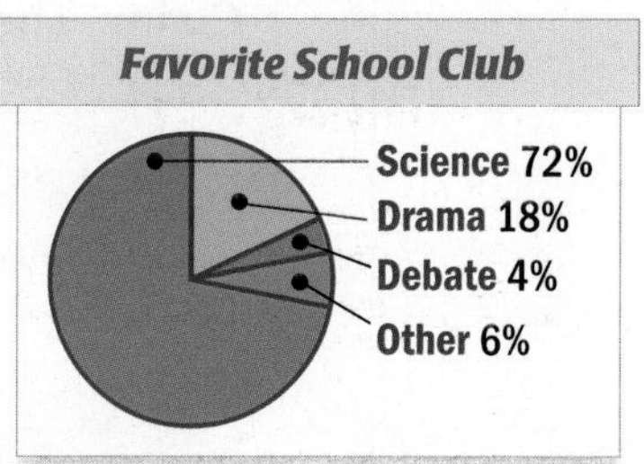

31. **CHALLENGE** Find a data display in a newspaper or a magazine that could potentially be misinterpreted. *Explain* why the display could be misinterpreted.

◆ CALIFORNIA STANDARDS SPIRAL REVIEW

SDAP 1.1 32. What is the median of 78, 54, 29, 45, 64, 81, 38, 58, and 67? ***(p. 364)***

Ⓐ 52 Ⓑ 57 Ⓒ 58 Ⓓ 64

AF 1.1 33. What is the value of y in the equation $\frac{3}{5}y = 75$? ***(p. 234)***

Ⓐ 25 Ⓑ 45 Ⓒ 125 Ⓓ 210

NS 1.3 34. It takes 12 pounds of fertilizer to cover 3000 square feet. How many pounds of fertilizer are needed to cover 2200 square feet? ***(p. 266)***

Ⓐ 7.4 Ⓑ 8 Ⓒ 8.8 Ⓓ 16.4

QUIZ *for Lessons 7.5–7.7*

1. **WORK WEEK** The hours worked during a week by each employee at a music store are listed below.

   29, 26, 23, 10, 17, 42, 38, 9, 29, 22, 16, 11, 39, 38, 26, 14

   Make a histogram of the data. Use 0–9 as the first interval. Then make a conclusion about the data. ***(p. 379)***

2. **PETS** The table shows the results of a survey that asked people their favorite pet. Display the data in a circle graph. ***(p. 387)***

Pet	Dog	Cat	Bird	Other
People	35%	30%	20%	15%

3. **TRAVEL** Which line graph might lead someone to make an invalid claim about train travel costs? *Explain* why that particular graph might be misinterpreted. Then make a valid claim about train travel costs. ***(p. 392)***

A.

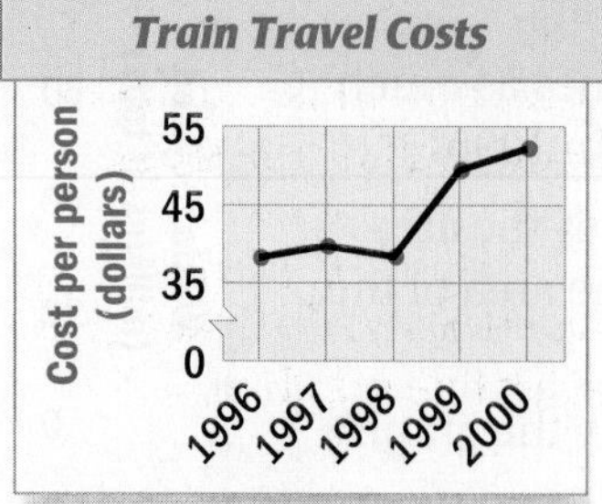

B.

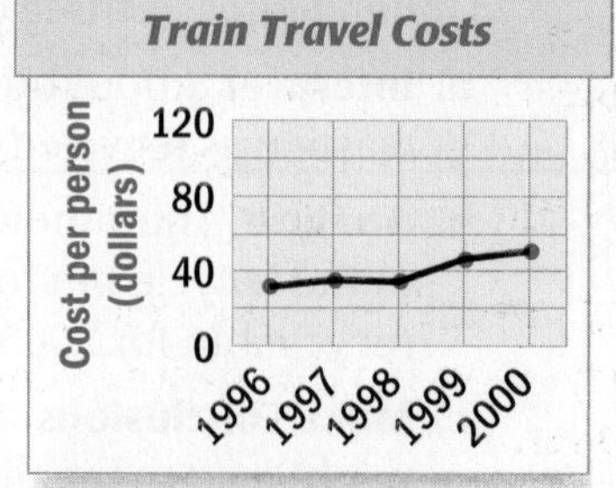

Technology **ACTIVITY** *Use after Lesson 7.7*

> **Standards Preparation**
> **Grade 5 SDAP 1.2**
> **Organize and display single-variable data in appropriate graphs and representations** (e.g., histogram, circle graphs) and explain which types of graphs are appropriate for various data sets.

7.7 Making Data Displays

QUESTION How can you use a spreadsheet to display data?

EXAMPLE **The daily mean temperature for each month in Chicago is shown at the right. Use spreadsheet software to make a line graph of the data.**

	A	B
1	Month	Temperature (°F)
2	Jan.	22
3	Feb.	27
4	Mar.	37.3
5	Apr.	47.8
6	May	58.7
7	Jun.	68.2
8	Jul.	73.3
9	Aug.	71.7
10	Sep.	63.8
11	Oct.	52.1
12	Nov.	39.3
13	Dec.	27.4

STEP 1 **Enter** the data in the first two columns of a spreadsheet, as shown at the right.

STEP 2 **Highlight** the data in cells A2:B13. The expression A2:B13 refers to the rectangular array of cells that has A2 and B13 at the corners.

STEP 3 **Use** the Insert menu to insert a graph, or *chart*. Select a line graph as the type of graph. Then choose the options for your graph, such as the titles and axis labels.

STEP 4 **Change** features of your graph by double clicking on the part of the graph that you wish to change and adjusting the formatting.

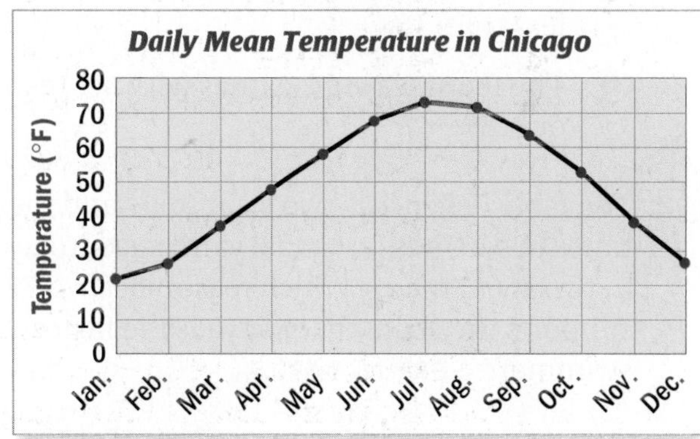

PRACTICE

Use spreadsheet software.

1. **CAR BUYING** The table shows the results of a survey that asked people in the United States what type of car they buy. Make a circle graph and then a bar graph of the data. To do this, follow the steps above but select the appropriate graph in Step 3.

Car Type	*People*
Luxury	86
Large	35
Midsize	242
Small	142

2. **TICKET PRICES** Do research to find the average U.S. movie ticket prices for each of the past 10 years. Then make a line graph of the data.

MIXED REVIEW *of Skills and Problem Solving*

Multiple Choice Practice for Lessons 7.5–7.7

1. The histogram shows the points scored in all the games played by a football team over the past several years. Which of the following claims about the team *must* be true? **SDAP 2.5**

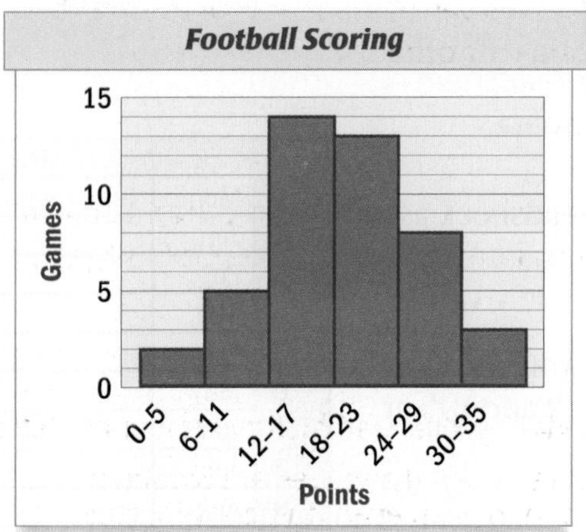

Ⓐ The team scored 13 points in one game.

Ⓑ The team scored 5 points in one game.

Ⓒ The team played 21 games with scores less than 18.

Ⓓ The team played 2 games with scores over 32.

2. The table below lists two swimmers and their times in seconds for the 50 yard backstroke in two swim meets. Which reason best supports the claim that Sonya is the faster swimmer? **SDAP 2.5, MR 2.5**

	Meet 1	*Meet 2*
Sonya	35	35.8
Louise	36.6	35.4

Ⓐ Sonya was faster in the first meet.

Ⓑ Sonya was slower in the second meet.

Ⓒ Sonya's mean time is less than Louise's mean time.

Ⓓ Sonya's time increased from the first meet to the second meet.

In Exercises 3 and 4, use the graph below, which shows the value of a plot of land over four years.

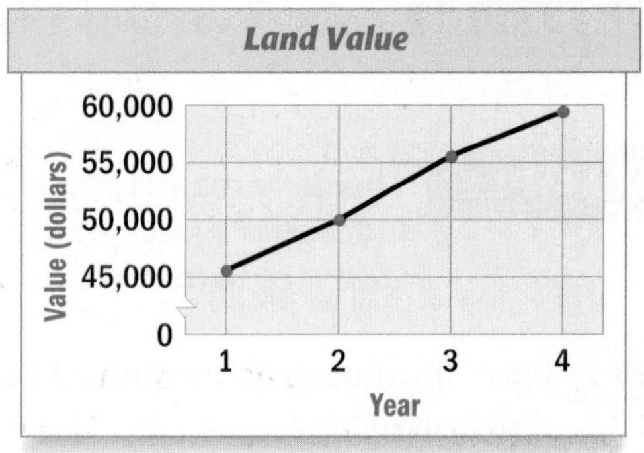

3. A person concludes that the land is worth about four times as much in year 4 as it was worth in year 1. What is the most likely reason the graph could lead to this invalid conclusion? **SDAP 2.3, MR 2.4**

Ⓐ The scale on the vertical axis goes too high.

Ⓑ The break in the vertical scale distorts the relative heights of data points.

Ⓒ The scale on the horizontal axis is too spread out.

Ⓓ The scale on the vertical axis is not spread out enough to estimate the data values.

4. Which of these claims about the land value data is *not* valid based on the graph? **SDAP 2.5, MR 2.3**

Ⓐ The land value in year 3 is two times the land value in year 1.

Ⓑ The land value in year 4 is about \$10,000 more than the land value in year 2.

Ⓒ The land value in year 5 will probably be greater than the land value in year 3.

Ⓓ The land value in year 5 will probably be about \$5000 greater than the land value in year 4.

7 CHAPTER SUMMARY

Standards
SDAP 1.1–1.4, 2.1–2.5, Gr. 5 SDAP 1.2

BIG IDEAS

For Your Notebook

Big Idea 1

Evaluating Sampling Methods and Validity of Claims

Information about a population can be found by surveying a *sample* of the population. Sampling methods include *random, systematic, convenience,* and *self-selected sampling*. Random sampling is most likely to produce a representative sample. Claims based on survey results may not be valid, due to a biased sample, a biased question, or other sampling errors.

Big Idea 2

Computing and Analyzing Statistics

You can use statistical measures to describe the center and the spread of a data set. An *outlier* can affect these measures, especially by distorting the mean and the range.

Measures of Central Tendency	
Mean	The sum of the values in a data set divided by the number of values
Median	The middle value in a data set when the values are written in numerical order. If the data set has an even number of values, the median is the mean of the two middle values.
Mode	The value in a data set that occurs most often

Describing the Spread of Data	
Extremes	The least and greatest values in a data set
Quartiles	The medians of the lower half and upper half of a data set
Range	The difference between the upper and lower extremes
Interquartile range	The difference between the upper and lower quartiles

Big Idea 3

Making and Analyzing Data Displays

Appropriate use of the data displays below can help you make meaningful and valid conclusions about data.

- Line plot
- Bar graph
- Line graph
- Circle graph
- Box-and-whisker plot
- Histogram

Some reasons data can be misinterpreted are:

- A break in the scale of a bar graph can exaggerate differences in bar lengths.
- Large increments on a line graph can compress the data vertically.
- Small intervals on a histogram can make it less clear how the data are clustered.

CHAPTER PROBLEM

Standards
SDAP 1.1–1.4
SDAP 2.1–2.5

APPLYING THE BIG IDEAS

Big Idea 1
You evaluate sampling methods in **Ex. 1.**

Big Idea 2
You compute and analyze statistics in **Step 3** and **Ex. 5.**

Big Idea 3
You make and analyze data displays in **Step 4, Ex. 2, Ex. 3,** and **Ex. 4.**

PROBLEM How can you use what you learned about surveys, statistics, and data displays to conduct a survey and analyze the results?

STEP 1 **Plan a survey.**

Plan how you will conduct a survey to find the average number of minutes students in your math class spend on homework each night.

Decide whether to ask students directly or have them write their responses on a survey form.

Use random sampling and one other sampling method to select two samples from your class to answer the survey.

STEP 2 **Conduct the survey.**

Conduct your survey using each sample and record the results. Then identify the population. Your teacher will survey the entire population and share the results with the class.

STEP 3 **Compute statistics.**

Find the mean of each sample and of the population. Compare the mean of each sample with the mean of the population. Find the median, mode, extremes, quartiles, range, and interquartile range for the population.

STEP 4 **Choose an appropriate data display.**

Which data display(s) can be used to display the data found for the population? Choose a data display and make a graph of the population data. Make a valid claim about the results for the population.

Extending the Problem

Use your results from the problem above to complete the exercises.

1. Identify possible bias in the sampling methods, survey question, or survey methods. Does sampling make sense in this situation?
2. Create an appropriate data display for each of your samples.
3. Use the data displays to compare the results based on your random sample to the results for the population.
4. Use the data displays to compare the results based on your other sample to the results for the population.
5. Are there are outliers in the population data? If there are, describe how their *exclusion* affects the mean, median, and mode(s).

7 CHAPTER REVIEW

California @HomeTutor
classzone.com
• Multi-Language Visual Glossary
• Vocabulary practice

REVIEW KEY VOCABULARY

- population, *p. 354*
- sample, *p. 354*
- random sampling, *p. 355*
- systematic sampling, *p. 355*
- convenience sampling, *p. 355*
- self-selected sampling, *p. 355*
- biased sample, *p. 355*
- mean, median, mode, *p. 364*
- lower extreme, *p. 372*
- upper extreme, *p. 372*
- lower quartile, *p. 372*
- upper quartile, *p. 372*
- range, *p. 372*
- interquartile range, *p. 372*
- outlier, *p. 373*
- box-and-whisker plot, *p. 374*
- frequency table, *p. 379*
- frequency, *p. 379*
- histogram, *p. 380*
- circle graph, *p. 387*
- angle, *p. 387*
- vertex, *p. 387*
- degrees (°), *p. 387*

VOCABULARY EXERCISES

Copy and complete the statement.

1. The middle value of an ordered set of data is the __?__.
2. The difference between the upper quartile and the lower quartile of a data set is the __?__.
3. **NOTETAKING SKILLS** Use a *notetaking organizer* like the one on page 352 to organize your notes about sampling methods.

REVIEW EXAMPLES AND EXERCISES

7.1 Sampling Methods *pp. 354–358*

SDAP 2.1, SDAP 2.2

EXAMPLE

CITY BUDGET You conduct a survey to find out how registered voters in your city think the city's money should be spent. You survey people as they enter a theater to watch a play. Identify the population, sample, and sampling method. Does sampling make sense? Are the results likely to be biased?

▶ **Answer** The population is the registered voters living in your city, the sample is the people entering the theater, and the sampling method is convenience sampling. Sampling does make sense because the population is too large to survey. The results are likely to be biased because the voters going to a play may not be representative of the entire population.

EXERCISES

SEE EXAMPLES 2 AND 3 on pp. 355–356 for Ex. 4

4. **SCHOOL ASSEMBLY** Students are asked if they would prefer a pep rally for the school football team or a concert by the school orchestra. *Describe* a sampling method that is not likely to result in a biased sample.

7.2 Sampling Methods

pp. 359–363

SDAP 2.3, SDAP 2.4

EXAMPLE

NEWSPAPER The publishers of a newspaper want to find out the section people most enjoy reading. They conduct a survey using the question "Do you most enjoy reading our newly enhanced entertainment section or some other section?" *Explain* why the results of the survey are likely to be biased.

▶ **Answer** This question is biased because it encourages people to name the entertainment section as their favorite.

EXERCISES

SEE EXAMPLES 1, 2, 3, AND 4 on pp. 359–360 for Exs. 5–7

***Explain* why the results of the survey are likely to be biased.**

5. The survey asks "Would you rather go to the park in the morning when it is quiet and peaceful or in the evening when it is noisy and busy?"

6. A principal surveys members of the school soccer team to determine if the school's students would attend after-school tutoring.

7. A math teacher asks his or her students to write their favorite school subjects on a piece of paper and include their names.

7.3 Mean, Median, and Mode

pp. 364–369

SDAP 1.1, SDAP 1.2, SDAP 1.4

EXAMPLE

Find the mean, median, and mode(s) of the data.

5, 6, 11, 11, 16, 18, 19, 21, 21, 23, 24, 29

Mean: $\frac{5 + 6 + 11 + 11 + 16 + 18 + 19 + 21 + 21 + 23 + 24 + 29}{12} = 17$

Median: $\frac{18 + 19}{2} = 18.5$ **Modes:** 11 and 21 both occur twice.

EXERCISES

SEE EXAMPLES 1, 2, AND 3 on pp. 364–365 for Ex. 8

8. **BASKETBALL** Michael's point totals in 15 basketball games are shown.

   12, 9, 15, 19, 14, 20, 15, 8, 11, 20, 12, 18, 20, 11, 21

   a. Find the mean, median, and mode(s).

   b. Which measure(s) is most useful for describing a typical point total? *Explain* your reasoning.

   c. How will a point total of 20 in a sixteenth game affect the mean, median, and mode(s)? *Explain* your reasoning.

7.4 Range and Outliers
pp. 372–377

SDAP 1.1, SDAP 1.3

EXAMPLE

Find the median, range, and interquartile range of the data.

32 37 **38** 41 **45** 47 65

Median: The middle number of the 7 numbers is 41.

Range: Upper extreme − lower extreme = 65 − 32 = 33

Interquartile Range: Upper quartile − lower quartile = 47 − 37 = 10

EXERCISES

SEE EXAMPLES 1 AND 2 on pp. 372–373 for Exs. 9–10

9. Find the median, range, and interquartile range of the data.

   28, 32, 26, 31, 35, 27, 11, 23, 32, 30

10. *Describe* how *excluding* the outlier in Exercise 9 affects the mean, median, mode(s), and range.

7.5 Histograms
pp. 379–384

Grade 5 SDAP 1.2

EXAMPLE

PRICES The frequency table shows the prices of shoes in a shoe store. Make a histogram of the data.

Price (dollars)	10–19	20–29	30–39	40–49
Frequency	10	22	16	11

STEP 1 **Draw** and label the axes.

- List the intervals along the horizontal axis.
- The greatest frequency is 22. Start the vertical axis at 0 and end at 25, using increments of 5.

STEP 2 **Draw** bars of the same width for each interval. Leave no gap between bars.

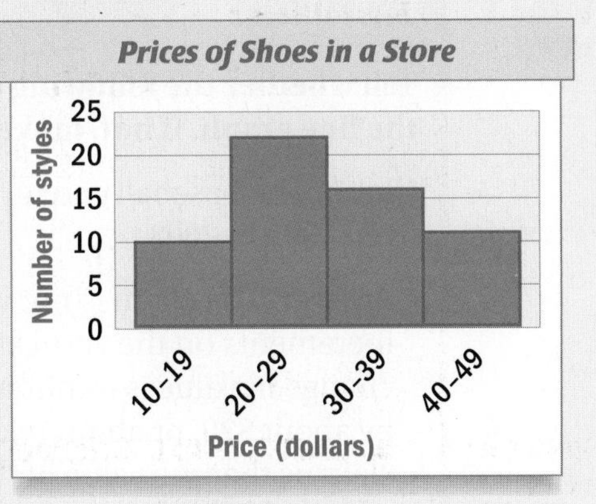

EXERCISES

SEE EXAMPLES 1 AND 2 on pp. 379–380 for Ex. 11

11. **CITY CLEANUP** The pounds of trash collected at 20 sites for a city cleanup project are below. Make a frequency table and a histogram of the data.

    65, 29, 38, 50, 60, 43, 27, 48, 29, 79, 37, 45, 48, 32, 57, 35, 54, 53, 37, 47

7.6 Circle Graphs

pp. 387–391

Grade 5 SDAP 1.2

EXAMPLE

COLORS A survey asked 120 teens their favorite color. Forty said red, 55 said green, and 25 said blue. Display the data in a circle graph.

Red $\frac{40}{120} \times 360° = \frac{1}{3} \times 360° = 120°$

Green $\frac{55}{120} \times 360° = \frac{11}{24} \times 360° = 165°$

Blue $\frac{25}{120} \times 360° = \frac{5}{24} \times 360° = 75°$

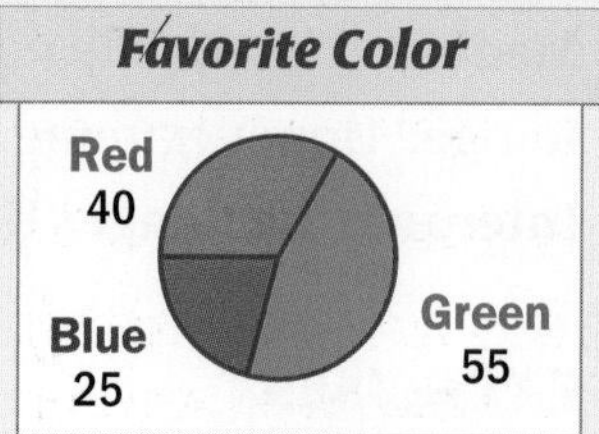

EXERCISES

SEE EXAMPLES 1 AND 2 on pp. 387–388 for Exs. 12–13

12. **PET SURVEY** In a survey, dog owners were asked where their dogs sleep. The results are shown. What percent of owners did *not* say "Dog Bed"?

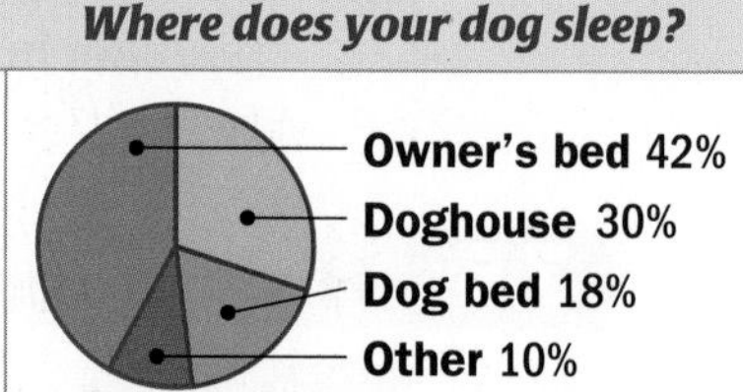

13. **TRANSPORTATION** A survey of how 150 adults get to work showed 20% walk, 50% drive, and 30% take a bus. Display the data in a circle graph.

7.7 Choosing and Analyzing Data Displays

pp. 392–398

SDAP 2.3, SDAP 2.5

EXAMPLE

Tell whether the following claim is valid based on the line graph. If not, make a valid claim.

Claim: The baseball card only slightly increased in value from 1999 to 2003.

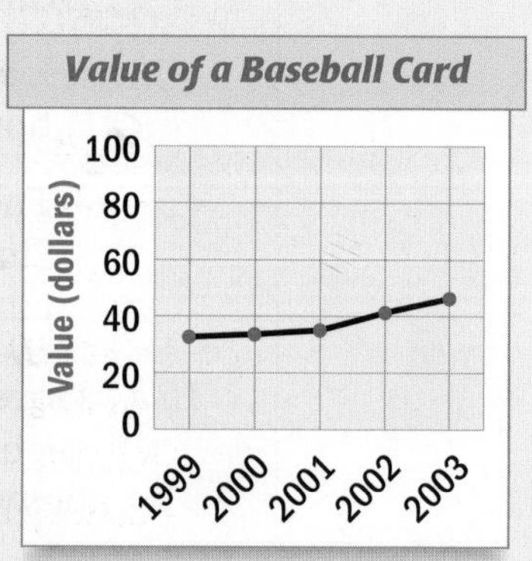

▸ **Answer** The claim is not valid. The graph has large increments on the vertical axis, making it appear that the change in value is minimal. The value actually increases by about \$20, or about two thirds of its value. A valid claim is that the value of the card increased more from 2001 to 2003 than from 1999 to 2001.

EXERCISES

SEE EXAMPLE 2 on pp. 392–393 for Ex. 14

14. **BASEBALL CARDS** Choose a scale for the vertical axis of the line graph above that would make a valid claim more likely. Then make a valid claim about the value of the card.

7 CHAPTER TEST

1. **VOCABULARY** *Contrast* random sampling and convenience sampling.

2. **VOCABULARY** *Explain* what the range tells you about a data set.

FUNDRAISING The data below show the numbers of tins of popcorn sold by members of a school band.

40, 32, 16, 14, 11, 16, 11, 12, 26, 1, 15, 9, 6, 3, 27, 5, 12, 18, 23, 33, 17, 50

3. Find the mean, median, mode(s), range, and interquartile range. Which measure is most useful for describing a typical number of tins?

4. Make a histogram of the data.

5. **STUDENT AGES** Which measure, mean or median, best describes the data below when the outlier is included? excluded? *Explain.*
   Ages of piano students: 4, 4, 5, 6, 8, 9, 10, 11, 14, 16, 45

BASEBALL The bar graph at the right shows the wins and losses for the Baltimore Orioles over three seasons.

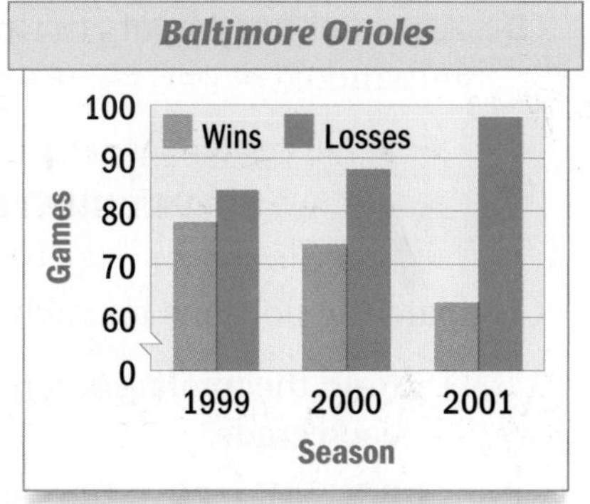

6. *Explain* why the graph appears to show that the Orioles had twice as many wins in 1999 as they did in 2001.

7. Make a valid claim about the data.

8. **MUSIC** You want to conduct a survey to find the favorite pop singer for students in your school. Identify the population. *Describe* a sampling method that is likely to result in a representative sample.

9. **COMPUTERS** The table shows a computer's price over time. Make a line graph of the data. Then make a conclusion about the data.

Month	1	2	3	4	5	6
Price	\$699	\$699	\$649	\$629	\$599	\$499

10. **RESTAURANTS** On a night when the special is chicken, a restaurant owner asks customers whether their favorite special is steak or moist, delicious chicken. The results of the survey show that 90% of the customers favor chicken. Are these results likely to be biased? If so, identify and correct the problems with the survey.

11. **ZOO ANIMALS** Choose two appropriate data displays for the data. Then make both graphs and compare what they show you.

Favorite Zoo Animal	Monkey	Elephant	Lion	Tiger	Giraffe
Students	26%	23%	18%	17%	16%

7 ◆ MULTIPLE CHOICE STRATEGIES

STRATEGIES YOU'LL USE:
- **SOLVE DIRECTLY**
- **ELIMINATE CHOICES**

Standards
SDAP 1.2
SDAP 2.5

If you have trouble solving a multiple choice problem directly, you may be able to use another approach to eliminate incorrect answer choices and obtain the correct answer.

PROBLEM 1

All 6th and 7th graders at one school were asked to name their favorite after school activity. The number of students in each grade who favor each activity are shown. Which claim is valid?

Ⓐ A greater portion of 6th than 7th graders favor sports.

Ⓑ A greater portion of 6th than 7th graders favor band or theater.

Ⓒ A greater portion of 7th than 6th graders favor band.

Ⓓ A greater portion of 7th than 6th graders favor clubs or band.

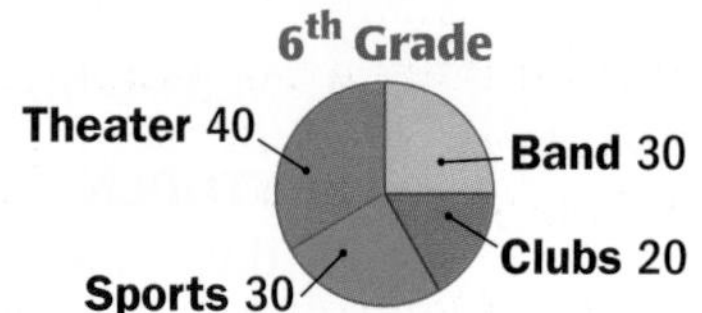

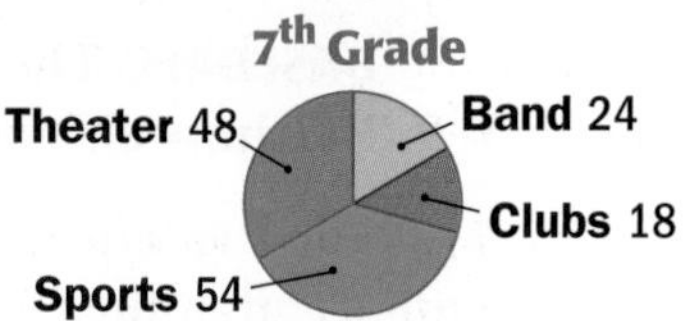

Strategy 1 SOLVE DIRECTLY

Compare the portions for each grade.

STEP 1 **Find** the total number of students in each grade.

6th grade: $30 + 20 + 30 + 40 = 120$
7th grade: $24 + 18 + 54 + 48 = 144$

STEP 2 **Calculate** and compare the percent of students who favor each activity or combination of activities.

	6th grade	7th grade
Choice A	$\frac{30}{120} = 25\%$	$\frac{54}{144} \approx 38\%$
Choice B	$\frac{30 + 40}{120} \approx 58\%$	$\frac{24 + 48}{144} = 50\%$
Choice C	$\frac{30}{120} = 25\%$	$\frac{24}{144} \approx 17\%$
Choice D	$\frac{20 + 30}{120} \approx 42\%$	$\frac{18 + 24}{144} \approx 29\%$

The correct answer is B. Ⓐ Ⓑ Ⓒ Ⓓ

Strategy 2 ELIMINATE CHOICES

You can compare the sizes of the colored regions on the circle graph.

The region representing sports is larger on the 7th grade graph than on the 6th grade graph. You can eliminate choice A.

The region representing band is larger on the 6th grade graph than on the 7th grade graph. You can eliminate choice C.

The regions representing clubs and band together are larger on the 6th grade graph than on the 7th grade graph. You can eliminate choice D.

The correct answer is B. Ⓐ Ⓑ Ⓒ Ⓓ

PROBLEM 2

Paul found the mode of the numbers 5, 7, 7, 9, and 14. If the number 9 were added to the list of numbers, then

Ⓐ there would be no mode. Ⓑ the mode would stay 7.

Ⓒ the mode would change to 9. Ⓓ the modes would be 7 and 9.

Strategy 1 **SOLVE DIRECTLY**

First, find the mode of the original numbers. Then find the mode when 9 is included with the numbers.

STEP 1 **Find** the mode of the original data. The mode of the numbers 5, 7, 7, 9, and 14 is 7 because it occurs most often in the list of numbers.

STEP 2 **Find** the mode when 9 is included with the numbers. The list of numbers is now 5, 7, 7, 9, 9, and 14. The modes are 7 and 9 because they each occur twice in the list of numbers.

The correct answer is D. Ⓐ Ⓑ Ⓒ Ⓓ

Strategy 2 **ELIMINATE CHOICES**

You can use reasoning and the definition of mode to consider the choices.

The original list of numbers has only one repeated number, the mode 7. When you add one more number to the list, 7 will still be a mode. You can eliminate choices A and C.

When you add 9 to the list, 7 and 9 each occur twice. Now the list has two modes. You can eliminate choice B.

The correct answer is D. Ⓐ Ⓑ Ⓒ Ⓓ

STRATEGY PRACTICE

Explain why you can eliminate the highlighted answer choice.

1. The numbers of goals scored by a soccer team in each game over a season are listed below. What is the mean number of goals?

   6, 2, 1, 2, 5, 1, 3, 4, 4, 3, 7, 2, 1, 3, 0, 4

   Ⓐ 0 Ⓑ 2 Ⓒ 3 Ⓓ ✗ **8**

2. What data display should a farmer use to see how the weights of dairy cows are distributed, without displaying individual data?

   Ⓐ ✗ **line plot** Ⓑ line graph Ⓒ bar graph Ⓓ histogram

3. What is the interquartile range of the data below?

   27, 32, 37, 41 49, 53, 56, 62, 68, 71, 75, 84

   Ⓐ 27 Ⓑ 30.5 Ⓒ 34 Ⓓ ✗ **57**

7 ◆ MULTIPLE CHOICE PRACTICE

1. The data below give the times, in minutes, it takes students in one class to get to school. Which measure is most useful for describing a typical time? **SDAP 1.4**

   14, 40, 47, 37, 15, 8, 27, 24, 40, 5, 10, 9

   (A) Mean

   (B) Median

   (C) Mode

   (D) Both the median and the mode

2. Which survey question would most likely produce biased results? **SDAP 2.4**

   (A) What is your favorite television show?

   (B) How many times did you use the school library last month?

   (C) Do you approve of the job done by our very successful mayor?

   (D) What do you prefer to do after school?

3. The graph shows the longest vertical drops for the three highest waterfalls in the world. Which of the following claims about the waterfalls is valid? **SDAP 2.5**

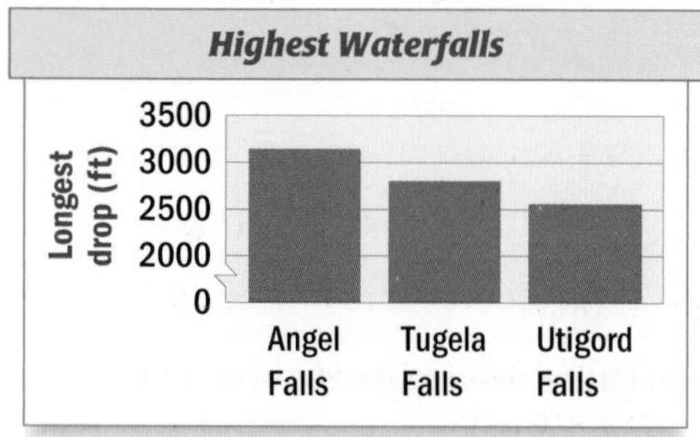

   (A) The longest vertical drop of Tugela Falls is about 2250 feet.

   (B) The difference between the longest vertical drops of Angel Falls and Utigord Falls is less than 400 feet.

   (C) The longest vertical drop of Tugela Falls is about 250 feet more than that of Utigord Falls.

   (D) The longest vertical drops of all 3 are between 2500 and 3000 feet.

4. Four years of home-opener attendance for a baseball and a hockey team are shown in the bar graph. Which prediction for hockey home-opener attendance in year 5 is best supported by the data? **SDAP 2.5, MR 2.3**

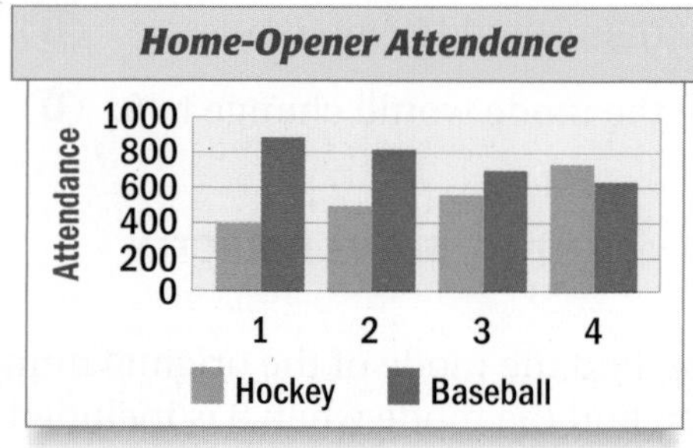

   (A) Hockey attendance will be greater than baseball attendance.

   (B) Hockey attendance will be less than baseball attendance.

   (C) Hockey attendance will be the same as baseball attendance.

   (D) Hockey attendance will triple that of year 1.

5. You want to display the results of a survey in which students named their favorite type of music. Which data display is most appropriate? **Gr. 5 SDAP 1.2**

   (A) Bar graph

   (B) Line graph

   (C) Histogram

   (D) Box-and-whisker plot

6. In which of the following survey situations would it make the most sense to survey a sample? **SDAP 2.1, MR 3.1**

   (A) The favorite movies of students in a classroom of 30 students

   (B) The average number of cars owned per family on a street of 20 families

   (C) The favorite animals of six zoo employees

   (D) The average number of cars owned per family in California

7. You want to know how many hours of chores students at a large school do each week. You survey the school's jazz band to get a sample. The data are shown below. How does the sample mean compare with the population mean of 4 hours? **SDAP 2.1**

Hours of Chores
1.5, 2.5, 2.5, 3, 3.5, 4, 4.5, 5,
5, 5.5, 6, 6.5, 6.5, 7

Ⓐ The mean for the sample is greater.

Ⓑ The mean for the population is greater.

Ⓒ The means are the same.

Ⓓ The means cannot be compared.

8. A restaurant invites customers to fill out and mail in a survey about menu choices. Which sampling method is being used? **SDAP 2.2**

Ⓐ Convenience

Ⓑ Random

Ⓒ Self-selected

Ⓓ Systematic

9. You are making a circle graph of the data below. What angle measure would represent the section labeled *Summer*? **Gr. 5 SDAP 1.2**

Ⓐ 75°

Ⓑ 90°

Ⓒ 150°

Ⓓ 300°

FAVORITE SEASON

Season	Winter	Spring	Summer	Fall
Votes	25	125	75	75

10. Which statement is *not* valid if the number 40 is added to the list of numbers? **SDAP 1.2**

10, 5, 23, 21, 28, 16, 5, 14, 22

Ⓐ The mean increases.

Ⓑ The median increases.

Ⓒ The mode increases.

Ⓓ The range increases.

11. Which average decreases when the outlier is excluded from the data? **SDAP 1.3**

0, 4, 8, 8, 8, 9, 20

Ⓐ Mean

Ⓑ Median

Ⓒ Mode

Ⓓ No outlier exists.

12. The histogram shows the times, in minutes, that it took students to run 1 mile. The track coach concludes that 3 times as many students run a mile in 11–12.9 minutes than in 13–14.9 minutes. What is the most likely reason the graph could lead to this invalid conclusion? **SDAP 2.3, MR 2.4**

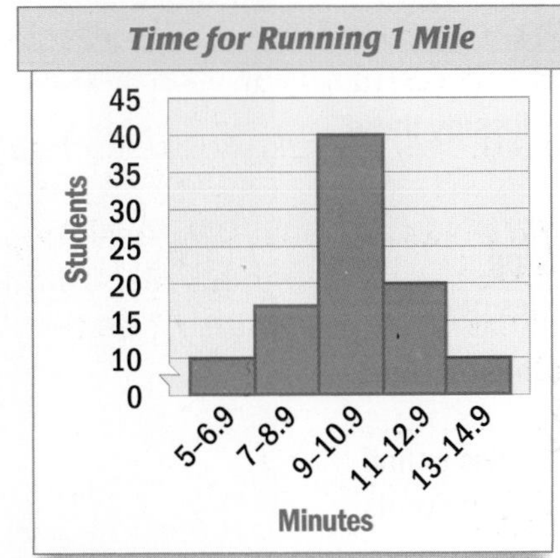

Ⓐ The intervals are too large.

Ⓑ The intervals are too small.

Ⓒ The break in the scale is on the wrong axis.

Ⓓ The break in the vertical scale distorts the relative bar heights.

13. What is the range of the numbers of lifts at the 10 ski resorts listed below? **SDAP 1.1**

11, 17, 25, 11, 8, 13, 16, 9, 11, 19

Ⓐ 8

Ⓑ 11

Ⓒ 14

Ⓓ 17

8 Probability

Before

In previous courses and chapters, you learned the following skills, which you'll use in Chapter 8:

- Using Venn diagrams
- Writing fractions and decimals as percents
- Performing operations with fractions

Now

In Chapter 8 you'll study these ***Big Ideas:***

1. Representing probabilities of events
2. Representing outcomes
3. Using formulas to find probabilities of events

Why?

So you can solve real-world problems about . . .

- Piano keys, p. 418
- Game pieces, p. 419
- Batting averages, p. 425
- Chess, p. 431
- School lunches, p. 438
- Experiments, p. 445

at *classzone.com*

Get-Ready Games

Scale the Cliff

California Standards

Review comparing fractions. *Gr. 6 NS 1.1*
Prepare for representing probabilities. *Gr. 6 SDAP 3.3*

$\frac{7}{32}$	$\frac{1}{3}$	$\frac{2}{7}$	$\frac{3}{11}$
$\frac{7}{17}$	$\frac{4}{9}$	$\frac{4}{15}$	$\frac{11}{25}$
$\frac{6}{11}$	$\frac{13}{21}$	$\frac{4}{7}$	$\frac{3}{8}$
$\frac{1}{2}$	$\frac{5}{8}$	$\frac{7}{11}$	$\frac{9}{14}$
$\frac{3}{4}$	$\frac{5}{6}$	$\frac{3}{5}$	$\frac{5}{7}$
	$\frac{2}{3}$		

How to Play

Each ratio above represents a "climbing hold". Beginning with the support labeled $\frac{2}{3}$, find the path of climbing holds that you can use to scale the cliff.

- Each hold that you choose must have a value less than that of the hold you used previously.

CALIFORNIA STANDARDS

- **Gr. 6 SDAP 3.0 Students determine theoretical and experimental probabilities and use these to make predictions about events.** ***(Lessons 8.1, 8.2, 8.3, 8.4, 8.5)***

Tangled Fractions

California Standards

Review comparing fractions. ***Gr. 6 NS 1.1***

Prepare for representing probabilities. ***Gr. 6 SDAP 3.3***

How to Play

Find a piece of equipment a rock climber needs.

- Choose the fraction in each column that is equivalent to the fraction at the top of that column.
- The letters associated with the fractions you choose will spell the answer.

Games Wrap-Up

Draw Conclusions

Complete these exercises after playing the games.

1. WRITING *Describe* the steps you take to decide whether fractions with different denominators are equivalent.

2. REASONING A student playing *Scale the Cliff* claims that all of the climbing supports in the row above $\frac{2}{3}$ are possible choices, because the denominators of the fractions are all greater than 3. *Describe* and correct the student's error.

8 Getting Ready

Prerequisite Skills

California @HomeTutor
Prerequisite skills practice at classzone.com

REVIEW VOCABULARY
- **percent,** *p. 301*
- **fraction,** *p. 672*
- **decimal,** *p. 672*
- **Venn diagram,** *p. 691*

VOCABULARY CHECK

Copy and complete using a review term from the list at the left.

1. A(n) __?__ uses shapes to show how sets are related.
2. A number written in the form $\frac{a}{b}$ $(b \neq 0)$ is a(n) __?__.
3. A ratio whose denominator is 100 is a(n) __?__.

SKILL CHECK

Use the Venn diagram to tell whether the statement is *true* or *false*. ***(p. 691)***

4. Lisa plays basketball.
5. Two students play soccer but not basketball.
6. More students play basketball than play soccer.

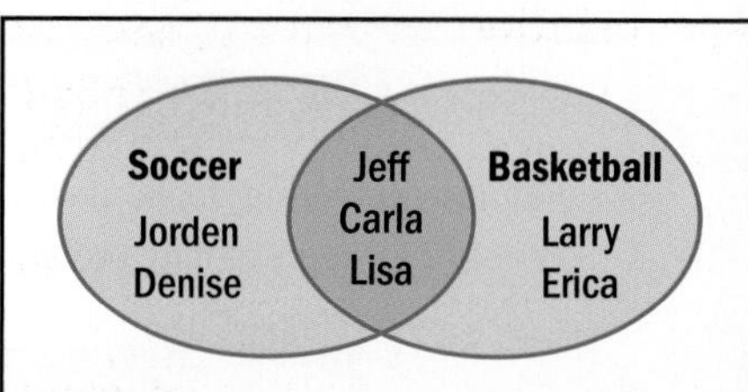

Write the fraction as a decimal and as a percent. ***(pp. 40, 301)***

7. $\frac{7}{10}$ 8. $\frac{13}{20}$ 9. $\frac{7}{16}$ 10. $\frac{1}{80}$

Notetaking Skills

NOW YOU TRY
Make a *Y chart* that compares writing ratios as decimals and writing ratios as percents.

Focus on Graphic Organizers

Use a *Y chart* to compare two concepts, such as using convenience and self-selected samples. Highlight similar characteristics in the branches. List similarities in the lower box.

USING CONVENIENCE AND SELF-SELECTED SAMPLES

USE A CONVENIENCE SAMPLE	USE A SELF-SELECTED SAMPLE
Easily reached members of a population are selected. This type of sample is likely to be biased.	Members of a population volunteer to be part of the sample. This type of sample is likely to be biased.

SIMILARITIES
Sample is likely to be biased.

8.1 Introduction to Probability

Math and SPORTS
Ex. 29, p. 419

Standards **SDAP 3.3 Represent probabilities as ratios, proportions, decimals between 0 and 1, and percentages between 0 and 100 and verify that the probabilities computed are reasonable**; know that if *P* is the probability of an event, 1 − *P* is the probability of an event not occurring.

Connect ***Before*** you wrote fractions and decimals as percents. ***Now*** you will represent probabilities as decimals and percents.

KEY VOCABULARY
- outcomes
- event
- favorable outcomes
- probability

When you perform an *experiment*, such as rolling a number cube, the possible results (1, 2, 3, 4, 5, and 6) are called **outcomes**. A specific outcome or group of outcomes, such as "roll an even number", is called an **event**. Outcomes for a specified event are called **favorable outcomes**.

The **probability** of an event is a measure of the likelihood that the event will occur. When all of the outcomes of an event are equally likely, the probability *P* of the event is the following ratio.

$$P(\text{event}) = \frac{\text{Number of favorable outcomes}}{\text{Total number of outcomes}}$$

You can write probabilities as fractions, decimals, or percents.

EXAMPLE 1 Finding a Probability

Find the probability of randomly choosing a blue marble from the marbles shown at the right.

$P(\text{blue}) = \frac{3}{10}$ ← There are 3 blue marbles. / ← There are 10 marbles in all.

▶ **Answer** The probability of choosing a blue marble is $\frac{3}{10}$, 0.3, or 30%.

CHECK 5 out of 10 is 50%, so 3 out of 10 must be less than 50%. ✓

AVOID ERRORS
Although there are only 3 colors of marbles in Example 1, there are 10 marbles to choose from. The total number of outcomes is 10.

Probabilities can range from 0 to 1. The closer the probability of an event is to 1, the more likely it is that the event will occur.

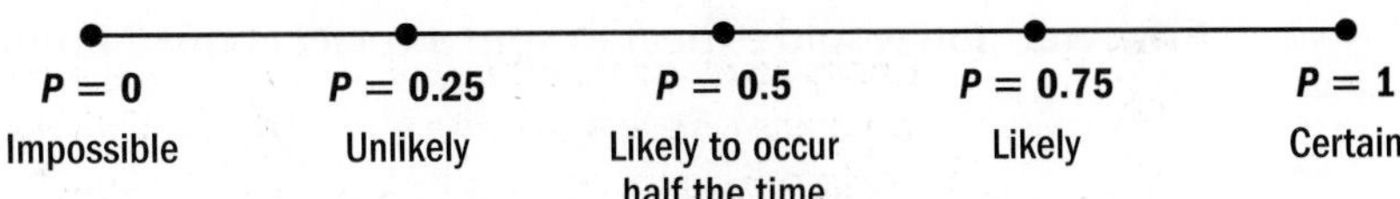

✓ GUIDED PRACTICE for Example 1

1. **WHAT IF?** In Example 1, suppose you randomly choose a green marble. Find the probability of this event. Check for reasonableness.

EXAMPLE 2 ◆ Multiple Choice Practice

Craig has 6 black, 4 blue, and 10 white pairs of socks in a drawer. What is the probability that, without looking, he will pick a pair of blue socks from the drawer?

Ⓐ 20% Ⓑ 30% Ⓒ 50% Ⓓ 80%

ELIMINATE CHOICES
Because fewer than half the pairs of socks are blue, choices C and D are not reasonable, and can be eliminated.

SOLUTION

$$P(\text{blue}) = \frac{\text{Number of favorable outcomes}}{\text{Total number of outcomes}}$$

$P(\text{blue}) = \frac{4}{20}$ ← There are 4 blue pairs of socks. / There are 20 pairs of socks in all.

$= \frac{1}{5}$ **Simplify fraction.**

$= 20\%$ **Write ratio as a percent.**

The probability that Craig will pick a blue pair of socks is 20%.

▶ **Answer** The correct answer is A. Ⓐ Ⓑ Ⓒ Ⓓ

PREDICTIONS Once you find the probability of an event, you can write the probability as a ratio. You can then use this ratio to predict the results of an experiment that is repeated multiple times.

EXAMPLE 3 Making Predictions

The outcomes on the spinner at the right are equally likely. You spin the spinner 60 times. Predict the number of spins that will be vowels.

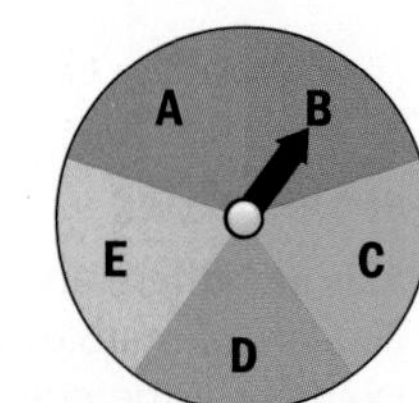

SOLUTION

$$\frac{\text{Number of vowels}}{\text{Total number of outcomes}} = \frac{\text{Number of vowels predicted}}{\text{Number of spins}}$$

$$\frac{2}{5} = \frac{n}{60}$$

$$2 \cdot 60 = 5n$$

$$24 = n$$

ANOTHER WAY
Because the probability of spinning a vowel in 1 spin is $\frac{2}{5}$, the number of times you can expect to spin a vowel in 60 spins is  $\frac{2}{5}(60) = 24$.

▶ **Answer** You would expect to spin a vowel about 24 times out of 60 spins.

✓ GUIDED PRACTICE for Examples 2 and 3

2. **WHAT IF?** In Example 2, find the probability that, without looking, Craig will pick a pair of white socks from the drawer. Check for reasonableness.

3. Predict how many spins out of 40 will be consonants in Example 3.

8.1 EXERCISES

HOMEWORK KEY ◆ = **MULTIPLE CHOICE PRACTICE** Exs. 12, 13, 30, 36–38
○ = **HINTS AND HOMEWORK HELP** for Exs. 9, 17, 29 at classzone.com

SKILLS • PROBLEM SOLVING • REASONING

VOCABULARY **Copy and complete the statement.**

1. A measure of the likelihood that an event will occur is its __?__.

2. The possible results of an experiment are called __?__.

3. **WRITING** *Describe* how to calculate the probability of rolling an even number when you roll a number cube.

SEE EXAMPLE 1 on p. 415 for Exs. 4–12

MATCHING **The spinner at the right is divided into equal parts. You spin the spinner. Match the event with the letter on the number line that indicates the probability of the event.**

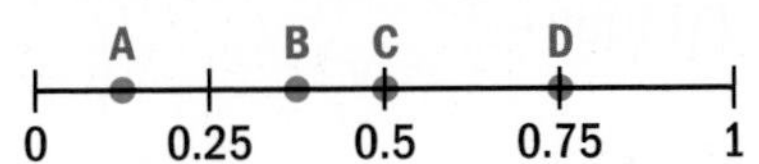

4. Pointer lands on green.
5. Pointer lands on 7.
6. Pointer lands on an even number.
7. Pointer lands on a prime number.

FINDING PROBABILITY **You randomly choose a marble from the marbles below. Write the probability of choosing a marble of the given color as a fraction, a decimal, and a percent. Check for reasonableness.**

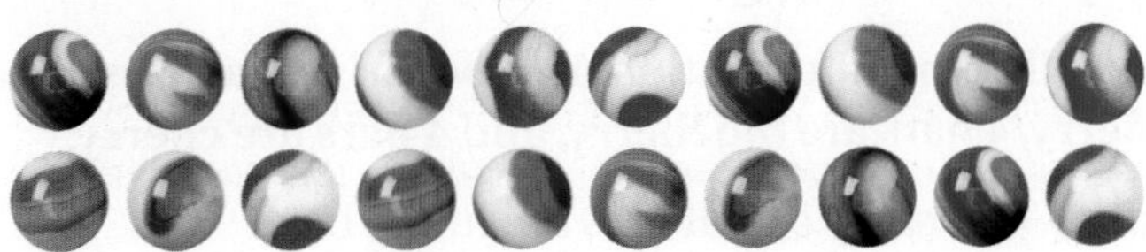

8. Blue
9. Red
10. Green
11. Yellow

12. ◆ **MULTIPLE CHOICE** What is the probability that you randomly choose a green ticket from a bag containing 3 red, 2 green, and 5 blue tickets?

Ⓐ $\frac{1}{5}$ Ⓑ $\frac{1}{4}$ Ⓒ $\frac{1}{3}$ Ⓓ $\frac{4}{5}$

SEE EXAMPLE 2 on p. 416 for Exs. 13–14

13. ◆ **MULTIPLE CHOICE** A bag contains 26 tiles, each labeled with a different letter of the alphabet. To the nearest percent, what is the probability that a tile chosen at random is a consonant? (include y)

Ⓐ 19% Ⓑ 23% Ⓒ 77% Ⓓ 81%

14. **ERROR ANALYSIS** *Describe* and correct the error made in finding the probability of randomly choosing a gray shirt from a drawer containing 6 white, 5 gray, and 3 red shirts.

$$P(\text{gray}) = \frac{\text{Number of shirts chosen}}{\text{Number of gray shirts}} = \frac{1}{5}$$ ✗

SEE EXAMPLES 1 AND 2 on pp. 415–416 for Ex. 15

15. ERROR ANALYSIS *Describe* and correct the error made in finding the probability of randomly choosing a red bean from a bag containing 5 red beans and 9 blue beans.

$$P(\text{red}) = \frac{\text{Number of red beans}}{\text{Number of blue beans}} = \frac{5}{9} \quad \times$$

SEE EXAMPLE 3 on p. 416 for Exs. 16–21

MAKING PREDICTIONS You roll a number cube. Write the probability of the event as a fraction and as a decimal rounded to the nearest hundredth. *Predict* the number of times the event will occur in 200 rolls.

16. You roll a multiple of 3.

17. You roll a 9.

18. You roll a positive number.

19. You roll a prime number.

20. You roll a multiple of 2.

21. You roll a number less than 4.

22. UNDERSTANDING PROBABILITIES Sketch a copy of the spinner shown below. Then color it so that all of the given probabilities hold true for one spin of the spinner.

$P(\text{red}) = \frac{1}{6}$ $\quad P(\text{blue}) = \frac{1}{2}$

$P(\text{yellow}) = \frac{1}{3}$ $\quad P(\text{green}) = 0$

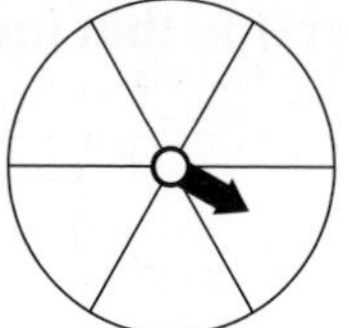

23. REASONING Is it possible to correctly color the spinner in Exercise 22 in more than one way? *Explain* why or why not.

CONNECT SKILLS TO PROBLEM SOLVING Exercises 24–27 will help you prepare for problem solving.

Use the following information: In a box of cereal bars, 8 bars are strawberry, 4 bars are blueberry, and 4 bars are cherry.

24. How many blueberry cereal bars are in the box?

25. What is the total number of cereal bars in the box?

26. What is the probability of randomly choosing a blueberry cereal bar?

27. Check the probability you found in Exercise 26 for reasonableness.

SEE EXAMPLES 1 AND 2 on pp. 415–416 for Exs. 28–30

28. PIANO KEYS The eight keys labeled C on the piano below are all the keys that produce a C tone. There are 52 white keys and 36 black keys in all. You randomly play one key. Find the probability that the key you play produces a C tone. Check the probability for reasonableness.

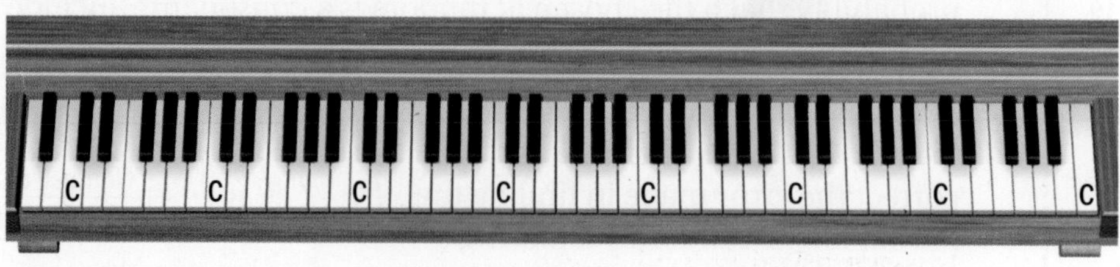

California @HomeTutor for problem solving help at classzone.com

29. **FOOTBALL** In a football game, the team that wins the coin toss decides which team receives the football first. One team calls "heads." How likely is it that this team wins the toss?

California @HomeTutor for problem solving help at classzone.com

30. ◆ **MULTIPLE CHOICE** Tanya decides to listen to a CD with 12 songs. Three of these are her favorites. If the songs play in random order, what is the probability that the first song played is one of her favorites?

(A) $\frac{1}{12}$ (B) $\frac{1}{4}$ (C) $\frac{1}{3}$ (D) $\frac{3}{4}$

31. **GAME PIECES** A bag contains red and blue marbles. The probability of randomly choosing a red marble is 25%, and the probability of randomly choosing a blue marble is 75%. There are 33 blue marbles in the bag. What is the total number of marbles in the bag?

32. **GEOMETRY** *Geometric probability* is based on areas of geometric regions. You can find geometric probability using the following formula.

$$P(\text{event}) = \frac{\text{Area of favorable outcomes}}{\text{Area of possible outcomes}}$$

You randomly toss a bean bag 36 times. Predict the number of times you will hit the red target shown.

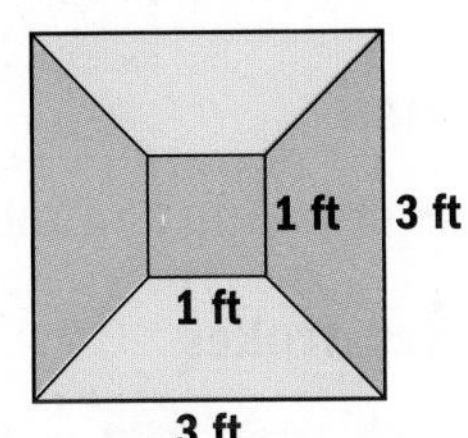

33. **REASONING** Seven people are choosing straws from a bundle of 6 long straws and 1 short straw without looking. *Describe* how the probability of choosing the short straw changes as each person removes a straw.

34. **CHALLENGE** You roll two number cubes. What is the probability that the sum of the numbers is less than 5? *Explain* your reasoning.

35. **CHALLENGE** A bus stops at the end of your street every 30 minutes. You arrive at the bus stop at a randomly chosen time. What is the probability that you wait less than 10 minutes? *Explain* your reasoning.

◆ CALIFORNIA STANDARDS SPIRAL REVIEW

NS 2.1 36. What is the value of $4\frac{3}{4} + 2\frac{8}{15}$? *(p. 81)*

(A) $6\frac{11}{60}$ (B) $6\frac{17}{60}$ (C) $6\frac{11}{19}$ (D) $7\frac{17}{60}$

SDAP 1.1 37. What is the range of the data shown below? *(p. 372)*

24, 45, 64, 19, 31, 44, 17, 55, 35, 14, 57

(A) 11 (B) 33 (C) 36 (D) 50

NS 1.4 38. You buy a lounge chair that is 35% off the original price of $45. What is the sale price? *(p. 325)*

(A) $15.75 (B) $27 (C) $29.25 (D) $60.75

8.1 Testing Probabilities

Standards

SDAP 3.3 Represent probabilities as ratios, proportions, decimals between 0 and 1, and percentages between 0 and 100 **and verify that the probabilities computed are reasonable;** know that if *P* is the probability of an event, 1 − *P* is the probability of an event not occurring.

QUESTION How can you use a calculator to construct a list of random data so you can test probabilities?

EXAMPLE Use the random integer feature to construct a list of random integers.

Construct a list of random data to model the results of 10 rolls on a number cube. Then compare your results to the probability of rolling an odd number.

SOLUTION

To model rolling a number cube, use the random integer feature **RANDI**.

Keystrokes	Display
PRB ◀ = 1 2nd [,] 6)	RANDI(1, 6)

This will produce a set of random integers from 1 to 6.

Press = 10 times to model the results of rolling a number cube 10 times. Record your results as you find them. Suppose you find the following numbers:

2, 4, 5, 6, 3, 1, 3, 4, 3, and 5

In the list, 6 of the 10 results are odd numbers.

▶ **Answer** You listed an odd number $\frac{6}{10}$, or $\frac{3}{5}$, of the time. This is slightly greater than the probability of rolling an odd number, $\frac{1}{2}$.

PRACTICE

Use a calculator to solve the problems below.

1. Construct a list of random data to show the results of rolling a number cube 18 times. How do your results compare to the probability of rolling a 1?
2. Let 1 represent heads and 2 represent tails. Construct a list of random data to model the results of 15 coin tosses. How do your results compare to the probability of landing on heads?
3. A spinner is divided into three equal sections. Let 1 and 2 represent red and 3 represent green. Construct a list of random data to show the results of 24 spins. How do your results compare to the probability of spinning green?

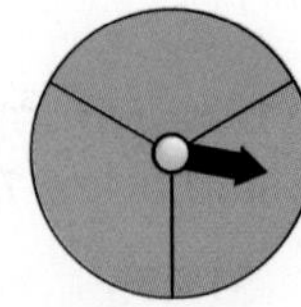

8.2 Investigating Probability

MATERIALS • two number cubes

> **Standards**
> **SDAP 3.2 Use data to estimate the probability of future events** (e.g., batting averages or number of accidents per mile driven).

QUESTION **How can you use an experiment to estimate the probability of an event?**

You can conduct an experiment to estimate the probability of an event. Probability that is estimated using repeated trials of an experiment is called *experimental probability.*

EXPLORE **Two number cubes are rolled. Estimate the probability that the sum of the resulting numbers is 7.**

STEP 1 **Roll** two number cubes 50 times. Record the sums of the resulting numbers and the corresponding frequencies in a frequency table like the one shown below. Note that the sums are not equally likely.

Sum	2	3	4	5	6	7	8	9	10	11	12
Tally	?	?	?	?	?	?	?	?	?	?	?
Frequency	?	?	?	?	?	?	?	?	?	?	?

STEP 2 **Find** the experimental probability of rolling a sum of 7. Divide the number of rolls that have a sum of 7 by the total number of rolls.

$$\text{Experimental probability of a sum of 7} = \frac{\text{Number of rolls that have a sum of 7}}{\text{Total number of rolls}}$$

DRAW CONCLUSIONS **Use your observations to complete these exercises.**

1. To find all the possible sums when rolling two number cubes, copy and complete the table at the right.

	1	2	3	4	5	6
1	2	3	?	?	?	?
2	3	4	?	?	?	?
3	?	?	?	?	?	?
4	?	?	?	?	?	?
5	?	?	?	?	?	?
6	?	?	?	?	?	?

2. Use your completed table from Exercise 1 to find the probability of rolling a sum of 7. Use this probability to predict the number of times you will get a sum of 7 in 50 rolls.

3. **REASONING** Compare the results of Exercise 2 with the results of Steps 1 and 2 above. *Explain* any differences.

8.2 Experimental Probability

Standards SDAP 3.2 **Use data to estimate the probability of future events (e.g., batting averages or number of accidents per mile driven).**

Connect ***Before*** you found probabilities. ***Now*** you will find experimental probabilities.

Math and **AMUSEMENT PARKS**
Example 2, p. 423

KEY VOCABULARY
- **theoretical probability**
- **experimental probability**

The probability discussed in Lesson 8.1 is **theoretical probability** because it is based on knowing all of the equally likely outcomes.

Probability that is based on repeated *trials* of an experiment is called **experimental probability**. Each trial in which the event occurs is a *success*. You can use the formula below to find an experimental probability.

$$\textbf{Experimental probability of an event} = \frac{\textbf{Number of successes}}{\textbf{Number of trials}}$$

EXAMPLE 1 Finding an Experimental Probability

ANIMAL TRAINING A cat that knows the shake command offers one of its front paws to shake. The table shows the number of times the cat offered each of its paws when asked to shake.

Paw Offered to Shake	
Left paw	38
Right paw	12

What is the experimental probability that the cat will offer its right paw when asked to shake?

AnimatedMath
For an interactive example of finding experimental probability go to **classzone.com.**

SOLUTION

STEP 1 **Determine** the number of successes and the number of trials.

Because a success is offering a right paw, there are **12** successes.

There are 38 + 12 = **50** trials.

STEP 2 **Find** the experimental probability.

$P(\text{right paw}) = \frac{12}{50}$ ← **There are 12 successes.** ← **There are 50 trials.**

$= \frac{6}{25}$ **Simplify.**

▶ **Answer** The experimental probability that the cat will offer its right paw when asked to shake is $\frac{6}{25}$, 0.24, or 24%.

✓ GUIDED PRACTICE for Example 1

1. **WHAT IF?** In Example 1, what is the experimental probability that the cat will offer its left paw when asked to shake?

EXAMPLE 2 Making Predictions

PACIFIC PARK In a survey at Santa Monica Pier, 24 out of 200 students said the Pacific Wheel is their favorite ride at Pacific Park. Predict how many students out of 500 at the Pier would say the Pacific Wheel is their favorite.

SOLUTION

MAKING PREDICTIONS

Predictions made based on probability are always estimates. Any prediction is *always* an estimate.

You can solve the problem by using ratios to form a proportion.

$$\frac{\text{Number who chose the Wheel}}{200} = \frac{\text{Predicted number of Wheel choices}}{500}$$

$$\frac{24}{200} = \frac{x}{500}$$

$$24 \cdot 500 = 200x$$

$$60 = x$$

▶ **Answer** About 60 students out of 500 would choose the Pacific Wheel.

EXAMPLE 3 Comparing Probabilities

You roll a number cube 80 times. The results are shown in the table at the right. Compare the theoretical probability to the experimental probability of rolling an even number.

Result	1	2	3	4	5	6
Times rolled	12	15	13	11	19	10

SOLUTION

STEP 1 **Find** the theoretical probability of rolling an even number.

$P(\text{even number}) = \frac{3}{6}$ — **There are 3 favorable outcomes. There are 6 possible outcomes.**

$= 0.5 \text{ or } 50\%$ — **Write as a decimal and as a percent.**

STEP 2 **Find** the experimental probability of rolling an even number.

$P(\text{even number}) = \frac{36}{80}$ — **There are 36 successes. There are 80 trials.**

$= 0.45 \text{ or } 45\%$ — **Write as a decimal and as a percent.**

▶ **Answer** The experimental probability is less than the theoretical probability. The two probabilities will usually become closer with more trials.

✓ GUIDED PRACTICE for Examples 2 and 3

2. **WHAT IF?** In Example 2, predict how many students out of 700 at the Pier would choose the Pacific Wheel as their favorite ride.
3. **WHAT IF?** In Example 3, compare the theoretical and experimental probabilities of rolling a number greater than 4.

8.2 EXERCISES

HOMEWORK KEY ◆ = **MULTIPLE CHOICE PRACTICE** Exs. 6, 12, 21, 27–29

○ = **HINTS AND HOMEWORK HELP** for Exs. 3, 7, 21 at classzone.com

SKILLS • PROBLEM SOLVING • REASONING

1. **VOCABULARY** Copy and complete: Probability that is based on repeated trials of an experiment is called _?_.

2. **NOTETAKING SKILLS** Make a *Y chart* like the one on page 414 that compares theoretical probability to experimental probability.

SEE EXAMPLE 1 on p. 422 for Exs. 3–6

EXPERIMENTAL PROBABILITY A bag contains red, blue, and green tiles. You randomly choose a tile from the bag, record the result, and then replace it. The table shows the results of several trials. Write the probability of the event as a fraction, decimal, and percent.

Tile color	red	blue	green
Times chosen	9	5	6

3. You choose a red tile.
4. You choose a blue tile.
5. You choose a green tile.

6. ◆ **MULTIPLE CHOICE** The table at the right shows the results of tossing a coin 30 times. What is the experimental probability that the coin lands on tails?

Result	heads	tails
Times tossed	18	12

Ⓐ $\frac{2}{5}$ Ⓑ $\frac{1}{2}$ Ⓒ $\frac{3}{5}$ Ⓓ $2\frac{1}{2}$

SEE EXAMPLE 2 on p. 423 for Exs. 7–12

MAKING PREDICTIONS A spinner is divided into 10 sections labeled as shown in the table below. The table shows the results of 50 spins. Use the table to predict the number of times the event would occur in 200 spins.

Section	1	2	3	5	8	13	16	21	28	45
Times landed	3	2	7	6	7	4	5	9	5	2

7. Pointer lands on 16.
8. Pointer lands on 13.
9. Pointer lands on an odd number.
10. Pointer lands on a multiple of 4.

11. **ERROR ANALYSIS** Use the table in Exercises 7–10. *Describe* and correct the error made in predicting the number of times the pointer would land on a prime number in 150 spins.

$\frac{4}{50} = \frac{x}{150}$

You would expect the pointer to land on a prime number 51 times. ✗

12. ◆ **MULTIPLE CHOICE** Use the table in Exercises 7–10. About how many times would you expect to land on a multiple of 3 in 300 spins?

Ⓐ 66 Ⓑ 72 Ⓒ 96 Ⓓ 108

SEE EXAMPLE 3
on p. 423
for Exs. 13–15

COMPARING PROBABILITIES A bag contains 12 brown, 12 black, and 12 silver marbles. You randomly choose a marble from the bag, record the result, and then replace it. The table below shows the results of your trials. Compare the theoretical probability to the experimental probability of the event.

Marble color	brown	black	silver
Times chosen	17	24	19

13. You choose a brown marble.

14. You choose a black marble.

15. You choose a silver marble.

CONNECT SKILLS TO PROBLEM SOLVING Exercises 16–18 will help you prepare for problem solving.

Use the following information: The only types of fish in a pond are bluegill, bass, and perch. Today, 120 fish have been caught thus far: 42 bluegills, 33 bass, and 45 perch. After a fish is caught, it is released back into the pond.

16. What is the probability that the next fish caught is a bluegill?

17. What is the probability that the next fish caught is a bass?

18. What is the probability that the next fish caught is a perch?

SEE EXAMPLES 1 AND 2
on p. 422–423
for Exs. 19–21

19. GENETICS The ability to roll your tongue into a U-shape is inherited from your parents.

a. You ask 80 students chosen at random if they can roll their tongues, and 64 students say yes. Find the probability that a student can roll his or her tongue.

b. Predict the number of students out of 2500 that can roll their tongues.

California @HomeTutor for problem solving help at classzone.com

20. BATTING AVERAGES During one baseball season, Ichiro Suzuki had 206 hits out of 679 at bats. Suppose in a later season he has 550 at bats. Predict the number of hits Ichiro Suzuki will have in that season.

California @HomeTutor for problem solving help at classzone.com

21. ◆ **MULTIPLE CHOICE** The table at the right shows the number of crashes that damaged only property for four types of vehicles in the United States in a recent year. Estimate how many of the next 1 million such crashes for these vehicles will involve light trucks.

Vehicle Type	*Crashes*
Large trucks	324,000
Light trucks	2,886,000
Motorcycles	13,000
Passenger cars	4,216,000

Ⓐ 390,000 Ⓑ 430,000

Ⓒ 570,000 Ⓓ 630,000

22. OPEN-ENDED *Describe* a real-world situation that has two possible outcomes that are not equally likely. *Explain* how to use an experiment to estimate the probability of each outcome.

23. SHORT RESPONSE Flip a coin 20 times and record the outcomes. Find the experimental probability of getting "tails" and compare it to the theoretical probability. Must the theoretical and experimental probabilities be different? *Explain.*

Flipping a coin

24. MULTI-STEP PROBLEM *Rock, Paper, Scissors* is a popular hand game involving two players. To play, each player taps his or her fist in the palm of his or her hand two times. Then, both players simultaneously extend a hand in the shape of a rock, a piece of paper, or a pair of scissors. The winner is decided as follows: rock beats scissors, scissors beats paper, and paper beats rock.

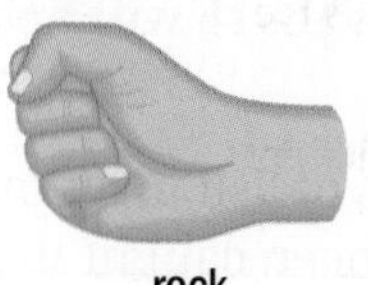
rock

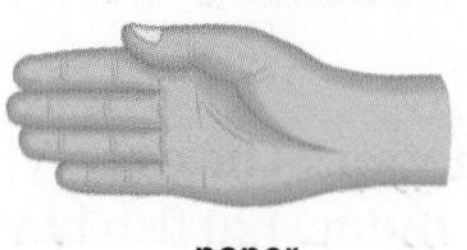
paper

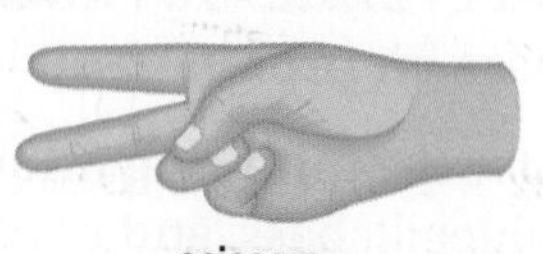
scissors

a. One outcome for this game is "rock" for Player 1 and "rock" for Player 2. Find all nine possible outcomes for this game.

b. Find the theoretical probability of a tie.

c. The table shows the results of 155 trials. Find the experimental probability of a tie.

d. Compare the theoretical and experimental probabilites of a tie.

Frequency Table	
Player 1 wins	51
Player 2 wins	53
Tie	51

25. CHALLENGE A game is considered fair if each player is equally likely to win. Is the game Rock, Paper, Scissors described in Exercise 24 a fair game, or is a player more likely to win by always choosing the same gesture while the other chooses randomly? *Justify* your answer.

26. CHALLENGE You roll two number cubes. What is the probability that you roll a sum less than 6? Make a table showing 5 trials to test your result. Make a table showing 20 trials to test your result. What can you conclude about the number of trials and the accuracy of the experimental probability compared to the theoretical probability?

◆ CALIFORNIA STANDARDS SPIRAL REVIEW

SDAP 3.3 **27.** A jar contains 4 red, 2 blue, and 2 white marbles. What is the probability of randomly choosing a white marble from the jar? *(p. 415)*

Ⓐ 0.25 Ⓑ 0.3 Ⓒ 0.5 Ⓓ 0.75

AF 3.2 **28.** A rectangle has a width of 12 meters and a perimeter of P meters. Which equation can you use to find the length, l, of the rectangle? *(p. 212)*

Ⓐ $P = l - 12$ Ⓑ $P = l + 12$ Ⓒ $P = 2l + 12$ Ⓓ $P = 2l + 24$

NS 1.4 **29.** You deposit $300 into a bank account that earns 4% simple annual interest. How much is in the account after 6 months? *(p. 331)*

Ⓐ $6 Ⓑ $306 Ⓒ $372 Ⓓ $720

8.3 Disjoint Events

Math and RECREATION
Exs. 36–39, p. 431

Standards **SDAP 3.3** **Represent probabilities as ratios, proportions, decimals between 0 and 1, and percentages between 0 and 100** and verify that the probabilities computed are reasonable; **know that if *P* is the probability of an event, 1 − *P* is the probability of an event not occurring.**

SDAP 3.4 **Understand that the probability of either of two disjoint events occurring is the sum of the two individual probabilities** and that the probability of one event following another, in independent trials, is the product of the two probabilities.

Connect ***Before*** you found the probability of single events. ***Now*** you will find the probability that either of two disjoint events occurs.

KEY VOCABULARY
- **disjoint events**
- **overlapping events**
- **complementary events**

Disjoint events are events that have no outcomes in common. Events that have one or more outcomes in common are **overlapping events**. The Venn diagrams below relate some events involving rolling a number cube.

Disjoint events

Event A: Roll an odd number.

Event B: Roll a 4.

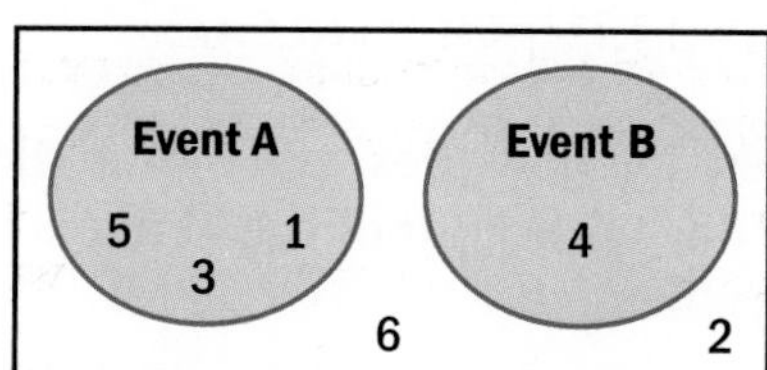

Overlapping events

Event C: Roll a number less than 3.

Event D: Roll an even number.

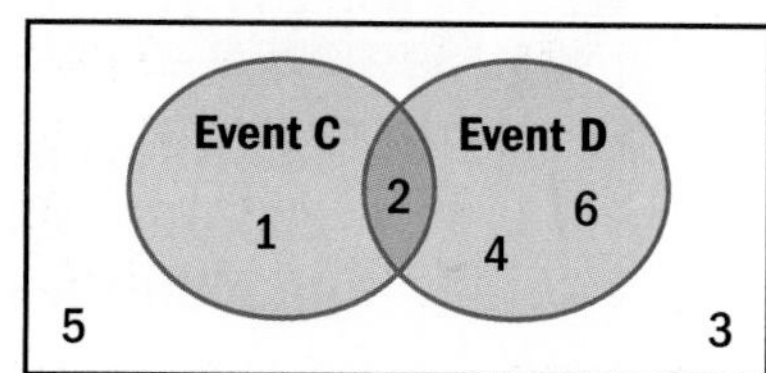

EXAMPLE 1 Disjoint and Overlapping Events

Tell whether the events involving the spinner are *disjoint* or *overlapping*.

Event R: Spin an odd number.

Event S: Spin a prime number.

2 7 15 8 3 4 6 9

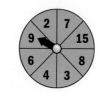

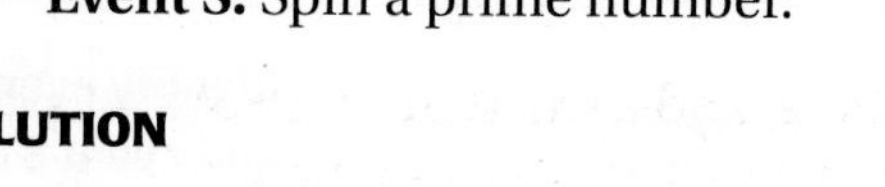

SOLUTION

Event R: 3, 7, 9, 15 **List the odd numbers.**

Event S: 2, 3, 7 **List the prime numbers.**

▶ **Answer** There are outcomes in common, so the events are overlapping.

Animated Math
For an interactive example of identifying disjoint and overlapping events go to **classzone.com.**

✓ GUIDED PRACTICE for Example 1

1. **WHAT IF?** In Example 1, suppose event R is "spin a number divisible by 4." Are the events R and S *disjoint* or *overlapping*? *Explain.*

PROBABILITY OF DISJOINT EVENTS The Venn diagram at the right shows two disjoint events that involve rolling a number cube.

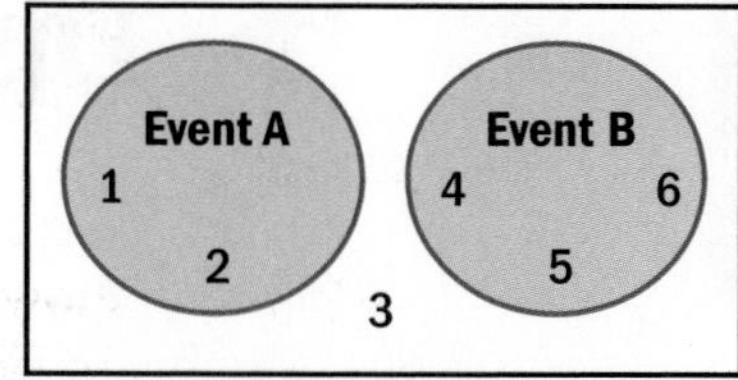

Event A: Roll a number less than 3.

Event B: Roll a number greater than 3.

The probability of event A *or* event B is $\frac{5}{6}$ because there are 5 favorable outcomes out of 6 possible outcomes. Notice that $\frac{5}{6}$ is the sum of the individual probabilities for events A and B, because the events have no outcomes in common: $\frac{2}{6} + \frac{3}{6} = \frac{5}{6}$.

KEY CONCEPT *For Your Notebook*

Probability of Disjoint Events

Words For two disjoint events, the probability that *either* of the events occurs is the sum of the probabilities of the events.

Algebra If A and B are disjoint events, then $P(\text{A } or \text{ B}) = P(\text{A}) + P(\text{B})$.

EXAMPLE 2 ◆ Multiple Choice Practice

Malcolm has 2 green tiles, 4 yellow tiles, and 3 blue tiles in a bag. He chooses 1 tile out of the bag without looking. What is the probability that the tile is green or yellow?

Ⓐ $\frac{2}{9}$ Ⓑ $\frac{4}{9}$ Ⓒ $\frac{1}{2}$ Ⓓ $\frac{2}{3}$

ELIMINATE CHOICES

Because $\frac{2}{9}$ is the probability of choosing a green tile and $\frac{4}{9}$ is the probability of choosing a yellow tile, you can eliminate choices A and B.

SOLUTION

Let event A be "choose green" and event B be "choose yellow." The events are disjoint because they do not have any outcomes in common.

$P(\text{A or B}) = P(\text{A}) + P(\text{B})$ **Events A and B are disjoint.**

$= P(\text{green}) + P(\text{yellow})$ **Identify event A as green and event B as yellow.**

$= \frac{2}{9} + \frac{4}{9}$ **Find probabilities.**

$= \frac{6}{9}$ **Add fractions.**

$= \frac{2}{3}$ **Simplify.**

▶ **Answer** The probability that the tile Malcolm chooses is green or yellow is $\frac{2}{3}$. The correct answer is D. Ⓐ Ⓑ Ⓒ Ⓓ

COMPLEMENTARY EVENTS Two disjoint events in which one or the other must occur are called **complementary events**. For example, when you roll a number cube, the events A and "*not* A" shown are complementary. Together they make up all possible outcomes, without any overlap.

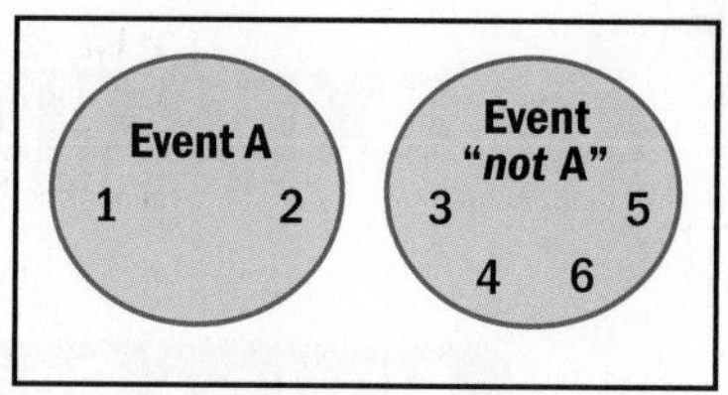

Two events A and "*not* A" are complements. The sum of their probabilities is 1.

$$P(\text{A}) + P(\textit{not}\ \text{A}) = 1 \qquad P(\text{A}) = 1 - P(\textit{not}\ \text{A}) \qquad P(\textit{not}\ \text{A}) = 1 - P(\text{A})$$

EXAMPLE 3 Probability of Complementary Events

SIGN LANGUAGE At a school, 3% of the students know sign language.

a. What is the probability that a randomly chosen student does *not* know sign language?

b. There are 267 sixth graders at the school. About how many sixth graders do *not* know sign language?

Three percent of students know sign language.

SOLUTION

a. $P(\text{does not know}) = 1 - P(\text{knows})$ **Use complementary events.**

$= 1 - 0.03$ **Substitute 3%, or 0.03, for *P*(knows).**

$= 0.97$ **Subtract.**

▸ **Answer** The probability that a randomly chosen student does not know sign language is 0.97, or 97%.

ANOTHER WAY

You can also use a proportion to find the answer in part (b).

$$\frac{97}{100} = \frac{x}{267}$$

$$97 \cdot 267 = 100x$$

$$25{,}899 = 100x$$

$$259 \approx x$$

b. From part (a), you know that 97% of students do not know sign language. You need to find 97% of 267.

$a = p\% \cdot b$ **Write percent equation.**

$= 97\% \cdot 267$ **Substitute 97 for *p* and 267 for *b*.**

$= 0.97 \cdot 267$ **Write percent as decimal.**

≈ 259 **Multiply. Round to a whole number.**

▸ **Answer** About 259 sixth graders do not know sign language.

✓ GUIDED PRACTICE for Examples 2 and 3

2. **WHAT IF?** In Example 2, what is the probability that Malcolm will choose a green tile or a blue tile?

3. **SUBWAYS** On a subway, 30% of the riders have briefcases. What is the probability that a randomly chosen rider does *not* have a briefcase? About how many riders out of 350 would *not* have a briefcase?

8.3 EXERCISES

HOMEWORK KEY

◆ = **MULTIPLE CHOICE PRACTICE**
Exs. 12, 13, 35, 45–47

○ = **HINTS AND HOMEWORK HELP**
for Exs. 9, 15, 37 at classzone.com

SKILLS • PROBLEM SOLVING • REASONING

1. **VOCABULARY** Copy and complete: Two disjoint events in which one or the other must occur are called ___?___.

2. **WRITING** *Describe* the difference between disjoint events and overlapping events.

SEE EXAMPLE 1
on p. 427
for Exs. 3–5

IDENTIFYING EVENTS **Use a list or Venn diagram to tell whether the events involving rolls of a number cube are *disjoint* or *overlapping*. *Explain* your reasoning.**

3. **Event A:** Roll a 4.
Event B: Roll a number less than 4.

4. **Event A:** Roll an odd number.
Event B: Roll a prime number.

5. **Event A:** Roll a multiple of 2.
Event B: Roll a number greater than 3.

SEE EXAMPLE 2
on p. 428
for Exs. 6–13

FINDING PROBABILITY **Events A and B are disjoint events. Find P(A or B).**

6. $P(\text{A}) = 0.3$
$P(\text{B}) = 0.2$

7. $P(\text{A}) = 0.25$
$P(\text{B}) = 0.35$

8. $P(\text{A}) = 33\%$
$P(\text{B}) = 8\%$

9. $P(\text{A}) = 16.1\%$
$P(\text{B}) = 28.2\%$

10. $P(\text{A}) = \frac{6}{25}$
$P(\text{B}) = \frac{37}{100}$

11. $P(\text{A}) = \frac{3}{25}$
$P(\text{B}) = \frac{3}{10}$

12. ◆ **MULTIPLE CHOICE** You roll a number cube. What is the probability of rolling an even number or a 3?

Ⓐ $\frac{1}{3}$ Ⓑ $\frac{1}{2}$ Ⓒ $\frac{2}{3}$ Ⓓ $\frac{5}{6}$

13. ◆ **MULTIPLE CHOICE** The spinner at the right is divided into equal parts. What is the probability that the spinner lands on green or on an odd number?

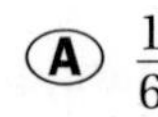

Ⓐ $\frac{1}{6}$ Ⓑ $\frac{1}{3}$ Ⓒ $\frac{1}{2}$ Ⓓ $\frac{5}{6}$

SEE EXAMPLE 3
on p. 429
for Exs. 14–20

FINDING PROBABILITY **Use P(A) to find P(*not* A).**

14. $P(\text{A}) = 0.4$

15. $P(\text{A}) = 64\%$

16. $P(\text{A}) = 23\%$

17. $P(\text{A}) = 0.51$

18. $P(\text{A}) = \frac{2}{5}$

19. $P(\text{A}) = \frac{3}{4}$

20. **MENTAL MATH** You have made 15 out of 35 basketball shots so far. Use mental math to estimate the probability of missing your next shot.

SEE EXAMPLE 3 on p. 429 for Ex. 21

21. **ERROR ANALYSIS** You roll a number cube. Your friend says that the events "roll an odd number" and "roll a number less than 4" are complementary, because the sum of their probabilities is 1. *Describe* and correct the error.

COMPARING PROBABILITIES You randomly choose a letter from the word EXAGGERATE. Compare the probabilities of the events using <, >, or =.

22. $P(\text{T})$? $P(\text{E})$
23. $P(\text{E})$? $P(\text{A or R})$
24. $P(\text{E or R})$? $P(\text{A or T})$
25. $P(\text{E})$? $P(\textit{not}\ \text{E})$
26. $P(\text{P})$? $P(\text{G or A})$
27. $P(\textit{not}\ \text{E})$? $P(\textit{not}\ \text{X})$

REASONING Tell whether the statement is *always, sometimes,* or *never* true. *Explain* your reasoning.

28. Two disjoint events are complementary.
29. Two overlapping events are disjoint.
30. Two complementary events are overlapping.

CONNECT SKILLS TO PROBLEM SOLVING Exercises 31–33 will help you prepare for problem solving.

Use the following information: You randomly choose a book from a shelf where 10% of the books are biographies and 40% are fantasy.

31. Are the events "choose a biography" and "choose a fantasy" disjoint?
32. Are the events in Exercise 31 complementary? *Explain* why or why not.
33. Find the probability of *not* choosing a fantasy book.

SEE EXAMPLES 2 AND 3 on pp. 428–429 for Exs. 34–39

34. **CHESS** You can move one of ten pieces on your first move in a chess game. Eight of these pieces are pawns. You choose one of these pieces at random for your first move. What is the probability that you do *not* choose a pawn?

California @HomeTutor for problem solving help at classzone.com

35. ◆ **MULTIPLE CHOICE** At a school, 53% of the students are boys. What is the probability that a randomly selected student is a girl?

Ⓐ 0.47 Ⓑ 0.53 Ⓒ 0.57 Ⓓ 0.63

California @HomeTutor for problem solving help at classzone.com

RECREATION Use the survey results in the circle graph. Find the probability that a randomly chosen person who answered the survey responded as indicated.

36. Chose horseback riding or fishing
37. Chose hiking or camping
38. Did *not* choose horseback riding
39. Did *not* choose fishing

What is your favorite activity on the Mendocino Coast?

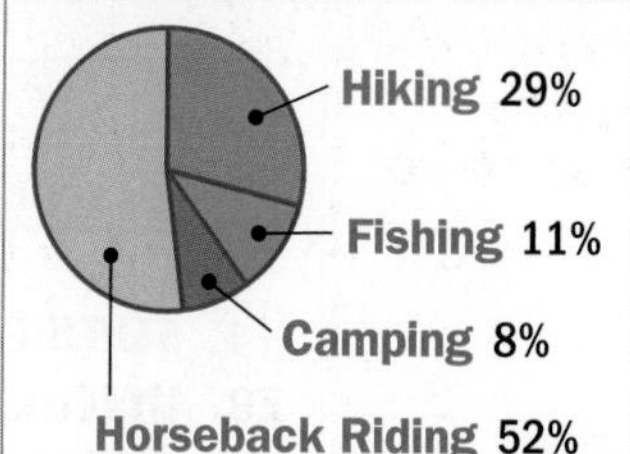

40. **BAKERY** A bakery offers blueberry, cranberry, bran, corn, and carrot muffins. You randomly choose a muffin from a bag that contains one of each kind of muffin.

   a. Are the events "choose carrot" and "choose corn" disjoint? *Explain.*

   b. What is the probability that you choose a muffin with berries?

   c. What is the complementary event of "choosing a muffin with berries"? What is the probability of the complementary event?

41. **CHALLENGE** A clearance-sale rack holds a total of 84 comedy, drama, and action DVDs. If you randomly choose a DVD, then *P*(comedy or drama) = *P*(action or drama). If the probability of *not* choosing a drama DVD is $\frac{5}{21}$, how many comedy DVDs are on the clearance-sale rack?

42. **CHALLENGE** Events A and B are disjoint events, and events B and C are disjoint events. Must events A and C be disjoint events? *Explain.*

◆ CALIFORNIA STANDARDS SPIRAL REVIEW

NS 2.1 43. What is the value of $\frac{7}{8} \times \frac{10}{21}$? ***(p. 88)***

Ⓐ $\frac{5}{168}$ Ⓑ $\frac{1}{4}$ Ⓒ $\frac{1}{3}$ Ⓓ $\frac{5}{12}$

SDAP 1.1 44. What is the mean of the data: 11, 15, 15, 15, 18, 16, 22, and 24? ***(p. 364)***

Ⓐ 15 Ⓑ 15.5 Ⓒ 16.5 Ⓓ 17

AF 2.3 45. Mark walks on a treadmill at a rate of 3 miles per hour. He walks for 45 minutes. How many miles does he walk? ***(p. 260)***

Ⓐ 2 Ⓑ 2.25 Ⓒ 2.5 Ⓓ 2.75

QUIZ *for Lessons 8.1–8.3*

1. What is the probability of rolling an odd number when rolling a number cube? Write your answer as a fraction, decimal, and percent. ***(p. 415)***

2. You roll a number cube 75 times and a 4 appears 14 times. Find your experimental probability of rolling a 4. About how many 4's would you have expected to roll using the theoretical probability? ***(pp. 415, 422)***

3. **AGES** The estimated distribution by age of the U.S. population in 2010 is shown in the table. Estimate the probability that, in 2010, a randomly chosen person is in the age group 15–19 *or* 60 and over. ***(p. 427)***

Age Group	14 and under	15–19	20–24	25–39	40–59	60 and over
Percent	20.0%	6.9%	7.0%	20.0%	27.6%	18.4%

4. **SUBJECTS** At your school, 275 students were surveyed and about 23% said that math was their favorite subject. Estimate the number of students who said that a subject other than math was their favorite. ***(p. 427)***

MIXED REVIEW *of Skills and Problem Solving*

Multiple Choice Practice for Lessons 8.1–8.3

1. The circle graph shows the most common materials used for the exteriors of new homes in the United States. Which equation can you use to predict the number of new homes that will be made of brick in a neighborhood of 50 new homes? **SDAP 3.2, MR 2.4**

Materials for New Homes

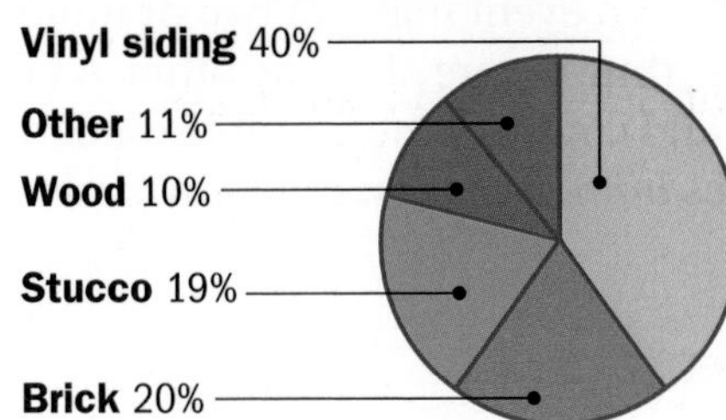

Ⓐ $\frac{x}{50} = \frac{20}{100}$ Ⓑ $\frac{50}{80} = \frac{x}{100}$

Ⓒ $\frac{x}{50} = \frac{80}{100}$ Ⓓ $\frac{50}{x} = \frac{80}{100}$

2. A spinner is divided into five sections, labeled from 1 to 5. The table below shows the results of several spins. In 100 spins, how many times would you expect to land on section 5? **SDAP 3.2**

Section	1	2	3	4	5
Times landed	1	3	5	5	6

Ⓐ 20 Ⓑ 30

Ⓒ 43 Ⓓ 60

3. In a middle school, 70 students take French, 144 students take Spanish, and the remaining 166 students do not take a language. No student takes both. What is the probability, rounded to the nearest percent, that a student chosen at random takes Spanish? **SDAP 3.3**

Ⓐ 18% Ⓑ 38%

Ⓒ 48% Ⓓ 61%

4. In one city, the probability that a March day is rainy is 0.38. What is the probability that a March day is *not* rainy? **SDAP 3.3**

Ⓐ 0.12 Ⓑ 0.38

Ⓒ 0.62 Ⓓ 1.38

5. A group of students volunteer to clean up the grounds at a community center. The table shows the number of students who are randomly assigned to work in each area. What is the probability that a student is assigned to clean the front yard or the back yard? **SDAP 3.4, MR 2.2**

Job and work area	*Volunteers*
Clean front yard	6
Clean back yard	6
Clean playground	4
Paint playground	2

Ⓐ 0 Ⓑ $\frac{1}{3}$

Ⓒ $\frac{2}{3}$ Ⓓ $\frac{3}{4}$

6. Events A and B are disjoint events. The probability of A is 0.2 and the probability of B is 0.55. What is the probability of A or B? **SDAP 3.4**

Ⓐ 0.11 Ⓑ 0.35

Ⓒ 0.57 Ⓓ 0.75

7. A bag contains yellow, orange, and blue stickers. The table lists the number of stickers of each color in the bag. You randomly choose a sticker from the bag. What is the probability that you choose an orange sticker? **SDAP 3.3**

Sticker color	yellow	orange	blue
Number	7	5	13

Ⓐ 0.2 Ⓑ 0.25

Ⓒ 0.28 Ⓓ 0.52

8.4 Compound Events

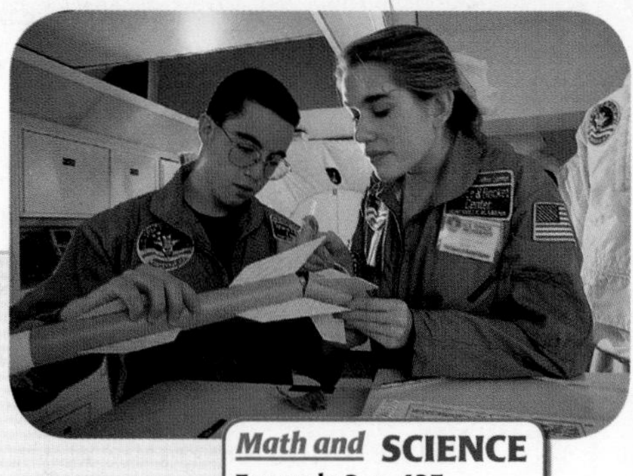

Math and SCIENCE
Example 2, p. 435

Standards **SDAP 3.1 Represent all possible outcomes for compound events in an organized way (e.g., tables, grids, tree diagrams) and express the theoretical probability of each outcome.**

Connect ***Before*** you listed outcomes to find a probability. ***Now*** you will use tree diagrams, tables, and grids to list outcomes and find probabilities.

KEY VOCABULARY
- **compound events**
- **tree diagram**

COMPOUND EVENTS A **compound event** is an event made of two or more events that can happen either at the same time or one after the other. A table or a **tree diagram** can help you identify and count all the possible outcomes of a compound event. A tree diagram uses *branches* to list different choices.

EXAMPLE 1 Representing Outcomes

FRUIT DRINKS You are ordering a fruit drink. You can choose a small or large drink in one of the following flavors: strawberry, banana, or orange. How many different choices of fruit drinks do you have?

AnimatedMath
For an interactive example on listing outcomes go to **classzone.com.**

METHOD 1 Make a table to list all possible choices of fruit drinks. List the sizes in the first column and the fruits in the first row.

	Strawberry	*Banana*	*Orange*
Small	small strawberry	small banana	small orange
Large	large strawberry	large banana	large orange

METHOD 2 Make a tree diagram to list all possible choices of fruit drinks. List the sizes on one column of branches and the fruits on another.

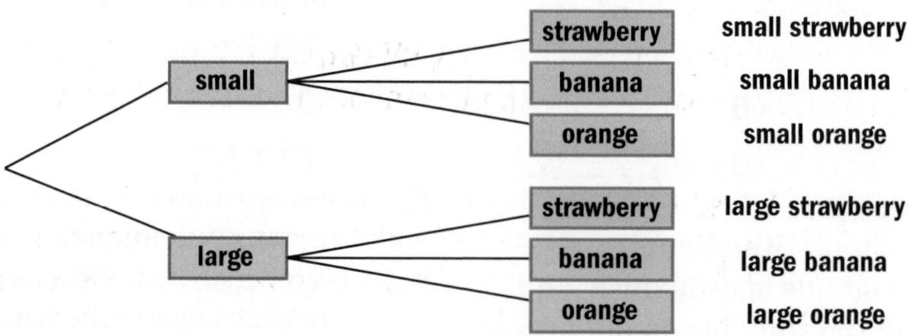

▶ **Answer** You have 6 different choices of fruit drinks.

✓ GUIDED PRACTICE for Example 1

1. **REFRESHMENTS** Popcorn at a movie theater comes in regular, medium, and large sizes, and it comes either plain or buttered. How many choices of popcorn do you have?

A *set* is a collection of distinct objects. Braces "{ }" indicate that the items in the list make up a set (or group), as in Example 2.

EXAMPLE 2 ◆ Multiple Choice Practice

You are going to two sessions at a science camp. At each session, you will be placed in one of the groups listed.

Session 1	Red (R)	Green (G)	Blue (B)	Yellow (Y)
Session 2	Red (R)	Green (G)	Blue (B)	Yellow (Y)

You will not be placed in the same group for both sessions. Which set lists all of your possible group placements?

Ⓐ {RG, RB, RY, GB, GY, BY}

Ⓑ {RG, RB, RY, GR, GB, GY, BR, BG, BY}

Ⓒ {RG, RB, RY, GR, GB, GY, BR, BG, BY, YR, YG, YB}

Ⓓ {RR, RG, RB, RY, GG, GR, GB, GY, BB, BR, BG, BY, YY, YR, YG, YB}

About the Standards

You can apply the strategies used in Example 1 to a more complex problem like Example 2. This is part of Grade 6 Standard MR 2.2.

SOLUTION

Because you cannot be in the same group for both sessions, do not include the same group in both sessions in the tree diagram.

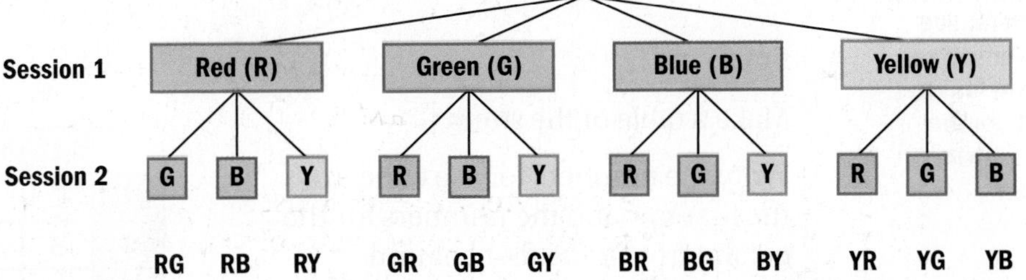

▶ **Answer** The set {RG, RB, RY, GR, GB, GY, BR, BG, BY, YR, YG, YB} lists all your possible group placements. The correct answer is C. Ⓐ Ⓑ Ⓒ Ⓓ

Notice in Example 2 that RG and GR represent different group placements. In RG, your first session is with the red group and your second session is with the green group. In GR, your group placements are in reverse order.

✓ GUIDED PRACTICE for Example 2

2. **SNACKS** You have a plum, a banana, an apple, an orange, and a pear. You eat one now with lunch and one later for a snack. List all the possible ways you can choose the fruits for your lunch and snack.

3. **WHAT IF?** In Example 2, how does the tree diagram change if you *can* be placed in the same color group for both sessions? *Explain.*

EXAMPLE 3 Using a Tree Diagram

Find the probability of landing on heads at least twice when flipping a coin 3 times.

Make a tree diagram to list the possible outcomes of the experiment. Circle the successful outcomes.

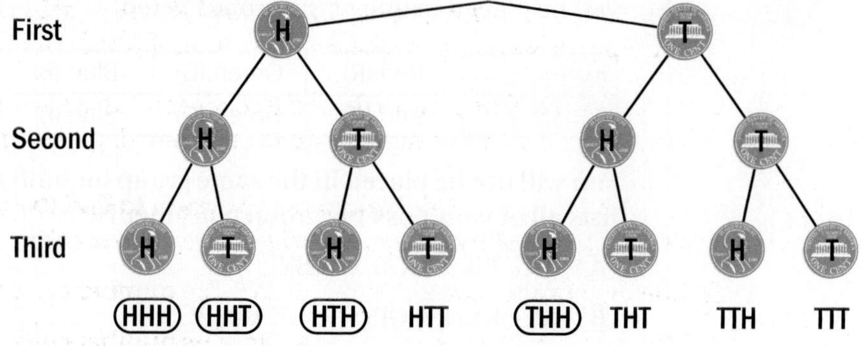

(HHH) (HHT) (HTH) HTT (THH) THT TTH TTT

▸ **Answer** Because 4 of the 8 outcomes have at least 2 heads, the probability is $\frac{4}{8}$, or $\frac{1}{2}$.

EXAMPLE 4 Using a Table

ANOTHER WAY

For an alternative method for solving Example 4, turn to page 440 for the **Problem Solving Workshop**.

You roll a cube numbered 1 through 6 and an octahedron numbered 1 through 8. Find the probability that the sum of the numbers rolled is 9.

SOLUTION

Make a table of the sums.

Write the numbers for the cube in the first row and the numbers for the octahedron in the first column.

Find the sums to complete the table.

The sum is 9 for 6 of the 48 outcomes.

$P(\text{sum is } 9) = \frac{6}{48} = \frac{1}{8} = 0.125 = 12.5\%$

▸ **Answer** The probability of rolling a sum of 9 when a number cube and a number octahedron are rolled is 12.5%.

Sums of the Numbers

	1	2	3	4	5	6
1	2	3	4	5	6	7
2	3	4	5	6	7	8
3	4	5	6	7	8	**9**
4	5	6	7	8	**9**	10
5	6	7	8	**9**	10	11
6	7	8	**9**	10	11	12
7	8	**9**	10	11	12	13
8	**9**	10	11	12	13	14

✓ GUIDED PRACTICE for Examples 3 and 4

4. You roll a number cube and flip a coin. Make a list of possible outcomes. What is the probability that you roll a 3 or 5 and land on tails?

5. **WHAT IF?** In Example 4, what is the probability that the sum of the numbers rolled is 5?

8.4 EXERCISES

HOMEWORK KEY

◆ = **MULTIPLE CHOICE PRACTICE**
Exs. 7, 13, 25, 32–34

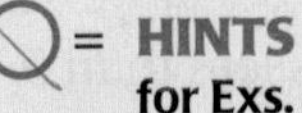

= **HINTS AND HOMEWORK HELP**
for Exs. 5, 11, 25 at classzone.com

SKILLS • PROBLEM SOLVING • REASONING

1. **VOCABULARY** Copy and complete: You can use a table or a tree diagram to help you list all the possible _?_ of a compound event.

2. **WRITING** *Explain* how to draw a tree diagram that shows the possible outcomes of rolling a number cube and choosing a letter from YES.

SEE EXAMPLE 1
on p. 434
for Exs. 3–7

MAKING TREE DIAGRAMS Make a tree diagram to find the number of possible outcomes involving a number cube and/or coin.

3. Roll the number cube twice.
4. Roll the number cube and flip the coin.
5. Flip the coin four times.
6. Roll the number cube once and flip the coin twice.

7. ◆ **MULTIPLE CHOICE** You randomly choose answer A, B, C, or D for each of 3 multiple choice questions. How many outcomes are possible?

   (A) 3 (B) 4 (C) 12 (D) 64

SEE EXAMPLES 1 AND 2
on pp. 434–435
for Exs. 8–14

LISTING CHOICES List the possible choices for pants and a shirt using the given colors and following restriction.

8. Pants: black, blue, brown, gray
   Shirts: black, red, blue, brown, orange
   Restriction: pant color = shirt color

9. Pants: blue, black, gray
   Shirts: blue, green, black
   Restriction: pant color ≠ shirt color

MAKING TABLES Each spinner is divided into equal parts. Make a table to find the number of possible outcomes for the experiment.

10. Spin spinner A two times.
11. Spin spinner B two times.
12. Spin spinner A and spinner B.

Spinner A

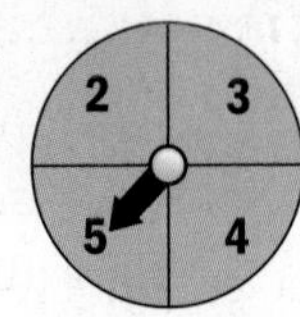

Spinner B

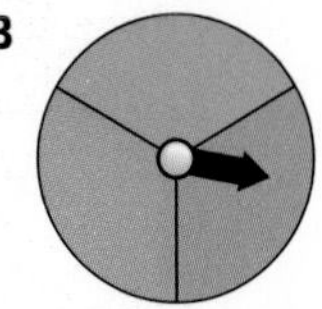

13. ◆ **MULTIPLE CHOICE** Which tree diagram can be used to find all two-digit numbers that can be formed using two different digits from {1, 3, 5}?

(A)

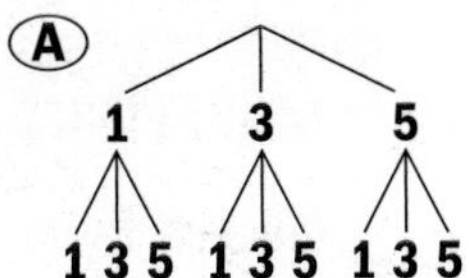

(B)

1 3 5
3 5 1 5 1 3

(C)

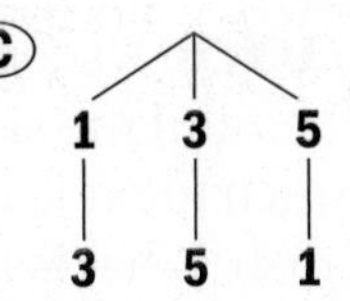

(D)

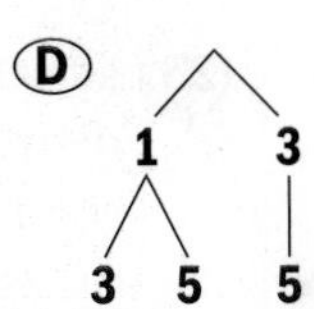

14. **ERROR ANALYSIS** A student must choose 2 electives for the next school year from the following: Spanish (S), art (A), and music (M). *Describe* and correct the error in finding the number of possible choices.

Spanish Art Music
A M S M A S
There are 6 choices of 2 electives.

SEE EXAMPLES 3 AND 4
on p. 436 for Exs. 15–18

PROBABILITY You roll two number cubes. Find the probability of the event.

15. You roll two odd numbers.

16. You roll two numbers less than 3.

17. The sum is less than 5.

18. The sum is 7.

CONNECT SKILLS TO PROBLEM SOLVING Exercises 19–21 will help you prepare for problem solving.

Use the following information: A store sells inflatable chairs in two styles: low-back and high-back. The chairs come in four colors: black, orange, lime, and purple. You randomly choose a chair.

19. List all the possible combinations of styles and colors you can choose.

20. Circle the combinations from Exercise 19 where the chair is black.

21. Find the probability that the chair you choose is black.

SEE EXAMPLE 1
on p. 434 for Exs. 22–23

22. **GIFTS** You are wrapping a gift. You can choose gold or silver wrapping paper with one of the following colored bows: red, blue, white, or green. Make a tree diagram or a table of all of the possible ways to wrap the gift.

California @HomeTutor for problem solving help at classzone.com

23. **MENUS** You are ordering a sandwich. You can choose turkey, ham, tuna, or egg made with either rye, wheat, or white bread. Make a table or tree diagram to list all of the possible sandwiches.

California @HomeTutor for problem solving help at classzone.com

SEE EXAMPLE 2
on p. 435 for Ex. 24

24. ◆ **MULTIPLE CHOICE** You randomly choose a mug from the shelf below, then randomly choose a second without replacing the first. Which set lists all color combinations for your first and second choices?

Ⓐ {RW, RB, WB}

Ⓑ {RR, RW, RB, WW, WB, BB}

Ⓒ {RW, RB, WR, WB, BR, BW}

Ⓓ {RW, RB, WR, WW, WB, BR, BW, BB}

SEE EXAMPLES 3 AND 4
on p. 436 for Ex. 25

25. **SCHOOL LUNCH** A school cafeteria offers the main dishes and the side dishes shown at the right. A lunch includes one main dish and one side dish. What is the probability that a lunch chosen at random will include a salad?

MAIN DISHES
Chicken fajita
Turkey sandwich
Yogurt with fresh fruit
SIDE DISHES
Broccoli
Potato wedges
Salad
Carrot sticks

26. **DRAW A DIAGRAM** Make a tree diagram for an experiment with these possible outcomes: A1X, A1Y, A2X, A2Y, A3X, A3Y, B1X, B1Y, B2X, B2Y, B3X, and B3Y.

READING IN MATH **Read the information below for Exercises 27–29.**

Arenas The floor surface of an arena can be modified to suit an event. Ice hockey games and ice shows use an ice surface. An insulated sub-floor can be placed over the ice for concerts or trade shows. Special surfaces can be placed over the sub-floor for events such as basketball or soccer games. One year at an arena, the following events took place the given number of times.

Event	Basketball	Ice hockey	Concert	Trade show	Ice show	Other
Days	36 days	34 days	24 days	17 days	12 days	27 days

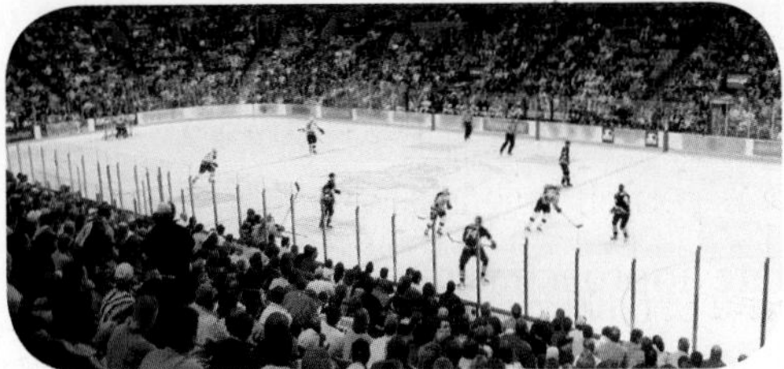

27. **Draw a diagram** Make a tree diagram to list the possible combinations of floor types (ice, sub-floor, special floor) and events from the table. Assume that "Other" events are evenly divided among the floor types.

28. **Calculate** Find the probability that the surface for a random event is the sub-floor. Use your tree diagram and the data above.

29. **Predict** Use your answer from Exercise 28 to predict the number of events that will use a sub-floor if 180 events take place at the arena.

30. **CHALLENGE** How many different odd two-digit numbers can you make using the digits 1, 4, 7, 8, and 9 if no digit appears more than once in a number?

31. xy **CHALLENGE** A number cube is rolled x times. What is the probability that all x of these rolls result in a number less than 3? *Explain.*

◆ CALIFORNIA STANDARDS SPIRAL REVIEW

NS 1.2 32. A restaurant has 45 gallons of apple juice and 80 gallons of orange juice. What is the ratio of apple juice to orange juice? ***(p. 255)***

Ⓐ 9 : 16 Ⓑ 16 : 9 Ⓒ 16 : 80 Ⓓ 80 : 45

NS 1.4 33. A stereo costs $156. The sales tax is 7.5%. What is the total cost to buy the stereo? ***(p. 325)***

Ⓐ $11.70 Ⓑ $113.88 Ⓒ $144.30 Ⓓ $167.70

SDAP 3.2 34. A kicker for a football team made 4 out of 5 field goal attempts in one game. How many field goals would you expect the kicker to make out of 30 attempts? ***(p. 422)***

Ⓐ 8 Ⓑ 13 Ⓒ 24 Ⓓ 37

Using ALTERNATIVE METHODS

Another Way to Solve Example 4, page 436

Standards
SDAP 3.1

In Example 4 on page 436, you saw how to solve the problem about rolling a number cube and a number octahedron by using a table. You can also solve the problem by using a grid.

PROBLEM

You roll a cube numbered 1 through 6 and an octahedron numbered 1 through 8. Find the probability that the sum of the numbers rolled is 9.

METHOD

Using a Grid An alternate approach is to use a grid.

STEP 1 **Draw** a grid. Let the vertical axis be the numbers on the octahedron and the horizontal axis be the numbers on the cube. Mark points on the grid to represent every possible sum.

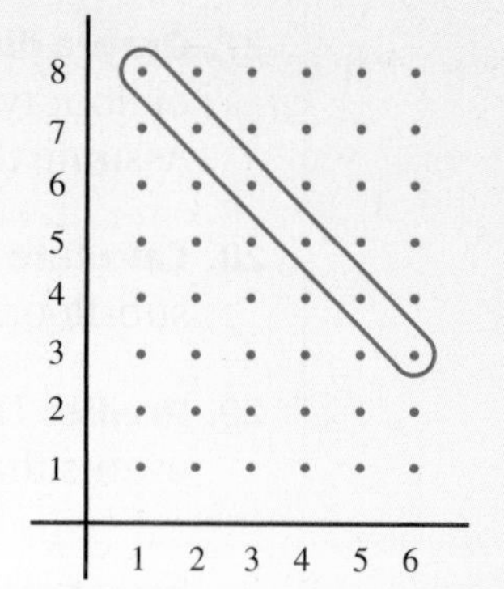

STEP 2 **Circle** the points that represent a sum of 9. There are 6 favorable outcomes.

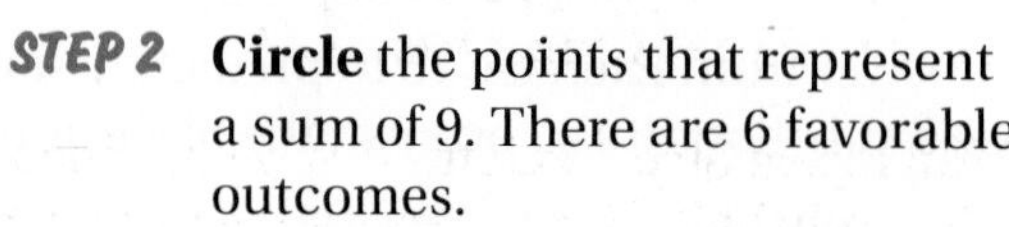

STEP 3 **Find** the probability that the sum of the resulting numbers is 9. There are 6 favorable outcomes and 48 possible outcomes.

$$P(\text{sum is } 9) = \frac{6}{48} = \frac{1}{8} = 0.125 = 12.5\%$$

▶ **Answer** The probability of rolling a sum of 9 when a number cube and a number octahedron are rolled is 12.5%.

PRACTICE

1. The outcomes on the spinners shown are equally likely. You spin each spinner once. Use a grid to find the probability that the sum of the two numbers is 15.

2. In the example above, what is the probability of rolling the same number on both the cube and on the octahedron?

3. You roll two octahedrons numbered 1 through 8. Use a grid to find the probability that the sum of the resulting numbers is 11.

8.5 Independent and Dependent Events

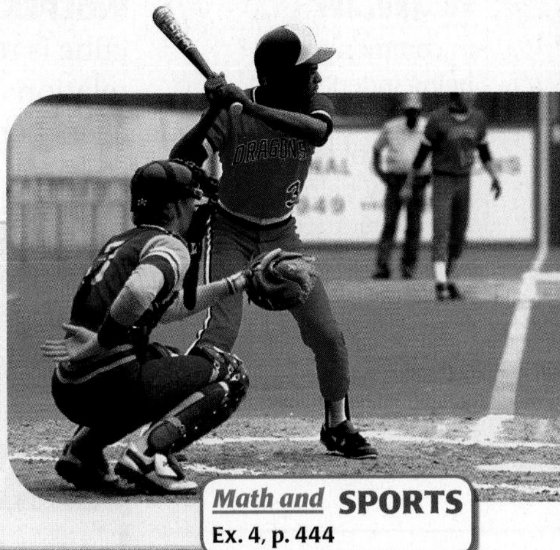

Math and SPORTS
Ex. 4, p. 444

Standards **SDAP 3.4 Understand that** the probability of either of two disjoint events occurring is the sum of the two individual probabilities and that **the probability of one event following another, in independent trials, is the product of the two probabilities.**

SDAP 3.5 Understand the difference between independent and dependent events.

Connect ***Before*** you listed outcomes to find probabilities. ***Now*** you will find the probabilities of compound events by using a formula.

KEY VOCABULARY
- **independent events**
- **dependent events**
- **compound events,** *p. 434*

ACTIVITY

You can find the probability of two events occurring.

STEP 1 A bag contains 5 pieces of paper that have an O and 4 pieces that have an X. You randomly choose a piece of paper from the bag, you get an O, and you don't put it back.

You randomly choose a second piece of paper. What is the probability that the second piece of paper has an X?

STEP 2 You repeat Step 1, but the first piece of paper has an X. What is the probability that the second piece of paper also has an X? Why is this probability different from the probability in Step 1?

DISTINGUISHING EVENTS Compound events are either *independent* or *dependent* events. They are **independent events** if the occurrence of one event does *not* affect the likelihood that the other event will occur. They are **dependent events** if the occurrence of one event *does* affect the likelihood that the other will occur.

EXAMPLE 1 Independent and Dependent Events

In Step 1 of the activity, you chose an O first and then an X, without putting the O back. Are these events *independent* or *dependent*?

In the activity, whether or not you choose an O first *does* affect the likelihood that you choose an X second. This is because the first piece of paper chosen is *not put back*. This affects the ratio of X's to O's in the bag when choosing the second letter.

▶ **Answer** The events are dependent.

VOCABULARY

In common usage, being independent means being free from the control of others. This may help you remember the meaning of *independent events*.

INDEPENDENT EVENTS A coin is flipped and a number cube is rolled. The table of outcomes helps you see the relationship between the probability of the compound events and the probabilities of the individual events.

	H	T
1	H, 1	T, 1
2	H, 2	T, 2
3	H, 3	T, 3
4	H, 4	T, 4
5	H, 5	T, 5
6	H, 6	T, 6

$$P(\text{H and odd}) = \frac{1 \cdot 3}{2 \cdot 6} \begin{array}{l}\leftarrow \textbf{favorable outcomes} \\ \leftarrow \textbf{total outcomes}\end{array}$$

$$= \frac{1}{2} \cdot \frac{3}{6}$$

$$= P(\text{H}) \cdot P(\text{odd})$$

KEY CONCEPT — *For Your Notebook*

Probability of Independent Events

Words For two independent events A and B, the probability that *both* events occur is the product of the probabilities of the events.

Algebra If A and B are independent events, then $P(\text{A } and \text{ B}) = P(\text{A}) \cdot P(\text{B})$.

EXAMPLE 2 Probability of Independent Events

About the Standards

In Example 2, you can break the problem into simpler parts. This is part of Grade 6 Standard MR 1.3.

GAME SHOW On a game show, you spin the wheel at the right. It is divided into 8 equal sections. Find the probability that you land on $200 on your first spin and go bankrupt on your second spin.

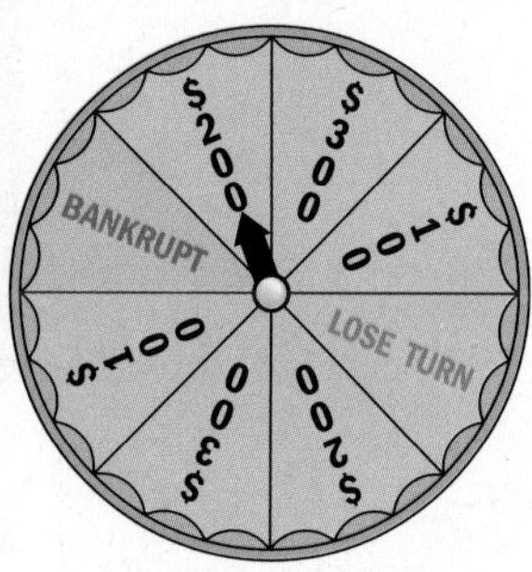

SOLUTION

STEP 1 **Find** the probability of each independent event.

$P(\$200) = \frac{2}{8} = \mathbf{0.25}$ **"$200" appears 2 times.**

$P(\text{bankrupt}) = \frac{1}{8} = \mathbf{0.125}$ **"Bankrupt" appears once.**

STEP 2 **Multiply** the probabilities, because the events are independent.

$P(\$200 \text{ and bankrupt}) = P(\$200) \times P(\text{bankrupt})$

$= \mathbf{0.25 \times 0.125}$

$= 0.03125$

▶ **Answer** The probability that you land on $200 on your first spin and go bankrupt on your second spin is 0.03125, or about 3%.

DEPENDENT EVENTS If A and B are dependent events, the probability that B occurs given A has occurred is *not* the same as the probability of B. The activity on page 441 suggests that the probability of B is affected by the occurence of event A. You need to use $P(\text{B given A})$ instead of $P(\text{B})$.

KEY CONCEPT — *For Your Notebook*

Probability of Dependent Events

Words For two dependent events, the probability that *both* events occur is the product of the probability of the first event and the probability of the second event given the first.

Algebra If A and B are dependent events, then
$P(\text{A } and \text{ B}) = P(\text{A}) \cdot P(\text{B given A})$.

EXAMPLE 3 Probability of Dependent Events

AQUARIUM You have 12 loaches, 7 barbs, and 6 tetras in your aquarium. You want to give 2 fish to a friend. You randomly choose 1 fish from the aquarium, and then randomly choose another fish without replacing the first. Find the probability that both are loaches.

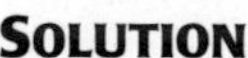

SOLUTION

The events are dependent. Find the probability of the first event and the probability of the second event given the first. Then multiply the probabilities.

STEP 1 $P(\text{loach}) = \frac{12}{25}$ — **Of the 25 fish, 12 are loaches.**

STEP 2 $P(\text{loach given loach}) = \frac{11}{24}$ — **Of the remaining 24 fish, 11 are loaches.**

STEP 3 $P(\text{loach and loach}) = \frac{12}{25} \times \frac{11}{24}$ — **Multiply probabilities.**

$= \frac{11}{50}$ — **Simplify.**

▶ **Answer** The probability that both fish are loaches is $\frac{11}{50}$, or 22%.

AVOID ERRORS
The probability of choosing the second loach is $\frac{11}{24}$, not $\frac{12}{25}$, because the first fish is not placed back into the tank.

✓ GUIDED PRACTICE for Examples 1, 2, and 3

1. From a jar of 5 red and 7 blue marbles, you randomly choose a marble, replace it, and then randomly choose another. Are the events "choose a red marble first" and "choose a blue marble second" *independent* or *dependent*? Find the probability that both events occur.

2. **KENNEL** You work at a kennel walking dogs. The 10 dogs being boarded on a given day include 3 black, 4 brown, 2 white, and 1 spotted dog. You randomly choose 1 dog to walk. When finished, you choose a different dog to walk. What is the probability that both dogs you walk are brown?

8.5 EXERCISES

HOMEWORK KEY ◆ = **MULTIPLE CHOICE PRACTICE** Exs. 12, 24, 25, 31–33
○ = **HINTS AND HOMEWORK HELP** for Exs. 5, 7, 25 at classzone.com

SKILLS • PROBLEM SOLVING • REASONING

VOCABULARY **Copy and complete the statement.**

1. Independent events and dependent events are types of _?_ events.
2. If A and B are independent events, then P(A and B) equals _?_.

SEE EXAMPLE 1 on p. 441 for Exs. 3–5

3. **WRITING** *Describe* a way to randomly choose one of the 6 lettered tiles, and then another, so that the events are independent.

CLASSIFYING EVENTS **Tell whether the events are *independent* or *dependent*.**

4. While you are watching a baseball game, the third batter in the lineup hits a home run. Then the fourth batter in the lineup hits a home run.
5. Your CD player randomly plays each song on a CD once. You hear track 3 first and track 1 second.

SEE EXAMPLE 2 on p. 442 for Exs. 6–8

INDEPENDENT EVENTS **Events A and B are independent. Find P(A and B).**

6. $P(A) = 0.3$, $P(B) = 0.7$
7. $P(A) = 0.5$, $P(B) = 0.5$
8. $P(A) = \frac{4}{5}$, $P(B) = \frac{1}{5}$

SEE EXAMPLE 3 on p. 443 for Exs. 9–12

DEPENDENT EVENTS **Events A and B are dependent. Find P(A and B).**

9. $P(A) = 0.6$, $P(B \text{ given } A) = 0.25$
10. $P(A) = \frac{9}{10}$, $P(B \text{ given } A) = \frac{1}{2}$
11. $P(A) = \frac{1}{4}$, $P(B \text{ given } A) = \frac{1}{5}$

12. ◆ **MULTIPLE CHOICE** A vendor is selling 7 pink, 8 yellow, and 5 white roses. Which expression can you evaluate to find the probability that a pink rose and then a yellow rose are randomly chosen and sold?

   Ⓐ $\frac{7}{20} + \frac{8}{19}$ Ⓑ $\frac{7}{19} \cdot \frac{8}{19}$ Ⓒ $\frac{7}{20} \cdot \frac{8}{19}$ Ⓓ $\frac{7}{20} \cdot \frac{8}{20}$

ALGEBRA **Events A and B are independent events. Find the unknown probability.**

13. $P(A) = 0.2$, $P(B) = \underline{?}$, $P(A \text{ and } B) = 0.08$
14. $P(A) = \underline{?}$, $P(B) = \frac{1}{2}$, $P(A \text{ and } B) = \frac{7}{20}$
15. $P(A) = \frac{3}{4}$, $P(B) = \underline{?}$, $P(A \text{ and } B) = \frac{1}{3}$

16. **ERROR ANALYSIS** *Describe* and correct the error made in finding the probability that you and your friend are the 2 people randomly chosen from a group of 10.

   ✗ $\frac{1}{10} \cdot \frac{1}{10} = \frac{1}{100}$

CONNECT SKILLS TO PROBLEM SOLVING **Exercises 17–20 will help you prepare for problem solving.**

Use the following information: A store has a display with 12 small, 24 medium, and 14 large T-shirts. You randomly choose one T-shirt and do not put it back. Then you randomly choose a second T-shirt.

17. If your first and second choices are both medium, are the events *independent* or *dependent*.

18. What is the probability that the first shirt you choose is small?

19. What is the probability that the second shirt you choose is large, given that the first shirt you choose is small?

20. What is the probability that the first shirt you choose is small and the second shirt you choose is large?

SEE EXAMPLES 2 AND 3 on pp. 442–443 for Exs. 21–26

SHOE PRODUCTION **The tables give data about the shoes produced at a factory during one day. Assume that the events are independent. Find the probability that a randomly chosen pair of shoes is the given type.**

21. Men's athletic shoes

22. Women's casual shoes

23. Men's casual shoes

Gender	Percent
men's	46%
women's	54%

Shoe Style	Percent
athletic	22%
casual	61%
dress	17%

California @HomeTutor for problem solving help at classzone.com

24. ◆ **MULTIPLE CHOICE** You have two state quarters and one that is not a state quarter. You randomly choose two of them. What is the probability that both coins are state quarters?

Ⓐ $\frac{1}{9}$ Ⓑ $\frac{1}{6}$ Ⓒ $\frac{1}{3}$ Ⓓ $\frac{2}{3}$

California @HomeTutor for problem solving help at classzone.com

25. ◆ **MULTIPLE CHOICE** The integers from 1 through 10 are written on separate pieces of paper. You randomly choose two numbers, one at a time, but you do not replace them. What is the probability that both numbers are odd?

Ⓐ $\frac{2}{9}$ Ⓑ $\frac{1}{4}$ Ⓒ $\frac{1}{2}$ Ⓓ $\frac{17}{18}$

26. **VENDING MACHINE** You deposit a quarter into the machine at the right, which gives you a randomly selected rubber ball. You repeat the process to get another rubber ball. What is the probability that both rubber balls are green?

27. **PERFORMING AN EXPERIMENT** Roll two number cubes 25 times. For each roll, record the sum of the two cubes. What is your experimental probability that the sum is less than 7? Use your results to predict the probability of getting a sum of less than 7 for (a) both and (b) neither of the next two rolls.

28. **REASONING** The 11 letters that spell the word PROBABILITY are written on slips of paper and put into a bag. You randomly choose two letters, one at a time, from the bag. Is the probability of choosing two B's greater if you replace the first letter chosen or if you don't replace it? *Explain.*

29. **CHALLENGE** A jar of coins includes 15 dimes. The probability of choosing a quarter is 20%. The probability of choosing a dime and then a quarter (after replacing the dime) is 6%. How many quarters are in the jar?

30. **CHALLENGE** The table shows the size and color of paper clips in a box. There are 65 in all. The probability of *not* randomly choosing a yellow paper clip is $\frac{7}{13}$. You randomly choose paper clips one at a time without replacing them. What is the probability that the first three paper clips you choose are small and yellow?

	Small	Large
Red	10	10
Blue	10	?
Yellow	?	15

◆ CALIFORNIA STANDARDS SPIRAL REVIEW

NS 1.4 31. The number 210 is 70% of what number? *(p. 319)*

Ⓐ 140 Ⓑ 147 Ⓒ 280 Ⓓ 300

AF 1.3 32. What is the value of $(8 - 3) \times (-4 + 13)$? *(p. 160)*

Ⓐ −45 Ⓑ −7 Ⓒ 17 Ⓓ 45

SDAP 3.3 33. On average, a baseball player gets 5 hits out of every 20 times at bat. What is the probability that the player does *not* get a hit? *(p. 427)*

Ⓐ 3.7% Ⓑ 19% Ⓒ 43% Ⓓ 75%

QUIZ *for Lessons 8.4–8.5*

1. You roll two number cubes. Use a table or grid to find the probability of rolling a sum of 7. *(p. 434)*

2. **VACATION** You are planning a family vacation. You have the choice of two modes of transportation: bus or train. You have the choice of four destinations: Las Vegas, San Francisco, Miami, or Denver. Make a tree diagram to find all of the possibilities. *(p. 434)*

Events A and B are dependent events. Find *P*(A and B). *(p. 441)*

3. $P(A) = 0.6$, $P(B \text{ given } A) = 0.3$

4. $P(A) = 0.11$, $P(B \text{ given } A) = 0.45$

5. $P(A) = \frac{2}{5}$, $P(B \text{ given } A) = \frac{1}{3}$

6. $P(A) = \frac{1}{8}$, $P(B \text{ given } A) = \frac{5}{6}$

7. **PASSWORDS** Your computer password has 5 randomly chosen letters that are lower case and do not repeat. What is the probability that the first letter of your password is "a" and the second letter is "c?" *(p. 441)*

MIXED REVIEW of Skills and Problem Solving

Multiple Choice Practice for Lessons 8.4–8.5

1. The circle graph shows the results of a survey asking students who usually helps them with homework. If 20% of the teachers who help the students are math teachers, what is the probability that a randomly selected student gets help from a math teacher? **SDAP 3.4**

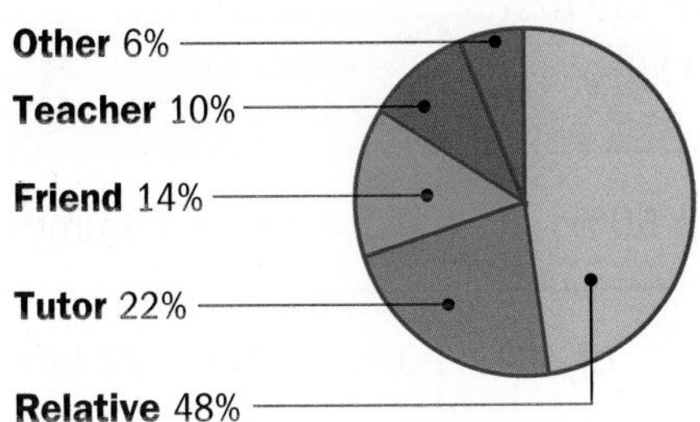

Ⓐ 2% Ⓑ 5% Ⓒ 20% Ⓓ 30%

2. Events A and B are independent. The probability of A is 0.25 and the probability of B is 0.3. What is the probability of A and B? **SDAP 3.4**

Ⓐ 5% Ⓑ 7.5% Ⓒ 45% Ⓓ 55%

3. You are playing a game in which you select tiles from a bag. The table shows the different shapes painted on the tiles and the number of tiles with those shapes. If you select two star (★) tiles, you win a prize.

Shape	♥	★	☺	⬅
No. of Tiles	6	4	12	8

You randomly choose a tile, but you don't replace it. Then you randomly choose another tile. Which expression gives the probability that you win a prize? **SDAP 3.5, MR 1.1**

Ⓐ $\frac{4 \cdot 4}{30 \cdot 30}$ Ⓑ $\frac{4 \cdot 3}{30 \cdot 30}$

Ⓒ $\frac{4 \cdot 4}{30 \cdot 29}$ Ⓓ $\frac{4 \cdot 3}{30 \cdot 29}$

4. A store has two shifts for 1 job position. The employees who work in this position are Adam, Emily, and Will. The same employee cannot work both shifts. Use a table or tree diagram to find which set gives all of the possible employee shift assignments. **SDAP 3.1, MR 2.4**

Ⓐ {AE, AW, EW}

Ⓑ {AA, AE, AW, EE, EW, WW}

Ⓒ {AE, AW, EA, EW, WA, WE}

Ⓓ {AA, AE, AW, EE, EA, EW, WW, WA, WE}

5. You own three animated movies and five action movies. You randomly choose two movies, one after the other, and both are action. Which type of events are your two choices? **SDAP 3.5**

Ⓐ Overlapping Ⓑ Complementary

Ⓒ Dependent Ⓓ Independent

6. You randomly choose a marble from the bag shown. You then put the marble back in the bag and randomly choose another marble. What is the probability that the first marble you choose is yellow and the second marble is orange? **SDAP 3.4**

Ⓐ $\frac{1}{12}$

Ⓑ $\frac{1}{11}$

Ⓒ $\frac{5}{48}$

Ⓓ 12

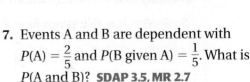

7. Events A and B are dependent with $P(\text{A}) = \frac{2}{5}$ and $P(\text{B given A}) = \frac{1}{5}$. What is $P(\text{A and B})$? **SDAP 3.5, MR 2.7**

Ⓐ $\frac{2}{25}$ Ⓑ $\frac{1}{5}$

Ⓒ $\frac{3}{10}$ Ⓓ $\frac{3}{5}$

8 CHAPTER SUMMARY

Standards
SDAP 3.1, 3.2, 3.3, 3.4, 3.5

BIG IDEAS

For Your Notebook

Big Idea 1 Representing Probabilities of Events

A spinner has six equal parts labeled from 1 to 6. You can find the theoretical probability of spinning each number or you can estimate the probability by performing an experiment.

Results of 50 spins						
Number	1	2	3	4	5	6
Times spun	10	7	8	9	8	8

Probability of spinning an even number	*Predicted times event will occur in 150 spins*
Theoretical $= \frac{\text{favorable outcomes}}{\text{total outcomes}} = \frac{3}{6} = \frac{1}{2}$, or 50%	$0.5 \times 150 = 75$ times
Experimental $= \frac{\text{number of successes}}{\text{number of trials}} = \frac{24}{50} = \frac{12}{25}$, or 48%	$0.48 \times 150 = 72$ times

Big Idea 2 Representing Outcomes

A table or a tree diagram can help you identify and count all of the possible outcomes of a compound event. All possible outcomes for ordering a lunch of either a ham or turkey sandwich along with either lemonade, orange juice, or apple juice are shown below.

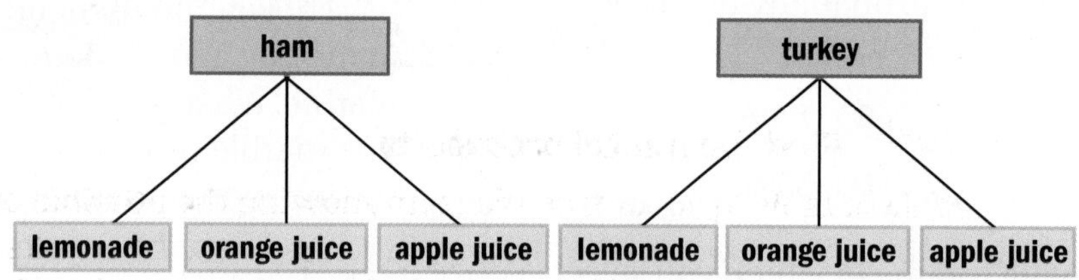

	Lemonade	*Orange Juice*	*Apple Juice*
Ham	ham/ lemonade	ham/ orange juice	ham/ apple juice
Turkey	turkey/ lemonade	turkey/ orange juice	turkey/ apple juice

Big Idea 3 Using Formulas to Find Probabilities of Events

Type of events	*Probability*
Disjoint	$P(\text{A or B}) = P(\text{A}) + P(\text{B})$
Complementary	$P(\text{A}) + P(\text{B}) = 1$, $P(\text{B}) = 1 - P(\text{A})$, $P(\text{A}) = 1 - P(\text{B})$
Independent	$P(\text{A and B}) = P(\text{A}) \cdot P(\text{B})$
Dependent	$P(\text{A and B}) = P(\text{A}) \cdot P(\text{B given A})$

CHAPTER PROBLEM

Standards
SDAP 3.1, 3.2, 3.3, 3.4, 3.5

APPLYING THE **BIG IDEAS**

Big Idea 1
You represent probabilities of events in **Step 3** and **Step 4.**

Big Idea 2
You represent outcomes in **Step 2.**

Big Idea 3
You recognize and find the probability of disjoint, complementary, and independent events in **Exercises 1, 2 and 3.**

PROBLEM What are the probabilities of the outcomes when rolling two number pyramids?

STEP 1 **Make two number pyramids.**

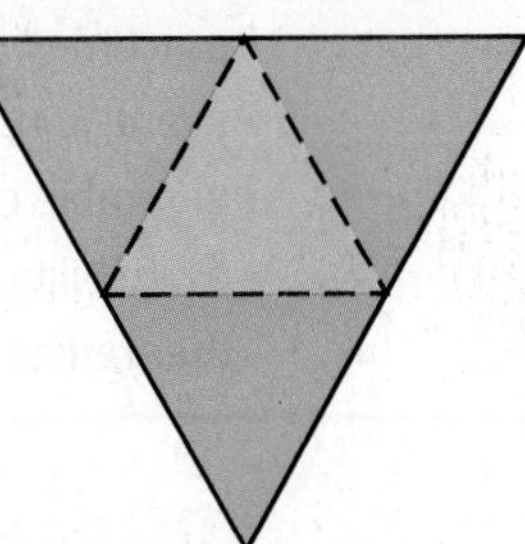

Using heavy paper and tape, make two number pyramids with faces that are the same size and shape. Use the pattern shown to help you.

Number the faces of each number pyramid. Use a different set of four consecutive numbers less than 16 for each number pyramid, such as 1–4 and 10–13.

STEP 2 **List outcomes.**

When rolling a number pyramid, a result is the sum of the numbers that are showing. The table below shows the possible results for one number pyramid numbered 1–4. List all the possible results for rolling each of your two number pyramids.

Number not showing	*Numbers showing*	*Results for one pyramid*
1	2, 3, 4	9
2	1, 3, 4	8
3	1, 2, 4	7
4	1, 2, 3	6

STEP 3 **Find theoretical probability.**

Make a table, grid, or tree diagram showing the possible outcomes when rolling your two number pyramids and adding the results. How many outcomes are there? How many different sums are there? Calculate the theoretical probability of each different outcome.

STEP 4 **Use data to estimate probability.**

Roll the two number pyramids 50 times. Compare your experimental probability of rolling each sum to the theoretical probability.

Extending the Problem

Use the outcomes and theoretical probabilities from Step 3 above.

1. Choose one of the possible outcomes. *Predict* the number of times this outcome will occur in 300 rolls.
2. *Describe* two disjoint events. Calculate the probability that one or the other events occurs.
3. *Describe* two independent events. Calculate the probability that both events occur and that neither do.

8 CHAPTER REVIEW

California @HomeTutor
classzone.com
• Multi-Language Visual Glossary
• Vocabulary practice

REVIEW KEY VOCABULARY

- outcomes, *p. 415*
- event, *p. 415*
- favorable outcomes, *p. 415*
- probability, *p. 415*
- theoretical probability, *p. 422*
- experimental probability, *p. 422*
- disjoint events, *p. 427*
- overlapping events, *p. 427*
- complementary events, *p. 429*
- compound events, *p. 434*
- tree diagram, *p. 434*
- independent events, *p. 441*
- dependent events, *p. 441*

VOCABULARY EXERCISES

Match the definition with a review word from the list above.

1. The possible results of an experiment
2. A specific outcome or collection of outcomes
3. A measure of the likelihood that an event will occur
4. A way to identify and count all possible outcomes
5. **NOTETAKING SKILLS** Make a *Y chart* like the one on page 414 that compares the probabilities of independent events and dependent events.

REVIEW EXAMPLES AND EXERCISES

8.1 Introduction to Probability *pp. 415–419*

SDAP 3.3

EXAMPLE

Each letter in PENNSYLVANIA is written on a separate piece of paper and put into a bag. You randomly choose a piece of paper from the bag. Find the probability of choosing an N. Write it as a fraction, decimal, and percent.

$$P(\text{N}) = \frac{\text{Number of favorable outcomes}}{\text{Total number of outcomes}} = \frac{3}{12} = \frac{1}{4}$$

▸ **Answer** The probability of choosing an N is $\frac{1}{4}$, 0.25, or 25%.

EXERCISES

SEE EXAMPLES 1, 2, AND 3 on pp. 415–416 for Exs. 6–8

You spin the spinner shown, which is divided into equal parts. Write the probability of the given event as a fraction, a decimal, and a percent.

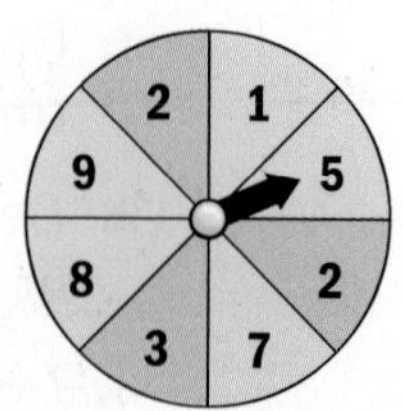

6. Landing on 5
7. Landing on yellow
8. How many spins out of 200 would you expect to land on an even number? Check for reasonableness.

8.2 Experimental Probability

pp. 422–426

SDAP 3.2

EXAMPLE

GROCERIES You select 12 ears of corn at a store. Of these, 8 are two-colored. In a bin of 80 ears, how many ears would you expect to be two-colored?

STEP 1 $P(\text{two-colored}) = \dfrac{\text{Number of successes}}{\text{Total number of trials}}$

$= \dfrac{8}{12} = \dfrac{2}{3}$

STEP 2 Number of ears $= \dfrac{2}{3} \cdot 80$

≈ 53

▶ **Answer** You would expect to find about 53 ears of two-colored corn in the bin.

EXERCISES

SEE EXAMPLES 1 AND 2 on pp. 422–423 for Exs. 9–10

A bag contains orange, purple, and yellow marbles. You randomly choose a marble and then replace it. The table shows the results of several trials.

Marble color	Orange	Purple	Yellow
Times chosen	11	24	15

9. What is the probability that you choose an orange marble?

10. How many times out of 300 trials would you expect to choose a yellow marble?

8.3 Disjoint Events

pp. 427–432

SDAP 3.3, SDAP 3.4

EXAMPLE

BLOOD TYPES The table shows the blood types of donors during a week at a hospital. What is the probability that a randomly selected donor has type O+ or type B+ blood?

Type	O	A	B	AB
+	38%	34%	9%	3%
–	7%	6%	2%	1%

The events are disjoint because a person can have only one blood type.

$P(\text{O+ or B+}) = P(\text{O+}) + P(\text{B+}) = 38\% + 9\% = 47\%$

▶ **Answer** The probability that a donor has type O+ or type B+ blood is 47%.

EXERCISES

SEE EXAMPLES 2 AND 3 on pp. 428–429 for Exs. 11–14

In Exercises 11–13, use the blood-type table above.

11. Find $P(\text{B– or O–})$.

12. Find $P(\text{A– or B–})$.

13. Find $P(\textit{not}\ \text{A–})$.

14. **FLOWERS** At a flower shop, 35% of the tulips are red. The shop needs 140 tulips to fill an order. Estimate how many tulips will *not* be red if the shop owner randomly chooses tulips to fill the order.

8.4 Compound Events

pp. 434–440

SDAP 3.1

EXAMPLE

SCHOOL NEWSPAPER The job openings for your school newspaper are for a reporter and an editor in each of the areas of sports, student government, and student life. Find the total number of job openings at the newspaper.

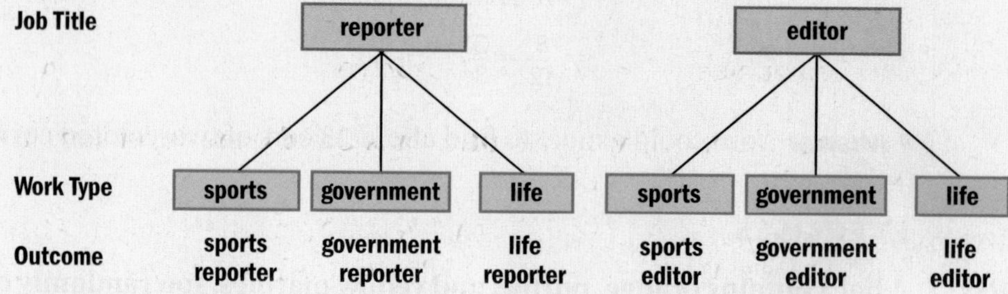

▶ **Answer** There are 6 job openings at the newspaper.

SEE EXAMPLE 3 on p. 436 for Ex. 15

EXERCISES

15. You flip a coin 3 times. Find the probability of landing on tails at least once.

8.5 Independent and Dependent Events

pp. 441–446

SDAP 3.4, SDAP 3.5

EXAMPLE

FRUIT A bowl contains 3 plums and 5 pears. A second bowl contains 2 plums and 4 pears. You randomly choose a piece of fruit from each bowl, and both are plums. Are the events *independent* or *dependent*? What is the probability that both choices are plums?

The choice you make from the first bowl does *not* affect the choice you make from the second bowl, so the events are independent.

$$P(\text{plum and plum}) = \frac{3}{8} \times \frac{2}{6} = \frac{\overset{1}{\cancel{3}} \times \overset{1}{\cancel{2}}}{\underset{4}{\cancel{8}} \times \underset{2}{\cancel{6}}} = \frac{1}{8}$$

▶ **Answer** The probability that both choices are plums is $\frac{1}{8}$, or 12.5%.

EXERCISES

SEE EXAMPLES 1 AND 3 on pp. 441–443 for Ex. 16

16. **WHAT IF?** In the Example above, you randomly choose a piece of fruit from the first bowl, and it is a pear. You replace it, and then randomly choose another pear from the same bowl. Are the events *independent* or *dependent*? What is the probability that both choices are pears?

8 CHAPTER TEST

1. **VOCABULARY** Probability that is based on repeated trials of an experiment is called _?_.

2. **VOCABULARY** Events that have no outcomes in common are _?_.

You have 6 red, 4 blue, and 2 green marbles in a bag. You randomly choose one marble. Write the probability of choosing a marble of the given color as a fraction, a decimal, and a percent. Check for reasonableness.

3. Red
4. *Not* blue
5. Blue or green
6. Red or blue
7. *Not* red
8. Green

Events A and B are independent. Events C and D are dependent. Find *P*(A and B) or *P*(C and D).

9. $P(\text{A}) = 0.2$
   $P(\text{B}) = 0.4$
10. $P(\text{C}) = 0.5$
    $P(\text{D given C}) = 0.2$
11. $P(\text{C}) = 0.3$
    $P(\text{D given C}) = 0.7$

ACTIVITIES The circle graph shows the results of a student survey. Find the probability that a randomly chosen student from those surveyed responded as indicated.

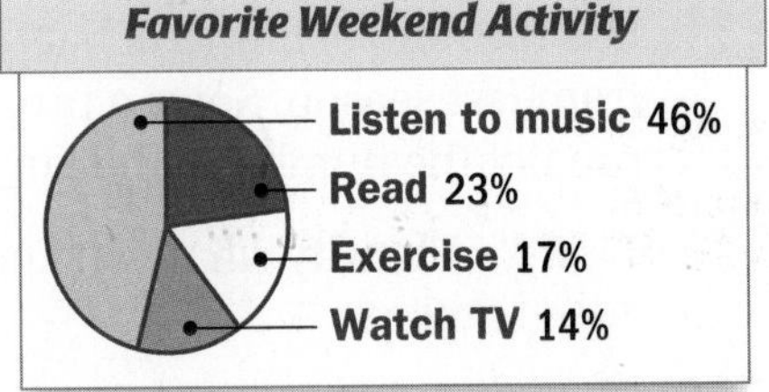

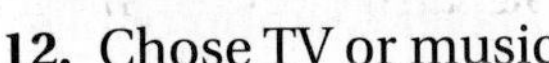

12. Chose TV or music
13. Chose music or reading
14. Did not choose exercise

SURVEYS You asked 60 randomly chosen classmates to name their favorite type of juice. Of the students surveyed, 42 chose orange juice.

15. What is the probability that a student did *not* choose orange juice as their favorite type of drink?

16. Predict how many randomly chosen classmates out of 210 would *not* choose orange juice.

You randomly choose a tile from a bag containing 7 green, 10 red, and 8 blue tiles. Then you randomly choose a second tile from the bag without replacing the first tile.

17. Are the events "choose a green tile first" and "choose a blue tile second" *independent* or *dependent*?

18. What is the probability of choosing a green tile first and a blue tile second? *Justify* your answer.

19. A spinner is divided into 3 equal parts labeled A, B, and C. You spin the spinner 3 times. Make a tree diagram to list all of the possible outcomes. What is the probability of landing on C at least twice?

8 ◆ MULTIPLE CHOICE STRATEGIES

STRATEGIES YOU'LL USE:
- **SOLVE DIRECTLY**
- **ELIMINATE CHOICES**

Standards
SDAP 3.2, 3.3

If you have trouble solving a multiple choice problem directly, you may be able to use another approach to eliminate incorrect answer choices.

PROBLEM 1

The table at the right shows the batting statistics of two baseball players at the end of last season. Suppose each player gets 600 at bats next season. *Predict* the number of hits Player A will have.

	At Bats	Hits
Player A	410	123
Player B	500	180

Ⓐ 110 Ⓑ 120 Ⓒ 180 Ⓓ 350

Strategy 1 SOLVE DIRECTLY

Use the ratio of hits to at bats (batting average) from last season. Solve a proportion to predict the number of hits next season.

STEP 1 **Identify** what you know about player A.

$$\frac{\text{Hits last season}}{\text{At bats last season}} = \frac{123}{410}$$

At bats next season = 600

STEP 2 **Write** a proportion using what you know about Player A. Let x represent the number of hits next season.

$$\frac{\text{Hits last season}}{\text{At bats last season}} = \frac{\text{Hits next season}}{\text{At bats next season}}$$

$$\frac{123}{410} = \frac{x}{600}$$

STEP 3 **Solve** the proportion.

$$\frac{123}{410} = \frac{x}{600}$$

$$410x = 73{,}800$$

$$x = 180$$

Player A should have about 180 hits next season.

The correct answer is C. Ⓐ Ⓑ Ⓒ Ⓓ

Strategy 2 ELIMINATE CHOICES

You can often use estimation to identify incorrect answer choices.

Because Player A had 123 hits out of 410 at bats, Player A's ratio of hits to at bats (batting average) is $\frac{123}{410}$, which is slightly greater than $\frac{1}{4}$.

Check each answer choice to see which batting average is slightly greater than $\frac{1}{4}$.

Choice A: Because $\frac{110}{600} \approx \frac{1}{6}$, and $\frac{1}{6} < \frac{1}{4}$, choice A can be eliminated. ✗

Choice B: Because $\frac{120}{600} = \frac{1}{5}$, and $\frac{1}{5} < \frac{1}{4}$, choice B can be eliminated. ✗

Choice C: Because $\frac{180}{600} = \frac{3}{10}$, and $\frac{3}{10} > \frac{1}{4}$, choice C is a possibility.

Choice D: Because $\frac{350}{600} > \frac{1}{2}$, which is much greater than $\frac{1}{4}$, choice D can be eliminated. ✗

The correct answer is C. Ⓐ Ⓑ Ⓒ Ⓓ

PROBLEM 2

The table shows the number of marbles of each color that are in a jar. You choose a marble at random. What is the probability that the marble is red?

Color	Blue	Green	Red	Yellow	Total
Number of marbles	1	4	5	15	25

Ⓐ 20% Ⓑ 25% Ⓒ 60% Ⓓ 80%

Strategy 1 SOLVE DIRECTLY

STEP 1 **Identify** the number of red marbles and the total number of marbles. There are 25 marbles. Five are red.

STEP 2 **Find** the probability of choosing a red marble.

$$P(\text{red}) = \frac{\text{Number of red marbles}}{\text{Total number of marbles}}$$
$$= \frac{5}{25}$$
$$= \frac{1}{5}$$
$$= 0.2$$

The probability of choosing a red marble is 0.2, or 20%.

The correct answer is A. Ⓐ Ⓑ Ⓒ Ⓓ

Strategy 2 ELIMINATE CHOICES

You can often use reasoning to identify incorrect answer choices.

A jar contains 5 red marbles, which is less than half of the total 25 marbles. So, the probability of choosing a red marble is less than 50%. You can eliminate choices C and D. ✗

To find 25% of 25, you need to find the product $0.25 \times 25 = 6.25$. You cannot choose one quarter of a marble, so you can eliminate choice B. ✗

The correct answer is A. Ⓐ Ⓑ Ⓒ Ⓓ

STRATEGY PRACTICE

Explain why you can eliminate the highlighted answer choice.

1. You can win a prize listed inside the bottle cap of a sports drink. The probability that you win a prize is $\frac{1}{12}$. What is the probability that you do *not* win a prize?

   Ⓐ $\frac{1}{12}$ Ⓑ $\frac{1}{2}$ Ⓒ $\frac{11}{12}$ Ⓓ ✗ **1**

2. You roll two number cubes. What is the probability of rolling two 5s?

   Ⓐ 0 Ⓑ $\frac{1}{36}$ Ⓒ $\frac{1}{12}$ Ⓓ ✗ $\mathbf{\frac{1}{3}}$

8 ◆ MULTIPLE CHOICE PRACTICE

1. The circle graph below shows the portion of new cars of each color in the Unites States.

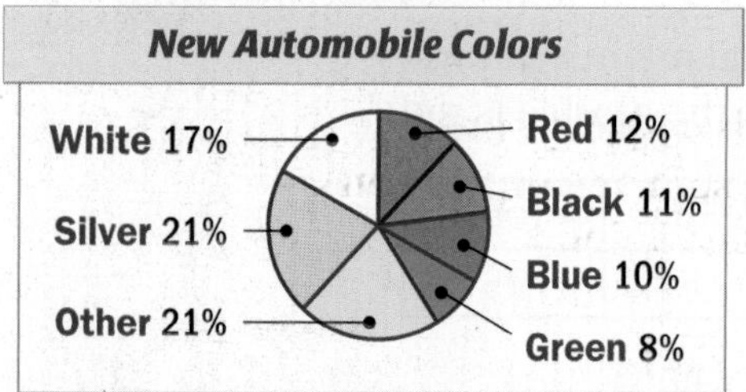

Out of 200 randomly choosen new cars, how many would you expect to be blue or black? **SDAP 3.2**

Ⓐ 2

Ⓑ 42

Ⓒ 110

Ⓓ 158

2. The types of disposable cameras a store sells are shown in the tree diagram. A coupon for a camera is given to 20% of randomly chosen customers. Coupons for each type of camera are equally likely.

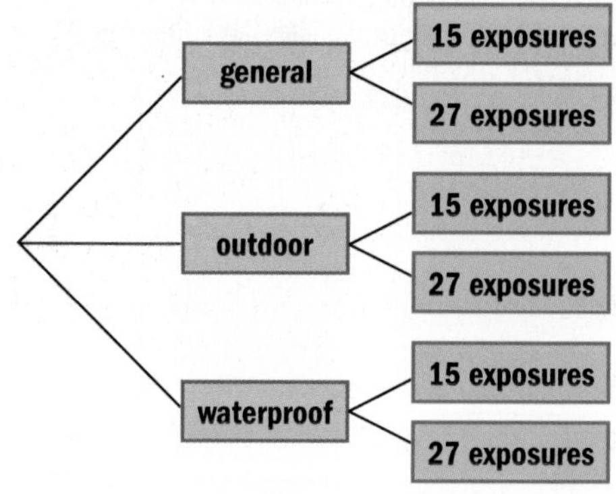

What is the probability a customer receives a coupon for a 27-exposure waterproof camera? **SDAP 3.4, MR 2.4**

Ⓐ $\frac{1}{30}$

Ⓑ $\frac{1}{6}$

Ⓒ $\frac{11}{30}$

Ⓓ $\frac{5}{6}$

3. At your school, 43% of the students play a sport. What is the probability that a randomly selected student does *not* play a sport? **SDAP 3.3**

Ⓐ 0.42

Ⓑ 0.43

Ⓒ 0.57

Ⓓ 0.67

4. You want to remodel your kitchen by painting the walls, replacing the countertop, and replacing the floor tiles. Your color choices for each item are given in the table.

Item	*Available colors*
Walls	white, tan, blue
Countertops	white, green, blue, gray, tan
Floor tiles	white, tan

Suppose you choose the color of each item at random. What is the probability that all three items are the same color? **SDAP 3.1**

Ⓐ $\frac{1}{30}$

Ⓑ $\frac{1}{15}$

Ⓒ $\frac{1}{7}$

Ⓓ $\frac{3}{10}$

5. You randomly choose the answers for 3 True/False questions. Which set shows all the possibles choices? **SDAP 3.1**

Ⓐ {TTT, FFF, TFT, TFF, FFT}

Ⓑ {TTF, TFT, TFF, FTT, FTT, FTF, FFT}

Ⓒ {TTT, FFF, TFF, FTT, FTF, FFT}

Ⓓ {TTT, TTF, TFT, TFF, FTT, FTF, FFT, FFF}

6. A bag contains 12 red tiles, 4 blue tiles, and 6 green tiles. Which of the following statements describes two independent events? **SDAP 3.5, MR 2.5**

Ⓐ Draw one green tile, set it aside, and then draw a second green tile.

Ⓑ Draw one red tile, put it back in the bag, and then draw a blue tile.

Ⓒ Draw one green tile and then draw one blue tile, without replacing the first.

Ⓓ Draw one red tile and then draw one green tile, without replacing the first.

7. A jar contains 3 red and 6 green marbles. Another jar contains 2 red and 3 blue marbles. You randomly choose a marble from each jar. What is the probability that both marbles are red? **SDAP 3.4**

Ⓐ $\frac{1}{45}$

Ⓑ $\frac{2}{15}$

Ⓒ $\frac{5}{14}$

Ⓓ $\frac{11}{15}$

8. The spinners below are divided into equal parts. You spin each spinner once.

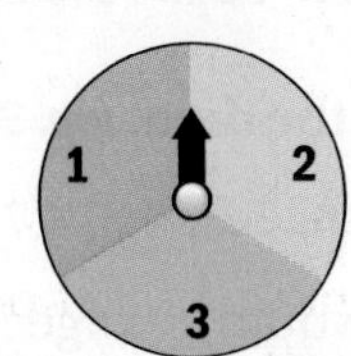

What is the probability that the sum of the results is an even number? **SDAP 3.1**

Ⓐ $\frac{2}{5}$

Ⓑ $\frac{7}{15}$

Ⓒ $\frac{8}{15}$

Ⓓ $\frac{3}{5}$

9. You spin the spinner at the right twice. It is divided into 10 equal parts. What is the probability that the pointer lands on yellow on your first spin and on blue on your second spin? **SDAP 3.5, MR 1.1**

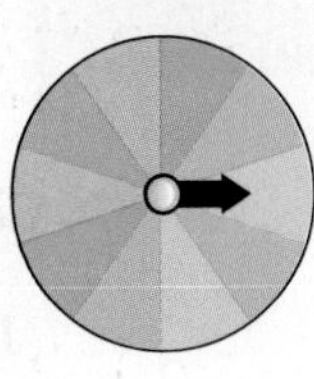

Ⓐ $\frac{1}{25}$

Ⓑ $\frac{1}{20}$

Ⓒ $\frac{3}{50}$

Ⓓ $\frac{2}{5}$

10. The table below shows the number and types of pitches thrown by a pitcher out of 200 pitches. What is the probability that the next pitch thrown will be a knuckleball? **SDAP 3.2**

Change up	*Curveball*	*Knuckleball*
54	56	90

Ⓐ 33%

Ⓑ 45%

Ⓒ 55%

Ⓓ 82%

11. A bag contains 3 red, 6 blue, and 9 green marbles. What is the probability of randomly choosing a red marble? **SDAP 3.3**

Ⓐ $\frac{1}{6}$

Ⓑ $\frac{1}{5}$

Ⓒ $\frac{1}{3}$

Ⓓ $\frac{1}{2}$

8 CUMULATIVE REVIEW Chapters 1–8

Compare the fractions, mixed numbers, and decimals. Use <, >, or =. *(p. 40)*

1. $5\frac{1}{8} \underline{?} \frac{47}{9}$ **2.** $7\frac{3}{16} \underline{?} \frac{65}{8}$ **3.** $0.75 \underline{?} \frac{7}{8}$ **4.** $0.62 \underline{?} \frac{3}{5}$

Evaluate the expression. Simplify if possible.

5. $\frac{8}{9} + \frac{1}{2}$ *(p. 69)* **6.** $\frac{11}{12} - \frac{1}{4}$ *(p. 69)* **7.** $8\frac{4}{7} - 4\frac{1}{3}$ *(p. 81)* **8.** $9\frac{4}{5} + 2\frac{7}{8}$ *(p. 81)*

9. $\frac{9}{10} \times \frac{2}{7}$ *(p. 88)* **10.** $7\frac{1}{6} \times 3\frac{3}{8}$ *(p. 88)* **11.** $6\frac{3}{4} \div \frac{5}{8}$ *(p. 95)* **12.** $\frac{7}{10} \div \frac{1}{5}$ *(p. 95)*

Evaluate the expression.

13. $54 + (-5)$ *(p. 135)* **14.** $-12 - (-3)$ *(p. 143)* **15.** $-17 - 3$ *(p. 143)*

16. $6 \cdot (-15)$ *(p. 148)* **17.** $-4 \cdot (-32)$ *(p. 148)* **18.** $-76 \div (-4)$ *(p. 154)*

Convert the temperatures to degrees Celsius or degrees Farenheit. *(p. 212)*

19. 40°C **20.** 30°C **21.** 14°F **22.** 58°F

Solve the equation. *(p. 219)*

23. $x - 2 = 8$ **24.** $3s = 42$ **25.** $\frac{y}{8} = 32$ **26.** $t + 32 = 56$

Solve the proportion. *(p. 274)*

27. $\frac{x}{2} = \frac{8}{32}$ **28.** $\frac{5}{s} = \frac{75}{3}$ **29.** $\frac{y}{8} = \frac{32}{2}$ **30.** $\frac{30}{2} = \frac{t}{6}$

Use the percent equation or a proportion to solve. *(pp. 306, 319)*

31. 2 is 8% of what number? **32.** What number is 1% of 44?

33. 51 is what percent of 60? **34.** 39 is 75% of what number?

Find the mean, median, mode(s), and range of the data. *(pp. 364, 372)*

35. 0, 1, 2, 4, 4, 5, 7, 8, 10, 12, 13 **36.** 5.5, 6.3, 4.7, 4.6, 4.6, 7.1, 6.3, 7.4, 6, 7.5

37. *Explain* how the mean, median, and mode would change if the number 24 were added to the data in Exercise 35.

Find the median, quartiles, range, and interquartile range of the data. *(p. 372)*

38. Ages of siblings: 5, 9, 16, 8, 6, 15, 14, 15, 5, 15, 12

39. Heights of trees (in feet): 10, 17, 23, 14, 56, 43, 32, 34, 51, 35

A bag contains 8 blue marbles, 7 red marbles, and 5 green marbles. You randomly choose a marble from the bag. Find the probability of choosing a marble of the given color. *(pp. 415, 427)*

40. Red **41.** Green **42.** Blue or Green **43.** Green or Red

Events A and B are complementary events. Find $P(A)$. ***(p. 427)***

44. $P(not\ A) = 0.57$ **45.** $P(not\ A) = 0.38$ **46.** $P(not\ A) = 26\%$

47. $P(not\ A) = 91\%$ **48.** $P(not\ A) = \frac{7}{10}$ **49.** $P(not\ A) = \frac{6}{25}$

Events A and B are independent events. Find $P(A \text{ and } B)$. ***(p. 441)***

50. $P(A) = 0.4; P(B) = 0.6$ **51.** $P(A) = 0.5; P(B) = 0.3$

52. $P(A) = \frac{1}{5}; P(B) = \frac{2}{3}$ **53.** $P(A) = \frac{1}{3}; P(B) = \frac{3}{8}$

The table at the right lists the box sizes and prices for two brands of cereal. ***(p. 107)***

Brand	A		B	
Size	10 oz.	14 oz.	12 oz.	16 oz.
Price	$2.79	$3.29	$2.99	$3.59

54. Which brand and size is the best buy?

55. Which brand and size is the worst buy?

56. DINING You and your family are eating at a restaurant. The food bill is $40. Your family chooses to leave a 20% tip before tax. The sales tax is 6%. What is the total cost of the meal? ***(p. 325)***

SURVEYS You want to know if students in your school are in favor of creating a new hockey team. Identify the sampling method. Tell whether the sample is likely to be biased. ***(pp. 354, 359)***

57. Survey five students randomly chosen from each homeroom.

58. Survey every fifth student entering the cafeteria during lunch.

59. Survey all students on any sports team.

TELEPHONE CALLS A recent survey asked 100 students how many telephone calls they made the day before. The results are shown in the histogram. ***(p. 379)***

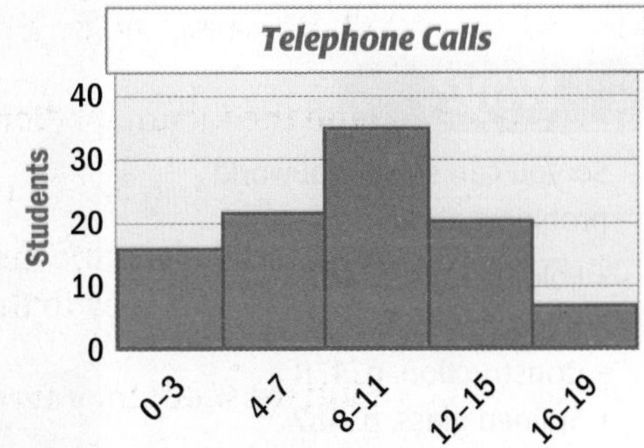

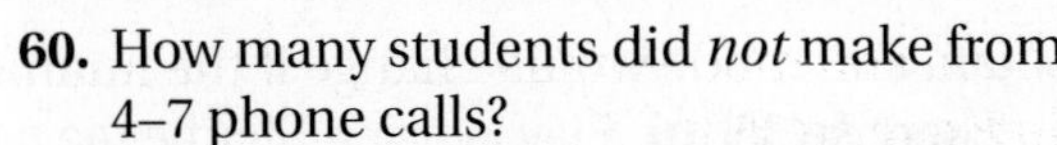
60. How many students did *not* make from 4–7 phone calls?

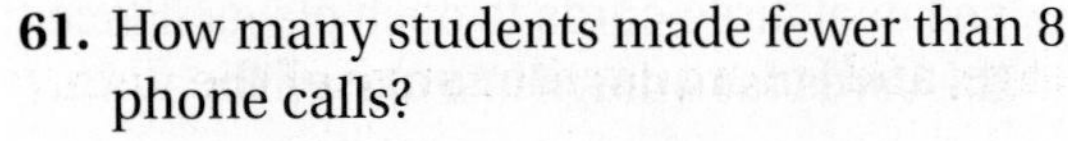
61. How many students made fewer than 8 phone calls?

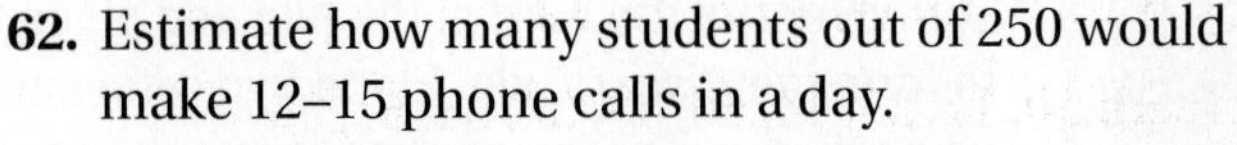
62. Estimate how many students out of 250 would make 12–15 phone calls in a day.

63. BREAKFAST The results of a survey that asked students to choose their favorite breakfast are shown. Display the results in a circle graph. ***(p. 387)***

Food	Eggs	Cold cereal	Pancakes	French toast	Other
Students	27.5%	45%	15%	7.5%	5%

9 Geometric Figures

Before

In previous chapters, you learned the following skills, which you'll use in Chapter 9:

- Performing operations with whole numbers and decimals
- Solving equations
- Solving proportions

Now

In Chapter 9 you'll study these **Big Ideas:**

1. Identifying and using special angle relationships
2. Drawing triangles and quadrilaterals from given information
3. Using ratios and proportions with similar polygons

Why?

So you can solve real-world problems about . . .

- Folding fans, p. 467
- Kites, p. 467
- Construction, p. 478
- Stained glass, p. 487
- Photo stickers, p. 493

California Standards

Review using ratios. ***Gr. 6 NS 1.2***

Prepare for using proportions in similar polygons. ***Gr. 6 NS 1.3***

Materials

- One deck of ratio cards
- One deck of number cards

Ratio Cards $\frac{1}{4}$ $\frac{4}{5}$ $\frac{5}{6}$ $\frac{2}{3}$ $\frac{1}{2}$

Number Cards 8

How to Play Play in pairs. Shuffle the number cards and deal three cards to each player. Place the rest of the cards face down in a *draw* pile.

Turn over the top card in the pile and place it face up to form the *discard* pile. Place five ratio cards face up so that you and your opponent can both see them.

Players should take turns following the steps on the next page.

California Standards

- **Gr. 6 NS 1.2 Interpret and use ratios in different contexts** (e.g., batting averages, miles per hour) **to show the relative sizes of two quantities,** using appropriate notations (a/b, a to b, a:b). ***(Lesson 9.5)***
- **Gr. 6 MG 2.2 Use the properties of complementary and supplementary angles and the sum of the angles of a triangle to solve problems involving an unknown angle.** ***(Lessons 9.1, 9.2, 9.3)***

1 Draw the top card from either the draw pile or the discard pile.

2 Decide whether you can use two of your cards to form a ratio that is equivalent to one of the displayed ratios. If you can, then place that ratio card and your pair of number cards face up in front of you.

3 Finish your turn by either drawing a card or discarding a card, so that you have exactly three number cards in your hand again.

Games Wrap-Up

How To Win Be the first player to collect three ratio cards.

Draw Conclusions

Complete these exercises after playing the game.

1. **WRITING** *Explain* how you decided which cards to discard at the end of your turn in *Rapid Ratios.*
2. **REASONING** Based on the number cards you saw as you played *Rapid Ratios*, which ratio do you think is easier to form, $\frac{8}{9}$ or $\frac{1}{2}$? *Explain* your reasoning.

9 Getting Ready

Prerequisite Skills

California @HomeTutor
Prerequisite skills practice at classzone.com

REVIEW VOCABULARY

- **angle,** *p. 387*
- **vertex,** *p. 387*
- **degrees,** *p. 387*
- **ray,** *p. 683*
- **square,** *p. 684*
- **rectangle,** *p. 684*

VOCABULARY CHECK

Copy and complete using a review term from the list at the left.

1. A rectangle with all four sides the same length is a(n) _?_.
2. A part of a line that begins at a point and extends in one direction without end is a(n) _?_.
3. A(n) _?_ consists of two rays that begin at a common point, called the _?_.

SKILL CHECK

Solve the equation. *(p. 226)*

4. $x + 6 = 8$
5. $x - 2 = 7$
6. $29 = 17 + x$
7. $5 + x = 13$

Solve the proportion using cross products. *(p. 274)*

8. $\frac{3}{a} = \frac{4}{9}$
9. $\frac{2}{3} = \frac{9}{m}$
10. $\frac{6}{21} = \frac{p}{35}$
11. $\frac{b}{55} = \frac{12}{15}$

Use a protractor to draw an angle with the given measure. *(p. 385)*

12. 45°
13. 135°
14. 155°
15. 75°

Notetaking Skills

NOW YOU TRY
Make an *examples and non-examples chart* for *proportions.* Include units in your proportions.

Focus on Graphic Organizers

Use an *examples and non-examples chart* to organize details about a vocabulary word, such as *equation.*

EQUATION	
EXAMPLES	NON-EXAMPLES
$2 + 2 = 4$	$3x$
$2x = 8$	$2 \geq 4$
$1 - x = 9$	$3 + x$
$x = 8$	$2 - 1$

9.1 Angles

Math and DESIGN
Ex. 44, p. 467

Standards **MG 2.1 Identify angles as** vertical, adjacent, **complementary, or supplementary and provide descriptions of these terms.**

MG 2.2 Use the properties of complementary and supplementary angles and the sum of the angles of a triangle **to solve problems involving an unknown angle.**

Connect ***Before*** you found angle measures to make circle graphs. ***Now*** you will classify angles as complementary or supplementary and apply their properties.

KEY VOCABULARY
- **acute angle**
- **right angle**
- **obtuse angle**
- **straight angle**
- **complementary**
- **supplementary**

GYMNASTICS The gymnast's arm makes a *right angle* with his body as he performs on the rings. A right angle has a measure of 90°.

Angles are classified by their measures. The notation $\angle A$ is read "angle *A*," and the notation $m\angle A$ is read "the measure of angle *A*."

KEY CONCEPT — *For Your Notebook*

Classifying Angles

An **acute angle** is an angle whose measure is less than 90°.

A **right angle** is an angle whose measure is exactly 90°.

Indicates a right angle

An **obtuse angle** is an angle whose measure is between 90° and 180°.

A **straight angle** is an angle whose measure is exactly 180°.

EXAMPLE 1 Classifying an Angle

Estimate the angle measure to classify the angle as *acute, right, obtuse,* or *straight*.

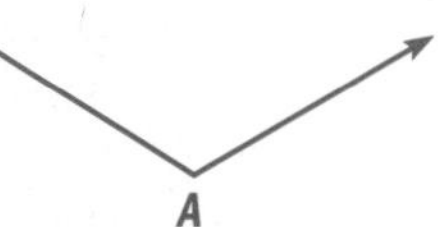

The angle measure of a corner of a piece of paper is 90°. Because $m\angle A$ is greater than the angle measure of a corner of a piece of paper, $\angle A$ is obtuse.

Animated Math
For an interactive example of classifying angles go to **classzone.com**.

ANGLE PAIRS Two angles are **complementary** if the sum of their measures is 90°. Two angles are **supplementary** if the sum of their measures is 180°.

EXAMPLE 2 Complementary and Supplementary Angles

READING MATH
The angle below can be named in several ways: $\angle ABC$, $\angle CBA$, $\angle B$, $\angle 1$.

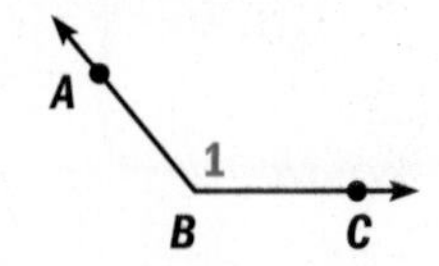

The vertex label must be the middle or only letter used in the name.

Tell whether the angles are *complementary*, *supplementary*, or *neither*.

a.

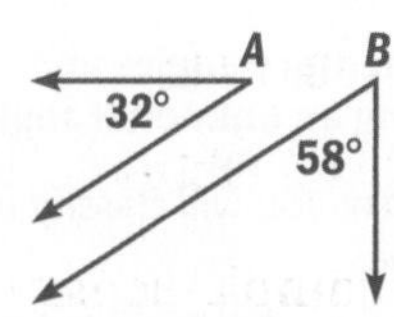

b.

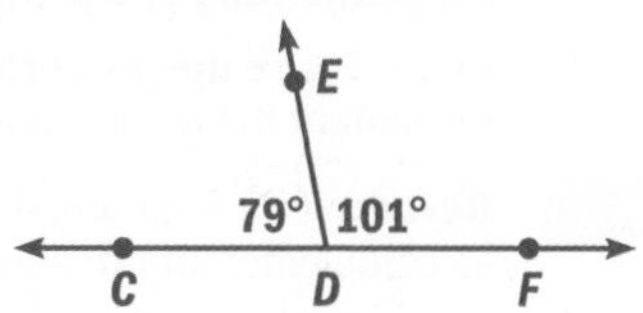

SOLUTION

a. $32° + 58° = 90°$ $\angle A$ and $\angle B$ are complementary.

b. $79° + 101° = 180°$ $\angle CDE$ and $\angle EDF$ are supplementary.

✓ GUIDED PRACTICE for Examples 1 and 2

Classify the angle as *acute, right, obtuse,* or *straight.* Then tell whether the angle and $\angle E$, where $m\angle E = 62°$, are *complementary, supplementary,* or *neither.*

1. $m\angle A = 90°$ **2.** $m\angle B = 118°$ **3.** $m\angle C = 180°$ **4.** $m\angle D = 28°$

EXAMPLE 3 ◆ Multiple Choice Practice

For the lounge chair at the right, $\angle 1$ and $\angle 2$ are supplementary. If $m\angle 1$ is 130°, what is $m\angle 2$?

Ⓐ 40° Ⓑ 50°

Ⓒ 130° Ⓓ 180°

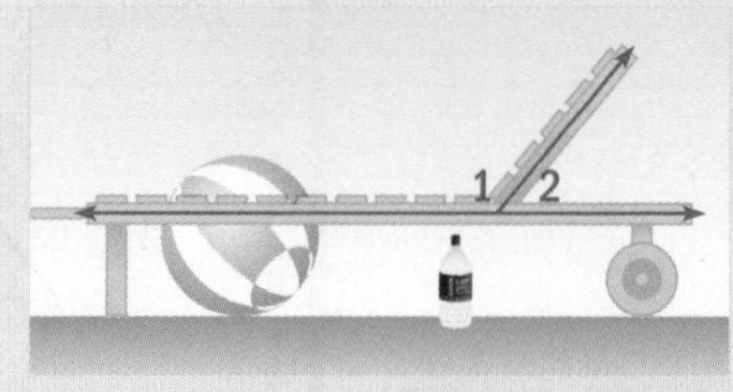

SOLUTION

$m\angle 1 + m\angle 2 = 180°$ **Definition of supplementary angles**

$130° + m\angle 2 = 180°$ **Substitute 130° for $m\angle 1$.**

$m\angle 2 = 50°$ **Subtract 130° from each side.**

▶ **Answer** The measure of $\angle 2$ is 50°. The correct answer is B. Ⓐ Ⓑ Ⓒ Ⓓ

✓ GUIDED PRACTICE for Example 3

5. $\angle D$ and $\angle E$ are supplementary, and $m\angle D = 84°$. Find $m\angle E$.

6. $\angle R$ and $\angle S$ are complementary, and $m\angle S = 9°$. Find $m\angle R$.

9.1 EXERCISES

HOMEWORK KEY
◆ = **MULTIPLE CHOICE PRACTICE** Exs. 10, 24, 43, 52–54
○ = **HINTS AND HOMEWORK HELP** for Exs. 11, 15, 45 at classzone.com

VOCABULARY **Match the angle measure with its classification.**

1. 78° **2.** 90° **3.** 168° **4.** 180°

A. Right **B.** Straight **C.** Obtuse **D.** Acute

5. WRITING *Explain* the difference between complementary and supplementary angles.

SEE EXAMPLE 1 on p. 463 for Exs. 6–10

CLASSIFYING ANGLES **Classify the angle as *acute, right, obtuse,* or *straight.***

6.

7.
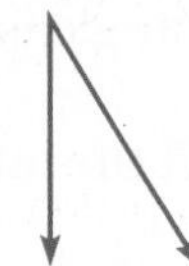

8.
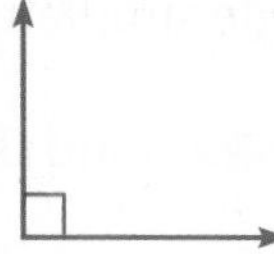

9.
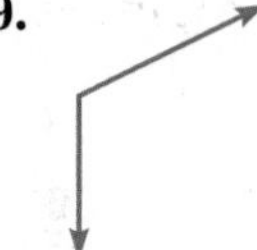

10. ◆ **MULTIPLE CHOICE** What type of angle is $\angle RST$ if $m\angle RST = 56°$?

Ⓐ Acute Ⓑ Right Ⓒ Obtuse Ⓓ Straight

SEE EXAMPLE 2 on p. 464 for Exs. 11–13

COMPLEMENTARY AND SUPPLEMENTARY ANGLES **Tell whether the angles are *complementary, supplementary,* or *neither*. *Explain* your reasoning.**

(11.)
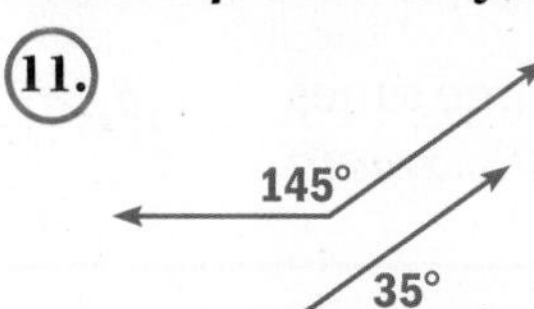

12.
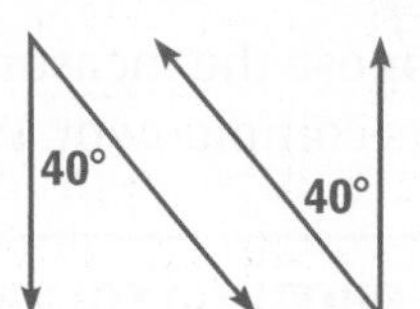

13.
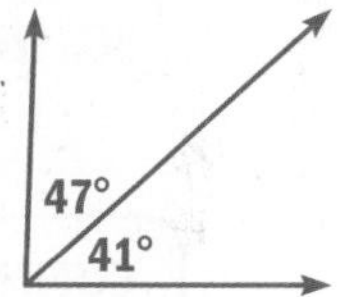

Animated Math at classzone.com

SEE EXAMPLE 3 on p. 464 for Exs. 14–23

FINDING ANGLE MEASURES **For the given angle measure, find the measure of a supplementary angle and the measure of a complementary angle, if possible.**

14. 19° **(15.)** 73° **16.** 122° **17.** 90°

18. 22° **19.** 162° **20.** 180° **21.** 3°

ERROR ANALYSIS ***Describe*** **and correct the error made in finding the unknown angle measure.**

22. $\angle A$ and $\angle B$ are supplementary angles, and $m\angle A = 70°$.

✗
$m\angle A + m\angle B = 360°$
$70° + m\angle B = 360°$
$m\angle B = 290°$

23. $\angle A$ and $\angle B$ are complementary angles, $m\angle B = 56°$.

✗
$m\angle A + m\angle B = 180°$
$m\angle A + 56° = 180°$
$m\angle A = 124°$

SEE EXAMPLE 3
on p. 464
for Ex. 24

24. ◆ **MULTIPLE CHOICE** $\angle C$ and $\angle D$ are supplementary angles, and $m\angle C = 26°$. What is $m\angle D$?

Ⓐ 64° Ⓑ 116° Ⓒ 154° Ⓓ 180°

INTERPRETING A DIAGRAM **In Exercises 25–28, refer to the diagram at the right.**

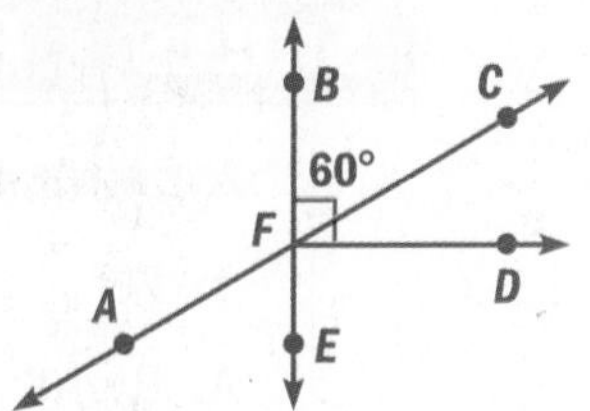

25. Find $m\angle CFD$. **26.** Find $m\angle AFB$.

27. Find $m\angle AFE$. **28.** Find $m\angle AFD$.

REASONING **Copy and complete the statement using *always, sometimes,* or *never*. *Justify* your reasoning.**

29. An angle complementary to an acute angle is __?__ acute.

30. An angle supplementary to an acute angle is __?__ acute.

31. An angle supplementary to a right angle is __?__ a right angle.

ALGEBRA **Find the measures of all the labeled angles.**

32.

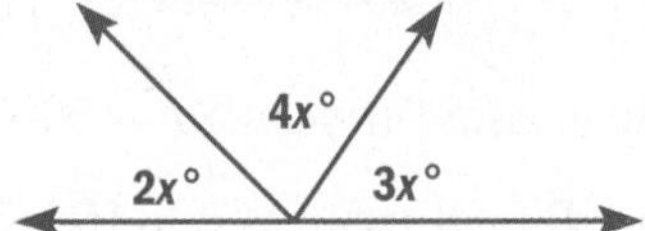

33.

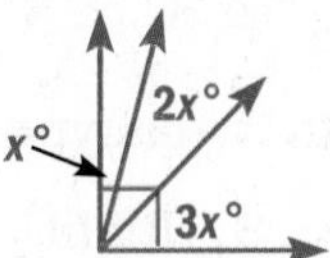

34.

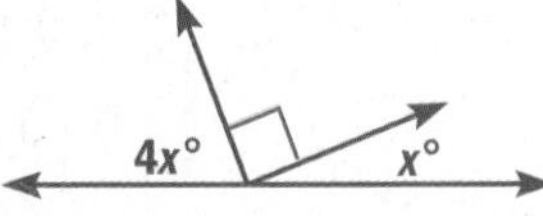

ALGEBRA **Write an expression for the angle measure.**

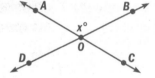

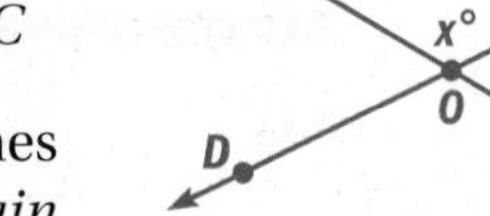

35. $m\angle BOC$ **36.** $m\angle AOD$ **37.** $m\angle DOC$

38. **REASONING** Suppose the measure of $\angle RST$ is three times the measure of its complement. What is $m\angle RST$? *Explain.*

CONNECT SKILLS TO PROBLEM SOLVING **Exercises 39–42 will help you prepare for problem solving.**

Use the diagram of a book resting on a bookshelf.

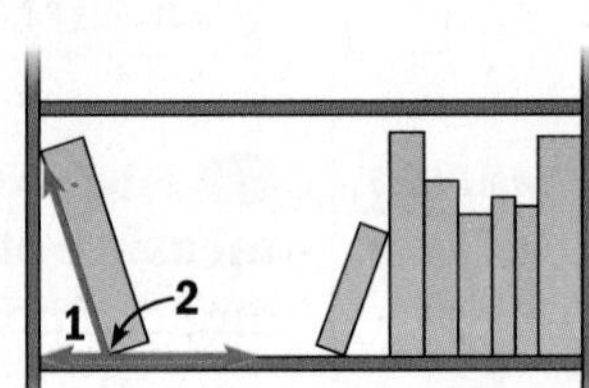

39. Classify $\angle 2$ as *acute, right, obtuse,* or *straight*.

40. Tell whether $\angle 1$ and $\angle 2$ are *complementary, supplementary,* or *neither*.

41. What is $m\angle 1 + m\angle 2$?

42. Write an equation that can be used to find $m\angle 2$, given $m\angle 1 = 72°$.

SEE EXAMPLE 3
on p. 464
for Ex. 43

43. ◆ **MULTIPLE CHOICE** Angles 1 and 2, on the roof support at the right, are complementary. The measure of $\angle 1$ is 50°. What is the measure of $\angle 2$?

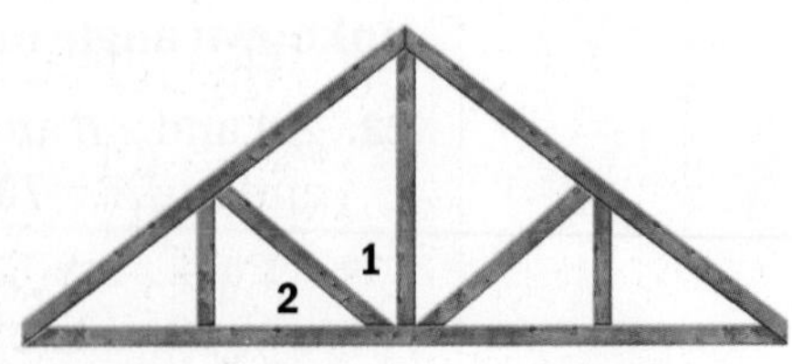

Ⓐ 40° Ⓑ 50°

Ⓒ 130° Ⓓ 140°

California @HomeTutor for problem solving help at classzone.com

SEE EXAMPLE 3
on p. 464
for Exs. 44–45

44. FOLDING FAN Many believe that the first folding fan was designed in Japan and introduced to China in the 9th century. A folding fan forms a straight angle when fully opened. If a fan is opened to a 138° angle, how many more degrees of unfolding does it need to be fully opened?

California @HomeTutor for problem solving help at classzone.com

45. HOCKEY STICK The *lie* is the angle the blade of a hockey stick makes with the shaft. The diagram shows a stick with a lie of 135°. Find the value of x.

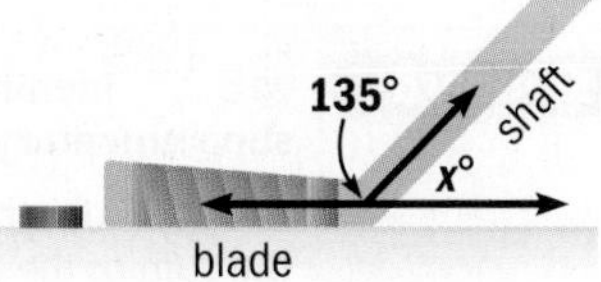

46. SHORT RESPONSE Which has a greater measure, an angle complementary to an angle measuring 15° or an angle supplementary to an angle measuring 125°? *Explain.*

47. KITES The line of a kite is tied to the ground as shown. Name the two supplementary angles. Then find $m\angle LMK$.

48. ERROR ANALYSIS John said that $m\angle M = 75°$ in the diagram at the right. What is wrong with this statement?

49. REASONING Make a table with three columns. Use the headings "$m\angle A$," "Complement of $\angle A$," and "Supplement of $\angle A$." Complete the table for five acute angles A. *Describe* the relationship between the measures of the complement and supplement of each acute angle A.

50. CHALLENGE $\angle DCG$ is a straight angle. $\angle ECF$ is a right angle and $m\angle DCE = 40.7°$. What are the possible measures of $\angle FCG$?

51. CHALLENGE Draw five points A, B, C, D, and E such that the following statements are true. What type of angle is $\angle DBA$?

- $\angle DBE$ is a straight angle.
- $\angle DBC$ is a right angle.
- $\angle ABE$ is an obtuse angle.

◆ CALIFORNIA STANDARDS SPIRAL REVIEW

NS 2.3 **52.** What is the value of $665 \div (-19)$? *(p. 154)*

Ⓐ −35 Ⓑ −0.03 Ⓒ 0.03 Ⓓ 35

AF 2.1 **53.** What is 15°C in degrees Fahrenheit? *(p. 212)*

Ⓐ −9°F Ⓑ 35°F Ⓒ 47°F Ⓓ 59°F

NS 1.4 **54.** You deposit \$200 into a new savings account that earns 4.2% simple annual interest. If you make no deposits or withdrawals, which amount is closest to your balance after 10 months? *(p. 331)*

Ⓐ \$207 Ⓑ \$221 Ⓒ \$270 Ⓓ \$284

9.2 Special Pairs of Angles

Standards **MG 2.1 Identify angles as vertical, adjacent,** complementary, **or supplementary and provide descriptions of these terms.**

MG 2.2 Use the properties of complementary and **supplementary angles** and the sum of the angles of a triangle **to solve problems involving an unknown angle.**

Connect ***Before*** you classified angles according to their measures. ***Now*** you will identify special pairs of angles and lines.

Math and **MAP READING** Example 3, p. 470

KEY VOCABULARY

- **adjacent angles**
- **vertical angles**
- **congruent angles**
- **plane**
- **intersecting lines, parallel lines, perpendicular lines**
- **corresponding angles**

ACTIVITY

You can find angle relationships when lines meet.

STEP 1 **Draw** and label $\overleftrightarrow{AB}$, the line containing points A and B, using a ruler. Then draw $\overleftrightarrow{CD}$ so it meets $\overleftrightarrow{AB}$ as shown.

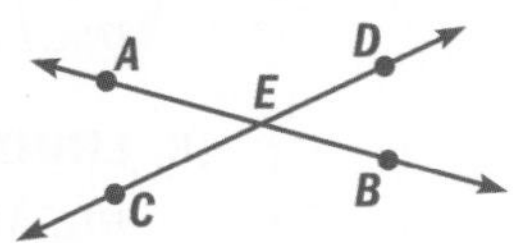

STEP 2 **Measure** each angle to the nearest degree using a protractor. Record the results.

STEP 3 **Make** a conclusion about the angles that are opposite each other.

STEP 4 **Draw** and label another pair of lines. Then repeat Step 2. Is your conclusion from Step 3 still true?

Two angles on a flat surface that share a common side and a vertex and do not overlap are called **adjacent angles**. When two lines meet at a point, as in the activity, adjacent angles are supplementary.

EXAMPLE 1 Identifying Adjacent Angles

Name all pairs of adjacent, supplementary angles.

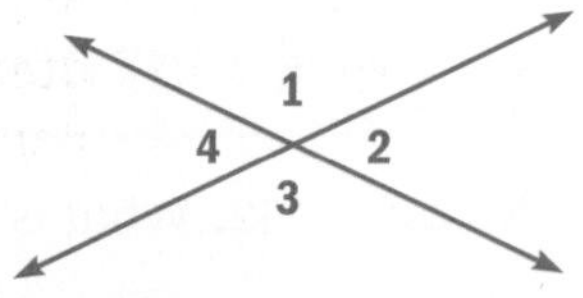

$\angle 1$ and $\angle 2$ $\angle 2$ and $\angle 3$

$\angle 3$ and $\angle 4$ $\angle 1$ and $\angle 4$

VERTICAL ANGLES When two lines meet at a point, as in the activity, the angles that are opposite each other are called **vertical angles**. Vertical angles are **congruent angles**, meaning they have the same measure.

READING
The symbol $\cong$ indicates congruence and is read "is congruent to."

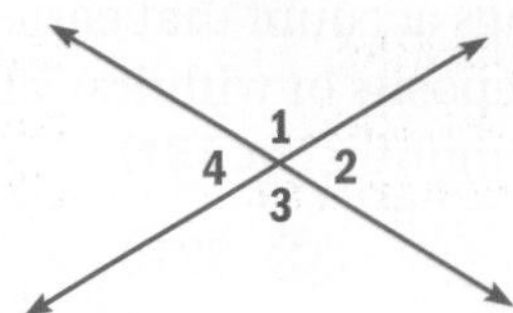

Vertical angles: $\angle 1 \cong \angle 3$

Vertical angles: $\angle 2 \cong \angle 4$

EXAMPLE 2 Using Vertical Angles

ANOTHER WAY

You can also find $m\angle 2$ using supplementary angles. Apply the definition first to $\angle 1$ and $\angle 4$, and then to $\angle 1$ and $\angle 2$.

Given that $m\angle 4 = 105°$, find $m\angle 2$.

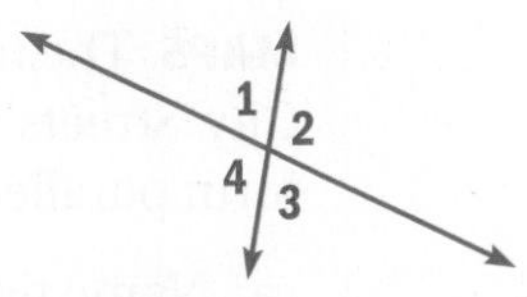

SOLUTION

Because $\angle 4$ and $\angle 2$ are vertical angles, they are congruent. So, $m\angle 2 = m\angle 4 = 105°$.

GUIDED PRACTICE for Examples 1 and 2

Refer to the diagram in Example 2.

1. Name all pairs of adjacent, supplementary angles.
2. Given that $m\angle 4 = 105°$, find $m\angle 1$.
3. Use your answer from Exercise 2 to find $m\angle 3$.

LINES IN A PLANE You can think of a **plane** as a flat surface that extends without end. In diagrams, planes appear as shown at the right. Two lines that meet at a point, as shown, are called **intersecting lines**.

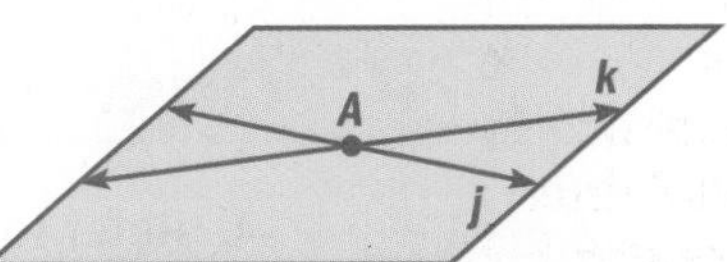

Two lines in the same plane that do not intersect are called **parallel lines**. **Perpendicular lines** intersect to form four right angles. The symbol ∥ is used to indicate parallel lines, and the symbol ⊥ is used to indicate perpendicular lines.

UNDERSTAND SYMBOLS

Arrowheads within lines are used to indicate that the lines are parallel.

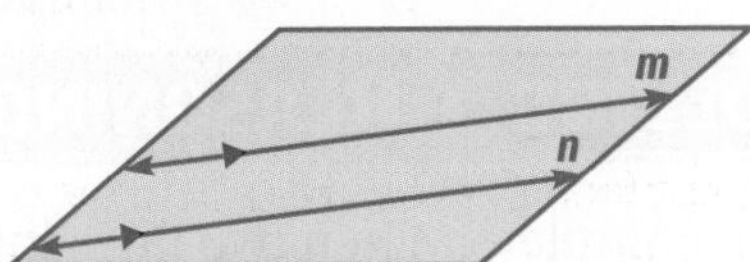

Parallel lines in a plane ($m \parallel n$)

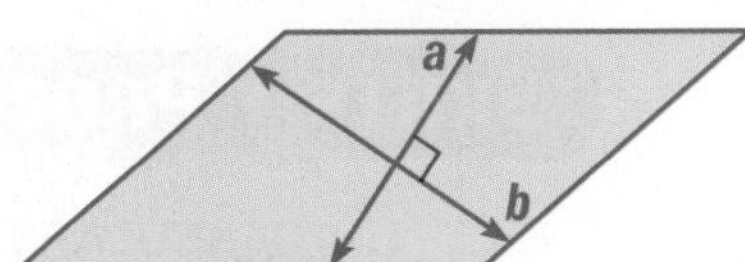

Perpendicular lines in a plane ($a \perp b$)

Angles that occupy corresponding positions when a line intersects two other lines are called **corresponding angles**. When a line intersects two parallel lines, corresponding angles are congruent.

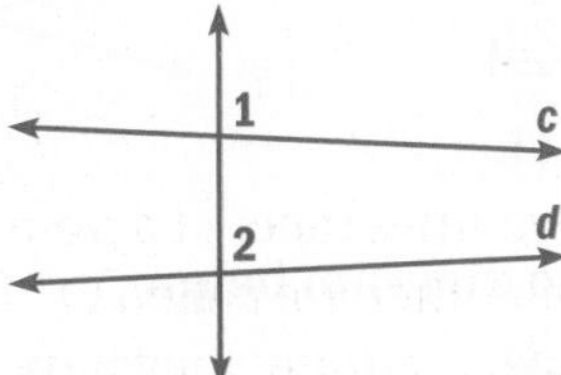

Lines c and d are not parallel, so corresponding angles, such as $\angle 1$ and $\angle 2$, are *not* congruent.

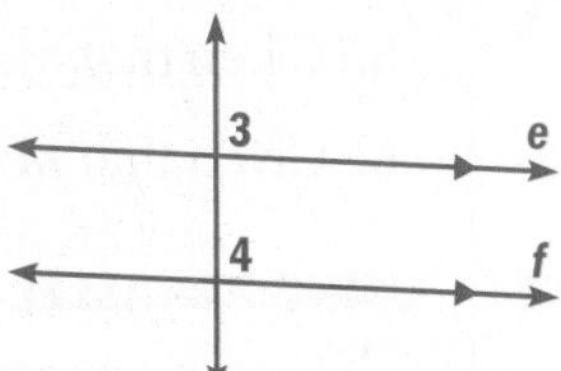

Lines e and f are parallel, so corresponding angles, such as $\angle 3$ and $\angle 4$, are congruent.

EXAMPLE 3 Using Corresponding Angles

MAPS The map shows a section of New York City. Streets shown on maps often appear to form parallel or intersecting lines.

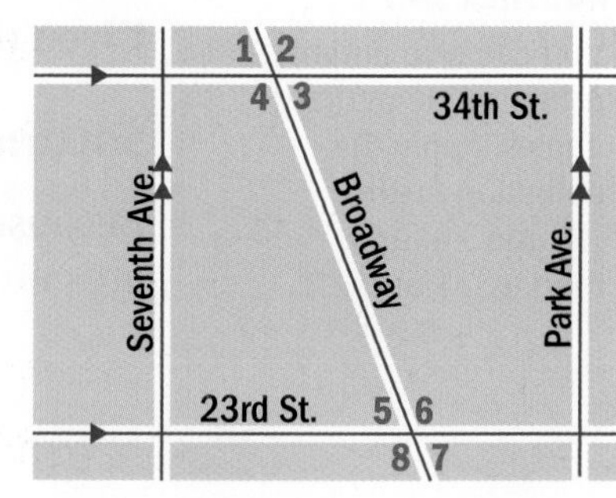

a. Name two streets that are parallel and two streets that intersect.

b. Given that $m\angle 7 = 68°$, find $m\angle 1$.

SOLUTION

a. Several answers are possible. For example, 34th Street is parallel to 23rd Street, and 34th Street intersects Broadway.

b. Because $\angle 7$ and $\angle 5$ are vertical angles, $m\angle 5 = m\angle 7 = 68°$. Because 34th Street and 23rd Street are parallel lines, $\angle 5$ and $\angle 1$ are congruent corresponding angles. So, $m\angle 1 = m\angle 5 = 68°$.

GUIDED PRACTICE for Example 3

4. Refer to the map above. Find $m\angle 6$ and $m\angle 2$. *Explain* your reasoning.

9.2 EXERCISES

HOMEWORK KEY

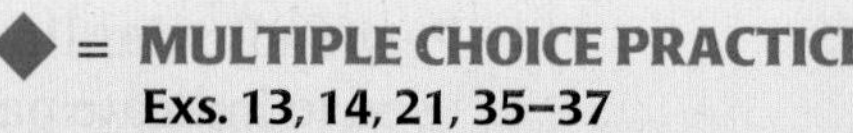

◆ = **MULTIPLE CHOICE PRACTICE** Exs. 13, 14, 21, 35–37

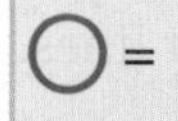

○ = **HINTS AND HOMEWORK HELP** for Exs. 5, 7, 29 at classzone.com

SKILLS • PROBLEM SOLVING • REASONING

1. VOCABULARY Copy and complete: When two lines intersect to form four right angles, the lines are _?_.

2. WRITING *Explain* the difference between adjacent and vertical angles.

SEE EXAMPLES 1 AND 2 on pp. 468–469 for Exs. 3–6

USING INTERSECTING LINES **Refer to the diagram below.**

3. Name all pairs of adjacent, supplementary angles.

4. Name all pairs of vertical angles.

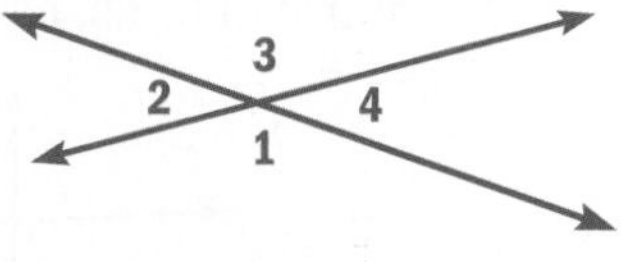

5. Given that $m\angle 3 = 147°$, find $m\angle 2$.

6. Given that $m\angle 3 = 147°$, find $m\angle 1$.

SEE EXAMPLES 2 AND 3 on pp. 469–470 for Exs. 7–13

USING PARALLEL LINES **Refer to the diagram below.**

7. Name two pairs of vertical angles.

8. Name two pairs of corresponding angles.

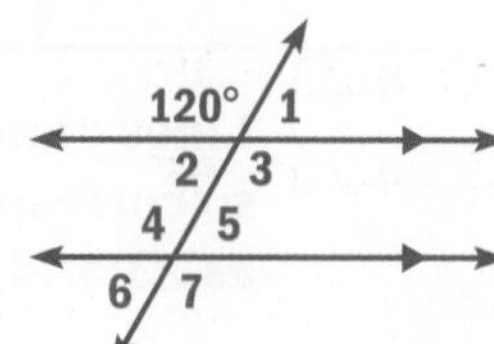

9. Find $m\angle 3$.

10. Find $m\angle 7$.

11. Find $m\angle 4$.

12. Find $m\angle 6$.

13. ◆ **MULTIPLE CHOICE** Which of the following pairs of angles are congruent?

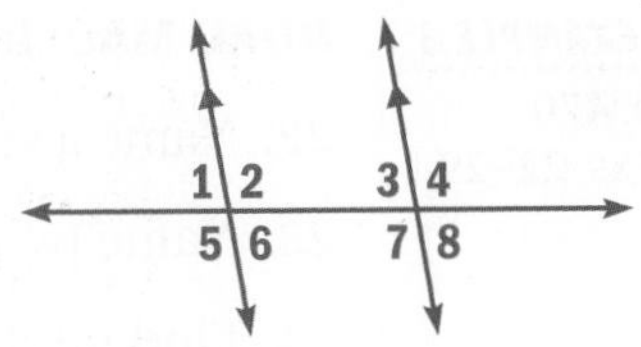

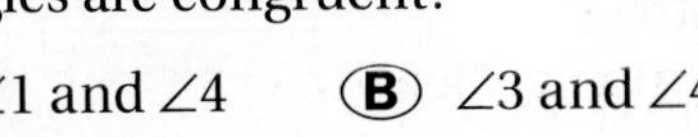

Ⓐ $\angle 1$ and $\angle 4$ Ⓑ $\angle 3$ and $\angle 4$

Ⓒ $\angle 4$ and $\angle 8$ Ⓓ $\angle 6$ and $\angle 8$

SEE EXAMPLES 1 AND 2 on pp. 468–469 for Exs. 14–15

14. ◆ **MULTIPLE CHOICE** Which of the following statements about the diagram in Exercise 13 is true?

Ⓐ $\angle 1$ and $\angle 2$ are vertical angles. Ⓑ $\angle 2$ and $\angle 4$ are vertical angles.

Ⓒ $\angle 1$ and $\angle 6$ are adjacent angles. Ⓓ $\angle 3$ and $\angle 7$ are adjacent angles.

15. **ERROR ANALYSIS** In the diagram at the right, $m\angle 1 = 38°$. *Describe* and correct the error made in finding $m\angle 3$.

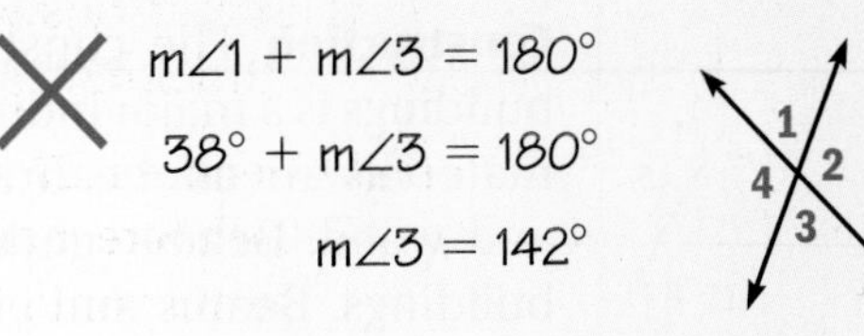

16. **OPEN-ENDED** Draw two parallel lines and a third line that intersects them. Label all the angles. Identify all the congruent angles.

CONNECT SKILLS TO PROBLEM SOLVING **Exercises 17–19 will help you prepare for problem solving.**

17. Name all pairs of adjacent, supplementary angles in the diagram.

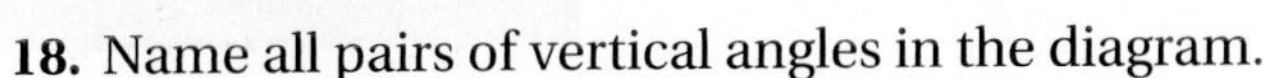

18. Name all pairs of vertical angles in the diagram.

19. In the diagram, $m\angle 3 = 96°$. Find $m\angle 1$, $m\angle 2$, and $m\angle 4$.

SEE EXAMPLES 2 AND 3 on pp. 469–470 for Exs. 20–21

20. **REASONING** Can vertical angles be supplementary angles? *Explain* your reasoning.

California @HomeTutor for problem solving help at classzone.com

21. ◆ **MULTIPLE CHOICE** In the diagram of the *zip line*, lines *a* and *b* are parallel, and $m\angle 2 = 95°$. Which statement about the diagram is *not* true?

Ⓐ $m\angle 3 = 85°$ Ⓑ $m\angle 7 = 95°$

Ⓒ $m\angle 8 = 85°$ Ⓓ $m\angle 10 = 95°$

California @HomeTutor for problem solving help at classzone.com

SEE EXAMPLE 3 on p. 470 for Exs. 22–29

ROAD MAP Refer to the road map.

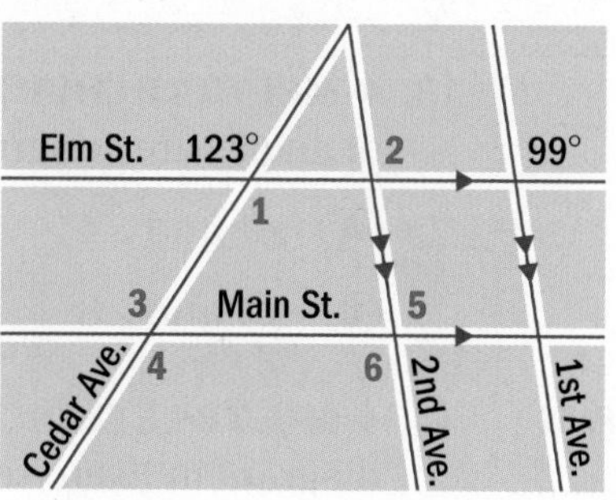

22. Name a street parallel to Elm Street.
23. Name two streets that intersect 1st Ave.
24. Find $m\angle 1$.
25. Find $m\angle 2$.
26. Find $m\angle 3$.
27. Find $m\angle 4$.
28. Find $m\angle 5$.
29. Find $m\angle 6$.

READING *IN* MATH **Read the information below for Exercises 30–33.**

Construction The construction of homes and buildings is a major industry. Common building materials are adobe, brick, cement, glass, iron, and wood. Beams, girders, and posts support buildings. Beams and girders run horizontally, and posts are vertical supports.

30. **Describe** *Describe* the relationship between any two posts.
31. **Describe** *Describe* the relationship between any post and a beam.
32. **Identify** Name five angles that have a measure of 53°.
33. **Calculate** What is $m\angle ADJ$? *Explain* how you found your answer.

34. **CHALLENGE** Write and solve an equation to find the values of x and $3x$. Then find $m\angle 1$ and $m\angle 2$. *Explain* how you found your answers.

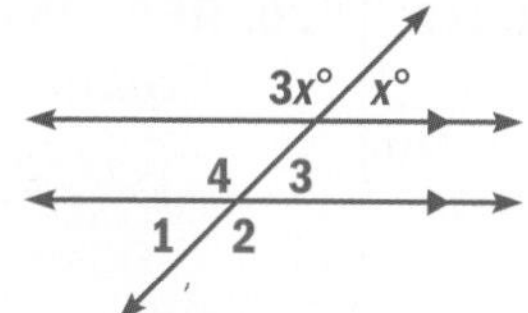

◆ CALIFORNIA STANDARDS SPIRAL REVIEW

NS 2.4 35. What is the least common multiple of 6 and 34? ***(p. 21)***

Ⓐ 68 Ⓑ 102 Ⓒ 136 Ⓓ 204

AF 3.1 36. A rectangle has a length of 6 units and a width of $(x - 3)$ units. Which expression could you use to find the area of the rectangle? ***(p. 212)***

Ⓐ $6x - 3$ Ⓑ $x - 18$ Ⓒ $6x - 18$ Ⓓ $2x + 6$

NS 1.3 37. You can buy 2 pounds of ground beef for \$4.50. Approximately how many pounds of ground beef can you buy for \$20? ***(p. 266)***

Ⓐ 6 lb Ⓑ 9 lb Ⓒ 12 lb Ⓓ 15 lb

9.3 Investigating Angles of a Triangle

Standards Preparation

Gr. 5 MG 2.2 **Know that the sum of the angles of any triangle is 180°** and the sum of the angles of any quadrilateral is 360° and use this information to solve problems.

MATERIALS • paper • ruler • scissors • protractor

QUESTION **How can you find the sum of the angle measures of a triangle?**

You can cut out triangles to investigate the sum of the angle measures of a triangle.

EXPLORE **Find the sum of the angle measures of a triangle.**

STEP 1 **Draw** a triangle on a piece of paper and cut it out. Make each side at least 3 inches long.

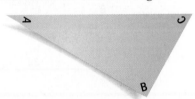

STEP 2 **Tear** off the three corners as shown.

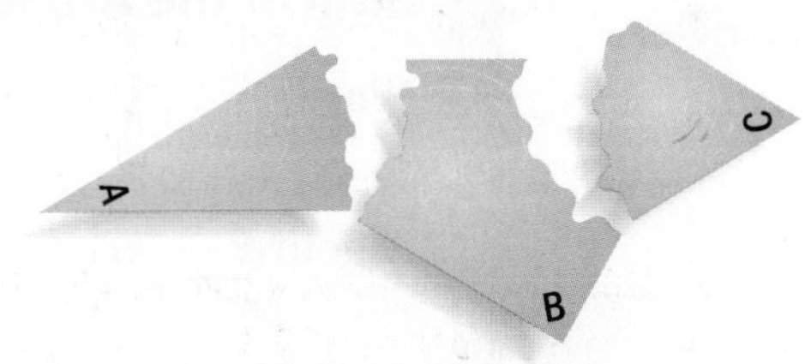

STEP 3 **Arrange** the three corners as shown. What type of angle do they appear to form?

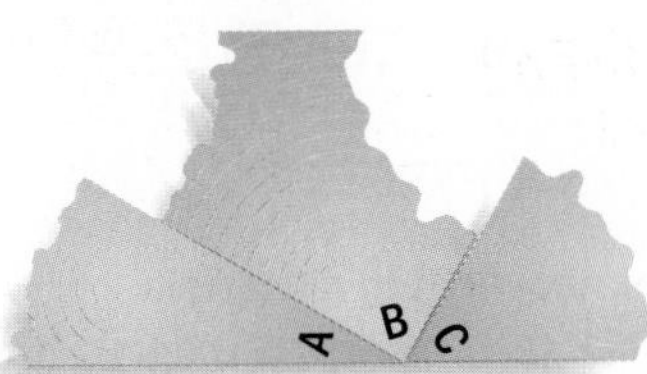

STEP 4 **Repeat** steps 1–3 with a different triangle. Compare your results with the results for the first triangle.

DRAW CONCLUSIONS **Use your observations to complete these exercises.**

Tell whether the three angle measures could be the angle measures of a triangle. *Explain* your reasoning.

1. 5°, 80°, 90° **2.** 30°, 70°, 80° **3.** 40°, 54°, 86° **4.** 37°, 42°, 102°

5. **REASONING** Choose three angles that you think could form a triangle. *Explain* how you chose the angles. Then draw a triangle with these angles using a protractor.

6. **WRITING** Make a generalization about the sum of the angle measures of any triangle.

9.3 Triangles

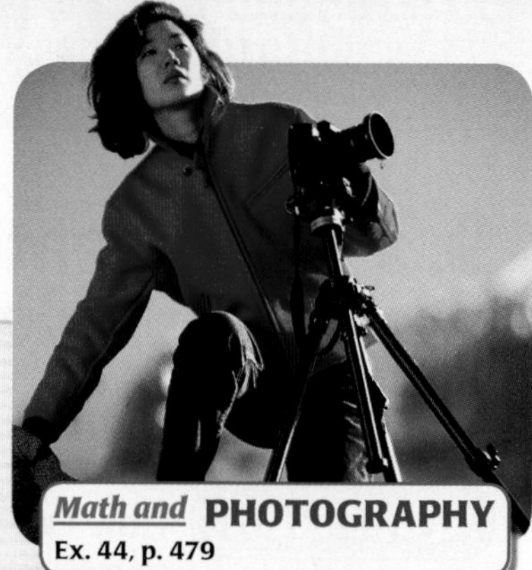

Standards **MG 2.2** **Use** the properties of complementary and supplementary angles and **the sum of the angles of a triangle to solve problems involving an unknown angle.**

MG 2.3 **Draw** quadrilaterals and **triangles from given information about them** (e.g., a quadrilateral having equal sides but no right angles, **a right isosceles triangle**).

Connect ***Before*** you classified angles. ***Now*** you will find unknown angles and draw triangles.

KEY VOCABULARY
- **acute, right, obtuse triangle**
- **congruent sides**
- **equilateral, isosceles, scalene triangle**

The activity on page 473 suggests that the measures of the angles of any triangle add up to 180°. You will prove this later in a geometry course.

KEY CONCEPT *For Your Notebook*

Sum of the Angle Measures of a Triangle

Words The sum of the angle measures of a triangle is 180°.

Algebra $m\angle A + m\angle B + m\angle C = 180°$

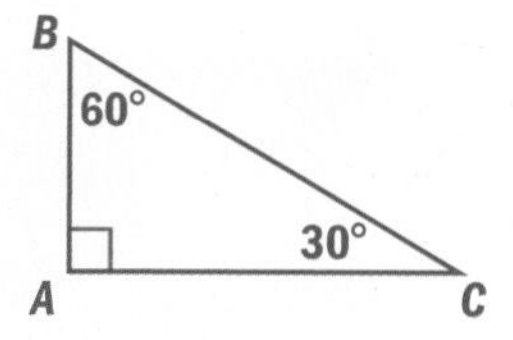

You can use the sum of the angle measures of a triangle to solve for an unknown angle measure.

EXAMPLE 1 Finding an Angle Measure in a Triangle

Find the value of x in the triangle.

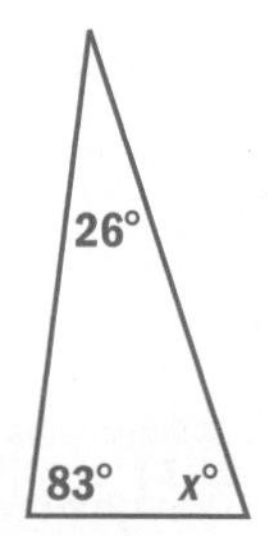

$x° + 83° + 26° = 180°$ **Sum of angle measures in a triangle is 180°.**

$x + 109 = 180$ **Simplify.**

$x = 71$ **Subtract 109 from each side.**

▶ **Answer** The value of x is 71.

✓ GUIDED PRACTICE for Example 1

Find the value of x or y.

1. 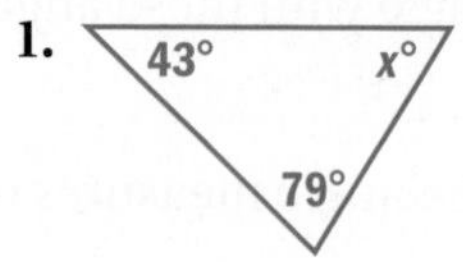

2. 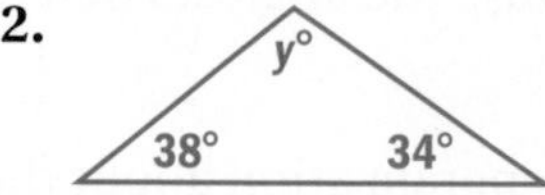

3. 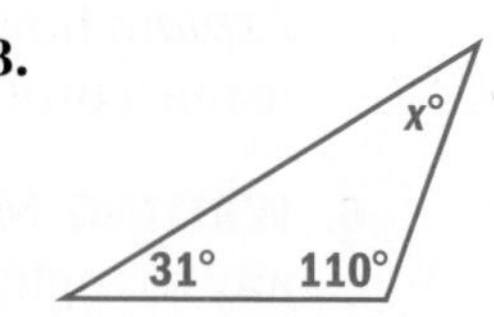

CLASSIFYING TRIANGLES You can classify a triangle by its angle measures. When you classify a triangle, be as specific as possible.

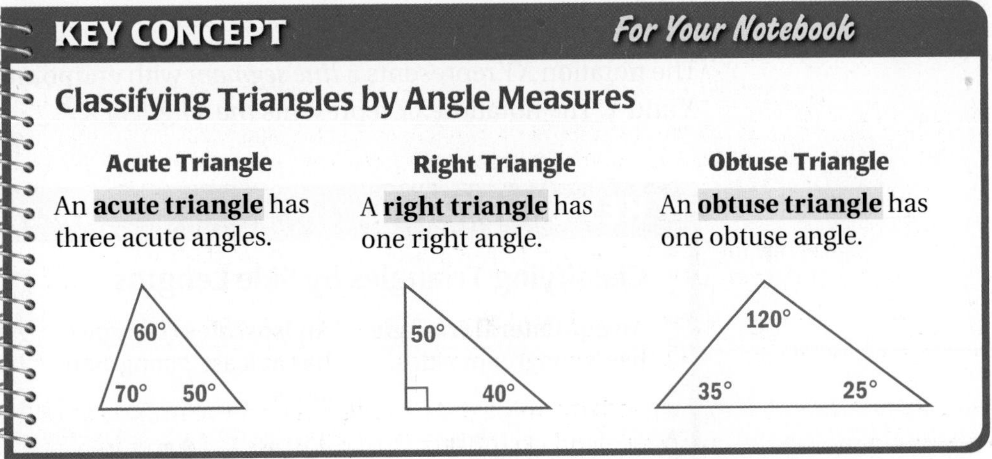

KEY CONCEPT
For Your Notebook
Classifying Triangles by Angle Measures
Acute Triangle
An acute triangle has three acute angles.
Right Triangle
A right triangle has one right angle.
Obtuse Triangle
An obtuse triangle has one obtuse angle.
60°
70°
50°
50°
40°
120°
35°
25°

EXAMPLE 2 ◆ Multiple Choice Practice

ELIMINATE CHOICES

The figure in choice B is a right triangle because it has a right angle mark. Choice B can be eliminated.

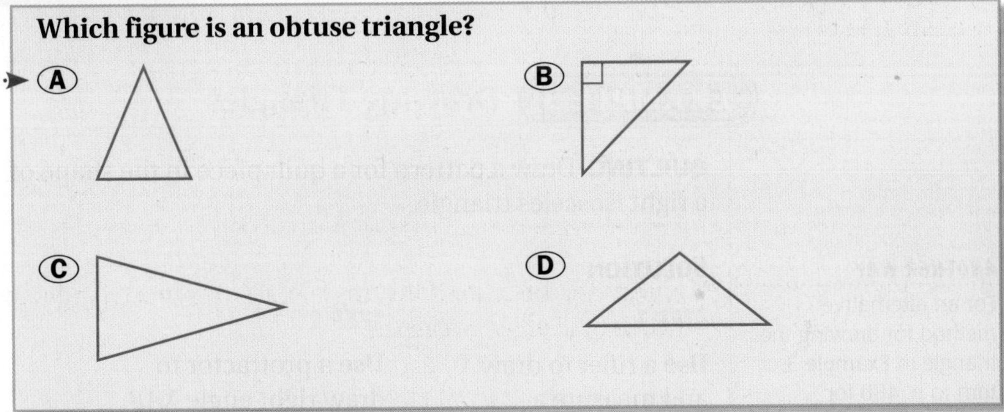

SOLUTION

Compare the angles of the triangles to a corner of a piece of paper, which has a measure of 90°. All angles in choices A and C have measures less than 90°. One angle in choice B has a measure of 90°. One angle in choice D has a measure greater than 90°.

▶ **Answer** The figure in choice D is an obtuse triangle.
The correct answer is D. Ⓐ Ⓑ Ⓒ Ⓓ

✓ GUIDED PRACTICE for Example 2

Classify the triangle by its angle measures.

4. 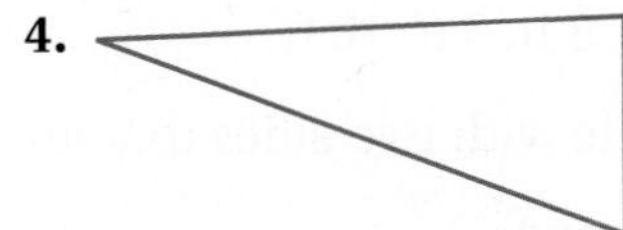

5. 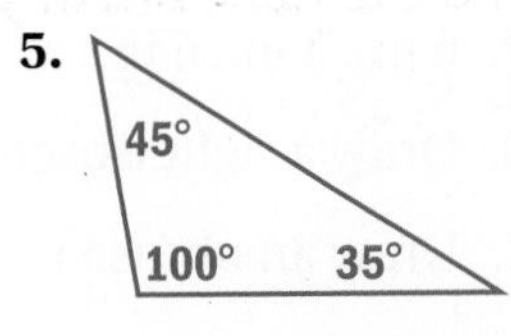

6. 37°, 53°, 90°

READING

A triangle is identified by its vertices. The triangle XYZ can be written $\triangle XYZ$.

CONGRUENT SIDES Sides of a figure that have the same length are **congruent sides**. The two marks on the sides of the triangle at the right indicate that sides $\overline{XY}$ and $\overline{XZ}$ are congruent. You can write this as $\overline{XY} \cong \overline{XZ}$.

The notation $\overline{XY}$ represents a *line segment* with endpoints X and Y. The notation XY represents *the length of* $\overline{XY}$.

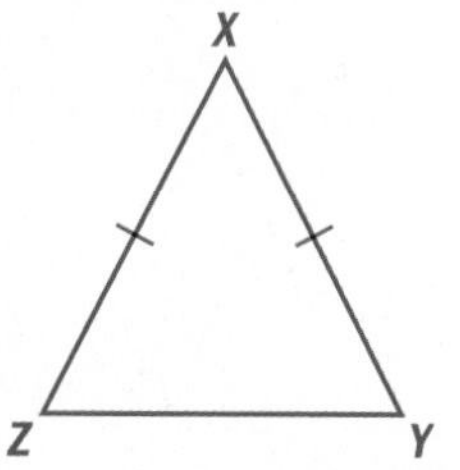

KEY CONCEPT — *For Your Notebook*

Classifying Triangles by Side Lengths

An **equilateral triangle** has 3 congruent sides.

9 in.
9 in.
9 in.

An **isosceles triangle** has at least 2 congruent sides.

8 m
5 m
8 m

A **scalene triangle** has no congruent sides.

5 ft
14 ft
11 ft

EXAMPLE 3 Drawing Triangles

QUILTING Draw a pattern for a quilt piece in the shape of a right isosceles triangle.

ANOTHER WAY

For an alternative method for drawing the triangle in Example 3, turn to p. 480 for the **Problem Solving Workshop**.

SOLUTION

STEP 1

Use a ruler to draw and measure a segment, $\overline{AB}$.

A B

STEP 2

Use a protractor to draw right angle XAB as shown.

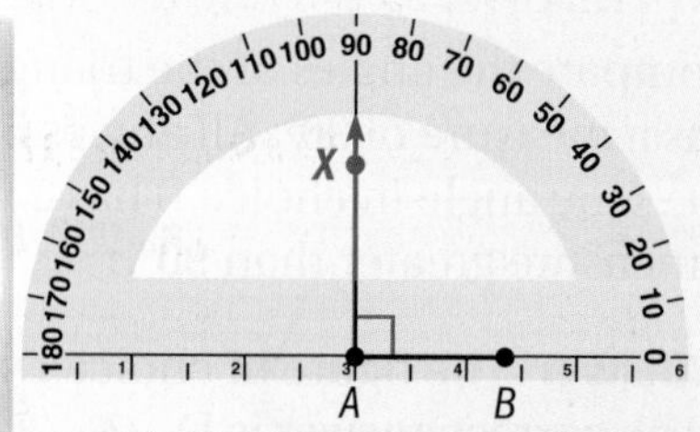

STEP 3

Draw point C on $\overrightarrow{AX}$ such that $AC = AB$. Then connect B and C.

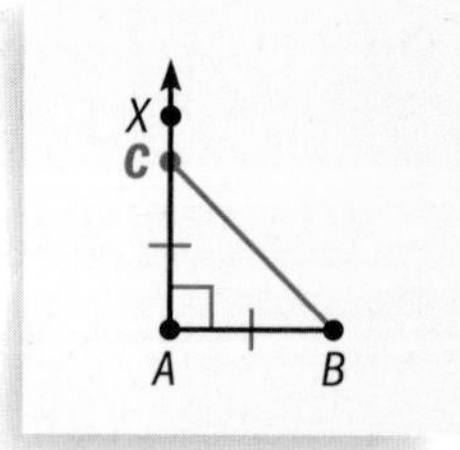

✓ GUIDED PRACTICE for Example 3

Classify the triangle by its side lengths.

7. 6 in., 8 in., 6 in.

8. 3 ft, 9 ft, 10 ft

9. 4 cm, 4 cm, 4 cm

10. Draw a right isosceles triangle with two sides that are 1.5 inches long.

11. Draw an obtuse isosceles triangle.

9.3 EXERCISES

HOMEWORK KEY ◆ = **MULTIPLE CHOICE PRACTICE** Exs. 9, 30, 37, 48–50
○ = **HINTS AND HOMEWORK HELP** for Exs. 3, 27, 43 at classzone.com

SKILLS • PROBLEM SOLVING • REASONING

1. **VOCABULARY** Copy and complete: A triangle with one angle measure greater than 90° is a(n) _?_ triangle.

2. **WRITING** Tell whether the following statement is *true* or *false*: An equilateral triangle can also be classified as an isosceles triangle. *Explain* your reasoning.

SEE EXAMPLES 1 AND 2 on pp. 474–475 for Exs. 3–10

ALGEBRA Find the value of x. Classify the triangle by angle measures.

3. 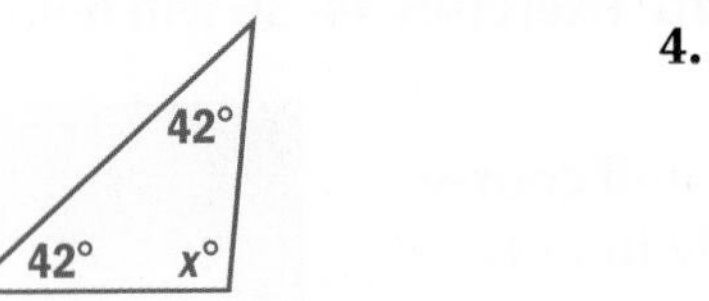

4. 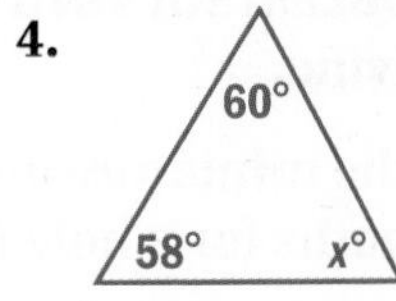

5. 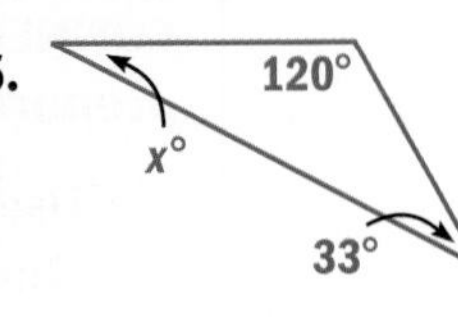

6. 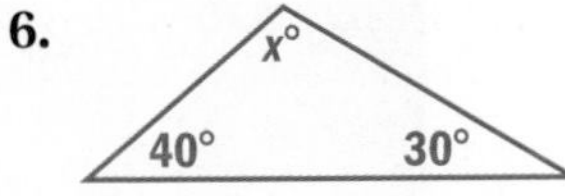

7. 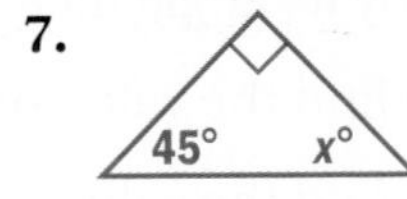

8. 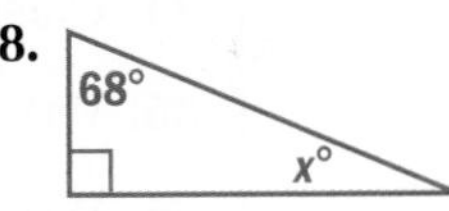

9. ◆ **MULTIPLE CHOICE** What is the value of x in the triangle at the right?

   Ⓐ 19 Ⓑ 34

   Ⓒ 53 Ⓓ 56

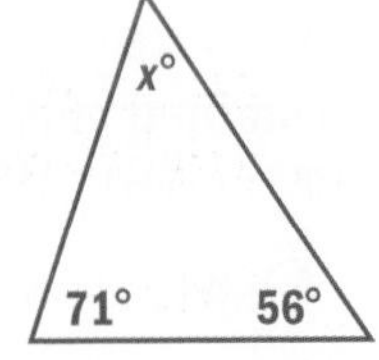

10. **ERROR ANALYSIS** *Describe* and correct the error made in finding the value of x.

SEE EXAMPLE 2 on p. 475 for Exs. 11–17

11. **ERROR ANALYSIS** *Describe* and correct the error made in classifying the triangle.

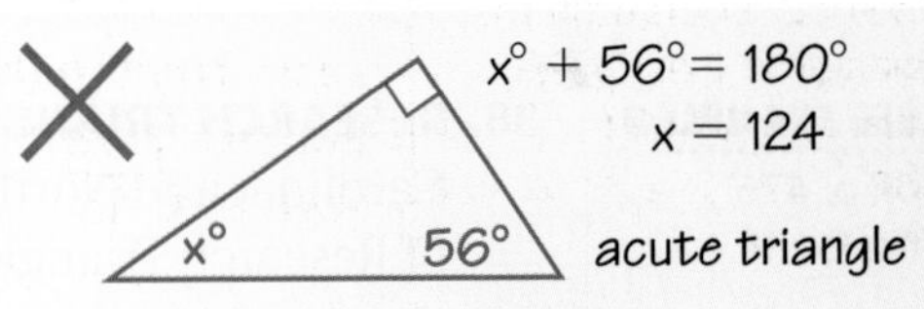

CLASSIFYING BY ANGLES Classify the triangle by its angle measures.

12. 68°, 22°, 90°
13. 82°, 64°, 34°
14. 135°, 24°, 21°
15. 17°, 60°, 103°
16. 58°, 49°, 73°
17. 54°, 90°, 36°

SEE EXAMPLE 3 on p. 476 for Exs. 18–29

CLASSIFYING BY SIDES Classify the triangle by its side lengths.

18. 12 cm, 6 cm, 11 cm
19. 6 m, 6 m, 6 m
20. 11 ft, 6 ft, 11 ft
21. 15 in., 15 in., 12 in.
22. 2 mm, 2 mm, 2 mm
23. 19 cm, 7 cm, 21 cm

DRAWING TRIANGLES Draw the triangle using a protractor and a ruler.

24. A scalene triangle
25. An isosceles triangle
26. An equilateral triangle
27. An obtuse scalene triangle
28. A right scalene triangle
29. An acute isosceles triangle

SEE EXAMPLES 2 AND 3
on pp. 475–476
for Ex. 30

30. ◆ **MULTIPLE CHOICE** Which of the following describes the triangle at the right?

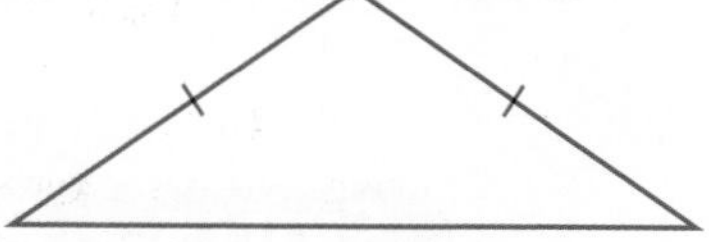

Ⓐ Right scalene Ⓑ Obtuse isosceles

Ⓒ Acute isosceles Ⓓ Acute equilateral

ALGEBRA Find the values of *x* and *y*.

31. 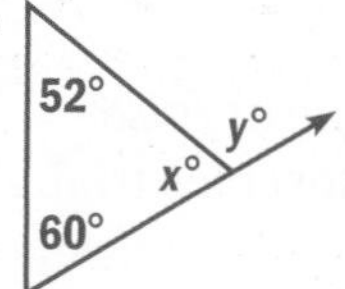

32. 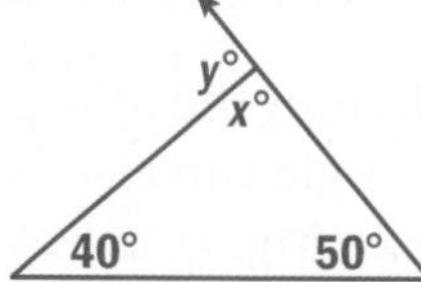

33. 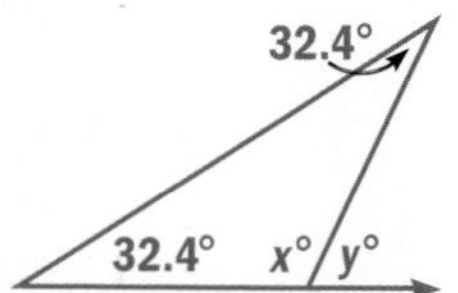

CONNECT SKILLS TO PROBLEM SOLVING Exercises 34–36 will help you prepare for problem solving.

Use the diagram of the miniature golf course showing 2 possible paths for a hole in one.

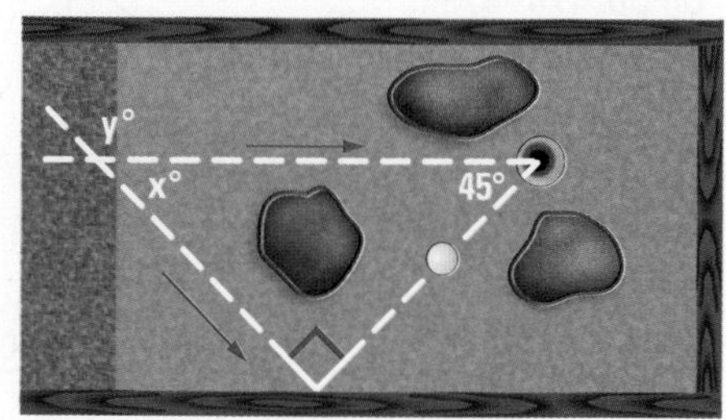

34. Classify the triangle by its angle measures.

35. Write an equation to find the value of x.

36. Write an equation to find the value of y.

SEE EXAMPLE 1
on p. 474
for Ex. 37

37. ◆ **MULTIPLE CHOICE** You are cutting a triangular piece of glass for a stained glass window. Two of the angles of the triangle measure 65° and 61°. What is the measure of the third angle?

Ⓐ 54° Ⓑ 63° Ⓒ 65° Ⓓ 126°

California @HomeTutor for problem solving help at classzone.com

SEE EXAMPLE 3
on p. 476
for Ex. 38

38. **RESEARCH TRIANGLE PARK** Duke University, the University of North Carolina, and North Carolina State University make up the three vertices of Research Triangle Park in North Carolina. The distances between the three universities are 9 miles, 21 miles, and 23 miles. Classify Research Triangle Park by its side lengths.

California @HomeTutor for problem solving help at classzone.com

REASONING Copy and complete the statement using *always, sometimes,* or *never. Justify* your reasoning.

39. An isosceles triangle is __?__ a right triangle.

40. An obtuse triangle is __?__ an equilateral triangle.

41. An equilateral triangle is __?__ an acute triangle.

42. A scalene triangle is __?__ an acute triangle.

43. **CONSTRUCTION** Wall posts and ceiling beams are connected by support braces as shown. Find the values of x and y. Classify the triangle by its angles.

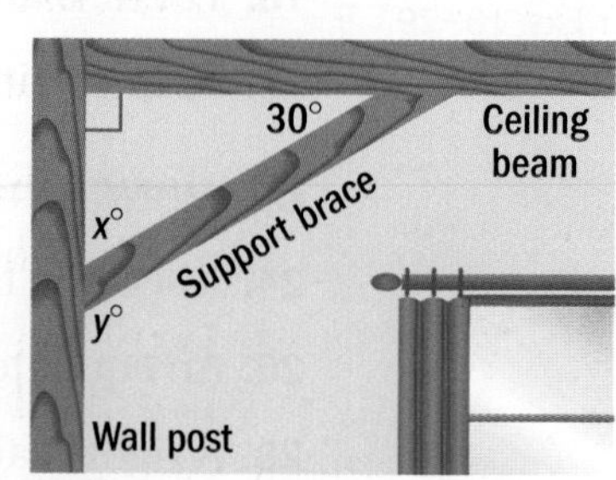

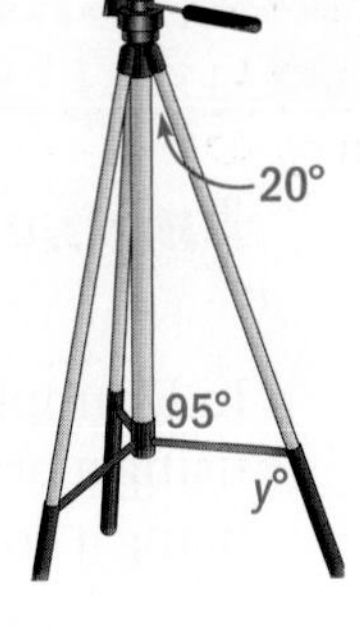

44. **CAMERA TRIPOD** A tripod keeps a camera steady. A tripod has three legs that are each connected to a vertical bar. Find the value of y.

45. **REASONING** Draw two different isosceles triangles. Then use a protractor to measure the angles. How many angles are congruent? How are these angles related to the congruent sides? What does this suggest about the angles of an equilateral triangle? *Explain.*

46. **CHALLENGE** The measure of one angle in a triangle is $x°$. The other two angles are congruent to each other. Write an expression for the measure of each of the other angles. *Explain* your reasoning.

47. **CHALLENGE** *Explain* how to make a precise drawing of a triangle with side lengths 10 centimeters, 12 centimeters, and 15 centimeters.

◆ CALIFORNIA STANDARDS SPIRAL REVIEW

NS 1.1 48. Which of the following lists the numbers in order from least to greatest? ***(p. 40)***

Ⓐ $3\frac{2}{3}, 3.7, 3\frac{5}{7}$ Ⓑ $3\frac{2}{3}, 3\frac{5}{7}, 3.7$ Ⓒ $3\frac{5}{7}, 3.7, 3\frac{2}{3}$ Ⓓ $3.7, 3\frac{2}{3}, 3\frac{5}{7}$

NS 2.2 49. What is the value of $8\frac{3}{4} \div 2\frac{1}{8}$? ***(p. 95)***

Ⓐ 4 Ⓑ $4\frac{2}{17}$ Ⓒ $4\frac{7}{17}$ Ⓓ $4\frac{1}{2}$

AF 2.3 50. You are driving at a constant speed of 65 miles per hour. You are currently 156 miles from your destination. If you maintain your current speed, how long will it take you to get to your destination? ***(p. 234)***

Ⓐ 2 h 5 min Ⓑ 2 h 15 min

Ⓒ 2 h 24 min Ⓓ 2 h 36 min

QUIZ *for Lessons 9.1–9.3*

In Exercises 1–4, use the diagram shown at the right.

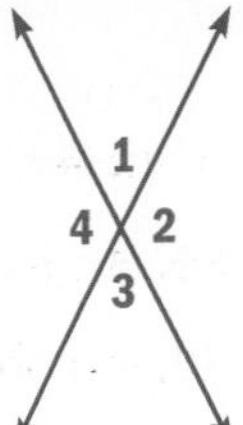

1. Name all pairs of adjacent, supplementary angles. ***(p. 468)***
2. Name all pairs of vertical angles. ***(p. 468)***
3. Given that $m\angle 2 = 125°$, find $m\angle 3$. ***(p. 463)***
4. Given that $m\angle 2 = 125°$, find $m\angle 4$. ***(p. 468)***

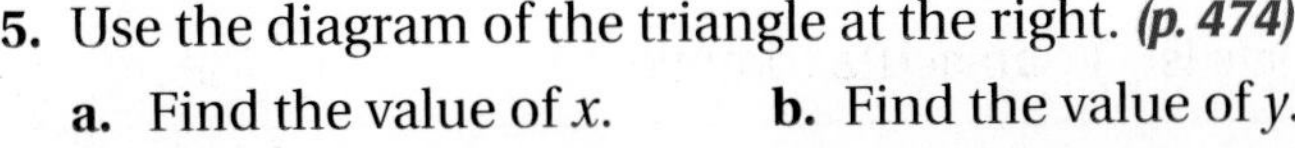

5. Use the diagram of the triangle at the right. ***(p. 474)***
   a. Find the value of x. b. Find the value of y.

95°
y° x° 35°

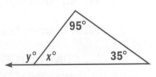

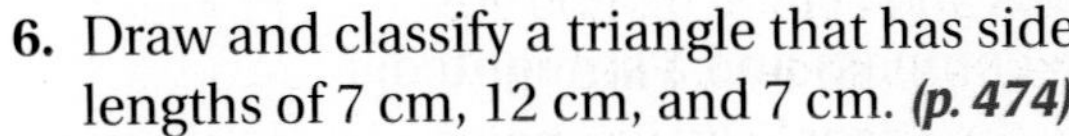

6. Draw and classify a triangle that has side lengths of 7 cm, 12 cm, and 7 cm. ***(p. 474)***
7. Can corresponding angles be complementary? *Explain.* ***(pp. 463, 468)***

PROBLEM SOLVING WORKSHOP
LESSON 9.3

Using ALTERNATIVE METHODS

Another Way to Solve Example 3, page 476

Standards
MG 2.3

In Example 3 on page 476, you saw how to draw a right isosceles triangle using a protractor and a ruler. You can also draw a right isosceles triangle using a compass and a straightedge.

PROBLEM

QUILTING Draw a pattern for a quilt piece in the shape of a right isosceles triangle.

METHOD

Using a Compass and a Straightedge An alternate approach is to use a compass and a straightedge to draw a right isosceles triangle.

STEP 1 **Draw** any line *AB*. Open the compass to a distance equal to the length of $\overline{AB}$. Then place the compass point at *A* and draw an arc as shown. Label the intersection of the line and the arc as *P*.

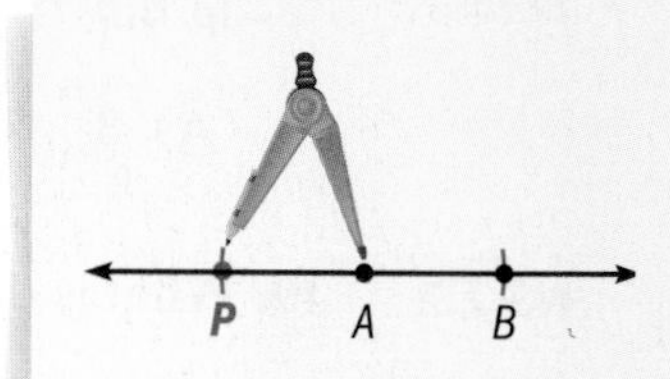

STEP 2 **Open** the compass wider than the length of $\overline{PA}$. Place the compass point at *P* and draw an arc above the line. Then place the compass point at *B*. Using the same compass setting, draw an arc above the line. Label the point where these two arcs intersect as *X*. Draw $\overrightarrow{AX}$.

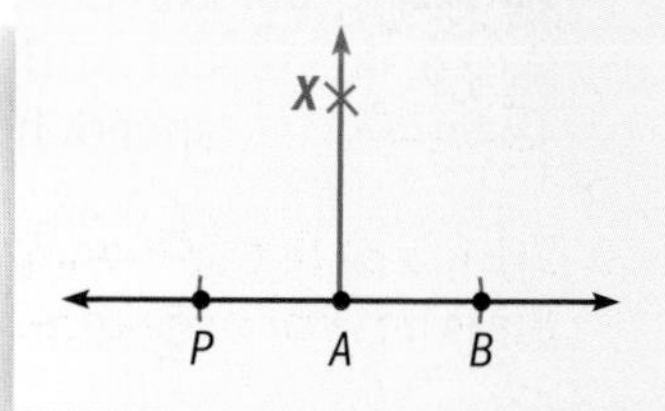

STEP 3 **Open** the compass to a distance equal to the length of $\overline{AB}$. Place the compass point on *A* and draw an arc on $\overrightarrow{AX}$. Label the intersection of $\overrightarrow{AX}$ and this arc *C*. Draw $\overline{BC}$.

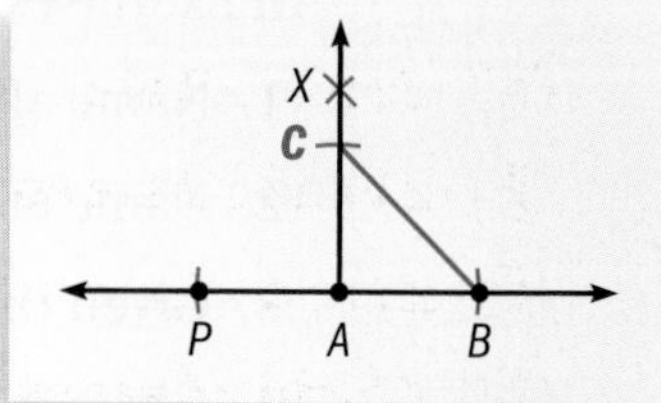

PRACTICE

1. Draw a right scalene triangle using a compass and a straightedge.
2. Draw an equilateral triangle using a compass and a straightedge.

MIXED REVIEW *of Skills and Problem Solving*

Multiple Choice Practice for Lessons 9.1–9.3

1. In the diagram below, which pair of angles are vertical angles? **MG 2.1, MR 1.1**

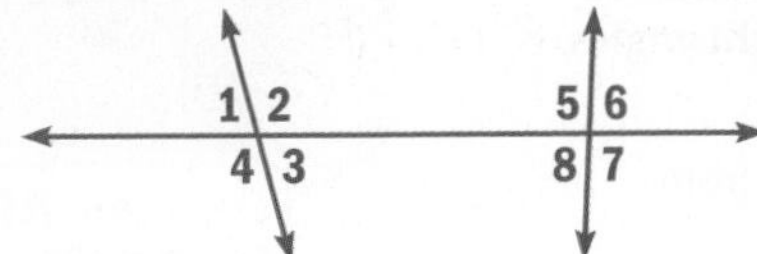

Ⓐ $\angle 1$ and $\angle 2$

Ⓑ $\angle 3$ and $\angle 8$

Ⓒ $\angle 4$ and $\angle 6$

Ⓓ $\angle 5$ and $\angle 7$

2. What is the value of x in the stained glass below? **MG 2.2**

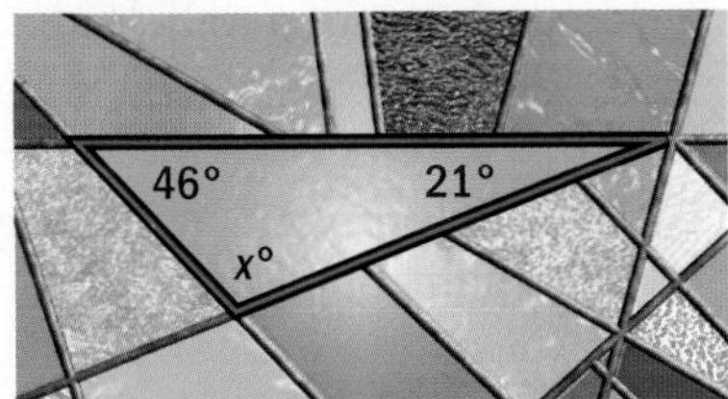

Ⓐ 23 Ⓑ 33

Ⓒ 113 Ⓓ 293

3. Which of the following statements about the diagram below is true? **MG 2.1**

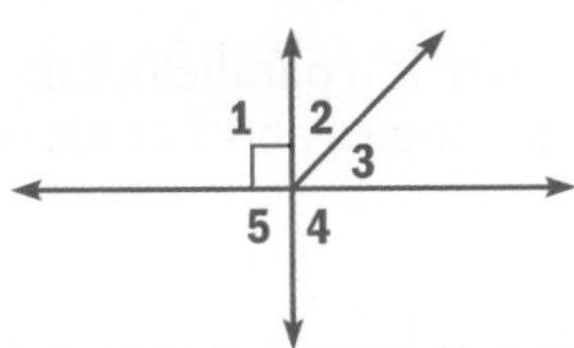

Ⓐ $\angle 2$ and $\angle 3$ are congruent.

Ⓑ $\angle 1$ and $\angle 2$ are congruent.

Ⓒ $\angle 1$ and $\angle 5$ are supplementary.

Ⓓ $\angle 2$ and $\angle 3$ are supplementary.

4. $\angle F$ and $\angle G$ are supplementary angles, and $m\angle F = 57°$. What is $m\angle G$? **MG 2.2**

Ⓐ 33° Ⓑ 57°

Ⓒ 123° Ⓓ 147°

5. In the diagram, $m\angle 4 = 29°$. Which process will *not* tell you the measure of $\angle 1$? **MG 2.2**

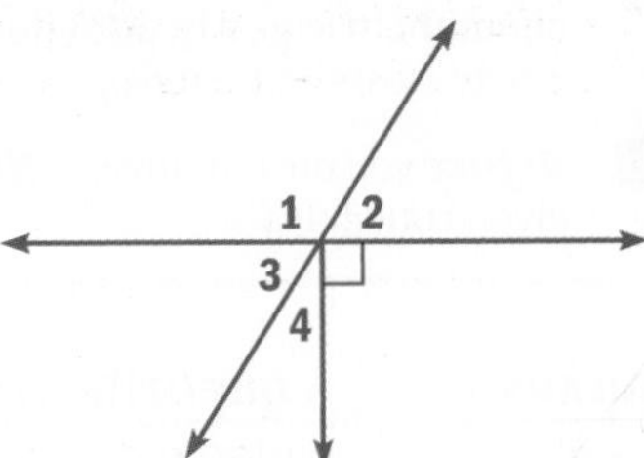

Ⓐ Find the complement of $\angle 4$ and subtract its angle measure from 180°.

Ⓑ Subtract $(m\angle 4 + 90°)$ from 180° and find the supplement of the resulting angle.

Ⓒ Add $m\angle 4$ and 90°.

Ⓓ Find the supplement of $\angle 4$ and subtract 90° from its angle measure.

6. A yield sign has the shape of a triangle as shown. Which of the following best describes the triangle? **MG 2.3**

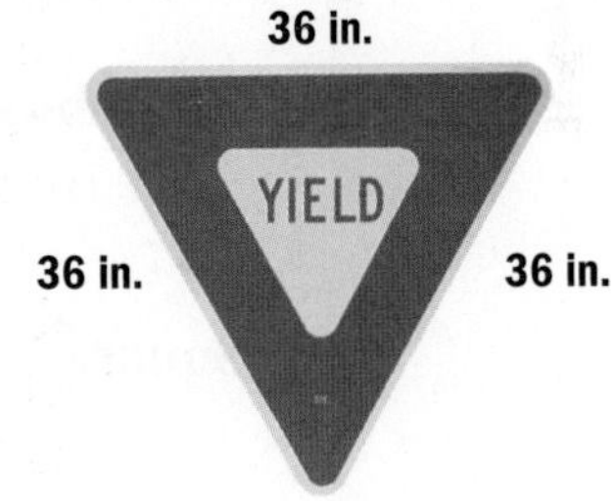

Ⓐ Right

Ⓑ Equilateral

Ⓒ Scalene

Ⓓ Obtuse

7. The measures of two angles of a triangle are 52° and 62°. What is the measure of an angle complementary to the third angle of the triangle? **MG 2.2, MR 1.3**

Ⓐ 24° Ⓑ 28°

Ⓒ 66° Ⓓ 114°

9.4 Quadrilaterals and Other Polygons

Math and ART
Ex. 40, p. 487

Standards MG 2.3 **Draw quadrilaterals** and triangles **from given information about them (e.g., a quadrilateral having equal sides but no right angles,** a right isosceles triangle).

Connect ***Before*** you drew triangles. ***Now*** you will draw quadrilaterals from given conditions.

KEY VOCABULARY
- quadrilateral
- trapezoid
- parallelogram
- rhombus
- polygon
- pentagon
- hexagon
- octagon
- diagonal
- rectangle, *p. 684*
- square, *p. 684*

A **quadrilateral** is a geometric figure that is made up of four line segments, called sides, which intersect only at their endpoints.

KEY CONCEPT *For Your Notebook*

Special Quadrilaterals

Trapezoid A **trapezoid** is a quadrilateral with exactly 1 pair of parallel sides.

Parallelogram A **parallelogram** is a quadrilateral with 2 pairs of parallel sides.

Rectangle A rectangle is a parallelogram with 4 right angles.

Rhombus A **rhombus** is a parallelogram with 4 congruent sides.

Square A square is a parallelogram with 4 right angles and 4 congruent sides.

EXAMPLE 1 Classifying a Quadrilateral

Give the most specific name for the quadrilateral shown.

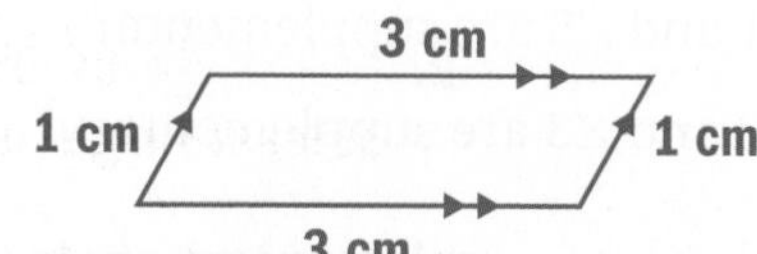

SOLUTION

The quadrilateral is a parallelogram because it has 2 pairs of parallel sides. It is not a rectangle or a square because it does not have 4 right angles. It is also not a rhombus because all 4 sides are not congruent.

▶ **Answer** The quadrilateral is a parallelogram.

EXAMPLE 2 Drawing Quadrilaterals

Draw a quadrilateral with equal sides and no right angles.

STEP 1 **Draw** two sides of the same length. The angle between the two sides should not be 90°.

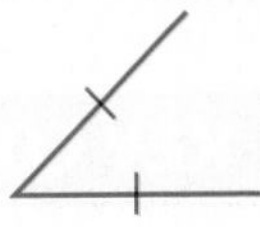

STEP 2 **Draw** two sides parallel to the sides in Step 1 to complete the figure. The figure drawn is a rhombus.

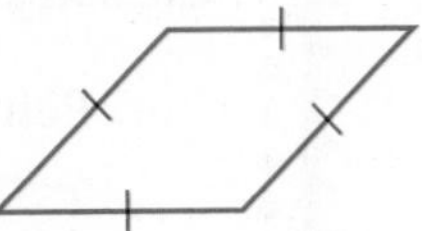

> **About the Standards**
>
> When you use what you know about triangles to find angle measures of other figures, you are applying Grade 6 Standard MR 2.2.

ANGLE MEASURES Notice that you can divide a quadrilateral into two triangles. This means that the sum of the angle measures of a quadrilateral is 360°. You will prove this in a future course.

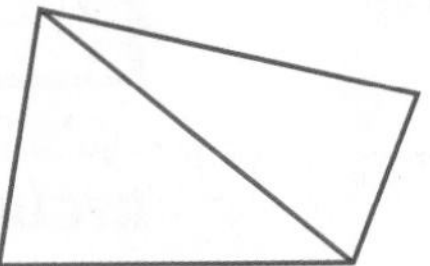

EXAMPLE 3 Finding Unknown Angle Measures

Find the value of x in the diagram shown.

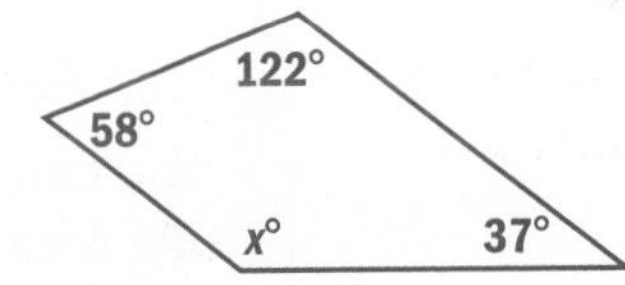

SOLUTION

The sum of the measures of the angles of a quadrilateral is 360°. Write an equation involving x and then solve the equation.

$x° + 37° + 122° + 58° = 360°$	**Write an equation.**
$x + 217 = 360$	**Combine like terms.**
$x = 143$	**Subtract 217 from each side.**

▶ **Answer** The value of x is 143.

✓ GUIDED PRACTICE for Examples 1, 2, and 3

1. A quadrilateral has 4 right angles, 4 congruent sides of length 2.5 centimeters, and 2 pairs of parallel sides. Classify the quadrilateral. Then use a ruler and a protractor to draw it.

2. **WHAT IF?** In Example 2, suppose the quadrilateral has equal sides and at least 1 right angle. Give the most specific name for the quadrilateral.

Find the value of x.

3.

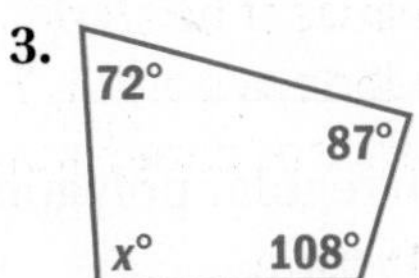

4.

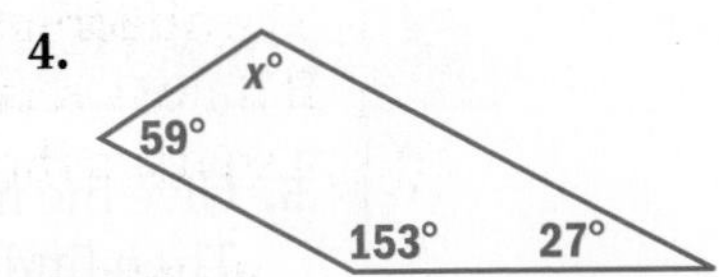

POLYGONS A **polygon** is a closed plane figure that is made up of three or more line segments, called sides, that intersect only at their endpoints. The number of sides determines the name of the polygon. Some common polygons are shown below.

VOCABULARY

The prefix used in the name of a polygon tells you the number of sides the figure has.

Prefix	Meaning
penta-	five
hexa-	six
octa-	eight

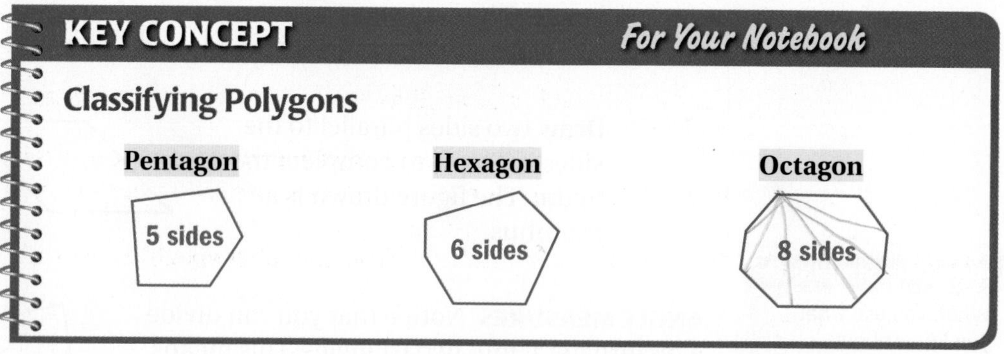

REGULAR POLYGONS A *regular polygon* is a polygon with all sides equal in length and all angles equal in measure. Matching angle marks indicate that the angles are congruent. The figures below are regular polygons.

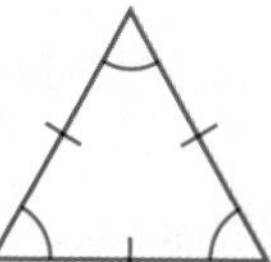

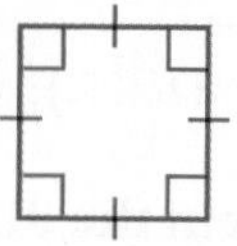

You can draw *diagonals* to divide polygons into triangles to find the sum of the measures of their angles. A **diagonal** of a polygon is a segment, other than a side, that connects two vertices of the polygon.

EXAMPLE 4 Angle Measures of a Regular Polygon

a. Give the most specific name for the polygon.

b. Find the sum of the angle measures.

SOLUTION

a. The polygon has 6 sides. All sides are equal in length and all angles are equal in measure.

▸ **Answer** The polygon is a regular hexagon.

b. Draw all diagonals from one vertex. They form 4 triangles.

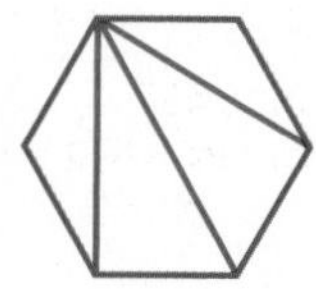

▸ **Answer** The sum of the angle measures of each of the 4 triangles is 180°. The sum of the angle measures of a hexagon is $4 \times 180° = 720°$.

AVOID ERRORS

A polygon with all sides congruent is not necessarily a regular polygon. All angles must also be congruent.

GUIDED PRACTICE for Example 4

5. Give the most specific name for each regular polygon above Example 4. Then find the sum of its angle measures.

9.4 EXERCISES

HOMEWORK KEY

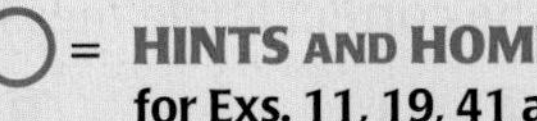

◆ = **MULTIPLE CHOICE PRACTICE** Exs. 22, 30, 41, 44–46

○ = **HINTS AND HOMEWORK HELP** for Exs. 11, 19, 41 at classzone.com

SKILLS • PROBLEM SOLVING • REASONING

1. **VOCABULARY** What is another name for a regular quadrilateral?

2. **NOTETAKING SKILLS** Make an *examples and non-examples chart* like the one on page 462 for *quadrilaterals*. Use sketches in your chart.

SEE EXAMPLE 1 on p. 482 for Exs. 3–9

CLASSIFYING QUADRILATERALS Give the most specific name for the figure.

3. 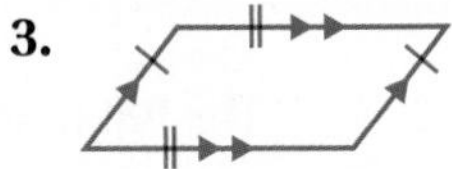

4. 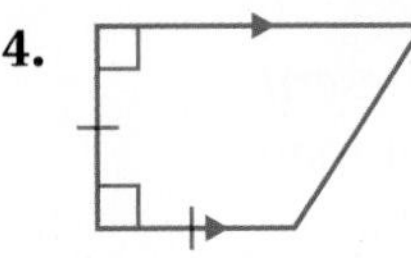

5. 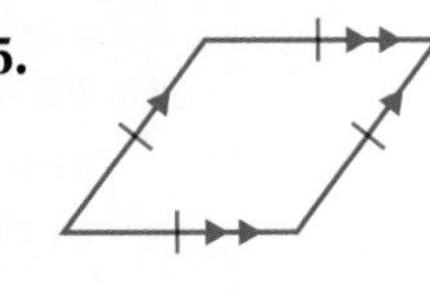

6. 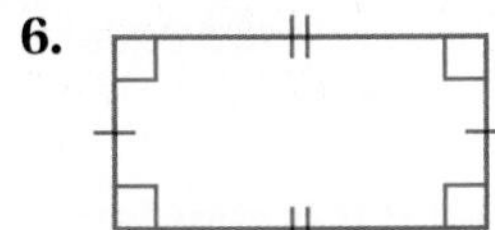

7. 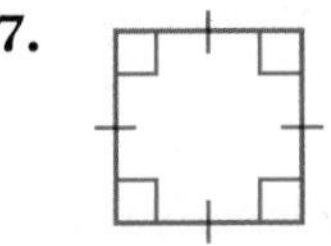

8. 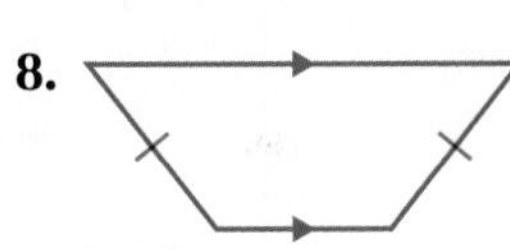

9. **ERROR ANALYSIS** Your friend said, "Because all squares are rhombuses, all rhombuses are squares." *Describe* and correct your friend's error.

SEE EXAMPLES 1 AND 2 on pp. 482–483 for Exs. 10–15

DRAWING QUADRILATERALS Use the clues to classify the quadrilateral. Then use a ruler and a protractor to draw it.

10. This figure has four right angles. Not all of the sides are the same length.

11. This figure's opposite sides are parallel. Not all of the angles are congruent.

12. This figure has exactly one pair of opposite sides that are parallel.

13. This figure has at least one right angle and its opposite sides are parallel. All the sides are the same length.

14. This figure has an acute angle. Its opposite sides are parallel and congruent.

15. This figure has an obtuse angle and exactly one pair of opposite sides that are parallel.

SEE EXAMPLE 3 on p. 483 for Exs. 16–21

ALGEBRA Find the value of x.

16. 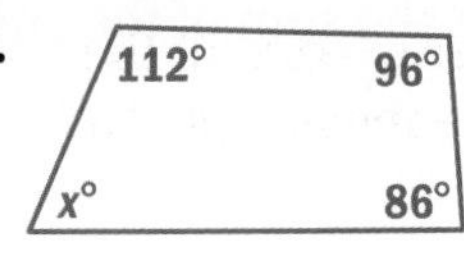

17. 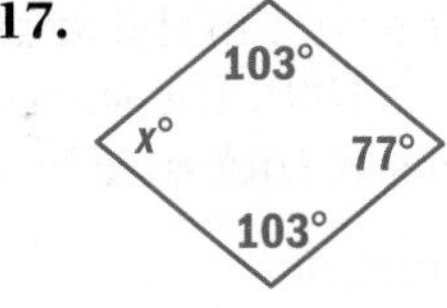

18. 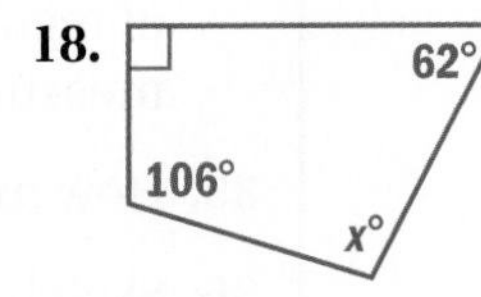

19. 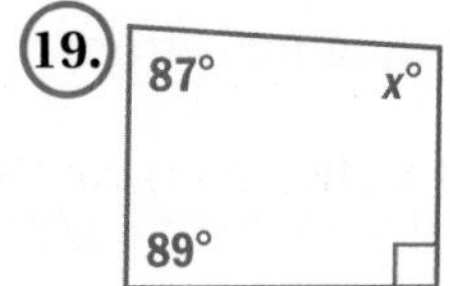

20. 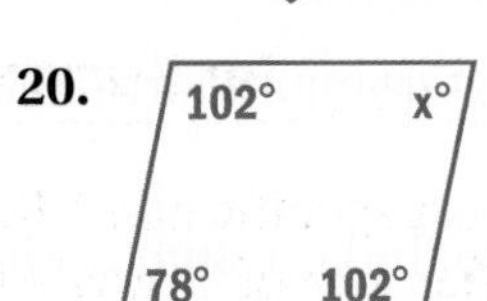

21. 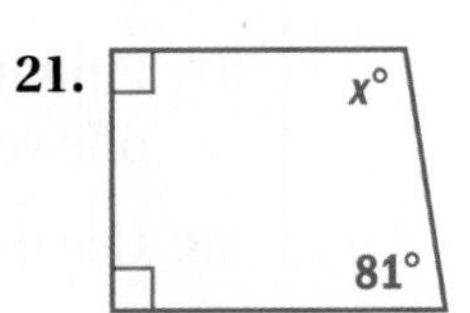

SEE EXAMPLE 3
on p. 483
for Ex. 22

22. ◆ **MULTIPLE CHOICE** The acute angle in the quadrilateral is labeled incorrectly. What is the correct angle measure?

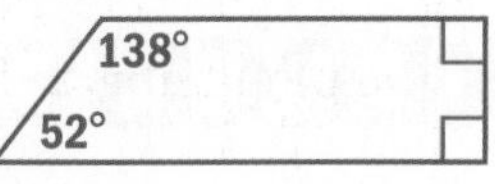

Ⓐ 38° Ⓑ 42° Ⓒ 128° Ⓓ 222°

SEE EXAMPLE 4
on p. 484
for Exs. 23–30

MATCHING Match the polygon with its classification.

23. 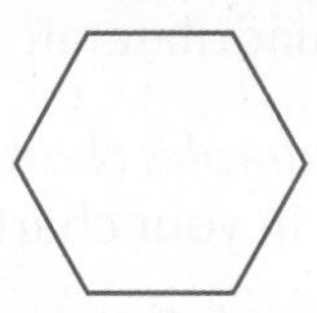

24. 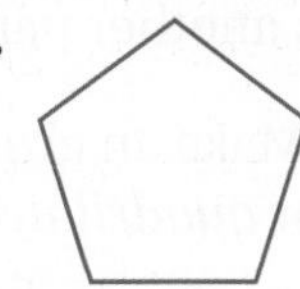

25. 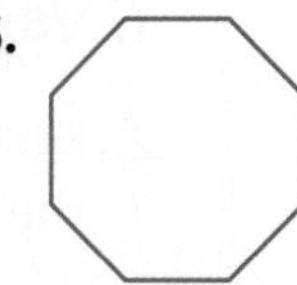

A. Pentagon **B.** Octagon **C.** Hexagon

26. **ERROR ANALYSIS** *Describe* and correct the error made in classifying the figure.

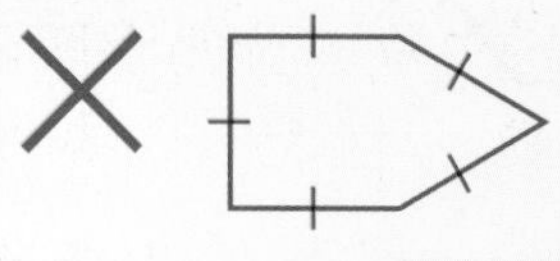

The figure is a regular pentagon because the lengths of all five sides are equal.

CLASSIFYING POLYGONS Classify the polygon and tell if it is regular. If it is not regular, explain why not.

27. 

28. 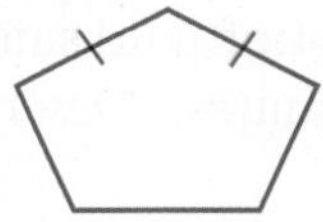

29. 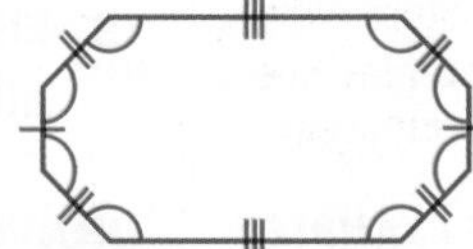

30. ◆ **MULTIPLE CHOICE** Which figure cannot be a regular polygon?

Ⓐ Rectangle Ⓑ Rhombus

Ⓒ Isosceles triangle Ⓓ Scalene triangle

REASONING Tell whether the statement is *true* or *false*. *Explain*.

31. All squares are rectangles.

32. A scalene triangle is regular.

33. A trapezoid is a parallelogram.

34. Every rectangle is a square.

CONNECT SKILLS TO PROBLEM SOLVING Exercises 35–38 will help you prepare for problem solving.

Use the following question: A blanket design has a repeated pattern of regular octagons and other polygons. What is the sum of the angle measures in an octagon?

35. How many sides does an octagon have?

36. Sketch a regular octagon.

37. Find the number of triangles formed by drawing all diagonals from one vertex.

38. Use the triangles to find the sum of the angle measures in an octagon.

39. SHORT RESPONSE Is a square always a rectangle, a rhombus, a parallelogram, and a quadrilateral? *Explain* your answer.

California @HomeTutor for problem solving help at classzone.com

40. STAINED GLASS WINDOW Sketch and classify four different quadrilaterals contained in the stained glass window at the right. Do any of the quadrilaterals appear to be regular quadrilaterals? *Explain* your reasoning.

California @HomeTutor for problem solving help at classzone.com

41. ◆ **MULTIPLE CHOICE** You are designing a patio in the shape of a quadrilateral. Its opposite sides are parallel, its adjacent sides are of equal length, and at least one of its angles is obtuse. Which term best describes the shape of the patio?

Ⓐ Square Ⓑ Rectangle Ⓒ Rhombus Ⓓ Parallelogram

42. MULTI-STEP PROBLEM Complete parts (a)–(c) to examine the angle measures of polygons.

REVIEW STRATEGIES
For help with problem solving strategies, see pp. 689–690.

a. **Break into Parts** Copy and complete the table below.

Polygons	*Triangle*	*Quadrilateral*	*Pentagon*	*Hexagon*
Sum of angle measures	?	?	?	?
Measure of each angle in a regular polygon	?	?	?	?

b. **Look for a Pattern** *Describe* a pattern in the sum of the angle measures in the table.

c. **Predict** Use the pattern you identified in part (b) to predict the sum of the angle measures in a 7 sided polygon. What do you predict is the measure of each angle in a regular 7 sided polygon?

43. CHALLENGE Find the values of a, b, c, and d in the diagram.

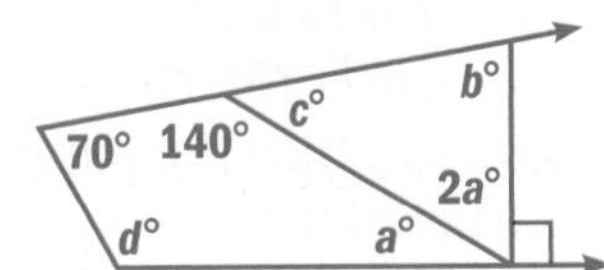

◆ CALIFORNIA STANDARDS SPIRAL REVIEW

NS 1.4 **44.** What number is 45% of 180? *(p. 301)*

Ⓐ 4 Ⓑ 25 Ⓒ 81 Ⓓ 400

AF 1.3 **45.** What is the value of $12\left(\frac{5}{12} + \frac{1}{6}\right)$? *(p. 173)*

Ⓐ 4 Ⓑ $5\frac{1}{6}$ Ⓒ 6 Ⓓ 7

AF 1.2 **46.** You have 20 baseball cards. You buy a pack of 6 cards each day. Which expression represents how many cards you have after x days? *(p. 202)*

Ⓐ $26x$ Ⓑ $20x + 6$ Ⓒ $6x$ Ⓓ $20 + 6x$

9.4 Drawing Quadrilaterals

Standards

MG 2.3
Draw quadrilaterals and triangles **from given information about them** (e.g., a quadrilateral having equal sides but no right angles, a right isosceles triangle).

QUESTION **How can you draw quadrilaterals using drawing software?**

EXAMPLE **Draw a quadrilateral with two pairs of parallel sides.**

STEP 1 **Construct** $\overleftrightarrow{AB}$ and a line parallel to $\overleftrightarrow{AB}$ through point C.

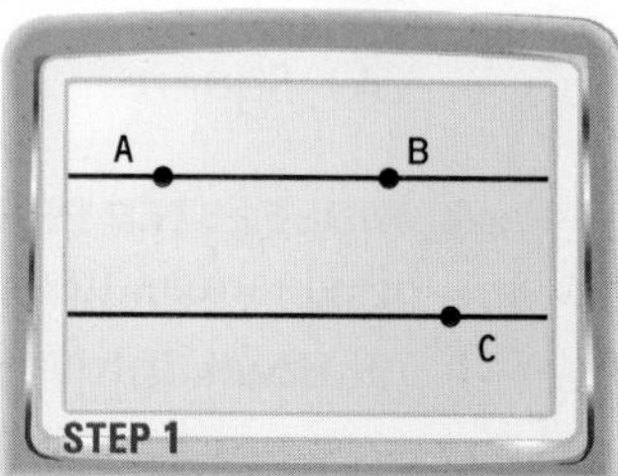

STEP 2 **Construct** $\overleftrightarrow{BC}$ and a line parallel to $\overleftrightarrow{BC}$ through point A.

STEP 3 **Construct** a point D at the intersection of the line drawn parallel to $\overleftrightarrow{AB}$ and the line drawn parallel to $\overleftrightarrow{BC}$.

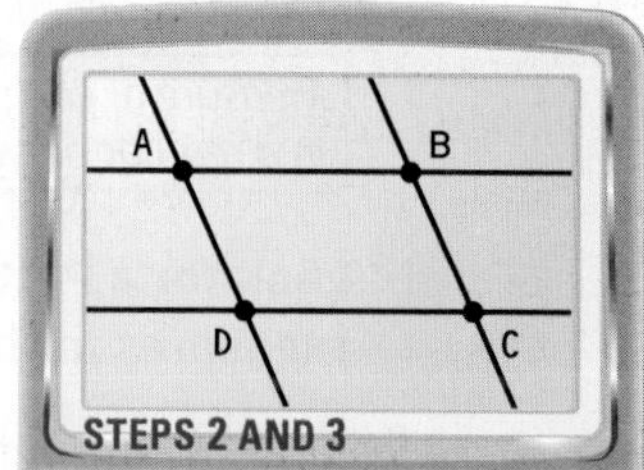

STEP 4 **Construct** segments to form the sides of quadrilateral $ABCD$. After you construct $\overline{AB}$, $\overline{BC}$, $\overline{CD}$, and $\overline{DA}$, hide the parallel lines that you constructed in Steps 1 and 2.

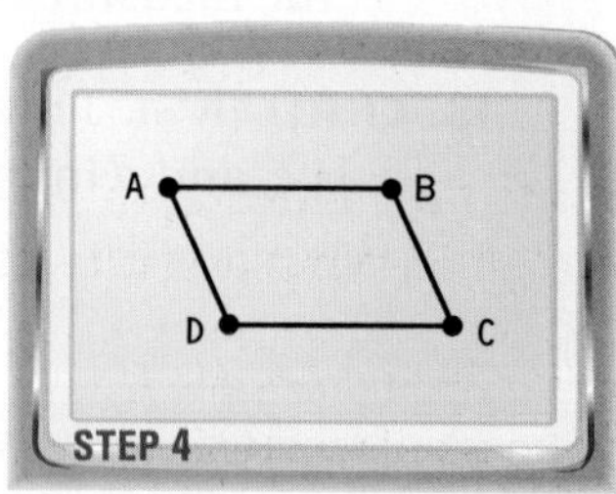

PRACTICE

Use drawing software to draw a quadrilateral with the given conditions.

1. Two pairs of parallel sides and at least one right angle
2. Exactly one pair of parallel sides
3. Exactly one pair of parallel sides and exactly two right angles

Standards

NS 1.2 Interpret and use ratios in different contexts (e.g., batting averages, miles per hour) **to show the relative sizes of two quantities,** using appropriate notations (a/b, a to b, $a : b$).

9.5 Comparing Rectangles

MATERIALS • graph paper • ruler

QUESTION How can you compare rectangles?

When you reduce or enlarge a rectangle, you create another rectangle of the same shape, but different size. You can draw rectangles of the same shape on graph paper to compare these rectangles.

EXPLORE Compare the lengths and widths of same-shaped rectangles using ratios.

STEP 1 **Draw** a rectangle on a piece of graph paper. Use a ruler to draw a diagonal line segment through two opposite vertices, as shown.

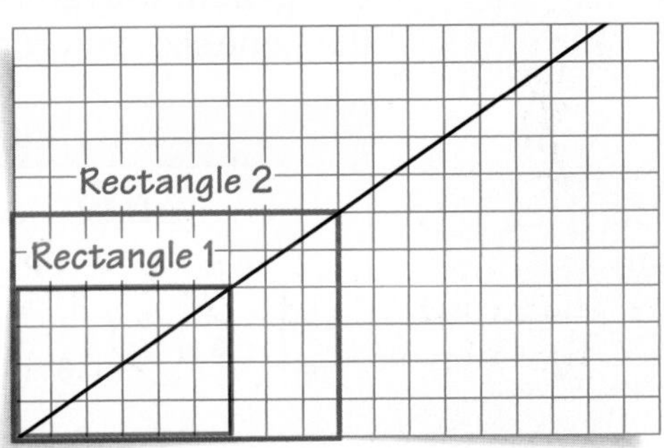

STEP 2 **Draw** a second rectangle that shares the lower left vertex. The opposite vertex should be on the diagonal line, as shown. This rectangle is an enlargement of the rectangle from Step 1.

STEP 3 **Copy** and complete the table by recording the length and width of each rectangle.

	Rectangle 1	Rectangle 2
Length	?	?
Width	?	?

STEP 4 **Write** the following ratios using the data in the table. What do you notice?

$$\frac{\text{Length of rectangle 1}}{\text{Length of rectangle 2}} \qquad \frac{\text{Width of rectangle 1}}{\text{Width of rectangle 2}}$$

DRAW CONCLUSIONS Use your observations to complete these exercises.

1. **LOOK FOR A PATTERN** Draw a third rectangle that shares the lower left corner and diagonal line with the rectangle from Step 1. Then repeat Steps 3 and 4, comparing the first rectangle and the third rectangle. *Describe* any relationships.

2. **REASONING** Rectangle A has the same shape as rectangle B. Rectangle B is 21 units long and 7 units wide. If rectangle A has a width of 6 units, how long is rectangle A? *Explain* your reasoning.

9.5 Similar and Congruent Polygons

Math and SAILING
Exs. 19–21, p. 493

Standards **NS 1.2** **Interpret and use ratios in different contexts** (e.g., batting averages, miles per hour) **to show the relative sizes of two quantities,** using appropriate notations (a/b, a to b, $a : b$).

Connect ***Before*** you used ratios to interpret scale drawings. ***Now*** you will use ratios to show relative sizes of similar polygons.

KEY VOCABULARY
- **similar polygons**
- **congruent polygons**

Two polygons that have the same shape but not necessarily the same size are **similar polygons**. The activity on page 489 suggests that side lengths of similar figures are proportional, as summarized below. The symbol $\sim$ indicates that two polygons are similar.

Congruent polygons are similar polygons that have the same shape *and* the same size. Polygons can be congruent even if they are rotated or flipped.

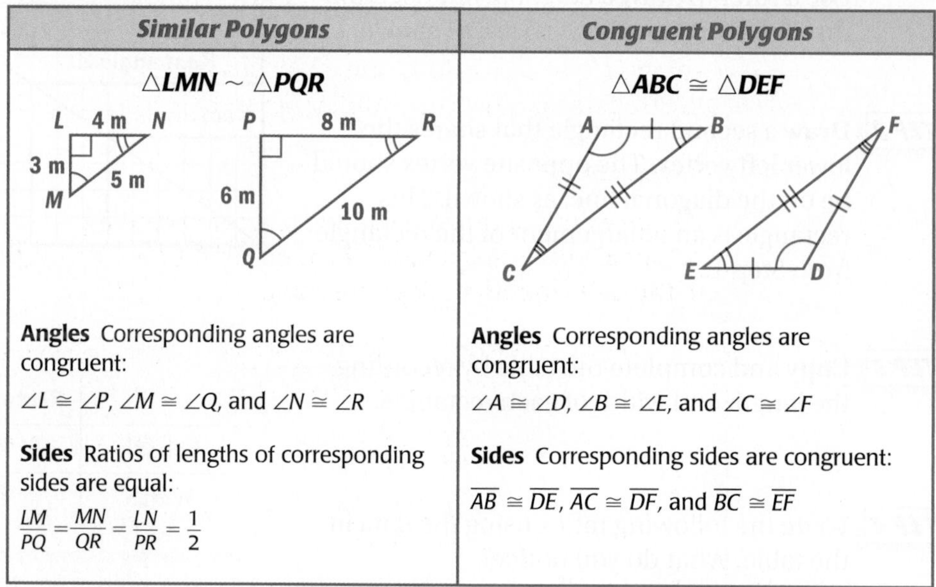

Similar Polygons	*Congruent Polygons*
$\triangle LMN \sim \triangle PQR$	$\triangle ABC \cong \triangle DEF$
Angles Corresponding angles are congruent: $\angle L \cong \angle P$, $\angle M \cong \angle Q$, and $\angle N \cong \angle R$	**Angles** Corresponding angles are congruent: $\angle A \cong \angle D$, $\angle B \cong \angle E$, and $\angle C \cong \angle F$
Sides Ratios of lengths of corresponding sides are equal: $\frac{LM}{PQ} = \frac{MN}{QR} = \frac{LN}{PR} = \frac{1}{2}$	**Sides** Corresponding sides are congruent: $\overline{AB} \cong \overline{DE}$, $\overline{AC} \cong \overline{DF}$, and $\overline{BC} \cong \overline{EF}$

EXAMPLE 1 Finding Measures of Congruent Polygons

AVOID ERRORS
When naming congruent or similar polygons, be sure to list the letters for the corresponding vertices in the same order.

$\triangle RST$ is congruent to $\triangle XYZ$. Name the corresponding sides and the corresponding angles. Then find XY.

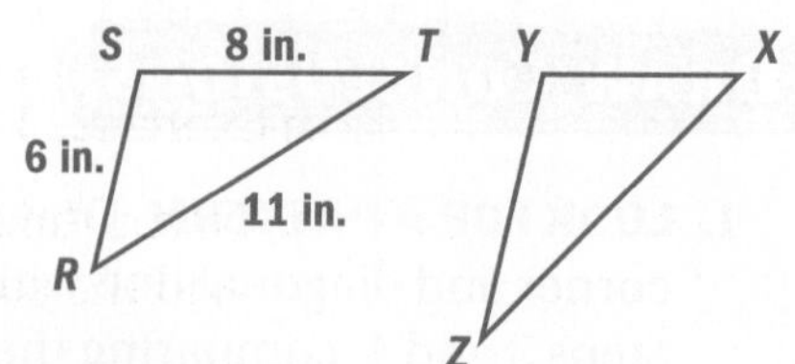

SOLUTION

Corresponding sides: $\overline{RS}$ and $\overline{XY}$, $\overline{RT}$ and $\overline{XZ}$, $\overline{ST}$ and $\overline{YZ}$

Corresponding angles: $\angle R$ and $\angle X$, $\angle S$ and $\angle Y$, $\angle T$ and $\angle Z$

Because $\overline{XY}$ and $\overline{RS}$ are corresponding sides, they are equal in length. So, $XY = RS = 6$ inches.

EXAMPLE 2 Finding the Ratio of Lengths

Given that $\triangle ABC \sim \triangle DEF$, find the ratio of the lengths of the corresponding sides of $\triangle ABC$ to $\triangle DEF$.

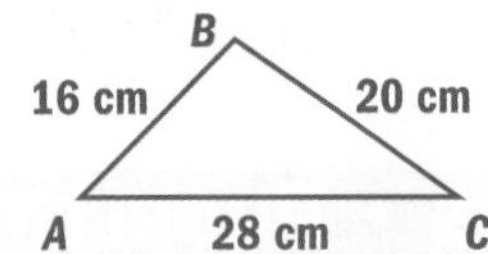

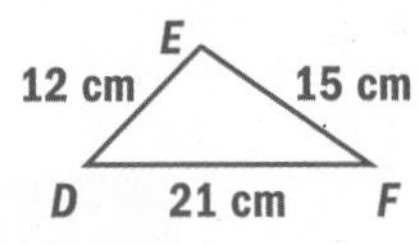

AVOID ERRORS

When you write the ratios, be sure you compare the sides of $\triangle ABC$ to $\triangle DEF$, not $\triangle DEF$ to $\triangle ABC$.

SOLUTION

Write a ratio for each pair of corresponding sides. Then substitute the lengths of the sides and simplify each ratio.

$$\frac{AB}{DE} = \frac{16}{12} = \frac{4}{3} \qquad \frac{BC}{EF} = \frac{20}{15} = \frac{4}{3} \qquad \frac{AC}{DF} = \frac{28}{21} = \frac{4}{3}$$

▶ **Answer** The ratio of the lengths of the corresponding sides is $\frac{4}{3}$.

EXAMPLE 3 Checking for Similarity

DRAWING An art student is copying a detail of a rectangular painting. The copy is 48 inches long and 36 inches wide. The rectangular region she is copying is 16 inches long and 12 inches wide. Are the original and the copy similar figures?

The copy is 48 in. by 36 in.

SOLUTION

Because both figures are rectangles, corresponding angles are congruent. See if the ratios of the lengths of the corresponding sides are equal.

$$\frac{\text{Length of original}}{\text{Length of copy}} \stackrel{?}{=} \frac{\text{Width of original}}{\text{Width of copy}}$$ Write ratios for lengths of corresponding sides.

$$\frac{16}{48} \stackrel{?}{=} \frac{12}{36}$$ Substitute values.

$$\frac{1}{3} = \frac{1}{3} \checkmark$$ Simplify.

▶ **Answer** The corresponding angles are congruent and the ratios of the lengths of the corresponding sides are equal, so the figures are similar.

✓ GUIDED PRACTICE for Examples 1, 2, and 3

In Exercises 1 and 2, use the fact that $ABCD \cong EFGH$.

1. Name the corresponding sides and the corresponding angles.

2. Find the unknown angle measures.

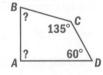

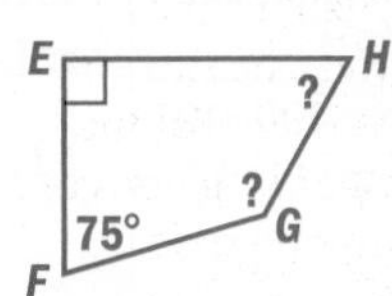

3. **WHAT IF?** In Example 3, suppose the copy is 44 inches long and 27 inches wide. Are the original and the copy similar figures?

9.5 EXERCISES

HOMEWORK KEY
◆ = **MULTIPLE CHOICE PRACTICE** Exs. 9, 10, 25, 30–32
○ = **HINTS AND HOMEWORK HELP** for Exs. 11, 13, 25 at classzone.com

SKILLS • PROBLEM SOLVING • REASONING

1. **VOCABULARY** Copy and complete: Two polygons that have the same shape but not necessarily the same size are __?__.

2. **WRITING** Are all squares similar? Are they all congruent? *Explain.*

SEE EXAMPLE 1 on p. 490 for Exs. 3–9

IDENTIFYING CORRESPONDING PARTS Given $\triangle UVW \cong \triangle XYZ$, name the part of $\triangle UVW$ corresponding to the given part of $\triangle XYZ$.

3. $\angle X$ 4. $\angle ZYX$ 5. $\overline{XZ}$ 6. $\overline{ZY}$

FINDING MEASURES Name the corresponding sides and the corresponding angles of the congruent polygons. Then find the unknown measures.

7. $KLMN \cong QRST$

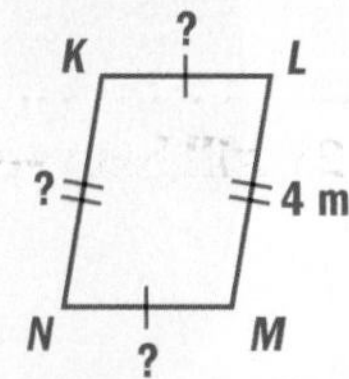

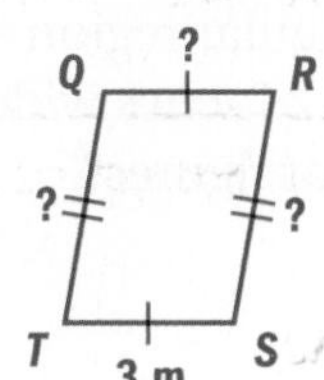

8. $\triangle FGH \cong \triangle JKL$

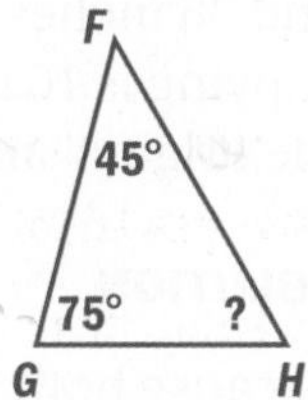

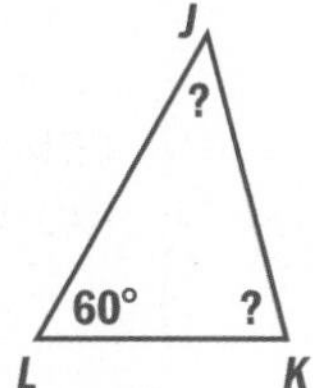

9. ◆ **MULTIPLE CHOICE** Suppose that $\triangle LMN \cong \triangle XYZ$ and both triangles are scalene. Which of the following statements is *not* true?

Ⓐ $\overline{LN} \cong \overline{XZ}$ Ⓑ $\overline{LM} \cong \overline{YZ}$ Ⓒ $\angle M \cong \angle Y$ Ⓓ $\angle N \cong \angle Z$

SEE EXAMPLE 2 on p. 491 for Ex. 10

10. ◆ **MULTIPLE CHOICE** Rectangles *ABCD* and *EFGH* are similar. What is the ratio of the lengths of the corresponding sides of *ABCD* to *EFGH*?

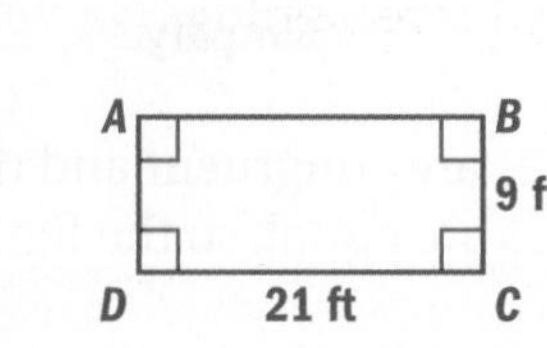

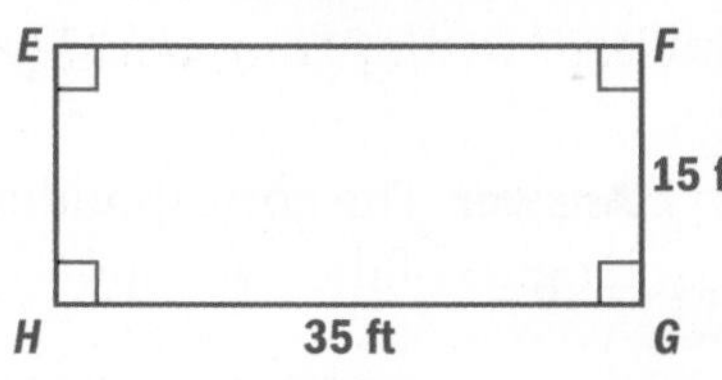

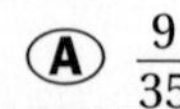

Ⓐ $\frac{9}{35}$ Ⓑ $\frac{3}{5}$ Ⓒ $\frac{7}{5}$ Ⓓ $\frac{5}{3}$

SEE EXAMPLES 1 AND 3 on pp. 490–491 for Exs. 11–12

ERROR ANALYSIS *Describe* and correct the error made in identifying the relationship between the figures.

11.

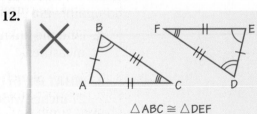

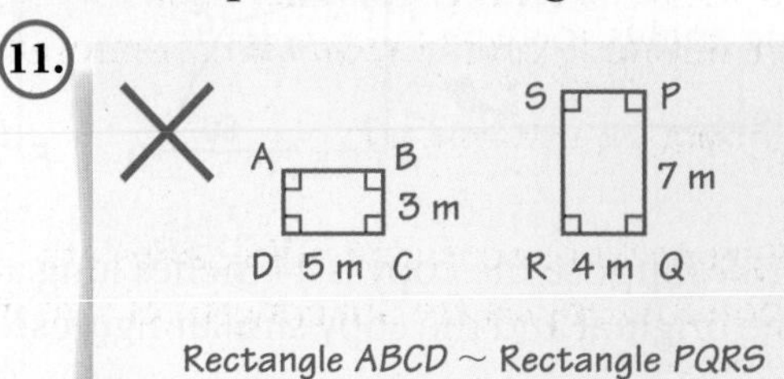

12.

B F E A C D

$\triangle ABC \cong \triangle DEF$

SEE EXAMPLES 2 AND 3
on p. 491 for Exs. 13–16

RATIOS **Tell whether the two polygons are similar. If they are, find the ratio of the lengths of the corresponding sides of figure A to figure B.**

13.
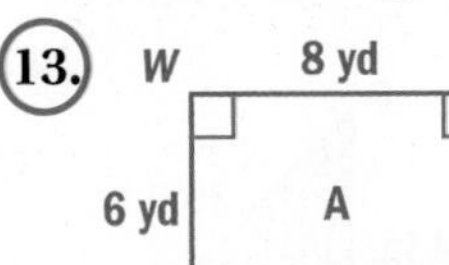

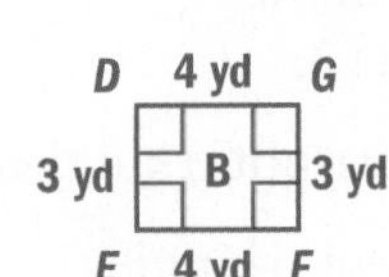

14.
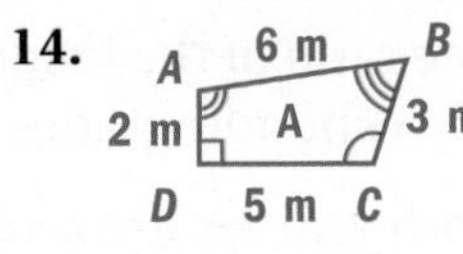

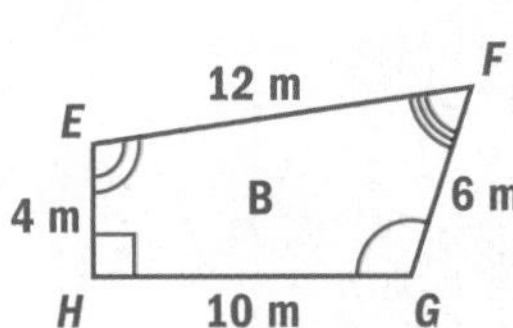

15.
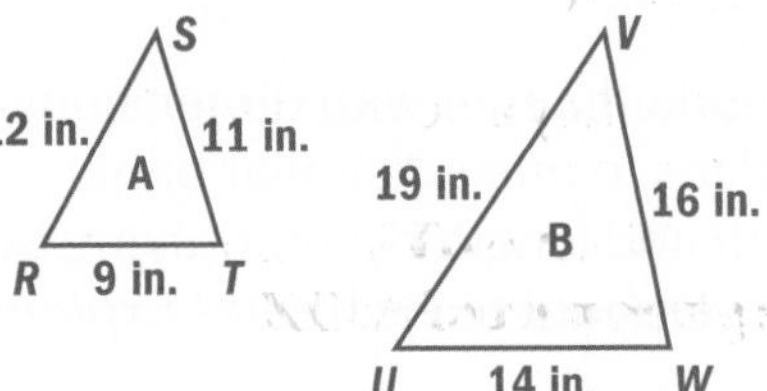

16.
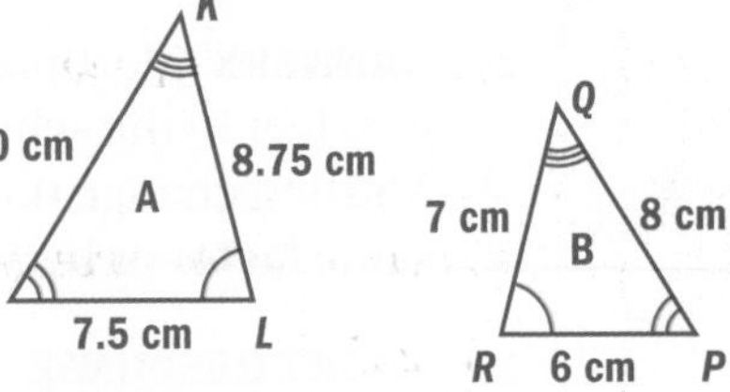

REASONING **Tell whether the statement is *true* or *false*. If false, explain why.**

17. Two rectangles are congruent if they have the same perimeter.

18. Two squares are congruent if they have the same perimeter.

CONNECT SKILLS TO PROBLEM SOLVING **Exercises 19–21 will help you prepare for problem solving.**

In the diagram of the two sailboats, $\triangle ABC \sim \triangle DEF$.

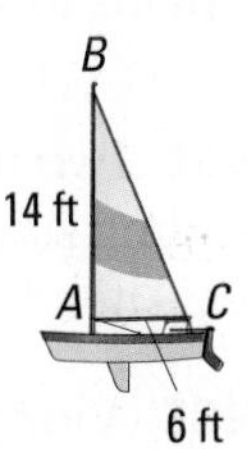

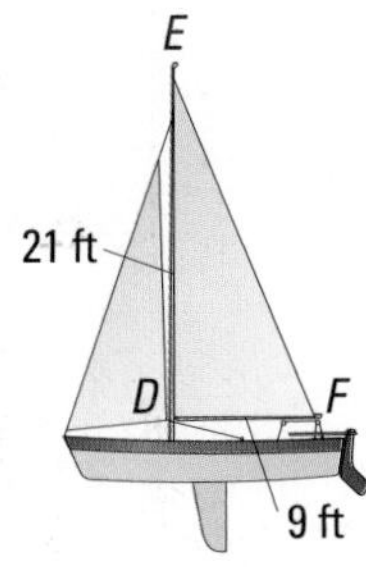

19. Name the corresponding sides.

20. Name the corresponding angles.

21. Find the ratio of the lengths of the corresponding sides of $\triangle ABC$ to $\triangle DEF$.

SEE EXAMPLES 1 AND 3
on pp. 490–491 for Exs. 22–23

22. **SHORT RESPONSE** Are the colored blocks shown below similar? Are they congruent? *Explain* your reasoning.

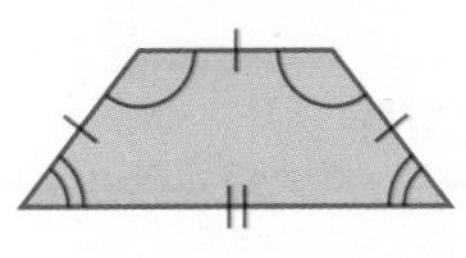
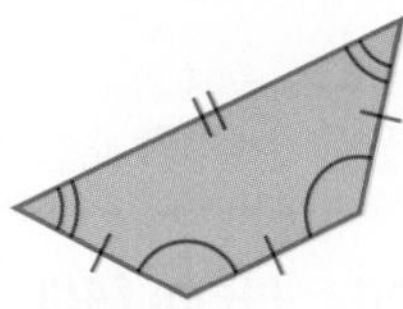

California @HomeTutor for problem solving help at classzone.com

23. **PHOTO STICKERS** A rectangular photograph measures 6 inches by 4 inches. A rectangular photo sticker is 1.4 inches by 0.9 inch. Are the photograph and photo sticker similar figures? *Explain* your reasoning.

California @HomeTutor for problem solving help at classzone.com

24. **OPEN-ENDED** Sketch two polygons whose corresponding sides are congruent but whose corresponding angles are not congruent. Are the polygons similar? Why or why not?

25. ◆ **MULTIPLE CHOICE** Which statement about the triangular scarves is true?

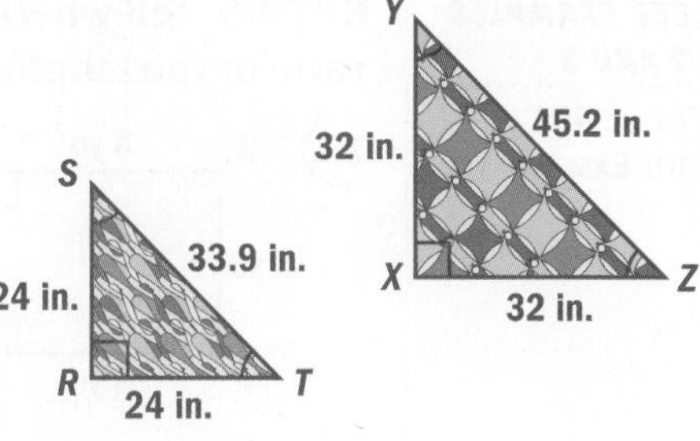

Ⓐ The ratio of the lengths of the corresponding sides is 2 : 3.

Ⓑ Both scarves are scalene right triangles.

Ⓒ The scarves are congruent triangles.

Ⓓ $\triangle RST \sim \triangle XYZ$

26. **BANNERS** Martina hung a rectangular banner with dimensions 2 feet by 8 feet in the school gym. She plans to make 3 similar banners. Should Martina change the banner's width and length by multiplying by the same factor or by adding the same amount to each side? *Explain.*

27. **SHORT RESPONSE** A college football field has a width of 160 feet and a length of 360 feet. A college soccer field can vary from 195 feet to 240 feet in width and from 330 feet to 360 feet in length.

    a. Can college football and soccer fields ever be similar rectangles? *Explain.*

    b. A tennis court is 78 feet long by 36 feet wide. Is this similar to either of the fields in part (a)? *Explain.*

Football field at UC Berkeley

28. **CHALLENGE** Two rectangles are similar. The ratio of the lengths of their corresponding sides is 1 : 2. Find the ratio of the perimeters of the two rectangles. Then find the ratio of the areas. *Explain* your answers.

29. **CHALLENGE** A long and narrow rectangular painting is matted with a border 2.5 inches wide all the way around the edges of the painting. Is the inner rectangle of the border similar to the outer rectangle of the border? *Explain.*

◆ CALIFORNIA STANDARDS SPIRAL REVIEW

NS 2.3 30. What is the product of 27 and −44? *(p. 148)*

Ⓐ −1188 Ⓑ −71 Ⓒ 17 Ⓓ 1188

MG 2.2 31. The measures of two angles of a triangle are 36° and 41°. What is the measure of the third angle? *(p. 474)*

Ⓐ 13° Ⓑ 93° Ⓒ 103° Ⓓ 283°

AF 1.2 32. Grapes cost $1.19 per pound and cherries cost $1.79 per pound. Which expression gives the total cost for x pounds of grapes and y pounds of cherries? *(p. 202)*

Ⓐ $1.19x \times 1.79y$ Ⓑ $1.19x + 1.79y$ Ⓒ $1.19x - 1.79y$ Ⓓ $2.98(x + y)$

9.6 Using Proportions with Similar Polygons

Standards **NS 1.3 Use proportions to solve problems (e.g.,** determine the value of *N* if $\frac{4}{7} = \frac{N}{21}$, **find the length of a side of a polygon similar to a known polygon).** Use cross-multiplication as a method for solving such problems, understanding it as the multiplication of both sides of an equation by a multiplicative inverse.

Connect ***Before*** you solved proportions. ***Now*** you will use proportions to find side lengths of similar polygons.

KEY VOCABULARY
- **proportion,** *p. 266*
- **similar polygons,** *p. 490*

You know that the lengths of corresponding sides of similar polygons are proportional. When two polygons are similar, you can use proportions to find unknown lengths.

EXAMPLE 1 ◆ Multiple Choice Practice

Quadrilaterals *ABCD* and *EFGH* are similar. What is the length of $\overline{FG}$?

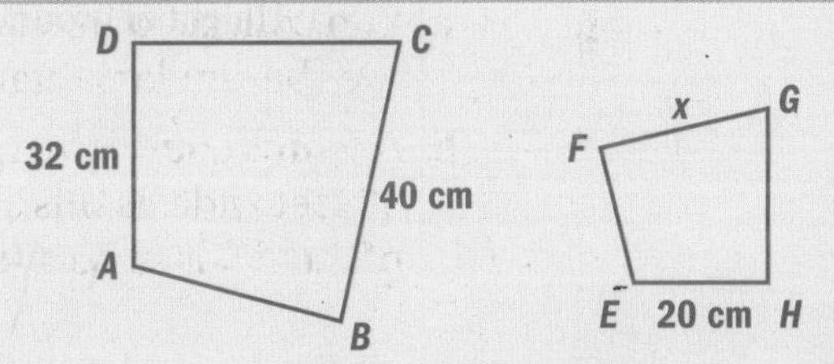

Ⓐ 25 cm Ⓑ 28 cm

Ⓒ 32 cm Ⓓ 44 cm

ELIMINATE CHOICES
You know that *EFGH* is smaller than *ABCD*. This means that the length of $\overline{FG}$ must be less than 40 cm. You can eliminate choice D.

SOLUTION

Use the ratios of the lengths of corresponding sides to write a proportion involving three known lengths and the unknown length.

$\frac{AD}{EH} = \frac{BC}{FG}$ **Write a proportion involving *FG*.**

$\frac{32}{20} = \frac{40}{x}$ **Substitute known values.**

$32x = 20 \cdot 40$ **Use cross products property.**

$x = 25$ **Divide each side by 32.**

▶ **Answer** The length of $\overline{FG}$ is 25 centimeters.
The correct answer is A. Ⓐ Ⓑ Ⓒ Ⓓ

✓ GUIDED PRACTICE for Example 1

1. Find the unknown length *x*, given that the polygons are similar.

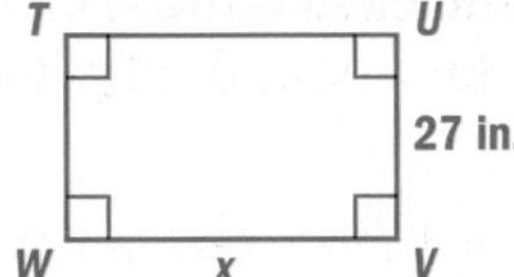

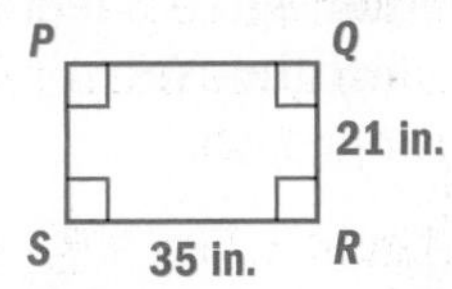

INDIRECT MEASUREMENT The sun's rays hit objects that are perpendicular to the ground at the same angle. The heights of these objects and the lengths of their shadows form similar triangles. You can use these similar triangles to find lengths that are difficult to measure directly.

EXAMPLE 2 Making an Indirect Measurement

TREE HEIGHT A 16 inch tall groundhog emerges on Groundhog Day near a tree and sees its shadow. The length of the groundhog's shadow is 5 inches, and the length of the tree's shadow is 35 inches. What is the height of the tree?

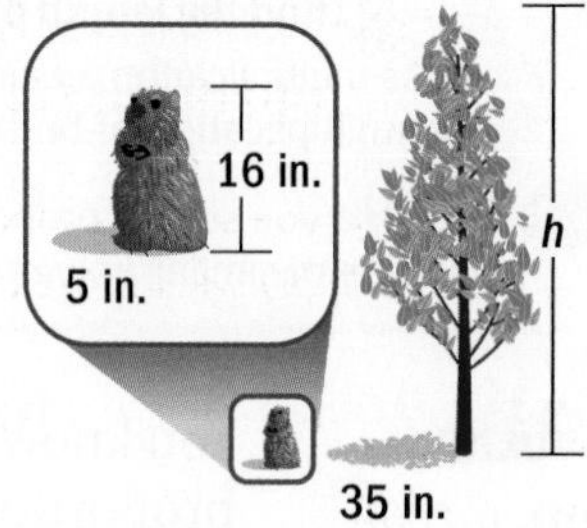

SOLUTION

Use the ratios of the lengths of corresponding parts. Write a proportion involving the unknown height h.

$$\frac{\text{Height of tree}}{\text{Height of groundhog}} = \frac{\text{Length of tree's shadow}}{\text{Length of groundhog's shadow}}$$

$\frac{h}{16} = \frac{35}{5}$ **Substitute known values.**

$16 \cdot \frac{h}{16} = 16 \cdot \frac{35}{5}$ **Multiply each side by 16.**

$h = 16 \cdot 7$ **Simplify.**

$h = 112$ **Multiply.**

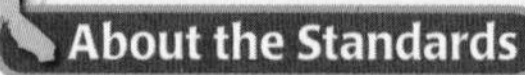
About the Standards

Note that Grade 6 Standard MR 2.1 asks you to use estimation to verify the reasonableness of calculated results.

▸ **Answer** The tree has a height of 112 inches, or 9 feet 4 inches.

CHECK You can estimate to check that your answer is reasonable. The groundhog is slightly taller than 3 times its shadow, so the tree should be slightly taller than 3 times its shadow. Because $3 \times 35 = 105$, the height of 112 inches is reasonable.

✓ GUIDED PRACTICE for Example 2

2. **WHAT IF?** In Example 2, suppose the groundhog emerges and sees its shadow next to a building. The length of the groundhog's shadow is 5 inches, and the length of the building's shadow is 95 inches. Draw a diagram for the situation. Then find the height of the building.

3. **LIGHTHOUSE HEIGHT** The shadow cast by a lighthouse is 30 feet long. At the same time, the shadow cast by a 4 foot tall sign is 3 feet long. How tall is the lighthouse?

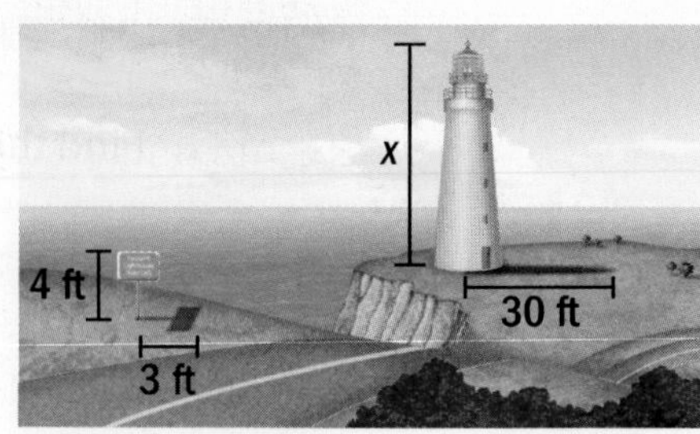

9.6 EXERCISES

HOMEWORK KEY ◆ = **MULTIPLE CHOICE PRACTICE** Exs. 8, 11, 19, 23–25

○ = **HINTS AND HOMEWORK HELP** for Exs. 3, 5, 21 at classzone.com

SKILLS • PROBLEM SOLVING • REASONING

1. **VOCABULARY** Copy and complete: You can use a(n) __?__ to find unknown side lengths in similar figures.

2. **WRITING** *Explain* why you agree or disagree with each of the following: (a) All congruent figures are similar; (b) All similar figures are congruent.

SEE EXAMPLE 1 on p. 495 for Exs. 3–8

FINDING LENGTHS **Find length *x*, given that the polygons are similar.**

3.

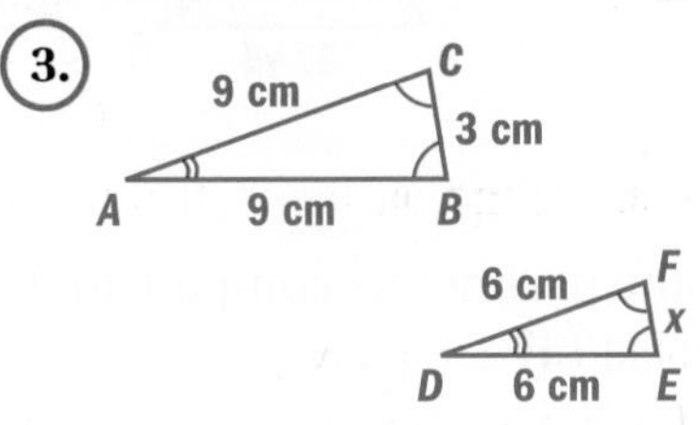

4.

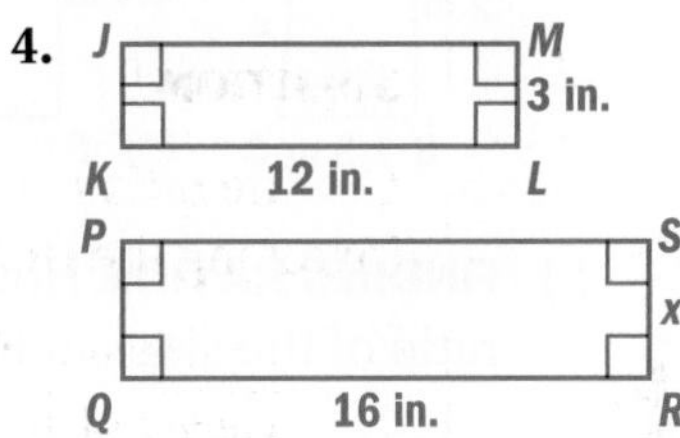

5.

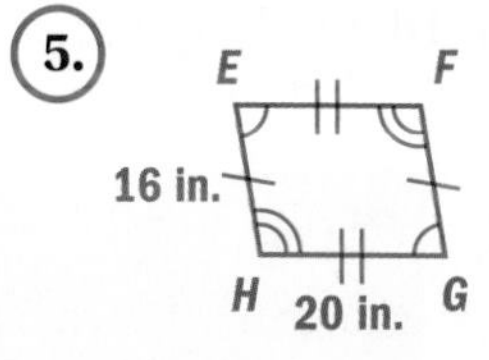

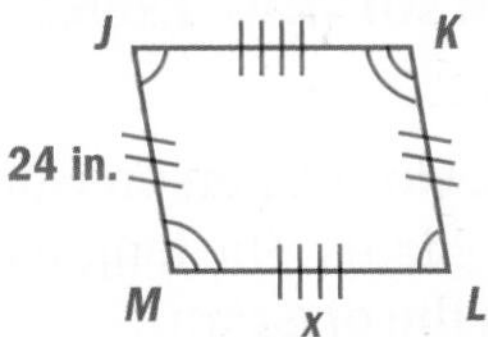

6.

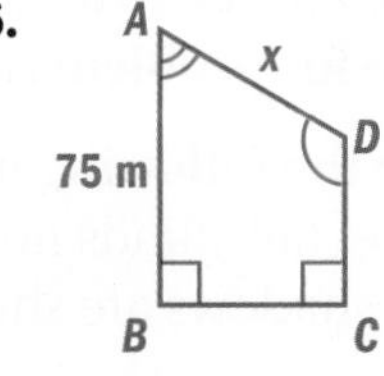

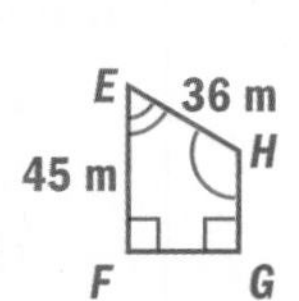

7. **ERROR ANALYSIS** Quadrilaterals *ABCD* and *QRST* are similar. *Describe* and correct the error made in finding the value of *x*.

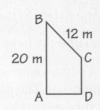

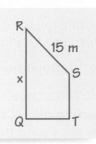

$$\frac{20}{15} = \frac{12}{x}$$

$20x = 180$

$x = 9$ meters

B, 12 m, C, 20 m, A, D; R, 15 m, S, x, Q, T

8. ◆ **MULTIPLE CHOICE** Rectangles *RSTU* and *LMNP* are similar and $RS = 7$ cm, $ST = 4$ cm, and $LM = 21$ cm. Which proportion can you use to find the width of rectangle *LMNP*?

Ⓐ $\frac{7}{21} = \frac{MN}{4}$ Ⓑ $\frac{7}{21} = \frac{4}{MN}$ Ⓒ $\frac{21}{7} = \frac{4}{MN}$ Ⓓ $\frac{21}{7} = \frac{7}{MN}$

FINDING AREAS **Find the area of the smaller, similar rectangle.**

9. 10.

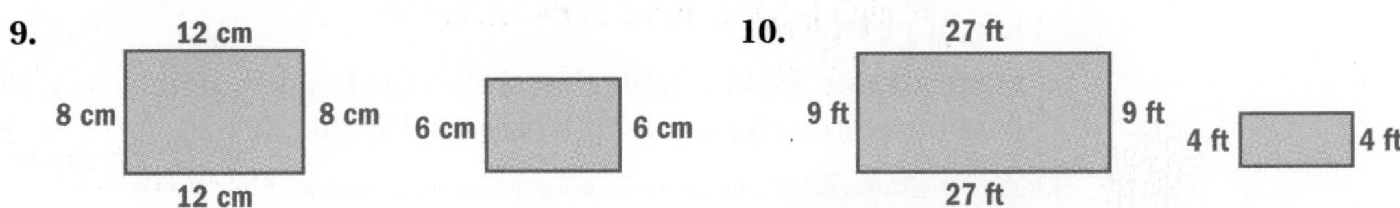

11. ◆ **MULTIPLE CHOICE** $\triangle FGH$ and $\triangle JKL$ are similar. What is the perimeter of $\triangle JKL$?

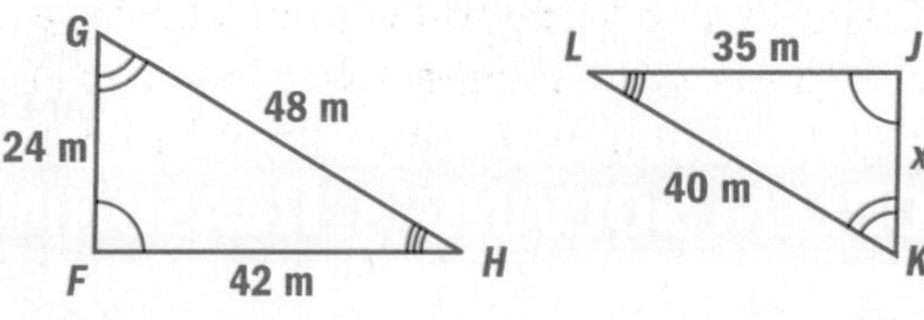

Ⓐ 20 m　　Ⓑ 40 m　　Ⓒ 95 m　　Ⓓ 114 m

FINDING PERIMETERS **Find the perimeters of the similar polygons.**

12.

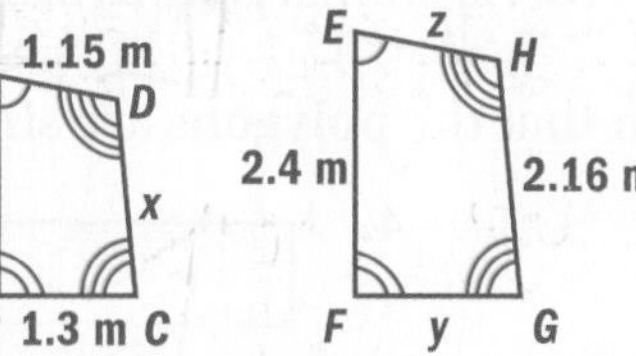

13.

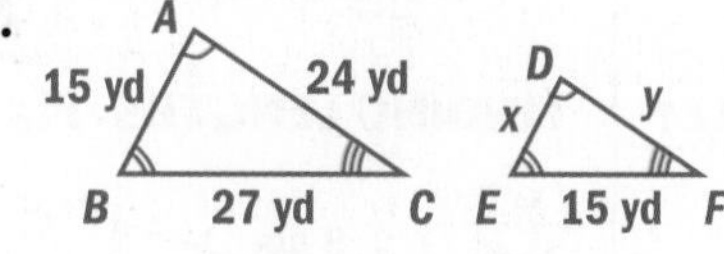

14. **FINDING RATIOS** How does the ratio of the perimeters compare to the ratio of the sides in Exercise 12? in Exercise 13?

CONNECT SKILLS TO PROBLEM SOLVING **Exercises 15–18 will help you prepare for problem solving.**

Use the following information: A person who is 5 feet tall stands next to a cactus. The lengths of the shadows are shown in the diagram.

15. Draw triangles to represent the situation.

16. Write a proportion, using words, involving the unknown height of the cactus.

17. Substitute the given heights and lengths in your proportion. Use x for the height of the cactus.

18. Solve the proportion to find the height of the cactus.

SEE EXAMPLE 2 on p. 496 for Exs. 19–21

19. ◆ **MULTIPLE CHOICE** A person who is 6 feet tall stands next to a life-sized model of a dinosaur. The person's shadow is 4 feet long. At the same time, the shadow cast by the dinosaur model is 12 feet long. How tall is the dinosaur model?

Ⓐ 8 feet　　Ⓑ 14 feet　　Ⓒ 18 feet　　Ⓓ 48 feet

California @HomeTutor for problem solving help at classzone.com

20. **MULTI-STEP PROBLEM** A flagpole is 24 feet tall and casts a 20 foot shadow. A tree next to the flagpole casts a shadow x feet long.

 a. **Write a Proportion** Write a proportion you can use to find the height y of the tree.

 b. **Make a Table** Make a table that shows the heights of trees next to the flagpole whose shadow lengths are 10, 15, and 20 feet.

California @HomeTutor for problem solving help at classzone.com

21. **BUILDING HEIGHT** A girl places a mirror on the ground and stands so that she can just see the top of a building. If she measures the distance x from the base of the building to the mirror and the distance y from where she is standing to the mirror, how can she use a proportion with her own height h to find the height z of the building?

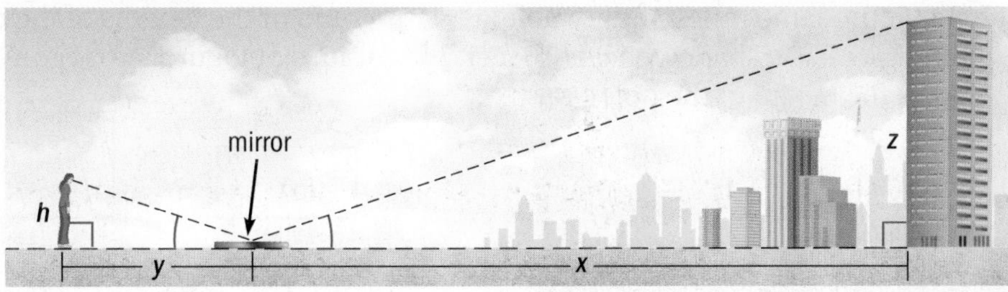

22. **CHALLENGE** In the figure, $\triangle RST \sim \triangle QSP$.

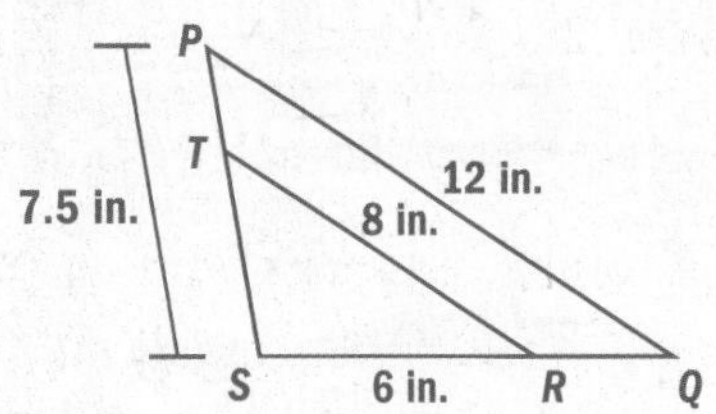

a. Find RQ, ST, and TP.

b. Does $\frac{ST}{TP} = \frac{SR}{RQ}$? Does $\frac{ST}{TP} = \frac{TR}{PQ}$? *Explain.*

◆ CALIFORNIA STANDARDS SPIRAL REVIEW

NS 2.2 23. What is the product of $2\frac{7}{8}$ and $6\frac{2}{9}$? ***(p. 88)***

Ⓐ $14\frac{5}{8}$ Ⓑ $15\frac{5}{9}$ Ⓒ $16\frac{3}{8}$ Ⓓ $17\frac{8}{9}$

MG 2.2 24. $\angle X$ and $\angle Y$ are complementary, and $m\angle X = 63°$. What is $m\angle Y$? ***(p. 463)***

Ⓐ 27° Ⓑ 63° Ⓒ 117° Ⓓ 153°

AF 2.3 25. You complete a crossword puzzle in 25 minutes. At that rate, how long will it take you to complete 5 crossword puzzles? ***(p. 266)***

Ⓐ 1 h 25 min Ⓑ 1 h 40 min Ⓒ 2 h 5 min Ⓓ 2 h 25 min

QUIZ *for Lessons 9.4–9.6*

Give the most specific name for the polygon. Then find the sum of the angle measures. *(p. 482)*

1. 6 m, 3 m, 3 m, 6 m

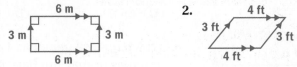

2. 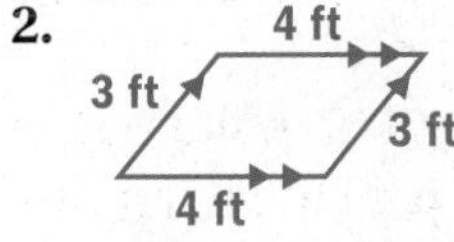

3. 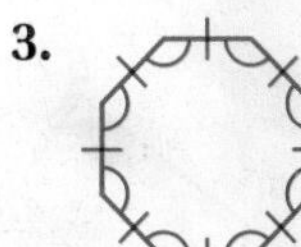

4. Draw a quadrilateral with 2 acute angles and 2 obtuse angles. ***(p. 482)***

5. Use the fact that $\triangle FGH \sim \triangle KLM$. Name the corresponding sides and the corresponding angles. Suppose $FH = 7$ ft, $GH = 8$ ft, and $LM = 6$ ft. Find KM. ***(pp. 490, 495)***

Multiple Choice Practice for Lessons 9.4–9.6

1. The sign shown casts a shadow that is 2 feet long. At the same time, a utility pole next to the sign casts a shadow that is 16 feet long. What is the height of the pole? **NS 1.3**

   Ⓐ 14 ft Ⓑ 32 ft
   Ⓒ 49 ft Ⓓ 56 ft

2. The ratio of the perimeters of two squares is 2 : 5. The perimeter of the smaller square is 12 inches. What is the ratio of the areas of the squares? **NS 1.2, MR 2.2**

   Ⓐ 2 : 5 Ⓑ 2 : 10
   Ⓒ 4 : 10 Ⓓ 4 : 25

3. Which of the following would you draw to show a parallelogram with 4 right angles and 4 congruent sides? **MG 2.3**

   Ⓐ Rectangle Ⓑ Rhombus
   Ⓒ Square Ⓓ Trapezoid

4. Given that $\triangle ABC$ is similar to $\triangle DEF$, what is the unknown length x? **NS 1.3**

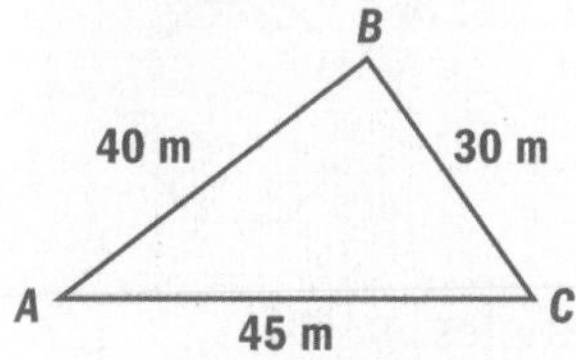

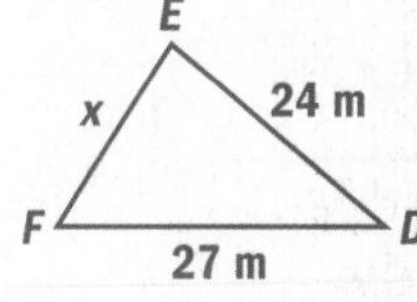

   Ⓐ 18 m Ⓑ 24 m
   Ⓒ 32 m Ⓓ 50 m

5. Figure A is similar to Figure B. What is the ratio of the lengths of the corresponding sides of Figure A to Figure B? **NS 1.2**

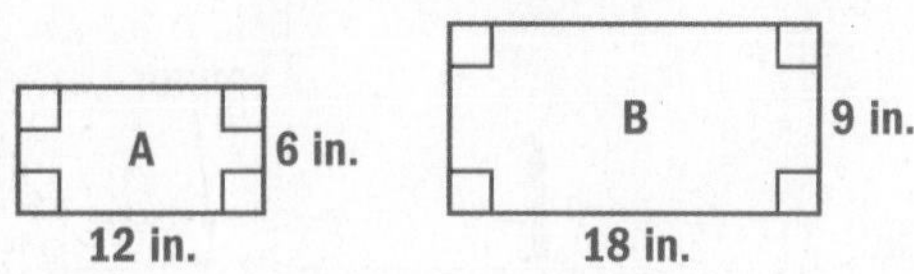

   Ⓐ $\frac{1}{3}$ Ⓑ $\frac{1}{2}$ Ⓒ $\frac{2}{3}$ Ⓓ $\frac{3}{4}$

6. Rectangles *PQRS* and *JKLM* are similar. Rectangle *PQRS* has a length of 18 feet and a width of 10 feet. Rectangle *JKLM* has a width of 25 feet. What is the length of rectangle *JKLM*? **NS 1.3**

   Ⓐ 7.2 ft Ⓑ 13.9 ft
   Ⓒ 33 ft Ⓓ 45 ft

7. A hiker looks up at a natural rock arch. The hiker is 5 feet tall and casts a shadow that is 7.5 feet long. The length of the opening in the arch's shadow is 67.5 feet. What is the height of the opening in the rock arch? **NS 1.3, MR 1.1**

   Ⓐ 37.5 ft Ⓑ 45 ft
   Ⓒ 65 ft Ⓓ 101.25 ft

8. Which quadrilateral has 4 congruent sides and may or may not have right angles? **MG 2.3**

   Ⓐ Rectangle Ⓑ Rhombus
   Ⓒ Square Ⓓ Trapezoid

9 CHAPTER SUMMARY

Standards
NS 1.2, NS 1.3,
MG 2.1, MG 2.2, MG 2.3

BIG IDEAS

For Your Notebook

Big Idea 1

Identifying and Using Special Angle Relationships

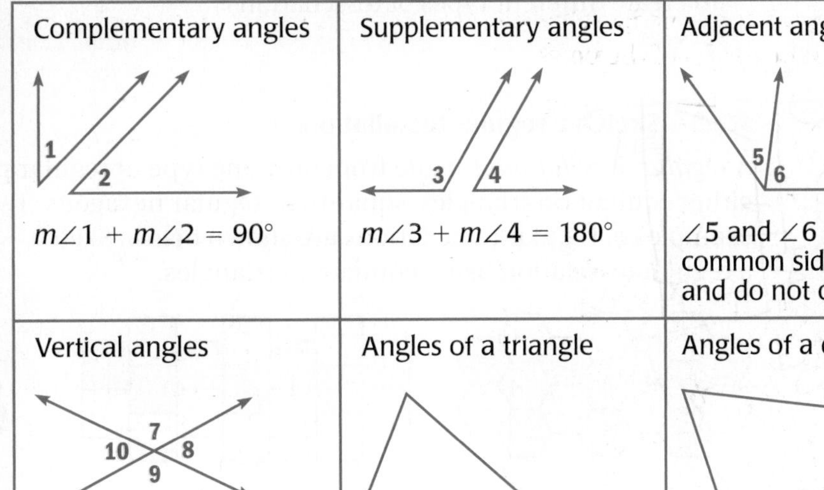

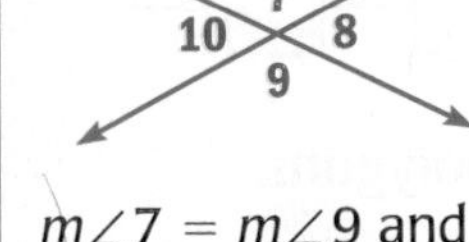

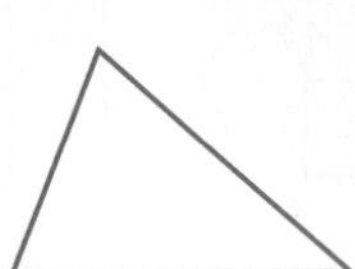

Complementary angles	Supplementary angles	Adjacent angles
$m\angle 1 + m\angle 2 = 90°$	$m\angle 3 + m\angle 4 = 180°$	$\angle 5$ and $\angle 6$ share a common side and vertex and do not overlap.
Vertical angles	**Angles of a triangle**	**Angles of a quadrilateral**
$m\angle 7 = m\angle 9$ and $m\angle 8 = m\angle 10$	The sum of the angle measures is 180°.	The sum of the angle measures is 360°.

Big Idea 2

Drawing Triangles and Quadrilaterals from Given Information

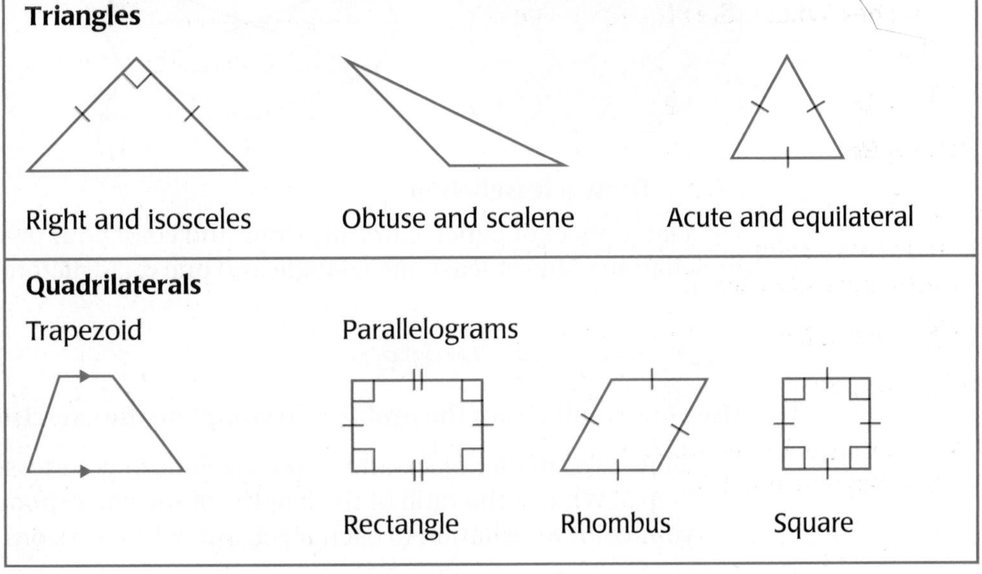

Triangles

Right and isosceles | Obtuse and scalene | Acute and equilateral

Quadrilaterals

Trapezoid

Parallelograms

Rectangle | Rhombus | Square

Big Idea 3

Using Ratios and Proportions with Similar Polygons

To find the height of the sign, use the following proportion.

$$\frac{\text{Height of sign}}{\text{Height of hydrant}} = \frac{\text{Length of sign's shadow}}{\text{Length of hydrant's shadow}}$$

NO PARKING

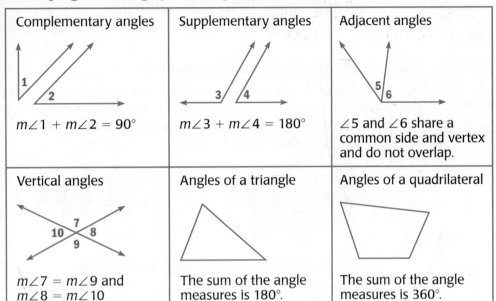

CHAPTER PROBLEM

Standards
NS 1.2, NS 1.3,
MG 2.1, MG 2.2, MG 2.3

APPLYING THE
BIG IDEAS

Big Idea 1
You identify and use special angle relationships in **Ex. 2** and **Ex. 3.**

Big Idea 2
You draw triangles and quadrilaterals in **Step 1** and **Step 3.**

Big Idea 3
You use ratios and proportions in **Ex. 1.**

PROBLEM A *tessellation* is a repeating pattern of figures that fill a plane with no gaps or overlaps. You may have noticed these types of patterns in wallpaper, fabric, or ceramic tiles. Follow the steps below to create different types of tessellations.

STEP 1 **Sketch a regular tessellation.**

A *regular tessellation* is made from only one type of regular polygon, either equilateral triangles, squares, or regular hexagons. Two examples of regular tessellations are shown below. Sketch a regular tesselation using equilateral triangles.

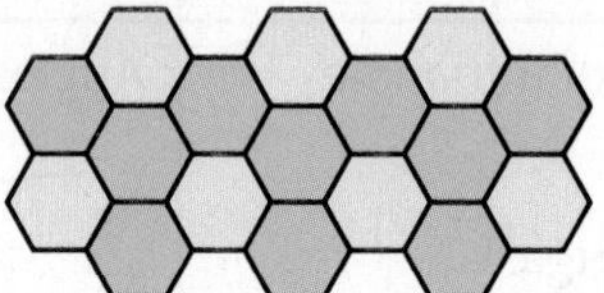

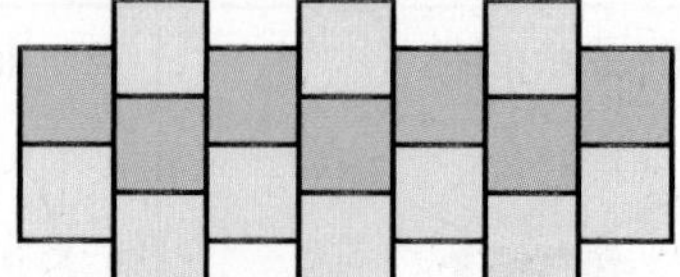

STEP 2 **Sketch a tessellation using two polygons.**

Tessellations can also be formed using more than one regular polygon or one or more nonregular polygons, as shown. Sketch a tessellation using two nonregular polygons.

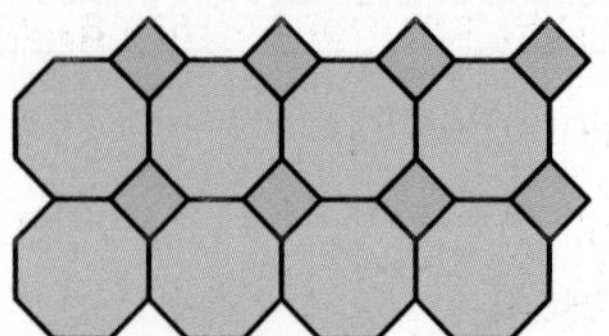

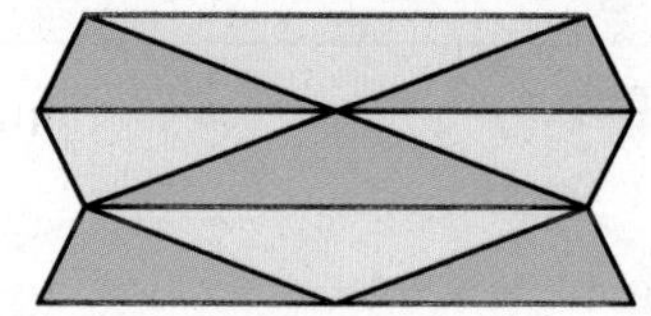

STEP 3 **Draw a tessellation.**

On a large sheet of paper, carefully draw and color your own tessellation using at least one triangle and one quadrilateral.

Extending the Problem

Use your results from the problem to complete the exercises.

1. Draw two smaller black-and-white versions of your tessellation from Step 3. What is the ratio of the lengths of the corresponding sides of your color tessellation to each black-and-white version?
2. On one black-and-white version, find a point where three or more polygons come together. Number each of the angles at this point. Find the measure of each of the numbered angles and then find the sum of these measures. Compare your results with a classmate's results.
3. On the other black-and-white version, number each of the angles in the repeating pattern in the tesselation. Identify any supplementary angles, complementary angles, adjacent angles, and vertical angles.

9 CHAPTER REVIEW

California @HomeTutor
classzone.com
- Multi-Language Visual Glossary
- Vocabulary practice

REVIEW KEY VOCABULARY

- angles: acute, right, obtuse, straight, *p. 463*
- complementary angles, *p. 464*
- supplementary angles, *p. 464*
- adjacent angles, *p. 468*
- vertical angles, *p. 468*
- congruent angles, *p. 468*
- plane, *p. 469*
- lines: intersecting, parallel, perpendicular, *p. 469*
- corresponding angles, *p. 469*
- triangles: acute, right, obtuse, *p. 475*
- congruent sides, *p. 476*
- triangles: equilateral, isosceles, scalene, *p. 476*
- quadrilaterals: trapezoid, parallelogram, rectangle, rhombus, square, *p. 482*
- polygons: pentagon, hexagon, octagon, *p. 484*
- diagonal, *p. 484*
- similar polygons, *p. 490*
- congruent polygons, *p. 490*

VOCABULARY EXERCISES

1. What is the measure of a straight angle?
2. How are parallel lines different from perpendicular lines?
3. How many congruent sides does a scalene triangle have?
4. Which type of special quadrilateral is not a parallelogram? *Explain* why it is not.
5. What is the sum of the measures of two supplementary angles?
6. How many diagonals does a pentagon have?
7. **NOTETAKING SKILLS** Make an *examples and non-examples chart* like the one on page 462 for *congruent figures*. Use sketches in your chart.

REVIEW EXAMPLES AND EXERCISES

9.1 Angles

pp. 463–467

MG 2.1, MG 2.2

EXAMPLE 1

Tell whether the angles are *complementary*, *supplementary*, or *neither*.

a.

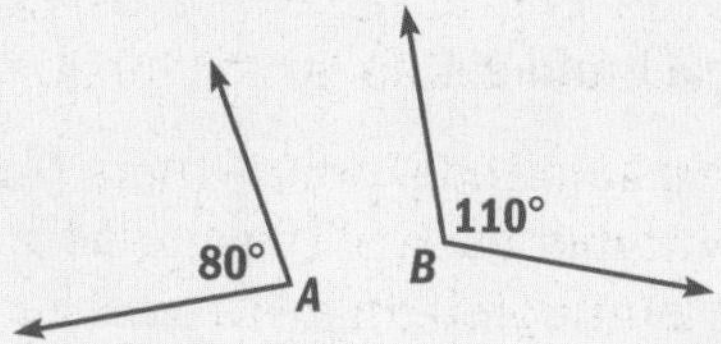

Because $80° + 110° = 190°$, $\angle A$ and $\angle B$ are neither complementary nor supplementary.

b.

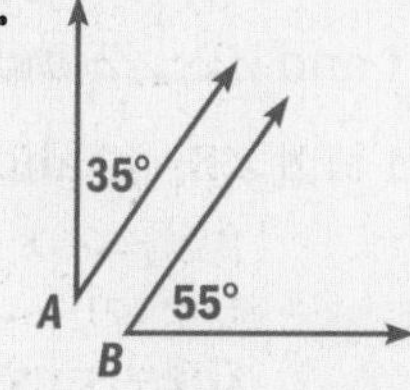

Because $35° + 55° = 90°$, $\angle A$ and $\angle B$ are complementary.

EXAMPLE 2

Find the unknown angle measure.

a. $\angle A$ and $\angle B$ are complementary, and $m\angle A = 44°$. What is $m\angle B$?

b. $\angle C$ and $\angle D$ are supplementary, and $m\angle D = 112°$. What is $m\angle C$?

SOLUTION

a. $m\angle A + m\angle B = 90°$

$44° + m\angle B = 90°$

$m\angle B = 46°$

b. $m\angle C + m\angle D = 180°$

$m\angle C + 112° = 180°$

$m\angle C = 68°$

EXERCISES

SEE EXAMPLES 1, 2, AND 3 on pp. 463–464 for Exs. 8–15

Classify the angle as *acute, right, obtuse,* or *straight*.

8. $m\angle A = 65°$ **9.** $m\angle A = 125°$ **10.** $m\angle A = 90°$ **11.** $m\angle A = 180°$

Tell whether $\angle C$ and $\angle D$ are *complementary, supplementary,* or *neither*.

12. $m\angle C = 42°, m\angle D = 48°$ **13.** $m\angle C = 113°, m\angle D = 67°$

14. $\angle F$ and $\angle G$ are complementary, and $m\angle F = 24°$. What is $m\angle G$?

15. $\angle R$ and $\angle S$ are supplementary, and $m\angle S = 74°$. What is $m\angle R$?

9.2 Special Pairs of Angles

pp. 468–472

MG 2.1
MG 2.2

EXAMPLE

Name all pairs of the given type of angles among the labeled angles.

a. Adjacent, supplementary angles

b. Vertical angles

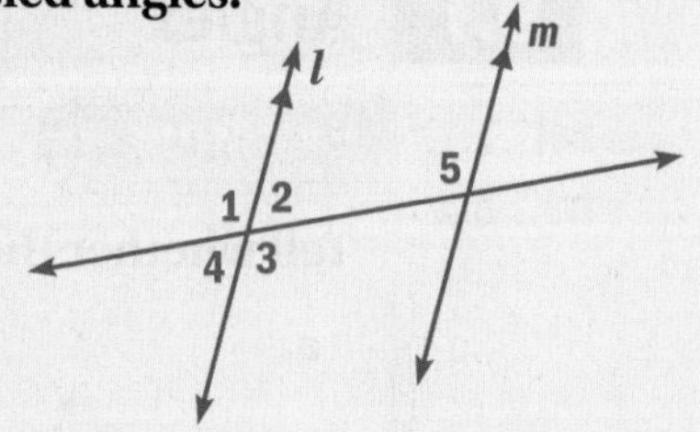

SOLUTION

a. $\angle 1$ and $\angle 2$, $\angle 2$ and $\angle 3$, $\angle 3$ and $\angle 4$, $\angle 1$ and $\angle 4$

b. $\angle 1$ and $\angle 3$, $\angle 2$ and $\angle 4$

EXERCISES

SEE EXAMPLES 1, 2, AND 3 on pp. 468–470 for Exs. 16–19

In the diagram above $m\angle 1 = 115°$. Find the measure of the given angle. *Explain* your reasoning.

16. $\angle 2$ **17.** $\angle 3$ **18.** $\angle 4$ **19.** $\angle 5$

9.3 Triangles

pp. 474–479

MG 2.2, MG 2.3

EXAMPLE

Find the value of y. Then classify the triangle by its angle measures.

$$90° + 55° + y° = 180°$$
$$y = 180 - 145$$
$$y = 35$$

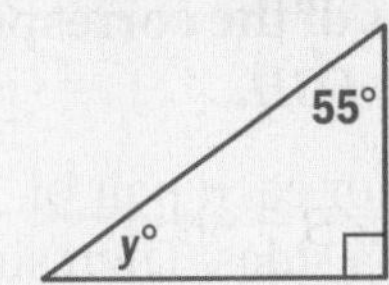

▶ **Answer** The value of y is 35. The triangle is a right triangle.

EXERCISES

SEE EXAMPLES 1, 2, AND 3 on pp. 474–476 for Exs. 20–23

Find the value of x. Then classify the triangle by its angle measures.

20. 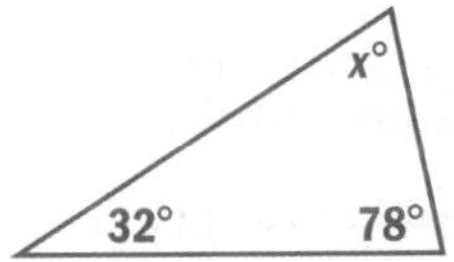

21. 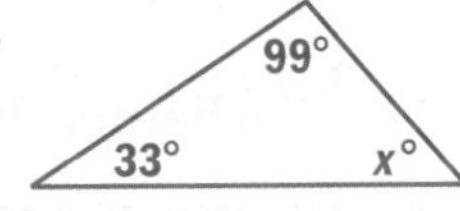

22. 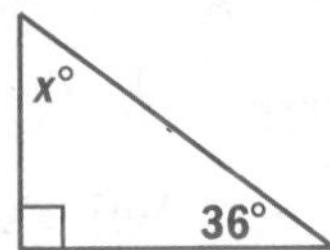

23. Draw a right isosceles triangle with two sides of length 2.5 inches.

9.4 Quadrilaterals and Other Polygons

pp. 482–487

MG 2.3

EXAMPLE

Draw a quadrilateral with exactly one pair of parallel sides.

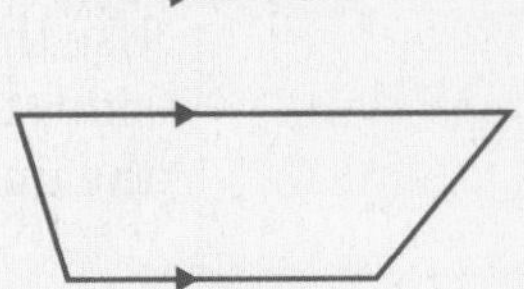

STEP 1 **Draw** two sides of different lengths that are parallel to each other.

STEP 2 **Connect** endpoints to complete the figure. The figure drawn is a trapezoid.

EXERCISES

SEE EXAMPLES 1, 2, AND 4 on pp. 482–484 for Exs. 24–27

Give the most specific name for the polygon and tell if it is regular. Then find the sum of its angle measures.

24. 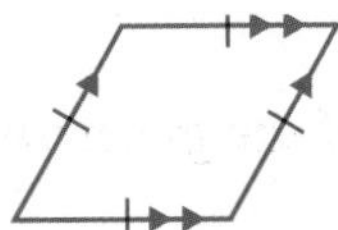

25. 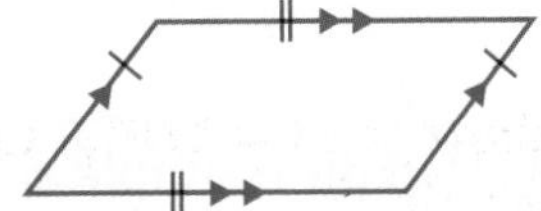

26. 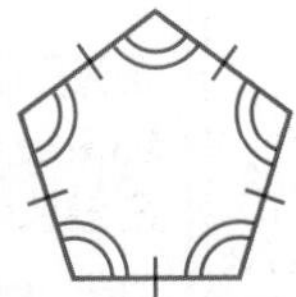

27. Draw a quadrilateral with 4 congruent sides and at least one right angle.

9.5 Similar and Congruent Polygons

pp. 490–494

NS 1.2

EXAMPLE

Given that $\triangle BCD \sim \triangle FGH$, find the ratio of the lengths of the corresponding sides of $\triangle BCD$ to $\triangle FGH$.

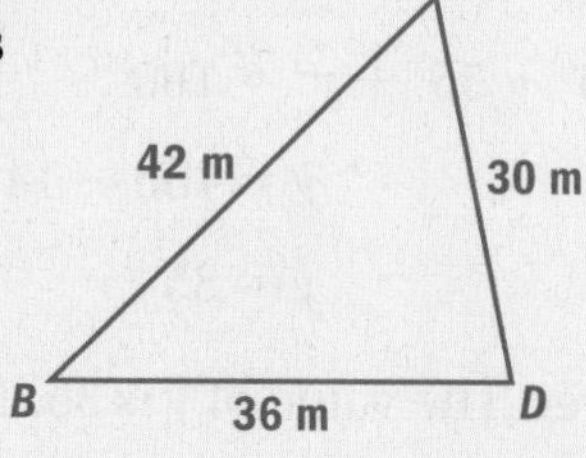

Write a ratio for each pair of corresponding sides. Then substitute the lengths of the sides and simplify each ratio.

$$\frac{BC}{FG} = \frac{42}{10.5} = \frac{4}{1} \qquad \frac{CD}{GH} = \frac{30}{7.5} = \frac{4}{1} \qquad \frac{BD}{FH} = \frac{36}{9} = \frac{4}{1}$$

EXERCISES

SEE EXAMPLES 1 AND 3 on pp. 490–491 for Exs. 28–30

In Exercises 28 and 29, tell whether the rectangles are similar.

28. *QRST* is 8 inches by 6 inches. *CDFG* is 20 inches by 15 inches.

29. *JKLM* is 10 meters by 4 meters. *PQRS* is 5 meters by 3 meters.

30. $\triangle ABC \cong \triangle TUV$. Find *TV*, given that $AB = 9$ feet, $BC = 6$ feet, and $AC = 4$ feet.

9.6 Using Proportions with Similar Polygons

pp. 495–499

NS 1.3

EXAMPLE

Quadrilaterals *JKLM* and *WXYZ* are similar. Find *YZ*.

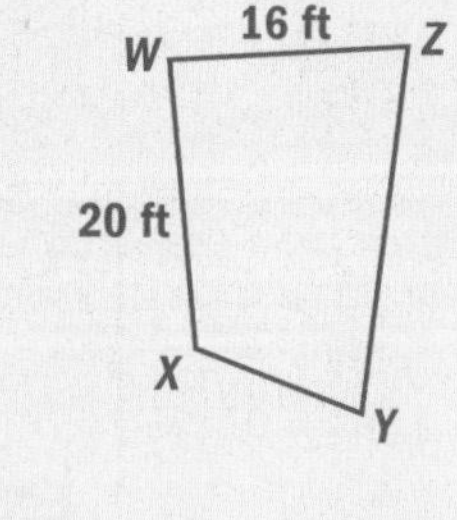

Use the ratios of the lengths of corresponding sides to write and solve a proportion involving the unknown length.

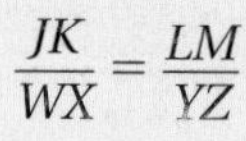

$\frac{JK}{WX} = \frac{LM}{YZ}$ **Write a proportion involving YZ.**

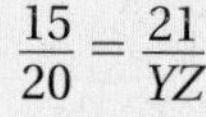

$\frac{15}{20} = \frac{21}{YZ}$ **Substitute known values.**

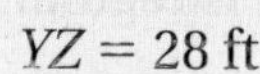

$YZ = 28$ ft **Use cross products property and simplify.**

EXERCISES

SEE EXAMPLES 1 AND 2 on pp. 495–496 for Exs. 31–32

31. Find *XY* and *JM* in the example above.

32. **TOWER HEIGHT** A cell phone tower casts a 130 foot shadow at the same time a 5 foot tall person casts a 4.5 foot shadow. How tall is the tower?

9 CHAPTER TEST

1. **VOCABULARY** The sum of the angle measures of two __?__ angles is 90°.

2. **VOCABULARY** Angles in a plane that share a common side and a vertex and do not overlap are __?__ angles.

Classify the angle as *acute, right, obtuse,* or *straight.*

3.

4. 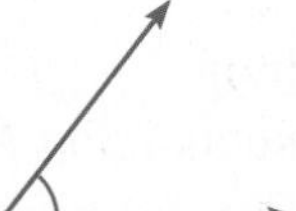

5. 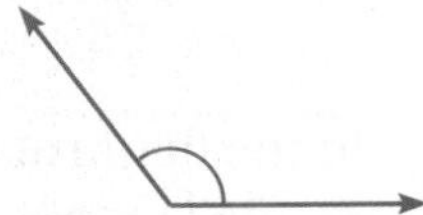

Tell whether $\angle A$ and $\angle B$ are *complementary, supplementary,* or *neither.* *Explain* your reasoning.

6. $m\angle A = 21°$, $m\angle B = 79°$

7. $m\angle A = 45°$, $m\angle B = 135°$

8. $m\angle A = 19°$, $m\angle B = 71°$

Find the angle measures of the numbered angles.

9. 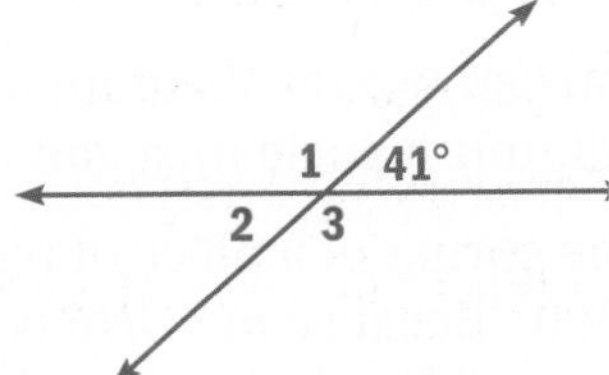

10. 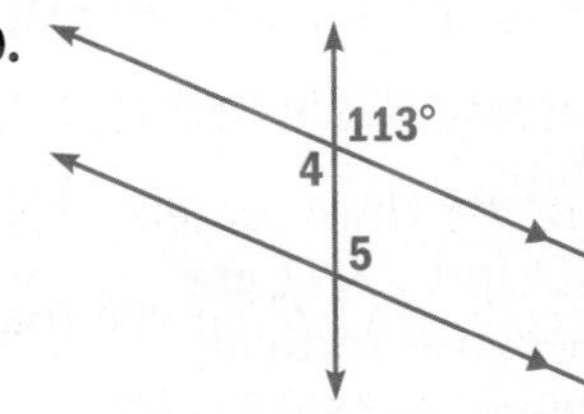

11. 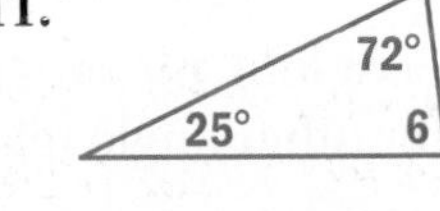

12. $\angle A$ and $\angle B$ are complementary, and $m\angle B = 37°$. What is $m\angle A$?

Give the most specific name for the polygon and tell if it is regular.

13. 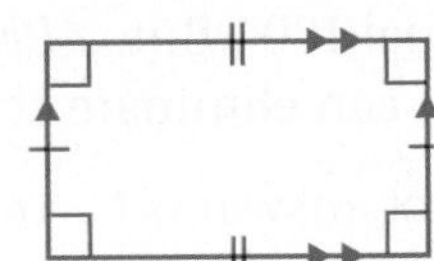

14. 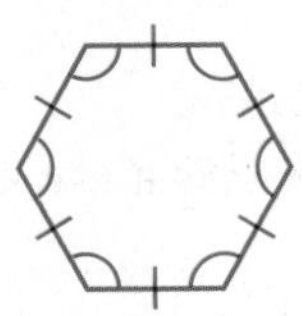

15. 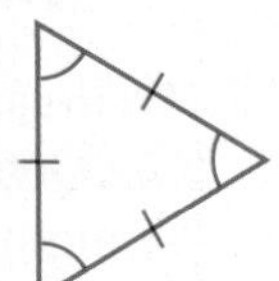

16. Given that $\triangle QRS \cong \triangle XYZ$, name the corresponding sides and the corresponding angles. Next find the ratio of QR to XY. Then find XZ and YZ.

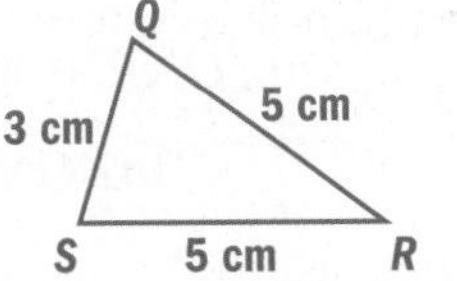

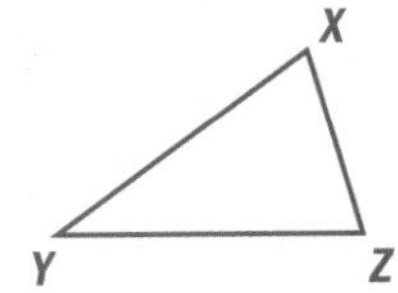

17. The measures of two angles of a triangle are 63° and 26°. Find the measure of the third angle. Then classify the triangle by its angle measures.

18. A figure has 4 congruent sides and not all of the angles are congruent. Use a ruler and a protractor to draw the figure. Then identify it.

19. **BUILDING HEIGHT** A building casts a 50 foot shadow at the same time that an 8 foot sign casts a 2.5 foot shadow. How tall is the building?

9 ◆ MULTIPLE CHOICE STRATEGIES

STRATEGIES YOU'LL USE:
- **SOLVE DIRECTLY**
- **ELIMINATE CHOICES**

Standards
MG 2.1, MG 2.2

If you have trouble solving a multiple choice problem directly, you may be able to use another approach to eliminate incorrect answer choices and obtain the correct answer.

PROBLEM 1

In the figure at the right, $\overleftrightarrow{QT}$ intersects $\overleftrightarrow{PS}$ at N, $m\angle PNQ = 40°$, and $\angle RNS \cong \angle SNT$. What is $m\angle QNR$?

Ⓐ 40° Ⓑ 50°

Ⓒ 100° Ⓓ 140°

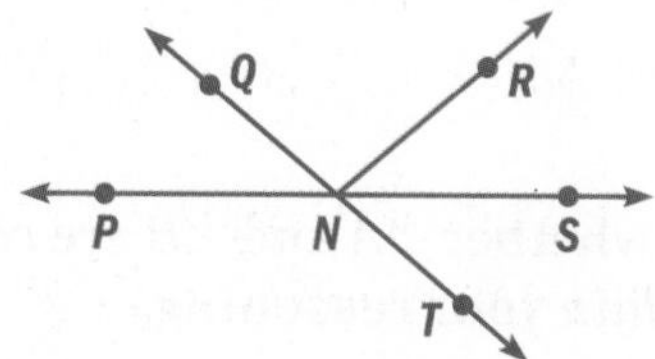

Strategy 1 SOLVE DIRECTLY

First look for congruent angles. Then look for other angle relationships.

STEP 1 **Notice** that $\angle PNQ$ and $\angle SNT$ are vertical angles. Because vertical angles are congruent, $m\angle SNT = 40°$.

STEP 2 **Use** the fact that $\angle RNS \cong \angle SNT$. Because $m\angle SNT = 40°$ from Step 1, $m\angle RNS = 40°$.

STEP 3 **Write** an equation that involves $m\angle QNR$. Use the fact that $\overleftrightarrow{QT}$ is a straight line.

$$m\angle QNR + m\angle RNS + m\angle SNT = 180°$$
$$m\angle QNR + 40° + 40° = 180°$$
$$m\angle QNR + 80° = 180°$$
$$m\angle QNR = 100°$$

The correct answer is C. Ⓐ Ⓑ Ⓒ Ⓓ

Strategy 2 ELIMINATE CHOICES

You can use the diagram to estimate a minimum angle measure.

The corner of a piece of paper has a measure of 90°. Because $m\angle QNR$ is greater than the angle measure of a corner of a piece of paper, $\angle QNR$ is obtuse. You can eliminate choices A and B.

If $m\angle QNR = 140°$, then $m\angle PNQ + m\angle QNR$ would equal 180°. But, $\angle PNR$ is not a straight angle. You can eliminate choice D.

The correct answer is C. Ⓐ Ⓑ Ⓒ Ⓓ

PROBLEM 2

Which is a true statement about ∠1 and ∠6 in the diagram, given ∠1 ≅ ∠3?

Ⓐ They are vertical angles.

Ⓑ They are adjacent angles.

Ⓒ ∠1 is supplementary to ∠6.

Ⓓ ∠1 is complementary to ∠6 .

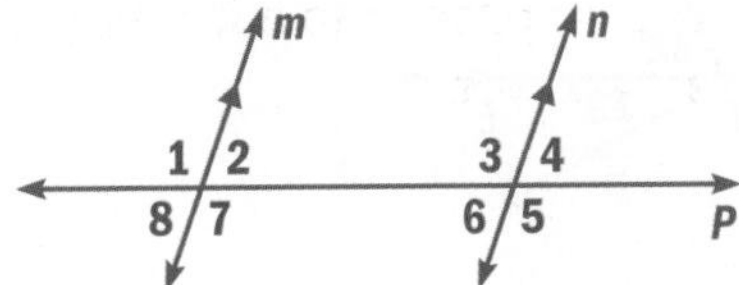

Strategy 1 **SOLVE DIRECTLY**

Use the fact that ∠1 ≅ ∠3 and what you know about special pairs of angles to solve the problem.

By looking at the diagram, you know that ∠3 and ∠6 are supplementary. By substituting ∠1 for ∠3, you can conclude that ∠1 and ∠6 are supplementary.

The correct answer is C. Ⓐ Ⓑ Ⓒ Ⓓ

Strategy 2 **ELIMINATE CHOICES**

Look at the diagram to get information for considering each answer choice.

∠1 and ∠6 are not formed by the same lines meeting at a point, so they are not vertical angles. You can eliminate choice A.

∠1 does not share a side with ∠6 so they are not adjacent angles. You can eliminate choice B.

Because ∠1 is obtuse, its measure is greater than 90°. So you know that ∠1 and ∠6 can not be complementary. You can eliminate choice D.

The correct answer is C. Ⓐ Ⓑ Ⓒ Ⓓ

STRATEGY PRACTICE

Explain why you can eliminate the highlighted answer choice.

1. What is the side length of a regular pentagon that has a perimeter of 6 feet?

Ⓐ 1 foot Ⓑ 1.2 feet Ⓒ 1.5 feet Ⓓ ✕ **30 feet**

2. ∠*A* and ∠*B* are supplementary, and *m*∠*A* = 63°. What is *m*∠*B*?

Ⓐ ✕ **27°** Ⓑ 37° Ⓒ 117° Ⓓ 137°

3. What is *m*∠1?

Ⓐ 20° Ⓑ ✕ **70°**

Ⓒ 110° Ⓓ 130°

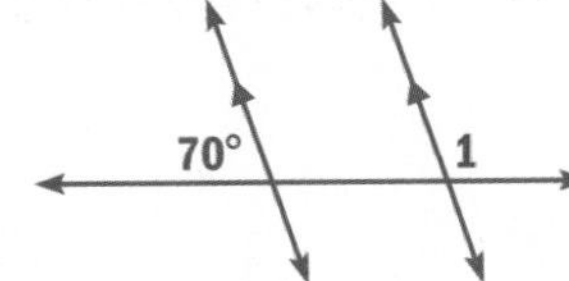

9 ◆ MULTIPLE CHOICE PRACTICE

1. Which angles are complementary? **MG 2.1**

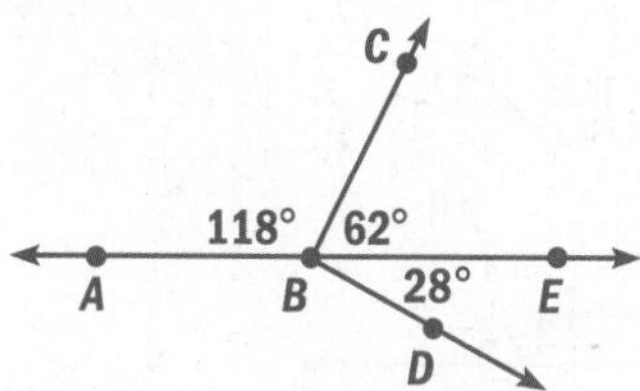

Ⓐ $\angle ABC$ and $\angle CBE$

Ⓑ $\angle CBE$ and $\angle EBD$

Ⓒ $\angle CBD$ and $\angle EBD$

Ⓓ $\angle CBD$ and $\angle CBE$

2. What is the value of x? **MG 2.2**

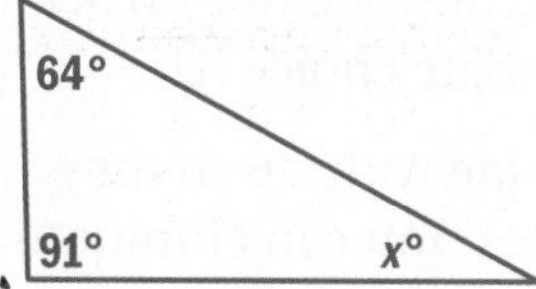

Ⓐ 25

Ⓑ 26

Ⓒ 64

Ⓓ 65

3. You are asked to draw a quadrilateral with 4 right angles. Which quadrilateral could *not* fit this description? **MG 2.3**

Ⓐ Rhombus

Ⓑ Rectangle

Ⓒ Parallelogram

Ⓓ Trapezoid

4. Two angles have measures of 84° and 96°. Which word describes the angles? **MG 2.1**

Ⓐ Supplementary

Ⓑ Complementary

Ⓒ Congruent

Ⓓ Vertical

5. A rectangular map is 3 feet long and 2 feet wide. A smaller version of the map on the cover of a map booklet is 2.7 inches wide. The maps are similar. What is the perimeter of the smaller map? **NS 1.3, MR 1.3**

Ⓐ 4.05 in.

Ⓑ 9 in.

Ⓒ 10 in.

Ⓓ 13.5 in.

6. A flagpole is 14 feet tall and casts a 10 foot shadow as shown. What is the length of the shadow cast by the building? **NS 1.3**

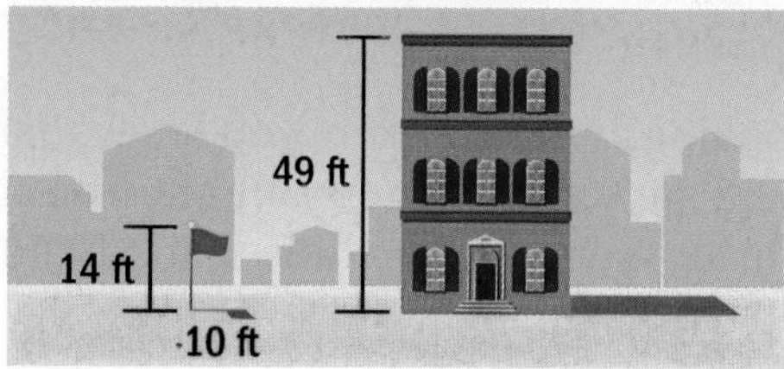

Ⓐ 30 ft

Ⓑ 35 ft

Ⓒ 40 ft

Ⓓ 45 ft

7. Which figure is an obtuse isosceles triangle? **MG 2.3**

Ⓐ

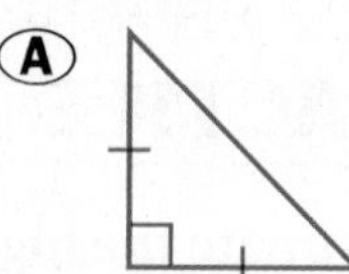

Ⓑ

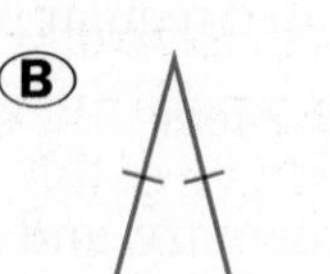

Ⓒ

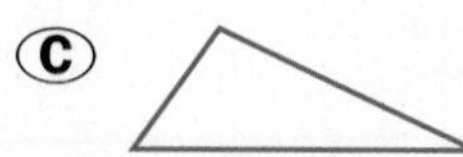

Ⓓ

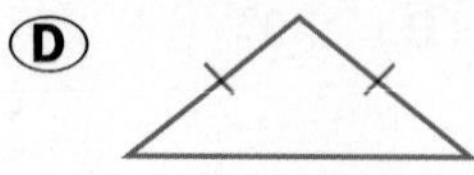

8. The measure of $\angle J$ is 3 times the measure of $\angle K$. The angles are supplementary. What is the measure of $\angle K$? **MG 2.2**

Ⓐ 22.5°

Ⓑ 45°

Ⓒ 67.5°

Ⓓ 135°

9. In the diagram below, which of the following pairs of angles are adjacent angles? **MG 2.1, MR 1.1**

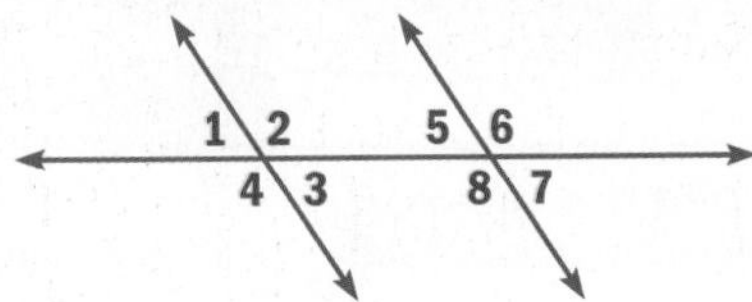

Ⓐ $\angle 1$ and $\angle 3$

Ⓑ $\angle 1$ and $\angle 4$

Ⓒ $\angle 2$ and $\angle 5$

Ⓓ $\angle 3$ and $\angle 6$

10. Rectangle *ABCD* is similar to rectangle *EFGH*. *ABCD* has a length of 12 inches and a width of 6 inches. *EFGH* has a length of 8 inches. What is the width of *EFGH*? **NS 1.3**

Ⓐ 4 in.

Ⓑ 8 in.

Ⓒ 9 in.

Ⓓ 16 in.

11. The measures of two angles of a triangle are 21° and 46°. What is the measure of an angle supplementary to the third angle of the triangle? **MG 2.2, MR 1.3**

Ⓐ 23°

Ⓑ 67°

Ⓒ 113°

Ⓓ 157°

12. Which number represents the value of x in the diagram of the quilt? **MG 2.2**

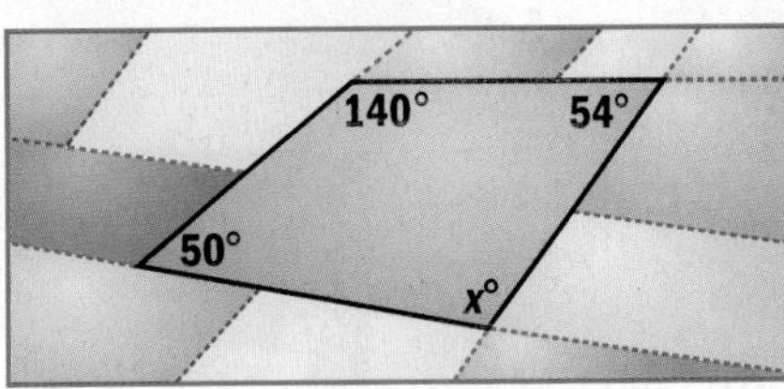

Ⓐ 16

Ⓑ 116

Ⓒ 140

Ⓓ 244

13. A triangle has two sides of length 5 feet. One of the angles of the triangle measures 90°. Which of the following describes the triangle? **MG 2.3**

Ⓐ Acute scalene

Ⓑ Acute isosceles

Ⓒ Right scalene

Ⓓ Right isosceles

14. $\triangle ABC$ is similar to $\triangle DEF$. What is the ratio of the lengths of the corresponding sides of $\triangle ABC$ to $\triangle DEF$? **NS 1.2**

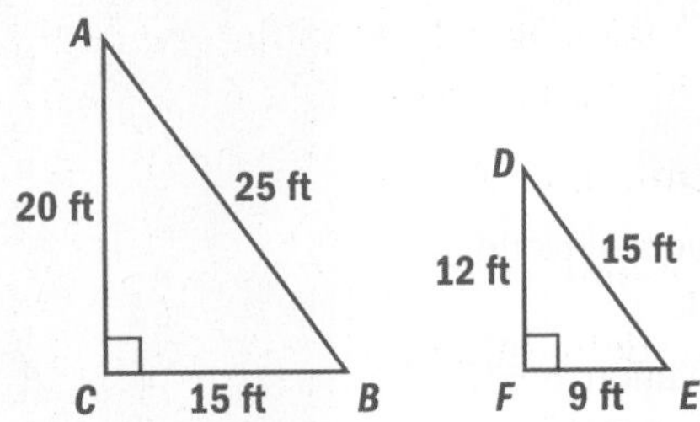

Ⓐ 2 : 5

Ⓑ 5 : 4

Ⓒ 5 : 3

Ⓓ 5 : 2

10 Measurement and Area

Before

In previous courses and chapters, you learned the following skills, which you'll use in Chapter 10:

- Converting units of time and temperature
- Finding areas of rectangles and squares
- Writing and evaluating expressions

Now

In Chapter 10 you'll study these ***Big Ideas:***

1. Converting one unit of measurement to another
2. Using variables in geometric expressions
3. Using estimates of π to calculate circumference and area of circles

Why?

So you can solve real-world problems about . . .

- Water conservation, p. 519
- Gorilla growth, p. 519
- Pyramids of Egypt, p. 524
- Hiking trails, p. 530
- Unicycles, p. 553
- Calendars, p. 558

at classzone.com

Get-Ready Games

Exponent Spotlight

California Standards

Review evaluating expressions. *Gr. 6 AF 1.2*

Prepare for calculating areas. *Gr. 6 MG 1.2*

A 13^2 N 9^2 K 30^2 M 3^3 L 10^2 E 2^5

P 12^2 J 80^2 N 60^2 R 6^3 O 5^3

How to Play

What is the name of the research lab in which Thomas Edison experimented with the light bulb? In what state was the lab located?

- Evaluate the powers. Write the answers in order from least to greatest.
- Write the letters associated with the powers in the same order as the powers.

CALIFORNIA STANDARDS

- **Gr. 6 AF 2.1** Convert one unit of measurement to another (e.g., from feet to miles, from centimeters to inches). *(Lessons 10.1, 10.2, 10.3)*
- **Gr. 6 MG 1.1** Understand the concept of a constant such as π; know the formulas for the circumference and area of a circle. *(Lessons 10.6, 10.7)*

California Standards

Review properties of figures. *Gr. 6 MG 2.0*
Prepare for using variables in expressions describing geometric quantities. *Gr. 6 AF 3.1*

How to Play

In the drawing, all line segments in the design above the stage that appear to be equal in length are equal in length. All segments of the same color are parallel.

- Copy the design above the stage.
- Identify at least 20 triangles, 3 rectangles, 9 parallelograms, and 13 trapezoids.

Games Wrap-Up

Draw Conclusions

Complete these exercises after playing the games.

1. **WRITING** *Describe* two situations where you can compare two powers without evaluating them.
2. **REASONING** *Describe* one parallelogram in *Stage Design*. *Explain* how you can be sure that it is a parallelogram.

10 Getting Ready

Prerequisite Skills

California @HomeTutor
Prerequisite skills practice at classzone.com

REVIEW VOCABULARY

- **trapezoid,** *p. 482*
- **parallelogram,** *p. 482*
- **length, mass, weight, capacity,** *p. 680*
- **perimeter,** *p. 684*
- **area,** *p. 685*

VOCABULARY CHECK

Copy and complete using a review term from the list at the left.

1. The distance around a figure is the __?__ of the figure.
2. The gram (g) is the basic metric unit of __?__.
3. A quadrilateral with exactly one pair of parallel sides is a(n) __?__.

SKILL CHECK

Evaluate the expression when $x = -4$, $y = 6$, and $z = 1.2$. *(p. 197)*

4. $2x + y$
5. $3y - 4z$
6. $5z - x^2$
7. $4(3x + y)$

Write and simplify expressions for the perimeter and area of the rectangle. *(p. 212)*

8. 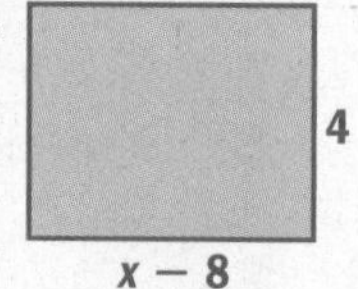

9. 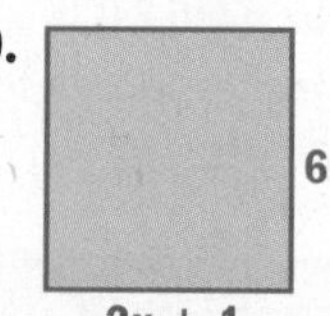

10. 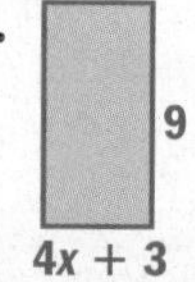

Copy and complete the statement with the appropriate metric unit. *(p. 680)*

11. A mug can hold 400 __?__.
12. A building is 100 __?__ high.

Copy and complete the statement with the appropriate customary unit. *(p. 680)*

13. The capacity of a can is 19 __?__.
14. An airplane weighs 455 __?__.

Notetaking Skills

NOW YOU TRY

Make an *information wheel* for *rectangle.* You may want to use colored pencils.

Focus on Graphic Organizers

Use an *information wheel* to organize ideas related to a vocabulary word, such as *square.*

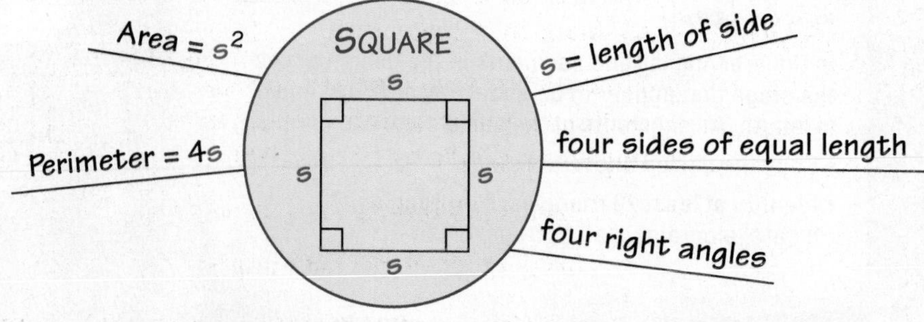

10.1 Converting Metric Units

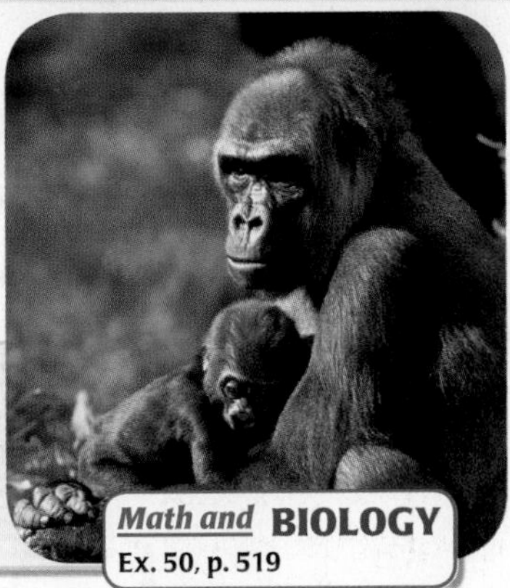

Math and BIOLOGY
Ex. 50, p. 519

Standards AF 2.1 **Convert one unit of measurement to another** (e.g., from feet to miles, from centimeters to inches).

Connect ***Before*** you used metric units of length, mass, and capacity. ***Now*** you will convert between metric units.

KEY VOCABULARY
- **metric system,** *p. 680*
- **length,** *p. 680*
- **mass,** *p. 680*
- **capacity,** *p. 680*

RUNNING In the 4×800 meter relay race, four teammates each run 800 meters. The total length of the race is 3200 meters. How many kilometers long is the race?

The metric system is a base-ten system. Metric prefixes relate each unit to the base unit, such as meter, gram, or liter.

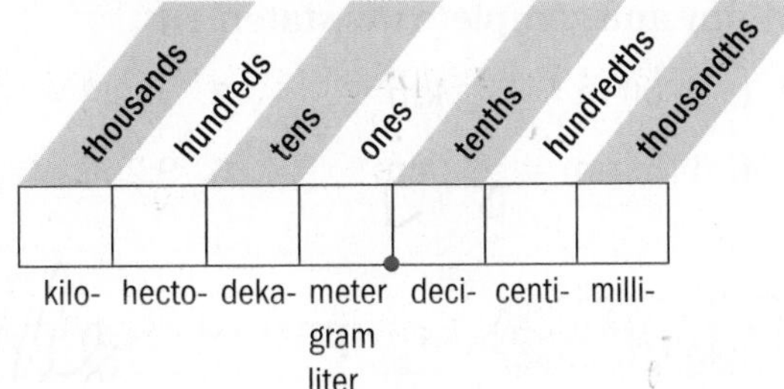

To convert between metric units n decimal places apart, multiply or divide as follows.

Multiply by 10^n.

larger unit → smaller unit

smaller unit → larger unit

Divide by 10^n.

EXAMPLE 1 Converting Metric Units of Length

To find the length (in kilometers) of the relay race described above, convert 3200 meters to kilometers.

SOLUTION

You are converting from a smaller unit (meters) to a larger unit (kilometers), so *divide* by a power of 10.

From meters to kilometers, the decimal point is moved **3 places** to the left, so divide by 10^3, or 1000.

3	2	0	0
kilo-	hecto-	deka-	meter

$3200 \div 1000 = 3.2$

3200 meters = 3.2 kilometers

▶ **Answer** The 4×800 meter relay race is 3.2 kilometers long.

EXAMPLE 2 Converting Units of Mass and Capacity

Copy and complete the statement.

a. 15 g = __?__ mg

b. 590 mL = __?__ L

SOLUTION

a. To convert from grams to milligrams, multiply by 1000.

$15 \times 1000 = 15{,}000$, so 15 g = 15,000 mg

b. To convert from milliliters to liters, divide by 1000.

$590 \div 1000 = 0.59$, so 590 mL = 0.59 L

✓ GUIDED PRACTICE for Examples 1 and 2

Copy and complete the statement.

1. 6800 m = __?__ km

2. 100 g = __?__ kg

3. 830 cm = __?__ m

4. 115 mm = __?__ cm

5. 9.25 kL = __?__ L

6. 0.5 kg = __?__ mg

EXAMPLE 3 Comparing Metric Measures

Copy and complete the statement using <, >, or =.

a. 320 cm __?__ 32 m

b. 0.2 kg __?__ 184 g

SOLUTION

AVOID ERRORS

To compare two measures that have different units, convert one of the measures so that both measures have the *same* units.

a. 320 cm __?__ 32 m	**Strategy: Convert meters to centimeters.**
320 cm __?__ 3200 cm	**32 × 100 = 3200, so 32 m = 3200 cm.**
320 cm < 3200 cm	**Compare.**

▸ **Answer** 320 cm < 32 m

b. 0.2 kg __?__ 184 g	**Strategy: Convert kilograms to grams.**
200 g __?__ 184 g	**0.2 × 1000 = 200, so 0.2 kg = 200 g.**
200 g > 184 g	**Compare.**

▸ **Answer** 0.2 kg > 184 g

GUIDED PRACTICE for Example 3

Copy and complete the statement using <, >, or =.

7. 1.4 kL __?__ 1400 L

8. 150 mg __?__ 1.5 g

9. 580 mm __?__ 5.8 cm

10. 4.9 m __?__ 500 cm

11. 8.3 kg __?__ 83,500 mg

12. 7.2 L __?__ 7100 mL

EXAMPLE 4 Solve a Multi-Step Problem

Sandwich is 720 meters long.

FOOD SERVICE In 2004, more than 700 people helped make a sandwich that was 720 meters long. Suppose the sandwich were cut into pieces that were each 40 centimeters long. How many pieces would the sandwich make?

About the Standards

In Example 4, you convert one unit of length to the other before dividing. You will use this method to solve similar problems on pages 518–519, as called for in Grade 6 Standard MR 3.2.

SOLUTION

STEP 1 **Convert** 720 meters to centimeters by multiplying by 100.

$720 \times 100 = 72{,}000$, so $720 \text{ m} = 72{,}000 \text{ cm}$

STEP 2 **Divide** the total length of the sandwich by the length of each piece to find the number of pieces.

$72{,}000 \text{ cm} \div 40 \text{ cm} = 1800$

▶ **Answer** The sandwich would make 1800 pieces.

✓ GUIDED PRACTICE for Example 4

13. **WHAT IF?** In Example 4, suppose the sandwich were cut into pieces that were each 37.5 centimeters long. How many pieces would it make?

10.1 EXERCISES

HOMEWORK KEY

◆ = **MULTIPLE CHOICE PRACTICE** Exs. 18, 30, 49, 56–58

= **HINTS AND HOMEWORK HELP** for Exs. 11, 21, 49 at classzone.com

SKILLS • PROBLEM SOLVING • REASONING

1. **VOCABULARY** How many milliliters are in 1 liter?

2. **WRITING** *Describe* how you would convert from a larger metric unit to a smaller metric unit.

SEE EXAMPLES 1 AND 2 on pp. 515–516 for Exs. 3–18

CONVERTING UNITS Copy and complete the statement.

3. 72 mg = __?__ g
4. 49 m = __?__ cm
5. 890 mL = __?__ L
6. 470 mL = __?__ L
7. 1.25 km = __?__ m
8. 3.75 kg = __?__ g
9. 0.28 cm = __?__ mm
10. 0.75 L = __?__ mL
11. 1540 m = __?__ km
12. 3528 mm = __?__ cm
13. 45.25 kg = __?__ g
14. 840,000 mg = __?__ g
15. 2.42 kL = __?__ mL
16. 1.28 kg = __?__ mg
17. 1,250,000 mm = __?__ km

18. ◆ **MULTIPLE CHOICE** Which measure is equivalent to 1300 liters?

Ⓐ 1.3 mL　Ⓑ 1,300,000 mL　Ⓒ 13 kL　Ⓓ 1,300,000 kL

SEE EXAMPLE 2
on p. 516
for Ex. 19

19. ERROR ANALYSIS *Describe* and correct the error made in converting 50 milligrams to grams.

> ✗ $50 \times 1000 = 50{,}000$
> So, 50 mg = 50,000 g.

SEE EXAMPLE 3
on p. 516
for Exs. 20–30

COMPARING MEASURES **Copy and complete using $<$, $>$, or $=$.**

20. 160 mg _?_ 16 g	**(21.)** 740 L _?_ 0.74 kL	**22.** 2 km _?_ 2000 m
23. 4.1 g _?_ 410 mg	**24.** 6.5 m _?_ 65 cm	**25.** 9.6 L _?_ 9600 mL
26. 2300 g _?_ 2 kg	**27.** 6.9 cm _?_ 70 mm	**28.** 880 mL _?_ 0.89 L

29. ERROR ANALYSIS *Describe* and correct the error made in comparing 20 meters to 115 centimeters.

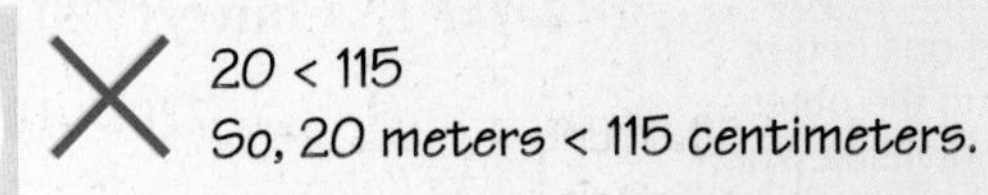
20 $<$ 115
So, 20 meters $<$ 115 centimeters.

30. ◆ **MULTIPLE CHOICE** Which measure is greater than 13 grams?

Ⓐ 1300 mg Ⓑ 130,000 mg Ⓒ 0.0013 kg Ⓓ 0.013 kg

ORDERING MEASURES **Order the measures from least to greatest.**

31. 60 g, 69 mg, 9.5 mg, 0.04 kg, 45 g

32. 15 L, 1.5 mL, 1500 mL, 1.5 kL, 0.15 kL

EXPRESSIONS WITH UNITS **Find the sum or difference. Write your answer using the smallest unit of measurement.**

33. 3 cm + 11 mm	**34.** 4 L − 35 mL	**35.** 6000 g − 3.5 kg
36. 25 mg + 1 kg − 893 g	**37.** 3 kL + 2550 mL − 3001 L	**38.** 95 m + 0.4 km − 225 mm

PERIMETER AND AREA **Find the perimeter (in centimeters) of the rectangle. Then find the area (in square centimeters) of the rectangle.**

39. 14 mm, 2 cm

40. 8 mm, 2.5 cm

41. 1.5 cm, 5 mm

CONNECT SKILLS TO PROBLEM SOLVING **Exercises 42–45 will help you prepare for problem solving.**

42. The capacity of a pitcher is 1250 milliliters. What is the capacity in liters?

43. The length of an iguana is 1.75 meters. What is the length in centimeters?

44. The distance from the center of Earth to its surface is about 6378 kilometers. What is the distance in meters?

45. The mass of a staple is 31 milligrams. What is the mass in grams?

SEE EXAMPLE 4
on p. 517
for Exs. 46–48

46. MEASUREMENT A chain of paper clips linked end to end is 2.7 meters long. Each paper clip is 4.5 centimeters long. About how many paper clips make up the chain?

California @HomeTutor for problem solving help at classzone.com

47. **WATER CONSERVATION** A leaky faucet drips 23.64 liters per day. How many milliliters of water does the faucet drip in one hour?

California @HomeTutor for problem solving help at classzone.com

48. **SHORT RESPONSE** A can of juice has a capacity of 355 milliliters. How many cans of juice does it take for their capacity to exceed the capacity of seven two liter bottles? *Explain* your reasoning.

49. ◆ **MULTIPLE CHOICE** Stefan builds a rectangular deck that is 6 meters long and 8 meters wide. What is the perimeter of the deck?

(A) 1400 cm (B) 2800 cm (C) 4800 cm (D) 9600 cm

50. **GORILLA GROWTH** A baby gorilla has a mass of about 2620 grams at birth. Baby gorillas grow at a fairly steady rate for the first month after birth.

a. Find the average rate (in grams per day) the baby gorilla grows each day for the first 30 days.

b. What is the approximate mass (in kilograms) of a 30 day old gorilla?

CHALLENGE Find the side length (in millimeters) of a square with the given area.

51. 9 cm^2 52. 36 cm^2 53. 100 cm^2 54. 256 cm^2

55. **CHALLENGE** Show two ways to find the area (in square centimeters) of a rectangle with a length of 4.5 meters and a width of 2.25 meters.

◆ CALIFORNIA STANDARDS SPIRAL REVIEW

NS 1.3 56. $\triangle ABC$ is similar to $\triangle DEF$. What is the length of $\overline{DF}$? ***(p. 495)***

(A) 6.7 cm (B) 7.5 cm

(C) 9.6 cm (D) 15 cm

8 cm
12 cm
A 10 cm C
B
D
E
F

MG 2.2 57. $\angle J$ and $\angle K$ are supplementary, and $m\angle J = 18°$. What is $m\angle K$? ***(p. 463)***

(A) 18° (B) 72° (C) 82° (D) 162°

SDAP 3.4 58. You roll a number cube and toss a coin. What is the probability of rolling a 4 and tossing heads? ***(p. 441)***

(A) $\frac{1}{12}$ (B) $\frac{1}{8}$ (C) $\frac{1}{4}$ (D) $\frac{2}{3}$

10.2 Converting Customary Units

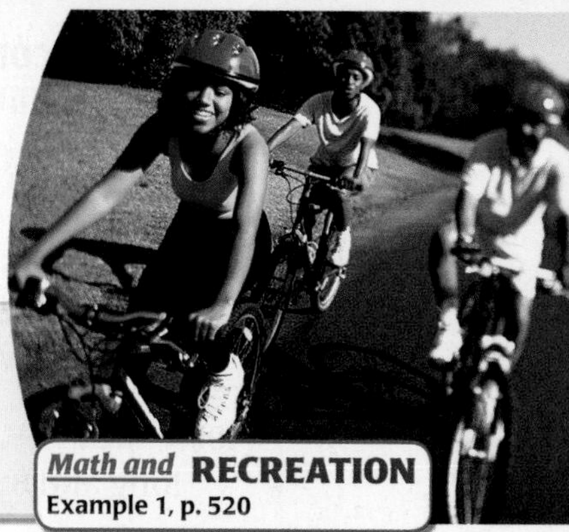

Math and RECREATION
Example 1, p. 520

Standards **AF 2.1 Convert one unit of measurement to another (e.g., from feet to miles**, from centimeters to inches).

Connect ***Before*** you converted between metric units. ***Now*** you will convert between U.S. customary units.

KEY VOCABULARY
- **U.S. customary system,** *p. 680*
- **length,** *p. 680*
- **weight,** *p. 680*
- **capacity,** *p. 680*

BICYCLING Yesterday you and your friends biked 6600 feet from your house to a park. What was the length (in miles) of your bike ride? You can use the relationships below to help you convert between U.S. customary units.

KEY CONCEPT *For Your Notebook*

U.S. Customary Units of Measure

Length	Weight	Capacity
1 ft = 12 in.	1 lb = 16 oz	1 c = 8 fl oz
1 yd = 3 ft = 36 in.	1 T = 2000 lb	1 pt = 2 c
1 mi = 1760 yd = 5280 ft		1 qt = 2 pt
		1 gal = 4 qt

To convert between customary units, the relationships above can be used to multiply by a convenient form of 1. For example, you can convert between inches and feet by using the rules below.

- To convert from inches to feet, multiply by $\frac{1 \text{ ft}}{12 \text{ in.}}$.
- To convert from feet to inches, multiply by $\frac{12 \text{ in.}}{1 \text{ ft}}$.

EXAMPLE 1 Converting Customary Units of Length

To find the distance (in miles) of the bike ride described above, convert 6600 feet to miles. Use the fact that 1 mi = 5280 ft.

$$6600 \text{ ft} \times \frac{1 \text{ mi}}{5280 \text{ ft}} = \frac{\overset{5}{\cancel{6600 \text{ ft}}} \times 1 \text{ mi}}{\underset{4}{\cancel{5280 \text{ ft}}}}$$ **Use rule for multiplying fractions. Divide out GCF of 1320 and unit "ft."**

$$= 1\frac{1}{4} \text{ mi}$$ **Simplify.**

▶ **Answer** The length of your bike ride was $1\frac{1}{4}$ miles.

About the Standards

Make sure you have the correct units after simplifying. Checking units is one way to evaluate the reasonableness of a solution, as called for in Grade 6 Standard MR 3.1.

EXAMPLE 2 Converting Customary Units of Weight

WHALES A humpback whale weighs $33\frac{1}{2}$ tons. How many pounds does the whale weigh?

Whale weighs $33\frac{1}{2}$ tons.

ANOTHER WAY

For alternative methods for converting customary units of weight in Example 2, turn to p. 526 for the **Problem Solving Workshop**.

SOLUTION

Use the fact that 1 T = 2000 lb.

$$33\frac{1}{2}\text{ T} \times \frac{2000\text{ lb}}{1\text{ T}} = \frac{33\frac{1}{2}\cancel{\text{T}} \times 2000\text{ lb}}{1\cancel{\text{T}}} = 67{,}000\text{ lb}$$

▶ **Answer** The whale weighs 67,000 pounds.

EXAMPLE 3 ◆ Multiple Choice Practice

How many pints are in 25 fluid ounces?

Ⓐ $1\frac{1}{4}$ pints Ⓑ $1\frac{9}{16}$ pints Ⓒ $6\frac{1}{4}$ pints Ⓓ 100 pints

SOLUTION

$$25\text{ fl oz} \times \frac{1\text{ c}}{8\text{ fl oz}} \times \frac{1\text{ pt}}{2\text{ c}} = \frac{25\cancel{\text{fl oz}} \times 1\cancel{\text{c}} \times 1\text{ pt}}{8\cancel{\text{fl oz}} \times 2\cancel{\text{c}}} = \frac{25}{16}\text{ pt, or } 1\frac{9}{16}\text{ pt}$$

▶ **Answer** There are $1\frac{9}{16}$ pints in 25 fluid ounces.

The correct answer is B. Ⓐ Ⓑ Ⓒ Ⓓ

EXAMPLE 4 Solve a Multi-Step Problem

Convert 26 fluid ounces to cups and fluid ounces.

STEP 1 **Convert** 26 fluid ounces to cups.

$$26\text{ fl oz} \times \frac{1\text{ c}}{8\text{ fl oz}} = \frac{\overset{13}{\cancel{26}}\cancel{\text{fl oz}} \times 1\text{ c}}{\underset{4}{\cancel{8}}\cancel{\text{fl oz}}} = \frac{13}{4}\text{ c, or } 3\frac{1}{4}\text{ c}$$

STEP 2 **Convert** the fractional part from cups to fluid ounces.

$$\frac{1\text{ c}}{4} \times \frac{8\text{ fl oz}}{1\text{ c}} = \frac{1\cancel{\text{c}} \times \overset{2}{\cancel{8}}\text{ fl oz}}{\underset{1}{\cancel{4}} \times 1\cancel{\text{c}}} = 2\text{ fl oz}$$

▶ **Answer** 26 fluid ounces = 3 cups 2 fluid ounces

Animated Math

For an interactive example of converting customary units go to **classzone.com**.

✓ GUIDED PRACTICE for Examples 1, 2, 3, and 4

Copy and complete the statement.

1. 10 yd = __?__ in.
2. 3000 lb = __?__ T
3. $6\frac{1}{2}$ qt = __?__ c
4. 9000 ft = __?__ mi __?__ ft
5. 35 oz = __?__ lb __?__ oz
6. 5 pt = __?__ qt __?__ pt

MIXED UNITS When adding or subtracting measures given in mixed units, you may need to rename some units.

EXAMPLE 5 Adding and Subtracting with Mixed Units

WAKEBOARDS One wakeboard weighs 7 pounds 6 ounces. Another wakeboard weighs 6 pounds 14 ounces.

a. Find the sum of the weights.

b. Find the difference of the weights.

One wakeboard weighs 7 lb 6 oz.

SOLUTION

a. Add. Then rename the sum.

$$\begin{array}{r} 7\text{ lb } \ 6\text{ oz} \\ +\ 6\text{ lb } 14\text{ oz} \\ \hline 13\text{ lb } 20\text{ oz} \end{array}$$

13 lb 20 oz = 13 lb + 1 lb 4 oz

▸ **Answer** The sum is 14 lb 4 oz.

b. Rename 7 lb 6 oz. Then subtract.

$$\begin{array}{r} 7\text{ lb } \ 6\text{ oz} \\ -\ 6\text{ lb } 14\text{ oz} \\ \hline \end{array} \rightarrow \begin{array}{r} 6\text{ lb } 22\text{ oz} \\ -\ 6\text{ lb } 14\text{ oz} \\ \hline 8\text{ oz} \end{array}$$

▸ **Answer** The difference is 8 oz.

RENAME UNITS
16 oz = 1 lb, so 20 oz is equal to 1 lb + 4 oz.

✓ GUIDED PRACTICE for Example 5

7. **WHAT IF?** In Example 5, suppose the weights of the wakeboards are 6 lb 15 oz and 7 lb 4 oz. Find the sum and difference of the weights.

10.2 EXERCISES

HOMEWORK KEY

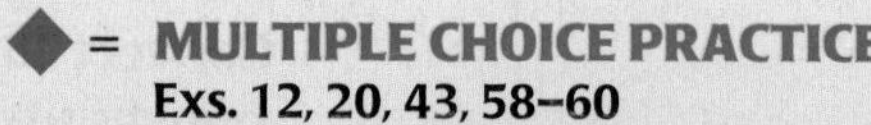

◆ = **MULTIPLE CHOICE PRACTICE** Exs. 12, 20, 43, 58–60

○ = **HINTS AND HOMEWORK HELP** for Exs. 3, 17, 45 at classzone.com

SKILLS • PROBLEM SOLVING • REASONING

1. **VOCABULARY** Copy and complete: 1 mi = 1760 __?__ and 1 lb = 16 __?__.

2. **WRITING** *Describe* how you would convert quarts to pints.

SEE EXAMPLES 1, 2, AND 3
on pp. 520–521 for Exs. 3–13

CONVERTING UNITS Copy and complete the statement.

3. 15 qt = __?__ pt
4. 24 oz = __?__ lb
5. 35 in. = __?__ ft
6. 5 yd = __?__ in.
7. $4\frac{5}{8}$ lb = __?__ oz
8. $3\frac{3}{4}$ c = __?__ fl oz
9. $1\frac{1}{4}$ T = __?__ lb
10. $2\frac{1}{2}$ mi = __?__ in.
11. 30 pt = __?__ fl oz

12. ◆ **MULTIPLE CHOICE** How many gallons are in 37 pints?

(A) $2\frac{5}{16}$ gal (B) $4\frac{5}{8}$ gal (C) $6\frac{1}{6}$ gal (D) $9\frac{1}{4}$ gal

13. **ERROR ANALYSIS** *Describe* and correct the error made in converting 30 feet to inches.

$$30 \text{ ft} \times \frac{1 \text{ in.}}{12 \text{ ft}} = \frac{\overset{5}{\cancel{30}} \cancel{\text{ft}} \times 1 \text{ in.}}{\underset{2}{\cancel{12}} \cancel{\text{ft}}} = \frac{5}{2} \text{ in.}$$

SEE EXAMPLE 4 on p. 521 for Exs. 14–20

WRITING MIXED UNITS **Copy and complete the statement.**

14. 40 in. = _?_ ft _?_ in.

15. 11 c = _?_ pt _?_ c

16. 2200 lb = _?_ T _?_ lb

17. 39 in. = _?_ yd _?_ in.

18. 9 qt = _?_ gal _?_ qt

19. 23,760 ft = _?_ mi _?_ ft

20. ◆ **MULTIPLE CHOICE** Which measure is equal to 130 ounces?

(A) 8 lb 2 oz (B) 8 lb 2 fl oz (C) 1 gal 2 oz (D) 1 gal 2 fl oz

SEE EXAMPLE 5 on p. 522 for Exs. 21–26

ADDING AND SUBTRACTING MEASURES **Find the sum or difference.**

21. 3 c 5 fl oz + 8 c 6 fl oz

22. 6 lb 7 oz + 8 lb 9 oz

23. 45 lb 9 oz − 17 lb 13 oz

24. 6 ft 2 in. − 2 ft 11 in.

25. 10 ft 3 in. − 4 ft 9 in.

26. 12 mi 500 ft + 27 mi 5250 ft

COMPARING MEASURES **Copy and complete the statement using <, >, or =.**

27. 36 in. _?_ 3 ft

28. 10 pt _?_ 2 gal

29. 10 lb _?_ 64 oz

30. 3 yd _?_ 10 ft

31. 10 c _?_ 20 fl oz

32. 2 T _?_ 5000 lb

ORDERING MEASURES **Order the measures from least to greatest.**

33. $\frac{1}{4}$ lb, 7 oz, $\frac{5}{8}$ lb, 0.5 lb, $\frac{32}{3}$ oz

34. 0.75 ft, 8.7 in., $\frac{37}{5}$ in., $\frac{5}{6}$ ft, $7\frac{3}{4}$ in.

ALGEBRA **Copy and complete the statement.**

35. There are _?_ mile(s) in x inches.

36. There are _?_ hour(s) in y seconds.

CONNECT SKILLS TO PROBLEM SOLVING **Exercises 37–40 will help you prepare for problem solving.**

Use the following information: A recipe calls for 3 cups of milk. The measuring container that you have only measures fluid ounces.

37. What is the relationship between cups and fluid ounces?

38. What form of 1 do you need to use to convert from cups to fluid ounces?

39. Write the expression you would use to convert 3 cups to fluid ounces.

40. Evaluate the expression to find how many fluid ounces of milk you need.

SEE EXAMPLE 4 on p. 521 for Ex. 41

41. **CONTAINERS** A container holds 20 fluid ounces of liquid. Convert this measure to cups and fluid ounces.

California @HomeTutor for problem solving help at classzone.com

42. **MULTI-STEP PROBLEM** You have 10 jugs and 18 bottles. Each jug contains 1 gallon of water. Each bottle contains 12 fluid ounces of water.
    a. How many cups of water do you have in the jugs?
    b. How many cups of water do you have in the bottles?
    c. How many cups of water do you have altogether?

California @HomeTutor for problem solving help at classzone.com

SEE EXAMPLE 1 on p. 520 for Ex. 43

43. ◆ **MULTIPLE CHOICE** One lap of the racecar event Indianapolis 500 is $2\frac{1}{2}$ miles long. How many feet are in three laps?

    (A) 1250 ft (B) 13,200 ft (C) 39,600 ft (D) 79,200 ft

44. **REFRESHMENTS** Nina needs 14 cups of orange juice to make fruit punch for a party. If she buys a one gallon jug of orange juice, will she have enough orange juice for the punch? *Explain* your reasoning.

45. **SHORT RESPONSE** In some areas, fishing regulations set weight limits. If you catch more than $7\frac{1}{2}$ pounds of fish in a day, you must return fish into the water. Suppose you catch a 4 pound 4 ounce rainbow trout and a 3 pound 5 ounce brook trout. Do you have to return any fish into the water? *Explain* your reasoning.

46. **REASONING** When converting from pounds to ounces, will the number of ounces be *greater than* or *less than* the number of pounds? *Explain.*

READING *IN* MATH **Read the information below for Exercises 47–51.**

Pyramids of Giza The three pyramids of Giza, Egypt, and their original heights and base widths are listed in the table. The tallest of these pyramids is called the Great Pyramid.

Khafre is 157 yards high.

Pyramid	Height	Base width
Khafre	157 yd	8484 in.
Menkaure	2618 in.	356 ft
Khufu	486 ft	254 yd

47. **Convert** What are the heights of the pyramids in yards? in feet?

48. **Reasoning** Which pyramid is the Great Pyramid? *Explain* your reasoning.

49. **Calculate** How many yards taller is the tallest pyramid than the shortest pyramid? how many feet taller?

50. **Compare** Which pyramid has the least base width?

51. **Reasoning** Are the heights of the pyramids all less than their base widths? *Justify* your answer.

52. **TRAVEL** Carl is taking a seaplane to an island. The weight limit for luggage is 24 pounds. His suitcase weighs 6 pounds 4 ounces and contains the items listed below. Is the total weight of his suitcase and its items over 24 pounds? If so, by how many pounds is it over? If not, how many more pounds can he add without going over the limit?

Item	shirts	pants	shoes	toiletries
Weight	6 lb 7 oz	3 lb 11 oz	4 lb 10 oz	2 lb 11 oz

53. **WRITING** You are subtracting two weights given in pounds and ounces. *Explain* how you can tell whether you need to rename one of the weights.

54. **MULTI-STEP PROBLEM** You are building a CD rack with 3 shelves that are each 1 foot 3 inches long. Each end piece is 2 inches long.

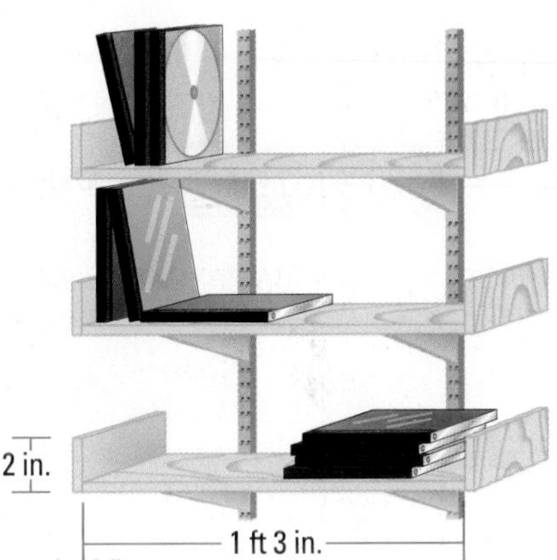

a. How many feet of wood will you need to buy for the shelves and six end pieces?

b. Each CD case has a width of $\frac{7}{16}$ inch. Estimate the number of CD cases in one inch. Predict the number of CD cases that will fit on a shelf. Calculate to find the exact number.

c. Your brother asks you to build a CD rack for him. He has a collection of 100 CD cases. How long should you make each of the 3 shelves?

CHALLENGE Copy and complete the statement.

55. 60 miles/hour = __?__ feet/second

56. 15 ounces/cup = __?__ pounds/gallon

57. (xy) **CHALLENGE** A rectangular driveway has a length of 12 yards and a width of $5\frac{1}{2}$ yards. Pavement sealer comes in containers that cover x square feet. Write an expression that represents the number of containers needed. How many containers are needed if $x = 400$?

◆ CALIFORNIA STANDARDS SPIRAL REVIEW

NS 2.4 58. What is the least common multiple of 36, 40, and 60? ***(p. 21)***

Ⓐ 4 Ⓑ 120 Ⓒ 180 Ⓓ 360

NS 1.4 59. You buy a chair that is on sale for 25% off the original price of $110. What is the sale price of the chair? ***(p. 325)***

Ⓐ $27.50 Ⓑ $82.50 Ⓒ $85.00 Ⓓ $137.50

AF 2.1 60. The length of a race is 250 meters. What is the length (in centimeters) of the race? ***(p. 515)***

Ⓐ 0.25 cm Ⓑ 2.5 cm Ⓒ 25,000 cm Ⓓ 250,000 cm

PROBLEM SOLVING WORKSHOP
LESSON 10.2

Using ALTERNATIVE METHODS

Another Way to Solve Example 2, page 521

Standards
AF 2.1

In Example 2 on page 521, you saw how to solve the problem about the weight of a humpback whale by converting customary units. You can also solve the problem by using a proportion or number sense.

PROBLEM

WHALES A humpback whale weighs $33\frac{1}{2}$ tons. How many pounds does the whale weigh?

METHOD 1

Using a Proportion One alternate approach is to use a proportion.

Use the fact that 1 T = 2000 lb to write the ratio $\frac{1}{2000}$.

Let x represent the weight (in pounds).

$$\frac{1}{2000} = \frac{33\frac{1}{2}}{x} \quad \begin{array}{l}\leftarrow \textbf{tons} \\ \leftarrow \textbf{pounds}\end{array}$$

$1 \cdot x = 2000 \cdot 33\frac{1}{2}$ **Use cross products property.**

$x = 67{,}000$ **Simplify.**

▶ **Answer** The whale weighs 67,000 pounds.

METHOD 2

Using Number Sense Another alternate approach is to use number sense.

Use the relationship 1 T = 2000 lb.

$1 \text{ T} = 2000 \text{ lb}$ **Write relationship between units.**

$33\frac{1}{2} \cdot (1 \text{ T}) = 33\frac{1}{2} \cdot (2000 \text{ lb})$ **Multiply each side by $33\frac{1}{2}$.**

$33\frac{1}{2} \text{ T} = 67{,}000 \text{ lb}$ **Simplify.**

▶ **Answer** The whale weighs 67,000 pounds.

PRACTICE

1. **BIOLOGY** You buy a 0.75 cup bottle of plant food. How many fluid ounces of plant food does the bottle contain? Solve this problem using two different methods.

2. **CLOTHING** You have 6.5 yards of ribbon to make an outfit. How many inches of ribbon do you have? Solve this problem using two different methods.

10.3 Converting Between Systems

Math and GEOGRAPHY
Ex. 44, p. 530

Standards **AF 2.1** **Convert one unit of measurement to another (e.g.,** from feet to miles, **from centimeters to inches).**

Connect ***Before*** you converted units within the metric and U.S. customary systems of measurement. ***Now*** you will convert between systems.

KEY VOCABULARY
- **length,** *p. 680*
- **mass,** *p. 680*
- **weight,** *p. 680*
- **capacity,** *p. 680*

Converting between metric and U.S. customary units is similar to converting units within the U.S. customary system, because in both procedures you multiply by a convenient form of 1. Converting between metric and U.S. customary units may use the relationships below.

KEY CONCEPT *For Your Notebook*

Units of Measure

Length	Weight/Mass	Capacity
1 in. = 2.54 cm	1 oz ≈ 28.35 g	1 fl oz ≈ 29.573 mL
1 ft = 0.3048 m	1 lb ≈ 0.454 kg	1 qt ≈ 0.946 L
1 mi ≈ 1.609 km		1 gal ≈ 3.785 L

EXAMPLE 1 Converting Units of Measurement

Copy and complete the statement. Round to the nearest whole number.

a. 68 cm ≈ ? in. **b.** 16 fl oz ≈ ? mL

SOLUTION

a. $68 \text{ cm} \times \frac{1 \text{ in.}}{2.54 \text{ cm}} = \frac{68 \cancel{\text{cm}} \times 1 \text{ in.}}{2.54 \cancel{\text{cm}}} \approx 26.77 \text{ in.} \approx 27 \text{ in.}$

▶ **Answer** 68 cm ≈ 27 in.

b. $16 \text{ fl oz} \times \frac{29.573 \text{ mL}}{1 \text{ fl oz}} = \frac{16 \cancel{\text{fl oz}} \times 29.573 \text{ mL}}{1 \cancel{\text{fl oz}}} \approx 473.168 \text{ mL} \approx 473 \text{ mL}$

▶ **Answer** 16 fl oz ≈ 473 mL

✓ **GUIDED PRACTICE** for Example 1

Copy and complete the statement. Round to the nearest whole number.

1. 7 mi ≈ ? km **2.** 134 g ≈ ? oz **3.** 10 L ≈ ? qt

EXAMPLE 2 Comparing Measures

Copy and complete using <, >, or =: 90 m _?_ 300 ft.

90 m _?_ 300 ft	**Strategy: Convert feet to meters.**
90 m _?_ 91.44 m	**300 × 0.3048 = 91.44, so 300 ft = 91.44 m.**
90 m < 91.44 m	**Compare.**

▶ **Answer** 90 m < 300 ft

CURRENCY People may need to convert currency when traveling to another country. The *exchange rate* between two currencies describes how much one currency is worth in a different currency.

EXAMPLE 3 Converting Currency

Use the exchange rate between U.S. dollars and British pounds shown in the graph.

a. A picture frame costs 2 British pounds in London. The same frame costs $5.75 in San Diego. In which city is the frame cheaper?

b. About how many U.S. dollars are 12 British pounds worth?

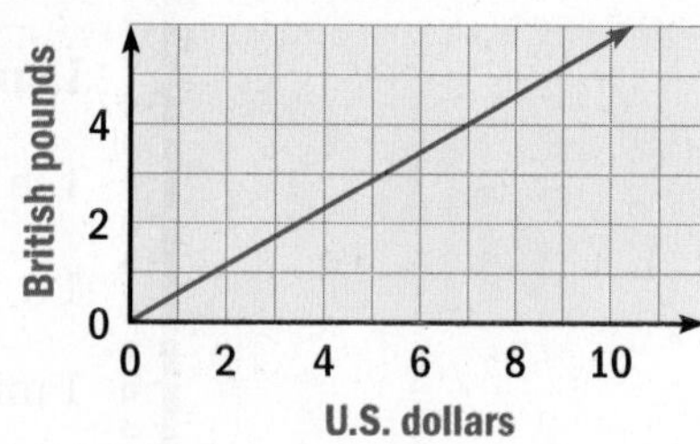

About the Standards

In Example 3, you analyzed a graph to solve a problem involving rates, as called for in Grade 6 Standard AF 2.0.

SOLUTION

a. The graph shows that 2 British pounds are worth between $3 and $4. The picture frame is cheaper in London.

b. The graph shows that 4 British pounds are worth about $7. The exchange rate is 1 British pound ≈ $1.75.

$$12 \text{ British pounds} \times \frac{\$1.75}{1 \text{ British pound}} = \frac{12 \cancel{\text{ British pounds}} \times \$1.75}{1 \cancel{\text{ British pound}}} = \$21$$

12 British pounds are worth about $21.

✓ GUIDED PRACTICE for Examples 2 and 3

Copy and complete the statement using <, >, or =.

4. 264 cm _?_ 110 in. **5.** 200 mL _?_ 7 fl oz **6.** 155 lb _?_ 74 kg

7. **WHAT IF?** In Example 3, suppose that a frame costs $12. How many British pounds would the frame cost? Round to the nearest pound.

Copy and complete the statement using the exchange rate 1 euro ≈ 1.22 U.S. dollars. Round to the nearest whole number.

8. 25 euros ≈ _?_ U.S. dollars **9.** 50 U.S. dollars ≈ _?_ euros

10.3 EXERCISES

HOMEWORK KEY

◆ = **MULTIPLE CHOICE PRACTICE** Exs. 16, 17, 42, 49–51

○ = **HINTS AND HOMEWORK HELP** for Exs. 3, 21, 43 at classzone.com

SKILLS • PROBLEM SOLVING • REASONING

1. **VOCABULARY** Copy and complete: 1 ft = 0.3048 _?_ and 1 qt ≈ 0.946 _?_.

2. **WRITING** *Describe* how you would convert from pounds to kilograms.

SEE EXAMPLE 1 on p. 527 for Exs. 3–16

CONVERTING UNITS Copy and complete the statement. Round to the nearest whole number.

3. 32 m ≈ _?_ ft	4. 450 g ≈ _?_ oz	5. 155 mL ≈ _?_ fl oz
6. 62 lb ≈ _?_ kg	7. 500 gal ≈ _?_ L	8. 24 km ≈ _?_ mi
9. 22 qt ≈ _?_ L	10. 3 in. ≈ _?_ cm	11. 7 oz ≈ _?_ g
12. 4 mi ≈ _?_ km	13. 110 kg ≈ _?_ lb	14. 46 fl oz ≈ _?_ mL

15. **ERROR ANALYSIS** *Describe* and correct the error made in converting 185 kilometers to miles.

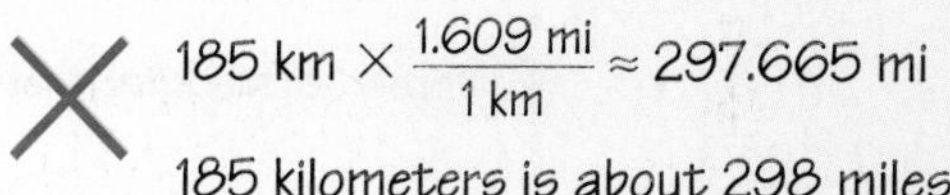

16. ◆ **MULTIPLE CHOICE** About how many grams are in 44 ounces?

(A) 2 g (B) 97 g (C) 1247 g (D) 1302 g

SEE EXAMPLE 2 on p. 528 for Exs. 17–25

17. ◆ **MULTIPLE CHOICE** Which statement is correct?

(A) 25 m > 86 ft (B) 154 lb < 60 kg

(C) 500 mL < 18 fl oz (D) 600 km > 400 mi

COMPARING MEASURES Copy and complete using <, >, or =.

18. 18 in. _?_ 44 cm	19. 45 kg _?_ 102 lb
20. 700 mL _?_ 24 fl oz	21. 90 g _?_ 3 oz
22. 78 qt _?_ 70 L	23. 7 m _?_ 25 ft
24. 70 mi _?_ 116 km	25. 200 L _?_ 528 gal

SEE EXAMPLE 3 on p. 528 for Exs. 26–30

CONVERTING CURRENCY Copy and complete using the exchange rate 1 U.S. dollar ≈ 118 Japanese yen. Round to the nearest whole number.

26. 12 U.S. dollars ≈ _?_ Japanese yen	27. 22 U.S. dollars ≈ _?_ Japanese yen
28. 210 Japanese yen ≈ _?_ U.S. dollars	29. 1200 Japanese yen ≈ _?_ U.S. dollars

30. **ERROR ANALYSIS** *Describe* and correct the error made in converting 145 euros to Canadian dollars. (1 euro ≈ 1.39 Canadian dollars)

✗ 145 euros × $\frac{\text{1 Canadian dollar}}{\text{1.39 euros}}$ ≈ 104.32 Canadian dollars

145 euros are about 104 Canadian dollars.

CONVERTING UNITS **Copy and complete the statement. Round to the nearest whole number.**

31. 2 L ≈ ? c
32. 1.2 kg ≈ ? oz
33. 115 mi ≈ ? m
34. 2200 kg ≈ ? T
35. 140 cm ≈ ? yd
36. 7 gal ≈ ? mL

CONNECT SKILLS TO PROBLEM SOLVING **Exercises 37–40 will help you prepare for problem solving.**

37. A newborn baby weighs 7 pounds. What is the mass in grams?

38. The length of a bridge is 1.7 miles. What is the length in kilometers?

39. A bench has a length of 150 centimeters. What is the length in inches?

40. A punch bowl has a capacity of 11 quarts. What is the capacity in liters?

SEE EXAMPLE 1 on p. 527 for Exs. 41–42

41. MULTI-STEP PROBLEM Heidi drinks 1.44 liters of water per day.

a. How many milliliters equal 1.44 liters?
b. How many fluid ounces equal the number of milliliters from part (a)?
c. How many 8 fluid ounce glasses does Heidi drink per day?

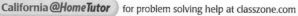

California @HomeTutor for problem solving help at classzone.com

42. ◆ **MULTIPLE CHOICE** A San Francisco cable car travels at a constant speed of 9.5 miles per hour. How many meters does a cable car travel in one hour?

Ⓐ 169 m Ⓑ 1823 m
Ⓒ 15,286 m Ⓓ 164,525 m

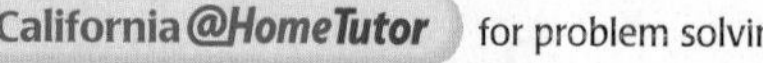
for problem solving help at classzone.com

Cable car travels at 9.5 mi/h.

43. **ZOOS** The rain forest habitat at a zoo is rectangular. The perimeter of the habitat is 375 feet. Its length is 1.5 times its width. What are the length and width in meters? What is the area in square meters?

44. HIKING TRAILS The Pacific Crest Trail is a 2650 mile scenic trail that passes through California, Oregon, and Washington. The units on the map are given in kilometers.

a. About how many miles of the trail are in Washington? in Oregon?
b. Write and solve an equation to find the number of miles of the trail in California.
c. The trail in California is divided into the northern, central, and southern sections. The northern section is 913 kilometers long. The central section is 813 kilometers long. About how many kilometers long is the southern section?

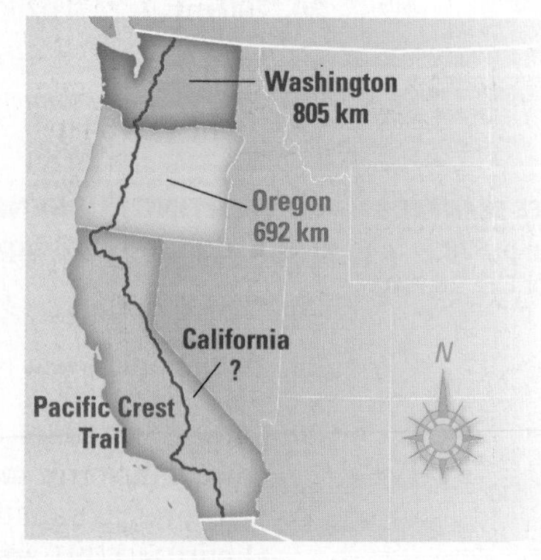

SEE EXAMPLE 3 on p. 528 for Ex. 45

45. **CURRENCY** Use the exchange rate between U.S. dollars and Canadian dollars shown in the graph.

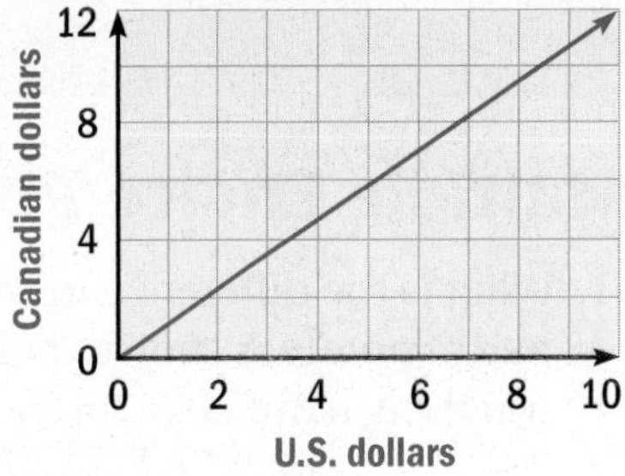

a. A shirt costs 6 U.S. dollars. The same shirt costs 8 Canadian dollars. In which country is the shirt cheaper? *Justify* your answer.

b. A used car is worth 7200 Canadian dollars. To the nearest hundred, how much is the car worth in U.S. dollars?

CHALLENGE Copy and complete. Round to the nearest whole number.

46. 24 meters/pound ≈ _?_ inches/gram

47. 70 liters/hour ≈ _?_ cups/minute

48. **CHALLENGE** The speed of light is 3×10^8 meters per second. Write this speed in miles per hour. The Sun is about 887 million miles from Saturn. How long (in hours) does light travel from the Sun to Saturn?

◆ CALIFORNIA STANDARDS SPIRAL REVIEW

AF 2.1 49. How many pints are in 7 gallons? *(p. 520)*

Ⓐ 14 pt Ⓑ 28 pt Ⓒ 56 pt Ⓓ 112 pt

SDAP 3.1 50. You roll a number cube twice. What is the probability of rolling a number less than 3 twice? *(p. 434)*

Ⓐ $\frac{1}{9}$ Ⓑ $\frac{1}{4}$ Ⓒ $\frac{5}{18}$ Ⓓ $\frac{2}{3}$

SDAP 1.4 51. The scores of 10 singers in a talent contest are: 7, 10, 10, 6, 9, 5, 8, 7, 5, and 5. Which measure supports the claim that a score of 7 is above average? *(p. 364)*

Ⓐ Mean Ⓑ Median Ⓒ Mode Ⓓ Range

QUIZ *for Lessons 10.1–10.3*

Copy and complete the statement.

1. 3200 mg = _?_ g *(p. 515)*
2. 57 cm = _?_ mm *(p. 515)*
3. $46\frac{2}{3}$ yd = _?_ ft *(p. 520)*
4. 22 qt = _?_ gal _?_ qt *(p. 520)*
5. 700 g ≈ _?_ oz *(p. 527)*
6. 500 mi ≈ _?_ km *(p. 527)*

Find the sum or difference. *(p. 520)*

7. 6 gal 3 qt
 + 2 gal 2 qt

8. 52 lb 8 oz
 − 27 lb 13 oz

9. 12 yd 2 ft
 + 4 yd 1 ft

10. **PUMPKINS** A pumpkin contest is held at a county fair. The pumpkin with the greatest weight is the winner. Which pumpkin is the winner? *(p. 527)*

Pumpkin	Orange 1	Happy Face	Pie Guy	Pumped Up
Mass/Weight	635 oz	45 kg	40,000 g	82.5 lb

MIXED REVIEW of Skills and Problem Solving

Multiple Choice Practice for Lessons 10.1–10.3

1. What is the difference in weight between the bag of potatoes shown and a single potato weighing 6 ounces? **AF 2.1**

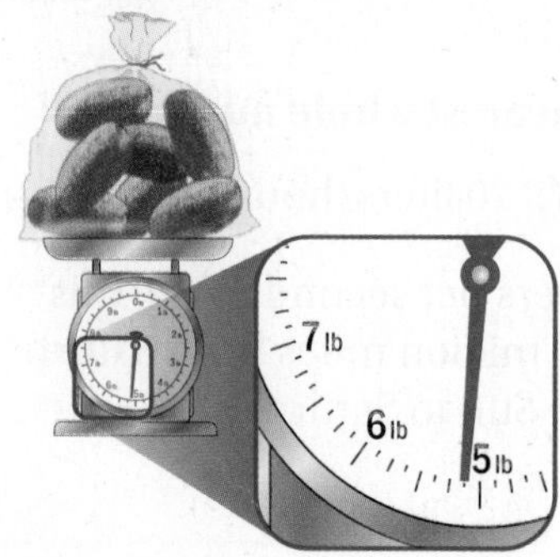

Ⓐ $\frac{3}{8}$ lb Ⓑ $4\frac{3}{4}$ lb

Ⓒ $5\frac{1}{4}$ lb Ⓓ $6\frac{1}{2}$ lb

2. About how many inches are in 15 centimeters? **AF 2.1, MR 2.1**

Ⓐ 17 in. Ⓑ 8 in.

Ⓒ 6 in. Ⓓ 5 in.

3. What is the area of the garden below? **AF 2.1**

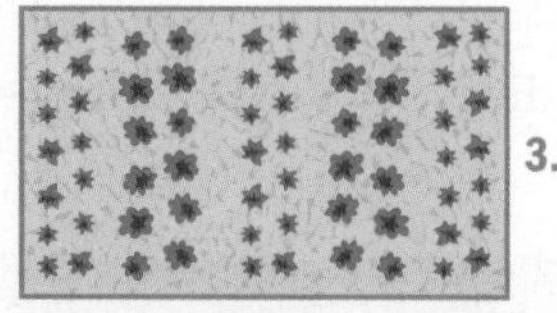

Ⓐ 24.05 cm^2 Ⓑ 2405 cm^2

Ⓒ $24{,}050\text{ cm}^2$ Ⓓ $240{,}500\text{ cm}^2$

4. What is the sum of 8640 feet and 7280 feet? **AF 2.1**

Ⓐ 3 mi 80 ft Ⓑ 3 mi

Ⓒ 2 mi 80 ft Ⓓ 1360 ft

5. The Boston Marathon is approximately 42.2 kilometers long. About how many miles long is the marathon? **AF 2.1, MR 2.1**

Ⓐ 4.2 mi Ⓑ 23.3 mi

Ⓒ 26.2 mi Ⓓ 67.9 mi

6. Suppose that $\$1 \approx 0.85$ euro. How much are 11 euros worth in U.S. dollars? **AF 2.1**

Ⓐ $.08 Ⓑ $9.35

Ⓒ $11.85 Ⓓ $12.94

7. A teenager's diet should include 1.2 grams of calcium each day. Four foods and the amounts of calcium they contain are shown in the table. Which combination of foods exceeds the daily recommended amount of calcium for a teenager? **AF 2.1**

Food	*Calcium (mg)*
1 cup of milk	300
1 cup of cooked broccoli	70
1 slice of cheese	200
6 oz yogurt	275

Ⓐ 2 cups of milk, 2 cups of broccoli, 1 slice of cheese, 6 ounces of yogurt

Ⓑ 1 cup of milk, 2 cups of broccoli, 2 slices of cheese, 6 ounces of yogurt

Ⓒ 1 cup of milk, 3 cups of broccoli, 2 slices of cheese, 6 ounces of yogurt

Ⓓ 1 cup of milk, 1 cup of broccoli, 1 slice of cheese, 12 ounces of yogurt

8. Which is less than 24 kilometers? **AF 2.1**

Ⓐ 240 km Ⓑ 24,000 m

Ⓒ 240,000 cm Ⓓ 24,000,000 mm

9. About how many milliliters of liquid are in the measuring cup below? **AF 2.1**

Ⓐ 2.25 mL Ⓑ 18 mL

Ⓒ 66 mL Ⓓ 532 mL

10.4 Investigating Area

MATERIALS • graph paper • scissors

Standards

AF 3.1 Use variables in expressions describing geometric quantities (e.g., $P = 2w + 2l$, $A = \frac{1}{2}bh$, $C = \pi d$ – the formulas for the perimeter of a rectangle, the area of a triangle, and the circumference of a circle, respectively).

QUESTION How can you compare the area of a parallelogram with the area of a rectangle?

EXPLORE Find the area of a parallelogram by finding the area of a related rectangle.

STEP 1 **Draw** a parallelogram like the one shown below on graph paper. Cut out the parallelogram.

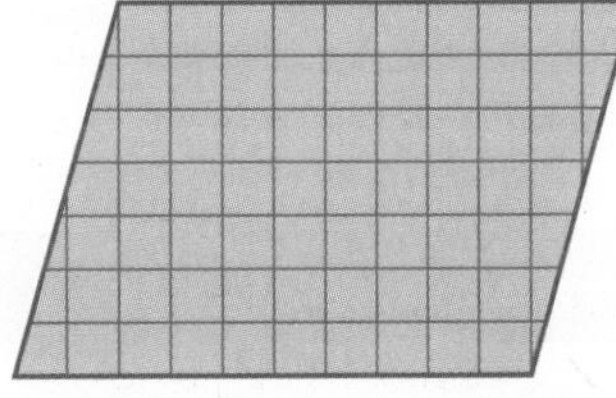

STEP 2 **Draw** a line to make a right triangle as shown. Cut out the triangle.

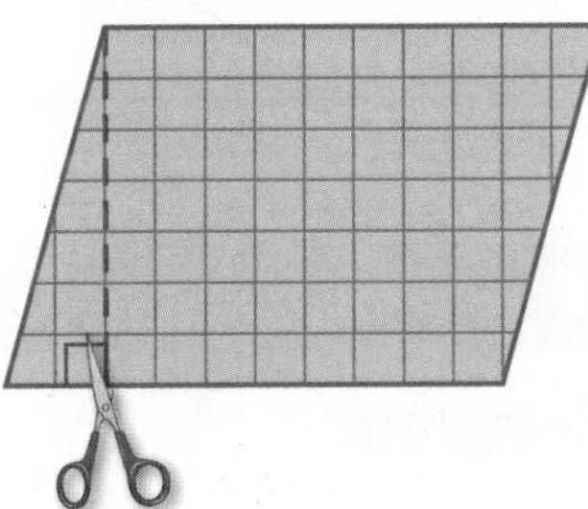

STEP 3 **Move** the triangle to the other side of the parallelogram to form a rectangle.

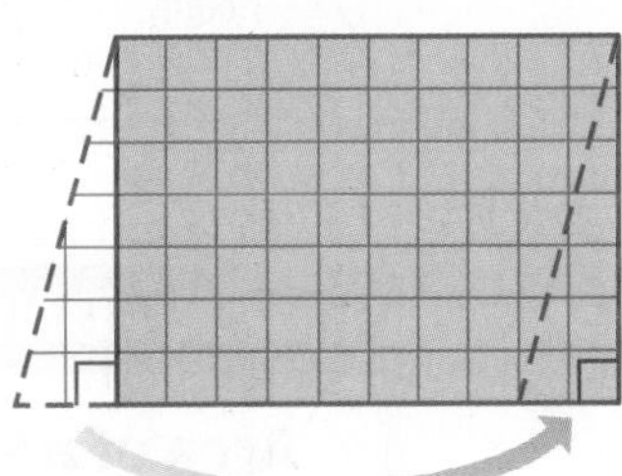

STEP 4 **Find** the area of the rectangle. Use the grid lines and the area formula for rectangles.

$$A = lw = 10 \times 7 = 70$$

The area of the parallelogram is 70 square units.

DRAW CONCLUSIONS Use your observations to complete these exercises.

Follow the steps above to find the area of the parallelogram.

1.

2.

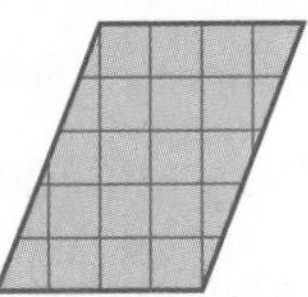

3. REASONING How does the area of a rectangle compare with the area of a parallelogram with the same base and height? *Explain.*

4. REASONING A parallelogram has a length of $(x + 5)$ units and a height of 3 units. Write an expression for the area of the parallelogram in terms of x. Find the area when $x = 7$.

10.4 Area of a Parallelogram

Standards **AF 3.1 Use variables in expressions describing geometric quantities** (e.g., $P = 2w + 2l$, $A = \frac{1}{2}bh$, $C = \pi d$ – the formulas for the perimeter of a rectangle, the area of a triangle, and the circumference of a circle, respectively).

AF 3.2 Express in symbolic form simple relationships arising from geometry.

Connect ***Before*** you found the areas of rectangles and squares. ***Now*** you will find the areas of parallelograms.

KEY VOCABULARY
- **base of a parallelogram**
- **height of a parallelogram**

The **base of a parallelogram** is the length of any one of the sides. The **height of a parallelogram** is the perpendicular distance between the side whose length is the base and the opposite side. The activity on page 533 suggests a formula to find the area of a parallelogram.

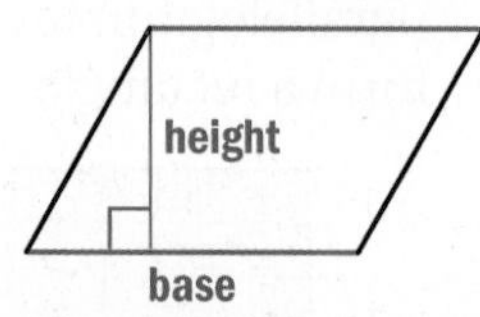

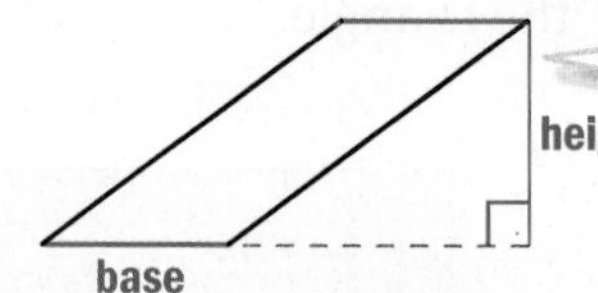

The height can lie outside the parallelogram.

KEY CONCEPT — *For Your Notebook*

Area of a Parallelogram

Words The area of a parallelogram is the product of a base and the corresponding height.

Algebra $A = bh$

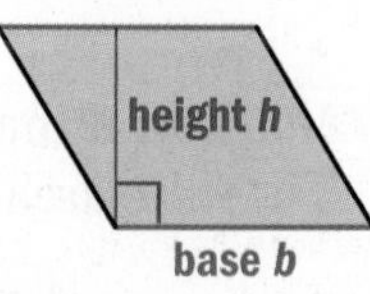

EXAMPLE 1 Finding the Area of a Parallelogram

Find the area of the parallelogram.

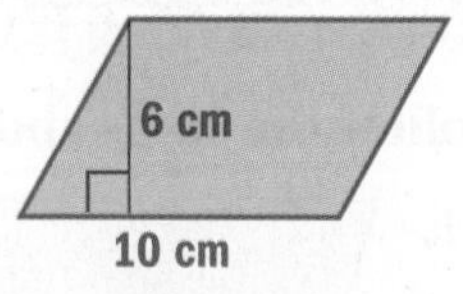

$A = bh$	**Write formula for area.**
$= 10(6)$	**Substitute 10 for *b* and 6 for *h*.**
$= 60$	**Multiply.**

▶ **Answer** The area of the parallelogram is 60 square centimeters.

AVOID ERRORS
Area is measured in square units, *not* linear units.

GUIDED PRACTICE for Example 1

Find the area of the parallelogram with the given base *b* and height *h*.

1. $b = 8$ in., $h = 11$ in. **2.** $b = 9.3$ m, $h = 7$ m **3.** $b = 3.25$ ft, $h = 12$ ft

EXAMPLE 2 Finding the Base of a Parallelogram

FITNESS A treadmill's belt is in the shape of a parallelogram before its ends are joined to form a loop. The belt's area is 2052 square inches. The belt's width, which is the height of the parallelogram, is 18 inches. Find the length of the belt, which is the base of the parallelogram.

Not drawn to scale

$A = bh$	**Write formula for area of a parallelogram.**
$2052 = b(18)$	**Substitute 2052 for *A* and 18 for *h*.**
$\frac{2052}{18} = \frac{b(18)}{18}$	**Divide each side by 18.**
$114 = b$	**Simplify.**

▶ **Answer** The length of the belt is 114 inches.

EXAMPLE 3 Comparing Areas of Parallelograms

A parallelogram has base 9 feet and height 4 feet. Its dimensions are tripled. Compare the areas of the original and enlarged parallelograms.

Original parallelogram

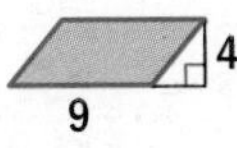

$A = bh$

$= 9(4)$

$= 36$

Enlarged parallelogram

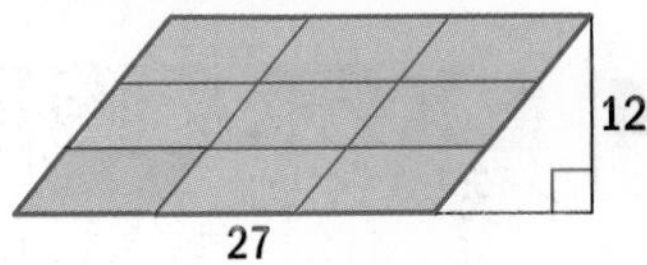

$A = bh$

$= 27(12)$

$= 324$

▶ **Answer** Because $\frac{324}{36} = 9$, the area of the enlarged parallelogram is 9 times the area of the original parallelogram.

ANOTHER WAY

You can also compare the areas without finding the actual areas.

Original area: $A = bh$

Enlarged area:

$A = 3b \cdot 3h$

$= (3)(3)bh$

$= 9bh$

✓ GUIDED PRACTICE for Examples 2 and 3

Use the area *A* of the parallelogram to find its base *b* or height *h*.

4. $A = 56 \text{ in.}^2$
   $b = \underline{?}$
   $h = 8$ in.

5. $A = 36 \text{ mm}^2$
   $b = \underline{?}$
   $h = 4.5$ mm

6. $A = 54 \text{ cm}^2$
   $b = 9$ cm
   $h = \underline{?}$

7. **WHAT IF?** In Example 3, suppose the dimensions of the original parallelogram are multiplied by 0.5. *Compare* the areas.

EXAMPLE 4 ◆ Multiple Choice Practice

A parallelogram with a base of 5 and a height of x is inside a parallelogram with a base of 12 and a height of 8, as shown. Which expression represents the area of the shaded region in terms of x?

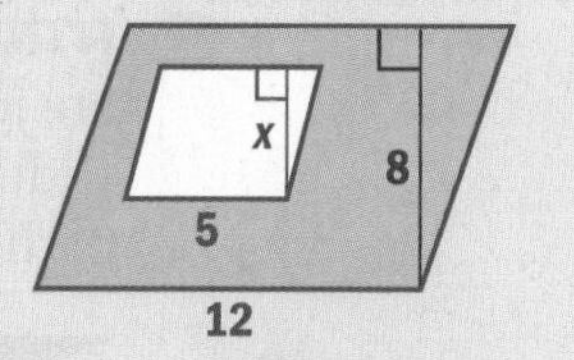

ELIMINATE CHOICES
In Example 4, you *subtract* the area of the smaller parallelogram from the area of the larger parallelogram. You can eliminate choice D.

Ⓐ $60 - 8x$ Ⓑ $60 + 8x$ Ⓒ $96 - 5x$ Ⓓ $96 + 5x$

SOLUTION

The area of the shaded region equals the area of the larger parallelogram minus the area of the smaller one. The area of the larger parallelogram is $A = bh = (12)(8) = 96$. The area of the smaller parallelogram is $A = bh = 5x$. The area of the shaded region is $96 - 5x$.

▶ **Answer** The correct answer is C. Ⓐ Ⓑ Ⓒ Ⓓ

GUIDED PRACTICE for Example 4

8. **WHAT IF?** In Example 4, suppose the larger parallelogram has a base of 14 and a height of x, and the smaller parallelogram has a base of 7 and a height of 6. What expression represents the area of the shaded region?

10.4 EXERCISES

HOMEWORK KEY
◆ = **MULTIPLE CHOICE PRACTICE** Exs. 17, 19, 28, 31–33
○ = **HINTS AND HOMEWORK HELP** for Exs. 7, 11, 27 at classzone.com

SKILLS • PROBLEM SOLVING • REASONING

1. **VOCABULARY** Draw a parallelogram. Label a base and the height.

2. **NOTETAKING SKILLS** Make an *information wheel* like the one on page 514 for *parallelogram*.

SEE EXAMPLE 1
on p. 534
for Exs. 3–9

FINDING AREA Find the area of the parallelogram.

3.
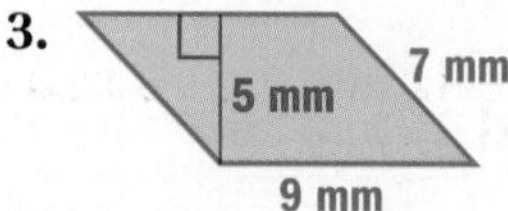

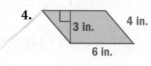

4.
3 in.
4 in.
6 in.

5.
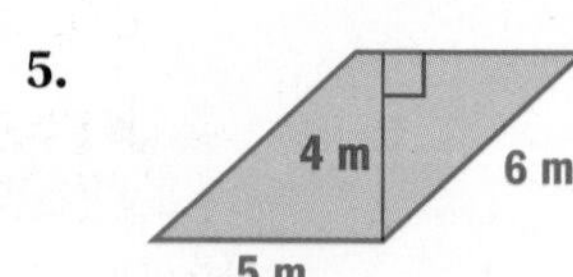

6.
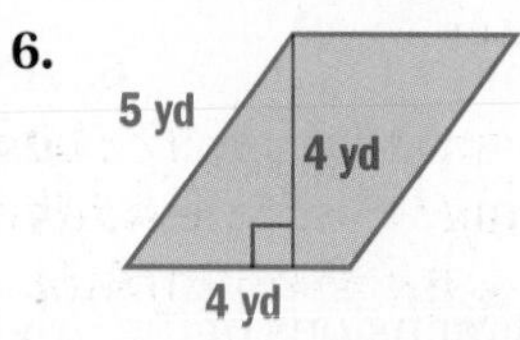

7.
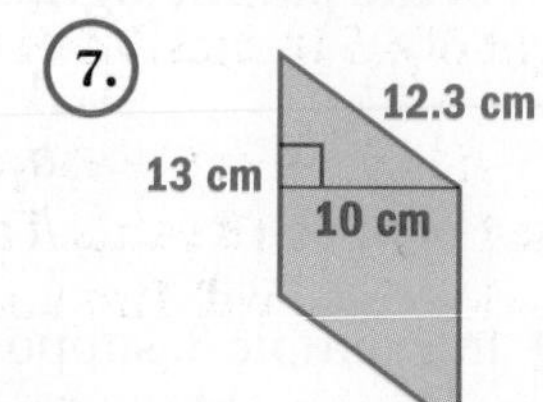

8.
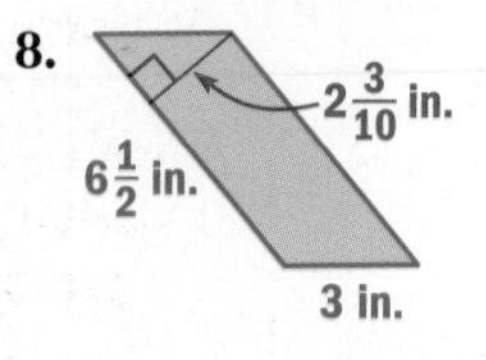

9. **ERROR ANALYSIS** *Describe* and correct the error made in finding the area of the parallelogram.

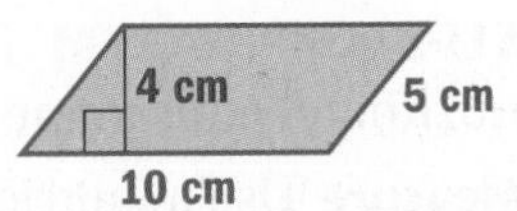

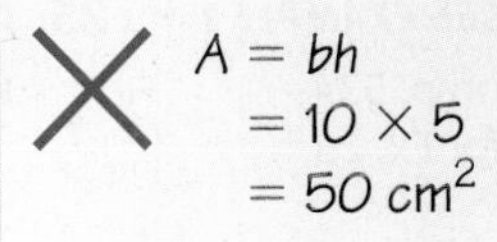

SEE EXAMPLE 2 on p. 535 for Exs. 10–13

FINDING THE BASE OR HEIGHT Use the area A of the parallelogram to find its base b or height h.

10. $A = 48\text{ cm}^2$, $b = 12$ cm, $h =$?

11. $A = 117\text{ ft}^2$, $b =$?, $h = 9$ ft

12. $A = 80\text{ m}^2$, $b =$?, $h = 15$ m

13. $A = 15\text{ in.}^2$, $b = \frac{5}{6}$ in., $h =$?

SEE EXAMPLE 3 on p. 535 for Exs. 14–18

COMPARING AREAS Find the ratio of the areas of parallelograms P and Q with the given base b and height h.

14. P: $b = 5$ m; $h = 3$ m
Q: $b = 20$ m; $h = 12$ m

15. P: $b = 6$ in.; $h = 9$ in.
Q: $b = 2$ in.; $h = 3$ in.

16. P: $b = 4$ cm; $h = 7$ cm
Q: $b = 12$ cm; $h = 21$ cm

17. ◆ **MULTIPLE CHOICE** The area of the larger parallelogram is twice the area of the smaller parallelogram. What is the value of x?

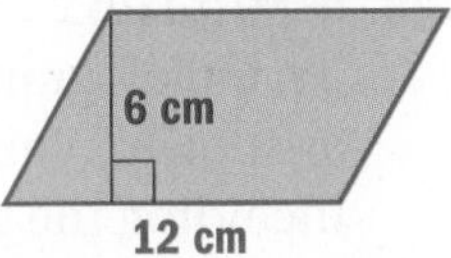

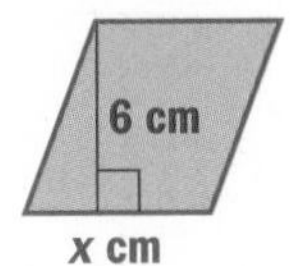

Ⓐ 3 Ⓑ 6 Ⓒ 12 Ⓓ 24

18. **ERROR ANALYSIS** The dimensions of one parallelogram are 4 times the dimensions of another parallelogram. Veronica says that the area of the larger parallelogram is 4 times the area of the smaller parallelogram. *Describe* and correct Veronica's error.

SEE EXAMPLE 4 on p. 536 for Ex. 19

19. ◆ **MULTIPLE CHOICE** A parallelogram with a base of 11 and a height of 9 is inside a parallelogram with a base of x and a height of 15, as shown. Which expression represents the area of the shaded region in terms of x?

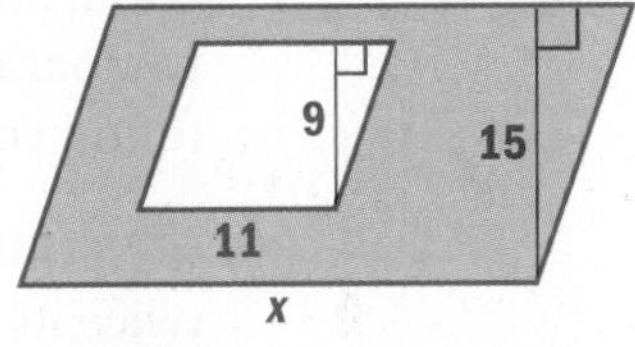

Ⓐ $99 + 15x$ Ⓑ $35 + x$ Ⓒ $15x - 99$ Ⓓ $99 - 15x$

CONNECT SKILLS TO PROBLEM SOLVING Exercises 20–23 will help you prepare for problem solving.

20. A floor tile in the shape of a parallelogram has a base of 26 centimeters and a height of 17 centimeters. What is its area?

21. A table top in the shape of a parallelogram has a base of 23.5 inches and a height of 18.4 inches. What is its area?

22. A piece of wall paneling in the shape of a parallelogram has an area of 117 square feet and a base of 13 feet. What is its height?

23. A parallelogram in a stained glass window has an area of 71.5 square inches and a height of 6.5 inches. What is its base?

24. **SHORT RESPONSE** A lawn is in the shape of a parallelogram. The base is 50 yards and the height is 18 yards. Tim can mow 15 square yards of grass per minute. How long will Tim take to mow the lawn? *Explain.*

California @HomeTutor for problem solving help at classzone.com

SEE EXAMPLE 1
on p. 534
for Ex. 25

25. MULTI-STEP PROBLEM The state of Missouri has approximately the shape of a parallelogram, as shown.

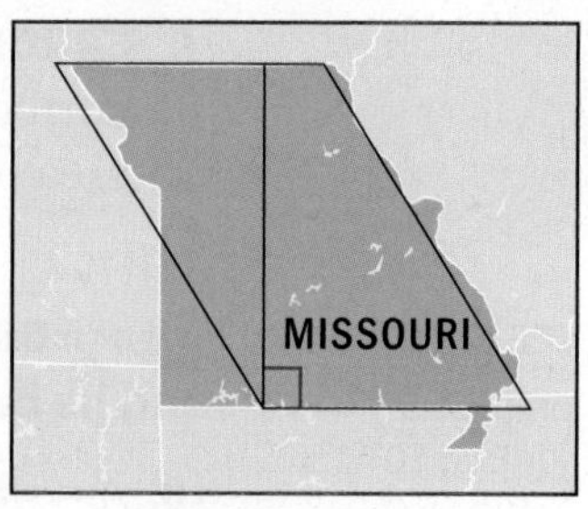

a. Measure Use a metric ruler to measure the base and height (in centimeters) of the parallelogram.

b. Estimate Use the scale 1 cm : 120 mi to estimate the area (in square miles) of Missouri.

for problem solving help at classzone.com

26. WRITING Two parallelograms have the same area. Do they need to have the same base and height? *Explain* your reasoning.

SEE EXAMPLE 3
on p. 535
for Ex. 27

27. REASONING The base of a parallelogram is 24.5 feet. Its height is 10 feet. If you divide the base and the height by 4, how does the area of the parallelogram change? *Explain* your reasoning.

28. ◆ MULTIPLE CHOICE A garden in the shape of a parallelogram is inside a rectangular lawn, as shown. What is the area of the lawn, *not* including the garden?

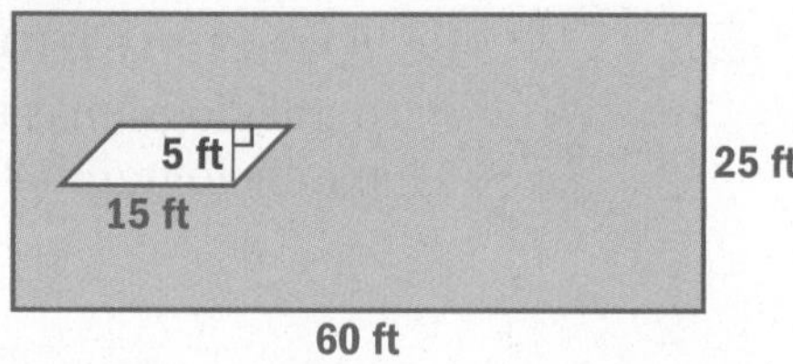

Ⓐ 1350 ft^2 Ⓑ 1425 ft^2

Ⓒ 1500 ft^2 Ⓓ 1575 ft^2

29. CHALLENGE A regular hexagon can be divided into 3 congruent parallelograms, as shown. The area of the regular hexagon shown is about 509.2 square inches. Find the distance x (in inches) between two parallel sides. Round to the nearest tenth. *Explain* how you found your answer.

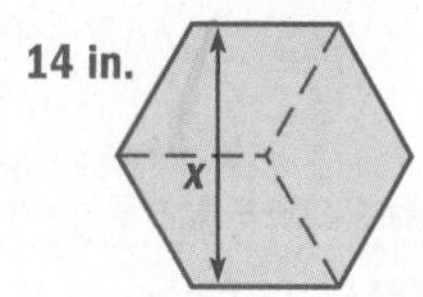

30. xy CHALLENGE The base of a parallelogram is 10 inches longer than twice its height h. Write an expression for the area in terms of h.

◆ CALIFORNIA STANDARDS SPIRAL REVIEW

Gr. 5 NS 1.4

31. What is the prime factorization of 40? ***(p. 5)***

Ⓐ $2^4 \times 5$ Ⓑ 2×5^2 Ⓒ $2^3 \times 5$ Ⓓ $2 \times 3 \times 5$

AF 3.1

32. Which expression represents the perimeter of the rectangle? ***(p. 212)***

Ⓐ $5x$ Ⓑ $6x$

Ⓒ $10x$ Ⓓ $6x^2$

NS 2.1

33. A recipe calls for $1\frac{3}{4}$ cups of flour. You want to make one third of the recipe. How many cups of flour should you use? ***(p. 95)***

Ⓐ $\frac{4}{21}$ c Ⓑ $\frac{7}{12}$ c Ⓒ $1\frac{1}{6}$ c Ⓓ $5\frac{1}{4}$ c

10.5 Modeling Areas of Triangles and Trapezoids

MATERIALS • graph paper • scissors

Standards

AF 3.1 Use variables in expressions describing geometric quantities (e.g., $P = 2w + 2l$, $\mathbf{A = \frac{1}{2}bh}$, $C = \pi d$ **– the formulas for** the perimeter of a rectangle, **the area of a triangle**, and the circumference of a circle, respectively).

QUESTION How can you use graph paper to find the areas of triangles and trapezoids?

EXPLORE 1 Find the area of the triangle shown.

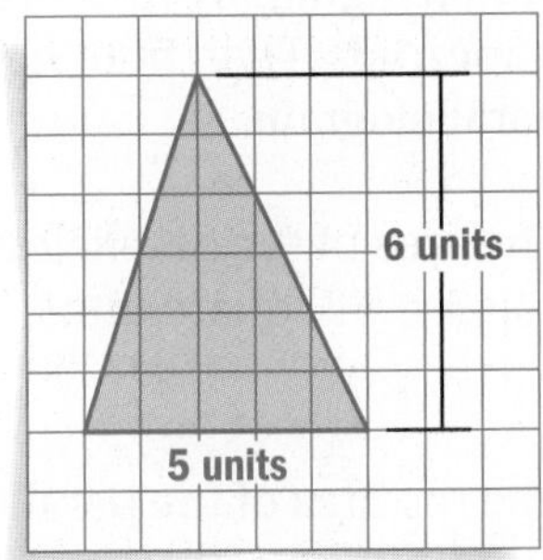

STEP 1 **Use** graph paper to draw two triangles that are congruent to the one shown. Cut out both triangles.

STEP 2 **Fit** the triangles together to form a parallelogram by rotating one of the triangles. Then find the area of the parallelogram.

The area of the parallelogram is $5 \cdot 6 = 30$ square units.

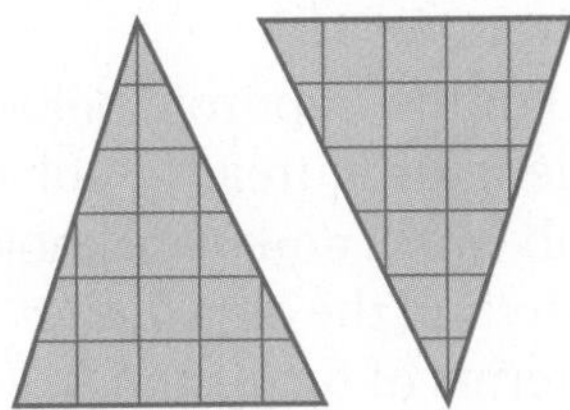

STEP 3 **Use** the area of the parallelogram to find the area of one triangle. Because two congruent triangles make up the parallelogram, the area of the triangle is $\frac{1}{2} \cdot 30 = 15$ square units.

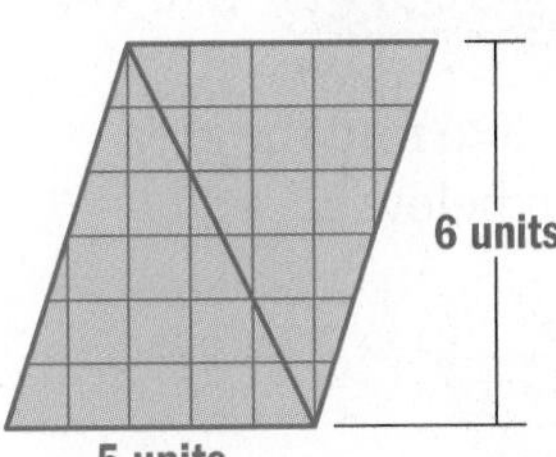

DRAW CONCLUSIONS Use your observations to complete these exercises.

1. Repeat Steps 1–3 to find the area of the triangle below.

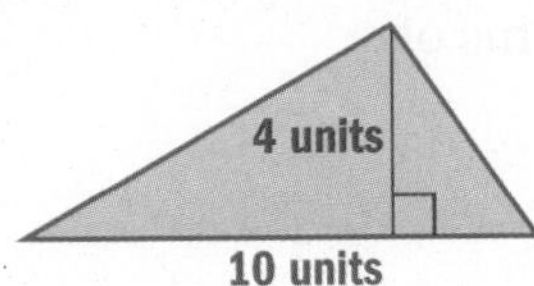

2. **REASONING** For the triangle below, suppose the lengths b and h are known. *Explain* how to find the area of the triangle in terms of b and h.

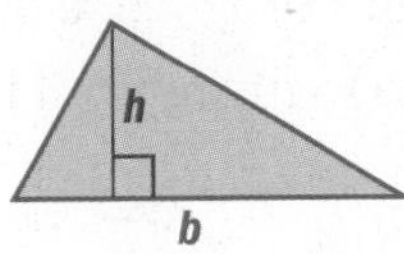

Continued on next page

Continued from the previous page

EXPLORE 2 Find the area of the trapezoid shown.

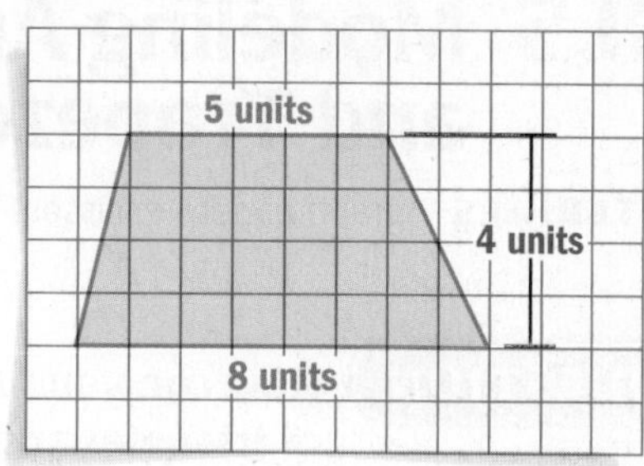

STEP 1 **Use** graph paper to draw two trapezoids that are congruent to the one shown. Cut out both trapezoids.

STEP 2 **Fit** the trapezoids together to form a parallelogram by rotating one of the trapezoids. Then find the area of the parallelogram.

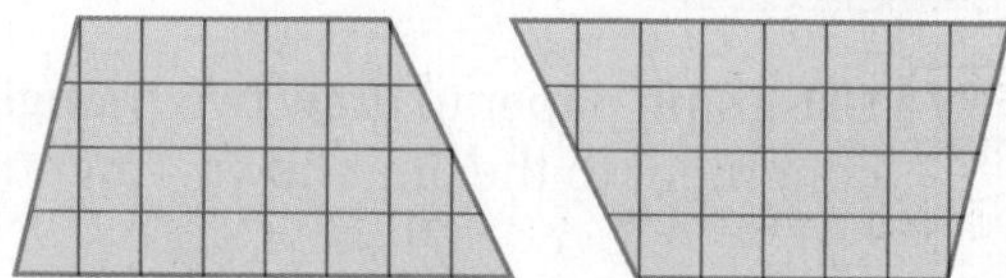

The area of the parallelogram is $13 \cdot 4 = 52$ square units.

STEP 3 **Use** the area of the parallelogram to find the area of one trapezoid. Because two congruent trapezoids make up the parallelogram, the area of the trapezoid is $\frac{1}{2} \cdot 52 = 26$ square units.

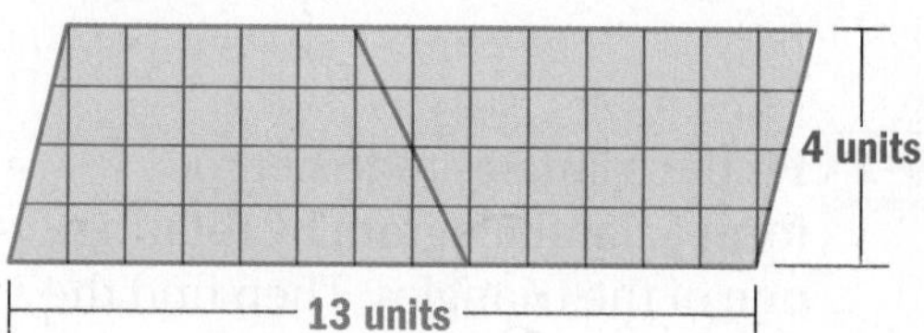

DRAW CONCLUSIONS Use your observations to complete these exercises.

3. Repeat Steps 1–3 to find the area of the trapezoid below.

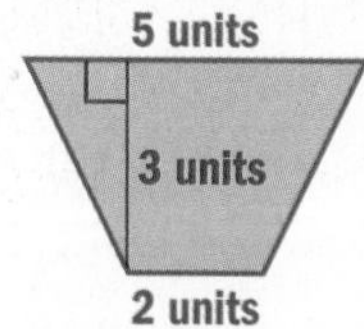

4. **REASONING** For the trapezoid below, suppose the lengths b_1 (read "b sub one"), b_2 (read "b sub two"), and h are known. *Explain* how to find the area of the trapezoid in terms of b_1, b_2, and h.

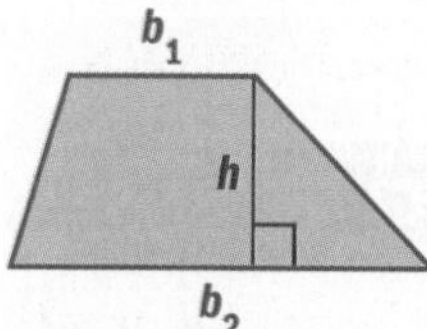

5. **REASONING** The bases of a trapezoid are $7x$ units and $3x$ units. The height is 12 units. Write an expression for the area of the trapezoid in terms of x. Find the area when $x = 8$.

10.5 Areas of Triangles and Trapezoids

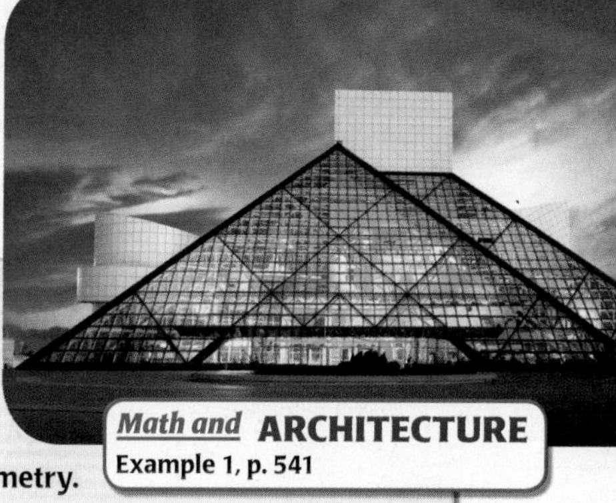

Math and **ARCHITECTURE**
Example 1, p. 541

Standards **AF 3.1** **Use variables in expressions describing geometric quantities (e.g.,** $P = 2w + 2l$, $A = \frac{1}{2}bh$, $C = \pi d$ – **the formulas for** the perimeter of a rectangle, **the area of a triangle**, and the circumference of a circle, respectively).

AF 3.2 **Express in symbolic form simple relationships arising from geometry.**

Connect ***Before*** you found the areas of parallelograms. ***Now*** you will find the areas of triangles and trapezoids.

KEY VOCABULARY
- **base of a triangle, height of a triangle**
- **bases of a trapezoid, height of a trapezoid**

The **base of a triangle** is the length of any one of the sides. The **height of a triangle** is the perpendicular distance between the side whose length is the base and the vertex opposite that side. The activity on pages 539–540 suggests a formula to find the area of a triangle.

KEY CONCEPT *For Your Notebook*

Area of a Triangle

Words The area of a triangle is half the product of a base and the corresponding height.

Algebra $A = \frac{1}{2}bh$

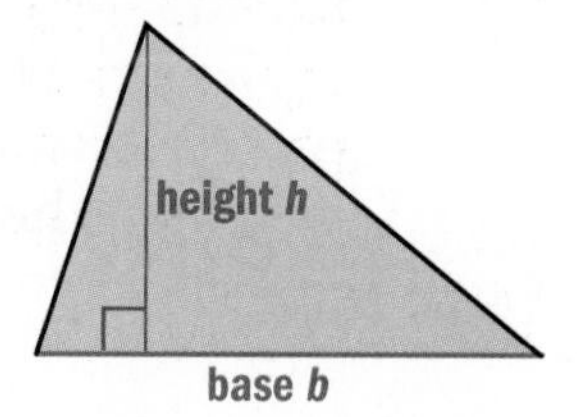

EXAMPLE 1 Finding the Area of a Triangle

MUSEUMS The Rock and Roll Hall of Fame and Museum in Cleveland, Ohio, has a triangular shaped wall, as shown. What is the area of the wall?

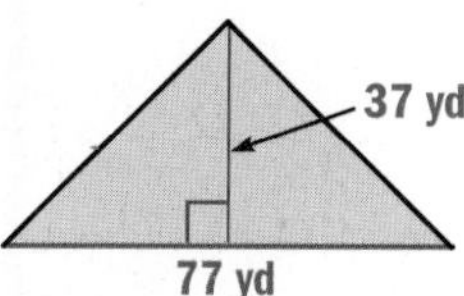

SOLUTION

$A = \frac{1}{2}bh$ **Write formula for area of a triangle.**

$= \frac{1}{2}(77)(37)$ **Substitute 77 for *b* and 37 for *h*.**

$= 1424.5$ **Multiply.**

▶ **Answer** The area of the wall is 1424.5 square yards.

***Animated* Math**
For an interactive example of finding the area of a triangle go to **classzone.com.**

✓ **GUIDED PRACTICE** **for Example 1**

1. Find the area of a triangle with base 6.4 inches and height 14 inches.

EXAMPLE 2 Finding the Base of a Triangle

FLATIRON BUILDING From above, the Flatiron Building in New York City has a shape that can be approximated by a right triangle with a height of 87 feet. The area of the triangle is 7525.5 square feet. Find its base.

Top view

$A = \frac{1}{2}bh$	Write formula for area of a triangle.
$7525.5 = \frac{1}{2}b(87)$	Substitute 7525.5 for *A* and 87 for *h*.
$7525.5 = 43.5b$	Simplify.
$173 = b$	Divide each side by 43.5.

▶ **Answer** The base of the triangle is about 173 feet.

✓ GUIDED PRACTICE for Example 2

Find the unknown base *b* or height *h* of the triangle.

2. $A = 61.6\text{ m}^2$, $b = 11\text{ m}$, $h = \underline{\ ?\ }$

3. $A = 108.5\text{ ft}^2$, $b = \underline{\ ?\ }$, $h = 14\text{ ft}$

TRAPEZOIDS The **bases of a trapezoid** are the lengths of the parallel sides of a trapezoid. The perpendicular distance between the bases is the **height of a trapezoid**. The activity on pages 539–540 suggests a formula to find the area of a trapezoid.

KEY CONCEPT — *For Your Notebook*

Area of a Trapezoid

Words The area of a trapezoid is half the product of the sum of the bases and the height.

Algebra $A = \frac{1}{2}(b_1 + b_2)h$

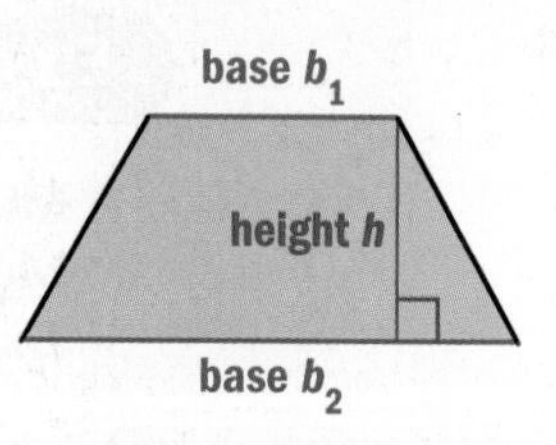

EXAMPLE 3 Finding the Area of a Trapezoid

Find the area of the trapezoid shown.

$A = \frac{1}{2}(b_1 + b_2)h$	Write formula for area of a trapezoid.
$= \frac{1}{2}(5 + 10)(8)$	Substitute 5 for b_1, 10 for b_2, and 8 for *h*.
$= 60$	Simplify.

▶ **Answer** The area of the trapezoid is 60 square feet.

READING
Because a trapezoid has two bases, they are usually labeled b_1 and b_2. You read b_1 as "*b* sub one."

EXAMPLE 4 Finding the Height of a Trapezoid

A trapezoid has an area of 66 square meters. The bases are 8 meters and 14 meters. Find the height.

Animated Math

For an interactive example of finding the height of a trapezoid go to **classzone.com**.

$A = \frac{1}{2}(b_1 + b_2)h$	**Write formula for area of a trapezoid.**
$66 = \frac{1}{2}(8 + 14)h$	**Substitute 66 for *A*, 8 for b_1, and 14 for b_2.**
$66 = \frac{1}{2}(22)h$	**Add.**
$66 = 11h$	**Multiply.**
$6 = h$	**Divide each side by 11.**

▶ **Answer** The height of the trapezoid is 6 meters.

EXAMPLE 5 Writing an Expression for the Area of a Trapezoid

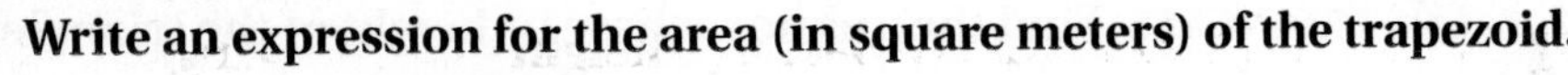

Write an expression for the area (in square meters) of the trapezoid.

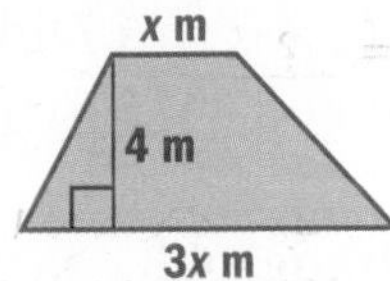

SOLUTION

$A = \frac{1}{2}(b_1 + b_2)h$	**Write formula for area of a trapezoid.**
$= \frac{1}{2}(x + 3x)4$	**Substitute *x* for b_1, 3*x* for b_2, and 4 for *h*.**
$= \frac{1}{2}(4x)4$	**Combine like terms.**
$= 8x$	**Multiply.**

▶ **Answer** An expression for the area of the trapezoid is $8x$.

✓ GUIDED PRACTICE for Examples 3, 4, and 5

4. A trapezoid has a height of 6 inches. The bases are 3 inches and 15 inches. Find the area of the trapezoid.

5. A trapezoid has an area of 216 centimeters. The bases are 11 centimeters and 13 centimeters. Find the height of the trapezoid.

Write an expression for the area of the triangle or trapezoid.

6.

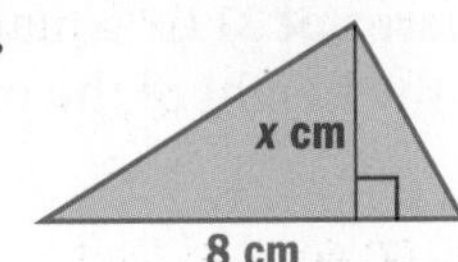

7.

5x in.
10 in.
2x in.

10.5 EXERCISES

HOMEWORK KEY

◆ = **MULTIPLE CHOICE PRACTICE** Exs. 17, 24, 32, 40–42

○ = **HINTS AND HOMEWORK HELP** for Exs. 7, 15, 33 at classzone.com

SKILLS • PROBLEM SOLVING • REASONING

1. **VOCABULARY** Draw a triangle and a trapezoid. Label the bases and heights.

2. **WRITING** *Describe* how the base, height, and area of a triangle are related. *Describe* how the bases, height, and area of a trapezoid are related.

SEE EXAMPLE 1 on p. 541 for Exs. 3–5

FINDING AREA **Find the area of the triangle.**

3. 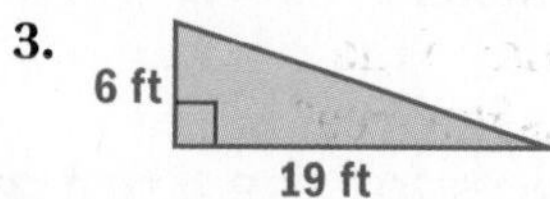

4. 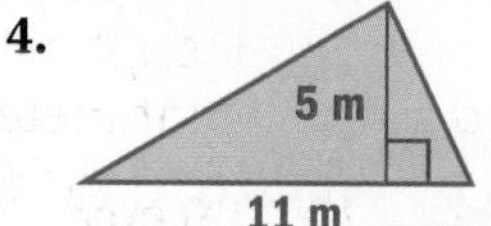

5. 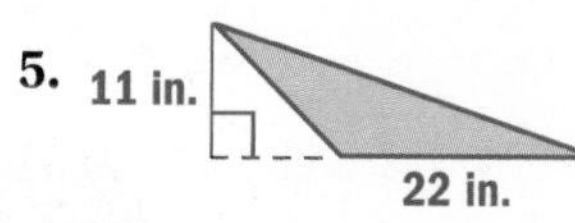

SEE EXAMPLE 2 on p. 542 for Exs. 6–9

TRIANGLES **Find the unknown base or height of the triangle.**

6. $A = 71.5\text{ mm}^2$, $b = 11$ mm, $h =$ __?__

7. $A = 45\text{ km}^2$, $b =$ __?__, $h = 15$ km

8. $A = 13\text{ cm}^2$, $b =$ __?__, $h = 2.5$ cm

9. $A = 98\text{ mi}^2$, $b = 21$ mi, $h =$ __?__

SEE EXAMPLE 3 on p. 542 for Exs. 10–13

FINDING AREA **Find the area of the trapezoid.**

10. 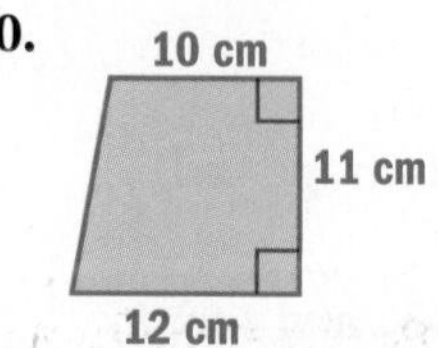

11. 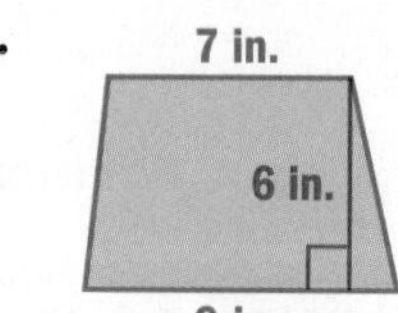

12. 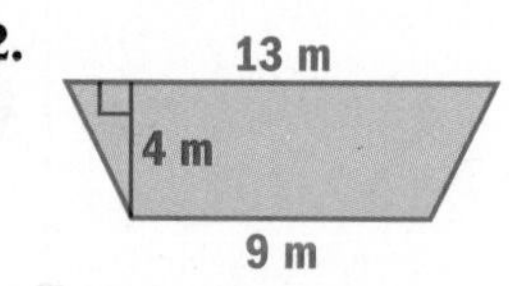

13. **ERROR ANALYSIS** *Describe* and correct the error made in finding the area of the trapezoid below.

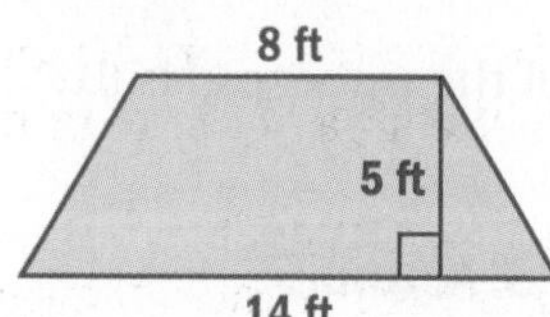

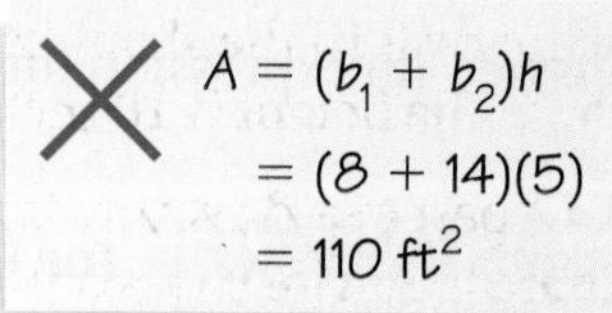

SEE EXAMPLE 4 on p. 543 for Exs. 14–17

TRAPEZOIDS **Find the unknown height of the trapezoid.**

14. $A = 180\text{ ft}^2$, $b_1 = 14$ ft, $b_2 = 26$ ft, $h =$ __?__

15. $A = 444.5\text{ m}^2$, $b_1 = 18$ m, $b_2 = 17$ m, $h =$ __?__

16. $A = 114\text{ cm}^2$, $b_1 = 13$ cm, $b_2 = 6$ cm, $h =$ __?__

17. ◆ **MULTIPLE CHOICE** A trapezoid has an area of 311.2 square feet. The bases are 25.2 feet and 13.7 feet. What is the height of the trapezoid?

Ⓐ 8 ft   Ⓑ 16 ft   Ⓒ 24 ft   Ⓓ 32 ft

SEE EXAMPLE 5
on p. 543
for Exs. 18–23

WRITING EXPRESSIONS **Write an expression for the area of the triangle or trapezoid.**

18.

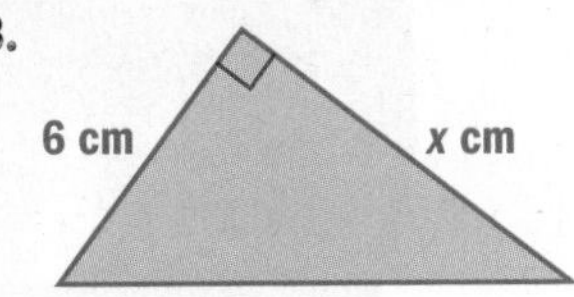

19.

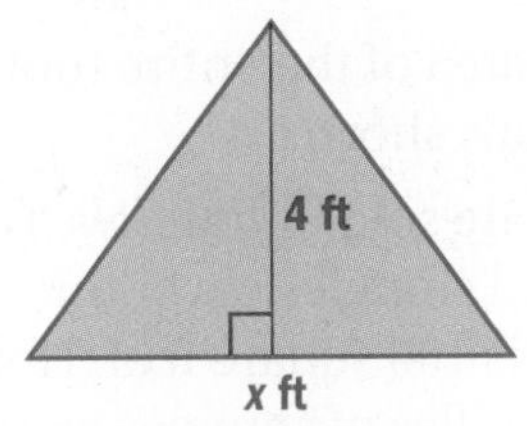

20.

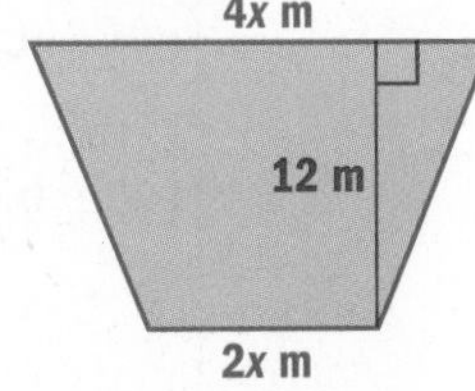

21.

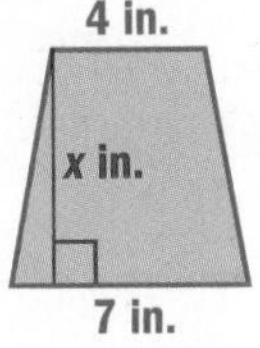

22.

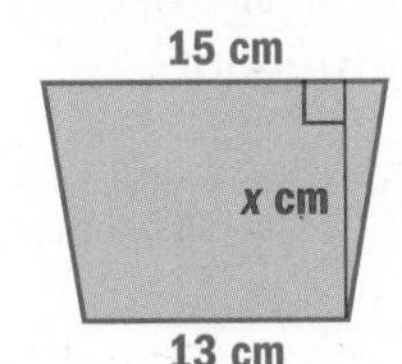

23.

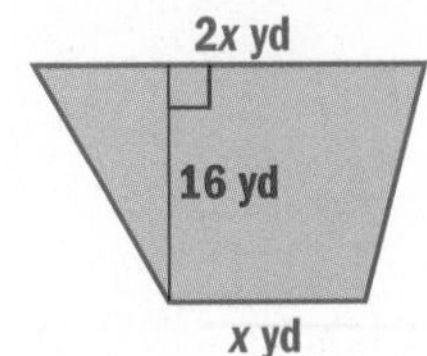

24. ◆ **MULTIPLE CHOICE** The length of the diagonal of the quadrilateral shown is 25 centimeters. What is the area?

Ⓐ 200 cm^2 Ⓑ 400 cm^2

Ⓒ 750 cm^2 Ⓓ 1500 cm^2

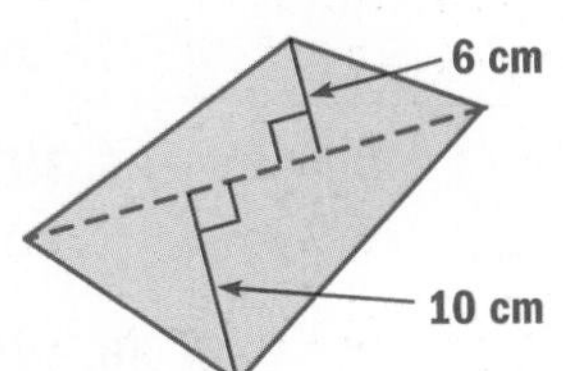

FINDING AREA **Find the area of the figure.**

25.

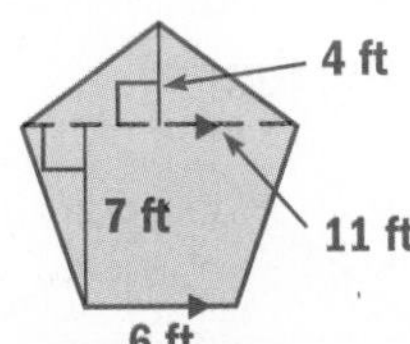

26.

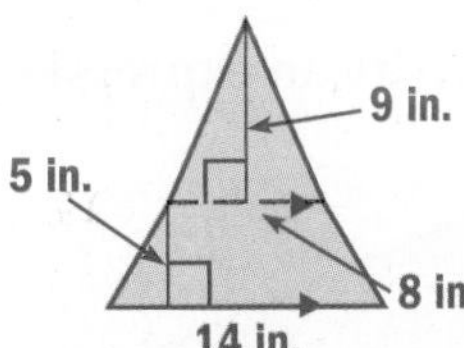

27.

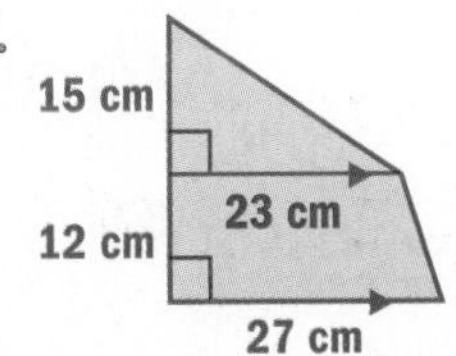

CONNECT SKILLS TO PROBLEM SOLVING **Exercises 28–31 will help you prepare for problem solving.**

28. A reflective patch for a backpack is in the shape of a triangle. Its base is 12 centimeters. Its height is 6 centimeters. What is the area of the patch?

29. A car window is in the shape of a trapezoid. The bases are 10 inches and 24 inches. The height is 18 inches. What is the area of the window?

30. The front part of a driveway is in the shape of a trapezoid. The area is 176 square feet. The bases are 10 feet and 12 feet. What is the height?

31. A triangular garden has an area of 204 square meters and a height of 24 meters. What is the base of the garden?

SEE EXAMPLE 4
on p. 543
for Ex. 32

32. ◆ **MULTIPLE CHOICE** The top of a table is shaped like the trapezoid shown. The area of the trapezoid is 1131 square inches. What is the height h of the trapezoid?

Ⓐ 6.5 in. Ⓑ 15.7 in.

Ⓒ 26 in. Ⓓ 83.8 in.

57 in.
h
30 in.

California @HomeTutor for problem solving help at classzone.com

33. **HIP ROOFS** A hip roof consists of four polygons. The front and back of the roof are congruent trapezoids. The sides are congruent triangles.

  a. Find the area of the entire roof using the dimensions shown.

  b. Shingles are sold in *bundles*. Three bundles of shingles cover one *square*. A square is 100 square feet. How many whole bundles of shingles would you need to cover the roof?

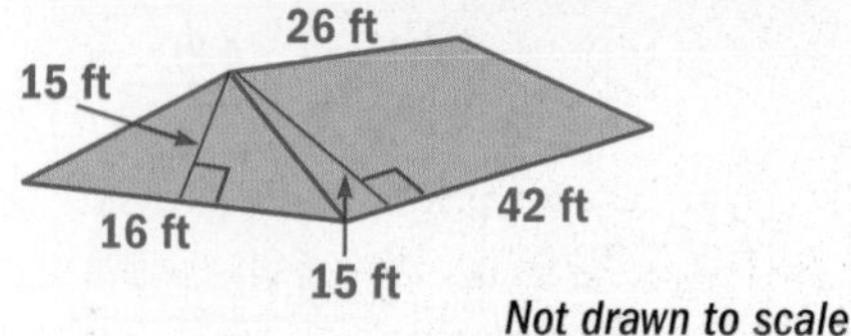

Not drawn to scale

California @HomeTutor for problem solving help at classzone.com

34. **OPEN-ENDED** Sketch two triangles and two trapezoids that each have an area of 24 square centimeters.

35. **REASONING** *Explain* why triangles *ADE, BDE,* and *CDE* have the same area.

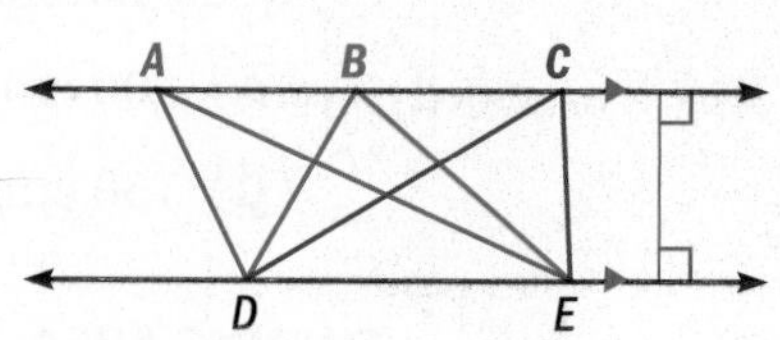

36. **WRITING** The base b and height h of a triangle are both doubled. How does the area change? *Justify* your reasoning.

CHALLENGE Write an expression for the area of the figure.

37.

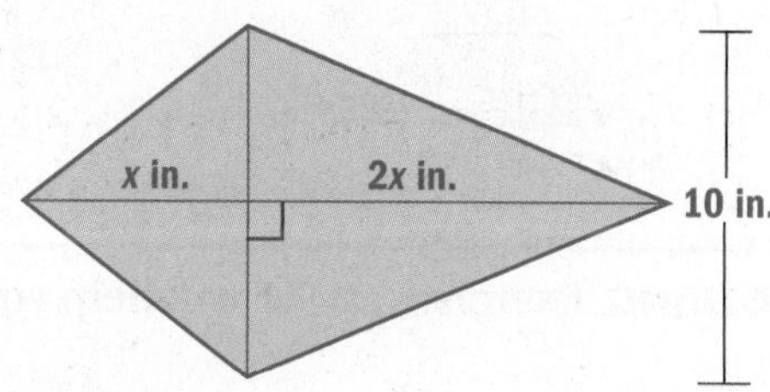

38.

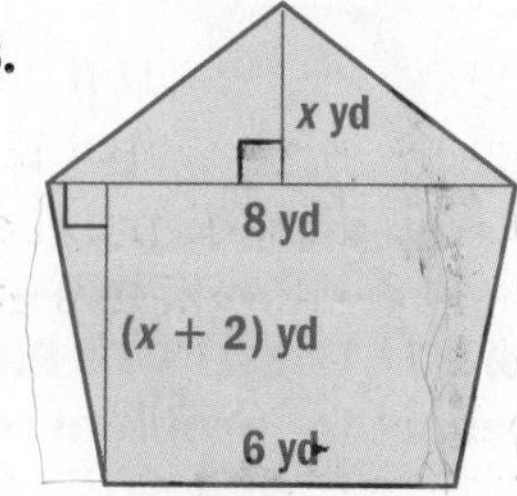

39. **CHALLENGE** In a trapezoid, b_2 is 3 times b_1, and the height h is twice b_1. Write an expression for the area of the trapezoid in terms of b_1.

◆ CALIFORNIA STANDARDS SPIRAL REVIEW

AF 2.1 40. What is 20°C in degrees Fahrenheit? *(p. 212)*

Ⓐ 52°F   Ⓑ 68°F   Ⓒ 80°F   Ⓓ 100°F

AF 1.2 41. What is the value of $4x^2 + 39$ when $x = -5$? *(p. 197)*

Ⓐ −61   Ⓑ −1   Ⓒ 79   Ⓓ 139

NS 1.2 42. Thirty-six of the 60 animals at an animal shelter are cats. What is the ratio of cats to other animals at the shelter? *(p. 255)*

Ⓐ $\frac{3}{5}$ Ⓑ $\frac{2}{3}$ Ⓒ $\frac{3}{2}$ Ⓓ $\frac{5}{3}$

10.6 Investigating Circumference

MATERIALS • ruler • compass • string • scissors

Standards

MG 1.1 Understand the concept of a constant such as π; know the formulas for the circumference and area **of a circle.**

QUESTION **How can you investigate the circumference of a circle?**

In this activity, you will construct circles with a given *radius,* the distance from the center to any point on the circle. Then you will use the constructions to investigate the relationship between the *diameter,* the distance across the circle through its center, and the *circumference,* the distance around the circle.

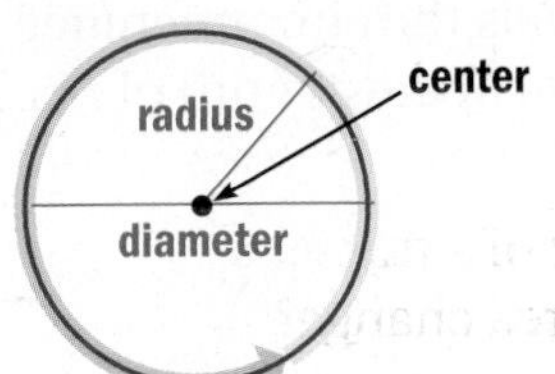

EXPLORE 1 **Use a compass to draw a circle with a radius of 2 centimeters.**

STEP 1 **Open** the compass so that the distance between the point and the pencil is 2 centimeters on a metric ruler.

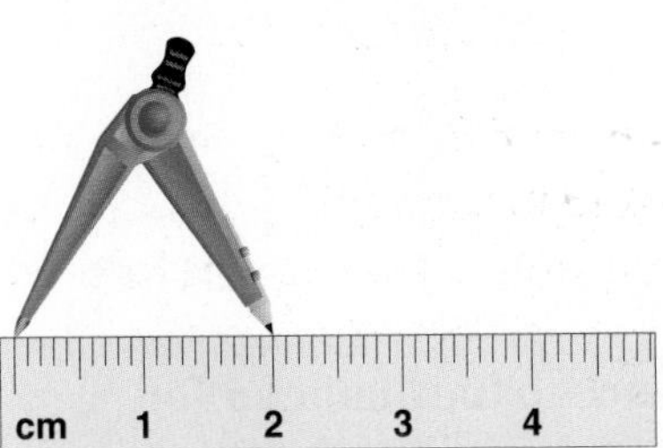

STEP 2 **Place** the point on a piece of paper and rotate the pencil around the point to draw a circle.

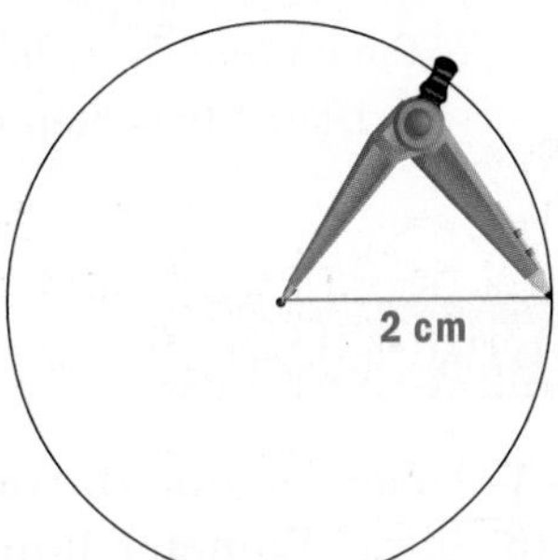

DRAW CONCLUSIONS **Use your observations to complete these exercises.**

Use a compass to draw a circle with the given radius.

1. 2.5 centimeters **2.** 3 centimeters **3.** 5 centimeters

4. WRITING *Explain* how you can use a compass to draw a circle when you are given only its diameter. Then draw a circle with a diameter of 7 centimeters.

Continued on next page

Continued from the previous page

EXPLORE 2 **Find the ratio of the circumference of a circle to the diameter of the circle.**

STEP 1 **Use** a compass to draw a circle with a diameter of 8 centimeters. You will need to set the opening of your compass to 4 centimeters.

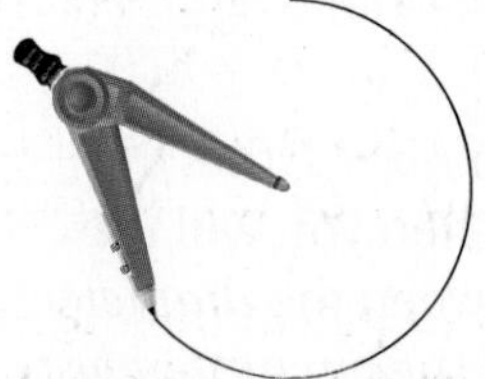

STEP 2 **Cut** a piece of string so that the length equals the circumference of the circle. Then measure the string to the nearest tenth of a centimeter.

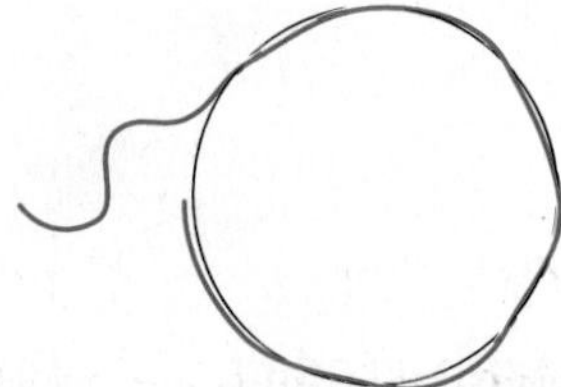

STEP 3 **Find** the ratio of the circumference to the diameter by dividing the circumference in Step 2 by the diameter given in Step 1. Round your answer to the nearest hundredth.

$$\frac{\text{Circumference in Step 2}}{\text{Diameter in Step 1}} \approx \frac{25.1}{8} \approx 3.14$$

DRAW CONCLUSIONS **Use your observations to complete these exercises.**

Repeat Steps 1–3 above to find the ratio of the circumference to the diameter for a circle with the given diameter. Round your answer to the nearest hundredth.

5. 4 cm **6.** 5 cm **7.** 6 cm

8. 3 in. **9.** 4 in. **10.** 5 in.

11. **WRITING** *Compare* the ratios in Exercises 5–10. What do the ratios tell you about the relationship between the circumference and diameter of a circle?

12. **REASONING** *Describe* how you can find the circumference of a circle if you know its diameter. Then find the circumference of a circle with a diameter of 9 centimeters. Confirm your result by following Steps 1 and 2 in Explore 2 above for a circle with a diameter of 9 centimeters.

10.6 Circumference of a Circle

Standards **MG 1.1 Understand the concept of a constant such as π; know the formulas for the circumference** and area **of a circle.**

MG 1.2 Know common estimates of π $\left(3.14; \frac{22}{7}\right)$ and use these values to estimate and calculate the circumference and the area **of circles; compare with actual measurements.**

Math and **RECREATION**
Ex. 29, p. 553

Connect ***Before*** you found the perimeters of polygons. ***Now*** you will find the circumferences of circles.

KEY VOCABULARY
- circle
- center
- radius
- diameter
- circumference

A **circle** is the set of all points in a plane that are the same distance from a fixed point called the **center**. The distance from the center to any point on the circle is the **radius**. The distance across the circle through the center is the **diameter**. The **circumference** is the distance around the circle.

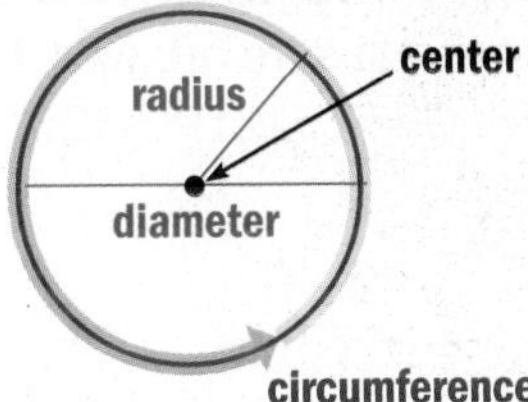

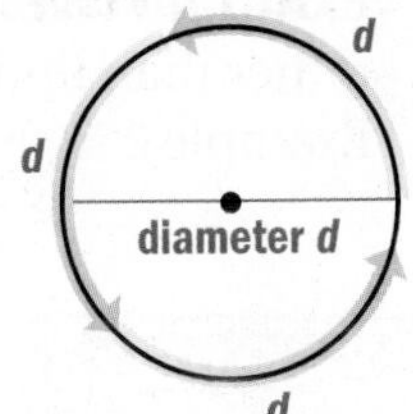

The activity on pages 547–548 suggests that the ratio of the circumference of a circle to its diameter is about 3.14. The exact ratio is represented by the Greek letter π (*pi*). The values 3.14 and $\frac{22}{7}$ are often used to approximate π.

KEY CONCEPT *For Your Notebook*

Circumference of a Circle

Words The circumference of a circle is the product of π and the diameter, or twice the product of π and the radius.

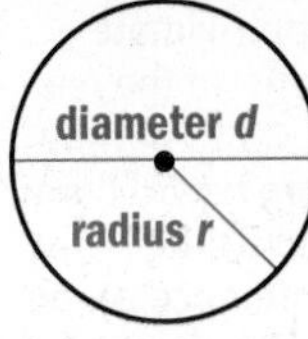

Algebra $C = \pi d \quad C = 2\pi r$

EXAMPLE 1 Finding the Circumference of a Circle

Find the circumference of a circle with a diameter of 8 feet. Use 3.14 for π.

$C = \pi d$ **Write formula for circumference.**

$\approx (3.14)(8)$ **Substitute 3.14 for π and 8 for d.**

$= 25.12$ **Multiply.**

▶ **Answer** The circumference of the circle is about 25.12 feet.

CHOOSING APPROXIMATIONS When the radius or diameter of a circle is divisible by 7, use $\frac{22}{7}$ as the approximation for π.

EXAMPLE 2 Finding the Circumference of a Circle

Find the circumference of the circle. Use $\frac{22}{7}$ for π.

21 in.

SOLUTION

$C = 2\pi r$	Write formula for circumference.
$\approx 2\left(\frac{22}{7}\right)(21)$	Substitute $\frac{22}{7}$ for π and 21 for r.
$= 132$	Multiply.

▸ **Answer** The circumference of the circle is about 132 inches.

EXACT ANSWERS You may be asked to leave your answers in terms of π rather than finding an approximate answer. For example, the answer to Example 2 in terms of π is $C = 2\pi(21) = 42\pi$.

EXAMPLE 3 ◆ Multiple Choice Practice

A clock has a diameter of 25 centimeters. Which equation can be used to find its circumference, C, in centimeters?

Ⓐ $C = 12.5 \times \pi$ Ⓑ $C = 25 \times \pi$

Ⓒ $C = 2 \times 25 \times \pi$ Ⓓ $C = 25^2 \times \pi$

About the Standards

Grade 6 Standard MR 2.6 asks for advantages of exact and approximate solutions. In the real world, 78.5 cm may be more useful than 25π cm as the circumference of the clock in Example 3.

SOLUTION

$C = \pi d$	Write formula for circumference.
$= \pi(25)$	Substitute 25 for d.

▸ **Answer** The equation $C = \pi(25)$, or $C = 25 \times \pi$, can be used to find the circumference. The correct answer is B. Ⓐ Ⓑ Ⓒ Ⓓ

GUIDED PRACTICE for Examples 1, 2, and 3

Find the circumference of the circle with the given radius r or diameter d. Use $\frac{22}{7}$ or 3.14 for π.

1. $r = 18$ m
2. $r = 24$ mm
3. $d = 35$ ft
4. **MOUNTAIN BIKES** A wheel of a mountain bike has a radius of 26 inches. Write an equation that can be used to find the circumference C (in inches) of the wheel.

EXAMPLE 4 Finding the Diameter of a Circle

TREES The largest living tree in the U.S. is a giant sequoia in Sequoia National Park in California. Its trunk is fairly circular and has a circumference of about 1231 inches at ground level. What is the trunk's diameter at ground level?

About the Standards

Grade 6 Standard AF 3.1 calls for using variables in expressions describing geometric quantities. In Example 4, you used the formula $C = \pi d$ to find the diameter of a circle.

SOLUTION

$C = \pi d$	**Write formula for circumference.**
$1231 \approx 3.14d$	**Substitute 1231 for C and 3.14 for π.**
$\frac{1231}{3.14} \approx \frac{3.14d}{3.14}$	**Divide each side by 3.14.**
$392 \approx d$	**Simplify.**

▶ **Answer** The trunk's diameter is about 392 inches, or $32\frac{2}{3}$ feet, at ground level.

GUIDED PRACTICE for Example 4

5. **TREES** In Example 4, the circumference of the tree's largest limb at its widest point is about 256 inches. Find the diameter.

10.6 EXERCISES

HOMEWORK KEY

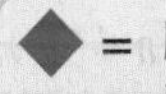 = **MULTIPLE CHOICE PRACTICE** Exs. 13, 20, 24, 34–36

 = **HINTS AND HOMEWORK HELP** for Exs. 3, 15, 27 at classzone.com

SKILLS • PROBLEM SOLVING • REASONING

1. **VOCABULARY** Sketch a circle. Label its diameter, center, and radius.

2. **WRITING** *Describe* how you would find the circumference of a circle with a diameter of 15 inches.

SEE EXAMPLES 1 AND 2 on pp. 549–550 for Exs. 3–8

CIRCUMFERENCE Find the circumference of the circle. Use $\frac{22}{7}$ or 3.14 for π.

3. $d = 9$ in.

4. $d = 30$ in.

5. $d = 6.5$ cm

6. $r = 3.5$ in.

7. $r = 14$ cm

8. $d = 1.205$ in.

SEE EXAMPLE 3 on p. 550 for Exs. 9–13

Find the circumference of the circle in terms of π.

9. 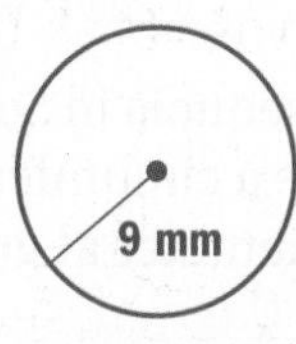

10. 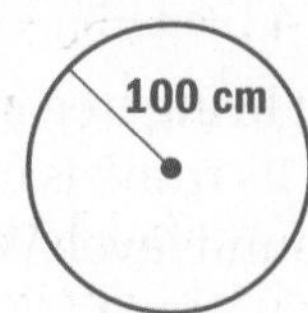

11. 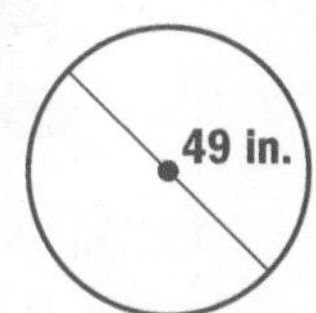

12. **ERROR ANALYSIS** Hakim says that the circumference of a circle with a radius of 5 meters is 5π meters. *Describe* and correct Hakim's error.

13. ◆ **MULTIPLE CHOICE** The radius of a circle is 40 feet. Which equation can be used to find the circumference C (in feet)?

Ⓐ $C = 20 \times \pi$ Ⓑ $C = 40 \times \pi$ Ⓒ $C = 40^2 \times \pi$ Ⓓ $C = 2 \times 40 \times \pi$

SEE EXAMPLE 4 on p. 551 for Exs. 14–19

FINDING DIAMETER AND RADIUS Find the diameter and the radius of the circle with the given circumference C. Use $\frac{22}{7}$ or 3.14 for π.

14. $C = 28.26$ in. **15.** $C = 119.32$ m **16.** $C = 81.64$ mm

17. $C = 42.39$ km **18.** $C = 37\frac{5}{7}$ cm **19.** $C = 14\frac{1}{7}$ ft

20. ◆ **MULTIPLE CHOICE** A circle has a circumference of 252π inches. What is its radius in yards?

Ⓐ 3.5 yd Ⓑ 7 yd Ⓒ 10.5 yd Ⓓ 126 yd

CONNECT SKILLS TO PROBLEM SOLVING **Exercises 21–23 will help you prepare for problem solving.**

21. The diameter of a circular mirror is 16 inches. What equation can be used to find the circumference of the mirror?

22. The radius of a circular swimming pool is 16.5 feet. What is the circumference of the swimming pool?

23. The circumference of a circular tree trunk is 44 centimeters. What is the diameter of the tree trunk?

SEE EXAMPLE 1 on p. 549 for Ex. 24

24. ◆ **MULTIPLE CHOICE** The Astrodome in Houston, Texas, is circular and has a diameter of 710 feet. What is its approximate circumference?

Ⓐ 1110 ft Ⓑ 2230 ft
Ⓒ 4460 ft Ⓓ 15,600 ft

California @HomeTutor for problem solving help at classzone.com

25. **ARCHITECTURE** The London Eye is a circular observation wheel whose outer rim rotates at a speed of about 0.26 meter per second. Its diameter is 135 meters. What is its circumference? About how many minutes does 1 full rotation take?

Diameter of London Eye is 135 meters.

California @HomeTutor for problem solving help at classzone.com

26. **REASONING** To 9 decimal places, the number π is 3.141592654. To how many decimal places is $\frac{22}{7}$ an accurate approximation of π? Is 3.14 or $\frac{22}{7}$ a more accurate approximation? *Explain* your answer.

27. **SHORT RESPONSE** The ends of the track shown are approximately semicircles.

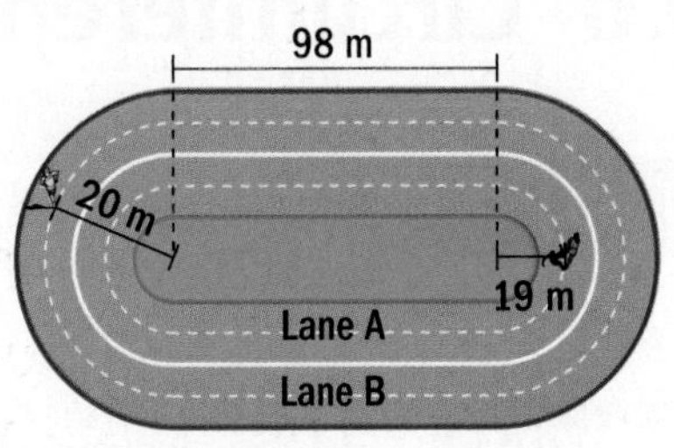

a. How far do you run in one lap in the center of lane A? lane B?

b. How much farther would you run in 10 laps in the center of lane B than if you ran in the center of lane A? *Explain.*

28. **OPEN-ENDED** Find a circular object in your house. Measure the diameter and the circumference of the object. Then find the circumference using the formula $C = \pi d$. *Compare* your results.

29. **UNICYCLES** A giant unicycle wheel has a diameter of 7 feet. What is the circumference of the wheel? Use $\frac{22}{7}$ for π. How many rotations does the wheel take to travel 176 feet? *Explain* your reasoning.

30. **AUTO MECHANICS** A car tire rotates 15 times when it travels 78.5 feet. Find the radius (in inches) of the tire. Use 3.14 for π.

xy **CHALLENGE** **The figure is a section of a circle graph. Find the value of x to the nearest tenth.**

31.

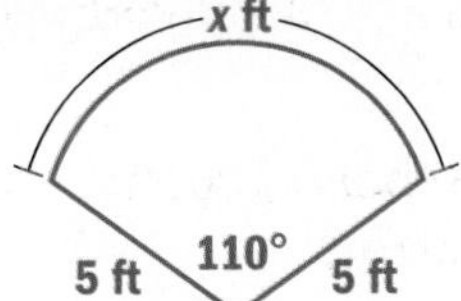

32.

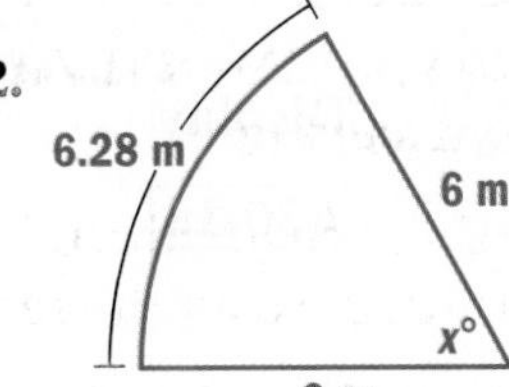

33.

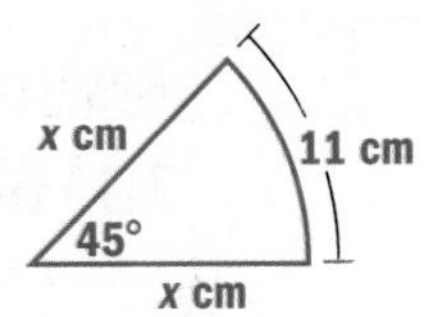

◆ CALIFORNIA STANDARDS SPIRAL REVIEW

NS 1.3 34. The scale on a map is 1 in. : 30 mi. How many inches represent 135 miles on the map? ***(p. 281)***

(A) 3.5 in. (B) 4 in. (C) 4.5 in. (D) 5 in.

AF 2.2 35. Jackie can type 55 words per minute. At this rate, how long would Jackie take to type a report that contains 4400 words? ***(p. 260)***

(A) 1 h 5 min (B) 1 h 10 min (C) 1 h 15 min (D) 1 h 20 min

MG 2.3 36. Which terms describe the triangle shown? ***(p. 474)***

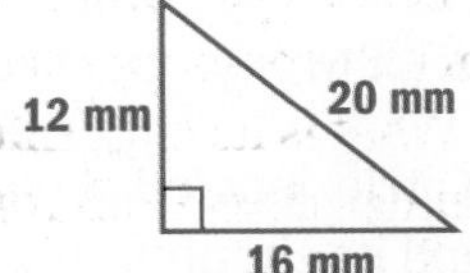

(A) Right, scalene

(B) Right, isosceles

(C) Acute, scalene

(D) Acute, isosceles

10.6 Circumference of a Circle

Standards

MG. 1.1 Understand the concept of a constant such as π; know the formulas for the circumference and area of a circle.

QUESTION **How can you use a calculator to find the circumference of a circle?**

EXAMPLE **Find the circumference of a circle using the pi key on a calculator.**

The *Place Charles de Gaulle*, a traffic circle which surrounds the Arc de Triomphe in Paris, has a diameter of about 137 meters. What is the circumference of the *Place Charles de Gaulle*?

SOLUTION

Use the formula $C = \pi d$ to find the circumference of a circle. To enter π on a calculator, you can use the approximation 3.14 or you can use the pi key, [π]. Although both methods give approximately the same answer, using the pi key gives a slightly more accurate answer.

METHOD 1 Use 3.14 for π.

Keystrokes	Display
3.14 [×] 137 [=]	**430.18**

METHOD 2 Use the [π] key.

Keystrokes	Display
[π] [×] 137 [=]	**430.398194**

▶ **Answer** The circumference of the *Place Charles de Gaulle* is about 430 meters.

PRACTICE

Use a calculator to find the circumference of the circle described. Round your answer to the nearest whole number.

1. $d = 12$ ft **2.** $d = 86$ in. **3.** $d = 341$ cm **4.** $d = 7.95$ m

5. $r = 15$ km **6.** $r = 54$ in. **7.** $r = 0.8$ m **8.** $r = 30.57$ mi

9. GEOGRAPHY The Arctic Circle, located at 66.5°N latitude, has a radius of about 2543 kilometers. Find its circumference to the nearest kilometer. Use the method that gives the more accurate approximation.

10.7 Area of a Circle

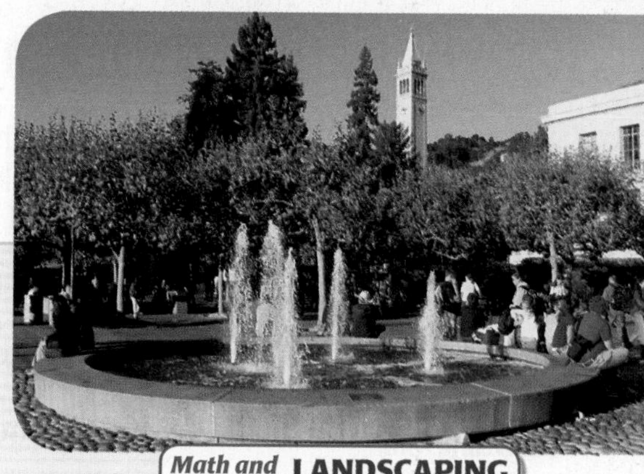

Standards **MG 1.1 Understand the concept of a constant such as π; know the formulas for the** circumference and **area of a circle.**
MG 1.2 Know common estimates of $\pi \left(3.14; \frac{22}{7}\right)$ and use these values to estimate and calculate the circumference and **the area of circles; compare with actual measurements.**

Connect ***Before*** you found the areas of polygons. ***Now*** you will find the areas of circles.

***Math and* LANDSCAPING**
Ex. 31, p. 558

KEY VOCABULARY
- **radius,** *p. 549*
- **diameter,** *p. 549*

The circle shown has a radius of 3 units. To estimate the area of the circle, you can count the number of squares entirely inside the circle, almost entirely inside the circle, and about halfway inside the circle.

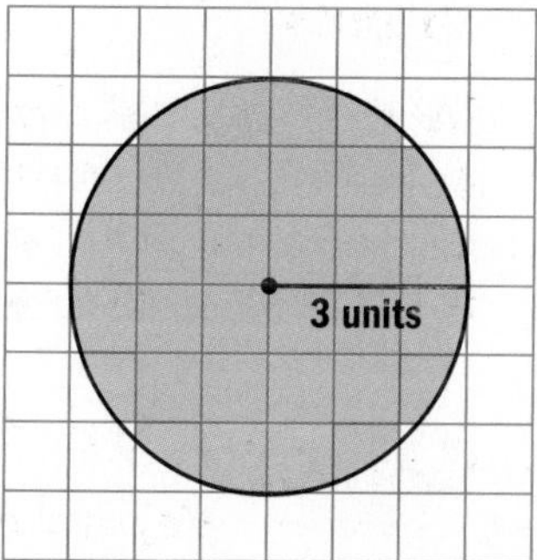

- **16** squares are *entirely* inside the circle.
- **8** squares are *almost entirely* in the circle.
- **8** squares are about *halfway* inside the circle.

You can then estimate the area of the circle.

$$\text{Area} \approx \mathbf{16} + \mathbf{8} + \frac{1}{2}(\mathbf{8}) = 28 \text{ square units}$$

Notice that 28 square units is a little less than π times the radius squared: $\pi \times 3^2 \approx 3.14 \times 9 = 28.26$. This comparison suggests the relationship below.

JUSTIFY FORMULA

In Grade 7, you will see how to derive the formula for the area of a circle by relating it to the formula for the area of a parallelogram.

KEY CONCEPT *For Your Notebook*

Area of a Circle

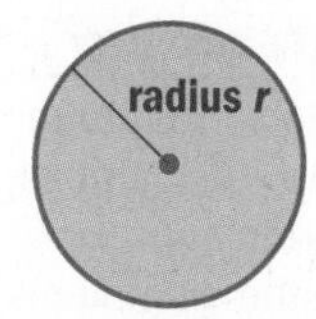

Words The area of a circle is the product of π and the square of the radius.

Algebra $A = \pi r^2$

EXAMPLE 1 Finding the Area of a Circle

Find the area of a circle with a radius of 5 meters.

$A = \pi r^2$	**Write formula for area of a circle.**
$\approx (3.14)(5)^2$	**Substitute 3.14 for π and 5 for r.**
$= 78.5$	**Simplify.**

▸ **Answer** The area of the circle is about 78.5 square meters.

EXAMPLE 2 Finding the Area of a Circle

CIRCUS RING The central performance area at a circus is a circular ring with a diameter of 42 feet. Find the area of the ring.

Diameter of ring is 42 feet.

Animated Math

For an interactive example of finding the area of a circle go to **classzone.com.**

SOLUTION

STEP 1 Find the radius: $r = \frac{d}{2} = \frac{42}{2} = 21$ ft

STEP 2 Find the area.

$A = \pi r^2$ — Write formula for area of a circle.

$\approx \frac{22}{7}(21)^2$ — Substitute $\frac{22}{7}$ for π and 21 for r.

$= 1386$ — Simplify.

▸ **Answer** The area of the ring is about 1386 square feet.

✓ GUIDED PRACTICE for Examples 1 and 2

Find the area of the circle with the given radius r or diameter d. Use $\frac{22}{7}$ or 3.14 for π.

1. $r = 8$ mm
2. $r = 11$ ft
3. $d = 14$ in.
4. **CONSUMER GOODS** The circular top of a yogurt container has a diameter of 7.5 centimeters. Find the area of the circular top.

EXAMPLE 3 ◆ Multiple Choice Practice

Which equation can be used to find the area A in square feet of a circle with a radius of 6 feet?

Ⓐ $A = 6 \times \pi$ Ⓑ $A = 12 \times \pi$ Ⓒ $A = \pi \times 6^2$ Ⓓ $A = \pi \times 12^2$

ELIMINATE CHOICES

Be sure to substitute the *radius,* not the diameter, in the formula $A = \pi r^2$. Because the diameter is 12 ft, you can eliminate choice D.

SOLUTION

$A = \pi r^2$ — Write formula for area of a circle.

$= \pi(6)^2$ — Substitute 6 for r.

$= \pi(36)$ — Simplify.

▸ **Answer** The equation for the area of the circle is $A = \pi(36)$, or $A = \pi \times 6^2$. The correct answer is C. Ⓐ Ⓑ Ⓒ Ⓓ

✓ GUIDED PRACTICE for Example 3

5. **WHAT IF?** In Example 3, suppose the circle has a radius of 7 feet. Write an equation for the area A (in square feet) of the circle.

10.7 EXERCISES

HOMEWORK KEY

◆ = **MULTIPLE CHOICE PRACTICE** Exs. 23, 29, 37–39

○ = **HINTS AND HOMEWORK HELP** for Exs. 7, 13, 29 at classzone.com

SKILLS • PROBLEM SOLVING • REASONING

1. **VOCABULARY** Copy and complete: The distance from the center of a circle to any point on the circle is the _?_. The distance across the circle through the center is the _?_.

2. **WRITING** *Describe* how you would find the area of a circle if you knew its diameter.

SEE EXAMPLES 1 AND 2 on pp. 555–556 for Exs. 3–10

FINDING AREA **Find the area of the circle. Use $\frac{22}{7}$ or 3.14 for π.**

3. $d = 13$ in.

4. $r = 3$ in.

5. $r = 7$ in.

6. $d = 28$ mm

7. $d = 26.5$ mm

8. $r = 1.3$ in.

ERROR ANALYSIS ***Describe*** **and correct the error made in finding the area of a circle with the given diameter.**

9. $d = 4$ in.

$A = \pi r^2$
$\approx (3.14)(4)^2$
$= 50.24 \text{ in.}^2$

10. $d = 10$ cm

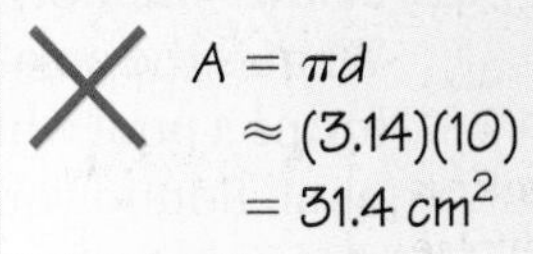

SEE EXAMPLE 3 on p. 556 for Exs. 11–16

FINDING AREA **Find the area of the circle with the given radius *r* or diameter *d*. Write your answer in terms of π.**

11. $r = 4$ in.
12. $r = 7.3$ mm
13. $d = 24.8$ cm
14. $d = 96$ ft
15. $r = 9.1$ yd
16. $d = 35$ m

USING CIRCUMFERENCE **Find the area of the circle with the given circumference. Use 3.14 for π.**

17. $C = 15.7$ mm
18. $C = 18.84$ m
19. $C = 62.8$ ft
20. $C = 9.42$ in.
21. $C = 37.68$ cm
22. $C = 21.98$ yd

23. ◆ **MULTIPLE CHOICE** The circumference of a circle is 25 centimeters. Which estimate is closest to the area of the circle?

Ⓐ 8 cm^2　Ⓑ 16 cm^2　Ⓒ 50 cm^2　Ⓓ 156 cm^2

CONNECT SKILLS TO PROBLEM SOLVING Exercises 24–27 will help you prepare for problem solving.

24. A circular world map at the U.S. Navy Memorial in Washington, D.C., has a radius of 50 feet. What is the area of the world map?

25. A circular patio thermometer has a diameter of 460 millimeters. What is the area of the thermometer?

26. A circular dessert tray has a radius of 15 centimeters. What equation can be used to find the area of the tray?

27. A circular table top has a diameter of 48 inches. What equation can be used to find the area of the table top?

SEE EXAMPLES 1 AND 2 on pp. 555–556 for Exs. 28–29

28. **CALENDARS** The top of an Aztec calendar stone is a circle with a diameter of 12 feet. What is the area of the top of the stone? Use 3.14 for π.

California @HomeTutor for problem solving help at classzone.com

Diameter of stone is 12 feet.

29. ◆ **MULTIPLE CHOICE** A penny has a diameter of 19.05 millimeters. What is the approximate area of one side of the penny?

Ⓐ 19.05π mm^2　Ⓑ 38.1π mm^2

Ⓒ 90.7π mm^2　Ⓓ 362.9π mm^2

California @HomeTutor for problem solving help at classzone.com

30. **WRITING** *Explain* how to find the area of a circle if you know its circumference.

31. **SHORT RESPONSE** A circular fountain has a diameter of 8.5 meters. What is the area of the fountain? The outermost meter of the fountain forms a pool where water collects and recirculates. What is the area of the pool? Round your answers to the nearest tenth. *Explain* how you found your answers.

32. **REASONING** Construct a circle on graph paper. Estimate the area of the circle by counting squares, as was done on page 555. Then find the area using the formula $A = \pi r^2$. *Compare* your results.

CHALLENGE Find the area of the shaded region. Use 3.14 for π.

33. 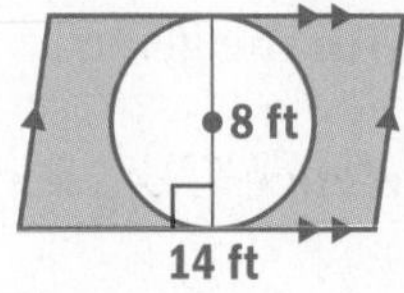

34. 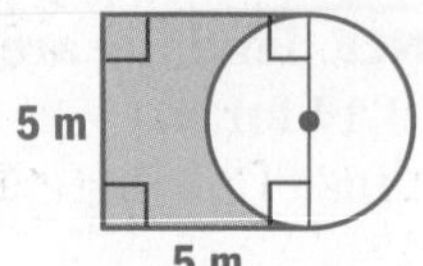

35. 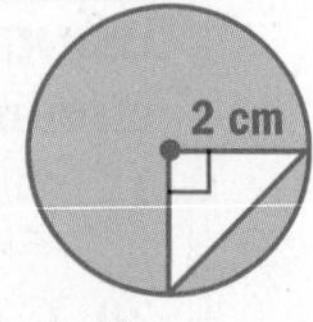

36. **CHALLENGE** All of the circles on the target have the same center. The distance between circles is 2 inches. The area of the red circle is π square inches.

a. What is the area of the blue portion? the green portion?

b. What percent of the target is green or blue? Round to the nearest percent.

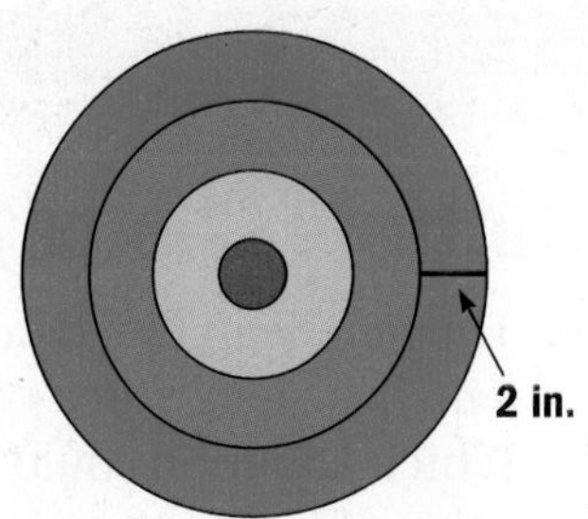

◆ CALIFORNIA STANDARDS SPIRAL REVIEW

AF 1.4 37. What is the value of $40 \div (7 - 3) + 4^2$? *(p. 160)*

Ⓐ 2　Ⓑ 5　Ⓒ 14　Ⓓ 26

SDAP 1.1 38. What is the mean of the numbers below? *(p. 364)*

11, 17, 14, 12, 17

Ⓐ 14　Ⓑ 14.2　Ⓒ 16.8　Ⓓ 17

MG 2.1 39. Which two angles are vertical angles? *(p. 468)*

Ⓐ $\angle 1$ and $\angle 5$　Ⓑ $\angle 2$ and $\angle 8$

Ⓒ $\angle 3$ and $\angle 4$　Ⓓ $\angle 6$ and $\angle 7$

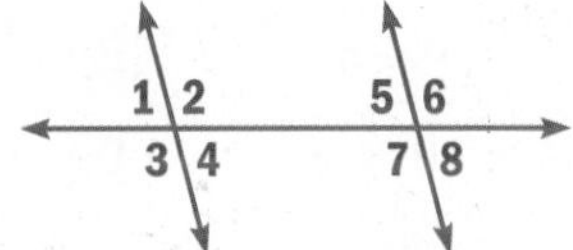

QUIZ *for Lessons 10.4–10.7*

Find the area of the triangle, trapezoid, or circle. Use 3.14 for π.

1. *(p. 541)*

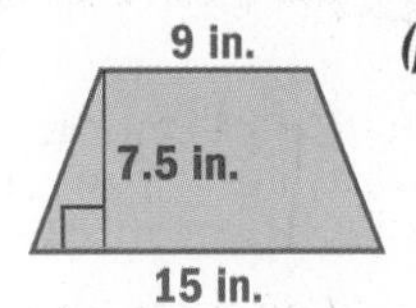

2. *(p. 541)*

3. *(p. 555)*

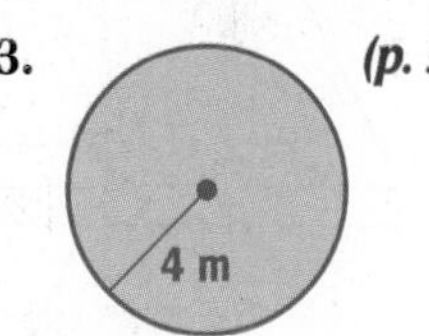

4. **WRISTWATCH** The face of a wristwatch is a parallelogram. The base is 2.75 centimeters, and the height is 2 centimeters. Find the area. *(p. 534)*

Find the unknown height or diameter of the figure. Use 3.14 for π.

5. $A = 11.7 \text{ m}^2$ *(p. 534)*

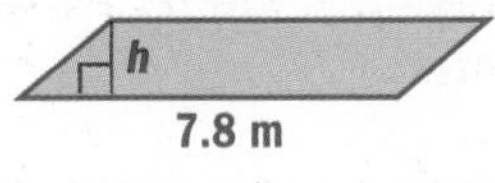

6. $A = 10.72 \text{ mm}^2$ *(p. 541)*

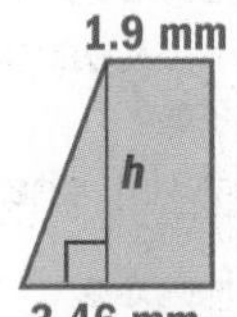

7. $C = 396$ cm *(p. 549)*

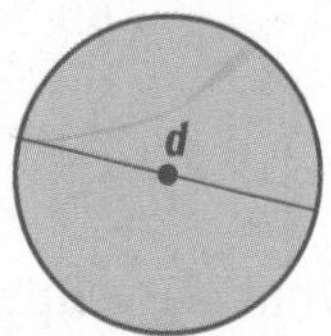

8. A circle has a radius of 8.3 feet. Find the circumference of the circle in terms of π. *(p. 549)*

MIXED REVIEW of Skills and Problem Solving

Multiple Choice Practice for Lessons 10.4–10.7

1. The parallelogram below has a height of 9 inches and an area of A square inches. Which equation could be used to find the value of b? **AF 3.2**

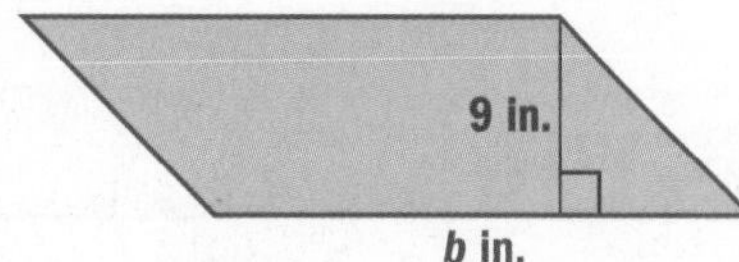

Ⓐ $A = 9b$ Ⓑ $A = \frac{1}{2}(9b)$

Ⓒ $A = 2b + 18$ Ⓓ $A = b + 9$

2. Which equation could be used to find the area A (in square centimeters) of a circle with a diameter of 10 centimeters? **MG 1.1**

Ⓐ $A = 5 \times \pi$ Ⓑ $A = 5^2 \times \pi$

Ⓒ $A = 10 \times \pi$ Ⓓ $A = 10^2 \times \pi$

3. You create the figure below by folding a piece of paper. Which equation does *not* give the area A of the figure? **AF 3.2, MR 3.3**

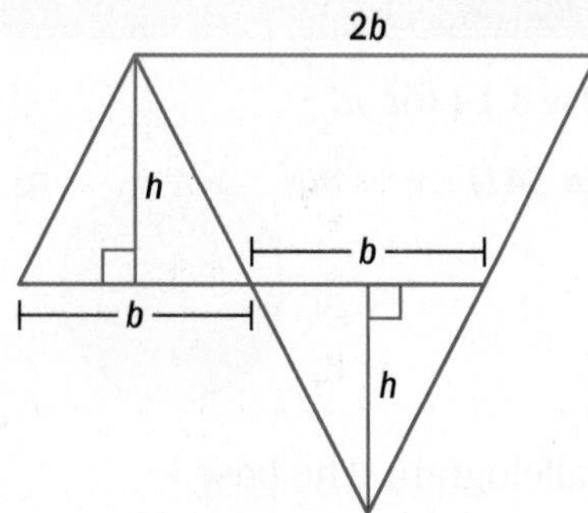

Ⓐ $A = \frac{1}{2}(b + 2b)(h) + 2\left(\frac{1}{2}\right)bh$

Ⓑ $A = 2bh + \frac{1}{2}bh$

Ⓒ $A = \frac{1}{2}bh + \frac{1}{2}(2b)(2h)$

Ⓓ $A = (2b)(2h) + 2\left(\frac{1}{2}\right)bh$

4. What is the approximate circumference of a circle with a radius of 2 meters? **MG 1.2**

Ⓐ 6.3 m Ⓑ 12.6 m

Ⓒ 18.9 m Ⓓ 20 m

5. Which expression represents the area (in square inches) of a triangle with base 8 inches and height $(x - 5)$ inches? **AF 3.1**

Ⓐ $8x - 40$ Ⓑ $4x - 20$

Ⓒ $x + 3$ Ⓓ $4x - 5$

6. A target has three colored regions: a red circle surrounded by two colored rings. What does the expression 12π represent? **MG 1.1**

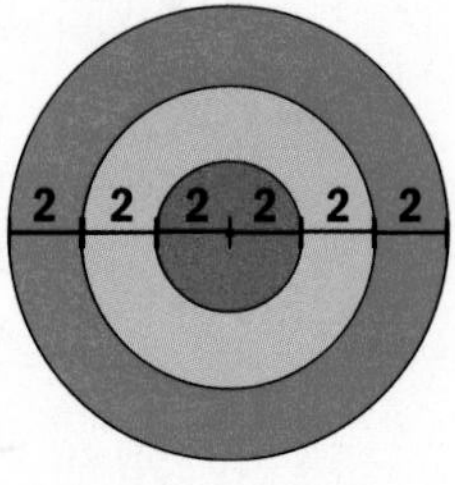

Ⓐ The circumference of the red circle

Ⓑ The circumference of the beige ring

Ⓒ The circumference of the blue ring

Ⓓ The area of the red circle

7. A baseball player may stand in the on-deck circle while waiting for a turn at bat. The circle has a radius of 2.5 feet. What is the approximate area of the circle? **MG 1.2**

Ⓐ 6.3 ft^2 Ⓑ 15.7 ft^2

Ⓒ 19.6 ft^2 Ⓓ 78.5 ft^2

8. Part of a shuffleboard court is shown. What is the area of the figure? **AF 3.1, MR 1.3**

Ⓐ 30.75 ft^2

Ⓑ 31.5 ft^2

Ⓒ 35.25 ft^2

Ⓓ 36.75 ft^2

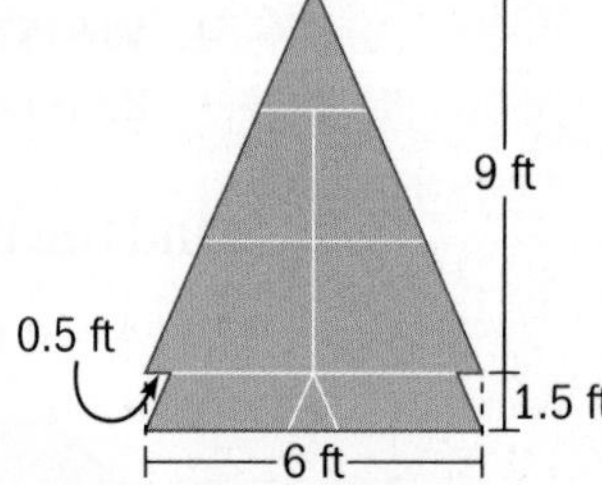

9. Which expression represents the area (in square feet) of a trapezoid with bases $5x$ feet and $3x$ feet and height 10 feet? **AF 3.1**

Ⓐ $8x + 10$ Ⓑ $10x$

Ⓒ $150x^2$ Ⓓ $40x$

10 CHAPTER SUMMARY

Standards
AF 2.1, AF 3.1, AF 3.2, MG 1.1, MG 1.2

BIG IDEAS

For Your Notebook

Big Idea 1

Converting One Unit of Measurement to Another

You can use powers of 10 to convert between metric units. You can use conversion factors to convert between customary units and to convert between systems of measurement.

Metric conversions	Multiply or divide by a power of 10.	$8 \text{ m} = 8 \cdot 100 \text{ cm}$ $= 800 \text{ cm}$
U.S. customary conversions	Multiply by a form of 1, such as $\frac{1 \text{ ft}}{12 \text{ in.}}$.	$4 \text{ yd} \cdot \frac{3 \text{ ft}}{1 \text{ yd}} = 12 \text{ ft}$
Conversions between systems	Multiply by a form of 1, such as $\frac{1 \text{ qt}}{0.946 \text{ L}}$.	$12 \text{ lb} \cdot \frac{0.454 \text{ kg}}{1 \text{ lb}} \approx 5.45 \text{ kg}$

Big Idea 2

Using Variables in Geometric Expressions

Parallelogram	*Triangle*	*Trapezoid*
$x + 3$; 5	y; 6	z; 4; $3z$
$A = bh$ $= 5(x + 3)$ $= 5x + 15$	$A = \frac{1}{2}bh$ $= \frac{1}{2}(6)(y)$ $= 3y$	$A = \frac{1}{2}(b_1 + b_2)h$ $= \frac{1}{2}(z + 3z)(4)$ $= 8z$

Big Idea 3

Using Estimates of π to Calculate Circumference and Area of Circles

Circumference		*Area*
14 cm	6 in.	5 ft
$C = \pi d$ $\approx \left(\frac{22}{7}\right)(14)$ $= 44 \text{ cm}$	$C = 2\pi r$ $\approx 2(3.14)(6)$ $= 37.68 \text{ in.}$	$A = \pi r^2$ $\approx (3.14)(5)^2$ $= 78.5 \text{ ft}^2$

CHAPTER PROBLEM

Standards
AF 2.1, AF 3.1, AF 3.2, MG 1.1, MG 1.2

APPLYING THE BIG IDEAS

Big Idea 1
You convert units of measurement in **Ex. 1.**

Big Idea 2
You use variables in geometric expressions in **Step 2** and in **Ex. 2.**

Big Idea 3
You use estimates of π to calculate the circumference and area of a circle in **Ex. 2.**

PROBLEM The designs on many world flags include basic geometric shapes, such as parallelograms, triangles, trapezoids, and circles. How can you use area formulas to write a percent that relates the area of a part of a flag to the area of the entire flag?

STEP 1 **Choose a flag.**

Research flags from different countries. Find a picture of a flag that includes any combination of parallelograms, triangles, trapezoids, and circles. For example, the national flag of the Philippines below includes one triangle, two trapezoids, and one circle.

Philippine flag includes one triangle, two trapezoids, and one circle.

STEP 2 **Find areas.**

Use a ruler to measure the length and width of the flag and the dimensions (in inches) of the geometric shapes. Then find the areas (in square inches) of the flag and of the shapes.

STEP 3 **Calculate percents.**

Find the percent of the total area that is made up of each geometric shape.

Extending the Problem

Use your results from the problem to complete the exercises.

1. Convert the dimensions that you found in Step 2 to centimeters. Then find the area (in square centimeters) of each shape.
2. Design a flag so that it includes one circle and one triangle.
   a. What is the radius (in millimeters) of the circle? What are the base and height (in millimeters) of the triangle?
   b. Find the circumference and area of the circle. *Describe* how doubling the radius affects the circumference and area.
   c. Suppose you increase the height of the triangle by x millimeters. Write an expression that represents the area of the new triangle. *Describe* how increasing the height by 4 millimeters affects the percent of the total area that is made up of the triangle.

10 CHAPTER REVIEW

California @HomeTutor
classzone.com
• Multi-Language Visual Glossary
• Vocabulary practice

REVIEW KEY VOCABULARY

- base of a parallelogram, *p. 534*
- height of a parallelogram, *p. 534*
- base of a triangle, *p. 541*
- height of a triangle, *p. 541*
- base of a trapezoid, *p. 542*
- height of a trapezoid, *p. 542*
- circle, *p. 549*
- center, *p. 549*
- radius, *p. 549*
- diameter, *p. 549*
- circumference, *p. 549*

VOCABULARY EXERCISES

In Exercises 1–6, copy and complete the statement.

1. 1 gram = 1000 _?_

2. 1 gallon ≈ _?_ liters

3. 1 mile = _?_ feet

4. The area of a triangle is one half the product of a _?_ and the corresponding height.

5. The perpendicular distance between the bases of a trapezoid is the _?_ of the trapezoid.

6. The distance across a circle through the center is its _?_.

7. **NOTETAKING SKILLS** Make an *information wheel* like the one on page 514 for *circle*.

REVIEW EXAMPLES AND EXERCISES

10.1 Converting Metric Units *pp. 515–519*

AF. 2.1

EXAMPLE

Copy and complete the statement.

a. 32 g = _?_ mg

To convert from grams to milligrams, multiply by 1000.

$32 \times 1000 = 32{,}000$

32 g = 32,000 mg

b. 1300 mL = _?_ L

To convert from milliliters to liters, divide by 1000.

$1300 \div 1000 = 1.3$

1300 mL = 1.3 L

EXERCISES

SEE EXAMPLES 1 AND 2 on pp. 515–516 for Exs. 8–13

Copy and complete the statement.

8. 7 cm = _?_ m

9. 802 L = _?_ mL

10. 9.4 mg = _?_ kg

11. 18 kg = _?_ g

12. 2000 mL = _?_ L

13. 4.2 m = _?_ mm

10.2 Converting Customary Units

pp. 520–525

AF. 2.1

EXAMPLE

Convert 5720 yards to miles.

Use the fact that 1 mi = 1760 yd.

$$5720 \text{ yd} \times \frac{1 \text{ mi}}{1760 \text{ yd}} = \frac{\overset{13}{\cancel{5720}} \cancel{\text{yd}} \times 1 \text{ mi}}{\underset{4}{\cancel{1760}} \cancel{\text{yd}}}$$ **Use rule for multiplying fractions. Divide out GCF of 440 and unit "yd."**

$$= \frac{13}{4} \text{ mi}$$ **Simplify.**

$$= 3\frac{1}{4} \text{ mi}$$ **Rewrite improper fraction as a mixed number.**

EXERCISES

SEE EXAMPLES 1, 2, 3, AND 4 on pp. 520–522 for Exs. 14–17

Copy and complete the statement.

14. 19 yd = ? in.

15. 8500 lb = ? T

16. 47 c = ? qt ? c

17. REFRESHMENTS Monique needs to make 16 one-cup servings of fruit punch for a party. How many quarts of punch does she need to make?

10.3 Converting Between Systems

pp. 527–531

AF 2.1

EXAMPLE

Convert 75 grams to ounces. Round to the nearest whole number.

$$75 \text{ g} \times \frac{1 \text{ oz}}{28.35 \text{ g}} = \frac{75 \cancel{\text{g}} \times 1 \text{ oz}}{28.35 \cancel{\text{g}}}$$

$$\approx 2.6455 \text{ oz}$$

$$\approx 3 \text{ oz}$$

EXERCISES

SEE EXAMPLES 1 AND 3 on pp. 527–528 for Exs. 18–24

Copy and complete the statement. Round to the nearest whole number.

18. 4 L ≈ ? qt

19. 4 m ≈ ? ft

20. 72 mi ≈ ? km

21. 23 lb ≈ ? kg

22. 12 gal ≈ ? L

23. 24 cm ≈ ? in.

24. TRAVEL Manuel is traveling to China. He wants to exchange $1200 for Chinese yuan. The exchange rate is $1 ≈ 8.0132 yuan. How many yuan will Manuel receive? Round your answer to the nearest whole number.

10.4 Area of a Parallelogram

pp. 534–538

AF 3.1, AF 3.2

EXAMPLE

Find the area of the parallelogram.

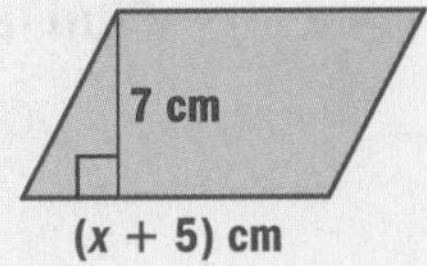

$A = bh$ — **Write formula for area of a parallelogram.**

$= (x + 5)(7)$ — **Substitute (x + 5) for b and 7 for h.**

$= (7x + 35)\text{ cm}^2$ — **Multiply.**

EXERCISES

SEE EXAMPLES 1 AND 4 on pp. 534, 536 for Exs. 25–26

Find the area of the parallelogram for the given base and height.

25. $b = 6$ in., $h = 10.5$ in.

26. $b = 11.2$ m, $h = (3x - 4)$ m

10.5 Areas of Triangles and Trapezoids

pp. 541–546

AF 3.1, AF 3.2

EXAMPLE

Find the area of the triangle or trapezoid.

a.

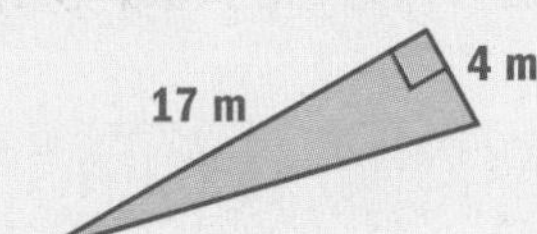

$A = \frac{1}{2}bh$

$= \frac{1}{2}(4)(17)$

$= 34\text{ m}^2$

b.

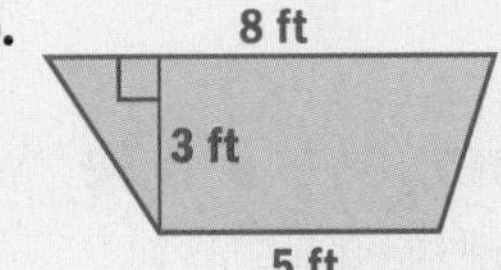

$A = \frac{1}{2}(b_1 + b_2)h$

$= \frac{1}{2}(8 + 5)3$

$= 19.5\text{ ft}^2$

EXERCISES

SEE EXAMPLES 1, 3, AND 5 on pp. 541–543 for Exs. 27–31

Find the area of the triangle or trapezoid.

27.

28.

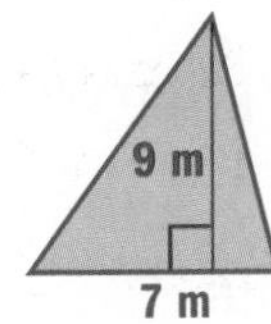

29.

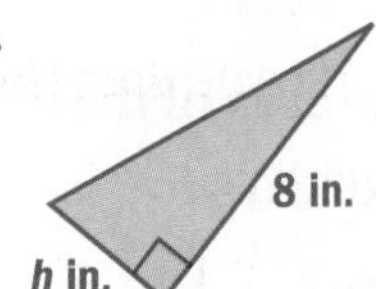

30.

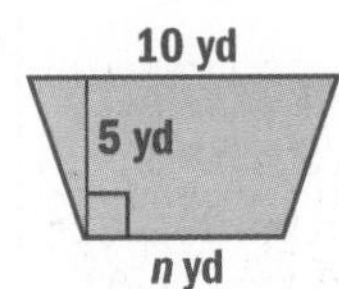

31. WINDOWS A triangular window has a base of 8 feet and a height of 7 feet. What is the area of the window?

10.6 Circumference of a Circle

pp. 549–553

MG 1.1, MG 1.2

EXAMPLE

Find the circumference of the circle. Use 3.14 for π.

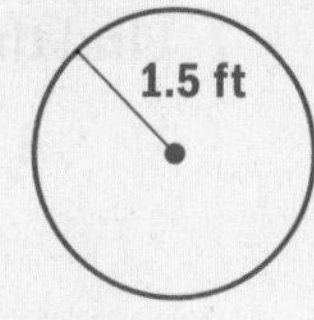

$C = 2\pi r$	**Write formula for circumference of a circle.**
$\approx 2(3.14)(1.5)$	**Substitute 3.14 for π and 1.5 for r.**
$= 9.42$ ft	**Multiply.**

▸ **Answer** The circumference of the circle is about 9.42 feet.

EXERCISES

SEE EXAMPLES 1 AND 2 on pp. 549–550 for Exs. 32–36

Find the circumference of the circle with the given radius r or diameter d. Use $\frac{22}{7}$ or 3.14 for π.

32. $d = 19$ mm **33.** $d = 42$ cm **34.** $r = 28$ in. **35.** $r = 17$ m

36. Find an object that has a face in the shape of a circle. Measure the circumference of the circle. Then find the circumference using the formula $C = 2\pi r$. *Compare* your results.

10.7 Area of a Circle

pp. 555–559

MG 1.1, MG 1.2

EXAMPLE

Find the area of the circle. Use 3.14 for π.

1.5 ft

$A = \pi r^2$	**Write formula for area of a circle.**
$\approx 3.14(1.5)^2$	**Substitute 3.14 for π and 1.5 for r.**
$= 7.065$ ft^2	**Multiply.**

▸ **Answer** The area of the circle is about 7.065 square feet.

EXERCISES

SEE EXAMPLES 1, 2, AND 3 on pp. 555–556 for Exs. 37–41

Find the area of the circle with the given radius r or diameter d. Use $\frac{22}{7}$ or 3.14 for π.

37. $r = 7$ km **38.** $r = 13$ mm **39.** $d = 34$ in. **40.** $d = 14$ mi

41. GARDENING Shonda is putting a circular tulip bed in her backyard. The radius is 3.2 feet. What is the area of the tulip bed? Write your answer in terms of π.

10 CHAPTER TEST

VOCABULARY Copy and complete the statement.

1. The distance from the center of a circle to any point on the circle is the _?_.

2. The area of a trapezoid is half the product of the sum of the _?_ and the _?_.

Copy and complete the statement.

3. 8.7 cm = _?_ mm
4. 28 kL = _?_ L
5. 20 T = _?_ lb
6. 34 oz = _?_ lb _?_ oz
7. 75.7 L ≈ _?_ gal
8. 5 ft = _?_ m

Suppose that the exchange rate between U.S. dollars and euros is $1 ≈ 0.81 euro. Find the amount in dollars or euros. Round to the nearest whole number.

9. 450 euros
10. $630
11. 1000 euros

Find the area of the parallelogram, triangle, or trapezoid.

12. 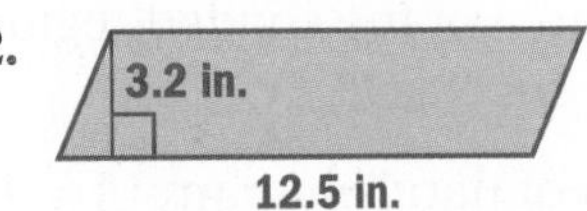

13. 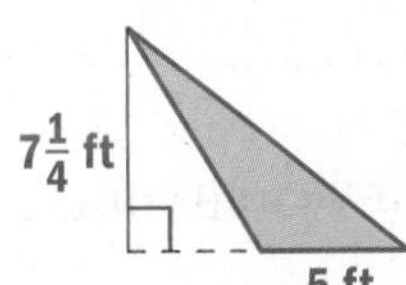

14. 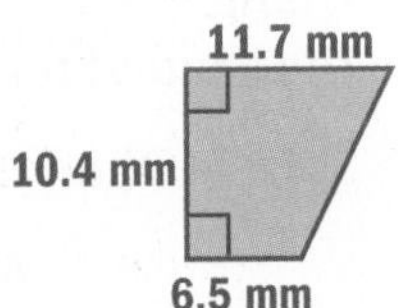

Write an expression for the area of the figure described.

15. Parallelogram
$b = 5$ ft
$h = (x - 8)$ ft

16. Triangle
$b = (x + 4)$ in.
$h = 12$ in.

17. Trapezoid
$b_1 = x$ cm
$b_2 = 7x$ cm
$h = 8$ cm

Find the circumference and the area of the circle with the given radius r or diameter d. Use $\frac{22}{7}$ or 3.14 for π.

18. $r = 20$ ft
19. $r = 0.4$ mm
20. $d = 28$ in.

21. Construct a circle with a radius of 7 units on graph paper. Estimate the area of the circle by counting squares. Then find the area using the formula $A = \pi r^2$. *Compare* your results.

22. **CLOTHING** A sweater costs 50 Canadian dollars. Suppose that the exchange rate is 1 U.S. dollar ≈ 1.12 Canadian dollars. How much does the sweater cost in U.S. dollars? Round to the nearest dollar.

23. **PARTIES** Marcus offers to bring juice for 30 people at a party. How many 2 liter bottles of juice does he need to bring so that all 30 people can each have two 300 milliliter glasses? *Explain* your answer.

10 ◆ MULTIPLE CHOICE STRATEGIES

STRATEGIES YOU'LL USE:
- **SOLVE DIRECTLY**
- **ELIMINATE CHOICES**

Standards
AF 3.1, MG 1.2

If you have difficulty solving a multiple choice problem directly, you may be able to use another approach to eliminate incorrect answer choices.

PROBLEM 1

A triangle with a base of 8 and a height of x is inside a parallelogram with a base of 12 and a height of 10, as shown at the right. Which expression represents the area of the shaded region in terms of x?

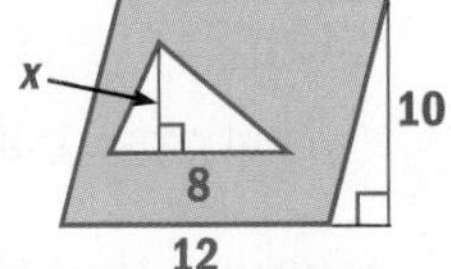

Ⓐ $120 - 8x$ Ⓑ $120 - 4x$ Ⓒ $8x - 120$ Ⓓ $4x - 120$

Strategy 1 SOLVE DIRECTLY

First, find the areas of the parallelogram and triangle. Then subtract to find the area of the shaded region.

STEP 1 **Find** the area of the parallelogram.

$A = bh$

$= 12(10)$

$= 120$

STEP 2 **Find** the area of the triangle.

$A = \frac{1}{2}bh$

$= \frac{1}{2}(8)(x)$

$= 4x$

STEP 3 **Subtract** the area of the triangle from the area of the parallelogram.

$120 - 4x$

An expression for the area of the shaded region is $120 - 4x$.

The correct answer is B. Ⓐ Ⓑ Ⓒ Ⓓ

Strategy 2 ELIMINATE CHOICES

Compare the value of each answer choice to the area of the shaded region for one value of x, such as 2.

Area of parallelogram: $A = bh$

$= (12)(10)$

$= 120$

Area of triangle: $A = \frac{1}{2}bh$

$= \frac{1}{2}(8)(x)$

$= \frac{1}{2}(8)(2)$, or 8

Area of shaded region: $120 - 8 = 112$

Choice A: $120 - 8x = 120 - 8(2)$

$= 104$ ✗

Choice B: $120 - 4x = 120 - 4(2)$

$= 112$ ✓

Choice C: $8x - 120 = 8(2) - 120$

$= -104$ ✗

Choice D: $4x - 120 = 4(2) - 120$

$= -112$ ✗

The correct answer is B. Ⓐ Ⓑ Ⓒ Ⓓ

PROBLEM 2

A can of fruit is shaped like a cylinder, as shown. The can has a circular top with a diameter of 8.5 centimeters.

Which measure is *closest* to the length of the label that goes around the outside of the can?

Ⓐ 13.4 cm   Ⓑ 17.0 cm

Ⓒ 26.7 cm   Ⓓ 38.5 cm

Strategy 1 SOLVE DIRECTLY

First, identify the geometric formula you would use to solve the problem. Then use the formula to calculate the result.

STEP 1 **Choose** the formula. The length of the label is the circumference of the circular top. Use the formula $C = \pi d$.

STEP 2 **Find** the circumference.

$$C = \pi d$$
$$= \pi \cdot 8.5$$
$$\approx 3.14 \cdot 8.5$$
$$= 26.69$$

The circumference is about 26.7 centimeters.

The correct answer is C. Ⓐ Ⓑ Ⓒ Ⓓ

Strategy 2 ELIMINATE CHOICES

Use estimation to evaluate the reasonableness of the solution in the context of the situation.

The length of the label is the circumference of the circular top, so use the formula $C = \pi d$.

Choices A and B: 13.4 cm and 17.0 cm
Find a low estimate of the circumference.

$$C = \pi d \approx 3 \cdot 8 = 24$$

The circumference is greater than 24 cm. You can eliminate choices A and B.

Choice D: 38.5 cm
Find a high estimate of the circumference.

$$C = \pi d \approx 4 \cdot 9 = 36$$

The circumference is less than 36 cm. You can eliminate choice D.

The correct answer is C. Ⓐ Ⓑ Ⓒ Ⓓ

STRATEGY PRACTICE

Explain why you can eliminate the highlighted answer choice.

1. Two square tiles, identical to the one shown at the right, are placed side by side. What is the perimeter of the resulting rectangle?

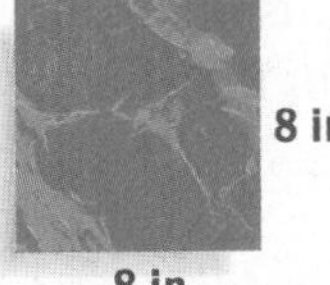

Ⓐ 4 ft   Ⓑ $4\frac{2}{3}$ ft   Ⓒ ✗ **$5\frac{1}{3}$ ft**   Ⓓ 6 ft

2. A piece of fabric 1.5 yards long is cut into sections that are each 5 inches long. How much fabric is left over?

Ⓐ ✗ **0 in.**   Ⓑ 0.8 in.   Ⓒ 4 in.   Ⓓ 10 in.

10 ◆ MULTIPLE CHOICE PRACTICE

1. What is the combined area of the two right triangles? **AF 3.1**

Ⓐ 13.44 m^2

Ⓑ 11.52 m^2

Ⓒ 7.68 m^2

Ⓓ 1.92 m^2

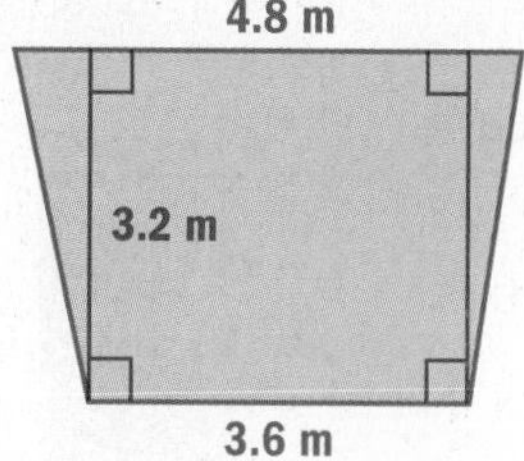

2. Which expression represents the area (in square inches) of the trapezoid below? **AF 3.1**

Ⓐ $15x$

Ⓑ $20x$

Ⓒ $30x$

Ⓓ $40x$

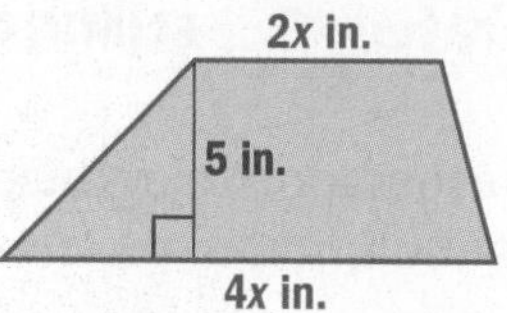

3. Which expression could be used to find the circumference (in centimeters) of the circle below? **MG 1.1**

Ⓐ $2 \times 18 \times \pi$

Ⓑ $2 \times 36 \times \pi$

Ⓒ $18 \times 18 \times \pi$

Ⓓ $36 \times 36 \times \pi$

36 cm

4. Which expression represents the area (in square feet) of the triangle below? **AF 3.1**

Ⓐ $8x + 40$

Ⓑ $8x + 5$

Ⓒ $4x + 5$

Ⓓ $4x + 20$

8 ft

$(x + 5)$ ft

5. The radius of the larger circle is a diameter of the smaller circle. The larger circle has a radius of 4 feet. What is the approximate area of the shaded region? **MG 1.2**

Ⓐ 6.28 ft^2

Ⓑ 9.42 ft^2

Ⓒ 37.7 ft^2

Ⓓ 62.8 ft^2

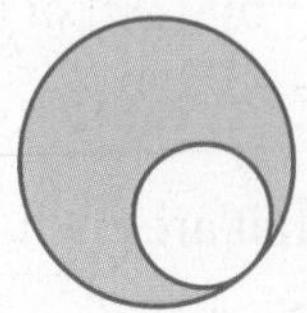

6. You have a punch recipe that calls for 1.5 liters of pineapple juice. A store sells only small bottles labeled as shown at the right. How many bottles do you need to buy? **AF 2.1, MR 3.2**

100% Pineapple Juice

473 mL

Ⓐ 1

Ⓑ 2

Ⓒ 3

Ⓓ 4

7. The circular base of a candle has a diameter of 6 centimeters. Which measure is *closest* to the circumference of the base? **MG 1.2**

Ⓐ 9.4 cm

Ⓑ 18.8 cm

Ⓒ 28.3 cm

Ⓓ 113.0 cm

8. The table below shows the heights and weights of two kinds of dinosaurs. Which statement is true? **AF 2.1**

Dinosaur	*Height*	*Weight*
Ankylosaurus	66 inches	3.5 tons
Stegosaurus	11 feet	4000 pounds

Ⓐ The Ankylosaurus was taller and weighed more than the Stegosaurus.

Ⓑ The Stegosaurus was taller but the Ankylosaurus weighed more.

Ⓒ The Stegosaurus was taller and weighed more than the Ankylosaurus.

Ⓓ The Ankylosaurus was taller but the Stegosaurus weighed more.

9. How many miles are in 29,040 feet? **AF 2.1**

Ⓐ 1 mi

Ⓑ 5 mi

Ⓒ 5.5 mi

Ⓓ 9680 mi

10. Circle A has radius 10 ft. Circle B has radius 5 ft. What is the ratio of the area of circle A to the area of circle B? **MG 1.2, MR 2.6**

Ⓐ 1 : 4

Ⓑ 1 : 2

Ⓒ 2 : 1

Ⓓ 4 : 1

11. Use the exchange rate between U.S. dollars and euros shown in the graph. A jacket in Paris costs 48 euros. How much does the jacket cost in Los Angeles? **AF 2.1, MR 2.3**

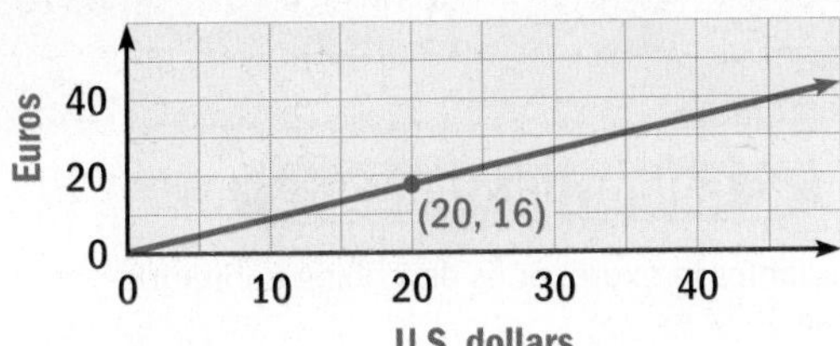

Ⓐ \$38.40

Ⓑ \$48.00

Ⓒ \$60.00

Ⓓ \$96.00

12. Peanuts cost \$3.45 per kilogram. Andre places a bag of peanuts on the scale below. What is the approximate cost of the bag of peanuts? **AF 2.1, MR 1.3**

Ⓐ \$4.00

Ⓑ \$4.50

Ⓒ \$5.00

Ⓓ \$5.50

3.20 lb

13. A parallelogram is inside a triangle, as shown below. Which expression represents the area of the shaded region in terms of x? **AF 3.1**

Ⓐ $66 - 10x$

Ⓑ $132 - 5x$

Ⓒ $132 - 10x$

Ⓓ $66 - 5x$

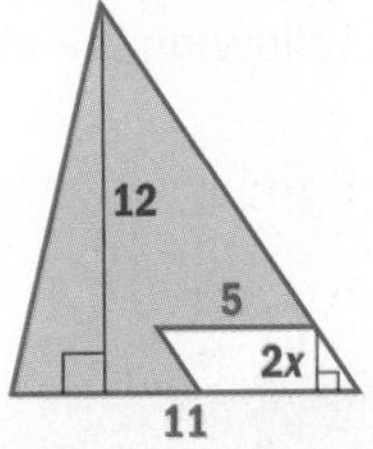

14. Which expression gives the area (in square inches) of the parallelogram below? **AF 3.1**

Ⓐ $2x + 3$

Ⓑ $14x - 4$

Ⓒ $7x - 14$

Ⓓ $14x - 28$

(2x − 4) in.
7 in.

15. Which equation could be used to find the area A (in square centimeters) of the circular front bicycle wheel below? **MG 1.1**

Ⓐ $A = 31 \times \pi$

Ⓑ $A = 62 \times \pi$

Ⓒ $A = 31^2 \times \pi$

Ⓓ $A = 62^2 \times \pi$

16. Approximately how many inches are in 35 centimeters? **AF 2.1**

Ⓐ 3 in.

Ⓑ 14 in.

Ⓒ 38 in.

Ⓓ 89 in.

17. A parallelogram has an area of A square meters and a base of 18 meters. Which equation could be used to find the height h (in meters) of the parallelogram? **AF 3.2**

Ⓐ $A = 9h$

Ⓑ $A = 18h$

Ⓒ $A = 18 + h$

Ⓓ $A = 36 + 2h$

11 Surface Area and Volume

Before

In previous courses and chapters, you learned the following skills, which you'll use in Chapter 11:

- Finding the areas of rectangles and triangles
- Using the order of operations
- Finding the circumference and area of circles

Why?

In Chapter 11 you'll study these **Big Ideas:**

1. Classifying and sketching views of solids
2. Finding surface areas of prisms and cylinders
3. Finding volumes of prisms and cylinders

Why?

So you can solve real-world problems about . . .

- Architecture, p. 579
- Photo cubes, p. 585
- Doghouses p. 585
- Painting, p. 592
- Watermelons, p. 599
- Biosphere, p. 604

Get-Ready Games

TWO OF A KIND

California Standards

Review using variables in expressions describing geometric quantities. ***Gr. 6 AF 3.1***

Prepare for using formulas for volume. ***Gr. 6 MG 1.3***

Materials

- One deck of *Two of a Kind* cards

How to Play Play in groups of three or four. Shuffle the deck of cards and deal eight cards to each player. Players should not show each other their cards.

Place the remaining deck face down where all players can reach it. This is the *draw* pile. Turn the top card over and place it face up beside the deck. This is the *discard* pile. Players should take turns following the steps on the next page.

CALIFORNIA STANDARDS

- **Gr. 6 AF 3.1 Use variables in expressions describing geometric quantities (e.g.,** $P = 2w + 2l$, $A = \frac{1}{2}bh$, $C = \pi d$ **– the formulas for** the perimeter of a rectangle, the area of a triangle, and **the circumference of a circle, respectively).** ***(Lesson 11.3)***
- **Gr. 6 MG 1.3 Know and use the formulas for the volume of triangular prisms and cylinders (area of base × height); compare these formulas and explain the similarity between them and the formula for the volume of a rectangular solid.** ***(Lessons 11.4, 11.5)***

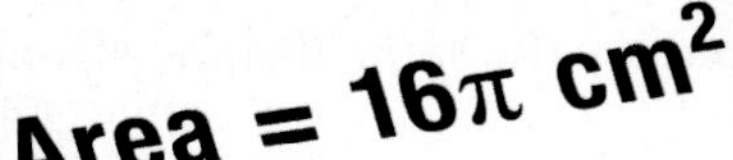

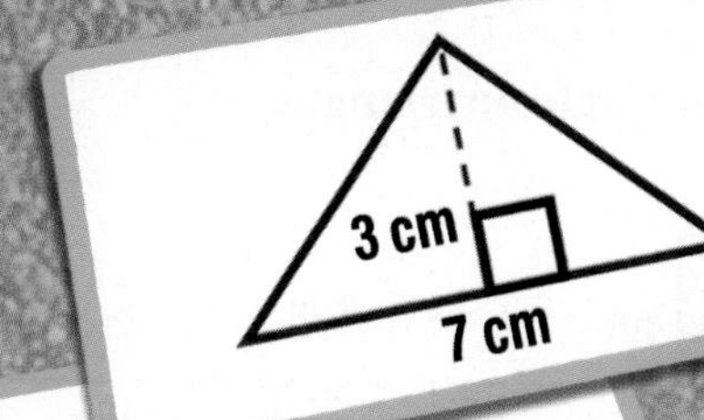

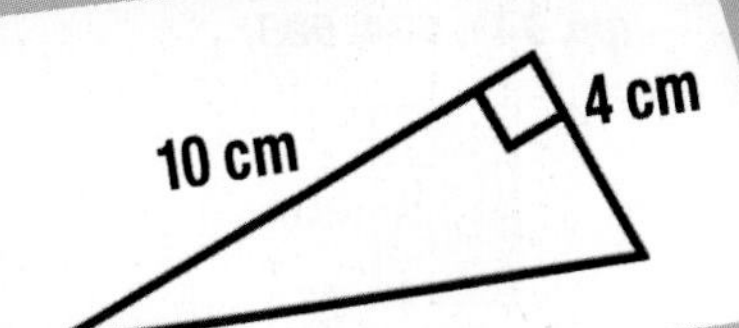

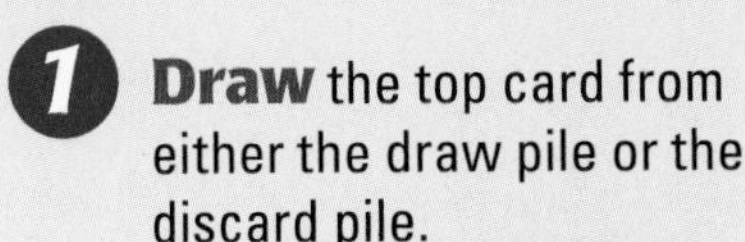

Area = 20 cm²

1 Draw the top card from either the draw pile or the discard pile.

2 Decide whether you have a pair of cards that show a figure and that figure's area. If you do, then place those cards face up in front of you.

3 Remove one card from those remaining in your hand and place it face up on top of the discard pile.

Games Wrap-Up

How To Win Be the first player to put down 3 pairs of matching cards.

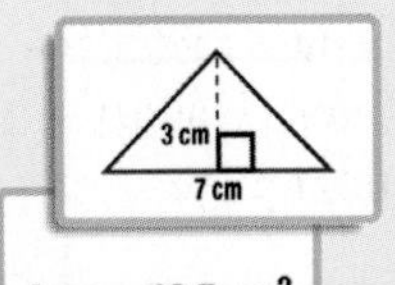

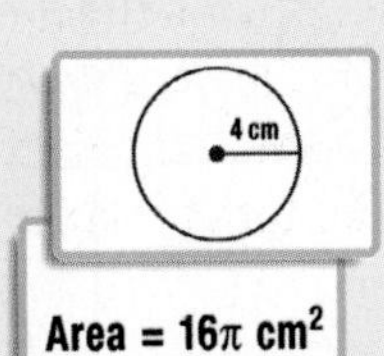

4 cm

Area = 16π cm²

Draw Conclusions

Complete these exercises after playing the game.

1. **WRITING** A student matches a card showing a triangle with a base of 6 cm and a height of 5 cm with a card showing an area of 30 cm^2. *Describe* and correct the student's error.
2. **REASONING** Consider the area cards that you found for the circles in the game. How can you tell whether the area is an exact number or an approximation?

Prerequisite Skills

California @HomeTutor
Prerequisite skills practice at classzone.com

REVIEW VOCABULARY

- **circle,** *p. 549*
- **radius,** *p. 549*
- **diameter,** *p. 549*
- **circumference,** *p. 549*
- **rectangle,** *p. 684*
- **triangle,** *p. 684*
- **perimeter,** *p. 684*
- **area,** *p. 685*

VOCABULARY CHECK

Copy and complete using a review term from the list at the left.

1. The set of points in a plane that are the same distance from a fixed point is a(n) __?__.
2. The distance around a circle is called its __?__.
3. The sum of the lengths of the sides of a rectangle is the __?__.

SKILL CHECK

Find the perimeter and the area of the rectangle or triangle. ***(pp. 541, 684, 685)***

4. 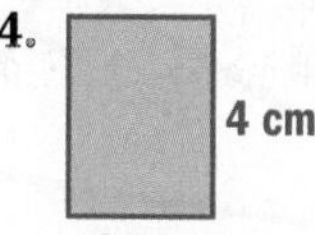

5. 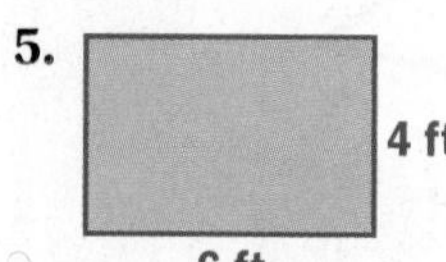

6. 8 in., 15 in., 17 in.

Find the circumference and the area of the circle with the given radius r or diameter d. Use 3.14 or $\frac{22}{7}$ for π. ***(pp. 549, 555)***

7. $r = 5$ m
8. $r = 11$ cm
9. $d = 28$ ft

Notetaking Skills

NOW YOU TRY
Make a *four square diagram* for *triangle.*

Focus on Graphic Organizers

Use a *four square diagram* to organize information about a vocabulary word, such as *polygon.*

Definition: A closed plane figure made up of 3 or more line segments, called sides, that intersect only at their endpoints.	*Vocabulary:* A polygon can have many sides. *Poly* means more than one.
POLYGON	
Examples:	*Non-Examples:* 

11.1 Visualizing Solids

Standards Preparation Grade 5 MG 2.3 **Visualize and draw two-dimensional views of three-dimensional objects made from rectangular solids.**

Connect ***Before*** you classified two-dimensional figures. ***Now*** you will classify and sketch views of solids to prepare for Grade 6 Standard MG 1.3.

Math and **SPORTS**
Ex. 1, p. 576

KEY VOCABULARY

- **solid**
- **face, edge, vertex**
- **prism**
- **pyramid**
- **cylinder**
- **cone**
- **sphere**
- **cube**

A **solid** is a three-dimensional figure that encloses a part of space. When polygons form the sides of a solid, the sides are called **faces**. The segments where the faces meet are **edges**. A point where the edges meet is a **vertex**.

Classifying Solids	
bases	A **prism** is a solid with two congruent parallel bases that are polygons. The remaining edges join corresponding vertices of the bases so that the remaining faces are rectangles.
base	A **pyramid** is a solid with a polygonal base lying in one plane and an additional vertex not lying in that plane. The remaining edges join the additional vertex to the vertices of the base so that the remaining faces are triangles.
bases	A **cylinder** is a solid with two congruent parallel circular bases. The remaining surface of the cylinder consists of all parallel circles of the same radius as the bases whose centers lie on the segment joining the centers of the bases.
base	A **cone** is a solid with a circular base lying in one plane and a vertex not lying in that plane. The remaining surface of the cone consists of all line segments joining the vertex to the circle that forms the base.
center	A **sphere** is a solid formed by all points in space that are the same distance from a fixed point called the center.

EXAMPLE 1 Classifying Solids

Classify the solid as a *prism, pyramid, cylinder, cone,* or *sphere*.

a.  pyramid

b.  cylinder

VIEWS OF SOLIDS One way to represent a three-dimensional figure using a two-dimensional drawing is to sketch three different views of the figure: a *top* view, a *side* view, and a *front* view.

EXAMPLE 2 Sketching Three Views of a Solid

Sketch the top, side, and front views of the square pyramid.

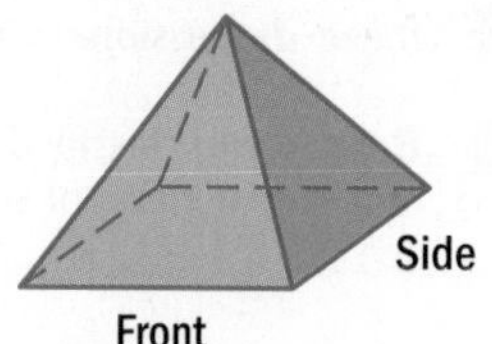

VOCABULARY
You can name a prism or pyramid by using the shape of its base. In Example 2, the base is a square, so the solid is called a *square pyramid*.

SOLUTION

The top view is a square.

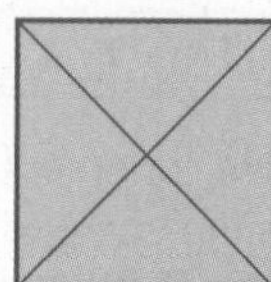

The side view is a triangle.

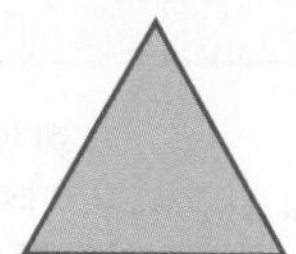

The front view is also a triangle.

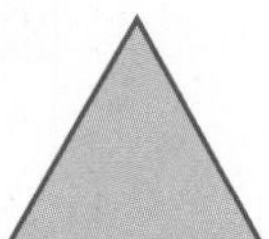

✓ GUIDED PRACTICE for Examples 1 and 2

1. **SPORTS** Classify the softball in the photograph at the top of page 575.

Classify the solid. Be as specific as possible. Then sketch the top, side, and front views.

2.

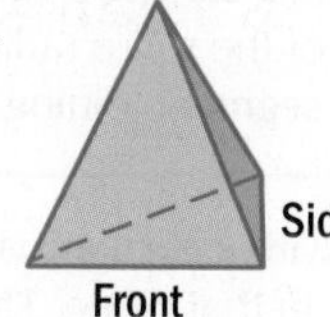

3.

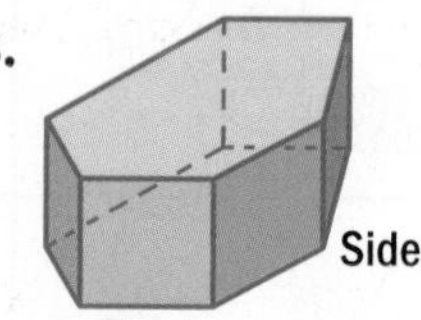

4.

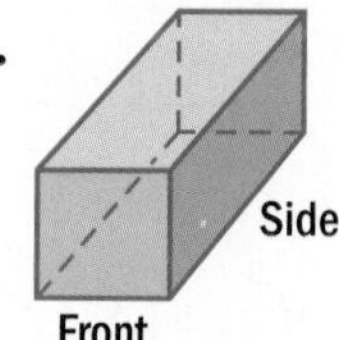

RECTANGULAR SOLIDS The solid shown below can be built using unit cubes. A **cube** is a rectangular prism with 6 congruent square faces. There are 9 unit cubes on the bottom layer and 3 unit cubes on the top layer.

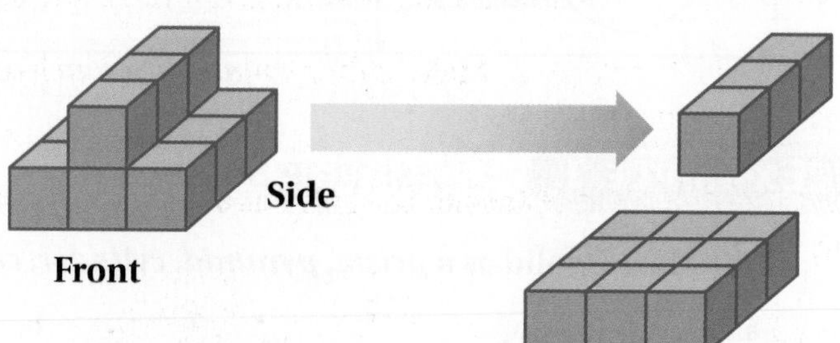

Modeling with unit cubes can help you visualize and identify the top, side, and front views of a solid.

EXAMPLE 3 Drawing Top, Side, and Front Views

VIEWING SOLIDS
For the solids in this textbook, assume there are no hidden cubes except those supporting the cubes you can see.

Draw the top, side, and front views of the solid at the bottom of page 576.

SOLUTION

STEP 1 To draw the top view, imagine what you would see if you were looking at the solid from directly above.

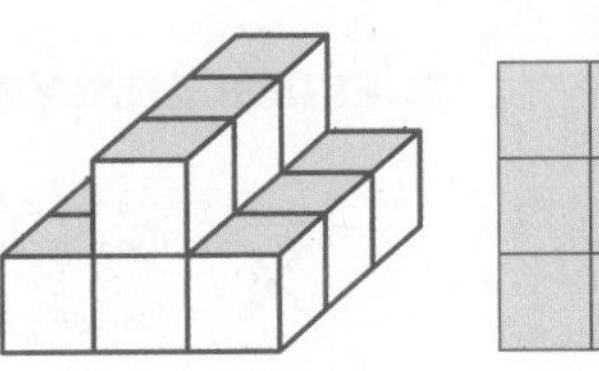

Top

STEP 2 To draw the side view, imagine what you would see if you were looking directly at one of the sides.

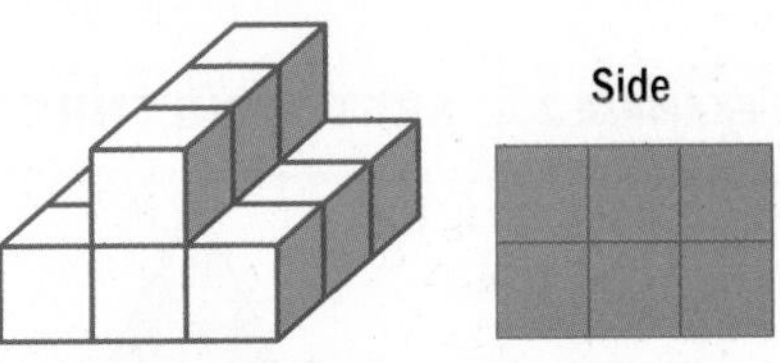

Side

STEP 3 To draw the front view, imagine what you would see if you were looking directly at the front.

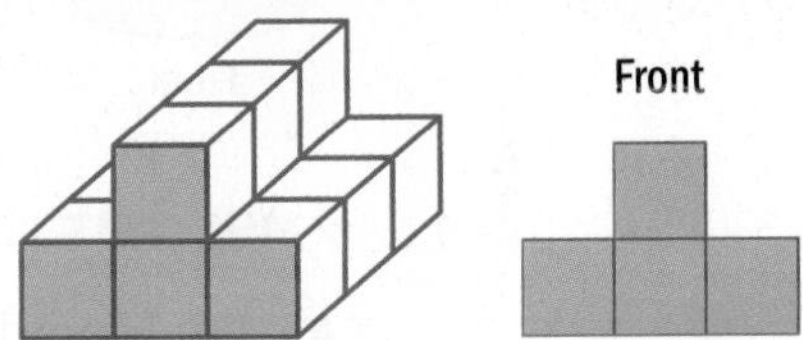

Front

GUIDED PRACTICE for Example 3

5. **WHAT IF?** In Example 3, suppose that a third layer is added by placing a unit cube on each of the 3 unit cubes in the top layer. Draw the top, side, and front views of the solid. Which view(s) did not change?

11.1 EXERCISES

HOMEWORK KEY
◆ = **MULTIPLE CHOICE PRACTICE** Exs. 6, 11, 24, 27–29
○ = **HINTS AND HOMEWORK HELP** for Exs. 3, 9, 23 at classzone.com

SKILLS • PROBLEM SOLVING • REASONING

1. **VOCABULARY** Name a solid that does not have any faces or edges.

2. **NOTETAKING SKILLS** Make a *four square diagram* like the one on page 574 for *solid*.

SEE EXAMPLE 1 on p. 575 for Exs. 3–5

CLASSIFYING SOLIDS Classify the solid as a *prism, pyramid, cylinder, cone,* or *sphere.*

3.

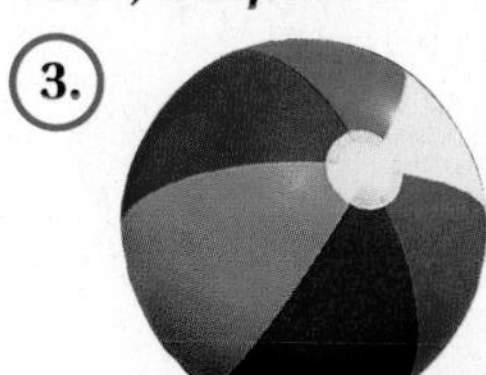

4.

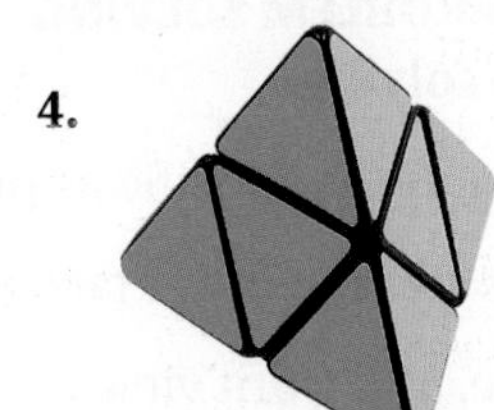

5.

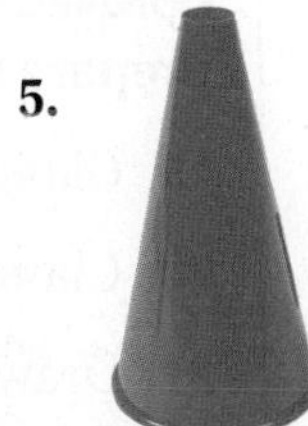

SEE EXAMPLE 1
on p. 575
for Exs. 6–7

6. ◆ **MULTIPLE CHOICE** What is the name of the solid shown?

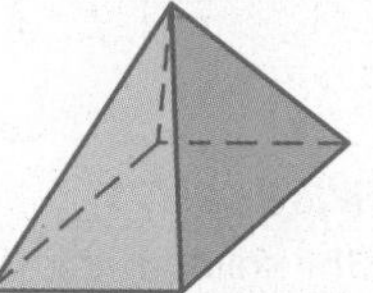

(A) Rectangular prism (B) Rectangular pyramid
(C) Triangular prism (D) Triangular pyramid

7. **ERROR ANALYSIS** *Describe* and correct the error in classifying the solid.

The solid has rectangular faces, so it is a rectangular prism.

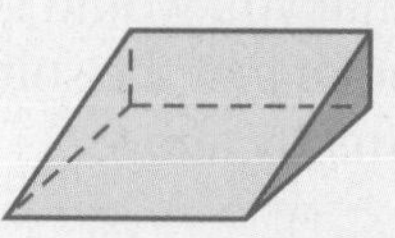

SEE EXAMPLE 2
on p. 576
for Exs. 8–11

SKETCHING THREE VIEWS Sketch the top, side, and front views of the solid.

8.

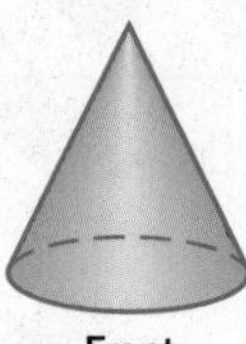

9.

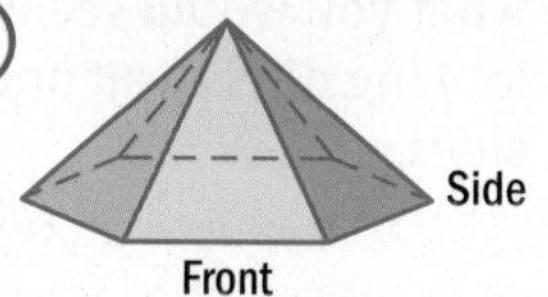

10.

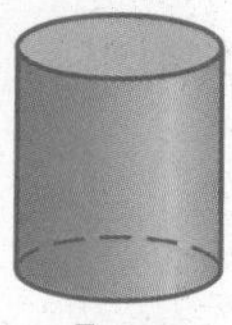

11. ◆ **MULTIPLE CHOICE** Which solid has the three views shown?

(A) Rectangular prism
(B) Rectangular pyramid
(C) Triangular prism
(D) Triangular pyramid

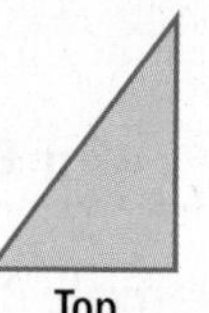

Side

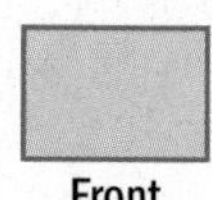

SEE EXAMPLE 3
on p. 577
for Exs. 12–14

DRAWING Draw the top, side, and front views of the solid. Assume that there are no hidden cubes except those supporting the cubes you can see.

12.

13.

14.

REASONING In Exercises 15–18, tell whether the statement is *true* or *false*. If it is false, change one word in the statement to make it true.

15. A prism has one base that is a polygon.
16. A cube has twelve square faces.
17. A cylinder has two congruent circular bases.
18. Any pair of opposite faces of a rectangular prism can be the bases.

CONNECT SKILLS TO PROBLEM SOLVING Exercises 19–21 will help you prepare for problem solving.

19. Classify the object. Be as specific as possible.
20. Classify the bases and the other faces.
21. Draw the top, side, and front views.

SEE EXAMPLES 1 AND 2 on pp. 575–576 for Ex. 22

22. **ARCHITECTURE** Classify the solid represented by the house shown. Be as specific as possible. Then sketch the top, side, and front views.

California @HomeTutor for problem solving help at classzone.com

23. **WRITING** *Compare* and contrast a cylinder and a cone. Then *compare* and contrast a pyramid and a prism.

California @HomeTutor for problem solving help at classzone.com

24. ◆ **MULTIPLE CHOICE** The solid at the right is made up of unit cubes. There are no hidden cubes. What are the dimensions (in units) of the top view of the solid?

Ⓐ 1×3 Ⓑ 4×1 Ⓒ 4×2 Ⓓ 4×3

25. **CHALLENGE** The ice cube tray shown below makes ice cubes whose faces are slanted outward on four sides for easier removal from the tray. Are the ice cubes prisms? *Explain* your reasoning.

Side view

Front view

26. **CHALLENGE** Two different solids may have the same top, side, and front views. Use the three views of a solid shown to draw two different solids.

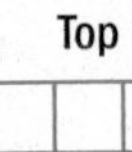

Top

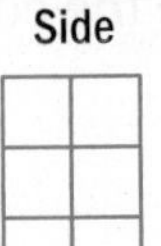

Side

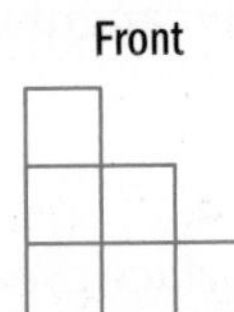

Front

◆ CALIFORNIA STANDARDS SPIRAL REVIEW

AF 3.2

27. A triangle with an area of A square inches has a base of 8 inches. Which equation can you use to find the height h of the triangle? ***(p. 541)***

Ⓐ $A = 4h$ Ⓑ $A = 8h$ Ⓒ $A = 16h$ Ⓓ $A = 64h$

SDAP 1.3

28. If the outliers are excluded from the data set below, which statement will be true? ***(p. 372)***

10, 31, 35, 39, 41, 44, 73

Ⓐ The mean increases. Ⓑ The mean decreases.

Ⓒ The median increases. Ⓓ The median decreases.

SDAP 2.2

29. Olivia wants to know if her classmates will support a field trip to Catalina Island. She surveys every fourth student from a list of all of her classmates. Which sampling method is she using? ***(p. 354)***

Ⓐ Convenience Ⓑ Random Ⓒ Self-selected Ⓓ Systematic

11.2 Surface Area of Prisms

MATERIALS • graph paper • ruler • scissors

Standards Preparation

Grade 5 MG 1.2 Construct a cube and rectangular box from two-dimensional patterns and use these patterns to compute the surface area for these objects.

QUESTION How can you find the surface area of a prism from a two-dimensional pattern?

A *net* is a two-dimensional representation of a solid. The *surface area* of a solid is the sum of the areas of its outside surfaces.

EXPLORE Use graph paper to find the surface area of a prism.

STEP 1 **Copy** the net at the right on graph paper.

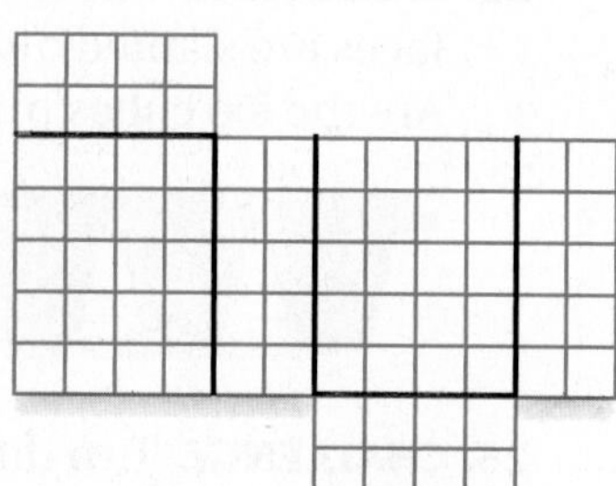

STEP 2 **Find** the area of the net by counting the number of unit squares that make up the net.

STEP 3 **Cut** out the net and fold it along the black lines to form a rectangular prism. Tape the edges together.

STEP 4 **Find** the surface area of the rectangular prism by counting the number of squares on each face and adding.

DRAW CONCLUSIONS Use your observations to complete these exercises.

1. **COMPARE** *Compare* the area of the net found in Step 2 with the surface area of the rectangular prism found in Step 4.

Copy the net on graph paper. Then cut out the net and fold it along the black lines to form a prism. Find the surface area of the prism.

2. 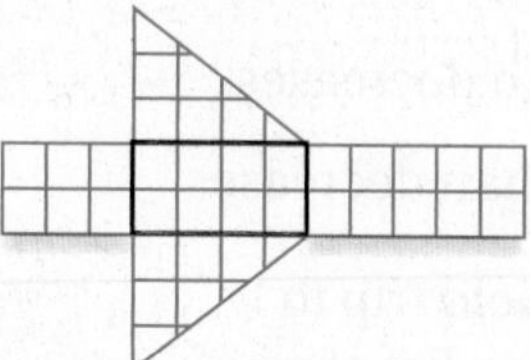

3. 

4. **REASONING** *Describe* how to find the surface area of a solid whose faces are polygons.

11.2 Surface Area of Prisms

Standards **AF 3.2 Express in symbolic form simple relationships arising from geometry.**

Connect ***Before*** you found the areas of two-dimensional figures. ***Now*** you will find surface areas of prisms.

KEY VOCABULARY
- **surface area**
- **net**

The **surface area** of a solid is the sum of the areas of its outside surfaces. A two-dimensional pattern that forms a solid when it is folded is called a **net**. The activity on page 580 suggests that the surface area of a rectangular prism is equal to the area of its net.

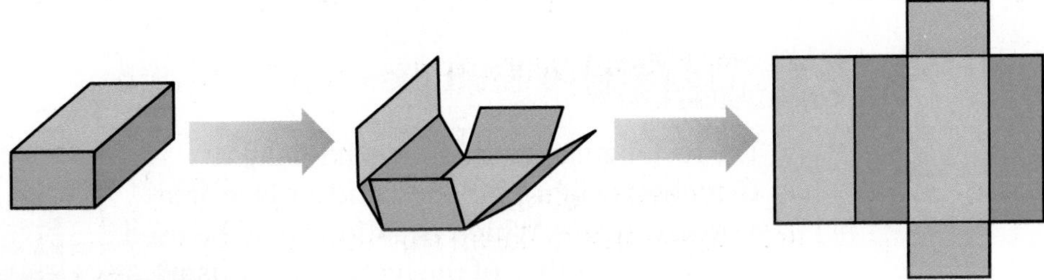

EXAMPLE 1 Finding Surface Area Using a Net

Find the surface area of the rectangular prism.

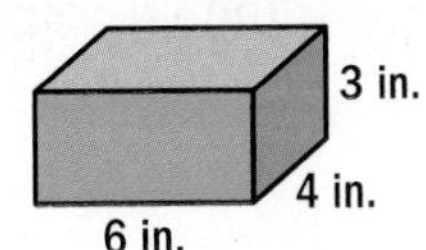

VOCABULARY
In this book, every prism is also a *right prism*, which means that the edges connecting the bases are perpendicular to the bases.

STEP 1 **Draw** a net and find the area of each face.

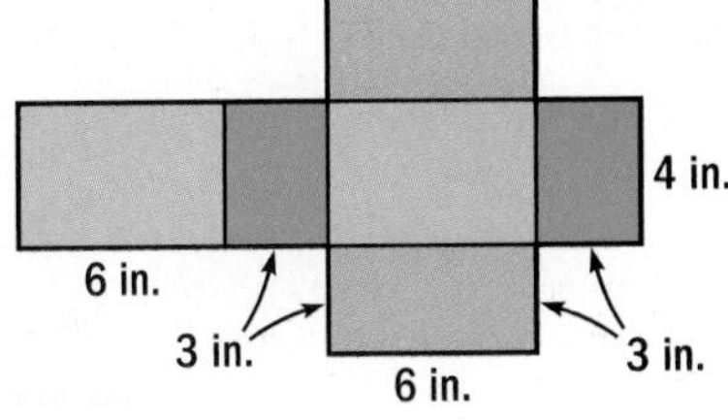

Area of top or bottom: $6 \times 4 = 24$

Area of front or back: $6 \times 3 = 18$

Area of either side: $4 \times 3 = 12$

STEP 2 **Add** the areas of all six faces.

$24 + 24 + 18 + 18 + 12 + 12 = 108$

▶ **Answer** The surface area of the prism is 108 square inches.

KEY CONCEPT *For Your Notebook*

Surface Area of a Rectangular Prism

Words The surface area of a rectangular prism is the sum of the areas of its faces.

Algebra $S = 2lw + 2lh + 2wh$

h w l

EXAMPLE 2 Finding Surface Area Using a Formula

Find the surface area of the stadium cushion.

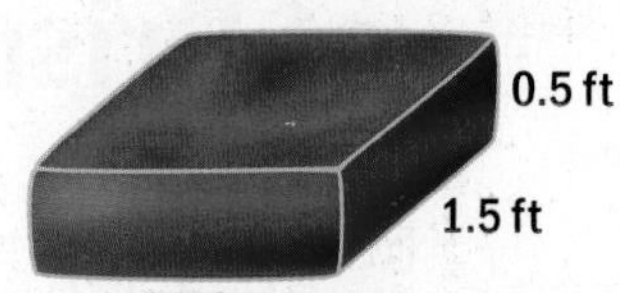

SOLUTION

$S = 2lw + 2lh + 2wh$	Write formula for surface area.
$= 2(1.5)(1.5) + 2(1.5)(0.5) + 2(1.5)(0.5)$	Substitute 1.5 for *l*, 1.5 for *w*, and 0.5 for *h*.
$= 4.5 + 1.5 + 1.5$	Multiply.
$= 7.5$	Add.

▸ **Answer** The surface area of the stadium cushion is 7.5 square feet.

EXAMPLE 3 ◆ Multiple Choice Practice

The rectangular prism shown has length 15 inches, height 12 inches, and surface area *S* square inches. Which equation could be used to find the width *w* of the rectangular prism?

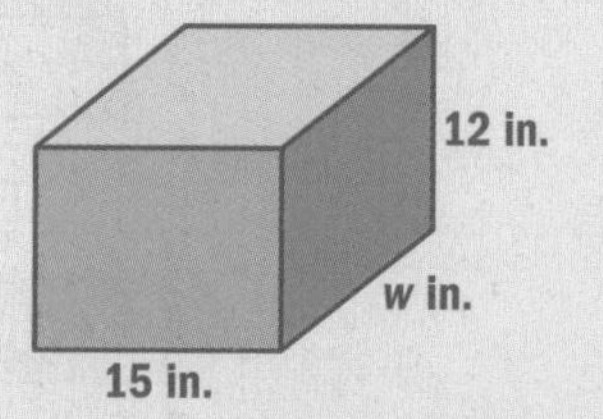

Ⓐ $S = 24w + 360$ Ⓑ $S = 27w + 180$

Ⓒ $S = 54w + 180$ Ⓓ $S = 54w + 360$

ELIMINATE CHOICES
The total area of the front and back faces is 2(15)(12), or 360 square inches. The areas of the other faces are expressed in terms of *w*. You can eliminate choices B and C.

SOLUTION

$S = 2lw + 2lh + 2wh$	Write formula for surface area.
$= 2(15)w + 2(15)(12) + 2w(12)$	Substitute 15 for *l* and 12 for *h*.
$= 30w + 360 + 24w$	Multiply.
$= 54w + 360$	Combine like terms.

▸ **Answer** The equation $S = 54w + 360$ could be used to find the width. The correct answer is D. Ⓐ Ⓑ Ⓒ Ⓓ

✓ GUIDED PRACTICE for Examples 1, 2, and 3

Find the surface area of the rectangular prism.

1.

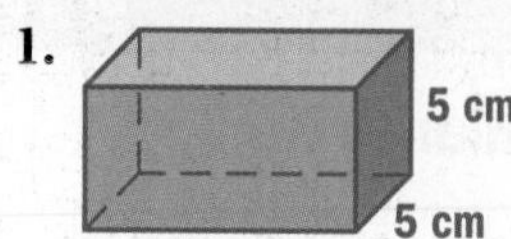

2.

1 mm
3 mm
5 mm

3.

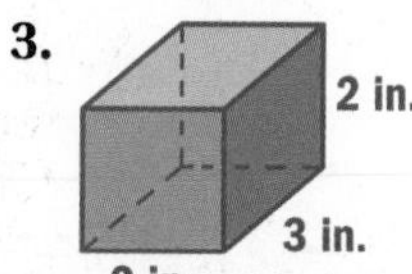

4. A rectangular prism has length 13 meters, width 7 meters, and height *h* meters. Write an equation for the surface area *S* of the prism.

EXAMPLE 4 Finding Surface Area of a Triangular Prism

Find the surface area of the triangular glass prism. The area of a base is about 10.8 cm².

ANOTHER WAY
For an alternative method for solving the problem in Example 4, turn to p. 587 for the Problem Solving Workshop.

SOLUTION

STEP 1 **Find** the area of each face.

Area of base: 10.8 cm^2

Area of rectangular face: $14 \times 5 = 70 \text{ cm}^2$

STEP 2 **Add** the areas of all the faces.

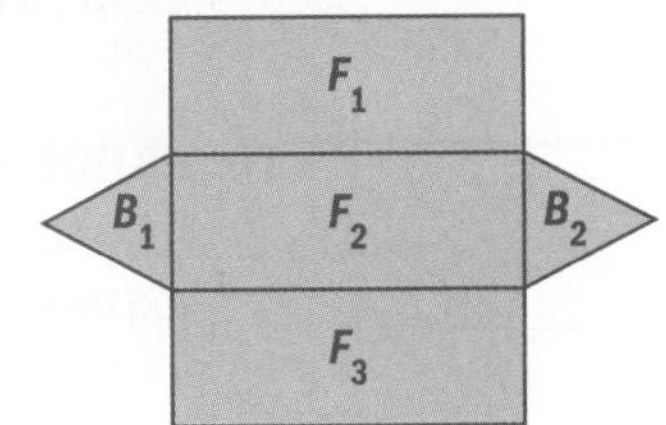

$$S = B_1 + B_2 + F_1 + F_2 + F_3$$
$$\approx 10.8 + 10.8 + 70 + 70 + 70$$
$$= 231.6$$

▶ **Answer** The surface area is about 231.6 square centimeters.

✓ GUIDED PRACTICE for Example 4

Find the surface area of the triangular prism.

5. 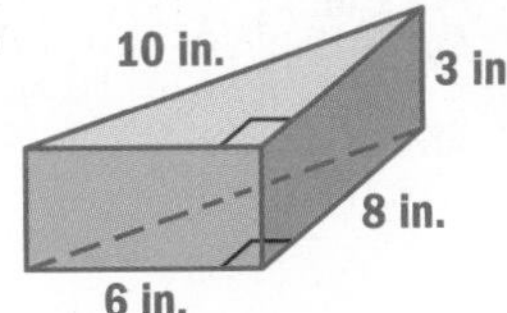

6. 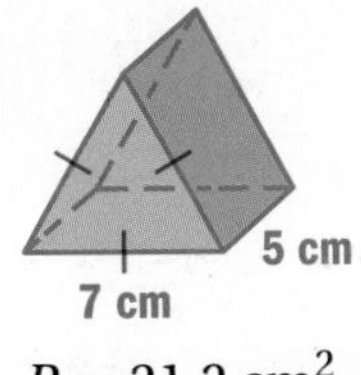

$B \approx 21.2 \text{ cm}^2$

11.2 EXERCISES

HOMEWORK KEY
◆ = **MULTIPLE CHOICE PRACTICE** Exs. 11, 19, 28, 40–42
○ = **HINTS AND HOMEWORK HELP** for Exs. 7, 15, 29 at classzone.com

SKILLS • PROBLEM SOLVING • REASONING

1. **VOCABULARY** Copy and complete: A two-dimensional pattern that forms a solid when it is folded is called a(n) __?__.

2. **WRITING** *Describe* two ways that you could find the surface area of a rectangular prism.

SEE EXAMPLE 1
on p. 581 for Ex. 3

3. **USING NETS** Find the surface area of the rectangular prism whose net is shown.

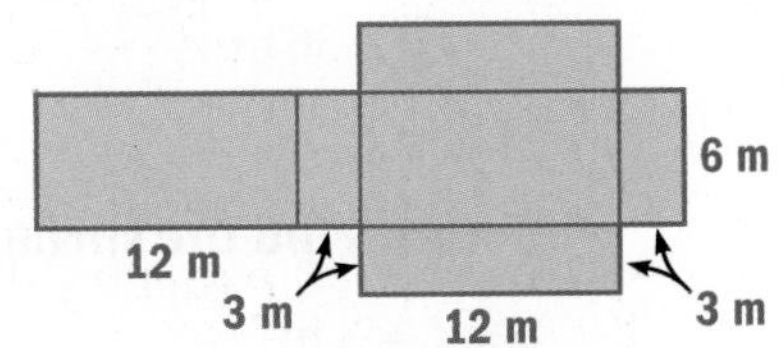

SEE EXAMPLE 2 on p. 582 for Exs. 4–11

FINDING SURFACE AREA **Find the surface area of the rectangular prism.**

4. 6 cm, 6 cm, 10 cm

5.

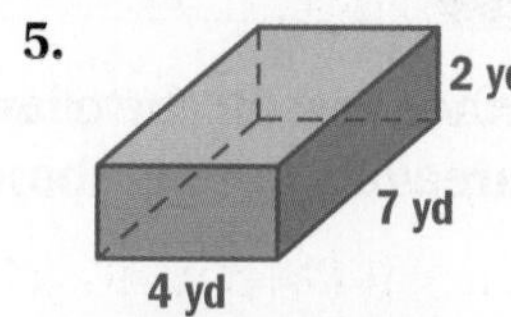

6.

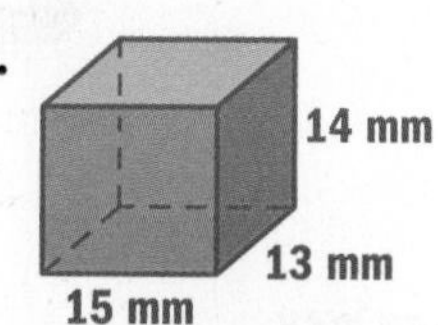

7.

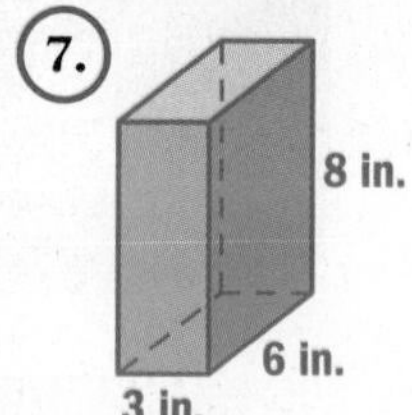

8.

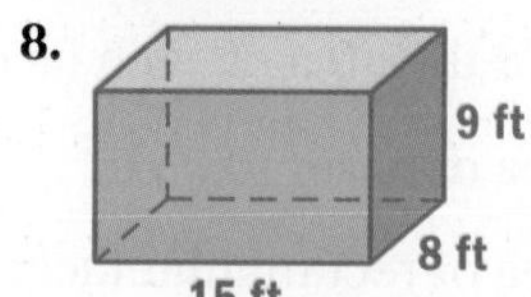

9.

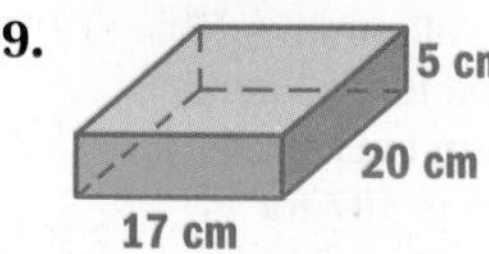

10. **ERROR ANALYSIS** A rectangular prism has dimensions 6 feet by 2 feet by 8 feet. Lana found the surface area of the prism by evaluating the expression $(6 \times 8) + (6 \times 2) + (8 \times 2)$. *Describe* and correct her error.

11. ◆ **MULTIPLE CHOICE** What is the surface area of a rectangular prism that is 16 inches long, 2 inches wide, and 12 inches high?

Ⓐ 248 in.^{2} Ⓑ 304 in.^{2} Ⓒ 384 in.^{2} Ⓓ 496 in.^{2}

SEE EXAMPLE 3 on p. 582 for Exs. 12–14

WRITING EQUATIONS **Write an equation for the surface area S of the rectangular prism.**

12.

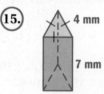

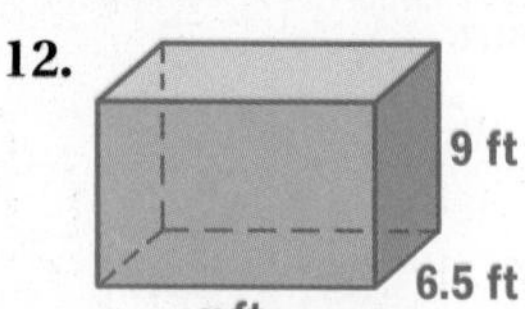

13.

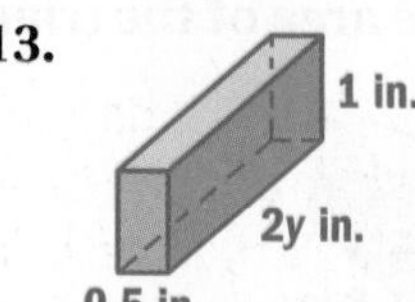

14.

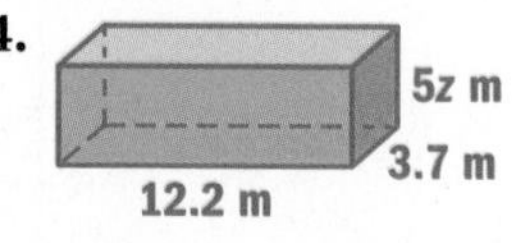

SEE EXAMPLE 4 on p. 583 for Exs. 15–19

FINDING SURFACE AREA **Find the surface area of the triangular prism.**

15.

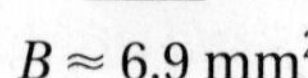

$B \approx 6.9 \text{ mm}^2$

16.

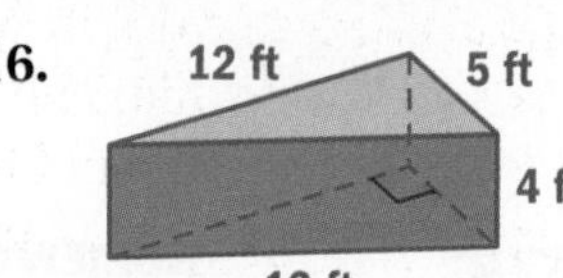

17.

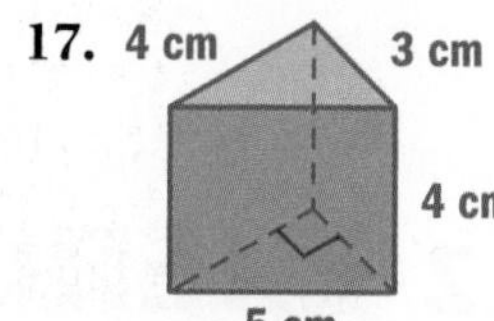

18. **ERROR ANALYSIS** The rectangular faces of a triangular prism each have a length of 15 yards and a width of 8 yards. The area of a base is 27.7 square yards. William found the surface area of the prism by evaluating $27.7 + 120 + 120 + 120$. *Describe* and correct his error.

19. ◆ **MULTIPLE CHOICE** What is the surface area of the triangular prism?

Ⓐ 24 cm^2 Ⓑ 30 cm^2

Ⓒ 36 cm^2 Ⓓ 72 cm^2

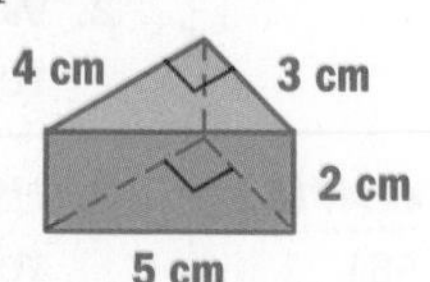

CUBES **Find the surface area of a cube with the given edge length s.**

20. $s = 3$ in. 21. $s = 1.5$ ft 22. $s = 4.5$ cm 23. $s = 0.75$ mm

CONNECT SKILLS TO PROBLEM SOLVING **Exercises 24–26 will help you prepare for problem solving.**

Find the surface area of the object described. Each object is in the shape of a rectangular prism.

24. A box with length 20 inches, width 14 inches, and height 18 inches

25. A brick with length 8 inches, width 4 inches, and height 2 inches

26. A cabinet with length 2 feet, width 1.5 feet, and height 1.8 feet

SEE EXAMPLE 4 on p. 583 for Ex. 27

27. **BIRDHOUSES** Cheryl is building a birdhouse out of plywood using the dimensions shown. Plywood costs an average of $.012 per square inch. She cuts the opening after buying the wood. Find the total cost of the plywood.

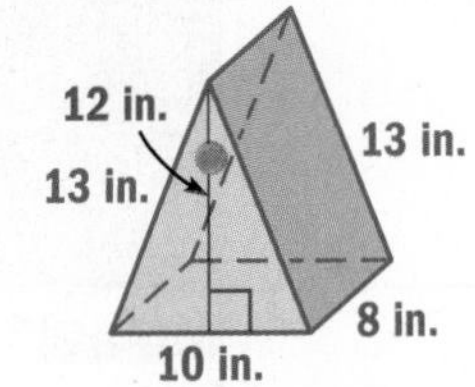

California @HomeTutor for problem solving help at classzone.com

28. ◆ **MULTIPLE CHOICE** A room is in the shape of a rectangular prism. The room is 13 feet long, 11 feet wide, and 10 feet high. One gallon of paint covers 320 square feet. How much paint do you need to cover the four walls of the room?

Ⓐ 1 gal Ⓑ 1.5 gal Ⓒ 2 gal Ⓓ 2.5 gal

California @HomeTutor for problem solving help at classzone.com

29. **PHOTO DISPLAYS** The edge length of a photo cube is 3 inches. Does the photo cube have *more* or *less* viewing surface than a flat rectangular photograph that is 8 inches wide and 10 inches long? *Explain.*

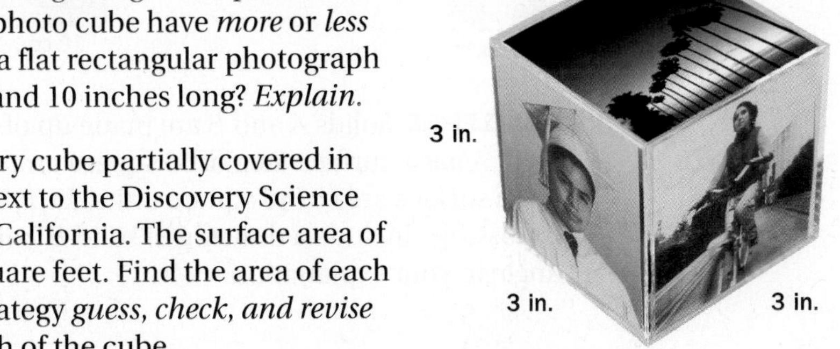

30. **SOLAR CUBE** A 10 story cube partially covered in solar panels stands next to the Discovery Science Center in Santa Ana, California. The surface area of the cube is 24,576 square feet. Find the area of each face. Then use the strategy *guess, check, and revise* to find the edge length of the cube.

31. **WRITING** Write a formula for the surface area S of a cube with edge length s. *Explain* how you derived the formula. Then use the formula to find the surface area of a cube with edge length 14 millimeters.

32. **DOGHOUSES** The doghouse shown is composed of a rectangular prism and a triangular prism. Find the surface area of the doghouse (including the floor) before the hole for the entrance was cut out.

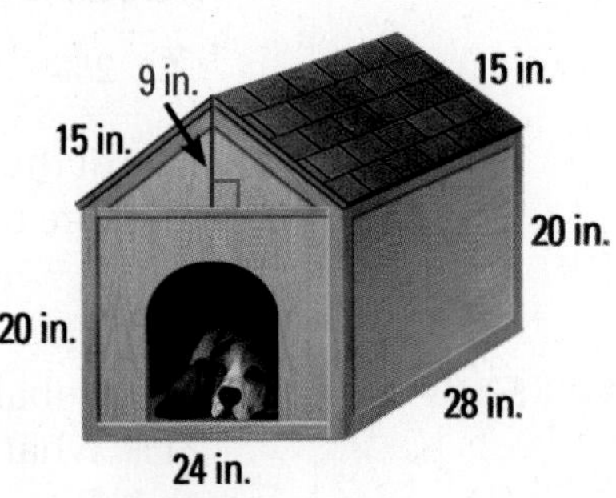

33. **REASONING** Another formula for the surface area S of a rectangular prism is $S = 2B + Ph$ where B is the area of a base, P is the perimeter of a base, and h is the height of the prism. Use the distributive property to show that $2lw + 2lh + 2wh = 2B + Ph$.

34. **BUILDINGS** The building below is made up of three rectangular prisms. What is the total area of the outside surfaces of the building, including doors and windows but *not* the bottom surface?

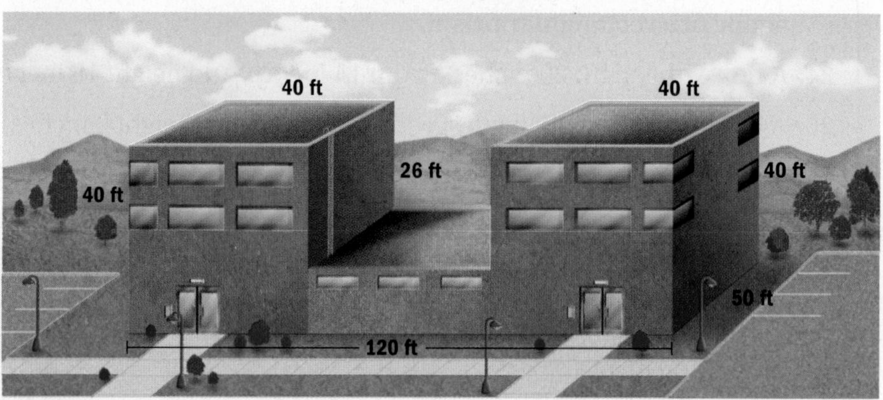

35. **REASONING** The surface area of a triangular prism is 376.4 square feet. The height of the prism is 8 feet. The side lengths of a triangular base are 9 feet, 12 feet, and 13 feet. What is the area of a base? *Explain.*

CHALLENGE Write an equation for the surface area S of the prism.

36. $B \approx 10.4 \text{ mm}^2$

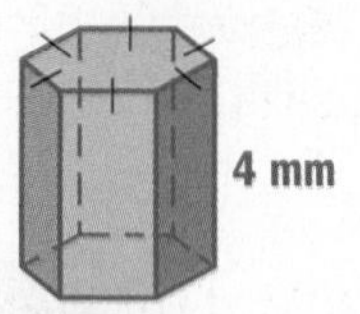

37. $B = 28 \text{ cm}^2$

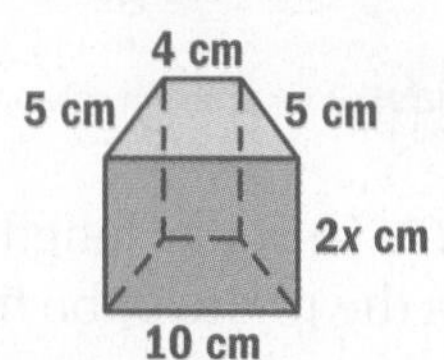

38. $B = 19 \text{ ft}^2$

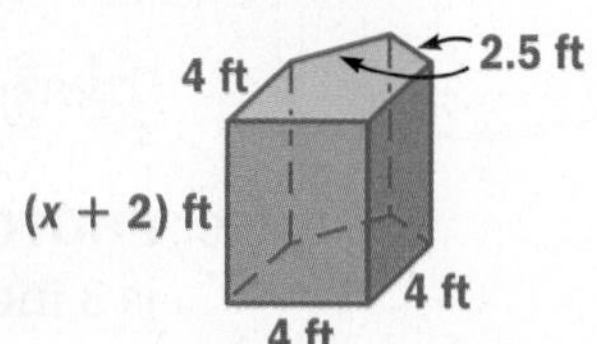

39. **CHALLENGE** Solids A and B are made up of unit cubes. Solid A has a surface area of 36 square units. Solid B has a surface area of 40 square units. *Explain* how this is possible. Include a drawing of solid B from a different angle in your explanation.

◆ CALIFORNIA STANDARDS SPIRAL REVIEW

Gr. 5 NS 1.2 40. On opening day of trout season, 8 out of every 10 people fishing caught a trout. What percent did *not* catch a trout? *(p. 301)*

Ⓐ 2% Ⓑ 8% Ⓒ 20% Ⓓ 80%

MG 2.2 41. One of the angles of a right triangle has a measure of 54°. What is the measure of the other acute angle of the triangle? *(p. 474)*

Ⓐ 6° Ⓑ 36° Ⓒ 54° Ⓓ 126°

SDAP 3.3 42. The probability of randomly choosing a red ball out of a box of balls is 21%. What is the probability of randomly choosing a ball that is *not* red? *(p. 427)*

Ⓐ 21% Ⓑ 29% Ⓒ 69% Ⓓ 79%

PROBLEM SOLVING WORKSHOP
LESSON 11.2

Using ALTERNATIVE METHODS

Another Way to Solve Example 4, page 583

Standards
AF 3.2

In Example 4 on page 583, you saw how to solve the problem about the surface area of the glass prism by using a net. You can also solve the problem by using a formula.

PROBLEM

Find the surface area of the triangular glass prism. The area of a base is about 10.8 cm^2.

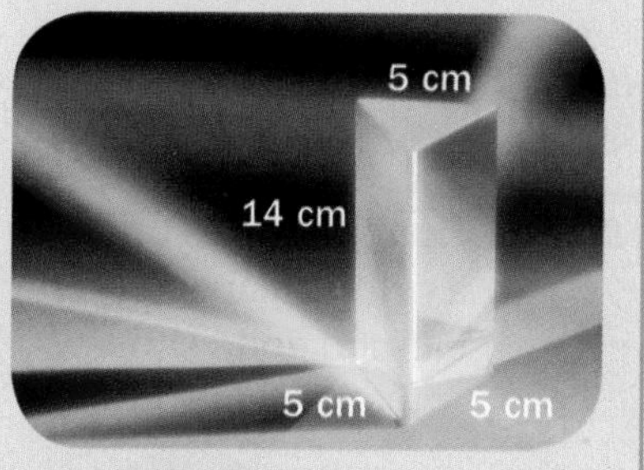

METHOD

Use a Formula An alternative approach is to use a formula.

To find the surface area of a prism, you can use the formula $S = 2B + Ph$ where B is the area of a base of the prism, P is the perimeter of a base, and h is the height of the prism.

STEP 1 **Find** the perimeter P of a base. Each side of the base is 5 centimeters long. The perimeter is $P = 5 + 5 + 5 = 15$ centimeters.

STEP 2 **Use** the formula $S = 2B + Ph$ to find the surface area.

$S = 2B + Ph$ **Write formula.**

$\approx 2(\mathbf{10.8}) + (\mathbf{15})(\mathbf{14})$ **Substitute values.**

$= 21.6 + 210$ **Multiply.**

$= 231.6$ **Add.**

▶ **Answer** The surface area is about 231.6 square centimeters.

PRACTICE

1. **RAMPS** Find the surface area of the ramp using two different methods.

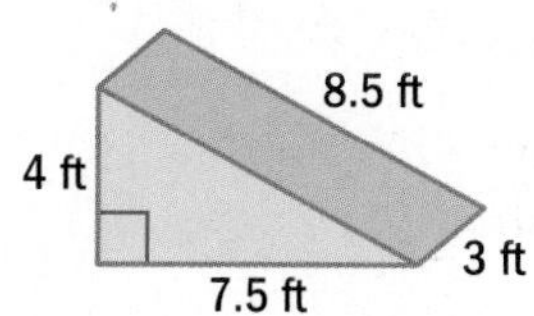

2. **CANDLES** Find the surface area of the candle using two different methods. The area of each regular pentagon is about 6.9 square centimeters.

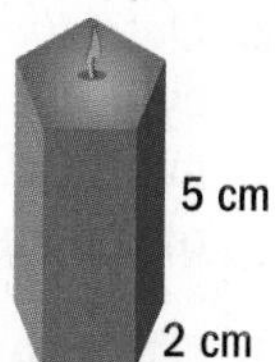

11.3 Surface Area of Cylinders

MATERIALS • cylindrical object • paper • ruler • scissors

Standards

MG 1.2 Know common estimates of $\pi\left(3.14; \frac{22}{7}\right)$ and use these values to estimate and calculate the circumference and the area of circles; compare with actual measurements.

QUESTION **How can you find the surface area of a cylinder?**

EXPLORE **Use a net to find the surface area of a cylinder.**

STEP 1 **Cut** out pieces of paper to cover a cylindrical object, such as the canned good shown.

STEP 2 **Use** a separate sheet of paper. Trace the pieces of paper you cut out in Step 1 to make a net of the can.

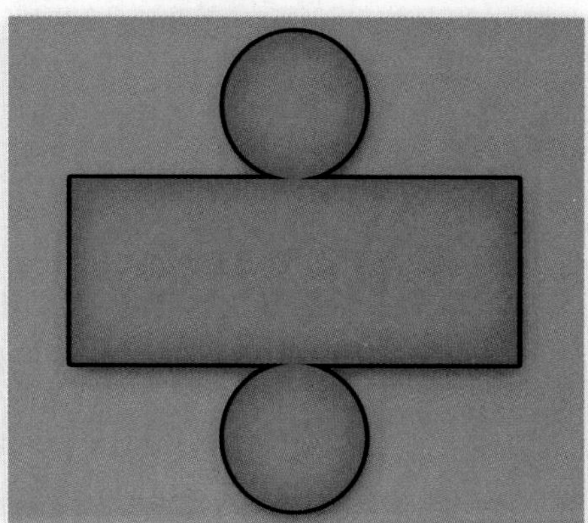

STEP 3 **Use** a ruler to measure the radius of each circle and the length and width of the rectangle in the net.

STEP 4 **Find** the surface area of the object.

DRAW CONCLUSIONS **Use your observations to complete these exercises.**

Let r represent the radius of a base of a cylinder. Let h represent its height.

1. Write an expression (in terms of π and r) for the total area of the bases of a cylinder.
2. *Describe* the relationship between the circumference of a base of a cylinder and the length of the rectangle that covers the side of the cylinder. Then write an expression (in terms of π, r, and h) for the area of the curved surface of a cylinder.
3. **REASONING** Write a formula that you can use to find the surface area S of a cylinder. *Explain* your reasoning.

11.3 Surface Area of Cylinders

Standards **AF 3.1 Use variables in expressions describing geometric quantities (e.g.,** $P = 2w + 2l$, $A = \frac{1}{2}bh$, $C = \pi d$ **– the formulas for** the perimeter of a rectangle, the area of a triangle, and **the circumference of a circle, respectively).**

Connect ***Before*** you found surface areas of rectangular and triangular prisms. ***Now*** you will use the circumference formula to find surface areas of cylinders.

Math and **RECREATION** Ex. 18, p. 592

KEY VOCABULARY
- **cylinder,** *p. 575*
- **surface area,** *p. 581*
- **net,** *p. 581*

As shown in the activity on page 588, the net of a cylinder consists of two circles that form the bases and a rectangle that forms the curved (or lateral) surface of the cylinder. The circumference of a base, $2\pi r$, is equal to the length of the rectangle.

VOCABULARY
In this book, all cylinders are *right cylinders,* which means that the line connecting the centers of the bases is perpendicular to the bases.

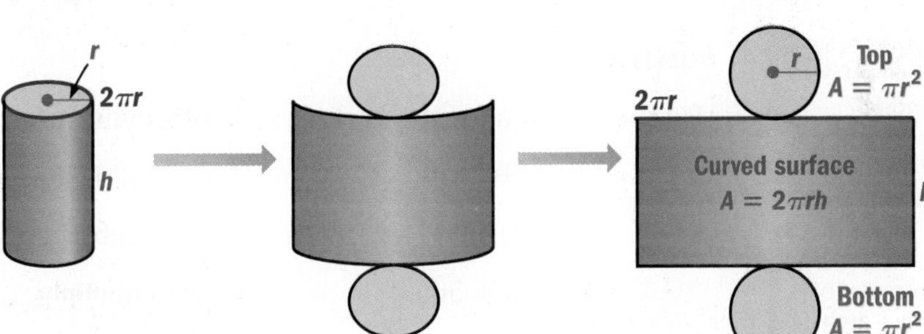

EXAMPLE 1 Finding the Surface Area of a Cylinder

Find the surface area of the cylinder at the right. Use 3.14 for π.

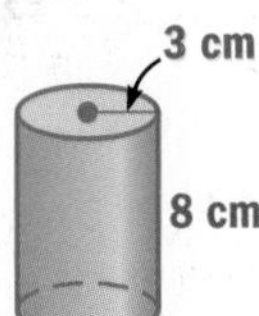

SOLUTION

Use a net to find the surface area.

AVOID ERRORS
When finding the surface area of a cylinder, don't forget to add the areas of *both* bases.

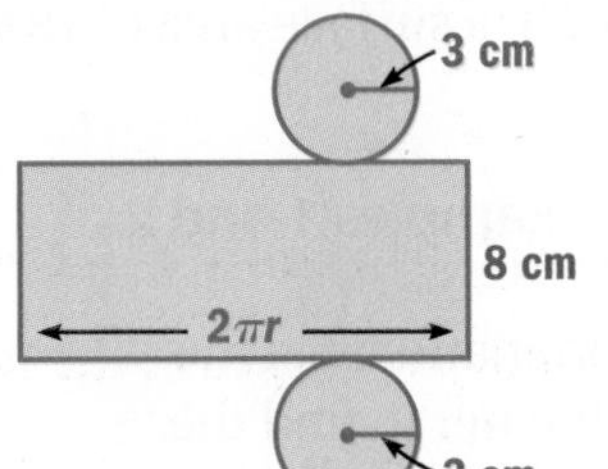

Area of base: $A = \pi r^2$

$\approx 3.14(3)^2$

$= 28.26$

Area of curved surface: $A = 2\pi rh$

$\approx 2(3.14)(3)(8)$

$= 150.72$

Surface area: $S = 28.26 + 28.26 + 150.72$

$= 207.24$

▸ **Answer** The surface area is about 207.24 square centimeters.

In Example 1, you saw that the surface area of a cylinder is the sum of twice the area of a base and the area of the curved surface. The formula for the surface area of a cylinder is summarized below.

KEY CONCEPT *For Your Notebook*

Surface Area of a Cylinder

Words The surface area of a cylinder is the sum of twice the area of a base and the product of the base's circumference and height.

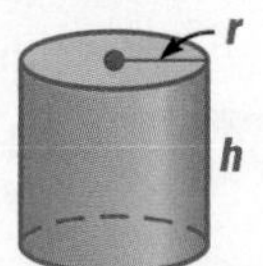

Algebra $S = 2\pi r^2 + 2\pi rh$

EXAMPLE 2 Finding Surface Area Using a Formula

Find the surface area of the cylinder at the right. Use 3.14 for π.

6 cm
15 cm

About the Standards

Grade 6 Standard MR 2.4 calls for using a variety of methods to explain reasoning. Examples 1 and 2 show how you can use a net or a formula to find the surface area of a cylinder.

SOLUTION

Use the formula for the surface area of a cylinder.

$S = 2\pi r^2 + 2\pi rh$ **Write formula for surface area.**

$\approx 2(3.14)(6)^2 + 2(3.14)(6)(15)$ **Substitute values.**

$= 226.08 + 565.2$ **Multiply.**

$= 791.28$ **Add.**

▶ **Answer** The surface area is about 791.28 square centimeters.

CHECK To check that your answer is reasonable, use 3 for π.

$S \approx 2(3)(6)^2 + 2(3)(6)(15)$ **Substitute values.**

$= 216 + 540$ **Multiply.**

$= 756$ **Add.**

Because 756 is close to 791.28, a surface area of 791.28 cm^2 is reasonable.

✓ GUIDED PRACTICE for Examples 1 and 2

1. Draw a net for the cylinder and label the dimensions. Then use the net to find the surface area of the cylinder. Use 3.14 for π.

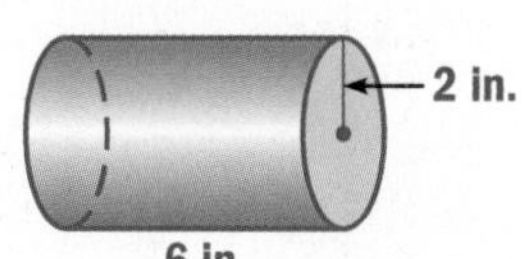

Find the surface area of the cylinder. Use 3.14 for π.

2. 5 mm, 3 mm

3.

4.

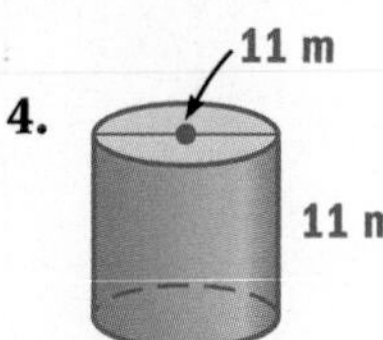

11.3 EXERCISES

HOMEWORK KEY ◆ = **MULTIPLE CHOICE PRACTICE** Exs. 6, 10, 22, 27–29

○ = **HINTS AND HOMEWORK HELP** for Exs. 3, 9, 23 at classzone.com

SKILLS • PROBLEM SOLVING • REASONING

1. **VOCABULARY** Copy and complete: The net for a cylinder consists of two _?_ and a(n) _?_.

2. **WRITING** *Describe* how you could find the surface area of a cylinder if you know its height and the diameter of a base.

SEE EXAMPLE 1 on p. 589 for Exs. 3–6

DRAWING NETS Draw a net for the cylinder and label the dimensions. Then use the net to find the surface area of the cylinder. Use 3.14 for π.

3. 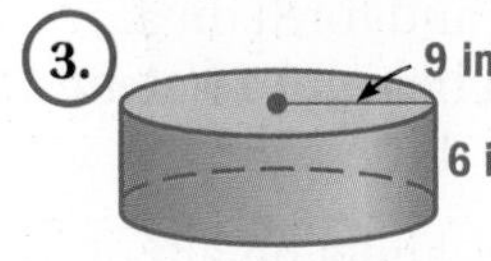

4. 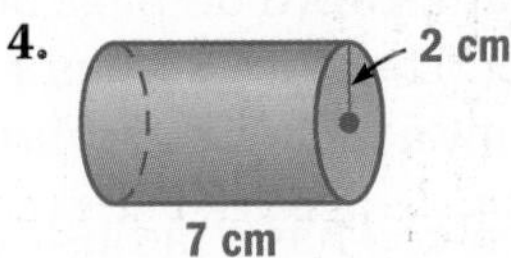

5. 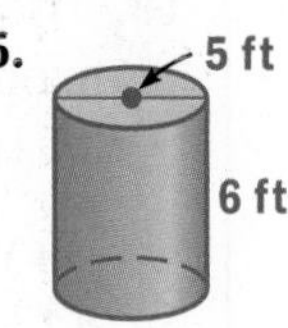

6. ◆ **MULTIPLE CHOICE** Which of the following is a net for a cylinder?

Ⓐ 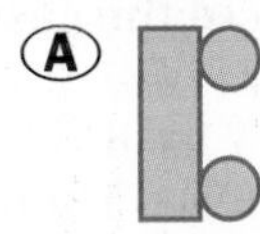
Ⓑ 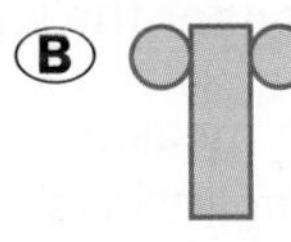
Ⓒ 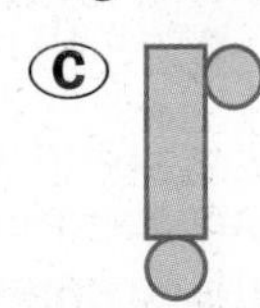
Ⓓ 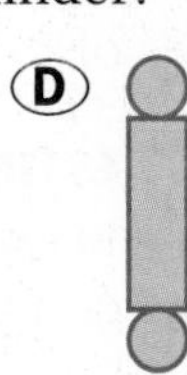

SEE EXAMPLE 2 on p. 590 for Exs. 7–12

SURFACE AREA Find the surface area of the cylindrical object. Use 3.14 for π.

7. 

8. 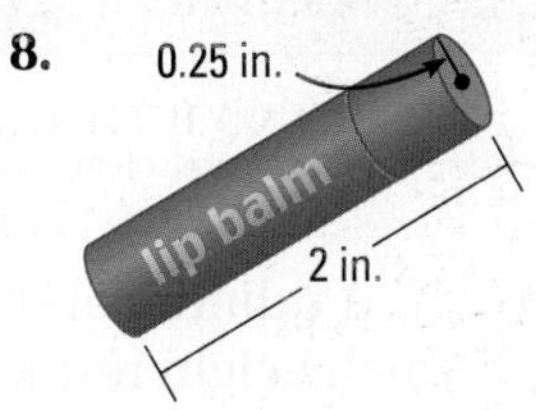

9. 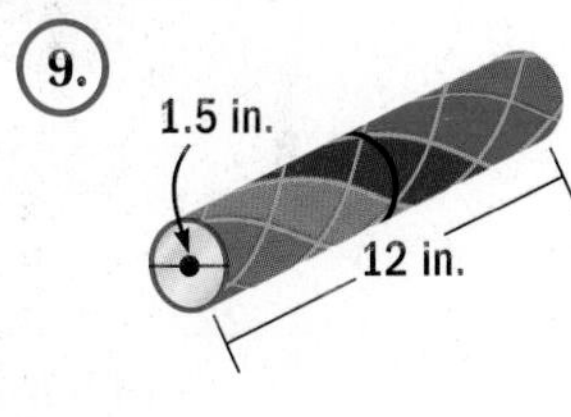

10. ◆ **MULTIPLE CHOICE** A cylinder has a radius of 8 feet and a height of 13 feet. What is the approximate surface area of the cylinder? Use 3.14 for π.

Ⓐ 703 ft^2 Ⓑ 754 ft^2 Ⓒ 854 ft^2 Ⓓ 1055 ft^2

ERROR ANALYSIS The diameter of a cylinder is 5 feet and the height is 10 feet. *Describe* and correct the error made in finding the surface area.

11.
$S = 2\pi r^2 + 2\pi rh$
$\approx 2(3.14)(5)^2 + 2(3.14)(5)(10)$
$= 157 + 314$
$= 471$
The surface area is about 471 ft^2. ✗

12.
$S = 2\pi r^2 + \pi rh$
$\approx 2(3.14)(2.5)^2 + (3.14)(2.5)(10)$
$= 39.25 + 78.5$
$= 117.75$
The surface area is about 117.75 ft^2. ✗

SURFACE AREA Find the surface area of a cylinder with the given dimensions. Use 3.14 for π. *Compare* the results to the surface area of a cylinder with radius 1 cm and height 2 cm.

13. radius: 3 cm
height: 6 cm

14. radius: 6 cm
height: 12 cm

15. radius: 9 cm
height: 18 cm

16. REASONING Use your answers to Exercises 13–15. How does a change in the dimensions of a cylinder by a factor of x affect the surface area?

CONNECT SKILLS TO PROBLEM SOLVING Exercises 17–20 will help you prepare for problem solving.

17. A cylindrical cheese wheel has a diameter of 8 inches and a height of 5 inches. Draw a net for the cylinder. Label the dimensions.

18. The balance board shown on page 589 rocks back and forth on a wooden cylinder. The cylinder has a radius of 3 inches and a height of 10 inches. Draw a net for the cylinder. Label the dimensions.

19. A cylindrical steel rod has a radius of 2 centimeters and a height of 11 centimeters. Write an expression for the surface area of the rod.

20. A cylindrical cosmetics case has a radius of 3 centimeters and a height of 1 centimeter. Write an expression for the surface area of the case.

SEE EXAMPLE 2 on p. 590 for Ex. 21

21. ESTIMATION Use a metric ruler to measure each battery in order to estimate its surface area to the nearest square centimeter. Then compare the surface areas of the batteries.

California @HomeTutor for problem solving help at classzone.com

22. ◆ MULTIPLE CHOICE A cylindrical keychain flashlight has a diameter of 8 millimeters. Which height results in a surface area of about 1608 square millimeters?

Ⓐ 12 mm Ⓑ 24 mm Ⓒ 30 mm Ⓓ 60 mm

California @HomeTutor for problem solving help at classzone.com

(23.) SHORT RESPONSE Cylinder A has a radius of 3 meters and a height of 6 meters. Cylinder B has a radius of 6 meters and a height of 3 meters. Which cylinder has the greater surface area? *Explain.*

24. PAINTING Jerome is using a cylindrical paint roller to paint a wall. The roller has a radius of 1 inch and a height of 9 inches. He makes one swipe with the roller to paint a rectangle that has a length of 28 inches and a width of 9 inches. About how many times did the roller revolve to make the rectangle?

25. **CHALLENGE** *Describe* a method to find the surface area of the solid at the right, *not* including the surface created by the circular hole. Then use your method to find the surface area.

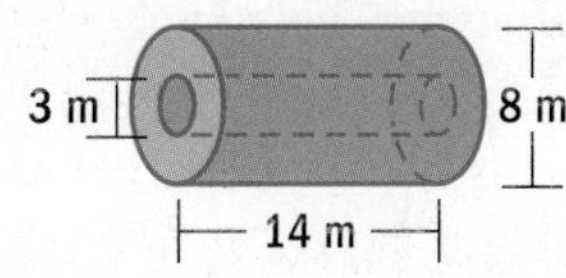

26. **CHALLENGE** A cylinder is inside a cube with edge length 1 inch, as shown. The cylinder is the largest possible cylinder that can fit inside the cube. Find the surface area of the cylinder. *Explain* your answer.

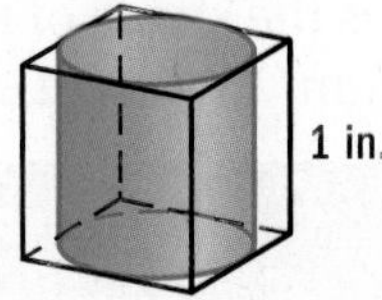

◆ CALIFORNIA STANDARDS SPIRAL REVIEW

MG 1.2 27. What is the area of a circle with radius 13 meters? Use 3.14 for π. ***(p. 555)***

Ⓐ 40.82 m^2 Ⓑ 81.64 m^2 Ⓒ 530.66 m^2 Ⓓ 1061.32 m^2

AF 3.1 28. A trapezoid has bases x inches and $3x$ inches and height 8 inches. Which expression represents the area of the trapezoid? ***(p. 541)***

Ⓐ $16x$ Ⓑ $32x$ Ⓒ $24x^2$ Ⓓ $4x + 8$

SDAP 2.2 29. Deanna wants to survey people in her town to see if they are satisfied with the condition of the roads. She surveys people at a birthday party that she attends. Which sampling method is she using? ***(p. 354)***

Ⓐ Convenience Ⓑ Random Ⓒ Self-selected Ⓓ Systematic

QUIZ *for Lessons 11.1–11.3*

Classify the solid, if possible. Then sketch the top, side, and front views. Assume that there are no hidden cubes except those supporting the cubes you can see. ***(p. 575)***

1.

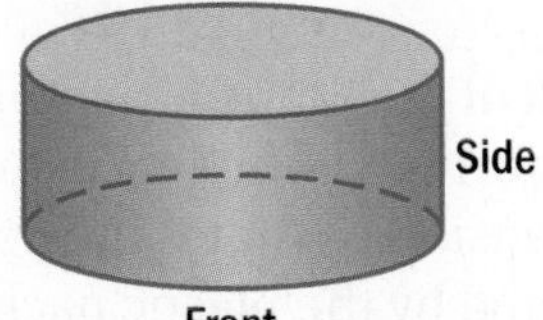

2.

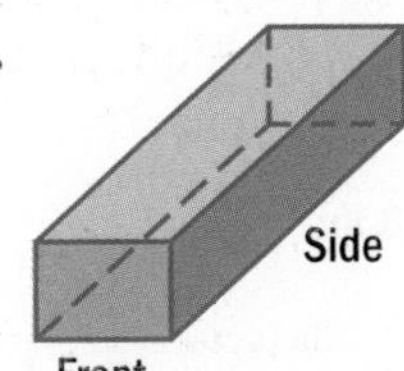

3.

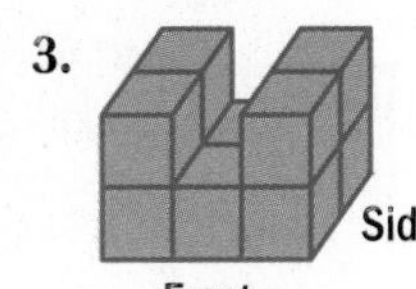

Find the surface area of the solid. Use 3.14 for π. ***(pp. 581, 589)***

4.

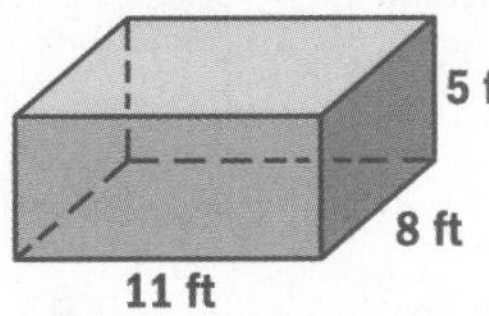

5.

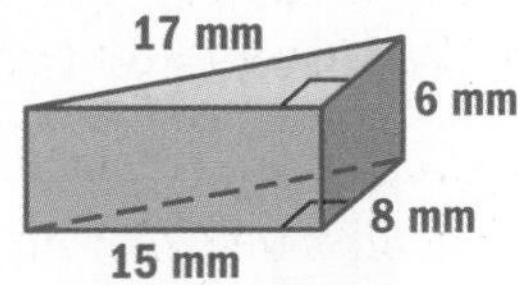

6.

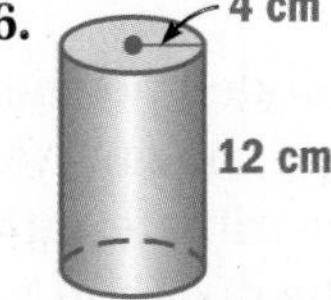

7. **SET DESIGN** Isaac is making a raised platform for a school play. The platform is a rectangular prism, as shown. He paints all of the faces except the bottom surface. What is the total area painted? ***(p. 581)***

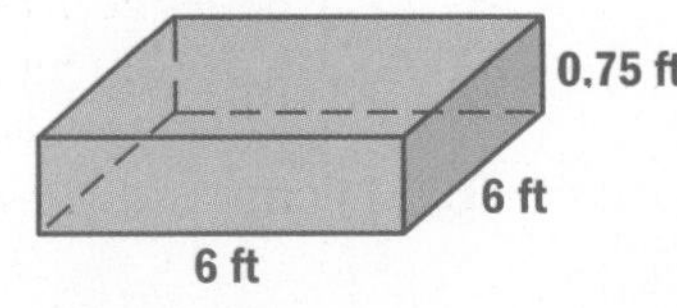

MIXED REVIEW of Skills and Problem Solving

Multiple Choice Practice for Lessons 11.1–11.3

1. The coliseum below is shaped like a cylinder. What is the shape of the front view of the coliseum? **Gr. 5 MG 2.3**

Ⓐ Circle Ⓑ Oval

Ⓒ Triangle Ⓓ Rectangle

2. Which view of the solid is shown? **Gr. 5 MG 2.3**

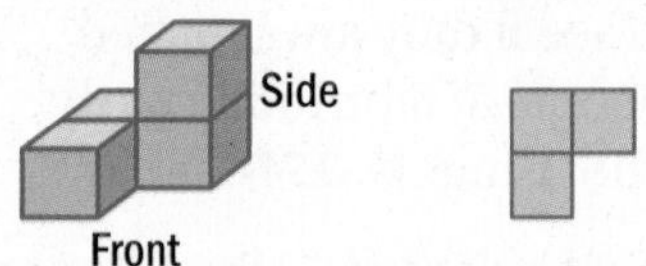

Ⓐ Top view Ⓑ Side view

Ⓒ Front view Ⓓ No view

3. The net of a triangular prism is shown below. Which equation represents the surface area S (in square inches) of the prism? **AF 3.2, MR 2.2**

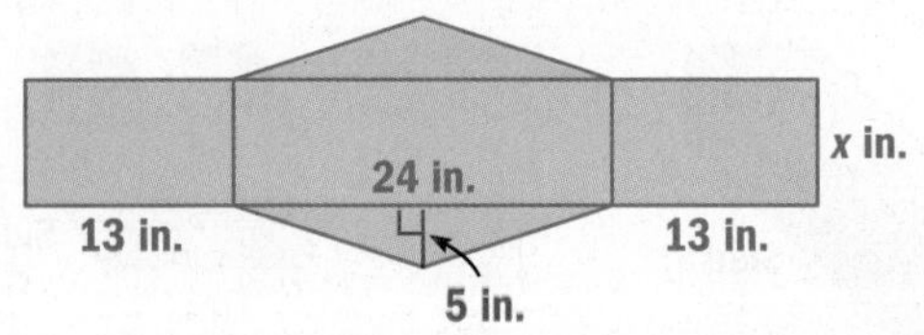

Ⓐ $S = 2x + 104$ Ⓑ $S = 50x + 60$

Ⓒ $S = 50x + 120$ Ⓓ $S = 170x$

4. A wooden peg has the shape shown. What is the approximate surface area of the peg? Use 3.14 for π. **AF 3.1**

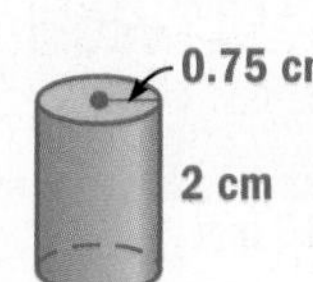

Ⓐ 12 cm^2 Ⓑ 13 cm^2

Ⓒ 14 cm^2 Ⓓ 15 cm^2

5. A rectangular prism is 30 centimeters wide, 45 centimeters long, and x centimeters high. Which equation represents the surface area S (in square centimeters)? **AF 3.2**

Ⓐ $S = 2850x$ Ⓑ $S = 150x + 2700$

Ⓒ $S = 1350x$ Ⓓ $S = 150x + 1350$

6. The dimensions of two wooden crates are shown. The prices of the crates are based on the amount of wood used to make them. Which statement is true about the costs of the crates? **AF 3.1, MR 1.2**

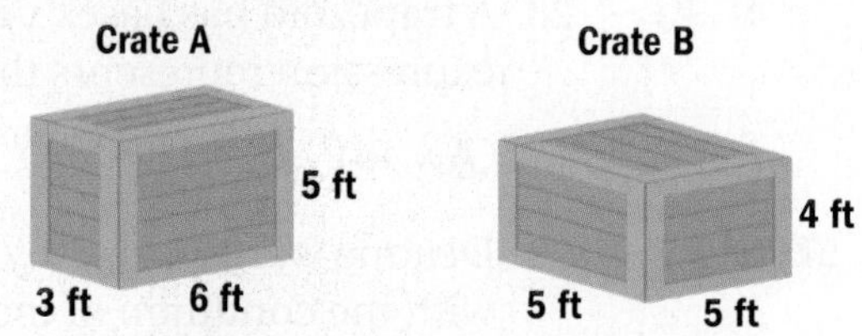

Ⓐ Crate A is less expensive because it has less surface area than Crate B.

Ⓑ Crate A is less expensive because it is not as long as Crate B.

Ⓒ Crate B is less expensive because it is not as high as Crate A.

Ⓓ Crate B is less expensive because it has less surface area than Crate A.

7. A roll of duct tape is packaged in plastic that forms a complete cylinder of the same dimensions. What is the approximate area covered by the plastic packaging? Use 3.14 for π. **AF 3.1**

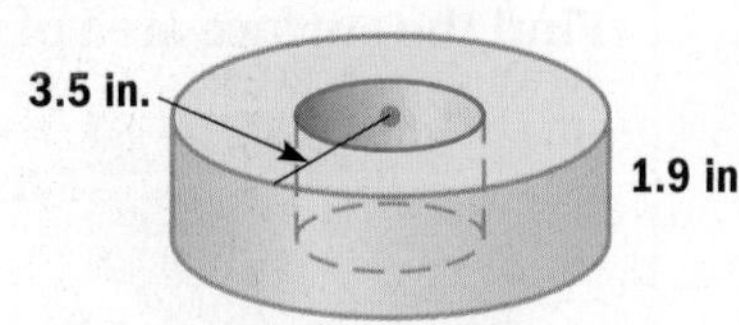

Ⓐ 40 $in.^2$ Ⓑ 64 $in.^2$

Ⓒ 119 $in.^2$ Ⓓ 391 $in.^2$

11.4 Investigating Volume

MATERIALS • unit cubes

Standards Preparation

Grade 5 MG 1.3
Understand the concept of volume and use the appropriate units in common measuring systems (i.e., cubic centimeter [cm³], cubic meter [m³], cubic inch [in.³], cubic yard [yd.³]) **to compute the volume of rectangular solids.**

QUESTION **How can you find the volumes of rectangular prisms?**

The *volume* of a solid is a measure of how much space it occupies. Volume is measured in cubic units. You can use unit cubes to build rectangular prisms and find their volumes.

EXPLORE **Find the volume of a rectangular prism that is 4 units long, 2 units wide, and 1 unit high.**

STEP 1 **Build** a rectangular prism that is 4 units long, 2 units wide, and 1 unit high. Use unit cubes.

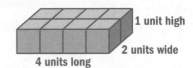

1 unit high
2 units wide
4 units long

STEP 2 **Count** the number of unit cubes used to build the prism. The rectangular prism is made up of 8 unit cubes. This means that the rectangular prism has a volume of 8 cubic units.

DRAW CONCLUSIONS **Use your observations to complete these exercises.**

1. Copy the table. Build the rectangular prisms whose dimensions are given in the table. Then find the volume of each prism by counting the number of unit cubes used to build the prism. Record your results in the table.

Length l	Width w	Height h	Volume V
4	2	1	8
2	1	5	?
1	1	7	?
2	2	3	?

2. Use 12 unit cubes to build three different rectangular prisms. What are the length, width, height, and volume of each prism? Include your results in the table.

3. **REASONING** How are the length l and the width w related to the area B of the base of a rectangular prism?

4. **REASONING** Look for a pattern in the table above. Then use your answer to Exercise 3 to write a formula that relates the volume V, area B of the base, and height h of a rectangular prism.

11.4 Volume of Prisms

Math and HOBBIES
Ex. 25, p. 600

Standards **MG 1.3** **Know and use the formulas for the volume of triangular prisms** and cylinders **(area of base × height)**; compare these formulas and **explain the similarity between them and the formula for the volume of a rectangular solid.**

Connect ***Before*** you found surface areas of prisms. ***Now*** you will find volumes of prisms.

KEY VOCABULARY
- **volume**
- **prism,** *p. 575*

The **volume** of a solid is the amount of space that the solid occupies. Volume is measured in cubic units, such as cubic feet (ft^3) and cubic meters (m^3). The activity on page 595 suggests that the volume of a rectangular prism is given by $V = lwh$ or $V = Bh$. The formula $V = Bh$ can be applied to all prisms.

KEY CONCEPT — *For Your Notebook*

Volume of a Prism

Words The volume of a prism is the product of the area of the base and the height.

Algebra $V = Bh$

h B h B w l

EXAMPLE 1 Finding the Volume of a Rectangular Prism

A rectangular prism has a length of 12 centimeters, a width of 6 centimeters, and a height of 10 centimeters. What is the volume?

SOLUTION

$V = Bh$	**Write formula for volume of prism.**
$= (12 \cdot 6)(10)$	**Substitute (12 · 6) for *B*, and 10 for *h*.**
$= 720$	**Multiply.**

▶ **Answer** The volume is 720 cubic centimeters.

AnimatedMath For an interactive example of finding the volumes of rectangular prisms go to **classzone.com**.

✓ **GUIDED PRACTICE** for Example 1

Find the volume of the rectangular prism.

1. 10 in. 6 in. 16 in.

2. 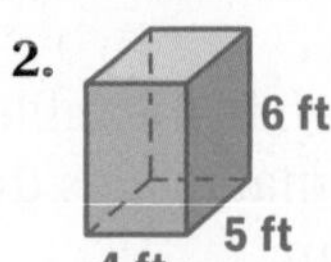

3. 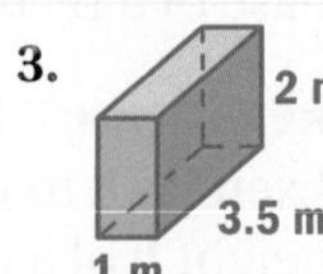

EXAMPLE 2 Finding the Volume of a Triangular Prism

What is the volume of the triangular prism shown?

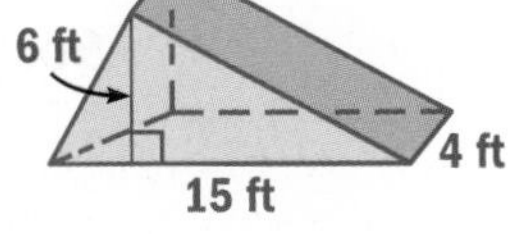

SOLUTION

AVOID ERRORS
The base of a prism is not always the bottom face. In Example 2, the bases are vertical.

STEP 1 **Find** the area of the triangular base.

$$B = \frac{1}{2}(15)(6) = 45$$

STEP 2 **Find** the volume of the prism.

$V = Bh$	**Write formula for volume of prism.**
$= (45)(4)$	**Substitute 45 for *B* and 4 for *h*.**
$= 180$	**Multiply.**

▸ **Answer** The volume is 180 cubic feet.

EXAMPLE 3 ◆ Multiple Choice Practice

The triangular prism shown at the right has volume *V* cubic inches. Which equation could be used to find the height *h* of the prism?

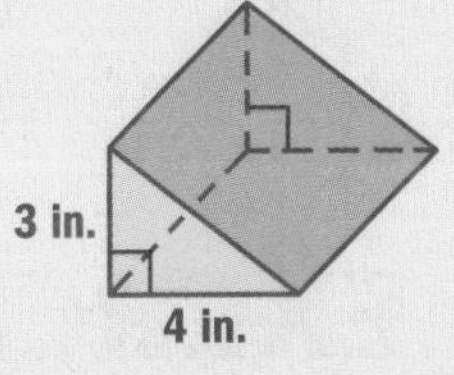

Ⓐ $V = 6h$　Ⓑ $V = 12h$

Ⓒ $V = 18h$　Ⓓ $V = 24h$

About the Standards
In Example 3, you expressed in symbolic form the relationship between the volume and the height of a triangular prism. This is part of Grade 6 Standard AF 3.2.

SOLUTION

STEP 1 **Find** the area of the triangular base.

$$B = \frac{1}{2}(4)(3) = 6$$

STEP 2 **Find** the equation for the volume of the prism.

$V = Bh$	**Write formula for volume of prism.**
$= 6h$	**Substitute 6 for *B*.**

▸ **Answer** The equation $V = 6h$ could be used to find the height of the prism. The correct answer is A. Ⓐ Ⓑ Ⓒ Ⓓ

✓ GUIDED PRACTICE for Examples 2 and 3

4. Find the volume of the triangular prism below.

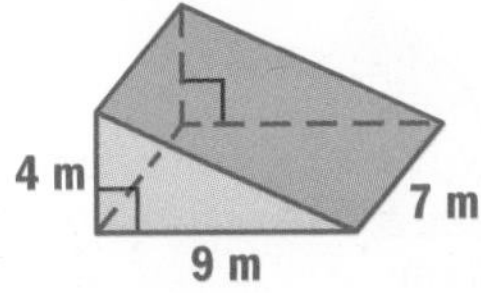

5. Find an equation for the volume *V* of the triangular prism below.

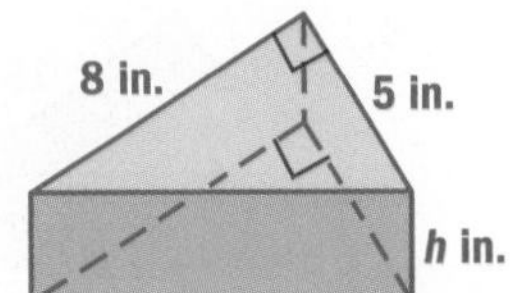

EXAMPLE 4 Finding the Height of a Rectangular Prism

The rectangular prism has a volume of 1440 cubic millimeters. Find the height of the prism.

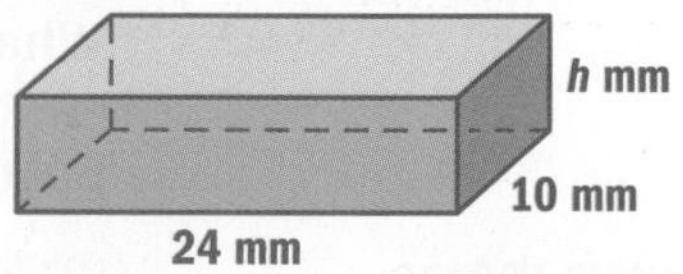

SOLUTION

$V = Bh$	**Write formula for volume of prism.**
$1440 = (24 \cdot 10)h$	**Substitute 1440 for *V* and (24 · 10) for *B*.**
$1440 = 240h$	**Multiply.**
$\frac{1440}{240} = \frac{240h}{240}$	**Divide each side by 240.**
$6 = h$	**Simplify.**

▸ **Answer** The height of the prism is 6 millimeters.

AVOID ERRORS

Make sure you use the correct units when writing your answer. Use linear units to describe the length, width, or height of an object.

✓ GUIDED PRACTICE for Example 4

6. A rectangular prism has a length of 18 inches, a width of 6 inches, and a volume of 864 cubic inches. What is the height of the prism?

11.4 EXERCISES

HOMEWORK KEY

= **MULTIPLE CHOICE PRACTICE** Exs. 14, 18, 26, 32–34

= **HINTS AND HOMEWORK HELP** for Exs. 3, 9, 25 at classzone.com

SKILLS • PROBLEM SOLVING • REASONING

1. **VOCABULARY** *Describe* how to find the volume of a prism.

2. **WRITING** *Explain* the difference between volume and surface area.

SEE EXAMPLES 1 AND 2 on pp. 596–597 for Exs. 3–11

FINDING VOLUME Find the volume of the prism.

3.
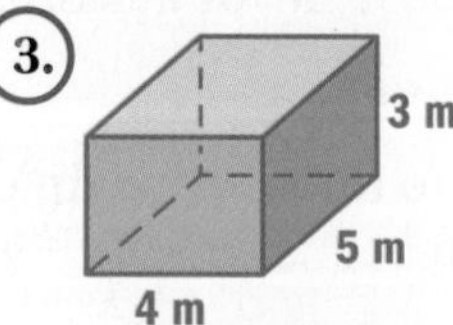

4.
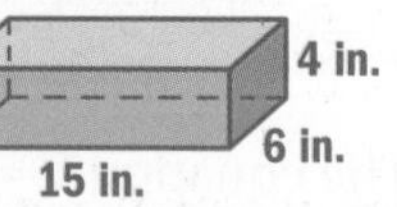

5.
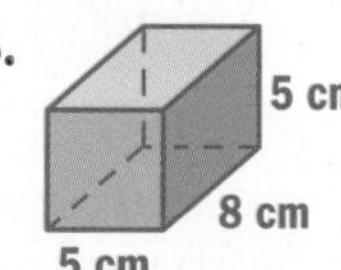

6.
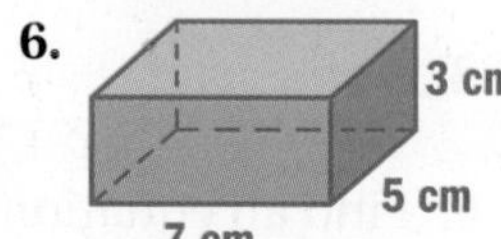

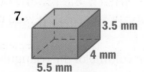

7. 3.5 mm, 4 mm, 5.5 mm

8.
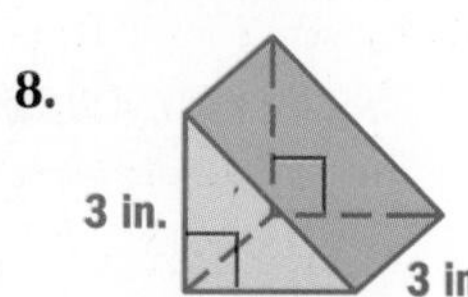

9.
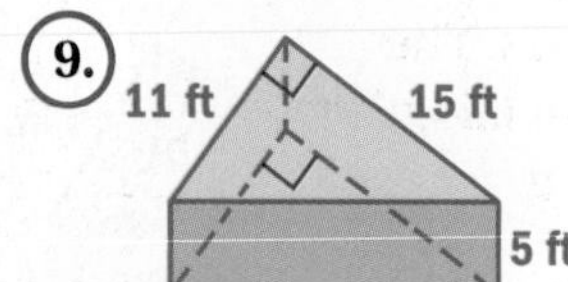

10.
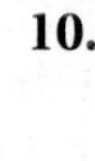
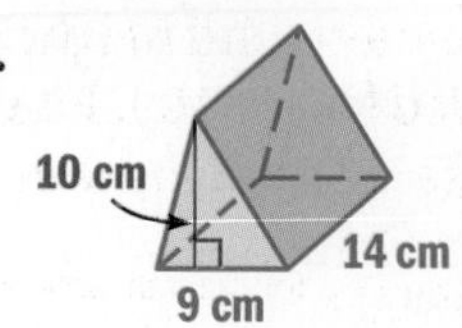

11.

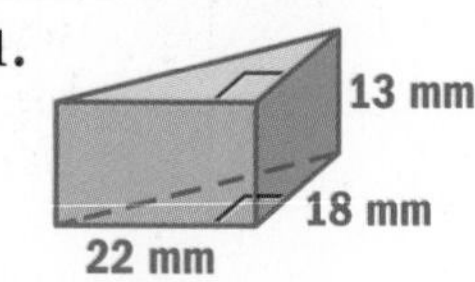

SEE EXAMPLES 1 AND 2
on pp. 596–597
for Exs. 12–13

ERROR ANALYSIS ***Describe*** **and correct the error in finding the volume.**

12.

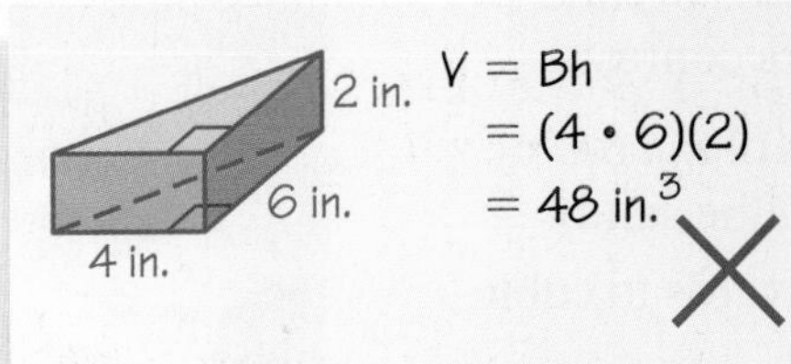

13.

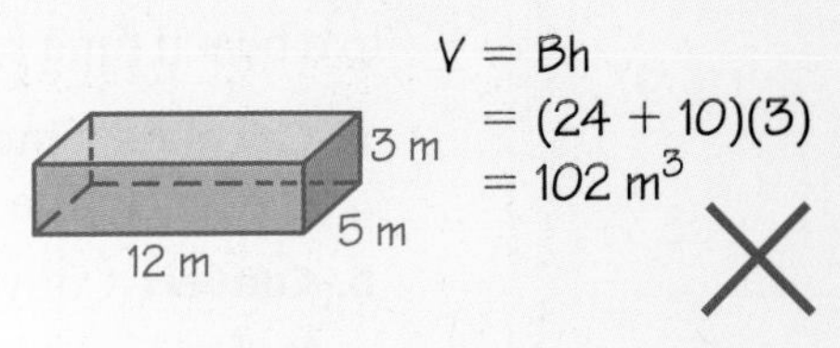

SEE EXAMPLE 3
on p. 597
for Ex. 14

14. ◆ **MULTIPLE CHOICE** A rectangular prism has length 10 feet, height 7 feet, and volume V cubic feet. Which equation could be used to find the width w of the prism (in feet)?

Ⓐ $V = 17w$ Ⓑ $V = 35w$ Ⓒ $V = 70w$ Ⓓ $V = 140w$

SEE EXAMPLE 4
on p. 598
for Exs. 15–18

ALGEBRA **Find the height of the prism with the given volume V.**

15. $V = 560 \text{ ft}^3$

16. $V = 420 \text{ cm}^3$

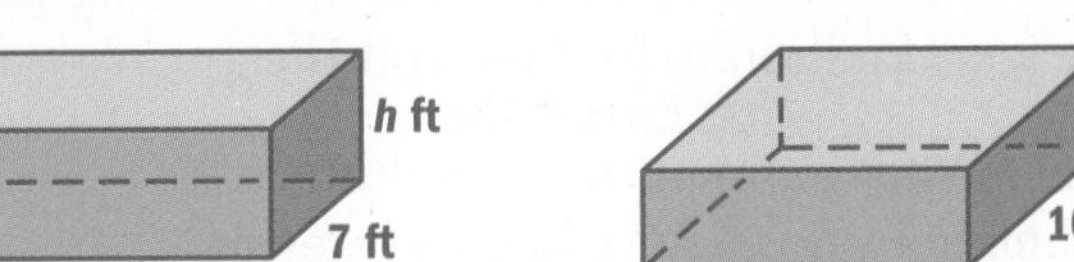

17. $V = 924 \text{ mm}^3$

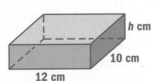

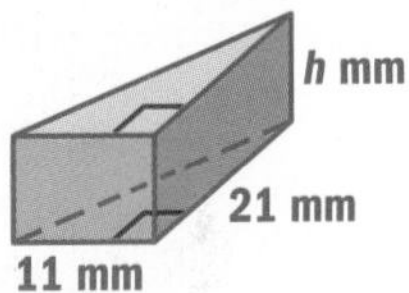

18. ◆ **MULTIPLE CHOICE** A rectangular prism has a volume of 432 cubic feet. Its bases are squares with side lengths of 6 feet. What is its height?

Ⓐ 3 ft Ⓑ 6 ft Ⓒ 12 ft Ⓓ 72 ft

19. **OPEN-ENDED** A rectangular prism has dimensions 3 in. by 4 in. by 5 in. *Describe* a rectangular prism with the same volume but less surface area.

CONNECT SKILLS TO PROBLEM SOLVING **Exercises 20–22 will help you prepare for problem solving.**

Tell whether you would find the surface area or the volume of the object.

20. You want to know how much paint you need to paint the outside of a box.

21. You want to know how much space is inside a glass cage for a lizard.

22. You want to know how much glitter will fit in a container.

SEE EXAMPLE 1
on p. 596
for Ex. 23

23. **WATERMELONS** In Japan, some farmers grow watermelons in glass cubes, so the fruit fits better in refrigerators. What is the volume of a cubic watermelon whose edge length is 18 centimeters?

California @HomeTutor for problem solving help at classzone.com

Edge length of cube: 18 cm

24. **MEASUREMENT** An aquarium has length 51 centimeters, width 25 centimeters, and height 30 centimeters. The aquarium is filled with water. Find the mass (in kilograms) of the water. Use this fact for water: $1 \text{ cm}^3 = 1 \text{ g}$.

California @HomeTutor for problem solving help at classzone.com

25. **MULTI-STEP PROBLEM** The truck at the right must deliver 15 cubic yards of sand to a beach for a sand sculpture contest.

a. **Calculate** Find the volume of the *bed* of the truck (the part holding the sand).

b. **Convert** Convert 15 cubic yards to cubic feet.

c. **Analyze** How many trips to the beach must the truck make? *Justify* your answer.

26. ◆ **MULTIPLE CHOICE** A refrigerator has a length of 36 inches, a width of 33 inches, and a height of 72 inches. What is its volume in cubic feet?

(A) 24.75 ft^3 (B) 49.5 ft^3 (C) $41{,}472\text{ ft}^3$ (D) $82{,}944\text{ ft}^3$

27. **REASONING** *Explain* how you can find the volume of the triangular prism at the right by first finding the volume of a rectangular prism. Then use your method to find the volume.

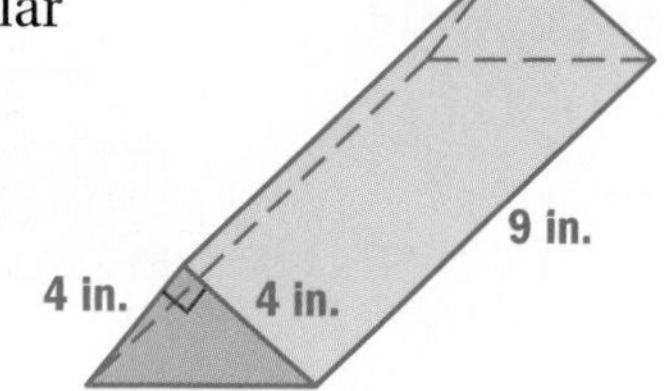

28. **SHORT RESPONSE** What happens to the volume of a prism when its height is doubled? when the area of the base is doubled? *Explain* your reasoning and give examples to support your answers.

29. **PUZZLE PROBLEM** A woodworker needs to design a cabinet in the shape of a rectangular prism with at most 300 square inches of wood. What whole number dimensions will give the cabinet the greatest volume?

30. **CHALLENGE** Find the volume of the hexagonal prism at the right. *Explain* how you found your answer.

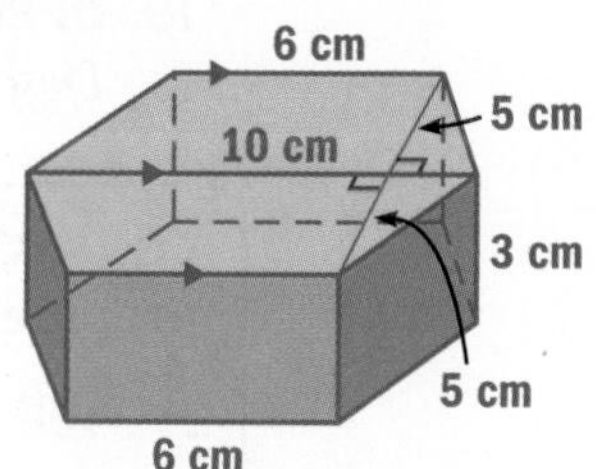

31. (xy) **CHALLENGE** A rectangular prism is built from 40 red cubes and 3 green cubes. The green cubes are twice as wide as the red cubes. Find the volume of the prism in terms of the width x of a red cube. Simplify the expression.

◆ CALIFORNIA STANDARDS SPIRAL REVIEW

MG 1.1 32. Which equation could be used to find the area A (in square inches) of a circle with a diameter of 24 inches? *(p. 555)*

(A) $A = 24\pi$ (B) $A = 48\pi$ (C) $A = 144\pi$ (D) $A = 576\pi$

MG 2.3 33. A quadrilateral has four congruent sides and no right angles. Which term most precisely describes the quadrilateral? *(p. 482)*

(A) Parallelogram (B) Rhombus (C) Square (D) Trapezoid

SDAP 2.4 34. When conducting a survey you ask, "Do you support our successful governor in his bid for reelection?" Which word makes the question potentially biased? *(p. 359)*

(A) Support (B) Successful (C) Bid (D) Reelection

11.5 Volume of Cylinders

Math and MUSIC
Ex. 22, p. 604

Standards **MG 1.3 Know and use the formulas for the volume of** triangular prisms and **cylinders (area of base × height); compare these formulas and explain the similarity between them and the formula for the volume of a rectangular solid.**

Connect ***Before*** you found volumes of prisms. ***Now*** you will find volumes of cylinders.

KEY VOCABULARY
- **cylinder,** *p. 575*
- **volume,** *p. 596*

The activity on page 595 suggests that the volume of a prism is the product of the area of a base and the height. The volume of a cylinder can be found the same way.

The area of the base is the number of unit squares that cover the base.

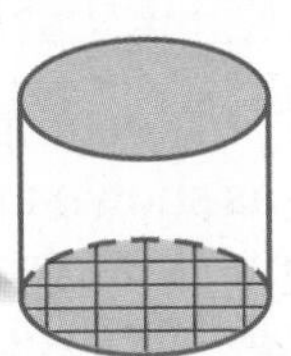

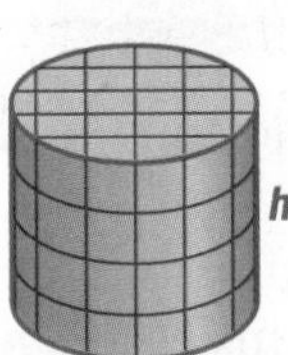

The height is the number of layers of unit cubes that fit in the solid.

KEY CONCEPT *For Your Notebook*

Volume of a Cylinder

Words The volume of a cylinder is the product of the area of a base and the height.

Algebra $V = Bh = \pi r^2 h$

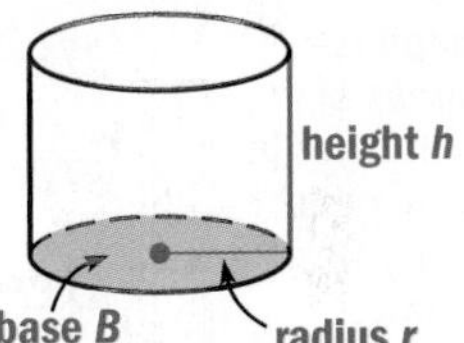

EXAMPLE 1 Finding the Volume of a Cylinder

Find the volume of the cylinder. Use 3.14 for π.

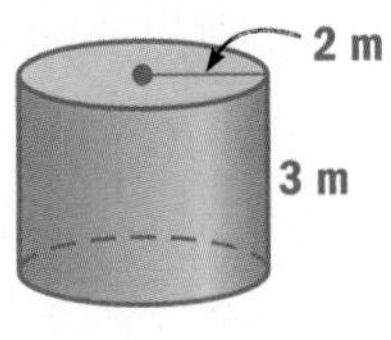

$V = \pi r^2 h$	**Write formula for volume of cylinder.**
$\approx (3.14)(2)^2(3)$	**Substitute values.**
$= 37.68$	**Multiply.**

▸ **Answer** The volume of the cylinder is about 37.68 cubic meters.

CHECK To check that your answer is reasonable, use 3 for π.

$V \approx (3)(2)^2(3)$	**Substitute values.**
$= 36$	**Multiply.**

Because 36 is close to 37.68, a volume of 37.68 cubic meters is reasonable.

About the Standards

In Example 1, you use estimation to verify the reasonableness of the calculated result, as expected in Grade 6 Standard MR 2.1.

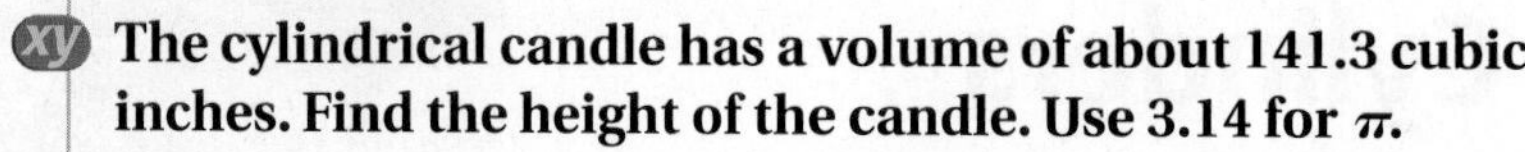

EXAMPLE 2 Finding the Height of a Cylinder

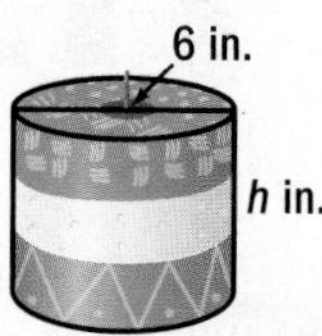

The cylindrical candle has a volume of about 141.3 cubic inches. Find the height of the candle. Use 3.14 for π.

AVOID ERRORS

Be sure to use the radius, *not* the diameter, in the formula for the volume of a cylinder.

The radius of the candle is half the diameter, or 3 inches.

$V = \pi r^2 h$	**Write formula for volume of cylinder.**
$141.3 \approx (3.14)(3)^2 h$	**Substitute values.**
$141.3 \approx 28.26h$	**Multiply.**
$5 \approx h$	**Divide each side by 28.26.**

▶ **Answer** The height of the candle is about 5 inches.

EXAMPLE 3 ◆ Multiple Choice Practice

A hole in the shape of a rectangular prism is cut through a cylinder, as shown at the right. Which expression represents the volume of the solid in terms of the height h? Use 3.14 for π.

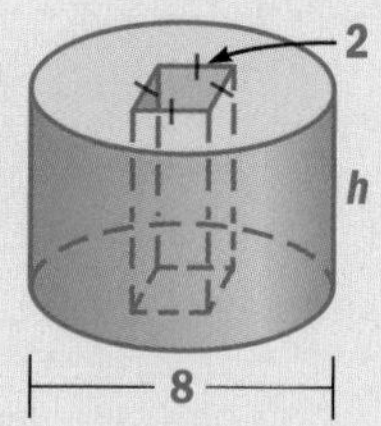

Ⓐ $46.24h$ Ⓑ $50.24h$

Ⓒ $196.96h$ Ⓓ $200.96h$

About the Standards

In earlier chapters, you found areas of polygons with holes in them. You can apply strategies from those problems to ones like Example 3, as expected in Grade 6 Standard MR 2.2.

SOLUTION

STEP 1 The volume of the cylinder is $\pi r^2 h \approx (3.14)(4^2)h = 50.24h$.

STEP 2 The volume of the hole is $Bh = (2 \cdot 2)h = 4h$.

STEP 3 Find the difference of the volumes: $50.24h - 4h = 46.24h$.

▶ **Answer** The expression $46.24h$ represents the volume of the solid. The correct answer is A. Ⓐ Ⓑ Ⓒ Ⓓ

✓ **GUIDED PRACTICE** for Examples 1, 2, and 3

Find the volume of the cylinder. Use 3.14 for π.

1. 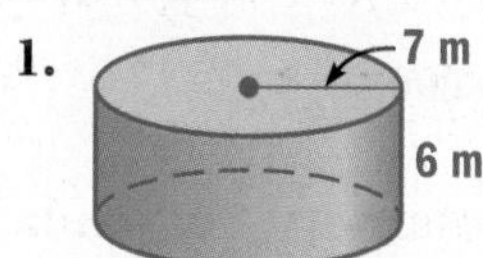

2. 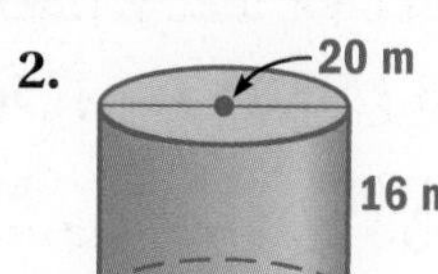

3. 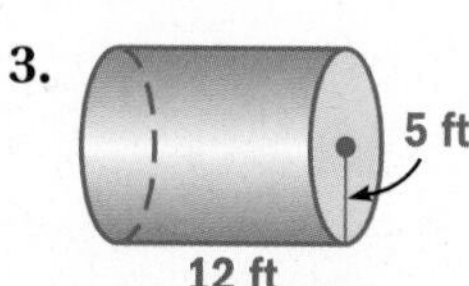

4. A cylinder has a radius of 4 inches and a volume of 251.2 cubic inches. Find the height of the cylinder. Use 3.14 for π.

5. **WHAT IF?** In Example 3, suppose that the cylinder has a diameter of 12 and that the hole has a length of 5 and a width of 3. Write an expression for the volume of the solid in terms of the height h.

11.5 EXERCISES

HOMEWORK KEY ◆ = **MULTIPLE CHOICE PRACTICE** Exs. 11, 15, 22, 31–33
○ = **HINTS AND HOMEWORK HELP** for Exs. 3, 13, 25 at classzone.com

SKILLS • PROBLEM SOLVING • REASONING

1. **VOCABULARY** Copy and complete: To find the volume of a cylinder, multiply the area of a(n) _?_ and the _?_.

2. **WRITING** *Compare* the formula for the volume of a triangular prism with the formula for the volume of a cylinder. How are they similar to the formula for the volume of a rectangular prism?

SEE EXAMPLE 1 on p. 601 for Exs. 3–11

FINDING VOLUME Find the volume of the cylinder. Use 3.14 for π.

3. 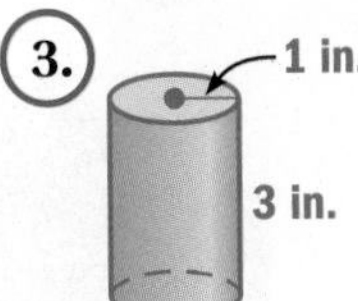

4. 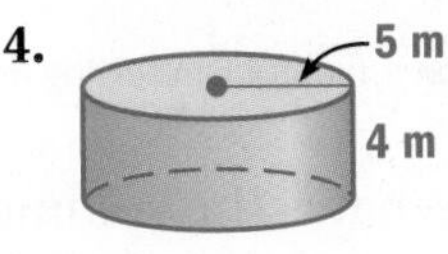

5. 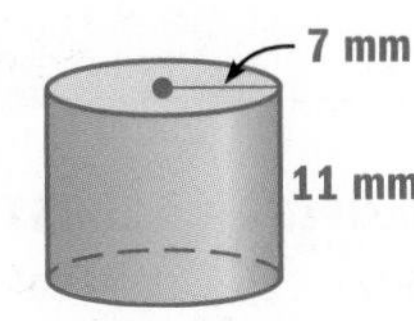

6. $r = 8$ ft, $h = 8$ ft

7. $d = 6$ in., $h = 4$ in.

8. $d = 8$ cm, $h = 9$ cm

ERROR ANALYSIS ***Describe*** **and correct the error in finding the volume.**

9. 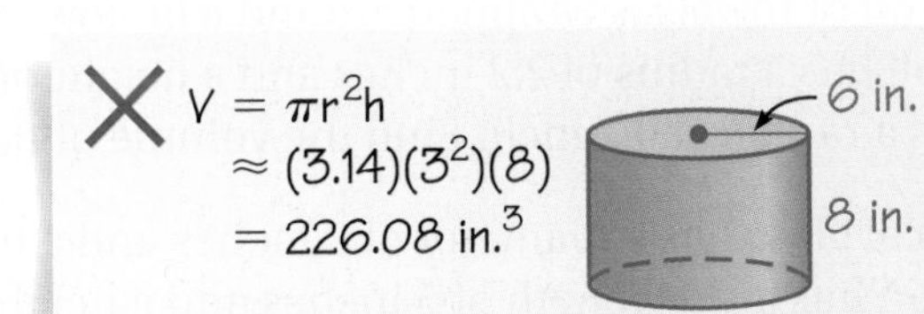

10. 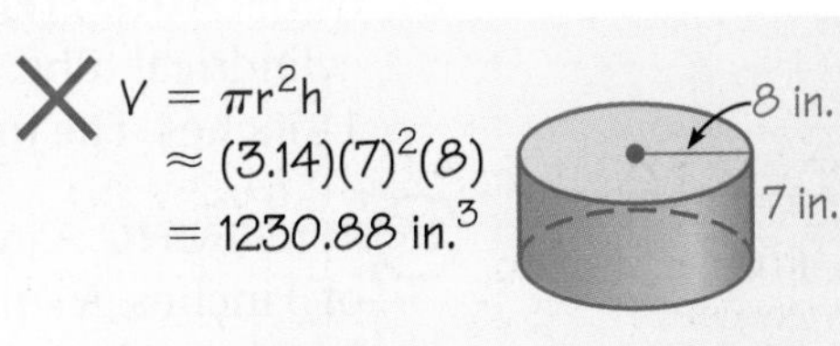

11. ◆ **MULTIPLE CHOICE** Which of the following are possible dimensions of a cylinder that has a volume of about 250 cubic units?

Ⓐ $r = 8, h = 10$ Ⓑ $r = 1, h = 4$ Ⓒ $r = 2, h = 6$ Ⓓ $r = 3, h = 9$

SEE EXAMPLE 2 on p. 602 for Exs. 12–15

ALGEBRA Find the height of the cylinder. Use 3.14 for π.

12. $V = 25.12 \text{ cm}^3, r = 1 \text{ cm}$

13. $V = 5024 \text{ in.}^3, d = 16 \text{ in.}$

14. $V = 5338 \text{ ft}^3, d = 20 \text{ ft}$

15. ◆ **MULTIPLE CHOICE** A cylinder has a radius of 9 feet and a volume of about 1907.55 cubic feet. What is its approximate height? Use 3.14 for π.

Ⓐ 3 ft Ⓑ 7.5 ft Ⓒ 23.55 ft Ⓓ 67.5 ft

SEE EXAMPLE 3 on p. 602 for Exs. 16–18

ALGEBRA Write an expression for the volume of the solid.

16. 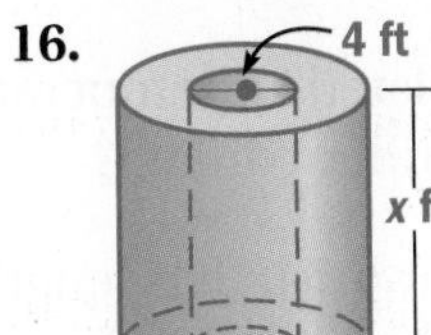

17. 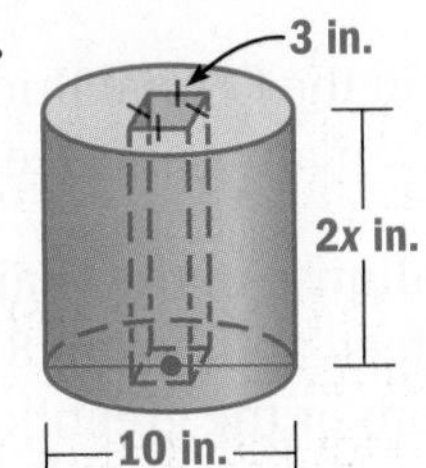

18. 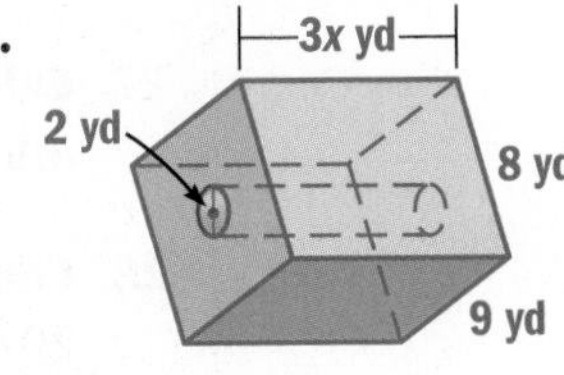

CONNECT SKILLS TO PROBLEM SOLVING **Exercises 19–21 will help you prepare for problem solving.**

Use the following information: A cylindrical glass bead is 10 millimeters long and has a radius of 2 millimeters. A cylindrical hole that passes through the bead has a radius of 0.25 millimeter.

19. Find the volume of the bead, including the hole.

20. Find the volume of the hole.

21. How much glass is in the actual bead?

SEE EXAMPLE 1 on p. 601 for Ex. 22

22. ◆ **MULTIPLE CHOICE** A cylindrical drum has a diameter of 14 inches and a height of 5.5 inches. What is the approximate volume of the drum?

Ⓐ 665 in.^{3} Ⓑ 847 in.^{3} Ⓒ 1370 in.^{3} Ⓓ 3385 in.^{3}

California @HomeTutor for problem solving help at classzone.com

SEE EXAMPLE 3 on p. 602 for Exs. 23–24

23. STORAGE UNITS What is the volume of the chest at the right? *Explain* how you found your answer. Check using estimation.

California @HomeTutor for problem solving help at classzone.com

24. HOUSEHOLD ITEMS A roll of towels is wrapped around a hollow cylindrical tube. The roll has a radius of 2.2 inches and a height of 11 inches. The tube has a radius of 0.7 inch. Find the volume of the roll.

(25.) REASONING A cylindrical glass has a diameter of 2 inches and a height of 3 inches. A square pan has a side length of 5 inches and a height of 3 inches. About how many glasses of water fill the pan? *Explain.*

READING *IN* MATH **Read the information below for Exercises 26–28.**

Biosphere The Myriad Gardens Crystal Bridge is a nature conservatory in Oklahoma City. The bridge is composed of two solids. The building is shaped approximately like a cylinder with a diameter of 70 feet and a height of 224 feet. A small cylindrical biosphere room that houses rainforest reptiles is attached to one end of the bridge. This room has a diameter of 10 feet and a height of 20 feet.

26. Calculate Find the surface area of the Myriad Gardens Crystal Bridge, including the biosphere room.

27. Calculate The air in the Crystal Bridge has to be regulated for temperature and humidity. How many cubic feet of air does the bridge contain?

28. Compare A greenhouse in the shape of a rectangular prism has length 20 feet, width 10 feet, and height 8 feet. Which has the greater volume, the biosphere room or the greenhouse? *Justify* your answer.

29. **REASONING** A cylinder fits snugly inside a rectangular prism with a square base. The heights of the cylinder and the prism are both 8 inches. The diameter of the cylinder is equal to the side length of the base of the prism. Find the ratio of the volume of the cylinder to the volume of the prism when the diameter is 4, 5, and 6 inches. *Compare* the ratios.

30. **CHALLENGE** Three tennis balls fit tightly in a can. Find the volume of the can. Round to the nearest cubic centimeter.

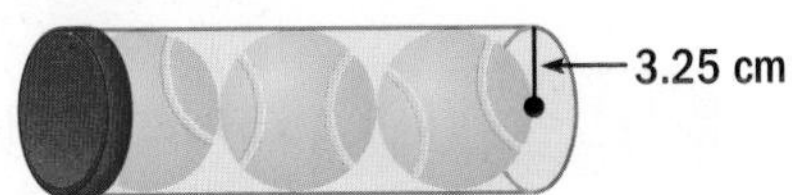

◆ CALIFORNIA STANDARDS SPIRAL REVIEW

MG 2.1 31. Angles A and B do not share a side. The measure of $\angle A$ is 34° and the measure of $\angle B$ is 56°. What kind of angles are $\angle A$ and $\angle B$? ***(p. 463)***

Ⓐ Adjacent Ⓑ Complementary

Ⓒ Supplementary Ⓓ Vertical

AF 3.2 32. A trapezoid has one base of 6 inches and a height of 10 inches. Which equation can you use to find the length b of the other base? ***(p. 541)***

Ⓐ $A = 5b + 30$ Ⓑ $A = 5b + 60$ Ⓒ $A = 10b + 30$ Ⓓ $A = 10b + 60$

SDAP 1.1 33. The data below show the ages of 10 people attending an art class. Which statement about the ages of the 10 people is true? ***(p. 364)***

21, 24, 28, 28, 31, 33, 36, 42, 45, 46

Ⓐ The mean is 33. Ⓑ The mode is 28.

Ⓒ The mean and mode are equal. Ⓓ The median is 31.

QUIZ *for Lessons 11.4–11.5*

Find the volume of the prism. *(p. 596)*

1.

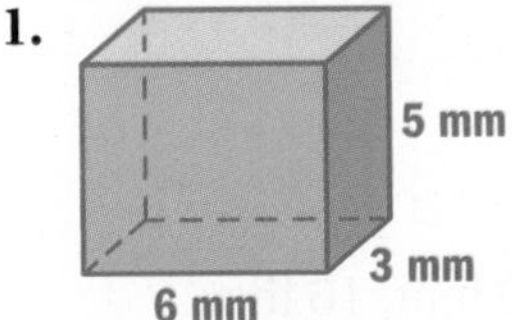

2.

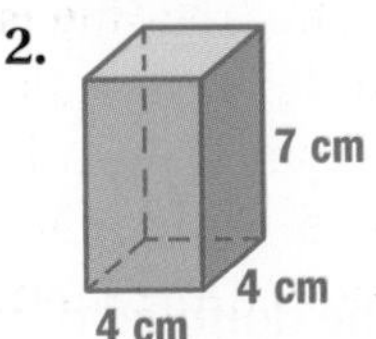

3.

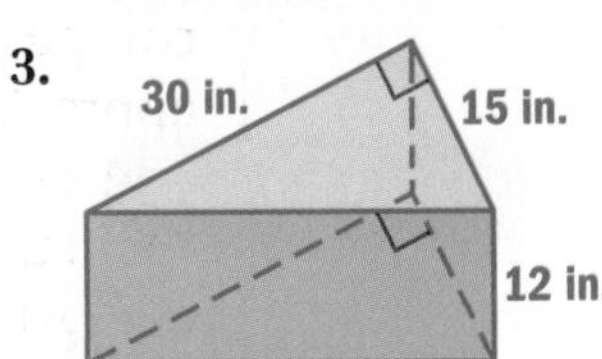

Find the volume of the cylinder. Use 3.14 for π. *(p 601)*

4.

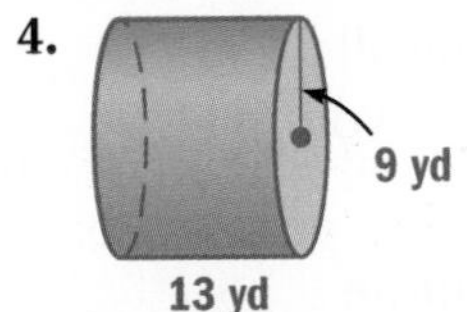

5.

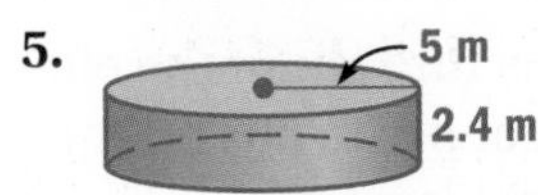

6.

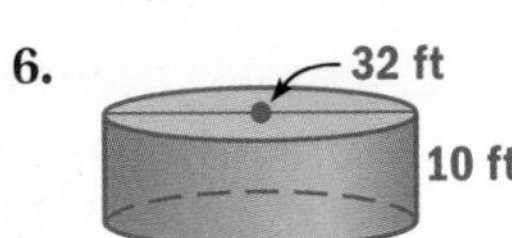

7. **BUILDING MATERIALS** A brick has a length of 8 inches, a width of 3.75 inches, and a volume of 67.5 cubic inches. Find the height of the brick. ***(p. 596)***

Technology **ACTIVITY** *Use after Lesson 11.5*

Standards

MR 1.2 Formulate and justify mathematical conjectures based on a general description of the mathematical question or problem posed.

11.5 Surface Area and Volume

QUESTION How can you use spreadsheet software to test conjectures about the effect of changing dimensions on surface area and volume?

EXAMPLE Describe the effect on the surface area and volume of the prism shown when all the dimensions are doubled.

Animated Math at classzone.com

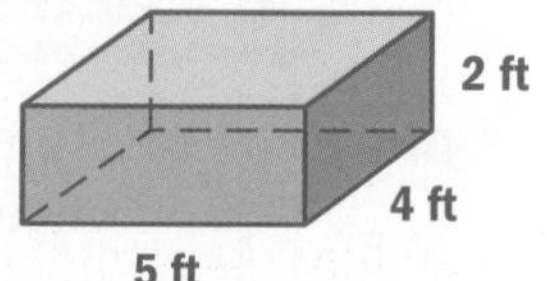

STEP 1 **Label** five columns in the first row of a spreadsheet as shown. Then enter the dimensions of the original prism and the formulas for surface area and volume as shown. Use * for multiplication.

	A	B	C	D	E
1	Length	Width	Height	Surface area	Volume
2	5	4	2	=2*A2*B2+2*A2*C2+2*B2*C2	=A2*B2*C2

STEP 2 **Enter** the doubled dimensions as shown. Then use the *Fill down* feature to have the spreadsheet calculate the surface area and volume of the new prism.

	A	B	C	D	E
1	Length	Width	Height	Surface area	Volume
2	5	4	2	76	40
3	10	8	4	304	320

STEP 3 **Compare** the calculated values for surface area and for volume. The surface area of the new prism is 4 times the surface area of the original prism. Its volume is 8 times the volume of the original.

PRACTICE

1. Repeat steps 2 and 3, entering the doubled dimensions 20 feet, 16 feet, and 8 feet into a new row. Then predict the surface area and volume of a rectangular prism with dimensions 40 feet, 32 feet, and 16 feet.

2. **REASONING** Make a conjecture about the effect that doubling all three dimensions of a rectangular prism has on the surface area and volume of the prism. *Justify* your reasoning.

3. Create a spreadsheet that calculates the surface area and volume of a cylinder for a given radius and height. Use PI() for π and ^2 for squaring. Make a conjecture about the effect on the surface area and volume of a cylinder when the radius and height are doubled or tripled.

MIXED REVIEW of Skills and Problem Solving

Multiple Choice Practice for Lessons 11.4–11.5

1. A block of cheese in the shape of a rectangular prism has dimensions 7.5 centimeters by 7.5 centimeters by 4 centimeters. What is the volume? **MG 1.3**

   Ⓐ 19 cm^3 Ⓑ 116.25 cm^3
   Ⓒ 225 cm^3 Ⓓ 232.5 cm^3

2. The triangular prism below has a volume of V cubic feet. Which equation could be used to find the length b? **AF 3.2**

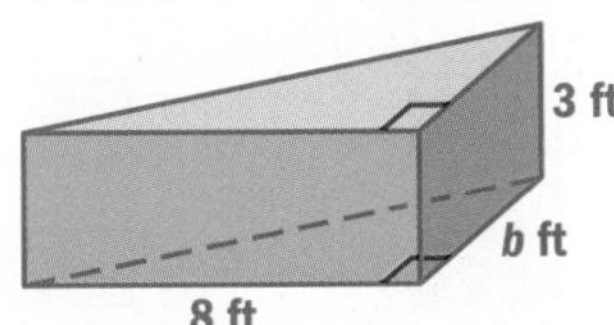

   Ⓐ $V = 4b$ Ⓑ $V = 8b$
   Ⓒ $V = 12b$ Ⓓ $V = 24b$

3. A rectangular prism has a length of 13 feet, a width of 8 feet, and a volume of 468 cubic feet. What is the height of the prism? **MG 1.3**

   Ⓐ 4.5 ft Ⓑ 4.75 ft
   Ⓒ 5 ft Ⓓ 5.25 ft

4. The paper lantern below is in the shape of a rectangular prism. What is the volume of the lantern? **MG 1.3**

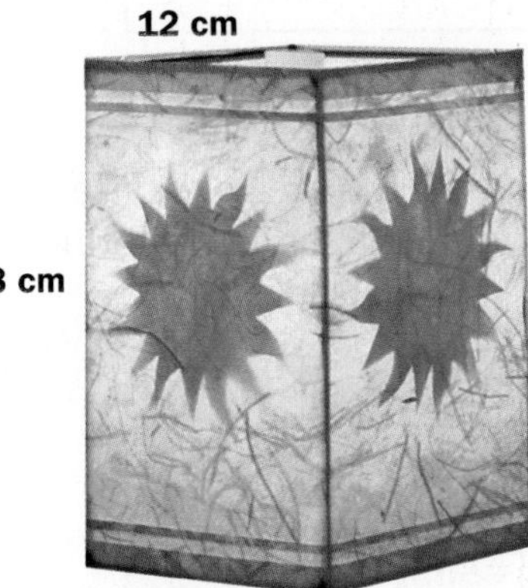

   Ⓐ 55 cm^3 Ⓑ 756 cm^3
   Ⓒ 1872 cm^3 Ⓓ 5040 cm^3

5. What is the volume of the triangular prism below? **MG 1.3**

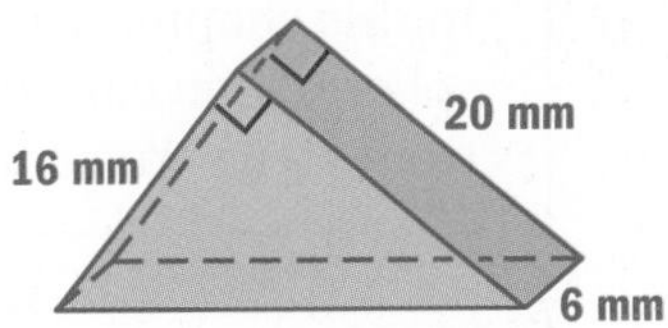

   Ⓐ 480 mm^3 Ⓑ 960 mm^3
   Ⓒ 1440 mm^3 Ⓓ 1920 mm^3

6. A box has the shape of a square prism with a height of 8 inches and square bases that are 4 inches by 4 inches. A cylinder fits snugly inside the box. What is the volume of the cylinder? **MG 1.3, MR 2.4**

   Ⓐ $32\pi\text{ in.}^3$ Ⓑ $40\pi\text{ in.}^3$
   Ⓒ $96\pi\text{ in.}^3$ Ⓓ $128\pi\text{ in.}^3$

7. A rectangular prism is cut out of a cylinder, as shown below. Which equation represents the volume V (in cubic inches) of the solid in terms of h? Use 3.14 for π. **AF 3.2, MR 2.2**

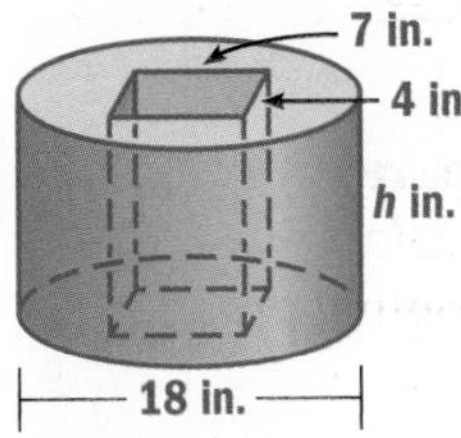

   Ⓐ $V = 226.34h$
   Ⓑ $V = 254.34h$
   Ⓒ $V = 989.36h$
   Ⓓ $V = 1017.36h$

8. A block of ice is in the shape of a cube. It has a surface area of 96 square centimeters. What is its volume? **MG 1.3, MR 2.5**

   Ⓐ 16 cm^3 Ⓑ 36 cm^3
   Ⓒ 64 cm^3 Ⓓ 256 cm^3

11 CHAPTER SUMMARY

Standards
AF 3.1, AF 3.2, MG 1.3, Gr. 5 MG 2.3

BIG IDEAS

For Your Notebook

Big Idea 1 Classifying and Sketching Views of Solids

In this chapter, you classified prisms, pyramids, cylinders, cones, and spheres. You can represent these solids by sketching the top, side, and front views. You can also sketch views of solids made from unit cubes.

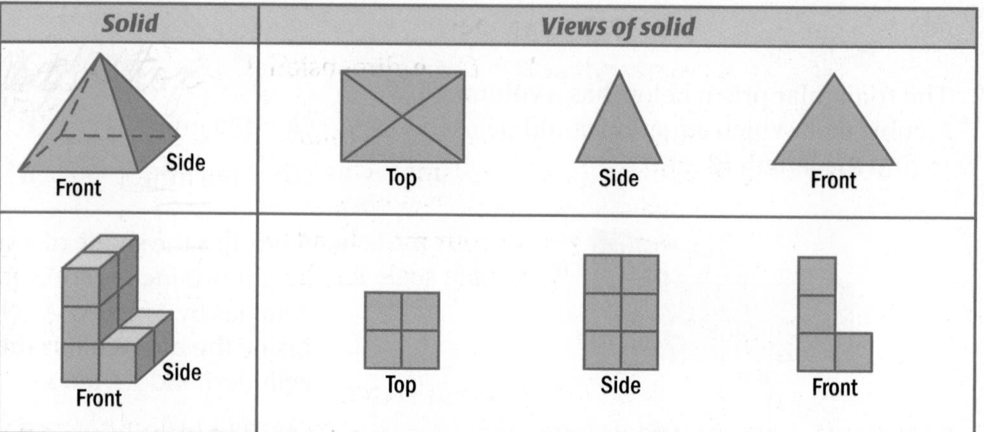

Big Idea 2 Finding Surface Areas of Prisms and Cylinders

The surface area of a solid is the sum of the areas of its outside surfaces. You can use a net or a formula to find the surface area of a rectangular prism or a cylinder.

Rectangular prism	*Cylinder*
h, w, l	r, h
$S = 2lw + 2lh + 2wh$	$S = 2\pi r^2 + 2\pi rh$

Big Idea 3 Finding Volumes of Prisms and Cylinders

The volume of a prism or cylinder is the product of the area of a base and the height. You can use the formulas for volume to write algebraic equations and to find the height of a prism or cylinder.

Prism		*Cylinder*
h, B	h, B, w, l	h, B, r
$V = Bh$	$V = lwh$	$V = Bh = \pi r^2 h$

CHAPTER PROBLEM

Standards
AF 3.1, AF 3.2, MG 1.3, Gr. 5 MG 2.3

APPLYING THE
BIG IDEAS

Big Idea 1
You sketch views of solids in **Step 2.**

Big Idea 2
You find surface areas of prisms and cylinders in **Step 3** and **Ex. 1.**

Big Idea 3
You find volumes of prisms and cylinders in **Step 3** and **Ex. 1.**

PROBLEM Architects sometimes use solids other than rectangular prisms in the designs of buildings, such as in the San Francisco Museum of Modern Art shown below. How can you represent a building using two- and three-dimensional models and find its surface area and volume?

STEP 1 **Make a model.**

Design and make a three-dimensional model of a building that is composed of any combination of rectangular prisms, triangular prisms, cylinders, and partial cylinders. Then measure the dimensions of your model and choose an appropriate scale for the actual building.

STEP 2 **Sketch different views.**

Sketch the top, side, and front views of your building. For example, these shapes are the top, side, and front views of the building shown above.

Top

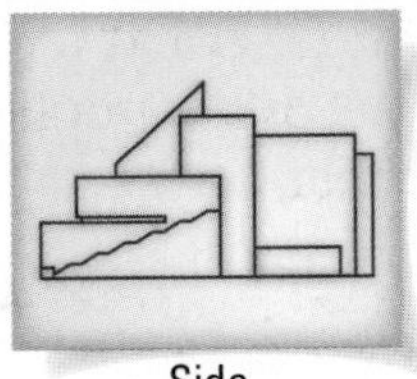
Side

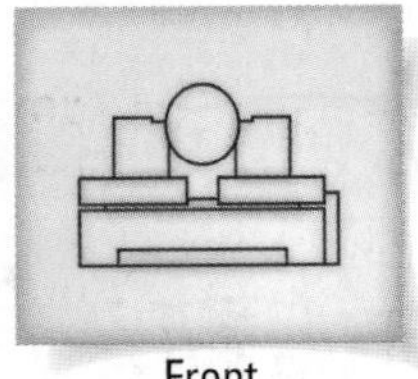
Front

STEP 3 **Find surface area and volume.**

Find the actual dimensions of your building using the scale that you chose in Step 1. Then find the surface area and volume of your building.

Extending the Problem

Use your results from the problem above to complete the exercises.

1. Double the dimensions of your building. Do the surface area and volume of your building also double? *Explain* your answers.
2. A building's ratio of surface area to volume measures how well the building retains heat. Buildings with lesser ratios retain heat better.
   a. Find the ratio of surface area to volume of your building.
   b. Compare your building's ratio with the ratio of a classmate's building. Whose building would retain heat better? *Explain.*

11 CHAPTER REVIEW

California @HomeTutor
classzone.com
- Multi-Language Visual Glossary
- Vocabulary practice

REVIEW KEY VOCABULARY

- solid, *p. 575*
- face, edge, vertex, *p. 575*
- prism, *p. 575*
- pyramid, *p. 575*
- cylinder, *p. 575*
- cone, *p. 575*
- sphere, *p. 575*
- cube, *p. 576*
- surface area, *p. 581*
- net, *p. 581*
- volume, *p. 596*

VOCABULARY EXERCISES

In Exercises 1–3, copy and complete the statement.

1. The sum of the areas of the faces of a solid is the __?__ of the solid.
2. The amount of space that a solid occupies is the __?__ of the solid.
3. A rectangular prism with 6 congruent square faces is called a(n) __?__.
4. **NOTETAKING SKILLS** Make a *four square diagram* like the one on page 574 for *prism*.

REVIEW EXAMPLES AND EXERCISES

11.1 Visualizing Solids *pp. 575–579*

Gr. 5 MG 2.3

EXAMPLE

Classify the solid. Then sketch the top, side, and front views.

Side

Front

The solid has 2 congruent parallel circular bases.
The solid is a cylinder.

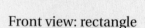

Top view: rectangle

Side view: circle

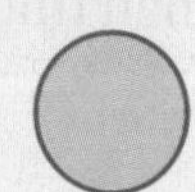

Front view: rectangle

EXERCISES

SEE EXAMPLES 1, 2, AND 3 on pp. 575–577 for Exs. 5–7

Classify the solid, if possible. Then sketch the top, side, and front views. Assume that there are no hidden cubes besides those supporting the cubes you can see.

5.
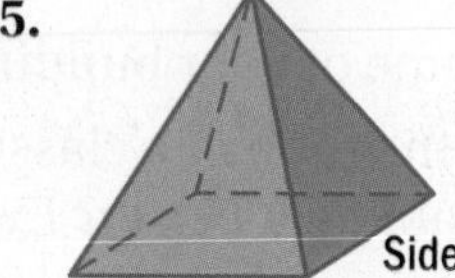

6.
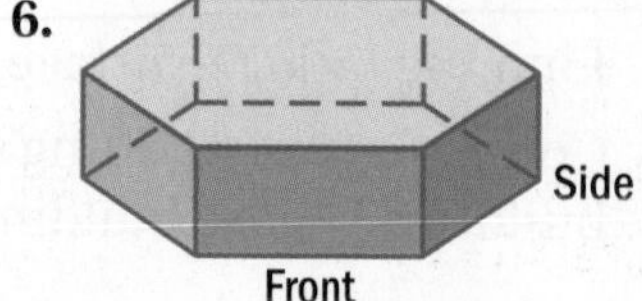

7.
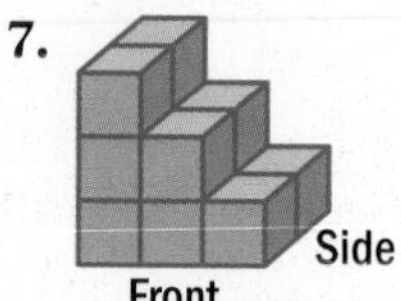

11.2 Surface Area of Prisms

pp. 581–586

AF 3.2

EXAMPLE

Write an equation for the surface area S (in square inches) of the rectangular prism.

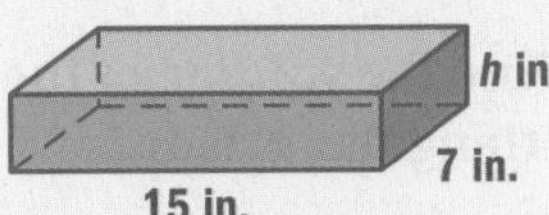

$S = 2lw + 2lh + 2wh$ **Write formula for surface area.**

$= 2(15)(7) + 2(15)h + 2(7)h$ **Substitute values.**

$= 210 + 30h + 14h$ **Multiply.**

$= 210 + 44h$ **Simplify.**

EXERCISES

SEE EXAMPLES 1, 2, 3, AND 4 on pp. 581–583 for Exs. 8–11

Find the surface area of the prism.

8. 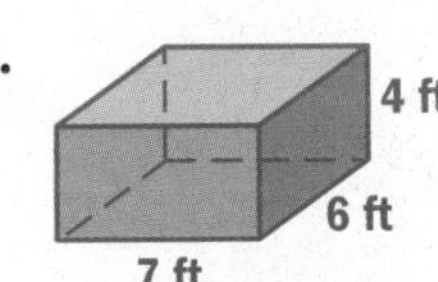

9. 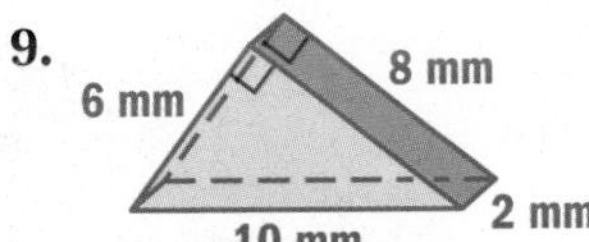

10. 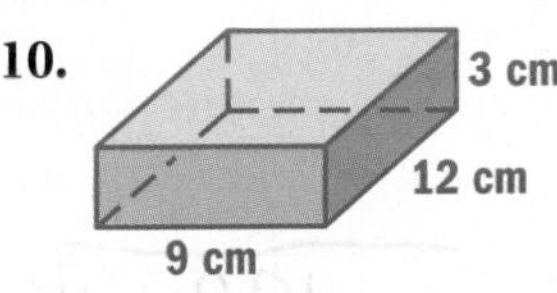

11. Write an equation for the surface area S (in square inches) of a rectangular prism with length 6 inches, width 3.5 inches, and height h inches.

11.3 Surface Area of Cylinders

pp. 589–593

AF 3.1

EXAMPLE

Find the surface area of the cylinder. Use 3.14 for π.

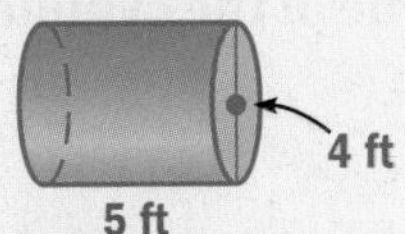

Because the diameter is 4 feet, the radius is 2 feet.

$S = 2\pi r^2 + 2\pi rh$ **Write formula for surface area.**

$\approx 2(3.14)(2)^2 + 2(3.14)(2)(5)$ **Substitute values.**

$= 87.92 \text{ ft}^2$ **Simplify.**

EXERCISES

SEE EXAMPLE 2 on p. 590 for Ex. 12

12. Find the surface area of the cylinder. Use 3.14 for π.

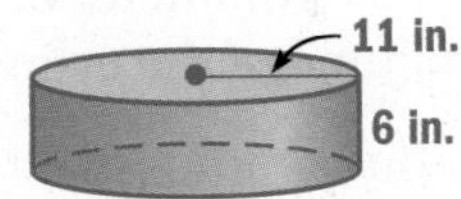

11.4 Volume of Prisms

pp. 596–600

MG 1.3

EXAMPLE

Find the volume of the triangular prism.

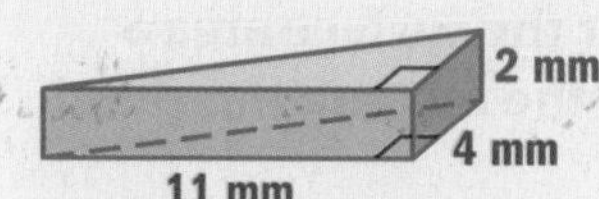

$V = Bh$ **Write formula for volume.**

$= \left(\frac{1}{2}(11)(4)\right)(2)$ **Substitute values.**

$= 44 \text{ mm}^3$ **Multiply.**

EXERCISES

SEE EXAMPLES 1, 2, AND 4 on pp. 596–598 for Exs. 13–16

Find the volume of the prism.

13.

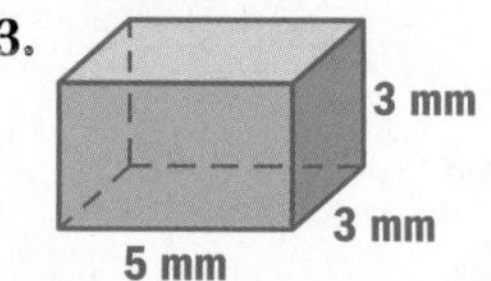

14.

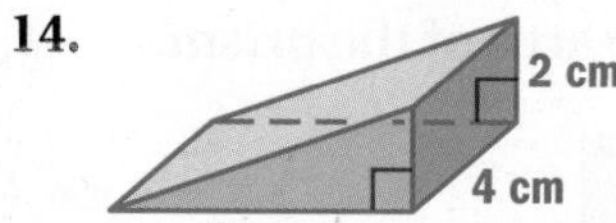

15.

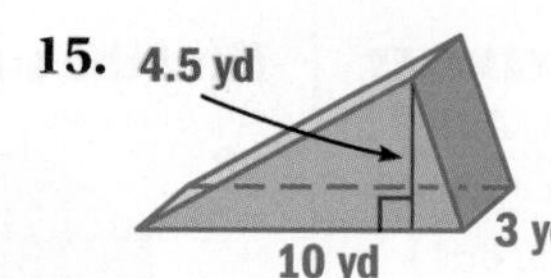

16. A rectangular prism has a length of 8 yards, a width of 12 yards, and a volume of 1344 cubic yards. Find the height of the prism.

11.5 Volume of Cylinders

pp. 601–605

MG 1.3

EXAMPLE

Find the volume of the cylinder. Use 3.14 for π.

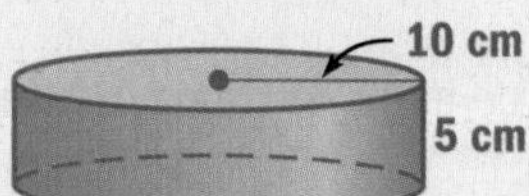

$V = \pi r^2 h$ **Write formula for volume.**

$\approx (3.14)(10)^2(5)$ **Substitute values.**

$= 1570 \text{ cm}^3$ **Simplify.**

EXERCISES

SEE EXAMPLES 1 AND 2 on pp. 601–602 for Exs. 17–18

17. A cylinder has a diameter of 6 meters and a height of 6.5 meters. Find the volume of the cylinder. Use 3.14 for π.

18. A cylinder has a radius of 20 feet and a volume of 11,304 cubic feet. Find the height of the cylinder. Use 3.14 for π.

11 CHAPTER TEST

VOCABULARY Copy and complete the statement.

1. A three-dimensional figure that encloses a part of space is a(n) __?__.
2. The net of a(n) __?__ consists of two circles and a rectangle.

Classify the solid, if possible. Then sketch the top, side, and front views of the solid. Assume that there are no hidden cubes besides those supporting the cubes you can see.

3. 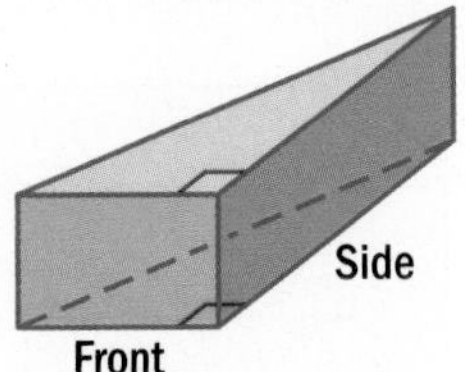

4. 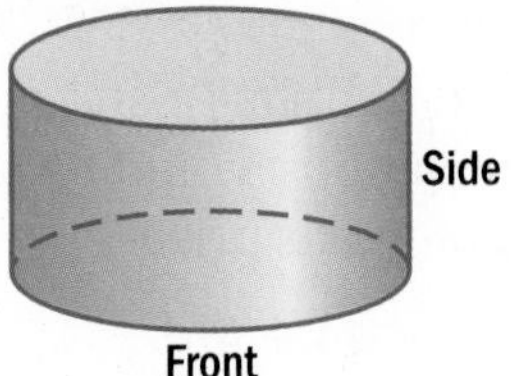

5. 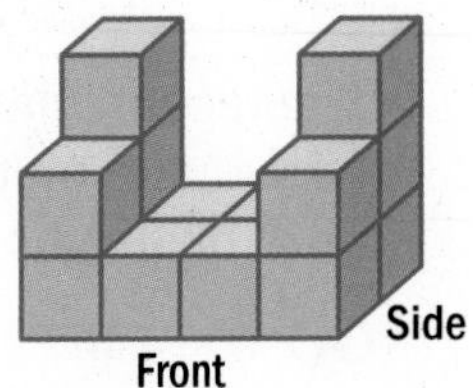

Find the surface area and volume of the prism.

6. 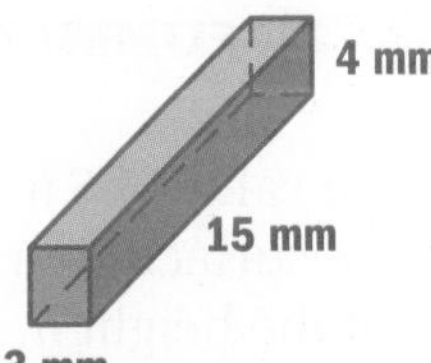

7. 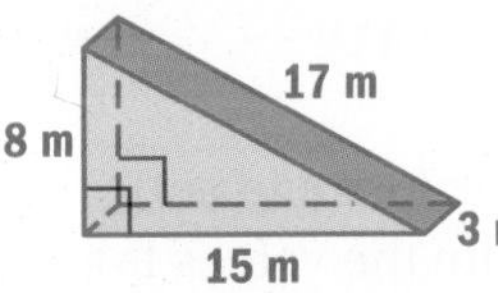

8. 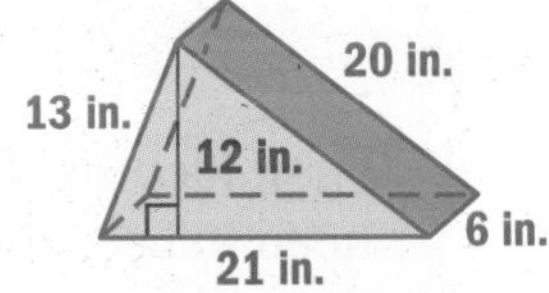

Find the surface area and volume of the cylinder. Use 3.14 for π.

9. 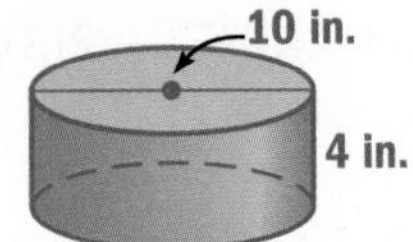

10. 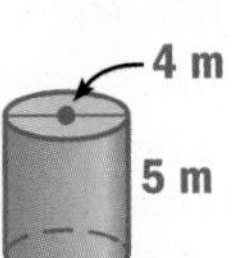

11. 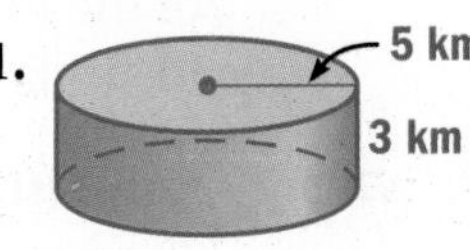

12. **WRITING** *Describe* the similarities among the formulas for the volumes of a rectangular prism, a triangular prism, and a cylinder. *Describe* the differences among these formulas.

13. A rectangular prism has a width of 4.5 inches, a length of 5 inches, and a volume of 135 cubic inches. Find the height of the prism.

14. A rectangular prism has a length of 9 centimeters, a width of 7 centimeters, and a height of $2n$ centimeters. Write an equation for the surface area S (in square centimeters) of the rectangular prism.

15. **DRUMS** Find the surface area and volume of the cylindrical drum at the right. Use 3.14 for π.

16. **DVD CASE** A standard DVD case is a rectangular prism that is 19 centimeters long, 13.5 centimeters wide, and 1.4 centimeters high. Find the surface area and volume of the DVD case.

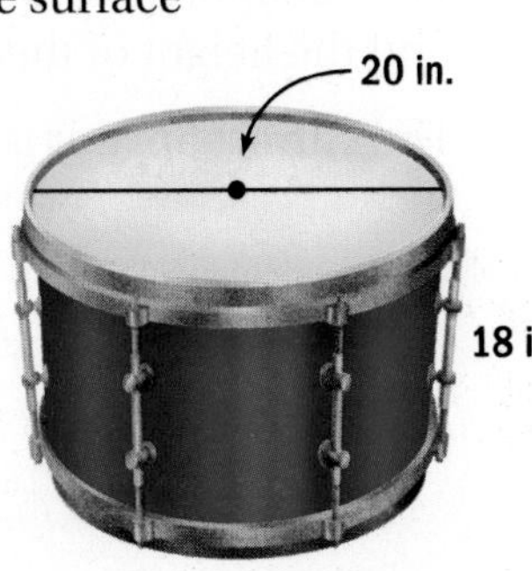

11 ◆ MULTIPLE CHOICE STRATEGIES

STRATEGIES YOU'LL USE:
- **SOLVE DIRECTLY**
- **ELIMINATE CHOICES**

Standards
AF 3.1, AF 3.2

If you have trouble solving a multiple choice problem directly, you may be able to use another approach to eliminate incorrect answer choices and obtain the correct answer.

PROBLEM 1

The rectangular prism at the right has a surface area of S square meters. Which equation could be used to find the height h of the rectangular prism?

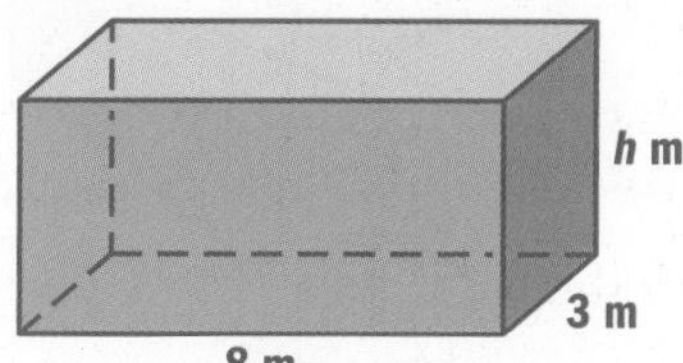

Ⓐ $S = 24h$ Ⓑ $S = 44 + 4h^2$

Ⓒ $S = 24 + 22h$ Ⓓ $S = 48 + 22h$

Strategy 1 SOLVE DIRECTLY

First, identify the geometric formula you need to use. Then substitute the values for the variables and simplify.

STEP 1 **Choose** the formula to use. You want to describe the surface area of the rectangular prism, so use the formula $S = 2lw + 2lh + 2wh$.

STEP 2 **Substitute** 8 for l and 3 for w. Then simplify the right side of the equation.

$S = 2lw + 2lh + 2wh$

$= 2(8)(3) + 2(8)h + 2(3)h$

$= 48 + 16h + 6h$

$= 48 + 22h$

The equation $S = 48 + 22h$ can be used to find the height of the rectangular prism.

The correct answer is D. Ⓐ Ⓑ Ⓒ Ⓓ

Strategy 2 ELIMINATE CHOICES

Compare the value of S in each answer choice to the surface area of the prism for one value of the height h, such as 5.

Surface area of rectangular prism:

$S = 2lw + 2lh + 2wh$

$= 2(8)(3) + 2(8)(5) + 2(3)(5)$

$= 48 + 80 + 30$, or 158

Choice A: $S = 24h$

$= 24(5)$, or 120 ✗

Choice B: $S = 44 + 4h^2$

$= 44 + 4(5)^2$

$= 44 + 100$, or 144 ✗

Choice C: $S = 24 + 22h$

$= 24 + 22(5)$

$= 24 + 110$, or 134 ✗

Choice D: $S = 48 + 22h$

$= 48 + 22(5)$

$= 48 + 110$, or 158 ✓

The correct answer is D. Ⓐ Ⓑ Ⓒ Ⓓ

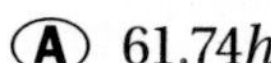

PROBLEM 2

A cylindrical hole is cut through a triangular prism, as shown at the right. Which expression represents the volume of the solid in terms of h? Use 3.14 for π.

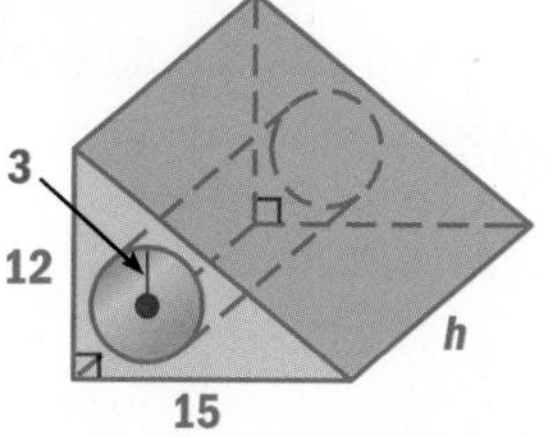

Ⓐ $61.74h$ Ⓑ $80.58h$ Ⓒ $118.26h$ Ⓓ $151.74h$

Strategy 1 SOLVE DIRECTLY

Subtract the volume of the cylindrical hole from the volume of the triangular prism.

STEP 1 **Find** the volume of the prism.

$$V = Bh = \left(\frac{1}{2}(15)(12)\right)h = 90h$$

STEP 2 **Find** the volume of the hole.

$$V = \pi r^2 h$$
$$\approx (3.14)(3)^2 h$$
$$= 28.26h$$

STEP 3 **Subtract** the volumes.

$$V \approx 90h - 28.26h = 61.74h$$

The volume of the solid is about $61.74h$.

The correct answer is A. Ⓐ Ⓑ Ⓒ Ⓓ

Strategy 2 ELIMINATE CHOICES

Evaluate the reasonableness of the solutions in the context of the original situation.

Choices C and D: $118.26h$ and $151.74h$
Find the volume of the triangular prism.

$$V = Bh = \left(\frac{1}{2}(15)(12)\right)h = 90h$$

Because the prism has a hole, the volume of the solid is less than $90h$. You can eliminate choices C and D.

Choice B: $80.58h$
Estimate the volume of the hole.

$$V = \pi r^2 h \approx (3)(3)^2 h = 27h$$

The volume of the solid is about $90h - 27h$, or $63h$. This expression is closer to $61.74h$ than to $80.58h$. You can eliminate choice B.

The correct answer is A. Ⓐ Ⓑ Ⓒ Ⓓ

STRATEGY PRACTICE

Explain why you can eliminate the highlighted answer choice.

1. A cylindrical hole is cut through a rectangular prism, as shown at the right. Which expression represents the volume (in cubic inches) of the solid in terms of h? Use 3.14 for π.

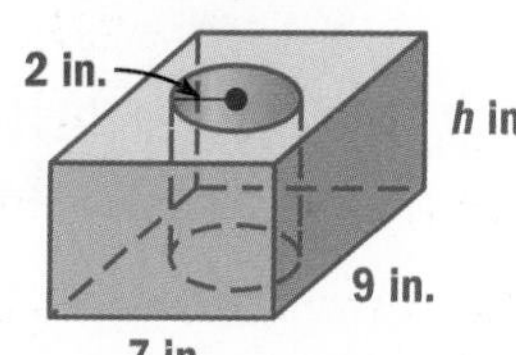

Ⓐ $19.44h$ Ⓑ $50.44h$ Ⓒ $56.72h$ Ⓓ ✗ **$75.56h$**

2. A rectangular prism has a length of 2 yards, a width of 3 yards, and a height of h yards. Which expression represents the surface area (in square yards) of the prism?

Ⓐ $5 + h$ Ⓑ $6 + 5h$ Ⓒ $12 + 10h$ Ⓓ ✗ **$6h$**

11 ◆ MULTIPLE CHOICE PRACTICE

1. The net is a representation of which solid? **Gr. 5 MG 2.3**

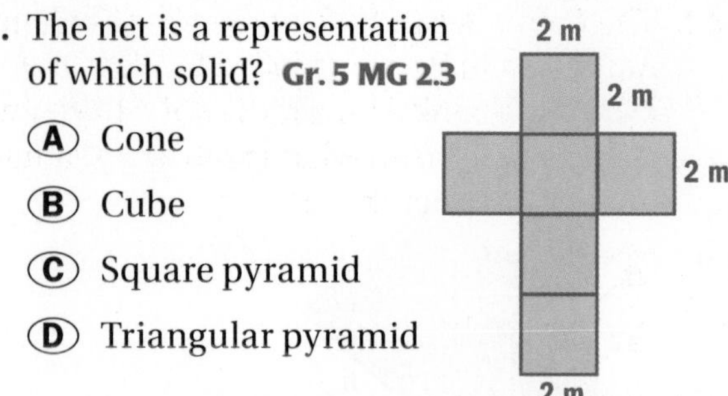

Ⓐ Cone

Ⓑ Cube

Ⓒ Square pyramid

Ⓓ Triangular pyramid

2. You want to paint the inside and outside of the prism below. What is the total area the paint must cover? **AF 3.1**

Ⓐ 24 in.^2

Ⓑ 48 in.^2

Ⓒ 52 in.^2

Ⓓ 104 in.^2

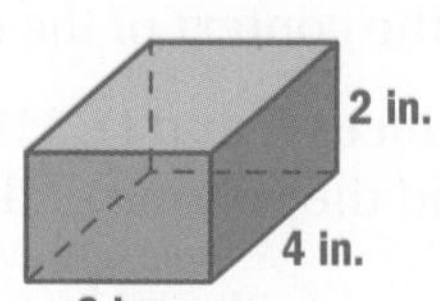

3. What is the surface area of the triangular prism below? **AF 3.1**

Ⓐ 120 cm^2

Ⓑ 144 cm^2

Ⓒ 168 cm^2

Ⓓ 216 cm^2

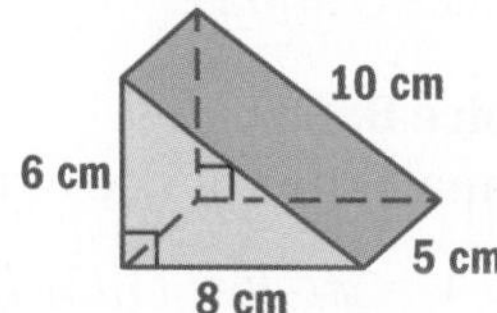

4. Layla wants to cover the outside of the jewelry box below with varnish. How much surface area does the varnish have to cover? **AF 3.1**

Ⓐ 18.5 in.^2

Ⓑ 106.5 in.^2

Ⓒ 180 in.^2

Ⓓ 213 in.^2

5. Jamal is pouring water from a cylindrical can into an empty cylindrical pan, as shown. What is the greatest number of full cans of water that he could pour into the pan without overflowing? **MG 1.3, MR 2.1**

Ⓐ 1

Ⓑ 2

Ⓒ 3

Ⓓ 4

6. A rectangular prism is 10 feet long, 5 feet wide, and 5 feet high. What is the volume of the prism? **MG 1.3**

Ⓐ 125 ft^3

Ⓑ 250 ft^3

Ⓒ 375 ft^3

Ⓓ 500 ft^3

7. A cylinder has a radius of 5 inches and a volume of about 628 cubic inches. What is the approximate height of the cylinder? Use 3.14 for π. **MG 1.3**

Ⓐ 6 in.

Ⓑ 8 in.

Ⓒ 10 in.

Ⓓ 12 in.

8. What is the approximate volume of the cylindrical container below? Use 3.14 for π. **MG 1.3**

Ⓐ 301 cm^3

Ⓑ 402 cm^3

Ⓒ 804 cm^3

Ⓓ 1608 cm^3

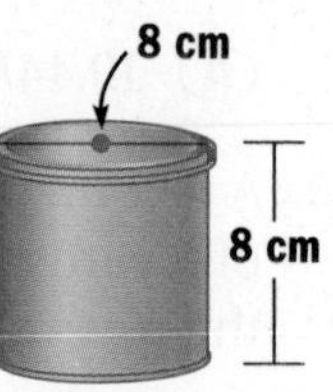

9. Which solid has the three views shown? **MR 1.2, Gr. 5 MG 2.3**

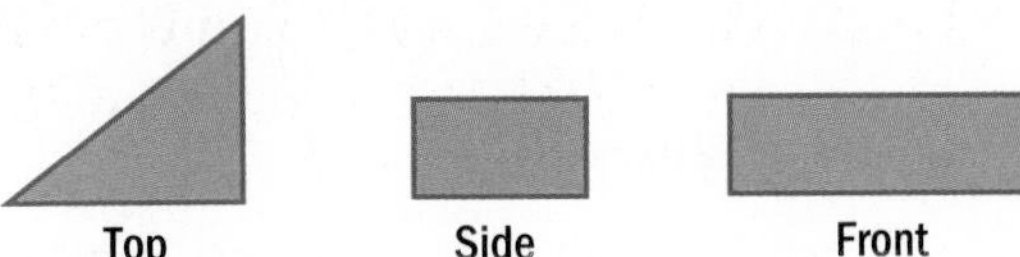

Ⓐ Rectangular prism

Ⓑ Rectangular pyramid

Ⓒ Triangular prism

Ⓓ Triangular pyramid

10. A rectangular prism has a surface area of 35.4 square feet, a length of 2 feet, and a width of 1.5 feet. What is the height? **AF 3.1**

Ⓐ 4.2 ft

Ⓑ 5.9 ft

Ⓒ 11.8 ft

Ⓓ 29.4 ft

11. What is the approximate volume of the glue stick below? **MG 1.3**

Ⓐ 57 cm^3

Ⓑ 85 cm^3

Ⓒ 113 cm^3

Ⓓ 339 cm^3

12. A hole in the shape of a rectangular prism is cut through a cylinder. Which expression represents the volume (in cubic feet) of the solid? Use 3.14 for π. **AF 3.2, MR 2.2**

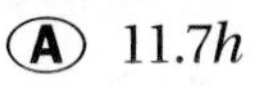
Ⓐ $11.7h$

Ⓑ $27.4h$

Ⓒ $74.5h$

Ⓓ $310h$

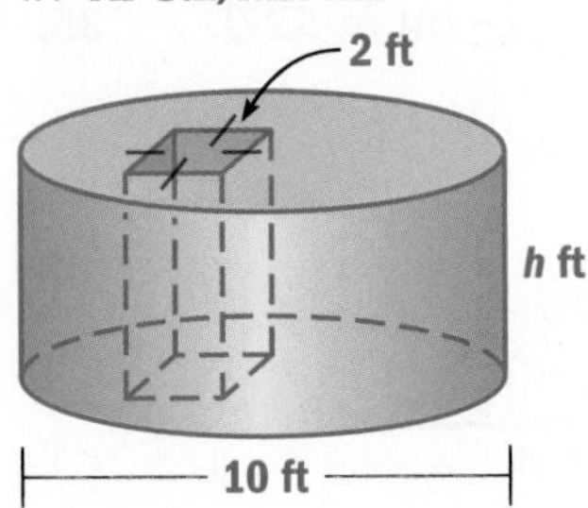

13. The Giant Ocean Tank at the New England Aquarium in Boston, Massachusetts, is a cylindrical tank with a radius of 20 feet and a height of 24 feet. What is the approximate volume of the tank? **MG 1.3**

Ⓐ 754 ft^3

Ⓑ 5526 ft^3

Ⓒ 30,144 ft^3

Ⓓ 36,172 ft^3

14. Which view of the solid below represents the side view? **Gr. 5 MG 2.3**

Ⓐ 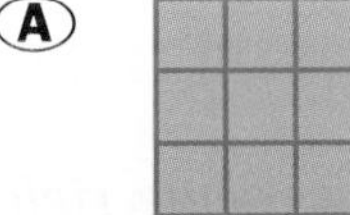

Ⓑ 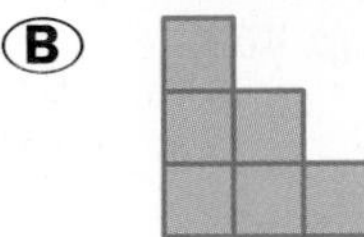

Ⓒ 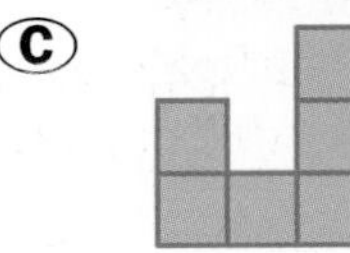

Ⓓ 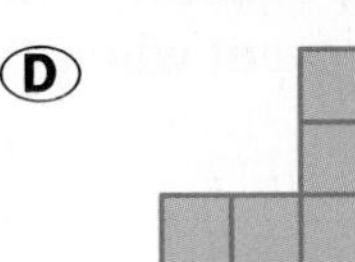

15. A rectangular prism has length 5 feet, width 2 feet, and surface area S square feet. Which equation could be used to find the height h (in feet) of the rectangular prism? **AF 3.2, MR 3.2**

Ⓐ $S = 7 + h$

Ⓑ $S = 20 + 14h$

Ⓒ $S = 10 + 7h$

Ⓓ $S = 10h$

11 CUMULATIVE REVIEW Chapters 1–11

Simplify the expression. ***(pp. 160, 207)***

1. $4(5) - 7(-12)$ **2.** $-20 - (8 + 3)$ **3.** $3^2 + 2(6 - 10)$ **4.** $\frac{2^5 - 5}{3}$

5. $3y - 6 + 4y - 2$ **6.** $16a - 8 - 1 + 4a$ **7.** $7 + 3(z - 8) + 6$ **8.** $6(x - 5) + 9$

Order the numbers from least to greatest. ***(p. 167)***

9. $-1.5, -1\frac{2}{3}, \frac{1}{5}, 1.005, -1.25$ **10.** $-3, \frac{-10}{3}, -3.25, 2.8, -2\frac{9}{10}$

Solve the equation or proportion.

11. $m + 6 = 4$ ***(p. 226)*** **12.** $9r = -72$ ***(p. 234)*** **13.** $\frac{7}{8} = \frac{n}{40}$ ***(p. 274)*** **14.** $\frac{1.6}{x} = \frac{5}{8}$ ***(p. 274)***

Use the percent equation or a proportion to solve. ***(pp. 306, 319)***

15. 2 is 8% of what number? **16.** What number is 1% of 44?

Find the mean, median, mode(s), range, and interquartile range of the data. ***(pp. 364, 372)***

17. 0, 1, 2, 4, 4, 5, 7, 8, 10, 12, 13 **18.** 5.5, 6.3, 4.7, 4.6, 4.6, 7.1, 6.3, 7.4, 6, 7.5

Classify the angle as *acute, right, obtuse,* or *straight.* Then find the measure of a supplementary angle and the measure of a complementary angle, if possible. ***(p. 463)***

19. $m\angle A = 25°$ **20.** $m\angle B = 140°$ **21.** $m\angle C = 5°$ **22.** $m\angle D = 90°$

The measures of two angles of $\triangle ABC$ are given. Find $m\angle C$. ***(p. 474)***

23. $m\angle A = 18°$, $m\angle B = 110°$ **24.** $m\angle A = 57°$, $m\angle B = 83°$ **25.** $m\angle A = 90°$, $m\angle B = 24°$ **26.** $m\angle A = 121°$, $m\angle B = 50°$

Events A and B are disjoint, and events B and C are independent. Find the probability of the event when $P(A) = 0.2$, $P(B) = 0.4$, and $P(C) = 0.3$.

27. Not A ***(p. 427)*** **28.** A or B ***(p. 427)*** **29.** B and C ***(p. 441)***

Copy and complete the statement.

30. 500 mL = __?__ L ***(p. 515)*** **31.** 8 m = __?__ cm ***(p. 515)*** **32.** 2.5 T = __?__ lb ***(p. 520)***

33. $5\frac{1}{2}$ gal = __?__ qt ***(p. 520)*** **34.** 5 km ≈ __?__ mi ***(p. 527)*** **35.** 10 lb ≈ __?__ kg ***(p. 527)***

Find the area of the figure. ***(pp. 534, 541)***

36.

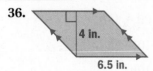

4 in.

6.5 in.

37.

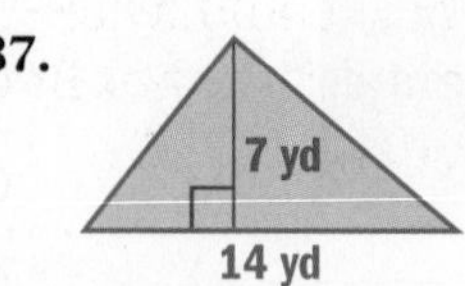

38.

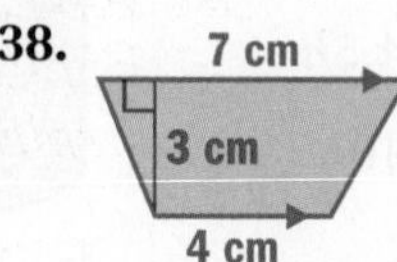

Find the surface area and volume of the solid. ***(pp. 581, 589, 596, 601)***

39. 4 in. 5 in. 20 in.

40. 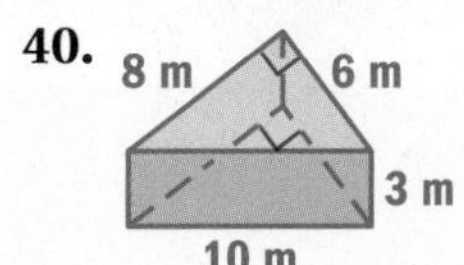

41. 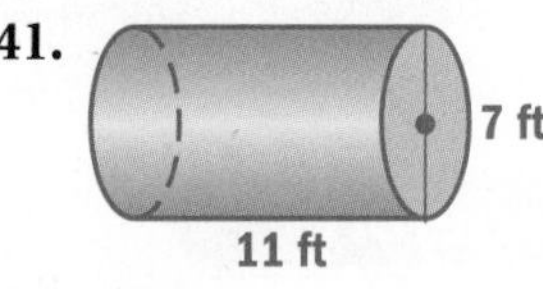

42. **DINING** You and your family are eating at a restaurant. The food bill is \$40. Your family chooses to leave a 20% tip before tax. The sales tax is 6%. What is the total cost of the meal? ***(p. 325)***

43. **MUSIC** Daniel conducts a survey to find the number of music CDs that students at his school buy each month. He surveys all of the students in his marching band. Based on his results, he claims that most students buy 5 CDs each month. Identify the sample and the sampling method. Explain why his claim may be invalid. ***(p. 359)***

44. **BREAKFAST FOODS** The table below shows the results of a survey asking 200 students what they usually eat for breakfast. Display the results in a circle graph. ***(p. 387)***

Food	eggs	cold cereal	pancakes	French toast	other
Students	55	90	30	15	10

CAR COLORS As you wait for the bus, you keep track of the color of each passing car, as shown in the table. Find the experimental probability that the next car will have the given description. ***(pp. 422, 427)***

45. White
46. Blue
47. Blue or red
48. Not black
49. Green or black
50. Yellow

Color	white	blue	green	red	black
Cars	5	14	6	7	18

51. **CLOTHING** You are deciding on a shirt and pants to wear. You can wear a red shirt, a blue shirt, or a white shirt. You can wear jeans, khakis, or slacks. Make a tree diagram to find all the possible outfits. ***(p. 424)***

52. **MOVIE POSTERS** A rectangular movie poster has a length of 28 inches and a width of 22 inches. A print of the poster is similar to the original and has a length of 14 inches. What is the width of the print? ***(p. 495)***

53. **BASKETBALL** The radius of the rim of a basketball hoop is 9 inches. What is the circumference of the rim? Use 3.14 for π. ***(p. 549)***

54. **PACKAGING** Can box A hold twice as much packing material as box B? *Explain* your reasoning. ***(p. 596)***

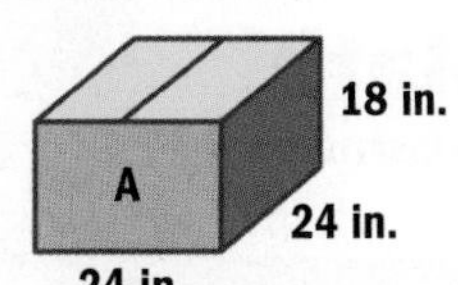

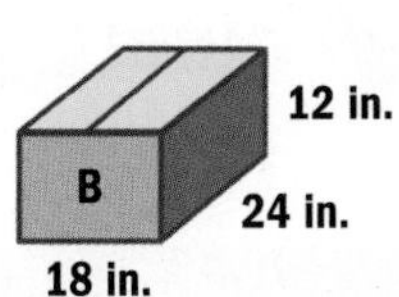

12 Graphing: Review and Preview

Before

In previous chapters, you learned the following skills, which you'll use in Chapter 12:

- Graphing numbers on a number line
- Evaluating expressions
- Writing equations
- Writing ratios

Now

In Chapter 12 you'll study these
Big Ideas:

1. Identifying and plotting ordered pairs
2. Writing and graphing linear functions
3. Using and interpreting slope

Why?

So you can solve real-world problems about . . .

- Shipwrecks, p. 628
- Radio broadcasts, p. 629
- Scuba diving, p. 633
- Skiing, p. 633
- Exercise, p. 639
- Unicycles, p. 639
- Sea turtles, p. 646

at classzone.com

Get-Ready Games

CAPTURE THE CORNERS

California Standards

Review evaluating an algebraic expression. *Gr. 6 AF 1.2*

Prepare for graphing functions. *Gr. 7 AF 3.3*

Materials

- One *Capture the Corners* game board
- One deck of *Capture the Corners* cards
- 6 markers, 3 each of two colors

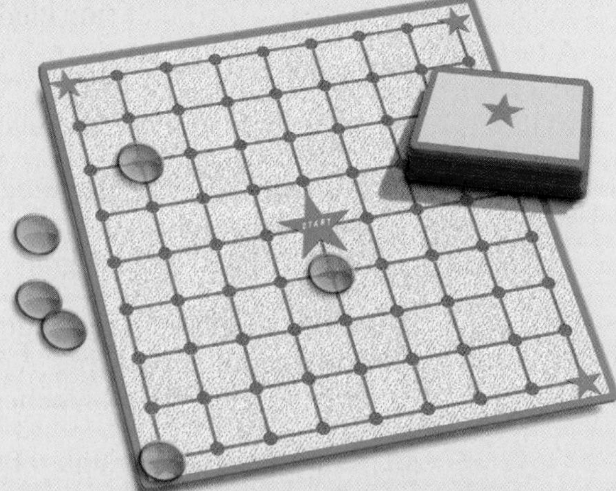

How to Play Play in pairs. Each player chooses 3 markers of one color. Shuffle the cards and place them face down in a pile. Players should take turns following the steps on the next page.

CALIFORNIA STANDARDS

- **Gr. 5 AF 1.5 Solve problems involving linear functions with integer values; write the equation; and graph the resulting ordered pairs of integers on a grid.** ***(Lessons 12.1, 12.2)***
- **Gr. 7 AF 3.3 Graph linear functions, noting that the vertical change (change in *y*-value) per unit of horizontal change (change in *x*-value) is always the same and know that the ratio ("rise over run") is called the slope of a graph.** ***(Lessons 12.3, 12.4)***

1 **Draw** the top card from the pile. On your first turn, place a marker on *Start*. After the first turn, you may use a marker already on the board or place a new marker on *Start*.

2 **Evaluate** the expression on your card. A negative value on a horizontal card indicates a move to the left. A negative value on a vertical card indicates a move downward.

3 **Move** one of your markers according to the value of the expression and the direction. If you can't move a marker, you must wait until your next turn. Markers must rest on points or stars. No two markers may occupy the same point.

How To Win Be the first player to have markers on two different corners of the board.

Games Wrap-Up

Draw Conclusions

Complete these exercises after playing the game.

1. WRITING *Describe* a situation in which you would choose to place your third marker on *Start*.

2. REASONING Suppose that all of the cards read either "vertical $x + 4$ when $x = -6$" or "horizontal $x + 2$ when $x = -1$." What is the fewest number of turns you would need to win the game? *Explain* your answer.

Prerequisite Skills

California @HomeTutor
Prerequisite skills practice at classzone.com

REVIEW VOCABULARY

- **evaluate,** *p. 70*
- **absolute value,** *p. 136*
- **coefficient,** *p. 207*
- **constant term,** *p. 207*
- **equation,** *p. 212*
- **area,** *p. 685*

VOCABULARY CHECK

Copy and complete using a review term from the list at the left.

1. In an algebraic expression, a term that has a number but no variable is called a(n) __?__.
2. The distance between a number and 0 on a number line is the __?__ of the number.
3. A mathematical sentence formed by setting two expressions equal is called a(n) __?__.
4. The number of square units needed to cover a figure is the __?__ of the figure.

SKILL CHECK

Evaluate the expression when $p = 2$ and $q = 6$. *(p. 197)*

5. q^3
6. $p^2 - q$
7. $-4p + 5q$
8. p^2q
9. $\frac{3p}{7} - \frac{q}{9}$
10. $p^3 + 3pq$
11. $\frac{4q}{7p}$
12. $\frac{7}{p} + 3q$

Solve the equation. *(p. 234)*

13. $12b = 144$
14. $3.5k = 21$
15. $5m = 21.6$
16. $2.3y = 9.2$
17. $\frac{7}{9}g = 35$
18. $\frac{t}{7} = 14$
19. $\frac{x}{4} = 7.62$
20. $\frac{2}{3}s = 9$

Notetaking Skills

NOW YOU TRY
Make a *definition and examples chart* for *formula.*

Focus on Graphic Organizers

Use a *definition and examples chart* to organize information about a vocabulary word, such as *ratio*.

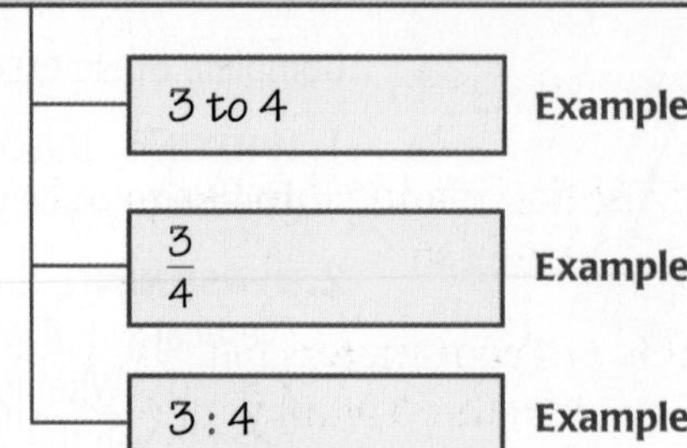

12.1 Graphing Paired Data

MATERIALS • metric tape measure • graph paper

Standards Review

Gr. 5 AF 1.4 Identify and graph ordered pairs in the four quadrants of the coordinate plane.

QUESTION How can you graph paired data values?

A *scatter plot* is a way to represent paired data visually. Each point on a scatter plot represents one data pair.

EXPLORE **Work in a group of six people. Make a scatter plot that shows the relationship between each person's height and lower-arm length.**

STEP 1 **Make** a table like the one shown. Measure and record the height and lower-arm length of each person in your group to the nearest centimeter. Your lower-arm length is the distance from your elbow to your fingertips.

Name	Height (cm)	Lower-Arm Length (cm)
Damon	155	40
?	?	?

STEP 2 **Graph** your group's data by plotting each person's height and lower-arm length as a data pair. Label the axes and plot the points as shown.

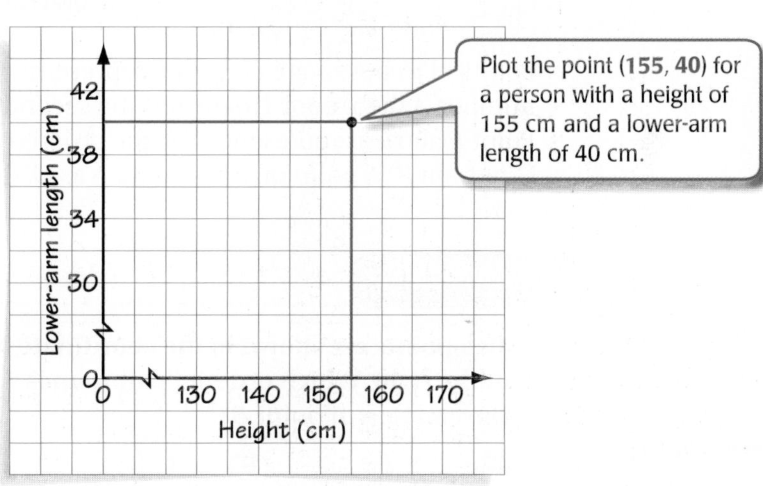

DRAW CONCLUSIONS **Use your observations to complete these exercises.**

1. **LOOK FOR A PATTERN** *Describe* the relationship between height and lower-arm length that the graph suggests.

2. **PREDICT** Suppose a student is 170 centimeters tall. Use your scatter plot to predict the student's lower-arm length. *Explain* your reasoning.

12.1 The Coordinate Plane

Standards Review Gr. 5 AF 1.4 **Identify and graph ordered pairs in the four quadrants of the coordinate plane.**

Connect *Before* you graphed numbers on a number line. *Now* you will identify and plot points in a coordinate plane to review Grade 5 Standard AF 1.4.

Math and **BROADCASTING**
Exs. 52–53, p. 629

KEY VOCABULARY
- **coordinate plane**
- **origin**
- **quadrant**
- **ordered pair**
- ***x*-coordinate**
- ***y*-coordinate**
- **scatter plot**

A **coordinate plane** is formed by the intersection of a horizontal number line, called the *x-axis*, and a vertical number line, called the *y-axis*. The *x*-axis and the *y*-axis meet at a point called the **origin**. The axes divide the coordinate plane into four **quadrants**.

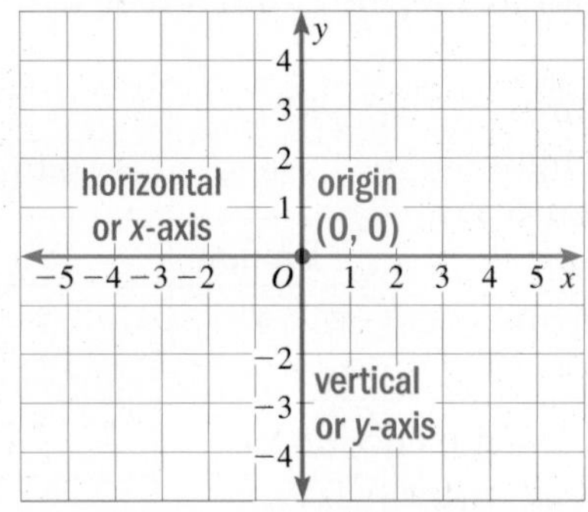

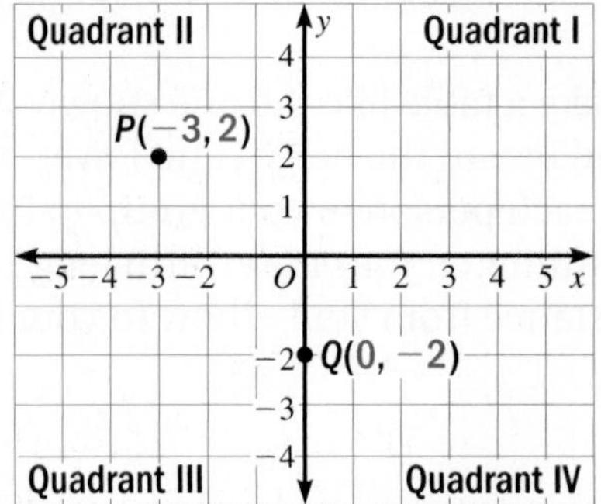

Points in a coordinate plane are represented by **ordered pairs.** The first number is the ***x*-coordinate** and the second number is the ***y*-coordinate.** Point P above is represented by the ordered pair $(-3, 2)$ and lies in Quadrant II. A point on an axis, such as Q, does not lie in any quadrant.

EXAMPLE 1 ◆ Multiple Choice Practice

Two points are shown in the coordinate plane at the right. Which ordered pair names the location of point *B*?

Ⓐ $(-3, 1)$ Ⓑ $(-1, 3)$

Ⓒ $(1, -3)$ Ⓓ $(3, -1)$

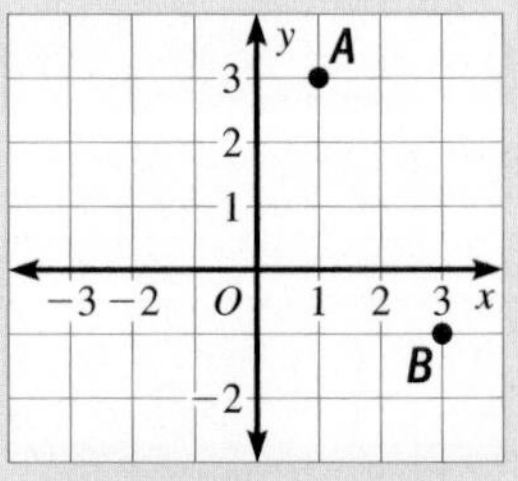

ELIMINATE CHOICES The *x*-coordinate describes the position left or right of the *y*-axis. Point *B* is to the right of the *y*-axis, so the *x*-coordinate is positive. You can eliminate choices A and B.

SOLUTION

Point B is 3 units to the right of the origin and 1 unit down, so the x-coordinate is 3 and the y-coordinate is -1. Point B is located at $(3, -1)$.

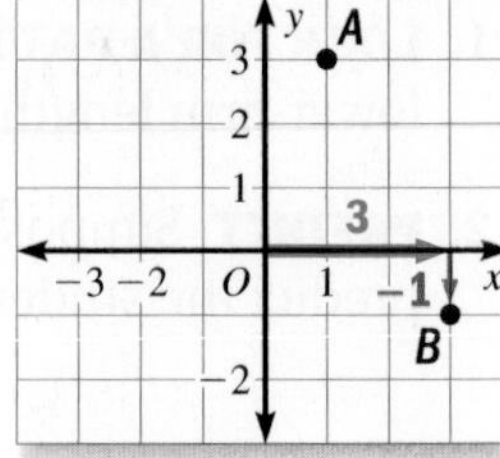

▶ **Answer** The correct answer is D. Ⓐ Ⓑ Ⓒ Ⓓ

EXAMPLE 2 Plotting Points in a Coordinate Plane

Plot the point and describe its location.

READING The notation $P(3, -4)$ means that point P is represented by the ordered pair $(3, -4)$.

a. $P(3, -4)$ **b.** $Q(-1, -3)$ **c.** $R(0, 2)$

SOLUTION

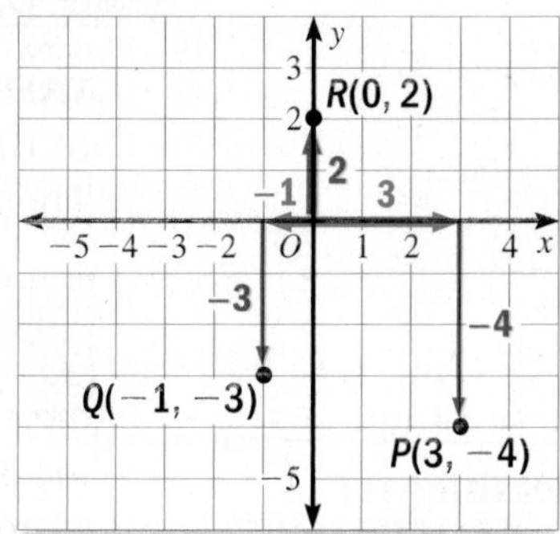

a. Begin at the origin. Move 3 units right, then 4 units down. Point P lies in Quadrant IV.

b. Begin at the origin. Move 1 unit left, then 3 units down. Point Q lies in Quadrant III.

c. Begin at the origin. Move 2 units up. Point R lies on the y-axis. It does not lie in any quadrant.

EXAMPLE 3 Finding Segment Lengths and Area

Find the length, width, and area of rectangle $ABCD$.

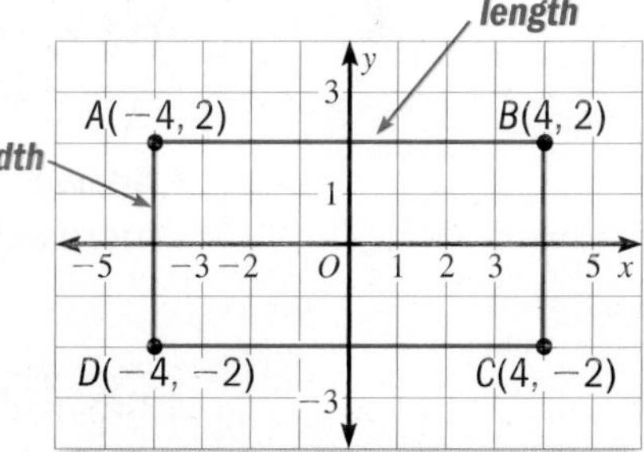

SOLUTION

The length of rectangle $ABCD$ is the *horizontal* distance between A and B. This distance is the absolute value of the difference between their x-coordinates.

ABSOLUTE VALUE For help with absolute value, see p. 135.

$$\textbf{Length} = |x\text{-coordinate of } A - x\text{-coordinate of } B|$$
$$= |-4 - 4| = |-8| = 8 \text{ units}$$

The width of rectangle $ABCD$ is the *vertical* distance between A and D. This distance is the absolute value of the difference between their y-coordinates.

$$\textbf{Width} = |y\text{-coordinate of } A - y\text{-coordinate of } D|$$
$$= |2 - (-2)| = |4| = 4 \text{ units}$$

The area of the rectangle is found by multiplying the length and width.

Area $= lw = 8(4) =$ **32 square units**

✓ GUIDED PRACTICE for Examples 1, 2, and 3

1. Name the ordered pair that represents point A in Example 1.

Plot the point and describe its location.

2. $A(-3, 4)$ **3.** $B(3, 4)$ **4.** $C(3, -3)$ **5.** $D(-3, -3)$

6. Find the length, width, and area of rectangle $ABCD$ in Exercises 2–5.

SCATTER PLOTS You can use a coordinate plane to make a **scatter plot** of paired data. Each data pair is plotted as a point. From the plotted points, you can sometimes recognize patterns and make predictions.

EXAMPLE 4 Making a Scatter Plot

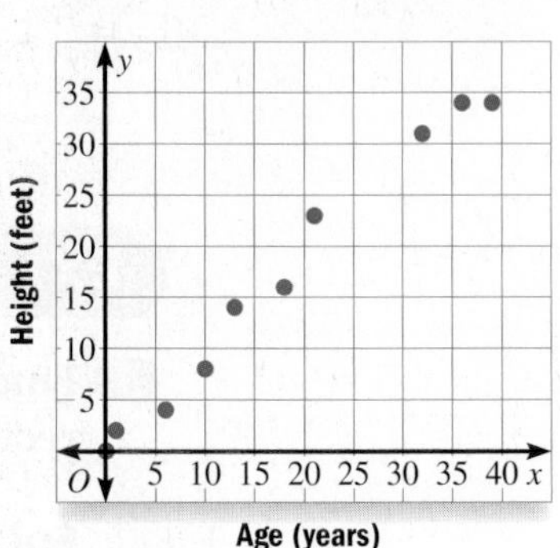

TREE GROWTH The table gives the ages and heights of 10 evergreen trees. Make a scatter plot of the data. Then make a conclusion about the data.

Age (years)	0	1	6	10	13	18	21	32	36	39
Height (feet)	0	2	4	8	14	16	23	31	34	34

DRAWING THE COORDINATE PLANE

Because none of the data values are negative, you need to draw only the first quadrant of a coordinate plane.

STEP 1 **Draw** a coordinate plane with ages on the x-axis and heights on the y-axis.

STEP 2 **Interpret** each column of data as an ordered pair: (age, height). Plot the ordered pairs.

STEP 3 **Look** for a pattern. The points tend to rise from left to right.

y
35
30
25
20
15
10
5
O 5 10 15 20 25 30 35 40 x
Height (feet)
Age (years)

▶ **Answer** As the age of an evergreen tree increases, its height tends to increase as well.

✓ **GUIDED PRACTICE** for Example 4

7. **WHAT IF?** Predict the height of a 27-year-old tree in Example 4.

12.1 EXERCISES

HOMEWORK KEY

◆ = **MULTIPLE CHOICE PRACTICE** Exs. 23, 25, 45, 55–57

○ = **HINTS AND HOMEWORK HELP** for Exs. 11, 27, 49 at classzone.com

SKILLS • PROBLEM SOLVING • REASONING

1. **VOCABULARY** Name the y-coordinate in the ordered pair $(5, -3)$.

2. **WRITING** *Describe* how to plot the points $A(2, -7)$ and $B(0, -5)$.

SEE EXAMPLE 1
on p. 624
for Exs. 3–10

NAMING ORDERED PAIRS **Name the ordered pair that represents the point.**

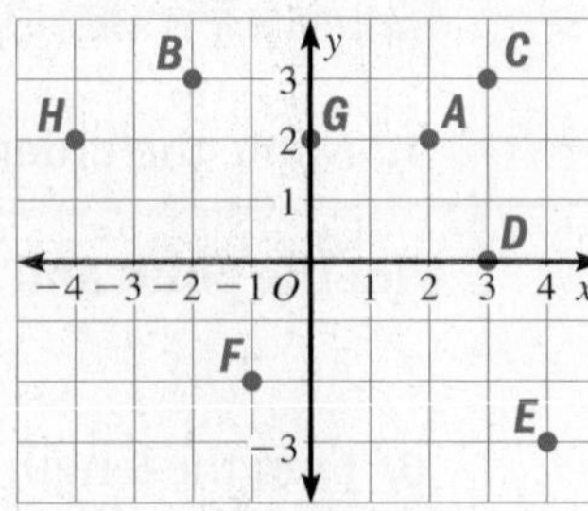

3. A
4. B
5. C
6. D
7. E
8. F
9. G
10. H

SEE EXAMPLE 2
on p. 625
for Exs. 11–24

PLOTTING POINTS Plot and label the point in a coordinate plane. *Describe* the location of the point.

11. $L(-6, 6)$
12. $M(0, -3)$
13. $N(-2, -4)$
14. $P(4, 1)$
15. $R(-2, 5)$
16. $S(7, 0)$
17. $T(-1, -8)$
18. $U(6, 3)$
19. $V(4, -2)$
20. $W(-4, -5)$
21. $X(0, -4)$
22. $Y(5, -7)$

23. ◆ **MULTIPLE CHOICE** Beginning at the origin, where should you plot the point $P(6, -3)$?

Ⓐ 6 units right, 3 units left Ⓑ 6 units up, 3 units left

Ⓒ 6 units right, 3 units down Ⓓ 6 units left, 3 units down

24. **ERROR ANALYSIS** A student plots the point $A(4, -6)$ by moving 4 units up from the origin, then 6 units left. *Describe* and correct the error.

SEE EXAMPLE 3
on p. 625
for Exs. 25–32

25. ◆ **MULTIPLE CHOICE** What is the length of $\overline{GH}$, that has endpoints $G(3, 3)$ and $H(3, -4)$?

Ⓐ −7 units Ⓑ 0 units Ⓒ 3 units Ⓓ 7 units

FINDING SEGMENT LENGTHS AND AREA Plot and connect the points to form a rectangle. Then find the length, width, and area of the rectangle.

26. $A(0, 0), B(6, 0), C(6, 2), D(0, 2)$
27. $M(7, 1), N(7, 5), U(8, 5), P(8, 1)$
28. $W(3, -4), X(-1, -4), Y(-1, 5), Z(3, 5)$
29. $I(-2, 2), J(8, 2), K(8, -1), L(-2, -1)$
30. $E(3, 4), F(-5, 4), G(-5, 2), H(3, 2)$
31. $Q(-4, 2), R(-4, 4), S(2, 4), T(2, 2)$

32. **ERROR ANALYSIS** *Describe* and correct the error made in finding the distance between A and B using the points $A(3, -14)$ and $B(3, -6)$.

✗ Distance = −14 − (−6)
= −14 + 6
= −8

SEE EXAMPLE 4
on p. 626
for Ex. 33

33. **REASONING** Make a scatter plot using the data in the table below. Then make a conclusion about the data.

x	0	1	2	3	4	5	6	7
y	16	14	12	12	9	10	8	6

ALGEBRA Tell what you know about the values of x and y, given the location of the point (x, y).

34. The point is in Quadrant I.
35. The point is in Quadrant IV.
36. The point is on the x-axis.
37. The point is on the y-axis.
38. The point is in Quadrant II.
39. The point is in Quadrant III.

40. **GRAPHING EQUIVALENT FRACTIONS** List 5 fractions equivalent to $\frac{2}{3}$. Use the list to graph 5 ordered pairs of the form (numerator, denominator). What conclusion can you make from this scatter plot?

CONNECT SKILLS TO PROBLEM SOLVING **Exercises 41–44 will help you prepare for problem solving.**

The coordinate plane at the right shows a map of a neighborhood.

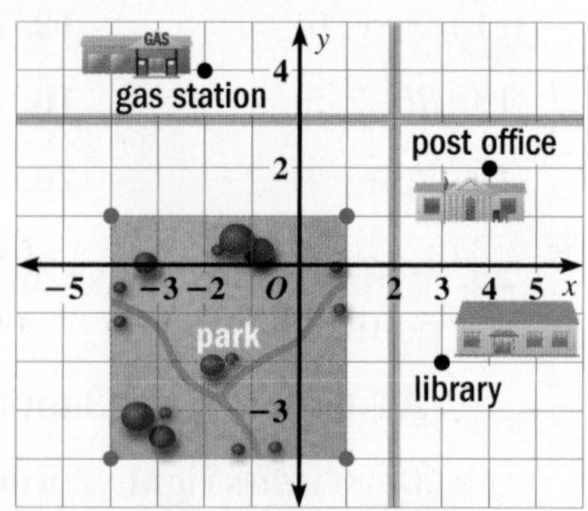

41. Name the ordered pair that represents the gas station.

42. Name the building located at (4, 2).

43. Is the point (−3, 2) inside the park?

44. Name the four ordered pairs that represent the corners of the park.

SEE EXAMPLES 2 AND 3 on p. 625 for Exs. 45–48

45. ◆ **MULTIPLE CHOICE** In a coordinate plane, your house is located at point (3, 6). Your school is plotted in the same coordinate plane. The length of the segment between your house and school is 4 units. Which point could *not* be the location of your school?

Ⓐ (−1, 6) Ⓑ (−3, 6) Ⓒ (3, 2) Ⓓ (7, 6)

California @HomeTutor for problem solving help at classzone.com

46. PATTERNS Plot and connect the points (−10, 2), (−10, 4), (−8, 4), (−8, 6), and (−6, 6) to create a series of steps. If you continue this pattern, what will be the coordinates when you reach the *y*-axis?

California @HomeTutor for problem solving help at classzone.com

47. SHIPWRECKS A researcher uses a coordinate plane to record the locations of shipwrecks. The research station is represented by the origin, and the positive *y*-axis represents north. Each unit is equal to 1 mile.

a. A shipwreck is 15 miles west and 8 miles south of the station. What ordered pair can be used to represent the location?

b. Another shipwreck is located 7 miles east and 8 miles south of the station. What is the distance between the two shipwrecks?

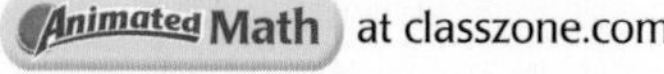

One shipwreck is 15 miles west and 8 miles south of the station.

48. OPEN-ENDED Draw a vertical line segment in a coordinate grid. Label the coordinates of the endpoints. Show how to calculate the length of the segment.

SEE EXAMPLE 4 on p. 626 for Ex. 49

(49.) SHORT RESPONSE The ordered pairs show the total head-to-tail length (in feet) and the weight (in pounds) of 15 red foxes found in a state park. Make a scatter plot of the data. Then make a conclusion about the data.

(3, 8), (3.4, 11), (3.1, 8.5), (3.5, 13), (3.5, 12.5), (3, 9), (3.7, 15), (3.7, 14.5), (3.4, 10), (3.3, 12), (3.2, 9), (3.2, 11.5), (3.6, 14.5), (3.6, 15), (3.5, 14)

SEE EXAMPLE 4 on p. 626 for Exs. 50–51

FUEL ECONOMY Use the table below that shows the engine size in liters and highway mileage in miles per gallon for 12 cars.

Engine Size (L)	3	5	1	6	2	2	4	3	3	2	4	5
Highway Mileage (mi/gal)	28	23	47	19	33	31	25	24	25	37	24	22

50. Make a scatter plot of the data. What pattern do the data suggest?

51. Predict the highway mileage for a 5.5 liter engine.

RADIO BROADCASTS The coordinate plane shows the broadcast area of a low power radio station as a circle and its interior.

52. Which of the house(s) located at the following points are in the station's broadcast area?

$A(-5, 5)$, $B(-6, -6)$, $C(4, -5)$, $D(-2, 7)$

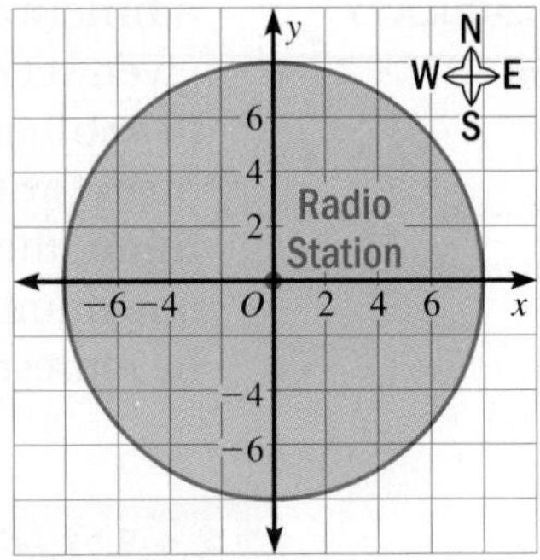

53. **CHALLENGE** Each unit on the coordinate plane shown is equal to one quarter mile. How far does the broadcast reach in a northeast direction from the station? *Explain.*

54. **CHALLENGE** Let a and b be nonzero integers. If you plot $O(0, 0)$, $P(a, b)$, and $Q(-b, a)$, you can connect these points to form $\angle POQ$. What type of angle is $\angle POQ$? Does the type of angle depend on the values of a and b? *Explain.*

◆ California Standards Spiral Review

MG 1.3 **55.** A triangular prism has a base area of 96 square inches and a height of 8 inches. What is the volume of the triangular prism? ***(p. 596)***

Ⓐ 384 in.^{2} Ⓑ 384 in.^{3} Ⓒ 768 in.^{2} Ⓓ 768 in.^{3}

SDAP 2.3 **56.** The line graph shows the average price of a movie ticket in the United States by year. Which change to the graph will make the price increase appear more dramatic? ***(p. 392)***

Ⓐ Use a vertical scale from 0 to 10.

Ⓑ Use a vertical scale from 4 to 5.

Ⓒ Delete data from 1999.

Ⓓ Use a broken horizontal axis.

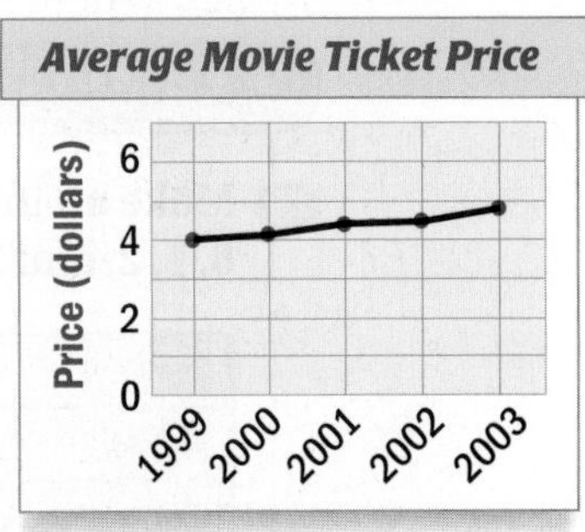

SDAP 3.3 **57.** In a school, 85 students take French, 140 take Spanish, and the remaining 170 students do not take a language. No student can take both languages. What is the probability that a student chosen at random takes French? ***(p. 427)***

Ⓐ $\frac{17}{79}$ Ⓑ $\frac{17}{45}$ Ⓒ $\frac{1}{2}$ Ⓓ $\frac{17}{28}$

12.2 Functions and Equations

Standards Review **Gr. 5 AF 1.5 Solve problems involving linear functions with integer values; write the equation**; and graph the resulting ordered pairs of integers on a grid.

Connect ***Before*** you wrote and evaluated expressions. ***Now*** you will write equations to represent linear functions to review Grade 5 Standard AF 1.5.

KEY VOCABULARY
- **function**
- **input**
- **output**
- **domain**
- **range**

A **function** is a pairing of each number in a given set of numbers with exactly one number in another set. A *set* is a collection of distinct objects. Starting with a number called an **input**, the function associates it with exactly one number called an **output**. A function can be represented by a rule, a table, or a graph.

EXAMPLE 1 Evaluating a Function

Evaluate the function $y = 5x$ when $x = 7$.

$y = 5x$ **Write rule for function.**

$= 5(7)$ **Substitute 7 for *x*.**

$= 35$ **Multiply.**

DOMAIN AND RANGE The set of all input values is the **domain** of a function. The set of all output values is the **range** of a function.

EXAMPLE 2 Making an Input-Output Table

Make an input-output table for the function $y = x + 6$ using the domain 0, 1, 2, and 3. Then state the range of the function.

Input x	0	1	2	3
Substitution	$y = 0 + 6$	$y = 1 + 6$	$y = 2 + 6$	$y = 3 + 6$
Output y	6	7	8	9

The range of the function is the set of outputs 6, 7, 8, and 9.

GUIDED PRACTICE for Examples 1 and 2

1. Make an input-output table for the function $y = 2x + 2$ using the domain -2, -1, 0, 1, and 2. Then state the range of the function.

EXAMPLE 3 ◆ Multiple Choice Practice

Which equation shows the relationship between x and y?

Input x	−2	−1	0	1	2	3	4
Output y	−8	−4	0	4	8	12	16

Ⓐ $y = x - 6$ Ⓑ $x = y - 6$ Ⓒ $y = 4x$ Ⓓ $x = 4y$

About the Standards

In Example 3, you are observing a pattern to solve the problem. This skill is part of Grade 6 Standard MR 1.1.

SOLUTION

Compare each output value to its corresponding input value. Notice that each output value is the input value multiplied by 4. The equation $y = 4x$ shows the relationship.

▸ **Answer** The correct answer is C. Ⓐ Ⓑ Ⓒ Ⓓ

EXAMPLE 4 Solve a Multi-Step Problem

SERVINGS The diagram below shows cuts made across the center to make servings of cheese. An input c, the number of cuts, results in an output s, the number of servings made. How many servings will 9 cuts make?

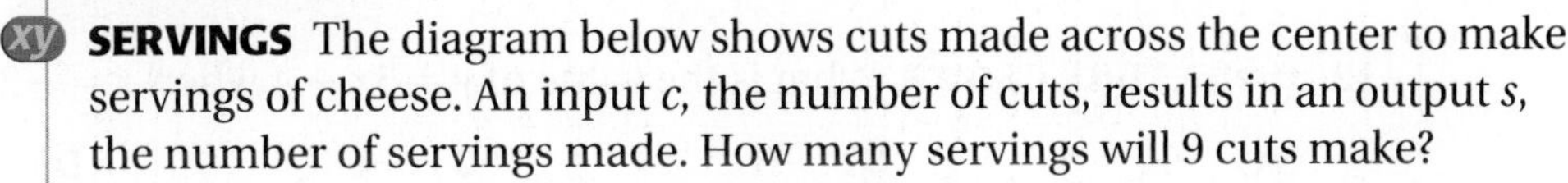

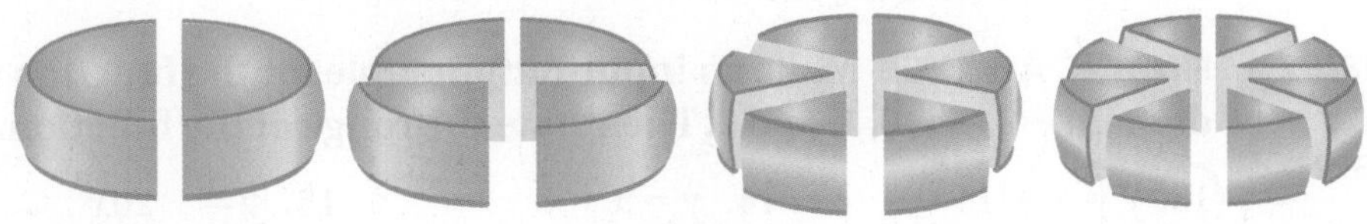

ANOTHER WAY

For an alternative method for solving the problem in Example 4, turn to page 635 for the **Problem Solving Workshop**.

SOLUTION

STEP 1 **Make** an input-output table.

Input c	1	2	3	4
Output s	2	4	6	8

STEP 2 **Write** a function rule. Notice that each output value is twice the input value. A rule for the function is $s = 2c$.

STEP 3 **Evaluate** the function when $c = 9$ to find the number of pieces 9 cuts will make. When $c = 9$, $s = 2(9) = 18$.

▸ **Answer** Nine cuts will make 18 servings of cheese.

✓ GUIDED PRACTICE for Examples 3 and 4

Write a function rule for the input-output table. Then use the rule to find the output y when $x = 12$.

2.

Input x	−1	0	1	2
Output y	−4	−3	−2	−1

3.

Input x	2	4	6	8
Output y	−2	−4	−6	−8

12.2 EXERCISES

HOMEWORK KEY

◆ = **MULTIPLE CHOICE PRACTICE** Exs. 12, 22, 34, 42–44

○ = **HINTS AND HOMEWORK HELP** for Exs. 13, 25, 37 at classzone.com

SKILLS • PROBLEM SOLVING • REASONING

VOCABULARY Copy and complete the statement.

1. A function starts with a number called a(n) _?_ and associates it with exactly one number called a(n) _?_.

2. For a given function, the set of all input values is called the _?_ and the set of all output values is called the _?_.

3. **NOTETAKING SKILLS** Make a *definitions and examples chart* like the one shown on page 622 for *function*.

SEE EXAMPLE 1 on p. 630 for Exs. 4–12

FUNCTIONS Evaluate the function $y = 3x - 2$ for the given value of x.

4. 4 5. 0 6. 1 7. 3

8. −7 9. −3 10. −2 11. −1

12. ◆ **MULTIPLE CHOICE** What is the value of $y = 5x - 4$ when $x = -2$?

Ⓐ −14 Ⓑ −6 Ⓒ −1 Ⓓ 6

SEE EXAMPLE 2 on p. 630 for Exs. 13–21

FINDING A RANGE Make an input-output table for the function using the domain −2, −1, 0, 1, and 2. Then state the range of the function.

13. $y = x + 11$ 14. $y = x - 5$ 15. $y = -20x$ 16. $y = 7x$

17. $y = 15 - 2x$ 18. $y = 6x - 4$ 19. $y = -9x + 7$ 20. $y = -5 + 2x$

21. **ERROR ANALYSIS** *Describe* and correct the error made in making an input-output table for the function.

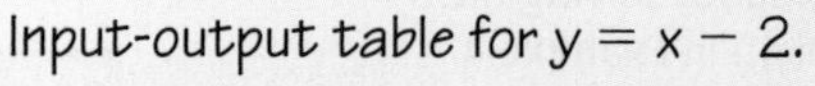

Input x	−2	−1	0	1
Output y	0	1	2	3

SEE EXAMPLE 3 on p. 631 for Exs. 22–24

22. ◆ **MULTIPLE CHOICE** The input x of a function is a number of inches. The output y is the equivalent number of feet. Which rule represents the function?

Ⓐ $y = 12x$ Ⓑ $y = \frac{x}{12}$ Ⓒ $y = 12 + x$ Ⓓ $y = 12 - x$

23. **ERROR ANALYSIS** *Describe* and correct the error made in writing a function rule for the table.

Input x	−2	−1	0	1
Output y	−6	−3	0	3

The rule for the table is $y = x - 4$.

24. **WRITING** *Describe* how to write a function rule to represent the unit conversion of years to months.

SEE EXAMPLE 3
on p. 631
for Ex. 25–30

FUNCTION RULES **Write a function rule for the input-output table.**

25.

Input x	1	2	3	4
Output y	5	10	15	20

26.

Input x	−2	−1	0	1
Output y	13	14	15	16

27.

Input x	2	3	4	5
Output y	−5	−4	−3	−2

28.

Input x	−1	0	1	2
Output y	4	0	−4	−8

29.

Input p	1	2	3	4
Output q	4	7	10	13

30.

Input m	3	4	5	6
Output n	−3	−5	−7	−9

Animated Math at classzone.com

CONNECT SKILLS TO PROBLEM SOLVING **Exercises 31–33 will help you prepare for problem solving.**

Make an input-output table for the given situation.

31. Alphonso is exactly 3 years older than his sister Julia. Use a domain of 10, 12, 14, and 16 for Alphonso's age a to find Julia's age j.

32. A package contains 12 pens. Use a domain of 2, 3, 4, 5, and 6 for the number of packages n to find the total number of pens p.

33. You burn about 440 calories per hour of biking. Use a domain of 1, 2, 3, and 4 for the number of hours n to find the total calories burned c.

SEE EXAMPLES 1 AND 2
on p. 630
for Exs. 34–35

34. ◆ **MULTIPLE CHOICE** The time t (in minutes) it takes to fill a neighbor's wading pool to various depths d (in inches) is given by the function $t = 2d$. How long will it take to fill the pool to a depth of 9 inches?

Ⓐ 4.5 min Ⓑ 7 min Ⓒ 11 min Ⓓ 18 min

California @HomeTutor for problem solving help at classzone.com

35. **SCUBA DIVING** The amount of pressure on a scuba diver is given by the function $p = 64d + 2112$, where p is the pressure (in pounds per square foot) and d is the depth (in feet). Make an input-output table for depths of 0, 20, 40, 60, 80, and 100 feet. As the depth increases, how does the pressure change?

California @HomeTutor for problem solving help at classzone.com

Pressure on a scuba diver changes with depth.

SEE EXAMPLE 4
on p. 631
for Ex. 36

36. **SKIING** At one ski resort, it costs \$415 to rent a cabin for a weekend. Each weekend lift pass costs \$72.

a. Make an input-output table using the domain 1, 2, 3, 4, 5, and 6. Use the table to write a function rule for the total cost c (in dollars) for n people. What is the total cost for 10 people?

b. At another resort, it costs \$450 to rent a cabin for a weekend, and each weekend lift pass costs \$64. Which resort is the better deal? Does it depend on the number of people? *Explain.*

SEE EXAMPLE 4 on p. 631 for Ex. 37

37. MULTI-STEP PROBLEM The diagram shows a folded piece of string being cut. Let c be the number of cuts across the folded string. Let p be the total number of pieces of string after making the cut(s).

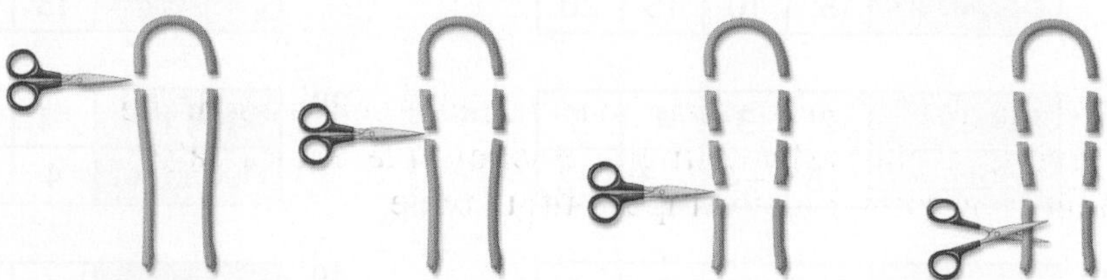

a. **Model** Make an input-output table with an input c and an output p.

b. **Interpret** Write a statement in words that shows the relationship between c and p. Then write a function rule relating c and p.

c. **Calculate** How many pieces do you have if you make 18 cuts?

CHALLENGE Write three different functions for the given input-output pair.

38. input: −3; output: 15 **39.** input: 6; output: −18 **40.** input: −4; output: −11

41. CHALLENGE A store sells used DVDs for $12 each and new DVDs for $18 each. Is the relationship between the total number of DVDs you buy and the total cost a function? *Explain* your reasoning.

◆ CALIFORNIA STANDARDS SPIRAL REVIEW

AF 2.1 **42.** About how many meters are in 66 feet? *(p. 527)*

Ⓐ 20 m Ⓑ 26 m Ⓒ 69 m Ⓓ 216 m

AF 3.1 **43.** The length of a rectangle is twice its width w. What is its area? *(p. 212)*

Ⓐ $3w$ Ⓑ $2w^2$ Ⓒ $6w$ Ⓓ $9w^2$

SDAP 3.5 **44.** A jar contains 6 red, 9 blue, and 5 green marbles. You randomly choose a marble from the jar. Without replacing the first, you randomly choose another. What is the probability that both marbles are blue? *(p. 441)*

Ⓐ $\frac{9}{50}$ Ⓑ $\frac{18}{95}$ Ⓒ $\frac{81}{400}$ Ⓓ $\frac{9}{20}$

QUIZ *for Lessons 12.1–12.2*

1. Plot and connect the points $A(-5, 4)$, $B(2, 4)$, $C(2, -2)$, and $D(-5, -2)$ to form rectangle $ABCD$. Then find its length, width, and area. *(p. 624)*

Make an input-output table for the function using the domain −2, −1, 0, and 2. Then state the range of the function. *(p. 630)*

2. $y = -2x + 5$ **3.** $y = 3 - 4x$ **4.** $y = 6x - 1$

5. Write a function rule for the input-output table. Then use the rule to find the output y when $x = -5$. *(p. 630)*

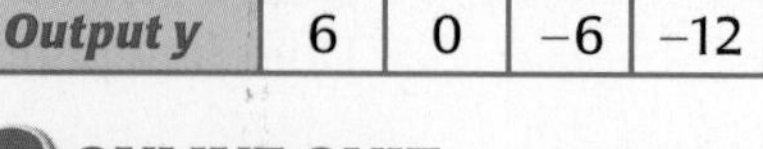

Input x	−2	0	2	4
Output y	6	0	−6	−12

PROBLEM SOLVING WORKSHOP
LESSON 12.2

Using ALTERNATIVE METHODS

Another Way to Solve Example 4, page 631

Standards Review
Gr. 5 AF 1.5

In Example 4 on page 631, you saw how to solve the problem about the number of servings of cheese by writing a function rule. You can also solve the problem by extending the input-output table.

PROBLEM

SERVINGS The diagram below shows cuts made across the center to make servings of cheese. An input *c*, the number of cuts, results in an output *s*, the number of servings made. How many servings will 9 cuts make?

METHOD

Extending the Table An alternative approach is to extend the input-output table.

Make an input-output table. Extend the table until you reach an input value of 9.

Input c	1	2	3	4	5	6	7	8	9
Output s	2	4	6	8	10	12	14	16	18

▶ **Answer** Nine cuts will make 18 servings of cheese.

PRACTICE

1. **GEOMETRY** Make an input-output table using the number of squares *s* as the input and the number of triangles *t* as the output. Extend the table to find the number of triangles made from 7 squares.

1
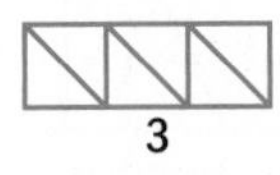
2
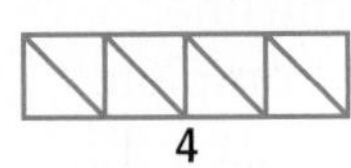
3

4

2. **PATTERNS** Copy the table below. Then extend the table to find *y* when $x = 8$.

x	1	2	3	4
y	3	6	12	24

3. **DISTANCE** In the table below, the input *t* is the number of hours traveled and the output *d* is the distance traveled (in miles) by a car driven at a constant speed. How far does the car travel in 11 hours? Solve the problem using two methods.

Hours t	1	2	3	4
Distance d	40	80	120	160

4. **REASONING** *Explain* why sometimes it may be more reasonable to write a function rule than to extend an input-output table to solve a problem. Give an example.

12.3 Graphing Functions

Standards Preview **Gr. 7 AF 3.3 Graph linear functions, noting that the vertical change (change in *y*-value) per unit of horizontal change (change in *x*-value) is always the same** and know that the ratio ("rise over run") is called the slope of a graph.

Connect ***Before*** you graphed ordered pairs in a coordinate plane. ***Now*** you will graph linear functions in a coordinate plane to preview Grade 7 Standard AF 3.3.

Math and **FITNESS**
Ex. 29, p. 639

KEY VOCABULARY
- **linear function**
- **domain,** *p. 630*

FABRIC COSTS You are in a craft shop choosing fabric for a sewing project. The fabric you choose costs \$2.50 for each yard. In Example 2, you will write and graph a function to represent this situation.

You can graph a function by creating an input-output table, forming ordered pairs, and then plotting the ordered pairs. The graph represents all of the solutions of the equation

EXAMPLE 1 Graphing a Function

Graph the function $y = 2x + 1$.

CHOOSE A DOMAIN
When the domain of a function is not given, assume that it includes every *x*-value for which the function can produce a corresponding *y*-value.

STEP 1 **Make** an input-output table by choosing several input values and finding the output values.

x	*Substitution*	*y*
−2	$y = 2(-2) + 1$	−3
−1	$y = 2(-1) + 1$	−1
0	$y = 2(0) + 1$	1
1	$y = 2(1) + 1$	3
2	$y = 2(2) + 1$	5

STEP 2 **Use** the table to write a list of ordered pairs:
$(-2, -3), (-1, -1), (0, 1),$
$(1, 3), (2, 5)$

STEP 3 **Plot** the ordered pairs in a coordinate plane.

STEP 4 **Connect** the points as shown. Notice that all of the points lie on a line. Any other ordered pair (x, y) that is a solution of the equation $y = 2x + 1$ also lies on the line. The line represents the complete graph of the function $y = 2x + 1$.

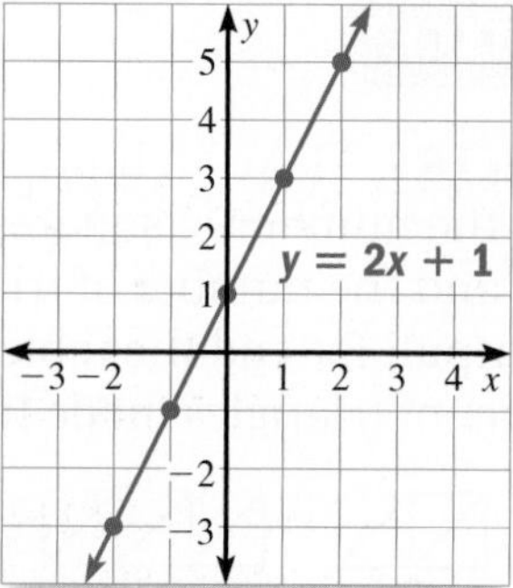

Animated Math
For an interactive example of graphing a function go to **classzone.com.**

✓ GUIDED PRACTICE for Example 1

Graph the function.

1. $y = x - 3$ **2.** $y = 2x - 3$ **3.** $y = -3x$ **4.** $y = -x + 4$

LINEAR FUNCTIONS The graphs in this chapter are graphs of *linear functions*. A graph of a **linear function** is a line or part of a line. The vertical change per unit of horizontal change is always the same for a linear function. You will learn more about this in Lesson 12.4. Not all graphs are lines, nor do all graphs represent functions, as you will see in later courses.

EXAMPLE 2 Writing and Graphing a Function

In the situation described on page 636, each yard of fabric costs \$2.50. You can represent the situation with a table, a graph, and a function rule.

About the Standards

You can use the graph in Example 2 to estimate the cost of 4 yards of fabric. You could also extend the table or use the function to find the cost. These skills are part of Grade 6 Standard MR 2.3.

STEP 1 **Make** an input-output table. The domain is nonnegative numbers.

Input x (yards)	*Output y (cost)*
0	0
1	2.50
2	5.00
3	7.50

STEP 2 **Plot** the ordered pairs. Connect them as shown.

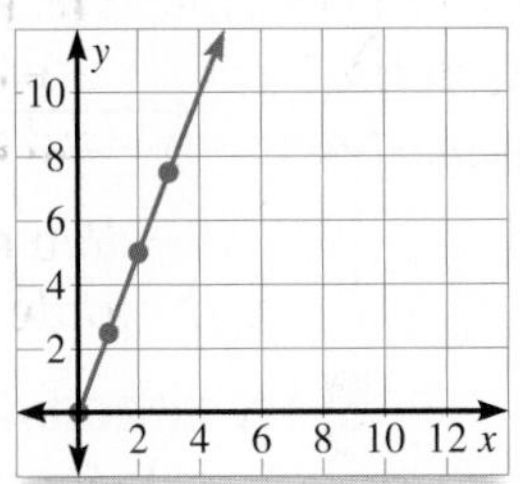

STEP 3 **Write** a function rule. Notice that each output is 2.5 times the input value. A rule for the function is $y = 2.5x$.

✓ GUIDED PRACTICE for Example 2

5. **COST** Write and graph a function for the total cost y of x ounces of raisins that cost \$.25 per ounce.

12.3 EXERCISES

HOMEWORK KEY

◆ = **MULTIPLE CHOICE PRACTICE** Exs. 13, 30, 40–42

○ = **HINTS AND HOMEWORK HELP** for Exs. 3, 15, 31 at classzone.com

SKILLS • PROBLEM SOLVING • REASONING

1. **VOCABULARY** Copy and complete: A function whose graph is a line or part of a line is a(n) __?__.

2. **WRITING** *Explain* how graphing a linear function is similar to making a scatter plot. How is it different?

SEE EXAMPLE 1 on p. 636 for Exs. 3–11

GRAPHING FUNCTIONS **Graph the function.**

3. $y = x$
4. $y = 10 - x$
5. $y = -2x$
6. $y = x + 3$
7. $y = 3x - 5$
8. $y = -4x + 1$
9. $y = -x + 2$
10. $y = -5x - 2$
11. $y = -x - 4$

SEE EXAMPLE 1 on p. 636 for Exs. 12–13

12. **ERROR ANALYSIS** Your friend says that the point (2, 0) lies on the graph of the function $y = -3x + 2$. *Describe* and correct the error.

13. ◆ **MULTIPLE CHOICE** Which function is graphed at the right?

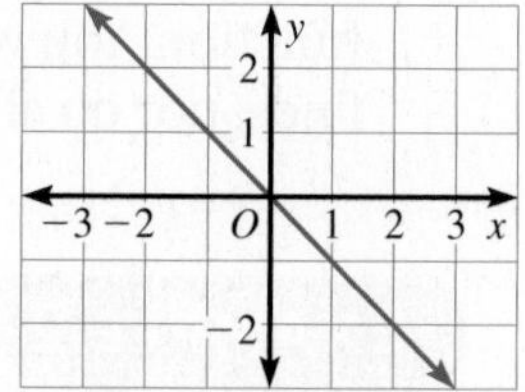

Ⓐ $y = -x$ Ⓑ $y = x$

Ⓒ $y = x - 1$ Ⓓ $y = x - 2$

SEE EXAMPLE 2 on p. 637 for Exs. 14–17

MAKING TABLES Make an input-output table from the graph. Then write a rule for the function.

14. 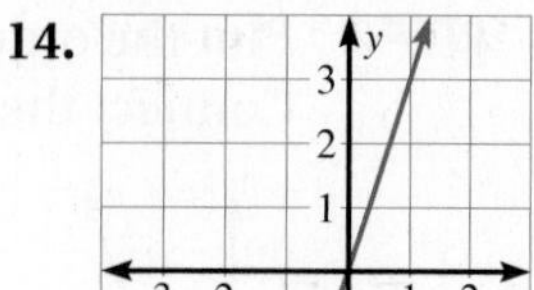

15. 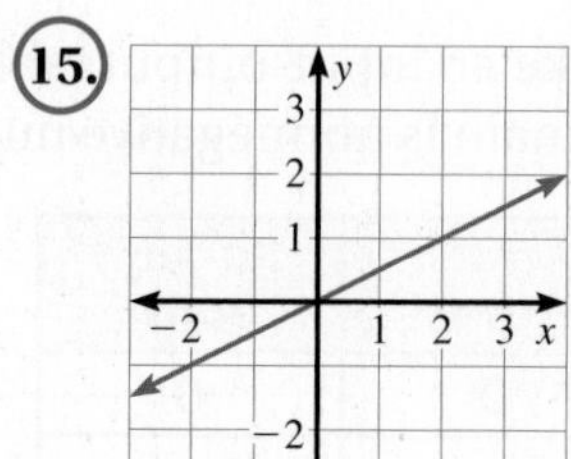

16. 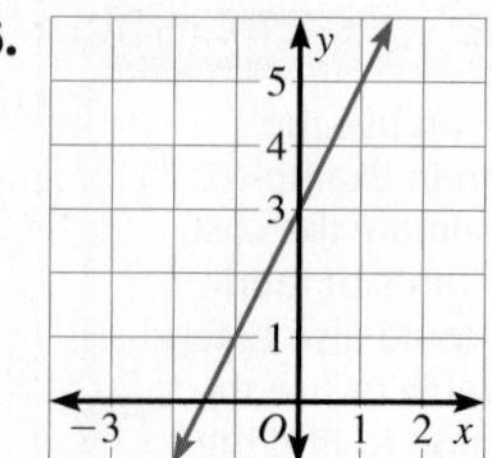

17. **ERROR ANALYSIS** A student states that the rule for the function graphed at the right is $y = x - 3$. *Describe* and correct the error.

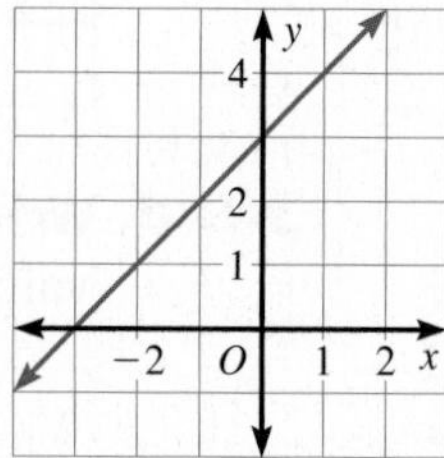

MEASUREMENT Write and graph a function that converts the units.

18. x days to y weeks

19. x yards to y feet

20. x pints to y cups

21. x millimeters to y centimeters

INTERSECTING LINES Graph the two functions in the same coordinate plane. Then name the point where they intersect.

22. $y = x$ and $y = 3x - 4$

23. $y = 5 - x$ and $y = 2x + 2$

24. $y = -x - 3$ and $y = 3x + 1$

25. $y = x + 1$ and $y = 3x - 1$

CONNECT SKILLS TO PROBLEM SOLVING Exercises 26–28 will help you prepare for problem solving.

Use the following information: Papayas cost $1.50 per pound. You can use the function $y = 1.5x$ to find the total cost y of x pounds of papayas.

26. Use the function to make an input-output table to find the cost of 1, 2, 5, and 10 pounds of papayas.

27. Use the table to make a list of ordered pairs.

28. Plot the ordered pairs in a coordinate plane and draw a line through the points.

SEE EXAMPLE 2 on p. 637 for Exs. 29–31

29. **EXERCISE** When you walk quickly, your body burns about 5 calories per minute. Write and graph a function to model the situation, where y is the number of calories burned and x is the number of minutes you walk.

California @HomeTutor for problem solving help at classzone.com

30. ◆ **MULTIPLE CHOICE** Which ordered pair lies on the graph of the function converting x gallons to y quarts?

Ⓐ (4, 32) Ⓑ (6, 24) Ⓒ (16, 4) Ⓓ (24, 3)

California @HomeTutor for problem solving help at classzone.com

31. **TEMPERATURE** You can use the function $y = 1.8x + 32$ to convert x degrees Celsius to y degrees Fahrenheit.

a. Copy and complete the table below.

Degrees Celsius x	−20	−10	0	10	20
Degrees Fahrenheit y	?	?	?	?	?

b. Use the table to make a list of ordered pairs. Then graph the function.

c. Use your graph from part (b) to estimate the equivalent Fahrenheit temperature of −15°C. Then use the function rule to find the actual Fahrenheit temperature. Compare your results.

32. **SHORT RESPONSE** A cable company charges $50 as a one-time installation fee and $30 per month for service. Write and graph a function that models the total cost y after x months of cable service. After how many months will cable costs total $230? *Explain.*

33. **OPEN-ENDED** *Describe* a real-world function whose output is always less than its input. Write and graph a rule for your function.

34. **UNICYCLES** A rider travels on a unicycle as shown below. The wheel on the unicycle has a diameter of 28 inches.

a. **Reasoning** What do you need to know in order to find the distance the rider travels in one rotation of the wheel?

b. **Write an Equation** Write a function rule that estimates the distance y (in inches) that the unicycle rider travels in x rotations. Use $\frac{22}{7}$ for π.

c. **Make a Table** Use the domain 0, 4, 8, 12, 16, and 20 rotations to make an input-output table. Use the table to make a list of ordered pairs.

d. **Draw a Graph** Graph the function. Use the graph, then the function, to find the distance traveled in 6.5 rotations. Compare your results.

READING IN MATH **Read the information below for Exercises 35–37.**

Physics The amount of force needed to move an object depends on its *mass* and its *acceleration*. Mass is a measure of the amount of material an object is made of. Acceleration is how quickly an object's velocity (speed) is changing.

Object	Mass m (kg)	Force F (Newtons)
Bowling ball	7	70
Large rock	4.5	45
Math book	1	10
Baseball	0.15	1.5

Gravity is a force that causes objects near Earth to fall toward the surface. The acceleration due to gravity for such objects is about 10 meters per second per second, or 10 m/s^2. The table shows the mass m (in kilograms) of several everyday objects and the gravitational force F (in *Newtons)* that acts upon the objects as they fall.

35. **Graphing** Use the table to write a list of ordered pairs of the form (mass, force), then plot and connect the points. Use the graph to estimate the force acting upon a 0.35 kilogram sneaker as it falls.

36. **Write a Rule** Use the table to write a function rule relating force F and mass m. How did you include acceleration due to gravity in your rule?

37. **Newton's Second Law** Based on your rule, write a formula relating force F, mass m, and acceleration a.

38. **CHALLENGE** The graphs of two functions intersect at a point. *Explain* how you could use input-output tables to find the coordinates of the point of intersection without graphing the functions.

39. **CHALLENGE** You are planning a vegetable garden. In a sketch of the garden, 3 inches represents 4 feet. Write a function rule that gives a, the actual dimensions (in feet), in terms of the sketch dimensions s (in inches). *Explain* the meaning of a domain of 0 to 6 for s. Then graph the function using this domain.

◆ CALIFORNIA STANDARDS SPIRAL REVIEW

MG 1.3 40. A cylinder has a diameter of 12 inches and a height of 18 inches. What is its volume? *(p. 601)*

Ⓐ 216π in.^{3} Ⓑ 486π in.^{3} Ⓒ 648π in.^{3} Ⓓ 2592π in.^{3}

SDAP 1.2 41. A data set consists of the numbers 19, 32, 37, and 44. If the number 16 is included in the data, which measure of the original set increases? *(p. 372)*

Ⓐ Mean Ⓑ Median Ⓒ Mode Ⓓ Range

NS 1.2 42. You used 5 cups of pasta for a pasta salad and 7 cups of pasta for a meal. What is the ratio of the amount of pasta used for the pasta salad to the amount of pasta used for the meal? *(p. 255)*

Ⓐ $\frac{5}{12}$ Ⓑ $\frac{5}{7}$ Ⓒ $\frac{7}{5}$ Ⓓ $\frac{12}{5}$

12.3 Graphing Functions

Standards Preview

Gr. 7 AF 3.3
Graph linear functions, noting that the vertical change (change in y-value) per unit of horizontal change (change in x-value) is always the same and know that the ratio ("rise over run") is called the slope of a graph.

QUESTION How can you graph functions using a graphing calculator?

EXAMPLE Graph $y = 3x - 2$ and find ordered pairs using the trace feature on your graphing calculator.

SOLUTION

STEP 1 Select Y= to enter the function $y = 3x - 2$ into the graphing calculator.

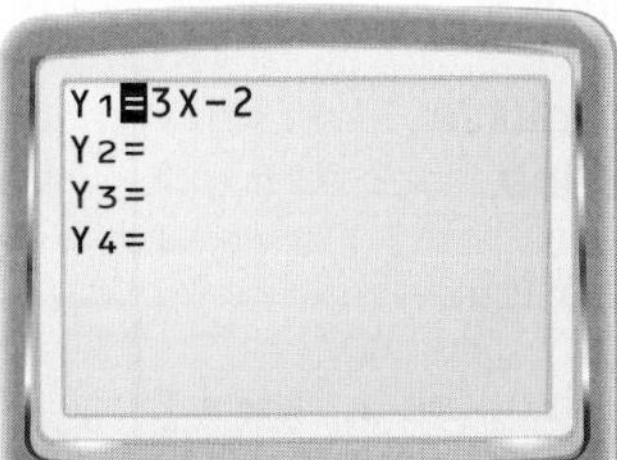

STEP 2 Select WINDOW and set up the window for the graph of $y = 3x - 2$ as shown.

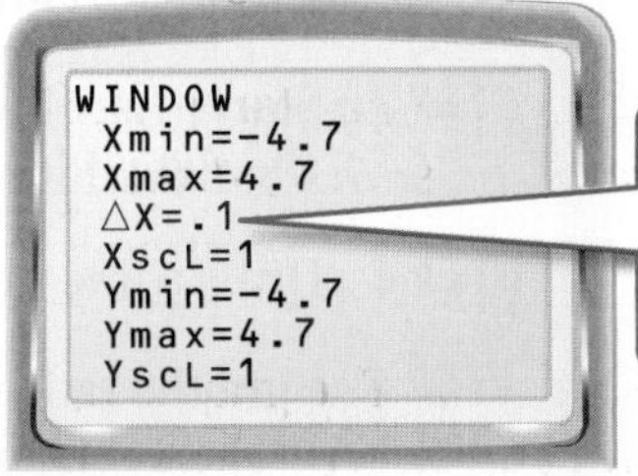

This determines the increment between x-values that you see using the trace feature.

STEP 3 Select GRAPH to view the graph of the function. Then select TRACE to see the coordinates of points on the graph. Use the left and right arrows to move the cursor along the graph.

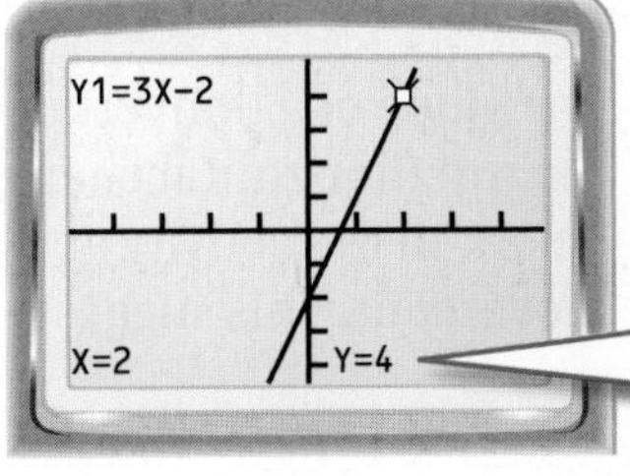

Notice that X = 2 and Y = 4 correspond to the indicated ordered pair, (2, 4).

PRACTICE

Use a graphing calculator to graph the function and find the unknown values in the given ordered pairs.

1. $y = 2x$, (? , 1.6) and (2.1, ?)
2. $y = -x$, (−4.3, ?) and (? , 0)
3. $y = -3x + 1$, (? , −2) and (−2, ?)
4. $y = 5x - \frac{1}{2}$, (4.5, ?) and (? , 1.5)
5. $y = -3x - 1$, (? , 0.8) and (0.2, ?)
6. $y = 2x + 2.3$, (0, ?) and (? , 5.5)
7. **INTERSECTIONS** Use a graphing calculator to graph $y = 2x + 5$ and $y = -x + 2$ in the same coordinate plane. Tell where they intersect. Check your answer by substituting the values into each equation.

12.4 Slope

Standards Preparation

Gr. 7 AF 3.3 Graph linear functions, noting that the vertical change (change in y-value) per unit of horizontal change (change in x-value) is always the same and know that the ratio ("rise over run") is called the slope of a graph.

Connect

Before you used a table to graph a linear function. ***Now*** you will find the slope of a line to preview Grade 7 Standard AF 3.3.

***Math and* EARNINGS**
Ex. 30–33, p. 645

KEY VOCABULARY

- **slope**

ACTIVITY

You can use ratios to describe the slope of a line.

STEP 1 **Start** at the origin in a coordinate plane. Move 3 units up and 2 units to the right, as shown. Plot this point and label it A.

STEP 2 **Start** at A. Move 6 units up and 4 units to the right. Plot this point and label it B.

STEP 3 **Draw** a line through A, B, and the origin.

STEP 4 **Find** the ratio of rise to run for each of the movements between points described in Steps 1 and 2. How do the ratios compare?

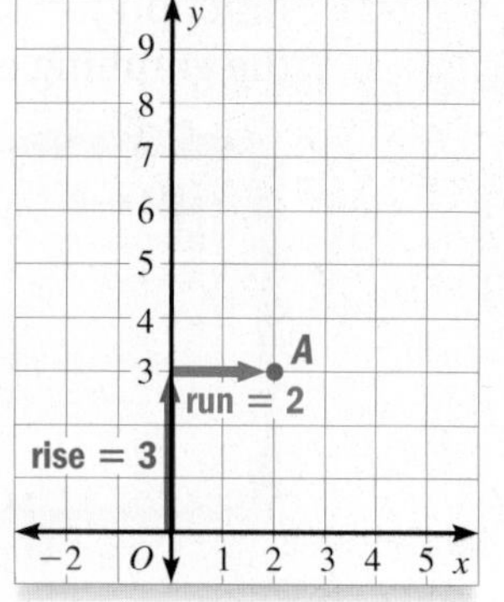

The **slope** of a nonvertical line is the ratio of the rise (vertical change) to the run (horizontal change) between any two points on the line as shown below. In the activity above, the ratio of rise to run was equal for each movement. This suggests that a line has a constant slope.

RISE AND RUN

Rise is positive when moving up and negative when moving down. Run is positive when moving to the right and negative when moving to the left.

$$\text{slope} = \frac{\textbf{rise}}{\textbf{run}} = \frac{-1}{5} = -\frac{1}{5}$$

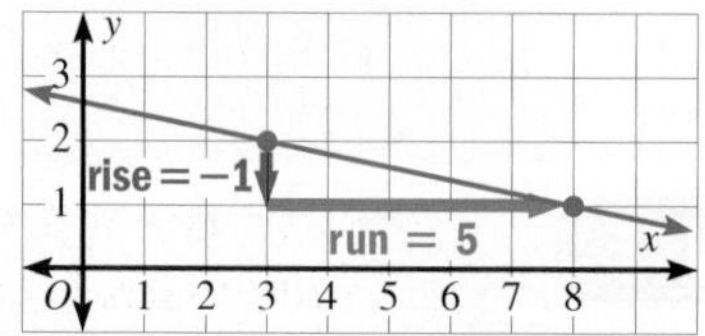

Examples of lines with positive, negative, and zero slopes are shown below. The slope of a vertical line is undefined.

A **positive** slope rises from left to right.

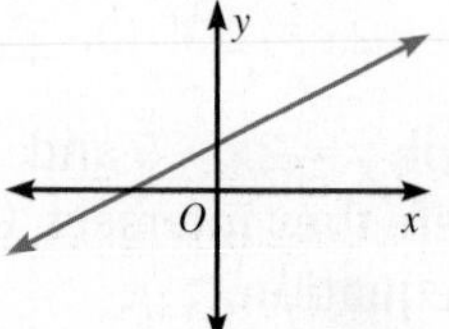

A **negative** slope falls from left to right.

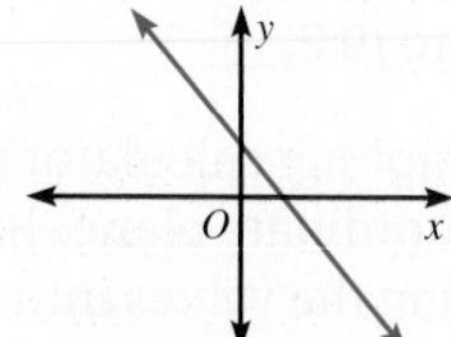

A horizontal line has a **slope of 0**.

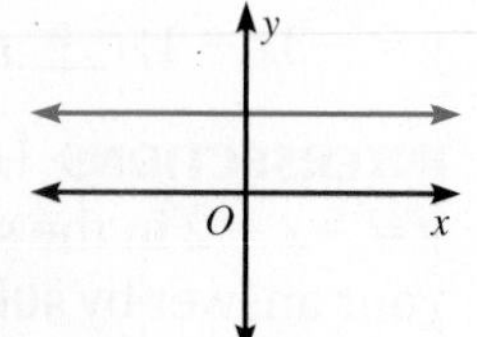

EXAMPLE 1 Finding the Slope of a Line

Find the slope of the line by finding the ratio of the rise to the run between any two points on the line.

a.

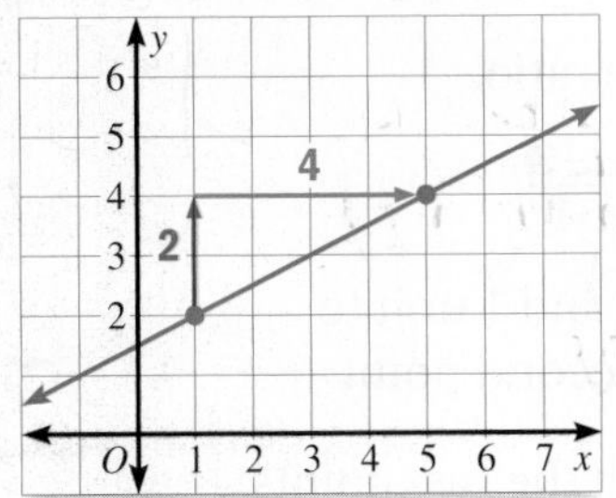

$$\text{slope} = \frac{\text{rise}}{\text{run}} = \frac{2}{4} = \frac{1}{2}$$

b.

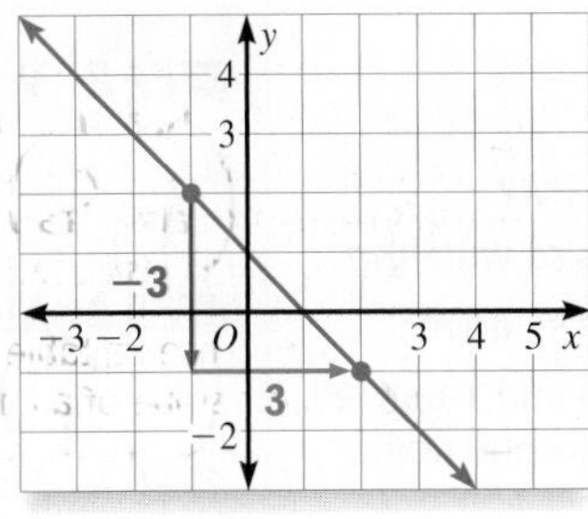

$$\text{slope} = \frac{\text{rise}}{\text{run}} = \frac{-3}{3} = -1$$

AVOID ERRORS

Be sure not to confuse the rise and the run, or you may calculate the reciprocal of the actual slope.

SLOPE AS A RATE When the graph of a line represents a real-world situation, the slope of a line can often be interpreted as a *rate of change*. You can write the slope as a unit rate to help interpret the situation.

EXAMPLE 2 Interpreting Slope as a Rate

VOLCANOES The graph represents the average distance traveled by a lava flow over time. To find the speed of the lava flow, find the slope of the line.

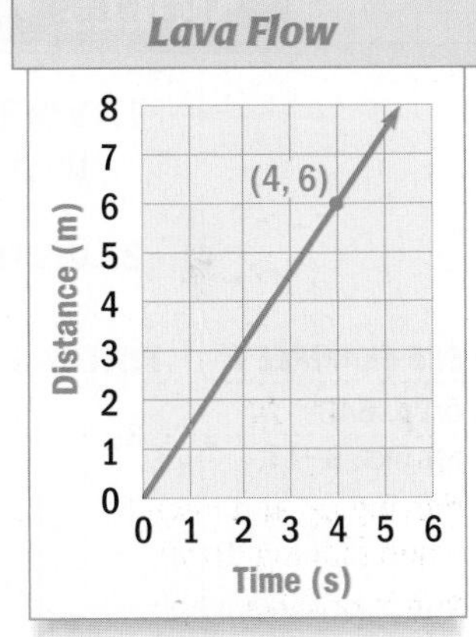

AnimatedMath

For an interactive example of interpreting slope go to **classzone.com.**

SOLUTION

$\text{slope} = \frac{\text{rise}}{\text{run}}$	**Write definition of slope.**
$= \frac{6 \text{ m}}{4 \text{ s}}$	**Rise from (0, 0) to (4, 6) is 6. Run from (0, 0) to (4, 6) is 4.**
$= \frac{1.5 \text{ m}}{1 \text{ s}}$	**Find unit rate.**

▶ **Answer** The speed of the lava flow is 1.5 meters per second.

✓ **GUIDED PRACTICE** for Examples 1 and 2

1. Plot the points (3, 4) and (6, 3). Then find the slope of the line that passes through the points.

2. **WHAT IF?** In Example 2, suppose a similar graph represents a different lava flow and the line passes through (3, 6). Find the speed of the lava flow.

EXAMPLE 3 Using Slope to Draw a Line

Draw the line that has a slope of −3 and that passes through (2, 5).

STEP 1 **Plot** (2, 5).

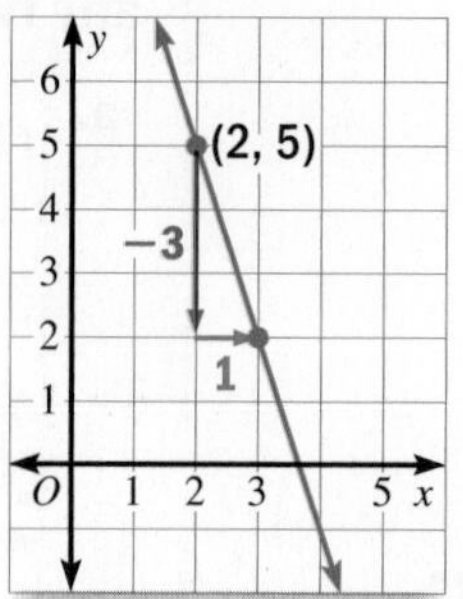

STEP 2 **Write** the slope as a ratio.

$$\text{slope} = \frac{\textbf{rise}}{\textbf{run}} = \frac{-3}{1}$$

STEP 3 **Move** 3 units down and 1 unit to the right to plot a second point.

STEP 4 **Draw** a line through the two points.

ANOTHER WAY

You can also write the slope as $\frac{3}{-1}$. Move 3 units up and 1 unit left to plot a second point.

✓ GUIDED PRACTICE for Example 3

3. Draw the line that has a slope of $\frac{1}{3}$ and passes through (−1, −3).

12.4 EXERCISES

HOMEWORK KEY

◆ = **MULTIPLE CHOICE PRACTICE** Exs. 12, 13, 34, 48–50

○ = **HINTS AND HOMEWORK HELP** for Exs. 5, 17, 39 at classzone.com

SKILLS • PROBLEM SOLVING • REASONING

1. **VOCABULARY** Copy and complete: The slope of a nonvertical line is the ratio of the __?__ to the __?__ between any two points on the line.

2. **WRITING** *Explain* why the slope of a horizontal line is zero.

SEE EXAMPLE 1 on p. 643 for Exs. 3–11

FINDING SLOPE **Find the slope of the line.**

3.

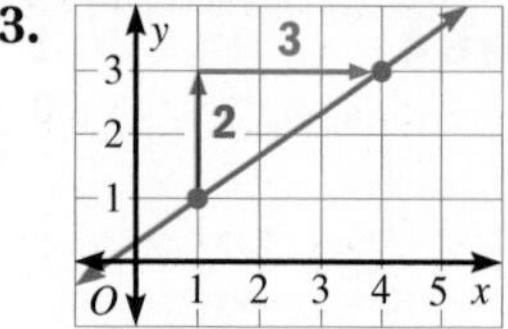

4.

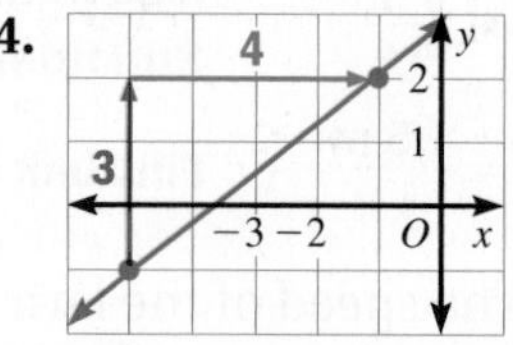

5.

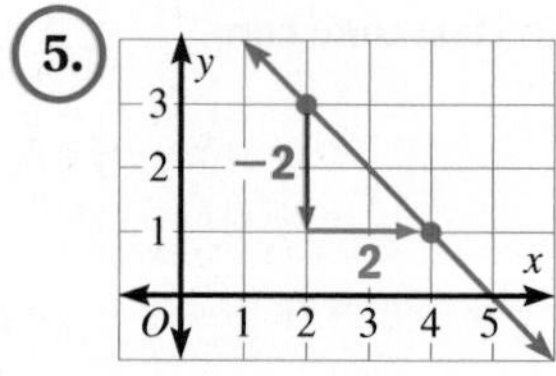

6.

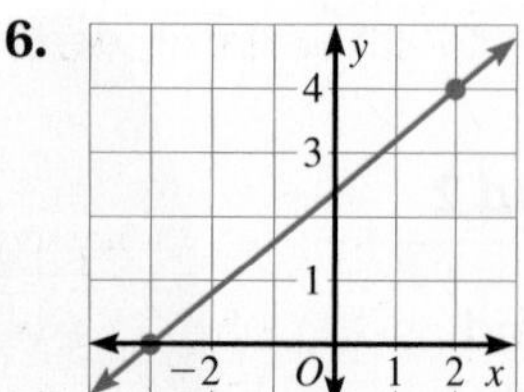

7.

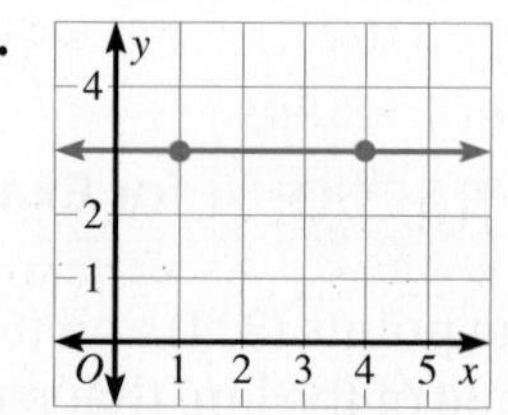

8.

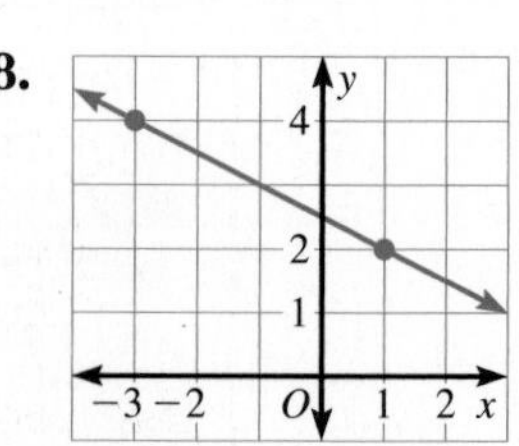

DRAWING LINES **Draw the graph of the line that passes through the points. Then find the slope of the line.**

9. (3, 4), (5, 6)

10. (2, 5), (5, −2)

11. (−5, −2), (3, −4)

SEE EXAMPLE 1
on p. 643
for Exs. 12–15

12. ◆ **MULTIPLE CHOICE** What is the slope of the blue line?

Ⓐ $-\frac{3}{2}$ Ⓑ $-\frac{2}{3}$ Ⓒ $\frac{2}{3}$ Ⓓ $\frac{3}{2}$

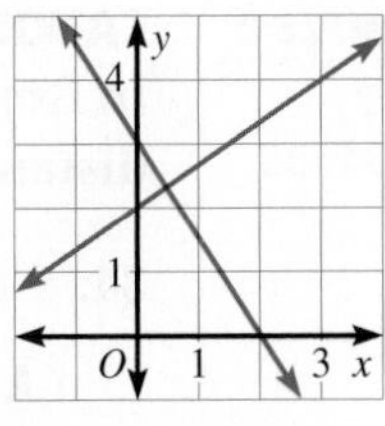

13. ◆ **MULTIPLE CHOICE** What is the slope of the red line?

Ⓐ $-\frac{3}{2}$ Ⓑ $-\frac{2}{3}$ Ⓒ $\frac{2}{3}$ Ⓓ $\frac{3}{2}$

ERROR ANALYSIS ***Describe*** **and correct the error made in finding the slope of the line passing through the given points.**

14. (0, 0), (3, 7)
$\text{slope} = \frac{\text{rise}}{\text{run}} = \frac{3}{7}$

15. (4, 6), (7, 2)
$\text{slope} = \frac{\text{rise}}{\text{run}} = \frac{4}{3}$

SEE EXAMPLE 3
on p. 644
for Exs. 16–21

USING SLOPE Draw the line that has the given slope and that passes through the given point.

16. slope = 3, (3, −1)
17. slope = 1, (0, −1)
18. slope = −2, (4, 0)
19. slope = $\frac{2}{3}$, (−2, −2)
20. slope = $\frac{3}{4}$, (−2, −1)
21. slope = $-\frac{5}{6}$, (5, 5)

COMPARING SLOPES Use the information given below to copy and complete the statement using <, >, or =.

Line a passes through the points (1, −3) and (2, 0).
Line b passes through the points (1, 1) and (7, 3).
Line c has a slope of $\frac{1}{3}$ and passes through the point (−2, 5).

22. slope of line a _?_ slope of line b
23. slope of line b _?_ slope of line c
24. slope of line c _?_ slope of line a
25. slope of line b _?_ slope of a horizontal line

xy ALGEBRA Use the points and slope of the line to find the value of *a*.

26. slope = $\frac{a}{2}$, (−2, −1), (2, 5)
27. slope = $\frac{-3}{a}$, (−3, −1), (1, 5)
28. slope = $-\frac{4}{3}$, (−3, 4), (6, a)
29. slope = $\frac{9}{4}$, (a, 7), (2, −11)

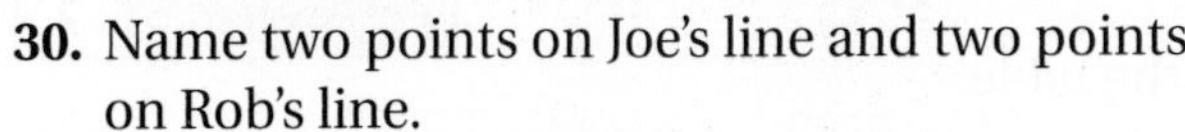

CONNECT SKILLS TO PROBLEM SOLVING Exercises 30–33 will help you prepare for problem solving.

Use the graph, which shows the amount earned over time by two different babysitters.

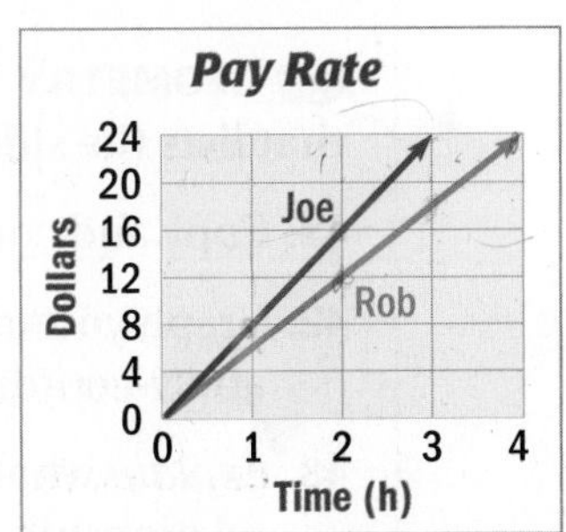

30. Name two points on Joe's line and two points on Rob's line.
31. Use the points to find the slope of each line.
32. Write the slopes as unit pay rates.
33. Who has the greater pay rate? How much greater?

SEE EXAMPLE 2
on p. 643
for Exs. 34–35

CANOEING **On Saturday, you go canoeing for 2 hours. In Exercises 34 and 35, use the graph representing the distance that you travel over time.**

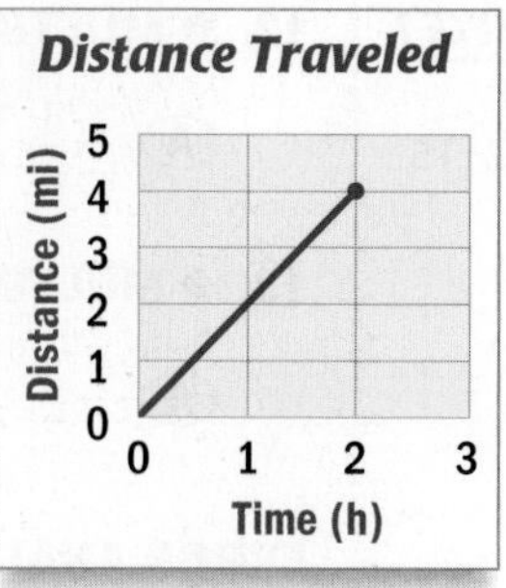

34. ◆ **MULTIPLE CHOICE** What is your speed?

Ⓐ 1 mile per hour Ⓑ 2 miles per hour

Ⓒ 3 miles per hour Ⓓ 4 miles per hour

for problem solving help at classzone.com

35. **SHORT RESPONSE** You go canoeing again on Sunday and travel 3.5 miles in 1.75 hours. How does this compare to your speed on Saturday? *Explain.*

California @HomeTutor for problem solving help at classzone.com

36. **REASONING** A line passing through the origin has a negative slope. Through which quadrant(s) does the line pass? *Explain.*

REASONING **In Exercises 37–39, use the graph representing the distance you are from home and the time since you left home while out for a walk.**

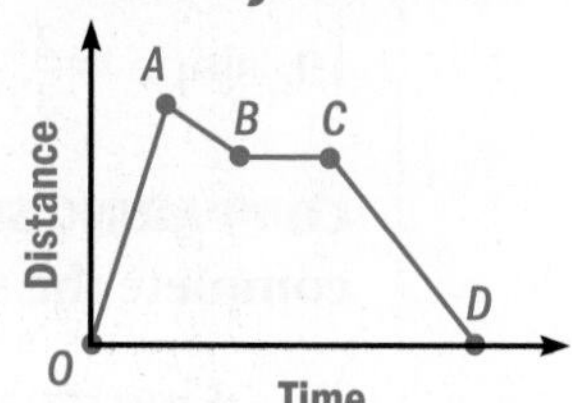

37. Between which two points do you walk fastest?

38. What could explain the slope of the line segment between points B and C?

39. The slope between points O and A is positive. The slope between points C and D is negative. *Interpret* the meaning of the positive and negative slopes.

40. **SEA TURTLES** Use the graph showing the distances that two sea turtles travel over time.

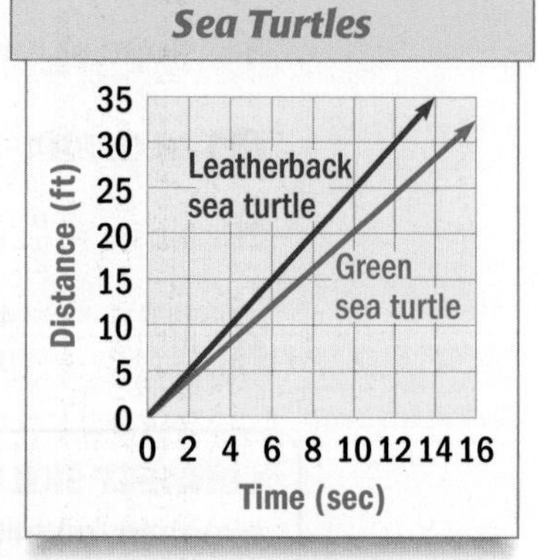

a. Which turtle swims at a greater speed? *Explain.*

b. About how many more feet per second does the faster sea turtle swim than the slower sea turtle? *Explain* how you found your answer.

c. A third turtle swims at a rate of 135 feet per minute. How does the swimming rate of the third turtle compare with the rates of the other two turtles? *Explain* your reasoning.

GEOMETRY **In Exercises 41–43, use the table that lists the side lengths of four squares.**

Side length	1	2	3	4
Perimeter	?	?	?	?

41. Copy and complete the table.

42. Graph your results as points whose x-coordinates are the side lengths and y-coordinates are the perimeters. Draw a line through the points.

43. *Explain* what the slope of the line in Exercise 42 tells about the relationship between the side length of a square and its perimeter.

44. **WRITING** You are given a graph of a line that shows the number of times y that your heart beats in x minutes. *Describe* two methods that you can use to find the number of beats per minute.

45. **OPEN-ENDED** Give a real-world example of a function describing a relationship that can be represented as a line in a coordinate plane with a negative slope. *Explain* your example.

46. **CHALLENGE** Use a rise of $\frac{1}{3}$ and a run of $-\frac{5}{6}$ to find the slope of a line. Graph the line with this slope that passes through $\left(-\frac{1}{3}, 4\frac{1}{3}\right)$. Name two points on the line whose coordinates are whole numbers.

47. xy **CHALLENGE** The points $(x - 4, y)$ and $(x, y + b)$ lie on a line. Find the slope of the line.

◆ CALIFORNIA STANDARDS SPIRAL REVIEW

AF 2.2 48. What is $\frac{\$5.60}{7 \text{ lb}}$ written as a unit rate? *(p. 260)*

Ⓐ $\frac{\$.08}{1 \text{ lb}}$ Ⓑ $\frac{\$.80}{1 \text{ lb}}$ Ⓒ $\frac{\$8}{10 \text{ lb}}$ Ⓓ $\frac{\$8}{1 \text{ lb}}$

AF 1.3 49. What is the value of $5(6 - 8)^2 + 7$? *(p. 160)*

Ⓐ −13 Ⓑ 27 Ⓒ 107 Ⓓ 491

MG 1.2 50. The bottom of a circular baking pan has a diameter of 12 inches. What is the area of the bottom of the pan? Use 3.14 for π. *(p. 555)*

Ⓐ 37.68 in.^{2} Ⓑ 75.36 in.^{2} Ⓒ 113.04 in.^{2} Ⓓ 452.16 in.^{2}

QUIZ *for Lessons 12.3–12.4*

Graph the function. *(p. 636)*

1. $y = -6x + 4$
2. $y = 12 - 3x$
3. $y = 4x - 9$

Draw the graph of the line that passes through the points. Then find the slope of the line. *(p. 642)*

4. (3, 4), (0, −2)
5. (1, 1), (−3, −3)
6. (−5, 5), (−1, 3)

7. Draw the line that has a slope of $-\frac{2}{3}$ and that passes through (−1, −3). *(p. 642)*

8. **UNIT RATES** The graph at the right shows the total cost y (in dollars) of x ounces of almonds. Find the cost per ounce of almonds. *(p. 642)*

9. **EROSION** A beach erodes 8 feet every year. Write and graph a function that relates the amount of erosion y (in feet) after x years. Estimate the erosion (in feet) after $9\frac{1}{2}$ years. *(p. 636)*

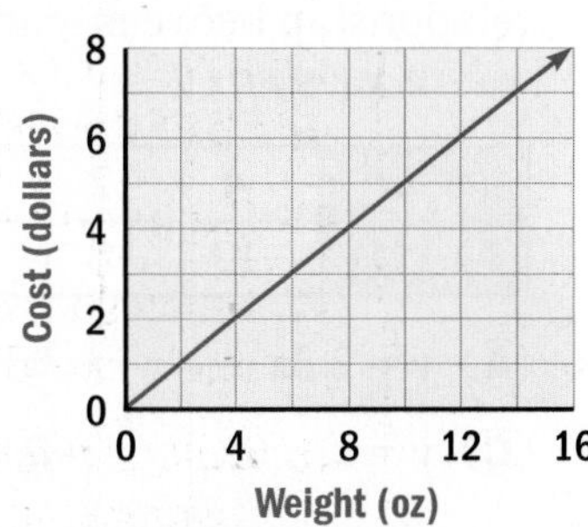

Multiple Choice Practice for Lessons 12.1–12.4

1. Two battery-operated toy cars were tested to see how fast they travel. The data are shown in the graph. What is the speed of each car? **Gr. 7 AF 3.3**

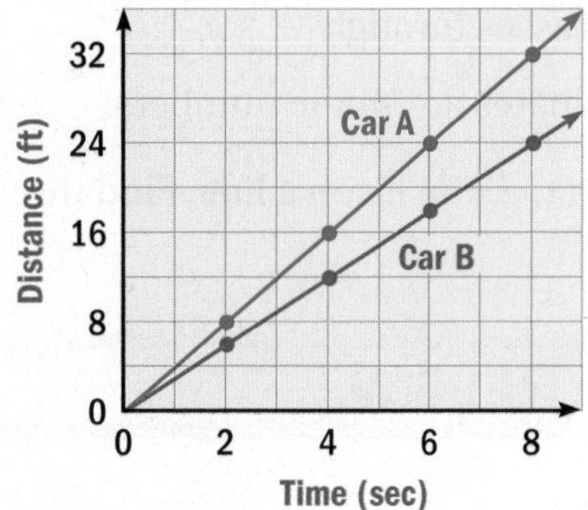

Ⓐ Car A: 4 ft/sec; Car B: 3 ft/sec

Ⓑ Car A: 3 ft/sec; Car B: 4 ft/sec

Ⓒ Car A: 32 ft/sec; Car B: 24 ft/sec

Ⓓ Car A: 24 ft/sec; Car B: 32 ft/sec

2. Which function has a graph with a negative slope? **Gr. 7 AF 3.3**

Ⓐ $y = x - 15$ Ⓑ $y = 6x - 4$

Ⓒ $y = 8 - 3x$ Ⓓ $y = 12 + x$

3. Monique is exactly 5 years younger than Jamie. Which function rule can be used to find Monique's age m when Jamie is j years old? **Gr. 5 AF 1.5**

Ⓐ $m = j + 5$ Ⓑ $j = m - 5$

Ⓒ $m = j - 5$ Ⓓ $j = \frac{m}{5}$

4. In the table below, which equation shows the relationship between x and y? **MR 1.1, Gr. 5 AF 1.5**

Input x	−4	−2	0	2	4
Output y	−10	−8	−6	−4	−2

Ⓐ $y = 2.5x$ Ⓑ $y = x + 6$

Ⓒ $y = x - 6$ Ⓓ $y = 2x - 2$

5. Every time you do yard work for a neighbor, you get a $5 tip after the first hour of work. You record the number of hours you work and the amount of money you earn each day. Which function relates the number of hours x that you work and the amount y that you earn after working for at least one hour? **Gr. 7 AF 3.3**

Ⓐ $y = 10x$

Ⓑ $y = 10x - 5$

Ⓒ $y = x + 5$

Ⓓ $y = 5x + 5$

MY TIME SHEET

Thurs.	1 h	$10
Fri.	2 h	$15
Sat.	3 h	$20
Sun.	4 h	$25

6. Terence used the following process to find the slope of the line passing through (2, 4) and (6, 1).

STEP 1: Write the definition of slope. $\text{slope} = \frac{\text{rise}}{\text{run}}$

STEP 2: Substitute for the rise and the run. $\text{slope} = \frac{1-4}{6-2}$

STEP 3: Simplify. $\text{slope} = -\frac{3}{4}$

According to Terence's method, which expression can you use to find the slope of the line passing through the points $A(a, 3)$ and $B(5, b)$? **MR 3.2, Gr. 7 AF 3.3**

Ⓐ $\frac{a-b}{2}$ Ⓑ $\frac{b-3}{5-a}$

Ⓒ $\frac{b-3}{a-5}$ Ⓓ $\frac{b-a}{2}$

7. Which point is located in Quadrant III? **Gr. 5 AF 1.4**

Ⓐ $A(-3, -3)$ Ⓑ $B(-3, 0)$

Ⓒ $C(0, -3)$ Ⓓ $D(3, -3)$

12 CHAPTER SUMMARY

Standards
Gr. 5 AF 1.4, Gr. 5 AF 1.5, Gr. 7 AF 3.3

BIG IDEAS

For Your Notebook

Big Idea 1

Identifying and Plotting Ordered Pairs

In the ordered pair (4, −1), the x-coordinate is 4 and the y-coordinate is −1. To plot the point $P(4, -1)$, you move 4 units right of the origin and 1 unit down.

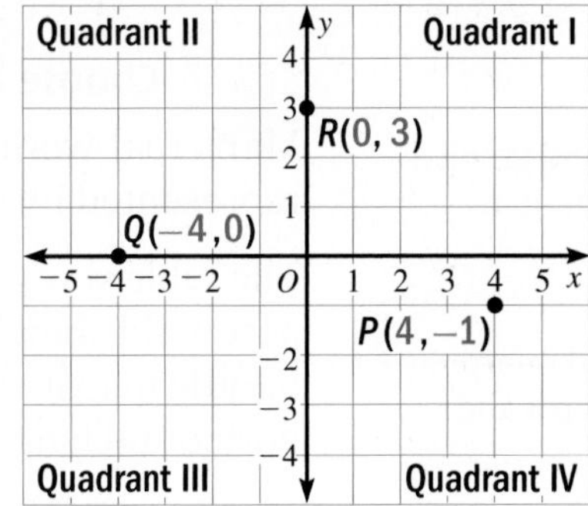

Point $P(4, -1)$ lies in Quadrant IV. Point $Q(-4, 0)$ lies on the x-axis and point $R(0, 3)$ lies on the y-axis. Points Q and R do not lie in any quadrant.

Big Idea 2

Writing and Graphing Linear Functions

A function pairs each number in one set with exactly one number in another set. The set of all input values is the domain and the set of all output values is the range.

The table and graph below relate the amount of time x (in hours) that you rent a kayak to the total cost y (in dollars). Because the situation involves a cost per hour, neither the domain nor the range can be less than zero.

Input x	0	2	4	6	8
Output y	0	15	30	45	60

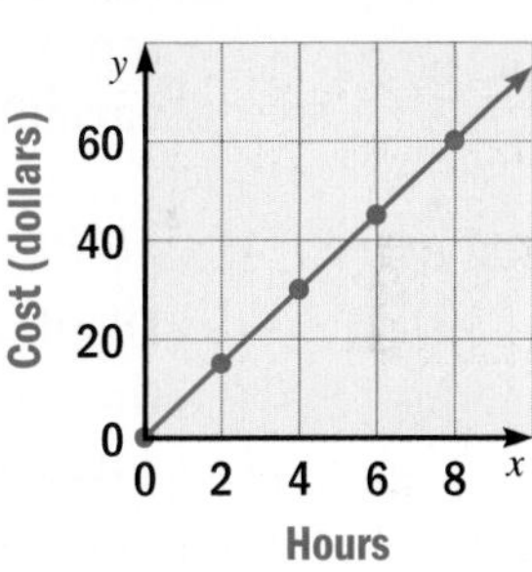

You can graph the function by plotting points from the table above and drawing a line through them, as shown at the right. You can also write a rule for the function by comparing each output to its input. Each output is 7.5 times the input. The rule for the function is $y = 7.5x$.

Big Idea 3

Using and Interpreting Slope

The slope of a nonvertical line is the ratio of the rise (vertical change) to the run (horizontal change) between any two points on the line. When written as a unit rate, slope can describe a rate of change.

The graph at the right represents the distance traveled by a car over time. To find the speed of the car, use the the given points to find the slope of the graph.

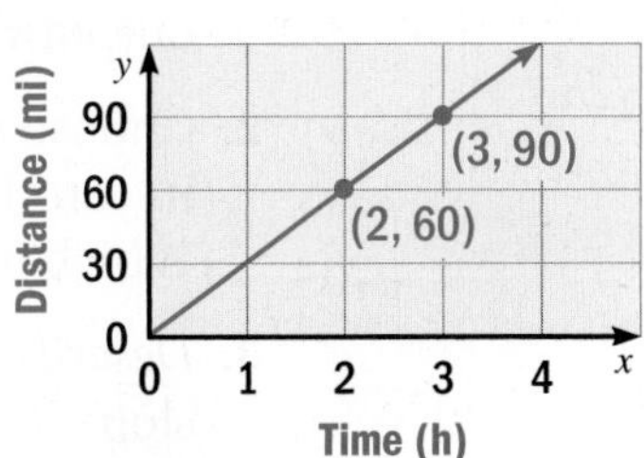

$$\text{slope} = \frac{\text{rise}}{\text{run}} = \frac{30}{1} = 30$$

The speed of the car is 30 miles per hour.

CHAPTER PROBLEM

Standards
Gr. 5 AF 1.4,
Gr. 5 AF 1.5,
Gr. 7 AF 3.3

APPLYING THE
BIG IDEAS

Big Idea 1
You identify and plot ordered pairs in **Step 2** and **Ex. 1.**

Big Idea 2
You write and graph a linear function in **Step 2.**

Big Idea 3
You use and interpret slope in **Step 3** and **Ex. 3.**

PROBLEM How can you use what you know about functions and slope to represent real-world situations mathematically?

STEP 1 **Choose a real-world situation.**

Many real-world situations can be represented by linear functions.

The table shows maximum acceptable heights h (in feet) of handicap exit ramps for given horizontal lengths l (in feet).

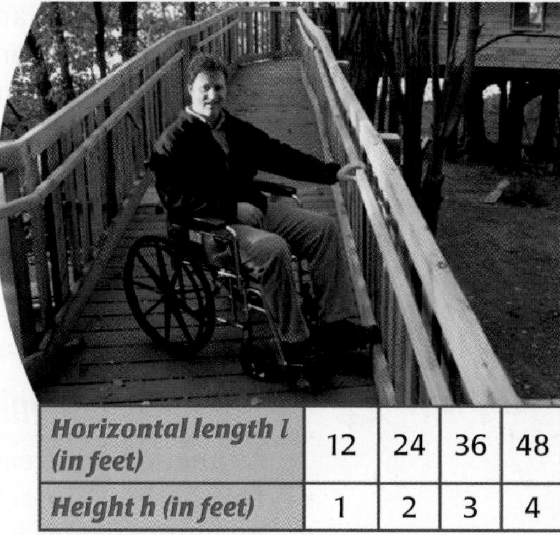

Horizontal length l (in feet)	12	24	36	48
Height h (in feet)	1	2	3	4

Choose a real-world situation that can be represented by a linear function. Examples include calories burned over time for various forms of exercise or gallons of gasoline used to travel different distances.

STEP 2 **Write a rule and graph the function.**

Make an input-output table to represent your function. Be sure to use a domain that makes sense for the situation. Write a rule to represent the function and graph the function. Identify what each variable represents.

STEP 3 **Interpret and display your results.**

Display your table, rule, and graph on a poster. Write a paragraph that summarizes your real-world situation. In your paragraph, be sure to discuss the slope of your graph and its meaning in the real-world situation.

Extending the Problem

Use your results to complete the exercises.

1. Choose an input value for your function that is between two values in your table and on your graph. *Explain* how to use the table, graph, and function rule to find the corresponding output value. Find the output value with each method and compare your results.
2. Choose an input value for your function that is greater than the values in your table and on your graph. Find the corresponding output value. Which method did you use and why?
3. *Describe* a function similar to the one you chose but with a different slope. *Explain* how the graphs of the two functions would compare.

12 CHAPTER REVIEW

California @HomeTutor
classzone.com
• Multi-Language Visual Glossary
• Vocabulary practice

REVIEW KEY VOCABULARY

coordinate plane, *p. 624*	*y*-coordinate, *p. 624*	domain, *p. 630*
origin, *p. 624*	scatter plot, *p. 626*	range, *p. 630*
quadrant, *p. 624*	function, *p. 630*	linear function, *p. 637*
ordered pair, *p. 624*	input, *p. 630*	slope, *p. 642*
x-coordinate, *p. 624*	output, *p.630*	

VOCABULARY EXERCISES

Copy and complete the statement.

1. The _?_ describes a point's position left or right of the *y*-axis.
2. The _?_ describes a point's position up or down from the *x*-axis.
3. The set of all output values is called the _?_ of a function.
4. A point in a coordinate plane is represented by a(n) _?_.
5. The ratio of the rise to the run between two points on a nonvertical line is called the _?_ of the line.
6. **NOTETAKING SKILLS** Make a *definitions and examples chart* like the one shown on page 622 for *slope*.

12.1 The Coordinate Plane

pp. 624–629

Gr. 5 AF 1.4

EXAMPLE

Name the ordered pair that represents the point.

a. *A* **b.** *B* **c.** *C*

SOLUTION

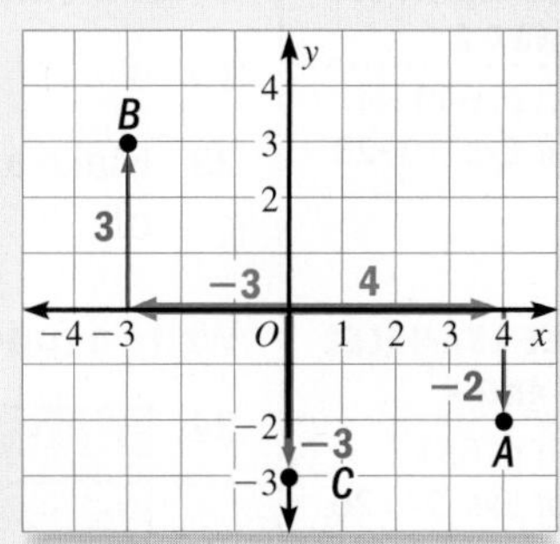

a. Point *A* is 4 units to the right of the origin and 2 units down. The *x*-coordinate is 4 and the *y*-coordinate is -2. Point *A* is represented by the ordered pair $(4, -2)$.

b. Point *B* is 3 units to the left of the origin and 3 units up. The *x*-coordinate is -3 and the *y*-coordinate is 3. Point *B* is represented by the ordered pair $(-3, 3)$.

c. Point *C* is neither left nor right of the origin. It is 3 units down. The *x*-coordinate is 0 and the *y*-coordinate is -3. Point *C* is represented by the ordered pair $(0, -3)$.

EXERCISES

SEE EXAMPLES 1 AND 2 on pp. 624–625 for Exs. 7–16

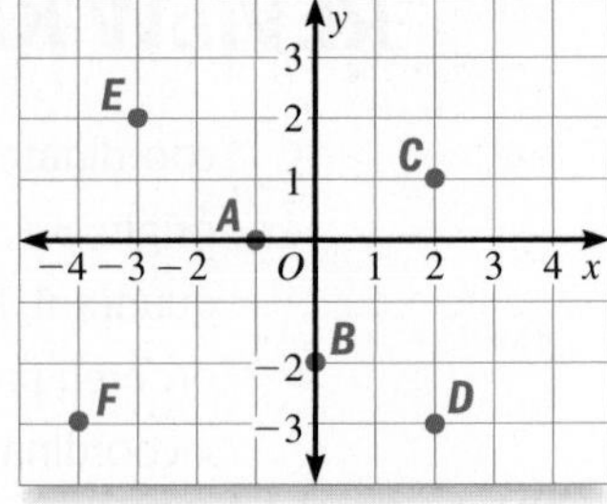

Name the ordered pair that represents the point.

7. *A*   **8.** *B*   **9.** *C*

10. *D*   **11.** *E*   **12.** *F*

Plot and label the points in the same coordinate plane.
***Describe* the location of each point.**

13. $P(-6, 2)$ **14.** $Q(3, 2)$ **15.** $R(3, -7)$ **16.** $S(-6, -7)$

SEE EXAMPLES 3 AND 4 on pp. 625–626 for Exs. 17–18

17. Find the length, width, and area of rectangle *PQRS* in Exercises 13–16.

18. **BIOLOGY** The ordered pairs show the widths and lengths (in centimeters) of seven butter-clam shells. Make a scatter plot of the data. Then make a conclusion about the data.

(2.1, 2.7), (3.1, 4.1), (3.0, 4.0), (2.8, 3.8), (2.8, 3.5), (2.6, 3.5), (2.4, 3.2)

12.2 Functions and Equations

pp. 630–634

Gr. 5 AF 1.5

EXAMPLE

Write a function rule for the input-output table.

Input x	−4	−3	−2	−1	0	1	2
Output y	2	3	4	5	6	7	8

Each output value is 6 more than the input value. The function rule for the table is $y = x + 6$.

EXERCISES

SEE EXAMPLES 1 AND 2 on p. 630 for Exs. 19–23

Evaluate the function $y = 3x - 7$ for the given value of x.

19. 4   **20.** 5   **21.** −3   **22.** −7

23. Make an input-output table for the function $y = -9x + 2$. Use a domain of −2, −1, 0, 1, and 2. Then state the range of the function.

SEE EXAMPLES 3 AND 4 on p. 631 for Exs. 24–26

Write a function rule for the input-output table.

24.

Input x	0	1	2	3
Output y	4	5	6	7

25.

Input x	−2	0	2	4
Output y	8	0	−8	−16

26. **DRIVING SPEED** A car travels at a constant speed of 45 miles per hour. Write a function rule to find the number of miles n traveled in t hours. How many miles does the car travel in 2.5 hours?

12.3 Graphing Functions   pp. 636–640

Gr. 7 AF 3.3

EXAMPLE

SOCCER You burn about 8 calories per minute while playing soccer. Write and graph a function to represent the number of calories burned y after playing soccer for x minutes.

STEP 1 **Make** an input-output table for the function. Choose several values for x. Note that playing for a negative number of minutes does not make sense, so the domain does not include negative numbers.

Input x (minutes)	0	1	2	3	4
Output y (calories)	0	8	16	24	32

STEP 2 **Use** the table to make a list of ordered pairs:

(0, 0), (1, 8), (2, 16), (3, 24), (4, 32)

Plot the ordered pairs and connect them as shown.

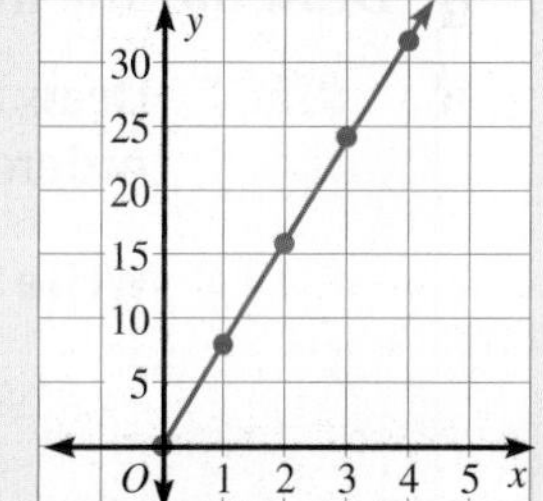

STEP 3 **Write** a function rule to represent the situation.

For every minute of playing soccer, you burn 8 calories. In x minutes of playing soccer, you will burn $8x$ calories.

A rule for the function is $y = 8x$.

EXERCISES

Graph the function.

SEE EXAMPLES 1 AND 2 on pp. 636–637 for Exs. 27–36

27. $y = x - 5$ **28.** $y = x + 4$ **29.** $y = -4x$

30. $y = 3x$ **31.** $y = 3x + 3$ **32.** $y = 2x - 4$

In Exercises 33–34, use the graph at the right.

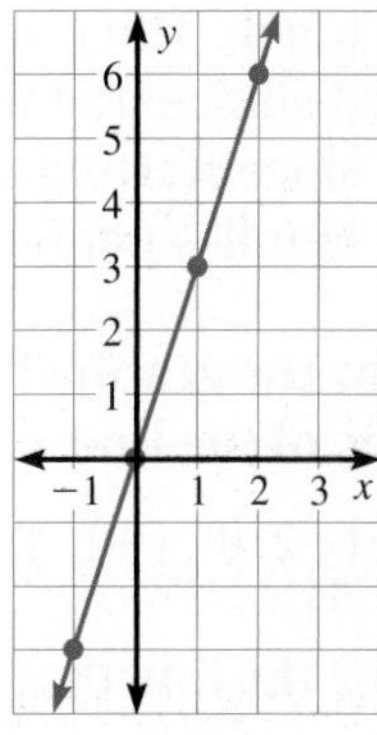

33. Make an input-output table from the graph.

34. Write a rule for the function.

35. HEALTH CLUBS A health club charges \$25 as a one-time registration fee and \$20 per month. Write and graph a function for the total cost y of a membership lasting x months.

36. Use your graph in Exercise 35 to predict the total cost of a ten-month membership.

12.4 Slope

pp.642–647

Gr. 7 AF 3.3

EXAMPLE 1

Find the slope of the line in the graph at the right.

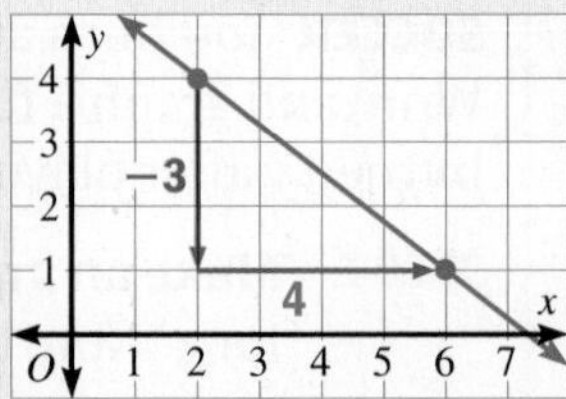

To find the slope of a line, find the ratio of the rise to the run between any two points on the line. Two points on the line are (2, 4) and (6, 1).

$$\text{slope} = \frac{\textbf{rise}}{\textbf{run}} = \frac{-3}{4} = -\frac{3}{4}$$

EXAMPLE 2

Draw the line that has a slope of −4 and that passes through (2, 2).

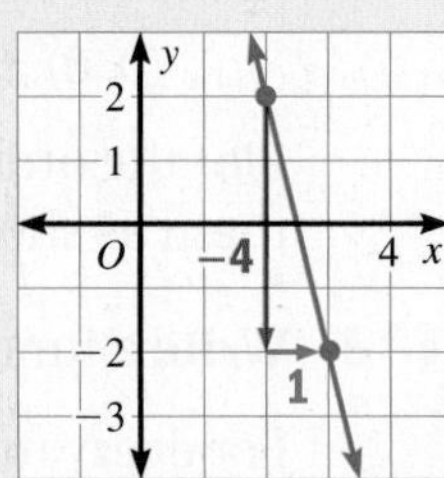

STEP 1 **Draw** a coordinate plane. Plot the ordered pair (2, 2).

STEP 2 **Write** the slope as a fraction.

$$\text{slope} = \frac{\textbf{rise}}{\textbf{run}} = \frac{-4}{1}$$

STEP 3 **Move** 4 units down and 1 unit to the right to plot a second point.

STEP 4 **Draw** a line through the two points.

EXERCISES

SEE EXAMPLES 1, 2, AND 3 on pp. 642–643 for Exs. 37–43

37. ROAD TRIP On a trip to visit relatives, your family stops for lunch after driving 60 miles. In the graph at the right, the x-values represent the amount of time that you travel at a constant speed after lunch. The y-values represent the total distance that your family has traveled since starting the trip. Find your speed in miles per hour.

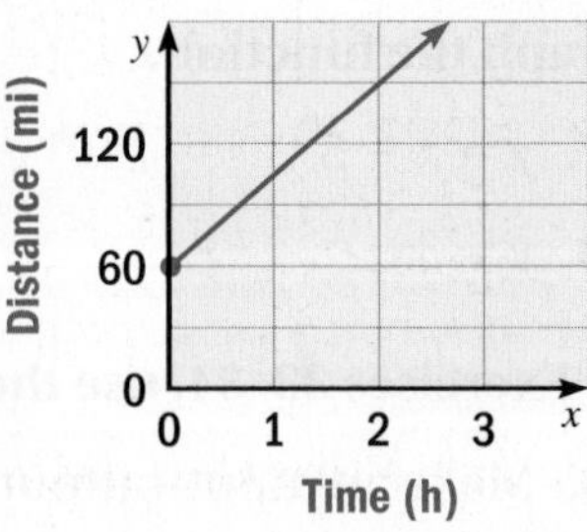

Draw the graph of the line that passes through the points. Then find the slope of the line.

38. (−2, 0), (−1, 4) **39.** (−1, 6), (3, 8) **40.** (−3, −2), (5, −5)

Draw the line that has the given slope and that passes through the given point.

41. slope = 3, (−2, −7) **42.** slope = −2, (0, 5) **43.** slope = $\frac{3}{4}$, (−1, 2)

12 CHAPTER TEST

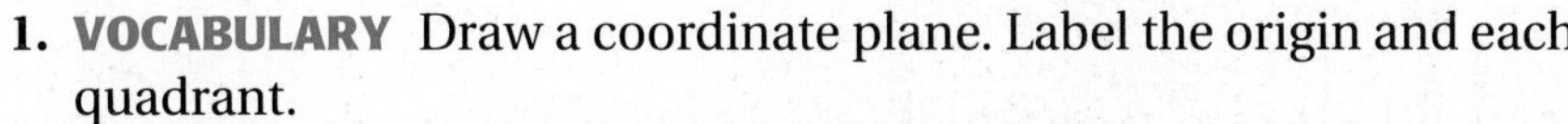

1. **VOCABULARY** Draw a coordinate plane. Label the origin and each quadrant.

2. **VOCABULARY** *Explain* the meaning of the x-coordinate and y-coordinate in an ordered pair. *Describe* where to plot $(-4, 4)$ in a coordinate plane.

Plot and label the points in the same coordinate plane. *Describe* the location of each point.

3. $P(-2, 5)$
4. $Q(0, 9)$
5. $R(6, -1)$
6. $S(-7, -3)$

7. Plot and connect the points $C(-6, 0)$, $D(-1, 0)$, $E(-1, -3)$, and $F(-6, -3)$ to form a rectangle. Find the length, width, and area of rectangle $CDEF$.

8. Make an input-output table for the function $y = -8x - 3$. Use a domain of $-4, -2, 0, 2$, and 4. Then state the range.

Write a function rule for the input-output table.

9.

Input x	−2	0	2	4
Output y	−20	0	20	40

10.

Input x	−2	−1	0	1
Output y	10	11	12	13

11.

Input x	−3	0	3	6
Output y	−8	−5	−2	1

12.

Input x	−5	−3	0	3
Output y	20	12	0	−12

Graph the function.

13. $y = 5x + 2$
14. $y = x - 7$
15. $y = 2x - 2$
16. $y = -9x + 1$

17. Write and graph a function to convert x feet to y yards.

18. **MUSIC** You buy a set of speakers for \$30. You also need to buy speaker wire, which costs \$.40 per foot. Write and graph a function to find the total cost y to buy the speakers and x feet of speaker wire. Find the total cost to buy the speakers and 12 feet of speaker wire.

Graph the line that passes through the points. Then find the slope of the line.

19. $(1, -2), (2, 1)$
20. $(-3, -4), (0, 0)$
21. $(-1, -6), (3, -4)$
22. $(5, 0), (1, 1)$

23. **PROTEIN** The graph at the right represents the amount of protein y (in grams) in x ounces of a certain brand of yogurt. Find the slope of the line in the graph and interpret its meaning.

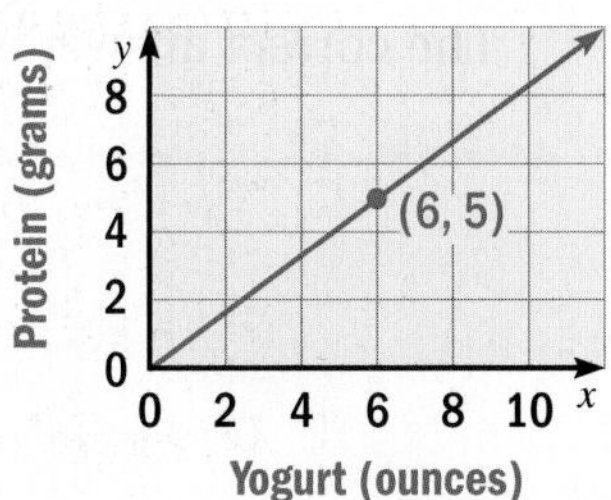

24. Draw the line that has a slope of $-\frac{3}{4}$ and that passes through $(6, 3)$.

12 ◆ MULTIPLE CHOICE STRATEGIES

STRATEGIES YOU'LL USE:
- **SOLVE DIRECTLY**
- **ELIMINATE CHOICES**

If you have difficulty solving a multiple choice problem directly, you may be able to use another approach to eliminate incorrect answer choices and obtain the correct answer.

PROBLEM 1

Which statement is true about the slope of $\overleftrightarrow{PR}$?

Ⓐ The slope between points P and R is greater than the slope between points Q and R.

Ⓑ The slope between points P and R is less than the slope between points Q and R.

Ⓒ The slope between points P and R is equal to the sum of the slope between points P and Q and the slope between points Q and R.

Ⓓ The slope between points P and R is equal to the slope between points Q and R.

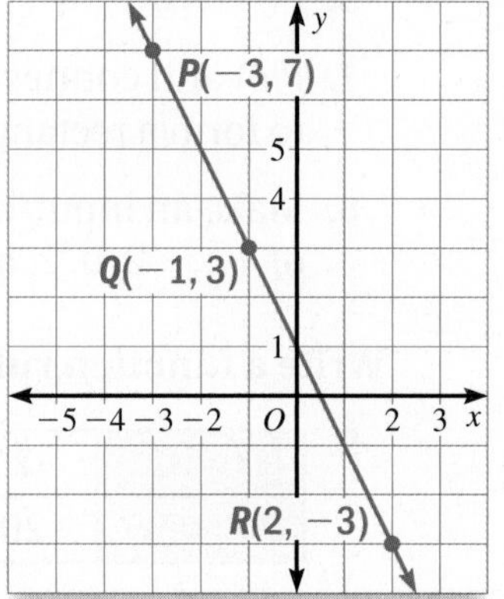

Strategy 1 SOLVE DIRECTLY

Find the slope between points P and R and the slope between points Q and R. Compare the results.

STEP 1 **Find** the slope between P and R.

$$\text{slope} = \frac{\text{rise}}{\text{run}} = \frac{-10}{5} = -2$$

STEP 2 **Find** the slope between Q and R.

$$\text{slope} = \frac{\text{rise}}{\text{run}} = \frac{-6}{3} = -2$$

STEP 3 **Compare** the slopes. The slope between points P and R is equal to the slope between points Q and R.

The correct answer is D. Ⓐ Ⓑ Ⓒ Ⓓ

Strategy 2 ELIMINATE CHOICES

Use the graph to help eliminate choices.

Points P, Q, and R are on the same line. A line has a constant slope, which means the slope between any two points on the line is always the same. You can eliminate choices A and B.

By looking at the graph, you can see that the slope of the line is not 0. This is the only possible way that the sum of two slopes between two different pairs of points on a line can equal the slope of the line. You can eliminate choice C.

The correct answer is D. Ⓐ Ⓑ Ⓒ Ⓓ

PROBLEM 2

Line k is represented by the function $y = -2$. Which ordered pair is located on line k?

Ⓐ (0, 0) Ⓑ (−2, 0)

Ⓒ (−2, 3) Ⓓ (3, −2)

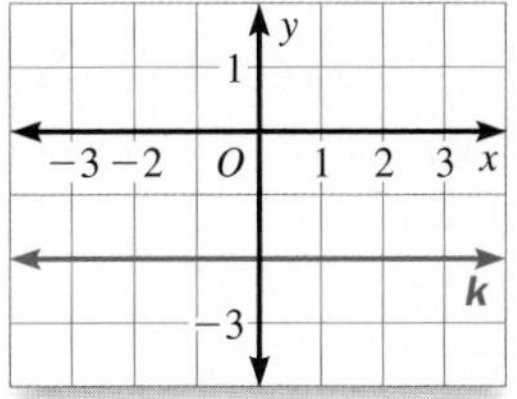

Strategy 1 SOLVE DIRECTLY

Plot the four points.

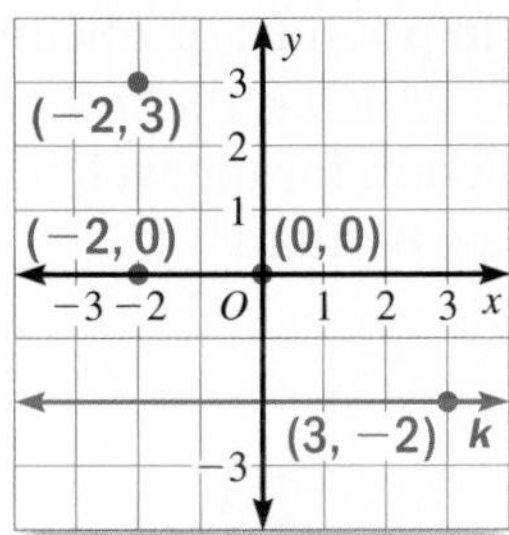

The correct answer is D. Ⓐ Ⓑ Ⓒ Ⓓ

Strategy 2 ELIMINATE CHOICES

Use the graph to help eliminate choices.

Looking at the graph, you can see that line k is a horizontal line that lies below the x-axis. This means that every point on the line must have the same y-coordinate and it must be negative.

The first three choices do not have a negative y-coordinate. You can eliminate choices A, B, and C.

The correct answer is D. Ⓐ Ⓑ Ⓒ Ⓓ

STRATEGY PRACTICE

Explain why you can eliminate the highlighted answer choice.

1. What is the equation of the line that has a slope of 2 and that passes through the point (−3, −5)?

   Ⓐ $y = 2x + 7$ Ⓑ $y = 2x + 1$ Ⓒ $y = 2x - 5$ Ⓓ ✗ $\mathbf{y = 3x - 5}$

2. Which point lies on the line that has a slope of −2 and that passes through the point (6, 4)?

   Ⓐ ✗ **(2, 4)** Ⓑ (4, 0) Ⓒ (4, 8) Ⓓ (8, 2)

3. Which equation shows the relationship between x and y?

Input x	−2	−1	0	1	2
Output y	−4	−1	2	5	8

   Ⓐ $y = 3x + 2$ Ⓑ ✗ $\mathbf{y = 2x}$ Ⓒ $y = x - 2$ Ⓓ $y = -3x + 2$

12 ◆ MULTIPLE CHOICE PRACTICE

1. The point $(x, 4)$ is located in Quadrant II. Where is the point $(-x, 4)$ located? **MR 2.2, Gr. 5 AF 1.4**

   Ⓐ Quadrant I

   Ⓑ Quadrant II

   Ⓒ Quadrant III

   Ⓓ Quadrant IV

2. Which line has the greatest slope? **Gr. 7 AF 3.3**

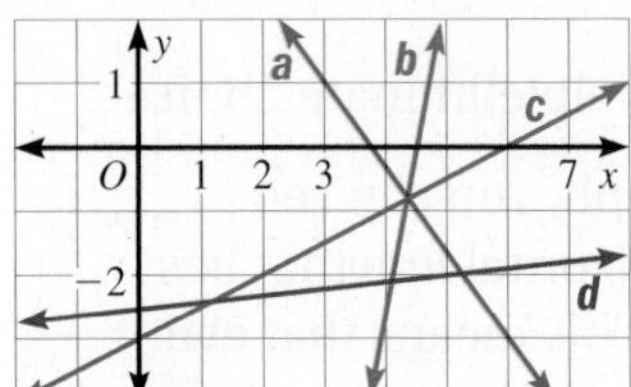

   Ⓐ Line a

   Ⓑ Line b

   Ⓒ Line c

   Ⓓ Line d

3. What is the slope of the graph of the line $y = 6x - 4$? **Gr. 7 AF 3.3**

   Ⓐ -4

   Ⓑ -2

   Ⓒ $\frac{1}{6}$

   Ⓓ 6

4. You join a tennis club with the fees shown below. Which function rule can you use to find the total cost c for a membership lasting m months? **Gr. 5 AF 1.5**

   Ⓐ $c = 32m - 50$

   Ⓑ $c = 32m + 50$

   Ⓒ $c = 50m + 32$

   Ⓓ $c = 82m$

5. In the table below, which equation shows the relationship between x and y? **Gr. 5 AF 1.5**

Input x	−4	−2	2	4
Output y	−12	−10	−6	−4

   Ⓐ $y = -3x$

   Ⓑ $y = 3x$

   Ⓒ $y = x + 8$

   Ⓓ $y = x - 8$

6. The scatter plot shows the age (in weeks) and the weight (in pounds) of 7 Saint Bernard puppies. Which is the most reasonable prediction for the weight of a 4-week-old Saint Bernard? **MR 2.3, Gr. 5 AF 1.4**

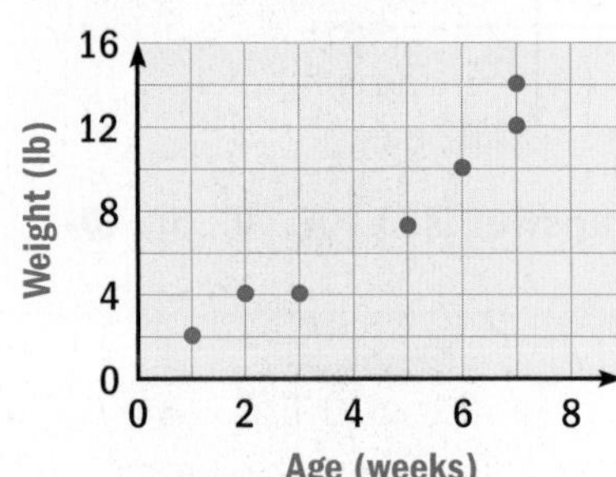

   Ⓐ 2 pounds

   Ⓑ 6 pounds

   Ⓒ 9 pounds

   Ⓓ 10 pounds

7. The input-output table below represents a linear function. What is the value of y when $x = 9$? **Gr. 5 AF 1.5**

Input x	−5	2	3	6
Output y	35	−14	−21	−42

   Ⓐ -84

   Ⓑ -70

   Ⓒ -63

   Ⓓ -49

8. The figures below form a pattern. Which function rule relates the number x below a figure and y, the number of squares in the figure? **Gr. 5 AF 1.5**

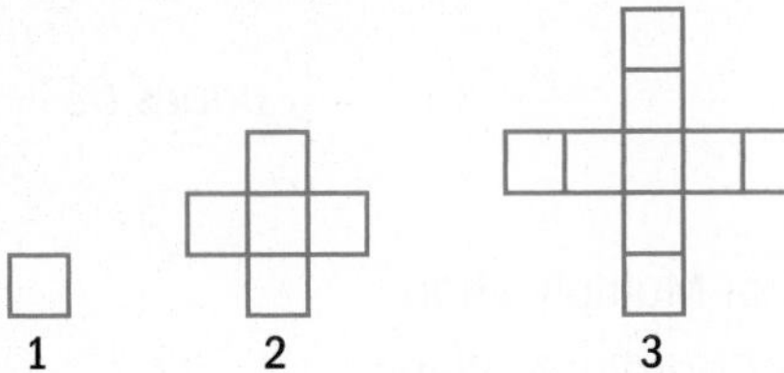

(A) $y = 4x$

(B) $y = 4x + 3$

(C) $y = 4x - 3$

(D) $y = 4x - 4$

9. The graph of which function is shown? **Gr. 7 AF 3.3**

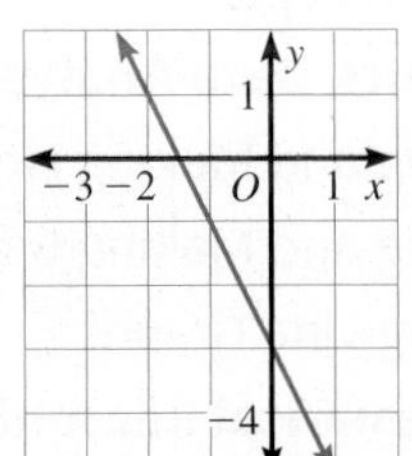

(A) 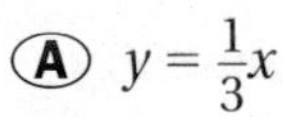 $y = \frac{1}{3}x$

(B) $y = -2x$

(C) 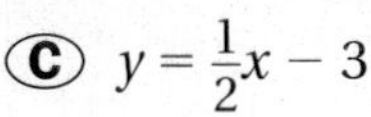 $y = \frac{1}{2}x - 3$

(D) $y = -2x - 3$

10. You have \$10 before you start babysitting for a neighbor. The table below shows the amount of money y you have after babysitting a total of x hours. How can you find your hourly pay rate? **MR 3.2, Gr. 7 AF 3.3**

Input x	2	3	4	5
Output y	23	29.5	36	42.5

(A) Divide 23 by 2.

(B) Draw the line passing through each point (x, y) and find the y-coordinate when $x = 1$.

(C) Draw the line passing through each point (x, y) and find the x-coordinate when $y = 1$.

(D) Draw the line passing through each point (x, y) and find its slope.

11. The table shows the x-coordinates and y-coordinates of four points. Three of the points lie on the same line. Which point does *not* lie on the same line as the other three? **Gr. 7 AF 3.3**

(A) Point P

(B) Point Q

(C) Point R

(D) Point S

Point	x	y
P	8	21
Q	4	11
R	−2	−6
S	−6	−14

12. A scale model of a rectangular garden is plotted on the coordinate plane below. Each unit on the graph represents one half foot. What is the area of the garden? **MR 1.3, Gr. 5 AF 1.4**

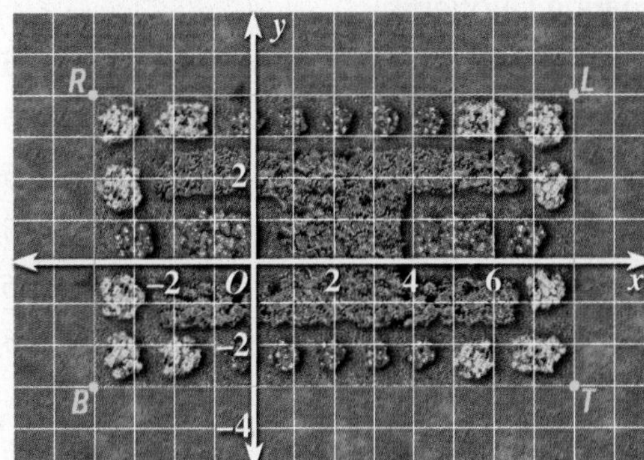

(A) 19 ft^2

(B) 21 ft^2

(C) 42 ft^2

(D) 84 ft^2

13. The graph shows the amount you earn d (in dollars) for t hours of mowing lawns. How much do you earn per hour? **Gr. 7 AF 3.3**

(A) \$.19

(B) \$2.75

(C) \$5.50

(D) \$11

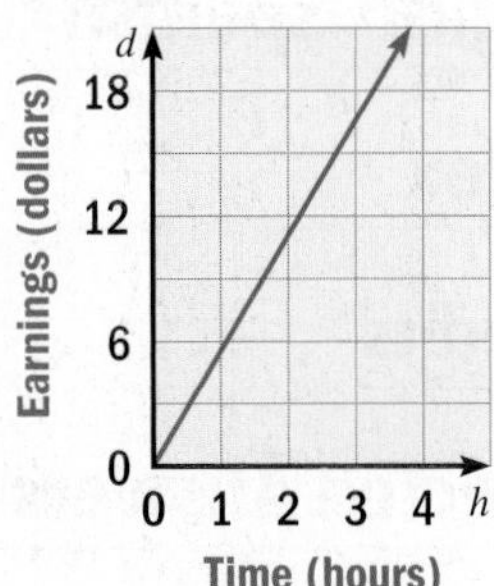

Contents of Student Resources

Adding and Subtracting Whole Numbers

Gr. 3 NS 2.1, Gr. 4 NS 3.1

The **whole numbers** are the numbers 0, 1, 2, 3, ... A **digit** is any of the numbers 0, 1, 2, 3, 4, 5, 6, 7, 8, or 9.

A **sum** is the result when you add two or more numbers. A **difference** is the result when you subtract two numbers. To add and subtract whole numbers, start with the digits in the ones' place. Moving to the left, add or subtract the digits one place value at a time, regrouping as needed.

EXAMPLE 1

Find the sum 329 + 75.

STEP 1 Add the ones. Regroup 14 ones as 1 ten and 4 ones.

```
   1
  329
+  75
-----
    4
```

STEP 2 Add the tens. Regroup 10 tens as 1 hundred and 0 tens.

```
  11
  329
+  75
-----
   04
```

STEP 3 Add the hundreds.

```
  11
  329
+  75
-----
  404
```

EXAMPLE 2

Find the difference 402 − 235.

STEP 1 Start with the ones. There are not enough ones in 402 to subtract 5.

```
  402
− 235
-----
```

STEP 2 Move to the tens. There are no tens in 402, so regroup 1 hundred as 9 tens and 10 ones.

```
     9
  3 10 12
  4  0  2
+ 2  3  5
---------
```

STEP 3 Subtract.

```
     9
  3 10 12
  4  0  2
− 2  3  5
---------
  1  6  7
```

CHECK Because addition and subtraction are inverse operations, you can check your answer by adding: 167 + 235 = 402.

PRACTICE

Find the sum or difference.

1. 79 + 23 **2.** 53 + 38 **3.** 312 − 27 **4.** 283 − 195

5. 4259 + 57 **6.** 1207 − 78 **7.** 2725 − 807 **8.** 3052 + 958

9. 12,235 + 876 **10.** 10,782 − 927 **11.** 23,008 + 6913 **12.** 27,091 − 3493

Multiplying Whole Numbers 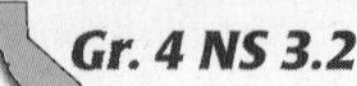 *Gr. 4 NS 3.2*

When whole numbers other than zero are multiplied together, the result is the **product** and each whole number is a **factor** of the product.

To multiply two whole numbers, multiply the entire first number by the digit in each place value of the second number to obtain partial products. To find the product of the original numbers, add the partial products.

EXAMPLE 1

Find the product 935 × 306.

STEP 1 Multiply 935 by the ones' digit in 306.

```
  23
  935
× 306
 5610
```

STEP 2 Skip the 0 in the tens' place, and multiply by the hundreds' digit. Start the partial product in the hundreds' place.

```
  11
  935
× 306
 5610
2805
```

STEP 3 Add the partial products.

```
    935
×   306
   5610
  2805
286,110
```

To multiply a whole number by a *power of 10,* such as 10, 100, or 1000, write the number followed by the number of zeros in the power. Because multiplying by such powers of 10 shifts each digit of the number to a greater place value, the zeros are needed as placeholders.

EXAMPLE 2

Find the product.

a. 823 × 100

b. 4200 × 1000

SOLUTION

a. 100 is a power of 10 with 2 zeros, so write 2 zeros after 823.

823 × 100 = 82,300

b. 1000 is a power of 10 with 3 zeros, so write 3 zeros after 4200.

4200 × 1000 = 4,200,000

PRACTICE

Find the product.

1. 89 × 54 **2.** 326 × 12 **3.** 452 × 708 **4.** 6290 × 2050

5. 167 × 100 **6.** 52 × 10,000 **7.** 970 × 1000 **8.** 2000 × 100

Powers and Exponents *Gr. 5 NS 1.3*

You can use a **power** to write a product that has a repeated factor. The **base** of the power is the repeated factor, and the **exponent** is the number of times the factor is used.

base exponent

$7^4 = 7 \times 7 \times 7 \times 7$

power 7 is a factor 4 times.

The power is read "seven to the fourth power."

EXAMPLE 1

Write the product 8 × 8 × 8 × 8 × 8 as a power.

SOLUTION

There are 5 factors of 8 in the product, so $8 \times 8 \times 8 \times 8 \times 8 = 8^5$.

When powers have an exponent of 2, the base is "squared." When powers have an exponent of 3, the base is "cubed." Numbers raised to the first power, such as 5^1, are usually written without the exponent.

EXAMPLE 2

a. Find the value of six cubed.

$6^3 = 6 \times 6 \times 6 = 216$

b. Find the value of three to the sixth power.

$3^6 = 3 \times 3 \times 3 \times 3 \times 3 \times 3 = 729$

PRACTICE

Write the product as a power.

1. $10 \times 10 \times 10$

2. 14×14

3. $9 \times 9 \times 9 \times 9 \times 9 \times 9$

4. $2 \times 2 \times 2 \times 2$

5. $17 \times 17 \times 17 \times 17 \times 17$

6. $25 \times 25 \times 25$

Find the value of the power.

7. 5^3

8. 11^2

9. 1^8

10. 10^5

11. 13^2

12. 2^4

13. 0^5

14. 10^4

15. 2^6

16. 3^3

17. 4^6

18. 30^4

19. 7 squared

20. 5 squared

21. 12 cubed

22. 9 cubed

23. four to the seventh power

24. three to the eighth power

Dividing of Whole Numbers

In a division problem, the number being divided is called the **dividend** and the number it is being divided by is called the **divisor**. The result of the division is called the **quotient**. To **divide** two whole numbers, you use the following pattern: divide, multiply, subtract, bring down.

EXAMPLE 1

Find the quotient 236 ÷ 4.

STEP 1

Decide where to write the first digit of the quotient. Because 4 is between 2 and 23, place the first digit above the 3.

□ ← first digit of quotient

divisor → 4)236

↑ dividend

STEP 2

Because 23 ÷ 4 is between 5 and 6, multiply 4 by **5**. Then subtract **20** from 23. Be sure the difference is less than the divisor.

5
4)236
20
3

STEP 3

Bring down the next digit, **6**. Divide 36 by 4. Because 36 ÷ 4 = **9**, multiply 4 by **9**. Subtract **36**. The remainder is 0.

59
4)236
20
36
36
0

Sometimes a whole number divided by a whole number does not divide evenly. Use number sense to decide the placement of the decimal point.

EXAMPLE 2

Find the quotient (a) 75 ÷ 6 and (b) 31 ÷ 4.

a.

12.5
6)75.0 ← Write zero in dividend as place holder.
6
15
12
30
30
0

b.

7.75 ← The quotient is between 7 and 8, because 4 × 7 = 28 and 4 × 8 = 32.
4)31.00
28
30
28
20
20
0

PRACTICE

Find the quotient.

1. 6)852 **2.** 5)650 **3.** 7)378 **4.** 7)126

5. 3645 ÷ 9 **6.** 2388 ÷ 4 **7.** 580 ÷ 10 **8.** 783 ÷ 12

9. 31 ÷ 2 **10.** 84 ÷ 5 **w.** 26 ÷ 8 **12.** 258 ÷ 16

Rounding Whole Numbers 

To **round** a whole number means to approximate the number to a given *place value.*

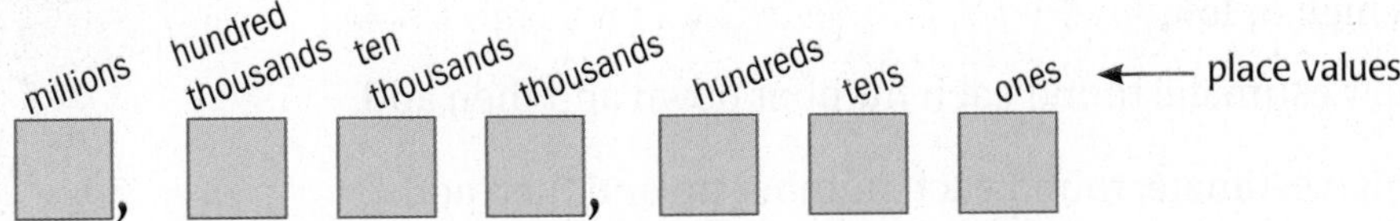

When rounding, look at the digit to the right of the given place value. If the digit to the right is *less than* 5 (0, 1, 2, 3, or 4), round *down.* If the digit to the right is *5 or greater* (5, 6, 7, 8, or 9), round *up.*

EXAMPLE 1

Round the number to the place value of the red digit.

a. 7839 **b.** 19,712 **c.** 3995

SOLUTION

a. Because 8 is in the hundreds' place, round 7839 to the nearest hundred. Because 7839 is between 7800 and 7900, it will round to one of these two numbers.

The digit to the right of the hundreds' place is the 3 in the tens' place. Because 3 is less than 5, round down.

▸ **Answer** 7839 rounded to the nearest hundred is 7800.

b. Because 9 is in the thousands' place, round 19,712 to the nearest thousand. Because 19,712 is between 19,000 and 20,000, it will round to one of these two numbers.

The digit to the right of the thousands' place is the 7 in the hundreds' place. Because 7 is 5 or greater, round up.

▸ **Answer** 19,712 rounded to the nearest thousand is 20,000.

c. Because 5 is in the ones' place, round up.

▸ **Answer** 3995 rounded to the nearest ten is 4000.

PRACTICE

Round the number to the place value of the red digit.

1. 342 **2.** 8351 **3.** 27,945 **4.** 184,920

5. 9388 **6.** 652 **7.** 298,725 **8.** 644,087

9. 58,920 **10.** 349,657 **11.** 5205 **12.** 24,618

13. 27,830,643 **14.** 156,970 **15.** 1,463,562 **16.** 509,726,310

STANDARDS REVIEW HANDBOOK

Estimating Sums Gr. 5 NS 2.1

To **estimate** the solution of a problem means to find an approximate answer. You can use the following steps to round numbers so that you get an estimate that is high or low.

STEP 1 To find a low estimate, round each number down and then add.

STEP 2 To find a high estimate, round each number up and then add.

EXAMPLE 1

You want to paint three rooms. The rooms cover 360 square feet, 210 square feet, and 190 square feet. To know how much paint to buy, find a low and a high estimate for the total area.

STEP 1 Find a low estimate: $300 + 200 + 100 = 600$

STEP 2 Find a high estimate: $400 + 300 + 200 = 900$

A low estimate for the area is 600 square feet and a high estimate is 900 square feet.

When numbers have about the same value, you can use *clustering* to estimate their sum.

EXAMPLE 2

Estimate the sum 72 + 68 + 65.

The numbers all cluster around the value 70.

$$\begin{array}{r} 72 \\ 68 \\ +\ 65 \\ \hline \end{array} \quad \longrightarrow \quad \begin{array}{r} 70 \\ 70 \\ +\ 70 \\ \hline \end{array} \qquad 3 \times 70 = 210$$

▸ **Answer** The sum $72 + 68 + 65$ is *about* 210.

PRACTICE

Find a low estimate and a high estimate.

1. $32 + 68 + 25 + 14$

2. $800 + 652 + 384 + 421$

3. \$7.59 + \$6.50 + \$1.27

4. \$129 + \$132 + \$275 + \$560

Estimate the sum.

5. $30 + 32 + 28 + 33$

6. $482 + 529 + 498$

7. $274 + 292 + 307 + 315$

8. $689 + 719 + 684$

9. $1100 + 1115 + 1088$

10. $6966 + 7044 + 6975$

Estimating Differences 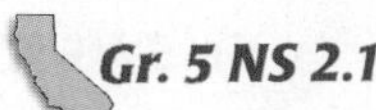

One way to estimate a difference is to use **front-end estimation**. First subtract the digits in the greatest place. Then round the remaining parts of the numbers and subtract the lesser number from the greater number. Finally, combine the two differences using addition or subtraction as shown below.

EXAMPLE 1

Estimate the difference.

a. $46{,}398 - 21{,}759$

b. $7276 - 3814$

SOLUTION

a. First subtract the digits in the ten thousands' place.

$$\begin{array}{r} \mathbf{46{,}398} \\ -\ \mathbf{21{,}759} \\ \hline \end{array} \longrightarrow \begin{array}{r} 40{,}000 \\ -\ 20{,}000 \\ \hline 20{,}000 \end{array}$$

Then round the remaining parts to the nearest thousand. Subtract the lesser number from the greater number.

$$\begin{array}{r} \mathbf{6{,}000} \\ -\ \mathbf{2{,}000} \\ \hline 4{,}000 \end{array}$$

Because the greater remaining number was originally on the *top*, you *add* the differences. $20{,}000 + 4{,}000 = 24{,}000$

▸ **Answer** The difference 46,398 − 21,759 is *about* 24,000.

b. First subtract the digits in the thousands' place.

$$\begin{array}{r} \mathbf{7276} \\ -\ \mathbf{3814} \\ \hline \end{array} \longrightarrow \begin{array}{r} 7000 \\ -\ 3000 \\ \hline 4000 \end{array}$$

Then round the remaining parts to the nearest hundred. Subtract the lesser number from the greater number.

$$\begin{array}{r} \mathbf{800} \\ -\ \mathbf{300} \\ \hline 500 \end{array}$$

Because the greater remaining number was originally on the *bottom*, you *subtract* the differences. $4000 - 500 = 3500$

▸ **Answer** The difference 7276 − 3814 is *about* 3500.

PRACTICE

Estimate the difference.

1. 891 − 252

2. 921 − 542

3. 587 − 175

4. 674 − 328

5. 3245 − 1097

6. 7658 − 3109

7. 9123 − 2345

8. 55,903 − 14,872

Estimating Products 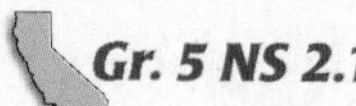

One way to estimate a product is to find a range for the product by finding a low estimate and a high estimate.

EXAMPLE 1

Find a low and high estimate for the product 47 × 34.

For the low estimate, round both factors *down*.

$$\begin{array}{r} 40 \\ \times\ 30 \\ \hline 1200 \end{array}$$

For the high estimate, round both factors *up*.

$$\begin{array}{r} 50 \\ \times\ 40 \\ \hline 2000 \end{array}$$

▶ **Answer** The product 47 × 34 is between 1200 and 2000.

Another way to estimate a product is to round to the leading digit.

EXAMPLE 2

Estimate the product 345 × 18 by rounding to the leading digit.

$$\begin{array}{r} 320 \\ \times\ 18 \\ \hline \end{array}$$

Round 320 to 300. → **Round 18 to 20.** →

$$\begin{array}{r} 300 \\ \times\ 20 \\ \hline 6000 \end{array}$$

▶ **Answer** The product 345 × 18 is *about* 6000.

PRACTICE

Find a low and high estimate for the product.

1. $\begin{array}{r} 28 \\ \times\ 12 \\ \hline \end{array}$ **2.** $\begin{array}{r} 46 \\ \times\ 81 \\ \hline \end{array}$ **3.** $\begin{array}{r} 56 \\ \times\ 29 \\ \hline \end{array}$ **4.** $\begin{array}{r} 74 \\ \times\ 32 \\ \hline \end{array}$

5. $\begin{array}{r} 387 \\ \times\ 21 \\ \hline \end{array}$ **6.** $\begin{array}{r} 640 \\ \times\ 74 \\ \hline \end{array}$ **7.** $\begin{array}{r} 183 \\ \times\ 27 \\ \hline \end{array}$ **8.** $\begin{array}{r} 819 \\ \times\ 55 \\ \hline \end{array}$

Estimate the product by rounding to the leading digit.

9. 452 × 153

10. 389 × 173

11. 628 × 921

12. 476 × 293

13. 807 × 504

14. 127 × 836

15. 6509 × 23

16. 7091 × 98

17. 3811 × 45

18. 9399 × 72

Estimating Quotients 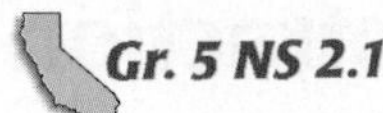

One way to estimate a quotient is to find a low estimate and a high estimate by using numbers that divide with no remainder.

EXAMPLE 1

Find a low and high estimate for the quotient 14,682 ÷ 63.

When the divisor has more than one digit, round it as described below.

For a *low* estimate, round the divisor *up* and replace 14,682 with a number that is divisible by 70 and is *less* than 14,682.

$$70\overline{)14{,}000} = 200$$

For a *high* estimate, round the divisor *down* and replace 14,682 with a number that is divisible by 60 and is *greater* than 14,682.

$$60\overline{)18{,}000} = 300$$

▶ **Answer** The quotient 14,682 ÷ 63 is between 200 and 300.

Another way to estimate a quotient is to use **compatible numbers**, which are numbers that make a calculation easier.

EXAMPLE 2

Use compatible numbers to estimate the quotient 152 ÷ 22.

Look for numbers close to 152 and 22 that divide evenly.

$$22\overline{)152} \longrightarrow 20\overline{)160} = 8$$

▶ **Answer** The quotient 152 ÷ 22 is *about* 8.

PRACTICE

Find a low and high estimate for the quotient.

1. 133 ÷ 4 **2.** 2397 ÷ 6 **3.** 1580 ÷ 6 **4.** 1957 ÷ 8

5. 528 ÷ 28 **6.** 8091 ÷ 92 **7.** 1735 ÷ 34 **8.** 3196 ÷ 42

9. 14,453 ÷ 6 **10.** 21,895 ÷ 9 **11.** 55,912 ÷ 59 **12.** 29,021 ÷ 74

Use compatible numbers to estimate the quotient.

13. 238 ÷ 5 **14.** 8319 ÷ 9 **15.** 4175 ÷ 7 **16.** 3214 ÷ 4

17. 633 ÷ 32 **18.** 4332 ÷ 78 **19.** 1462 ÷ 53 **20.** 2581 ÷ 83

21. 36,012 ÷ 8 **22.** 13,906 ÷ 3 **23.** 32,164 ÷ 62 **24.** 67,428 ÷ 76

Using Addition and Subtraction

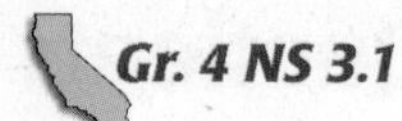

Sometimes you can solve a word problem by writing and evaluating a *numerical expression.* A **numerical expression** consists of numbers and operations to be performed. Use the following guidelines to decide whether to use addition or subtraction to solve a word problem.

- Use addition when you need to combine, join, or find a total.
- Use subtraction when you need to separate, compare, take away, find how many are left, or find how many more are needed.

EXAMPLE 1

You paid $14 for a CD and $30 for a DVD. How much did you pay in all?

You need to find a total, so you need to add.

$14 + $30 = $44

▸ **Answer** You paid $44 in all.

EXAMPLE 2

You have 25 invitations to your birthday party. You hand out 16 invitations. How many invitations do you have left?

You need to find how many are left, so you need to subtract.

$25 - 16 = 9$

▸ **Answer** You have 9 invitations left.

PRACTICE

Solve the problem by writing and evaluating a numerical expression.

1. You have $18 to spend. You buy a book for $6. How much money do you have left?
2. You spend $25 for a shirt and $35 for a pair of jeans. How much more did you spend for the jeans?
3. You invited 18 boys and 26 girls to your party. How many people did you invite in all?
4. Costumes for a school play cost $112, and scenery costs $54. How much do costumes and scenery cost altogether?
5. You have $35. Your sister gives you $9 more. How much money do you have now?
6. You have 200 sheets of notebook paper. You give your friend 65 sheets. How many sheets do you have left?

Using Multiplication and Division

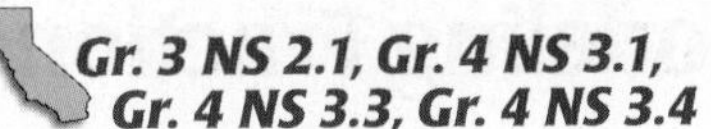

You can use the following guidelines to tell whether to use multiplication or division to solve a word problem.

- Use multiplication when you need to find the total number of objects that are in groups of equal size.
- Use division when you need to find the number of equal groups or find the number in each equal group.

EXAMPLE 1

You bought 3 packages of socks. Each package contains 6 pairs of socks. How many pairs of socks did you buy?

You need to find the total number of objects, so you need to multiply.

$3 \times 6 = 18$

▶ **Answer** You bought 18 pairs of socks.

EXAMPLE 2

You have 36 baseball cards. You put the same number of baseball cards in 9 plastic sheets. How many baseball cards do you put in each sheet?

You need to find the number in each equal group, so you need to divide.

$36 \div 9 = 4$

▶ **Answer** You put 4 cards in each sheet.

PRACTICE

Solve the problem by writing and evaluating a numerical expression.

1. You order 3 packages of pencils for the school store. Each package contains 12 pencils. How many pencils do you get?
2. You bought 4 bags of apples. Each bag contains 6 apples. How many apples did you buy?
3. You bought 6 packages of muffins and have a total of 24 muffins. How many muffins are in a package?
4. You have 5 boxes of dog biscuits. Each box contains 10 dog biscuits. How many dog biscuits do you have?
5. You split a deck of 52 playing cards evenly among 4 people. How many cards does each person get?

STANDARDS REVIEW HANDBOOK

Modeling Fractions

A **fraction** is a number of the form $\frac{a}{b}$ where $b \neq 0$. A fraction is used to describe one or more parts of a set or a whole. Each part must have the same size. A **mixed number** is a sum of a whole number and a fraction.

A **decimal** is a number that is written using the base-ten place value system. A decimal point separates the ones' and tenths' digits.

EXAMPLE 1

Write a fraction to represent the shaded part of the set.

There are 9 objects in this set, and 5 of the objects are shaded.

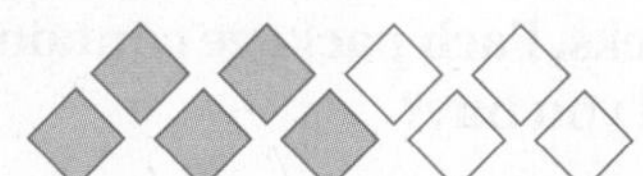

▶ **Answer** The fraction that represents the shaded part of the set is $\frac{5}{9}$.

EXAMPLE 2

Write the number modeled as a mixed number and as a decimal.

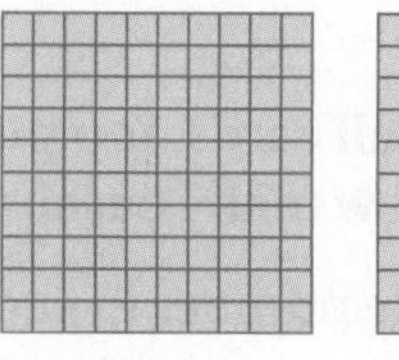

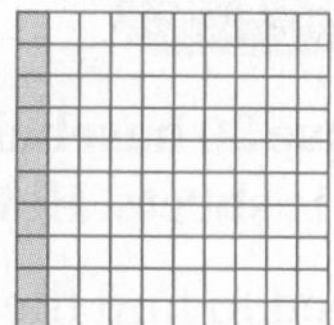

Each whole square represents 1 whole. The square is divided into 100 equal parts, or hundredths. The base-ten pieces represent 1 one and 10 hundredths.

▶ **Answer** The model represents the mixed number $1\frac{10}{100}$ and the decimal 1.10.

PRACTICE

Write a fraction to represent the shaded part of a set or region.

1.

2.

3.

4.

5.

6.

Write the number modeled as a fraction or a mixed number and as a decimal.

7.

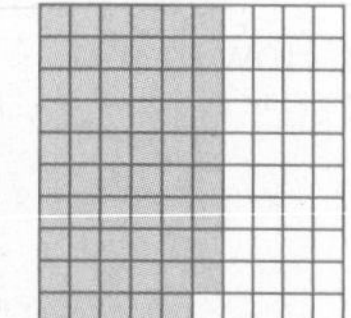

8.

Graphing Decimals and Fractions

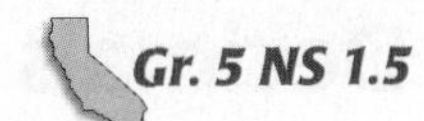

A **number line** is a line whose points are associated with numbers. The numbers on a number line increase from left to right.

EXAMPLE 1

Identify points *A* and *B* on the number line.

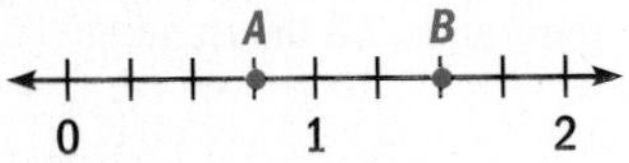

A B
0 1 2

Each unit is divided into 4 equal parts, or fourths.

▸ **Answer** *A* represents $\frac{3}{4}$ and *B* represents $1\frac{2}{4}$, or $1\frac{1}{2}$.

EXAMPLE 2

Graph the numbers 2.1 and 2.225 on a number line.

Draw a line. Mark off tenths from 2.0 to 2.3. Hundredths divide each tenth into ten equal parts. So 5 thousandths is halfway between the two nearest hundredths.

▸ **Answer**

PRACTICE

Identify the points on the number line.

1. 8 9

2. 0 1 2

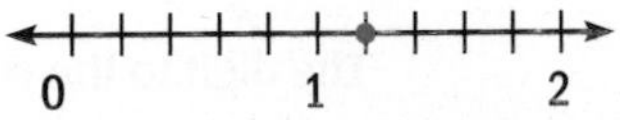

3. 6.3 6.4

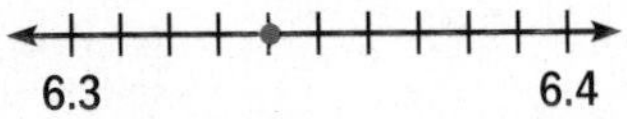

4. 8.1 8.2

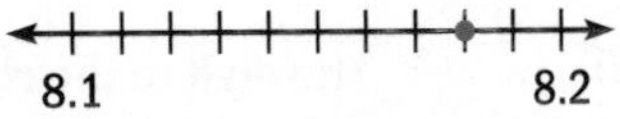

Graph the numbers on a number line.

5. 0.7 and 1.2

6. 10 and 11.2

7. 2.05 and 2.15

8. 8 and 7.95

9. 5.3 and 5.45

10. 3.55 and 3.65

11. $\frac{2}{3}$ and $2\frac{1}{3}$

12. $\frac{3}{5}$ and $3\frac{4}{5}$

13. $3\frac{1}{4}$ and 6

14. $2\frac{1}{8}$ and $3\frac{7}{8}$

15. $\frac{2}{6}$ and $\frac{5}{6}$

16. $3\frac{3}{8}$ and $5\frac{2}{8}$

Rounding Decimals 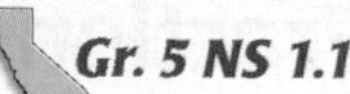 *Gr. 5 NS 1.1*

To round a decimal is to approximate the number to a given place. The names of the decimal place values are shown at the right.

To read the decimal part of a number such as 4.058, first identify the last decimal place, thousandths. The decimal's digits, 058, tell how many thousandths there are. So the decimal part is read as *58 thousandths.* The complete number is shown at the right.

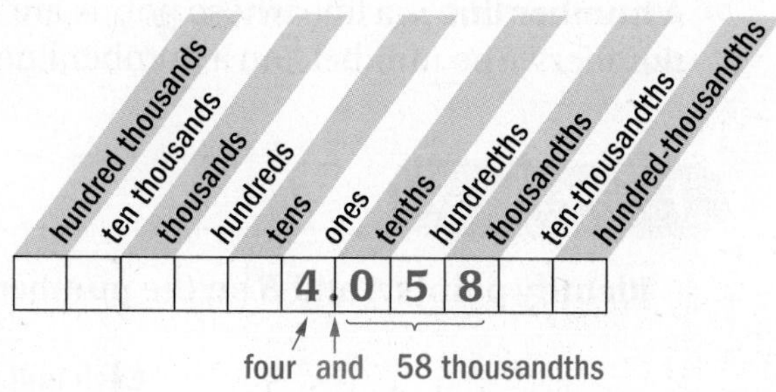

EXAMPLE 1

Use a number line to round 5.26 to the nearest tenth.

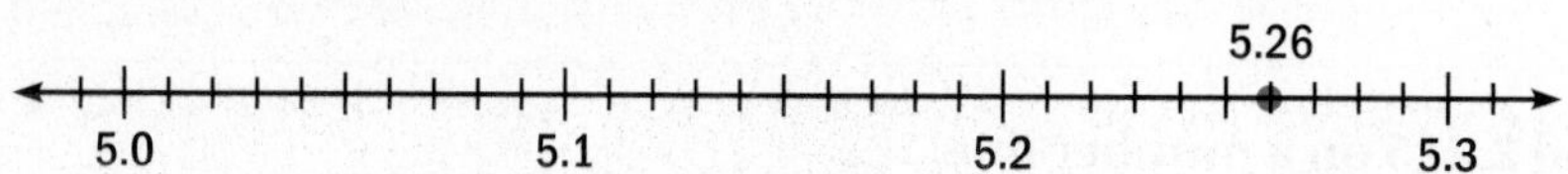

The decimal 5.26 is closer to 5.3 than to 5.2.

▶ **Answer** 5.26 to the nearest tenth is 5.3.

When rounding, look at the digit to the right of the given place value. If the digit to the right is *less than 5,* round *down.* If the digit to the right is *5 or greater,* round *up.*

EXAMPLE 2

Round the decimal to the place value of the red digit.

a. 7.143 → 7.1 — **The digit to the right of 1 is 4, so round down.**

b. 8.17052 → 8.171 — **The digit to the right of 0 is 5, so round up.**

c. 0.9783 → 1.0 — **The digit to the right of 9 is 7, so round up.**

PRACTICE

Use a number line to round each decimal to the given place value.

1. 5.92 (tenths) **2.** 2.5 (ones) **3.** 0.897 (hundredths)

Round the decimal to the place value of the red digit.

4. 16.187 **5.** 7.5 **6.** 0.413 **7.** 28.13

8. 3.507 **9.** 9.249 **10.** 31.825 **11.** 0.5796

12. 4.38047 **13.** 4.38047 **14.** 1.99 **15.** 6.61262

Comparing Decimals 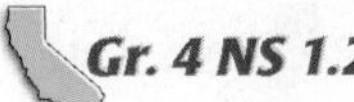 *Gr. 4 NS 1.2*

When you compare decimals, remember that the symbol < means *is less than* and the symbol > means *is greater than.*

EXAMPLE 1

Use the expanded form of the decimals to compare 8.7 and 8.70.

$8.7 \ \ = 8 \times 1 + 7 \times 0.1$

$8.70 = 8 \times 1 + 7 \times 0.1 + 0 \times 0.001$

▸ **Answer** Because 0×0.001 equals 0, $8.7 = 8.70$.

EXAMPLE 2

Copy and complete the statement with <, >, or =.

0.54 _?_ 0.543

STEP 1 Write the decimals in a column, lining up the decimal places.

0.540 ⟵ **Write a 0 as a placeholder, so both decimals**
0.543   **have the same number of decimal places.**

STEP 2 Compare place values from left to right.

The tenths' and hundredths' digits are the same.

The thousandths' digits are different: $0 < 3$.

▸ **Answer** $0.54 < 0.543$

You can check your answer to the Example by graphing, as shown at the right.

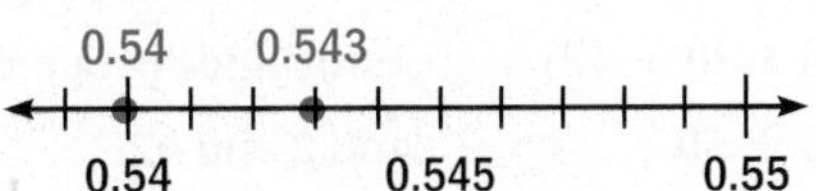

PRACTICE

Copy and complete the statement with <, >, or =.

1. 5.35 _?_ 5.53	**2.** 6.2 _?_ 6.20	**3.** 7.24 _?_ 7.21
4. 0.590 _?_ 0.59	**5.** 0.2 _?_ 0.019	**6.** 6.640 _?_ 6.64
7. 0.7 _?_ 0.713	**8.** 3.00 _?_ 3	**9.** 1.04 _?_ 1.40
10. 11.43 _?_ 12.15	**11.** 9.415 _?_ 9.145	**12.** 1.88 _?_ 1.880
13. 7.1 _?_ 7.107	**14.** 0.25 _?_ 0.2500	**15.** 34.1 _?_ 29.9
16. 8.075 _?_ 8.05	**17.** 0.002 _?_ 0.0020	**18.** 4.513 _?_ 4.5109

Properties of Addition 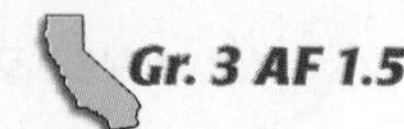

The properties below can help you add numbers.

Commutative Property of Addition		Associative Property of Addition	
Words	In a sum, you can add numbers in any order.	**Words**	Changing the grouping of the numbers in a sum does not change the sum.
Numbers	$2 + 4 = 4 + 2$	**Numbers**	$(3 + 8) + 6 = 3 + (8 + 6)$
Algebra	$a + b = b + a$	**Algebra**	$(a + b) + c = a + (b + c)$

EXAMPLE 1 Identifying Properties of Addition

Identify the property that the statement illustrates.

a. $(43 + 9) + 7 = (9 + 43) + 7$

b. $13 + (7 + 15) = (13 + 7) + 15$

SOLUTION

a. The order of two of the numbers in the sum has changed. This illustrates the commutative property of addition.

b. The grouping of the numbers in the sum has changed. This illustrates the associative property of addition.

EXAMPLE 2 Using Properties of Addition

Evaluate the expression 8 + 16 + 42. Justify each step.

$8 + 16 + 42 = (8 + 16) + 42$	Use order of operations.
$= (16 + 8) + 42$	Commutative property of addition
$= 16 + (8 + 42)$	Associative property of addition
$= 16 + 50$	Add 8 and 42.
$= 66$	Add 16 and 50.

PRACTICE

Identify the property that the statement illustrates.

1. $(77 + 20) + 50 = 77 + (20 + 50)$

2. $(8 + 15 + 2) + 1 = (15 + 8 + 2) + 1$

Evaluate the expression. *Justify* each step.

3. $5 + (15 + 21)$

4. $44 + (16 + 12)$

5. $(7 + 61) + 13$

6. $(98 + 36) + 12$

7. $16 + 19 + 4$

8. $3 + 11 + 97$

Properties of Multiplication Gr. 3 AF 1.5

The properties below can help you multiply numbers.

Commutative Property of Multiplication		Associative Property of Multiplication	
Words	In a product, you can multiply the factors in any order.	**Words**	Changing the grouping of the factors in a product does not change the product.
Numbers	$9 \times 3 = 3 \times 9$	**Numbers**	$(7 \times 2) \times 4 = 7 \times (2 \times 4)$
Algebra	$a \times b = b \times a$	**Algebra**	$(a \times b) \times c = a \times (b \times c)$

EXAMPLE 1 Identifying Properties of Multiplication

Identify the property that the statement illustrates.

a. $(2 \times 11) \times 13 = 2 \times (11 \times 13)$

b. $(8 \times 21) \times 9 = (21 \times 8) \times 9$

SOLUTION

a. The grouping of the factors in the product has changed. This illustrates the associative property of multiplication.

b. The order of two of the factors in the product has changed. This illustrates the commutative property of multiplication.

EXAMPLE 2 Using Properties of Multiplication

Evaluate the expression 5 × 34 × 4. Justify each step.

$5 \times 34 \times 4 = (5 \times 34) \times 4$	**Use order of operations.**
$= (34 \times 5) \times 4$	**Commutative property of multiplication**
$= 34 \times (5 \times 4)$	**Associative property of multiplication**
$= 34 \times 20$	**Multiply 5 and 4.**
$= 680$	**Multiply 34 and 20.**

PRACTICE

Identify the property that the statement illustrates.

1. $2 \times 3 \times 8 \times 12 = 3 \times 2 \times 8 \times 12$

2. $(3 \times 25) \times 4 = 3 \times (25 \times 4)$

Evaluate the expression. *Justify* each step.

3. $(9 \times 15) \times 2$

4. $(32 \times 6) \times 5$

5. $2 \times 41 \times 5$

6. $25 \times 26 \times 4$

7. $10 \times 47 \times 10$

8. $25 \times 16 \times 8$

STANDARDS REVIEW HANDBOOK

Points in a Coordinate Plane 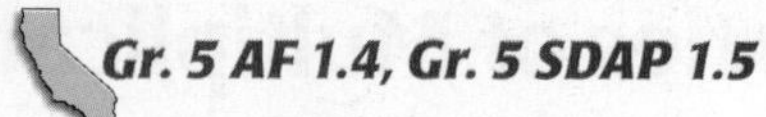

A **coordinate plane** is formed by a horizontal number line, called the x-axis, and a vertical number line, called the y-axis. The x-axis and y-axis intersect at the **origin.** You can plot points in a coordinate plane by using **ordered pairs** such as (3, 5). The numbers are the **coordinates** of the point. The origin has coordinates (0, 0).

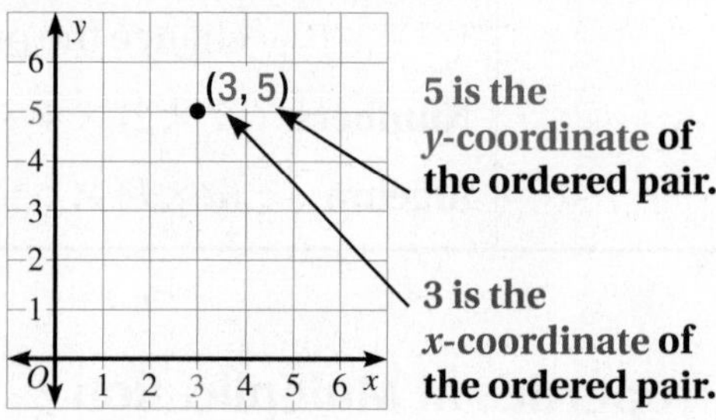

EXAMPLE 1

a. Plot point $M(6, 2)$ in a coordinate plane. Start at (0, 0). Move **6** units to the right and **2** units up.

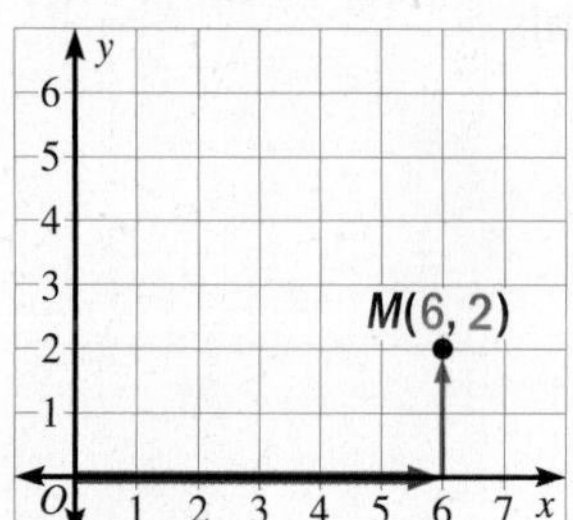

b. Plot point $N(0, 2)$ in a coordinate plane. Start at (0, 0). Move **0** units to the right and **2** units up.

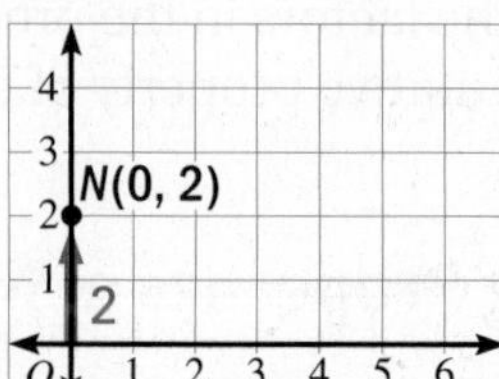

PRACTICE

Name the ordered pair that represents the point.

1. A **2.** B **3.** C

4. D **5.** E **6.** F

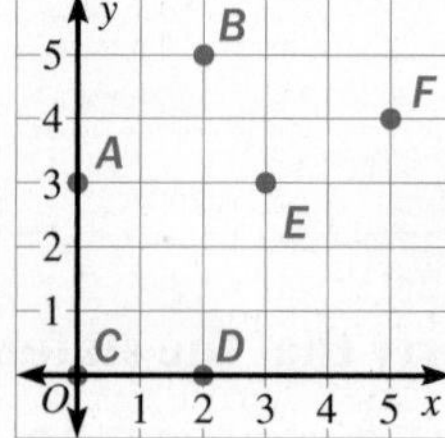

Plot and label the points in the same coordinate plane.

7. $P(5, 2)$ **8.** $Q(0, 0)$ **9.** $R(1, 4)$ **10.** $S(6, 0)$

11. $T(1, 6)$ **12.** $U(7, 5)$ **13.** $V(0, 3)$ **14.** $W(4, 4)$

Units of Time 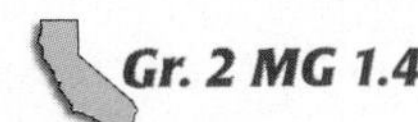

To convert from a longer unit of time to a shorter unit, *multiply*. To convert from a shorter unit of time to a longer unit, *divide*. To find the number to multiply or divide by, use the table at the right.

1 week (wk) = 7 days (d)
1 day (d) = 24 hours (h)
1 hour (h) = 60 minutes (min)
1 minute (min) = 60 seconds (sec)

EXAMPLE 1

Copy and complete: 21 d = ? wk

SOLUTION

You are converting days to weeks, a smaller unit to a larger unit. There are 7 days in one week, so divide by 7.

$$21 \text{ d} = (21 \div 7) \text{ wk}$$
$$= 3 \text{ wk}$$

The amount of time between a start time and an end time is called *elapsed* time.

EXAMPLE 2

A study session began at 10:40 A.M. and ended at 12:10 P.M. How long did the it last?

STEP 1 Find the time until noon:
10:40 → 11:40 = 1 h; 11:40 → 12:00 = 20 min

STEP 2 Find the time after noon:
12:00 → 12:10 = 10 min

STEP 3 Add the elapsed times: 1 h 20 min + 10 min = 1 h 30 min

▸ **Answer** The study session lasted 1 h 30 min.

PRACTICE

Copy and complete.

1. 120 sec = ? min
2. 3 d = ? h
3. 1 min 15 sec = ? sec
4. 14 wk 2 d = ? d
5. 75 h = ? d ? h
6. 265 min = ? h ? min

Find the elapsed time.

7. 8:35 A.M. to 11:56 A.M.
8. 5:38 A.M. to 11:42 A.M.
9. 6:15 A.M. to 1:23 P.M.
10. 10:44 P.M. to 1:02 A.M.
11. 7:45 A.M. to 12:15 A.M.
12. 10:05 A.M. to 8:25 P.M.

Units of Measure 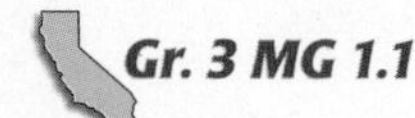 *Gr. 3 MG 1.1*

The **mass** of an object is the amount of matter it has. The **capacity** of a container is the amount that it can hold.

Units of Measure

Type of Measure	U.S. Customary System Units and Benchmarks		Metric System Units and Benchmarks	
Length	**Inch (in.)**	Length of small paper clip	**Millimeter (mm)**	Thickness of a dime
	Foot (ft)	Length of an adult's foot	**Centimeter (cm)**	Width of little finger
	Yard (yd)	Width of a door	**Meter (m)**	Width of a door
	Mile (mi)	Length of 8 city blocks	**Kilometer (km)**	Length of 5 city blocks
Weight or Mass	**Ounce (oz)**	Weight of a slice of bread	**Milligram (mg)**	Mass of a grain of sugar
	Pound (lb)	Weight of a soccer ball	**Gram (g)**	Mass of a small paper clip
	Ton (t)	Weight of a compact car	**Kilogram (kg)**	Mass of a textbook
Capacity	**Fluid ounce (fl oz)**	Capacity of a serving spoon	**Milliliter (mL)**	Capacity of an eyedropper
	Cup (c)	Capacity of a drinking glass	**Liter (L)**	Capacity of a large water bottle
	Pint (pt)	A large mug	**Kiloliter (kL)**	Capacity of 8 large trash cans
	Quart (qt)	Capacity of a large water bottle		
	Gallon (gal)	Capacity of a large milk container		

EXAMPLE 1

a. You could use ounces to measure the weight of a peach and grams to measure its mass.

b. You could use feet, yards, or meters to measure the length of a desk.

PRACTICE

Choose an appropriate customary unit and metric unit to measure the length, weight and mass, or capacity of the object.

1. distance between two cities
2. capacity of a cereal bowl
3. weight/mass of an elephant
4. length of a pencil
5. height of an office building
6. weight/mass of a hockey skate
7. capacity of a bottle of glue
8. weight/mass of a feather
9. diameter of a marble
10. capacity of a swimming pool

Using a Ruler *Gr. 5 MG 2.1*

An **inch ruler** has markings for inches, halves of an inch, fourths of an inch, eighths of an inch, and sixteenths of an inch. As the lengths get shorter, so do the markings.

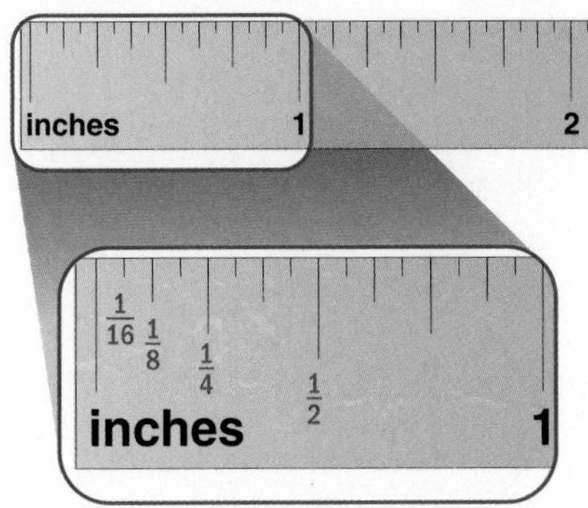

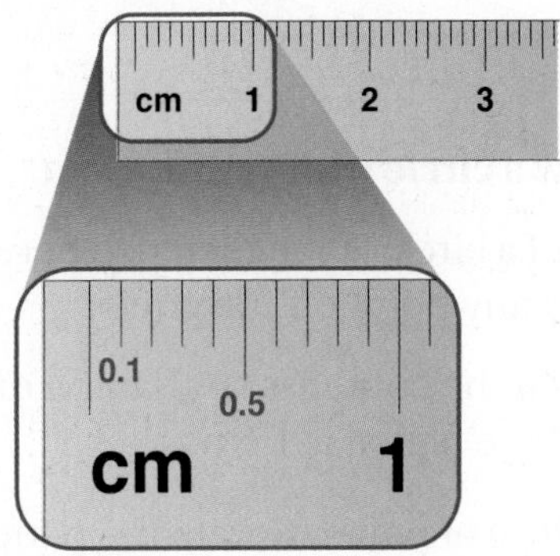

A **centimeter ruler** has markings for centimeters, halves of a centimeter, and tenths of a centimeter (also called *millimeters*). Like an inch ruler, as the lengths get shorter, so do the markings.

EXAMPLE 1

Use a ruler to draw a segment with the given length.

a. $1\frac{3}{4}$ inches

b. 2.9 centimeters

SOLUTION

a.

Start at the leftmost mark on the ruler.

inches 1 2

Draw a segment so that the other end is at the $1\frac{3}{4}$ in. mark.

b.

Start at the leftmost mark on the ruler.

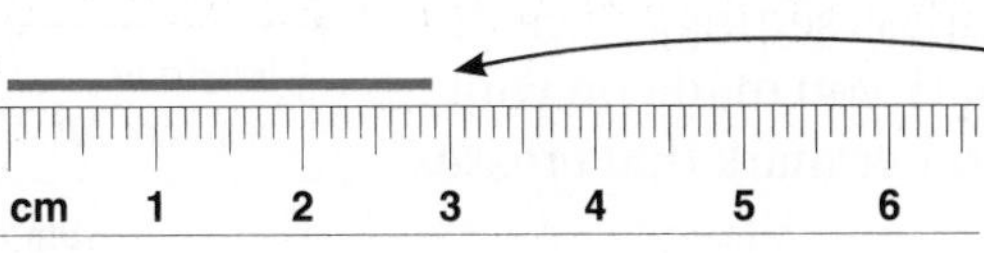

Draw a segment so that the other end is at the 2.9 cm mark.

PRACTICE

Use a ruler to draw a segment with the given length.

1. $\frac{9}{16}$ inch

2. $4\frac{1}{4}$ inches

3. 1.8 centimeters

4. 6.2 centimeters

5. $3\frac{7}{8}$ inches

6. 2.3 centimeters

7. 5.5 centimeters

8. $1\frac{1}{2}$ inches

Using a Compass Gr. 5 NS 2.1

A **compass** is a tool used to draw circles. A **straightedge** is any tool that can be used to draw a segment.

EXAMPLE 1

Use a compass to draw a circle with radius 1 cm.

Recall that the *radius* of a circle is the distance between the center of the circle and any point on the circle.

Use a metric ruler. Open the compass so that the distance between the point and the pencil is 1 cm.

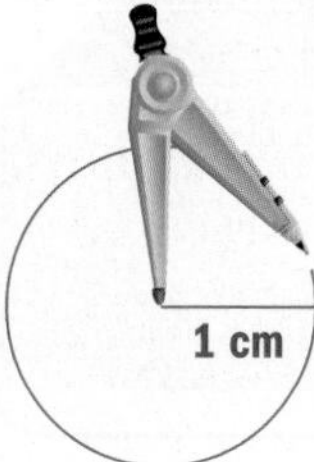

Place the point on a piece of paper. Rotate the pencil around the point to draw the circle.

EXAMPLE 2

Use a straightedge and a compass to draw a segment whose length is the sum of the lengths of $\overline{AB}$ and $\overline{CD}$.

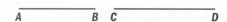

A ——— B C ——— D

SOLUTION

STEP 1 Use a straightedge to draw a segment longer than both segments.

STEP 2 Open your compass to measure segment *AB*. Using this compass setting, place the point at the left end of your segment. Make a mark that crosses your segment.

STEP 3 Open your compass to measure segment *CD*. Using this compass setting, place the point at the first mark you made on your segment. Make another mark that crosses your segment.

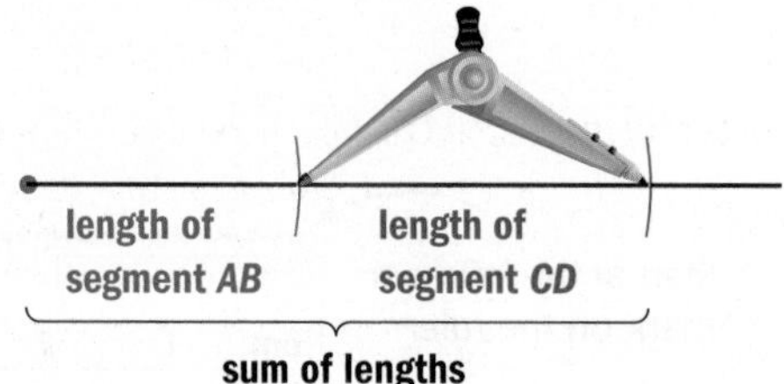

PRACTICE

1. Use a compass to draw a circle with radius 5 centimeters.
2. Use a compass to draw a circle with radius 1 inch.
3. Use a straightedge and a compass to draw a segment whose length is the *sum* of the lengths of the two segments at the right.

4. Use a straightedge and a compass to draw a segment whose length is the *difference* of the lengths of the two given segments in Exercise 3.

Points and Lines   *Gr. 5 MG 2.1*

In geometry, a **point** is usually labeled with an uppercase letter, such as A or B. Points are used to name *lines, rays,* and *segments.*

Words	*Diagram*	*Symbols*
A **line** extends without end in two *opposite* directions.	X Y	$\overleftrightarrow{XY}$ or $\overleftrightarrow{YX}$
A **ray** has one **endpoint** and extends without end in *one* direction.	X Y	$\overrightarrow{XY}$
A **segment** is a part of a line that consists of two endpoints and all the points between them.	X Y	$\overline{XY}$ or $\overline{YX}$

EXAMPLE 1

Identify and name the *line, ray,* or *segment.*

a. A B

b. 

c. 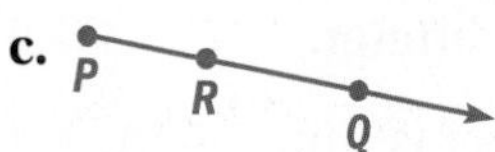

SOLUTION

a. The figure is a segment that can be named $\overline{AB}$ or $\overline{BA}$.

b. The figure is a line that can be named $\overleftrightarrow{MN}$, $\overleftrightarrow{NM}$, $\overleftrightarrow{LN}$, $\overleftrightarrow{NL}$, $\overleftrightarrow{LM}$, or $\overleftrightarrow{ML}$.

c. The figure is a ray that can be named $\overrightarrow{PQ}$ or $\overrightarrow{PR}$, but not $\overrightarrow{RQ}$. The endpoint of $\overrightarrow{RQ}$ is R, not P.

PRACTICE

Match the name with the correct figure.

1. $\overline{CD}$ **2.** $\overleftrightarrow{CD}$ **3.** $\overrightarrow{CD}$

A. D C

B. 

C. 

In Exercises 4–7, use the diagram.

U S V R T

4. Name three points.

5. Name two rays.

6. Name two lines.

7. Name a segment that has S as an endpoint.

8. Name a ray that has U as an endpoint.

Perimeter Concepts

A **triangle** is a geometric figure having 3 sides and 3 angles.

side

angle

A **rectangle** has 4 sides and 4 right angles. Opposite sides have the same length.

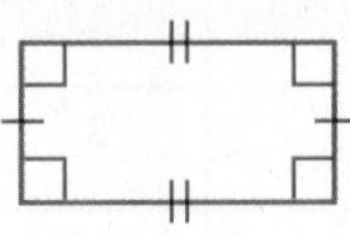

A **square** is a rectangle with all four sides the same length.

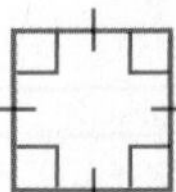

The distance around a figure is called its **perimeter**. You measure perimeter in linear units, such as inches. To find perimeter, add the lengths of the sides.

EXAMPLE 1

Find the perimeter.

The perimeter is 5 in. + 4 in. + 4 in. = 13 in.

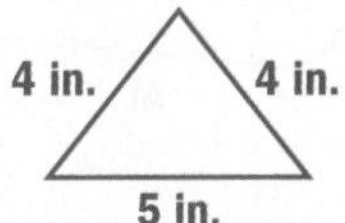

EXAMPLE 2

Draw and label a rectangle with a length of 3 cm and a width of 2 cm. Then find its perimeter.

Draw a horizontal side 3 cm long. Then draw the two vertical sides 2 cm long. Finally, draw the second horizontal side 3 cm long.

The perimeter is 3 cm + 2 cm + 3 cm + 2 cm = 10 cm.

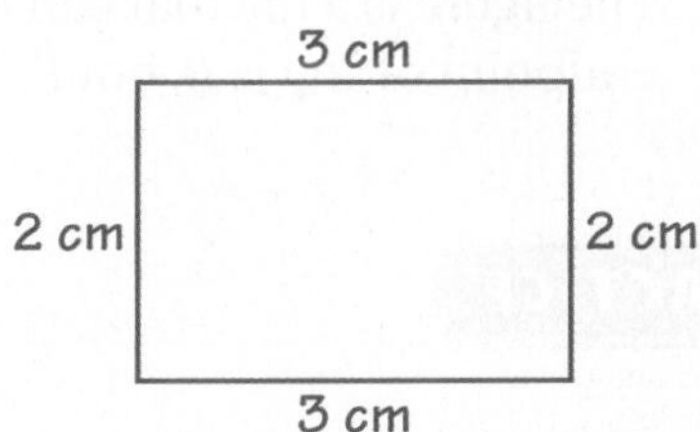

PRACTICE

Find the perimeter.

1. 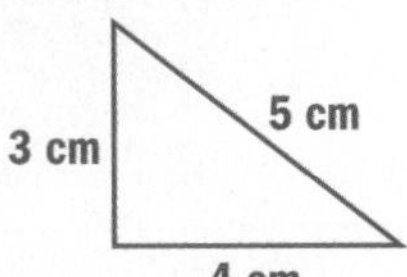

2. 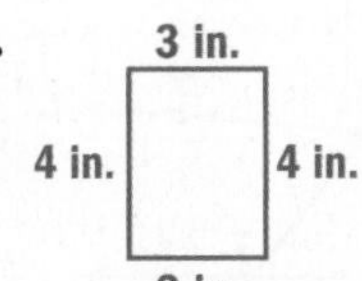

3. 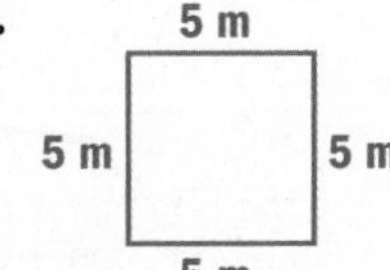

4. 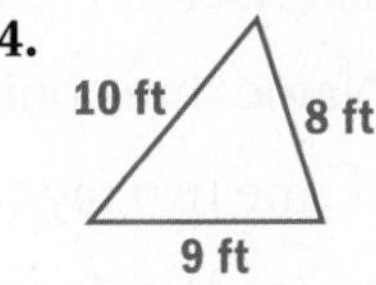

Draw and label the figure described. Then find its perimeter.

5. A square with sides 1 in. long
6. A square with sides 4 cm long
7. A rectangle with a length of 4 cm and a width of 3 cm
8. A rectangle with a length of 2 in. and a width of 1 in.

Area Concepts 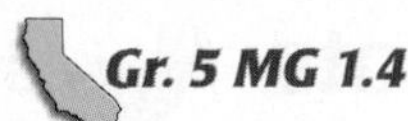

The **area** of a figure is the amount of surface covered by the figure. Areas are measured in square units such as square inches.

EXAMPLE 1

Find or estimate the area.

a.

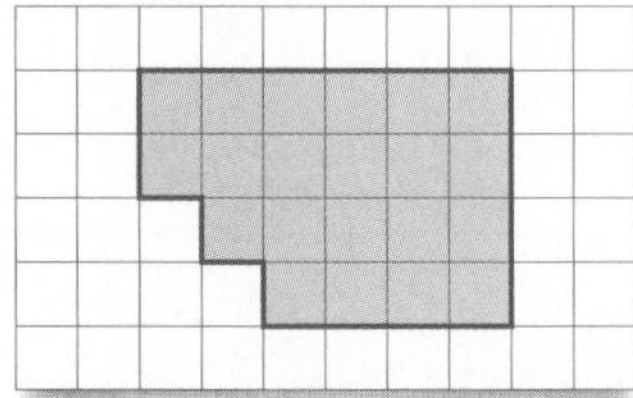

Find the area by counting the number of squares inside the figure. There are 21 squares. So the area is 21 square units.

b.

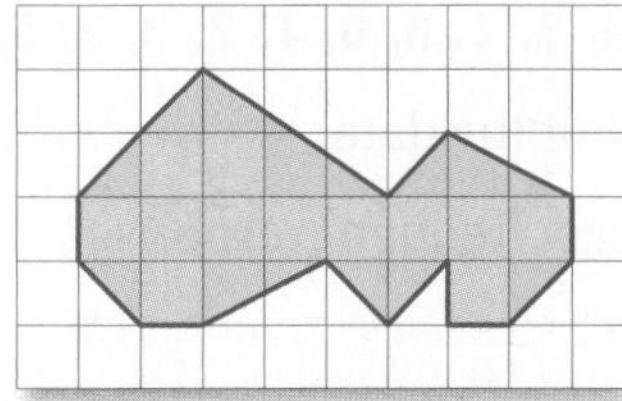

Count the **whole squares**: 12. Estimate how many more whole squares can be covered by the **partial squares**: 8. The total area is about $12 + 8 = 20$ square units.

PRACTICE

Find or estimate the area.

1.

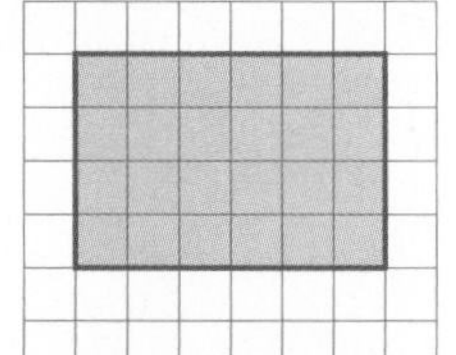

2.

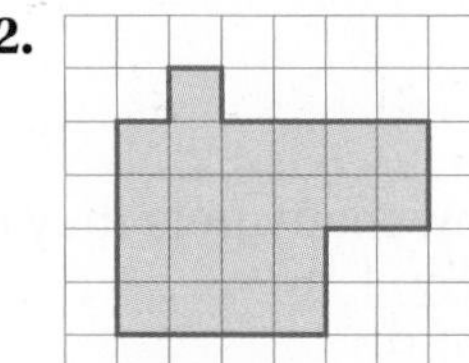

3.

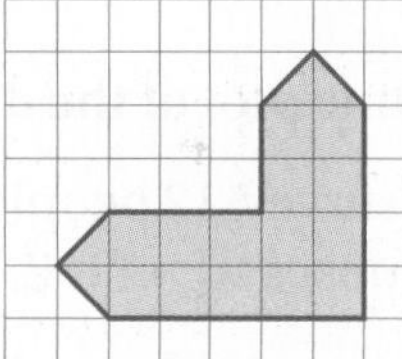

4.

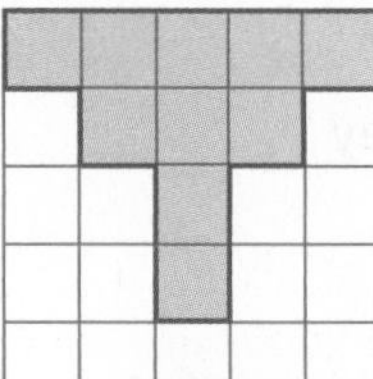

5.

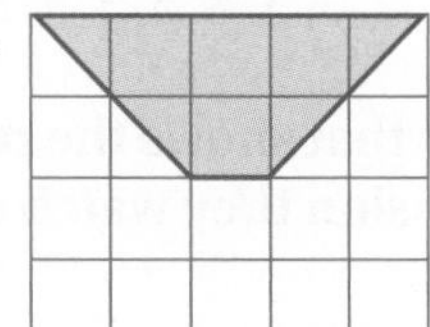

6.

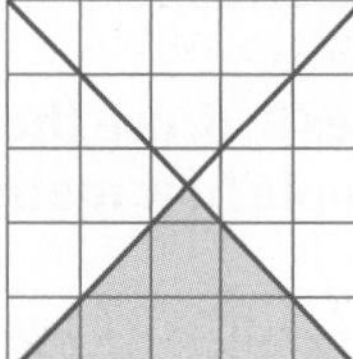

7.

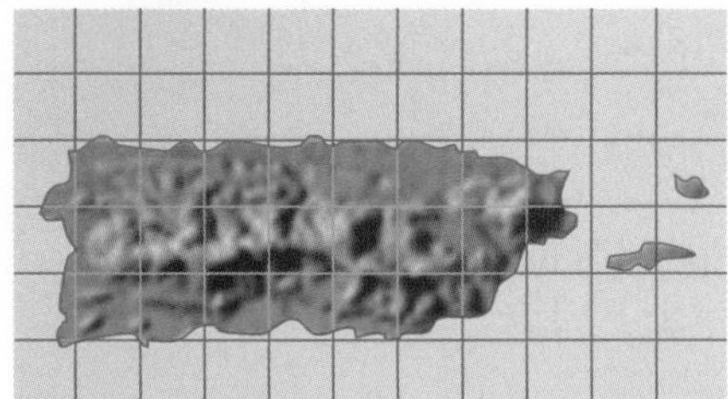

8.

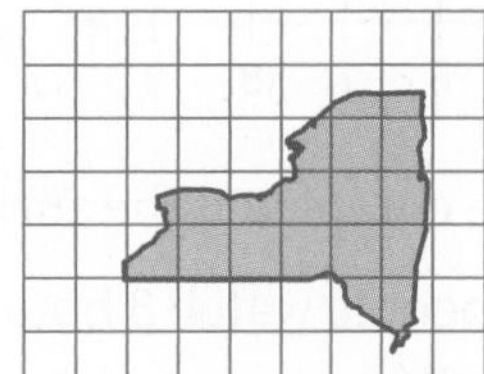

STANDARDS REVIEW HANDBOOK

Reading and Making Line Plots

Gr. 5 SDAP 1.0, Gr. 5 SDAP 1.2

A **line plot** uses a number line to show how often data values occur.

EXAMPLE 1

You surveyed 15 of your neighbors and asked them how many brothers and sisters they have. Their responses were:

5, 3, 2, 1, 0, 6, 3, 4, 3, 0, 1, 2, 3, 2, 5, 3, 4

a. Make a line plot of the data.

b. What was the least frequent response?

SOLUTION

a.

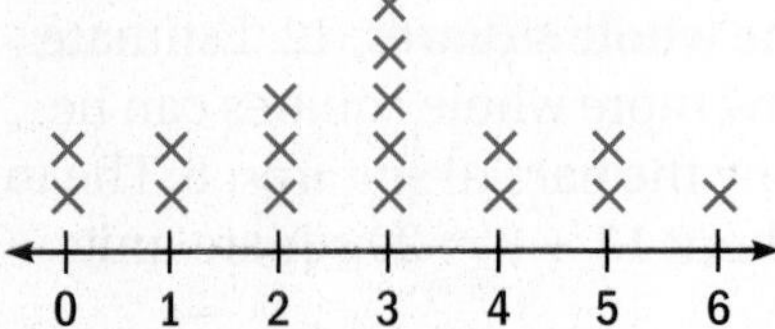

b. There is only one × above 6, so 6 was the least frequent response.

PRACTICE

Make a line plot of the data.

1. In a survey, 12 people were asked how many pets they own. Their responses were: 1, 2, 1, 1, 0, 4, 1, 0, 0, 2, 1, 3.

2. In a survey, 16 people were asked how many times they exercise during a week. Their responses were: 1, 3, 4, 2, 3, 3, 3, 5, 3, 4, 5, 2, 3, 3, 5, 6.

In Exercises 3–5, use the line plot below that shows the results of a survey asking people how many hours of television they watch each week.

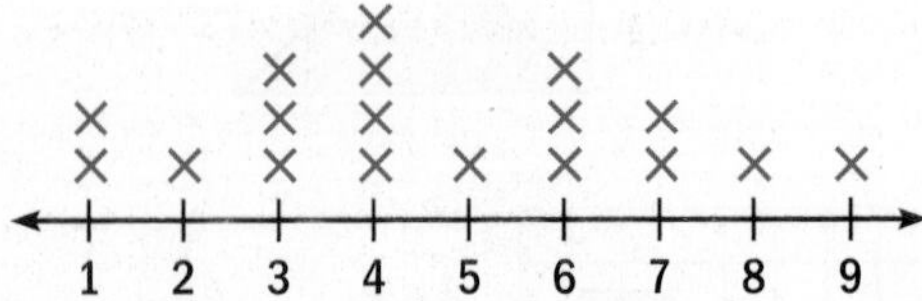

3. How many people completed the survey?

4. How many more people watch 3 hours of television each week than watch 5 hours of television?

5. How many people watch less than 4 hours of television each week?

6. How many people watch 7 or more hours of television each week?

Reading and Making Bar Graphs

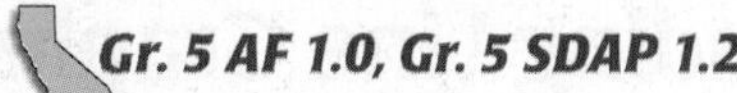

Data are numbers or facts. A **bar graph** is one way to display data. A bar graph uses bars to show how quantities in categories compare.

EXAMPLE 1

The bar graph shows the results of a survey on favorite pizza toppings. Which topping is chosen the most? Which topping was chosen the least?

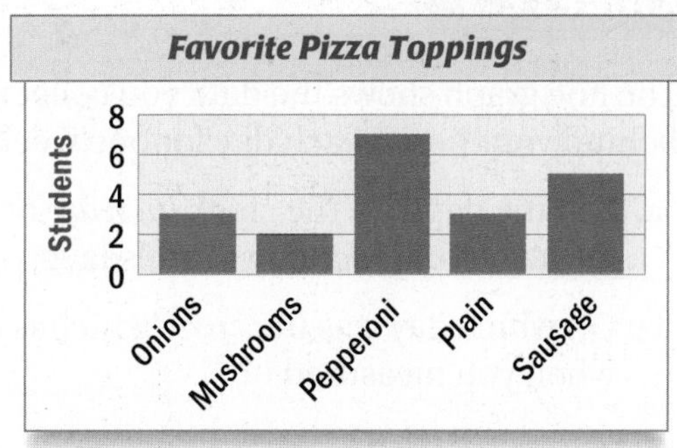

SOLUTION

The longest bar on the graph represents the 7 people who chose pepperoni, the topping chosen the most. The shortest bar represents the 2 students who chose mushrooms, the topping chosen the least.

EXAMPLE 2

Draw a bar graph for the data showing students' favorite subject.

Subject	Students
Math	8
English	15
History	20
Science	16

SOLUTION

Choose a scale that extends slightly beyond the greatest data value, 20. The scale should also be easily divided into intervals. A scale that goes to 25 works well.

Then draw and label the two axes. Draw four bars of equal width to show the data. Finish the graph by writing its title.

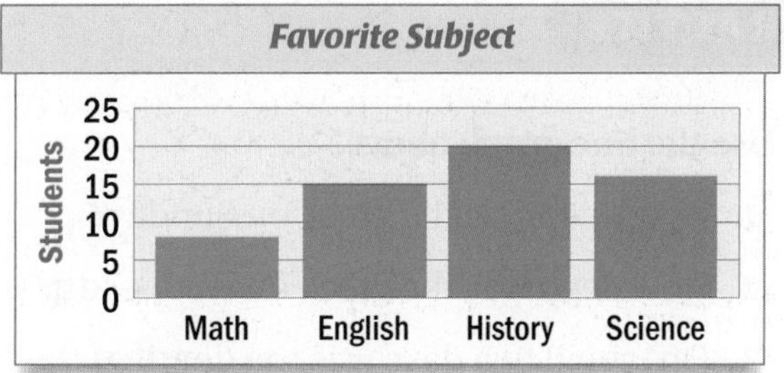

PRACTICE

In Exercises 1–3, use the bar graph of pizza toppings.

1. How many students chose sausage as a favorite pizza topping?
2. How many students chose onions as a favorite topping?
3. Which two toppings were chosen by the same number of students?
4. Suppose 8 more students took the survey shown in the second example. Draw a new bar graph if 3 of the students chose math, 4 chose history, and 1 chose science.

Reading Line Graphs Gr. 5 SDAP 1.2

A **line graph** is a graph in which points representing data pairs are connected by line segments. You can use a line graph to show how quantities change over time.

EXAMPLE 1

The line graph shows the data you collected on the depth of a creek behind your house each day for one week.

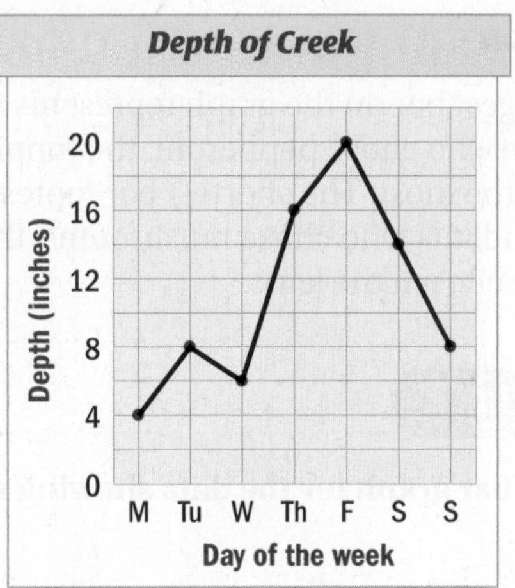

a. Did the depth of the creek *increase* or *decrease* from Monday to Tuesday?

b. On which day was the creek 6 inches deep when you measured it?

SOLUTION

a. If the line rises from left to right, the data increase. If the line falls from left to right, the data decrease. Because the line from Monday to Tuesday rises, the depth of the creek increased.

b. Look at the vertical scale and locate 6. Then find the data point on this horizontal line with the value of 6.The creek was 6 inches deep when you measured it on Wednesday.

PRACTICE

Use the line graph above.

1. How deep was the creek on Sunday?
2. How deep was the creek on Wednesday?
3. On which two days was the depth of the creek the same when you measured it?
4. Did the depth of the creek *increase* or *decrease* from Friday to Saturday?
5. Did the depth of the creek *increase* or *decrease* from Thursday to Friday?
6. On which day was the creek 16 inches deep when you measured it?
7. On which day was the creek the deepest?
8. On which day was the creek the shallowest?
9. Between which two days did the depth of the creek decrease by 2 inches?
10. Between which two days did the depth of the creek increase the most? How much was the increase?

Problem Solving Strategies

To be successful in mathematics, you need to be a good problem solver. The following strategies can help you solve word problems.

Strategy	Use when you . . .
Draw a diagram	can represent the conditions in the problem visually.
Look for a pattern	are given a series of numbers or diagrams to analyze.
Guess, check, and revise	want a place to start or you want to see what happens for a particular number.
Act it out	when you can represent a problem with physical objects or movement.
Make a list or table	want to systematically record, generate, or organize information.
Solve a simpler or related problem	can make a difficult problem easier by using simpler numbers or conditions.
Work backward	know an end result and you need to find beginning conditions.
Break into parts	cannot solve a problem all at once, but can solve it in parts or stages.

A problem may include facts that are not needed to solve the problem. Information that is not needed is called *irrelevant information.* Some problems cannot be solved because they do not contain enough information.

EXAMPLE 1

You are baking cookies that require 6 cups of cereal for each batch. Use the information found on the cereal box, shown at the right.

Nutrition Facts

Serving size: 1.5 cups (40 g)

Servings per package: 10

a. Find the number of boxes of cereal you will need to make 3 batches of cookies.

b. Find the number of cookies you can make.

SOLUTION

a. Each box has 1.5 cups/serving, and there are 10 servings per box.

1.5 cups/serving $\times$ 10 servings per box = 15 cups per box

You need 6 cups per batch $\times$ 3 batches = 18 cups. So you need 2 boxes.

b. There is not enough information to find how many cookies can be made. Notice that the serving size in grams is irrelevant information.

PRACTICE

Identify any irrelevant information. Then solve the problem if possible. If there is not enough information to solve the problem, tell what information is needed.

1. The deli makes 5 types of sandwiches. You can order each sandwich with mayonnaise, mustard, lettuce, and tomatoes. In how many different ways can you order a turkey sandwich with at least two toppings?

2. The lengths of 3 sticks are 6 inches, 10 inches, and 18 inches. How can you use these sticks to mark off a length of 14 inches?

3. You buy 6 pounds of grapes at $1 per pound, a loaf of bread for $2, and cheese at $5 per pound. You give the cashier a $20 bill. How much change do you receive?

4. During regular season games, a hockey team earns 2 points for a win, 1 point for a tie, and 0 points for a loss. Out of 82 games played, a hockey team won 48 games and tied 3 games. How many points did the team earn for the 82 games?

5. Cans of corn are stacked with 1 can in the top row, 3 cans in the second row, 5 cans in the third row, 7 cans in the fourth row, and so on. There are 15 rows in all. How many cans are in the stack?

6. In how many different ways can three different postage stamps be arranged so that equal sides match up?

7. You type 32 words per minute and your friend types 36 words per minute. How long will it take you to type an essay that is 10 handwritten pages long?

8. A rectangular corral is 40 feet long and 20 feet wide. You want to enclose the corral with posts placed 10 feet apart. How many posts will be needed?

9. You have saved $1200 to buy a new computer. You plan to buy a computer for $1020, plus a sales tax of $51. The first payment will be $150, and the rest of the cost will be paid in 3 equal payments. *Describe* how you can find the amount of each equal payment.

10. You are on a three-day hiking trip. The trail is 36 miles long. On the first day you hike 10 miles at 2 miles per hour. On the second day you hike 11 miles at 3 miles per hour. How far and how long will you hike on the third day?

11. A horse eats the rest of a 50 pound bag of feed in a day. How much feed does the horse eat in a day?

12. You are making balloon bunches for a party. You have 80 red balloons, 120 blue balloons, and 100 yellow balloons. If each bunch of balloons is identical, and there are no leftover balloons, what is the greatest number of bunches you can make?

Venn Diagrams and Logical Reasoning

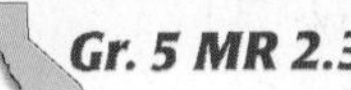

A **Venn diagram** uses shapes to show how sets are related.

EXAMPLE 1

Draw and use a Venn diagram.

a. Draw a Venn diagram of the whole numbers between 10 and 20 where set *A* consists of odd numbers and set *B* consists of multiples of 3.

b. Is the following statement *true* or *false*? Explain.
No odd whole number between 10 and 20 is a multiple of 3.

c. Is the following statement *always, sometimes,* or *never* true? Explain.
A multiple of 3 between 10 and 20 is even.

SOLUTION

a.

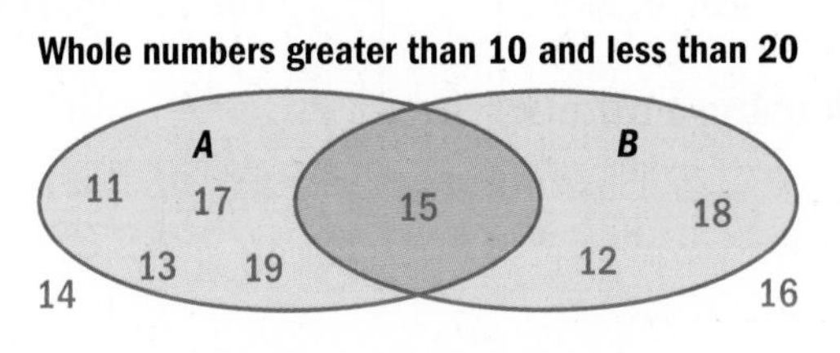

b. False. 15 is an odd whole number that is a multiple of 3.

c. Sometimes. It is true that 12 and 18 are multiples of 3 that are even, but 15 is a multiple of 3 that is odd.

STANDARDS REVIEW HANDBOOK

PRACTICE

Draw a Venn diagram of the sets described.

1. Of the whole numbers less than 10, set *A* consists of numbers that are greater than 7 and set *B* consists of even numbers.

2. Of the whole numbers less than 15, set *C* consists of multiples of 4 and set *D* consists of odd numbers.

Use the Venn diagrams from Exercises 1 and 2 to answer the question. *Explain* your reasoning.

3. Is the following statement *true* or *false*? *There is only one even number greater than 7 and less than 10.*

4. Is the following statement *true* or *false*? *The number 6 is an even whole number greater than 7.*

5. Is the following statement *always, sometimes,* or *never* true? *A whole number less than 15 is both a multiple of 4 and odd.*

Extra Practice

Chapter 1

1.1 **Tell whether the number is *prime* or *composite*. *Explain* your reasoning. If the number is composite, write the prime factorization.**

1. 50 **2.** 71 **3.** 84 **4.** 225

1.2 **Find the greatest common factor of the numbers. Use prime factorization.**

5. 72, 96 **6.** 35, 105 **7.** 36, 78, 84 **8.** 30, 51, 175

1.3 **Write the fractions in simplest form. Tell whether they are equivalent.**

9. $\frac{20}{24}, \frac{30}{36}$ **10.** $\frac{21}{56}, \frac{28}{84}$ **11.** $\frac{12}{16}, \frac{14}{18}$ **12.** $\frac{14}{35}, \frac{22}{55}$

1.4 **Find the least common multiple of the numbers by listing multiples.**

13. 12, 16 **14.** 20, 25 **15.** 4, 6, 9 **16.** 32, 96, 160

1.5 **Copy and complete using <, >, or =. Check using a number line.**

17. $\frac{5}{6} \underline{?} \frac{3}{4}$ **18.** $\frac{14}{56} \underline{?} \frac{18}{72}$ **19.** $\frac{7}{18} \underline{?} \frac{7}{10}$ **20.** $\frac{22}{25} \underline{?} \frac{9}{10}$

Order the fractions from least to greatest.

21. $\frac{1}{3}, \frac{1}{5}, \frac{4}{15}, \frac{11}{45}$ **22.** $\frac{11}{12}, \frac{7}{9}, \frac{2}{3}, \frac{5}{6}$ **23.** $\frac{7}{8}, \frac{13}{18}, \frac{3}{4}, \frac{19}{24}$

1.6 **Copy and complete the statement using <, >, or =.**

24. $7\frac{1}{6} \underline{?} \frac{43}{6}$ **25.** $\frac{33}{8} \underline{?} 4\frac{3}{8}$ **26.** $5\frac{4}{9} \underline{?} \frac{16}{3}$ **27.** $\frac{19}{7} \underline{?} 2\frac{7}{10}$

Order the numbers from least to greatest.

28. $\frac{34}{5}, 3\frac{40}{55}, \frac{11}{15}, 3\frac{4}{5}$ **29.** $\frac{16}{16}, \frac{17}{10}, \frac{13}{8}, 1\frac{1}{6}$ **30.** $8\frac{1}{3}, 8, \frac{26}{3}, \frac{23}{8}$

1.7 **Copy and complete the statement using <, >, or =.**

31. $\frac{7}{9} \underline{?} 0.68$ **32.** $8\frac{9}{10} \underline{?} 8.925$ **33.** $0.5 \underline{?} \frac{63}{126}$ **34.** $\frac{43}{12} \underline{?} 3.625$

Order the numbers from least to greatest.

35. $5, \frac{59}{11}, 4.99, 5\frac{1}{7}$ **36.** $2\frac{7}{9}, 2.33, \frac{15}{6}, 2.45$ **37.** $1, \frac{8}{5}, 0, 0.923, 1\frac{5}{6}$

1.8 **38.** There are 5 tennis players in a tournament. If each tennis player plays every other player once, how many games will be played?

39. The items that Frank needs to buy for his cookout are given in the table. If Frank spends $7, how much does each ear of corn cost?

Item	*Total Cost*
1 package of ground beef	$3
1 bag of rolls	$2
4 ears of corn	?

Chapter 2

2.1 Find the sum or difference.

1. $\frac{5}{8}+\frac{1}{8}$ 2. $\frac{8}{11}-\frac{3}{11}$ 3. $\frac{3}{7}+\frac{5}{7}$ 4. $\frac{11}{12}-\frac{7}{12}$

Evaluate the expression for the given value of the variable.

5. $\frac{4}{11}+m$ when $m=\frac{3}{11}$ 6. $k-\frac{5}{9}$ when $k=\frac{7}{9}$ 7. $\frac{8}{23}-x$ when $x=\frac{4}{23}$

2.2 Evaluate the expression. Simplify if possible.

8. $\frac{1}{6}+\frac{5}{12}$ 9. $\frac{8}{9}-\frac{5}{6}$ 10. $\frac{7}{18}+\frac{1}{3}$ 11. $\frac{13}{15}-\frac{1}{5}$

2.3 12. $3\frac{1}{4}+3\frac{3}{4}$ 13. $8\frac{7}{9}+1\frac{8}{9}$ 14. $2\frac{2}{5}+4\frac{3}{10}$ 15. $7\frac{3}{4}+1\frac{5}{6}$

16. $11\frac{3}{5}-8\frac{4}{5}$ 17. $5\frac{1}{2}-3\frac{3}{8}$ 18. $6-5\frac{4}{7}$ 19. $8\frac{3}{8}-3\frac{2}{3}$

2.4 20. $\frac{7}{9}\times\frac{3}{4}$ 21. $\frac{7}{10}\times 24$ 22. $3\frac{1}{5}\times 1\frac{1}{4}$ 23. $\frac{5}{8}\times 4\frac{4}{9}$

24. $12\times\frac{1}{6}$ 25. $\frac{7}{24}\times\frac{8}{14}$ 26. $4\frac{2}{5}\times\frac{2}{11}$ 27. $10\frac{1}{2}\times 5\frac{1}{3}$

2.5 28. $\frac{3}{4}\div\frac{7}{8}$ 29. $\frac{6}{25}\div 4$ 30. $7\frac{4}{5}\div\frac{13}{15}$ 31. $2\frac{1}{6}\div 1\frac{1}{3}$

In Exercises 32–33, find the solution and explain which operation you used and why.

32. You are using a sheet of cardboard that is $10\frac{1}{2}$ in. long to make bookmarks for a craft fair. You divide the cardboard into 6 equal bookmarks. How wide is each bookmark?

33. You drink $\frac{1}{3}$ liter of water after every lap you run on a track. If you run 8 laps, how many liters of water will you drink?

2.6 Find the sum or difference. Use estimation to check your answer.

34. $8.33-7.41$ 35. $16.7+129.413$ 36. $702.85+35.2$ 37. $42.9-26.74$

Evaluate the expression when $a = 13.2$ and $b = 7.49$.

38. $6.4+a$ 39. $a+b$ 40. $8.613-b$ 41. $8+a-b$

2.7 Evaluate the expression. Then check that your answer is reasonable.

42. 2.7×0.8 43. 3.05×0.26 44. 1.48×0.037 45. 46×2.718

46. 0.89×8.76 47. 3.5×6.3 48. 6.4×9.05 49. 0.006×1.2

50. $84.14\div 7$ 51 $19.98\div 27$ 52. $6.4\div 0.08$ 53. $0.115\div 5.75$

54. $0.126\div 2.8$ 55. $0.884\div 0.26$ 56. $23.24\div 1.12$ 57. $3.91\div 34$

58. Find $18\div 3.21$. Round your answer to the nearest hundredth.

EXTRA PRACTICE

Chapter 3

3.1 Order the integers from least to greatest by graphing on a number line.

1. $-3, 0, 6, -10, 3$ **2.** $63, -48, -9, 32, -106$ **3.** $71, -70, 15, 99, -10, -84$

3.2 Evaluate the expression.

4. $-18 + 14$ **5.** $75 + (-38)$ **6.** $22 + (-7)$ **7.** $0 + (-11)$

8. $12 + 27 + (-12)$ **9.** $-8 + (-5) + 6$ **10.** $-9 + 23 + (-1)$ **11.** $-3 + (-17) + (-6)$

3.3 **12.** $7 - 11$ **13.** $-9 - 36$ **14.** $-25 - 10$ **15.** $64 - (-15)$

16. $-8 - (-9)$ **17.** $12 - (-12)$ **18.** $-13 - (-13)$ **19.** $0 - (-12)$

3.4 **20.** $20(-7)$ **21.** $-4(15)$ **22.** $-9(-8)$ **23.** $1(-47)$

24. $-6(5)(3)$ **25.** $11(7)(-2)$ **26.** $-3(-4)(-1)$ **27.** $6(0)(-100)$

3.5 **28.** $65 \div (-5)$ **29.** $0 \div (-3)$ **30.** $-42 \div (-14)$ **31.** $-60 \div 12$

Find the mean of the integers.

32. $-3, 6, -12, 17$ **33.** $-11, 5, 14, -20$ **34.** $15, -4, 4, -15, 0$

3.6 Evalute the expression.

35. $1 + (7 - 3)^3$ **36.** $\frac{36 - 8}{2 + 5}$ **37.** $72 \div 4 \div 3$ **38.** $(3^3 - 2)(1 + 2)$

39. You are training to run a 12 mile race. When you start training, you run 12 miles in 108 minutes. By the time of the race, you run each mile 2 minutes faster than when you started training. Write and evaluate an expression to find how many minutes it takes you to run the race.

3.7 Graph the numbers on a number line. Then compare them using <, >, or =.

40. $-\frac{9}{11}, -0.9$ **41.** $-3.625, -3\frac{5}{8}$ **42.** $-\frac{6}{13}, -\frac{5}{12}$

Show that each number is rational by writing it in $\frac{a}{b}$ form. Then order the numbers from least to greatest.

43. $-6, -\frac{70}{11}, -5.99, -6\frac{1}{7}$ **44.** $-1, -\frac{8}{5}, 0, -0.83, 1\frac{2}{3}$ **45.** $-\frac{7}{9}, 1.33, \frac{7}{6}, -1.45, 0.13$

Evaluate the expression. *Justify* each step.

46. $-3 + 7 + 3$ **47.** $6 \cdot 10 \cdot \frac{1}{6}$ **48.** $50 \cdot 13 \cdot 2$ **49.** $66 + 47 + 34$

3.8 Use the distributive property to evaluate the expression.

50. $8(9.1) + 8(0.9)$ **51.** $11\left(\frac{5}{9}\right) + 11\left(\frac{4}{9}\right)$ **52.** $12\left(\frac{5}{8}\right) - 12\left(\frac{1}{8}\right)$ **53.** $6(4.8)$

54. You buy 4 teddy bears for $24.95 each. Write an expression that will allow you to use the distributive property to find the total cost of the teddy bears. Then evaluate the expression.

55. Evaluate the expression $5(9) + 5(-8) + 3$ and justify your steps.

Chapter 4

4.1 Evaluate the expression when $a = 3$, $b = -5$, and $c = \frac{1}{4}$.

1. $7.5a$
2. $26 - 4b$
3. $8c + 6$
4. $12a - 14\left(c + \frac{3}{4}\right)$
5. $b^2 + 16c$
6. $\frac{12c}{ab}$
7. The expression $60h$ can be used to find the number of minutes in h hours. Find the number of minutes in 9.5 hours.

4.2 Write the verbal phrase as an algebraic expression. Let x represent the number.

8. 17 times a number
9. The quotient of a number and 7
10. A number added to -1
11. 5 more than the square of a number

Write the phrase as an algebraic expression.

12. The sum of n and the product of 3 and m
13. The quotient of 23 minus r and s

4.3 Simplify the expression.

14. $-r + 4 - 2 + r$
15. $6 + z + 3z - 4$
16. $6y + 12 - 4y$
17. $8a - 2(3 + 4a)$
18. $2(3 - x) - 12 - 3x$
19. $3(2t - 5) + 4t$

4.4

20. Find the perimeter and area of a rectangular garden with a length of 13 feet and a width of 8 feet.
21. Ramon jogs at a rate of 5 miles per hour. How far does he jog in 1.5 hours?
22. Find the side length of a square that has a perimeter of 32 centimeters.

4.5 Tell whether the number is a solution of the equation.

23. $7m = 15; 2$
24. $4 = h - 3; 7$
25. $\frac{y}{9} = 5; 45$

Solve the equation using mental math.

26. $x + 6 = 13$
27. $\frac{z}{8} = 2$
28. $1 = 10 - p$
29. $280 = 20t$

4.6 Solve the equation. Check your solution.

30. $n + 6 = -4$
31. $15 = d - 3$
32. $1.4 = 3.8 + w$
33. $z - (-7) = 3$
34. $-22 = 28 + f - 19$
35. $2.7 + z + 4.3 = 15.4$

4.7 Solve the equation. Check your solution.

36. $17t = 119$
37. $-49 = -7y$
38. $10c = 110$
39. $\frac{g}{3} = -7$
40. $18 = \frac{2}{3}m$
41. $\frac{5}{6}q = 20$
42. $1.2 = \frac{k}{4}$
43. $26k = -52$

EXTRA PRACTICE

Chapter 5

5.1 **In the 2001–2002 season, the Michigan State men's hockey team had 18 wins, 6 losses, and 4 ties in their conference. Use this information to write the ratio as a fraction, a decimal, and a percent.**

1. Wins to losses　**2.** Wins to games played　**3.** Losses to games played

Write the ratio as a fraction in simplest form.

4. 30 : 36　**5.** 12 to 48　**6.** 28 to 70

5.2 **Find the unit rate.**

7. $11.89 for 8.2 gallons　**8.** $370 for 40 hours　**9.** 432 words in 12 minutes

10. 120 miles for 2.5 hours　**11.** 14 pounds in 8 months　**12.** $15.30 for 8.5 feet

13. Find the average speed of a runner who completes a 1500 meter race in 4 minutes 10 seconds.

14. Determine which bottle of shampoo is the better buy: 15 fluid ounces for $2.59 or 20 fluid ounces for $3.59.

5.3 **Solve the proportion using equivalent ratios or algebra.**

15. $\frac{x}{30} = \frac{5}{6}$　**16.** $\frac{28}{24} = \frac{r}{6}$　**17.** $\frac{t}{36} = \frac{3}{4}$　**18.** $\frac{12}{15} = \frac{c}{10}$

19. $\frac{18}{b} = \frac{6}{13}$　**20.** $\frac{15}{36} = \frac{5}{s}$　**21.** $\frac{32}{12} = \frac{96}{n}$　**22.** $\frac{7}{6} = \frac{63}{g}$

5.4 **Solve the proportion using the cross products property.**

23. $\frac{30}{12} = \frac{6}{z}$　**24.** $\frac{9}{x} = \frac{5}{14}$　**25.** $\frac{2.4}{9} = \frac{n}{1.5}$　**26.** $\frac{a}{39} = \frac{6.5}{13}$

27. $\frac{3}{p} = \frac{12}{26}$　**28.** $\frac{15}{40} = \frac{c}{18}$　**29.** $\frac{x}{8.5} = \frac{6}{30}$　**30.** $\frac{1.5}{9} = \frac{3.4}{m}$

31. A 30 gram serving of walnuts has 180 calories. How many calories are in a 100 gram serving of walnuts?

32. The length of a scale model is 4 inches. The actual length is 80 inches. What is the model's scale?

5.5 **In Exercises 33–36, use the fact that a floor plan of a house is drawn using a scale of 1 in. : 8 ft.**

33. Find the actual dimensions of a rectangular kitchen that is 2.5 inches long and 1.25 inches wide on the floor plan.

34. Find the actual dimensions of a rectangular deck that is 3.75 inches long and 1.875 inches wide on the floor plan.

35. Find the dimensions on the floor plan of a rectangular bedroom with an actual length of 22 feet and an actual width of 14 feet.

36. Find the dimensions on the floor plan of a rectangular dining room with an actual length of 19 feet and an actual width of 17 feet.

Chapter 6

6.1 **Write the percent as a fraction.**

1. 60%
2. 49%
3. 84%
4. 56%

Write the fraction as a percent.

5. $\frac{2}{5}$
6. $\frac{9}{10}$
7. $\frac{1}{4}$
8. $\frac{17}{25}$

6.2 **Use a proportion to answer the question.**

9. What percent of 25 is 16?
10. 54 is 75% of what number?
11. What number is 27% of 250?
12. What percent of 32 is 12?
13. What number is 30% of 600?
14. 11 is 44% of what number?

6.3 **Write the percent as a decimal.**

15. 24%
16. 2%
17. 10.6%
18. 3.94%

Write the decimal as a percent.

19. 0.575
20. 0.082
21. 0.0012
22. 4.2

Find the percent of the number.

23. 0.004% of 500
24. 0.17% of 230
25. 250% of 46
26. 1525% of 12

6.4 **Use the percent equation to answer the question.**

27. 57 is 125% of what number?
28. What number is 3% of 18?
29. What percent of 64 is 20?
30. 60 is 40% of what number?
31. What number is 70% of 700?
32. What percent of 118 is 59?

6.5 **Use the given information to find the new price.**

33. Wholesale price: $96
    Markup: 120%
34. Original price: $58
    Discount: 25%
35. Food bill before tax: $62
    Sales tax: 7%
36. Food bill before tax: $27
    Tip: 20%
37. Original price: $126
    Discount: 33%
38. Wholesale price: $38
    Markup: 15%

6.6 **In Exercises 39–41, find the interest and the balance of the account that earns simple annual interest.**

39. $250 at 2.5% for 2 years
40. $1000 at 3% for 8 months
41. $600 at 4.4% for 1 month
42. Suppose you deposit $500 into an account that earns 4% simple annual interest. How long will it take to earn $10 in interest?
43. Suppose you deposit $800 into a savings account that earns 2.5% simple annual interest. How long will it take to earn $40 in interest?

EXTRA PRACTICE

Chapter 7

7.1 **A survey asks people to name their favorite type of movie. Identify the sampling method. Tell whether the sample is likely to be biased.**

1. Survey people as they walk out of the theater after seeing a horror film.
2. Survey every fifth person that enters a video store.

7.2 **Tell whether the question could produce biased results. *Explain.***

3. Would you rather watch an exciting soccer game or a long, boring baseball game?
4. How many hours do you spend practicing a musical instrument each week?

7.3 **Find the mean, median, and mode(s) of the data.**

5. 7, 7.5, 7.1, 7.9, 7.5, 7, 7.3, 7.5
6. 94, 108, 145, 171, 162, 197, 186, 76, 88, 143
7. The record low temperatures in July in 8 cities are 43°F, 69°F, 35°F, 51°F, 40°F, 35°F, 44°F, and 35°F. Which measure of central tendency is most useful for describing a typical data value? *Explain* your reasoning.

7.4 **In Exercises 8–9, use the prices (in dollars) of several DVD players and VCRs listed below.**

DVD PLAYERS 250, 200, 160, 180, 160, 300, 185, 190, 130, 95, 250, 160, 200, 180

VCRS 130, 100, 80, 200, 100, 100, 100, 90, 90, 120, 140, 230

8. Find the median, extremes, quartiles, range and interquartile range of each data set.

7.5 9. Make a frequency table and a histogram of each data set using the intervals 70–109, 110–149, 150–189, 190–229, 230–269, and 270–309.

7.6 10. The table shows Jake's work schedule at a video store during the week. Display the data in a circle graph.

Day	Monday	Tuesday	Wednesday	Thursday	Friday
Hours	3.5	5	6	3	2.5

11. In a circle graph, what angle measure corresponds to 60%? 40%?

7.7 12. A student makes the claim that AA batteries cost approximately twice as much in the United States as in France or in Germany. Tell whether this is a valid claim based on the data shown in the graph. *Explain* your reasoning.

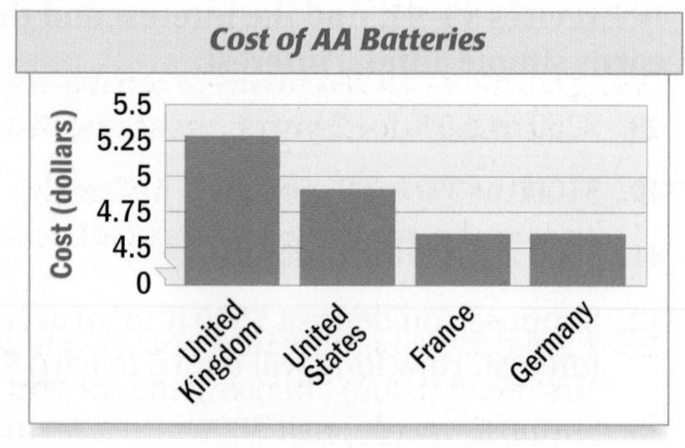

Chapter 8

8.1 **Each number from 1 to 20 is written on a separate card and put in a bag. You randomly choose a card from the bag. Find the probability of the event. Write the probability as a fraction, a decimal, and a percent.**

1. You choose a multiple of 6.
2. You choose a factor of 12.
3. You choose an even number.
4. You choose a prime number.

8.2

5. When a bottle cap is tossed, it lands top side down 36 times and top side up 14 times. Find the experimental probability that the next time the bottle cap is tossed, it will land top side down.

6. A survey of 500 teens asked, "Where would you like to live?" Of the 500 teens, 155 answered "a large city." Predict how many teens out of 2000 would like to live in a large city.

7. In 7 basketball games, Charlie scores a total of 84 points. Predict how many points Charlie will score in a 20 game season.

8.3 **Events A and B are disjoint events. Find *P*(A or B).**

8. $P(\text{A}) = 0.15$, $P(\text{B}) = 0.45$
9. $P(\text{A}) = 27.3\%$, $P(\text{B}) = 18.6\%$
10. $P(\text{A}) = \frac{1}{3}$, $P(\text{B}) = \frac{5}{8}$
11. $P(\text{A}) = \frac{9}{25}$, $P(\text{B}) = \frac{3}{100}$

You randomly choose one of the letters A to Z, excluding Y. Find the probability of the event.

12. The letter is a vowel or a B.
13. The letter is *not* in the word MATH.

8.4

14. A store sells sweatshirts in blue, black, and white. The sizes available are small, medium, large, and extra large. Make a tree diagram to find all the possible sweatshirt choices you have to choose from.

15. Suppose a pitcher can throw a fastball, a curve ball, or a slider. If the pitcher chooses any two pitches at random, what is the probability that one pitch is a fastball and one is a slider?

8.5 **Events A and B are independent. Find *P*(A and B).**

16. $P(\text{A}) = 0.4$, $P(\text{B}) = 0.6$
17. $P(\text{A}) = 0.83$, $P(\text{B}) = 0.17$
18. $P(\text{A}) = \frac{7}{8}$, $P(\text{B}) = \frac{1}{8}$
19. $P(\text{A}) = \frac{1}{5}$, $P(\text{B}) = \frac{3}{25}$

A bag contains 10 red beads and 6 white beads. You randomly choose one bead, and then randomly choose another bead.

20. Find the probability that both beads are red if you replace the first bead before choosing the second bead. Is this an *independent* or a *dependent* event?

21. Find the probability that both beads are red if you do not replace the first bead before choosing the second bead. Is this an *independent* or a *dependent* event?

Chapter 9

9.1 **For the given angle measure, find the measure of a supplementary angle and the measure of a complementary angle, if possible.**

1. 86° **2.** 151° **3.** 90° **4.** 7°

9.2 **Find the measures of ∠1 and ∠2. Tell whether they form *adjacent* or *vertical* angles.**

5.

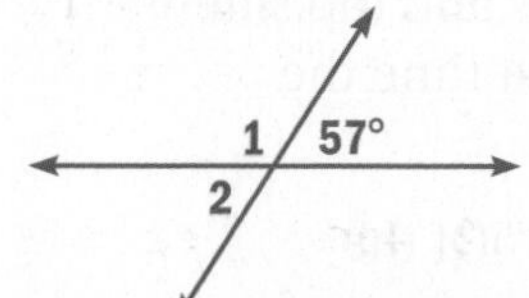

6.

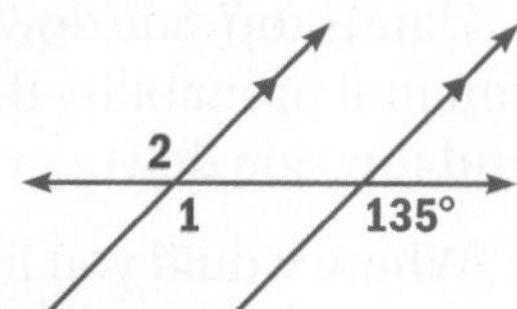

7.

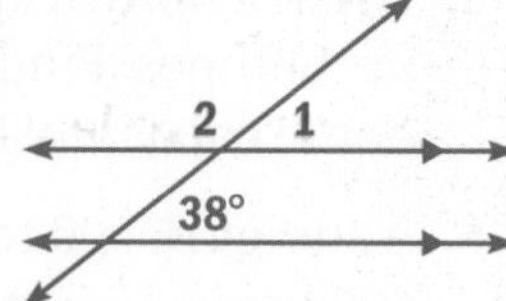

9.3 **Classify the triangle by its angle measures.**

8. 18°, 44°, 118° **9.** 66°, 37°, 77° **10.** 45°, 91°, 44°

11. The measures of two angles in a triangle are 52° and 38°. Find the measure of the third angle. Then classify the triangle by its angle measures.

Classify the triangle by its side lengths.

12. 3 m, 4 m, 5 m **13.** 11 ft, 8 ft, 11 ft **14.** 48 mm, 48 mm, 48 mm

15. Draw a right triangle with 2 sides that are 3.5 in. long.

9.4 **16.** Sketch a parallelogram that is both a rectangle and a rhombus. Then give the most specific name to classify the quadrilateral.

17. Find the sum of the angle measures of an octagon.

18. Find the number of triangles formed by drawing all diagonals from one vertex of a hexagon. Use the triangles to find the sum of the angle measures in a hexagon.

9.5 **19.** Given that $\triangle ABC \cong \triangle DEF$, name the corresponding sides and the corresponding angles.

20. One square has a side length of 8 meters, and another square has a side length of 10 meters. Are the squares similar? *Explain.*

21. Given that $\triangle ABC \sim \triangle XYZ$, $AB = 15$ m, and $XY = 10$ m, find the ratio of the lengths of the corresponding sides of $\triangle ABC$ and $\triangle XYZ$.

9.6 **22.** Rectangles $WXYZ$ and $PQRS$ are similar and $WX = 24$ m, $XY = 9$ m, and $QR = 3$ m. What is the length of PQ?

23. Find the unknown lengths given that the triangles are similar.

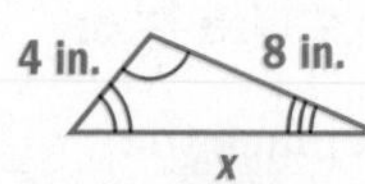

24. The shadow cast by a tree is 18 feet long. At the same time, a girl who is 5 feet tall casts a 3 foot long shadow. How tall is the tree?

Chapter 10

10.1 Copy and complete the statement.

1. 24 cm = ? mm   **2.** 0.4 g = ? mg   **3.** 795 g = ? kg

4. 120 L = ? kL   **5.** 0.07 kL = ? mL   **6.** 36,100 mm = ? km

Copy and complete using <, >, or =.

7. 3 km ? 3200 m   **8.** 9450 g ? 9.45 kg   **9.** 5.4 L ? 540 mL

10.2 Copy and complete the statement.

10. 3 yd = ? in.   **11.** 5 pt = ? c   **12.** 4 lb = ? oz

13. 8000 lb = ? T   **14.** 19 qt = ? gal ? qt   **15.** 13,200 ft = ? mi ? ft

Find the sum or difference.

16. 7 qt 1 pt + 2 qt 1 pt

17. 3 ft 7 in. + 1 ft 9 in.

18. 3 T 100 lb − 1 T 400 lb

10.3 Copy and complete the statement. Round to the nearest whole number.

19. 4 m ≈ ? ft   **20.** 19 fl oz ≈ ? mL   **21.** 85 kg ≈ ? lb

Copy and complete using <, >, or =.

22. 53 qt ? 50 L   **23.** 73 mi ? 120 km   **24.** 420 g ? 13 oz

10.4 Find the unknown area, base, or height of the parallelogram.

25. $b = 14$ cm, $h = 9$ cm, $A =$?   **26.** $A = 96$ ft^2, $b = 12$ ft, $h =$?

27. $A = 20$ in.^{2}, $b =$?, $h = 1.6$ in.   **28.** $b = 8$ m, $h = 4$ m, $A =$?

10.5 Find the area of the triangle or trapezoid.

29.

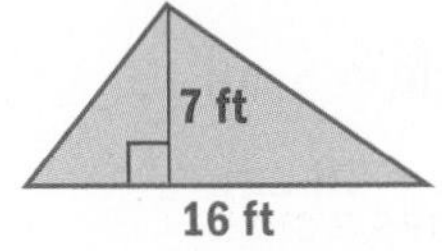

30.

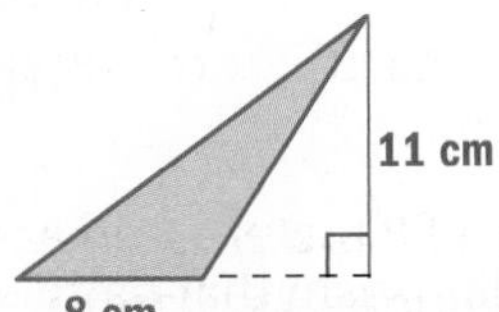

31.

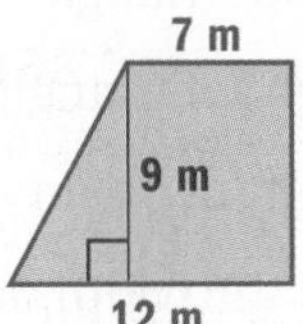

10.6 Find the circumference of the circle with the given radius r or diameter d. Use $\frac{22}{7}$ or 3.14 for π.

32. $r = 42$ mi   **33.** $r = 12$ in.   **34.** $r = 50$ cm   **35.** $d = 35$ mm

36. $d = 20$ m   **37.** $d = 5.5$ in.   **38.** $r = 14$ ft   **39.** $r = 0.4$ cm

10.7 Find the area of the circle with the given radius r or diameter d. Use $\frac{22}{7}$ or 3.14 for π.

40. $r = 40$ yd   **41.** $r = 84$ m   **42.** $d = 14$ ft   **43.** $d = 0.2$ km

44. $d = 28$ ft   **45.** $r = 9$ mi   **46.** $r = 10$ in.   **47.** $d = 24$ m

EXTRA PRACTICE

Chapter 11

11.1 Classify the solid. Be as specific as possible.

1. 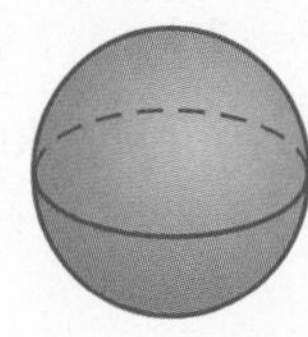

2. 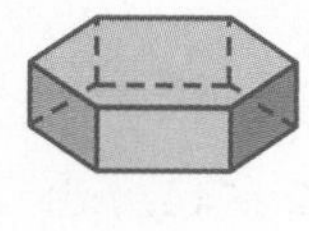

3. 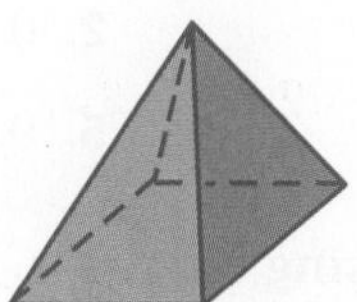

4. 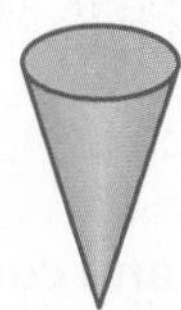

5. Sketch the top, side, and front views of the cylinder shown at the right.

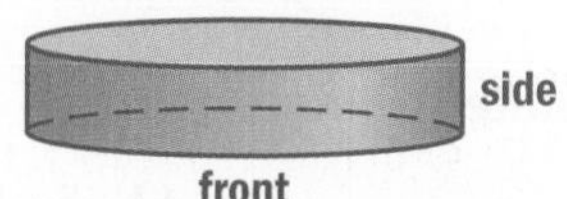

11.2 Find the surface area of the rectangular prism.

6. 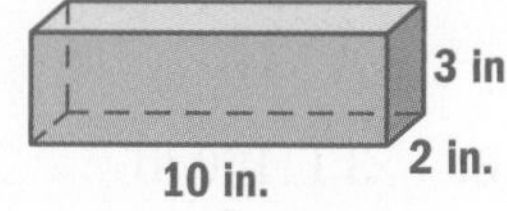

7. 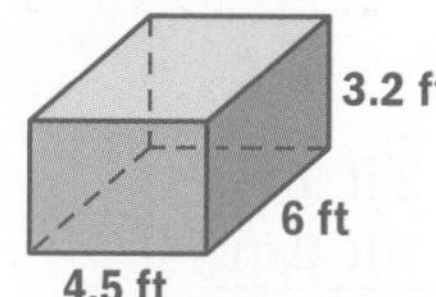

8. 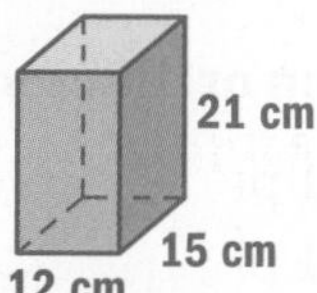

11.3 Find the surface area of the cylinder. Use 3.14 for π.

9. 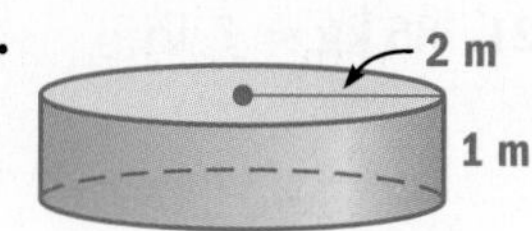

10. 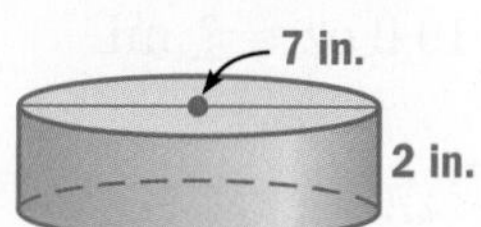

11. 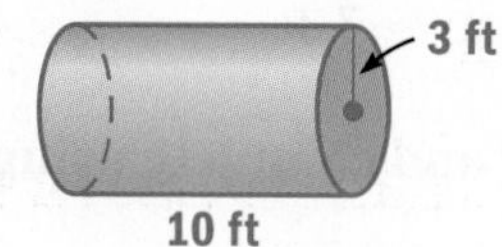

11.4 Find the volume of the rectangular prism with the given dimensions.

12. 3 m by 4 m by 0.5 m

13. 14 in. by 10 in. by 2 in.

14. 7 ft by 7 ft by 3.5 ft

15. 5 cm by 2.5 cm by 11 cm

Find the volume of the triangular prism with the given dimensions.

16. Base of triangle = 6 in.
Height of triangle = 8 in.
Height of prism = 3 in.

17. Base of triangle = 2 cm
Height of triangle = 5 cm
Height of prism = 10 cm

18. Find the width of a rectangular prism that has a length of 15 meters, a height of 9 meters, and a volume of 1080 cubic meters.

11.5 Find the unknown volume, radius, or height of the cylinder. Use 3.14 for π.

19. $V =$?
$r = 6$ in.
$h = 10$ in.

20. $V = 25.12\ \text{cm}^3$
$r = 2$ cm
$h =$?

21. $V =$?
$d = 10$ ft
$h = 0.5$ ft

22. $V = 28.26\ \text{m}^3$
$r =$?
$h = 1$ m

23. $V =$?
$d = 4$ in.
$h = 15$ in.

24. $V = 2210.56\ \text{cm}^3$
$r = 8$ cm
$h =$? cm

Chapter 12

12.1 Plot and label the points in the same coordinate plane. *Describe* the location of each point.

1. $W(-3, -4)$
2. $Z(0, 2)$
3. $N(6, -1)$
4. $L(-1, 6)$
5. $A(5, 0)$
6. $X(2, 3)$
7. $C(4, -3)$
8. $P(-2, -1)$
9. Plot and connect the points $P(-4, 5)$, $Q(-4, 1)$, $R(2, 1)$, and $S(2, 5)$ to form a rectangle. Find the length, width, and area of the rectangle.
10. The table shows the pressures at various depths underwater. Make a scatter plot of the data. Then make a conclusion about the data.

Depth (ft)	5	10	15	20	25	30	35
Pressure (lb/in.^{2})	17	19	21	23.5	26	28	30

12.2 Evaluate the function $y = 6x + 18$ for the given value of x.

11. -3
12. 0
13. 1
14. 6

Make an input-output table for the function using the domain $-4, -2, 0, 2$, and 4. Then state the range of the function.

15. $y = x - 3$
16. $y = -9x$
17. $y = 8 - x$
18. $y = 4x + 1$

Write a function rule for the input-output table.

19.

Input x	−2	−1	0	1
Output y	−8	−7	−6	−5

20.

Input x	−2	0	2	4
Output y	4	0	−4	−8

21.

Input x	−1	0	1	2
Output y	5	2	−1	−4

22.

Input x	−3	−1	1	3
Output y	0	14	28	42

12.3 Graph the function.

23. $y = 5x$
24. $y = -x$
25. $y = 6 - x$
26. $y = 3 - 4x$
27. $y = 2x + 3$
28. $y = -2 + 6x$
29. $y = -5x + 12$
30. $y = -7x - 10$

12.4 Draw the graph of the line that passes through the points. Then find the slope of the line.

31. $(7, 2), (-5, 4)$
32. $(-6, 0), (-5, 1)$
33. $(3, 4), (5, 9)$
34. $(-2, -3), (1, -3)$
35. $(-4, 2), (4, -3)$
36. $(-1, 5), (-1, -2)$

Draw the line that has the given slope and passes through the given point.

37. slope $= -2$, $(0, 5)$
38. slope $= 1$, $(1, -1)$
39. slope $= \frac{1}{4}$, $(-2, 1)$
40. slope $= -\frac{8}{7}$, $(2, -3)$
41. slope $= 0$, $(3, -5)$
42. slope $= -\frac{5}{3}$, $(-1, 4)$

EXTRA PRACTICE

Table of Symbols

Symbol	Meaning	Page
$=$	equals, is equal to	**5, 219**
4^3	4 to the third power, or $4 \times 4 \times 4$	**6**
28.6	decimal point	**9**
$\frac{14}{2}$	14 divided 2	**15**
$\neq$	is not equal to	**16, 219**
$\ldots$	continues on	**21**
$<$	is less than	**27, 675**
$>$	is greater than	**27, 675**
$1.1\overline{6}$	repeating decimal 1.16666 . . .	**40**
$\approx$	is approximately equal to	**48**
$3 \cdot x$ $3(x)$ $3x$	3 times x	**88, 149, 197**
-3	the opposite of 3	**129**
-3	negative 3	**129**
$\lvert a \rvert$	the absolute value of a number a	**136**
( )	parentheses—a grouping symbol	**161**
[ ]	brackets—a grouping symbol	**161**
$\geq$	is greater than or equal to	**210**
∟	right angle	**212**
$\stackrel{?}{=}$	is equal to?	**219**
$a : b, \frac{a}{b}$	ratio of a to b	**255**
%	percent	**301**
$^\circ$	degree(s)	**385**
{ }	braces —items in the list make up of a set or group	**435**
$m\angle B$	measure of angle B	**463**
$\angle PQR$	angle PQR	**464**
$\cong$	is congruent to	**468**
$\overleftrightarrow{AB}$	line AB	**468**
⇉	parallel lines	**469**
$\parallel$	is parallel to	**469**
$\perp$	is perpendicular to	**469**
$\triangle ABC$	triangle with vertices A, B, and C	**476**
$\overline{AB}$	line segment AB	**476**
AB	the length of line segment AB	**476**
$\overrightarrow{AB}$	ray AB	**476**
$\sim$	is similar to	**490**
π	pi—a number approximately equal to 3.14 or $\frac{22}{7}$	**549**
(x, y)	ordered pair	**624**

Table of Measures

Time

60 seconds (sec) = 1 minute (min)	365 days, 52 weeks (approx.), 12 months = 1 year
60 minutes = 1 hour (h)	10 years = 1 decade
24 hours = 1 day (d)	100 years = 1 century
7 days = 1 week (wk)	
4 weeks ≈ 1 month	

Metric

Length

10 millimeters (mm) = 1 centimeter (cm)
100 cm, 1000 mm = 1 meter (m)
1000 m = 1 kilometer (km)

Area

100 square millimeters (mm^2) = 1 square centimeter (cm^2)
10,000 cm^2 = 1 square meter (m^2)
10,000 m^2 = 1 hectare (ha)

Volume

1000 cubic millimeters (mm^3) = 1 cubic centimeter (cm^3)
1,000,000 cm^3 = 1 cubic meter (m^3)

Capacity

1000 milliliters (mL), 1000 cubic centimeters (cm^3) = 1 liter (L)
1000 L = 1 kiloliter (kL)

Mass

1000 milligrams (mg) = 1 gram (g)
1000 g = 1 kilogram (kg)
1000 kg = 1 metric ton (t)

United States Customary

Length

12 inches (in.) = 1 foot (ft)
36 in., 3 ft = 1 yard (yd)
5280 ft, 1760 yd = 1 mile (mi)

Area

144 square inches ($in.^2$) = 1 square foot (ft^2)
9 ft^2 = 1 square yard (yd^2)
43,560 ft^2, 4840 yd^2 = 1 acre (A)

Volume

1728 cubic inches ($in.^3$) = 1 cubic foot (ft^3)
27 ft^3 = 1 cubic yard (yd^3)

Capacity

8 fluid ounces (fl oz) = 1 cup (c)
2 c = 1 pint (pt)
2 pt = 1 quart (qt)
4 qt = 1 gallon (gal)

Weight

16 ounces (oz) = 1 pound (lb)
2000 lb = 1 ton

Conversions Between Systems

Length	1 in. = 2.54 cm	1 ft = 0.3048 m	1 mi ≈ 1.609 km
Capacity	1 fl oz ≈ 29.573 mL	1 qt ≈ 0.946 L	1 gal ≈ 3.785 L
Mass/Weight	1 oz ≈ 28.35 g	1 lb ≈ 0.454 kg	

Table of Formulas

Geometric Formulas

Rectangle *(p. 212)*

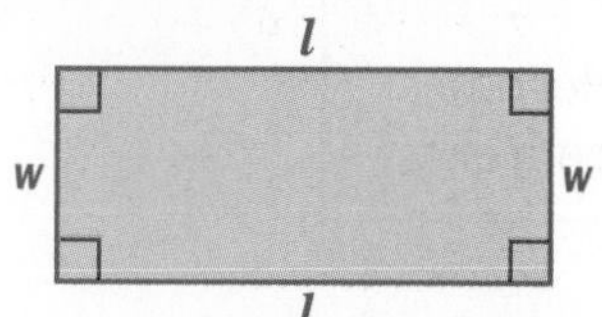

Area
$A = lw$

Perimeter
$P = 2l + 2w$

Square *(p. 212)*

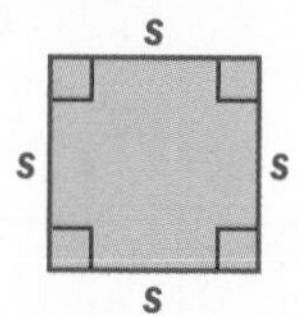

Area
$A = s^2$

Perimeter
$P = 4s$

Parallelogram *(p. 534)*

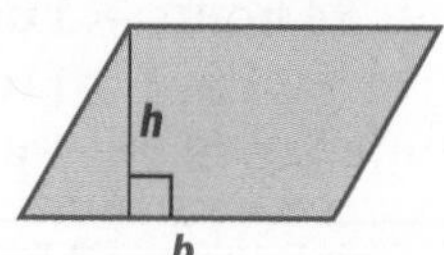

Area
$A = bh$

Triangle *(p. 541)*

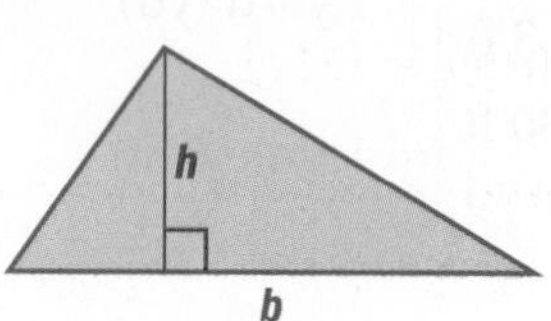

Area
$A = \frac{1}{2}bh$

Trapezoid *(p. 542)*

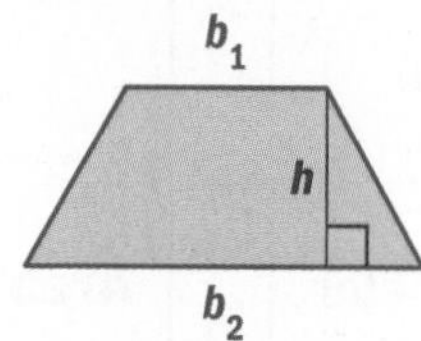

Area
$A = \frac{1}{2}(b_1 + b_2)h$

Circle *(pp. 549, 555)*

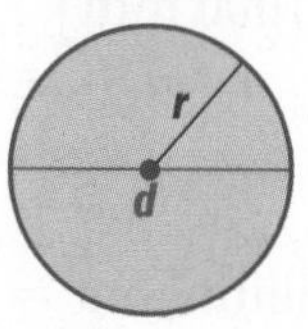

Area
$A = \pi r^2$

Circumference
$C = \pi d$ or
$C = 2\pi r$

Rectangular Prism *(pp. 581, 596)*

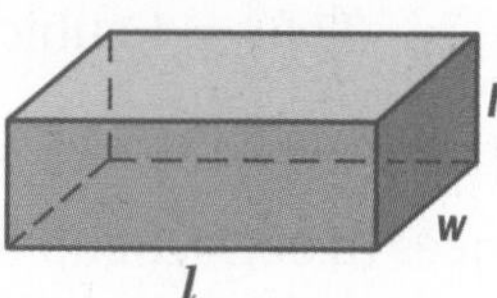

Surface Area
$S = 2lw + 2lh + 2wh$

Volume
$V = lwh$

Cylinder *(pp. 590, 601)*

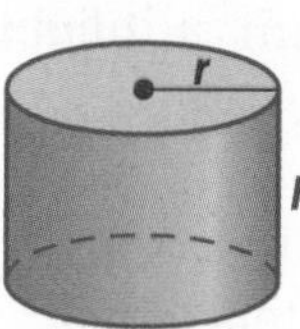

Surface Area
$S = 2\pi r^2 + 2\pi rh$

Volume
$V = \pi r^2 h$

Other Formulas

Distance traveled *(p. 213)*	$d = rt$ where d = distance, r = rate, and t = time
Temperature *(p. 214)*	$F = \frac{9}{5}C + 32$ and $C = \frac{5}{9}(F - 32)$ where F = degrees Fahrenheit and C = degrees Celsius
Simple interest *(p. 331)*	$I = Prt$ where I = simple interest, P = principal, r = annual interest rate, and t = time in years

Table of Properties

Number Properties	
Commutative Property of Addition *(p. 168)* In a sum, you can add terms in any order.	**Numbers** $-2 + 5 = 5 + (-2)$ **Algebra** $a + b = b + a$
Commutative Property of Multiplication *(p. 168)* In a product, you can multiply factors in any order.	**Numbers** $3(-6) = -6(3)$ **Algebra** $ab = ba$
Associative Property of Addition *(p. 168)* Changing the grouping of terms in a sum will not change the sum.	**Numbers** $(2 + 4) + 6 = 2 + (4 + 6)$ **Algebra** $(a + b) + c = a + (b + c)$
Associative Property of Multiplication *(p. 168)* Changing the grouping of factors in a product will not change the product.	**Numbers** $(6 \times 2.5) \times 4 = 6 \times (2.5 \times 4)$ **Algebra** $(ab)c = a(bc)$
Inverse Property of Addition *(p. 168)* The sum of a number and its additive inverse, or opposite, is 0.	**Numbers** $4 + (-4) = 0$ **Algebra** $a + (-a) = 0$
Identity Property of Addition *(p. 168)* The sum of a number and the additive identity, 0, is the number.	**Numbers** $7 + 0 = 7$ **Algebra** $a + 0 = a$
Inverse Property of Multiplication *(p. 168)* The product of a nonzero number and its multiplicative inverse, or reciprocal, is 1.	**Numbers** $\frac{2}{3} \cdot \frac{3}{2} = 1$ **Algebra** For any nonzero integers a and b, $\frac{a}{b} \cdot \frac{b}{a} = 1$.
Identity Property of Multiplication *(p. 168)* The product of a number and the multiplicative identity, 1, is the number.	**Numbers** $3 \cdot 1 = 3$ **Algebra** $a \cdot 1 = a$
Distributive Property *(p. 173)* You can multiply a number and a sum by multiplying each term of the sum by the number and then adding these products. The same property applies to subtraction.	**Numbers** $3(4 + 6) = 3(4) + 3(6)$ $2(8 - 5) = 2(8) - 2(5)$ **Algebra** $a(b + c) = a(b) + a(c)$ $a(b - c) = a(b) - a(c)$
Cross Products Property *(p. 308)* The cross products of a proportion are equal.	**Numbers** If $\frac{3}{4} = \frac{6}{8}$, then $3 \cdot 8 = 4 \cdot 6$. **Algebra** If $\frac{a}{b} = \frac{c}{d}$ and b and d do not equal 0, then $ad = bc$.

TABLES

Finding Squares and Square Roots

EXAMPLE 1 Finding a Square

Find 54^2.

Find 54 in the column labeled *No.* (an abbreviation for *Number*). Read across to the column labeled *Square.*

No.	Square	Sq. Root
51	2601	7.141
52	2704	7.211
53	2809	7.280
54	2916	7.348
55	3025	7.416

▸ **Answer** So, $54^2 = 2916$.

EXAMPLE 2 Finding a Square Root

Find a decimal approximation of $\sqrt{54}$.

Find 54 in the column labeled *No.* Read across to the column labeled *Sq. Root.*

No.	Square	Sq. Root
51	2601	7.141
52	2704	7.211
53	2809	7.280
54	2916	7.348
55	3025	7.416

▸ **Answer** So, to the nearest thousandth, $\sqrt{54} \approx 7.348$.

EXAMPLE 3 Finding a Square Root

Find a decimal approximation of $\sqrt{3000}$.

Find the two numbers in the *Square* column that 3000 is between. Read across to the column labeled *No.*; $\sqrt{3000}$ is between 54 and 55, but closer to 55.

No.	Square	Sq. Root
51	2601	7.141
52	2704	7.211
53	2809	7.280
54	2916	7.348
55	3025	7.416

▸ **Answer** So, $\sqrt{3000} \approx 55$. A more accurate approximation can be found using a calculator: 54.772256.

Table of Squares and Square Roots

No.	Square	Sq. Root	No.	Square	Sq. Root	No.	Square	Sq. Root
1	1	1.000	***51***	2601	7.141	***101***	10,201	10.050
2	4	1.414	***52***	2704	7.211	***102***	10,404	10.100
3	9	1.732	***53***	2809	7.280	***103***	10,609	10.149
4	16	2.000	***54***	2916	7.348	***104***	10,816	10.198
5	25	2.236	***55***	3025	7.416	***105***	11,025	10.247
6	36	2.449	***56***	3136	7.483	***106***	11,236	10.296
7	49	2.646	***57***	3249	7.550	***107***	11,449	10.344
8	64	2.828	***58***	3364	7.616	***108***	11,664	10.392
9	81	3.000	***59***	3481	7.681	***109***	11,881	10.440
10	100	3.162	***60***	3600	7.746	***110***	12,100	10.488
11	121	3.317	***61***	3721	7.810	***111***	12,321	10.536
12	144	3.464	***62***	3844	7.874	***112***	12,544	10.583
13	169	3.606	***63***	3969	7.937	***113***	12,769	10.630
14	196	3.742	***64***	4096	8.000	***114***	12,996	10.677
15	225	3.873	***65***	4225	8.062	***115***	13,225	10.724
16	256	4.000	***66***	4356	8.124	***116***	13,456	10.770
17	289	4.123	***67***	4489	8.185	***117***	13,689	10.817
18	324	4.243	***68***	4624	8.246	***118***	13,924	10.863
19	361	4.359	***69***	4761	8.307	***119***	14,161	10.909
20	400	4.472	***70***	4900	8.367	***120***	14,400	10.954
21	441	4.583	***71***	5041	8.426	***121***	14,641	11.000
22	484	4.690	***72***	5184	8.485	***122***	14,884	11.045
23	529	4.796	***73***	5329	8.544	***123***	15,129	11.091
24	576	4.899	***74***	5476	8.602	***124***	15,376	11.136
25	625	5.000	***75***	5625	8.660	***125***	15,625	11.180
26	676	5.099	***76***	5776	8.718	***126***	15,876	11.225
27	729	5.196	***77***	5929	8.775	***127***	16,129	11.269
28	784	5.292	***78***	6084	8.832	***128***	16,384	11.314
29	841	5.385	***79***	6241	8.888	***129***	16,641	11.358
30	900	5.477	***80***	6400	8.944	***130***	16,900	11.402
31	961	5.568	***81***	6561	9.000	***131***	17,161	11.446
32	1024	5.657	***82***	6724	9.055	***132***	17,424	11.489
33	1089	5.745	***83***	6889	9.110	***133***	17,689	11.533
34	1156	5.831	***84***	7056	9.165	***134***	17,956	11.576
35	1225	5.916	***85***	7225	9.220	***135***	18,225	11.619
36	1296	6.000	***86***	7396	9.274	***136***	18,496	11.662
37	1369	6.083	***87***	7569	9.327	***137***	18,769	11.705
38	1444	6.164	***88***	7744	9.381	***138***	19,044	11.747
39	1521	6.245	***89***	7921	9.434	***139***	19,321	11.790
40	1600	6.325	***90***	8100	9.487	***140***	19,600	11.832
41	1681	6.403	***91***	8281	9.539	***141***	19,881	11.874
42	1764	6.481	***92***	8464	9.592	***142***	20,164	11.916
43	1849	6.557	***93***	8649	9.644	***143***	20,449	11.958
44	1936	6.633	***94***	8836	9.695	***144***	20,736	12.000
45	2025	6.708	***95***	9025	9.747	***145***	21,025	12.042
46	2116	6.782	***96***	9216	9.798	***146***	21,316	12.083
47	2209	6.856	***97***	9409	9.849	***147***	21,609	12.124
48	2304	6.928	***98***	9604	9.899	***148***	21,904	12.166
49	2401	7.000	***99***	9801	9.950	***149***	22,201	12.207
50	2500	7.071	***100***	10,000	10.000	***150***	22,500	12.247

English-Spanish Glossary

A

absolute value (p. 136) The absolute value of a number a is the distance between a and 0 on a number line. The absolute value of a is written $\|a\|$. **valor absoluto** (pág. 136) El valor absoluto de un número a es la distancia entre a y 0 en una recta numérica. El valor absoluto de a se escribe $\|a\|$.	$\|4\| = 4$ $\|-7\| = 7$ $\|0\| = 0$
acute angle (p. 463) An angle whose measure is less than 90°. **ángulo agudo** (pág. 463) Un ángulo que mide menos de 90°.	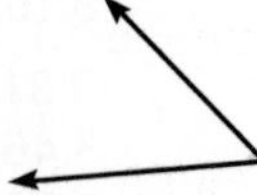
acute triangle (p. 475) A triangle with three acute angles. **triángulo acutángulo** (pág. 475) Un triángulo que tiene tres ángulos agudos.	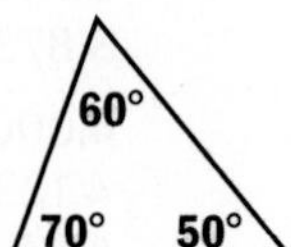
additive identity (p. 168) The number 0 is the additive identity because the sum of any number and 0 is the original number. **identidad de la suma** (pág. 168) El número 0 es la identidad de la suma porque la suma de cualquier número y 0 es el número original.	$-7 + 0 = -7$ $a + 0 = a$
additive inverse (p. 168) The additive inverse of a number a is the opposite of the number, or $-a$. The sum of a number and its additive inverse is 0. **inverso aditivo** (pág. 168) El inverso aditivo de un número a es el opuesto del número, o $-a$. La suma de un número y su inverso aditivo es 0.	The *additive inverse* of 6 is -6, so $6 + (-6) = 0$. El *inverso aditivo* de 6 es -6, por lo tanto $6 + (-6) = 0$.
adjacent angles (p. 468) Two angles in a plane that share a common side and a vertex and do not overlap. **ángulos adyacentes** (pág. 468) Dos ángulos en un plano que comparten un lado común y un vértice y no se superponen.	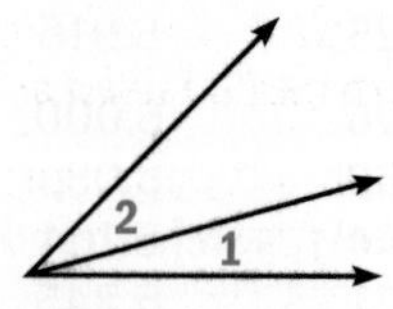 $\angle 1$ and $\angle 2$ are *adjacent angles.* $\angle 1$ y $\angle 2$ son *ángulos adyacentes.*
algebraic expression (p. 70) An expression that consists of numbers, variables, and operations. **expresión algebraica** (pág. 70) Expresión compuesta por números, variables y operaciones.	$n - 3$ and $\frac{1}{3} \div z$ are *algebraic expressions.* $n - 3$ y $\frac{1}{3} \div z$ son *expresiones algebraicas.*

angle (p. 387) A figure formed by two rays that begin at a common point, called a vertex. **ángulo** (pág. 387) Figura formada por dos semirrectas que comienzan en un punto común, llamado vértice.	vertex/vértice ray/semirrecta ray/semirrecta
annual interest rate (p. 331) The percent of the principal earned or paid per year. **tasa de interés anual** (pág. 331) El porcentaje sobre el capital ganado o pagado por año.	*See* simple interest. *Véase* interés simple.
area (p. 685) The number of square units needed to cover a figure. **área** (pág. 685) La cantidad de unidades cuadradas que se necesitan para cubrir una figura.	3 units 3 unidades 7 units 7 unidades *Area* = 21 square units *Área* = 21 unidades cuadradas

B

balance (p. 331) The sum of the interest and the principal. **balance** (pág. 331) La suma del interés y el capital.	*See* simple interest. *Véase* interés simple.
bar graph (p. 687) A type of graph in which the lengths of bars are used to represent and compare data. **gráfica de barras** (pág. 687) Un tipo de gráfica en el que las longitudes de las barras se usan para representar y comparar datos.	Annual Sales at an Automobile Dealership Ventas anuales en concesionario automotriz Automobiles / Automóviles 400 300 200 100 0 Cars / Carros Trucks / Camiones SUVs / SUVs
base of a parallelogram (p. 534) The length of any side of the parallelogram can be used as the base. **base de un paralelogramo** (pág. 534) La longitud de cualquier lado del paralelogramo puede usarse como la base.	height/altura base/base
base of a power (p. 663) The number or expression that is used as a factor in a repeated multiplication. **base de una potencia** (pág. 663) El número o la expresión que se usa como factor en una multiplicación repetida.	In the power 5^3, the *base* is 5. La *base* de la potencia 5^3 es 5.

base of a triangle (p. 541) The length of any side of the triangle can be used as the base.

base de un triángulo (pág. 541) La longitud de cualquier lado de un triángulo puede usarse como base.

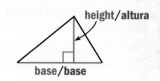

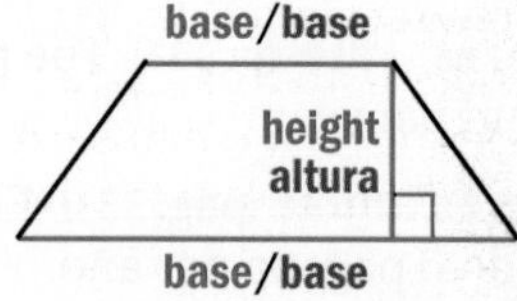

bases of a trapezoid (p. 542) The lengths of the parallel sides of the trapezoid.

bases de un trapecio (pág. 542) Las longitudes de los lados paralelos del trapecio.

base/base

height
altura

base/base

biased sample (p. 355) A sample that is not representative of the population from which it is selected.

muestra parcial (pág. 355) Una muestra que no es representativa de la población de la cual fue seleccionada.

The members of a football team are a *biased sample* if you want to determine the average amount of time students spend playing sports each week.

Los miembros de un equipo de fútbol son una *muestra parcial* para determinar la cantidad promedio de tiempo a la semana que los estudiantes practican deportes.

box-and-whisker plot (p. 374) A data display that divides a data set into four parts using the lower extreme, lower quartile, median, upper quartile, and upper extreme.

diagrama de líneas y bloques (pág. 374) Diagrama que divide un conjunto de datos en cuatro partes usando el extremo inferior, el cuartil inferior, la mediana, el cuartil superior y el extremo superior.

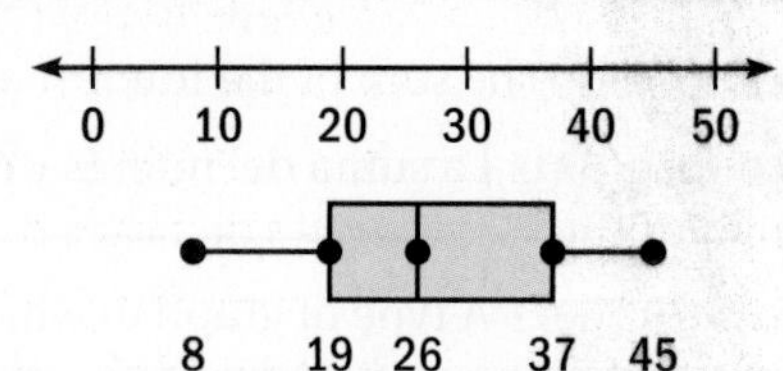

C

center of a circle (p. 549) The point inside the circle that is the same distance from all points on the circle.

centro de un círculo (pág. 549) El punto en el interior del círculo que está a la misma distancia de todos los puntos del círculo.

See circle.

Véase círculo.

circle (p. 549) The set of all points in a plane that are the same distance, called the radius, from a fixed point, called the center.

círculo (pág. 549) El conjunto de todos los puntos en un plano que están a la misma distancia, llamada radio, de un punto fijo, llamado centro.

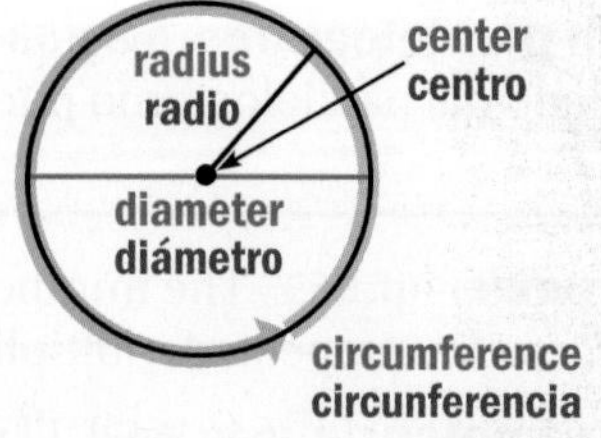

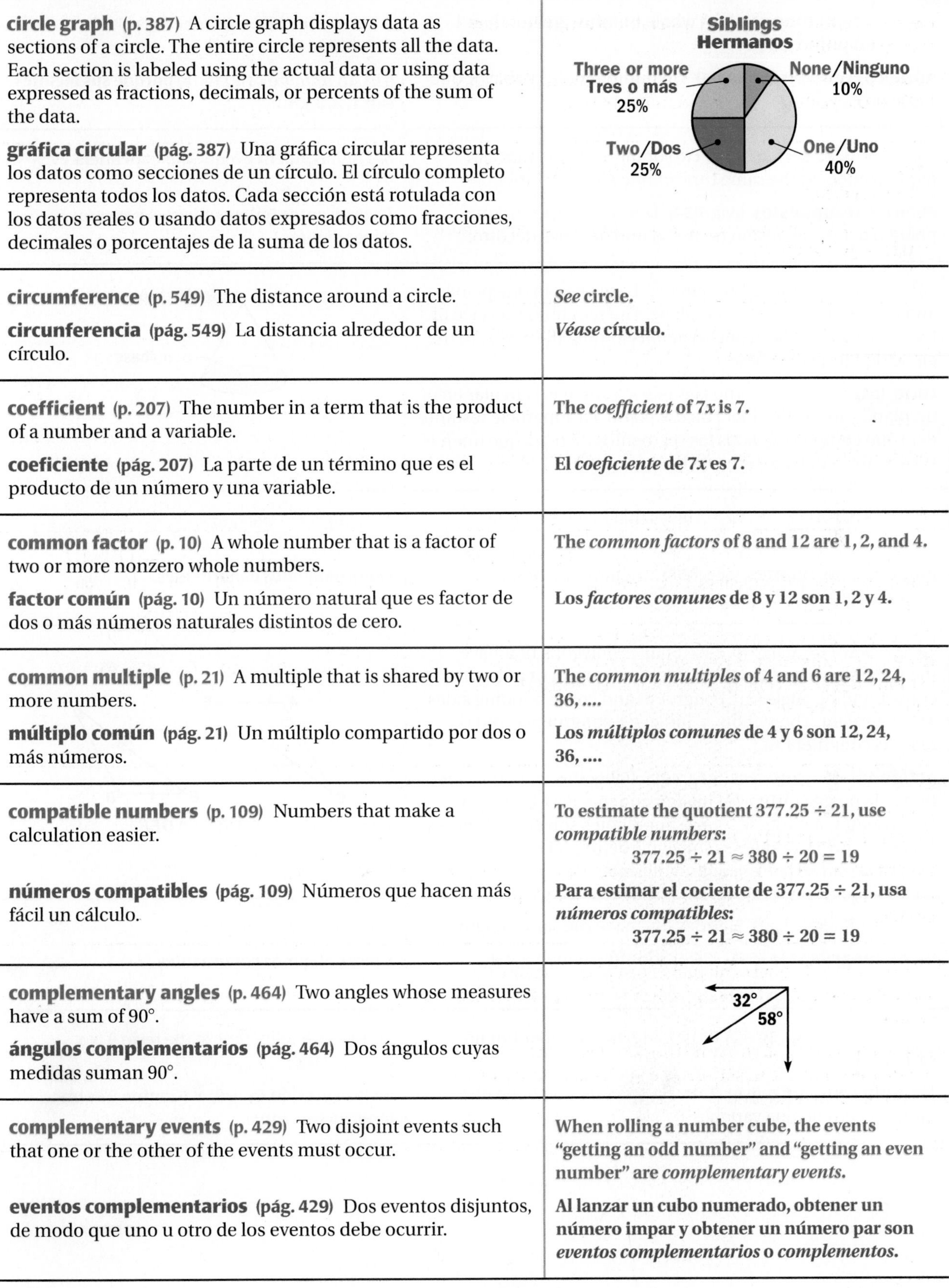

circle graph (p. 387) A circle graph displays data as sections of a circle. The entire circle represents all the data. Each section is labeled using the actual data or using data expressed as fractions, decimals, or percents of the sum of the data. **gráfica circular** (pág. 387) Una gráfica circular representa los datos como secciones de un círculo. El círculo completo representa todos los datos. Cada sección está rotulada con los datos reales o usando datos expresados como fracciones, decimales o porcentajes de la suma de los datos.	
circumference (p. 549) The distance around a circle. **circunferencia** (pág. 549) La distancia alrededor de un círculo.	*See* circle. *Véase* círculo.
coefficient (p. 207) The number in a term that is the product of a number and a variable. **coeficiente** (pág. 207) La parte de un término que es el producto de un número y una variable.	The *coefficient* of $7x$ is 7. El *coeficiente* de $7x$ es 7.
common factor (p. 10) A whole number that is a factor of two or more nonzero whole numbers. **factor común** (pág. 10) Un número natural que es factor de dos o más números naturales distintos de cero.	The *common factors* of 8 and 12 are 1, 2, and 4. Los *factores comunes* de 8 y 12 son 1, 2 y 4.
common multiple (p. 21) A multiple that is shared by two or more numbers. **múltiplo común** (pág. 21) Un múltiplo compartido por dos o más números.	The *common multiples* of 4 and 6 are 12, 24, 36, ... Los *múltiplos comunes* de 4 y 6 son 12, 24, 36, ...
compatible numbers (p. 109) Numbers that make a calculation easier. **números compatibles** (pág. 109) Números que hacen más fácil un cálculo.	To estimate the quotient $377.25 \div 21$, use *compatible numbers*: $377.25 \div 21 \approx 380 \div 20 = 19$ Para estimar el cociente de $377.25 \div 21$, usa *números compatibles*: $377.25 \div 21 \approx 380 \div 20 = 19$
complementary angles (p. 464) Two angles whose measures have a sum of 90°. **ángulos complementarios** (pág. 464) Dos ángulos cuyas medidas suman 90°.	
complementary events (p. 429) Two disjoint events such that one or the other of the events must occur. **eventos complementarios** (pág. 429) Dos eventos disjuntos, de modo que uno u otro de los eventos debe ocurrir.	When rolling a number cube, the events "getting an odd number" and "getting an even number" are *complementary events.* Al lanzar un cubo numerado, obtener un número impar y obtener un número par son *eventos complementarios* o *complementos.*

composite number (p. 5) A whole number greater than 1 that is not prime. **número compuesto** (pág. 5) Un número natural mayor que 1 que no es primo.	6 is a *composite number* because its factors are 1, 2, 3, and 6. 6 es un *número compuesto* porque sus factores son 1, 2, 3 y 6.
compound events (p. 434) Two or more events that can happen either at the same time or one after the other. **eventos compuestos** (pág. 434) Dos o más eventos que pueden ocurrir al mismo tiempo o uno después del otro.	*See* independent events *and* dependent events. *Véase* eventos independientes *y* eventos dependientes.
cone (p. 575) A solid with a circular base lying in one plane and a vertex not lying in that plane. The remaining surface of the cone consists of all line segments joining the vertex to the circle that forms the base. **cono** (pág. 575) Un cuerpo geométrico con base circular en un plano y un vértice fuera de ese plano. La superficie restante del cono consiste en todos los segmentos de recta que unen el vértice al círculo que forma la base.	vertex/vértice base/base
congruent angles (p. 468) Angles that have the same measure. **ángulos congruentes** (pág. 468) Ángulos que tienen medidas iguales.	*See* congruent polygons. *Véase* polígonos congruentes.
congruent polygons (p. 490) Similar polygons that have the same shape and the same size. For congruent polygons, corresponding angles are congruent and corresponding sides are congruent. The symbol ≅ indicates congruence and is read "is congruent to." **polígonos congruentes** (pág. 490) Polígonos similares que tienen la misma forma y el mismo tamaño. Para polígonos congruentes, los ángulos correspondientes son congruentes y los lados correspondientes son congruentes. El signo ≅ indica congruencia y se lee "es congruente con".	A B F C E D $\triangle ABC \cong \triangle DEF$
congruent sides (p. 476) Sides that have the same length. **lados congruentes** (pág. 476) Lados que tienen igual longitud.	*See* congruent polygons. *Véase* polígonos congruentes.
constant term (p. 207) A term that has a number but no variable. **término constante** (pág. 207) Un término que tiene un número pero no una variable.	In the expression $5y + 9$, the term 9 is a *constant term*. En la expresión $5y + 9$, el término 9 es un *término constante*.

convenience sampling (p. 355) A sampling method in which easy to reach members of a population are selected. **muestreo de conveniencia** (pág. 355) Un método de muestreo en el cual se seleccionan miembros de la población fácilmente accesibles.	**Conducting a poll of the students you sit with every day at lunch will result in a *convenience sampling.*** **Conducir una encuesta a estudiantes que se sientan contigo todos los días a la hora del almuerzo será un *muestreo de conveniencia.***
coordinate plane (p. 624) A coordinate system formed by the intersection of a horizontal number line, called the x-axis, and a vertical number line, called the y-axis. **plano de coordenadas** (pág. 624) Un sistema de coordenadas formado por la intersección de una recta numérica horizontal, llamada eje x, y una recta numérica vertical, llamada eje y.	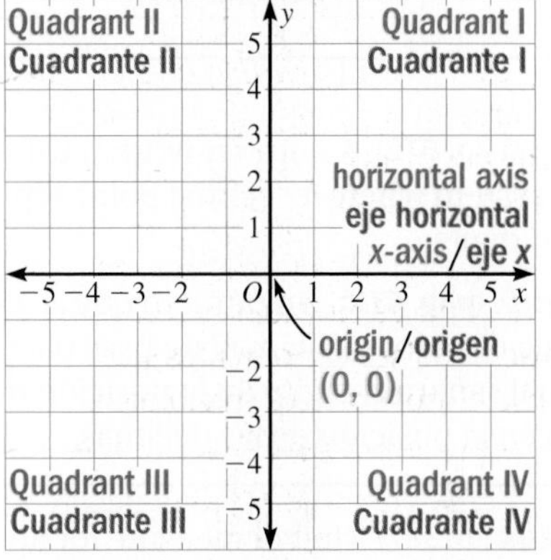
corresponding angles (p. 469) Angles that occupy corresponding positions when a line intersects two other lines. **ángulos correspondientes** (pág. 469) Ángulos que ocupan posiciones correspondientes cuando una recta interseca otras dos rectas.	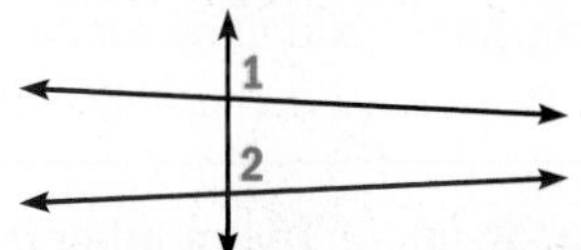 **∠1 and ∠2 are *corresponding angles.*** **∠1 y ∠2 son *ángulos correspondientes.***
cross products (p. 274) For the proportion $\frac{a}{b} = \frac{c}{d}$, where $b \neq 0$ and $d \neq 0$, the cross products are ad and bc. **productos cruzados** (pág. 274) Para la proporción $\frac{a}{b} = \frac{c}{d}$, donde $b \neq 0$ y $d \neq 0$, los productos cruzados son ad y bc.	**The *cross products* of the proportion $\frac{2}{3} = \frac{4}{6}$ are $2 \cdot 6$ and $3 \cdot 4$.** **Los *productos cruzados* de la proporción $\frac{2}{3} = \frac{4}{6}$ son $2 \cdot 6$ y $3 \cdot 4$.**
cube (p. 576) A rectangular prism with 6 congruent square faces. **cubo** (pág. 576) Un prisma rectangular que tiene 6 caras cuadradas congruentes.	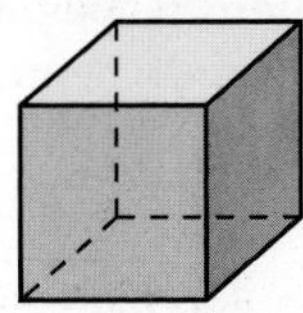

ENGLISH-SPANISH GLOSSARY

cylinder (p. 575) A solid with two congruent parallel circular bases. The remaining surface of the cylinder consists of all parallel circles of the same radius as the bases whose centers lie on the segment joining the centers of the bases. **cilindro** (pág. 575) Un cuerpo geométrico con dos bases circulares paralelas congruentes. La superficie restante del cilindro consiste en todos los círculos paralelos del mismo radio que las bases cuyos centros se sitúan en el segmento que une los centros de las bases.	bases/bases

D

decimal (p. 672) A number written using the base-ten place value system where a decimal point separates the ones' and tenths' digits.	**2.6 and 7.053 are *decimals*.**
decimal (pág. 672) Un número que se escribe usando el sistema de valor posicional de base diez en el que un punto decimal separa el dígito en la posición de las unidades del dígito en la posición de las décimas.	**2.6 y 7.053 son *decimales*.**
degrees (p. 387) Unit of measure for angles. The symbol for degrees is °. There are 360° in a circle. **grados** (pág. 387) Unidad de medida para ángulos. El símbolo para los grados es °. Hay 360° en un círculo.	A 58°
denominator (p. 16) The number b in the fraction $\frac{a}{b}$ where $b \neq 0$.	**The *denominator* of $\frac{7}{13}$ is 13.**
denominador (pág. 16) El número b en la fracción $\frac{a}{b}$ donde $b \neq 0$.	**El *denominador* de $\frac{7}{13}$ es 13.**
dependent events (p. 441) Two events such that the occurrence of one affects the likelihood that the other will occur.	**A bag contains 5 red and 8 blue marbles. You randomly choose a marble, do not replace it, then randomly choose another marble. The events "first marble is red" and "second marble is red" are *dependent events*.**
eventos dependientes (pág. 441) Dos eventos tales que la ocurrencia de uno afecta la probabilidad de que ocurra el otro.	**Una bolsa contiene 5 canicas rojas y 8 azules. Tomas una canica al azar y no la reemplazas, luego tomas otra canica al azar. Los eventos "primera canica es roja" y "segunda canica es roja" son *eventos dependientes*.**
diagonal (p. 484) A segment, other than a side, that connects two vertices of a polygon. **diagonal** (pág. 484) Un segmento, distinto de un lado, que conecta dos vértices de un polígono.	diagonals/ diagonales

diameter of a circle (p. 549) The distance across the circle through its center. **diámetro de un círculo** (pág. 549) La distancia que atraviesa el círculo por el centro.	*See* circle. *Véase* círculo.
difference (p. 661) The result when one number is subtracted from another. **diferencia** (pág. 661) El resultado cuando un número se resta de otro número.	The *difference* of 7 and 3 is $7 - 3$, or 4. La *diferencia* de 7 y 3 es $7 - 3$, ó 4.
disjoint events (p. 427) Events that have no outcomes in common. **eventos disjuntos** (pág. 427) Eventos que no tienen resultados en común.	When rolling a number cube, the events "getting an odd number" and "getting a 4" are *disjoint events.* Al lanzar un cubo numerado, los eventos "obtener un número impar" y "obtener 4" son *eventos disjuntos.*
dividend (p. 664) A number that is divided by another number. **dividendo** (pág. 664) Un número que es dividido por otro número.	In $18 \div 6 = 3$, the *dividend* is 18. En $18 \div 6 = 3$, el *dividendo* es 18.
divisor (p. 664) The number by which another number is divided. **divisor** (pág. 664) El número por el que otro número es dividido.	In $18 \div 6 = 3$, the *divisor* is 6. En $18 \div 6 = 3$, el *divisor* es 6.
domain of a function (p. 630) The set of all input values for the function. **dominio de una función** (pág. 630) El conjunto de todos los valores de entrada para la función.	*See* function. *Véase* función.

E

edge of a solid (p. 575) A line segment where two faces of the solid meet. **arista de un cuerpo geométrico** (pág. 575) Un segmento de recta donde se encuentran dos caras del cuerpo geométrico.	face cara edge arista vertex vértice
equation (p. 212) A mathematical sentence formed by setting two expressions equal. **ecuación** (pág. 212) Un enunciado matemático que se forma al establecer como iguales dos expresiones.	$3 \cdot 6 = 18$ and $x + 7 = 12$ are *equations.* $3 \cdot 6 = 18$ y $x + 7 = 12$ son *ecuaciones.*

equilateral triangle (p. 476) A triangle with three congruent sides. **triángulo equilátero** (pág. 476) Un triángulo que tiene tres lados congruentes.	
equivalent equations (p. 226) Equations that have the same solution(s). **ecuaciones equivalentes** (pág. 226) Ecuaciones que tienen la misma solución o soluciones.	$2x - 6 = 0$ and $2x = 6$ are *equivalent equations* because the solution of both equations is 3. $2x - 6 = 0$ y $2x = 6$ son *ecuaciones equivalentes* porque la solución de ambas ecuaciones es 3.
equivalent expressions (p. 173) Expressions that have the same value when simplified. **expresiones equivalentes** (pág. 173) Expresiones que tienen el mismo valor cuando se las simplifica.	$4(3 + 5)$ and $4(3) + 4(5)$ are *equivalent expressions* because $4(3 + 5) = 4(8) = 32$ and $4(3) + 4(5) = 12 + 20 = 32$. $4(3 + 5)$ y $4(3) + 4(5)$ son *expresiones equivalentes* porque $4(3 + 5) = 4(8) = 32$ y $4(3) + 4(5) = 12 + 20 = 32$.
equivalent fractions (p. 16) Fractions that represent the same part-to-whole relationship. Equivalent fractions have the same simplest form. **fracciones equivalentes** (pág. 16) Fracciones que representan la misma relación entre la parte y el todo. Las fracciones equivalentes tienen la misma mínima expresión.	$\frac{6}{8}$ and $\frac{9}{12}$ are *equivalent fractions* that both represent $\frac{3}{4}$. $\frac{6}{8}$ y $\frac{9}{12}$ son *fracciones equivalentes* porque ambas representan $\frac{3}{4}$.
equivalent ratios (p. 255) Ratios that have the same value. **razones equivalentes** (pág. 255) Razones que tienen el mismo valor.	$\frac{15}{12}$ and $\frac{25}{20}$ are *equivalent ratios* because $\frac{15}{12} = 1.25$ and $\frac{25}{20} = 1.25$. $\frac{15}{12}$ y $\frac{25}{20}$ son *razones equivalentes* porque $\frac{15}{12} = 1.25$ y $\frac{25}{20} = 1.25$.
evaluating an algebraic expression (p. 70) Substituting a value for each variable in the expression and simplifying the resulting numerical expression. **hallar el valor de una expresión algebraica** (pág. 70) Sustituir con un valor cada variable de la expresión y simplificar la expresión numérica resultante.	*Evaluating* $2x + 3y$ when $x = 1$ and $y = 4$ gives $2(1) + 3(4) = 2 + 12 = 14$. Al *hallar* el valor de $2x + 3y$ cuando $x = 1$ e $y = 4$ se obtiene $2(1) + 3(4) = 2 + 12 = 14$.
event (p. 415) A collection of outcomes of an experiment. **evento** (pág. 415) Un conjunto de resultados de un experimento.	An *event* that involves tossing a coin is "getting heads." Al lanzar una moneda, "obtener cara" es un *evento*.

experimental probability (p. 422) A probability based on repeated trials of an experiment. The experimental probability of an event is given by: $P(\text{event}) = \dfrac{\text{Number of successes}}{\text{Number of trials}}$	**During one month, your school bus is on time 17 out of 22 school days. The *experimental probability* that the bus is on time is: $P(\text{bus is on time}) = \frac{17}{22} \approx 0.773$**
probabilidad experimental (pág. 422) Una probabilidad basada en el número de ensayos de un experimento. La probabilidad experimental de un evento se expresa: $P(\text{evento}) = \dfrac{\text{Número de éxitos}}{\text{Número de ensayos}}$	**Durante un mes, tu autobús llega a tiempo 17 de 22 días escolares. La *probabilidad experimental* de que el autobús llegue a tiempo es: $P(\text{autobús a tiempo}) = \frac{17}{22} \approx 0.773$**
exponent (p. 663) A number that represents how many times a base is used as a factor in a repeated multiplication.	**In the power 5^3, the *exponent* is 3.**
exponente (pág. 663) Un número que representa cuántas veces una base se usa como factor en una multiplicación repetida.	**El *exponente* de la potencia 5^3 es 3.**

F

face of a solid (p. 575) A polygon that is a side of the solid.	***See* edge of a solid.**
cara de un cuerpo geométrico (pág. 575) Un polígono que forma un lado del cuerpo geométrico.	***Véase* arista de un cuerpo geométrico.**
factor (p. 662) When whole numbers other than zero are multiplied together, each number is a factor of the product.	**Because $2 \times 3 \times 7 = 42$, 2, 3, and 7 are *factors* of 42.**
factor (pág. 662) Cuando los números naturales distintos de cero se multiplican entre sí, cada número es un factor del producto.	**Como $2 \times 3 \times 7 = 42$, 2, 3 y 7 son *factores* de 42.**
factor tree (p. 6) A diagram that can be used to write the prime factorization of a number. **árbol de factores** (pág. 6) Un diagrama que puede usarse para escribir la descomposición de un número en factores primos.	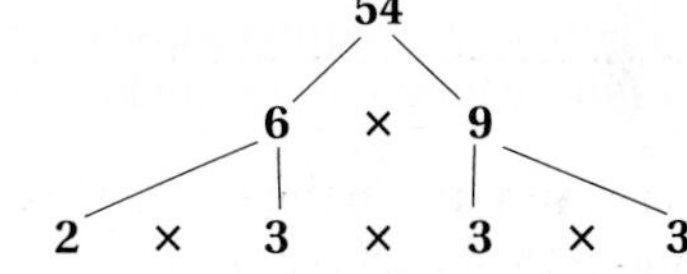
favorable outcomes (p. 415) Outcomes corresponding to a specified event.	**When rolling a number cube, the *favorable outcomes* for the event "getting a number greater than 4" are 5 and 6.**
resultados favorables (pág. 415) Los resultados correspondientes a un evento determinado.	**Al lanzar un cubo numerado, los *resultados favorables* para el evento "obtener un número mayor que 4" son 5 y 6.**
formula (p. 212) An equation that relates two or more quantities such as perimeter, length, and width.	$P = 2l + 2w$
fórmula (pág. 212) Una ecuación que relaciona dos a más cantidades tales como perímetro, longitud y ancho.	$P = 2l + 2a$

fraction (p. 674) A number of the form $\frac{a}{b}$ where both a and b are integers and $b \neq 0$.

fracción (pág. 674) Un número de la forma $\frac{a}{b}$ donde tanto a como b son números enteros y $b \neq 0$.

$\frac{5}{7}$ and $\frac{18}{10}$ are *fractions*.

$\frac{5}{7}$ y $\frac{18}{10}$ son *fracciones*.

---

frequency (p. 379) The number of data values that lie in an interval of a frequency table or histogram.

frecuencia (pág. 379) El número de valores en un conjunto de datos que se ubican en un intervalo de una tabla de frecuencias o histograma.

***See* frequency table *and* histogram.**

***Véase* tabla de frecuencias *e* histograma.**

---

frequency table (p. 379) A table used to group data values into intervals.

tabla de frecuencias (pág. 379) Una tabla que se usa para agrupar valores de un conjunto de datos en intervalos.

Interval Intervalo	Tally Marca	Frequency Frecuencia
0–9	II	2
10–19	IIII	4
20–29	~~IIII~~	5
30–39	III	3
40–49	IIII	4

---

front-end estimation (p. 103) A method for estimating the sum of two or more numbers. In this method, you add the front-end digits, estimate the sum of the remaining digits, and then add the results.

estimación por la izquierda (pág. 103) Un método para estimar la suma de dos o más números. En este método, se suman los dígitos de la izquierda, se estima la suma de los dígitos restantes y luego se suman los resultados.

To estimate $3.81 + 1.32 + 5.74$, first add the front-end digits: $3 + 1 + 5 = 9$. Then estimate the sum of the remaining digits: $0.81 + (0.32 + 0.74) \approx 1 + 1 = 2$. The sum is about $9 + 2 = 11$.

Para estimar la suma de $3.81 + 1.32 + 5.74$, suma primero los dígitos de la izquierda: $3 + 1 + 5 = 9$. Luego estima la suma de los dígitos restantes: $0.81 + (0.32 + 0.74) \approx 1 + 1 = 2$. La suma es aproximadamente $9 + 2 = 11$.

---

function (p. 630) A pairing of each number in a given set with exactly one number in another set. Starting with a number called an input, the function associates with it exactly one number called an output.

función (pág. 630) La asociación de cada número en un conjunto dado con exactamente un número de otro conjunto. Comenzando con un número llamado de entrada, la función asocia con él exactamente un número llamado de salida.

Input/Entrada, x	1	2	3	4
Output/Salida, y	2	4	6	8

The input-output table above represents a *function*.

La tabla anterior de entrada y salida representa una *función*.

G

greatest common factor (GCF) (p. 10) The greatest whole number that is a factor of two or more nonzero whole numbers.

máximo común divisor (MCD) (pág. 10) El mayor número natural que es un factor de dos o mas números naturales distintos de cero.

The *GCF* of 18 and 27 is 9.
The *GCF* of 48, 24, and 36 is 12.

El *MCD* de 18 y 27 es 9.
El *MCD* de 48, 24 y 36 es 12.

H

height of a parallelogram (p. 534) The perpendicular distance between the side whose length is the base and the opposite side.

altura de un paralelogramo (pág. 534) La distancia perpendicular entre el lado cuya longitud es la base y el lado opuesto.

See base of a parallelogram.

Véase base de un paralelogramo.

height of a trapezoid (p. 542) The perpendicular distance between the bases of the trapezoid.

altura de un trapecio (pág. 542) La distancia perpendicular entre las bases de un trapecio.

See bases of a trapezoid.

Véase bases de un trapecio.

height of a triangle (p. 541) The perpendicular distance between the side whose length is the base and the vertex opposite that side.

altura de un triángulo (pág. 541) La distancia perpendicular entre el lado cuya longitud es la base y el vértice opuesto a ese lado.

See base of a triangle.

Véase base de un triángulo.

hexagon (p. 484) A polygon with six sides.

hexágono (pág. 484) Polígono que tiene seis lados.

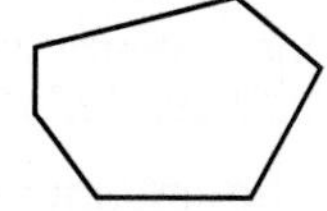

histogram (p. 380) A graph that displays data from a frequency table. A histogram has one bar for each interval of the table that contains data values. The length of the bar indicates the frequency for the interval.

histograma (pág. 380) Una gráfica que muestra datos de una tabla de frecuencias. Un histograma tiene una barra para cada intervalo de la tabla que contiene valores de datos. La longitud de la barra indica la frecuencia para el intervalo.

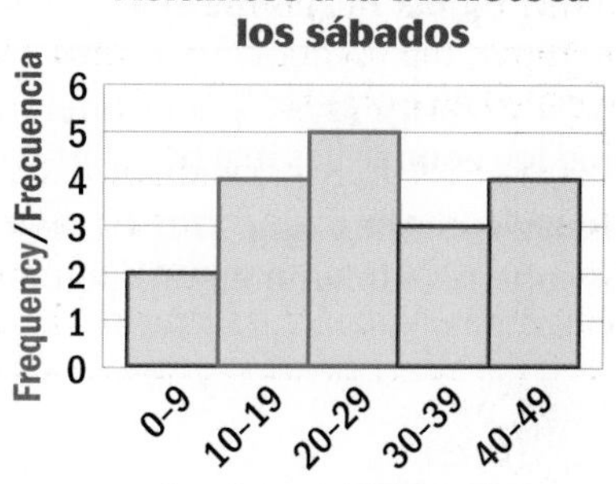

horizontal axis (p. 687) The horizontal number line of a graph.	*See* **coordinate plane.**
eje horizontal (pág. 687) La recta numérica horizontal de una gráfica.	***Véase* plano de coordenadas.**

I

improper fraction (p. 35) A fraction whose numerator is greater than or equal to its denominator.	$\frac{8}{7}$ **is an *improper fraction.***
fracción impropia (pág. 35) Una fracción en la cual el numerador es mayor que el denominador o igual a él.	$\frac{8}{7}$ **es una *fracción impropia.***
independent events (p. 441) Two events such that the occurrence of one event does not affect the likelihood that the other will occur.	**You toss a coin and roll a number cube. The events "getting heads" and "getting a 6" are *independent events.***
eventos independientes (pág. 441) Dos eventos tales que la ocurrencia de uno no afecta la probabilidad de que ocurra el otro.	**Lanzas una moneda y después lanzas un cubo numerado. Los eventos "obtener cara" y "obtener 6" son *eventos independientes.***
input (p. 630) A number on which a function operates. An input value is in the domain of the function.	*See* **function.**
entrada (pág. 630) Número sobre el que opera una función. Un valor de entrada está en el dominio de la función.	***Véase* función.**
integers (p. 129) The numbers . . . , $-4, -3, -2, -1, 0, 1, 2, 3, 4,$ . . . consisting of the negative integers, zero, and the positive integers.	**-8 and 14 are *integers.*** **$-8\frac{1}{3}$ and 14.5 are not *integers.***
números enteros (pág. 129) Los números ..., $-4, -3, -2, -1, 0, 1, 2, 3, 4,$ ... que constan de los números enteros negativos, cero y los números enteros positivos.	**-8 y 14 son *números enteros.*** **$-8\frac{1}{3}$ y 14.5 no son *números enteros.***
interest (p. 331) The amount earned or paid for the use of money.	*See* **simple interest.**
interés (pág. 331) La cantidad ganada o pagada por el uso de dinero.	***Véase* interés simple.**
interquartile range (p. 372) The difference between the upper and lower quartiles in a box-and-whisker plot.	0 10 20 30 40 50 8 19 26 37 45 **The *interquartile range* is $37 - 19$, or 18.**
rango entre cuartiles (pág. 372) La diferencia entre los cuartiles superior e inferior en un diagrama de líneas y bloques.	**El *rango entre cuartiles* es $37 - 19$, ó 18.**

intersecting lines (p. 469) Two lines that meet at a point. **rectas secantes** (pág. 469) Dos rectas que se encuentran en un punto.	
inverse operations (p. 226) Operations that "undo" each other. **operaciones inversas** (pág. 226) Operaciones que se "deshacen" mutuamente.	**Addition and subtraction are *inverse operations.*** **Multiplication and division are also *inverse operations.*** **La suma y la resta son *operaciones inversas.*** **La multiplicación y la división también son *operaciones inversas.***
isosceles triangle (p. 476) A triangle with at least two congruent sides. **triángulo isósceles** (pág. 476) Un triángulo que tiene al menos dos lados congruentes.	

L

leading digit (p. 107) The first nonzero digit in a number. **dígito dominante** (pág. 107) El primer dígito distinto de cero en un número.	**The *leading digit* of 725 is 7.** **The *leading digit* of 0.002638 is 2.** **El *dígito dominante* de 725 es 7.** **El *dígito dominante* de 0.002638 es 2.**
least common denominator (LCD) (p. 29) The least common multiple of the denominators of two or more fractions. **mínimo común denominador (m.c.d.)** (pág. 29) El mínimo común múltiplo de los denominadores de dos o más fracciones.	**The *LCD* of $\frac{7}{10}$ and $\frac{3}{4}$ is 20, the least common multiple of 10 and 4.** **El *m.c.d.* de $\frac{7}{10}$ y $\frac{3}{4}$ es 20, que es el mínimo común múltiplo de 10 y 4.**
least common multiple (LCM) (p. 21) The least number that is a common multiple of two or more numbers. **mínimo común múltiplo (m.c.m.)** (pág. 21) El menor de los múltiplos comunes de dos o más números.	**The *LCM* of 4 and 6 is 12.** **The *LCM* of 3, 5, and 10 is 30.** **El *m.c.m.* de 4 y 6 es 12.** **El *m.c.m.* de 3, 5 y 10 es 30.**
like terms (p. 207) Terms that have identical variable parts with corresponding variables raised to the same power. (Two or more constant terms are considered like terms.) **términos semejantes** (pág. 207) Términos que tienen partes variables idénticas con las variables correspondientes elevadas a la misma potencia. (Dos o más términos constantes se consideran términos semejantes.)	**In the expression $x + 4 - 2x + 1$, x and $-2x$ are *like terms,* and 4 and 1 are *like terms.*** **En la expresión $x + 4 - 2x + 1$, x y $-2x$ son *términos semejantes,* y 4 y 1 son *términos semejantes.***

ENGLISH-SPANISH GLOSSARY

line graph (p. 392) A type of graph in which points representing data pairs are connected by line segments. **gráfica lineal** (pág. 392) Un tipo de gráfica en la que los puntos que representan pares de datos se conectan por segmentos de recta.	 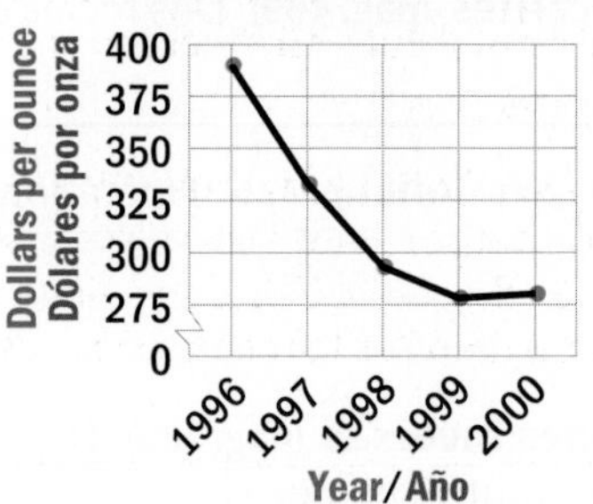
line plot (p. 686) A number line diagram that uses X marks to show the frequencies of items or categories being tallied. **diagrama lineal** (pág. 686) Un diagrama de recta numérica que usa marcas X para mostrar las frecuencias con las que se marcan artículos o categorías.	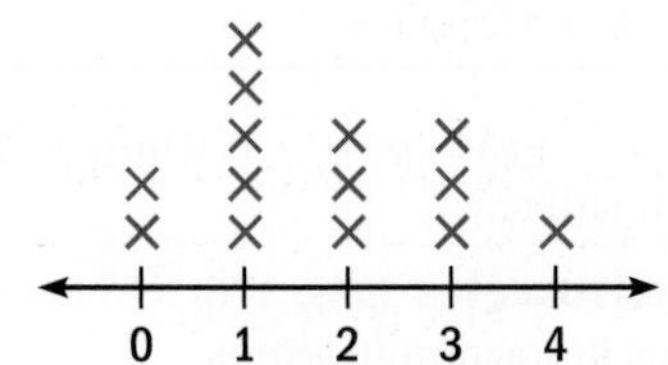
linear function (p. 637) A function whose graph is a line or part of a line. **función lineal** (pág. 637) Una función cuya gráfica es una recta o parte de una recta.	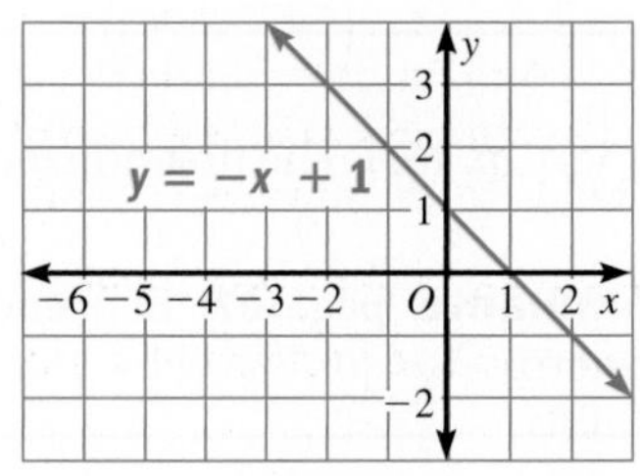
lower extreme (p. 372) The least value in a data set. **extremo inferior** (pág. 372) El menor valor en un conjunto de datos.	*See* box-and-whisker plot. *Véase* diagrama de líneas y bloques.
lower quartile (p. 372) The median of the lower half of a data set. **cuartil inferior** (pág. 372) La mediana de la mitad inferior de un conjunto de datos.	*See* box-and-whisker plot. *Véase* diagrama de líneas y bloques.

M

mean (pp. 156, 364) The sum of the values in a data set divided by the number of values. **media** (págs. 156, 364) La suma de los valores en un conjunto de datos dividida por el número de valores.	The *mean* of the data set 85, 59, 97, 71 is $\frac{85+59+97+71}{4} = \frac{312}{4} = 78$. La *media* del conjunto de datos 85, 59, 97, 71 es $\frac{85+59+97+71}{4} = \frac{312}{4} = 78$.

median (p. 364) The middle value in a data set when the values are written in numerical order. If the data set has an even number of values, the median is the mean of the two middle values. **mediana** (pág. 364) El valor que está en el medio de un conjunto de datos cuando los valores están escritos en orden numérico. Si el conjunto de datos tiene un número par de valores, la mediana es la media de los dos valores que están en el medio.	**The *median* of the data set** **8, 17, 21, 23, 26, 29, 34, 40, 45** **is the middle value, 26.** **La *mediana* del conjunto de datos** **8, 17, 21, 23, 26, 29, 34, 40, 45** **es 26, el valor que está en el medio.**
mixed number (p. 35) A number that has a whole number part and a fraction part. **número mixto** (pág. 35) Un número que tiene una parte que es un número natural y una parte que es una fracción.	**$3\frac{2}{5}$ is a *mixed number*.** **$3\frac{2}{5}$ es un *número mixto*.**
mode (p. 364) The value in a data set that occurs most often. A data set can have no mode, one mode, or more than one mode. **moda** (pág. 364) En un conjunto de datos, el valor que ocurre con mayor frecuencia. Un conjunto de datos puede no tener moda, o puede tener una moda o más de una moda.	**The *mode* of the data set** **73, 42, 55, 77, 61, 55, 68** **is 55 because it occurs most often.** **La *moda* del conjunto de datos** **73, 42, 55, 77, 61, 55, 68** **es 55 porque es el valor que aparece más veces.**
multiple (p. 21) The product of a number and any nonzero whole number. **múltiplo** (pág. 21) El producto de un número y cualquier número natural distinto de cero.	**The *multiples* of 3 are 3, 6, 9, ...** **Los *múltiplos* de 3 son 3, 6, 9, ...**
multiplicative identity (p. 168) The number 1 is the multiplicative identity because the product of any number and 1 is the original number. **identidad de la multiplicación** (pág. 168) El número 1 es la identidad de la multiplicación porque el producto de cualquier número y 1 es el número original.	$9 \cdot 1 = 9$ $a \cdot 1 = a$
multiplicative inverse (p. 168) The multiplicative inverse of a number $\frac{a}{b}$ $(a, b \neq 0)$ is the reciprocal of the number, or $\frac{b}{a}$. The product of a number and its multiplicative inverse is 1. **inverso multiplicativo** (pág. 168) El inverso multiplicativo de un número $\frac{a}{b}$ $(a, b \neq 0)$ es el recíproco de dicho número, es decir, $\frac{b}{a}$. El producto de un número y su inverso multiplicativo es 1.	**The *multiplicative inverse* of $\frac{3}{2}$ is $\frac{2}{3}$, so $\frac{3}{2} \cdot \frac{2}{3} = 1$.** **El *inverso multiplicativo* de $\frac{3}{2}$ es $\frac{2}{3}$, por lo tanto $\frac{3}{2} \cdot \frac{2}{3} = 1$.**

N

negative integers **(p. 129)** The integers that are less than zero.

números enteros negativos **(pág. 129)** Números enteros menores que cero.

The *negative integers* are −1, −2, −3, −4, ...

Los *números enteros negativos* son −1, −2, −3, −4, ...

net **(p. 581)** A two-dimensional pattern that forms a solid when it is folded.

red **(pág. 581)** Un patrón bidimensional que puede doblarse para formar un cuerpo geométrico.

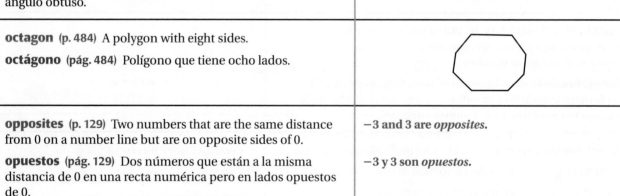

numerator **(p. 16)** The number a in the fraction $\frac{a}{b}$.

numerador **(pág. 16)** El número a en la fracción $\frac{a}{b}$.

The *numerator* of $\frac{7}{13}$ is 7.

El *numerador* de $\frac{7}{13}$ es 7.

O

obtuse angle **(p. 463)** An angle whose measure is between 90° and 180°.

ángulo obtuso **(pág. 463)** Ángulo cuya medida es mayor que 90° y menor que 180°.

obtuse triangle **(p. 475)** A triangle with one obtuse angle.

triángulo obtusángulo **(pág. 475)** Triángulo que tiene un ángulo obtuso.

120° 35° 25°

octagon **(p. 484)** A polygon with eight sides.

octágono **(pág. 484)** Polígono que tiene ocho lados.

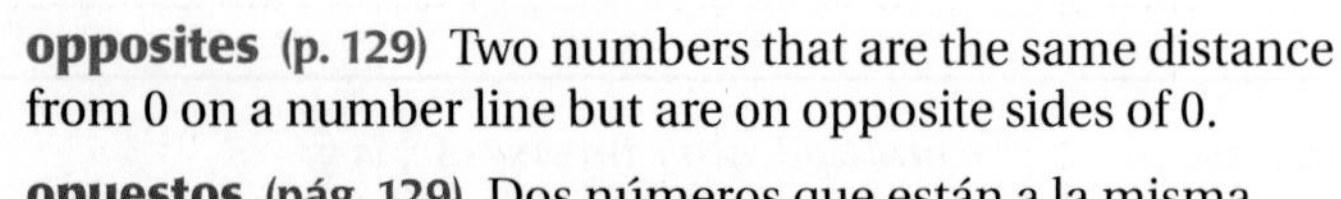

opposites **(p. 129)** Two numbers that are the same distance from 0 on a number line but are on opposite sides of 0.

opuestos **(pág. 129)** Dos números que están a la misma distancia de 0 en una recta numérica pero en lados opuestos de 0.

−3 and 3 are *opposites*.

−3 y 3 son *opuestos*.

order of operations **(p. 160)** A set of rules for evaluating an expression involving more than one operation.

orden de las operaciones **(pág. 160)** Conjunto de reglas para hallar el valor de una expresión que tiene más de una operación.

To evaluate $3 + 2 \cdot 4$, you perform the multiplication before the addition:

$$3 + 2 \cdot 4 = 3 + 8 = 11$$

Para hallar el valor de $3 + 2 \cdot 4$, haz la multiplicación antes que la suma:

$$3 + 2 \cdot 4 = 3 + 8 = 11$$

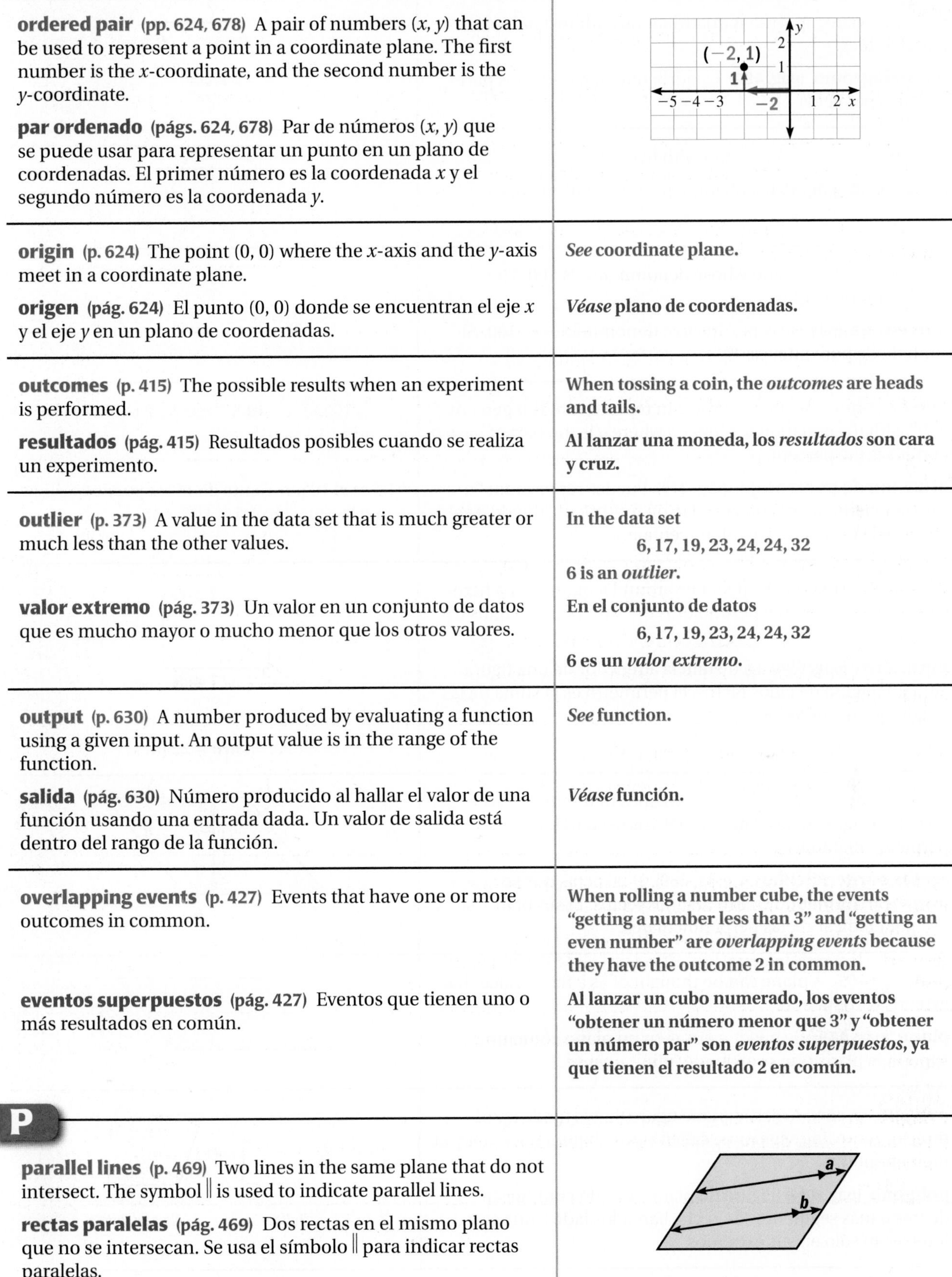

ordered pair (pp. 624, 678) A pair of numbers (x, y) that can be used to represent a point in a coordinate plane. The first number is the x-coordinate, and the second number is the y-coordinate. **par ordenado** (págs. 624, 678) Par de números (x, y) que se puede usar para representar un punto en un plano de coordenadas. El primer número es la coordenada x y el segundo número es la coordenada y.	
origin (p. 624) The point (0, 0) where the x-axis and the y-axis meet in a coordinate plane. **origen** (pág. 624) El punto (0, 0) donde se encuentran el eje x y el eje y en un plano de coordenadas.	*See* coordinate plane. *Véase* plano de coordenadas.
outcomes (p. 415) The possible results when an experiment is performed. **resultados** (pág. 415) Resultados posibles cuando se realiza un experimento.	When tossing a coin, the *outcomes* are heads and tails. Al lanzar una moneda, los *resultados* son cara y cruz.
outlier (p. 373) A value in the data set that is much greater or much less than the other values. **valor extremo** (pág. 373) Un valor en un conjunto de datos que es mucho mayor o mucho menor que los otros valores.	In the data set 6, 17, 19, 23, 24, 24, 32 6 is an *outlier.* En el conjunto de datos 6, 17, 19, 23, 24, 24, 32 6 es un *valor extremo.*
output (p. 630) A number produced by evaluating a function using a given input. An output value is in the range of the function. **salida** (pág. 630) Número producido al hallar el valor de una función usando una entrada dada. Un valor de salida está dentro del rango de la función.	*See* function. *Véase* función.
overlapping events (p. 427) Events that have one or more outcomes in common. **eventos superpuestos** (pág. 427) Eventos que tienen uno o más resultados en común.	When rolling a number cube, the events "getting a number less than 3" and "getting an even number" are *overlapping events* because they have the outcome 2 in common. Al lanzar un cubo numerado, los eventos "obtener un número menor que 3" y "obtener un número par" son *eventos superpuestos,* ya que tienen el resultado 2 en común.

P

parallel lines (p. 469) Two lines in the same plane that do not intersect. The symbol ‖ is used to indicate parallel lines. **rectas paralelas** (pág. 469) Dos rectas en el mismo plano que no se intersecan. Se usa el símbolo ‖ para indicar rectas paralelas.	

parallelogram **(p. 482)** A quadrilateral with two pairs of parallel sides. **paralelogramo** **(pág. 482)** Cuadrilátero que tiene dos pares de lados paralelos.	
pentagon **(p. 484)** A polygon with five sides. **pentágono** **(pág. 484)** Polígono que tiene cinco lados.	
percent **(p. 301)** A ratio whose denominator is 100. The symbol for percent is %. **porcentaje** **(pág. 301)** Razón cuyo denominador es 100. El símbolo de porcentaje es %.	$\frac{17}{20} = \frac{17 \cdot 5}{20 \cdot 5} = \frac{85}{100} = 85\%$
percent equation **(p. 319)** You can represent "*a* is *p* percent of *b*" with the equation $a = p\% \cdot b$ where *a* is the part of base *b* and *p*% is the percent. **ecuación de porcentaje** **(pág. 319)** Puedes representar "*a* es *p* por ciento de *b*" con la ecuación $a = p\% \cdot b$, donde *a* es parte de la base *b* y *p*% es el porcentaje.	**"4.5 is 10 percent of 45" can be written as the equation 4.5 = 10% • 45.** **"4.5 es el 10 por ciento de 45" se puede escribir como la ecuación 4.5 = 10% • 45.**
perimeter **(p. 684)** The distance around a figure. For a figure with straight sides, the perimeter is the sum of the lengths of the sides. **perímetro** **(pág. 684)** La distancia alrededor de una figura. Para una figura de lados rectos, el perímetro es la suma de las longitudes de los lados.	7 ft/7 pies 4 ft/4 pies 4 ft/4 pies 7 ft/7 pies *Perimeter* = 22 ft *Perímetro* = 22 pies
perpendicular lines **(p. 469)** Two lines that intersect to form four right angles. The symbol ⊥ is used to indicate perpendicular lines. **rectas perpendiculares** **(pág. 469)** Dos rectas que se intersecan formando cuatro ángulos rectos. El símbolo ⊥ se usa para indicar rectas perpendiculares.	a b $a \perp b$
plane **(p. 469)** A plane can be thought of as a flat surface that extends without end. **plano** **(pág. 469)** Se puede pensar en un plano como una superficie plana que se extiende infinitamente.	
polygon **(p. 484)** A closed plane figure that is made up of three or more line segments, called sides, that intersect only at their endpoints. **polígono** **(pág. 484)** Figura de plano cerrado compuesta de tres o más segmentos de recta, llamados lados, que se intersecan sólo en sus extremos.	Polygon Polígono Not a polygon No polígono

population (p. 354) In statistics, the entire group of people or objects about which you want information. **población** (pág. 354) En estadística, todo el grupo de personas u objetos sobre los que se busca información.	If a biologist wants to determine the average age of the elephants in a wildlife refuge, the *population* consists of every elephant in the refuge. Si un biólogo quiere determinar la edad promedio de los elefantes de un santuario animal, la *población* consiste en cada elefante del santuario.
positive integers (p. 129) The integers that are greater than zero. **números enteros positivos** (pág. 129) Números enteros mayores que cero.	The *positive integers* are 1, 2, 3, 4, ... Los *números enteros positivos* son 1, 2, 3, 4, ...
power (p. 663) A product formed from repeated multiplication by the same number or expression. A power consists of a base and an exponent. **potencia** (pág. 663) Producto que se obtiene de la multiplicación repetida por el mismo número o expresión. Una potencia está compuesta de una base y un exponente.	2^4 is a *power* with base 2 and exponent 4. 2^4 es una *potencia* con base 2 y exponente 4.
prime factorization (p. 6) Expressing a whole number as a product of prime numbers. **descomposición en factores primos** (pág. 6) Expresar un número natural como producto de números primos.	The *prime factorization* of 54 is $54 = 2 \times 3 \times 3 \times 3 = 2 \times 3^3$. La *descomposición en factores primos* de 54 es $54 = 2 \times 3 \times 3 \times 3 = 2 \times 3^3$.
prime number (p. 5) A whole number greater than 1 whose only whole number factors are 1 and itself. **número primo** (pág. 5) Número natural mayor que 1 cuyos únicos factores que son números naturales son 1 y él mismo.	5 is a *prime number* because its only whole number factors are 1 and 5. 5 es un *número primo*, porque sus únicos factores que son números naturales son 1 y 5.
principal (p. 331) An amount of money that is deposited or borrowed. **capital** (pág. 331) Una cantidad de dinero que se deposita o se solicita en préstamo.	*See* simple interest. *Véase* interés simple.
prism (p. 575) A solid with two congruent parallel polygonal bases. The remaining edges join corresponding vertices of the bases so that the remaining faces are rectangles. **prisma** (pág. 575) Un cuerpo geométrico con dos bases poligonales congruentes paralelas. Las aristas restantes unen los vértices correspondientes de las bases de modo que las caras restantes son rectángulos.	bases/bases Rectangular prism / Prisma rectangular Triangular prism / Prisma triangular
probability of an event (p. 415) A number from 0 to 1 that measures the likelihood that the event will occur. **probabilidad de un evento** (pág. 415) Número de 0 a 1 que mide la posibilidad de que ocurra un evento.	*See* experimental probability *and* theoretical probability. *Véase* probabilidad experimental *y* probabilidad teórica.

product (p. 662) The result when two or more numbers are multiplied. **producto** (pág. 662) Resultado cuando se multiplican dos o más números.	The *product* of 3 and 4 is 3×4, or 12. El *producto* de 3 y 4 es 3×4, ó 12.
proper fraction (p. 35) A fraction whose numerator is less than its denominator. **fracción propia** (pág. 35) Una fracción cuyo numerador es menor que su denominador.	$\frac{7}{8}$ is a *proper fraction.* $\frac{7}{8}$ es una *fracción propia.*
proportion (p. 266) An equation stating that two ratios are equivalent. **proporción** (pág. 266) Una ecuación que establece que dos razones son equivalentes.	$\frac{3}{5} = \frac{6}{10}$ and $\frac{x}{12} = \frac{25}{30}$ are *proportions.* $\frac{3}{5} = \frac{6}{10}$ y $\frac{x}{12} = \frac{25}{30}$ son *proporciones.*
pyramid (p. 575) A solid with a polygonal base lying in one plane and an additional vertex not lying in that plane. The remaining edges join the additional vertex to the vertices of the base so that the remaining faces are triangles. **pirámide** (pág. 575) Un cuerpo geométrico con una base poligonal en un plano y un vértice adicional fuera de ese plano. Las aristas restantes unen el vértice adicional a los vértices de la base de modo que las caras restantes son triángulos.	base/base

Q

quadrant (p. 624) One of the four regions that a coordinate plane is divided into by the x-axis and the y-axis. **cuadrante** (pág. 624) Una de las cuatro regiones en las que el eje x y el eje y dividen un plano de coordenadas.	*See* coordinate plane. *Véase* plano de coordenadas.
quadrilateral (p. 482) A geometric figure made up of four line segments, called sides, that intersect only at their endpoints; a polygon with four sides. **cuadrilátero** (pág. 482) Figura geométrica formada por cuatro segmentos de recta, llamados lados, que se intersecan sólo en sus extremos; polígono de cuatro lados.	
quotient (p. 664) The result of a division. **cociente** (pág. 664) Resultado de una división.	The *quotient* of 18 and 6 is $18 \div 6$, or 3. El *cociente* de 18 y 6 es $18 \div 6$, ó 3.

R

radius of a circle (p. 549) The distance between the center and any point on the circle. **radio de un círculo** (pág. 549) Distancia entre cualquier punto del círculo y su centro.	*See* circle. *Véase* círculo.

random sampling (p. 355) A sampling method in which each person or object in a population has an equally likely chance of being selected. **muestreo al azar** (pág. 355) Un método de muestreo en el cual cada persona u objeto en una población tiene una posibilidad equivalente de ser seleccionado.	**A sample of 5 sixth graders being selected by putting the names of all sixth graders in a hat and drawing 5 names without looking is a *random sampling*.** **Un ejemplo de *muestreo al azar* sería la selección de 5 alumnos de sexto grado después de colocar el nombre de todos los alumnos de sexto grado en un sombrero y habiendo extraído 5 nombres sin mirar.**
range of a data set (p. 372) The difference of the greatest and least values in the data set. **rango de un conjunto de datos** (pág. 372) La diferencia entre el valor mayor y el valor menor en un conjunto de datos.	**The *range of the data set*** $60, 35, 22, 46, 81, 39$ **is** $81 - 22 = 59$. **El *rango del conjunto* de datos** $60, 35, 22, 46, 81, 39$ **es** $81 - 22 = 59$.
range of a function (p. 630) The set of all output values for the function. **rango de una función** (pág. 630) Conjunto de todos los valores de salida posibles para la función.	***See* function.** ***Véase* función.**
rate (p. 260) A ratio of two quantities measured in different units. **tasa** (pág. 260) Razón entre dos cantidades medidas en unidades diferentes.	**An airplane climbs 18,000 feet in 12 minutes. The airplane's *rate* of climb is** $\frac{18{,}000 \text{ ft}}{12 \text{ min}} = 1500 \text{ ft/min}$. **Un avión asciende 18,000 pies en 12 minutos. La *tasa* de ascenso del avión es** $\frac{18{,}000 \text{ pies}}{12 \text{ min}} = 1500 \text{ pies/min}$.
ratio (p. 255) A comparison of two numbers using division. The ratio of a to b (where $b \neq 0$) can be written as a to b, as $\frac{a}{b}$, or as $a : b$. **razón** (pág. 255) Comparación entre dos números usando la división. La razón de a a b (donde $b \neq 0$) puede escribirse como a a b, como $\frac{a}{b}$ o como $a : b$.	**The *ratio* of 17 to 12 can be written as 17 to 12, as** $\frac{17}{12}$, **or as** $17 : 12$. **La *razón* de 17 a 12 puede escribirse como 17 a 12, como** $\frac{17}{12}$ **o como** $17 : 12$.
rational number (p. 167) A number that can be written as $\frac{a}{b}$ where a and b are integers and $b \neq 0$. **número racional** (pág. 167) Un número que se puede escribir como $\frac{a}{b}$ donde a y b son números enteros y $b \neq 0$.	$6 = \frac{6}{1}$, $-\frac{3}{5} = \frac{-3}{5}$, $0.75 = \frac{3}{4}$, **and** $2\frac{1}{3} = \frac{7}{3}$ **are all *rational numbers*.** $6 = \frac{6}{1}$, $-\frac{3}{5} = \frac{-3}{5}$, $0.75 = \frac{3}{4}$ **y** $2\frac{1}{3} = \frac{7}{3}$ **son todos *números racionales*.**

ENGLISH-SPANISH GLOSSARY

ray (p. 683) A part of a line that begins at a point and extends in one direction without end.

semirrecta (pág. 683) Una parte de una recta que comienza en un punto y se extiende infinitamente en una dirección.

B A

reciprocals (p. 95) Two nonzero numbers whose product is 1.

recíprocos (pág. 95) Dos números distintos de cero cuyo producto es 1.

$\frac{2}{3}$ and $\frac{3}{2}$ are *reciprocals.*

$\frac{2}{3}$ y $\frac{3}{2}$ son *recíprocos.*

regular polygon (p. 484) A polygon with all sides equal in length and all angles equal in measure.

polígono regular (pág. 484) Un polígono cuyos lados tienen igual longitud y cuyos ángulos tienen la misma medida.

Regular pentagon
Pentágono regular

repeating decimal (p. 40) A decimal that has one or more digits that repeat without end.

decimal periódico (pág. 40) Decimal que tiene uno o más dígitos que se repiten infinitamente.

$0.7777\ldots$ and $1.\overline{29}$ are *repeating decimals.*

$0.7777\ldots$ y $1.\overline{29}$ son *decimales periódicos.*

rhombus (p. 482) A parallelogram with four congruent sides.

rombo (pág. 482) Paralelogramo que tiene cuatro lados congruentes.

right angle (p. 463) An angle whose measure is exactly 90°.

ángulo recto (pág. 463) Un ángulo que mide exactamente 90°.

right triangle (p. 475) A triangle with one right angle.

triángulo rectángulo (pág. 475) Un triángulo que tiene un ángulo recto.

50°
40°

S

sample (p. 354) A part of a population.

muestra (pág. 354) Una parte de una población.

To predict the results of an election, a survey is given to a *sample* of voters.

Para predecir los resultados de unas elecciones, se encuesta a una *muestra* de votantes.

scale (p. 281) In a scale drawing, the scale gives the relationship between the drawing's dimensions and the actual dimensions.

escala (pág. 281) En un dibujo a escala, la escala muestra la relación entre las dimensiones del dibujo y las dimensiones reales.

The *scale* "1 in. : 10 ft" means that 1 inch in the scale drawing represents an actual distance of 10 feet.

La *escala* "1 pulg. : 10 pies" significa que una pulgada en el dibujo a escala representa una distancia real de 10 pies.

---

scale drawing (p. 281) A diagram of an object in which the dimensions are in proportion to the actual dimensions of the object.

dibujo a escala (pág. 281) Un diagrama de un objeto cuyas dimensiones están en proporción con las dimensiones reales del objeto.

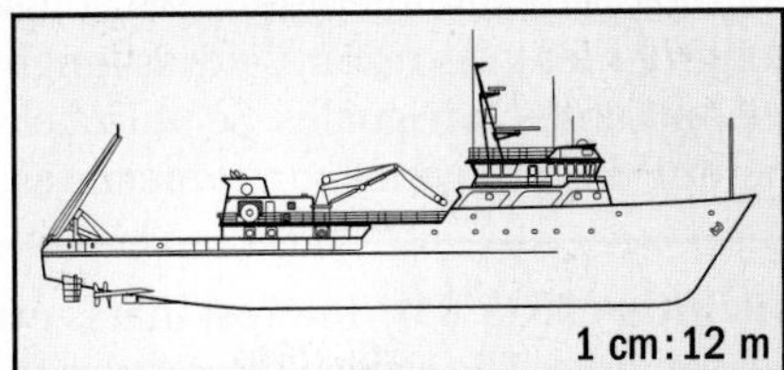

---

scale model (p. 282) A model of an object in which the dimensions are in proportion to the actual dimensions of the object.

modelo a escala (pág. 282) Un modelo de un objeto cuyas dimensiones están en proporción con las dimensiones reales del objeto.

A *scale model* of the White House has been displayed at various museums across the country. The scale of the model is 1:12.

Un *modelo a escala* de la Casa Blanca ha sido exhibida en varios museos del país. La escala del modelo es 1:12.

---

scalene triangle (p. 476) A triangle with no congruent sides.

triángulo escaleno (pág. 476) Un triángulo cuyos lados no son congruentes.

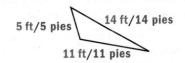

5 ft/5 pies

14 ft/14 pies

11 ft/11 pies

---

scatter plot (p. 626) The graph of a set of a data pairs (x, y), which is a collection of points in a coordinate plane.

diagrama de dispersión (pág. 626) La gráfica de un conjunto de pares de datos (x, y), que es un grupo de puntos en un plano de coordenadas.

Pine Tree Growth
Crecimiento del pino

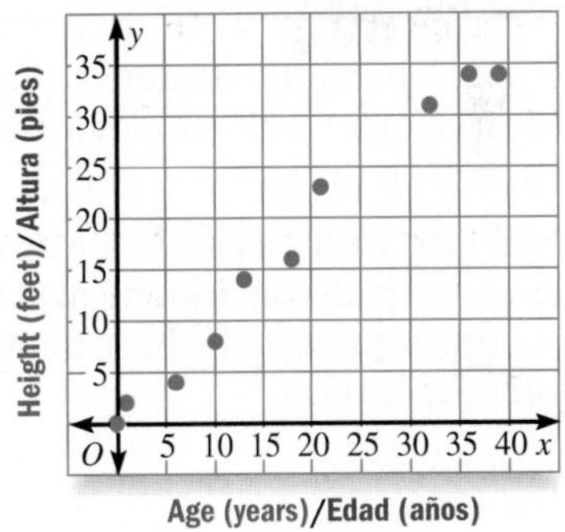

---

self-selected sampling (p. 355) A sampling method in which members of a population volunteer to be part of the sample.

muestreo de auto selección (pág. 355) Un método de muestreo en el cual los miembros de una población se ofrecen voluntariamente para ser partes de ese muestreo.

A questionnaire is mailed out to students. Those who choose to respond will create a *self-selected sampling*.

Se envía por correo un cuestionario a los estudiantes. Aquellos que decidan responder crearán un *muestreo de auto selección*.

similar polygons (p. 490) Polygons that have the same shape but not necessarily the same size. Corresponding angles of similar polygons are congruent, and the ratios of the lengths of corresponding sides are equal. The symbol ~ is used to indicate that two polygons are similar.

polígonos semejantes (pág. 490) Polígonos que tienen la misma forma pero no necesariamente el mismo tamaño. Los ángulos correspondientes de los polígonos semejantes son congruentes y las razones de las longitudes de los lados correspondientes son iguales. Se utiliza el símbolo ~ para indicar que dos polígonos son semejantes.

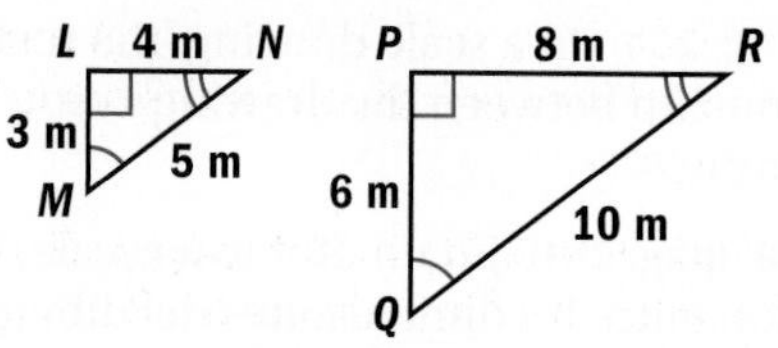

$\triangle LMN \sim \triangle PQR$

simple interest (p. 331) Interest that is earned or paid only on the principal. The simple interest I is the product of the principal P, the annual interest rate r written as a decimal, and the time t in years: $I = Prt$.

interés simple (pág. 331) El interés ganado o pagado sólo sobre el capital. El interés simple I es el producto del capital C, la tasa de interés anual t escrita en forma decimal y el tiempo a en años: $I = Cta$.

Suppose you deposit $700 into a savings account. The account earns 3% *simple annual interest.* After 5 years, the interest is $I = Prt = (700)(0.03)(5) = \$105$, and your account balance is $700 + $105 = $805.

Imagina que depositas $700 en una cuenta de ahorros. La cuenta genera un *interés anual simple* del 3%. Después de 5 años, el interés es $I = Cta = (700)(0.03)(5) = \$105$, y el saldo de tu cuenta es $700 + $105 = $805.

simplest form of a fraction (p. 17) A fraction is in simplest form if its numerator and denominator have a greatest common factor of 1.

mínima expresión de una fracción (pág. 17) Una fracción está en su mínima expresión si el máximo común divisor del numerador y del denominador es 1.

The *simplest form of the fraction* $\frac{6}{8}$ is $\frac{3}{4}$.

La *mínima expresión de la fracción* $\frac{6}{8}$ es $\frac{3}{4}$.

slope (p. 642) The slope of a nonvertical line is the ratio of the rise (vertical change) to the run (horizontal change) between any two points on the line.

pendiente (pág. 642) La pendiente de una recta no vertical es la razón entre la distancia vertical (cambio vertical) y la distancia horizontal (cambio horizontal) entre dos puntos cualesquiera de la recta.

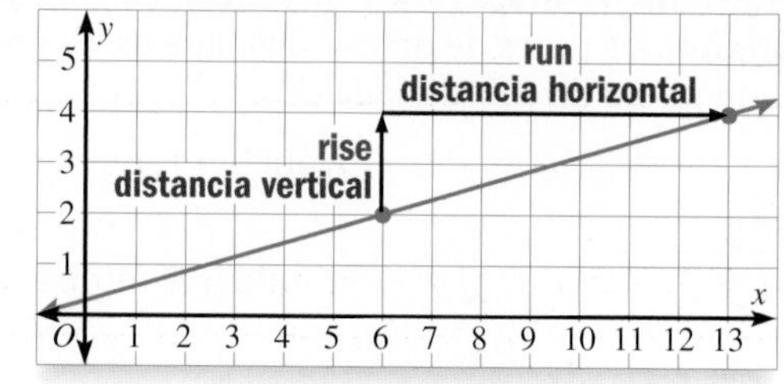

The *slope* of the line above is:

$$\text{slope} = \frac{\text{rise}}{\text{run}} = \frac{2}{7}$$

La *pendiente* de la recta anterior es:

$$\text{pendiente} = \frac{\text{distancia vertical}}{\text{distancia horizontal}} = \frac{2}{7}$$

solid (p. 575) A three-dimensional figure that encloses a part of space.

cuerpo geométrico (pág. 575) Figura tridimensional que encierra una parte del espacio.

***See* cone, cylinder, prism, pyramid, sphere, *and* cube.**

***Véase* cono, cilindro, prisma, pirámide, esfera *y* cubo.**

solution of an equation (p. 219) A number that, when substituted for the variable in the equation, makes the equation true. **solución de una ecuación** (pág. 219) Número que, cuando sustituye la variable en la ecuación, hace verdadera la ecuación.	The *solution of the equation* $n - 3 = 4$ is 7. La *solución de la ecuación* $n - 3 = 4$ es 7.
solving an equation (p. 220) Finding all solutions of the equation. **resolver una ecuación** (pág. 220) Hallar todas las soluciones de la ecuación.	To *solve the equation* $4x = 20$, find the number that can be multiplied by 4 to equal 20; $4(5) = 20$, so the solution is 5. Para *resolver la ecuación* $4x = 20$, halla el número que multiplicado por 4 sea igual a 20; $4(5) = 20$, por lo tanto la solución es 5.
sphere (p. 575) A solid formed by all points in space that are the same distance from a fixed point called the center. **esfera** (pág. 575) Cuerpo geométrico formado por todos los puntos en el espacio que se encuentran a la misma distancia de un punto fijo llamado centro.	center centro
stem-and-leaf plot (p. 369) A data display that helps you see how data values are distributed. Each data value is separated into a leaf (the last digit) and a stem (the remaining digits). In an ordered stem-and-leaf plot, the leaves for each stem are listed in order from least to greatest. **diagrama de tallo y hojas** (pág. 369) Diagrama que muestra cómo se distribuyen los valores en un conjunto de datos. Cada valor está separado en una hoja (el último dígito) y un tallo (los dígitos restantes). En un diagrama de tallo y hojas ordenado, las hojas para cada tallo están en orden de menor a mayor.	stems/tallos leaves/hojas 10 | 8 11 | 2 2 5 12 | 1 3 4 7 13 | 0 6 Key/Clave: 10 | 8 = 108
straight angle (p. 463) An angle whose measure is exactly 180°. **ángulo llano** (pág. 463) Ángulo que mide exactamente 180°.	
sum (p. 661) The result when two or more numbers are added. **suma** (pág. 661) El resultado cuando se suman dos o más números.	The *sum* of 2 and 5 is 2 + 5, or 7. La *suma* de 2 y 5 es 2 + 5, ó 7.
supplementary angles (p. 464) Two angles whose measures have a sum of 180°. **ángulos suplementarios** (pág. 464) Dos ángulos cuyas medidas suman 180°.	79° 101°

surface area of a solid (p. 581) The sum of the areas of the outside surfaces of the solid. **área de la superficie de un cuerpo geométrico** (pág. 581) La suma de las áreas de las superficies exteriores del cuerpo geométrico.	3 in./3 pulg. 4 in./4 pulg. 6 in./6 pulg. ***Surface area*** **= 2(6)(4) + 2(6)(3) + 2(4)(3) = 108 in.**^{2} ***Área de la superficie*** **= 2(6)(4) + 2(6)(3) + 2(4)(3) = 108 pulg.**^{2}
systematic sampling (p. 355) A sampling method in which a pattern is used to select members of a population. **muestreo sistemático** (pág. 355) Un método de muestreo en el cual se usa un patrón para seleccionar a miembros de una población.	**Surveying every fourth student walking into school in the morning will result in a *systematic sampling.*** **Entrevistar a uno de cada cuatro estudiantes que entran a la escuela por la mañana sería un ejemplo de *muestreo sistemático.***

T

terminating decimal (p. 40) A decimal that has a final digit. **decimal exacto** (pág. 40) Decimal que tiene un dígito final.	**0.4 and 3.6125 are *terminating decimals.*** **0.4 y 3.6125 son *decimales exactos.***
terms of an algebraic expression (p. 207) The parts of an algebraic expression that are added together. **términos de una expresión algebraica** (pág. 207) Las partes de una expresión algebraica que se suman entre sí.	**The *terms* of $2x + 3$ are $2x$ and 3.** **Los *términos* de $2x + 3$ son $2x$ y 3.**
theoretical probability (p. 422) A probability based on all of the equally likely outcomes of an experiment. The theoretical probability of an event is given by: $P(\text{event}) = \frac{\text{Number of favorable outcomes}}{\text{Total number of outcomes}}$ **probabilidad teórica** (pág. 422) Probabilidad basada en que todos los resultados de un experimento son igualmente probables; la probabilidad de un evento se expresa como: $P(\text{evento}) = \frac{\text{Número de resultados favorables}}{\text{Número total de resultados}}$	**A bag of 20 marbles contains 7 red marbles. The *theoretical probability* of randomly choosing a red marble is:** $P(\text{red}) = \frac{7}{20} = 0.35$ **Una bolsa de 20 canicas contiene 7 canicas rojas. La *probabilidad teórica* de tomar al azar una canica roja es:** $P(\text{roja}) = \frac{7}{20} = 0.35$
trapezoid (p. 482) A quadrilateral with exactly one pair of parallel sides. **trapecio** (pág. 482) Cuadrilátero que tiene exactamente un par de lados paralelos.	
tree diagram (p. 434) A branching diagram that shows all the possible outcomes of a process carried out in several stages. **diagrama de árbol** (pág. 434) Diagrama ramificado que muestra todos los resultados posibles de un proceso llevado a cabo en varias etapas.	H T H T H T

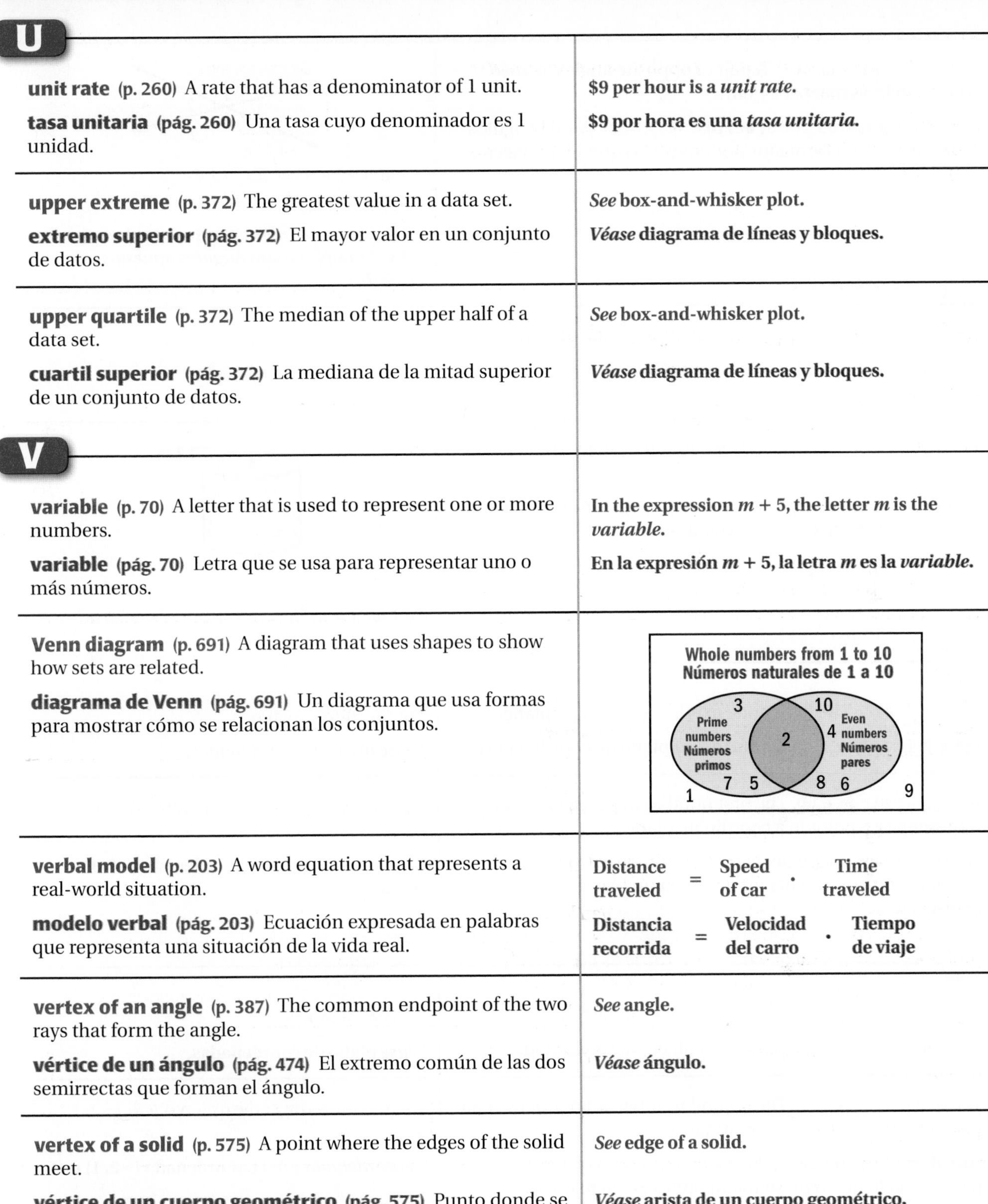

U

unit rate (p. 260) A rate that has a denominator of 1 unit.	**$9 per hour is a *unit rate*.**
tasa unitaria (pág. 260) Una tasa cuyo denominador es 1 unidad.	**$9 por hora es una *tasa unitaria*.**
upper extreme (p. 372) The greatest value in a data set.	***See* box-and-whisker plot.**
extremo superior (pág. 372) El mayor valor en un conjunto de datos.	***Véase* diagrama de líneas y bloques.**
upper quartile (p. 372) The median of the upper half of a data set.	***See* box-and-whisker plot.**
cuartil superior (pág. 372) La mediana de la mitad superior de un conjunto de datos.	***Véase* diagrama de líneas y bloques.**

V

variable (p. 70) A letter that is used to represent one or more numbers.	**In the expression $m + 5$, the letter m is the *variable*.**
variable (pág. 70) Letra que se usa para representar uno o más números.	**En la expresión $m + 5$, la letra m es la *variable*.**
Venn diagram (p. 691) A diagram that uses shapes to show how sets are related.	
diagrama de Venn (pág. 691) Un diagrama que usa formas para mostrar cómo se relacionan los conjuntos.	
verbal model (p. 203) A word equation that represents a real-world situation.	**Distance traveled = Speed of car · Time traveled**
modelo verbal (pág. 203) Ecuación expresada en palabras que representa una situación de la vida real.	**Distancia recorrida = Velocidad del carro · Tiempo de viaje**
vertex of an angle (p. 387) The common endpoint of the two rays that form the angle.	***See* angle.**
vértice de un ángulo (pág. 474) El extremo común de las dos semirrectas que forman el ángulo.	***Véase* ángulo.**
vertex of a solid (p. 575) A point where the edges of the solid meet.	***See* edge of a solid.**
vértice de un cuerpo geométrico (pág. 575) Punto donde se encuentran las aristas de un cuerpo geométrico.	***Véase* arista de un cuerpo geométrico.**

vertical angles **(p. 468)** A pair of opposite angles formed when two lines meet at a point. **ángulos opuestos por el vértice** **(pág. 468)** Par de ángulos opuestos entre sí formados por dos rectas que se intersecan.	1 2 3 4 **$\angle 1$ and $\angle 3$ are *vertical angles.* $\angle 2$ and $\angle 4$ are also *vertical angles.*** **$\angle 1$ y $\angle 3$ son *ángulos opuestos por el vértice.* $\angle 2$ y $\angle 4$ también son *ángulos opuestos por el vértice.***
vertical axis **(p. 687)** The vertical number line of a graph. **eje vertical** **(pág. 687)** La recta numérica vertical de una gráfica.	***See* coordinate plane.** ***Véase* plano de coordenadas.**
volume of a solid **(p. 596)** The amount of space the solid occupies. **volumen de un cuerpo geométrico** **(pág. 596)** Cantidad de espacio que ocupa el cuerpo geométrico.	2 m 3 m ***Volume*** $= \pi r^2 h \approx (3.14)(2)^2(3) \approx 37.7\ \text{m}^3$ ***Volumen*** $= \pi r^2 h \approx (3.14)(2)^2(3) \approx 37.7\ \text{m}^3$

X

x*-axis** **(p. 678)** The horizontal axis in a coordinate plane. **eje *x **(pág. 678)** Eje horizontal de un plano de coordenadas.	***See* coordinate plane.** ***Véase* plano de coordenadas.**
x*-coordinate** **(p. 624)** The first number in an ordered pair representing a point in a coordinate plane. **coordenada *x **(pág. 624)** El primer número en un par ordenado que representa un punto en un plano de coordenadas.	**The *x-coordinate* of the ordered pair $(-2, 1)$ is -2.** **La *coordenada x* del par ordenado $(-2, 1)$ es -2.**

Y

y*-axis** **(p. 678)** The vertical axis in a coordinate plane. **eje *y **(pág. 678)** Eje vertical en un plano de coordenadas.	***See* coordinate plane.** ***Véase* plano de coordenadas.**
y*-coordinate** **(p. 624)** The second number in an ordered pair representing a point in a coordinate plane. **coordenada *y **(pág. 624)** El segundo número de un par ordenado que representa un punto en un plano de coordenadas.	**The *y-coordinate* of the ordered pair $(-2, 1)$ is 1.** **La *coordenada y* del par ordenado $(-2, 1)$ es 1.**

Index

A

C

D

INDEX

G

H

I

INDEX

N

INDEX

INDEX

S

Credits

Photographs

Cover
Lori Adamski Peek/Getty Images

Authors, Teacher Advisors, and Reviewers
Aguilar Maritza Chang/Fantastic Shots; *Austin* Jostens Photography/Lifetouch; *Birbeck* Thomas Birbeck; *Boswell* Robert C. Jenks, Jenks Studio; *Bryson* Margaret L. Kidd; *Carter* Lifetouch; *Chavez* Courtesy of Mark Chavez; *Cliffe* Timothy Cliffe; *Davis* Shawn Davis; *Duffy* Courtesy of Ellen Duffy; *Fox* Courtesy of Barry Fox ; *Kanold* McDougal Littell/Houghton Mifflin Co.; *Kohn* Sharon Kohn; *Kuykendall* Courtesy of Brent Kuykendall; *Larson* Meridian Creative Group; *Martinez* Courtesy of Chris Martinez; *Miyata* Courtesy of Greg Miyata; *Okamoto* Akiko Okamoto; *Pacheco* Nila Pacheco; *Phair* James F. Phair; *Sass* Courtesy of Rudy Sass; *Smith* Jessica Smith; *Stiff* Jerry Head Jr.; *Walker-Jennels* Courtesy of Gwendolyn Walker-Jennels.

TOC1 Royalty-Free/Corbis; **TOC2** Matthias Kulka/Corbis; **TOC3** Ryuhei Shindo/Getty Images; **TOC4** Chris van Lennep/Getty Images; **TOC5** Richard Cummins/Corbis; **TOC6** David Butow/Corbis; **TOC7** Justin Pumfrey/Getty Images; **TOC8** Theo Allofs/Corbis; **TOC9** Gerald French/Getty Images; **TOC10** Michael Caulfield/AP Images; **TOC11** Klaus Hackenberg/Corbis; **TOC12** Kevin Fleming/Corbis; **TOC13** Bill Ross/Corbis; **SG1** Royalty-Free/Corbis; **SG27** Royalty Free/PhotoSpin; **SG27** McDougal Littell/Houghton Mifflin Co.; **5** David Sanger Photography/Alamy; **9** Mary Kate Denny/PhotoEdit; **10** Photograph by Jonathan Wiggs. Republished with permission of Globe Newspaper Company, Inc, from the 7/25/01 issue of The Boston Globe, 2001; **11** Royalty-Free/Artville; **13** Vince Bucci/AFP/Getty Images; **14** Monika Graff/The Image Works; **16** Jeff Greenberg/Alamy; **19** Maxine Hall/Corbis; **21** Tony Freeman/PhotoEdit; **22** Seb Agudelo/Alamy; **24** Michael T. Sedam/Corbis; **29** Mike Brinson/Getty Images; **32** Peter Gridley/Getty Images; **33** Barbara Stitzer/PhotoEdit; **35** The News Press/AP Images; **37** Dennis MacDonald/Royalty-Free/Alamy; **39** Dennis MacDonald/PhotoEdit; **40** Tim Flach/Getty Images; **44** Ric Ergenbright/Corbis; **47** Paul A. Souders/Corbis; **48** David Young-Wolff/PhotoEdit; **50** Royalty-Free/Getty Images; **53** Royalty-Free/Index Stock Imagery; **55** David Young-Wolff/PhotoEdit; **69** Tony Freeman/PhotoEdit; **70** Mike Yoder/Lawrence Journal-World/AP Images; **75** Scott Manchester/The Press Democrat; **79** Jeffrey L. Rotman/Corbis; **81** Jed Jacobsohn/Getty Images; **84** Michal Heron; **88** Steven J. Kazlowski/Alamy; **91** A. Ramey/PhotoEdit; **92** Ken O'Donoghue/McDougal Littell/Houghton Mifflin Co.; **95** Jose Carillo/PhotoEdit; **99** Terry Husebye/The Image Bank/Getty Images; **102** David Young-Wolff/Getty Images; **105** Courtesy of the MAiZE, www.cornfieldmaze.com; **107** Paul Barton/Corbis; **108** Royalty-Free/Corbis; **112** Richard Drew/AP Images; **116** SUNNYphotography.com/Alamy; **126** Kent Porter/The Press Democrat; **127** David Madison/Allsport/Getty Images; **129** Jeff Gross/Getty Images; **130** Bruno Morandi/Getty Images; **132** Chuck Savage/Corbis; **135** Peter Mason/The Image Bank/Getty Images; **140** Ken O'Donoghue/McDougal Littell/Houghton Mifflin Co.; **143** Keren Su/Corbis; **144** Alan Puzey/Getty Images; **146** Cydney Conger/Corbis; **148** age fotostock/SuperStock; **149** Steve Hutton/Lonely Planet Images; **151** Norbert Wu/Minden Pictures; **152** Danny Lehman/Corbis; **154** Fritz Polking/Peter Arnold, Inc.; **157** Michael Freeman/Corbis; **160** Myrleen Ferguson Cate/PhotoEdit; **163** Brandon Cole/Bruce Coleman Inc.; **164** Pedro Ugarte/Getty Images; **167** Ricardo Mazalan/AP Images; **171** E. Schlegel/Dallas Morning News/Corbis; **172** Chris Hondros/Getty Images; **173** Brigid Davis; **174** Michael Newman/PhotoEdit; **177** Bob Daemmrich/PhotoEdit; **181** Michael Newman/PhotoEdit; **191** Craig Aurness/Corbis; **195** Ken O'Donoghue/McDougal Littell/Houghton Mifflin Co.; **197** Michelle D. Bridwell/PhotoEdit; **198** Thinkstock/Royalty-Free/Alamy; **200** Keren Su/Corbis; **202** Michael Nichols/National Geographic Society Image Collection; **205** John Kelly/The Image Bank/Getty Images; **207** Billy E. Barnes/PhotoEdit; **208** Walter Hodges/Getty Images; **210** Ryan McVay/Getty Images; **212** David Young-Wolff/PhotoEdit; **214** Rachel Epstein/PhotoEdit; **217** Jeff Greenberg/PhotoEdit; **219** Gail Mooney/Masterfile; **221** Bembaron Jeremy/Corbis; **223** Index Stock Imagery; **224** Jeff Christensen/Reuters; **226** Courtesy of NASA; **228** Courtesy of NASA; **231** R. Holz/zefa/Corbis; **234** Getty Images; **238** Michael Geissinger/The Image Works; **253** Ken O'Donoghue/McDougal Littell/Houghton Mifflin Co.; **255** Brian Kersey/AP Images; **256** Joe McBride/Getty Images; **258** Duncan Smith/Getty Images; **260** NASA/AP Images; **261** Jerry Lampen/Reuters; **263** Royalty-Free/Corbis; **266** Scott Markewitz/Taxi/Getty Images; **268** Lee White/Corbis; **269** Brand X Pictures/Royalty-Free/Alamy; **273** Patti Murray/Animals Animals; **274** Mitsuaki Iwago/Minden Pictures; **276** Frans Lanting/Minden Pictures; **279** National Zoo/AP Images; **281** Royalty-Free/Corbis; **282** © Bruce Mathews/Harry S. Truman Museum and Library; **287** Tony Gutierrez/AP Images; **289** Richard Cummins/Corbis; **301** Bob Child/AP Images; **304** Stephen McBrady/PhotoEdit; **306** Peter Wilson/AP Images; **307** Royalty-Free/Corbis; **310** SW Productions/Royalty-Free/Getty Images; **311** Frans Lanting/Minden Pictures; **312** Index Stock Imagery; **314** NASA/USGS/Stockli, Nelson, Hasler/Laboratory for Atmospheres/Goddard Space Flight Center; **316** HOT WHEELS ® trademark owned by and used with permission from Mattel, Inc. © 2002 Mattel, Inc. All Rights Reserved. Cougar trademark used under license to Mattel, Inc. from Ford Motor Company. Photograph courtesy of David Williamson, ToyCarCollector.com; **317** Royalty-Free/Corbis; **319** *top right* Annie Griffiths Belt/Corbis; *bottom* Mary Terriberry/Shutterstock; **322** Mike Blake/Reuters/Corbis; **323** Bob Krist/Corbis; **325** Ellen Senisi/The Image Works; **326** Bob Daemmrich/PhotoEdit; **328** PhotoDisc/Getty Images; **331** Thomas Florian/Index Stock Imagery; **332** Comstock; **334** Roy Ooms/Masterfile; **338** Richard Levine/Alamy; **346** PhotoDisc; **350** *baseballs* Royalty-Free/Corbis; *field* Joseph Sohm/ChromoSohm Inc./Corbis; **354** Lars Klove Photo Service/Getty Images; **357** Visions of America, LLC/Alamy; **358** PhotoDisc; **359** Gavin Hellier/Getty Images; **362** Ariel Skelley/Corbis; **364** Mary Kate Denny/PhotoEdit; **365** Kevin Cooley/Getty Images; **367** Donald Miralle/Getty Images; **368** Ralph Clevenger/Corbis;

371 Frank Siteman/McDougal Littell/Houghton Mifflin Co.; **372** Royalty-Free/Corbis; **374** Pierre Ducharme/Reuters/Corbis; **376** CSA Plastock/Getty Images; **379** *top right* Jim Sugar/Corbis; *center left* Spencer Jones/Getty Images; **381** *top right* Royalty-Free/PhotoSpin; *top center* Svetlana Larina/Shutterstock; **383** Joseph Sohm/ChromoSohm Inc./Corbis; **384** Douglas Peebles/Corbis; **387** Chris Mellor/Lonely Planet Images; **391** Reza Estakhrian/Getty Images; **392** Dana White/PhotoEdit; **396** *1961* Illustration by Morgan-Cain & Associates/McDougal Littell/HMCo, based on 50 Star Flag stamp image © 1960 United States Postal Service. All Rights Reserved. Used with Permission; *1969* Illustration by Morgan-Cain & Associates/McDougal Littell/HMCo, based on Dwight D. Eisenhower stamp image © 1970 United States Postal Service. All Rights Reserved. Used with Permission; *1980* Illustration by Morgan-Cain & Associates/McDougal Littell/HMCo, based on Education stamp image © 1980 United States Postal Service. All Rights Reserved. Used with Permission; *1989* Illustration by Morgan-Cain & Associates/McDougal Littell/HMCo, based on Best Wishes stamp image © 1980 United States Postal Service. All Rights Reserved. Used with Permission; *2000* Illustration by Morgan-Cain & Associates/McDougal Littell/HMCo, based on Flag and Chalkboard stamp image © 1980 United States Postal Service. All Rights Reserved. Used with Permission; *2005* Illustration by Dan Stuckenschneider/McDougal Littell/HMCo, based on Spring Flowers-Iris stamp image © 2005 United States Postal Service. All Rights Reserved. Used with Permission; **402** Spencer Grant/PhotoEdit; **412** David Brooks/Corbis; **413** Don Mason/Corbis; **415** *center right* Royalty-Free/Corbis; *top right* Steve Skjold/Skjold Stock Photography; **417** Royalty-Free/Corbis; **422** Mitchell Funk/Getty Images; **425** Frank Siteman/McDougal Littell/Houghton Mifflin Co.; **426** Ron Avery/SuperStock; **427** Roger Ressmeyer/Corbis; **429** Myrleen Ferguson Cate/PhotoEdit; **431** Jonathan Nourok/PhotoEdit; **434** Richard T. Nowitz/National Geographic Image Collection; **439** *right* Ben Garvin 1999/The Christian Science Monitor; *left* Ben Garvin/The Christian Science Monitor; **441** Bob Daemmrich/The Image Works; **444** Ken O'Donoghue/McDougal Littell/Houghton Mifflin Co.; **445** *top* Quarter-dollar coin image from the United States Mint; *center right* Quarter-dollar coin image from the United States Mint; *center* Quarter-dollar coin image from the United States Mint; **449** Steve Gorton/DK Images; **463** *top right* Imagemore/SuperStock; *center right* Timothy Clary/AFP/Getty Images; **468** Digital Vision/age fotostock; **472** Harris ("Butterfly") House, 1997, designed by Samuel Mockbee and students, Rural Studio, Auburn University, AL. Photograph by Timothy Hursley; **474** Doug Menuez/PhotoDisc Green/Getty Images; **481** David Pollack/Corbis; **482** Jeff Greenberg/PhotoEdit; **487** Farrell Grehan/Corbis; ©2006 Frank Lloyd Wright Foundation, Scottsdale, AZ/Artists Rights Society (ARS), NY; **490** Morton Beebe/Corbis; **491** David Bartruff/Index Stock imagery; **494** Barrie Rokeach/The Image Bank/Getty Images; **495** B.A.E. Inc./Alamy; **500** *right* Laura Ciapponi/Photonica/Getty Images; *left* Royalty-Free/Corbis; **502** Philadelphia Museum of Art/Corbis; **515** Martin Harvey/Gallo Images/Corbis; **517** Jamal Saidi/Reuters; **520** Larry Dale Gordon/Getty Images; **521** Yukimasa Hirota/Getty Images; **522** Royalty-Free/Corbis; **524** Epix Photography/Getty Images; **527** Tomas Kaspar/Alamy; **530** Paul Sakuma/AP Images; **534** Roberto Candia/AP Images; **541** Photo courtesy of the Rock and Roll Hall of Fame and Museum; **542** Henry Westheim Photography/Alamy; **546** Linda Whitwam/DK Images; **549** Eric Sander; **550** Steve Shott/DK Images; **551** center, *bottom center, bottom left* PhotoDisc; *center right, bottom right* School Division/Houghton Mifflin Co.; *center left* John Miller/Getty Images; **552** Getty Images; **555** Geri Engberg/The Image Works; **556** Dean Conger/Corbis; **557** *top left, top right, center left, center right* McDougal Littell/Houghton Mifflin Co.; center Courtesy of the United States Mint; top center Royalty-Free/Artville; **558** McDougal Littell/Houghton Mifflin Co.; **571** Neil Tingle/actionplus/Icon SMI; **575** *bottom left* Dennis MacDonald/PhotoEdit; *bottom right* Ken O'Donoghue/McDougal Littell/Houghton Mifflin Co.; *top right* Ben Devries/The Daily Nonpareil/AP Images; **577** *bottom right, bottom center* Ken O'Donoghue/McDougal Littell/Houghton Mifflin Co.; *bottom left* Royalty-Free/Brand X Pictures; **578** Ken O'Donoghue/McDougal Littell/Houghton Mifflin Co.; **579** Lee Snider/Corbis; **581** The Discovery Science Center; **583** Elizabeth Simpson/Getty Images; **585** *center right* Ken O'Donoghue/McDougal Littell/Houghton Mifflin Co.; *graduate* PhotoDisc; *girl on bike* Digital Vision; *Palms* Gary Ortiz/Shutterstock; **587** Elizabeth Simpson/Getty Images; **589** Courtesy of IndoBoard.com Rider: Serena Brooke. Photograph by Tom Servais; **592** M. Deutsch/Corbis; **594** John Elk III/Lonely Planet Images; **596** Rich Pedroncelli/AP Images; **599** Koichi Kamoshida/Getty Images; **601** Mike DeVries/The Capital Times; **604** Tom Dietrich/Getty Images; **607** Diana Miller/DK Images; **609** William S. Heisel/Getty Images; **616** Tim Ridley/DK Images; **624** Nancy Sheehan/PhotoEdit; **626** Dale Sanders/Masterfile; **628** Jonathan Blair/Corbis; **630** Karl Weatherly/Corbis; **633** Stephen Frink/Corbis; **636** David Young-Wolff/PhotoEdit; **642** Mary Kate Denny/PhotoEdit; **643** G. Brad Lewis/Getty Images; **650** Toby Talbot/AP Wide World Photos.

Illustrations and Maps

Steve Cowden **457** *center right*; Stephen Durke **66** *center*, **67** *center*, **447** *bottom right*; Patrick Gnan **512** *center*, **513** *stage*; Steve McEntee **134** *center right*, **296** *center right*, **498** *center right*, **513** *scaffolding*; Dan Stuckenschneider **8** *bottom center*, **159** *bottom right*, **585** *bottom right*, **604** *top right*, **659** *center right*; Carol Zuber-Mallison **313** *bottom right*. All other illustrations by Morgan Cain/McDougal Littell/Houghton Mifflin Co. or McDougal Littell/Houghton Mifflin Co.

Chapter 1

1.1 Exercises (pp. 7–9) **1.** composite **3.** 1, 2, 4, 5, 10, 20 **5.** 1, 13 **7.** 1, 2, 4, 5, 10, 20, 25, 50, 100 **9.** *Sample answer:* Although 48 is an even number, it can have an odd factor; factors of 48: 1, 2, 3, 4, 6, 8, 12, 16, 24, 48. **11.** Prime; it's only factors are 1 and itself. **13.** Composite; it has more factors other than 1 and itself. **15.** Prime; it's only factors are 1 and itself. **17.** Composite; it has more factors other than 1 and itself. **19.** Composite; it has more factors other than 1 and itself. **21.** 7^2 **23.** 2×5^2 **25.** 2×13 **27.** $3^2 \times 5^2$ **29.** $2^2 \times 3^2 \times 17$ **33.** False; 1 is not prime. **35.** False. *Sample answer:* 1 and 3 are numbers, and 1×3 is a prime. **37.** 17, 19, 23, 29, 31 **39.** 109, 113, 127, 131 **41.** 233, 239, 241, 251, 257 **43.** possible group sizes: 1, 2, 4, 7, 14, 28 **45.** possible distances: 1, 2, 3, 6, 7, 14, 21, 42 **47.** Composite; the total number of stones is the product of the number of stones in a pouch times the number of pouches. It is divisible by at least 2, the minimum number of stones in each pouch. **55.** *Sample answer:* All the exponents in Group A are even, but not in Group B. Another number in Group A would be $2^2 \times 5^2 = 100$; another number in Group B would be $2^2 \times 5 = 20$.

1.2 Exercises (pp. 12–14) **1.** common factor **3.** 7 **5.** 11 **7.** 1 **9.** 5 **11.** 15 **13.** 6 **17.** In the prime factorization of 18, 9 is not a prime number; $18 = 2 \times 3 \times 3$, the GCF is 3. **19.** 14 **21.** 2 **23.** 18 **25.** 17 **27.** 24 **29.** 21 **31.** Sometimes. *Sample answer:* GCF of 2 and 4 is 2, but the GCF of 4 and 8 is 4. **33.** Always. *Sample answer:* By definition of prime numbers, 1 will be the GCF. **35.** *Sample answer:* 210, 217; I know that $7 \times 30 = 210$, so I used 7×30 and 7×31. **37.** *Sample answer:* 240, 248; I know that $8 \times 30 = 240$, so I used 8×30 and 8×31. **39.** 8 bags **41.** 16 tables **47.** 3 groups; 4 boys; 5 girls

1.3 Exercises (pp. 18–20) **1.** simplest form **3.** *Sample answer:* $\frac{1}{4}, \frac{2}{8}$ **5.** *Sample answer:* $\frac{2}{3}, \frac{16}{24}$ **7–15.** Sample answers are given. **7.** $\frac{6}{7}, \frac{12}{14}$ **9.** $\frac{15}{26}, \frac{45}{78}$ **11.** $\frac{7}{8}, \frac{21}{24}$ **13.** $\frac{9}{28}, \frac{108}{336}$ **15.** $\frac{3}{13}, \frac{6}{26}$ **17.** $\frac{4}{9}$ **19.** $\frac{5}{7}$ **21.** $\frac{7}{12}$ **23.** $\frac{3}{4}$ **25.** $\frac{7}{15}$ **29.** equivalent **31.** not equivalent **33.** not equivalent **35.** equivalent **37.** not equivalent **39.** 9 **41.** 42 **43.** 2 **45.** 10 **49.** *Sample answer:* $\frac{38}{42}, \frac{19}{21}$ **51.** *Sample answer:* $\frac{12}{40}, \frac{3}{10}$

1.4 Exercises (pp. 23–25) **1.** multiple **3.** 72 **5.** 80 **7.** 120 **9.** 126 **15.** 420 **17.** 2520 **19.** 2028 **21.** 10,800 **23.** 15, 990; they are the same. **25.** 6, 1188; they are the same. **27.** 5, 5; 10 and 15 **29.** 3, 3; 15 and 6 **31.** in 12 min **33.** at 60 in. apart **37.** *Sample answer:* Prime factorization; 32 and 49 are fairly large numbers, and it would be quicker to find the prime factorization for them than to list their multiples. **39.** No; a multiple of 15 has to have a factor of 5, and the given number doesn't.

1.5 Exercises (pp. 31–33) **1.** least common denominator **3.** > **5.** = **7.** < **9.** = **11.** = **13.** $\frac{2}{5}, \frac{5}{8}, \frac{7}{10}, \frac{3}{4}$ **15.** $\frac{1}{4}, \frac{9}{32}, \frac{5}{16}, \frac{3}{8}$ **17.** $\frac{17}{81}, \frac{13}{27}, \frac{5}{9}, \frac{2}{3}$ **19.** $\frac{15}{28}$ **21.** $\frac{40}{79}$ **23.** *Sample answer:* Numerators are only compared after making the denominators equal; use approximation instead. $\frac{15}{49} < \frac{1}{2}$ and $\frac{3}{4} > \frac{1}{2}$, so $\frac{3}{4} > \frac{15}{49}$. **29.** =. *Sample answer:* Mental math; $\frac{7}{21} = \frac{1}{3}$ **31.** >. *Sample answer:* Mental math; $\frac{5}{9} = \frac{10}{18}$ **33.** Molly **35.** tree with $\frac{7}{12}$ apples falling **37.** $\frac{3}{8}, \frac{7}{16}, \frac{1}{2}, \frac{5}{8}, \frac{11}{16}, \frac{3}{4}$ **43.** *Sample answer:* When fractions have the same numerator, that indicates that they have the same number of parts of their whole. The fraction with the larger denominator represents smaller pieces making it less than the fraction with the smaller denominator, so $\frac{11}{37} > \frac{11}{42}$.

1.6 Exercises (pp. 37–39) **1.** improper fraction **3.** mixed number **5.** proper fraction **7.** $\frac{16}{3}$ **9.** $\frac{91}{8}$ **11.** $\frac{69}{16}$ **13.** $15\frac{5}{6}$ **15.** 9 **17.** < **19.** = **21.** > **23.** > **27.** $\frac{40}{40}, \frac{22}{20}, 1\frac{1}{9}, \frac{49}{42}$ **29.** $\frac{65}{24}, \frac{43}{12}, 3\frac{11}{18}, 3\frac{3}{4}$ **31.** $2\frac{3}{8}, \frac{35}{14}, 2\frac{15}{28}, \frac{26}{7}$ **33.** The denominator was added instead of the numerator; $\frac{5 \times 3 + 2}{3} = \frac{17}{3}$. **35.** $\frac{3}{2}$ cups **37.** $\frac{839}{32}$ mi **39.** 25 quarter cups **41.** Improper fraction; an improper fraction is greater than or equal to 1, and a proper fraction is less than 1.

1.7 Exercises (pp. 42–45) **1.** repeating decimal **3.** 0.5 **5.** $1.\overline{3}$ **7.** $0.2\overline{7}$ **9.** 2.4 **11.** $3.\overline{4}$ **15.** 3.58 **17.** $2.\overline{358}$ **19.** $\frac{4}{5}$ **21.** $\frac{19}{40}$ **23.** $6\frac{6}{25}$ **25.** $2\frac{49}{200}$ **27.** < **29.** = **31.** > **33.** < **35.** $6\frac{1}{3} = 6.\overline{3}$, not 6.3; $6\frac{1}{3} > 6.32$. **37.** $\frac{16}{5}, 3\frac{2}{3}, 3.67, 3.6\overline{7}, 3\frac{4}{5}$ **39.** $\frac{15}{20}, \frac{6}{7}, 0.89, \frac{9}{10}, 0.\overline{90}$ **41.** $5\frac{4}{9}, \frac{11}{2}, 5.\overline{54}, 5\frac{7}{12}, 5.6$ **43.** C **45.** A **47.** Change $5\frac{3}{5}$ to a decimal; it is easier to use to compare. If you change 5.75 to a fraction, the denominators are not the same, so you would need to do more work. **49.** $7.\overline{81}$ lb **51.** 4.675 lb **55.** No; the normal black kangaroo is between 3.7 feet and 4.5 feet. **57.** $\frac{1}{8}$, 0.125; yes; 0.125 is 0.005 greater than 0.12.

1.8 Exercises (pp. 49–52) **1.** *Sample answer:* Step 1: Read the problem and identify the important information. Step 2: Pick a strategy to solve the problem. Step 3: Use the strategy to answer the problem. Step 4: Check your answer. **3.** know: 12 pens cost \$3; find: cost per pen **5.** The total cost of the tickets and snacks was \$22, so you have to subtract the cost of the snacks before you divide by 2; $(22 - 6) \div 2 = 8$, the tickets cost \$8 each. **7.** She makes 3 more each day; on day 7. **9.** Find the factors of 42. **11.** The answer is reasonable. **13.** 7:55 P.M.

15. 52 **17.** No; you only need one lantern on each corner; 26 lanterns. **19.** School song, songs A and B; school song, songs A and C; school song, songs B and C; school song, songs C and D; since the school song is 3 minutes long, the band can play other songs for 11 minutes. So, I found combinations of songs that totaled 11 minutes.
21. Emily, Ty, Rob, Marta. *Sample answer:* I drew a picture to visualize where they are standing.

Chapter Review (pp. 56 – 60) **1.** prime factorization **3.** greatest common factor **7.** 1, 43; prime **9.** 1, 31; prime **11.** 7×13 **13.** $2 \times 3 \times 11^2$ **15.** 1 **17.** 48 **19.** 11 **21.** 1 **23.** 12 **25.** 12 **27.** 1 **29.** 9 **31.** *Sample answer:* $\frac{6}{10}, \frac{9}{15}$ **33.** *Sample answer:* $\frac{1}{2}, \frac{2}{4}$ **35.** $\frac{23}{25}, \frac{9}{10}$; no; the fractions are not the same when they are in simplest form.
37. 42 **39.** 1872 **41.** 72 **43.** 770 **45.** $\frac{1}{2}, \frac{8}{15}, \frac{2}{3}, \frac{7}{10}$
47. $\frac{6}{13}, \frac{25}{39}, \frac{17}{26}, \frac{5}{6}$ **49.** $\frac{5}{12}, \frac{9}{20}, \frac{4}{7}, \frac{11}{18}$ **51.** $\frac{6}{7}, \frac{7}{8}, \frac{9}{10}, \frac{11}{12}$
53. > **55.** = **57.** $4.\overline{7}$ **59.** 11.6 **61.** $5\frac{1}{8}$ **63.** $2\frac{1}{4}$
65. $\frac{73}{12}$, 6.1, 6.24, $6\frac{1}{3}$ **67.** 3 buses

Chapter 2

2.1 Exercises (pp. 71–73) **1.** numerators, denominator
3. $\frac{3}{4} + \frac{1}{4} = 1$ **5.** $\frac{7}{9} - \frac{4}{9} = \frac{1}{3}$ **7.** $1\frac{1}{5}$ **9.** 1 **11.** $\frac{1}{3}$ **13.** $\frac{2}{5}$
15. $\frac{2}{3}$ **17.** $\frac{1}{3}$ **19.** $1\frac{11}{12}$ **21.** $1\frac{3}{14}$ **23.** $\frac{1}{2}$ **25.** $\frac{1}{4}$
27. The problem was not worked from left to right; $\frac{7}{9} - \frac{4}{9} - \frac{1}{9} = \frac{2}{9}$. **31.** $\frac{3}{7}, \frac{1}{7}$ **33.** $\frac{3}{26}$ **35.** $1\frac{5}{8}$ **37.** $\frac{16}{17}$ ft
39. $\frac{1}{4}$ c **41. a.** $\frac{2}{5}$ mi; $\frac{14}{25}$ mi; $\frac{19}{25}$ mi **b.** 0.8 mi; Runway B can at most be $\frac{3}{25}$ less than the maximum length of Runway A.
43. $1\frac{1}{4}$ ft; add the amount of snow that fell on Saturday and Sunday $\frac{3}{4} + \frac{3}{4} = 1\frac{1}{2}$ feet, then subtract $\frac{1}{4}$ foot.

2.2 Exercises (pp. 77–80) **1.** least common denominator
3. $\frac{9}{10}$ **5.** $\frac{27}{28}$ **7.** $1\frac{11}{60}$ **9.** $\frac{17}{48}$ **11.** $\frac{1}{6}$ **13.** $\frac{3}{8}$ **15.** $1\frac{9}{16}$
17. $\frac{1}{60}$ **21.** When changing $\frac{2}{7}$ into an equivalent fraction, the numerator must also be multiplied by 4; $\frac{9}{28} - \frac{8}{28} = \frac{1}{28}$.
23. $\frac{11}{14}$ **25.** $1\frac{1}{12}$ **27.** $1\frac{59}{270}$ **31–35.** Sample answers are given. **31.** >, mental math **33.** <, pencil and paper
35. <, estimation **37.** $\frac{3}{8} + \frac{19}{24}$ **39.** $1 - \frac{7}{10}$
41. $\frac{3}{4} + \frac{5}{12} = 1\frac{1}{6}$; use addition to find the alligators total length now. **47.** No; the sum is $\frac{1}{4} + \frac{1}{2} + 2 + \frac{3}{4} = 3\frac{1}{2}$ beats.

2.3 Exercise (pp. 83–85) **1.** When the fractional part of the second mixed number is greater than the fractional part of the first mixed number. **3.** $17\frac{4}{5}$ **5.** 13 **7.** $1\frac{1}{3}$
9. $3\frac{2}{9}$ **11.** The first mixed number needs to be renamed; $2\frac{7}{6} - 1\frac{5}{6} = 1\frac{1}{3}$. **13.** $7\frac{5}{8}$ **15.** $11\frac{5}{12}$ **17.** $17\frac{17}{30}$ **19.** $6\frac{1}{2}$
21. $3\frac{3}{8}$ **23.** $3\frac{7}{10}$ **27.** $9\frac{1}{5}$ **29.** $1\frac{2}{3}$ **31.** $17\frac{8}{45}$ **33.** $1\frac{9}{20}$
35–39. Sample answers are given. **35.** =; mental math **37.** <; mental math **39.** =; pencil and paper
41. Addition; you want to find the total weight of the meat.
43. Subtraction; you want to find the how much cornmeal is left. **47.** No; the width enclosed by the frame is $6\frac{1}{2} - \frac{3}{4} - \frac{3}{4} = 5$ inches, and the length enclosed by the frame is $8\frac{1}{4} - \frac{3}{4} - \frac{3}{4} = 6\frac{3}{4}$ inches, which is less than 7 inches.

2.4 Exercises (pp.90–92) **1.** simplest form **3.** $\frac{5}{14}$
5. $\frac{2}{45}$ **7.** 10 **9.** 2 **11.** $6\frac{1}{3}$ **13.** $\frac{3}{4}$ **15.** 6 **17.** 48
19. You can only divide out common factors between the numerator and denominator; $\frac{2}{3} \times \frac{5}{9} = \frac{10}{27}$. **23.** >; $1\frac{3}{25}$
25. <; $6\frac{3}{4}$ **27.** >; $12\frac{8}{15}$ **29.** Never. *Sample answer:* The product is less than the smaller fraction. **31.** 120 votes
33. $4\frac{4}{5}$ km **35.** $5\frac{1}{6}$ ft **39.** Multiply each amount by $1\frac{1}{3}$; $2\frac{2}{3}$ c baking mix, $2\frac{2}{3}$ apples, 4 eggs, $\frac{2}{3}$ c sugar, $1\frac{1}{3}$ c milk, $2\frac{2}{3}$ tsp cinnamon.

2.5 Exercises (pp. 97–99) **1.** $\frac{6}{5}$ **3.** 1 **5.** To divide fractions, multiply by the reciprocal of the divisor.
7. $2\frac{2}{5}$ **9.** $\frac{5}{8}$ **11.** $13\frac{1}{3}$ **13.** $2\frac{2}{5}$ **15.** $\frac{40}{51}$ **17.** $7\frac{1}{2}$ **19.** $1\frac{5}{16}$
21. $2\frac{1}{24}$ **23.** Multiply be the reciprocal of only the divisor; $\frac{12}{5} \times \frac{3}{8} = \frac{9}{10}$. **27.** $\frac{1}{16}$ **29.** $5\frac{1}{4}$ **31.** $\frac{16}{63}$ **33.** $\frac{8}{19}$
35. Division; you want to find how long $\frac{1}{5}$ of $2\frac{1}{3}$ is.
37. $\frac{1}{2}$ ft

2.5 Technology Activity (p. 100) **1.** $1\frac{23}{99}$ **3.** $\frac{1}{5}$ **5.** $2\frac{11}{14}$
7. $23\frac{2}{3}$ **9.** $1.70

2.6 Exercises (pp. 104–106) **1.** decimal points **3.** 23.4 **5.** 67.263 **7.** 82.5 **9.** 483.83 **11.** 43.95 **13.** 15.268
15. Write 13 as 13.00, line up the decimal points, then add; 3.48 + 13.00 = 16.48. **17.** 46.28 **19.** 12.582 **21.** 15.822
23–31. Sample answers are given. **23.** 15 **25.** 3 **27.** 17 **29.** 3 **31.** 13 **35.** > **37.** < **39.** < **41.** 74.35 − 68.72
43. 9.3 acres **45.** *Sample answer:* An estimate of the sum is $19, which is $0.21 higher than the exact sum.
47. your team; 2.35 min; 22.35 + 25.8 + 30.15 = 78.3 minutes, 80.65 − 78.3 = 2.35 minutes

2.7 Exercises (pp. 110–113) **1.** 4 **3.** 20 **5.** 56 and 7 **7.** 0.012 **9.** 2.4 **11.** 22.1 **13.** 3.549 **15.** 0.0126
17. 0.054 **19.** 0.000602 **21.** 98.8473 **25.** 0.46
27. 1.25 **29.** 1.88 **31.** 3.44 **33.** 0.05 **35.** 93.81
37. 5.05 **39.** 2.46 **41.** The decimal point must move the same number of places in the divisor and the dividend; 9.342 ÷ 2.7 = 93.42 ÷ 27 = 3.46. **43.** 270 **45.** 1000
47. 0.56 **49.** 0.2 **51.** 20 **53.** 1 **55.** 36 **57.** 4

59. 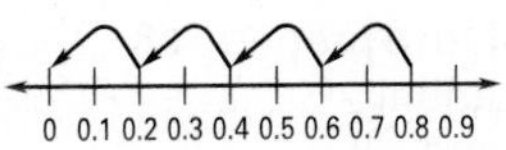 0 0.1 0.2 0.3 0.4 0.5 0.6 0.7 0.8 0.9

61. 1.008 **63.** 2.66112 **65.** 9.6 **67.** 10 **69.** Multiply the previous number by 5; 75, 375, 1875. **71.** Multiply the previous number by 1.5; 10.125, 15.1875, 22.78125. **73.** $779 \div 4.75$ **75.** 3×14.69 **77.** yes; 52 min; 45 pages; 36 min; $1.25 \times 60 = 75$ pages in 1 hour. $120 - 75 = 45$ pages left, $45 \div 1.25 = 36$ more minutes. **79.** 76.1 yr **83.** Yes; no; $27.75; $30.45 \div 8.7 =$ $3.50 per gallon, $32.19 \div 8.7 =$ $3.70 per gallon, $3.19 \times 8.7 =$ $27.75.

Chapter Review (pp. 117–120) **1.** least common denominator **3.** compatible numbers **7.** $\frac{1}{5}$ **9.** $\frac{4}{5}$ **11.** 1 **13.** $\frac{1}{4}$ **15.** $1\frac{1}{2}$ **17.** $\frac{1}{6}$ **19.** $1\frac{1}{8}$ **21.** $1\frac{13}{18}$ **23.** $\frac{1}{2}$ **25.** $\frac{7}{12}$ **27.** $5\frac{4}{5}$ **29.** $1\frac{1}{2}$ **31.** $7\frac{7}{8}$ in.; $36\frac{5}{8} - 28\frac{3}{4} = 7\frac{7}{8}$ **33.** $10\frac{1}{2}$ **35.** $11\frac{11}{12}$ **37.** $10\frac{1}{2}$ **39.** $5\frac{1}{3}$ **41.** 36 DVDs; $21\frac{1}{4} - \frac{1}{2} - \frac{1}{2} = 20\frac{1}{4}$, $20\frac{1}{4} \div \frac{9}{16} = 36$ **43.** 25.895 **45.** 34.822 **47.** 21.2 **49.** 19.27 **51.** 993.6 **53.** 65.344 **55.** 18.376092 **57.** 0.25 **59.** 9.4 **61.** 739.9 **63.** $.94 **65.** $2.83

Chapter 3

3.1 Exercises (pp. 131–133) **1.** −12 **3.** 1333; −1333 **5.** −9,000,000; 9,000,000

7. 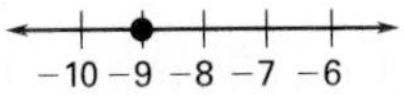 −10 −9 −8 −7 −6 **9.** −7 −6 −5 −4 −3

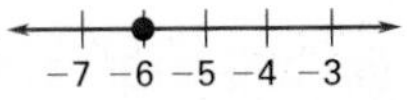

13. > **15.** > **17.** < **19.** > **21.** > **23.** > **25.** −28, −17, −12, 0, 7, 18 **27.** −435, −150, −75, 235, 345 **29.** −250, −19, 2, 15, 320 **31.** *Sample answer:* A number to the left on a number line is smaller; −12, −7, −3, −1.

37. no

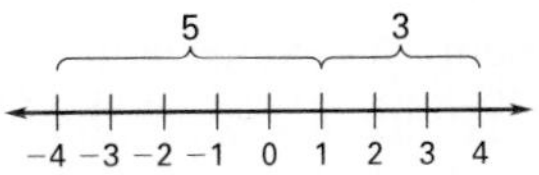

5 3
−4 −3 −2 −1 0 1 2 3 4

39–49. Sample answers are given. **39.** 20; 21 **41.** −8; −7 **43.** 3; 6 **45.** 8; −1 **47.** −21; −13 **49.** 53; 59 **51.** Fairbanks **53.** −75

3.2 Exercises (pp. 138–140) **1.** False; an absolute value is always positive or zero, regardless of the sign of the integer. **5.** $6 + (-1) = 5$ **7.** 12 **9.** 54 **11.** 37 **13.** 47 **15.** positive, 3 **17.** negative, −14 **19.** negative, −145 **21.** zero, 0 **23.** negative, −25 **25.** negative, −2 **29.** The sum did not use the sign of the number with the greater absolute value; $-36 + 15 = -21$. **31.** < **33.** < **35.** = **39.** −9 **41.** 4 **43.** −3 **45.** −4 **47.** > **49.** = **51.** −17 **53.** 16 **55.** −10 **57.** $40 + (-14)$; 26 **59.** $30 + 25 + (-20)$; 35 **61.** $-60 + 25 + (-10) + 25$; −20

3.3 Exercises (pp. 145–147) **1.** opposite **3.** C **5.** A **7.** 17 **9.** −2 **11.** 33 **13.** 20 **15.** 20 **17.** −84 **19.** The student subtracted 6, not the opposite of 6; $3 - (-6) = 3 + 6 = 9$. **23.** 20 **25.** 46 **27.** −65 **29.** > **31.** > **33.** = **35.** > **37.** < **39.** $300 - (-100)$ **41.** $75 - (-35)$ **45.** 11,331 ft **49. a.** 3830 years **b.** 1587 years **c.** 2476 years **d.** 233 years

3.4 Exercises (pp. 150–151) **1.** positive **5.** −33 **7.** 24 **9.** 0 **11.** −40 **13.** −30 **15.** 28 **17.** −32 **19.** −45 **21.** 288 **23.** −150 **25.** Rewrite (-3) as $(-1)(3)$; $5(-3) = 5(-1)(3) = -15$. **29.** 8 **31.** −6 **33.** 20 **35.** −140 **37.** −5 **39.** −4 **41.** −13 **43.** −1 **45.** 21, −567 **47.** 25, −125 **49.** −180 ft **51.** $5(-2) = -10$ **53.** 60 ft **55.** $10(-4)$; −40 ft **57.** −37; if you calculate all possible sums, you get: $1 + 36 = 37$, $2 + 18 = 20$, $3 + 12 = 15$, $4 + 9 = 13$, $6 + 6 = 12$, $-1 + (-36) = -37$, $-2 + (-18) = -20$, $-3 + (-12) = -15$, $-4 + (-9) = -13$, and $-6 + (-6) = -12$. **59.** $9(-3) = -27$; 45 ft

3.5 Exercises (pp. 156–158) **1.** negative **3.** undefined **5.** −4 **7.** −7 **9.** 4 **11.** 7 **13.** −3 **15.** 0 **17.** −3 **19.** −2 **21.** not defined **23.** −4 **27.** The quotient of two integers with different signs is negative; $-\frac{24}{12} = -2$. **29.** −1 **31.** −17 **33.** 7 **35.** < **37.** = **39.** $134 **41.** $26.80 **43.** −7°F

3.6 Exercises (pp. 162–165) **1.** before **5.** $11\frac{1}{3}$ **7.** 36 **9.** 40 **11.** −11 **13.** $\frac{1}{27}$ **15.** 6 **17.** −1 **19.** −23 **21.** $\frac{15}{4}$ **23.** 4 **25.** −7 **27.** 2 **29.** 600 **31.** 60.75 **33.** The student found $27 \div 3 = 9$ first rather than $3^2 = 9$. First evaluate powers: $27 \div 3^2 = 27 \div 9 = 3$. **37.** + **39.** × **41.** × **43.** − **45.** $(20 - 3^2) \cdot (2 + 8) = 110$ **47.** $(8 - 2) \cdot 6 \div 3^2 = 4$ **49.** 86, 98, 240 **55.** $15 + 4 \cdot 25 + 2 \cdot 20 = 155$ **57.** You get 6 discounts of $11: $66 \cdot 4 - 6 \cdot 11 = 264 - 66 = 198$. **61.** bowling + cake + soft drinks = $10 \cdot 5 + 10 \cdot 2 + 10 \cdot 1 =$ $80 **63.** Yes; at the per person rate, the cost for 17 people would be $17 \cdot (5 + 2 + 1) =$ $136. That is more than the cost for a deluxe birthday package, which would be $125.

3.6 Technology Activity (p. 166) **1.** 23 **3.** 4 **5.** 5 **7.** 13 **9.** about 1080

3.7 Exercises (pp. 170–172) **1.** 0; 1 **3.** $\frac{2}{5}$ **5.** $\frac{3}{1}$ **7.** $\frac{11}{5}$ **9.** $-\frac{29}{5}$ **11.** $-0.8 = -\frac{4}{5}$

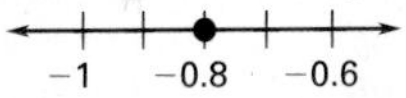

−1 −0.8 −0.6

13. $-\frac{6}{7} > -\frac{7}{6}$

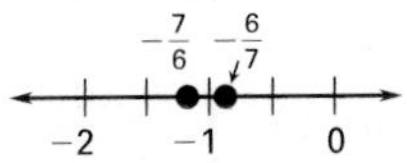

$-\frac{7}{6}$ $-\frac{6}{7}$
−2 −1 0

17. −4, −3.7, −1.25, 3, 4.31 **19.** −4, $-3\frac{3}{4}$, −3.7, $-\frac{10}{3}$, −3.1 **21.** $-1\frac{1}{3}$, −0.5, 0.02, $\frac{3}{10}$, 1 **23.** The student ordered them based on their absolute value; $-1\frac{1}{3}$, $-\frac{5}{6}$, $0.\overline{6}$, $\frac{1}{6}$, $\frac{1}{3}$

25. commutative property of addition

27. identity property of addition

29. commutative property of multiplication

31. $= 4 + (-4) + 17$ [Commutative property of addition]
$= 0 + 17$ [Inverse property of addition]
$= 17$ [Identity property of addition]

33. $= 7(-8 \cdot 5)$ [Associative property of multiplication]
$= 7(-40)$ [Multiply −8 and 5.]
$= -280$ [Multiply 7 and −40.]

35. $= 14 \cdot \frac{1}{14} \cdot \frac{2}{3}$ [Commutative property of multiplication]
$= \left(14 \cdot \frac{1}{14}\right) \cdot \frac{2}{3}$ [Associative property of multiplication]
$= 1 \cdot \frac{2}{3}$ [Inverse property of multiplication]
$= \frac{2}{3}$ [Identity property of multiplication]

39. $\frac{12}{12}$ **41.** $\frac{25}{25}$ **43.** −28.5 ft. **45.** $-8\frac{4}{25}, -\frac{631}{100}, -5.87$, 1.97; southeast **49.** lost \$54

51. = 5 + (−5) + 7 + (−7) [Commutative property of addition]
= [5 + (−5)] + [7 + (−7)] [Associative property of addition]
= 0 + 0 [Inverse property of addition]
= 0 [Identity property of addition]

53. 0

3.8 Exercises (pp. 175–178) **1.** equivalent **3.** 5(3) + 5(7) **5.** 7(3 + 4) **7.** $6\left(\frac{5}{12} - \frac{1}{12}\right)$ **11.** 101.1 **13.** 11 **15.** $\frac{9}{5}$ **17.** 44 **21.** The student wrote the outside term as 3 + 3 rather than 3; 3(9) + 3(7) = 3(9 + 7) = 3(16) = 48. **23.** inverse property of addition **25.** associative property of multiplication **27.** distributive property **29.** identity property of multiplication

31. $= 4\left(\frac{4}{5} + \frac{1}{5}\right) + (-4)$ [Distributive property]
= 4(1) + (−4) $\left[\text{Add } \frac{4}{5} \text{ and } \frac{1}{5}.\right]$
= 4 + (−4) [Identity property of multiplication]
= 0 [Inverse property of addition]

33. = 4(8) + 4(−8) − 20 [Commutative property of addition]
= 4[8 + (−8)] − 20 [Distributive property]
= 4(0) − 20 [Inverse property of addition]
= 0 − 20 [Zero product property]
= −20 [Identity property of addition]

35. = [2 + (−2)] + 39(8) + 39(−8)] [Commutative property of addition]
= [2 + (−2)] + 39(8 + (−8)] [Distributive property]
= 0 + 39(0) [Inverse property of addition]
= 0 + 0 [Zero product property]
= 0 [Identity property of addition]

39. 20, 0.30, 20, 0.30 **41.** 0.70(10 + 6); 0.70 • 10 + 0.70 • 6 **45.** 150 min **47.** $2(\ell + w)$; $2\ell + 2w = 2(14) + 2(12) = 28 + 24 = 52$; $2(\ell + w) = 2(14 + 12) = 2(26) = 52$ **49.** $x(3 + 1 + 1 + 3 + 1 + 3 + 1 + 1)$; $14x$; 5600 cm; 3959.2 cm

Chapter Review (pp. 182–186) **1.** integers: −4, 5, −2, 4; opposites: 2.3 and −2.3, −4 and 4 **3.** equivalent **7.** < **9.** > **11.** −350 **13.** −42 **15.** −38 **17.** −23 **19.** −95 **21.** −126 **23.** −7 **25.** −10 **27.** −22 **29.** −23 **31.** 12°F **33.** 0 **35.** −54 **37.** −114 **39.** 0 **41.** 36 **43.** −21 **45.** −4 **47.** 0 **49.** 2 **51.** −4 **53.** −3°C **55.** 32 **57.** 32 **59.** −48 **61.** 25 **63.** 1 **65.** 61 **67.** $\frac{12}{5}, \frac{-21}{10}, \frac{-14}{5}, \frac{2}{1}, \frac{19}{9}; -2\frac{4}{5}, -2.1, 2, 2\frac{1}{9}, 2.4$

69. $= -\frac{2}{3} + \left(-\frac{2}{3} + \frac{2}{3}\right)$ [Associative property of addition]
$= -\frac{2}{3} + 0$ [Inverse property of addition]
$= -\frac{2}{3}$ [Identity property of addition]

71. $= \left(\frac{3}{7} \cdot \frac{7}{3}\right)(-1)$ [Commutative property of multiplication and Associative property of multiplication]
= 1(−1) [Inverse property of multiplication]
= −1 [Identity property of multiplication]

73. = [(25)(−8)](−9) [Commutative property of multiplication]
= (−200)(−9) [Multiply 25 and −8.]
= 1800 [Multiply −200 and −9.]

75. $9\left(\frac{5}{12} + \frac{7}{12}\right)$; 9 **77.** 6(1 + 0.03); 6.18 **79.** 9(9 − 0.10); \$80.10

Chapter 4

4.1 Exercises (pp 199–200) **1.** c **3.** 2.5 **5.** 26 **7.** 3.5 **9.** 56 **11.** −45 **13.** 10.5 **15.** 103 **17.** 47 **19.** 1.5 **21.** 11 **23.** The a does not represent the ones digit, $2a$ means "2 • a"; $2a = 2(3) = 6$. **27.** > **29.** > **31.** < **33.** \$1,080 **37.** \$1,400

4.1 Technology Activity (p. 201) **1.** 2, 5, 8, 11, 14, 17 **3.** 17, 8, −1, −10, −19, −28 **5.** Use a separate column for the number of nickels, dimes, and quarters, and then use a fourth column for the value of the expression; \$1.85.

4.2 Exercises (pp. 204–206) **1.** verbal model **3.** B **5.** A **7.** $-7 + n$ **9.** $\frac{n+6}{3}$ **11.** $\frac{n}{6} + 2$ **15.** $\frac{a^3}{b}$ **17.** $s \cdot (1.2 - r)$ **19.** $f^9 + g + h$ **21–27.** Sample answers are given. **21.** the sum of 3 and a **23.** 1 plus the product of 5 and x **25.** n squared plus p **27.** the product of 2 and the sum of a plus b plus c **29.** 7 and x are misplaced; 7 less than a number should be written $x - 7$. **31.** $t + 3$; t = Theo's age **33.** $0.5 \cdot c$; c = class size **39.** $\frac{(b - c - d)}{2}$; 55 books

4.3 Exercises (pp. 209–210) **1.** 5, 2 **3.** coefficients: 3, −1; like terms: $3x$, $-x$; constant term: 4 **5.** coefficients: −4, 5; like terms: $-4y$, $5y$ and 10, −8; constant terms: 10, −8 **9.** $4b + 24$ **11.** $12t + 15$ **13.** $m - 1$ **15.** 20.68 **17.** 1 is not a like term with $4x$ and $3x$; $7x + 1$. **19.** $5z + 2$ **21.** $6s + 5$ **23.** $6b - 4$ **25.** $5m - 13$ **27.** $11r + 8$ **29.** $8t + \frac{4}{7}$ **31.** not equivalent **33.** equivalent **35.** $0.05x + 0.1x + 0.25x$; $0.4x$ **37.** $h + 0.5h$; $1.5h$ **39. a.** $10 + x + 2x$; $10 + 3x$ **b.** 46 photos

4.4 Exercises (pp. 215–217) **1.** formula **3.** $2(3c) + 2(2c)$, $10c$ **5.** $2(3z) + 2(z + 1)$, $8z + 2$ **7.** The wrong formula for perimeter was used; $P = 4s$, $= 4(4)$, $= 16$ m. **9.** $P = 2(2.7a) + 2(12a) = 29.4a$, $A = 2.7a(12a) = 32.4a^2$ **11.** $P = 2(d + 7) + 2(6) = 2d + 26$, $A = 6(d + 7) = 6d + 42$ **13.** $P = 2(2g - 3) + 2(8) = 4g + 10$, $A = 8(2g - 3) = 16g - 24$ **15.** 63 in. **17.** 145 mi **19.** $(118x - 236)$ ft **21.** $105x$ cm **25.** 0°C **27.** 68°F **29.** 64.4°F **31.** 149.5°F **33.** P = 48 in., A = 126 in.^{2} **35.** 264 ft **37.** 900 in.^{2} **39.** $P = 2(4c) + 2(c) = 10c$, $A = 4c(c) = 4c^2$ **41.** 2187°F

4.5 Exercises (pp. 221–224) **1.** solution **3.** solution **5.** not a solution **7.** not a solution **9.** $n + (-9) = 24$ **11.** $\frac{3}{n} = 2(23)$ **13.** The variable and the number 7 are written in the wrong order; $\frac{x}{7} = 28$. **15.** 6 **17.** 9 **19.** 17 **21.** 3 **23.** 4 **25.** 48 **29.** 25 **31.** 4 **33.** 2 **35.** 4

37. no **39.** no **41.** never **43.** sometimes **45.** $c - 12$; c = the number of CD's in Lily's collection **47.** $5c = 40$; 8 cars **49.** $48 + s = 64$; 16 empty seats **53. a.** $x - 200 = 1000$; 1200 ft **b.** 5 min; solve the equation $1200 = 240t$. **55. a.** $t + 15 = 512$ **b.** 497 min; 8 h 17 min

4.6 Exercises (pp. 228–231) **1.** *Sample answer:* Addition and subtraction **3.** 3 **5.** −17 **7.** −30 **9.** −20 **11.** −14 **13.** 20.7 **15.** 20.2 **17.** $\frac{1}{16}$ **19.** Subtract 8 from the right side instead of adding; 6. **23.** 8 **25.** 7 **27.** 21 **29.** 0 **31.** 7.7 **33.** 7 **35.** 4.2 **37.** $p - 5 = -17$; −12 **39.** $n + 6 = 13$; 7 **41.** $y - 11 = -16$; −5 **43.** $n + 2\frac{1}{3} = 4\frac{1}{2}$; $2\frac{1}{6}$ **47.** associative property of addition; commutative property of addition; associative property of addition; combine like terms; subtraction property of equality; combine like terms **49.** $a + 4 + 4 = 13$; 5 **51.** $d + 5.2 + 15.6 + 6.5 = 42.5$; 15.2 **53.** $r - 1.50 = 5.75$ **55.** $t - 45 = 23$

4.7 Exercises (pp. 236–239) **1.** inverse operations **3.** 3 **5.** 9 **7.** 16 **9.** −154 **11.** 7 **13.** 2.5 **15.** 2.16 **17.** 16 **19.** 9 **21.** 24 **23–26.** Methods may vary. **23.** Divide both sides by 3; 5. **25.** Multiply both sides by 9; −18. **29.** Divide both sides by −3 instead of 3; −16. **31.** $11n = -22$; −2 **33.** $\frac{n}{-11} = -7$; 77 **35.** $\frac{4}{13}n = 2$; 6.5 **39.** 7.5 **41.** 0.5 **43.** 2.25 **45.** $7.5w = 45$ **47.** $50t = 2400$; 48 h **51.** $s = \frac{309}{3}$; 103 strikes per min

Chapter Review (pp. 243–246) **1.** equivalent equations **3.** coefficient **5.** solution **9.** $\frac{2}{3}$ **11.** 11 **13.** 15 **15.** −3 **17.** $2(w + 4)$ **19.** $\frac{6}{w+5}$ **21.** $8x - 4$ **23.** $z - 6$ **25.** $7d - 18$ **27.** $(3 + 2r) + r$; $3 + 3r$ **29.** perimeter: $2(n + 3) + 2(0.5)$, $2n + 7$; area: $0.5(n + 3)$, $0.5n + 1.5$ **31.** 102.2°F **33.** $\frac{n}{7} = 3$ **35.** $n^2 + 3 = 7$ **37.** −12 **39.** 16 **41.** 1.8 **43.** 17.4 **45.** 73 cards **47.** 3 **49.** −40 **51.** 15

Chapter 5

5.1 Exercises (pp. 257–259) **1.** 2 cats **3.** 1 to 7, 1 : 7, $\frac{1}{7}$ **5.** 3 to 10, 3 : 10, $\frac{3}{10}$ **7.** $\frac{1}{2}$ **9.** $\frac{4}{7}$ **11.** $\frac{9}{5}$ **13.** $\frac{2}{3}$ **15.** $\frac{5}{32}$ **17.** $\frac{3}{4}$ **19.** $\frac{2}{7}$ **21.** $\frac{12}{35}$ **23.** The student wrote the ratio of 16 to the sum of 16 and 18, $\frac{16}{18} = \frac{8}{9}$. **25.** = **27.** > **29.** = **31.** 3 : 6, 5 : 8, 15 : 5 **33.** 1 : 7, 2 : 9, 3 : 8 **35.** 18 : 72, 20 : 75, 10 : 36 **39.** 11 : 8 **41.** 5 : 18 **43.** 3000 : 2900 or 30 : 29 **47.** 44 : 36 or 11 : 9 **49.** 36 : 80 or 9 : 20

5.2 Exercises (pp. 262–264) **1.** rate **5.** $7 per lb **7.** $3.50 per oz **9.** 16 students per teacher **11.** $20.75 per ticket **13.** $7.50 per plant **15.** 1.75 cups per serving **17.** 3 in. per year **21.** 60 mi/h **23.** 12 m/min or 0.2 m/sec **25.** 30 ft/min or 0.5 ft/sec **27.** 72 km/h or 1.2 km/min **29.** 180 yd/min or 3 yd/sec **31.** The units are switched. The rate is $ per bottle; $6.50 per bottle. **33.** 5 tomatoes per day **35.** 22.5 points per game **37.** $.89 per pen **41.** 17 oz for $3.40

5.3 Exercises (pp. 268–271) **1.** proportion **3.** 9 **5.** 5 **7.** 24 **9.** 44 **13.** 18 **15.** 15 **17.** 5.6 **19.** $\frac{40}{7}$ **21.** $\frac{8}{3} = \frac{w}{12}$; 32 **23.** $\frac{p}{30} = \frac{10}{12}$; 25 **25.** $\frac{4 \text{ qt}}{560 \text{ ft}^2} = \frac{x}{140 \text{ ft}^2}$ **27.** $\frac{280 \text{ ft}^2}{\$1,400} = \frac{x}{\$6,700}$ **29.** 285 lb **33.**

B	32	48	80
F	2	3	5

35. 159 calories **37.** 10.5 ft **45.** 56 min

5.4 Exercises (pp. 276–279) **1.** 70, 70 **3.** 25 **5.** 12 **7.** 8 **9.** 35 **11.** 8 **13.** 7 **15.** 6.25 **17.** 44 **21.** To find the cross products, multiply rather than add; $32 \cdot y = 8 \cdot 28$, $y = 7$. **23.** 4.8 lb **25.** 500 lb **27.** 30 boys, 50 girls **29.** 20 boys, 15 girls **31.** 49 boys, 21 girls **33.** 26 boys, 39 girls **37.** 2 **39.** $8\frac{1}{6}$ **41.** not a proportion **43.** proportion **45.** 45, $3p$ **51.** 180 CDs **55.** about 215 invertebrates

5.4 Technology Activity (p. 280) **1.** 32 **3.** 28 **5.** 12 **7.** 15 **9.** 217 girls

5.5 Exercises (pp. 283–286) **1.** scale model **3.** B **5.** A **7.** 75 mi **9.** 130 mi **11.** 0.2 m **13.** 0.8 m **15.** The wrong unit of measurement is used. The scale is 1 in : 5 ft, so the unit for x is inches; 3 in. **17.** 1 : 10 **19.** 24 : 5 **21.** 3 : 2 **23.** 1 : 10 **27.** Larger. *Sample answer:* If a length in the model is 1 m, then the corresponding length in the actual object would be 0.2 m. **29.** $\frac{1}{12} = \frac{w}{24}$ **31.** about 760 cm or 7.6 m

Chapter 5 Review (pp. 290–292) **1.** 12 **3.** proportion **5.** $\frac{1}{9}$, 1 : 9 **7.** $\frac{4}{7}$, 4 to 7 **9.** < **11.** 5 : 2 **13.** 5.5 oz per serving **15.** 5 ft/1 sec **17.** 16 oz for $3.89 **19.** 30 **21.** 2 **23.** 8 **25.** 13.5 **27.** $6.75 **29.** 1 in. : 1 ft

Chapter 6

6.1 Exercises (pp. 303–304) **1.** per hundred **3.** $\frac{11}{100}$ **5.** $\frac{41}{50}$ **7.** $\frac{2}{25}$ **9.** $\frac{17}{50}$ **11.** $\frac{7}{50}$ **13.** $\frac{11}{50}$ **15.** $\frac{9}{25}$ **17.** $\frac{8}{25}$ **19.** 52% **21.** 60% **23.** 44% **25.** 56% **27.** 35% **29.** 95% **31.** 18% **33.** 80% means 80 per 100, not 8 per 100; $\frac{80}{100} = \frac{4}{5}$. **35.** 44 **37.** 125 **39.** 15 **41.** 81 **45.** 10 **47.** 27 **49.** 60 **51.** 54 **53.** 4 : 5, 81%, $\frac{41}{50}$ **55.** 89%, $\frac{9}{10}$, 23 : 25 **57.** 12%, $\frac{7}{50}$, 3 : 20 **59.** $\frac{90}{100}$ **61.** 78%

6.2 Exercises (pp. 308–311) **1.** $\frac{18}{25}$ **7.** 94% **9.** 20 **11.** 150 **13.** 30% **15.** 54 **17.** 18 is part of the base; $\frac{18}{b} = \frac{24}{100}$, $b = 75$. **21.** 63% **23.** 44% **25.** 25% **27.** 105 **29.** 32 **31.** $20y$; if 5% of a number is y, then 100% of the number is $20y$ because 100% is 20 times 5%. **33.** $\frac{a}{72} = \frac{25}{100}$, a is the number of students who will audition. **35.** 125 people **37.** 9 problems **41.** 20,463 orangutans **43.** about 1500 volcanoes

6.3 Exercises (pp. 314–317) **1.** *Sample answer:* 1.02; 0.002 **3.** 0.47 **5.** 0.08 **7.** 0.425 **9.** 0.0165 **11.** 26% **13.** 20.5% **15.** 15% **17.** 85% **19.** 58.6 % **21.** 9.95% **25.** 61.9% **27.** 76.7% **29.** 19.2% **31.** 0.5% **33.** 0.0002; $\frac{1}{5000}$ **35.** 0.0071; $\frac{71}{1000}$ **37.** 0.0078; $\frac{39}{5000}$ **39.** 2.52; $2\frac{13}{25}$ **41.** 12.75; $12\frac{3}{4}$ **43.** 6.15; $6\frac{3}{20}$ **45.** Move the decimal point two places to the right instead of to the left; 1578%. **47.** 0.0165 **49.** 139.5 **51.** 0.216 **53.** 419.9 **55.** 334.65 **57.** 2.04 **59.** 3.25; 325% **61.** about 9.67; about 967% **63.** 13.7; 1370% **65.** 2.6; 260% **67.** $<$ **69.** $=$ **71.** $<$ **73.** $<$ **77.** 65% **79.** 0.02% **81.** $1,645,280 **85.** Not reasonable; 0.05% of 100 people is 0.05 people, you cannot have less than a person as an answer. **87.** About 194.6%; yes; to double means to multiply by 2 and 2 written as a percent is 200%. Since 194.6% is close to 200%, the typical price almost doubled in 3 years. **89.** 16; 24; 32; convert the percent to a decimal and multiply by 8.

6.4 Exercises (pp. 321–323) **1.** base **3.** 40 **5.** 180 **7.** 105 **9.** 100 **11.** 72 **13.** 70% **15.** 17% **17.** 72% **19.** 25% **23.** The percentage was not changed into a decimal; $a = 0.3 \cdot 180 = 54$. **25.** $=$ **27.** $>$ **29.** $=$ **31.** 20, 40, 60, 80, $20n$ **33.** base **35.** $230 **37.** 28 games **39.** 32.6% **41.** $250 **43.** By the multiplication property of equality, $\frac{a}{b} \cdot b = \frac{p}{100} \cdot b$, $a = \frac{p}{100} \cdot b$; the percent equation is the same except that p is written as a percent instead of a fraction. **45.** *Sample answer:* Skiing: 5.9 million, snowboarding: 9.0 million, ice skating: 2.4 million; since the sports are increasing or decreasing steadily, find the difference between the popularity in 1998 and 2003. Use this difference to find the number of people in 2008.

6.4 Technology Activity (p. 324) **1.** 7.2 **3.** 7.809 **5.** 24.057 **7.** 8.64 **9.** 60.45 **11.** 13.42 **13.** $16.50 **15.** 80 games

6.5 Exercises (pp. 327–329) **1.** $15 **3.** $15.75 **7.** $56 **9.** $19.20 **11.** $82.50 **13.** $92.25 **15.** $26.50 **17.** $54 **21.** *Sample answer:* $30 **23.** $.80 **25.** in-line skates: $164, skateboard: $225, sneakers: $69 **29.** No, because the discount is off the marked up price, so the final price is $60. **31.** $20

6.6 Exercises (pp. 333–335) **1.** interest **3.** $3, $33 **5.** $20, $70 **7.** $3.36, $255.36 **9.** $486.72, $6726.72 **11.** $75, $5075 **15.** Interest is written incorrectly; $I = (300) \cdot (0.06) \cdot (0.5) = \$9$. **17.** $600 **19.** 6 months **21.** 8 months **23.** $360 **25.** 5% **27.** 5 years **29.** Interest is reasonable, round 98 to 100 and then take 5% of 100. **31.** 0.025 **33.** $26.25 **35.** $3 **37.** 4% **39.** 4 yr

Chapter Review (pp.339–342) **1.** percent **3.** interest **7.** $\frac{13}{20}$ **9.** $\frac{49}{50}$ **11.** 8% **13.** 60% **15.** 85% **17.** 32.5 **19.** 25% **21.** 60% **23.** 15% **25.** 20 **27.** 18 **29.** 0.31 **31.** 0.0028 **33.** 124% **35.** 48 **37.** $63.75 **39.** $54.60 **41.** $50.40 **43.** $319 **45.** 0.25 year **47.** 4%

Chapter 7

7.1 Exercises (pp. 356–358) **1.** self-selected **3.** No; the population is small enough to ask each employee. **5.** Yes; the population is too large to ask each person. **7.** convenience sampling; likely to be biased **9.** systematic sampling; not likely to be biased **11.** The sampling method is incorrect; the sampling method is systematic sampling. **13.** Resident of a city. *Sample answer:* Ask every tenth person in the phone book. **15.** Biased. *Sample answer:* The sample is likely to be biased because the apartment building might not allow pets.

7.2 Exercises (pp. 361–363) **1.** biased sample **3.** not biased **5.** Biased; the question favors an answer of yes; should our city budget more money for trash cans? **7.** Biased; the question favors an answer of relax at home; would you rather be home or at a mall? **9.** Students are less likely to answer that they spend less than 45 minutes on math problems in front of their math teacher. **11.** Students in the math club are more likely to spend more time on math problems. **13.** The sample is biased. *Sample answer:* Your friend should survey 50 people randomly chosen from the phone book. **15.** How many DVD's do you watch each weekend?; no; the question is straightforward. **17.** No; the team is more likely to favor a suggestion by their own team member. **19.** No; the question is biased and favors an answer towards choosing national parks. **21.** Your friend's; your friend's survey is of a larger sample and is a systematic sampling, while your sample is smaller and is a convenience sampling.

7.3 Exercises (pp. 366–369) **1.** true **3.** The mean could increase, decrease, or remain the same depending on the numbers added. **5.** 437; 502; 502 **7.** 51; 46; 23 and 46 **9.** 8.32; 7.6; 7.6 **11.** The numbers need to be written in numerical order; the median is 24.

13. mean decreases; median stays the same; mode stays the same **15.** mean decreases; median stays the same; mode stays the same **17.** mean decreases, median decreases, mode stays the same **21.** mean **23.** 226.630; 225.608. *Sample answer:* The median is the better measure, because the two larger values distort the mean and make it too large to represent the data well. **25. a.** \$101.67; \$82.50; \$25 and \$170 **25. b.** *Sample answer:* The mean gives the most useful information because the median is distorted by the number of lower values. **27.** 37.5in.; 34.5 in.; 30 in. **29.** The median; the median increases from 34.5 to 39, and the mode stays the same. **33. a.** 26.9; 26; 5, 11, and 34 years old **33. b.** 26 years old **33. c.** 25.9 years old **33. d.** The mean increases from 26.9 to 29.6, the median increases from 26 to 27, while the mode stays the same.

7.4 Exercises (pp. 375–377) **1.** upper extreme, lower extreme **3.** 57; 50, 62; 55, 61; 12; 6 **5.** 6.15; 1.9, 9.2; 4.6, 7.95; 7.3; 3.35 **9.** The mean increases from 82.3 to 87.6, the median increases form 87 to 89, the mode does not change, and the range decreases from 55 to 28. **11.** The mean increases from 76.9 to 82.4, the median increases from 76 to 78.5, the mode does not change, and the range decreases from 87 to 56. **13.** The mode is not affected by outliers as often. The mode is only affected when the outliers are the mode; the mode is affected by outliers less than other measures of central tendency. **15.** 82; 43, 117; 58, 93; 74; 35 **17.** 54.7; 52; 60; 72 **19.** \$70.63; \$61.50; no mode; \$142; \$170; the mean decreases from \$70.63 to \$56.43, the median decreases from \$61.50 to \$55, the mode does not change, and the range decreases from \$142 to \$67. **21.** 361.5; 361; 358; 10; the mean decreases from 361.5 to 360.6, the median and mode do not change, and the range increases to 23.

7.5 Exercises (pp. 382–384) **1.** frequency

3.

Interval	Tally	Frequency
16–18	IIII	4
19–21	~~IIII~~	5
22–24	IIII	4
25–27	~~IIII~~	5

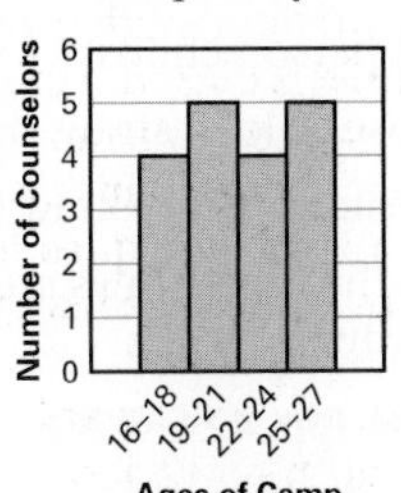

7. The intervals cannot overlap.

Interval	Tally	Frequency
100–149	IIII	4
150–199	~~IIII~~ I	6
200–249	II	2
250–299	IIII	4

9. Add up the bars from 1–15; there were 28 weeks when the dealership sold from 1 to 15 cars.

11.

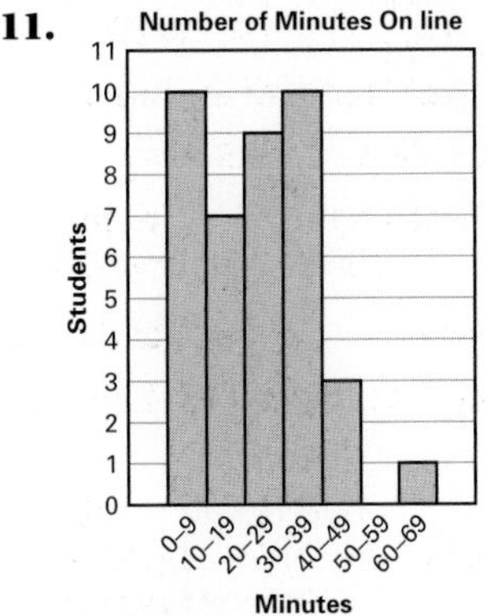

7.6 Exercises (pp. 389–391) **1.** degrees **3.** 195 hits **5.** 18° **7.** 162°

9. 24% is not equal to $\frac{1}{24}$; $0.24 \times 360° = 86.4°$.

13.

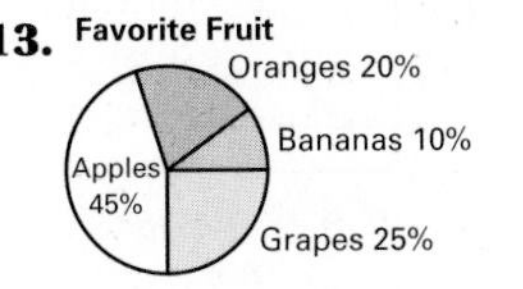

15.

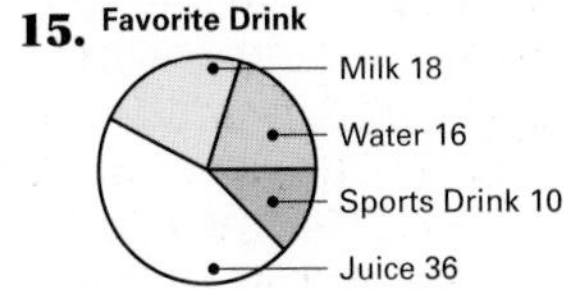

17. 10%

21.

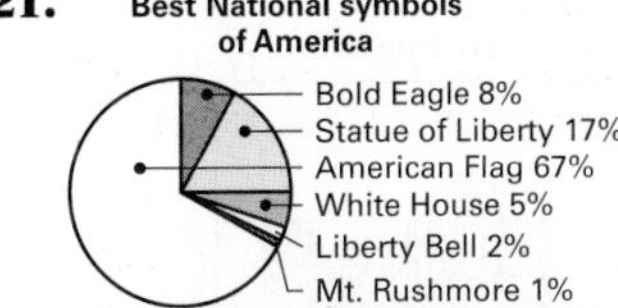

Sample answer: Most people think the American flag most symbolizes the United States.

7.7 Exercises (pp. 395–398) **1.** line graph **3.** Line graph; use a line graph to show change over time. **5.** Histogram, use a histogram to show frequency given for intervals.

9. no

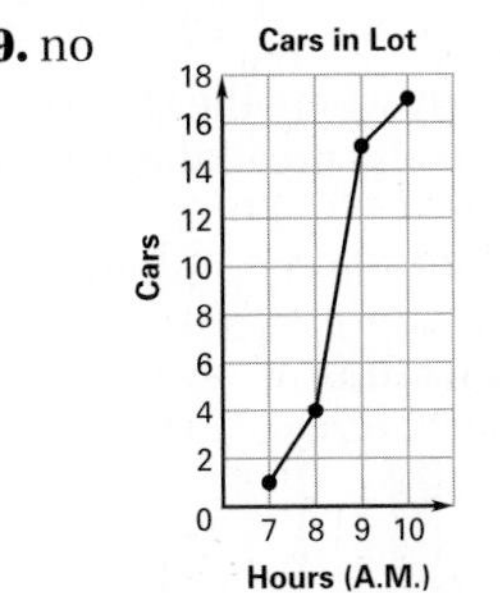

11. yes

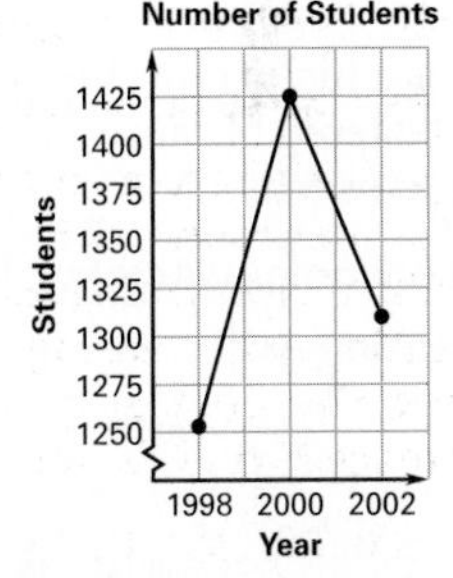

13. True; pasta and beef were chosen the same number of times. **15.** False; pasta was chosen 60 times and other was chosen 40 times. **17.** True; chicken was chosen 90 times and fish was chosen about 45 times. **19.** A circle graph represents data as part of a whole; use a line graph to represent change over time.

21.

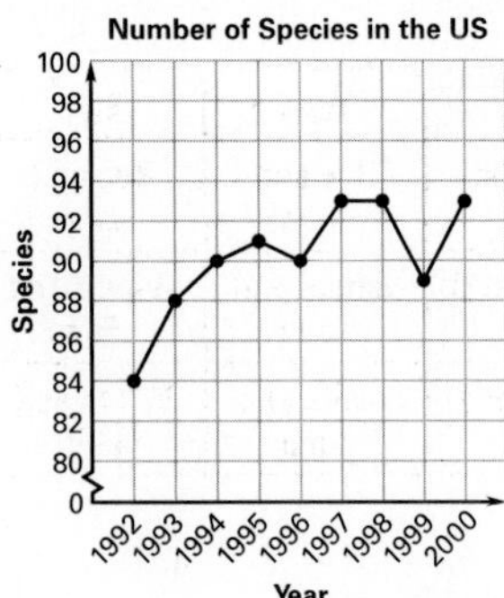

23. A line graph; choose a line graph because it shows data over time. *Sample answer:* The price of stamps increases over time.

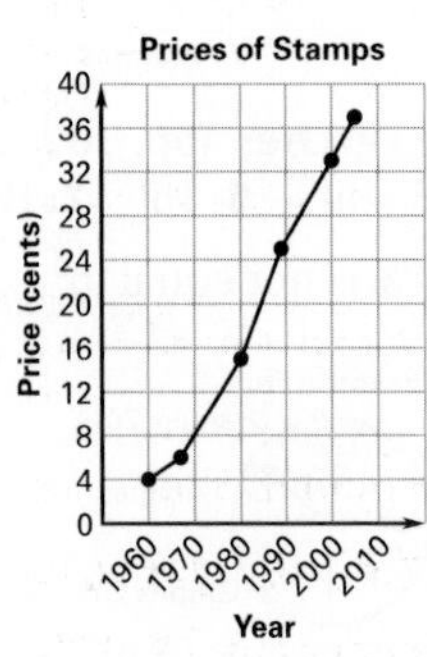

25. No. *Sample answer:* The sales increase the most between December and January.

27.

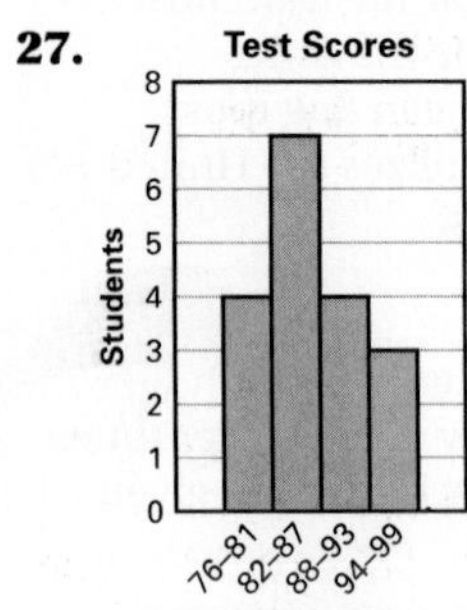

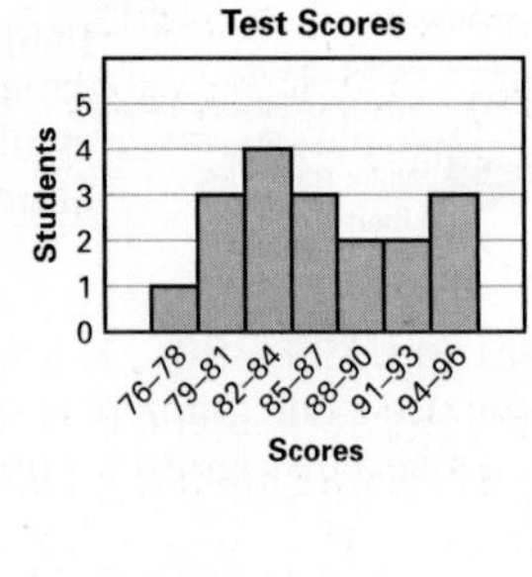

The first histogram shows more clearly where the scores are clustered because the small intervals spread the data out too much.

7.7 Technology Activity (p. 399)

1.

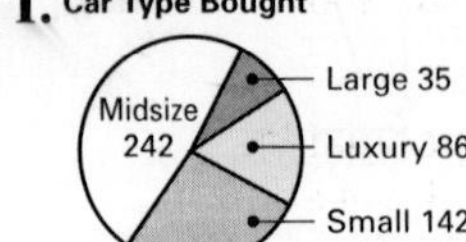

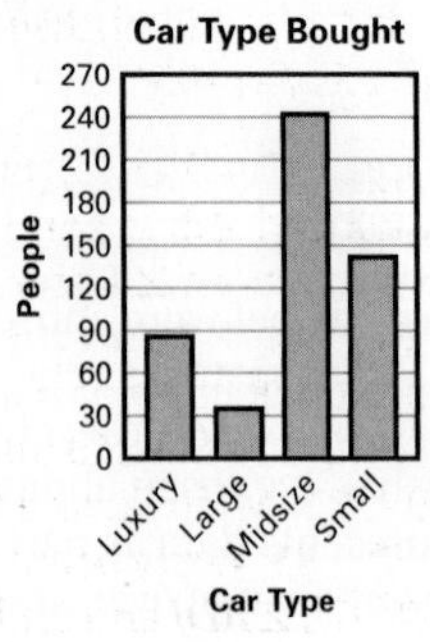

Chapter Review (pp. 403–406)

1. median **5.** The question is biased because is encourages people to say they prefer the park in the morning. **7.** The results are likely to be biased because students are more likely to tell their math teacher that their favorite subject is math. **9.** 29; 24; 6

11.

Interval	Frequency
20–29	3
30–39	5
40–49	5
50–59	4
60–69	2
70–79	1

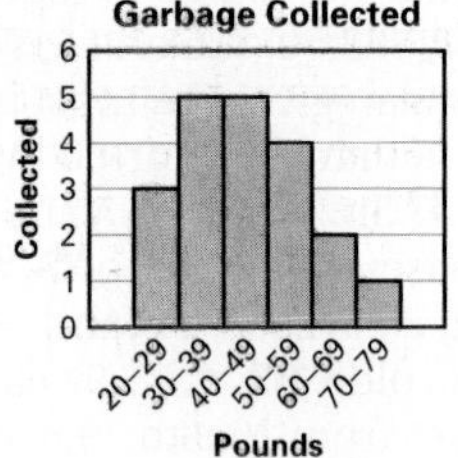

13.

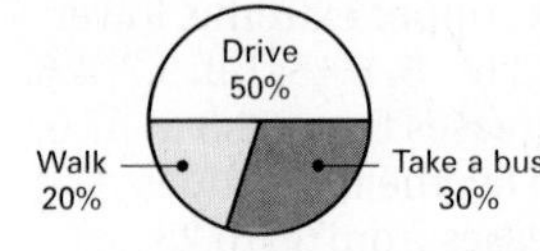

Chapter 8

8.1 Exercises (pp. 417–419)

1. probability **5.** A **7.** B **9.** $\frac{1}{2}$, 0.5, 50% **11.** $\frac{0}{20}$, 0, 0% **15.** The number of possible outcomes should be in the denominator, not the number of blue beans. The denominator is 14, not 9; $\frac{5}{14}$. **17.** $\frac{0}{6}$, 0; 0 **19.** $\frac{1}{2}$, 0.5; 100 **21.** $\frac{1}{2}$, 0.5; 100 **23.** Yes; the colors do not have to be in any particular order.

25. 16 cereal bars **27.** *Sample answer:* There are 16 bars in the box and there are 8 strawberry. Since 8 is half of 16, the probability of picking another flavor is less than 50%. **29.** $\frac{1}{2}$, 0.5, 50% **31.** 44 **33.** The probability that the first person chooses a short straw is $\frac{1}{7}$. If the first person chooses a long straw, the probability of the second person choosing a short straw is $\frac{1}{6}$. The probability increases as the long straws are removed and the short one is not drawn.

8.2 Exercises (pp. 424–426)

1. experimental probability **3.** $\frac{9}{20}$, 0.45 45% **5.** $\frac{3}{10}$, 0.3, 30% **7.** 20 times **9.** 124 times **11.** The number of sections labeled with prime numbers was found; you would expect to land on a prime number about 57 times. **13.** $\frac{17}{60}$ is slightly less than the theoretical probability of $\frac{1}{3}$. **15.** $\frac{19}{60}$ is slightly less than the theoretical probability of $\frac{1}{3}$. **17.** $\frac{11}{40}$, 0.275, or 27.5% **19. a.** $\frac{4}{5}$, 0.8, or 80% **19. b.** 2000 students

8.3 Exercises (pp. 430–432) **1.** complementary
3. Disjoint; the events cannot occur at the same time.
5. Overlapping; the events can occur at the same time, 4 and 6 are both multiples of 2 and greater than 3.
7. 0.6 **9.** 44.3% **11.** $\frac{21}{50}$ **15.** 36% **17.** 0.49 **19.** $\frac{1}{4}$
21. *Sample answer:* To be complementary, the events cannot overlap; the events are overlapping because the numbers 1 and 3 are in both sets. **23.** = **25.** < **27.** <
29. Never; if two events are overlapping, then they share an outcome. Disjoint events never share outcomes.
31. yes **33.** 60% **37.** 37% **39.** 89%

8.4 Exercises (pp. 437–439) **1.** outcomes

3. **5.**

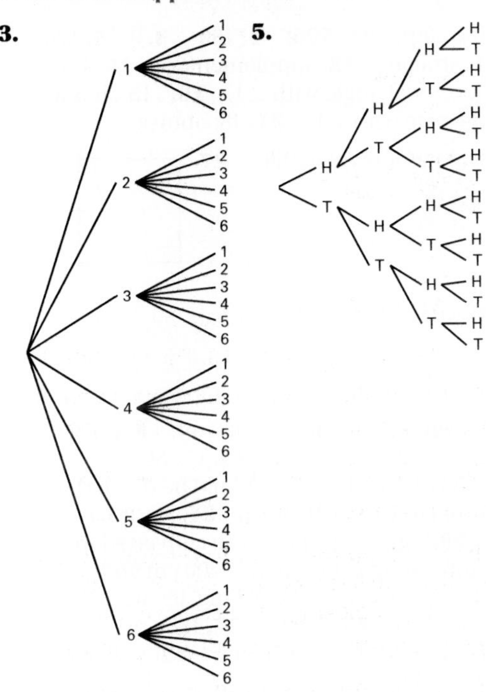

9. blue/green, blue/black, black/blue, black/green, gray/blue, gray/green, gray/black

11.

	Green	Red	Blue
Green	Green and Green	Green and Red	Green and Blue
Red	Red and Green	Red and Red	Red and Blue
Blue	Blue and Green	Blue and Red	Blue and Blue

15. $\frac{1}{4}$ **17.** $\frac{1}{6}$ **19.** low black, low orange, low lime, low purple, high black, high orange, high lime, high purple

21. $\frac{1}{4}$

23. *Sample:*

	Turkey	Ham	Tuna	Egg
Rye	Rye and Turkey	Rye and Ham	Rye and Tuna	Rye and Egg
Wheat	Wheat and Turkey	Wheat and Ham	Wheat and Tuna	Wheat and Egg
White	White and Turkey	White and Ham	White and Tuna	White and Egg

25. $\frac{1}{4}$

27.

29. about 60 events

8.5 Exercises (pp. 444–446) **1.** compound
5. dependent **7.** 0.25 **9.** 0.15 **11.** $\frac{1}{20}$ **13.** 0.4 **15.** $\frac{4}{9}$
17. dependent **19.** $\frac{14}{49}$ **21.** 10.12% **23.** 28.06%

Chapter Review (pp. 450–452) **1.** outcomes
3. probability **7.** $\frac{5}{8}$, 0.625, 62.5% **9.** $\frac{11}{50}$ **11.** 9%
13. 94% **15.** $\frac{7}{8}$

Chapter 9

9.1 Exercise (pp. 465–467) **1.** D **3.** C **7.** acute
9. obtuse **11.** supplementary; 145° + 35° = 180°
13. neither; 47° + 41° = 88° **15.** 107°; 17° **17.** 90°; none
19. 18°; none **21.** 177°; 87° **23.** The sum of the angles should be 90°; $m\angle A + m\angle B = 90$, $m\angle A + 56 = 90°$, $m\angle A = 34°$. **25.** 30° **27.** 60° **29.** Always; only measures of two acute angles will add up to 90°.
31. Always; a right angle has measure 90°, so the supplement will also be 90°. **33.** 15°, 30 °, 45°
35. 180° − x° **37.** x° **39.** obtuse **41.** 180° **45.** 45°
47. $\angle LMK$ and $\angle KMN$; 105°

9.2 Exercises (pp.470–472) **1.** perpendicular
3. ∠1 and ∠2; ∠2 and ∠3; ∠3 and ∠4; ∠4 and ∠1
5. 33° **7.** *Sample answer:* ∠4 and ∠7, ∠5 and ∠6
9. 120° **11.** 120° **15.** ∠1 and ∠3 are vertical angles and are congruent, not supplementary; $m\angle 3 = 38°$.
17. ∠1 and ∠2; ∠2 and ∠3; ∠3 and ∠4; ∠4 and ∠1
19. 96°; 84°; 84° **23.** Main St. and Elm St. **25.** 99°
27. 123° **29.** 99° **31.** Every beam is perpendicular to every post. **33.** 37°; $\angle ADJ$ and $\angle LDF$ are complementary.

9.3 Exercises (pp. 477–479) **1.** obtuse **3.** 96, obtuse **5.** 27, obtuse **7.** 45, right **11.** The triangle contains a right angle; right scalene triangle. **13.** acute **15.** obtuse **17.** right **19.** equilateral **21.** isosceles **23.** scalene

25. *Sample:*

27. *Sample:*

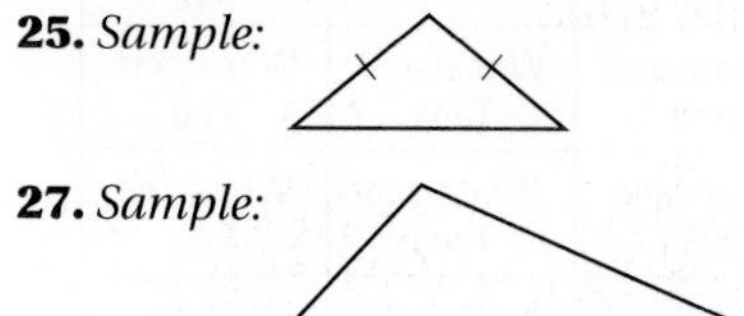

31. 68, 112 **33.** 115.2, 64.8 **35.** $180° - 90° - 45° = x$ **39.** Sometimes; if two sides are congruent, one of the angles of the triangle may or may not measure 90°. **41.** Always; an acute triangle has all angles less than 90° and an equilateral triangle has three angles which measure less than 90°. **43.** 60, 120; right

9.4 Exercises (pp. 485–487) **1.** square **3.** parallelogram **5.** rhombus **7.** square **9.** A rhombus does not have to have 4 right angles; all rhombuses are not necessarily squares.

11. parallelogram;

15. trapezoid;

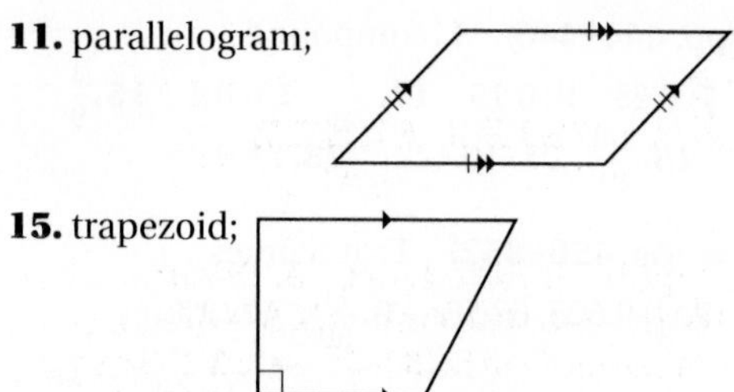

17. 77 **19.** 94 **21.** 99 **23.** C **25.** B **27.** hexagon; regular **29.** Pentagon; not regular, not all of the angles and sides are congruent. **31.** True; a square has 4 right angles. **33.** False; a trapezoid has only one pair of parallel sides. **35.** 8 **37.** 6 **39.** Yes, a square always has four right angles; yes, a square always has four congruent sides; yes, a square always has opposite sides parallel; yes, a square always has four sides.

9.4 Technology Activity (p. 488)

1. **3.**

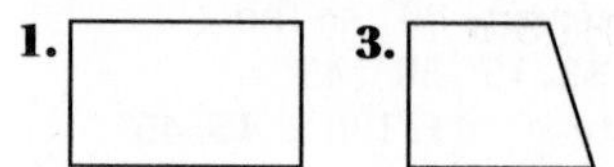

9.5 Exercises (pp. 492–494) **1.** similar **3.** $\angle U$ **5.** $\overline{UW}$ **7.** $\overline{KL}$ and $\overline{QR}$, $\overline{LM}$ and $\overline{RS}$, $\overline{MN}$ and $\overline{ST}$, $\overline{NK}$ and $\overline{TQ}$; $\angle K$ and $\angle Q$, $\angle L$ and $\angle R$, $\angle M$ and $\angle S$, $\angle N$ and $\angle T$; $KL = QR = NM = 3$ m; $KN = QT = RS = 4$ m **11.** The ratio of the lengths is not the same as the ratio of the widths; Rectangle *ABCD* and Rectangle *PQRS* are not similar.

13. similar; $\frac{2}{1}$ **15.** not similar **17.** False; if one rectangle has dimensions 2 by 3 and another has dimensions 1 by 4, the perimeters would be the same, but the rectangles would not be congruent. **19.** $\overline{AB}$ and $\overline{DE}$, $\overline{BC}$ and $\overline{EF}$, $\overline{AC}$ and $\overline{DF}$ **21.** $\frac{2}{3}$ **23.** No; the ratio of the lengths is not the same as the ratio of the widths, $\frac{6}{1.4} = \frac{60}{14} = 4\frac{2}{7}$ and $\frac{4}{0.9} = \frac{40}{9} = 4\frac{4}{9}$.

9.6 Exercises (pp. 497–499) **1.** proportion **3.** 2 cm **5.** 30 in. **7.** The proportion was not set up using corresponding parts; $\frac{20}{x} = \frac{12}{15}$, $12x = 300$, $x = 25$ meters. **9.** 54 cm^2 **13.** 66 yd, $36\frac{2}{3}$ yd **15.**

5 ft
2 ft
x ft
5 ft

17. $\frac{x}{5\text{ ft}} = \frac{5\text{ ft}}{2\text{ ft}}$ **21.** Write the proportion $\frac{h}{z} = \frac{y}{x}$. This can be solved for z, $z = \frac{hx}{y}$.

Chapter Review (pp. 503–506) **1.** 180° **3.** 0 **5.** 180° **9.** obtuse **11.** straight **13.** supplementary **15.** 106° **17.** 115°; it is a vertical angle with $\angle 1$. **19.** 115°; it is a corresponding angle with $\angle 1$. **21.** 48; obtuse

25. parallelogram; not regular; 360° **27.**

29. not similar **31.** $13\frac{1}{3}$ ft; 12 ft

Chapter 10

10.1 Exercises (pp. 517–519) **1.** 1000 mL **3.** 0.072 **5.** 0.89 **7.** 1250 **9.** 2.8 **11.** 1.54 **13.** 45,250 **15.** 2,420,000 **17.** 1.25 **19.** Fifty should be divided by 1000, not multiplied; 50 mg = 0.05 g. **21.** = **23.** > **25.** = **27.** < **29.** The units need to be converted to the same thing before comparing; 20 m = 200 cm and 200 > 115, so 20 m > 115 cm. **31.** 9.5 mg, 69 mg, 0.04 kg, 45 g, 60 g **33.** 41 mm **35.** 2500 g **37.** 1550 mL **39.** 6.8 cm; 2.8 cm^2 **41.** 4 cm; 0.75 cm^2 **43.** 175 cm **45.** 0.031 g **47.** 985 mL

10.2 Exercises (pp. 522–525) **1.** yd; oz **3.** 30 **5.** $2\frac{11}{12}$ **7.** 74 **9.** 2500 **11.** 480 **13.** You should multiply 30 ft by $\frac{12\text{ in.}}{1\text{ ft}}$; 360 in. **15.** 5; 1 **17.** 1; 3 **19.** 4; 2640 **21.** 12 c 3 fl oz **23.** 27 lb 12 oz **25.** 5 ft 6 in. **27.** = **29.** > **31.** > **33.** $\frac{1}{4}$ lb, 7 oz, 0.5 lb, $\frac{5}{8}$ lb, $\frac{32}{3}$ oz **35.** $\frac{x}{63{,}360}$ **37.** 1 c = 8 fl oz **39.** $3\text{ c} \times \frac{8\text{ fl oz}}{1\text{ c}}$ **41.** 2 c 4 fl oz

47. Khafre: 157 yd or 471 ft; Menkaure: $72\frac{13}{18}$ yd or $218\frac{1}{6}$ ft; Khufu: 162 yd or 486 ft **49.** $89\frac{5}{18}$ yd; $267\frac{15}{18}$ ft **51.** Yes. *Sample answer:* The heights are 471 feet, $218\frac{1}{6}$ feet, and 486 feet, while the bases are 707 feet, 356 feet, and 762 feet, respectively.

10.3 Exercises (pp. 529–531) **1.** m; L **3.** 105 **5.** 5 **7.** 1893 **9.** 21 **11.** 198 **13.** 242 **15.** 185 km should be multiplied by $\frac{1\text{ mi}}{1.609\text{ km}}$; about 115 mi. **19.** < **21.** > **23.** < **25.** < **27.** 2596 **29.** 10 **31.** 8 **33.** 185,035

35. 2 **37.** 3178 g **39.** about 59 in. **43.** 34.29 m, 22.86 m; 783.87 m^2 **45. a.** U.S. *Sample answer:* 6 U.S. dollars is equivalent to approximately 7 Canadian dollars.
45. b. 6000 US Dollars

10.4 Exercises (pp. 536–538)

1. 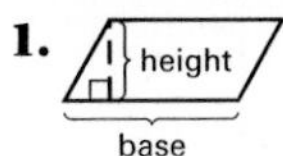

3. 45 mm^2 **5.** 20 m^2 **7.** 130 cm^2 **9.** Use the height, 4, rather than the side length of 5; $10 \times 4 = 40$ cm^2.
11. 13 ft **13.** 18 in. **15.** 9:1 **21.** 432.4 $in.^2$ **23.** 11 in.
27. The new area is $\frac{1}{16}$ of the original area. $\frac{24.5}{4} \times \frac{10}{4} = \frac{245}{16}$.

10.5 Exercises (pp. 544–546)

1. 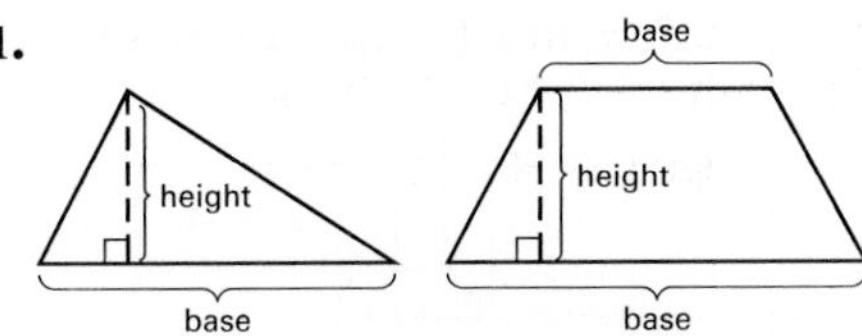

3. 57 ft^2 **5.** 121 $in.^2$ **7.** 6 km **9.** $9\frac{1}{3}$ mi **11.** 48 $in.^2$
13. The formula for area is incorrect; $A = \frac{1}{2}(b_1 + b_2)h = \frac{1}{2}(8 + 14) \cdot 5 = 55$ ft^2. **15.** 25.4 m **19.** $2x$ **21.** $5.5x$
23. $24x$ **25.** 81.5 ft^2 **27.** 472.5 cm^2 **29.** 306 $in.^2$
31. 17 m **33. a.** 1260 ft^2 **33. b.** 38 bundles
35. They all have the same base and height.

10.6 Exercises (pp. 551–553)

1. 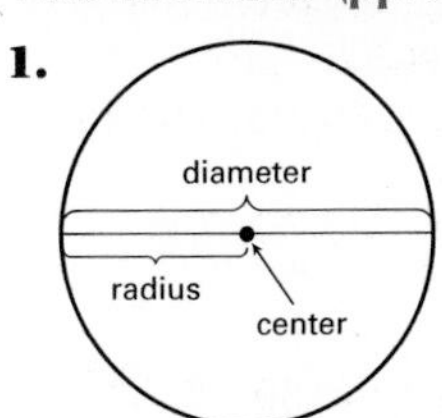

3. 28.26 in. **5.** 20.41 cm **7.** 88 cm **9.** 18π mm
11. 49π in. **15.** 38 m; 19 m **17.** 13.5 km; 6.75 km
19. 4.5 ft; 2.25 ft **21.** $C = 16\pi$ **23.** about 14 cm
25. 423.9 m; 27 min **29.** 22 ft; 8 rotations; $176 \div 22 = 8$

10.6 Technology Activity (p. 554)

1. 38 ft **3.** 1071 cm **5.** 94 km **7.** 5 m **9.** 15,978 km

10.7 Exercises (pp. 557–559)

1. radius; diameter
3. 132.67 $in.^2$ **5.** 154 $in.^2$ **7.** 551.27 mm^2 **9.** The radius is 2, not 4; $A = 3.14(2^2) = 12.56$ $in.^2$ **11.** 16π $in.^2$
13. 153.76π cm^2 **15.** 82.81π yd^2 **17.** 19.625 mm^2
19. 314 ft^2 **21.** 113.04 cm^2 **25.** 166,106 mm^2
27. $A = 576\pi$

Chapter Review (pp. 563–566)

1. milligrams
3. 5280 **5.** height **9.** 802,000 **11.** 18,000 **13.** 4200
15. 4.25 **17.** 4 qt **19.** 13 **21.** 10 **23.** 9 **25.** 63 $in.^2$
27. 120 ft^2 **29.** $4h$ $in.^2$ **31.** 28 ft^2 **33.** 132 cm
35. 106.76 m **37.** 154 km^2 **39.** 907.46 $in.^2$ **41.** 10.24π ft^2

Chapter 11

11.1 Exercises (pp. 577–579)

1. sphere **3.** sphere
5. cone **7.** The bases of the figure are triangles, not rectangles; it is a triangular prism.

9., **13.** 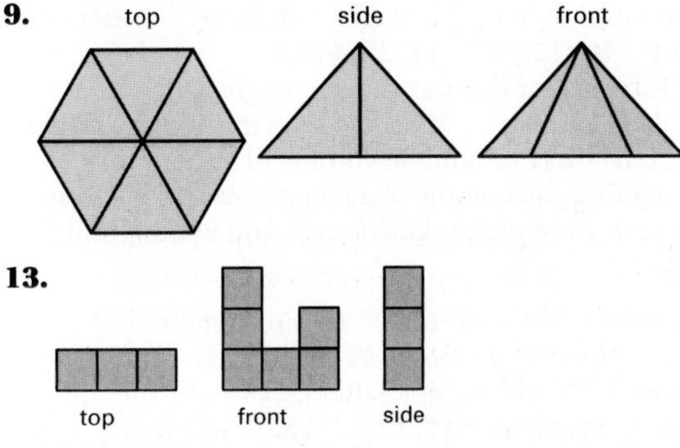

15. False. *Sample answer:* A pyramid has only one base that is a polygon. **17.** true **19.** rectangular prism

21. 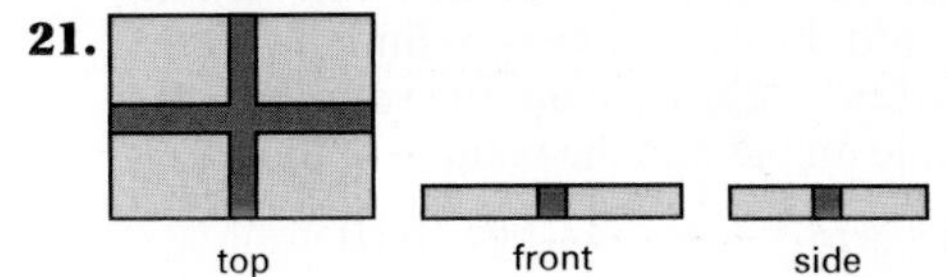

11.2 Exercises (pp. 583–586)

1. net **3.** 252 m^2
5. 100 yd^2 **7.** 180 $in.^2$ **9.** 1050 cm^2 **13.** $S = 6y + 1$
15. 97.8 mm^2 **17.** 60 cm^2 **21.** 13.5 ft^2 **23.** 3.375 mm^2
25. 112 $in.^2$ **27.** $4.90 **29.** Less; each face of the photo cube has an area of 9 square inches. There are 6 faces, so its total surface area is 54 square inches, which is less than the 80 square inches of the flat photograph.
33. $2\ell w = 2B$ and $2\ell h + 2wh = (2\ell + 2w)h = Ph$, so $2\ell w + 2\ell h + 2wh = 2B + Ph$ **35.** 52.2 ft^2; subtract the area of the three faces from 376.4 to get the total area of the two triangle bases. Divide by 2 to find the area of one triangle base.

11.3 Exercises (pp. 591–593)

1. circles, rectangle

3. 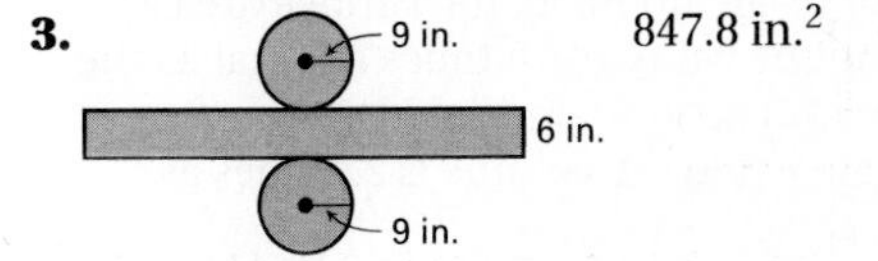

847.8 $in.^2$

5. 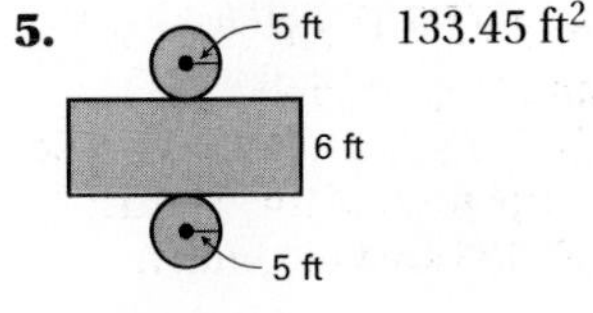

133.45 ft^2

7. 1356.5 cm^2 **9.** about 60.1 $in.^2$ **11.** The diameter was used instead of the radius; $S \approx 2(3.14)(2.5)^2 + 2(3.14)(2.5)(10) = 39.25 + 157 \approx 196$ ft^2. **13.** 169.56 cm^2; 9 times as large **15.** 1526.04 cm^2; 81 times as large

17. 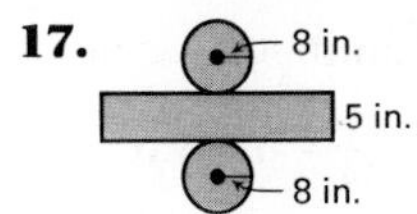

19. 52π cm^2 **21.** *Sample answer:* About 20 cm^2; about 15 cm^2; the surface area of the larger battery is about 5 square centimeters greater than the surface area of the smaller battery.

11.4 Exercises (pp. 598–600) **1.** Find the area of the base and multiply it by the height. **3.** 60 m^3 **5.** 200 cm^3 **7.** 77 mm^3 **9.** 412.5 ft^3 **11.** 2574 mm^3
13. The formula for the area of a rectangle is $B = \ell w$, (12)(5)(3), $V = 180$ m^3. **15.** 5 ft **17.** 8 mm **21.** volume **23.** 5832 cm^3 **27.** To find the volume of a triangular prism, first find the volume of a rectangular prism with a rectangular base of the same length and width, then divide by 2; $V = 72$ in.^{3}

11.5 Exercises (pp. 603–605) **1.** base, height **3.** 9.42 in.^{3} **5.** 1692.46 mm^3 **7.** 113.04 in.^{3} **9.** The radius is 6 inches, not 3 inches; $V \approx (3.14)(6^2)(8) \approx 904.32$ in.^{3} **13.** 25 in. **17.** $139x$ **19.** 125.6 mm^3 **21.** 123.6375 mm^3 **23.** 29,842.54 in.^{3}; find the volume of the rectangular prism on the bottom and find the volume of the lid using the formula for a cylinder and dividing it in half. Then add the two volumes to find the total volume of the chest. **25.** 8 glasses; the volume of the glass is 9.42 cubic inches and the volume of the pan is 75 cubic inches, $\frac{75}{9.42} = 7.96$. **27.** 863,186 ft^3

29. $\frac{100.48}{128}, \frac{157}{200}, \frac{226.08}{288}$; they are all equal.

11.5 Technology Activity (p. 606)

1.

Length	Width	Height	Surface area	Volume
20	16	8	1216	2560
40	32	16	4864	20,480

3.

	A	B	C	D
1	Radius	Height	Surface area	Volume
2			=2*PI()•A2^2+2*PI()*A2*B2	=PI()*A2^2*B2

When the dimensions are doubled, the surface area is 4 times as great and the volume is 8 times as great as the original. When the dimensions are tripled, the surface area is 9 times as great and the volume is 27 times as great as the original.

Chapter Review (pp. 610–612) **1.** surface area **3.** net

5. pyramid

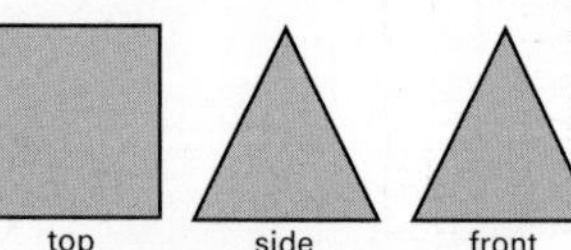

7. rectangular solid

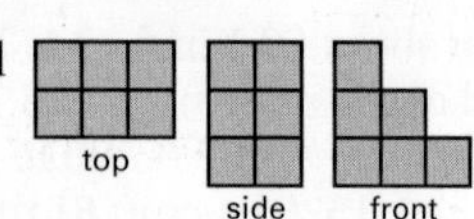

9. 96 mm^2 **11.** $(42 + 19h)$ in.^{2} **13.** 45 mm^3 **15.** 67.5 yd^3 **17.** 183.69 m^3

Chapter 12

12.1 Exercise (pp. 626–629) **1.** -3 **3.** (2, 2) **5.** (3, 3) **7.** (4, -3) **9.** (0, 2)

11. 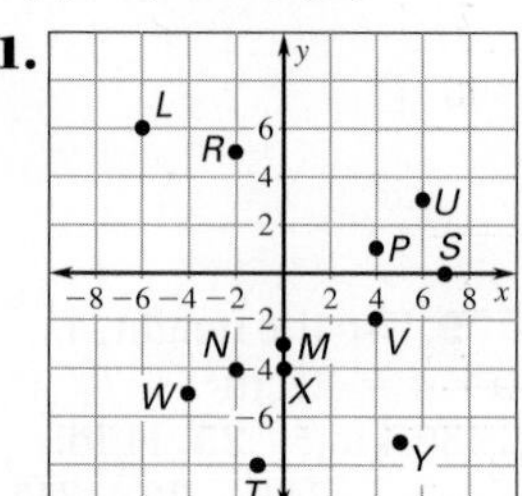 quadrant II

13. quadrant III

27. 4 units, 1 unit, 4 square units

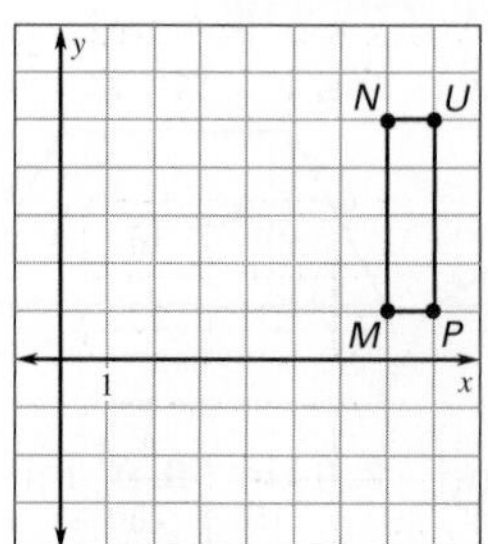

29. 10 units, 3 units, 30 square units

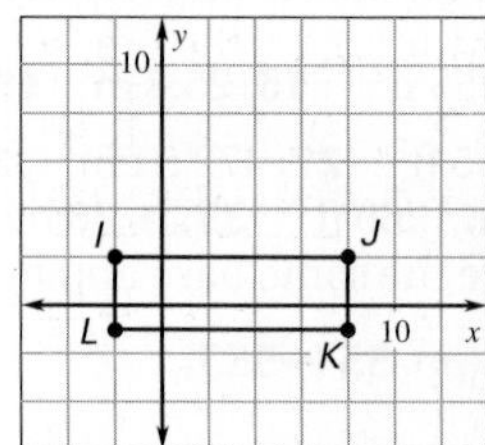

33. As x increases, y tends to decrease.

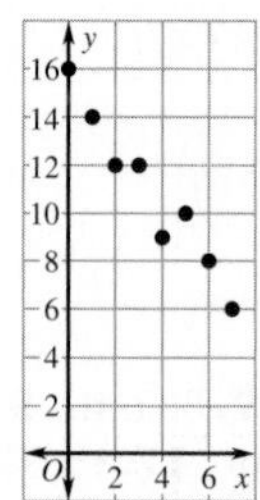

35. x is positive; y is negative. **37.** The x-coordinate is zero, and the y-coordinate is any number.
39. Both are negative. **41.** (-2, 4) **43.** no
47. a. (-15, -8); **b.** 22 mi **51.** *Sample answer:* 21 mi/gal

12.2 Exercises (pp. 632-634) **1.** input; output **5.** -2 **7.** 7 **9.** -11 **11.** -5
13. range 9, 10, 11, 12, 13

Input x	-2	-1	0	1	2
Output y	9	10	11	12	13

15. range 40, 20, 0, -20, -40

Input x	-2	-1	0	1	2
Output y	40	20	0	-20	-40

21. The input and output values in the table were swapped;

Input x	0	1	2	3
Output y	-2	-1	0	1

23. The rule must work for all x- and y-pairs, not just the first pair; $y = 3x$. **25.** $y = 5x$ **27.** $y = x - 7$
29. $q = 3p + 1$

31.

Input a	10	12	14	16
Output j	7	9	11	13

33.

Input h	1	2	3	4
Output c	440	880	1320	1760

35. As the depth increases, the pressure increases.

Input d	0	20	40	60	80	100
Output p	2112	3392	4672	5952	7232	8512

12.3 Exercises (pp. 637–640) **1.** linear function

3.

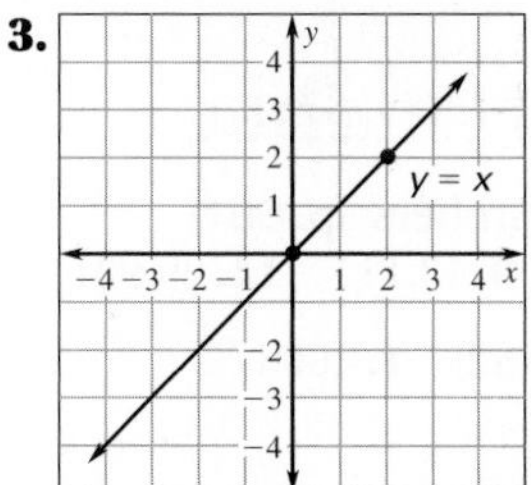

15.

Input x	-2	0	2
Output y	-1	0	1

$y = \frac{1}{2}x$

17. *Sample answer:* If the x- and y-coordinates were reversed, the function would be correct; $y = x + 3$.

19. $y = 3x$

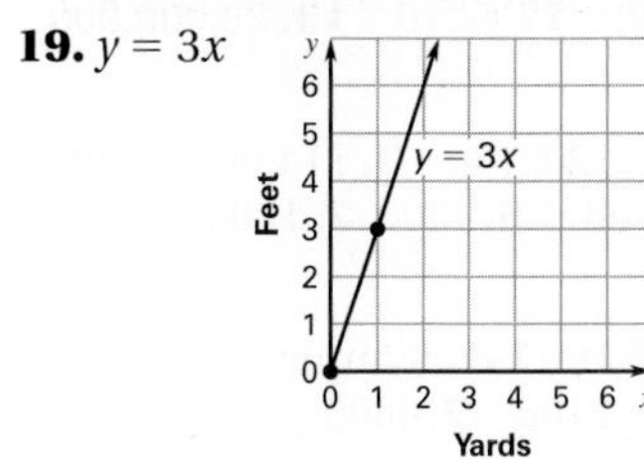

25. (1, 2)

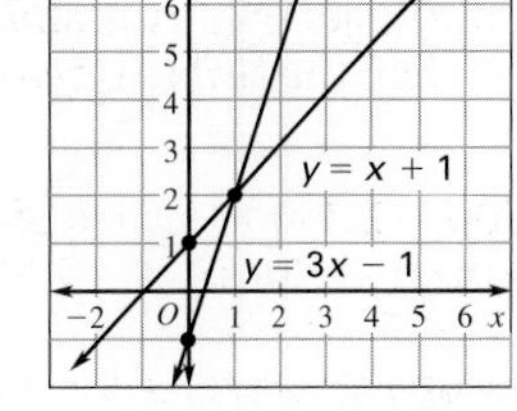

27. (1, 1.5), (2, 3), (5, 7.5), (10, 15)

29. $y = 5x$

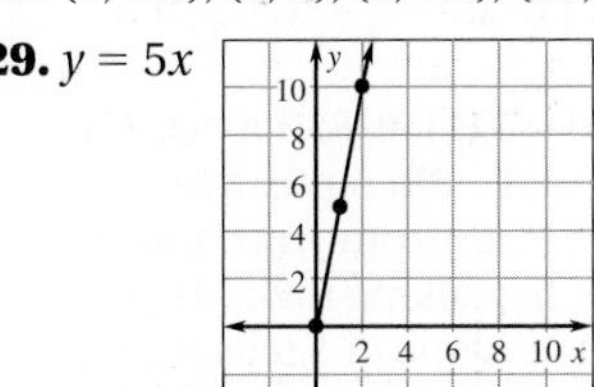

31. a.

Degrees Celsius x	-20	-10	0	10	20
Degrees Fahrenheit y	-4	14	32	50	68

b.

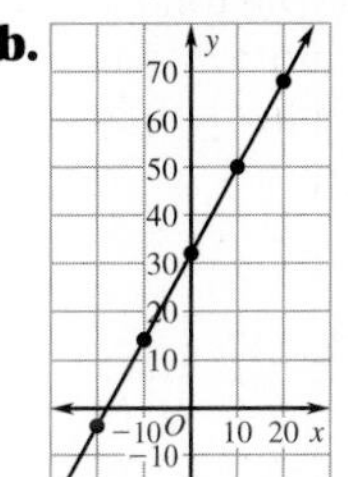

c. 5°C; the results are the same or nearly the same.

37. force = mass • acceleration

12.3 Technology Activity (p. 641)

1. 0.8; 4.2 **3.** 1; 7 **5.** -0.6; -1.6 **7.** $(-1, 3)$

12.4 Exercises (pp. 644–647) **1.** rise; run **3.** $\frac{2}{3}$

5. -1 **7.** 0 **9.** 1

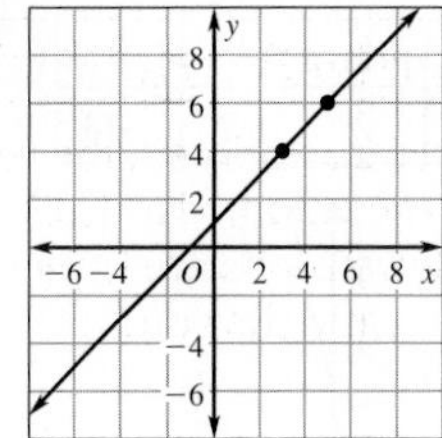

11. $-\frac{1}{4}$

15. The negative rise was not recorded; $-\frac{4}{3}$.

17.

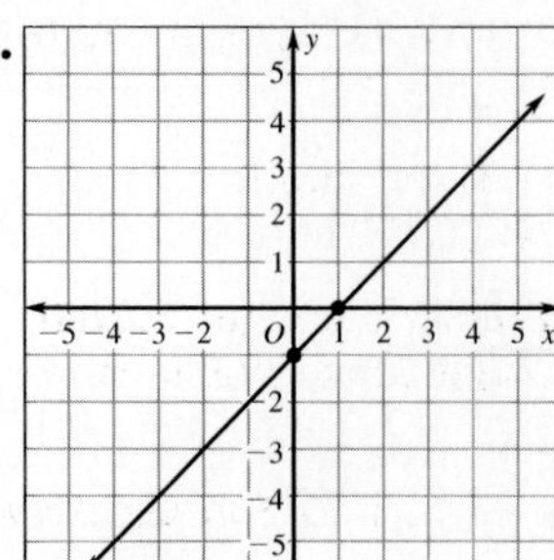

21.

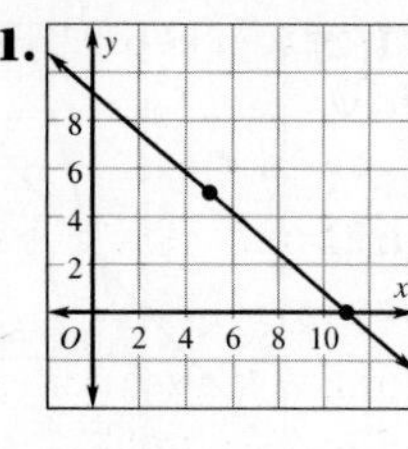

23. = **25.** > **27.** −2 **29.** 10 **31.** Joe: 8; Rob: 6 **33.** Joe; \$2 per hour **37.** *O* and *A* **39.** A positive slope means you were walking away from your house; a negative slope means you were walking towards your house. **41.** 4; 8; 12; 16 **43.** The slope of 4 tells that the perimeter of a square is four times the length of the side.

Chapter Review (pp. 651–654) **1.** *x*-coordinate **3.** range **5.** slope **7.** (−1, 0) **9.** (2, 1) **11.** (−3, 2)

13–16.

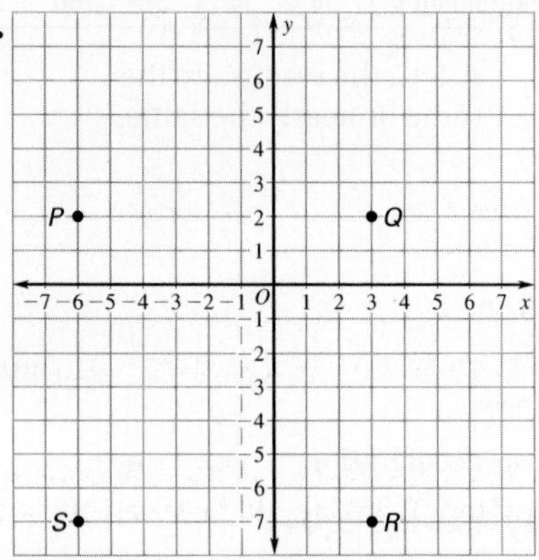

13. quadrant II **15.** quadrant IV **17.** 9 units; 9 units; 81 square units **19.** 5 **21.** −16 **23.** range −16, −7, 2, 11, 20

Input *x*	−2	−1	0	1	2
Output *y*	20	11	2	−7	−16

25. $y = -4x$ **29.**

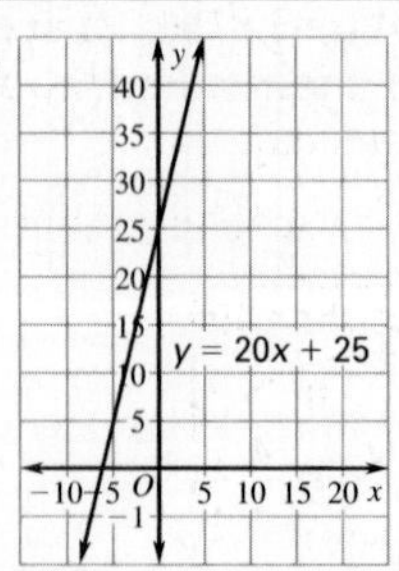

33.

Input *x*	−1	0	1	2
Output *y*	−3	0	3	6

35. $y = 20x + 25$

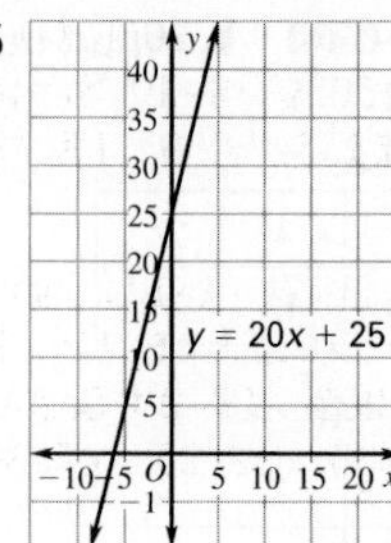

37. 45 mi/h

39. $\frac{1}{2}$

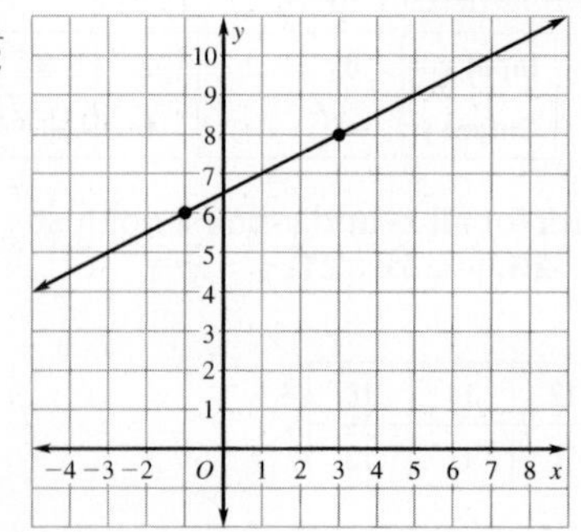

41.

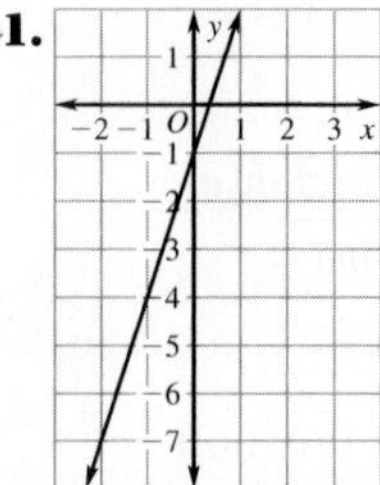

Standards Review Handbook

Adding and Subtracting Whole Numbers (p. 661) **1.** 102 **3.** 285 **5.** 4316 **7.** 1918 **9.** 13,111 **11.** 29,921

Multiplying Whole Numbers (p. 662) **1.** 4806 **3.** 320,016 **5.** 16,700 **7.** 970,000

Powers and Exponents (p. 663) **1.** 10^3 **3.** 9^6 **5.** 17^5 **7.** 125 **9.** 1 **11.** 169 **13.** 0 **15.** 64 **17.** 4096 **19.** 49 **21.** 1728 **23.** 16,384

Dividing Whole Numbers (p. 664) **1.** 142 **3.** 54 **5.** 405 **7.** 58 **9.** 15.5 **11.** 3.25

Rounding Whole Numbers (p. 665) **1.** 340 **3.** 28,000 **5.** 9000 **7.** 300,000 **9.** 58,900 **11.** 5210 **13.** 28,000,000 **15.** 1,500,000

Estimating Sums (p. 666) **1.** 120; 160 **3.** \$14.00; \$17.00 **5–9.** Sample estimates are given. **5.** 120 **7.** 1200 **9.** 3300

Estimating Differences (p. 667) **1–7.** Sample estimates are given. **1.** 640 **3.** 410 **5.** 2100 **7.** 6800

Estimating Products (p. 668) **1.** 200; 600 **3.** 1000; 1800 **5.** 6000; 12,000 **7.** 2000; 6000 **9–17.** Sample estimates are given. **9.** 100,000 **11.** 540,000 **13.** 400,000 **15.** 140,000 **17.** 200,000

Estimating Quotients (p. 669) **1–11.** Sample estimates are given. **1.** 32; 35 **3.** 250; 265 **5.** 17; 26 **7.** 40; 60 **9.** 2400; 3000 **11.** 850; 1200 **13–23.** Sample estimates are given. **13.** 48 **15.** 600 **17.** 20 **19.** 30 **21.** 5000 **23.** 600

Using Addition and Subtraction (p. 670) **1.** \$12 **3.** 44 people **5.** \$44

Using Multiplication and Division (p. 671) **1.** 36 pencils **3.** 4 muffins **5.** 13 cards

Modeling Fractions (p. 672) **1.** $\frac{7}{8}$ **3.** $\frac{2}{7}$ **5.** $\frac{5}{8}$ **7.** $1\frac{59}{100}$; 1.59

Graphing Decimals and Fractions (p. 673)
1. 8.5 **3.** 6.34

5.
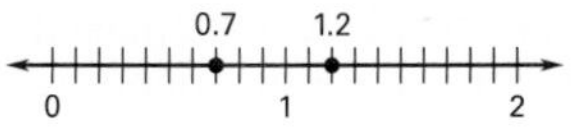

11.
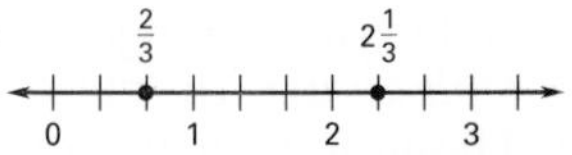

Rounding Decimals (p. 674)

1.
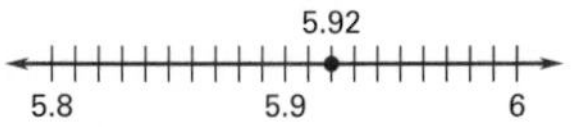

5.9

3.
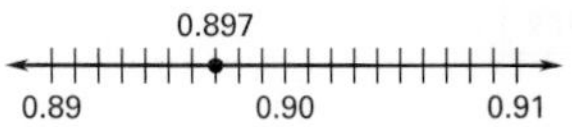

0.90

5. 8 **7.** 28 **9.** 9.25 **11.** 0.580 **13.** 4.380 **15.** 6.61

Comparing Decimals (p. 675) **1.** < **3.** > **5.** > **7.** < **9.** < **11.** > **13.** < **15.** > **17.** =

Properties of Addition (p. 676) **1.** associative property of addition **3.** (5 + 15) + 21, associative property; 20 + 21, addition; 41, addition **5.** (61 + 7) + 13, commutative property; 61 + (7 + 13), associative property; 61 + 20, addition; 81, addition **7.** 16 + 4 + 19, commutative property; 20 + 19, addition; 39, addition

Properties of Multiplication (p. 677) **1.** commutative property of multiplication **3.** 9 × (15 × 2), associative property; 9 × 30, multiplication; 270, multiplication **5.** 41 × 2 × 5, commutative property; 41 × 10, multiplication; 410, multiplication **7.** 47 × 10 × 10, commutative property; 47 × 100, multiplication; 4700, multiplication

Points in a Coordinate Plane (p. 678) **1.** (0, 3) **3.** (0, 0) **5.** (3, 3)

Units of Time (p. 679) **1.** 2 **3.** 75 **5.** 3; 3 **7.** 3 h 21 min **9.** 7 h 8 min **11.** 4 h 30 min

Units of Measure (p. 680) **1.** mile, kilometer **3.** ton, kilogram **5.** yard, meter **7.** fluid ounce, milliliter **9.** inch, centimeter

Points and Lines (p. 683) **1.** *B* **3.** *A* **5.** *Sample answer:* $\overrightarrow{SR}$, $\overrightarrow{ST}$ **7.** *Sample answer:* $\overline{US}$

Perimeter Concepts (p. 684) **1.** 12 cm **3.** 20 m

5.
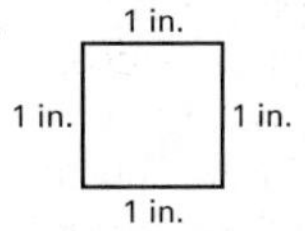

4 in.

7.
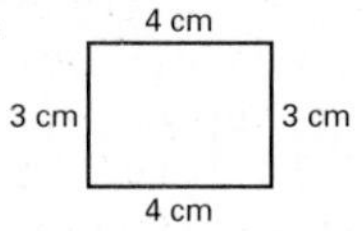

14 cm

Area Concepts (p. 685) **1.** 24 square units **3.** 16 square units **5.** 6 square units **7.** 21 square units

Reading and Making Line Plots (p. 686)

1.
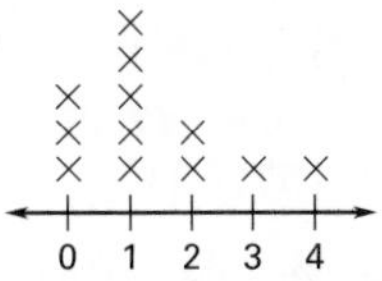

3. 18 people **5.** 6 people

Reading and Making Bar Graphs (p. 687) **1.** 5 students **3.** plain and onions

Reading Line Graphs (p. 688) **1.** 8 in. **3.** Tuesday and Sunday **5.** increase **7.** Friday **9.** between Tuesday and Wednesday

Problem Solving Strategies (p. 690) **1.** "The deli makes 5 types of sandwiches" is irrelevant; 11 ways. **3.** not enough information; how many pounds of cheese you bought **5.** 225 cans **7.** not enough information; how many words are on each page **9.** "You have saved \$1200 to buy a new computer" is irrelevant; find the sum of \$1020 and \$51, and subtract \$150. Then divide the result by 3. **11.** not enough information; the amount of feed in the bag at the start of the day

Venn Diagrams and Logical Reasoning (p. 691)

1.
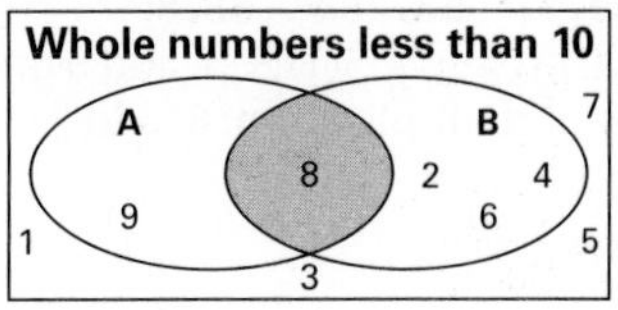

3. true **5.** never

Extra Practice

Chapter 1 (p. 692) **1.** Composite. *Sample answer:* The factors of 50 are 1, 2, 5, 10, and 50; $2 \cdot 5^2$. **3.** Composite. *Sample answer:* The factors of 84 are 1, 2, 3, 4, 6, 7, 12, 14, 21, 28, 42, and 84; $2^2 \cdot 3 \cdot 7$. **5.** 24 **7.** 6 **9.** $\frac{5}{6}; \frac{5}{6}$; equivalent **11.** $\frac{3}{4}; \frac{7}{9}$; not equivalent **13.** 48 **15.** 36 **17.** > **19.** < **21.** $\frac{1}{5}, \frac{11}{45}, \frac{4}{15}, \frac{1}{3}$ **23.** $\frac{13}{18}, \frac{3}{4}, \frac{19}{24}, \frac{7}{8}$ **25.** < **27.** > **29.** $\frac{16}{16}, 1\frac{1}{16}, \frac{13}{8}, \frac{17}{10}$ **31.** > **33.** = **35.** $4.99, 5, 5\frac{1}{7}, \frac{59}{11}$ **37.** $0, 0.923, 1, \frac{8}{5}, 1\frac{5}{6}$ **39.** \$0.50

Chapter 2 (p. 693) **1.** $\frac{3}{4}$ **3.** $1\frac{1}{7}$ **5.** $\frac{7}{11}$ **7.** $\frac{4}{23}$ **9.** $\frac{1}{18}$ **11.** $\frac{2}{3}$ **13.** $10\frac{2}{3}$ **15.** $9\frac{7}{12}$ **17.** $2\frac{1}{8}$ **19.** $4\frac{17}{24}$ **21.** $16\frac{4}{5}$ **23.** $2\frac{7}{9}$ **25.** $\frac{1}{6}$ **27.** 56 **29.** $\frac{3}{50}$ **31.** $1\frac{5}{8}$ **33.** $2\frac{2}{3}$ L; multiply $\frac{1}{3}$ by 8, since each lap you run you drink another $\frac{1}{3}$ liter of water. **35.** 146.113 **37.** 16.16 **39.** 20.69 **41.** 13.71 **43.** 0.793 **45.** 125.028 **47.** 22.05 **49.** 0.0072 **51.** 0.74 **53.** 0.02 **55.** 3.4 **57.** 0.115

Chapter 3 (p. 694) **1.** −10, −3, 0, 3, 6 **3.** −84, −70, −10, 15, 71, 99 **5.** 37 **7.** −11 **9.** −7 **11.** −26 **13.** −45 **15.** 79 **17.** 24 **19.** 12 **21.** −60 **23.** −47 **25.** −154 **27.** 0 **29.** 0 **31.** −5 **33.** −3 **35.** 65 **37.** 6 **39.** 108 − (12)(2) = 84 min

41. =

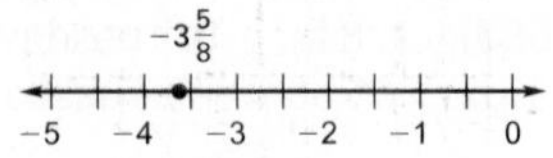

43. $-6 = \frac{-6}{1} - \frac{70}{11} = \frac{-70}{11}, -5.99 = \frac{-599}{100}, -6\frac{1}{7} = \frac{-43}{7}; \frac{-70}{11}, \frac{-43}{7}, \frac{-6}{1}, \frac{-599}{100}$ **45.** $-\frac{7}{9} = \frac{-7}{9}, 1.33 = \frac{133}{100}, \frac{7}{6}, -1.45 = \frac{-29}{20}, 0.13 = \frac{13}{100}; \frac{-29}{20}, \frac{-7}{9}, \frac{13}{100}, \frac{7}{6}, \frac{133}{100}$

47. 10; $-6 \cdot \left(-\frac{1}{6}\right) \cdot 10$, commutative property of multiplication; $1 \cdot 10$, inverse property of multiplication; 10, identity property of multiplication **49.** 66 + 34 + 47, commutative property of addition; (66 + 34) + 47, associative property of addition; 100 + 47, add 66 and 34; 147, add 100 and 47 **51.** 11 **53.** 28.8 **55.** 8; 5(9 + (−8)) + 3, distributive property; 5(1) + 3, add 9 and −8; 5 + 3, identity property of multiplication; 8, add 5 and 3

Chapter 4 (p. 695) **1.** 22.5 **3.** 8 **5.** 29 **7.** 570 min **9.** $\frac{x}{7}$ **11.** $x^2 + 5$ **13.** $\frac{23 - r}{s}$ **15.** $2 + 4z$ **17.** −6 **19.** $10t - 15$ **21.** 7.5 mi **23.** not a solution **25.** solution **27.** 16 **29.** 14 **31.** 18 **33.** −4 **35.** 8.4 **37.** 7 **39.** −21 **41.** 24 **43.** −2

Chapter 5 (p. 696) **1.** $\frac{3}{1}$, 3, 300% **3.** $\frac{3}{14}$, about 0.21, about 21% **5.** $\frac{1}{4}$ **7.** \$1.45 per gal **9.** 36 words per min **11.** 1.75 lb per month **13.** 6 m/sec **15.** 25 **17.** 27 **19.** 39 **21.** 36 **23.** 2.4 **25.** 0.4 **27.** 6.5 **29.** 1.7 **31.** 600 calories **33.** 20 ft long, 10 ft wide **35.** 2.75 in. long, 1.75 in. wide

Chapter 6 (p. 697) **1.** $\frac{3}{5}$ **3.** $\frac{21}{25}$ **5.** 40% **7.** 25% **9.** 64% **11.** 67.5 **13.** 180 **15.** 0.24 **17.** 0.106 **19.** 57.5% **21.** 0.12% **23.** 0.02 **25.** 115 **27.** 45.6 **29.** 31.25% **31.** 490 **33.** \$211.20 **35.** \$66.34 **37.** \$84.42 **39.** \$12.50, \$262.50 **41.** \$2.20, \$602.20 **43.** 2 yr

Chapter 7 (p. 698) **1.** convenience; likely to be biased **3.** Could produce biased results; the question encourages people to show a preference for soccer by describing soccer as exciting and baseball as long and boring. **5.** 7.35, 7.4, 7.5 **7.** Median. *Sample answer:* The mode is too low and will therefore not be an accurate measure of central tendency. The high value of 69°F distorts the mean. Therefore, the median reflects the data most accurately.
9. DVD Players:

Interval	Tally	Frequency
70–109	I	1
110–149	I	1
150–189	~~IIII~~ I	6
190–229	III	3
230–269	II	2
270–309	I	1

VCRS:

Interval	Tally	Frequency
70–109	𝍸 II	7
110–149	III	3
150–189		0
190–229	I	1
230–269	I	1
270–309		0

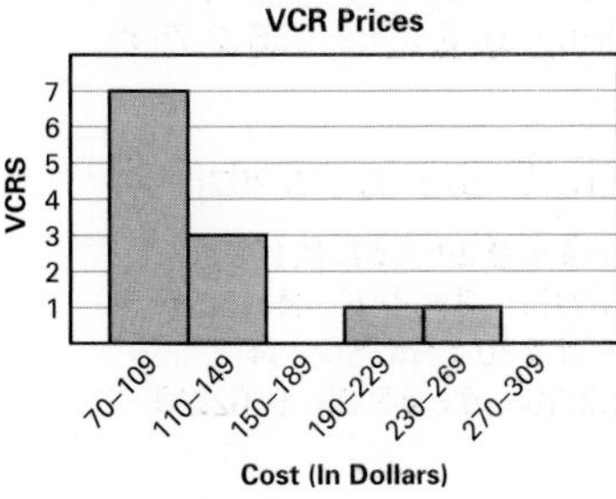

11. 216°, 144°

Chapter 8 (p. 699) **1.** $\frac{3}{20}$, 0.15, 15% **3.** $\frac{1}{2}$, 0.5, 50% **5.** 0.72 **7.** 240 points **9.** 45.9% **11.** $\frac{39}{100}$ **13.** $\frac{21}{25}$ or 0.84 **15.** $\frac{2}{9}$ **17.** 0.1411 **19.** $\frac{3}{125}$ **21.** $\frac{3}{8}$; dependent

Chapter 9 (p. 700) **1.** 94°, 4° **3.** 90° **5.** $m\angle 1 = 123°$, $m\angle 2 = 57°$; adjacent angles **7.** $m\angle 1 = 38°$, $m\angle 2 = 142°$; adjacent angles **9.** acute **11.** 90°; right **13.** isosceles

15.

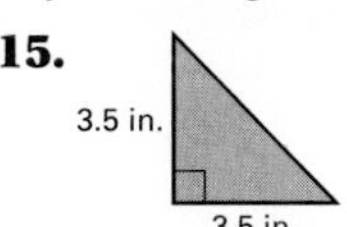

17. 1080° **19.** $\overline{AB} \cong \overline{DE}$, $\overline{AC} \cong \overline{DF}$, $\overline{BC} \cong \overline{EF}$; $\angle A \cong \angle D$, $\angle B \cong \angle E$, $\angle C \cong \angle F$ **21.** $\frac{3}{2}$ **23.** $x = 10$ in., $y = 12$ in.

Chapter 10 (p. 701) **1.** 240 **3.** 0.795 **5.** 70,000 **7.** < **9.** > **11.** 10 **13.** 4 **15.** 2, 2640 **17.** 5 ft 4 in. **19.** 13 ft **21.** 187 lb **23.** < **25.** 126 cm^2 **27.** 12.5 in. **29.** 56 ft^2 **31.** 85.5 m^2 **33.** 75.36 in. **35.** 109.9 mm **37.** 17.27 in. **39.** 2.512 cm **41.** 22,155.84 m^2 **43.** 0.0314 km^2 **45.** 254.34 mi^2 **47.** 452.16 m^2

Chapter 11 (p. 702) **1.** sphere **3.** rectangular pyramid

5.

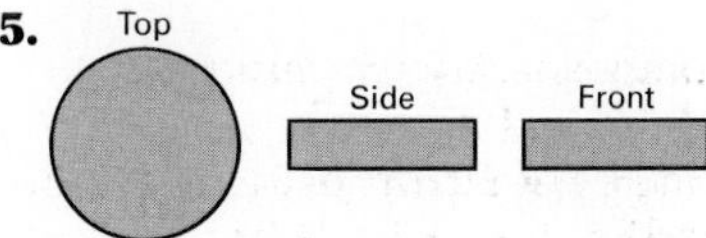

7. 121.2 ft^2 **9.** 37.68 m^2 **11.** 244.92 ft^2 **13.** 280 in.^{3} **15.** 137.5 cm^3 **17.** 50 cm^3 **19.** 1130.4 in.^{3} **21.** 39.25 ft^3 **23.** 188.4 in.^{3}

Chapter 12 (p. 703)

9.

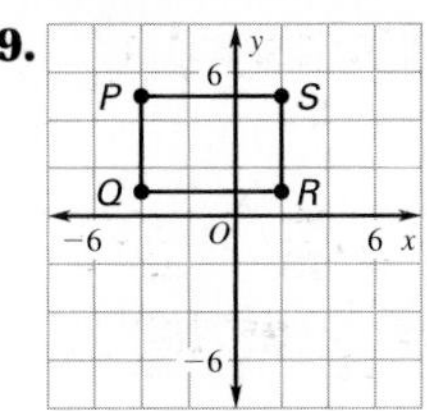

length: 6 units, width: 4 units; area: 24 units^2

11. 0 **13.** 24

15.

Input	Output
−4	−7
−2	−5
0	−3
2	−1
4	1

$\{-7, -5, -3, -1, 1\}$

19. $y = x - 6$ **21.** $y = -3x + 2$

23.

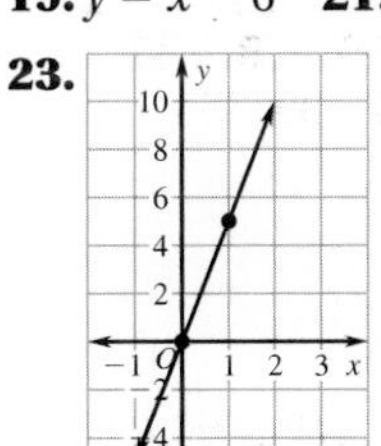

31. $-\frac{1}{6}$;

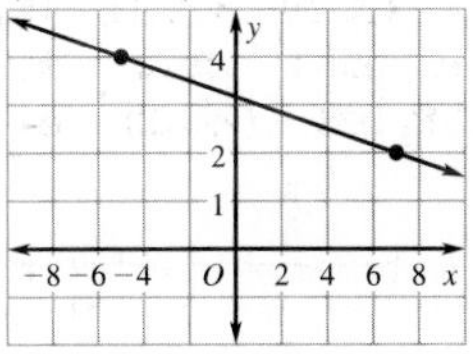

37.

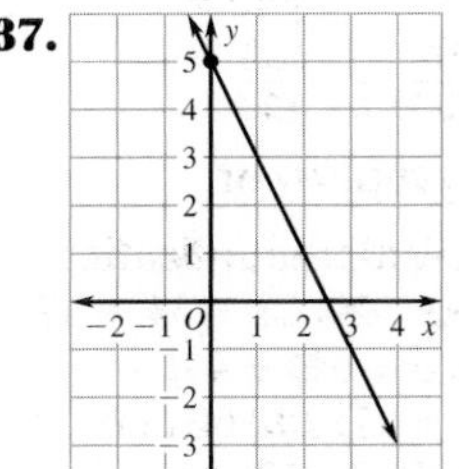

SELECTED ANSWERS